CORPORATE FINANCE

"Corporate Finance is a very useful reference book for students and practitioners both of whom will get great help in the present complex environment in understanding the principles of the financial markets and their practical application. The book's approach is both logical and sequential and presents some interesting cases that make study easier and more stimulating."

Gabriele Galateri, Chairman of Telecom Italia

"I opened my first Vernimmen in 1982. After having spent a just a few weekends reading it, I felt better equipped for my role in financial management at Paribas. Now at Apax, the Vernimmen remains my companion in my search for value creation (key in the private equity industry)."

Monique Cohen, Associated Director, Apax Partners

"Written in a fluent and readable style and supplemented by numerous real-world examples, Corporate Finance: Theory and Practice has served as an excellent aid to my studies of finance. The book's broad content has been indispensable in acquiring a better understanding of all the core areas of finance, ranging from the basics of financial analysis through to the workings of complex M&A transactions and cutting edge financial products."

Geoffrey Coombs, Student at ESCP Europe

"What sets the Vernimmen apart from other text books is its integration of practice and current affairs in a rigorous theoretical framework. Recipes and pontification are replaced by a scientific approach. And, thanks to the Newsletter, this is done practically in real time!"

Christophe Evers, Professor of Finance at the Solvay Brussels School, Executive Director of TEXAF

"Corporate finance is a lively subject that changes from day to day and evolves regularly, depending on new market developments. The Vernimmen is a true bible of corporate finance. With regular updates through their monthly newsletter and upgrades, the authors have made it applicable to any place, any time. This is pretty unique in the field."

Mehdi Sethom, Managing Director, Swicorp, Head of Advisory

Pierre Vernimmen

CORPORATE FINANCE

THEORY AND PRACTICE

Third Edition

Pascal Quiry
Maurizio Dallocchio
Yann Le Fur
Antonio Salvi

A John Wiley and Sons, Ltd, Publication

This edition first published 2011
© 2011 John Wiley & Sons, Ltd

Registered office
John Wiley & Sons Ltd, The Atrium, Southern Gate, Chichester, West Sussex, PO19 8SQ, United Kingdom

For details of our global editorial offices, for customer services and for information about how to apply for permission to reuse the copyright material in this book please see our website at www.wiley.com.

Library of Congress Cataloging-in-Publication Data
　　Corporate finance : theory and practice/Pascal Quiry . . . [et al.]—3rd ed
　　　p.　cm.
　　Rev. ed. of: Corporate finance: theory and practice/Pierre Vernimmen. 2005.
　　ISBN 978-1-119-97558-8 (pbk.)
　　　1. Corporations—Finance. 2. Business enterprises—Finance. I. Quiry, Pascal. II. Vernimmen,
Pierre. Corporate finance.
　HG4026. V467 2011
　658.15—dc23

2011024388

A catalogue record for this book is available from the British Library.

ISBN: 978-1-119-97558-8 (pbk) ISBN: 978-1-119-95184-1 (ebk)
ISBN: 978-1-119-96007-2 (ebk) ISBN: 978-1-119-96006-5 (ebk)

Typeset in 10/12pt Times by MPS Limited, a Macmillan Company, Chennai, India
Printed and bound in Great Britain by TJ International Ltd, Padstow, Cornwall

About the authors

Pascal Quiry is a professor of finance at the leading European business school HEC Paris, and a managing director in the Corporate Finance arm of BNP Paribas specialising in M&A.

Maurizio Dallocchio is Bocconi University Nomura Chair of Corporate Finance and Past Dean of SDA Bocconi, School of Management. He is also a board member of international and Italian institutions and is one of the most distinguished Italian authorities in finance.

Yann Le Fur is a corporate finance teacher at HEC Paris business school and an investment banker with Mediobanca in Paris after several years with Schroders and Citi.

Antonio Salvi is Full Professor of Corporate Finance at "Jean Monnet" University, Italy. He also teaches corporate finance at EM Lyon Business School and SDA Bocconi School of Management.

Pierre Vernimmen who died in 1996, was both an M&A dealmaker (he advised Louis Vuitton on its merger with Moët Henessy to create LVMH, the world luxury goods leader) and a finance teacher at HEC Paris. His book, *Finance d'Entreprise*, was and still is the top-selling financial textbook in French-speaking countries and is the forebear of *Corporate Finance: Theory and Practice*.

Summary

A detailed table of contents can be found on page 965

Introduction: Contrasts, Shocks, Threats and Opportunities

It's been a very long time indeed since we've seen such a contrast between macro-economics and company performances. We won't dwell on the macro-economics in order to avoid getting too depressed – something we're not used to at the Vernimmen. Suffice it to say, we have budget deficits that remain high at over 7% of GDP in many countries (and 10% in the USA), inflation that seems to be rising, high unemployment, economic depression in the so-called peripheral European countries (Greece, Ireland, Portugal), questions over the viability of the euro zone, persistence of monetary and trade imbalances, etc.

Alongside, and despite, the above, we have companies that have rarely been in such good health. In 2011, European companies listed on stock exchanges and, accordingly, examples of good companies could generate operating margins close to the historic high of over 11%:

OPERATING MARGIN FOR EUROPEAN LISTED COMPANIES EX-FINANCIALS

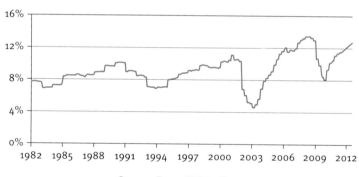

Source: Exane BNP Paribas.

1 *See page 693*
They have continued to deleverage. With an average Debt/EBITDA ratio of 1.2 times[1] we can't say that the situation is unhealthy, all the more so since most debt is concentrated on LBOs, diversified Spanish public works groups and real estate companies where lending is based on the value of assets and not on the basis of EBITDA.

At a European level, the situation for SMEs with over 20 employees is not very different, as most of them have a share of over 30% of equity capital on their balance sheets (except in Italy) while the share of debt is less than 20% (it was 30% in the early 2000s).

Another equally striking, but different, contrast is the contrast between young Europeans and Americans who believe that their personal future is promising but that the future of their countries is a lot less so (around 40 points), while the youth in emerging countries draw no distinction between their own future and that of their countries:

PROMISING

	My future is promising	The future of my country is promising
India	90%	83%
Brazil	87%	72%
Russia	81%	59%
United States	81%	37%
Finland	75%	61%
United Kingdom	74%	34%
China	73%	82%
Germany	56%	25%
France	53%	17%
Greece	43%	17%
Japan	43%	24%

Source: Les Echos / *Source*: Insee.

At the same time, the birth rate in France is the highest it has been since 1980 (828,000 births to be exact), which is a better indicator of optimism than any survey and paints a picture of a rosy future.[2]

New readers of the Vernimmen may be surprised to find references to happiness and the birth rate in the introduction to a textbook on finance. In addition to being very pro-children,[3] we believe that finance should help to make people happy. What else is it there for?

The last contrast we'd like to mention briefly is the fact that although bankers as a class are still largely derided, those interviewed state that they appreciate their personal bankers. It is true that traders rarely have much to do with the general public.

* * *

One of the most important contributions made by Benoît Mandelbrot, creator of fractals[4] who died on 14 October 2010, is to have shown that there is discontinuity in price variations, thus going against the notion of continuity and regularity as symbolised by normal law/the Gauss curve.

2 *And not only for the sales of the Vernimmen in 20 years!*

3 *"People are the only form of wealth"* wrote *Jean Bodin as early as the 16th century.*

4 *See page 268.*

If prices followed normal law, the Dow Jones would only vary by more than 7% per day once every 300,000 years. In the 20th century, 48 such variations, with two since 2000, were recorded. In other words, models based on this assumption (Black–Scholes, VaR, etc.) underestimate the risk of a stock market crash.[5] This is not news for readers of the Vernimmen, as it is discussed in the 1996 edition.

Having said that, shocks seem to have become a recurrent, and even normal, part of our lives, with the September 11 attacks, the collapse of Lehman Brothers and the Fukushima catastrophe. As Denis Kessler, CEO of the reinsurer SCOR said, "We should expect shocks of all sorts, which will interact and have increasingly complex consequences – the world has become a frenzied village!"[5]

5 *Le Monde*
5 May 2011.

We now understand better why companies have increased the share of cash and marketable securities on the asset side of their balance sheets, from 3.7% in 2002 to 7.5% in 2010.

**RATIO OF CASH AND MARKETABLE SECURITIES / TOTAL ASSETS FOR
THE 3000 LARGEST CAPS WORLDWIDE (70% OF WORLDWIDE CAPITALISATION)**

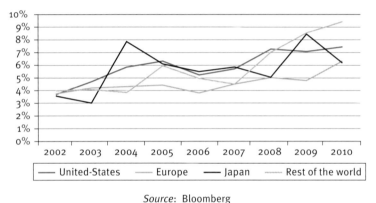

Source: Bloomberg

This is a fundamental trend which is unlikely to change very quickly.

* * *

What are the threats? We'll restrict ourselves to three.

- Substantial tightening of liquidity ratios by banks which could restrict them in granting medium- and long-term loans by requiring that they have as much in medium- and long-term resources as uses of funds of the same nature. Of course, the biggest companies will find a way of getting around this by tapping the bond markets, but not all companies will be in a position to do so. It would indeed be a paradox if the banking system, which was not responsible for the 2008 financial crisis, were to become a victim of measures intended to avoid a repeat scenario, and the markets—which were the main instigators of the crisis—were to end up benefiting from such moves.

  Similarly, the implementation of the Solvency II Directive in the insurance sector could severely penalise investment in equity capital by investors, who, however, have long-term resources at their disposal.

At this stage, these are only projects, even though they are well advanced and should be finalised by the close of 2011. We'll come back to them in the next edition of the Vernimmen.

- The level of margins and the difference between after-tax ROCE and the cost of capital, expected to be 3.7% in 2011 and 4.3% in 2012, are historically high in Europe[6] and are untenable. They cannot last and, what's more, the macro-economic environment in Europe is going to be far from euphoric.

  A part of government debt will have to be paid back as this is not debt that can be carried permanently, but the rest can continue to be renewed as has always been the case. As recent excess debt was often contracted to sustain consumption rather than for investment, it cannot be paid back out of income on investments which it did not finance, but will have to be paid back by savings made through the contraction of future consumption. This is clearly visible in Greece where, for example, sales of pharmaceutical drugs are down by 29% (2013 estimated/2009), private construction in 2010 by 32% in volume compared with 2009, and by January 2011, the drop had reached 73%.

- The growing imbalance in the distribution of wealth and income in developed countries, which is threatening the social contract. In the USA, every year, the 12,000 wealthiest families receive a share of the national income that is equal to the share received by the 24 million poorest families. When the wheels of social mobility are well-oiled, this can be said to be a motivating factor. When the wheels seem to get stuck, it becomes morally unacceptable and runs the risk of opening the door to events of all sorts, which include the best (Tunisia) and the worst (the rise of extremism).

* * *

Given our natural optimism, we'd like to conclude with opportunities. There has been no fundamental change in opportunities over the last year, and they still go by the name of emerging countries.

For the first time in history, 2010 saw sales of cars in emerging countries equal sales in developed countries. Is there a better symbol than that?

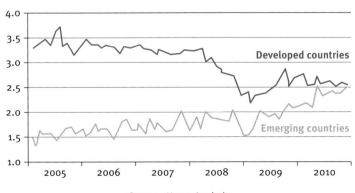

WORLDWIDE CAR SALES (MILLIONS OF UNITS PER MONTH)

Source: Haver Analytic

6 *See page 525.*

There will, of course, be other economic and financial crises and there is no guarantee that the impact on emerging countries will be as slight as it was in 2008–2009, but the trend is clear:

GDP IN CONSTANT (US$bn)

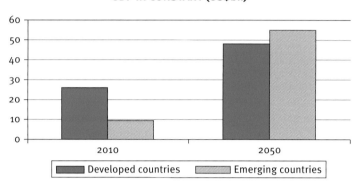

Source: HSBC

L'Oréal already sells more cosmetics in China than in Germany or in Italy, markets on which it has been active for over 60 years. The same can be said for SEB's sales in Brazil.

And this is clearly only the beginning.

7 *Les Echos 10 January 2011.*

Michel Cicurel[7] predicts the start of a long cycle of strong growth, driven by the expansion of the middle classes in emerging countries and an increase in the world's population by 3 billion over the next 50 years.

This will require considerable investments in terms of infrastructure, energy, in the field of agriculture, in the emerging countries themselves, but also in developed countries, in order to deal with the growing scarcity of certain raw materials and heavy restrictions on carbon emissions.

8 *Farewell to cheap capital? The implications of long-term shifts in global investment and saving. December 2010.*

McKinsey believes[8] that inadequate long-term savings could lead to a rise in the cost of capital of around 1.5%, given that investment requirements are so high. Is this situation unacceptable? No.

The very healthy financial structures that we mentioned at the beginning of this Introduction will enable canny or audacious entrepreneurs to seize opportunities without taking on excessive debt. Because what is the point of creating debt capacity if not to take out reasonable amounts of debt when the time is right? However, debts should be reasonable and not excessive, since in the troubled world in which we live, the only certainty is the fact of uncertainty. And debt does not like uncertainty.

As for the intellectual capacities required to cope in the area of finance, you'll find all of the answers you need in the following 964 pages.

Preface

This book aims to cover the full scope of corporate finance as it is practised today worldwide.

A way of thinking about finance

We are very pleased with the success of the first two editions of the book. It has encouraged us to retain the approach in order to explain corporate finance to students and professionals. There are four key features that distinguish this book from the many other corporate finance textbooks available on the market today:

- Our strong belief that financial analysis is part of corporate finance. Pierre Vernimmen, who was mentor and partner to some of us in the practice of corporate finance, understood very early on that a good financial manager must first be able to analyse a company's economic, financial and strategic situation, and then value it, while at the same time mastering the conceptual underpinnings of all financial decisions.
- *Corporate Finance* is neither a theoretical textbook nor a practical workbook. It is a book in which theory and practice are constantly set off against each other, in the same way as in our daily practice as investment bankers at BNP Paribas, DGPA and Mediobanca, as board members of several listed and unlisted companies, and as teachers at the Bocconi and HEC Paris business schools.
- Emphasis is placed on concepts, intended to give you an understanding of situations, rather than on techniques, which tend to shift and change over time. We confess to believing that the former will still be valid in 20 years' time, whereas the latter will, for the most part, be long forgotten!
- Financial concepts are international, but they are much easier to grasp when they are set in a familiar context. We have tried to give examples and statistics from all around the world to illustrate the concepts.

The five sections

This book starts with an introductory chapter reiterating the idea that corporate financiers are the bridge between the economy and the realm of finance. Increasingly, they must play the role of marketing managers and negotiators. Their products are financial securities that represent rights to the firm's cash flows. Their customers are bankers and investors. A good financial manager listens to customers and sells them good products at high prices. A good financial manager always thinks in terms of value rather than costs or earnings.

Section I goes over the basics of financial analysis, i.e. understanding the company based on a detailed analysis of its financial statements. We are amazed at the extent to which large numbers of investors neglected this approach during the latest stockmarket euphoria. When share prices everywhere are rising, why stick to a rigorous approach? For one thing, to avoid being caught in the crash that inevitably follows.

The return to reason has also returned financial analysis to its rightful place as a cornerstone of economic decision-making. To perform financial analysis, you must first understand the firm's basic financial mechanics (Chapters 2–5). Next you must master the basic techniques of accounting, including accounting principles, consolidation techniques and certain complexities (Chapters 6–7), based on international (IFRS) standards now mandatory in over 80 countries, including the EU (for listed companies), Australia, South Africa and accepted by the SEC for US listing. In order to make things easier for the newcomer to finance, we have structured the presentation of financial analysis itself around its guiding principle: in the long run, a company can survive only if it is solvent and creates value for its shareholders. To do so, it must generate wealth (Chapters 9 and 10), invest (Chapter 11), finance its investments (Chapter 12) and generate a sufficient return (Chapter 13). The illustrative financial analysis of the Italian appliance manufacturer Indesit will guide you throughout this section of the book.

Section II reviews the basic theoretical knowledge you will need to make an assessment of the value of the firm. Here again, the emphasis is on reasoning, which in many cases will become automatic (Chapters 15–20): efficient capital markets, the time value of money, the price of risk, volatility, arbitrage, return, portfolio theory, present value and future value, market risk, beta, etc. Then we review the major types of financial securities: equity, debt and options, for the purposes of valuation, along with the techniques for issuing and placing them (Chapters 21–26).

The **central section, the third one**, is devoted to value, to its theoretical foundations and to its computation. Value is the focus of any *financier*, both its measure and the way it is shared. Over the medium term, creating value is, most of the time, the first aim of managers (Chapters 27–32).

In **Section IV**, "Corporate financial policies", we analyse each financial decision in terms of:

- value in the context of the theory of efficient capital markets;
- balance of power between owners and managers, shareholders and debtholders (agency theory);
- communication (signal theory).

Such decisions include choosing a capital structure, investment decisions, cost of capital, dividend policy, share repurchases, capital increases, hybrid security issues, etc.

In this section, we draw your attention to today's obsession with earnings per share, return on equity and other measures whose underlying basis we have a tendency to forget and which may, in some cases, be only distantly related to value creation. We have devoted considerable space to the use of options (as a technique or a type of reasoning) in each financial decision (Chapters 33–39).

When you start reading **Section V**, "Financial management", you will be ready to examine and take the remaining decisions: how to organise a company's equity capital and its governance, buying and selling companies, mergers, demergers, LBOs, bankruptcy and restructuring (Chapters 40–46). Lastly, this section presents cash flow management, working capital management and the management of the firm's financial risks (Chapters 47–49).

Last but not least, the epilogue addresses the question of the links between finance and strategy

Suggestions for the reader

To make sure that you get the most out of your book, each chapter ends with a summary, a series of problems and questions (a total of 827, with the solutions provided). We've used the last page to provide a cribsheet (the nearly 1000 pages of this book summarised on one page!). For those interested in exploring the topics in greater depth, there is an end-of-chapter bibliography and suggestions for further reading, covering fundamental research papers, articles in the press, published books and websites. A large number of graphs and tables (over 100!) have been included in the body of the text and these can be used for comparative analyses. Finally, there is a fully comprehensive index.

The masculine pronoun has been used throughout this book simply for convenience and brevity. This use is not intended to be discriminatory in any way.

An Internet site with huge and diversified content

www.vernimmen.com provides free access to tools (formulas, tables, statistics, lexicons, glossaries), resources that supplement the book (articles, prospectuses of financial transactions, financial figures for over 16 000 European, North American and emerging countries listed companies, thesis topics, thematic links, a list of must-have books for your bookshelf, an Excel file providing detailed solutions to all of the problems set in the book), plus problems, case studies and quizzes for testing and improving your knowledge. There is a letterbox for your questions to the authors (we reply within 72 hours, unless, of course, you manage to stump us!). There are questions and answers and much more. The site has its own internal search engine, and new services are added regularly. The Internet site is already visited by over 1000 unique visitors a day.

A teachers' area provides teachers with free access to case studies, slides and an Instructor's Manual, which gives advice and ideas on how to teach all of the topics discussed in the *Vernimmen*.

A free monthly newsletter on corporate finance

Since (unfortunately) we can't bring out a new edition of the *Vernimmen* every month, we have set up the *Vernimmen.com Newsletter*, which is sent out free of charge to subscribers via the web. It contains:

* A conceptual look at a topical corporate finance problem (e.g. *accounting for operating and capital leases, what if inflation rises again?*).
* Statistics and tables that you are likely to find useful in the day-to-day practice of corporate finance (e.g. *corporate income tax rates, debt ratios in LBOs*).
* A critical review of a financial research paper with a concrete dimension (e.g. *the real effect of corporate cash, why don't US issuers demand European fees for their IPOs?*).
* A question left on the vernimmen.com site by a visitor plus a response (e.g. *why do successful groups have such a low debt level? what is an assimilation clause?*).

Subscribe to *www.vernimmen.com* and become one of the many readers of the Vernimmen. com Newsletter.

Many thanks

- To Damien Anzel, Adnan Bey, Patrice Carlean-Jones, Geoffrey Coombs, Matthew Cush, Deloitte IFRS MNC Advisory team, and in particular Elisabeth Baudin, for helping us on the first part of the book, Carlos Domingues, Pierre Foucry, Simon Gueguen, Daniel Hagge, Robert Killingsworth, Patrick Iweins, Eric Jakubowicz, Bertrand Jacquillat, Pierre Laur, Guillaume Mallen, Franck Megel, François Meunier, John Olds, Laetitia Remy, Gita Roux, Mehdi Sethom, Steven Sklar, Marc Vermeulen, Georges Watkinson-Yull, and students of the HEC Paris and Bocconi MBA programmes for their help in improving the manuscript.
- To Altimir Perrody, the vernimmen.com webmaster.
- To Isabelle Marié-Sall for her help in transforming our scribblings into a proper manuscript.
- And last but not least to Françoise, Anne-Valérie, Enrica and Annalisa; our children Paul, Claire, Pierre, Philippe, Soazic, Solène and Aymeric and our many friends who have had to endure our endless absences over the last years, and of course Catherine Vernimmen and her children for their everlasting and kind support.

We hope that you will gain as much enjoyment from your Vernimmen – whether you are a new student of corporate finance or are using it to revise and hone your financial skills – as we have had in editing this edition and in expanding the services and products that go with the book.

We wish you well in your studies!

Milan and Paris, July 2011

Pascal Quiry   *Maurizio Dallocchio*

Yann Le Fur   *Antonio Salvi*

Frequently used symbols

A_k^N	Annuity factor for N years and an interest rate of k
ABCP	Asset Backed Commercial Paper
ADR	American Depositary Receipt
APT	Arbitrage Pricing Theory
APV	Adjusted Present Value
BIMBO	Buy In Management Buy Out
BV	Book Value
Capex	Capital Expenditures
CAPM	Capital Asset Pricing Model
CB	Convertible Bond
CD	Certificate of Deposit
CE	Capital Employed
CFROI	Cash Flow Return On Investment
COV	Covariance
CVR	Contingent Value Right
D	Debt, net financial and banking debt
d	Payout ratio
DCF	Discounted Cash Flows
DDM	Dividend Discount Model
DECS	Debt Exchangeable for Common Stock; Dividend Enhanced Convertible Securities
Div	Dividend
DPS	Dividend Per Share
EBIT	Earnings Before Interest and Taxes
EBITDA	Earnings Before Interest, Taxes, Depreciation and Amortisation
ECP	European Commercial Paper
EGM	Extraordinary General Meeting
EMTN	Euro Medium-Term Note
ENPV	Expanded Net Present Value
EONIA	European Over Night Index Average
EPS	Earnings Per Share
$E(r)$	Expected return
ESOP	Employee Stock Ownership Programme
EURIBOR	EURopean Inter Bank Offer Rate
EV	Enterprise Value
EVA	Economic Value Added
f	Forward rate
F	Cash flow
FA	Fixed Assets
FASB	Financial Accounting Standards Board
FC	Fixed Costs
FCF	Free Cash Flow
FCFE	Free Cash Flow to Equity
FCFF	Free Cash Flow to Firm
FE	Financial Expenses
FIFO	First In, First Out

FRA	Forward Rate Agreement
g	Growth rate
GAAP	Generally Accepted Accounting Principles
GDR	Global Depositary Receipt
i	After-tax cost of debt
IASB	International Accounting Standards Board
IFRS	International Financial Reporting Standard
IPO	Initial Public Offering
IRR	Internal Rate of Return
IRS	Interest Rate Swap
IT	Income Taxes
k	Cost of capital, discount rate
k_D	Cost of debt
k_E	Cost of equity
K	Option strike price
LBO	Leveraged BuyOut
LBU	Leveraged Build Up
L/C	Letter of Credit
LIBOR	London Inter Bank Offer Rate
LIFO	Last In, First Out
LMBO	Leveraged Management BuyOut
ln	Naperian logarithm
LOI	Letter Of Intent
m	Contribution margin
MOU	Memorandum Of Understanding
MTN	Medium-Term Notes
MVA	Market Value Added
n	Years, periods
N	Number of years
$N(d)$	Cumulative standard normal distribution
NA	Not available
NAV	Net Asset Value
NM	Not Meaningful
NOPAT	Net Operating Profit After Tax
NPV	Net Present Value
OGM	Ordinary General Meeting
OTC	Over The Counter
P	Price
PBO	Projected Benefit Obligation
PBR	Price-to-Book Ratio
PBT	Profit Before Tax
P/E ratio	Price/Earnings ratio
PEPs	Personal Equity Plans
PERCS	Preferred Equity Redemption Cumulative Stock
PSR	Price-to-Sales Ratio
P to P	Public to Private
PV	Present Value
PVI	Present Value Index
QIB	Qualified Institutional Buyer
r	Rate of return, interest rate
r_F	Risk-free rate
r_M	Expected return of the market
RNAV	Restated Net Asset Value
ROA	Return On Assets
ROCE	Return On Capital Employed
ROE	Return On Equity
ROI	Return On Investment

RWA	Risk Weighted Assessment
S	Sales
SEC	Securities Exchange Commission
SEO	Seasoned Equity Offering
SPV	Special Purpose Vehicle
STEP	Short-Term European Paper
t	Interest rate, discount rate
T	Time remaining until maturity
T_c	Corporate tax rate
TSR	Total Shareholder Return
V	Value
V_D	Value of Debt
V_E	Value of Equity
$V(r)$	Variance of return
VAT	Value Added Tax
VC	Variable Cost
WACC	Weighted Average Cost of Capital
WC	Working Capital
y	Yield to maturity
YTM	Yield To Maturity
Z	Scoring function
ZBA	Zero Balance Account
β or β_E	Beta coefficient for a share or an equity instrument
β_A	Beta coefficient for an asset or unlevered beta
β_D	Beta coefficient of a debt instrument
$\sigma(r)$	Standard deviation of return
$\rho A,B$	Correlation coefficient of return between shares A and B

Chapter 1
WHAT IS CORPORATE FINANCE?

To whet your appetite . . .

The primary role of the financial manager is to ensure that his company has a sufficient supply of capital.

The financial manager is at the crossroads of the real **economy**, with its industries and services, and the world of **finance**, with its various financial markets and structures.

There are two ways of looking at the financial manager's role:

- a buyer of capital who seeks to minimise its cost, i.e. the traditional view;
- a seller of financial securities who tries to maximise their value. This is the view we will develop throughout this book. It corresponds, to a greater or lesser extent, to the situation that exists in a capital market economy, as opposed to a credit-based economy.

At the risk of oversimplifying, we will use the following terminology in this book:

- the **financial manager** or **chief financial officer** (CFO) is responsible for financing the firm and acts as an intermediary between the financial system's institutions and markets, on the one hand, and the company, on the other;
- the **business manager** invests in plants and equipment, undertakes research, hires staff and sells the firm's products, whether the firm is a manufacturer, a retailer or a service provider;
- the **financial investor** invests in financial securities. More generally, the financial investor provides the firm with financial resources, and may be either an equity investor or a lender.

Section 1.1
THE FINANCIAL MANAGER IS FIRST AND FOREMOST A SALESMAN . . .

1/ THE FINANCIAL MANAGER'S JOB IS NOT ONLY TO "BUY" FINANCIAL RESOURCES . . .

The financial manager is traditionally perceived as a buyer of capital. He negotiates with a variety of investors – bankers, shareholders, bond investors – to obtain funds at the lowest possible cost.

Transactions that take place on the **capital markets** are made up of the following elements:

- a commodity: money,
- a price: the interest rate in the case of debt; dividends and capital gains in the case of equities.

In the traditional view, the financial manager is responsible for the company's financial procurement. His job is to minimise the price of the **commodity** to be purchased, i.e. the **cost of the funds** he raises.

We have no intention of contesting this view of the world. It is obvious and is confirmed every day, in particular in the following types of negotiations:

- between corporate treasurers and bankers, regarding interest rates and value dates applied to bank balances (see Chapter 47);
- between chief financial officers and financial market intermediaries, where negotiation focuses on the commissions paid to arrangers of financial transactions (see Chapter 26).

2/ . . . BUT ALSO TO SELL FINANCIAL SECURITIES

That said, let's now take a look at the financial manager's job from a different angle:

- he is not a buyer but a **seller**;
- his aim is not to reduce the cost of the raw material he buys but to **maximise a selling price**;
- he practises his art not on the capital markets, but on the market for financial instruments, be they loans, bonds, shares, etc.

We are not changing the world here; we are merely looking at the same market from another point of view:

- the **supply** of financial securities corresponds to the demand for capital;
- the **demand** for financial securities corresponds to the supply of capital;
- the **price**, the point at which the supply and demand for financial securities are in equilibrium, is therefore the **value of security**. In contrast, the equilibrium price in the traditional view is considered to be the interest rate, or the cost of funds.

We can summarise these two ways of looking at the same capital market in the following table:

Analysis/Approach	Financial approach: financial manager as salesman	Traditional approach: financial manager as purchaser
Market	Securities	Capital
Supply	Issuer	Investor
Demand	Investor	Issuer
Price	Value of security	Interest rate

Depending on your point of view, i.e. traditional or financial, supply and demand are reversed, as follows:

- when the **cost of money** – the interest rate, for example – **rises**, demand for funds is greater than supply. In other words, the supply of financial securities is greater than the demand for financial securities, and **the value of the securities falls**;
- conversely, when **the cost of money falls**, the supply of funds is greater than demand. In other words, the demand for financial instruments is greater than their supply and **the value of the securities rises**.

The cost of capital and the value of the securities vary in opposite directions. We can summarise with the following theorem, fundamental to this entire book:

Minimising financing cost is synonymous with maximising the value of the underlying securities.

For two practical reasons, one minor and one major, we prefer to present the financial manager as a seller of financial securities.

The minor reason is that viewing the financial manager as a salesman trying to sell his products at the highest price casts his role in a different light. As the merchant does not want to sell low-quality products but products that respond to the needs of his customers, so the financial manager must understand his capital suppliers and satisfy their needs without putting the company or its other capital suppliers at a disadvantage. **He must sell high-quality products at high prices**. But he can also repackage his product to better meet investor expectations. Indeed, financial markets are subject to fashion: in one period convertible bonds (see Chapter 25) can be easily placed; in another period it will be syndicated loans (see Chapter 22) that investors will welcome.

The more important reason is that when a financial manager applies the traditional approach of minimising the cost of the company's financing too strictly, erroneous decisions may easily follow. The traditional approach can make the financial manager **short-sighted**, tempting him to take decisions that emphasise the short term to the detriment of the long term.

For instance, choosing between a capital increase, a bank loan and a bond issue with lowest cost as the only criterion reflects flawed reasoning. Why? Because suppliers of capital, i.e. the buyers of the corresponding instruments, do not all face the same level of risk.

The investor's risk must be taken into account in evaluating the cost of a source of financing.

The cost of two sources of financing can be compared only when the suppliers of the funds incur the same level of risk.

All too often we have seen managers or treasurers assume excessive risk when choosing a source of financing because they have based their decision on a single criterion: the respective cost of the different sources of funds. For example:

- increasing short-term debt, on the pretext that short-term interest rates are lower than long-term rates can be a serious mistake;
- granting a mortgage in return for a slight decrease in the interest rate on a loan can be very harmful for the future;
- increasing debt systematically on the sole pretext that debt costs less than equity capital jeopardises the company's prospects for long-term survival.

We will develop this theme further throughout the third part of this book, but we would like to warn you now of the pitfalls of faulty financial reasoning. **The most dangerous thing a financial manager can say is, "It doesn't cost anything." This sentence should be banished and replaced with the following question: "What is the impact of this action on value?"**

Section 1.2
. . . OF FINANCIAL SECURITIES . . .

Let's now take a look at the overall concept of a financial security, the product created by the financial manager.

1/ ISSUANCE OR CREATION OF SECURITIES

There is a great variety of financial instruments, each of which has the following characteristics:

- it is a contract . . .
- . . . executed over time,
- its value derives solely from the series of cash flows it represents.

Indeed, from a mathematical and more theoretical viewpoint, a financial instrument is defined as a **schedule of future cash flows**.

Holding a financial security is the same as holding the right to receive the cash flows, as defined in the terms and conditions of the issue that gave rise to the financial instrument. Conversely, for the issuer, creating a financial instrument is the same as committing to paying out a series of cash flows. In return for this right to receive cash flows or for taking on this commitment, the company will issue a security at a certain price, enabling it to raise the funds needed to run its business.

A financial security is a contract . . .

You've undoubtedly heard people say that the financial manager's stock-in-trade is "paper". Computerisation has now turned financial instruments from paper documents into intangible book entries, reducing them to the information they contain, i.e. the contract. The essence of finance is, and will always be, **negotiation** between an issuer seeking new funds and the investors interested in buying the instruments that represent the underlying obligations. And negotiation means markets, be they credit markets, bond markets, stock markets, etc.

. . . executed over time . . .

Time, or the term of the financial security, introduces the notion of **risk**. A debt instrument that promises cash flows over time, for example, entails risk, even if the borrower is very creditworthy. This seems strange to many people who consider that "a deal is a deal" or "a man's word is his bond". Yet, experience has shown that a wide variety of risks can affect the payment of those cash flows, including political risk, strikes, natural disasters and other events.

. . . and materialised by cash flows.

Further on in this book you will see that financial logic is used to analyse and choose among a firm's investment options. The financial manager transforms flows of goods and services, deriving from the company's industrial and other business assets, into cash flows. You will soon understand that the world of finance is one of **managing rights on the one hand and commitments on the other, both expressed in terms of cash flows**.

In a market for financial instruments, it is not the actual flows that are sold, but the rights associated with them. The investor, i.e. the buyer of the security, acquires the rights granted by the instrument. The issuing company assumes contractual obligations deriving from the instrument, regardless of who the owner of the instrument is.

For example, commodity futures markets make it possible to perform purely financial transactions. You can buy sugar "forward", via financial instruments called futures contracts, knowing full well that you will never take delivery of the sugar into your warehouse. Instead, you will close out the position prior to maturity. The financial manager thus trades on a market for real goods (sugar), using contracts that can be unwound prior to or at maturity.

A property investor acts similarly. After acquiring real property, the value of which fluctuates, he can lease it or resell it. Viewed this way, real property is as fungible as any other property and is akin to a financial asset.

Clearly, these assets exhibit different degrees of "financiality". To take the argument one step further, you turn a painting into a financial instrument when you put it in your safe in the hope of realising a gain when you sell it.

The distinction between a real asset and a financial asset is therefore subtle but fundamental. It lies either in the nature of the contract or in the investor's motivation, as in the example of the painting.

Lastly, the purchase of a financial security differs from the purchase of a durable good in that the financial security is undifferentiated. A large number of investors can buy the same financial security. In contrast, acquiring a specific office building or building an industrial plant is a very specific, unique investment.

In conclusion, every financial instrument represents a series of cash flows to be received according to a set timetable. Mathematically, it can be expressed as a series of future cash flows $F_1, F_2, F_3, F_4 \ldots, F_n$ over n periods.

2/ TYPES OF FINANCIAL SECURITIES

(a) Debt instruments (Chapters 21 and 22)

The simplest financial instrument is undoubtedly the contract that ties a lender (investor) to a borrower (company). It represents a very strong commitment, not only to repay, but to repay with interest. Loans become financial securities when they are made negotiable on a secondary market (see page 7) and "listed". Bonds and commercial paper fall into this category.

A bond is a negotiable debt security representing a fraction of a borrowing contracted by a company, a financial institution or a sovereign state (Gilts in the UK, Bunds in Germany, etc.).

Commercial paper is a negotiable debt security representing a fraction of a short-term borrowing (generally between 1 day and 2 years) contracted by a company. If the company is a bank, the security will be called a **certificate of deposit**. Short-term sovereign debt instruments go by different names depending on the country; in Spain, for example, they are called *Bonos del Estado*, while they are called *Treasury Bills* in the US.

Strictly speaking, investors in these securities do not assume any industrial risk. **Their return is set contractually** and may be fixed or floating (i.e. variable). If it is floating, it will be indexed on an interest rate and not on the results of the company.

In Chapter 14 we will see that the lender nevertheless assumes certain risks, namely the failure of the borrower to honour the debt contract.

(b) Equity securities (Chapter 23)

Equity represents the capital injected into a company by an investor who bears the full risk of the company's industrial undertakings in return for a share of the profits.

If the company is organised under a limited liability structure, the equity is divided into **shares**. The risk borne by the shareholders is limited to the amount they contribute to the firm. Unless otherwise noted, we will be dealing in this book with finance as it relates to the various forms of "limited companies".

Shareholders' equity is a source of financing for the enterprise, but the related financial security, the share, guarantees the investor neither a fixed level of income nor repayment. The shareholder can realise his investment only by selling it to someone else. The investor obtains certain corporate rights, however: a claim on the company's earnings and – via his voting rights – management oversight.

(c) Other securities (Chapter 25)

As you will discover in Chapter 25, financial engineering specialists have invented hybrid securities that combine the characteristics of the two categories discussed above. Some securities have the look and feel of equity from the point of view of the company, but the corresponding cash flows are fixed, at least partially. Others instruments have yields that are dependent on the performance of the company, but are considered loans, not equity capital. Financial imagination knows no bounds. Keep in mind that these instruments are peripheral to our primary focus in this book. As such, we won't burden you with them until Chapter 25!

There is a specific type of financial instrument, however, **the option,** whose associated cash flows are actually less "important" to the investor than the rights the option conveys. This instrument grants the right, but not the obligation, to do something.

In sum, financial instruments carry a wide spectrum of characteristics, which, from the investor's point of view, ranges from rights to commitments.

Section 1.3
. . . VALUED CONTINUOUSLY BY THE FINANCIAL MARKETS

Our view of finance can take shape only in the context of well-developed financial markets. But before examining the technical characteristics of markets (Section II of this book), let's spend a moment on definitions.

1/ FROM THE PRIMARY MARKET TO THE SECONDARY MARKET

Once launched by its issuer, a financial security lives a life of its own. It is sold from one investor to another, and it serves as support for other transactions. The instrument itself evolves, but the terms of the contract under which it was issued do not.

The life of a financial security is intimately connected with the fact that it can be bought or sold at any moment. For example, shares issued or created when a company is founded can later be floated on a stock exchange, just as long-term bonds may be used by speculators for short-term strategies.

The new issues market (i.e. creation of securities) is called the primary market. Subsequent transactions involving these securities take place on the **secondary market**. Both markets, like any market, are defined by two basic elements: the product (the security) and the price (its value).

From the point of view of the company, the distinction between the primary and secondary markets is fundamental. **The primary market is the market for "new" financial products**, from equity issues to bond issues and everything in between. It is the market for newly-minted financial securities.

Conversely, the secondary market is the market for "used" financial products. Securities bought and sold on this market have already been created and are now simply changing hands, without any new securities being created.

The primary market enables companies, financial institutions, governments and local authorities to obtain financial resources by issuing securities. These securities are then listed and traded on secondary markets. The job of the secondary market is to ensure that securities are properly priced and traded. This is the essence of **liquidity**: facilitating the purchase or sale of a security.

The distinction between primary and secondary markets is conceptual only. The two markets are not separated from each other. A given financial investor can buy either existing shares or new shares issued during a capital increase, for example.

If there is often more emphasis placed on the primary market, it is because the function of the financial markets is, first and foremost, to ensure equilibrium between financing needs and the sources of finance. Secondary markets, where securities can change hands, constitute a kind of financial "innovation".

2/ THE FUNCTION OF THE SECONDARY MARKET

Financial investors do not intend to remain invested in a particular asset indefinitely. From the moment they buy a security (or even before), they begin thinking about how they will **exit**. As a result, they are constantly evaluating whether they should buy or sell such and such an asset.

Monetising is relatively easy when the security is a short-term one. All the investor has to do is wait until maturity. The need for an exit strategy grows with the maturity of the investment and is greatest for equity investments, whose maturity is unlimited. The only way a shareholder can exit his investment is to sell his shares to someone else.

Similarly, the successful businessman who floats his company on the stock exchange, thereby bringing in new shareholders, diversifies his own portfolio, which before flotation was essentially concentrated in one investment.

The secondary market makes the investor's investments liquid.

Liquidity refers to the ability to convert an instrument into cash quickly and without loss of value. It affords the opportunity to trade a financial instrument at a "listed" price and in large quantities without disrupting the market. An investment is liquid when an investor can buy or sell it in large quantities without causing a change in its market price.

The secondary market is therefore a **zero-sum game** between investors, because what one investor buys, another investor sells. In principle, the secondary market operates completely independently from the issuer of the securities.

A company that issues a bond today knows that a certain amount of funds will remain available in each future year. This knowledge is based on the bond's amortisation schedule. During that time, however, the investors holding the bonds will have changed.

Secondary market transactions do not show up in macroeconomic statistics on capital formation, earning them the scorn of some observers who claim that the secondary market does nothing to further economic development, but only bails out the initial investors.

We believe this thinking is misguided and reflects great ignorance about the function of secondary markets in the economy. Remember that a financial investor is constantly comparing the primary and secondary markets. He cares little whether he is buying a "new" or a "used" security, so long as they have the same characteristics.

The secondary market plays the fundamental role of valuing securities.

In fact, the quality of a primary market for a security depends greatly on the quality of its secondary market. Think about it: who would want to buy a financial security on the primary market, knowing that it will be difficult to sell it on the secondary market?

Consequently, it makes no economic sense to grant tax advantages, for example, to investments in the primary market without offering the same advantages to investments in the secondary market. Otherwise, investors quickly realise that the advantage is fictitious, because they will lose out when they try to sell the investment in the secondary market.

The secondary market determines the price at which the company can issue its securities on the primary market, because investors are constantly deciding between existing investments and proposed new investments.

We have seen that it would be a mistake to think that a financial manager takes no interest in the secondary market for the securities issued by his company. On the contrary, it is on the secondary market that his company's financial "raw material" is priced every day. When the raw material is equities, there is another reason the company cannot afford to turn its back on the secondary market: this is where investors trade the voting rights in the company's affairs and, by extension, control of the company.

3/ DERIVATIVE MARKETS: FUTURES AND OPTIONS

Derivative markets are where securities that derive their value from another asset (share, bond, commodity or even climate index) are traded. There are two main types of derivative products: options (which we will develop in Chapter 24 as they have become a key matter in financial theory and practice) and futures (Chapter 49).

Derivatives are instruments for taking positions on other instruments, or "contracts" on "contracts". They let you take significant short or long positions on other assets with a limited outlay of funds.

Derivative instruments are tailored especially to the management of financial risk. By using derivatives, the financial manager chooses a price – expressed as an interest rate, an exchange rate or the price of a raw material – that is independent of the company's financing or investment term. Derivatives are also highly liquid. The financial manager can change his mind at any time at a minimal cost.

Section 1.4
MOST IMPORTANTLY, HE IS A NEGOTIATOR . . .

Let's return to our financial manager who has just created a financial security. Because the security is traded on a secondary market, he doesn't know who holds the securities. Nor does he know who has sold it, especially as, via the futures market, investors can sell the security without ever having bought it.

But what exactly is our financial manager selling? Or, put another way: how can the value of the financial security be determined?

From a practical standpoint, the financial manager "sells" management's reputation for integrity, its expertise, the quality of the company's assets, its overall financial health, its ability to generate a certain level of profitability over a given period and its commitment to more or less restrictive legal terms. Note that the quality of assets will be particularly important in the case of a loan tied to and often secured by specific assets, while the overall financial health will dominate when financing is not tied to specific assets.

Theoretically, the financial manager sells expected future cash flows that can derive only from the company's business operations.

A company cannot distribute more cash flow to its providers of funds than its business generates. A money-losing company pays its creditors only at the expense of its shareholders. When a company with sub-par profitability pays a dividend, it jeopardises its financial health.

The financial manager's role is to transform the company's commercial and industrial business assets and commitments into financial assets and commitments.

In so doing, he spreads the expected cash flows among many different investor groups: banks, financial investors, family shareholders, individual investors, etc.

Far from building castles in the sky, the corporate financial manager transforms the company's economic activity into cash flows that he offers (or rather sells) to financial investors.

Financial investors then turn these flows into negotiable instruments traded on an open market, which value the instruments in relation to other opportunities available on the market.

Underlying the securities is the market's evaluation of the company. A company considered to be poorly managed will see investors vote with their feet. Yields on the company's securities will rise to prohibitive levels and prices on them will fall. Financial difficulties, if not already present, will soon follow. The financial manager must therefore keep the market convinced at all times of the quality of his company, because that is what backs up the securities it issues!

The different financial partners hold a portion of the value of the company. This diversity gives rise to yet another job for the financial manager: **he must adroitly steer the company through the distribution of the overall value of the company.**

Like any dealmaker, he has something to sell, but he must also:

* assess his company's overall financial situation;
* understand the motivations of the various participants;
* analyse the relative powers of the parties involved.

Section 1.5
. . . WHO NEVER FORGETS TO DO AN OCCASIONAL REALITY CHECK!

The financial investors who buy the company's securities do so not out of altruism, but because they hope to realise a certain rate of return on their investment, in the form of interest, dividends or capital gains. In other words, in return for entrusting the company with their money via their purchase of the company's securities, they require a minimum return on their investment.

Consequently, the financial manager must make sure that over the medium term, the company makes investments with returns at least equal to the rate of return expected by the company's providers of capital. If so, all is well. If not, if the company is consistently falling short of this goal, it will destroy value, turning what was worth 100 into 90, or 80. This is corporate purgatory. On the other hand, if the profitability of its investments consistently exceeds investor demands, transforming 100 into 120 or more, the company deserves the kudos it will get. But it should also remain humble. With technological progress and deregulation advancing apace, repeat performances are becoming more and more challenging.

The financial manager must therefore analyse proposed investment projects and explain to his colleagues that some should not be undertaken because they are not profitable enough. In short, he sometimes has to be a "party-pooper". He is indirectly the spokesman of the financial investment community.

The financial manager must ensure that the company creates value, that the assets it has assembled will generate a rate of return into the medium term that is at least equal to the rate required by the investors whose capital has enabled the company to build those assets.

Section 1.6
. . . HE IS ALSO NOW A RISK MANAGER

Over the last 40 years, fluctuations in interest rates, currencies and the prices of raw materials have become so great that financial risks have become as important as industrial risks. Consider a Swiss company that buys copper in the world market, then processes it and sells it in Switzerland and abroad.

Its performance depends not only on the price of copper but also on the exchange rate of the US dollar vs. the Swiss franc, because it uses the dollar to make purchases abroad and receives payment in dollars for international sales. Lastly, interest rate fluctuations have an impact on the company's financial flows. A multi-headed dragon!

The company must manage its specific interest rate and exchange rate risks because doing nothing can also have serious consequences. As the bumper sticker says, "if you think education is expensive, try ignorance!"

Take an example of an economy with no derivative markets. A corporate treasurer anticipating a decline in long-term interest rates and whose company has long-term debt has no choice but to borrow short term, invest the proceeds long term, wait for interest rates to decline, pay off the short-term loans and borrow again. You will have no trouble understanding that this strategy has its limits. The balance sheet becomes inflated, intermediation costs rise, and so on. Derivative markets enable the treasurer to manage this long-term interest rate risk without touching his company's balance sheet.

Generally, the CFO is responsible for the identification, the assessment and the management of risks for the firm. This includes not only currency and interest rate risks but also liquidity and counterparty risk. Recent years have shown that a CFO with strong know-how in such matters will be highly appreciated.

How's that appetite?

We're going to leave you with these appetisers in the hope that you are now hungry for more. But beware of taking the principles briefly presented here and skipping directly to Section III of the book. If you are looking for high finance and get-rich-quick schemes, this book might not be for you. The menu we propose is as follows:

- First, an understanding of the firm, i.e. the source of all the cash flows that are the subject of our analysis (**Section I: Financial analysis**).
- Then an appreciation of markets, because it is they who are constantly valuing the firm (**Section II: Investors and markets**).
- Then an understanding of how value is created and how it is measured (**Section III: Value**).
- Followed by the major financial decisions of the firm, viewed in the light of both market theory and organisational theory (**Section IV: Corporate financial policies**).
- Finally, if you persevere through the foregoing, you will get to taste the dessert, as **Section V** presents several practical, current topics in financial management.

The summary of this chapter can be downloaded from www.vernimmen.com.

The financial manager has two roles:

SUMMARY

- To ensure the company has enough funds to finance its expansion and meet its obligations.

    To do this, the company issues securities (equity and debt) and the financial manager sells them to financial investors at the highest possible price. In today's capital market economy, the role of the financial manager is less a buyer of funds, with an objective to minimise cost, and more a seller of financial securities. By emphasising the financial security, we focus on its value, which combines the notions of return and risk. We thereby de-emphasise the importance of minimising the cost of financial resources, because this approach ignores the risk factor. Casting the financial manager in the role of salesman also underlines the marketing aspect of his job, which is far from theoretical. He has customers (investors) that he must convince to buy the securities his company issues. The better he understands their needs, the more successful he will be.

- To ensure that over the long run the company uses the resources investors put at its disposal to generate a rate of return at least equal to the rate of return the investors require. If it does, the company creates value. If it does not, it destroys value. If it continues to destroy value, investors will turn their backs on the company and the value of its securities will decline. Ultimately, the company will have to change its senior managers, or face bankruptcy.

In his first role, the financial manager transforms the company's real assets into financial assets. He must maximise the value of these financial assets while selling them to the various categories of investors.

His second role is a thankless one. He must be a "party-pooper", a "Mr No" who examines every proposed investment project under the microscope of expected returns and advises on whether to reject those that fall below the cost of funds available to the company.

QUESTIONS

1/ Should the unexpected announcement of a rise in interest rates automatically result in a drop in the stock market index?

2/ Would your answer be the same if the announcement had been anticipated by the market? So what is the most important factor when valuing securities?

3/ Other than the word "market", what in your view is the key word in corporate finance?

4/ How is it possible to sell something without actually having bought anything?

5/ You are offered a loan at 7.5% over 10 years without guarantee, and a loan at 7% over 10 years with guarantee. You need the loan. How should you go about deciding which loan to take out?

6/ Is a financial security a financial asset or a financial liability? Why?

7/ Can you define a financial security?

8/ Provide an example of something that was assumed to be a financial asset, but which proved on analysis to be a financial liability.

9/ How important is it to think in terms of an offer of and a demand for securities, and not in terms of an offer of and a demand for capital, for:

- ○ shares;
- ○ bonds;
- ○ medium-term syndicated loans;
- ○ bilateral bank loans.

Why?

10/ What other financial term should immediately spring to mind when you hear the word "returns"?

11/In your view, are more securities issued on the primary market or exchanged on the secondary market?

12/What other financial term should immediately spring to mind when you hear the word "risk"?

13/Which instrument carries the greater risk – a share or a bond? Why?

14/Explain how the poor performance of the secondary market can impact the primary market.

15/What are the two biggest flaws of a bad financial manager?

16/What are the two main types of securities issued by a firm?

17/Why do you believe management has to do some roadshows before issuing new shares or bonds?

18/Why would you finance a firm's investments with a very short term loan? What would the drawback be?

More questions are waiting for you at www.vernimmen.com.

1/*As an automatic reaction, yes as value moves in the opposite direction to interest rates.*

2/*The answer in this case would be no. The most important factor in valuing securities is anticipation.*

3/*Value.*

4/*On the futures market.*

5/*Is it worth providing a guarantee for a gain of 0.5%?*

6/*A financial asset if the present value of future flows is positive (which it is for the investor), and a liability if not (which is the case for the issuer).*

7/*A financial security is a tradable contract represented by a series of cash flows to be received according to a set timetable.*

8/*The inheritance of an estate, the debts of which exceed the value of the assets.*

9/*In order – 1 = very important; 2 = of moderate importance; 3 = unimportant: 1223, because they are more easily traded.*

10/*Risk.*

11/*No, far fewer securities are issued on the primary market than exchanged on the secondary market. In 2010, worldwide, listed companies issued $1012 bn worth of new shares, whereas the value of shares exchanged was $63 090 bn (source: World Federation of Exchanges).*

12/*Returns, the two are inextricably linked.*

13/*Shares, as returns are not guaranteed for the investor, and creditors are paid out before shareholders.*

14/*If the value of shares continues to decline long term, market pessimism descends, and investors become reluctant to subscribe shares on the primary market, as they are convinced that the value of such shares will fall once issued.*

15/*Shortsightedness and poor marketing skills.*

16/*Shares and debts (loans and bonds).*

17/ *This is called marketing: they are trying to sell at best one product which is a financial instrument in order to lower their cost of funding.*

18/ *To benefit from lower interest rates (as we will see in Chapter 20, short-term interest rates are generally lower than long-term interest rates). But in that case the firm will run a strong liquidity risk as it will constantly be subject to the availability of loans on the market. The firm would probably be better off taking a long-term financing.*

BIBLIOGRAPHY

S. Mian, On the choice and replacement of chief financial officers, *Journal of Financial Economics*, **60**(1), 143–175, April 2001.

R. Norton, *CFO Thought Leaders*, Strategy Business Books, 2005.

M. Scott, *Achieving Fair Value: How Companies Can Better Manage Their Relationships with Investors*, John Wiley & Sons, Ltd, 2005.

Section I
FINANCIAL ANALYSIS

PART ONE
FUNDAMENTAL CONCEPTS IN
FINANCIAL ANALYSIS

The following six chapters provide a gradual introduction to the foundations of financial analysis. They examine the concepts of cash flow, earnings, capital employed and invested capital, and look at the ways in which these concepts are linked.

Chapter 2

CASH FLOW

Let's work from A to Z (unless it turns out to be Z to A!)

In the introduction, we emphasised the importance of cash flows as the basic building block of securities. Likewise, we need to start our study of corporate finance by analysing company cash flows.

CLASSIFYING COMPANY CASH FLOWS

Let's consider, for example, the monthly account statement that individual customers receive from their bank. It is presented as a series of lines showing the various inflows and outflows of money on precise dates and in some cases the type of transaction (deposit of cheques, for instance).

Our first step is to trace the rationale for each of the entries on the statement, which could be everyday purchases, payment of a salary, automatic transfers, loan repayments or the receipt of bond coupons, to mention but a few examples.

The corresponding task for a financial manager is to reclassify company cash flows by category to draw up a cash flow document that can be used to:

- analyse past trends in cash flow (the document put together is generally known as a cash flow statement[1]); or
- project future trends in cash flow, over a shorter or longer period (the document needed is a cash flow budget or plan).

With this goal in mind, we will now demonstrate that cash flows can be classified into one of the following processes:

- Activities that form part of the industrial and commercial life of a company:

  ○ operating cycle;
  ○ investment cycle.

- Financing activities to fund these cycles:

  ○ the debt cycle;
  ○ the equity cycle.

1 *Or sometimes as a statement of changes in financial position.*

Section 2.1
OPERATING AND INVESTMENT CYCLES

1/ THE IMPORTANCE OF THE OPERATING CYCLE

Let's take the example of a greengrocer, who is "cashing up" one evening. What does he find? Firstly, he sees how much he spent in cash at the wholesale market in the morning and then the cash proceeds from fruit and vegetable sales during the day. If we assume that the greengrocer sold all the produce he bought in the morning at a mark-up, the balance of receipts and payments for the day will be a cash surplus.

Unfortunately, things are usually more complicated in practice. Rarely are all the goods bought in the morning sold by the evening, especially in the case of a manufacturing business.

A company processes raw materials as part of an operating cycle, the length of which varies tremendously, from a day in the newspaper sector to seven years in the cognac sector. There is, thus, a time lag between purchases of raw materials and the sale of the corresponding finished goods.

And this time lag is not the only complicating factor. It is unusual for companies to buy and sell in cash. Usually, their suppliers grant them extended payment periods, and they in turn grant their customers extended payment periods. The money received during the day does not necessarily come from sales made on the same day.

As a result of customer credit[2], supplier credit[3] and the time it takes to manufacture and sell products or services, the operating cycle of each and every company spans a certain period, **leading to timing differences between operating outflows and the corresponding operating inflows.**

Each business has its own operating cycle of a certain length that, from a cash flow standpoint, may lead to positive or negative cash flows at different times. Operating outflows and inflows from different cycles are analysed by period, e.g. by month or by year. The balance of these flows is called **operating cash flow**. Operating cash flow reflects the cash flows generated by operations during a given period.

In concrete terms, operating cash flow represents the cash flow generated by the company's day-to-day operations. Returning to our initial example of an individual looking at his bank statement, it represents the difference between the receipts and normal outgoings, such as food, electricity and car maintenance costs.

Naturally, unless there is a major timing difference caused by some unusual circumstances (startup period of a business, very strong growth, very strong seasonal fluctuations), the balance of operating receipts and payments should be positive.

Readers with accounting knowledge will note that operating cash flow is independent of any accounting policies, which makes sense since it relates only to cash flows. More specifically:

- neither the company's depreciation and provisioning policy,
- nor its inventory valuation method,
- nor the techniques used to defer costs over several periods have any impact on the figure.

However, the concept is affected by decisions about how to classify payments between investment and operating outlays, as we will now examine more closely.

2 *That is credit granted by the company to its customers, allowing them to pay the bill several days, weeks or in some countries, even several months, after receiving the invoice.*

3 *That is credit granted by suppliers to the company.*

2/ INVESTMENT AND OPERATING OUTFLOWS

Let's return to the example of our greengrocer, who now decides to add frozen food to his business.

The operating cycle will no longer be the same. The greengrocer may, for instance, begin receiving deliveries once a week only and will therefore have to run much larger inventories. Admittedly, the impact of the longer operating cycle due to much larger inventories may be offset by larger credit from his suppliers. The key point here is to recognise that the operating cycle will change.

The operating cycle is different for each business and, generally speaking, the more sophisticated the end product, the longer the operating cycle.

But most importantly, before he can start up this new activity, our greengrocer needs to invest in a chest freezer.

What difference is there, from solely a cash flow standpoint, between this investment and operating outlays?

The outlay on the chest freezer seems to be a prerequisite. It forms the basis for a new activity, the success of which is unknown. It appears to carry higher risks and will be beneficial only if overall operating cash flow generated by the greengrocer increases. Lastly, **investments are carried out from a long-term perspective and have a longer life than that of the operating cycle**. Indeed, they last for several operating cycles, even if they do not last forever given the fast pace of technological progress.

This justifies the distinction, from a cash flow perspective, between operating and investment outflows.

Normal outflows, from an individual's perspective, differ from an investment outflow in that they afford enjoyment, whereas investment represents abstinence. As we will see, this type of decision represents one of the vital underpinnings of finance. Only the very puritanically minded would take more pleasure from buying a microwave than from spending the same amount of money at a restaurant! One of these choices can only be an investment and the other an ordinary outflow. So what purpose do investments serve? Investment is worthwhile only if the decision to forgo normal spending, which gives instant pleasure, will subsequently lead to greater gratification.

From a cash flow standpoint, an investment is an outlay that is subsequently expected to increase operating cash flow such that overall the individual will be happy to have forsaken instant gratification.

This is the definition of the **return on investment** (be it industrial or financial) from a cash flow standpoint. We will use this definition throughout this book.

Like the operating cycle, the investment cycle is characterised by a series of inflows and outflows. But the length of the investment cycle is far longer than the length of the operating cycle.

The purpose of investment outlays (also frequently called capital expenditures) is to alter the operating cycle, e.g. to boost or enhance the cash flows that it generates.

The impact of investment outlays is spread over several operating cycles. Financially, capital expenditures are worthwhile only if inflows generated thanks to these expenditures exceed the outflows by an amount yielding at least the return on investment expected by the investor.

Note also that a company may sell some assets in which it has invested in the past. For instance, our greengrocer may decide after several years to trade in his freezer for a larger model. The proceeds would also be part of the investment cycle.

3/ FREE CASH FLOW

Before-tax free cash flow is defined as the difference between operating cash flow and capital expenditure net of fixed asset disposals.

As we shall see in Sections II and III of this book, free cash flow can be calculated before or after tax. It also forms the basis for the most important valuation technique. Operating cash flow is a concept that depends on how expenditure is classified between operating and investment outlays. Since this distinction is not always clear-cut, operating cash flow is not widely used in practice, with free cash flow being far more popular. If free cash flow turns negative, additional financial resources will have to be raised to cover the company's cash flow requirements.

Section 2.2
FINANCIAL RESOURCES

The operating and investment cycles give rise to a timing difference in cash flows. Employees and suppliers have to be paid before customers settle up. Likewise, investments have to be completed before they generate any receipts. Naturally, this cash flow deficit needs to be filled. This is the role of financial resources.

The purpose of financial resources is simple: they must cover the shortfalls resulting from these timing differences by providing the company with sufficient funds to balance its cash flow.

These financial resources are provided by investors: shareholders, debtholders, lenders, etc. These financial resources are not provided "no strings attached". In return for providing the funds, investors expect to be subsequently "rewarded" by receiving dividends or interest payments, registering capital gains, etc. This can happen only if the operating and investment cycles generate positive cash flows.

To the extent that the financial investors have made the investment and operating activities possible, they expect to receive, in various different forms, their fair share of the surplus cash flows generated by these cycles.

The financing cycle is therefore the "flip side" of the investment and operating cycles.

At its most basic, the principle would be to finance these shortfalls solely using capital that incurs the risk of the business. Such capital is known as **shareholders' equity**. This type of financial resource forms the cornerstone of the entire financial system. Its importance is such that shareholders providing it are granted decision-making powers and control over the business in various different ways. From a cash flow standpoint, the equity cycle comprises inflows from capital increases and outflows in the form of dividend payments to the shareholders.

Without casting any doubt on their managerial capabilities, all our readers have probably had to cope with cash flow shortfalls, if only as part of their personal financial affairs. The usual approach in such circumstances is to talk to a banker. Your banker will only give you a loan if he believes that you will be able to repay the loan with interest. Bank loans may be short term (overdraft facilities) or long term (e.g. a loan to buy an apartment).

Like individuals, a business may decide to ask lenders rather than shareholders to help it cover a cash flow shortage. Bankers will lend funds only after they have carefully analysed the company's financial health. They want to be nearly certain of being repaid and do not want exposure to the company's business risk. These cash flow shortages may be short term or long term, but lenders do not want to take on business risk. The capital they provide represents the company's **debt capital**.

The debt cycle is the following: the business arranges borrowings in return for a commitment to repay the capital and make interest payments regardless of trends in its operating and investment cycles. These undertakings represent firm commitments, ensuring that the lender is certain of recovering its funds provided that the commitments are met. This definition applies to both:

- financing for the investment cycle, with the increase in future net receipts set to cover capital repayments and interest payments on borrowings; and
- financing for the operating cycle, with credit making it possible to bring forward certain inflows or to defer certain outflows.

From a cash flow standpoint, the life of a business comprises an operating and an investment cycle, leading to a positive or negative free cash flow. If free cash flow is negative, the financing cycle covers the funding shortfall.

As the future is unknown, a distinction has to be drawn between:

- equity, where the only commitment is to enable the shareholders to benefit fully from the success of the venture;
- debt capital, where the only commitment is to meet the capital repayments and interest payments regardless of the success or failure of the venture.

The risk incurred by the lender is that this commitment will not be met. Theoretically speaking, debt may be regarded as an advance on future cash flows generated by the investments made and guaranteed by the company's shareholders' equity.

Although a business needs to raise funds to finance investments, it may also find, at a given point in time, that it has a cash surplus, i.e. the funds available exceed cash requirements.

These surplus funds are then invested in short-term investments and marketable securities that generate revenue, called financial income.

Although at first sight short-term financial investments (marketable securities) may be regarded as investments since they generate a rate of return, we advise readers to consider them instead as the opposite of debt. As we will see, company treasurers often have to raise additional debt just to reinvest those funds in short-term investments without speculating in any way.

These investments are generally realised with a view to ensuring the possibility of a very quick exit without any risk of losses.

Debt and short-term financial investments or marketable securities should not be considered independently of each other, but as inextricably linked. We suggest that readers **reason in terms of debt net of short-term financial investments** and **financial expense net of financial income**.

Putting all the individual pieces together, we arrive at the following simplified cash flow statement, with the balance reflecting the net decrease in the company's debt during a given period:

SIMPLIFIED CASH FLOW STATEMENT

	2010	2011	2012
Operating receipts			
− Operating payments			
= **Operating cash flow**			
− Capital expenditure			
+ Fixed asset disposals			
= **Free cash flow before tax**			
− Financial expense net of financial income			
− Corporate income tax			
+ Proceeds from share issue			
− Dividends paid			
= **Net decrease in debt**			
With:			
Repayments of borrowings			
− New bank and other borrowings			
+ Change in marketable securities			
+ Change in cash and cash equivalents			
= **Net decrease in debt**			

SUMMARY

The summary of this chapter can be downloaded from www.vernimmen.com.

The cash flows of a company can be divided into four categories, i.e. operating and investment flows, which are generated as part of its business activities, and debt and equity flows, which finance these activities.

The operating cycle is characterised by a time lag between the positive and negative cash flows deriving from the length of the production process (which varies from business to business) and the commercial policy (customer and supplier credit).

Operating cash flow, the balance of funds generated by the various operating cycles in progress, comprises the cash flows generated by a company's operations during a given period. It represents the (usually positive) difference between operating receipts and payments.

From a cash flow standpoint, capital expenditures must alter the operating cycle in such a way as to generate higher operating inflows going forward than would otherwise have been the case. Capital expenditures are intended to enhance the operating cycle by enabling it to achieve a higher level of profitability in the long term. This profitability can be measured only over several operating cycles, unlike operating payments, which belong to a single cycle. As a result, investors forgo immediate use of their funds in return for higher cash flows over several operating cycles.

Free cash flow can be defined as operating cash flow minus capital expenditure (investment outlays).

When a company's free cash flow is negative, it covers its funding shortfall through its financing cycle by raising equity and debt capital.

Since shareholders' equity is exposed to business risk, the returns paid on it are unpredictable and depend on the success of the venture. Where a business rounds out its financing with debt capital, it undertakes to make capital repayments and interest payments (financial expense) to its lenders regardless of the success of the venture. Accordingly, debt represents an advance on the operating receipts generated by the investment that is guaranteed by the company's shareholders' equity.

Short-term financial investment, the rationale for which differs from capital expenditures, and cash should be considered in conjunction with debt. We will always reason in terms of net debt (i.e. net of cash and of marketable securities, which are short-term financial investments) and net financial expense (i.e. net of financial income).

QUESTIONS

1/ What are the four basic cycles of a company?

2/ Why do we say that financial flows are the flip side of investment and operating flows?

3/ Define operating cash flow. Should the company be able to spend this surplus as it likes?

4/ Is operating cash flow an accounting profit?

5/ Why do we say that, as a general rule, operating cash flow should be positive? Provide a simple example that demonstrates that operating cash flow can be negative during periods of strong growth, startup periods and in the event of strong seasonal fluctuations.

6/ When a cash flow budget is drawn up for the purposes of assessing an investment, can free cash flows be negative? If so, is it more likely that this will be the case at the beginning or at the end of the business plan period? Why?

7/ Among the following different flows, which will be appropriated by both shareholders and lenders: operating receipts, operating cash flow, free cash flows? Who has priority, shareholders or lenders? Why?

8/ A feature of a supermarket chain such as Tesco or Ahold is a very fast rotation of food stocks (six days), cash payments by customers, long supplier credit periods (60 days) and very low administrative costs. Will the operating cycle generate cash requirements or a cash surplus?

9/ Should the cash outflows of launching a new perfume be considered as an operating outlay or an investment outlay?

10/ How is an investment decision analysed from a cash standpoint?

11/ After reading this chapter, can you guess how to define bankruptcy?

12/ Is debt capital risk free for the lender? Can you analyse what the risk is? Why do some borrowers default on loans?

More questions are waiting for you at www.vernimmen.com.

EXERCISES

1/ Boomwichers NV, a Dutch company financed by shareholders' equity only, decides, during the course of year n, to finance an investment project worth €200m using shareholders' equity (50%) and debt (50%). The loan it takes out (€100m) will be paid off in full in $n+5$, and the company will pay 5% interest per year over the period. At the end of the period, you are asked to complete the following simplified table (no further investments are to be made):

Period	n	$n+1$	$n+2$	$n+3$	$n+4$	$n+5$
Operating inflows	165	200	240	280	320	360
Operating outflows	165	175	180	185	180	190
Operating cash flows						
Investments	−200					
Free cash flows						
Flows . . .						
. . . *to creditors*						
. . . *to shareholders*						

What do you conclude from the above?

2/ Ellingham plc opens a Spanish subsidiary, which starts operating on 2 January 2011. On 2 January 2011 it has to buy a machine costing €30m, partly financed by a €20m bank loan repayable in instalments of €2m every 15 July and 15 January over 5 years. Financial expenses, payable on a half-yearly basis, are as follows:

2011		2012		2013		2014		2015	
June	Dec	June	Dec	June	Dec	June	Dec	June	Dec
1	0.9	0.8	0.7	0.6	0.5	0.4	0.3	0.2	0.1

Profits are tax free. Sales will be €12m per month. A month's inventory of finished products will have to be built up. Customers pay at 90 days.

The company is keen to have a month's worth of advance purchases and, accordingly, plans to buy two months' worth of supplies in January 2011. Requirements in a normal month amount to €4m.

The supplier grants the company a 90-day payment period. Other costs are:

○   personnel costs of €4m per month;
○   shipping, packaging and other costs amounting to €2m per month and paid at 30 days. These costs are incurred from 1 January 2011.

Draw up a monthly and an annual cash flow plan.

How much cash will the subsidiary need at the end of each month over the first year? And if operations are identical, how much will it need each month over 2012? What is the change in the cash position over 2012 (no additional investments are planned)?

Questions

1/ *Operating, investment, debt and equity cycles.*
2/ *Because negative free cash flows generated by operating and investment cycles must be compensated by resources from the financial cycle. When free cash flows are positive, they are entirely absorbed by the financial cycle (debts are repaid, dividends are paid, etc).*
3/ *It is the balance of the operating cycle. No, as it has to repay bank debts when they are due, for example.*
4/ *No, it is a cash flow, not an accounting profit.*
5/ *It measures flows generated by the company's operations, i.e. its business or "raison d'être". If it is not positive in the long term, the company will be in trouble. Major shortfall due to operating cycle, large inventories, operating losses on startup, heavy swings in operating cycle.*
6/ *Yes. At the beginning, an investment may need time to run at full speed.*
7/ *Free cash flows since all operating or investment outlays have been paid. The lenders because of contractual agreement.*
8/ *A cash surplus, as customer receipts come in before suppliers are paid.*
9/ *Investment outlays, from which the company will benefit over several financial years as the product is being put onto the market.*
10/ *Expenditure should generate inflows over several financial periods.*
11/ *The inability to find additional resources to meet the company's financial obligations.*
12/ *No. The risk is the borrowers' failure to honour contracts either because of inability to repay due to poor business conditions or because of bad faith.*

Exercises

A detailed Excel version of the solutions is available at www.vernimmen.com.

1/ *Boomwichers NV*

Period	n	n+1	n+2	n+3	n+4	n+5
Operating inflows	165	200	240	280	320	360
Operating outflows	165	175	180	185	180	190
Operating cash flows	0	25	60	95	140	170
Investments	−200	0	0	0	0	0
Free cash flows	−200	25	60	95	140	170
Flows . . .						
. . . to creditors	−100	5	5	5	5	105
. . . to shareholders	−100	20	55	90	135	65

The investment makes it possible to repay creditors and leave cash for shareholders.

2/ *Ellingham plc exercise, see page 70.*

BIBLIOGRAPHY

To learn more about cash flows:

G. Friedlob, R. Welton, *Keys to Reading an Annual Report*, 4th edn, Barrons Educational Series, 2008.
E. Helfert, *Techniques of Financial Analysis*, 11th edn, Irwin, 2002.

Chapter 3
EARNINGS

Time to put our accounting hat on!

Following our analysis of company cash flows, it is time to consider the issue of how a company creates wealth. In this chapter, we are going to study the income statement to show how the various cycles of a company create wealth.

Section 3.1
ADDITIONS TO WEALTH AND DEDUCTIONS FROM WEALTH

What would your spontaneous answer be to the following questions?

* Does purchasing an apartment make you richer or poorer?
* Would your answer change if you were to buy the apartment on credit?

There can be no doubt as to the correct answer. Provided that you pay the market price for the apartment, your wealth is not affected whether or not you buy it on credit. Our experience as university lecturers has shown us that students often confuse cash and wealth.

Cash and wealth are two of the fundamental concepts of corporate finance. It is vital to be able to juggle them around and thus be able to differentiate between them confidently.

Consequently, we advise readers to train their minds by analysing the impact of all transactions in terms of cash flows and wealth impacts.

For instance, when you buy an apartment, you become neither richer nor poorer, but your cash decreases. Arranging a loan makes you no richer or poorer than you were before (you owe the money), but your cash has increased. If a fire destroys your house and it was not insured, you are worse off, but your cash position has not changed, since you have not spent any money.

Raising debt is tantamount to increasing your financial resources and commitments at the same time. As a result, it has no impact on your net worth. Buying an apartment for cash results in a change in your assets (reduction in cash, increase in real estate assets) without any change in net worth. The possible examples are endless. **Spending money does not necessarily make you poorer. Likewise, receiving money does not necessarily make you richer.**

1 *Also called a
Profit and Loss
statement or
P&L account.*

The job of listing all the items that positively or negatively affect a company's wealth is performed by the **income statement**,[1] which shows all the additions to wealth (**revenues**) and all the deductions from wealth (**charges or expenses or costs**). The fundamental aim of all businesses is to increase wealth. Additions to wealth cannot be achieved without some deductions from wealth. In sum, earnings represent the difference between additions to and deductions from wealth.

	Revenues		Gross additions to wealth
−	Costs	−	gross deductions from wealth
=	Earnings	=	net additions to wealth (deductions from)

Earnings represent the difference between revenues and costs, leading to a change in net worth during a given period. Earnings are positive when wealth is created and negative when wealth is destroyed.

Since the rationale behind the income statement is not the same as for a cash flow statement, some cash flows do not appear on the income statement (those that neither generate nor destroy wealth). Likewise, some revenues and costs are not shown on the cash flow statement (because they have no impact on the company's cash position).

1/ Earnings and the operating cycle

The operating cycle forms the basis of the company's wealth. It consists of both:

- additions to wealth (products and services sold, i.e. products and services whose worth is recognised in the market); and
- deductions from wealth (consumption of raw materials or goods for resale, use of labour, use of external services such as transportation, taxes and other duties).

The very essence of a business is to increase wealth by means of its operating cycle.

Additions to wealth		Operating revenues
Deductions from wealth	−	Cash operating costs
	=	Earnings before interest, taxes, depreciation and amortisation (EBITDA)

Put another way, the result of the operating cycle is the balance of operating revenues and cash operating costs incurred to obtain these revenues. We will refer to it as gross operating profit or EBITDA (earnings before interest, taxes, depreciation and amortisation).

It may be described as gross insofar as it covers just the operating cycle and is calculated before non-cash expenses such as depreciation and amortisation, and before interest and taxes.

2/ EARNINGS AND THE INVESTING CYCLE

(a) Principles

Investing activities do not appear directly on the income statement. In a wealth-oriented approach, an investment represents a use of funds that retains some value.

To invest is to forgo liquid funds: an asset is purchased but no wealth is destroyed. As a result, investments never appear directly on the income statement.

That said, the value of investments may change during a financial year:

- it may decrease if they suffer wear and tear or become obsolete;
- it may increase if the market value of certain assets rises. Even so, by virtue of the principle of prudence, increases in value are recorded only if realised through the disposal of the asset.

(b) Accounting for a decrease in the value of fixed assets

The decrease in value of a fixed asset due to its use by the company is accounted for by means of **depreciation** and **amortisation**.[2]

Impairment losses or write-downs on fixed assets recognise the loss in value of an asset not related to its day-to-day use, i.e. the unforeseen diminution in the value of:

- an intangible asset (goodwill, patents, etc.);
- a tangible asset (property, plant and equipment);
- an investment in a subsidiary.

Depreciation and amortisation on fixed assets are so-called "non-cash" costs insofar as they merely reflect arbitrary accounting assessments of the loss in value.

As we shall see, there are other types of non-cash costs, such as impairment losses on fixed assets, write-downs on current assets (which are included in operating costs) and provisions.

2 Amortisation is sometimes used instead of depreciation, particularly in the context of intangible assets.

3/ THE DISTINCTION BETWEEN OPERATING COSTS AND FIXED ASSETS

Although we are easily able to define investment from a cash flow perspective, we recognise that our approach goes against the grain of the traditional presentation, especially as far as those familiar with accounting are concerned:

- Whatever is consumed as part of the operating cycle to create something new belongs to the operating cycle. Without wishing to philosophise, we note that the act of creation always entails some form of destruction.
- Whatever is used without being destroyed directly, thus retaining its value, belongs to the investment cycle. This represents an immutable asset or, in accounting terms, a fixed asset (a "non-current asset" in IFRS terminology).

For instance, to make bread, a baker uses flour, salt and water, all of which form part of the end product. The process also entails labour, which has a value only insofar as it transforms the raw material into the end product. At the same time, the baker also needs a bread oven, which is absolutely essential for the production process, but is not destroyed by it. Though this oven may experience wear and tear, it will be used many times over.

This is the major distinction that can be drawn between operating costs and fixed assets. It may look deceptively straightforward, but in practice is no clearer than the distinction between investment and operating outlays. For instance, does an advertising campaign represent a charge linked solely to one period with no impact on any other? Or does it represent the creation of an asset (e.g. a brand)?

4/ THE COMPANY'S OPERATING PROFIT

From EBITDA, which is linked to the operating cycle, we deduct non-cash costs, which comprise depreciation and amortisation and impairment losses or write-downs on fixed assets.

This gives us operating income or operating profit or EBIT (Earnings Before Interest and Taxes), which reflects the increase in wealth generated by the company's industrial and commercial activities.

Operating profit or EBIT represents the earnings generated by investment and operating cycles for a given period.

The term "operating" contrasts with the term "financial", reflecting the distinction between the real world and the realms of finance. Indeed, operating income is the product of the company's industrial and commercial activities before its financing operations are taken into account. Operating profit or EBIT may also be called operating income, trading profit or operating result.

5/ EARNINGS AND THE FINANCING CYCLE

(a) Debt capital

Repayments of borrowings do not constitute costs but, as their name suggests, merely repayments.

Just as common sense tells us that securing a loan does not increase wealth, neither does repaying a borrowing represent a charge.

The income statement shows only costs related to borrowings. It never shows the repayments of borrowings, which are deducted from the debt recorded on the balance sheet.

We emphasise this point because our experience tells us that many mistakes are made in this area.

Conversely, we should note that the interest payments made on borrowings lead to a decrease in the wealth of the company and thus represent an expense for the company. As a result, they are shown on the income statement.

The difference between financial income and financial expense is called **net financial expense/(income)**.

The difference between operating profit and net financial expense is called **profit before tax and non-recurring items**.[3]

3 *Or non-recurrent items.*

(b) Shareholders' equity

From a cash flow standpoint, shareholders' equity is formed through issuance of shares minus outflows in the form of dividends or share buy-backs. These cash inflows give rise to ownership rights over the company. The income statement measures the creation of wealth by the company; it therefore naturally ends with the net earnings (also called net profit). Whether the net earnings are paid in dividends or not is a simple choice of cash position made by the shareholder.

If we take a step back, we see that net earnings and financial interest are based on the same principle of distributing the wealth created by the company. Likewise, income tax represents earnings paid to the State in spite of the fact that it does not contribute any funds to the company.

6/ Recurrent and non-recurrent items: extraordinary and exceptional items, discontinued operations

We have now considered all the operations of a business that may be allocated to the operating, investing and financing cycles of a company. That said, it is not hard to imagine the difficulties involved in classifying the financial consequences of certain **extraordinary** events, such as losses incurred as a result of earthquakes, other natural disasters or the expropriation of assets by a government.

They are not expected to occur frequently or regularly and are beyond the control of a company's management – hence, the idea of creating a separate catch-all category for precisely such extraordinary items.

Among the many different types of **exceptional** events, we will briefly focus on asset disposals. Investing forms an integral part of the industrial and commercial activities of businesses. But it would be foolhardy to believe that investment is a one-way process. The best-laid plans may fail, while others may lead down a strategic impasse.

Put another way, disinvesting is also a key part of an entrepreneur's activities. It generates exceptional "asset disposal" inflows on the cash flow statement and capital gains and losses on the income statement, which may appear under exceptional items.

Lastly, when a company disposes of some segments of its activity or entire sections of a business, the corresponding gains or losses are recorded under **discontinued operations.**

One of the main puzzles for the financial analyst is to identify whether an extraordinary or exceptional item can be described as recurrent or non-recurrent. If it is recurrent, it will occur again and again in the future. If it is not recurrent, it is simply a one-off item.

Without any doubt, extraordinary items and results from discontinued operations are non-recurrent items.

Exceptional items are much more tricky to analyse. In large groups, closure of plants, provisions for restructuring, etc. tend to happen every year in different divisions or countries. In some sectors, exceptional items are an intrinsic part of the business. A car rental company renews its fleet of cars every nine months and regularly registers capital gains. Exceptional items should then be analysed as recurrent items and as such be included in the operating profit. For smaller companies, exceptional items tend to be one-off items and as such should be seen as non-recurrent items.

Depending on accounting principles, firms are allowed to include more or fewer items in the exceptional/extraordinary items line. The International Accounting Standards Board (IASB) has decided to include extraordinary and exceptional items within operating without identifying them as such. Nevertheless, the real need for such a distinction has led a large number of companies reporting in IFRS to present a "recurring operating profit" (or similar term) before the operating profit line.

By definition, it is easier to analyse and forecast profit before tax and non-recurrent items than **net income or net profit**, which is calculated after the impact of non-recurrent items and tax.

Section 3.2
DIFFERENT INCOME STATEMENT FORMATS

Two main formats of income statement are frequently used, which differ in the way they present revenues and expenses related to the operating and investment cycles. They may be presented either:

4 *Also called by-destination income statement.*

5 *Also called by-category income statement.*

- **by function,**[4] i.e. according to the way revenues and costs are used in the operating and investing cycle. This shows the cost of goods sold, selling and marketing costs, research and development costs and general and administrative costs; or
- **by nature,**[5] i.e. by type of expenditure or revenue which shows the change in inventories of finished goods and in work in progress (closing minus opening inventory), purchases of and changes in inventories (closing minus opening inventory) of goods for resale and raw materials, other external costs, personnel expenses, taxes and other duties, depreciation and amortisation.

Thankfully, operating profit works out to be the same, irrespective of the format used!

The two different income statement formats can be summarised by the following diagram:

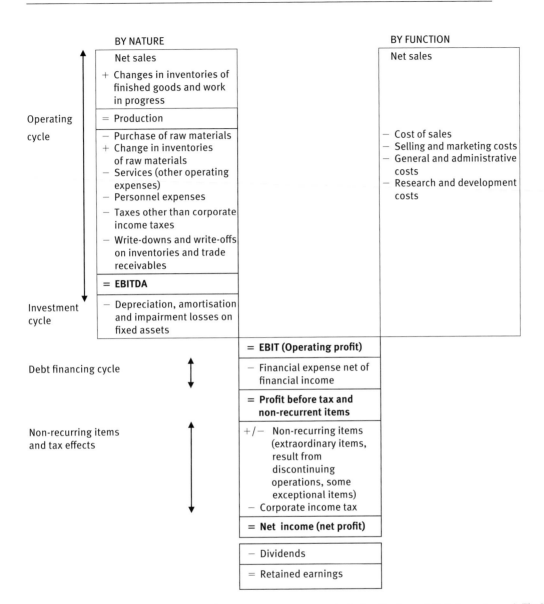

BY NATURE

	Net sales
+	Changes in inventories of finished goods and work in progress
=	Production
−	Purchase of raw materials
+	Change in inventories of raw materials
−	Services (other operating expenses)
−	Personnel expenses
−	Taxes other than corporate income taxes
−	Write-downs and write-offs on inventories and trade receivables
=	**EBITDA**
−	Depreciation, amortisation and impairment losses on fixed assets

Operating cycle

Investment cycle

BY FUNCTION

Net sales

− Cost of sales
− Selling and marketing costs
− General and administrative costs
− Research and development costs

=	**EBIT (Operating profit)**
−	Financial expense net of financial income
=	**Profit before tax and non-recurrent items**
+/−	Non-recurring items (extraordinary items, result from discontinuing operations, some exceptional items)
−	Corporate income tax
=	**Net income (net profit)**
−	Dividends
=	Retained earnings

Debt financing cycle

Non-recurring items and tax effects

The by-nature presentation predominates to a great extent in Italy, Spain and Belgium. In the US, the by-function presentation is used almost to the exclusion of any other form[6]

6 The US airline companies are an exception as most of them use the by-nature income statement.

Presentation	Brazil	China	France	Germany	India	Italy	Japan	Morocco	Russia	Switzerland	UK	US
By nature	23%	23%	33%	23%	90%	77%	17%	100%	33%	40%	33%	7%
By function	60%	73%	63%	77%	7%	23%	77%	0%	57%	53%	57%	67%
Other	17%	3%	3%	0%	3%	0%	7%	0%	10%	7%	10%	27%

Whereas in the past France, Germany, Switzerland and the UK tended to use systematically the by-nature or by-function format, the current situation is less clear-cut. Moreover, a new presentation is making some headway; it is mainly a by-function format but depreciation and amortisation is not included in the cost of goods sold, in selling and marketing costs, or research and development costs, but is isolated on a separate line.

1/ THE BY-FUNCTION INCOME STATEMENT FORMAT

This presentation is based on a management accounting approach, in which costs are allocated to the main corporate functions:

Function	Corresponding cost
Production	Cost of sales
Commercial	Selling and marketing costs
Research and development	Research and development costs
Administration	General and administrative costs

As a result, personnel expense is allocated to each of these four categories (or three where selling, general and administrative costs are pooled into a single category) depending on whether an individual employee works in production, sales, research or administration. Likewise, depreciation expense for a tangible fixed asset is allocated to production if it relates to production machinery, to selling and marketing costs if it concerns a car used by the sales team, to research and development costs if it relates to laboratory equipment, or to general and administrative costs in the case of the accounting department's computers, for example.

The underlying principle is very simple indeed. This format clearly shows that operating profit is the difference between sales and the cost of sales irrespective of their nature (i.e. production, sales, research and development, administration).

On the other hand, it does not differentiate between the operating and investment processes since depreciation and amortisation is not shown directly on the income statement (it is split up between the four main corporate functions), obliging analysts to track down the information in the cash flow statement or in the notes to the accounts.

2/ THE BY-NATURE INCOME STATEMENT FORMAT

This is the traditional presentation of income statements in many continental European countries, although some groups are dropping it in favour of the by-function format in their consolidated accounts.

The by-nature format is simple to apply, even for small companies, because no allocation of expenses is required. It offers a more detailed breakdown of costs.

Naturally, as in the previous approach, operating profit is still the difference between sales and the cost of sales.

In this format, costs are recognised as they are incurred rather than when the corresponding items are used. Showing on the income statement all purchases made and all invoices sent to customers during the same period would not be comparing like with like.

A business may transfer to the inventory some of the purchases made during a given year. The transfer of these purchases to the inventory does not destroy any wealth. Instead, it represents the formation of an asset, albeit probably a temporary one, but one that has real value at a given point in time. Secondly, some of the end products produced by the company may not be sold during the year and yet the corresponding costs appear on the income statement.

To compare like with like, it is necessary to:

- eliminate changes in inventories of raw materials and goods for resale from purchases to get raw materials and goods for resale used rather than simply purchased;
- add changes in the inventory of finished products and work in progress back to sales. As a result, the income statement shows **production** rather than just sales.

The by-nature format shows the amount spent on production for the period and not the total expenses under the accruals convention. It has the logical disadvantage that it seems to imply that changes in inventory are a revenue or an expense in their own right, which they are not. They are only an adjustment to purchases to obtain relevant costs.

Exercise 1 will help readers get to grips with the concept of changes in inventories of finished goods and work in progress.

To sum up, there are two different income statement formats:

- **the by-nature format** which is focused on production in which all the costs incurred during a given period are recorded. This amount then needs to be adjusted (for changes in inventories) so that it may be compared with products sold during the period;
- **the by-function format** which reasons directly in terms of the cost price of goods or services sold.

Either way, it is worth noting that EBITDA depends heavily on the inventory valuation methods used by the business. This emphasises the appeal of the by-nature format, which shows inventory changes on a separate line of the income statement and thus clearly indicates their order of magnitude.

Like operating cash flow, EBITDA is not influenced by the valuation methods applied to tangible and intangible fixed assets or the taxation system.

SUMMARY

The summary of this chapter can be downloaded from www.vernimmen.com.

A distinction needs to be made between cash and wealth. Spending money does not necessarily make you poorer and neither does receiving money necessarily make you any richer. Additions to wealth or deductions from wealth by a company are measured on the income statement. They are the difference between revenues and costs that increase a company's net worth during a given period.

From an accounting standpoint, operating costs reflect what is used up immediately in the operating cycle and somehow forms part of the end product. On the contrary, fixed assets are not destroyed directly during the production process and retain some of their value.

EBITDA (earnings before interest, taxes, depreciation and amortisation) shows the profit generated by the operating cycle (operating revenues – operating costs).

As part of the operating cycle, a business naturally builds up inventories, which are assets. These represent deferred costs, the impact of which needs to be eliminated in the calculation of EBITDA. In the by-nature format, this adjustment is made to operating revenues (by adding back changes in finished goods inventories) and to operating costs (by subtracting changes in inventories of raw materials and goods for resale from purchases). The by-function income statement shows merely sales and the cost of goods sold requiring no adjustment.

Capital expenditures never appear directly on the income statement, but they lead to an increase in the amount of fixed assets held. That said, an accounting assessment of impairment in the value of these investments leads to non-cash expenses, which are shown on the income statement (depreciation, amortisation and impairment losses on fixed assets).

EBIT (Earnings Before Interest and Taxes) shows the profit generated by the operating and investment cycles. In concrete terms, it represents the profit generated by the industrial and commercial activities of a business. It is allocated to:

- financial expense: only costs related to borrowings appear on the income statement, since capital repayments do not represent a destruction of wealth;

- corporate income tax;

- net income that is distributed to shareholders as dividends or transferred to the reserves (as retained earnings).

QUESTIONS

1/A company raises €500m in shareholders' equity for an R&D project. Has it become richer or poorer? By how much? What is your answer if the company spends half of the funds in the first two years, and the project does not produce results? In the third year, the company uses the remaining funds to acquire a competitor that is overvalued by 25%. But thanks to synergies with this new subsidiary, it is able to improve its earnings by €75m. Has it become richer or poorer? By how much?

2/What are the accounting items corresponding to additions to wealth for shareholders, lenders and the State?

3/In concrete terms, based on the diagram on page 35, by how much does a company create wealth over a given financial period? Why?

4/Comment on the following two statements: "This year, we're going to have to go into debt to cover our losses" and "We'll be able to buy out our main competitor, thanks to the profits we made this year".

5/In 2011, a company's free cash flow turns negative. Has the company created or destroyed wealth?

6/Is there a substantial difference between the income statement and the cash flow statement?

7/Does EBITDA always flow directly into a company's bank account?

8/Is it correct to say that a company's wealth is increased each year by the amount of EBITDA?

9/According to the terminology used in Chapter 2, is depreciation a cash outflow or a cost? What is the difference between these two concepts?

10/Analyse the similarities and the differences between cash and wealth, looking at, for example, investment in real estate and investment in research.

11/Will repayment of a loan always be recorded on the income statement? Will it always be recorded under a cash item?

12/Does the inflation-related increase in the nominal value of an asset appear on the income statement?

13/Why is the increase in inventories of raw materials deducted from purchases in the by-nature income statement format?

14/Why is change in finished goods inventories recorded under income in the by-nature income statement format?

15/Should the sale of a fixed asset be classified as part of the "ordinary course of business" of a company? How is it recorded on the income statement? Why under this heading?

16/Provide several examples illustrating the difference between cash receipts and revenues, cash expenses and costs.

17/What is a non-cash expense? What is a deferred charge? Describe their similarities and the differences between them.

More questions are waiting for you at www.vernimmen.com.

EXERCISES

1/ **Starjö AB**

You are asked by a Swedish company that assembles computers to draw up a by-nature and by-function income statement for year n. You are provided with the following information:

Retail price of a PC: €1500.

Cost of various components:

Parts	Price	Opening inventory	Closing inventory
Case	50	5	13
Mother board	200	8	2
Processor	300	4	11
Memory	100	6	4
Graphic card	50	1	13
Hard disk	150	5	10
Screen	200	3	3
DVD combo	50	7	19

Over the financial period, the company paid out €60 000 in salaries and social security contributions of 50% of that amount. The company produced 240 PCs. Closing stock of finished products was 27 units and opening stock 14 units.

At the end of the financial period, the manager of the company sells the premises that he had bought for €200 000 three years ago (which was depreciated over 40 years) for €230 000, it now occupies old premises that are fully depreciated, and pays off a €12 000 loan on which the company was paying interest at 5%. What impact do these transactions have on EBITDA, operating profits and net incomes? Tax is levied at a rate of 35%.

Over the course of the financial period, by how much did the company/the lenders/the company manager (who owns 50% of the shares) get richer/poorer?

2/ Ellingham plc

Draw up the income statement for 2011 in both the by-nature and by-function formats. Depreciation and amortisation come to €6m.

3/ Mumbai Oaks

Consider an Indian business that sells oak barrels to vineyards. At the start of the year, its inventory of finished products was zero. It sold 800 of the 900 barrels it had produced, leaving the closing inventory at 100 barrels. Each barrel sells for INR 10 000. To produce one barrel, the company spends INR 5000 on oak purchases and incurs INR 2000 in labour costs. In addition, the sales force generates costs of INR 450 000 per year and the fully outsourced administrative department incurs costs of INR 400 000 p.a. Annual depreciation expense related to the production facilities comes to INR 300 000. The opening inventory of raw materials was INR 400 000 and the closing inventory INR 500 000. In sum, the business spent INR 4 600 000 on raw materials.

Produce the by-nature income statement.

Assuming that depreciation breaks down into INR 200 000 for the production machinery, INR 70 000 for the sales facilities and INR 30 000 for the administrative facilities, produce the by-function income statement. Are you surprised that both formats give the same EBIT? Why? What do you think about Mumbai Oaks's EBIT margin?

4/ Singapore Kite Surf Magazine

You want to launch the first kite surf monthly magazine in Singapore. The economics are the following:

- For each issue you need to pay some friends for the articles $2000 (paid each month including social insurance charges);
- the magazine will be sold only by subscription, you know the universe of buyers and you believe you can sell 1500 subscriptions (no additional sales are expected in the short term);
- fabrication and delivery costs are $2 per magazine;

○ you believe you can sell the yearly subscription at $50;
○ you should benefit from income tax exemption for the first two years of operations.

You launch your project in September. You close your accounts in December. What will your income statement and cash-flow statement be for your first two financial years?

How can you finance your project?

ANSWERS

Questions

1/ *Neither. Zero, poorer by €250m. Richer by €25m: 75 − 250 × [25%/(1 + 25%)]*
2/ *Net income, financial expenses, corporate income tax.*
3/ *EBIT (Operating profit) + non-recurring items − corporate income tax. The wealth created is the wealth to be divided up between lenders (financial expenses), the State (corporate income tax) and shareholders (the balance).*
4/ *Confusion between additions to and deductions from wealth (which is an accounting issue) and cash: in the former, new borrowings do not add wealth to cover the losses; in the latter, profit is not the means used to finance an investment as it does not translate 100% in cash.*
5/ *There is nothing that tells us whether wealth has been destroyed or created as we do not know what net income for 2011 is.*
6/ *Yes. See flow chart in Chapter 5.*
7/ *No, because income and costs may not necessarily correspond to immediate cash receipts or expenses.*
8/ *No, because a company takes on costs that are deductible from EBITDA to form net income - depreciation, financial costs, etc.*
9/ *It is a non-cash charge, not a cash expense, i.e. a cost that is recorded, but which does not have to be cashed-out.*
10/ *From a cash standpoint, an investment in real estate is a cash expense which will only generate income on the day it is sold. From a wealth standpoint, real estate is an attractive asset. For investments in R&D, returns must be quicker from a cash standpoint. In terms of wealth, however, the disposal value of R&D is nil.*
11/ *No, only financial interest is recorded in the income statement. Yes, because debts are repaid in cash.*
12/ *No, because of the prudence principle.*
13/ *In order to obtain a figure for purchases consumed in the business in the current year.*
14/ *In order to counterbalance costs recorded in the income statement which should not affect this year's net income as they are related to unsold products.*
15/ *No, except if the company is in the business of regularly selling fixed assets, like a car rental company, for example. Capital gains or losses on the sale of a fixed asset will be recorded as exceptional gains/losses (if this category exists in the accounting system).*
16/ *Sales (revenues) and customer payments (cash receipts). Depreciation and amortisation (costs without cash expenses). Purchase of a machine (cash expense but not a charge).*

17/ *A non-cash expense is a charge which does not reflect a specific expense, but an accounting valuation of how much wealth has been destroyed. A deferred charge is one that is carried over to the next financial period. Common point: both are based on an accounting decision, resulting in a dilemma for the financial manager: have they been measured properly?*

EXERCISES

A detailed Excel version of the solutions is available at www.vernimmen.com.

1/ Starjö AB

Production sold	340 500	Sales	340 500
Change in finished goods and in-progress inventory	19 175		
Purchases of raw materials and goods for resale	267 050		
Change in raw materials and goods for resale	3050		
Personnel costs, including payroll taxes	90 000		
Other purchases and external costs, including lease payments	0		
EBITDA	5675		
Depreciation and amortisation	5000	Cost of goods sold	339 825
EBIT			675
Net interest and other financial costs			600
Non-recurring items			45 000
Tax			15 776
Net earnings			29 299

Sale of premises: capital gain of €45 000 shown as a non-recurring item gain.

Rental of premises: extra €12 000 in operating costs (recorded under "Other purchases and external costs"), and disappearance of depreciation and amortisation the following year.

Repayment of the loan: disappearance of €600 in interest expenses the following financial year.

Over the course of the financial year, and after booking these transactions, the company became richer by €29 299 (after tax), the creditors by €600 and the company manager by €14 649.

2/Ellingham plc: see Chapter 5.

3/Mumbai Oaks

By-nature income statement:

	Net sales	$800 \times INR\ 10\ 000 = 8\ 000\ 000$	
+	Closing inventory of finished products	$100 \times (5000 + 7000) = +700\ 000$	+ Changes in inventories of finished goods and work in progress
−	Opening inventory and work in progress	− 0	
=	Production for the year	$8\ 700\ 000$	
−	Purchases of raw materials and goods for resale	− 4 600 000	= Raw materials and goods for resale consumed
−	Opening inventory of raw materials and goods for resale	− 400 000	
+	Closing inventory of raw materials and goods for resale	+ 500 000	
=	Gross profit on raw materials and goods for resale used	4 200 000	
−	Personnel expenses	$900 \times INR\ 2000 + INR\ 450\ 000 = -2\ 250\ 000$	
−	Services (other operating expenses)	− 400 000	
−	Depreciation and amortisation	− 300 000	
=	EBIT (operating profit)	1 250 000	

By-function income statement:

Sales (products)	$800\ units \times 10\ 000 =$	INR 8 000 000
Cost of sales	$200\ 000 + 800\ units \times 7000 =$	INR 5 800 000
Selling and marketing costs	$70\ 000 + 450\ 000 =$	INR 520 000
General and administrative costs	$30\ 000 + 400\ 000 =$	INR 430 000
EBIT (operating profit)		INR 1 250 000

This corresponds exactly to the gross margin per unit of INR 3000 multiplied by the 800 units sold minus fixed costs of INR 450 000 (sales force), INR 400 000 (administration) and INR 300 000 (depreciation).

As by-nature and by-function formats differ only by presentation and not substance, it is quite logical that the different formats do not lead to a difference in reported EBIT!

Achieving an EBIT of INR 1 250 000 out of a turnover of INR 8 000 000 is a very nice margin (15.6%). Most industrial groups do not achieve this kind of margin. This may be due to the fact that in most small companies, owners prefer to be paid a low wage and receive higher dividends which are generally taxed at a lower rate than ordinary salaries.

4/ Singapore Kite Surf Magazine

Income statement

	FY1	FY2
Sales	$50 \times 1500/3 = 25\,000$	$50 \times 1500 = 75\,000$
Personnel cost	$4 \times 2000 = 8000$	$12 \times 2000 = 24\,000$
Fabrication and distribution	$1500 \times 2 \times 4 = 12\,000$	$1500 \times 2 \times 12 = 36\,000$
Net income	5000	15 000

Cash flow statement

	FY1	FY2
Operating cash inflow	$50 \times 1500 = 75\,000$	$50 \times 1500 = 75\,000$
Operating cash outflow	$4 \times 2000 + 1500 \times 2 \times 4 = 20\,000$	$12 \times 2000 + 1500 \times 2 \times 12 = 60\,000$
Cash flow from operations	55 000	15 000

If you can convince your clients to pay their subscription before they get the first issue, they will basically finance the project!

BIBLIOGRAPHY

For the basics of income statements:

F. Plewa, G. Friedlob, *Financial and Business Statements,* Barron's Business Library, 2006.

For a thorough explanation of the structure of the income statement:

C.R. Baker, Y. Ding, H. Stolowy, The statement of intermediate balance: a tool for international financial statement analysis based on income statement "by nature", an application to the airline industry, *Advances in International Accounting,* **18**, 2005.

H. Stolowy, M. Lebas, Y. Ding, *Financial Accounting and Reporting: A Global Perspective*, 3rd edn, Thomson, 2010.

On the relevancy of accounting measures from the income statement:

L.D. Brown, K. Sivakumar, Comparing the Value Relevance of Two Operating Income Measures, *Review of Accounting Studies,* **8**(4), 561–572, December 2003.

J.-F. Casta, S. Lin, O. Ramond, *Value relevance of summary accounting income measures*, Working Paper Florida University and Université Paris-Dauphine, February 2007.

Chapter 4
CAPITAL EMPLOYED AND INVESTED CAPITAL

The end-of-period snapshot

So far in our analysis, we have looked at inflows and outflows, or revenues and costs during a given period. We will now temporarily set aside this dynamic approach and place ourselves at the end of the period (rather than considering changes over a given period) and analyse the balances outstanding.

For instance, in addition to changes in net debt over a period, we also need to analyse net debt at a given point in time. Likewise, we will study here the wealth that has been accumulated up to a given point in time, rather than that generated over a period.

The balance represents a snapshot of the cumulative inflows and outflows previously generated by the business.

To summarise, we can make the following connections:

- an inflow or outflow represents a change in "stock", i.e. in the balance outstanding;
- a "stock" is the arithmetic sum of inflows and outflows since a given date (when the business started up) through to a given point in time. For instance, at any moment, shareholders' equity is equal to the sum of capital increases by shareholders and annual net income for past years not distributed in the form of dividends plus the original share capital.

Section 4.1
THE BALANCE SHEET: DEFINITIONS AND CONCEPTS

The purpose of a balance sheet is to list all the assets of a business and all of its financial resources at a given point in time.

1/ MAIN ITEMS ON A BALANCE SHEET

Assets on the balance sheet comprise:

- **fixed assets**,[1] i.e. everything required for the operating cycle that is not destroyed as part of it. These items retain some value (any loss in their value is accounted for through depreciation, amortisation and impairment losses). A distinction is

1 *"Non-current assets" in IFRS terminology.*

2 *Known as property, plant and equipment in the US.*

drawn between **tangible fixed assets** (land, buildings, machinery, etc.)[2], **intangible fixed assets** (brands, patents, goodwill, etc.) and **investments**. When a business holds shares in another company (in the long term), they are accounted for under investments;

- inventories and trade receivables, i.e. temporary assets created as part of the operating cycle;
- lastly, marketable securities and cash that belong to the company and are thus assets.

3 *Known as debtors in the UK.*

Inventories, receivables,[3] marketable securities and cash represent the **current assets**, a term reflecting the fact that these assets tend to "turn over" during the operating cycle.

Resources on the balance sheet comprise:

- capital provided by shareholders, plus retained earnings, known as **shareholders' equity**;
- borrowings of any kind that the business may have arranged, e.g. bank loans, supplier credits, etc., known as **liabilities**.

By definition, a company's assets and resources must be exactly equal. This is the fundamental principle of double-entry accounting. When an item is purchased, it is either capitalised or expensed. If it is capitalised, it will appear on the asset side of the balance sheet, and if expensed, it will lead to a reduction in earnings and thus shareholders' equity. The double-entry for this purchase is either a reduction in cash (i.e. a decrease in an asset) or a commitment (i.e. a liability) to the vendor (i.e. an increase in a liability). According to the algebra of accounting, assets and resources (equity and liabilities) always carry the opposite sign, so the equilibrium of the balance sheet is always maintained.

4 *Required by the European Fourth Directive.*

It is European practice to classify assets starting with fixed assets and to end with cash,[4] whereas it is North American and Japanese practice to start with cash. The same is true for the equity and liabilities side of the balance sheet: Europeans start with equity, whereas North Americans and Japanese end with it.

A "horizontal" format is common in continental Europe, with assets on the left and resources on the right. In the United Kingdom, the more common format is a "vertical" one, starting from fixed assets plus current assets and deducting liabilities to end up with equity. These are only choices of presentation.

THE BALANCE SHEET

FIXED ASSETS	SHAREHOLDERS' EQUITY
CURRENT ASSETS	LIABILITIES

2/ TWO WAYS OF ANALYSING THE BALANCE SHEET

A balance sheet can be analysed either from a capital-employed perspective or from a solvency-and-liquidity perspective.

In the capital-employed analysis, the balance sheet shows all the uses of funds for the company's operating cycle and analyses the origin of its sources of funds.

A capital-employed analysis of the balance sheet serves three main purposes:

- to understand how a company finances its operating assets (see Chapter 12);
- to compute the rate of return either on capital employed or on equity (see Chapter 13); and
- as a first step to valuing the equity of a company as a going concern (see Chapter 32).

In a solvency-and-liquidity analysis, a business is regarded as a set of assets and liabilities, the difference between them representing the book value of the equity provided by shareholders. From this perspective, the balance sheet lists everything that a company owns and everything that it owes.

A solvency-and-liquidity analysis of the balance sheet serves three purposes:

- to measure the solvency of a company (see Chapter 14);
- to measure the liquidity of a company (see Chapter 12); and
- as a first step to valuing its equity in a bankruptcy scenario.

CAPITAL-EMPLOYED ANALYSIS OF THE BALANCE SHEET		SOLVENCY-AND-LIQUIDITY ANALYSIS OF THE BALANCE SHEET	
All USES OF FUNDS (CAPITAL EMPLOYED)	Origin of SOURCES OF FUNDS (INVESTED CAPITAL)	List of all ASSETS	SHAREHOLDERS' EQUITY
			List of all LIABILITIES

Section 4.2

A CAPITAL-EMPLOYED ANALYSIS OF THE BALANCE SHEET

To gain a firm understanding of the capital-employed analysis of the balance sheet, we believe it is best approached in the same way as the analysis in the previous chapter, except that here we will be considering "stocks" rather than inflows and outflows.

The purpose of a capital-employed analysis of the balance sheet is to analyse the capital employed in the operating cycle and how this capital is financed.

More specifically, in a capital-employed analysis, a balance sheet is divided into the following main headings.

1/ FIXED ASSETS

These represent all the investments carried out by the business, based on our financial and accounting definition.

It is helpful to distinguish wherever possible between operating and non-operating assets that have nothing to do with the company's business activities, e.g. land, buildings and subsidiaries active in significantly different or non-core businesses. Non-operating assets can thus be excluded from the company's capital employed. By isolating non-operating assets, we can assess the resources the company may be able to call upon in hard times (i.e. through the disposal of non-operating assets).

The difference between operating and non-operating assets can be subtle in certain circumstances. For instance, how should a company's head office on Bond Street or on the Champs-Elysées be classified? Probably under operating assets for a fashion house or a car manufacturer, but under non-operating assets for an engineering or construction group which has no business reason to be on Bond Street (unlike Burberry or Jaguar).

2/ WORKING CAPITAL

Uses of funds comprise all the operating costs incurred but not yet used or sold (i.e. inventories) and all sales that have not yet been paid for (trade receivables).

Sources of funds comprise all charges incurred but not yet paid for (trade payables, social security and tax payables), as well as operating revenues from products that have not yet been delivered (advance payments on orders).

The net balance of operating uses and sources of funds is called the **working capital**.

If uses of funds exceed sources of funds, the balance is positive and working capital needs to be financed. This is the most frequent case. If negative, it represents a source of funds generated by the operating cycle. This is a nice – but rare – situation!

It is described as "working capital" because the figure reflects the cash required to cover financing shortfalls arising from day-to-day operations.

Sometimes working capital is defined as current assets minus current liabilities. This definition corresponds to our working capital definition + marketable securities and net cash – short-term borrowings. We think that this is an improper definition of working capital as it mixes items from the operating cycle (inventories, receivables, payables) and items from the financing cycle (marketable securities, net cash and short-term bank and financial borrowings). You may also find in some documents expressions such as "working capital needs" or "requirements in working capital". These are synonyms for working capital.

Working capital can be divided between operating working capital and non-operating working capital.

3/ OPERATING WORKING CAPITAL

Operating working capital comprises the following accounting entries:

	Inventories	Raw materials, goods for resale, products and work in progress, finished products
+	**Trade receivables**	Amounts owed by customers, prepayments to suppliers and other trade receivables
−	**Trade payables**	Amounts owed to trade suppliers, social security and tax payables, prepayments by customers and other trade payables
=	**Operating working capital**	

Only the normal amount of operating sources of funds is included in calculations of operating working capital. Unusually long payment periods granted by suppliers should not be included as a component of normal operating working capital.

Where it is permanent, the abnormal portion should be treated as a source of cash, with the suppliers thus being considered as playing the role of the company's banker.

Inventories of raw materials and goods for resale should be included only at their normal amount. Under no circumstances should an unusually large figure for inventories of raw materials and goods for resale be included in the calculation of operating working capital.

Where appropriate, the excess portion of inventories or the amount considered as inventory held for speculative purposes can be treated as a high-risk short-term investment.

Working capital is totally independent of the methods used to value fixed assets, depreciation, amortisation and impairment losses on fixed assets. However, it is influenced by:

- inventory valuation methods;
- deferred income and cost (over one or more years);
- the company's provisioning policy for current assets and operating liabilities and costs.

As we shall see in Chapter 5, working capital represents a key principle of financial analysis.

The amount of working capital depends on the accounting methods used to determine earnings, as well as the operating cycle.

4/ NON-OPERATING WORKING CAPITAL

Although we have considered the timing differences between inflows and outflows that arise during the operating cycle, we have, until now, always assumed that capital expenditures are paid for when purchased and that non-recurring costs are paid for when they are recognised in the income statement. Naturally, there may be timing differences here, giving rise to what is known as **non-operating working capital**.

Non-operating working capital, which is not a very robust concept from a theoretical perspective, is hard to predict and to analyse because it depends on individual transactions, unlike operating working capital which is recurring.

In practice, non-operating working capital is a catch-all category for items that cannot be classified anywhere else. It includes amounts due on fixed assets, extraordinary items, etc.

5/ Capital employed

Capital employed is the sum of a company's fixed assets and its working capital (i.e. operating and non-operating working capital). It is therefore equal to the sum of the net amounts devoted by a business to both the operating and investing cycles. It is also known as **operating assets**.

Capital employed is financed by two main types of funds: shareholders' equity and net debt, sometimes grouped together under the heading of **invested capital**.

6/ Shareholders' equity

Shareholders' equity comprises capital provided by shareholders when the company is initially formed and at subsequent capital increases, as well as capital left at the company's disposal in the form of earnings transferred to the reserves.

7/ Net debt

The company's gross debt comprises **debt financing**, irrespective of its maturity, i.e. medium- and long-term (various borrowings due in more than one year that have not yet been repaid), and short-term bank or financial borrowings (portion of long-term borrowings due in less than one year, discounted notes, bank overdrafts, etc.). A company's **net debt** goes further by deducting cash and equivalents (e.g. petty cash and bank accounts) and marketable securities which are the opposite of debt (the company lending money to banks or financial markets) that could be used to partially or totally reduce the gross debt.

All things considered, the equation is as follows:

	Medium- and long-term bank and other borrowings (bond issues, commitment under finance lease, etc.)
+	Short-term bank or financial borrowings (discounted notes, overdrafts, revolving credit facility, etc.)
−	Marketable securities (marketable securities)
−	Cash and equivalents (petty cash and bank accounts)
=	Net debt

A company's net debt can either be positive or negative. If it is negative, the company is said to have net cash.

In the previous paragraphs, we looked at the key accounting items, but some are a bit more complex to allocate (pensions, accruals, etc.) and we will develop these in Chapter 7.

From a capital-employed standpoint, a company balance sheet can be analysed as follows:

		2010	2011	2012
	Fixed assets (**A**)			
	Inventories			
+	Accounts receivable			
−	Accounts payable			
=	Operating working capital			
+	Non-operating working capital			
=	Working capital (**B**)			
Capital employed (A + B)				
	Shareholders' equity (**C**)			
	Short-, medium- and long-term bank and other borrowings			
−	Marketable securities			
−	Cash and equivalents			
=	Net debt (**D**)			
Invested capital (C+D)=Capital employed (A+B)				

Section 4.3
A SOLVENCY-AND-LIQUIDITY ANALYSIS OF THE BALANCE SHEET

The solvency-and-liquidity analysis of the balance sheet, which presents a statement of what is owned and what is owed by the company at the end of the year, can be used:

- by shareholders to list everything that the company owns and owes, bearing in mind that these amounts may need to be revalued;
- by creditors looking to assess the risk associated with loans granted to the company. In a capitalist system, shareholders' equity is the ultimate guarantee in the event of liquidation since the claims of creditors are met before those of shareholders.

Hence the importance attached to a solvency-and-liquidity analysis of the balance sheet in traditional financial analysis. As we shall see in detail in Chapters 12 and 14, it may be analysed from either a liquidity or solvency perspective.

1/ BALANCE SHEET LIQUIDITY

A classification of the balance sheet items needs to be carried out prior to the liquidity analysis. Liabilities are classified in the order in which they fall due for repayment. Since balance sheets are published annually, a distinction between the short term and long term turns on whether a liability is due in less than or more than one year. Accordingly, liabilities are classified into those due in the short term (less than one year), in the medium and long term (i.e. in more than one year) and those that are not due for repayment.

Likewise, what the company owns can also be classified by duration as follows:

- assets that will have disappeared from the balance sheet by the following year, which comprise current assets in the vast majority of cases;
- assets that will still appear on the balance sheet the following year, which comprise fixed assets in the vast majority of cases.

Consequently, from a liquidity perspective, we classify liabilities by their due date, investments by their maturity date and assets as follows:

Assets are regarded as liquid where, as part of the normal operating cycle, they will be monetised in the same year.

Thus they comprise (unless the operating cycle is unusually long) inventories and trade receivables.

Assets that, regardless of their nature (head office, plant, etc.), are not intended for sale during the normal course of business are regarded as fixed (non-current) and not liquid.

Balance sheet liquidity therefore derives from the fact that the turnover of assets (i.e. the speed at which they are monetised within the operating cycle) is faster than the turnover of liabilities (i.e. when they fall due). The maturity schedule of liabilities is known in advance because it is defined contractually. However, the liquidity of current assets is unpredictable (risk of sales flops or inventory write-downs, etc.). **Consequently, the clearly defined maturity structure of a company's liabilities contrasts with the unpredictable liquidity of its assets**.

Therefore, short-term creditors will take into account differences between a company's asset liquidity and its liability structure. They will require the company to maintain current assets at a level exceeding that of short-term liabilities to provide a margin of safety. Hence the sacrosanct rule in finance that each and every company must have assets due to be monetised in less than one year at least equal to its liabilities falling due within one year.

2/ SOLVENCY

Solvency reflects the ability of a company to honour its commitments in the event of liquidation, i.e. if its operations are wound up and are put up for sale.

In accounting terms, a company may be regarded as insolvent once its shareholders' equity turns negative. This means that it owes more than it owns.

3/ NET ASSET VALUE OR THE BOOK VALUE OF SHAREHOLDERS' EQUITY

This is a solvency-oriented concept that attempts to compute the funds invested by shareholders by valuing the company's various assets under deduction of liabilities. Net asset value is an accounting and, in some instances, tax-related term, rather than a financial one.

The book value of shareholders' equity is equal to everything a company owns less everything it already owes or may owe. Financiers often talk about net asset value, which leads to confusion among non-specialists, who can understand them as total assets net of depreciation, amortisation and impairment losses.

Book value of equity is thus equal to the sum of:

	fixed assets
+	current assets
−	all liabilities of any kind

When a company is sold, the buyer will be keen to adopt an even stricter approach:

- by factoring in contingent liabilities (that do not appear on the balance sheet);
- by excluding worthless assets, i.e. of zero value. This very often applies to most intangible assets owing to the complexity of the way in which they are accounted for (see Chapter 7).

Section 4.4
A DETAILED EXAMPLE OF A CAPITAL-EMPLOYED BALANCE SHEET

On the following page, you will find the capital-employed balance sheet of the Italian group Indesit. This balance sheet will be used in future chapters.

Items specific to consolidated accounts are highlighted in blue and will be described in detail in Chapter 6.

BALANCE SHEET FOR INDESIT

	in € m	2006	2007	2008	2009	2010
	Goodwill	326	298	208	223	230
+	Other intangible fixed assets	115	108	124	109	102
+	Tangible fixed assets	751	763	693	630	637
+	Equity in associated companies	13	1	1	1	1
+	Deferred tax asset	48	38	55	71	74
+	Other non-current assets	2	1	1	1	3
=	**NON-CURRENT ASSETS (FIXED ASSETS)**	**1254**	**1208**	**1080**	**1035**	**1046**
	Inventories of goods for resale	0	0	0	0	0
+	Inventories of raw materials and semi-finished parts	121	119	112	92	111
+	Finished goods inventories	232	216	262	189	215

in € m	2006	2007	2008	2009	2010
+ Trade receivables	573	523	456	392	498
+ Other operating receivables	116	141	138	87	87
− Trade payables	886	856	765	660	829
− Tax and social security liabilities	147	165	138	147	143
− Other operating payables	37	25	52	94	44
= **OPERATING WORKING CAPITAL (1)**	**−28**	**−48**	**13**	**−141**	**−105**
Non-operating receivables	0	0	0	0	0
− Non-operating payables	0	0	0	19	10
= **NON-OPERATING WORKING CAPITAL (2)**	**0**	**0**	**0**	**−19**	**−10**
= **WORKING CAPITAL (1+2)**	**−28**	**−48**	**13**	**−160**	**−115**
CAPITAL EMPLOYED = NON-CURRENT ASSETS + WORKING CAPITAL	**1226**	**1160**	**1093**	**875**	**931**
Share capital	93	93	93	93	93
+ Reserves and retained earnings	453	485	327	374	480
+ Reserve-like provisions	74	58	46	40	36
= **SHAREHOLDERS' EQUITY GROUP SHARE**	**620**	**636**	**466**	**506**	**609**
+ Minority interests in consolidated subsidiaries	7	2	3	2	0
= **TOTAL GROUP EQUITY**	**626**	**638**	**469**	**508**	**609**
Debt-like provisions	176	191	155	77	141
Medium- and long-term borrowings and liabilities	403	309	452	337	175
+ Bank overdrafts and short-term borrowings	296	276	250	170	246
− Marketable securities	90	68	53	26	17
− Cash and equivalents	185	187	178	191	223
= **NET DEBT**	**424**	**331**	**470**	**290**	**181**
ADJUSTED NET DEBT	**600**	**522**	**625**	**367**	**322**
INVESTED CAPITAL = (GROUP EQUITY + NET DEBT)	**1226**	**1160**	**1093**	**875**	**931**
= **CAPITAL EMPLOYED**					

SUMMARY

The summary of this chapter can be downloaded from www.vernimmen.com.

The balance sheet shows a snapshot of cumulative inflows and outflows from the company classified into assets and resources (liabilities and shareholders' equity).

Assets comprise fixed assets (intangible and tangible fixed assets and long-term investments) and current assets (inventories, accounts receivable, marketable securities and cash and equivalents). Resources comprise shareholders' equity and bank and financial borrowings, plus trade payables.

A capital-employed analysis of the balance sheet shows all the uses of funds by a company as part of the operating cycle and analyses the origin of the sources of a company's funds at a given point in time.

On the asset side, the capital-employed balance sheet has the following main headings:

• fixed assets, i.e. investments made by the company;

- operating working capital (inventories and trade receivables under deduction of trade payables). The size of the operating working capital depends on the operating cycle and the accounting methods used to determine earnings;

- non-operating working capital, a catch-all category for the rest.

The sum of fixed assets and working capital is called capital employed.

Capital employed is financed by capital invested, i.e. shareholders' equity and net debt.

Net debt is defined as bank and financial borrowings, be they short-, medium- or long-term, minus marketable securities (short-term investments) and cash and equivalents.

A solvency-and-liquidity analysis lists everything the company owns and everything that it owes, the balance being the book value of shareholders' equity or net asset value. It can be analysed from either a solvency or liquidity perspective.

Solvency measures the company's ability to honour its commitments in the event of liquidation, whereas liquidity measures its ability to meet its commitments up to a certain date by monetising assets in the ordinary course of business.

QUESTIONS

Questions

1/ When do we use a capital-employed analysis of the balance sheet? And when do we use a solvency-and-liquidity analysis of the balance sheet?

2/ Which approach to the balance sheet should you adopt:

- when giving a warranty on the balance sheet of a company being sold?
- when forecasting a company's working capital?

3/ Do liabilities that arise during the operating cycle always have a maturity of less than one year?

4/ Classify the following as "stocks", in/outflows, or change in in/outflows: sales, trade receivables, change in trade receivables, increase in dividends, financial expense, increase in sales, EBITDA.

5/ A company's sales clearly represent a source of funds. However, they do not appear on the balance sheet. Why?

6/ Classify the following balance sheet items under fixed assets, working capital, shareholders' equity or net debt: overdraft, retained earnings, brands, taxes payable, finished goods inventories, bonds.

7/ Is a company that is currently unable to pay its debts always insolvent?

8/ Assess the liquidity of the following assets: plant, unlisted securities, listed securities, head office building located in the centre of a large city, ships and aircraft, commercial paper, raw materials inventories, work-in-progress inventories.

9/ Give a synonym for net assets.

10/ What is another way of describing a difference in "stocks"?

11/What is the difference between liabilities and sources of funds?

12/What is another way of describing a cumulative inflow or outflow?

13/Give examples of businesses with positive working capital.

14/Give examples of businesses with negative working capital.

15/The main manufacturers of telephony equipment (Ericsson, Nokia, etc.) provided telecoms operators (Deutsche Telekom, Swisscom, etc.) with substantial supplier credit lines, in order to assist them in financing the construction of their UMTS networks. State your views.

16/Does the company operating Singapore Kite Surf Magazine (see previous chapter) have a positive or negative working capital?

More questions are waiting for you at www.vernimmen.com.

EXERCISE

Ellingham plc

Draw up the balance sheet showing capital-employed and invested capital (1 January 2011, end 2011, 2012) assuming that the company has equity of €40m.

ANSWERS

Questions

1/*Capital-employed analysis of the balance sheet: for understanding the company's use of funds and how they were financed. Solvency-and-liability analysis of the balance sheet: for listing all assets and liabilities.*
2/*The solvency-and-liquidity analysis, the capital-employed analysis.*
3/*No, in some industries, there is a long period between the invoice date and customer payment (e.g. movie rights).*
4/*Inflow, "stocks", inflow, change in outflow, outflow, change in inflow, inflow.*
5/*The balance resulting from the activity is what appears on the balance sheet, i.e. the profit or loss, not the activity itself measured by sales.*
6/*In order of listing: net debt, shareholders' equity, fixed assets, working capital, working capital, net debt.*
7/*In theory no, as the company may be facing a temporary credit crunch, but most of the time yes because it will have to dispose of assets quickly or stop its activities which will result in a big reduction in equity, and then in its solvency.*
8/*In order of decreasing liquidity: listed securities, commercial paper, raw materials inventories, head office, unlisted securities, ships and aircraft, work-in-progress inventories, plant.*
9/*Shareholders' equity.*
10/*An inflow or outflow.*
11/*Sources of funds include shareholders' equity (which does not have to be repaid and is consequently not a liability) and liabilities (which sooner or later have to be repaid).*

12/ *A "stock".*

13/ *Most businesses: publishers, appliances manufacturers, chemical industry, etc.*

14/ *Movie theatres (no inventories, cash payment from clients), pay TV (subscriptions paid in advance), public works (advance payment from clients).*

15/ *These are, in fact, merely financial loans and not operating loans, granted to enable the telecoms operator to buy the equipment made by the manufacturer. These loans should be treated as fixed assets on the manufacturer's balance sheet and as financial debts on the telecom operator's balance sheet.*

16/ *A negative working capital.*

Exercise

Ellingham plc – see Chapter 5.

BIBLIOGRAPHY

For a thorough explanation of the balance sheet:

G. Friedlob, R. Welton, *Keys to Reading an Annual Report*, 4th edn, Barrons Educational Series, 2008.

For more advanced topics on balance sheets:

H. Stolowy, M. Lebas, Y. Ding, *Financial Accounting and Reporting: A Global Perspective*, 3rd edn, Thomson, 2010.

Chapter 5
WALKING THROUGH FROM EARNINGS TO CASH FLOW

Or how to move mountains together!

Chapter 2 showed the structure of the cash flow statement, which brings together all the receipts and payments recorded during a given period and determines the change in net debt position.

Chapter 3 covered the structure of the income statement, which summarises all the revenues and charges during a period.

It may appear that these two radically different approaches have nothing in common. But common sense tells us that a rich woman will sooner or later have cash in her pocket, while a poor woman is likely to be strapped for cash – unless she should make her fortune along the way.

Although the complex workings of a business lead to differences between profits and cash, they converge at some point or another.

The aim of this chapter is to reconcile the cash flow and earnings approaches.

First of all, we will examine revenues and costs from a cash flow standpoint. Based on this analysis, we will establish a link between changes in wealth (earnings) and the change in net debt that bridges the two approaches.

We recommend that readers get to grips with this chapter, because understanding the transition from earnings to the change in net debt represents a key step in comprehending the financial workings of a business.

Section 5.1
ANALYSIS OF EARNINGS FROM A CASH FLOW PERSPECTIVE

This section is included merely for explanatory and conceptual purposes. Even so, it is vital to understand the basic financial workings of a company.

1/ Operating revenues

Operating receipts should correspond to sales for the same period, but they differ because:

- customers may be granted a payment period; and/or
- payments of invoices from the previous period may be received during the current period.

As a result, operating receipts are equal to sales only if sales are immediately paid in cash. Otherwise, they generate a change in trade receivables.

$$
\text{Sales for the period} \quad
\begin{cases}
- & \text{Increase in trade receivables} \\
 & \text{or} \\
+ & \text{Reduction in trade receivables}
\end{cases}
\quad = \quad \text{Operating receipts}
$$

2/ Changes in inventories of finished goods and work in progress

As we have already seen in by-nature income statements, the difference between production and sales is adjusted for through changes in inventories of finished goods and work in progress.[1] But this is merely an accounting entry to deduct from operating costs, costs that do not correspond to products sold. It has no impact from a cash standpoint.[2] As a result, changes in inventories need to be reversed in a cash flow analysis.

3/ Operating costs

Operating costs differ from operating payments in the same way as operating revenues differ from operating receipts. Operating payments are the same as operating costs for a given period only when adjusted for:

- timing differences arising from the company's payment terms (credit granted by its suppliers, etc.);
- the fact that some purchases are not used during the same period. The difference between purchases made and purchases used is adjusted for through change in inventories of raw materials.

These timing differences give rise to:

- changes in trade payables in the first case;
- discrepancies between raw materials used and purchases made, which are equal to change in inventories of raw materials and goods for resale.

$$
\begin{array}{l}
\text{Operating payments} \\
\quad = \\
\text{operating costs except} \\
\text{depreciation,} \\
\text{amortisation and} \\
\text{impairment losses}
\end{array}
\left\{
\begin{array}{l}
+ \quad \text{reduction in supplier credit} \\
\qquad \text{or} \\
- \quad \text{increase in supplier credit} \\
+ \quad \text{increase in inventories of raw materials and goods for resale} \\
\qquad \text{or} \\
- \quad \text{reduction in inventories of raw materials and goods for resale}
\end{array}
\right.
$$

1 *This adjustment is not necessary in by-function income statements, as explained in Chapter 3.*
2 *In accounting parlance, this is known as a "closing entry".*

The only differences between operating revenues and receipts and between operating charges and payments are timing differences deriving from deferred payments (payment terms) and deferred charges (changes in inventories).

The total amount of the timing differences between operating revenues and costs and between operating receipts and payments can thus be summarised as follows for by-nature and by-function income statements:

BY-NATURE INCOME STATEMENT	DIFFERENCE	CASH FLOW STATEMENT
Net sales	− Change in trade receivables (deferred payment)	= **Operating receipts**
+ **Changes in inventories of finished goods and work in progress**	− Changes in inventories of finished goods and work in progress (deferred charges) + Change in trade payables (deferred payments)	
− **Operating costs except depreciation, amortisation and impairment losses**	− Change in inventories of raw materials and goods for resale (deferred charges)	= − **Operating payments**
= **EBITDA**	− Change in operating working capital	= **Operating cash flows**

BY-FUNCTION INCOME STATEMENT	DIFFERENCE	CASH FLOW STATEMENT
Net sales	− Change in trade receivables (deferred payment) + Change in trade payables (deferred payments)	= **Operating receipts**
− **Operating costs except depreciation, amortisation and impairment losses**	− Change in inventories of finished goods, work in progress, raw materials and goods for resale (deferred changes)	= − **Operating payments**
= **EBITDA**	− Change in operating working capital	= **Operating cash flows**

Astute readers will have noticed that the items in the central column of the above table are the components of the change in operating working capital between two periods, as defined in Chapter 4.

Over a given period, the change in operating working capital represents a need for, or a source of, financing that must be added to or subtracted from the other financing requirements or resources.

The change in operating working capital accounts for the difference between EBITDA and operating cash flow.

If positive, it represents a financing requirement, and we refer to an increase in operating working capital. If negative, it represents a source of funds, and we refer to a reduction in operating working capital.

The change in working capital merely represents a straightforward timing difference between the balance of operating cash flows (operating cash flow) and the wealth created by the operating cycle (EBITDA). As we shall see, it is important to remember that timing differences may not necessarily be small, of limited importance, short or negligible in any way.

The analysis of changes in working capital is one of the pillars of financial analysis.

4/ CAPITAL EXPENDITURE

Capital expenditures[3] lead to a change in what the company owns without any immediate increase or decrease in its wealth. Consequently, they are not shown directly on the income statement. Conversely, capital expenditures have a direct impact on the cash flow statement.

3 Or investments in fixed assets.

From a capital expenditure perspective, there is a fundamental difference separating the income statement and the cash flow statement. The income statement spreads the capital expenditure charge over the entire life of the asset (through depreciation), while the cash flow statement records it only in the period in which it is purchased.

A company's capital expenditure process leads to both cash outflows that do not diminish its wealth at all and the accounting recognition of impairment in the purchased assets through depreciation and amortisation that does not reflect any cash outflows.

Accordingly, there is no direct link between cash flow and net income for the capital expenditure process, as we knew already.

5/ FINANCING

Financing is, by its very nature, a cycle that is specific to inflows and outflows. Sources of financing (new borrowings, capital increases, etc.) do not appear on the income statement, which shows only the remuneration paid on some of these resources, i.e. interest on borrowings but not dividends on equity.[4]

Outflows representing a return on sources of financing may be analysed as either costs (i.e. interest) or a distribution of wealth created by the company among its equity capital providers (i.e. dividends).

4 Except in the UK where companies deduct dividends from net income and end the income statement with "retained profit".

The distinction between capital and interest payments is not of paramount importance in the cash flow statement, but is essential in the income statement.

To keep things simple, assuming that there are no timing differences between the recognition of a cost and the corresponding cash outflow, a distinction needs to be drawn between:

- interest payments on debt financing (financial expense) and income tax which affect the company's cash position and its earnings;
- the remuneration paid to equity capital providers (dividends) which affects the company's cash position and earnings transferred to reserves;
- new borrowings and repayment of borrowings, capital increases and share buy-backs[5] which affect its cash position, but have no impact on earnings.

Lastly, corporate income tax represents a charge that appears on the income statement and a cash payment to the State which, though it may not provide any financing to the company, provides it with a range of free services and entitlements, e.g. police, education, roads, etc.

We can now finish off our table and walk through from earnings to decrease in net debt:

5 When a company buys back some of its shares from some of its shareholders. For more see Chapter 38.

FROM THE INCOME STATEMENT . . . TO THE CASH FLOW STATEMENT

INCOME STATEMENT		DIFFERENCE			CASH FLOW STATEMENT
	EBITDA	−	Change in operating working capital	= −	**Operating cash flow**
		−	Capital expenditure	= −	Capital expenditure
		+	Disposals	= +	Disposals
−	Depreciation, amortisation and impairment losses on fixed assets	+	Depreciation, amortisation and impairment losses on fixed assets (non-cash charges)	=	
=	**EBIT (Operating profit)**			= =	**Free cash flow before tax**
−	Financial expense net of financial income			−	Financial expense net of financial income
−	Corporate income tax			= −	Corporate income tax
		+	Proceeds from share issues	= +	Proceeds from share issues
		−	Share buy-backs	−	Share buy-backs
		−	Dividends paid	= −	Dividends paid
=	**Net income (net earnings)**	+	Column total	=	**Decrease in net debt**

Section 5.2
CASH FLOW STATEMENT

The same table enables us to move in the opposite direction and thus account for the decrease in net debt based on the income statement. To do so, we simply need to add back all the movements shown in the central column to net profit.

> **Net income**
> +   Depreciation, amortisation and impairment losses on fixed assets
> −   Change in operating working capital
> −   Capital expenditure net of asset disposals
> +   Disposals
> +   Proceeds from share issue
> −   Share buy-backs
> −   Dividends paid
> =   **Decrease in net debt**

The following reasoning may help our attempt to classify the various line items that enable us to make the transition from net income to decrease in net debt.

Net income should normally turn up in "cash at hand". That said, we also need to add back certain non-cash costs (depreciation, amortisation and impairment losses on fixed assets) that were deducted on the way down the income statement but have no cash impact, to arrive at what is known as **cash flow**.

Cash flow will appear in "cash at hand" only once the timing differences related to the operating cycle as measured by change in operating working capital have been taken into account.

Lastly, the investing and financing cycles give rise to uses and sources of funds that have no immediate impact on net income.

1/ FROM NET INCOME TO CASH FLOW

As we have just seen, depreciation, amortisation, impairment losses on fixed assets and provisions are non-cash costs that have no impact on a company's cash position. From a cash flow standpoint, they are no different from net income.

Consequently, they are added back to net income to show the total financing generated internally by the company.

These two items form the company's cash flow, which accountants allocate between net income on the one hand, and depreciation, amortisation and impairment losses on the other hand, according to the relevant accounting and tax legislation.

Cash flow can therefore be calculated by adding certain non-cash charges net of write-backs to net income.

The simplicity of the cash flow statement shown in Chapter 2 was probably evident to our readers, but it would not fail to shock traditional accountants, who would find it hard to accept that financial expense should be placed on a par with repayments of borrowings. Raising debt to pay financial expense is not the same as replacing one debt with another. The former makes the company poorer, whereas the latter constitutes liability management.

As a result, traditionalists have managed to establish the concept of cash flow. We need to point out that we would advise computing cash flow before any capital gains (or losses) on asset disposals and before non-recurring items, simply because they are non-recurrent items. Cash flow is only relevant in a cash flow statement if it is not made artificially volatile by inclusion of non-recurring items.

Cash flow is not as pure a concept as EBITDA. That said, a direct link may be established between these two concepts by deriving cash flow from the income statement using the top-down method:

	EBITDA
−	Financial expense net of financial income
−	Corporate income tax
=	Cash flow

or the bottom-up method:

	Net income
+	Depreciation, amortisation and impairment losses
+/−	Capital losses/gains on asset disposal
+/−	Other non-cash items
=	Cash flow

Cash flow is influenced by the same accounting policies as EBITDA. Likewise, it is not affected by the accounting policies applied to tangible and intangible fixed assets.

6 For details on consolidated accounts, see Chapter 6.

Note that the calculation method differs slightly for consolidated accounts[6] since the contribution to consolidated net profit made by equity-accounted income is replaced by the dividend payment received. This is attributable to the fact that the parent company does not actually receive the earnings of an associate company,[1] since it does not control it, but merely receives a dividend.

Furthermore, cash flow is calculated at group level without taking into account minority interests. This seems logical since the parent company has control of and allocates the cash flows of its fully-consolidated subsidiaries. In the cash flow statement, minority interests[6] in the controlled subsidiaries are reflected only through the dividend payments that they receive.

Lastly, readers should beware of cash flow as there are nearly as many definitions of cash flow as there are companies in the world!

The upper definition is widely used, but frequently free cash flows, cash flow from operating activities and operating cash flow are simply called "cash flow" by some professionals. So it is safest to check which cash flow they are talking about.

2/ FROM CASH FLOW TO CASH FLOW FROM OPERATING ACTIVITIES

In Chapter 2 we introduced the concept of cash flow from operating activities, which is not the same as cash flow.

To go from cash flow to cash flow from operating activities, we need to adjust for the timing differences in cash flows linked to the operating cycle.

This gives us the following equation:

Cash flow from operating activities = Cash flow − Change in operating working capital.

Note that the term "operating activities" is used here in a fairly broad sense of the term, since it includes financial expense and corporate income tax.

3/ OTHER MOVEMENTS IN CASH

We have now isolated the movements in cash deriving from the operating cycle, so we can proceed to allocate the other movements to the investment and financing cycles.

The investment cycle includes:

- capital expenditures (acquisitions of tangible and intangible assets);
- disposals of fixed assets, i.e. the price at which fixed assets are sold and not any capital gains or losses (which do not represent cash flows);
- changes in long-term investments (i.e. financial assets).

Where appropriate, we may also factor in the impact of timing differences in cash flows generated by this cycle, notably non-operating working capital (e.g. amount owed to a supplier of a fixed asset).

The financing cycle includes:

- capital increases in cash, the payment of dividends (i.e. payment out of the previous year's net profit) and share buy-backs;
- change in net debt resulting from the repayment of (short-, medium- and long-term) borrowings, new borrowings, changes in marketable securities (short-term investments) and changes in cash and equivalents.

This brings us back to the cash flow statement in Chapter 2, but using the indirect method, which starts with net income and classifies cash flows by cycle (i.e. operating, investing or financing activities; see next page):

This format calls for the following comments:

(a) Even though the order used in cash flow statements indicates the pre-eminence of operating activities, it is important to recognise that operating activities are, to some extent, a catch-all category containing all the items not allocated to investing or financing activities. Indeed, the scope of operating activities is, in most cases, different from the operating cycle in the strict sense of the term, as described in Chapter 2. Aside from the items falling within a narrower definition of the operating cycle, operating activities include financial expense and income tax, which logic dictates should appear under financing activities or be split among the three cycles.

Readers may legitimately ask whether the best indicator of the company's operating performance is:

- operating cash flow minus theoretical tax on operating profit; or
- cash flow minus the change in working capital, which is cash flow from operating activities.

CASH FLOW STATEMENT FOR INDESIT (€m)

		2006	2007	2008	2009	2010
	OPERATING ACTIVITIES					
	Net income	77	105	56	34	90
+	Depreciation, amortisation and impairment losses on fixed assets	143	141	130	141	126
+	Other non-cash items	(16)	2	(75)	(15)	(36)
=	**CASH FLOW**	**204**	**248**	**111**	**160**	**180**
−	Change in working capital	(40)	(20)	61	(173)	44
=	**CASH FLOW FROM OPERATING ACTIVITIES (A)**	**244**	**268**	**50**	**333**	**135**
	INVESTING ACTIVITIES					
	Capital expenditure	136	172	145	83	77
−	Disposal of fixed assets	5	20	8	7	2
+/−	Acquisition (disposal) of financial assets	(9)	(12)	0	0	0
+/−	Acquisition (disposal) of other LT assets	(6)	(2)	0	0	0
=	**CASH FLOW FROM INVESTING ACTIVITIES (B)**	**116**	**139**	**136**	**76**	**75**
=	**FREE CASH FLOW AFTER FINANCIAL EXPENSE (A − B)**	**128**	**129**	**(87)**	**257**	**61**
	FINANCING ACTIVITIES					
	Proceeds from share issues (C)	3	2	0	0	0
	Dividends paid (D)	37	40	53	0	16
	A − B + C − D = DECREASE/(INCREASE) IN NET DEBT	**94**	**92**	**(139)**	**257**	**45**
	Decrease in net debt can be broken down as follows:					
	Repayment of short-, medium- and long-term borrowings	110	113	(316)	272	22
−	New short-, medium- and long-term borrowings	5	0	200	0	0
+	Change in marketable securities (short-term investments)	(6)	(23)	(15)	(27)	(9)
+	Change in cash and equivalents	(15)	2	(8)	13	32
=	**DECREASE/(INCREASE) IN NET DEBT**	**94**	**92**	**(139)**	**257**	**45**

First of all, we note that the difference between these two indicators is attributable primarily to financial expense after tax, which is generally modest in a low-interest-rate environment.

In our view, operating cash flow minus theoretical tax on operating profit is the most useful because it is a key factor influencing both investment decisions (Chapter 29) and valuations (Chapter 32). However, most if not all cash flow statements define cash flow from operating activities as cash flow minus the change in working capital.

Cash flow is a relatively unclear concept because it is calculated before the return (dividends) paid on certain funds (i.e. shareholders' equity) but after that (financial expense) paid on other funds (i.e. debt).

(b)   Investing activities are shown as a financing requirement (or a surplus in rare cases), which is calculated as the difference between capital expenditure and disposals.

(c)   In practice, most companies publish a cash flow statement that starts with net income and moves down to changes in "cash and equivalents" or change in "cash", a poorly defined concept since certain companies include marketable securities while others deduct bank overdrafts and short-term borrowings.

Furthermore, net debt reflects the level of indebtedness of a company much better than cash and cash equivalents or than cash and cash equivalents minus short-term borrowings, since the latter are only a portion of the debt position of a company. On the one hand, one can infer relevant comments from changes in the net debt position of a company. On the other hand, changes in cash and cash equivalents are rarely relevant as it is so easy to increase cash on the balance sheet at the closing date: simply get into long-term debt and put the proceeds in a bank account! Cash on the balance sheet has increased but net debt is still the same.

As we will see in Chapter 36, net debt is managed globally and looking at only one side (cash and cash equivalents and marketable securities) is therefore of little interest.

SUMMARY

The summary of this chapter can be downloaded from www.vernimmen.com.

The first step in the process of moving from the income statement to a cash flow perspective is to recreate operating cash flows. The only differences between operating receipts and operating revenues and between operating costs and operating payments are timing differences related to payment terms (deferred payments) and changes in inventories (deferred charges).

The change in operating working capital accounts for the difference between operating cash flow and the generation of wealth within the operating cycle (EBITDA).

For capital expenditures, there is no direct link between cash flow and net income, since the former records capital expenditures as they are paid and the latter spreads the cost of capital expenditures over their whole useful life.

From a financing standpoint, the cash flow statement does not distinguish between capital and remuneration related to sources of financing, while the income statement shows only returns on debt financing (interest expenses) and corporate income tax.

Net income should normally appear in "cash at hand", along with certain non-cash charges that together form cash flow. Cash flow may be translated into an inflow or outflow of cash only once adjusted for the change in operating working capital to arrive at cash flow from operating activities in a broad sense of the term.

Lastly, factoring in the investment cycle, which gives rise to outflows sometimes offset by fixed asset disposals, and the equity financing cycle, we arrive at the decrease in net debt.

QUESTIONS

1/ Do inventories valuation methods influence:

- o   the company's net income?
- o   the company's cash position?

2/ Same question for the following:

- (a)   depreciation and amortisation
- (b)   corporate income tax
- (c)   equity issue through cash contribution
- (d)   cash purchase of fixed assets
- (e)   recognition and payment of salaries
- (f)   disposal for cash of an asset at its book value
- (g)   sale of goods on credit
- (h)   payment for these goods
- (i)   repayment of medium-term loan
- (j)   financial expenses.

3/ What differences are there between cash flow from operating activities and operating cash flow?

4/ What non-cash charges must be factored back into calculations of cash flow?

5/ Is cash flow a measure of an increase in wealth? Or an increase in cash?

6/ Why is the difference between EBITDA and operating cash flows equal to a change in working capital?

7/ What difference is there between sales in a financial year and operating receipts over the same period?

8/ What is the difference between cash flow and cash flow from operating activities?

9/ Why is a decrease in net debt more relevant than change in cash position or marketable securities?

10/ Make use of the cash flow statement to show how impairment losses on current assets have no impact on cash.

11/ Will a capital increase by way of incorporation of reserves appear on the cash flow statement?

More questions are waiting for you at www.vernimmen.com.

EXERCISE

Ellingham plc

Draw up a cash flow statement for Ellingham for 2011 and 2012. If you so wish, create a cash-earnings link at each level. What is your interpretation of these figures?

Questions

1/ *Yes, the lower inventories are valued, the lower net income for the current year. No, except for corporate income tax.*

2/ *(a) Yes, as depreciation and amortisation are expenses; no, except for corporate income tax, as depreciation and amortisation are non-cash expenses. (b) Yes and yes, as corporate income tax is a cash expense. (c) No, yes, as a source of financing is neither a revenue nor an expense. (d) No, yes, as the cash purchase of a fixed asset is not an expense but a cash payment. (e) Yes, yes, as salaries paid are cash expense. (f) No, yes, as no capital gain is registered. (g) Yes, no, as a revenue is registered but the cash receipt still has to be received (goods sold on credit). (h) No, yes, as the cash receipt is now received but the revenue has already been registered. (i) No, yes, as repayment of a loan does not modify the wealth of the company but its cash position. (j) Yes, yes, as financial expenses reduce the wealth of the company and its cash position.*

3/ *Unlike operating cash flow, cash flow from operating activities encompasses not only operations but also financial expense, tax and some exceptional items.*

4/ *Depreciation, amortisation and impairment losses on fixed assets and provisions for liabilities and charges.*

5/ *No, cash flow is not a measure of increase in wealth because it does not take into account depreciation, which reflects the wear and tear of fixed assets and thus a source of wealth destruction. No, because customers do not pay cash, because suppliers are not paid in cash.*

6/ *The difference between EBITDA and operating cash flow is nothing but new invoices received or sent but not yet paid either by the company or its customers, or variation in inventories, i.e. increase in working capital.*

7/ *Change in trade receivables.*

8/ *Changes in working capital.*

9/ *Because it is easier to modify the cash position of a company at year end than the net debt position which reflects its true level of indebtedness.*

10/ *Impairment losses reduce earnings, but also bring down working capital: they cancel each other out at the level of the cash flow from operating activities.*

11/ *No, it will not impact on the company's cash flow as it is a pure accounting entry.*

Exercise

A detailed Excel version of the solutions is available at www.vernimmen.com.

Ellingham plc

Cash forecast	Jan 2011	Feb 2011	Mar 2011	Apr 2011	May 2011	June 2011	July 2011	Aug 2011	Sept 2011	Oct 2011	Nov 2011	Dec 2011	2011	2012	2013
Operating inflows															
Sales					12	12	12	12	12	12	12	12	96	144	144
Operating outflows															
– Purchases				8	12	12	12	12	12	12	12	12	40	48	48
– Personnel costs	4	4	4	4	4	4	4	4	4	4	4	4	48	48	48
– Shipping		2	2	2	2	2	2	2	2	2	2	2	22	24	24
– Interest expense						1						0.9	1.9	1.5	1.1
– Capital expenditure	30												30		
+ New borrowings	20												20		
– Repayment of borrowings	2						3						4	4	4
Change in cash	–16	–6	–6	–14	2	1	0	2	2	2	2	1.1	–29.9	18.5	18.9
Cumulated balance	–16	–22	–28	–42	–40	–39	–39	–37	–35	–33	–33	–29.9	–29.9	–11.4	7.5

(N.B.: No sales in January 2011 in order to build up initial stock of finished goods.)

Income statement (by nature)	2011	2012	2013
Sales	132	144	144
+ Change in finished goods and in progress in inventory [1]	10	0	0
= Production for period	142	144	144
− Raw material used in the business [2]	48	48	48
− Payroll costs	48	48	48
− Shipping	24	24	24
= EBITDA	22	24	24
− Depreciation and amortisation	6	6	6
= Operating income	16	18	18
− Interest expense	1.9	1.5	1.1
= Net earnings	14.1	16.5	16.9

[1]Change in finished goods and in-progress inventory: €4m in raw materials + €4m in payroll costs + €2m in shipping costs = €10m.

[2]Breakdown of raw materials used in the business in year 1: €52m (purchases) − €4m (increase in raw materials inventories) = €48m.

Income statement (by function)	2011	2012	2013
Sales	32	144	144
− Cost of sales	116	126	126
= Operating income	16	18	18
− Interest expense	1.9	1.5	1.1
= Net earnings	14.1	16.5	16.9

Cash flows statement – Format 1	2011	2012	2013
EBITDA	22	24	24
− Change in working capital	36	0	0
= Operating cash flows	−14	24	24
− Capital expenditure	30	0	0
− Interest expense	1.9	1.5	1.1
= Net decrease in debt	−45.9	22.5	22.9
New borrowings	20	0	0
− Debt repayments	4	4	4
− Change in cash and equivalents	−29.9	18.5	18.9

Cash flows statement – Format 2	2011	2012	2013
Net income	14.1	16.5	16.9
– Depreciation and amortisation	6	6	6
= Cash flow	20.1	22.5	22.9
– Change in working capital	36	0	0
= Cash flow from operating activities	–15.9	22.5	22.9
– Capital expenditure	30	0	0
= Net decrease in debt	–45.9	22.5	22.9
New borrowings	20	0	0
– Debt repayments	4	4	4
– Change in cash and equivalents	–29.9	18.5	18.9

Balance sheet	2011	2012	2013
Fixed assets, net (A)	0	24	18
Inventories	0	14	14
+ Trade receivables	0	36	36
– Trade payables and other debts	0	14	14
= Working capital (B)	0	36	36
= Capital employed (A + B)	0	60	54
Shareholders' equity (C)	40	54.1	70.6
Bank and financial debts	0	16	12
– Marketable securities	0	0	0
– Cash and equivalents	40	10.1	28.6
= Net debt (D)	–40	5.9	–16.6
= Invested capital (C + D)	0	60	54

The creation of their Spanish subsidiary is a clever move. This outfit is profitable the first year, capital expenditure and increase in working capital (30 + 36) are nearly entirely paid back at end-2013 after only three years of activity. It is almost too good to be true!

BIBLIOGRAPHY

For more on the topics covered in this chapter:

K. Checkley, *Strategic Cash Flow Management*, Capstone Express, 2002.

J. Kinnunen, M. Koskela, Do cash flows reported by firms articulate with their income statements and balance sheets? Descriptive evidence from Finland, *The European Accounting Review*, **8**(4), 631–654, 1999.

H. Stolowy, M. Lebas, Y. Ding, *Financial Accounting and Reporting: A Global Perspective*, 3rd edn, Thomson, 2010.

O. Whitfield Broome, Statement of cash flows: Time for change! *Financial Analysts Journal*, **60**(2), 16–22, March–April 2004.

Chapter 6
GETTING TO GRIPS WITH CONSOLIDATED ACCOUNTS

A group-building exercise

The purpose of consolidated accounts is to present the financial situation of a group of companies as if they formed one single entity. This chapter deals with the basic aspects of consolidation that should be understood by anyone interested in corporate finance.

An analysis of the accounting documents of each individual company belonging to a group does not serve as a very accurate or useful guide to the economic health of the whole group. The accounts of a company reflect the other companies that it controls only through the book value of its shareholdings (revalued or written down, where appropriate) and the size of the dividends that it receives.

The purpose of consolidated accounts is to present the financial situation of a group of companies as if they formed one single entity.

The goal of this chapter is to familiarise readers with the problems arising from consolidation. Consequently, we present an example-based guide to the main aspects of consolidation in order to facilitate analysis of consolidated accounts.

In some cases, consolidated accounts take some time to come out or even do not exist.[1] That said, for various reasons, financial analysts may need to know some of the key consolidated figures, such as earnings and shareholders' equity, albeit only approximately.

The aggregation of accounts may give analysts this overview provided that they roughly apply the various preconsolidation adjustments explained in this chapter.

Section 6.1
CONSOLIDATION METHODS

Any firm that controls other companies exclusively or that exercises significant influence over them should prepare consolidated accounts and a management report for the group.[2]

Consolidated accounts must be certified by the statutory auditors and, together with the group's management report, made available to shareholders, debtholders and all other parties with a vested interest in the company.

1 *For example, it took nine months for Dutch supermarket group Ahold to produce its 2002 consolidated accounts after it had discovered accounting fraud in its US subsidiary.*

2 *Unless (i) the parent is itself a wholly-owned subsidiary or is virtually wholly owned and (ii) its securities are not listed or about to be and (iii) the immediate or ultimate parent issues consolidated accounts.*

Listed European companies have been required to use IFRS[3] accounting principles for their consolidated financial statements since 2005.[4]

The companies to be included in the preparation of consolidated accounts form what is known as the **scope of consolidation**. The scope of consolidation comprises:

- the parent company;
- the companies in which the parent company has a material influence (which is assumed when the parent company holds at least 20% of the voting rights).

However, a subsidiary should not be consolidated when its parent loses the power to gov-ern its financial and operating policies, for example when the subsidiary becomes subject to the control of a government, a court or an administration. Such subsidiaries should be accounted for at fair market value.

The basic principle behind consolidation consists of replacing the historical cost of the parent's investment in the company being consolidated with its assets, liabilities and equity.

For instance, let us consider a company with a subsidiary that appears on its balance sheet with an amount of 20. Consolidation entails replacing the historical cost of 20 with all or some of the assets, liabilities and equity of the company being consolidated.

There are three methods of consolidation which are used depending on the strength of the parent company's control or influence over its subsidiary:

Type of relationship	Type of company	Consolidation method
Control	Subsidiary	Full consolidation[5]
Joint control	Joint venture	Proportionate consolidation[6]
Significant influence	Associate	Equity method

We will now examine each of these three methods in terms of its impact on sales, net profit and shareholders' equity.

1/ FULL CONSOLIDATION

The accounts of a subsidiary are fully consolidated if the latter is controlled by its parent. Control is defined as the ability to direct the strategic financing and operating policies of an entity so as to access benefits. It is presumed to exist when the parent company:

- holds, directly or indirectly, over 50% of the voting rights in its subsidiary;
- holds, directly or indirectly, less than 50% of the voting rights but has power over more than 50% of the voting rights by virtue of an agreement with other investors;
- has power to govern the financial and operating policies of the subsidiary under a statute or an agreement;
- has power to cast the majority of votes at meetings of the board of directors; or
- has power to appoint or remove the majority of the members of the board.

The criterion of exclusive control is the key factor under IFRS standards. Under US GAAP, the determining factor is whether or not the parent company holds the majority of voting rights. Nevertheless, the definition is broader and can encompass companies in which only a minority is held (or even no shares at all!).

As its name suggests, full consolidation consists of transferring all the subsidiary's assets, liabilities and equity to the parent company's balance sheet and all the revenues and costs to the parent company's income statement.

The assets, liabilities and equity thus replace the investments held by the parent company, which therefore disappear from its balance sheet.

That said, when the subsidiary is not controlled exclusively by the parent company, the claims of the other "minority" shareholders on the subsidiary's equity and net income also need to be shown on the consolidated balance sheet and income statement of the group.

Assuming there is no difference between the book value of the parent's investment in the subsidiary and the share of the book value of the subsidiary's equity,[7] full consolidation works as follows:

- On the balance sheet:

  o the subsidiary's assets and liabilities are **added item by item** to the parent company's balance sheet;
  o the historical cost amount of the shares in the consolidated subsidiary held by the parent is eliminated from the parent company's balance sheet and the same amount is deducted from the parent company's reserves;
  o the subsidiary's equity (including net income) is added to the parent company's equity and then allocated between the interests of the parent company (added to its reserves) and those of minority investors in the subsidiary (if the parent company does not hold 100% of the capital), which is added to a special **minority interests** line below the line item showing the parent company's shareholders' equity.

- On the income statement, all the subsidiary's revenues and charges are added item by item to the parent company's income statement. The parent company's net income is then broken down into:

  o the portion attributable to the parent company, which is added to the parent company's net income on both the income statement and the balance sheet;
  o the portion attributable to third-party investors, which is shown on a separate line of the income statement under the heading "minority interests".

Minority interests represent the share attributable to minority shareholders in the shareholders' equity and net income of fully consolidated subsidiaries.

From a solvency standpoint, minority interests certainly represent shareholders' equity. But from a valuation standpoint, they add no value to the group since minority interests represent shareholders' equity and net profit attributable to third parties and not to shareholders of the parent company.

Right up until the penultimate line of the income statement, financial analysis assumes that the parent company owns 100% of the subsidiary's assets and liabilities and implicitly that all the liabilities finance all the assets. This is true from an economic, but not from a legal, perspective.

7 *Which means "no goodwill", a topic to which we will return.*

To illustrate the full consolidation method, consider the following example assuming that the parent company owns 75% of the subsidiary company.

The original balance sheets are as follows:

Parent company's balance sheet				Subsidiary's balance sheet			
Investment in the subsidiary[8]	15	Shareholders' equity	70	Assets	28	Shareholders' equity	20
Other assets	57	Liabilities	2			Liabilities	8

8 *Valued at historical cost less depreciation if any.*

In this scenario, the consolidated balance sheet would be as follows:

Consolidated balance sheet			
Investment in the subsidiary $(15-15)$	0	Shareholders' equity $(70+20-15)$	75
Assets $(57+28)$	85	Liabilities $(2+8)$	10

Or, in a more detailed form:

Consolidated balance sheet		
Assets	85	Shareholders' equity group share $(75-5)$ 70
		Minority interests $(20\times25\%)$ 5
		Liabilities 10

The original income statements are as follows:

Parent company's income statement				Subsidiary's income statement			
Costs	80	Net sales	100	Costs	30	Net sales	38
Net income	20			Net income	8		

In this scenario, the consolidated income statement would be as follows:

Consolidated income statement			
Costs $(80+30)$	110	Net sales $(100+38)$	138
Net income $(20+8)$	28		

Or, in a more detailed form:

Consolidated income statement		
Costs	110	Net sales 138
Net income:		
Group share	26	
Minority interest $(8\times25\%)$	2	

2/ EQUITY METHOD OF ACCOUNTING

When the parent company exercises significant influence over the operating and financial policy of its associate, the latter is accounted for under the equity method. Significant influence over the operating and financial policy of a company is assumed when the parent holds, directly or indirectly, at least 20% of the voting rights. Significant influence may be reflected by participation on the executive and supervisory bodies, participation in strategic decisions, the existence of major intercompany links, exchanges of management personnel and a relationship of dependence from a technical standpoint.

Equity accounting consists of replacing the carrying amount of the shares held in an associate (also known as an **equity affiliate** or **associated undertaking**) with the corresponding portion of the associate's shareholders' equity (including net income).

This method is purely financial. Both the group's investments and aggregate profit are thus reassessed on an annual basis. Accordingly, the IASB regards equity accounting as being more of a valuation method than a method of consolidation.

From a technical standpoint, equity accounting takes place as follows:

- the historical cost amount of shares held in the associate is subtracted from the parent company's investments and replaced by the share attributable to the parent company in the associate's shareholders' equity including net income for the year;
- the carrying value of the associate's shares is subtracted from the parent company's reserves, to which is added the share in the associate's shareholders' equity, **excluding** the associate's income attributable to the parent company;
- the portion of the associate's net income attributable to the parent company is added to its net income on the balance sheet and the income statement.

Investments in associates represent the share attributable to the parent company in associates' shareholders' equity.

The equity method of accounting therefore leads to an increase each year in the carrying amount of the shareholding on the consolidated balance sheet, by an amount equal to the net income transferred to reserves by the associate.

However, from a solvency standpoint, this method does not provide any clue to the group's risk exposure and liabilities *vis-à-vis* its associate. The implication is that the group's risk exposure is restricted to the value of its shareholding.

The equity method of accounting is more a method used to reevaluate certain participating interests than a genuine form of consolidation.

To illustrate the equity method of accounting, let us consider the following example based on the assumption that the parent company owns 20% of its associate:

The original balance sheets are as follows:

Parent company's balance sheet			Associate's balance sheet		
Investment in the associate	5	Shareholders' equity	60	Assets	35	Shareholders' equity	25
Other assets	57	Liabilities	2			Liabilities	10

In this scenario, the consolidated balance sheet would be as follows:

Consolidated balance sheet			
Investment in the associate (20%×25)	5	Shareholders' equity (60+5−5)	60
Other assets	57	Liabilities	2

The original income statements are as follows:

Parent company's income statement				Associate's income statement			
Costs	80	Net sales	100	Costs	30	Net sales	35
Net income	20			Net income	5		

In this scenario, the consolidated income statement would be as follows:

Consolidated income statement			
Costs	80	Net sales	100
Net income (20+5×20%)	21	Income from associates (5×20%)	1

3/ PROPORTIONATE CONSOLIDATION

A difficult question to solve when preparing the accounts is what method to use when the parent company exercises joint control with a limited number of partners over another company (joint ventures). The key factors determining joint control are: (i) a limited number of partners sharing control (without any partner able to claim exclusive control), and (ii) a contractual arrangement outlining and defining how this joint control is to be exercised.

IFRS used to allow the use of the **proportionate consolidation** method which was not permitted under US GAAP. Current changes in IFRS will probably lead to not allowing proportionate consolidation in the future, so the method to be used in the case of joint control will then be the equity method.

Similar to full consolidation, proportionate consolidation leads to the replacement of the investment held in the joint venture with the assets, liabilities and equity of the joint venture. As its name suggests, the key difference with respect to full consolidation is that assets and liabilities are transferred to the parent company's balance sheet **only in proportion to the parent company's interest in the joint venture**. Likewise, the joint venture's revenues and charges are added to those of the parent company on the consolidated income statement only in proportion to its participation in the joint venture.

From a technical standpoint, proportionate consolidation is carried out as follows:

- the joint venture's assets and liabilities are added to the parent company's assets and liabilities in proportion to the latter's interest in the joint venture;
- the carrying amount of the shares in the joint venture held by the parent company is subtracted from long-term investments and from reserves in the balance sheet;

- the parent company's share in the shareholders' equity of the joint venture excluding the latter's net income is added to the parent company's reserves;
- all the joint venture's revenues and charges are added in proportion to the level of the parent company's shareholding to the corresponding line items of the parent company's income statement;
- the portion of the joint venture's net income attributable to the parent company is added to its net income on the balance sheet and income statement.

Proportionate consolidation does not give rise to any minority interests.

One shortcoming of proportionate consolidation is that it appears to exaggerate the group's power since a portion of the turnover, cash flow, equity, fixed assets, etc. of joint ventures is included in the parent company's financial statements even if the group does not have exclusive control over those joint ventures.

Section 6.2
CONSOLIDATION-RELATED ISSUES

1/ SCOPE OF CONSOLIDATION

The scope of consolidation, i.e. the companies to be consolidated, is determined using the rules we presented in Section 6.1. To determine the scope of consolidation, one needs to establish the level of control exercised by the parent company over each of the companies in which it owns shares.

(a) Level of control and ownership level

The **level of control**[9] measures the strength of direct or indirect dependence that exists between the parent company and its subsidiaries, joint ventures or associates. Although control is assessed in a broader way in IFRS (see p. 74), the percentage of voting rights that the parent company controls (what we call here "level of control") will be a key indication to determine whether the subsidiary is controlled or significantly influenced.

> 9 *Or percentage control.*

To calculate the level of control, we must look at the percentage of voting rights held by all group companies in the subsidiary provided that the group companies are controlled directly or indirectly by the parent company.

Control is assumed when the percentage of voting rights held is 50% or higher or when a situation of *de facto* control exists at each link in the chain.

It is important not to confuse the level of control with the level of ownership. Generally speaking, these two concepts are different. The **ownership level**[10] is used to calculate the parent company's claims on its subsidiaries, joint ventures or associates. It reflects the proportion of their capital held directly or indirectly by the parent company. It is a financial concept, unlike the level of control which is a power-related concept.

> 10 *Or percentage interest.*

The ownership level is the sum of the product of the direct and indirect percentage stakes held by the parent company in a given company. The ownership level differs from the level of control which considers only the controlled subsidiaries.

Consider the following example:

SCOPE OF CONSOLIDATION

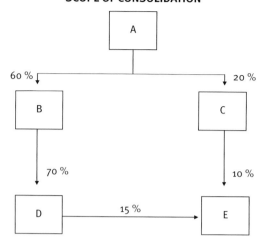

A controls 60% of B, B controls 70% of D, so A controls 70% of D. D and B are therefore considered as controlled and thus fully consolidated by A. But A does not own 70%, but 42% of D (i.e. 60% × 70%). The ownership level of A over D is then 42%: only 42% of D's net income is attributable to A.

Since C owns just 10% of E, C will not consolidate E. Neither will D as it only owns 15% of E. But since A controls 20% of C, A will account for C under the equity method and will show 20% of C's net income in its income statement.

The ownership level of A over E is 20% × 10% + 60% × 70% × 15% = 8.3%. The percentage of control of A over E is 15%.

How the ownership level is used varies from one consolidation method to another:

- with full consolidation, the **ownership level** is used only to allocate the subsidiary's reserves and net income between the parent company and minority interests in the subsidiary;
- with proportionate consolidation, all the joint venture's balance sheet and income statement items are added in proportion to the **ownership level** to the balance sheet and income statement items of the parent company;
- with the equity method of accounting, the **ownership level** is used to determine the portion of the subsidiary's shareholders' equity and net income attributable to the parent company.

(b) Changes in the scope of consolidation

It is important to analyse the scope of consolidation, especially with regard to what has changed and what is excluded. A decision not to consolidate a company means:

- neither its losses nor its shareholders' equity will appear on the balance sheet[11] of the group;
- its liabilities will not appear on the balance sheet of the group.

The equity method of accounting also means that not all the group's liabilities are shown on the balance sheet, as readers will see with the example of Coca Cola in Chapter 13.

11 *Unless the losses are such that the portion of the subsidiary's shareholders' equity attributable to the parent company is lower than the net book value of the shares in the subsidiary held by the parent. In which case, an impairment loss is recognised on the shareholding.*

Changes in the scope of consolidation require the preparation of **pro forma** financial statements. Pro forma statements enable analysts to compare the company's performances on a consistent basis. In these pro forma statements, the company may either:

- restate past accounts to make them comparable with the current scope of consolidation; or
- remove from the current scope of consolidation any item that was not present in the previous period to maintain its previous configuration. This latter option is, however, less interesting for financial analysts.

Finally certain techniques can be used to remove subsidiaries still controlled by the parent company from the scope of consolidation. These techniques have been developed to make certain consolidated accounts look more attractive. These techniques frequently involve a special-purpose vehicle (SPV). The SPV is a separate legal entity created specially to handle a venture on behalf of a company. In many cases, from a legal standpoint the SPV belongs to banks or to investors rather than to the company. That said, the IASB has stipulated that the company should consolidate the SPV if:

- it enjoys the majority of the benefits; or
- it incurs the residual risks arising from the SPV even if it does not own a single share of the SPV.

These rules now make it very difficult to use this type of scheme under IFRS.[12]

12 *The same is not true for US GAAP.*

2/ GOODWILL

It is very unusual for one company to acquire another for exactly its book value.

Generally speaking, there is a difference between the acquisition price, which may be paid in cash or in shares, and the portion of the target company's shareholders' equity attributable to the parent company. In most cases, this difference is positive as the price paid exceeds the target's book value.

(a) What does this difference represent?

In other words, why should a company agree to pay out more for another company than its book value? There are several possible explanations:

- the assets recorded on the acquired company's balance sheet are worth more than their historical cost. This situation may result from the prudence principle, which means that unrealised capital losses have to be taken into account, but not unrealised capital gains;
- it is perfectly conceivable that assets such as patents, licences and market shares that the company has accumulated over the years without wishing to, or even being able to, account for them, may not appear on the balance sheet. This situation is especially true if the company is highly profitable;
- the merger between the two companies may create synergies, either in the form of cost reductions and/or revenue enhancement. The buyer is likely to partly reflect them in the price offered to the seller;
- the buyer may be ready to pay a high price for a target just to prevent a new player from buying it, entering the market, and putting the current level of the buyer's profitability under pressure;
- finally, the buyer may quite simply have overpaid for the deal.

(b) How is goodwill accounted for?

Goodwill is shown under intangible fixed assets of the new group's balance sheet at an amount equal to the difference between the acquisition price and the share of the new subsidiary's equity adjusted for unrealised capital gains net of unrealised capital losses on assets and liabilities. Assets, liabilities and equity of the new subsidiary are transferred to the group's balance sheet at their estimated value rather than their book value. In this case, the intangible assets acquired, i.e. brands, patents, licences, landing slots, databases, etc., are recorded on the group's balance sheet even if they did not originally appear on the acquired company's balance sheet.

> The difference between the purchase cost and the fair market value of the assets and liabilities acquired with a company is called goodwill.

Goodwill is assessed each year to verify whether its value is at least equal to its net book value as shown on the group's balance sheet. This assessment is called an **impairment test**. If the market value of goodwill is below its book value, goodwill is written down to its fair market value and a corresponding impairment loss is recorded in the income statement.

This method is known as the **purchase method**. This is the method prescribed by US GAAP[13] since December 2001 and by IFRS from 1 January 2006. The **pooling of interest method** was abolished by the US authorities in December 2001 and by the IASB in 2006. It allowed the assets and liabilities of the newly acquired company to be included in the group's accounts at their book value without any goodwill being recorded.[14]

To illustrate the purchase method, let's analyse now how the electricity producer EDF accounted for the acquisition of its rival British Energy in early 2009.

Prior to the acquisition, EDF's balance sheet (in billions of €) can be summarised as follows:

Goodwill	7.7	Shareholders' equity	32.7
Other fixed assets	150.7	Provisions	89.3
Working capital	4.9	Net debt	41.3

While British Energy's balance sheet was as follows:

Goodwill	7.3	Shareholders' equity	9.6
Other fixed assets	7.9	Provisions	7.4
Working capital	1.2	Net debt	−0.6

EDF acquired 100% of British Energy for €13.5bn paid for in cash. Therefore, EDF paid €3.9bn[15] more than British Energy's equity. This amount is not equal to goodwill as EDF proceeded to a revaluation of assets and liabilities of British Energy as follows:

- intangible assets   − €6.6bn
- tangible assets   + €7.6bn
- inventories   + €0.6bn
- deferred tax liability[16] + €2.3bn
- net debt (fair value)   + €0.1bn
- operating liabilities   − €0.1bn
- provisions   + €1.2bn

13 *Generally Accepted Accounting Principles.*

14 *As the difference between the price paid for the shares and their book value was deducted from the acquiror's equity.*

15 *13.5 − 9.6 = 3.9*

16 *See Chapter 7.*

Total adjustments amount to $-€1.9$bn. Consequently, the amount of goodwill created was $€3.9$bn $+ €1.9$bn $= €5.8$bn. The simplified balance sheet of the combined entity was therefore as follows:

Goodwill	13.5[17]	Shareholders' equity	32.7
Other fixed assets	166.9[18]	Provisions	97.9[19]
Working capital	4.5[20]	Net debt	54.3[21]

[17] $7.7 + 5.8 = 13.5$

[18] $150.7 + 7.3 + 7.9 - 6.6 + 7.6 = 166.9$

[19] $89.3 + 7.4 + 1.2 = 97.9$

[20] $4.9 + 1.2 + 0.6 - 2.3 + 0.1 = 4.5$

[21] $41.3 - 0.6 + 0.1 + 13.5 = 54.3$

Finally, transactions may give rise to negative goodwill under certain circumstances. Under IFRS, negative goodwill is immediately recognised as a profit in the income statement of the new groups.

All in all, the difference between the purchase price and the share in equity is broken down into two portions. One reflects unrealised capital gains on the assets of the target company and is factored into the valuation of the consolidated assets. The other one, the residual portion, is called goodwill and is not accounted for by unrealised capital gains. This is called Purchase Price Allocation (or simply PPA).

The consolidated company's assets and liabilities are therefore revalued upon its first-time consolidation. Its accounts are adjusted to bring them into line with the accounting policies applied by its new parent company.

(c) How should financial analysts treat goodwill?

From a financial standpoint, it is sensible to regard goodwill as an asset like any other, which may suffer sudden falls in value that need to be recognised by means of an impairment charge.

Can it be argued that goodwill impairment losses do not reflect any decrease in the company's wealth because there is no outflow of cash? We do not think so.

Granted, goodwill impairment losses are a non-cash item, but it would be wrong to say that only decisions giving rise to cash flows affect a company's value. For instance, setting a maximum limit on voting rights or attributing 10 voting rights to certain categories of shares does not have any cash impact, but definitely reduces the value of shareholders' equity.

Recognising the impairment of goodwill related to a past acquisition is tantamount to admitting that the price paid was too high. But what if the acquisition was paid for in shares? This makes no difference whatsoever, irrespective of whether the buyer's shares were overvalued at the same time.

Had the company carried out a share issue rather than overpaying for an acquisition, it would have been able to capitalise on its lofty share price to the great benefit of existing shareholders. The cash raised through the share issue would have been used to make acquisitions at much more reasonable prices once the wave of euphoria had subsided. This is precisely the strategy adopted by Bouygues. It raised €1.5bn of new equity in March 2000 at a very high share price, refused to participate in the UMTS auctions and used its cash pile only in 2002 to buy out minority interests in its telecom subsidiary at a far lower level than the rumoured price in 2000.

It is essential to remember that shareholders in a company which pays for a deal in shares suffer dilution in their interest. They accept this dilution because they take the view that the size of the cake will grow at a faster rate (e.g. by 30%) than the number of guests invited to the party (e.g. by over 25%). Should it transpire that the cake grows at merely 10% rather than the expected 30% because the purchased assets prove to be worth less than anticipated, the number of guests at the party will unfortunately stay the same. Accordingly, the size of each guest's slice of the cake falls by 12% (110/125−1), so shareholders' wealth has certainly diminished.

Finally, testing each year whether the capital employed of each company segment is greater than its book value so as to determine whether the purchased goodwill needs to be written down is implicitly checking whether internally generated goodwill gradually replaces the purchased goodwill or not. As we know, goodwill has a limited lifespan in view of the competition prevailing in the business world that will, sooner or later, erode too high a profitability obtained after an acquisition.

(d) How should financial analysts treat "adjusted income"?

In certain specific sectors (like the pharmaceutical sector), following an acquisition, the acquirer publishes an "adjusted income" to neutralise the P&L impact of the revaluation of assets and liabilities of its newly-acquired subsidiary. Naturally, a P&L account is drawn up under normal standards, but it carries an audited table showing the impact of the switch to adjusted income.

As a matter of fact, by virtue of the revaluation of the target's inventories to their market value, the normal process of selling the inventories generates no profit. So how relevant will the P&L be in the first year after the merger? This issue becomes critical only when the production cycle is very long and therefore the revaluation of inventories (and potentially research and development capitalised) is material.

We believe that for those specific sectors, groups are right to show this adjusted P&L.

Section 6.3
TECHNICAL ASPECTS OF CONSOLIDATION

1/ HARMONISING ACCOUNTING DATA

Since consolidation consists of aggregating accounts give or take some adjustments, it is important to ensure that the accounting data used are consistent, i.e. based on the same principles.

Usually, the valuation methods used in individual company accounts are determined by accounting or tax issues specific to each subsidiary, especially when some of them are located outside the group's home country. This is particularly true for provisions, depreciation and amortisation, fixed assets, inventories and work in progress, deferred charges and shareholders' equity.

These differences need to be eliminated upon consolidation. This process is facilitated by the fact that most of the time consolidated accounts are not prepared to calculate taxable income, so groups may disregard the prevailing tax regulations.

Prior to consolidation, the consolidating company needs to restate the accounts of the to-be-consolidated companies. The consolidating company applies the same valuation principles and makes adjustments for the impact of the valuation differences that are justified on tax grounds, e.g. tax-regulated provisions, accelerated depreciation for tax purposes and so on.

2/ ELIMINATING INTRA-GROUP TRANSACTIONS

Consolidation entails more than the mere aggregation of accounts. Before the consolidation process as such can begin, intra-group transactions and their impact on net income have to be eliminated from the accounts of both the parent company and its consolidated companies.

Assume, for instance, that the parent company has sold to subsidiaries products at cost plus a margin. An entirely fictitious gain would show up in the group's accounts if the relevant products were merely held in stock by the subsidiaries rather than being sold on to third parties. Naturally, this fictitious gain, which would be a distortion of reality, needs to be eliminated.

Intra-group transactions to be eliminated upon consolidation can be broken down into two categories:

- Those that are very significant because they affect consolidated net income. It is therefore vital for such transactions to be reversed. The goal is to avoid showing two profits or showing the same profit twice in two different years. The reversal of these transactions upon consolidation leads primarily to the elimination of:

  o intra-group profits included in inventories;
  o capital gains arising on the transfer or contribution of investments;
  o dividends received from consolidated companies;
  o impairment losses on intra-group loans or investments; and
  o tax on intra-group profits.

- those that are not fundamental because they have no impact on consolidated net income or those affecting the assets or liabilities of the consolidated entities. These transactions are eliminated through netting, so as to show the real level of the group's debt. They include:

  o parent-to-subsidiary loans (advances to the subsidiary) and vice versa;
  o interest paid by the parent company to the consolidated companies (financial income of the latter) and vice versa.

3/ TRANSLATING THE ACCOUNTS OF FOREIGN SUBSIDIARIES

(a) The problem

The translation of the accounts of foreign companies is a tricky issue because of exchange rate fluctuations and the difference between inflation rates, which may distort the picture provided by company accounts.

For instance, a parent company located in the euro zone may own a subsidiary in a country with a soft currency.[22]

Using year-end exchange rates to convert the assets of its subsidiary into the parent company's currency understates their value. From an economic standpoint, all the assets do not suffer depreciation proportional to that of the subsidiary's home currency.

On the one hand, fixed assets are protected to some extent. Inflation means that it would cost more in the subsidiary's local currency to replace them after the devaluation in the currency than before. All in all, the inflation and devaluation phenomena may actually offset each other, so the value of the subsidiary's fixed assets in the parent company's currency is roughly stable. On the other hand, inventories, receivables and liabilities

22 A soft or weak currency is a currency that tends to fall in value because of political or economic uncertainty (high inflation rate).

(irrespective of their maturity) denominated in the devalued currency all depreciate in tandem with the currency.

If the subsidiary is located in a country with a hard currency (i.e. a stronger one than that of the parent company), the situation is similar, but the implications are reversed.

To present an accurate image of developments in the foreign subsidiary's situation, it is necessary to take into account:

- the impact on the consolidated accounts of the translation of the subsidiary's currency into the parent company's currency;
- the adjustment that would stem from translation of the foreign subsidiary's fixed assets into the local currency.

(b) Methods

Several methods may be used at the same time to translate different items in the balance sheet and income statement of foreign subsidiaries giving rise to currency translation differences.

- If the subsidiary is economically and financially independent of its parent company, which is the most common situation, the **closing rate method** is used.
- If the subsidiary is not independent of its parent company, because its operations are an integral part of another company, the **temporal method**[23] is used.
- Finally, if the subsidiary is based in a country with high inflation, a special method is used.

23 Based on the historical exchange rate method.

Under the **closing rate method**, all assets and liabilities are translated at the closing rate which is the rate of exchange at the balance sheet date.[24] IFRS recommend using the exchange rate prevailing on the transaction date to translate revenues and charges on the income statement or, failing this, the average exchange rate for the period, which is what most companies do. Currency translation differences are recorded under shareholders' equity, with a distinction being made between the group's share and that attributable to minority investors. This translation method is relatively comparable to the US standard.

*24 This method is also called the **current rate method**.*

The **temporal method** consists of translating:

- monetary items (i.e. cash and sums receivable or payable denominated in the foreign company's currency and determined in advance) at the closing rate;
- non-monetary items (fixed assets and the corresponding depreciation and amortisation,[25] inventories, prepayments, shareholders' equity, investments, etc.) at the exchange rate at the date to which the historical cost or valuation pertains;
- revenues and charges on the income statement theoretically at the exchange rate prevailing on the transaction date. In practice, however, they are usually translated at an average exchange rate for the period.

25 As an exception to this rule, goodwill is translated at the closing rate.

Under the temporal method, the difference between the net income on the balance sheet and that on the income statement is recorded on the income statement under foreign exchange gains and losses.

The temporal method is prescribed in the US.

(c) Translating the accounts of subsidiaries located in hyperinflationary countries

A hyperinflationary country is one where inflation is both chronic and out of control. In such circumstances, the previous methods are not suitable for translating the effects of inflation into the accounts.

Hence the use of a specific method based on restatements made by applying a general price index. Elements such as monetary items that are already stated at the measuring unit at the balance sheet date are not restated. Other elements are restated based on the change in the general price index between the date those items were acquired or incurred and the balance sheet consolidation. A gain or loss on the net monetary position is included in net income.

The summary of this chapter can be downloaded from www.vernimmen.com.

SUMMARY

Consolidation aims at presenting the financial position of a group of companies as if they formed one single entity. It is an obligation for companies that exclusively control other companies or exercise significant influence over them. The scope of consolidation encompasses the parent company and the companies in which the parent company holds at least 20% of the voting rights. The basic principle of consolidation is to replace the book value of investments on the parent company's balance sheet with the assets, liabilities and equity of the consolidated subsidiaries.

Full consolidation, which is generally applied when the parent company holds more than 50% of voting rights in its subsidiary, consists of replacing the investments on the parent company's balance sheet with all the subsidiary's assets, liabilities and equity, as well as adding all the revenues and charges from its income statement. This method gives rise to minority interests in the subsidiary's net income and shareholders' equity.

Where the parent company exercises significant influence (usually by holding over 20% of the voting rights) over another company (hence called an associate), the equity method of accounting is used. The book value of investments is replaced by the parent company's share in the associate's equity (including net income). This method is actually equivalent to an annual revaluation of these investments.

Proportionate consolidation can be used where the parent company shares control over a joint venture with a limited number of partners. The approach is the same as for full consolidation, but assets, liabilities, equity, revenues and charges are transferred only in proportion to the stake of the parent company in the joint venture.

From a financial standpoint, the ownership level, which represents the percentage of the capital held directly or indirectly by the parent company, is not equal to the level of control, which reflects the proportion of voting rights held. The level of control is used to determine which consolidation method is applied. The ownership level is used to separate the group's interests from minorities' interests in equity and net income.

A group often acquires a company by paying more than the book value of the company's equity. The difference is recorded as goodwill under intangible assets, minus any unrealised capital gains or losses on the acquired company's assets and liabilities. This goodwill arising on consolidation is compared each year with its estimated value and written down to fair market value, where appropriate.

When analysing a group, it is essential to ensure that the basic accounting data are consistent from one company to another. Likewise, intra-group transactions, especially those affecting consolidated net income (intra-group profits, dividends received from subsidiaries, etc.), must be eliminated upon consolidation.

Two methods are used to translate the accounts of foreign subsidiaries: the closing rate and the temporal method for currency exchange rate translations. In addition, specific currency translation methods are used for companies in hyperinflationary countries.

QUESTIONS

1/ Describe the three methods used for consolidating accounts.

2/ What criticism can be made of the equity method of accounting?

3/ What criticism can be made of proportionate consolidation?

4/ What is the difference between the proportion of voting rights held and the ownership level?

5/ On the consolidated income statement, what is the "share of earnings in companies accounted for under the equity method" similar to?

6/ In what circumstances should the group's share be separated from that attributable to minority investors?

7/ Will opening up the capital of a subsidiary to shareholders outside the group have an impact on the group's earnings? Is this a paradox? Explain.

8/ Why do dividends paid by subsidiaries have to be restated when consolidated accounts are drawn up?

9/ What is goodwill and how is it stated?

10/ What is the most frequently used method of consolidation? Why?

11/ In French, in the UK or in Italian GAAP (used for some non-listed companies) where goodwill is amortised linearly over a fixed period of time, does the rate at which goodwill is written down have an impact on the amount of tax paid by the group?

12/ Why have some groups judged it necessary to publish adjusted income?

13/ Why has the phasing-out of the pooling of interests method made accounts more rigorous?

More questions are waiting for you at www.vernimmen.com.

EXERCISE

The financial statements of company M and its subsidiary S are shown here (in €m).

Balance sheet

Assets	M	S	Equity and liabilities	M	S
Tangible and intangible fixed assets	100	30	Equity and share capital	40	10
Investment in subsidiary S	16	—	Reserves	80	10
Other investments	5	—	Net earnings	10	5
Current assets	200	70	Debt	191	75
Total	**321**	**100**	**Total**	**321**	**100**

Income statement

	M	S
Sales	200	90
− Purchases of raw materials	100	50
− Change in inventories	—	2
− Other external services	25	20
− Personnel costs	40	8
− Interest and other financial charges	10	1
+ Interest, dividends and other financial income	3	—
− Exceptional costs	9	—
+ Exceptional income	2	—
− Corporate income tax	11	4
= Net income	**10**	**5**

Draw up the consolidated accounts for the group M + S in the following circumstances:

(a) M has an 80% stake in S (full consolidation).
(b) M has a 50% stake in S (assuming the accounting principles allow for proportional consolidation).
(c) M has a 20% stake in S (equity method consolidation).

(N.B. It is assumed that there are no flows between M and S.)

ANSWERS

Questions

1/ *See chapter.*
2/ *It is not a consolidation method but a method for revaluing assets.*
3/ *It is misleading in the sense that, if you own a third of the joint venture, you do not own a third of the assets and are not liable for a third of liabilities.*
4/ *See chapter.*
5/ *Financial income on long-term investments.*
6/ *When valuing shares of the group because shareholders of the group have no claim whatsoever on stakes owned by minority interests in subsidiaries.*
7/ *Yes, it results in minority interests. This is a paradox since the group registers a profit or a loss without receiving cash. This is because of the increase or reduction in the group's share in shareholders' equity (see page 98).*

8/ *Because they are internal flows.*
9/ *Goodwill is the difference between the price paid for the subsidiary and the estimated value of its assets minus liabilities. Goodwill is an intangible asset, the value of which will be tested every year and impaired if need be.*
10/ *Full consolidation because groups tend to prefer exclusive control over joint control or significant influence.*
11/ *No, it is a consolidated accounting entry; and corporate income taxes are not computed on consolidated accounts but in individual accounts in France, in the UK and in Italy.*
12/ *To provide more accurate financial information in some specific cases.*
13/ *Because it is no longer possible to reduce capital employed and capital invested by writing-off goodwill against equity, artificially boosting return on equity or return on capital employed.*

Exercise

A detailed Excel version of the solutions is available at www.vernimmen.com.

M + S balance sheet (€M)	80%	50%	20%
Assets	130	115	100
Tangible and intangible fixed assets			5
Equity in associated companies	5	5	5
Investments	270	235	200
Total	405	355	310
Equity and liabilities			
Share capital	40	40	40
Reserves	80*	74	68
Minority interests in equity	4		
Net earnings (group share)	14	12.5	11
Minority interests in net earnings	1		
Debt	266	228.5	191
Total	405	335	310

*group share

SECTION 1

M + S income statement (€M)	80%	50%	20%
Sales	290	245	
− Purchase of raw materials	150	125	200
− Change in inventories	2	1	100
− Other external services	45	35	25
− Personnel costs	48	44	40
− Interest and other finance charges	11	10.5	10
+ Interest, dividends and other financial income	3	3	3
− Exceptional costs	9	9	9
+ Exceptional income	2	2	2
− Corporate income tax	15	13	11
+ Income from associates			1
= Net earnings	15	12.5	11
− Minority interests	1		
= Net earnings, group share	14		

BIBLIOGRAPHY

For more about consolidation techniques:

D. Alexander, C. Nobes, *Financial Accounting: An International Introduction*, 4th edn, Financial Times Prentice Hall, 2010.

H. Stolowy, M. Lebas, Y. Ding, *Financial Accounting and Reporting: A Global Perspective*, 3rd edn, Thomson, 2010.

To get the latest version of US and International GAAPs:

B. Epstein, E. Jermakowicz, *Interpretation and Application of International Accounting Standards*, John Wiley & Sons Inc., published every year.

www.fasb.org, the website of the US Accounting Standards Board.

www.ifrs.org, the website of the International Accounting Standards Board.

www.iasplus.com, Deloitte's website about IAS rules.

To understand how financial markets react to impairment losses in goodwill:

M. Hirschey, V. Richardson, Investor underreaction to goodwill write-offs, *Financial Analysts Journal*, **59**(6), 75–84, November–December 2003.

Chapter 7
HOW TO COPE WITH THE MOST COMPLEX POINTS IN FINANCIAL ACCOUNTS

Everything you always wanted to know but never dared to ask!

This chapter is rather different from the others. It is not intended to be read from start to finish, but consulted from time to time, whenever readers experience problems interpreting, analysing or processing a particular accounting item.

Each of these complex points will be analysed from these angles:

* **from an economic standpoint** so that readers gain a thorough understanding of its real substance;
* **from an accounting standpoint** to help readers understand the accounting treatment applied and how this treatment affects the published accounts;
* **from a financial standpoint** to draw a conclusion as to how best to deal with this problem.

Our experience tells us that this is the best way of getting to grips with and solving problems. The key point to understand in this chapter is the method we use to deal with complex issues since we cannot look at every single point here. When faced with a different problem, readers will have to come up with their own solutions using our methodology – unless they contact us through the vernimmen.com website.

The following bullet list shows, in alphabetical order, the main line items and principal problems that readers are likely to face.

* accruals
* construction contracts
* convertible bonds or loans
* currency translation adjustments
* deferred tax assets and liabilities
* dilution profits or losses
* exchangeable bonds
* goodwill
* impairment losses
* intangible fixed assets
* inventories

* leases
* mandatory convertible bonds
* off-balance sheet commitments
* pensions and other employee benefits
* perpetual subordinated loans or notes
* preference shares
* provisions
* stock options
* tangible fixed assets
* treasury shares

Section 7.1
ACCRUALS

1/ WHAT ARE ACCRUALS?

Accruals are used to recognise revenue and costs booked in one period but relating to another period. To accrue basically means to transfer revenue or costs from the P&L to the balance sheet.

2/ HOW ARE THEY ACCOUNTED FOR?

The main categories of accruals are:

- **prepaid costs**, i.e. costs relating to goods or services to be supplied later. For instance, three-quarters of a rental charge payable in advance for a 12-month period on 1 October each year will be recorded under prepaid costs on the asset side of the balance sheet at 31 December;[1]
- **deferred income**, i.e. income accounted for before the corresponding goods or services have been delivered or carried out. For instance, a cable company records three-quarters of the annual subscription payments it receives on 1 October under deferred income on the liabilities side of its balance sheet at 31 December.[1]

We should also mention accrued income and cost, which work in the same way as deferred income and prepaid cost, only in reverse. For example, a company can accrue R&D costs, i.e. consider that it should not appear in the P&L but as an intangible asset that will be amortised.

1 *If the company's financial year starts as of 1 January*

3/ HOW SHOULD FINANCIAL ANALYSTS TREAT THEM?

Deferred income and prepaid cost form part of operating working capital.

Accrued costs are either part of the working capital if short term or of fixed assets if they correspond to a long-term asset (e.g. R&D costs).

Section 7.2
CONSTRUCTION CONTRACTS

1/ WHAT ARE CONSTRUCTION CONTRACTS?

In some cases, it may take more than a year for a company to complete a project. For instance, a group that builds dams or ships may work for several years on a single project.

2/ HOW ARE THEY ACCOUNTED FOR?

Construction contracts are accounted for using the percentage of completion method, which consists of recognising at the end of each financial year the sales and profit/loss

2 *The completed contract method consists of recognising the sales and earnings on a project only when the project has been completed or the last batch delivered. Nonetheless, by virtue of the conservatism principle, any losses anticipated are fully provisioned. This method is thus equivalent to recognising only unrealised losses while the project is under way. It may be used in the US where the recommended method is the percentage of completion method.*

anticipated on the project in proportion to the percentage of the work completed at that time. US accounting rules recognise both the percentage of completion method and the completed contract method where revenue recognition is deferred until completion of the contract.[2]

3/ HOW SHOULD FINANCIAL ANALYSTS TREAT THEM?

Construction projects in progress are part of the operating working capital. The percentage of completion method results in less volatile profits as they are spread over several fiscal years even if the completed contract method may seem more prudent. Analysts should be aware of changes in accounting methods for construction contracts (which are not possible under IFRS) as such changes may indicate an attempt to improve artificially the published net income for a given year.

Section 7.3
CONVERTIBLE BONDS AND LOANS

1/ WHAT ARE CONVERTIBLE BONDS AND LOANS?

3 *See Chapter 25.*

Convertible bonds are bonds that may be converted at the request of their holders into shares in the issuing company. Conversion is thus initiated by the investor.[3]

2/ HOW ARE THEY ACCOUNTED FOR?

4 *This is known as "split accounting".*

When they are issued, convertible bonds and loans are allocated between debt and equity accounts[4] since they are analysed under IFRS standards as compound financial instruments made up of a straight bond and a call option (see Chapter 25). The present value of the coupons and reimbursement amount discounted at fair borrowing rate of the firm is accounted for as debt. The remainder is accounted for as equity. In addition, each year the company will account for the interest as it would be paid for a standard bond (part of this amount corresponding to the actual amount paid, the rest being a notional amount).

3/ HOW SHOULD FINANCIAL ANALYSTS TREAT THEM?

Some analysts take the view that convertible bonds lie halfway between equity and debt, so treat them as 50% shareholders' equity and 50% debt. We believe this to be a totally arbitrary and unjustified approach. The approach we recommend is to examine the conditions governing conversion of the bonds and to make the equity/debt classification based on the results of this analysis. For instance, if the share price already lies well above the conversion price, the bonds are very likely indeed to be converted, so they should be treated as equity. For valuation purposes, the related interest expense net of tax should be reversed out of the income statement, leading to an increase in net income. The number of shares should also be increased by those to be issued through the conversion of the convertible bonds.

On the other hand, if the share price is below the conversion price, convertible bonds should be treated as conventional bonds and stay classified as borrowings.

Section 7.4
Currency translation adjustments

See Chapter 6.

Section 7.5
Deferred tax assets and liabilities

1/ What are deferred tax assets and liabilities?

Deferred taxation giving rise to deferred tax assets or liabilities stems:

* either from differences in periods in which the income or cost is recognised for tax and accounting purposes;
* or from differences between the taxable and book values of assets and liabilities.

On the income statement, certain revenues and charges are recognised in different periods for the purpose of calculating pre-tax accounting profit and taxable profit.

In some cases, the difference may be temporary due to the method used to derive taxable profit from pre-tax accounting profit. For instance, a cost has been recognised in the accounts, but is not yet deductible for tax purposes (e.g. employee profit-sharing in some countries); or vice versa. The same may apply to certain types of revenue. Such differences are known as **timing differences**.

In other circumstances, the differences may be definitive or permanent, i.e. for revenue or charges that will never be taken into account in the computation of taxable profit (e.g. tax penalties or fines that are not deductible for tax purposes). Consequently, there is no deferred tax recognition.

On the balance sheet, the historical cost of an asset or liability may not be the same as its tax base, which creates a **temporary difference**. Depending on the situation, temporary differences may give rise to a future tax charge and thus deferred tax liabilities, while others may lead to future tax deductions and thus deferred tax assets. For instance, deferred tax liabilities may arise from:

* assets that give rise to tax deductions that are lower than their book value when sold or used. The most common example of this derives from the revaluation of assets upon the first-time consolidation of a subsidiary. Their value on the consolidated balance sheet is higher than the tax base used to calculate depreciation and amortisation or capital gains and losses;
* capitalised financial costs that are deductible immediately for tax purposes, but that are accounted for on the income statement over several years or deferred;
* revenues, the taxation of which is deferred, such as accrued financial income that becomes taxable only once it has been actually received.

Deferred tax assets may arise in various situations including costs that are expensed in the accounts but are deductible for tax purposes in later years only, such as:

- provisions that are deductible only when the stated risk or liability materialises (for retirement indemnities in certain countries);
- certain tax losses that may be offset against tax expense in the future (i.e. tax loss carryforwards, long-term capital losses).

Finally, if the company were to take certain decisions, it would have to pay additional tax. These taxes represent **contingent tax liabilities**, e.g. stemming from the distribution of reserves on which tax has not been paid at the standard rate.

2/ How are they accounted for?

It is mandatory for companies to recognise all their deferred tax liabilities in consolidated accounts. Deferred tax assets arising from tax losses should be recognised when it is probable that the deferred tax asset can be used to reduce tax to be paid.

Deferred tax liabilities are not recognised on goodwill where goodwill depreciation is not deductible for tax purposes, as is the case in the UK, Italy or France. Likewise, they are not recorded in respect of tax payable by the consolidating company on distributions (e.g. dividend withholding tax) since they are taken directly to shareholders' equity.

In some more unusual circumstances, the temporary difference relates to a transaction that directly affects shareholders' equity (e.g. a change in accounting method), in which case the temporary difference will also be set off against the company's shareholders' equity.

IFRS do not permit the discounting of deferred tax assets and liabilities to net present value.

Deferred tax is not the same as **contingent taxation**, which reflects the tax payable by the company if it takes certain decisions. For instance, tax charges payable if certain reserves are distributed (i.e. dividend withholding tax), or if assets are sold and a capital gain is registered, revenue qualifying for a lower rate of tax provided they are not distributed to shareholders (long-term capital gains in some countries, etc.). The principle governing contingent taxation is straightforward: it is not recorded on the balance sheet and no charge appears on the income statement.

3/ How should financial analysts treat them?

It is important to recognise that deferred taxation does not represent an amount of tax currently due to or from the tax authorities, but consists of accounting entries with, most of the time, no economic underpinnings and with no corresponding cash flows.

(a) The simple case of losses

A group makes a pre-tax book and tax loss of 100. From a **tax** point of view, the tax due is zero. From an **accounting** point of view, and if there is reason to believe that the company is likely to make profits in the future that will enable it to use this tax loss carryforward, the loss will be reduced by a tax credit of 34[5]. Accordingly, it will be booked at 66. In order to balance the books, a tax credit carryforward of 34 will be recognised in the balance sheet on the assets side.

The following year, if our group makes an accounting and taxable profit of 100, it will not pay any tax, as the tax loss carryforward created that year will be set off against the tax due. From an accounting point of view, we'll recognise a theoretical tax expense of 34 and reduce the deferred tax recognised previously in the balance sheet to 0.

This example clearly shows that the deferred tax credit was created by reducing the amount of the net accounting loss and thus increasing equity by the same amount. From a financial point of view, it is only of value if future operations are able to generate enough profits. But under no circumstances can it be considered as an ordinary asset that could be sold for cash. And it is most certainly not an element of working capital as it does not result from the time lapse between the billing date and the payment date. We'll consider it as a fixed asset. At worst, it could be reversed against shareholders' equity, if there are serious doubts about the company's future ability to make profits.

(b) The case of provisions that are not immediately tax deductible

In some countries, provisions for retirement benefits, restructuring and environmental risks are not tax deductible when they are recognised. They are only tax deductible when the related expense is paid. The accounting rule for consolidated accounts is different because allocations to these provisions are treated as tax deductible when they are recognised. This is what results in the gap between real flows and the accounting treatment.

Let's consider a group that is making pre-tax profits of 100 per year. This year, it must allocate 100 to a reserve to cover a risk that may materialise in three years. From a **tax point of view**, the net result is 66[6] as the reserve is not tax deductible and the tax recognised is 34. From an **accounting point of view**, as the reserve of 100 is a cost, the net result is 0. The tax effectively paid (34) appears on the income statement but is neutralised by a deferred tax income of 34 which, in order to balance the books, is also recorded on the assets side of the balance sheet. Finally, the net tax recorded on the income statement is 0.

In three years, all other things being equal, the net tax result is 0 since the cost is **tax deductible**, and the tax effectively paid that year is thus 0. From an **accounting point of view**, the written back provision cancels out the expense, so the pre-tax result is 100 − 100 (cost) + 100 (provision written back) = 100. The tax recognised by accountants is 34 which is split into 0 tax paid and 34 recognised through deduction from the deferred tax credit recognised in the balance sheet three years ago, which is thus used up.

The deferred tax credit carried on the balance sheet for three years has a cross-entry under equity capital that is higher by 34. This is tax that has already been paid but from an accounting point of view is considered as a future expense. Unlike inventories of raw materials which have been paid for and which are also a future expense, deferred tax has no monetary value.

You can now see why we started out by saying that deferred taxes are a "purely intellectual construction". You can also see how difficult it is for any analyst to deal with this "asset", which isn't really one, notwithstanding its name, and which only exists to set off an expense which has been paid (the tax), but which for arbitrary reasons is only recognised later in a group's consolidated financial statements.

The financial treatment we advocate is simple: it is cancelled from assets and deducted from the provision under liabilities (so that it appears after tax) or from equity to reverse the initial entry.

5 *At a corporation tax rate of 34%.*

6 *At a corporation tax rate of 34%.*

(c) Revaluing assets

7 *See Chapter 6.*

Revaluing an asset when it is first consolidated or subsequently (when tested for impairment)[7] has two consequences:

- The taxable capital gains if the asset is sold will be different from the book value of the capital gains recorded in the consolidated financial statements.
- The basis for depreciation will be different, and will thus generate deferred taxes.

A group acquires a new subsidiary which has land recorded on its balance sheet at its initial acquisition value of 100. This land is revalued in the consolidated financial statements at 150.

We will then book a deferred tax liability of (150 − 100) × 34% = 17 in the consolidated financial statements. What is this liability from an economic point of view? It is the difference that will be booked in the consolidated financial statements between the tax actually paid on the day when the land is sold at a price of P − (P − 100) × 34% and the tax that will be recognised (P − 150) × 34%. The cross-entry on the balance sheet for this deferred tax is a lesser reduction of goodwill, which is reduced not by 50 but by (50 − 17).

Is this a debt owed to the tax administration? Clearly not, since the land would have to be sold for a tax liability to appear and then for an amount of (P − 100) × 34% and probably not 17! How do we advise our readers to treat this deferred tax liability? Deduct it from goodwill.

So, what of the case of the asset that has been revalued but that is depreciable? There is an initial recognition of the deferred tax liability being gradually reduced over the duration of the residual life of the asset by deferred tax credits due to the difference between a tax depreciation calculated on the basis of 100 and book depreciation calculated on the basis of 150.

Lastly, contingent tax liabilities, which do not appear in company accounts, are of interest only for the computation of the net asset value of the company (see Chapter 32).

Section 7.6
DILUTION PROFIT AND LOSSES

1/ WHAT ARE DILUTION PROFIT AND LOSSES?

Where a parent company does not subscribe either at all or only partially to a capital increase by one of its subsidiaries that takes place above the subsidiary's book value, the parent company records a **dilution profit**.

Likewise, if the valuation of the subsidiary for the purpose of the capital increase is less than its book value, the parent company records a **dilution loss**.

2/ HOW ARE THEY ACCOUNTED FOR?

For instance, let us consider the case of a parent company that has paid 200 for a 50% shareholding in a subsidiary with shareholders' equity of 100. A capital increase of 80 then takes place, valuing the subsidiary at a total of 400. Since the parent company does not take up its allocation, its shareholding is diluted from 50% to 41.67%.

The parent company's share of the subsidiary's equity decreases from 50%×100=50 to 41.67%×(100+80)=75, which generates a non-recurrent gain of 75−50=25. This profit of 25 corresponds exactly to the profit that the parent company would have made by selling an interest of $50\% - 41.67\% = 8.33\%$ based on a valuation of 400 and a cost price of 100 for 100%, since $25 = 8.33\% \times (400 - 100)$.

3/ How should financial analysts treat them?

Dilution gains and losses generate an accounting profit, whereas the parent company has not received any cash payments. They are, by their very nature, non-recurring. Otherwise, the group would soon not have any subsidiaries left. Naturally, they do not form part of a company's normal earnings power and so they should be totally disregarded.

Section 7.7
EXCHANGEABLE BONDS

1/ What are exchangeable bonds?

Exchangeable bonds are bonds issued by a company that may be redeemed at the request of their holders into shares of a company other than the issuer of the bonds or in cash (see Chapter 26).

2/ How are they accounted for?

Exchangeable bonds are accounted for as financial debt.

3/ How should financial analysts treat them?

Financial analysts must treat exchangeable bonds as financial debt as they will be redeemed either in cash or in shares of a company other than the issuer, and never in shares of the issuer. They have no equity component at all.

Section 7.8
GOODWILL

See Chapter 6.

Section 7.9
IMPAIRMENT LOSSES

1/ What are impairment losses?

Impairment losses are set aside to cover capital losses or those that may be reasonably anticipated on assets. They can be incurred on goodwill, other intangible assets and tangible assets.

2/ HOW ARE THEY ACCOUNTED FOR?

Impairment losses are computed based on the value of Cash Generating Units (CGUs).[8] The firm needs to define a maximum number of largely independent CGUs and allocates assets for each one. Each year, the recoverable value of the CGU is computed if there is an indication that there might be a decrease in value or if it includes goodwill.[9] If the recoverable value of the CGU is lower than the carrying amount, an impairment loss needs to be recognised. Impairment is first allocated to goodwill (if any) and then between the other assets.

The recoverable value is defined as the highest of:

- the value in use, i.e. the present value of the cash flows expected to be realised from the asset;
- the net selling price, i.e. the amount obtainable from the sale of an asset in an arm's length transaction,[10] less the costs of disposal.

If the value of the CGU increases again, the impairment can be reversed on all assets but goodwill.

3/ HOW SHOULD FINANCIAL ANALYSTS TREAT THEM?

Impairment losses are netted off directly against assets, and provided that these losses are justified, there is no need for any restatements. Conversely, we regard impairment losses on tangible assets as non-recurring items. As discussed on page 83, we consider impairment losses on intangible fixed assets (including goodwill) as non-operating items to be excluded from EBITDA and EBIT.[11]

Section 7.10
INTANGIBLE FIXED ASSETS

These primarily encompass startup costs, capitalised development costs, patents, licences, concessions and similar rights, leasehold rights, brands, market share, software and goodwill arising on acquisitions (see Chapter 6).

Under IFRS, a company is required to recognise an intangible asset (at cost) if and only if:

- it is probable that the future economic benefits that are attributable to the asset will flow to the company; and if
- the cost of the asset can be reliably measured.

Internally generated goodwill, brands, mastheads, publishing titles and customer lists should not be recognised as intangible assets. Internally generated goodwill is expensed as incurred. Costs on starting up a business, on training, on advertising, on relocating or reorganising a company receive the same treatment.

This line item requires special attention since companies have some degree of latitude in treating these items that now represent a significant portion of companies' balance sheets.

8 *The CGU, as defined by the IASB, is the smallest identifiable group of assets that generates cash inflows from continuing use, these cash inflows being largely independent of the cash inflows from other assets or groups of assets.*

9 *An intangible asset with indefinite useful life to be precise.*

10 *A transaction done "at arm's length" designates a transaction where two entities have acted as if they had no pre-existing relations of any kind.*

11 *Earnings Before Interest and Taxes.*

1/ Startup costs

(a) What are startup costs?

Startup costs are costs incurred in relation to the creation and the development of a company, such as incorporation, customer canvassing and advertising costs incurred when the business first starts operating, together with capital increase, merger and conversion fees.

(b) How are they accounted for?

Startup costs are to be expensed as incurred under IFRS. In the US, pre-operating costs may be included in "Other non-current assets" and are generally amortised over 3–5 years.

(c) How should financial analysts treat them?

It is easy to analyse such costs from a financial perspective. They have no value and should thus be deducted from the company's shareholders' equity.

2/ Research and development costs

(a) What are research and development costs?

These costs are those incurred by a company on research and development **for its own benefit**.

(b) How are they accounted for?

Under IFRS, research costs are expensed as incurred in line with the conservatism principle governing the unpredictable nature of such activities.

Development costs should be capitalised on the balance sheet if the following conditions are met:

- the project or product is clearly identifiable and its costs measurable;
- the product's feasibility can be demonstrated;
- the company intends to produce, market or use the product or project;
- the existence of a market for the project or product can be demonstrated;
- the utility of the product for the company, where it is intended for internal use, can be demonstrated;
- the company has or will have the resources to see the project through to completion and use or market the end product.

Under US GAAP, research and development costs generally cannot be capitalised (except specific web developments).

(c) How should financial analysts treat them?

We recommend leaving development costs in intangible fixed assets, while monitoring closely any increases in this category, since those could represent an attempt to hide losses.

3/ BRANDS AND MARKET SHARE

(a) What are brands and market share?

These are brands or market share purchased from third parties and valued upon their first-time consolidation by their new parent company.

(b) How are they accounted for?

Brands are not valued in the accounts unless they have been acquired. This gives rise to an accounting deficiency, which is especially critical in the mass consumer (e.g. food, textiles, automotive sectors) and luxury goods industries, particularly from a valuation standpoint. Brands have considerable value, so it makes no sense whatsoever not to take them into account in a company valuation. As we saw in Chapter 6, the allocation of goodwill on first-time consolidation to brands and market share leads to an accumulation of such assets on groups' balance sheets. For instance, LVMH carries brands for €8.7 billion on its balance sheet, which thus account for one-quarter of its capital employed. Since the amortisation of brands is not tax deductible in most countries, it has become common practice not to amortise such assets all the more so as they have an indefinite life. Brands are at most written down, where appropriate.

Under IFRS, market share cannot be carried on the balance sheet unless the company has protection enabling it to protect or control its customer relationships (which is difficult to get and demonstrate).

(c) How should financial analysts treat them?

Some analysts, especially those working for lending banks, regard brands as having nil value from a financial standpoint. Such a view leads to deducting these items peremptorily from shareholders' equity. We beg to differ.

These items usually add considerably to a company's valuation, even though they may be intangible. For instance, what value would a top fashion house or a consumer goods company have without its brands?

4/ CONCLUSION

To sum up, our approach to intangible fixed items is as follows: the higher the book value of intangibles, the lower their market value is likely to be; and the lower their book value, the more valuable they are likely to be. This situation is attributable to the accounting and financial policy of a profitable company that seeks to minimise as much as possible its tax expense by expensing every possible cost. Conversely, an ailing company or one that has made a very large acquisition may seek to maximise its intangible assets in order to keep its net profit and shareholders' equity in positive territory.

From a financial standpoint, intangible fixed assets form a key part of a company's value. That said, we believe that their book value in a company's balance sheet has little to do with financial reality.

Readers familiar with traditional accounting must understand that no difference is now made between:

- intangible fixed assets that are, by nature, immune to wear and tear and thus not subject to amortisation, aside from write-downs in the event of a crisis; and
- tangible assets that are depreciated.

Intangible assets with finite lives are amortised over their useful life. The International Accounting Standards Board (IASB) also requires that intangible assets with indefinite life undergo an impairment test each year to verify that their net book value is consistent with the recoverable value of the corresponding assets (see section on Impairment losses).

US rules are very similar to the IASB's.

Depreciation and amortisation indicate a desire to reflect the turnover in fixed assets, be they tangible or intangible, and thus recognise the ephemeral nature of all assets.

Section 7.11
INVENTORIES

1/ WHAT ARE INVENTORIES?

Inventories include items used as part of the company's operating cycle. More specifically, they are:

- used up in the production process (inventories of raw materials);
- sold as they are (inventories of finished goods or goods for resale) or sold at the end of a transformation process that is either under way or will take place in the future (work in progress).

2/ HOW ARE THEY ACCOUNTED FOR?

(a) Costs that should be included in inventories

The way inventories are valued varies according to their nature: supplies of raw materials and goods for resale or finished products and work in progress. Supplies are valued at acquisition cost, including the purchase price before taxes, customs duties and costs related to the purchase and the delivery. Finished products and work in progress are valued at production cost, which includes the acquisition cost of raw materials used, direct and indirect production costs insofar as the latter may reasonably be allocated to the production of an item.

Costs must be calculated based on normal levels of activity, since allocating the costs of below-par business levels would be equivalent to deferring losses to future periods and artificially inflating profit for the current year. In practice, this calculation is not always properly performed, so we would advise readers to closely follow the cost allocation.

Financial charges, research and development costs and general and administrative costs are not usually included in the valuation of inventories unless specific operating

12 *Interest on capital borrowed to finance production.*

conditions justify such a decision. IFRS require interim interest payments[12] to be included in the cost of inventories; US GAAP allows interim interest payments to be included in inventories in certain cases.

In all sectors of activity where inventories account for a significant proportion of the assets, we would strongly urge readers to study closely the impact of inventory valuation methods on the company's net income.

(b) Valuation methods

Under IFRS, there are three main methods for valuing inventories:

* the weighted average cost method;
* the FIFO (first in, first out) method;
* the identified purchase cost method.

Weighted average cost consists of valuing items withdrawn from the inventory at their weighted average cost, which is equal to the total purchase cost divided by quantities purchased.

The **FIFO** (first in, first out) method values inventory withdrawals at the cost of the item that has been held in inventory for the longest.

The **identified purchase** cost is used for non-interchangeable items and goods or services produced and assigned to specific projects.

For items that are interchangeable, the IASB allows the weighted average cost and FIFO methods but no longer accepts the LIFO method (last in, first out) that values inventory withdrawals at the cost of the most recent addition to the inventory. US GAAP permits all methods (including LIFO) but the identified cost method.

During periods of inflation, the FIFO method enables a company to post a higher profit than under the LIFO method. The FIFO method values items withdrawn from the inventory at the purchase cost of the items that were held for longest and thus at the lowest cost, hence giving a higher net income. The LIFO method produces a smaller net income as it values items withdrawn from the inventory at the most recent, and thus the highest, purchase cost. The net income figure generated by the weighted average cost method lies midway between these two figures.

Analysts need to be particularly careful when a company changes its inventory valuation method. These changes, which must be disclosed and justified in the notes to the accounts, make it harder to carry out comparisons between periods and may artificially inflate net profit or help to curb a loss.

Finally, where the market value of an inventory item is less than its calculated carrying amount, the company is obliged to recognise an impairment loss for the difference (i.e. an impairment loss on current assets).

3/ HOW SHOULD FINANCIAL ANALYSTS TREAT THEM?

Firstly, let us reiterate the importance of inventories from a financial standpoint. Inventories are assets booked by recognising deferred costs. Assuming quantities remain unchanged, the higher the carrying amount of inventories, the lower future profits will be.

Put more precisely, assuming inventory volumes remain constant in real terms, **valuation methods do not affect net profit for a given period**. But, depending on the method used, inventory receives a higher or lower valuation, making shareholders' equity higher or lower accordingly.

When inventories are being built up, the higher the carrying amount of inventories, the faster profits will appear. The reverse is true when inventories are decreasing. Overvalued inventories that are being run down generate a fall in net income.

Hence the reluctance of certain managers to scale down their production even when demand contracts. Finally, we note that tax-related effects apart, inventory valuation methods have no impact on a company's cash position.

From a financial standpoint, it is true to say that the higher the level of inventories, the greater the vulnerability and uncertainty affecting net income for the given period. We recommend adopting a cash-oriented approach if, in addition, there is no market serving as a point of reference for valuing inventories, such as in the building and public infrastructure sectors, for instance. In such circumstances, cash generated by operating activities is a much more reliable indicator than net income, which is much too heavily influenced by the application of inventory valuation methods.

Inventories are merely accruals (deferred costs), which are always slightly speculative and arbitrary in nature, even when accounting rules are applied bona fide.

Consequently, **during inflationary periods**, inventories carry unrealised capital gains that are larger when inventories are moving more slowly. In the accounts, these gains will appear only as these inventories are being sold, even though these gains are there already. When prices are falling, inventories carry real losses that will appear only gradually in the accounts, unless the company writes down inventories.

The only financial approach that makes sense would be to work on a replacement cost basis and thus to recognise gains and losses incurred on inventories each year. In some sectors of activity where inventories move very slowly, this approach seems particularly important. In 1993, Champagne houses carried inventories at prices that were well above their replacement cost. We firmly believe that had inventories been written down to their replacement cost, the ensuing crisis in the sector would have been less severe. The companies would have recognised losses in one year and then posted decent profits the next instead of resorting to all kinds of creative solutions to defer losses. The same can be argued regarding the loan portfolios carried by the Japanese banks in the early 2000s. Banks with subprime credit portfolios did not make the same mistake in 2007–2008.

Section 7.12
LEASES

1/ WHAT ARE LEASES?

Leases allow a company to use some of its operating fixed assets (i.e. buildings, plant and other fixed assets) under a rental system. In certain cases, the company may purchase the asset at the end of the contract for a predetermined and usually very low amount (see page 414).

Leases raise two relatively complicated problems for external financial analysts:

- Firstly, leases are used by companies to finance the assets. Even if those items may not appear on the balance sheet, they may represent a considerable part of a company's assets.
- Secondly, they represent a commitment, the extent of which varies depending on the type of contract:
  - equipment leasing may be treated as similar to debt depending on the length of the period during which the agreement may not be terminated;
  - real estate leasing for buildings may not be treated as actual debt in view of the termination clause contained in the contract. Nonetheless, the utility of the leased property usually leads the company to see out the initially determined length of the lease and the termination of a lease may then be treated as the early repayment of a borrowing (financed by the sale of the relevant asset).

2/ HOW ARE THEY ACCOUNTED FOR?

13 *Capital lease in the United States.*
14 *IAS 17.*

A lease is either a **finance lease** or an **operating lease**.

A finance lease[13] according to IASB is "a lease that transfers substantially all the risk and rewards incident to ownership of an asset. Title may or may not eventually be transferred".[14] Indications of the financial nature of a lease include:

- the contract sets that the asset will be transferred at the end of the lease to the company;
- the lessee has the option to purchase the asset at an "attractive" price;
- the lease is for the major part of the economic life of the asset;
- the present value of the rents are close to the fair value of the leased asset at the beginning of the contract;
- the assets leased are so specific that only the company can use them without major changes being made.

Although the idea is similar, US GAAP follows a more directive approach to distinguish financial and operating leases:

CLASSIFICATION OF LEASES

Classification of leases under US GAAP

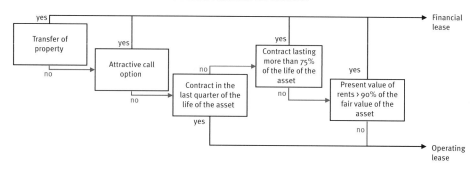

An operating lease is a lease that is not a finance lease.

Under IFRS, finance leases are capitalised which means they are recorded under fixed assets and a corresponding amount is booked under financial debt.

The lease payments to the lessor are treated partly as a repayment of financial debt and partly as financial expense. The capitalised asset under a finance lease is depreciated over its useful life. Accordingly, no rental costs are recorded on the income statement, merely financial and depreciation costs.

Operating leases are not capitalised and are treated as rents.

Sale and leaseback transactions, where an asset is sold only to be taken back immediately under a lease, are restated as follows: any capital gain on the disposal is deferred and recognised in income over the duration of the lease for finance leases or immediately for operating leases.

3/ HOW SHOULD FINANCIAL ANALYSTS TREAT THEM?

As the reader can see, the distinction between a finance lease and an operating lease is fairly vague; nonetheless, it remains a vital one for analysing the real level of a group's indebtedness.

US GAAP contain precise criteria. But they may be too precise as companies wanting to avoid capitalising leases in their balance sheet may artificially structure leases in a way to avoid being qualified as a finance lease so as not to show additional liabilities.

Eventually, accountants may decide that all leases are financial leases.[15] Such a decision is not as dramatic as it seems at first sight, since, when a lessee signs a contract with a lessor and pays him a rent, this commitment gives rise to a liability, at least from a financial point of view.

So the reader should beware of a company with large operating leases. They add fixed costs to its income statement and raise its breakeven point.

15 *The IASB and the FASB are currently considering this option*

Section 7.13
MANDATORY CONVERTIBLE BONDS

1/ WHAT ARE MANDATORY CONVERTIBLE BONDS?

Mandatory convertible bonds are bonds that initially pay a fixed interest rate (not linked to the company's earnings performance) and are redeemed in shares of the issuing company. For further details, please refer to Chapter 25 on hybrid securities.

2/ HOW ARE THEY ACCOUNTED FOR?

Proceeds from the issue of mandatory convertible bonds are allocated between debt (present value of interest) and equity (present value of shares to be issued to redeem the bonds). Such treatment is due to the IASB seeing mandatory convertible bonds as compound financial instruments made up of a straight bond and a deferred issue of shares.

3/ HOW SHOULD FINANCIAL ANALYSTS TREAT THEM?

We treat mandatory convertible bonds as equity, since this is what they are **certain** to become. For valuation purposes, interest payments net of tax should be reversed. This boosts net profit, and increases the number of shares outstanding to reflect those to be issued upon redemption of the bonds.

Section 7.14
OFF-BALANCE-SHEET COMMITMENTS

1/ WHAT ARE OFF-BALANCE-SHEET COMMITMENTS?

The balance sheet shows all the items resulting from transactions that were realised. But it is hard to show in company accounts transactions that have not yet been realised (e.g. the remaining payments due under an operating lease, orders placed but not yet recorded or paid for because the goods have not yet been delivered). And yet such items may have a significant impact on a company's financial position.

2/ HOW ARE THEY ACCOUNTED FOR?

These commitments may have:

- either a positive impact – they are not recorded on the balance sheet, but are stated in the notes to the accounts, hence the term "off-balance-sheet". These are known as **contingent assets**;
- or a negative impact that causes a provision to be set aside if likely to be realised, or gives rise to a note to the accounts if it remains a possibility only. These are called **contingent liabilities**.

3/ HOW SHOULD FINANCIAL ANALYSTS TREAT THEM?

Analysts should always be concerned that a company may show some items as off-balance entries while they should actually appear on the balance sheet. It is therefore very important to analyse off-balance-sheet items because they reflect:

- the degree of accounting ingenuity used by the company; this judgement provides the basis for an opinion about the quality of the published accounts;
- the subsequent arrival on the balance sheet of the effects of the commitments (purchase of fixed assets or purchase commitment that will have to be financed with debt, guarantees given to a failed third party that will lead to losses and payments with nothing received in return).

The key points to watch are as follows:

	Item	Comments
Financial commitments	Pledges and guarantees granted (including representations and warranties on disposal of an asset, product warranties).	Analyse the situation of the relevant entity to estimate the size of the commitment.
	Commitments given as partners, whether unlimited or not, put options written on assets.	
	Clawback commitments.	
Liabilities	Debts backed by tangible collateral.	Reflects bankers' confidence in the company.
Other	Orders to suppliers of fixed assets and other purchase commitments.	These will alter the balance sheet in the short term.

It should be noted that, since 2009, firms using IFRS have had to account for all potential liabilities and are no longer allowed to put forward the fact that the liability is hardly measurable to avoid accounting. In addition, detailed information has to be provided to justify the assessment of the amount.

Section 7.15
PENSIONS AND OTHER EMPLOYEE BENEFITS

1/ WHAT ARE PROVISIONS FOR EMPLOYEE BENEFITS AND PENSIONS?

Pension and related commitments include severance payments, early retirement and related payments, special retirement plans, top-up plans providing guaranteed resources and healthcare benefits, life insurance and similar entitlements that, in some cases, are granted under employment contracts and collective labour agreements.

A distinction is made between:

- **defined benefit plans** where the employer commits to the amount or guarantees the level of benefits defined by the agreement. This is a commitment to a certain level of performance, usually according to the final salary and length of service of the retiring employee. These plans may be managed internally or externally;
- **defined contribution plans** where the employer commits to making regular payments to an external organisation. Those payments are paid back to employees when they retire in the form of pensions together with the corresponding investment revenue. The size of the pension payments depends on the investment performance of the external organisation managing the plan. The employer does not guarantee the level of the pension paid (a resource-related obligation). This applies to most national social security systems.

2/ How are they accounted for?

Defined contribution plans are fairly simple to account for as contributions to these plans are expensed each year as they are incurred.

Defined benefit plans require detailed specific information disclosures in accounts. A defined benefit plan gives rise to a liability corresponding to the **actuarial present value of all the pension payments due at the balance sheet closing date** (Defined benefit obligation or, in US GAAP, Projected Benefit Obligation – PBO).

In countries where independent pension funds handle the company's commitments to its workforce, the market value of the pension fund's assets is set off against the actuarial value of the liability. The method used to assess the actuarial value is the projected unit credit method that models the benefits vested with the entire workforce of the company at the assessment date. It is based on certain demographics, staff turnover and other assumptions (resignations, redundancies, mortality rates, etc.).

Each year, changes in actuarial assumptions (especially the discount rate) and changes to retirement benefit plans give rise to adjustments in the calculation of pension liabilities. These adjustments may be recognised according to one of these three methods:

- immediately in the income statement;
- amortised on a straight-line basis over the remaining service life of employees for amounts exceeding 10% of the provision for retirement benefit plans (or 10% of assets if greater);[16]
- recorded entirely in equity (this last method has been authorised since 2004).

16 *This is called the "corridor method" and it will no longer be authorised from 2013 onwards*

Consequently, the net pension costs in the income statement for a given year are mainly composed of:

- a service cost, which represents the present value of benefits earned by employees during the year;
- an interest cost, which represents the increase in the present value of the pensions payments due at the balance sheet closing date since the previous year due to the passage of time; this is generally recognised in financial expense;
- an expected return on assets, which represents what management expects to earn on the pension plan assets;
- depending on the method used to record actuarial profit or losses, an amortisation of actuarial unrecognised profit or loss on the pension plan if it exceeds 10% of the projected benefit obligation or the fair value of plan assets, whichever is greater.

In a move that has broadened the debate, the IASB has stipulated that all benefits payable to employees, i.e. retirement savings, pensions, insurance and healthcare cover and severance payments should be accounted for. These standards state in detail how the employee liabilities deriving from these benefits should be calculated. US accounting standards also provide for the inclusion of retirement benefits and commitments other than just pension obligations, i.e. mainly the reimbursement of medical costs by companies during the active service life of employees.

3/ How should financial analysts treat them?

How, therefore, should we treat provisions for employees' benefits and pensions that may, in some cases, reach very high levels, as is often the case with German companies?

Our view is that provisions for retirement benefit plans are very similar to a financial liability *vis-à-vis* employees. This liability is adjusted each year to reflect the actuarial (and automatic) increase in employees' accrued benefits, just like a zero-coupon bond,[17] where the company recognises an annual financial charge that is not paid until the bond is redeemed. Consequently, we suggest treating such provisions minus the market value of the pension fund's assets as financial debt.

17 See p. 306.

In the income statement, we regard only pension service costs as operating costs and the balance of net pension costs (interest costs, notional return on pension assets, amortisation of various types, etc.) as financial charges. Consequently the balance of net pension costs must be deducted from EBITDA and EBIT and added to financial charges unless the company has already applied this rule in its accounts as sometimes happens.

Section 7.16
Perpetual subordinated loans and notes

1/ What are perpetual subordinated loans and notes?

As their name suggests, these instruments are never redeemable and thus continue to pay interest as long the borrower remains solvent.

They have no duration because there is no contractual undertaking for repayment, which may take place when the issuer so wishes. **Note that if the issuer is liquidated, holders rank for repayment after other creditors** (as they are subordinated loans) but before shareholders.

2/ How are they accounted for?

Perpetuals are booked under financial debt or equity depending on their characteristics (see Chapter 25).

3/ How should financial analysts treat them?

We regard perpetual subordinated notes as financial debt. They do not meet one of the three criteria needed to be ranked as equity: their returns are not linked to the company's earnings.

Section 7.17
Preference shares[18]

18 Also called preferred shares.

1/ What are preference shares?

Preference shares combine characteristics of shares and bonds. They may have a fixed dividend (bonds pay interest), a redemption price (bonds), and a redemption date (bonds). If the company were to be liquidated, the preference shareholders would be paid a given amount before the common shareholders would have a right to receive any of the proceeds. Sometimes the holders of preference shares may participate in earnings beyond the ordinary dividend rate, or have a cumulative feature allowing their dividends in arrears, if any, to be paid in full before shareholders can get a dividend, and so on.

Most of the time, in exchange for these financial advantages, the preference shares have no voting rights. They are known as *actions de préférence* in France, *Vorzugsaktien* in Germany, *azioni risparmio* in Italy, preferred stock in the US, etc.[19]

19 *For more details about preference shares, see Chapter 25.*

2/ How are they accounted for?

Under IFRS, preference shares are accounted for either as equity or financial debt, depending on the results of a "substance over form" analysis. If the preference share:

20 *Or determinable.*

- provides for mandatory redemption by the issuer at a fixed[20] date in the future; or
- if the holder has a put option allowing him to sell the preference share back to the issuer in the future; or
- if the preference share pays a fixed dividend regardless of the net income of the company,

it is financial debt.

Under US GAAP, preference shares are treated as equity.

3/ How should financial analysts treat them?

Let's call a spade a spade: if the preference share meets all our criteria for consideration as equity:

- returns linked solely to the company's earnings;
- no repayment commitment;
- claims on the company ranking last in the event of liquidation,

then it is equity. If not, it is a financial debt.

Section 7.18
Provisions

Provisions are set aside in anticipation of a future cost. Additions to provisions reduce net income in the year they are set aside and not in the year the corresponding cost will actually be incurred. Provisions will actually be written back the year the corresponding charge will be incurred, thereby neutralising the impact of recognising the charges in the income statement. Additions to provisions are therefore equivalent to an anticipation of costs.

1/ Restructuring provisions

(a) What are restructuring provisions?

Restructuring provisions consist of taking a heavy upfront charge against earnings in a given year to cover a restructuring programme (site closures, redundancies, etc.). The future costs of this restructuring programme are eliminated through the gradual write-back of the provision, thereby smoothing future earnings performance.

(b) How are they accounted for?

Restructuring costs represent a liability if they derive from an obligation for a company *vis-à-vis* third parties or members of its workforce. This liability must arise from a decision by the relevant authority and be confirmed prior to the end of the accounting period by the announcement of this decision to third parties and the affected members of the workforce. The company must not anticipate anything more from those third parties or members of its workforce. Conversely, a relocation leading to profits further ahead in the future should not give rise to such a provision.

(c) How should financial analysts treat them?

The whole crux of the matter boils down to whether restructuring provisions should be recorded under operating or non-operating items: the former are recurrent in nature, unlike the latter. Some groups consider productivity-enhancing restructuring charges as operating items and business shutdowns as non-recurrent items. This may be acceptable when the external analyst is able to verify the breakdown between these two categories. Other companies tend to treat the entire restructuring charge as a non-recurrent item.

Our view is that in today's world of rapid technological change and endless restructuring in one division or another, restructuring charges are usually structural in nature, which means they should be charged against operating profit. The situation may be different for SMEs,[21] where those charges are more likely to be of a non-operating nature.

21 *Small- and medium-sized enterprises.*

On the liability side of the balance sheet, we treat these restructuring provisions as comparable to financial debt.

2/ Provisions for decommissioning or restoration of sites

(a) What are provisions for decommissioning or restoration?

Some industrial groups may have commitments due to environmental constraints to decommission an industrial plant after use (nuclear plant, etc.) or restore the site after use (mine, polluted site, etc.).

(b) How are they accounted for?

In such cases, as these commitments are generally over the very long term, provisions will be booked as the net present value of future commitments.

(c) How should financial analysts treat them?

These provisions should be treated as net debt.

Section 7.19
Stock options

1/ What are stock options?

Stock options are options to buy existing or to subscribe to new shares at a fixed price. Their maturity is generally between 3 and 10 years after their issuance. They are granted free of charge to company employees, usually senior executives. Their purpose is to motivate executives to manage the company as efficiently as possible, thereby increasing its value and delivering them a financial gain when they exercise the stock options. As we will see in Chapter 27, they represent one of the ways of aligning the interests of managers with those of shareholders.

2/ How are they accounted for?

22 *Which means that stock options cannot be exercised for at least four years.*

Under IFRS, the issuance of fully-vested stock options is presumed to relate to past service, requiring the full amount of the grant-date fair value to be expensed immediately. The issuance of stock options to employees with, say, a four-year vesting period[22] is considered to relate to services over the vesting period. Therefore, the fair value of the share-based payment, determined at the grant date, should be expensed on the income statements over the vesting period. The corresponding entry is an increase in equity for the same amount.

23 *For more, see Chapter 24.*

Stock options are usually valued using standard option-pricing models[23] with some alterations or discounts to take into account cancellations of stock options during the vesting period (some holders may resign), conditions which may be attached to their exercise such as the share price reaching a minimum threshold or outperforming an index.

3/ How should financial analysts treat them?

We are not in favour of expensing stock options because:

- the issuance of stock options means that existing shareholders potentially transfer some of their ownership interests to employees without any loss for the company;
- there is no cost for the company itself, because stock option flows do not require the company to sacrifice any cash or other assets at any point in time;
- cost recognition is inconsistent with the definition of a cost. If services are received in a stock option payment, there is no transaction or event that meets the definition of a cost: there is no outflow of assets and no liability is incurred.

If the company has expensed stock options and if the amounts are material, we recommend reversing the relevant entries.

We treat the dilution issue of stock options for valuation purposes in Chapter 32.

Section 7.20
TANGIBLE ASSETS

1/ What are tangible assets?

24 *Known as PPE.*

Tangible assets (or property, plant and equipment)[24] comprise land, buildings, technical assets, industrial equipment and tools, other tangible assets and tangible assets in process.

Together with intangible assets, tangible assets form the backbone of a company, namely its **industrial and commercial base**.

2/ HOW ARE THEY ACCOUNTED FOR?

Tangible assets are booked at acquisition cost and depreciated over time (except for land). IFRS allows them to be revalued at fair value. The fair value option then has to be taken for a whole category of assets (e.g. real estate). This option is not widely used by companies (in particular because the annual measurement of fair values and booking of changes in fair value is complex)[25] except:

- on first implementation of IFRS;
- following an acquisition where it is required for the tangible assets of the purchased company.[26]

Some tangible assets may be very substantial; they may have increased in value (e.g. a head office, a store, a plant located in an urban centre) and thus become much more valuable than their historical costs suggest. Conversely, some tangible assets have virtually no value outside the company's operations. Though it may be an exaggeration, we can say that they have no more value than certain startup costs.

It is clear that showing assets at historical cost, in line with the historical cost principle, does not have any benefits for the analyst from a financial standpoint.

Note that certain companies also include interim financial expense into internally or externally produced fixed assets (provided that this cost is clearly identified). IFRS provides for the possibility of including borrowing costs related to the acquisition cost or the production of fixed assets when it is likely that they will give rise to future economic benefits for the company and that their cost may be assessed reliably. Under US GAAP, these financial costs must be included in the cost of fixed assets.

3/ HOW SHOULD FINANCIAL ANALYSTS TREAT THEM?

The accounting policies applied with respect to fixed assets may have a significant impact on various parameters, including the company's or group's net income and apparent solvency level.

For instance, a decision to capitalise a charge by recording it as an asset increases net income in the corresponding year, but depresses earnings performance in subsequent periods because it leads to higher depreciation charges.

The way tangible fixed assets are accounted for is:

- formal in a capital-employed analysis of the balance sheet;
- partial in an analysis seeking to establish the company's value or its solvency.

Accordingly, financial analysts need to take a much closer look at changes in fixed assets rather than fixed assets at a given point in time. The advantage of movements is that they are shown at their current value.

25 For tangible assets (except investment property) an increase in the value of the asset will directly impact on equity (except if it reverses a previous loss) and a loss will be accounted through the income statement.

26 See p. 81.

SECTION 1

Section 7.21
TREASURY SHARES

1/ WHAT ARE TREASURY SHARES?

Treasury shares are shares that a company or its subsidiaries owns in this company. We will examine the potential reasons for such a situation in Chapter 37.

2/ HOW ARE THEY ACCOUNTED FOR?

Under IFRS, treasury shares are systematically deducted from shareholders' equity. If they are sold by the company in the future, the disposal price will directly increase equity, no capital gain or loss will be recognised in the income statement.

3/ HOW SHOULD FINANCIAL ANALYSTS TREAT THEM?

Whatever their original purpose, we recommend deducting treasury shares from assets and from shareholders' equity if this has not yet been done by the accountants. From a financial standpoint, we believe that share repurchases are equivalent to a capital reduction, regardless of the legal treatment. Likewise, if the company sells the shares, we recommend that these sales be analysed as a capital increase.

Treasury shares must thus be subtracted from the number of shares outstanding when calculating earnings per share or valuing the equity.

BIBLIOGRAPHY

To better understand accounting rules:

B. Epstein, E. Jermakowicz, *Interpretation and Application of International Accounting Standards*, John Wiley & Sons Inc., published every year.
International Financial Reporting Standards, a yearly publication from the IASB.
www.fasb.org, the US accounting setter website.
www.ifrs.org, the IASB website.
www.iasplus.com, the Deloitte website dedicated to IFRS.

On financial versus operating leases:

Y. Le Fur, P. Quiry, Accounting for operating and capital leases – a step 30 years backwards?, *The vernimmen.com newsletter*, **55**, 1–4, December 2010.

APPENDIX 7A: MAIN DIFFERENCES BETWEEN INTERNATIONAL AND US ACCOUNTING STANDARDS

	IFRS	US GAAP
Consolidation policy for subsidiaries (1)	Control (look to governance). New standard will focus on the way it is exposed to variable interests from its involvement and has the ability to affect returns through its power	Majority of voting rights.
Joint ventures (2)	Consolidated using the equity method or proportionate consolidation. But the proportionate method will be forbidden (new standard).	Generally the equity method is used.
Special purpose entity (1)	Consolidated if controlled (look to risk & rewards). New standard should be applied to subsidiaries and SPE's and disclosures in line with US GAAP.	Consolidated if certain criteria are met.
Capitalisation of R&D costs	Research costs must be expensed. Development costs are recognised as intangible assets if a whole series of conditions are met related to: • the technical feasibility of completing the project such that the final asset may be used or sold, • the intention of completing the project, • the ability to sell or use the asset, • the way in which the asset will generate future economic benefits, • the ability to measure expenditure related to the project's development.	All R&D costs must be expensed as incurred (except some specific IT/web developments).
Tangible assets	Generally valued at historical costs but option to use fair value for investment properties.	Valued at historical costs.
Goodwill	Option to recognise goodwill related to non controlling interest (minority interest) at fair value.	Goodwill related to non controlling interest to be recognised at fair value.
Long-life asset impairment	One step impairment test (discounted cash flows).	Two step impairment test.
Impairment loss subsequent reversal	Required if certain criteria are met, except for goodwill.	Prohibited.
Construction contracts	The percentage of completion method is the only method accepted.	The percentage of completion method is preferred. The completed contract method may also be used.

**APPENDIX 7A: MAIN DIFFERENCES BETWEEN INTERNATIONAL
AND US ACCOUNTING STANDARDS (CONTINUED)**

	IFRS	US GAAP
Inventory cost	LIFO is prohibited.	LIFO is permitted.
Liabilities (3)	Best estimate to settle the obligation.	Low end of the range of possible amounts.
Convertible debt	Split the convertible debt into its debt and equity components at issuance.	Classified as a debt.
Spin off transactions	Non monetary assets distributed recorded at fair value (gain or loss).	Non monetary assets distributed recorded at carrying value (neither gain nor loss).
Financial instruments (4)		Greater use of fair value measurement but new standard still in process

(1) New IFRS standard issued in May 2011 reducing differences between standards (for year 2013)
(2) New IFRS standard issued in May 2011 in line with US GAAP (for year 2013)
(3) New IFRS standard planned to be issued in near term without convergence effect
(4) New IFRS and US Standards planned to be issued in near term without full convergence effect

PART TWO
FINANCIAL ANALYSIS
AND FORECASTING

In this section, we will gradually introduce more aspects of financial analysis, including how to analyse wealth creation, investments either in working capital or capital expenditure and their profitability. But first we need to look at how to carry out an economic and strategic analysis of a company.

Chapter 8

How to perform a financial analysis

Opening up the toolbox

Before embarking on an examination of a company's accounts, readers should take the time to:

- carry out a strategic and economic assessment, paying particular attention to the characteristics of the sector in which the company operates, the quality of its positions and how well its production model, distribution network and ownership structure fit with its business strategy;
- carefully read and critically analyse the auditors' report and the accounting rules and principles adopted by the company when preparing its accounts. These documents describe how the company's economic and financial situation is translated by means of a code (i.e. accounting) into tables of figures (accounts).

Since the aim of financial analysis is to portray a company's economic reality by going beyond just the figures, it is vital to think about what this reality is and how well it is reflected by the figures before embarking on an analysis of the accounts. Otherwise, the resulting analysis may be sterile, highly descriptive and contain very little insight. It would not identify problems until they have shown up in the numbers, i.e. after they have occurred and when it is too late for investors to sell their shares or reduce their credit exposure.

Once this preliminary task has been completed, readers can embark on the standard course of financial analysis that we suggest and use more sophisticated tools, such as credit scoring and ratings.

But first and foremost, we need to deal with the issue of what financial analysis actually is.

Section 8.1
What is financial analysis?

1/ What is financial analysis for?

Financial analysis is a tool used by existing and potential shareholders of a company, as well as lenders or rating agencies. For shareholders, financial analysis assesses whether the company is able to create value. It usually involves an analysis of the value of the share and ends with the formulation of a buy or a sell recommendation on the share. For lenders, financial analysis assesses the solvency and liquidity of a company, i.e. its ability to honour its commitments and repay its debts on time.

We should emphasise, however, that there are not two different sets of processes depending on whether an assessment is being carried out for shareholders or lenders. Even though the purposes are different, the techniques used are the same for the very simple reason that a value-creating company will be solvent and a value-destroying company will, sooner or later, face solvency problems. Nowadays, both lenders and shareholders look very carefully at a company's cash flow statement because it shows the company's ability to repay debts to lenders and to generate free cash flows, the key value driver for shareholders.

2/ FINANCIAL ANALYSIS IS MORE OF A PRACTICE THAN A THEORY

The purpose of financial analysis, which primarily involves dealing with economic and accounting data, is to provide insight into the reality of a company's situation on the basis of figures. Naturally, knowledge of an economic sector and a company and, more simply, some common sense may easily replace some of the financial analysis techniques. Very precise conclusions may be made without sophisticated analytical techniques.

Financial analysis should be regarded as a rigorous approach to the issues faced by a business that helps rationalise the study of economic and accounting data.

3/ IT REPRESENTS A RESOLUTELY GLOBAL VISION OF THE COMPANY

It is worth noting that although financial analysis carried out internally within a company and externally by an outside observer is based on different information, the logic behind it is the same in both cases. Financial analysis is intended to provide a global assessment of the company's current and future position.

Whether carrying out an internal or external analysis, an analyst should seek to study the company primarily from the standpoint of an outsider looking **to achieve a comprehensive assessment of abstract data, such as the company's strategy and its results**. Fundamentally, financial analysis is a method that helps to describe the company in broad terms on the basis of a few key points.

From a practical standpoint, the analyst has to match the policies adopted by the company and its real situation. Therefore, analysts' effectiveness is not measured by their use of sophisticated techniques but by their ability to uncover evidence of the inaccuracy of the accounting data or of serious problems being concealed. As an example, a company's earnings power may be maintained artificially through a revaluation or through asset disposals, while the company is experiencing serious cash flow problems. In such circumstances, competent analysts will cast doubt on the company's earnings power and track down the root cause of the deterioration in profitability.

We frequently see that external analysts are able to piece together the global economic model of a company and place it in the context of its main competitors. By analysing a company's economic model over the medium term, analysts are able to detect chronic weaknesses and separate them from temporary glitches. For instance, an isolated incident may be attributable to a precise and non-recurring factor, whereas a string of incidents caused by different factors will prompt an external analyst to look for more fundamental problems likely to affect the company as a whole.

Naturally, it is impossible to appreciate the finer points of financial analysis without grasping the fact that a set of accounts represents a compromise between different concerns. Let's consider, for instance, a company that is highly profitable because it has a very efficient operating structure, but also posts a non-recurrent profit that was "unavoidable". As a result, we see a slight deterioration in its operating ratios. In our view, it is important not to rush into making what may be overhasty judgements. The company probably attempted to adjust the size of the exceptional gain by being very strict in the way that it accounts for operating revenues and costs.

Section 8.2
ECONOMIC ANALYSIS OF COMPANIES

An economic analysis of a company does not require cutting-edge expertise in industrial economics or encyclopaedic knowledge of economic sectors. Instead, it entails straightforward reasoning and a good deal of common sense, with an emphasis on:

- analysing the company's market;
- understanding the company's position within its market;
- studying its production model;
- analysing its distribution networks;
- and, lastly, identifying what motivates the company's key people.

1/ ANALYSIS OF THE COMPANY'S MARKET

Understanding the company's market generally leads analysts to reach conclusions that are important for the analysis of the company as a whole.

(a) What is a market?

First of all, a market is not an economic sector as statistical institutes, central banks or professional associations would define it. Markets and economic sectors are two completely separate concepts.

What is the market for pay-TV operators such as BSkyB, Premiere, Telepiù or Canal+? It is the entertainment market, not just the TV market. Competition comes from cinema multiplexes, DVDs and live sporting events rather than from ITV, RTL TV, Rai Uno or TF1, which mainly sell advertising slots to advertisers seeking to target the legendary housewife below 50 years of age.

So what is a market? A market is defined by consistent behaviour, e.g. a product satisfying similar needs, purchased through a similar distribution network by the same customers.

A market is not the same as an economic sector. Rather, it is a niche or space in which a business has some industrial, commercial or service-oriented expertise. It is the arena in which it competes.

Once a market has been defined, it can then be segmented using geographical (i.e. local, regional, national, worldwide market) and sociological (luxury, mid-range, entry-level products) variables. This is also an obvious tactic adopted by companies seeking to gain protection from their rivals. If such a tactic succeeds, a company will create its own market in which it reigns supreme, such as RIM, which, with its Blackberry, has created a product that is neither a mobile phone nor a PDA but a unique product – the "Blackberry". But before readers get carried away and rush off to create their very own markets arenas, it should be remembered that a market always comes under threat, sooner or later.

Segmenting markets is never a problem for analysts, but it is vital to get the segmentation right! To say that a manufacturer of running shoes has a 30% share of the German running shoes market may be correct from a statistical standpoint but is totally irrelevant from an economic standpoint, because this is a worldwide market with global brands backed by marketing campaigns featuring international champions. Conversely, a 40% share of the northern Italian cement market is a meaningful number, because cement is a heavy product with a low unit value that cannot be stored for long and is not usually transported more than 150–200 km from the cement plants.

(b) Market growth

Once a financial analyst has studied and defined a market, his or her natural reflex is then to attempt to assess the growth opportunities and identify the risk factors. The simplest form of growth is organic volume growth, i.e. selling more and more products.

That said, it is worth noting that volume growth is not always as easy as it may sound in developed countries given the weak demographic growth (e.g. between −0.5% and +1% p.a. in Europe). Booming markets do exist (flat-screen TV sets), but others are rapidly contracting (nuclear power stations, daily newspapers) or are cyclical (transportation, paper production).

At the end of the day, the most important type of growth is value growth. Let's imagine that we sell a product satisfying a basic need, such as bread. Demand does not grow much and, if anything, appears to be declining. So we attempt to move upmarket by means of either marketing or packaging, or by innovating. As a result, we decide to switch from selling bread to providing a whole range of speciality products, such as baguettes, rye bread and farmhouse loaves, and we start charging €0.90, €1.10 or even €1.30, rather than €0.70 per item. The risk of pursuing this strategy is that our rivals may react by focusing on a narrow range of straightforward, unembellished products that sell for less than ours, e.g. a small shop that bakes pre-prepared dough in its ovens or the in-store bakeries at food superstores.

Once we have analysed the type of growth, we need to attempt to predict its duration, and this is no easy task. The famous 17th century letter-writer Mme de Sévigné once forecast that coffee was just a fad and would not last for more than a week . . . At the other end of the spectrum, it is not uncommon to hear entrepreneurs claiming that their products will revolutionise consumers' lifestyles and even outlast the wheel!

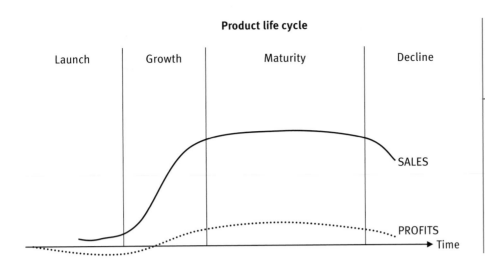

Product life cycle

| Launch | Growth | Maturity | Decline |

SALES

PROFITS

Time

To tackle the question of market growth, we need to look at the product lifecycle.

Growth drivers in a developed economy are often highly complex. They may include:

- technological advances, new products (e.g. TV on mobile phones);
- changes in the economic situation (e.g. expansion of air travel with the rise in living standards);
- changes in consumer lifestyles (e.g. eating out);
- changing fashions (e.g. snowboards, catamarans);
- demographic trends (e.g. popularity of cruises owing to the ageing of the population);
- environmental considerations (e.g. electric cars);
- delayed uptake of a product (e.g. mobile telephone in developing countries where the fixed line network was limited).

In its early days, the market evolves rapidly, as products are still poorly geared to consumers' needs. During the growth phase, the technological risk has disappeared, the market has become established and expands rapidly, being fairly insensitive to fluctuations in the economy at large. As the market reaches maturity, sales become sensitive to ups and downs in general economic conditions. And as the market ages and goes into decline, price competition increases, and certain market participants fall by the wayside. Those that remain may be able to post very attractive margins, and no more investment is required.

Lastly, readers should note that an expanding sector is not necessarily an attractive sector from a financial standpoint. Where future growth has been over-estimated, supply exceeds demand, even when growth is strong, and all market participants lose money (e.g. car manufacturers in China). For instance, after a false start in the 1980s (when the leading player Atari went bankrupt), the video games sector has experienced growth rates of well over 20%, but returns on capital employed of most companies are at best poor. Conversely, tobacco, which is one of the most mature markets in existence, generates a very high level of return on capital employed for the last few remaining companies operating in the sector.

(c) Market risk

Market risk varies according to whether the product in question is original equipment or a replacement item. A product sold as original equipment will seem more compelling in the eyes of consumers who do not already possess it. And it is the role of advertising to make sure this is how they feel. Conversely, should consumers already own a product, they will always be tempted to delay replacing it until their conditions improve and thus spend their limited funds on another new product. Needs come first! Put another way, replacement products are much more sensitive to general economic conditions than original equipment. For instance, sales in the European motor industry beat all existing records in 2000, when the economy was in excellent shape, but sales slumped to new lows in 2003 when the next recession kicked in. Sales picked up again to reach new highs in 2007 only to fall again sharply in 2009.

As a result, it is vital for an analyst to establish whether a company's products are acquired as original equipment or as part of a replacement cycle because this directly affects its sensitivity to general economic conditions.

All too often we have heard analysts claim that a particular sector, such as the food industry, does not carry any risk (because we will always need to eat!). These analysts either cannot see the risks or disregard them. Granted, we will always need to eat and drink, but not necessarily in the same way. For instance, eating out is on the increase, wine consumption is declining and fresh fruit juice is growing fast.

Risk also depends on the nature of barriers to entry to the company's market and whether or not alternative products exist. Nowadays barriers to entry tend to weaken constantly owing to:

- a powerful worldwide trend towards deregulation (there are fewer and fewer monopolies, e.g. in railways and postal services);
- technological advances (and in particular the Internet);
- a strong trend towards internationalisation.

All these factors have increased the number of potential competitors and made the barriers to entry erected by existing players far less sturdy.

For instance, the five record industry majors – Sony, Bertelsmann, Universal, Warner and EMI – had achieved worldwide domination of their market, with a combined market share of 80%. Nevertheless, they have seen their grip loosened by the development of the Internet and artists' ability to sell their products directly to consumers through music downloads, without even mentioning the impact of piracy!

(d) Market share

The position held by a company in its market is reflected by its market share, which indicates the share of business in the market (in volume or value terms) achieved by the company.

A company with substantial market share has the advantage of:

- some degree of loyalty among its customers, who regularly make purchases from the company. As a result, the company reduces the volatility of its business;
- a strong bargaining position *vis-à-vis* its customers and suppliers. Mass retailers are a perfect example of this;

- an attractive position which means that any small producer wishing to put itself up for sale, any inventor of a new product or new technique or any talented new graduate will usually come to see this market leader first, because a company with a large market share is a force to be reckoned with in its market.

That said, just because market share is quantifiable does not mean that the numbers are always relevant. For instance, market share is meaningless in the construction and public works market (and indeed is never calculated). Customers in this sector do not renew their purchases on a regular basis (e.g. town halls, swimming pools and roads have a long useful life). Even if they do, contracts are awarded through a bidding process, meaning that there is no special link between customers and suppliers. Likewise, building up market share by slashing prices without being able to hold onto the market share accumulated after prices are raised again is pointless. This inability demonstrates the second limit on the importance of market share: the acquisition of market share must create value, otherwise it serves no purpose.

Lastly, market share is not the same as size. For instance, a large share of a small market is far more valuable than middling sales in a vast market.

(e) The competition

If the market is expanding, it is better to have smaller rivals than several large ones with the financial and marketing clout to cream off all the market's expansion. Where possible, it is best not to try to compete against the likes of Google. Conversely, if the market has reached maturity, it is better for the few remaining companies which have specialised in particular niches to have large rivals that will not take the risk of attacking them because the potential gains would be too small. Conversely, a stable market with a large number of small rivals frequently degenerates into a price war that drives some players out of business.

But since a company cannot choose its rivals, it is important to understand what drives them. Some rivals may be pursuing power or scale-related targets (e.g. biggest turnover in the industry) that are frequently far from profitability targets. Consequently, it is very hard for groups pursuing profitability targets to grow in such conditions. So how can a company achieve profitability when its main rivals, e.g. farming cooperatives in the canned vegetables sector, are not profit-driven? It is very hard indeed because it will struggle to develop since it will generate weak profits and thus have few resources at its disposal.

(f) How does competition work?

Roughly speaking, competition is driven either by prices or by products:

- Where competition is price-driven, pricing is the main – if not the only – factor that clinches a purchase. Consequently, for example, costs need to be kept under tight control so that products are manufactured as cheaply as possible, product lines need to be streamlined to maximise economies of scale and the production process needs to be automated as far as possible. As a result, market share is a key success factor since higher sales volumes help keep down unit costs (see Boston Consulting Group's famous experience curve which shows that unit costs fall by 20% when total production volumes double in size). This is where engineers and financial controllers are most at home! It applies to markets such as petrol, milk, phone calls, and so on.

- Where competition is product-driven, customers make purchases based on after-sales service, quality, image, etc., which are not necessarily price-related. Therefore, companies attempt to set themselves apart from their rivals and pay close attention to their sales and customer loyalty techniques. This is where the marketing specialists are in demand! Think about Nespresso's quality of product and service, Harrods's atmosphere or, of course, Apple.

The real world is never quite as simple and competition is rarely only price- or product-driven, but is usually dominated by one or the other or may even be a combination of both, e.g. vitamin-enhanced milk, caller-display services for phone calls, bio wine, etc.

2/ PRODUCTION

(a) Value chain

A value chain comprises all the companies involved in the manufacturing process, from the raw materials to the end product. Depending on the exact circumstances, a value chain may encompass the processing of raw materials, R&D, secondary processing, trading activities, a third or fourth processing process, further trading and lastly the end distributor. Increasingly in our service-oriented society, grey matter is the raw material, and processing is replaced by a series of services involving some degree of added value, with distribution retaining its role.

The point of analysing a value chain is to understand the role played by the market participants, as well as their respective strengths and weaknesses. Naturally, in times of crisis, all participants in the value chain come under pressure. But some of them will suffer more than others, and some may even disappear altogether because they are structurally in a weak position within the value chain. Analysts need to determine where the structural weaknesses lie. They must be able to look beyond good performance when times are good because it may conceal such weaknesses. Analysts' ultimate goal is to identify where not to invest or not to lend within the value chain.

Let's consider the example of the film industry. The main players are:

- the production company, which plays both an artistic and a financial role. The producer writes or adapts the screenplay and brings together a director and actors. In addition, the production company finances the film using its own funds and by arranging contributions from third parties, such as co-producers and television companies that secure the right to broadcast the film, as well as by earning advances from film distribution companies (guaranteed minimum payment);
- the distributor, which also has a dual role assuming responsibility for logistics and financial aspects. It distributes the film reels to dozens, if not hundreds, of cinemas and promotes the film. In addition, it helps finance the film by guaranteeing the

producer minimum income from cinema operators, regardless of the actual level of box office receipts generated by the film;

• lastly, the cinema operator that owns or leases its cinemas, organises the screenings and collects the box-office receipts.

Going beyond a review of a particular value chain, additional insight can be gained into the balance of power by modelling the effects of a crisis and assessing the impact on the different players. During the 1980s, the number of box-office admissions fell right across Europe owing to the advent of new TV channels and video cassettes.

Which category of players was worst affected and has now generally lost its independence?

Cinema operators? Granted, the fall in box-office admissions led to a contraction in their sales. Some had to shut down cinemas, but since their properties were located in town and city centres, cinema operators that owned the premises had no trouble in finding buyers that were prepared to pay a decent price for these properties. The others modernised their theatres, increased the prices of tickets, built up their sales of confectionery that carry very high margins and have capitalised on the renewed growth in audiences across Europe over the past 10 years.

What about the production companies? Obviously, lower audiences meant lower box-office receipts but, at the same time, other media outlets developed for films (television channels, video cassettes/DVDs), generating new sources of revenue for film producers.

All things considered, film distribution companies were the worst hit. Some went bankrupt, while others were snapped up by film producers or cinema operators. Film distribution companies had only one source of revenue: box-office receipts. Unlike cinema operators, they had no bricks-and-mortar assets which could be redeveloped. Unlike film production companies, they had no access to the alternative sources of income (royalties from pay TV or video cassettes/DVDs) which caused the slump in the number of tickets sold. They had agreed to pay a guaranteed minimum to film production companies based on estimated box-office receipts but, given the steady decline in admissions, these estimates systematically proved overoptimistic. As a result, distributors failed to cover the guaranteed minimum and were doomed to failure.

When studying a value chain, analysts need to identify weaknesses where a particular category of player has no or very little room for manoeuvre (scope for developing new activities, for selling operating assets with value independent of their current use, etc.).

(b) Production models

In a service-dominated economy, the production models used by an industrial company are rarely analysed, even though we believe this is a very worthwhile exercise.

The first step is to establish whether the company assumes responsibility for or subcontracts the production function, whether production takes place locally or whether it has been transferred to low labour-cost countries and whether the labour force is made up of permanent or temporary staff, etc. This step allows the analyst to measure the flexibility of the income statement in the event of a recession or strong growth in the market.

In doing so, the analyst can detect any inconsistency between the product and the industrial organisation adopted to produce it. As indicated in the following chart, there are four different types of industrial organisations:

Processes: / Products:	Unique custom-made designed for the user	Multiple, differentiated not standardised produced on demand	Diversified but made up of standardised components high volumes	Unique complex very high volumes
Project: Specific and temporary organisation comprising experts	Pyramids in Egypt Cathedrals Hubble telescope			
Workshop: Flexibility through overcapacity, not very specialised equipment, multi-skilled workforce		Aerospace Catering Machine tools		
Mass production: Flexibility through semi-finished inventories not very qualified or multi-skilled workforce			Consumer appliances Shoes Textiles	
Process-specific: Total lack of flexibility but no semi-finished inventories, advanced automatisation, small and highly technical workforce				Automotive Energy Sugar production Chemicals

Source: Adapted from J.C. Tarondeau.

The **project**-type organisation falls outside the scope of financial analysis. Although it exists, its economic impact is very modest indeed.

The **workshop** model may be adopted by craftsmen, in the luxury goods sector or for research purposes, but as soon as a product starts to develop, the workshop model should be discarded as soon as possible.

Mass production is suitable for products with a low unit cost, but gives rise to very high working capital owing to the inventories of semi-finished goods that provide its flexibility. With this type of organisation, barriers to entry are low because as soon as a process designer develops an innovative method, it can be sold to all the market players. This type of production is frequently relocated to emerging markets.

Process-oriented production is a type of industrial organisation that took shape in the late 1970s and revolutionised production methods. It has led to a major decline in working capital because inventories of semi-finished goods have almost disappeared. It is a continuous production process from the raw material to the end product, which requires the suppliers, subcontractors and producers to be located close to each other and to work on a just-in-time basis. This type of production is hard to relocate to countries with low labour costs owing to its complexity (fine-tuning) and it does not provide any flexibility given the elimination of the inventories of semi-finished goods. A strike affecting a supplier or subcontractor may bring the entire group to a standstill.

Project	Workshop	Mass production	Process-oriented production
1900	1920	1980	

The natural tendency for all industries is to evolve gradually, mirroring trends in the motor industry during the 20th century.

But readers should not allow themselves to get carried away with the details of these industrial processes. Instead, they should examine the pros and cons of each process and consider how well the company's business strategy fits with its selected production model. Workshops will never be able to deliver the same volumes as mass production!

(c) Capital expenditure

A company should not invest too early in the production process. When a new product is launched on the market, there is an initial phase during which the product must show that it is well suited to consumers' needs. Then the product will evolve, more minor new features will be built in and its sales will increase.

From then on, the priority is to lower costs; all attention and attempts at innovation will then gradually shift from the product to the production model.

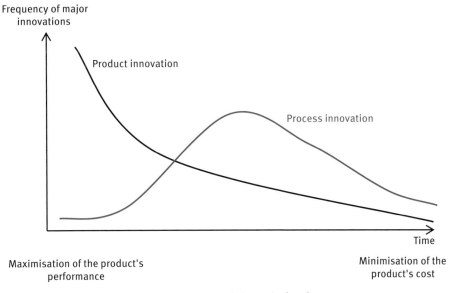

Source: Utterback and Abernathy (1975).

Investing too early in the production process is a mistake for two reasons. Firstly, money should not be invested in production facilities that are not yet stable and might even have to be abandoned. Secondly, it is preferable to use the same funds to anchor the product more firmly in its market through technical innovation and marketing campaigns. Consequently, it may be wiser to outsource the production process and not incur production-related risks on top of the product risk. Conversely, once the production process has stabilised, it is in the company's best interests to invest in securing a tighter grip over the production process and unlocking productivity gains that will lead to lower costs.

More and more, companies are looking to outsource their manufacturing or service operations, thereby reducing their core expertise to project design and management. Roughly speaking, companies in the past were geared mainly to production and had a vertical organisation structure because value was concentrated in the production function. Nowadays, in a large number of sectors (telecoms equipment, computer production, etc.), value lies primarily in the research, innovation and marketing functions.

Companies therefore have to be able to organise and coordinate production carried out externally. This outsourcing trend has given rise to companies such as Solectron, Flextronics and Celestica, the sole expertise of which is industrial manufacturing and which are able to secure low costs and prices by leveraging economies of scale because they produce items on behalf of several competing groups.

3/ DISTRIBUTION SYSTEMS

A distribution system usually plays three roles:

- **logistics**: displaying, delivering and storing products;
- **advice and services**: providing details about and promoting the product, providing after-sales service and circulating information between the producer and consumers, and vice versa;
- **financing**: making firm purchases of the product, i.e. assuming the risk of poor sales.

These three roles are vital, and where the distribution system does not fulfil them or does so only partially, the producer will find itself in a very difficult position and will struggle to expand.

Let's consider the example of the furniture retail sector. It does not perform the financing role because it does not carry any inventory aside from a few demonstration items. The logistics side merely entails displaying items, and advice is limited to say the least. As a result, the role of furniture producers is merely that of piece-workers which are unable to build their own brand (a proof of their weakness), the only well-known brands being private-label brands such as Ikea.

It is easy to say that producers and distributors have diverging interests, but this is not true. Their overriding goal is the same, i.e. that consumers buy the product. Inevitably, producers and distributors squabble over their respective share of the selling price, but that is a secondary issue. A producer will never be efficient if the distribution network is inefficient.

The risk of a distribution network is that it does not perform its role properly and that it restricts the flow of information between the producer and consumers, and vice versa.

So what type of distribution system should a company choose? Naturally, this is a key decision for companies. The closer they can get to their end customers, possibly even handling the distribution role themselves, the faster and more accurately will they find out what their customers want (pricing, product ranges, innovation, etc.). And the earlier they become aware of fluctuations in trading conditions, the sooner they will be able to adjust their output. But such choice requires special human skills, as well as investment in logistics and sales facilities and substantial working capital.

This approach makes more sense where the key factor motivating customer purchases is not pricing but the product's image, after-sales service and quality, which must be tightly controlled by the company itself rather than an external player. For instance, in recent years Puma has initiated a strategy to buy back the franchises and licences it had given in certain countries on its trademark.

Being far from end customers brings the opposite pros and cons. The requisite investment is minimal, but the company is less aware of its customers' preferences and the risks associated with cyclical ups and downs are amplified. If end customers slow down their purchases, it may take some time before the end retailer becomes aware of the trend and reduces its purchases from the wholesaler. The wholesaler will, in turn, suffer from an inertia effect before scaling down its purchases from the producer, which will not therefore have been made aware of the slowdown until several weeks or even months after it started. And when conditions pick up again, it is not unusual for distributors to run out of stock even though the producer still has vast inventories.

Where price competition predominates, it is better for the producer to focus its investment on production facilities to lower its costs, rather than to spread it thinly across a distribution network that requires different expertise from the production side. In this regard, the Internet can be a cost-effective distribution means.

4/ The company and its people

All too often, we have heard it said that a company's human resources are what really count. In certain cases, this is used to justify all kinds of strange decisions. There may be some truth to it in smaller companies, which do not have strategic positions and survive thanks to the personal qualities and charisma of their managers. Such a situation represents a major source of uncertainty for lenders and shareholders. To say that the men and women employed by a company are important may well be true, but management will still have to establish strategic positions and build up economic rents[1] that give some value to the company aside from its founder or manager.

(a) Shareholders

From a purely financial standpoint, the most important men and women of a company are its shareholders. They appoint its executives and determine its strategy. It is important to know who they are and what their aims are, as we will see in Chapter 40. There are two types of shareholder, namely inside and outside shareholders.

Inside shareholders are shareholders who also perform a role within the company, usually with management responsibilities. This fosters strong attachment to the company and sometimes leads to the pursuit of scale-, power- and prestige-related objectives that may have very little to do with financial targets. **Outside shareholders** do not work within the company and behave in a purely financial manner.

What sets inside shareholders apart is that they assume substantial personal risks because both their assets and income are dependent on the same source, i.e. the company. Consequently, inside shareholders usually pay closer attention than a manager who is not a shareholder and whose wealth is only partly tied up in the company. Nonetheless, the

1 *i.e earn a rate of return higher than justified by risk. See Chapter 27.*

danger is that inside shareholders may not take the right decisions, e.g. to shut down a unit, dispose of a business or discontinue an unsuccessful diversification venture, owing to emotional ties or out of obstinacy. The Kirch Group would probably have fared better during the early 2000s had the group's founder not clung on to his position as CEO well into retirement age and had groomed a successor.

Outside shareholders have a natural advantage. Because their behaviour is guided purely by financial criteria, they will serve as a very useful pointer for the group's strategy and financial policy. That said, if the company runs into problems, they may act very passively and show a lack of resolve that will not help managers very much.

Lastly, analysts should watch out for conflicts among shareholders that may paralyse the normal life of the company. As an example, disputes among the founding family members almost ruined Gucci.

(b) Managers

It is important to understand the managers' objectives and attitude *vis-à-vis* shareholders. The reader needs to bear in mind that the widespread development of share option-based incentive systems in particular has aligned the managers' financial interests with those of shareholders. We will examine this topic in greater depth in Chapter 27.

We would advise readers to be very cautious where incentive systems have been extended to include the majority of a company's employees. Firstly, stock options cannot yet be used to buy staple products and so salaries must remain the main source of income for unskilled employees. Secondly, should a company's position start to deteriorate, its top talent will be fairly quick to jump ship after having exercised their stock options before they become worthless. Those that remain on board may fail to grasp what is happening until it is too late, thereby losing precious time. This is what happened to so-called new economy companies, which distributed stock options as a standard form of remuneration. It is an ideal system when everything is going well, but highly dangerous in the event of a crisis because it exacerbates the company's difficulties.

(c) Corporate culture

Corporate culture is probably very difficult for an outside observer to assess. Nonetheless, it represents a key factor, particularly when a company embarks on acquisitions or diversification ventures. A monolithic and highly centralised company with specific expertise in a limited number of products will struggle to diversify its businesses because it will probably seek to apply the same methods to its target, thereby disrupting the latter's impetus.

For instance, Daimler of Germany acquired US car producer Chrysler, but the deal never really worked because Daimler's structured and hierarchical culture was far removed from the innovative and young culture prevailing in Chrysler at the time.

Section 8.3
AN ASSESSMENT OF A COMPANY'S ACCOUNTING POLICY

We cannot overemphasise the importance of analysing the auditors' report and considering the accounting principles adopted before embarking on a financial analysis of a group's accounts based on the guide that we will present in Section 8.4.

If a company's accounting principles are in line with practices, readers will be able to study the accounts with a fairly high level of assurance about their relevance, i.e. their ability to provide a decent reflection of the company's economic reality.

Conversely, if readers detect anomalies or accounting practices that depart from the norm, there is little need to examine the accounts because they provide a distorted picture of the company's economic reality. In such circumstances, we can only advise the lender not to lend or to dispose of its loans as soon as possible and the share-holder not to buy shares or to sell any already held as soon as possible. A company that adopts accounting principles that deviate from the usual standards does not do so by chance. In all likelihood the company will be seeking to window-dress a fairly grim reality.

To facilitate this task, the appendix to this chapter includes tables showing the main creative accounting techniques used to distort earnings, the shape of the income statement or the balance sheet.

Section 8.4
STANDARD FINANCIAL ANALYSIS PLAN

Experience has taught us that novices are often disconcerted when faced with the task of carrying out their first financial analysis because they do not know where to start and what to aim for. They risk producing a collection of mainly descriptive comments with-out connecting them or verifying their internal consistency, i.e. without establishing any causal links.

A financial analysis is an investigation that must be carried out in a logical order. It comprises parts that are interlinked and should not therefore be carried out in isolation. Financial analysts are detectives, constantly on the look-out for clues, seeking to establish a logical sequence, as well as looking for any disruptive factor that may be a prelude to problems in the future. The questions they most often need to ask are "Is this logical? Is this consistent with what I have already found? If so, why? If not, why not?"

We suggest that readers remember the following sentence, which can be used as the basis for all types of financial analysis:

Wealth creation requires investments that must be financed and provide sufficient return.

Let us analyse this sentence in more depth. A company will be able to remain viable and ultimately survive only if it manages to find customers ready to buy its goods or ser-vices in the long term at a price that enables it to post a sufficient operating profit. This forms the base for everything else. Consequently, it is important to look first at the struc-ture of the company's earnings. But the company needs to make capital expenditures to start operations: acquire equipment, buildings, patents, subsidiaries, etc. (which are fixed assets) and set aside amounts to cover working capital. Fixed assets and working capital jointly form its capital employed. Naturally, these outlays will have to be financed either through equity or bank loans and other borrowings.

Once these three factors (margins, capital employed and financing) have been exam-ined, the company's profitability, i.e. its efficiency, can be calculated, in terms of either its return on capital employed (ROCE) or its return on equity (ROE). This marks the end of the analyst's task and provides the answers to the original questions, i.e.: is the company able to honour the commitments it has made to its creditors? Is it able to create value for its shareholders?

Consequently, we have to study the company's:

- **wealth creation**, by focusing on:

  ○ trends in the company's sales, including an analysis of both prices and volumes. This is a key variable that sets the backdrop for a financial analysis. An expanding company does not face the same problems as a company in decline, in a recession, pursuing a recovery plan or experiencing exponential growth;

  ○ the impact of business trends, the strength of the cycle and its implications in terms of volumes and prices (gap vs. those seen at the top or bottom of the cycle);

  ○ trends in margins and particularly the EBITDA and EBIT margins;

  ○ an examination of the scissors effect (see Chapter 9) and the operating leverage (see Chapter 10), without which the analysis is not very robust from a conceptual standpoint.

- **capital employed policy**, i.e. capital expenditure and working capital (see Chapter 11);

- **financing policy**: This involves examining how the company has financed capital expenditure and working capital either by means of debt, equity or internally generated cash flow. The best way of doing so is to look at the cash flow statement for a dynamic analysis and the balance sheet for a snapshot of the situation at the company's year end (see Chapter 12).

- *profitability* by:

  ○ analysing its return on capital employed (ROCE) and return on equity (ROE), leverage effect and associated risk (see Chapter 13);

  ○ comparing actual profitability with the required rate of return (on capital employed or by shareholders) to determine whether the company is creating value and whether the company is solvent (see Chapter 14).

In the following chapters we use the case of the Indesit group as an example of how to carry out a financial analysis.

Indesit is one of the world's largest manufacturers of household appliances. It operates 18 facilities and sells washing machines, ovens, dish washers, etc. under the brand names Indesit, Ariston, Hotpoint and Scholtes.

Net sales in 2010 were €2.9 bn in four main lines of products: cooking, cooling, washing and services. It generates 62% of its sales in Western Europe.

Annual reports of Indesit from 2004 to 2010 are available on the website www. vernimmen.com.

Let's now see the various different techniques that can be used in financial analysis.

Overview of a standard plan for a financial analysis

Two preliminary tasks :

FIRSTLY, GET TO KNOW THE BUSINESS WELL...
■ *The market(s)* ■ *The product(s)* ■ *Production model(s)* ■ *Distribution network* ■ *Human resources*

...AS WELL AS THE COMPANY'S ACCOUNTING POLICIES
Auditors' reports *Accounting principles* ■ *Consolidation techniques* ■ *Goodwill, brands, etc.* ■ *Provisions* ■ *Inventories* ■ *Unconsolidated subsidiaries* ■ *etc.*

Four-stage plan:

WEALTH CREATION...

■ *Revenues analysis:*
  – External/internal growth
  – Price/volume growth
■ *Margin analysis:*
  – structure
  – scissors effect
  – breakeven effect

...REQUIRES INVESTMENT...
■ *Working capital* ■ *Capital expenditures*

...THAT MUST BE FINANCED
■ *Allocation of free cash flows* ■ *Equity/Debt* ■ *Liquidity, interest rate and currency risk*

...AND BE SUFFICIENTLY PROFITABLE

■ *Analysis of return on capital employed and return on equity: leverage effect*
 	
■ *Comparison between ROCE/rate of return required by shareholders and lenders*
    -> Value
    -> Solvency risk

Section 8.5
THE VARIOUS TECHNIQUES OF FINANCIAL ANALYSIS

1/ TREND ANALYSIS OR THE STUDY OF THE SAME COMPANY OVER SEVERAL PERIODS

Financial analysis always takes into account trends over several years because its role is to **look at the past to assess the present situation and to forecast the future**. It may also be applied to projected financial statements prepared by the company. The only way of teasing out trends is to look at performance over several years (usually at least three where the information is available).

Analysts need to bring to light any possible deterioration so that they can seize on any warning signals pointing to major problems facing the company. All too often we have seen lazy analysts look at the key profit indicators without bothering to take a step back and analyse trends. Nonetheless, this approach has two important drawbacks:

- trend analysis only makes sense when the data are roughly comparable from one year to the next. This is not the case if the company's business activities, business model (e.g. massive use of outsourcing) or scope of consolidation change partially or entirely, not to mention any changes in the accounting rules used to translate its economic reality;
- accounting information is always published with a delay. Broadly speaking, the accounts for a financial year are published between two and five months after the year end, and they may no longer bear any relation to the company's present situation. In this respect, external analysts stand at a disadvantage to their internal counterparts who are able to obtain data much more rapidly if the company has an efficient information system.

2/ COMPARATIVE ANALYSIS OR COMPARING SIMILAR COMPANIES

Comparative analysis consists of evaluating a company's key profit indicators and ratios so that they can be compared with the typical (median or average) indicators and ratios of companies operating in the same sector of activity. The basic idea is that one should not get up to any more nonsense than one's neighbours, particularly when it comes to a company's balance sheet. Why is that? Simply because during a recession, most of the lame ducks will be eliminated and only healthy companies will be left standing. **A company is not viable or unviable in absolute terms. It is merely more or less viable than others.**

The comparative method is often used by financial analysts to compare the financial performance of companies operating in the same sector, by certain companies to set customer payment periods, by banks to assess the abnormal nature of certain payment periods and of certain inventory turnover rates and by those examining a company's financial structure. It may be used systematically by drawing on the research published by organisations (such as Central Banks, Datastream, Standard & Poor's or Moody's, etc.) that compile the financial information supplied by a large number of companies. They publish the main financial characteristics in a standardised format of companies operating in different sectors of activity, as well as the norm (median or average) for each indicator or ratio in each sector. This is the realm of **benchmarking**.

This approach has two drawbacks:

- The concept of sector is a vague one and depends on the level of detail applied. This approach analyses a company based on rival firms, so to be of any value, the information compiled from the various companies in the sector must be consistent, and the sample must be sufficiently representative.
- There may be cases of mass delusion, leading to all the stocks in a particular sector being temporarily overvalued. Financial investors should then withdraw from the sector.

3/ Normative analysis and financial rules of thumb

Normative analysis represents an extension of comparative analysis. It is based on a comparison of certain company ratios or indicators with rules or standards derived from a vast sample of companies.

For instance, there are norms specific to certain industries:

- in the hotel sector, the bed/night cost must be at least 1/1000 of the cost of building the room, or the sales generated after three years should be at least one-third of the investment cost;
- the level of work in progress relative to the company's shareholders' equity in the construction sector;
- the level of sales generated per square metre in supermarkets, etc.

There are also some financial rules of thumb applicable to all companies regardless of the sector in which they operate and relating to their balance sheet structure:

- fixed assets should be financed by stable sources of funds;
- net debt should be no greater than around three times EBITDA;
- etc.

Readers should be careful not to set too much store by these norms which often are not very robust from a conceptual standpoint because they are determined from statistical studies. These ratios are hard to interpret, except perhaps where capital structure is concerned. After all, profitable companies can afford to do what they want, and some may indeed appear to be acting rather whimsically, but profitability is what really matters. Likewise, we will illustrate in Section IV of this book that there is no such thing as an ideal capital structure.

Section 8.6
Ratings

Credit ratings are the result of a continuous assessment of a borrower's solvency by a specialised agency (mainly Standard & Poor's, Moody's and Fitch), by banks for internal purposes to ensure that they meet prudential ratios and by credit insurers (e.g. Coface, Altradius, etc.). As we shall see in Chapter 21, this assessment leads to the award of a rating reflecting an opinion about the risk of a borrowing. The financial risk derives both from:

- the borrower's ability to honour the stipulated payments; and
- the specific characteristics of the borrowing, notably its guarantees and legal characteristics.

The rating is awarded at the end of a fairly lengthy process. Rating agencies assess the company's strategic risks by analysing its market position within the sector (market share, industrial efficiency, size, quality of management, etc.) and by conducting a financial analysis.

The main aspects considered include trends in the operating margin, trends and sustainability of return on capital employed, analysis of capital structure (and notably coverage of financial expense by operating profit and coverage of net debt by cash generated by operations or cash flow). We will deal with these ratios in more depth in Chapters 9 to 14.

Let us now deal with what may be described as "automated" financial analysis techniques, which we will not return to again.

Section 8.7
SCORING TECHNIQUES

1/ THE PRINCIPLES OF CREDIT SCORING

Credit scoring is an analytical technique intended to carry out a preemptive check-up of a company.

The basic idea is to prepare ratios from companies' accounts that are leading indicators (i.e. two or three years ahead) of potential difficulties. Once the ratios have been established, they merely have to be calculated for a given company and cross-checked against the values obtained for companies that are known to have run into problems or have failed. Comparisons are not made ratio by ratio, but globally. The ratios are combined in a function known as the Z-score that yields a score for each company. The equation for calculating Z-scores is as follows:

$$Z = a + \sum_{i=1}^{n} \beta_i \times R_i$$

where a is a constant, R_i the ratios, β_i the relative weighting applied to ratio R_i and n the number of ratios used.

Depending on whether a given company's Z-score is close to or a long way off normative values based on a set of companies that ran into trouble, the company in question is said to have a certain probability of experiencing trouble or remaining healthy over the following 2- or 3-year period. Originally developed in the US during the late 1960s by Edward Altman, the family of Z-scores has been highly popular, the latest version of the Z″ equation being:

$$Z'' = 6.6X_1 + 3.26X_2 + 6.72X_3 + 1.05X_4$$

where X_1 is working capital/total assets; X_2 is retained earnings/total assets; X_3 is operating profit/total assets; X_4 is shareholders' equity/net debt.

If Z'' is less than 1.1, the probability of corporate failure is high, and if Z'' is higher than 2.6, the probability of corporate failure is low, the grey area being values of between 1.1 and 2.6. The Z''-score has not yet been replaced by the Zeta score, which introduces into the equation the criteria of earnings stability, debt servicing and balance sheet liquidity.

The MKV firm (bought by Moody's in 2002) also developed its proprietary scoring model founded on an optional approach (see Chapter 35).

2/ Benefits and drawbacks of scoring techniques

Scoring techniques represent an enhancement of traditional ratio analysis, which is based on the isolated use of certain ratios. With scoring techniques, the problem of the relative importance to be attached to each ratio has been solved because each is weighted according to its ability to pick out the "bad" companies from the "good" ones.

That said, scoring techniques still have a number of drawbacks.

Some weaknesses derive from the statistical underpinnings of the scoring equation. The sample needs to be sufficiently large, the database accurate and consistent and the period considered sufficiently long to reveal trends in the behaviour of companies and to measure its impact.

The scoring equation has to be based on historical data from the fairly recent past and thus needs to be updated over time. Can the same equation be used several years later when the economic and financial environment in which companies operate may have changed considerably? It is thus vital for scoring equations **to be kept up to date**.

The design of scoring equations is heavily influenced by their designers' top priority, i.e. to measure the risk of failure for small and medium-sized enterprises. They are not well suited for any other purpose (e.g. predicting in advance which companies will be highly profitable) or for measuring the risk of failure for large groups. Scoring equations should thus be used only for companies where the business activities and size are on a par with those in the original sample.

Scoring techniques, which are a straightforward and rapid way of synthesising figures, have considerable appeal. Their development may even have perverse self-fulfilling effects. Prior awareness of the risk of failure (which scoring techniques aim to provide) may lead some of the companies' business partners to adopt behaviour that hastens their demise. Suppliers may refuse to provide credit, banks may call in their loans, customers may be harder to come by because they are worried about not receiving delivery of the goods they buy or not being able to rely on after-sales service.

It should be noted that the Basel 2 capital requirements for banks have given a new boost to credit-scoring models.

Section 8.8
Expert systems

Expert systems comprise software developed to carry out financial analysis using a knowledge base consisting of rules of financial analysis, enriched with the result of each analysis performed. The goal of expert systems is to develop lines of reasoning akin to those used by human analysts. This is the realm of artificial intelligence.

To begin with, the company's latest financial statements and certain market and social indicators are entered and serve as the basis for the expert system's analysis. It then poses certain questions about the company, its environment and its business activities to enrich the database. It proceeds on a step-by-step basis by activating the rules contained in its database.

Thirdly, the expert system produces a financial report that may comprise an assessment of the company, plus recommendations about certain measures that need to be considered.

The goal is to develop a tool providing early warnings of corporate failures, which can be used by, for instance, financial institutions.

APPENDIX 8A: ACCOUNTING PROCEDURES WITH AN IMPACT ON EARNINGS

Main items affected	Mechanism used	Impact on the accounts	Drawbacks
Fixed assets and financial expense	Financial expense included in the cost of fixed assets produced internally by the company	• Increase in earnings in the year when the charges are transferred • Decrease in earnings in the year of the transfer and following years through depreciation of the fixed asset produced	Procedure often regarded as exceptional in practice
Development costs	Development costs capitalised on the balance sheet	• Increase in earnings in the year the development costs are capitalised • Decrease in earnings in the year of the transfer and following years through amortisation of the fixed asset produced • Impact of the date chosen to start amortisation	• Conditions relating to individualised projects, technical feasibility and commercial profitability must be satisfied • Risk of a boomerang effect whereby development costs may have to be capitalised artificially to offset the impact of amortising past expenditure
Fixed assets	Sale and lease-back, i.e. the sale of a fixed asset, which is then leased back by the company	• A lease-back gain may be recorded on the sale • Leasing costs are recorded for the duration of the lease	• Artificial increase in earnings because the company undertakes to pay leasing costs for a certain period • Hence it is recommended that the capital gain should be spread over the relevant period
Depreciation and amortisation	When a depreciation schedule is drawn up, a company has numerous options: • Determine the likely useful life • Fix a residual value • Take into account the rate of use • Use physical working units, etc.	Depending on the option selected, the size of depreciation and amortisation allowances may change, leading to a change in the profile of depreciation and amortisation over time	• Need for a depreciation schedule • Methods to be applied consistently
Depreciation and fixed assets	Revise the depreciation schedule, e.g. by increasing (or decreasing) the residual depreciation period	Decrease/(increase) in future allowances over a longer (shorter) period.	Change in accounting method: disclosures required in the notes to the accounts

APPENDIX 8A: ACCOUNTING PROCEDURES WITH AN IMPACT ON EARNINGS (cont.)

Main items affected	Mechanism used	Impact on the accounts	Drawbacks
Depreciation and intangible assets or investment	Understatement/ (overstatement) of impairment losses on investment or intangible assets (goodwill), notably made possible by the existence of various different valuation methods	• Increase/(decrease) in earnings when the impairment losses are recognised • Opposite effect when the impairment losses are reversed	• Prudence principle • Boomerang effect when the impairment losses are reversed
Inventories	Financial expense included in the production cost of inventories	• Increase in earnings in the year when the charges are transferred • Decrease in earnings when the inventory is eliminated	Justification and amount of the relevant expenses must be disclosed in the notes to the accounts
Inventories	Change in inventory valuation method	Earnings modified as a result of the change	Change in accounting method: disclosures must be disclosed in the notes to the accounts
Inventories	Incorporation of costs related to below-normal activity in the valuation of items held in inventory	• Transfer of the loss arising from below-normal activity to the following year • Increase in earnings for the current year • Decrease in earnings for the following year	• IASB states that the cost of below-normal activity should not be taken into account in inventory valuations • It is hard to determine the normal level of production
Impairment losses and current assets	• Understatement/ (overstatement) of impairment losses on doubtful receivables • Understatement/ (overstatement) of impairment losses on inventories	• Increase/(decrease) in earnings when the impairment losses are recognised • Opposite effect when the impairment losses are reversed	• Conservatism principle • Boomerang effect when the impairment losses are reversed
Deferred costs and startup costs (especially pre-opening and research costs)	Change in accounting method: • Deferral of charges through amortisation whereas the charges were previously recorded in an earlier year • or vice versa	• Deferral of charges • Or, on the contrary, recognition of changes in a single period	• Consistency principle undermined • Disclosures required in the notes to the accounts
Costs related to the acquisition of fixed assets	Acquisition-related costs (which cannot be included in acquisition costs), e.g. professional fees, commission payments, registration fees left under costs or deferred costs	• Immediate decrease in earnings if left under costs • Deferral of costs if transferred to assets	Consistency principle (type of costs, amortisation period).

APPENDIX 8A: ACCOUNTING PROCEDURES WITH AN IMPACT ON EARNINGS (cont.)

Main items affected	Mechanism used	Impact on the accounts	Drawbacks
Grants and subsidies	• Investment subsidy added to shareholders' equity • Several possibilities for its inclusion on the income statement	• Affects return on invested capital calculations	Consistency principle
Provisions for restructuring	Several problems exist: • What is the decision date? • Degree of precision and impact on the valuation • Recognition of potential capital gains in the assessment of the provision	• Impact on earnings depends on the size of the provision • Opposite effect when reversed	• Consistency principle • Checked by auditors
Financial income	Artificial sale of securities, i.e. sale followed by repurchase	Unrealised capital gain turned into a real capital gain	• Transaction expenses • Neutral impact on cash
Financial income	Securities sold with a repurchase option at a fixed price (i.e. less accrued interest) for a certain period.	• Unrealised capital gain turned into a real capital gain • Shape of balance sheet improves: financing guaranteed by securities with no increase in debt • Payment of accrued interest and decrease in earnings in the year the option is exercised	• Where the parties intend to return the securities sold within the given period, the capital gain arising on the sale is eliminated and a provision set aside for the accrued interest
Goodwill	Goodwill allocated to non-depreciable items (i.e. brands, etc.) with no revaluation of depreciable items (i.e. fixed assets)	No reduction in consolidated earnings in future years except if impairment necessary	• Hard to establish the value of brands • Closely watched by auditors • Requires an annual impairment review and possibly recognition of impairment losses
Scope of consolidation	Change in scope of consolidation to include profitable subsidiaries. Use of the following options: • Concept of non-material subsidiaries • Fully consolidated when less than 50% owned	Change in earnings dependent on the change in the scope of consolidation	• Consistency principle • Disclosure of details adjusted for the change in scope of consolidation

APPENDIX 8A: ACCOUNTING PROCEDURES WITH AN IMPACT ON EARNINGS (cont.)

Main items affected	Mechanism used	Impact on the accounts	Drawbacks
Deferred taxation	Recognition of deferred tax assets	• Increase in consolidated earnings • Increase in shareholders' equity	• Conservatism principle • Restrictive conditions to be checked (in particular it must be probable that the company will return to profit). Hence the need for verifiable budgeted statements based on conservative and coherent assumptions
Accounting year end	Change in the year-end date	• The company may hope to increase its earnings during the additional months • Working capital may be more favourable depending on seasonality	Numerous drawbacks: organisation of accounting, consolidation and tax arrangements
Earnings generated by subsidiaries	Accelerate the transfer of subsidiaries' earnings. Profitable subsidiaries: • Interim dividends • Difference in year-end dates • Partnership status Loss-making subsidiaries: • Subsidies or debt waivers • Impairment losses proportional to the change in shareholders' equity • Partnership status	Positive or negative impact on earnings depending on the entry	Works for unconsolidated accounts

Source: Excerpt adapted from H. Stolowy, *Comptabilité Creative, Encyclopédie de Comptabilité, Contrôle de Gestion et Audit*, pp. 157–178, Economica, 2000.

APPENDIX 8B: ACCOUNTING PROCEDURES WITH AN IMPACT ON THE SHAPE OF THE BALANCE SHEET

Main items affected	Mechanism used	Impact on the accounts	Drawbacks
Fixed assets	Sale and lease-back,[1] i.e. the sale of a fixed asset, which is then leased back by the company	Reduction in debt	• Artificial improvement in financial situation • Restatement of the lease shows the real level of debt
Fixed assets and shareholders' equity	Revaluation of tangible fixed assets	• Increase in assets • Increase in shareholders' equity (an attractive way of building capital back up for thinly capitalised companies)	Revaluation gains may be liable to tax
Trade receivables	Discounting of a bill of exchange or promissory note	Accounting view: • Reduction in working capital • Reduction in debt	• After restatement: • No reduction in working capital • No reduction in debt
Trade receivables	Securitisation: sale of receivables to a mutual fund in return for cash	Reduction in working capital and debt	Need to be restated in financial analysis
Shareholders' equity	Issue of hybrid securities that are hard to classify between debt and equity	Change in gearing and return on equity	
Minority interests	Inclusion in shareholders' equity, with debt apportioned separately, or other solutions	Change in gearing and return on equity	
Borrowings	Use of sale and operating lease-back	Operating lease-related debt does not appear on the balance sheet	More likely than not to be restated in a financial analysis

1 *This mechanism also serves to alter the level of earnings (see Appendix 8A).*

Summary

The summary of this chapter can be downloaded from www.vernimmen.com.

The aim of financial analysis is to explain how a company can create value in the medium term (shareholders' viewpoint) or to determine whether it is solvent (lenders' standpoint). Either way, the techniques applied in financial analysis are the same.

First of all, financial analysis involves a detailed examination of the company's economics, i.e. the market in which it operates, its position within this market and the suitability of its production, distribution and human resources management systems to its strategy. Next, it entails a detailed analysis of the company's accounting principles to ensure that they reflect rather than distort the company's economic reality. Otherwise, there is no need to study the accounts, since they are not worth bothering with, and the company should be avoided like the plague, as far as shareholders, lenders and employees are concerned.

A standard financial analysis can be broken down into four stages:

- Wealth creation (sales trends, margin analysis) . . .

- . . . requires investments in capital employed (fixed assets, working capital) . . .

- . . . that must be financed (by internal financing, shareholders' equity or bank loans and borrowings) . . .

- . . . and provide sufficient returns (return on capital employed, return on equity, leverage effect).

Only then can the analyst come to a conclusion about the solvency of the company and its ability to create value.

Analysts may use: trend analysis, which uses past trends to assess the present and predict the future; comparative analysis, which uses comparisons with similar companies operating in the same sector as a point of reference; and normative analysis, which is based on financial rules of thumb.

Ratings represent an evaluation of a borrower's ability to repay its borrowings. Ratings are produced through a comprehensive financial analysis of groups, part of whose debt is traded on a market.

Scoring techniques are underpinned by a statistical analysis of the accounts of companies, which are compared with accounts of companies that have experienced problems, including bankruptcy in some cases. This automated process yields a probability of corporate failure. Scoring is primarily used for small and medium-sized companies.

Questions

1/ Do shareholders and lenders carry out financial analysis in the same way?

2/ What are the two prerequisites for financial analysis?

3/ Is a market an economic sector? Why?

4/ Why is there less risk on an original equipment market than on a replacement product market?

5/When a new product is launched, should the company invest in the production process or in the product itself? Why?

6/What is a standard financial analysis plan?

7/What standard ratios are applicable to all companies?

8/When is it possible to compare the EBIT margin of two companies?

9/What criticism can be directed at scoring techniques?

10/Why does the financial expense/EBITDA ratio play such a fundamental role in scoring techniques?

11/What are the strengths of a trends analysis?

12/Why start a financial analysis with a study of wealth creation?

13/Is financial analysis always doomed to be too late to be useful?

14/What is your view of the Italian proverb *traduttore, traditore* (to translate is to betray)?

15/Why will vertical integration be dismissed as being of little value after an analysis of the value chain?

16/What assumptions are made in a comparative financial analysis, especially on an international scale?

17/At the end of the day, what is the objective of the financial analyst?

More questions are waiting for you at www.vernimmen.com.

EXERCISES

1/Carry out an analysis of the frozen chicken value chain and decide which participants in the value chain are in a structurally weak position. The main participants in the chicken value chain are as follows:

○ Research: genetic selection of the best laying hens.
○ Breeding of laying hens: a laying hen lays eggs for 18 months nonstop, after which it is sold to the pet food industry.
○ Hatcheries: the eggs are placed in incubators stacked in batteries for an 18-day incubation period followed by a 3-day hatching period, and kept at the appropriate temperature and level of humidity.
○ Rearing: chickens are reared for around 40 days, until they reach a weight of 1.8 kg. This function provides additional income for a couple who, thanks to computerised equipment, only need to spend two to three hours/day attending to the chickens.
○ Feed: produced by animal feed groups, which develop subtle blends of wheat, maize and soya or rape seed proteins.
○ Slaughterhouses: 20 000 chickens are anaesthetised, decapitated, processed and frozen per hour, then exported mainly to the Middle East.

2/Guizzardi is one of the main Italian producers of synthetic raincoats. It sells two product ranges – the fashion and the classic raincoat – through supermarkets. Most of the Guizzardi workforce is paid the minimum wage.

Key figures (€m):

	2008	2009	2010
Sales	256	326	422
Raw materials used	78	104	143
Personnel cost	102	139	190
Operating income	41	52	59
Net income	23	27	30
Shareholders' equity	119	129	152
Net bank borrowings	42	125	150

(a) What is your view on the financial health of Guizzardi?

(b) Would you be of the same opinion if you had carried out an analysis beforehand of the company's value chain and simulated the impact of a crisis in 2011 (11% increase in labour costs due to the introduction of a shorter working week with no reduction in wages, 40% rise in cost of raw materials due to the drop in the value of the euro against the dollar and the 2011 hike in the price of oil), with a 17% drop in the price of cotton in 2011.

3/ **The table below appears on page 2 of the annual report of the Norne group.**

Key financials (unaudited, in millions of $, excluding earnings per share and dividends):

	1996	1997	1998	1999	2000
Sales	13 289	20 273	31 260	40 112	100 789
Net income:					
Recurring net income	493	515	698	957	1266
Items impacting comparability	91	−410	5	−64	−287
Total	584	105	703	893	979
Diluted earnings per share					
Recurring net income	0.91	0.87	1.00	1.18	147
Items impacting comparability	017	−0.71	0.01	−0.08	−0.35
Total	1.08	0.16	1.01	1.10	1.12
Dividend per share	0.43	0.46	0.48	0.50	0.50
Total assets	16 137	22 552	29 350	33 381	65 503
Cash from operating activities (excluding change in working capital)	742	276	1873	2228	3010
Capital expenditure	1483	2092	3564	3085	3314
Share price at 31 Dec	22	21	29	44	83

State your views.

Questions

1/ *Yes, because a company that creates value (for shareholders) will be solvent (for lenders).*
2/ *An understanding of the company's "economics" (market, competitive position, production and distribution system, staff) and the accounting principles used.*
3/ *No, a market is defined by consistent behaviour of customers who buy products in order to meet similar needs.*
4/ *The replacement products market is far more sensitive to general economic conditions, because when consumers already own a product, they can postpone replacing it until the economy picks up.*
5/ *When a product is launched, it is better to invest in the product and the marketing thereof than in the production facilities or process that could change in the future.*
6/ *Wealth creation requires investments that must be financed and be sufficiently profitable.*
7/ *None.*
8/ *When the companies operate in the same sector.*
9/ *To be effective, the sample must be sufficiently large and scores need to be updated regularly. Priority is to measure the risk of failure, which may have perverse self-fulfilling effects.*

10/ *Because it reveals both high levels of debt (substantial financial expense) and low returns (low EBITDA).*

11/ *It helps in understanding the company's strategy.*

12/ *Because this is the very reason why the company exists.*

13/ *In theory yes, if the analyst merely studies the company's financial statements. In practice no, if the analyst has factored in the "economics" of the company.*

14/ *This saying demonstrates why it is important to take a close look at the accounting principles used by the company.*

15/ *Because in a value chain, there are positions of structural weakness, where it is better to let others invest, even if it means handling them through supply contracts.*

16/ *Comparable accounting principles.*

17/ *Analyse the past to understand the present and forecast the future.*

Exercises

A detailed Excel version of the solutions is available at www.vernimmen.com.

1/ *Position of structural weakness:*

(a) *Breeding of laying hens: in times of crisis, all of the hens (which are unable to stop laying) have to be slaughtered and sold at a knock-down price to pet food manufacturers. The breeder thus loses her asset and her source of income.*

(b) *The hatchery and chicken rearing: no special skills or technology required.*

Position of strength:

(a) *Research and animal feed: many opportunities outside the chicken segment.*

(b) *The slaughterhouse: control over the whole of the chain upstream, through supply contracts and sales to the finished product.*

2/ *(a) Very good financial health, with a 20% return on equity in 2010 and 12% ROCE with sales growing briskly. (b) Guizzardi is in a position of structural weakness which is hidden by the good performance of the very volatile fashion range. It has no control over 92% of its costs (labour, oil, dollar). Its customers – supermarkets – would be reluctant to increase sales prices given that the competition (manufacturers of cotton raincoats) is not facing the same problems (drop in the price of cotton, rise in the price of oil). It is too small a business to expect any help from its suppliers (the big petrochemical groups).*

3/ *Why have these figures not been audited? Are the negative items impacting comparability really non-recurring (3 out of 5 years)? Should the presentation of the results not be improved? Why talk about cash flow from operating activities **excluding** changes in working capital, change in working capital is a natural constituent of cash flow from operating activities. The share is very highly valued (adjusted P/E of 56 (74 non-adjusted)). All of the above should set alarm bells ringing. These are, in fact, the financial statements for Enron, which went bankrupt with a big bang in 2001.*

BIBLIOGRAPHY

For more about the economic analysis of companies:

S. Chopra, P. Meindl, *Supply Chain Management*, 4th edn, Prentice Hall, 2009.

Ph. Kotler, Ph. Keller, *Marketing Management*, 13th edn, Prentice Hall, 2008.

B. Moingeon, G. Soenen, *Corporate and Organisational Identities*, Routledge, London, 2003.

M. Porter, *Competitive Strategy: Techniques for Analyzing Industries and Competitors*, Free Press, 1998.

W. Stevenson, *Operations Management*, 10th edn, McGraw-Hill/Irwin, 2008.

J.C. Tarondeau, *Stratégie Industrielle*, 2nd edn, Vuibert, 1998.

J.C. Utterback, W.J. Abernathy, A dynamic model of process and product innovations, *Omega*, **3**(6), 1975.

J. Woodward, *Industrial Organization: Theory and Practice*, 2nd edn, Oxford University Press, 1980.

For more about company accounting practices:

AIMR, *Financial Reporting in the 1990s and Beyond*, Association for Investment Management and Research, 1993.

AIMR, *Finding Reality in Reported Earnings*, Association for Investment Management and Research, 1997.

AIMR, *Closing the Gap between Financial Reporting and Reality*, Association for Investment Management and Research, 2003.

C. Mulford, E. Comiskey, *The Financial Number Game: Detecting Creative Accounting Practices*, John Wiley & Sons Inc., 2005.

T. O'Glove, *Quality of Earnings*, Free Press, 1998.

H. Schilit, *Financial Shenanigans: How to Detect Accounting Gimmicks and Fraud in Financial Reports*, 3rd edn, McGraw Hill, 2010.

For more on automated financial analysis:

E. Altman, Financial Ratios, Discriminant Analysis and the Prediction of Corporate Bankruptcy, *Journal of Finance*, **23**(4), 589–609, 1968.

E. Altman, *Bankruptcy, Credit Risk and High Yield Junk Bonds*, Blackwell, 2002.

Standard and Poor's, *Corporate Ratings Criteria*, (www.standardpoors.com/ratings).

Chapter 9
MARGIN ANALYSIS: STRUCTURE

If financial analysis were a puppet, company strategy would be pulling its strings

An analysis of a company's margins is the first step in any financial analysis. It is a key stage because a company that does not manage to sell its products or services for more than the corresponding production costs is clearly doomed to fail. But, as we shall see, positive margins are not sufficient on their own to create value or to escape bankruptcy.

Net income is what is left after all the revenues and charges shown on the income statement have been taken into account. Readers will not therefore be very surprised to learn that we will not spend too much time on analysing net income as such. A company's performance depends primarily on its operating performance, which explains why recurring operating profit (or EBIT) is the focus of analysts' attention. Financial and non-recurrent items are regarded as being almost "inevitable" or "automatic" and are thus less interesting, particularly when it comes to forecasting a company's future prospects.

For the purposes of this chapter, we will assume that the analyst has drawn up an income statement as shown on p. 170, which will serve as a point of reference. What's more, we will assume that additional information, such as average headcount, sales and production volumes, is also available, as well as industry data, such as prices in the sector and rivals' market share.

The first step in margin analysis is to examine the accounting practices used by the company to draw up its income statement. We dealt with this subject in Chapter 8 and shall not restate it here, except to stress how important it is. Given the emphasis placed by analysts on studying operating profit, there is a big temptation for companies to present an attractive recurring operating profit by transferring operating charges to financial or non-recurring items.

The next stage involves a trend analysis based on an examination of the revenues and charges that determined the company's operating performance. This is useful only insofar as it sheds light on the past to help predict the future. Therefore, it is based on historical data and should cover several financial years. Naturally, this exercise is based on the assumption that the company's business activities have not altered significantly during the period under consideration.

The main aim here is to calculate the rate of change in the main sources of revenue and the main costs, to examine their respective trends and thus to account for the relative change in the margins posted by the company over the period.

The main potential pitfall in this exercise is to adopt a purely descriptive approach, without much or any analytical input, e.g. statements such as "personnel cost increased by 10%, rising from 100 to 110 . . .".

Margin trends are a reflection of a company's:

* strategic position, which may be stronger or weaker depending on the scissors effect; and
* risk profile, which may be stronger or weaker depending on the breakeven effect that we will examine in Chapter 10.

All too often the strategic aspects are neglected, with the lion's share of the study being devoted to ratios and no assessment being made of what these figures tell us about a company's strategic position.

As we saw in Chapter 8, analysing a company's operating profit involves assessing what these figures tell us about its strategic position, which directly influences the size of its margins and its profitability:

* a company lacking any strategic power will, sooner or later, post a poor, if not a negative, operating performance;
* a company with strategic power will be more profitable than the other companies in its business sector.

In our income statement analysis, our approach therefore needs to be far more qualitative than quantitative.

Section 9.1
HOW OPERATING PROFIT IS FORMED

By-nature format income statements (raw material purchases, personnel cost, etc.), which predominate in continental Europe, provide a more in-depth analysis than the by-function format developed in the Anglo-Saxon tradition of accounting (cost of sales, selling and marketing costs, research and development costs, etc.). Granted, analysts only have to page through the notes to the accounts for the more detailed information they need to get to grips with the following questions. In most cases, they will be able to work back towards EBITDA[1] by using the depreciation and amortisation data that must be included in the notes or in the cash flow statement.

1 *Earnings before interest, taxes, depreciation and amortisation.*

1/ SALES

Sales trends are an essential factor in all financial analysis and company assessments. Companies where business activities are expanding rapidly, stagnating, growing slowly, turning lower or depressed will encounter different problems. An examination of sales trends sets the scene for an entire financial analysis. Sales growth forms the cornerstone for all financial analysis. Sales growth needs to be analysed in terms of volume (quantities sold) and price trends, organic and external growth (i.e. acquisition driven).

Before sales volumes can be analysed, external growth needs to be separated from the company's organic growth, so that like can be compared with like. This means analysing the company's performance (in terms of its volumes and prices) on a comparable structure basis and then assessing additions to and withdrawals from the scope of consolidation.

In practice, most groups publish **pro forma accounts** in the notes to their accounts showing the income statements for the relevant and previous periods based on the same scope of consolidation and using the same consolidation methods.

If a company is experiencing very brisk growth, analysts will need to look closely at the growth in operating costs and the financial requirements generated by this growth.

A company experiencing a period of stagnation will have to scale down its operating costs and financial requirements. As we shall see later in this chapter, production factors do not have the same flexibility profile when sales are growing as when sales are declining.

Where a company sells a single product, volume growth can easily be calculated as the difference between the overall increase in sales and that in the selling price of its product. Where it sells a variety of different products or services, analysts face a trickier task. In such circumstances, they have the option of either working along the same lines by studying the company's main products or calculating an average price increase, based on which the average growth in volumes can be estimated.

An analysis of price increases provides valuable insight into the extent to which overall growth in sales is attributable to inflation. This can be carried out by comparing trends in the company's prices with those in the general price index for its sector of activity. Account also needs to be taken of currency fluctuations and changes in the product mix, which may sometimes significantly affect sales, especially in consolidated accounts.

In turn, this process helps to shed light on the company's strategy, i.e.:

• whether its prices have increased through efforts to sell higher value-added products;
• whether they have been hiked owing to a lack of control on administrative overheads, which will gradually erode its sales performance;
• whether the company has lowered its prices in a bid to pass on efficiency gains to customers and thus to strengthen its market position;
• etc.

Key points and indicators:

• The rate of growth in sales is the key indicator that needs to be analysed.
• It should be broken down into volume and price trends, as well as into product and regional trends.
• These different rates of growth should then be compared with those for the market at large and (general and sectoral) price indices. Currency effects should be taken into account.
• The impact of changes in the scope of consolidation on sales needs to be studied.

2/ PRODUCTION

Sales represent what the company has been able to sell to its customers. Production represents what the company has produced during the year and is computed as follows:

	Production sold, i.e. sales
+	Changes in inventories of finished goods and work in progress at cost price
+	Production for own use, reflecting the work performed by the company for itself and carried at cost
=	**Production**

First and foremost, production provides a way of establishing a relationship between the materials used during a given period and the corresponding sales generated. As a result, it is particularly important where the company carries high levels of inventories or work in progress. Unfortunately, production is not entirely consistent insofar as it lumps together:

- production sold (sales), shown at the selling price;
- changes in inventories of finished goods and work in progress and production for own use, stated at cost price.

Consequently, production is primarily an accounting concept that depends on the methods used to value the company's inventories of finished goods and work in progress.

A faster rate of growth in production than in sales may be the result of serious problems:

- **overproduction**, which the company will have to absorb in the following year by curbing its activities, bringing additional costs;
- **overstatement of inventories' value**, which will gradually reduce the margins posted by the company in future periods.

Production for own use does not constitute a problem unless its size seems relatively large. From a tax standpoint, it is good practice to maximise the amount of capital expenditure that can be expensed, in which case production for own use is kept to a minimum. An unusually high amount may conceal problems and an effort by management to boost book profit superficially.

Key points and indicators:

- The growth rate in production and the production/sales ratio are the two key indicators.
- They naturally require an analysis of production volumes and inventory valuation methods.

3/ GROSS TRADING PROFIT

Gross trading profit is the difference between the selling price of goods for resale and their purchase cost. It is useful only in the retail, wholesale and trading sectors, where it is a crucial indicator and helps to shed light on a company's strategy. It is usually more stable than its components (i.e. sales and the cost of goods for resale sold).

4/ RAW MATERIALS USED AND OTHER OPERATING COSTS

This is another arena in which price and volume effects are at work, but it is almost impossible to separate them out because of the variety of items involved. At this general level, it is very hard to calculate productivity ratios for raw materials. Consequently, analysts may have to make do with a comparison between the growth rate in cost of sales and that in net sales (for by-function income statements), or the growth rate of raw material and other operating costs and that in production (by-nature income statements). A sustained difference between these figures may be attributable to changes in the products manufactured by the company or improvements (deterioration) in the production process.

Conversely, internal analysts may be able to calculate productivity ratios based on actual raw material costs used in the operating cycle since they have access to the company's management accounts.

Key points and indicators:

*   What are the main components of this item (raw materials, transportation costs, energy, advertising, etc.), and to what extent have they changed and are they forecast to change?
*   Has there been any major change in the price of each of these components?

5/ VALUE ADDED

This represents the value added by the company to goods and services purchased from third parties through its activities. It is equivalent to the sum of gross trading profit and profit on raw materials used minus other goods and services purchased from third parties.

It may thus be calculated as follows for by-nature income statements:

	Gross trading profit
+	Profit on raw materials used
−	Other operating costs purchased from third parties
=	**Value added**

Other operating costs comprise outsourcing costs, property or equipment rental charges, the cost of raw materials and supplies that cannot be held in inventory (i.e. water, energy, small items of equipment, maintenance-related items, administrative supplies, etc.), maintenance and repair work, insurance premiums, studies and research costs, fees payable to intermediaries and professional costs, advertising costs, transportation charges, travel costs, the cost of meetings and receptions, postal charges and bank charges (i.e. not interest on bank loans, which is booked under interest expense).

For by-function income statements, value added may be calculated as follows:

	Operating profit (EBIT)
+	Depreciation, amortisation and impairment losses on fixed assets
+	Personnel costs
+	Tax other than corporate income tax
=	**Value added**

At company level, value added is of interest only insofar as it provides valuable insight regarding the degree of a company's integration within its sector. It is not uncommon for an analyst to say that average value added in sector X stands at A, as opposed to B in sector Y. But such comparisons may be seriously flawed, especially if a company relies heavily on outsourcing.

Besides that, we do not regard the concept of value added as being very useful. In our view, it is not very helpful to make a distinction between what a company adds to a product or service internally and what it buys in from the outside. This is because all decisions of a company are tailored to the various markets in which it operates, i.e. the markets for labour, raw materials, capital and capital goods, to cite but a few. Against this backdrop, a company formulates a specific value-creation strategy, i.e. a way of differentiating its offering from that of its rivals in order to generate a revenue stream.

This is what really matters – not the internal/external distinction.

In addition, value added is only useful where a market-based relationship exists between the company and its suppliers in the broad sense of the term, e.g. suppliers of raw materials, capital providers and suppliers of labour. In the food sector, food processing companies usually establish special relationships with the farming industry. As a result, a company with a workforce of 1000 may actually keep 10 000 farmers in work. This raises the issue of what such a company's real value added is.

Where a company has established special contractual ties with its supplier base, the concept of value added loses its meaning.

Value added is a useful concept only where a market-based relationship exists between a company and its suppliers.

6/ PERSONNEL COST

This is a very important item because it is often high in relative terms. Although personnel cost is theoretically a variable cost, it actually represents a genuinely fixed cost item from a short-term perspective.

A financial analysis should focus both on volume and price effects (measured by the $\frac{\text{personnel expense}}{\text{average headcount}}$ ratio) as well as the employee productivity ratio, which is measured by the following ratios: $\frac{\text{sales}}{\text{average headcount}}$, $\frac{\text{production}}{\text{average headcount}}$ or $\frac{\text{value added}}{\text{average headcount}}$.

Since external analysts are unable to make more accurate calculations, they have to make a rough approximation of the actual situation. In general, productivity gains are limited and are thinly spread across most income statement items, making them hard to isolate.

Analysts should not neglect the inertia of personnel cost, as regards either increases or decreases in the headcount. If 100 additional staff members are hired throughout the year, this means that only 50% of their salary costs will appear in the first year, with the full amount showing up in the following period. The same applies if employees are laid off.

Key points and indicators:

Personnel cost should be analysed in terms of:

- productivity – sales/average headcount, value added/average headcount and production/average headcount;
- cost control – personnel cost/average headcount;
- growth.

7/ Gross profit

In by-function income statements, the production, gross trading profit or value added cannot be computed by the external analyst.

Nevertheless, he can compute the gross margin which is equal to sales less cost of good sold. This is an interesting concept to compute to measure the capacity of the firm to monitor its sales prices.

8/ An analysis of the EBITDA margin forms a natural conclusion to the points considered so far

As we saw in Chapter 3, EBITDA (earnings before interest, taxes, depreciation and amortisation) is a key concept in the analysis of income statements. The concepts we have just examined, i.e. value added and production, have more to do with macroeconomics, whereas EBITDA firmly belongs to the field of microeconomics.

We cannot stress strongly enough the importance of EBITDA in income statement analysis.

EBITDA represents the difference between operating revenues and cash operating charges. Consequently, it is computed as follows:

	Operating profit (EBIT)
+	Depreciation, amortisation and impairment losses on fixed assets
=	**EBITDA**

Alternatively, for by-nature income statements, EBITDA can be computed as follows:

	Value added
−	Taxes other than on income
−	Personnel cost and payroll charges
−	Impairment losses on current assets and additions to provisions
+	Other operating revenues
−	Other operating costs
=	**EBITDA**

Other operating costs comprise charges that are not used up as part of the production process and include items such as redundancy payments, recurring restructuring charges, payments relating to patents, licences, concessions, representation agreements and directors' fees. Other operating revenues include payments received in respect of patents, licences, concessions, representation agreements, directors' fees, operating subsidies received, etc.

Impairment losses on current assets include impairment losses related to receivables (doubtful receivables), inventories, work in progress and various other receivables related to the current or previous periods. Additions to provisions primarily include provisions for retirement benefit costs, litigation, major repairs and deferred costs, statutory leave, redundancy or pre-redundancy payments, early retirement, future under-activity, relocation, etc., provided that they relate to the company's normal business activities. In fact, these provisions represent losses for the company and should be deducted from its EBITDA.

Personnel expense and payroll charges also include employee incentive payments, stock options and profit-sharing.

Since it is unaffected by non-cash charges – i.e. depreciation, amortisation, impairment charges and provisions, which may leave analysts rather blind-sighted – trends in the EBITDA/sales ratio, commonly known as the **EBITDA margin**, form a central part of a financial analysis. All the points we have dealt with so far in this section should enable a financial analyst to explain why a group's EBITDA margin expanded or contracted by X points between one period and the next. The EBITDA margin change can be attributable to an overrun on production costs, to personnel cost, to the price effect on sales or to a combination of all these factors.

Our experience tells us that competitive pressures are making it increasingly hard for companies to keep their EBITDA margin moving in the right direction!

The following table shows trends in the EBITDA margins posted by various different sectors in Europe over the 1995–2010 period (2011 and 2012 are brokers' consensus estimates).

EBITDA MARGIN IN % OF SALES FOR LISTED GROUPS (EUROPEAN GROUPS)

Sector	1995	2000	2005	2006	2007	2008	2009	2010	2011e	2012e
Aerospace & Defence	9%	10%	11%	10%	11%	12%	11%	9%	10%	10%
Automotive	9%	8%	10%	10%	11%	9%	6%	11%	12%	12%
Building Materials	17%	17%	16%	17%	17%	15%	14%	14%	15%	16%
Capital Goods	10%	9%	11%	11%	14%	13%	12%	14%	15%	15%
Consumer Goods	18%	14%	15%	14%	15%	14%	13%	14%	14%	14%
Food Retail	6%	6%	6%	6%	7%	6%	6%	7%	7%	7%
IT Services	9%	12%	9%	9%	9%	10%	9%	9%	9%	10%
Luxury Goods	15%	16%	19%	19%	20%	20%	20%	23%	23%	24%
Media	8%	16%	21%	22%	22%	22%	21%	22%	23%	23%
Mining	17%	29%	41%	42%	41%	39%	34%	44%	47%	46%
Oil & Gas		19%	19%	20%	18%	18%	18%	17%	19%	20%
Pharmaceuticals	21%	26%	30%	32%	32%	33%	35%	36%	35%	34%
Steel		11%	16%	17%	16%	16%	8%	10%	11%	13%
Telecom Operators	40%	32%	35%	34%	33%	33%	34%	33%	33%	33%
Utilities	48%	16%	23%	22%	22%	20%	22%	21%	21%	21%

Source: Exane BNP Paribas

It clearly shows, among other things, the tiny but stable EBITDA margin of food retailers, and the very high EBITDA margin of telecom groups which was impacted by the Internet bubble blow out in 2000–2002. The highest margins are for the mining industry, which needs heavy investment, thus requiring high margins in order to get sufficient returns.

9/ Depreciation, amortisation

In a given period, this income statement item is relatively independent of the operating cycle. Aside from accounting policies, it depends on the company's investment policy, which we examine in greater detail in Chapter 11.

Now we come to the operating profit (EBIT), an indicator whose stock has risen substantially of late. Analysts usually refer to the operating profit/sales ratio as the **operating margin**, trends in which must also be explained.

10/ Operating profit or EBIT

Operating profit is EBITDA minus non-cash operating costs. It may thus be calculated as follows:

	EBITDA
−	Depreciation and amortisation
+	Write-backs of depreciation and amortisation
=	**Operating profit or EBIT**

Impairment losses on fixed assets relate to operating assets (i.e. brands, purchased goodwill, etc.) and are normally included with depreciation and amortisation by accountants. We beg to differ as impairment losses are normally non-recurring items and as such should be excluded by the analyst from the operating profit and relegated to the bottom of the income statement.

As we saw in Chapter 3, the by-function format directly reaches operating profit without passing through EBITDA:

	Sales
−	Cost of sales
−	Selling, general and administrative costs
−	Research and development costs
+/−	Other operating income and costs
=	**Operating profit (or EBIT)**

SECTION 1

The emphasis placed by analysts on operating performance over the past decade or so has led many companies to attempt to boost their operating profit artificially by excluding charges that should logically be included. These charges are usually to be found on the separate "Other income and costs" line, below operating profit, and are, of course, normally negative . . .

Other companies publish an operating profit figure and a separate EBIT figure, presented as being more significant than operating profit. Naturally, it is always higher, too . . .

For instance, we have seen foreign currency losses of a debt-free company,[2] recurring provisions for length-of-service awards and environmental liabilities, costs related to under-activity and anticipated losses on contracts excluded from operating profit. In other cases, capital gains on asset disposals have been included in recurring EBIT.

2 Which are necessarily related to the operating process and not the financing process as the company is debt free.

We believe it is vital for readers to avoid preconceptions and to analyse precisely what is included and what is not included in operating profit. In our opinion, the broader the operating profit definition, the better!

The following table shows trends in the operating margin posted by various different sectors over the 1995–2012 period.

The reader may notice, for example, how cyclical the steel sector is in stark contrast to the food retail sector.

OPERATING PROFIT IN % OF SALES FOR LISTED GROUPS
(EUROPEAN GROUPS PER SECTOR)

Sector	1995	2000	2005	2006	2007	2008	2009	2010	2011e	2012e
Aerospace & Defence	4%	6%	7%	7%	7%	9%	7%	6%	6%	7%
Automotive	3%	4%	4%	5%	6%	4%	1%	6%	7%	8%
Building Materials	11%	11%	11%	12%	12%	11%	8%	8%	10%	11%
Capital Goods	6%	6%	7%	8%	11%	10%	9%	10%	12%	12%
Consumer Goods	13%	11%	12%	11%	12%	11%	9%	10%	11%	11%
Food Retail	4%	4%	4%	4%	4%	4%	4%	4%	4%	5%
IT Services	6%	10%	6%	6%	7%	8%	7%	7%	7%	8%
Luxury Goods	13%	13%	15%	16%	17%	17%	16%	19%	19%	20%
Media	5%	11%	18%	18%	18%	17%	16%	17%	17%	18%
Mining	12%	21%	34%	35%	35%	32%	25%	37%	41%	40%
Oil & Gas		13%	15%	15%	14%	14%	11%	12%	14%	15%
Pharmaceuticals	16%	20%	25%	27%	28%	28%	30%	31%	30%	30%
Steel		6%	12%	13%	13%	12%	2%	6%	7%	9%
Telecom Operators	18%	15%	20%	18%	17%	17%	18%	17%	18%	18%
Utilities	31%	9%	15%	15%	15%	13%	14%	13%	13%	13%

Source: Exane BNP Paribas

Section 9.2
HOW OPERATING PROFIT IS ALLOCATED

1/ NET FINANCIAL EXPENSE/INCOME

It may seem strange to talk about net financial income for an industrial or service company whose activities are not primarily geared towards generating financial income. Since finance is merely supposed to be a form of financing a company's operating assets, financial items should normally show a negative balance, and this is generally the case. That said, some companies, particularly large groups generating substantial negative working capital (like big retailers, for instance), have financial aspirations and generate net financial income, to which their financial income makes a significant contribution.

Net financial expense thus equals financial expense minus financial income. Where financial income is greater than financial expense, we naturally refer to it as net financial income.

Financial income includes:

- income from securities and from loans recorded as long-term investments (fixed assets). This covers all income received from investments other than participating interests, i.e. dividends and interest on loans;
- other interests and related income, i.e. income from commercial and other loans, income from marketable securities, other financial income;
- write-backs of certain provisions and charges transferred, i.e. write-backs of provisions, of impairment losses on financial items and, lastly, write-backs of financial charges transferred;
- foreign exchange gains on debt;
- net income on the disposal of marketable securities, i.e. capital gains on the disposal of marketable securities.

Financial expense includes:

- interest and related charges;
- foreign exchange losses on debt;
- net expense on the disposal of marketable securities, i.e. capital losses on the disposal of marketable securities;
- amortisation of bond redemption premiums;
- additions to provisions for financial liabilities and charges and impairment losses on investments.

Where a company uses sophisticated financial liabilities and treasury management techniques, we advise readers to analyse its net financial income/(expense) carefully.

Net financial expense is not directly related to the operating cycle, but instead reflects the size of the company's debt burden and the level of interest rates. There is no volume or price effect to be seen at this level. Chapter 12, which is devoted to the issue of how companies are financed, covers the analysis of net financial expense in much greater detail.

Profit before tax is the difference between operating profit and financial expense net of financial income.

2/ INCOME FROM ASSOCIATES, MINORITY INTERESTS, INCOME TAX

Depending on its size, the share of net profits (losses) of associates[3] deserves special attention. Where these profits or losses account for a significant part of net income, either they should be separated out into operating, financial and non-recurring items to provide greater insight into the contribution made by the equity-accounted associates, or a separate financial analysis should be carried out of the relevant associate.

3 *For more on associates, see p. 77.*

Minority interests[4] are always an interesting subject and beg the following questions: Where do they come from? Which subsidiaries do they relate to? Do the minority investors finance losses or do they grab a large share of the profits? An analysis of minority interests often proves to be a useful way of working out which subsidiary(ies) generate(s) the group's profits.

4 *For more on minority interest, see p. 75.*

Last comes the corporate income tax line, which can be difficult to analyse owing to the effects of deferred taxation, the impact of foreign subsidiaries and tax loss carry-forwards. Analysts usually calculate the group's effective tax rate (i.e. corporate income tax divided by profit before tax), which they monitor over time to assess how well the company has managed its tax affairs.

3/ NON-RECURRING ITEMS

Non-recurring items are discussed in detail on page 33 and we remind the reader that IFRS has dropped the use of this category.

Non-recurring items are not an accounting entry but a category of items defined on a case-by-case basis by the analyst which includes some exceptional items, extraordinary items, impairment losses on fixed assets and results from discontinuing operations. It makes no sense to assess the current level of non-recurring items from the perspective of the company's profitability or to predict their future trends. Analysts should limit themselves to understanding their origin and why, for example, the company needed to write down the goodwill.

Section 9.3
COMPREHENSIVE INCOME

In 2007, IASB published revised requirements in presenting results.[5] The IASB leaves the option either to replace the income statement by a "statement of comprehensive income" or present that statement in addition to the traditional income statement.

5 *Revised IAS 1*

Comprehensive income is defined as the periodic change in equity capital, excluding any dealings with shareholders, i.e. payment of dividends and capital increases/decreases. It includes, in addition to net income in its IFRS version, all unrealised foreign exchange gains and losses, asset revaluations, cash flow hedging, changes in the fair value of financial instruments intended to be sold and actuarial gains and losses (if any) relating to pension fund commitments. Under this presentation, net income is merely an intermediary balance on the statement of change in equity, with the difference between this net income and CI being referred to as "other comprehensive income" (OCI).

We find little interest for the financial analyst in the other comprehensive income.

Section 9.4
Financial assessment

1/ The scissors effect

The scissors effect is, first and foremost, the product of a simple phenomenon.

The scissors effect is what takes place when revenues and costs move in diverging directions. It accounts for trends in profits and margins.

If revenues are growing by 5% p.a. and certain costs are growing at a faster rate, earnings naturally decrease. If this trend continues, earnings will decline further each year and ultimately the company will sink into the red. This is what is known as the scissors effect.

Whether or not a scissors effect is identified matters little. What really counts is establishing the causes of the phenomenon. A scissors effect may occur for all kinds of reasons (regulatory developments, intense competition, mismanagement in a sector, etc.) **that reflect the higher or lower quality of the company's strategic position in its market**. If it has a strong position, it will be able to pass on any increase in its costs to its customers by raising its selling prices and thus gradually widening its margins.

A scissors effect may arise in different situations, some examples of which are given above.

Where it reduces profits, the scissors effect may be attributable to:

- a statutory freeze on selling prices, making it impossible to pass on the rising cost of production factors;
- psychological reluctance to put up prices. During the 1970s, the impact of higher interest rates was very slow to be reflected in selling prices in certain debt-laden sectors;
- poor cost control, e.g. where a company does not have a tight grip on its cost base and may not be able to pass rising costs on in full to its selling prices. As a result, the company no longer grows, but its cost base continues to expand.

The impact of trends in the cost of production factors is especially important because these factors represent a key component of the cost price of products.

In such cases, analysts have to try to estimate the likely impact of a delayed adjustment in prices. This depends primarily on how the company and its rivals behave and on their relative strength within the marketplace.

But the scissors effect may also work to the company's benefit, as shown by the last two charts in the figure above.

A company's accounts are littered with potential pitfalls, which must be sidestepped to avoid errors of interpretation during an analysis. The main types of potential traps are as follows.

DIFFERENT EXAMPLES OF THE SCISSORS EFFECT

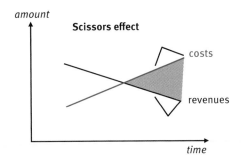

Ranging from carelessness

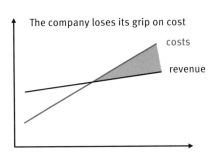

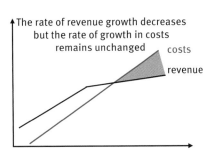

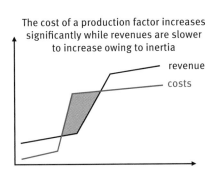

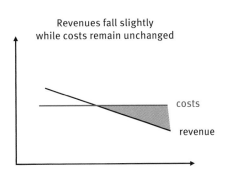

... to excellence

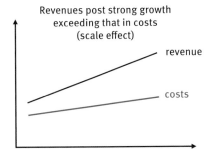

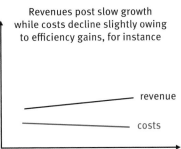

Profits   Losses

2/ THE STABILITY PRINCIPLE (WHICH PREVENTS ANY SIMPLISTIC REASONING)

This principle holds that a company's earnings are much more stable than we would expect. Net income is frequently a modest amount that remains when **charges are offset against revenues**. Net income represents an equilibrium that is not necessarily upset by external factors. Let's consider, for instance, a supermarket chain where the net income is roughly equal to the net financial income. It would be a mistake to say that if interest rates decline, the company's earnings will be wiped out. The key issue here is whether the company will be able to slightly raise its prices to offset the impact of lower interest rates, without eroding its competitiveness. It will probably be able to do so if all its rivals are in the same boat. But the company may be doomed to fail if more efficient distribution channels exist.

The situation is very similar for champagne houses. A poor harvest drives up the cost of grapes, and pushes up the selling price of champagne bottles. Here the key issues are when prices should be increased in view of the competition from sparkling wines, the likely emergence of an alternative product at some point in the future and consumers' ability to make do without champagne if it is too expensive.

It is important not to repeat the common mistake of establishing a direct link between two parameters and explaining one by trends in the other.

A company's margins also depend to a great extent on those of its rivals. The purpose of financial analysis is to understand why they are above or below those of its rivals.

That said, there are limits to the stability principle.

3/ REGULATORY CHANGES

These are controls imposed on a company by an authority (usually the government) that generally restricts the "natural" direction in which the company is moving. Examples include an aggressive devaluation, the introduction of a shorter working week or measures to reduce the opening hours of shops.

4/ EXTERNAL FACTORS

Like regulatory changes, these are imposed on the company. That said, they are more common and are specific to the company's sector of activity, e.g. pressures in a market, arrival (or sudden reawakening) of a very powerful competitor or changes to a collective bargaining agreement.

5/ PRE-EMPTIVE ACTION

Pre-emptive action is where a company immediately reflects expectations of an increase in the cost of a production factor by charging higher selling prices. This occurs in the champagne sector where the build-up of pressure in the raw materials market following a poor grape harvest very soon leads to an increase in prices per bottle. Such action is taken even though it will be another two or three years before the champagne comes onto the marketplace.

Pre-emptive action is particularly rapid where no alternative products exist in the short to medium term and competition in the sector is not very intense. It leads to gains or losses on inventories that can be established by valuing them only at their replacement cost.

6/ INERTIA EFFECTS

Inertia effects are much more common than those we have just described, and they work in the opposite direction. Owing to inertia, a company may struggle to pass on fluctuations in the cost of its production factors immediately by upping its selling prices. For instance, in a sector that is as competitive and has such low barriers to entry as the road haulage business, there usually is a delay before an increase in diesel fuel prices is passed on to customers in the form of higher shipping charges.

7/ INFLATION EFFECTS

Inflation distorts company earnings because it acts as an incentive for overinvestment and overproduction, particularly when it is high (e.g. during the 1970s and the early 1980s). A company that plans to expand the capacity of a plant four years in the future should decide to build it immediately; it will then save 30–40% of its cost in nominal terms, giving it a competitive advantage in terms of accounting costs. Building up excess inventories is another temptation in high-inflation environments because time increases the value of inventories, thereby offsetting the financial expense involved in carrying them and giving rise to inflation gains in the accounts.

Inflation gives rise to a whole series of similar temptations for artificial gains, and any players opting for a more cautious approach during such periods of madness may find themselves steamrollered out of existence. By refusing to build up their inventories to an excessively high level and missing out on inflation gains, they are unable to pass on a portion of them to consumers, as their competitors do. Consequently, during periods of inflation:

- depreciation and amortisation are in most cases insufficient to cover the replacement cost of an investment, the price of which has risen;
- inventories yield especially large nominal inflation gains where they are slow-moving.

Deflation leads to the opposite results.

8/ CAPITAL EXPENDITURE AND RESTRUCTURING

It is fairly common for major investments (e.g. the construction of a new plant) to depress operating performance and even lead to operating losses during the first few years after they enter service.

For instance, the construction of a new plant generally leads to:

- additional general and administrative costs, such as R&D and launch costs, professional fees, etc;

- financial costs that are not matched by any corresponding operating revenue until the investment comes on stream (this is a common phenomenon in the hotel sector given the length of the payback periods on investments). In certain cases, they may be capitalised and added to the cost of fixed assets but this is even more dangerous;
- additional personnel cost deriving from the early recruitment of line staff and managers, who have to be in place by the time the new plant enters service;
- lower productivity owing both to the time it takes to get the new plant and equipment running and the inexperience of staff at the new production facilities.

As a result of these factors, some of the investment spending finds its way onto the income statement, which is thus weighed down considerably by the implications of the investment programme.

Conversely, a company may deliberately decide to pursue a policy of underinvestment to enhance its bottom line (so as to be sold at an inflated price) and to maximise the profitability of investments it carried out some time ago. But this type of strategy of maximising margins jeopardises its scope for value creation in the future (it will not create any new product, it will not train sufficient staff to prepare for changes in its business, etc.).

Section 9.5
STANDARD INCOME STATEMENTS
(INDIVIDUAL AND CONSOLIDATED ACCOUNTS)

The following tables show two model income statements. The first has been adapted to the needs of non-consolidated (individual) company accounts and is based on the by-nature format. The second is based on the by-function format as it is used in the Indesit group's consolidated accounts.

BY-NATURE INCOME STATEMENT – INDIVIDUAL COMPANY ACCOUNTS

Periods	2009	2010	2011

NET SALES

+ Changes in inventories of finished goods and work in progress
+ Production for own use

= **PRODUCTION**

− Raw materials used
− Cost of goods for resale sold
= Profit on raw materials used/goods for resale sold
− Other purchases and external charges

= **VALUE ADDED**

− Personnel cost (incl. employee profit-sharing and incentives)
− Taxes other than on income
+ Operating subsidies
− Change in operating provisions[6]
+ Other operating income and cost

6 *Impairment losses on current assets operating and provisions.*

BY-NATURE INCOME STATEMENT – INDIVIDUAL COMPANY ACCOUNTS (CONTINUED)

Periods	2009	2010	2011

= EBITDA

− Depreciation and amortisation

= EBIT (OPERATING PROFIT) (A)

Financial expense
− Financial income
− Net capital gains/(losses) on the disposal of marketable securities
+ Change in financial provisions

= NET FINANCIAL EXPENSE (B)

(A) − (B) = PROFIT BEFORE TAX AND NON-RECURRING ITEMS

+/− Non-recurring items including impairment losses on fixed assets
− Corporate income tax

= NET INCOME (net profit)

BY-FUNCTION INCOME STATEMENT – CONSOLIDATED ACCOUNTS

	2006		2007		2008		2009		2010	
	€m	%	€m	%	€m	%	€m	%	€m	%
NET SALES	3249	+6%	3438	+6%	3155	−8%	2613	−17%	2879	+10%
− Cost of sales	2404		2543		2378		1939		2044	
= GROSS MARGIN	845	26.0%	895	27.5%	777	26.4%	674	25.8%	835	29.0%
− Selling and marketing costs	512		547		503		408		483	
− General and administrative costs	140		141		114		97		124	
± Other operating income and expense	6		13		0		0		0	
+ Income from associates	(2)		4		0		0		0	
= RECURRING OPERATING PROFIT	197	6.1%	224	6.9%	160	4.9%	169	6.5%	228	7.9%
± Non-recurring items	(39)		(27)		(19)		(50)		(44)	
= OPERATING PROFIT (EBIT)	158	4.9%	197	6.0%	141	4.3%	119	4.6%	184	6.4%
− Financial expense	41		46		58		53		36	
+ Financial income	14		16		13		2		2	
= PROFIT BEFORE TAX	132	4.1%	166	5.1%	95	2.9%	68	2.6%	150	5.2%
− Income tax	55		61		39		33		60	
− Minority interests	0		(0)		1		1		0	
= NET PROFIT ATTRIBUTABLE TO SHAREHOLDERS	76	2.4%	105	3.2%	56	1.7%	34	1.3%	90	3.1%

Section 9.6
CASE STUDY: INDESIT

In 2006 and 2007 sales grew thanks to volume effect (price and mix effect being close to 0 due to pressure on prices from Asian competition). Indesit has succeeded in developing sales in countries (mainly eastern Europe and Russia) where major domestic appliances are not yet widespread. But in Q4 2008, Indesit suffered from a sharp slow down in sales together with a drop in the pound (Indesit realises a significant part of its sales in the UK). In 2009 sales in eastern European countries and Russia dropped by 46% (!) due in particular to retailers' financial difficulties and devaluations. In 2010, activity picked up, led by emerging countries and, in particular, Russia (catch up effect).

Despite such volatility in sales, Indesit has succeeded in maintaining a decent operating margin thanks to the transfer of part of the production and to sourcing from low-cost countries (e.g. Poland). In 2009 Indesit reacted strongly by closing production units, thus substantially reducing its fixed costs base. The economic crisis led to a decrease in steel and plastic prices, which allowed Indesit partially to set off the impact of the drop in sales on the operating profit. In 2010, the group benefited from a lowered fixed costs base. In addition, Indesit did not suffer from the increase in raw material prices as it had signed a long-term contract with suppliers at the end of 2009. In 2010, the margin reached a level higher than that before the crisis.

SUMMARY

The summary of this chapter can be downloaded from www.vernimmen.com.

The first step in any financial analysis is to analyse a company's margins. This is absolutely vital because a company that fails to sell its products or services to its customers at above their cost is doomed.

An analysis of margins and their level relative to those of a company's competitors reveals a good deal about the strength of a company's strategic position in its sector.

Operating profit, which reflects the profits generated by the operating cycle, is a central figure in income statement analysis. First of all, we look at how the figure is formed based on the following factors:

- sales, which are broken down to show the rate of growth in volumes and prices, with trends being compared with growth rates in the market or the sector;

- production, which leads to an examination of the level of unsold products and the accounting method used to value inventories, with overproduction possibly heralding a serious crisis;

- raw materials used and other external charges, which need to be broken down into their main components (i.e. raw materials, transportation, distribution costs, advertising, etc.) and analysed in terms of their quantities and costs;

- personnel cost, which can be used to assess the workforce's productivity (sales/ average headcount, value-added/average headcount) and the company's grip on costs (personnel cost/average headcount);

- depreciation and amortisation, which reflect the company's investment policy.

Further down the income statement, operating profit is allocated as follows:

- net financial expense, which reflects the company's financial policy. Heavy financial expense is not sufficient to account for a company's problems, it merely indicates that its profitability is not sufficient to cover the risks it has taken;

- non-recurring items (extraordinary items, some exceptional items and results from discontinued operations) and the items specific to consolidated accounts (income or losses from associates, minority interests, impairment losses on fixed assets).

- corporate income tax.

Diverging trends in revenues and charges produce a scissors effect, which may be attributable to failures in the market in which the company operates, e.g. economic rents, monopolies, regulatory changes, pre-emptive action, inertia. Identifying the cause of the scissors effect provides valuable insight into the economic forces at work and the strength of the company's strategic position in its sector. We are able to understand why the company generates a profit, and get clues about its future prospects.

QUESTIONS

1/ If you had to analyse the non-consolidated accounts of a holding company of several industrial participations, which profit level would you focus on ? What are the important items on the income statement? Are the consolidated accounts of this holding company interesting?

2/ The industrial group HEEMS shows a net result, 80% of which is from extraordinary income. State your views.

3/ The industrial group VAN DAM shows a net result, 80% of which is from its financial income. State your views.

4/ Why can a direct link not be drawn between an increase in production costs and the corresponding drop in profits?

5/ What steps can be taken to help offset the impact of a negative scissors effect?

6/ Of the following companies, which would you define as making "a margin between the end market and an upstream market"?

- temporary employment agency;
- storage company (warehouse);
- slaughterhouse;
- furniture manufacturer;
- supermarket.

7/ What does the stability of a company's net profits depend on?

8/ Van Poucke NV has positive EBITDA and growth, but negative operating profit. State your views.

9/ What is your view of a company which has seen a huge increase in sales due to a significant drop in prices and a strong volume effect?

10/ Why analyse minority interests on the consolidated income statement?

11/ Why break down contributions made by associate companies into operating, financial and non-recurring items?

12/ In a growing company, would you expect margins to grow or to decrease?

More questions are waiting for you at www.vernimmen.com.

EXERCISES

1/ Identify the sector to which each of the following types of company belongs: electricity producer, supermarket, temporary employment agency, specialised retailer, construction and public infrastructure.

Company	1	2	3	4	5
Sales	100	100	100	100	100
Production	100	100	104	99	0
Trading profit	23.0	24.8	0	0	0
Raw materials used	0	0	} 46.6	23.6	0
Other external charges	7.8	7.0		46.9	14.1
Personnel cost	9.3	11.7	21.5	24.1	88.2
EBITDA	6.8	6.7	28.1	3.7	4.6
Depreciation and amortisation	2.6	0.9	14.4	1.2	0.7
Operating income	4.2	5.8	7.1	2.9	3.1

2/ Identify the sector to which each of the following types of company belongs: cement, luxury products, travel agency, stationery, telecom equipment.

Company	1	2	3	4	5
Sales	100	100	100	100	100
Cost of sales	35.9	84.0	67.7	44.3	52.2
Marketing and selling costs	37.0	4.4	14.0	23.1	21.8
Administrative costs	11.1	10.0	6.6	10.7	9.3
R&D costs	0	0	20.1	6.6	2.1
Operating income	16.0	1.6	− 8.3	15.3	14.6

ANSWERS

Questions

1/ *Focus on financial result. Administrative costs, corporate income tax. No, as consolidated accounts will only reflect the cumulated financial situation of very diverse activities.*

2/ *It is important to understand the nature of this extraordinary income as, by definition, it is not likely to be recurring.*

3/ *It is important to understand the nature of this financial income: is it due to excess cash or to withdrawal of provisions?*

4/ *Because of the very complex issues at work which will require further study.*

5/ *Be flexible: outsource, bring in temporary staff.*

6/ *Temporary employment agency: margin between the direct employment market and the temporary employment market. Warehouse: fixed costs although margins are linked to volumes of business. Slaughterhouses: margin between downstream and upstream. Manufacturer of furniture: margin between raw material, the wood and the sales price. Supermarkets: fixed costs although margins are linked to volumes of business.*

7/ *On the cyclical nature of sales, the flexibility of the company (fixed/variable cost split), and the margin in absolute value.*

8/ *Analyse the investments and amortisation policy, along with impairment losses on fixed assets.*

9/ *What is the impact on EBITDA?*

10/ *In order to find out which of the group's entities is making profits.*

11/ *To obtain a clearer view of the entirety of the income statement, especially operating income.*

12/ *Margins should increase in theory as the company should enjoy a scale effect. It is often the reverse as, in growing markets, gain of market share is made at the expense of margins by cutting prices.*

Exercises

1/ *Electricity production: 3 (large amount booked under depreciation and amortisation); supermarkets: 1 (lowest trading profits, it is a low margins business); temporary employment agency: 5 (high personnel cost); specialised retail: 2 (highest trading profits); building and public infrastructure: 4 (high outsourcing costs).*

2/ *Luxury products group: 1 (high operating income margin and high marketing costs); travel agency: 2 (very low operating income, very high cost of sales, no R&D); telecom equipment supplier: 3 (high R&D costs); stationery products group: 4 (high marketing costs but lower than for the luxury products group); Cement group: 5 (the last one! Limited R&D).*

Chapter 10
MARGIN ANALYSIS: RISKS

Costs are not like problems, people do not like them to be fixed

In Chapter 9, we compared the respective growth rates of revenues and costs. In this chapter, we will compare all company costs and key profit indicators as a percentage of sales (or production for companies that experience major swings in their inventories of finished goods and work in progress).

The purpose of this analysis is to avoid extrapolating into the future the rate of earnings growth recorded in the past. Just because profits grew by 30% p.a. for two years as a result of a number of factors, does not mean they will necessarily keep growing at the same pace going forward.

Earnings and sales may not grow at the same pace owing to the following factors:

- structural changes in production;
- the scissors effect (see Chapter 9);
- **simply a cyclical effect accentuated by the company's cost structure. This is what we will be examining in more detail in this chapter.**

Section 10.1
HOW OPERATING LEVERAGE WORKS

Operating leverage links variation in activity (measured by sales) with changes in result (either operating profit or net income). Operating leverage depends on the level and nature of the breakeven point.

1/ DEFINITION

Breakeven is the level of activity at which total revenue covers total costs. With business running at this level, earnings are thus zero.

Put another way:

- if the company does not reach breakeven (i.e. insufficient sales), the company posts losses;
- if sales are exactly equal to the breakeven point, profits are zero;
- if the company exceeds its breakeven point, it generates a profit.

A company's breakeven point depends on its cost structure.

2/ CALCULATING THE BREAKEVEN POINT

Before the breakeven point can be calculated, it is vital for costs to be divided up into fixed and variable costs. This classification depends on the period under consideration. For instance, it is legitimate to say that:

- in the long term, all costs are variable, irrespective of their nature. If a company is unable to adjust its cost base, it is not a viable company;
- in the very short term (less than three months), almost all costs are fixed, with the exception of certain direct costs (i.e. certain raw materials);
- from a medium-term perspective, certain costs can be considered variable, e.g. indirect personnel cost, etc.

The breakeven point cannot be defined in absolute terms. It depends first and foremost on the length of the period under consideration. It usually decreases as the period in question increases.

Before starting to calculate a company's breakeven point, it is wise to define which type of breakeven point is needed. This obvious step is all too commonly forgotten.
For instance, we may want to assess:

- the projected change in the company's earnings in the event of a partial recession with or without a reduction in the company's output;
- the sensitivity of earnings to particularly strong business levels at the end of the year;
- the breakeven point implied by a strategic plan, particularly that resulting from the launch of a new business venture.

The breakeven point can be presented graphically:

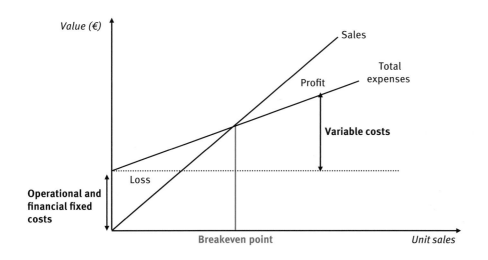

SECTION 1

The breakeven point is the level of sales at which fixed costs are equal to the contribution margin, which is defined as the difference between sales and variable costs. At the breakeven point, the following equation therefore holds true:

$$\text{Contribution margin} = \text{Fixed costs}$$
$$\text{or } m \times \text{Sales}_0 = \text{Fixed costs}$$
$$\text{i.e. Sales}_0 = \frac{\text{Fixed costs}}{m}$$
$$\text{with } m = \frac{\text{Sales} - \text{Variable costs}}{\text{Sales}}$$

where Sales_0 is the level of sales at the breakeven point and m is the contribution margin expressed as a percentage of sales.

Example   A company has sales of €150m, fixed costs of €90m and variable costs of €50m.

Its contribution margin is thus $150 - 50 = 100$, i.e. $100/150 = 66.67\%$ when expressed as a percentage of sales.

The breakeven point thus lies at: $90/0.6667 = €135$ m. In this example, the company is 11.1% above its breakeven point.

In 2010, BNP Paribas estimated that the typical European listed group with a revenue of €100 had €26.5 fixed costs, €61 variable costs and an operating profit of €11.6. Accordingly, a decrease of 1% in turnover results in a decrease of 3.5% in operating profit.

3/ THREE DIFFERENT BREAKEVEN POINTS

The breakeven point may be calculated before or after payments to the company's providers of funds. As a result, three different breakeven points may be calculated:

- **operating breakeven**, which is a function of the company's fixed and variable production costs that determine the stability of operating profit;
- **financial breakeven**, which takes into account the interest costs incurred by the company that determine the stability of profit before tax and non-recurring items.
- **total breakeven**, which takes into account all the returns required by the company's lenders **and** shareholders.

Operating breakeven is a dangerous concept because it disregards any return on capital invested in the company, while financial breakeven understates the actual breakeven point because it does not reflect any return on equity, which is the basis of all value creation.

Consequently, we recommend that readers calculate the breakeven point at which the company is able to generate not a zero net income but a positive net income high enough to provide shareholders with the return they require. To this end, we need to adjust the company's cost base by the profit before tax expected by shareholders. Below this breakeven point, the company might generate a profit, but will not (totally) satisfy the profitability requirements of its shareholders.

Interest charges represent a fixed cost at a given level of sales (and thus capital requirement). A company that experiences significant volatility in its operating profit may thus compensate partially for this instability through modest financial expense, i.e. by pursuing a strategy of limited debt. In any event, earnings instability is greater for a highly indebted company owing to its financial expense which represents a fixed cost.

To illustrate these concepts in concrete terms, we have prepared the following table calculating the various breakeven points for Indesit:[1]

1 *We analyse the table for Indesit in Section 10.4 of this chapter (see p. 185). We have assumed that costs of sales and selling and marketing costs are all variable costs and that other operating costs are fixed. This is evidently a rough cut but nevertheless gives a reasonable estimate.*

€m		2006	2007	2008	2009	2010
Sales		3249	3438	3155	2613	2879
Operating fixed costs	FC	658	701	617	505	607
Financial fixed costs	FiC	27	30	46	52	35
Variable costs	VC	2404	2543	2378	1939	2044
Contribution margin as a % of sales	$m = \dfrac{\text{Sales} - VC}{\text{Sales}}$	26%	26%	25%	26%	29%
Operating breakeven	$\text{Sales}_{op} = \dfrac{FC}{m}$	2530	2694	2505	1957	2093
Position of the company relative to operating breakeven as a %	$\dfrac{\text{Sales}}{\text{Sales}_{op}} - 1$	+28%	+28%	+26%	+33%	+38%
Financial breakeven	$\text{Sales}_f = \left(\dfrac{FC + FiC}{m} \right)$	2633	2810	2691	2158	2212
Position of the company relative to financial breakeven	$\dfrac{\text{Sales}}{\text{Sales}_f} - 1$	+23%	+22%	+17%	+21%	+30%
Total breakeven[1]	$\text{Sales}_t = \dfrac{FC + FiC + PBT}{m}$	3003	3187	3130	2749	2562
Position of the company relative to total breakeven	$\dfrac{\text{Sales}}{\text{Sales}_f} - 1$	+8%	+8%	+1%	−5%	+12%

(1): For Indesit, we have assumed a cost of equity (see Chapter 19) of 10% in 2006–2007 and 2010, 15% in 2008 and 2009 and a tax rate of 35% for 2006–2008, 50% for 2009 and 40% for 2010.

Based on these considerations, we see that the operating leverage depends on four key parameters:

- the three factors determining the stability of operating profit, i.e. the stability of sales, the structure of production costs and the company's position relative to its breakeven point;
- the level of interest expense, which is itself a function of the debt policy pursued by the company.

From our experience we have seen that, in practice, a company is in an unstable position when its sales are less than 10% above its financial breakeven point. Sales 20% above the financial breakeven point reflect a relatively stable situation and sales over 20% above the financial breakeven point for a given business structure indicate an exceptional and comfortable situation.

In the highly competitive and unstable conditions that we are currently experiencing, these figures may not be high enough in sectors with rapid technological changes.

Section 10.2
A MORE REFINED ANALYSIS PROVIDES GREATER INSIGHT

1/ ANALYSIS OF PAST SITUATIONS

Breakeven analysis (also known as cost–volume–profit analysis) may be used for three different purposes:

- to analyse earnings stability taking into account the characteristics of the market and the structure of production costs;
- to assess a company's real earnings power;
- to analyse the difference between forecasts and actual performance.

(a) Analysis of earnings stability

Here the level of the breakeven point in absolute terms matters much less than the company's position relative to its breakeven point.

The closer a company is to its breakeven point, the higher its earnings instability.

When a company is close to its breakeven point, a small change in sales triggers a steep change in its net income, so a strong rate of earnings growth may simply reflect a company's proximity to its breakeven point. This is the real problem affecting Japanese industry, the profitability of which is weak compared with that of industrial sectors in other countries.

Consider a company with the following manufacturing and sales characteristics:

Total fixed costs	=	€200 000
Variable costs per unit	=	€50
Unit selling price	=	€100

Its breakeven point stands at 4000 units. To make a profit, the company therefore has to sell at least 4000 units.

The following table shows a comparison of the relative increases (or reductions) in sales and earnings at five different sales volumes:

Sales volumes		Net income		Sensitivity
Number of units sold	% increase compared to previous level (*A*)	Amount	% increase compared to previous level (*B*)	(*A*)/(*B*)
4000		0		
5000	25%	50 000	Infinite	Infinite
6000	20%	100 000	100%	5
7200	20%	160 000	60%	3
8640	20%	232 000	45%	2.25

This table clearly shows that the closer the breakeven point, the higher the sensitivity of a company's earnings to changes in sales volumes. This phenomenon holds true both above and below the breakeven point.

We should be wary when profits are increasing much faster than sales for a company with low margins, since this phenomenon may be attributable to the operating leverage.

Consequently, breakeven analysis helps put into perspective a very strong rate of earnings growth during a good year. Rather than getting carried away with one good performance, analysts should attempt to assess the risks of subsequent downturns in reported profits.

For instance, Cemex and Lafarge posted similar sales trends, but completely different earnings trends, during 2009 because their proximity to breakeven point was very different. Lafarge was clearly farther from its breakeven point than Cemex, as can be seen by comparing the 2009 operating margins: 18% versus 11%.

	Sales	Operating income
Cemex	$14.5bn −19%	$1.2bn −38%
Lafarge	€15.9bn −17%	€2.5bn −26%

Likewise, the sensitivity of a company's earnings to changes in sales depends, to a great extent, on its cost structure. The higher a company's fixed costs, the greater the volatility of its earnings, as illustrated by the following example.

	Sales	Operating income
Tesco	£54.3bn (+9%)	£3.3bn (+10%)
SEB	€3.2bn (−2%)	€248m (−11%)
Lufthansa	€22.3bn (−10%)	€96m (−89%)

Tesco, the UK food retailer, has the lowest fixed costs of the three and Lufthansa the highest. A 10% decrease in Lufthansa's turnover drives its earnings down by 89%, whereas a 9% increase in sales leads to a similar increase in Tesco's operating income (10%). The situation of SEB (small appliances) stands in between the two extremes of retail (very limited fixed costs) and airlines (almost all costs are fixed).

(b) Assessment of normal earnings power

The operating leverage, which accelerates the pace of growth or contraction in a company's earnings triggered by changes in its sales performance, means that the significance of income statement-based margin analysis should be kept in perspective.

The reason for this is that an exceptionally high level of profits may be attributable to exceptionally good conditions that will not last. In such conditions good performance does not necessarily indicate a high level of structural profitability. This held true for a large number of companies in 2006–2007.

Consequently, an assessment of a company's earnings power deriving from its structural profitability drivers needs to take into account the operating leverage and cyclical trends, i.e. are we currently in an expansion phase of the cycle?

(c) Variance analysis

Breakeven analysis helps analysts account for differences between the budgeted and actual performance of a company over a given period.

The following table helps illustrate this:

	Value in absolute terms				Structure	
	Budget	Actual (A)	Change	% Difference	Actual sales/ Budgeted margin (B)	Difference (A) – (B)
Sales	240	180	−60	−25%	180	—
Variable costs	200	155	−45	−22.5%	150	+5
Contribution margin	40	25	−15	−37.5%	30	−5
Margin	16.7%	13.9%				
Fixed costs	20	25	+5	+25%	20	+5
Earnings	20	0	−20	−100%	10	−10

This table shows the collapse in the company's earnings of 20 is attributable to:

- the fall in sales (−25%);
- the surge in fixed costs (+25%);
- the surge in variable costs as a proportion of sales from 83.33% to 86.1%.

The cost structure effect accounts for 50% of the earnings decline (5 in higher fixed costs and 5 in higher variable costs), **with the impact of the sales contraction** accounting for the remaining 50% of the decline (10 lost in contribution margin).

2/ Strategic analysis

(a) Industrial strategy

A company's breakeven point is influenced by its industrial strategy.

A large number of companies operating in cyclical sectors made a mistake by raising their breakeven point through heavy investment. In fact, they should have been seeking to achieve the lowest possible operating leverage and, above all, the most flexible possible cost structure to curb the effects of major swings in business levels on their profitability.

For instance, integration has often turned out to be a costly mistake in the construction sector. Only companies that have maintained a lean cost structure through a strategy of outsourcing have been able to survive the successive cycles of boom and bust in the sector.

In highly capital-intensive sectors and those with high fixed costs (pulp, metal tubing, cement, etc.), it is in companies' interests to use equity financing. Such financing does not accentuate the impact of ups and downs in their sales on their bottom line through the leverage effect of debt, but in fact attenuates their impact on earnings.

A breakeven analysis provides a link between financial and industrial strategy.

When a company finds itself in a tight spot, its best financial strategy is to reduce its financial breakeven point by raising fresh equity rather than debt capital, since the latter actually increases its breakeven point, as we have seen. As an example of this policy, Cemex and CRH, the cement and building material producers, raised equity in 2009.

If the outlook for its market points to strong sales growth in the long term, a company may decide to pick up the gauntlet and invest. In doing so, it raises its breakeven point, while retaining substantial room for manoeuvre. It may thus decide to take on additional debt.

As we shall see in Chapter 36, the only real difference in terms of cost between debt and equity financing can be analysed in terms of a company's breakeven point.

(b) Restructuring

When a company falls below its breakeven point, it sinks into the red. It can return to the black only by increasing its sales, lowering its breakeven point or boosting its margins.

Increasing its sales is only a possibility if the company has real strategic clout in its marketplace. Otherwise, it is merely delaying the inevitable: sales will grow at the expense of the company's profitability, thereby creating an illusion of improvement for a while but inevitably precipitating cash problems.

Lowering the breakeven point entails restructuring industrial and commercial operations, e.g. modernisation, reductions in production capacity, cuts in overheads. The danger with this approach is that management may fall into the trap of believing that it is only reducing the company's breakeven point when actually it is shrinking its business. In many cases, **a vicious circle sets in, as the measures taken to lower breakeven trigger a major business contraction, compelling the company to lower its breakeven point further, thereby sparking another business contraction, etc.**

Boosting margins means improving management, enhancing the competitiveness of products, eliminating low- or zero-margin products and consolidating operations around their existing strengths.

(c) Analysis of cyclical risks

As we stated earlier, there is no such thing as an absolute breakeven point – there are as many breakeven points as there are periods of analysis. But first and foremost, the break-even point is a dynamic rather than static concept. If sales fall by 5%, the mathematical formulae will suggest that earnings may decline by 20%, 30% or more, depending on the exact circumstances. In fact, experience shows that earnings usually fall much further than breakeven analysis predicts.

A contraction in market volumes is often accompanied by a price war, leading to a decline in the contribution margin. In this situation, fixed costs may increase as customers are slower to pay; inventories build up leading to higher interest costs and higher oper-ating provisions. All these factors may trigger a larger reduction in earnings than that implied by the mathematical formulae of breakeven analysis.

During cyclical downturns, contribution margins tend to decline, while fixed costs are often higher than expected.

Consequently, breakeven point increases while sales decline, as many recent examples show. Any serious forecasting thus requires modelling based on a thorough analysis of the situation.

During the German property slump of the mid-1990s (after the reunification boom), a mere slowdown in growth halted the speculators in their tracks. Crippled by their inter-est expense, they were compelled to lower prices, which led to speculation of a fall in the market (purchases were delayed in expectation of an additional fall in prices).

Businesses such as shipping and paper production, which require substantial production capacity that takes time to set up, periodically experience production gluts or shortages. As readers are aware, if supply is inflexible, a volume glut (or shortage) of just 5% may be suf-ficient to trigger far larger price reductions (or hikes) (i.e. 30%, 50% and sometimes even more).

Here again, an analysis of competition (its strength, patterns and financial structure) is a key factor when assessing the scale of a crisis.

Section 10.3

FROM ANALYSIS TO FORECASTING: THE CONCEPT OF NORMATIVE MARGIN

Nowadays, a great deal of the analysis of financial statements for past periods is car-ried out for the purpose of preparing financial projections. These forecasts are based on the company's past and the decisions taken by management. This section contains some advice about how best to go about this type of exercise.

All too often, it is not sufficient to merely set up a spreadsheet, click on the main income statement items determining EBITDA (or operating profit if depreciation and amortisation are also to be forecast) and then grow all of these items at a fixed rate. This may be reasonable in itself, but implies unreasonable assumptions when applied system-atically. Trees do not grow to the sky!

Instead, readers should:

- gain a full understanding of the company and especially its key drivers and margins;
- build growth scenarios, as well as possible reactions by the competition, the environ-ment, international economic conditions, etc.;

• draw up projections and analyse the coherence of the company's economic (for example, is its investment sufficient?) and strategic policy.

To this end, financial analysts have developed the concept of normalised earnings, i.e. a given company in a given sector should achieve an operating margin of x% (i.e. operating profit/sales).

This type of approach is entirely consistent with financial theory, which states that in each sector profitability should be commensurate with the sector's risks and that, sooner or later, these margins will be achieved, even though adjustments may take some considerable time (i.e. five years or even more, in any case much longer than they do in the financial markets).

What factors influence the size of these margins? This question can be answered only in qualitative terms and by performing an analysis of the strategic strengths and weaknesses of a company, which are all related to the concept of barriers to entry:

• the degree of maturity of the business;
• the strength of competition and quality of other market players;
• the importance of commercial factors, such as market share, brands, distribution networks, etc.
• the type of industrial process and incremental productivity gains, etc.

This approach is helpful because it takes into consideration the economic underpinnings of margins. Its drawback lies in the fact that analysts may be tempted to overlook the company's actual margin and concentrate more on its future, theoretical margins.

We cannot overemphasise the importance of explicitly stating and verifying the significance of all forecasts.

Section 10.4
CASE STUDY: INDESIT[2]

2 *The breakeven table for Indesit is on p. 179.*

Most of the time the information provided by listed companies is not enough for an external analyst to be able to compute precisely the breakeven point.

A rough estimate may be made using linear regression of each cost against net sales to approximate the breakdown between fixed and variable costs. For Indesit, we have assumed that cost of sales were variable costs (which is probably a bit optimistic) whereas other operating costs were fixed (which seems a decent assumption looking at the evolution over the period).

In 2009, we saw the vigorous reaction of Indesit to the crisis with a strong reduction in fixed costs (−18%) which, together with the drop in raw material prices, allowed the group to remain way above its operating and financial breakeven.

In 2010, Indesit got far away from its breakeven point thanks to the increase in sales and strict cost control. In the future it is likely that, in a more favourable context, the group may not be able to remain in such tight cost control (deferred increase in raw material costs, political pressure to limit relocation of production to low-cost countries).

Without the active policy of driving fixed costs down, Indesit would have shown an operating loss of €27m in 2009 (against an actual operating profit of €169m). Net loss would then have been c. €130m, i.e. 28% of shareholders' equity. This would have seriously handicapped its solvency.

SUMMARY

The summary of this chapter can be downloaded from www.vernimmen.com.

The breakeven point is the level of business activity, measured in terms of sales, production or the quantity of goods sold, at which total revenues cover total costs. At this level of sales, a company makes zero profit.

The breakeven point is not an absolute level – it depends on the length of period being considered because the distinction between fixed and variable costs can be justified only by a set of assumptions and, sooner or later, any fixed cost can be made variable.

Three different breakeven points may be calculated:

- operating breakeven, which is a function of the company's fixed and variable production costs. It determines the stability of operating activities, but may lead to financing costs being overlooked;

- financial breakeven, which takes into account the interest expense incurred by the company, but not its cost of equity;

- total breakeven, which takes into account both interest expense and the net profit required by shareholders. As a result, it takes into account all the returns required by all of the company's providers of funds.

Operating breakeven is calculated by dividing a company's fixed costs by its contribution margin ((sales – variable costs)/sales). Financial breakeven is calculated by adding interest expense to the fixed costs in the previous formula. Total breakeven is computed by adding the net income required to cover the cost of equity to fixed operating costs and interest costs.

The calculation and a static analysis of a company's breakeven point can be used to assess the stability of its earnings, its normal earnings power and the actual importance of the differences between budgeted and actual performance. The further away a company lies from its breakeven point, the more stable its earnings and the more significant its earnings trends are. The higher its fixed costs as a share of total costs, the higher the breakeven point and the greater the operating leverage and the volatility of its earnings are.

An analysis of trends in the operating leverage over time reveals a good deal about the company's industrial strategy. An attempt to harness economies of scale will raise the breakeven point and thus make a company more sensitive to economic trends. Efforts to make its industrial base more flexible will lower its breakeven point, but may also reduce its potential earnings power.

QUESTIONS

1/ A company's net income, which was 0.2% of sales in year 1, leaps by 40% in year 2. State your views.

2/ Would it be better for an oil refinery to finance its needs using equity or debt?

3/ Would it be better for an Internet startup company to finance its needs using equity or debt?

4/ You are appointed financial director of a cement group which has no debts. What should you be concerned about?

5/ You are appointed financial director of a cement group which has a fairly substantial amount of debts. What should you be concerned about?

6/ Is personnel cost a variable or a fixed cost?

7/ A major investment bank announces the best half-year results it has ever achieved. State your views.

8/ On page 181, which of Cemex and Lafarge is the closer to breakeven?

9/ What is the operating leverage? What does it depend on? On page 181 (second table), which group has the lowest operating leverage?

10/ Are bonuses a fixed or variable cost?

More questions are waiting for you at www.vernimmen.com.

EXERCISES

1/ Below are the income statements of four companies with the same level of sales, but with different production costs and financial structures.

	A	B	C	D
Sales	100	100	100	100
Variable costs	65	55	36	30
Fixed costs	25	29	50	55
EBITDA	10	16	14	15
Depreciation and amortisation	2	8	4	6
EBIT	8	8	10	9
Financial expense	2	6	1.5	6
Profit before tax and non-recurring items	6	2	8.5	3

For each company, calculate the breakeven point, before and after financial costs, and the company's position relative to its breakeven point.

2/ Below are the income statements for the Spanish Hoyos group. The company asks you to analyse these statements and answer the following questions:

(a) What is your opinion of the company?

(b) Is the company moving closer towards or further away from breakeven point?

(c) In your view, is the company in a period of heavy capital expenditures?

(d) What choices are made with regard to cost control?

(e) Explain the rise in financial expense.

Grupo Hoyos	1	2	3
Sales	82 000	92 000	97 000
Change in finished goods and in-progress inventory	500	1400	2800
Production	82 500	93 400	99 800
Purchases of raw materials and goods for resale	24 800	27 400	29 900
Change in inventories	−1700	−500	−1600
Other external charges	20 200	23 000	23 500
Taxes	1200	1400	1500
Personnel cost	29 000	33 000	37 000
Depreciation and amortisation	5200	4900	4800
Provisions	100	200	−
Operating charges	78 800	89 400	95 100
Operating income	3700	4000	4700
Interest, dividends and other financial income	300	400	300
Interest and other finance charges	2300	2900	3900
Financial income	−2000	−2500	−3600
Exceptional income	− 100	− 100	+100
Tax	800	700	600
Net income	800	700	600

3/In January of year 0, the Swiss group Schmidheiny published the following projected figures:

	0	1	2	3
Production	70.2	106	132	161
Raw materials used	29.4	35.4	44.3	53.8
Personnel cost	22.2	29.4	36.7	41.1
Taxes	0.5	0.7	0.7	0.8
Other external services	13.7	19.8	24.6	30.5
Outsourcing	2.5	8.9	11.2	11.3
Depreciation and amortisation	1.4	2.7	3.6	5

(a) Calculate the breakeven point for each year. The cost structure is as follows:

○   variable costs: raw materials used, outsourcing, 50% of other external services;
○   fixed costs: all other costs.

(b) Schmidheiny is planning a capital expenditure programme which should increase its production capacity threefold. This programme, which is spread over years 0 to 1, includes the construction of four factories and the launch of new products. The income statements for years 1, 2 and 3 factor in these investments. State your views.

(c) The company will need to raise around €30m to finance this capital expenditure programme. Financial expense before this capital expenditure programme amounts to €1.6m, and Schmidheiny is planning to finance its new requirements using debt exclusively (average interest rate: 10% before tax). What is your view of the debt policy the company intends to pursue?

Questions

1/ *Low profit levels mean that any improvement in the economic situation will very quickly lead to higher profits (company close to breakeven point).*

2/ *A company with very cyclical activity: financing with equity.*

3/ *Shareholders' equity as it has a high fixed costs structure.*

4/ *Turn a maximum of costs into variable costs, and bring down fixed costs.*

5/ *The same concerns as Question 4, and get rid of your debts!*

6/ *It depends on whether the staff are permanent or temporary and on the breakdown of salaries between fixed salary and commissions/bonuses and on whether local rules allow you to fire people rapidly (as in the UK) or not (as in Germany or France).*

7/ *How much of this improvement can be attributed to an improvement in the economy, and how much to structural improvements?*

8/ *Cemex, as it is the most sensitive to a change in sales.*

9/ *Operating leverage indicates the sensitivity of profits to a change in sales. The more variable costs are, the lower the operating leverage will be. In the table, Tesco has the lowest operating leverage.*

10/ *Variable costs, but they become a source of scandal when they become fixed costs.*

Exercises

1/ *A detailed Excel version of the solutions is available at www.vernimmen.com.*

	A	B	C	D
Sales	100	100	100	100
Contribution	35	45	64	70
Contribution in % of sales	35%	45%	64%	7%
Breakeven point before financial expense[1]	77	82	84	87
Sales/breakeven	129.6%	121.6%	118.5%	114.8%
Breakeven point after financial expense	83	96	87	96
Sales/breakeven	120.7%	104.7%	115.3%	104.5%

[1] Total fixed costs = fixed operating costs + depreciation and amortisation

2/ *(a) Personnel cost will increasingly eat into EBITDA. Given the steep rise in financial expense, profit before tax and non-recurring items decreases in both absolute and relative value. The company is becoming less and less profitable, and accumulating more and more debts. One quarter of increased production is artificial, as it is tied up in inventories and finished products. The company is producing more but cannot shift its products.*

(b) With stable margins on purchases and an increase in other costs, the company is clearly approaching its breakeven point.

(c) With depreciation and amortisation down in absolute value, we can conclude that the company is not overinvesting in fixed assets.

(d) The management of Grupo Hoyos keeps tight control over raw materials, probably a reflection of a sound procurement policy. External charges are also well managed. Personnel cost, however, is out of control.

(e) The company is not investing and the explanation for the increase in financial expense probably lies in the rise in working capital (increase in inventories).

3/ (a) *Economic breakeven point*

Schmidheiny	0	1	2	3
Production	70.2	106	132	161
Variable costs	38.75	54.2	67.8	80.35
Contribution	31.45	51.8	64.2	80.65
Contribution as a % of sales	44.80%	48.87%	48.64%	50.09%
Fixed costs	30.95	42.7	53.3	62.15
Breakeven	69.08	87.38	109.59	124.07

(b) *A good investment: improvement in earnings with fixed costs rising at a slower pace than production. The company is moving further away from its breakeven point. Trebling production capacity only results in a doubling of fixed costs. Improvement in production or over-optimistic projections?*
(c) *Breakeven point after financial expense with the envisaged level of debt.*

	1	2	3
Breakeven point after financial expense	96.8	119.0	133.3

Debt capital significantly increases breakeven point and, accordingly, the risk.

BIBLIOGRAPHY

G. Buccino, K. McKinley, The importance of operating leverage in a turnaround, *Secured Lender*, 64–68, Sept./Oct. 1997.

Harvard Business School Press, *Breakeven Analysis and Operating Leverage:Understanding Cash Flows*, 2008.

Chapter 11

WORKING CAPITAL AND CAPITAL EXPENDITURES

Building the future

As we saw in the standard financial analysis, all value creation requires investment. In finance, investment means creating either new fixed assets or working capital. The latter, often high in continental Europe, deserves some explanation.

Section 11.1

THE NATURE OF WORKING CAPITAL

Every analyst intuitively tries to establish a percentage relationship between a company's working capital and one or more of the measures of the volume of its business activities. In most cases, the chosen measure is annual turnover or sales.

The ratio:

$$\frac{\text{Operating working capital}}{\text{Annual sales}}$$

reflects the fact that the operating cycle generates an operating working capital that includes:

- capital "frozen" in the form of inventories, representing procurement and production costs that have not yet resulted in the sale of the company's products;
- funds "frozen" in customer receivables, representing sales that customers have not yet paid for;
- accounts payable that the company owes to suppliers.

The balance of these three items represents the net amount of money tied up in the operating cycle of the company. In other words, if the working capital turnover ratio is 25% (which is high), this means that 25% of the company's annual sales volume is "frozen" in inventories and customer receivables not financed by supplier credit. This also means that, at any moment, the company needs to have on hand funds equal to a quarter of its annual sales to pay suppliers and employee salaries for materials and work performed on products or services that have not yet been manufactured, sold or paid for by customers.

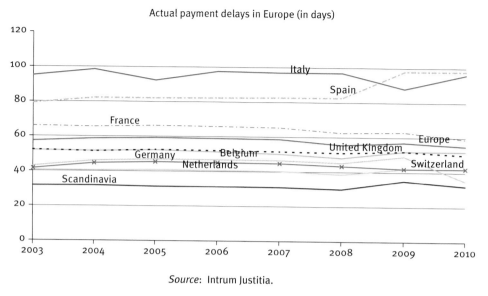

Source: Intrum Justitia.

The above chart shows trends in the actual payment periods in various geographical areas over the 2003–2010 period.

As we will see in Section 11.2, working capital is often expressed as a number of days of sales. This figure is derived by multiplying a percentage ratio by 365. In our example, a ratio of 25% indicates that working capital totals around 90 days of the company's sales.

1/ STEADY BUSINESS, PERMANENT WORKING CAPITAL

Calculated from the balance sheet, a company's working capital is the balance of the accounts directly related to the operating cycle. According to traditional financial theory, these amounts are very liquid; that is, they will either be collected or paid within a very short period of time. **But in fact, although it is liquid, working capital also reflects a permanent requirement.**

No matter when the books are closed, the balance sheet always shows working capital, although the amount changes depending on the statement date. The only exceptions are the rare companies whose operating cycle actually generates cash rather than absorbs it.

There is an apparent contradiction between the essentially liquid nature of working capital on the one hand and its permanence on the other.

Working capital is liquid in the sense that every element of it disappears in the ordinary course of business. Raw materials and inventories are consumed in the manufacturing process. Work in progress is gradually transformed into finished products. Finished products are (usually) sold. Receivables are (ordinarily) collected and become cash, bank balances, etc. Similarly, debts to suppliers become outflows of cash when they are paid.

As a result, if the production cycle is less than a year (which is usually the case) all of the components of working capital at the statement date will disappear in the course of the following year. But at the next statement date, other operating assets will have taken their place. **This is why we view working capital as a permanent requirement.**

Even if each component of working capital has a relatively short lifetime, the operating cycles are such that the contents of each are replaced by new contents. As a result, if the level of business activity is held constant, the various working capital accounts remain at a constant level.

All in all, at any given point in time, a company's working capital is indeed liquid. It represents the difference between some current assets and some current liabilities. But thinking in terms of "permanent working capital" introduces a radically different concept. It suggests that if business is stable, current (liquid) operating assets and current operating liabilities will be renewed and new funds will be tied up, constituting a permanent capital requirement as surely as fixed assets are a permanent capital requirement.

Working capital is two-sided. From the point of view of balance sheet value, it is liquid. From a going-concern point of view, it is permanent.

2/ SEASONAL BUSINESS ACTIVITY, PARTLY SEASONAL REQUIREMENT

When a business is seasonal, purchases, production and sales do not take place evenly throughout the year. As a result, working capital also varies during the course of the year, expanding then contracting.

The working capital of a seasonal business never falls to zero. Whether the company sells canned vegetables or raincoats, a minimum level of inventories is always needed to carry the company over to the next production cycle.

In our experience, companies in seasonal businesses often pay too much attention to the seasonal aspect of their working capital and ignore the fact that a significant part of it is permanent. As some costs are fixed, so are some parts of the working capital.

We have observed that in some very seasonal businesses, such as toys, the peak working capital is only twice the minimum. This means that half of the working capital is permanent, the other half is seasonal.

3/ CONCLUSION: PERMANENT WORKING CAPITAL AND THE COMPANY'S ONGOING NEEDS

An external analyst risks confusing the working capital on the balance sheet with the permanent working capital.

Approximately 36% of all companies close their books at a date other than 31 December. Bordeaux vineyards close on 30 September, Caribbean car rental companies on 30 April. They choose these dates because that is when the working capital requirement shown on their balance sheets is lowest. This is pure window dressing.

A company in trouble uses trade credit to the maximum possible extent. In this case, you must restate working capital by eliminating trade credit that is in excess of normal levels. Similarly, if inventory is unusually high at the end of the year because the company speculated that raw material prices would rise, then the excess over normal levels should be eliminated in the calculation of permanent working capital. Lastly, to avoid giving the impression that the company is too cash rich, some companies make an extra effort to pay their suppliers before the end of the year. This is more akin to investing cash balances than to managing working capital.

It may be rash to say that the working capital at fiscal year end is the company's permanent working capital.

Although the working capital on the balance sheet at year end can usually not be used as an indicator of the company's permanent requirement, its year-to-year change can still be informative. Calculated at the same date every year, there should be no seasonal impact. Analysing how the requirement has changed from year end to year end can shed light on whether the company's operations are improving or deteriorating.

The year-end working capital is informative only if compared with the working capital at other year-end dates.

You are therefore faced with a choice:

- if the company publishes quarterly financial statements, you can take the permanent working capital to be the lowest of the quarterly balances and estimate the average working capital requirement with the year average of the figures for each quarter;
- if the company publishes only year-end statements, you must reason in terms of year-to-year trends and comparisons with competitors.[1]

1 *Provided competitors have the same balance sheet closing date.*

Section 11.2
WORKING CAPITAL TURNOVER RATIOS

As financial analysis consists of uncovering hidden realities, let's simulate reality to help us understand the analytical tools.

Working capital accounts are composed of uncollected sales, unsold production and unpaid-for purchases, in other words, the business activities that took place during the days preceding the statement date. Specifically:

- if customers pay in 15 days, receivables represent the last 15 days of sales;
- if the company pays suppliers in 30 days, accounts payable represent the last 30 days of purchases;
- if the company stores raw materials for three weeks before consuming them in production, the inventory of raw materials represents the last three weeks of purchases.

These are the principles. Naturally, the reality is more complex, because:

- payment periods can change;
- business is often seasonal, so the year-end balance sheet may not be a real picture of the company;
- payment terms are not the same for all suppliers or all customers;
- the manufacturing process is not the same for all products.

Nevertheless, working capital turnover ratios calculated on the basis of accounting balances represent an attempt to see the reality behind the figures.

1/ THE MENU OF RATIOS

(a) Days' sales outstanding (DSO)

The days' sales outstanding (or days/receivables) ratio measures the average payment terms the company grants its customers (or the average actual payment period). It is calculated by dividing the receivables balance by the company's average daily sales, as follows:

$$\frac{\text{Receivables}}{\text{Annual sales (incl. VAT)}} \times 365 = \text{Days' sales outstanding}$$

As the receivables on the balance sheet are shown inclusive of VAT, for consistency, sales must be shown on the same basis. But the sales shown on the profit and loss statement are exclusive of VAT. You must therefore increase them by the applicable VAT rate for the products the company sells or by an average rate if it sells products taxed at different rates.

VAT RATES ACROSS EUROPE, JAPAN AND THE USA

	Normal rate	Reduced rate
France	19.6%	2.1 or 5.5%
Germany	19%	7%
India	12.5%	0–1–4%
Italy	20%	4–10%
Japan	5%	0%
Netherlands	19%	0–6%
Poland	22%	0–3–7%
Russia	18%	0–10%
Spain	16%	0–4–7%
Sweden	25%	0–6–12%
Switzerland	7.6%	0–2.4–3.6%
United Kingdom	20%	0–5%
United States of America	VAT does not exist in the USA. A sales tax is paid. Its rate varies across states.	

Receivables are calculated as follows:

	Customer receivables and related accounts
+	Outstanding bills discounted (if not already included in receivables)
−	Advances and deposits on orders being processed
=	Total receivables

(b) Days' payables outstanding (DPO)

The days/payables ratio measures the average payment terms granted to the company by its suppliers (or the average actual payment period). It is calculated by dividing accounts payable by average daily purchases, as follows:

$$\frac{\text{Accounts payable}}{\text{Annual purchases (incl. VAT)}} \times 365 = \text{Number of days of payables}$$

Accounts payable are calculated as follows:

	Accounts payable and related accounts
−	Advances and deposits paid on orders
=	Total accounts payable

To ensure consistency, purchases are valued inclusive of VAT. They are calculated as follows:

	Purchase of goods held for resale (incl. VAT)
+	Purchase of raw materials (incl. VAT)
+	Other external costs (incl. VAT)
=	Total purchases

The amounts shown on the profit and loss statement must be increased by the appropriate VAT rate.

When the figure for annual purchases is not available (mainly when the income statement is published in the by-function format), the days' payables ratio is approximated as:

$$\frac{\text{Accounts payable}}{\text{Sales (incl. VAT)}} \times 365 = \text{Payables in number of days of sales}$$

(c) Days' inventory outstanding (DIO)

The significance of the inventory turnover ratios depends on the quality of the available accounting information. If it is detailed enough, you can calculate true turnover ratios. If not, you will have to settle for approximations that compare dissimilar data.

You can start by calculating an overall turnover ratio, not meaningful in an absolute sense, but useful in analysing trends:

$$\frac{\text{Inventories and work in progress}}{\text{Annual sales (excl. VAT)}} \times 365 = \text{Approximate in number of days of inventory}$$

Depending on the available accounting information, you can also calculate the turnover of each component of inventory, in particular raw material and goods held for resale, and distil the following turnover ratios:

- **Days of raw material**, reflecting the number of days of purchases the inventory represents or, viewed the other way round, the number of days necessary for raw material on the balance sheet to be consumed:

$$\frac{\text{Inventory of raw material}}{\text{Annual purchases of raw material (excl. VAT)}} \times 365 = \text{Number of days of purchase}$$

- **Days of goods held for resale**, reflecting the period between the time the company purchases goods and the time it resells them:

$$\frac{\text{Inventory of goods held for resale}}{\text{Annual purchases of goods held for resale (excl. VAT)}} \times 365$$

$$= \text{Number of days of goods held for resale}$$

- **Days of finished goods inventory**, reflecting the time it takes the company to sell the products it manufactures, and calculated with respect to cost of goods sold:

$$\frac{\text{Inventory of finished goods}}{\text{Annual cost of goods sold}} \times 365 = \text{Number of days of finished goods inventory}$$

- If cost of goods sold is unavailable, it is calculated with respect to the sales price:

$$\frac{\text{Finished goods inventory}}{\text{Annual sales (excl. VAT)}} \times 365$$

- **Days of work in progress**, reflecting the time required for work in progress and semi-finished goods to be completed – in other words, the length of the production cycle:

$$\frac{(\text{Work in progress}) + (\text{semi-finished products})}{\text{Annual cost of goods sold}} \times 365 = \text{Length of production cycle}$$

For companies that present their profit and loss statement by nature, this last ratio can be calculated only from internal sources as cost of goods sold does not appear as such on the P&L. The calculation is therefore easier for companies that use the by-function presentation for their profit and loss statement.

2/ THE LIMITS OF RATIO ANALYSIS

Remember that, in calculating the foregoing ratios, you must follow two rules:

- make sure the base of comparison is the same: sales price or production cost, inclusive or exclusive of VAT;
- compare outstandings in the balance sheet with their corresponding cash flows.

Turnover ratios have their limitations:

- they can be completely misleading if the business of the company is seasonal. In this case, the calculated figures will be irrelevant. To take an extreme example, imagine a company that makes all its sales in a single month. If it grants payment terms of one month, its number of days' receivables at the end of that month will be 365;
- they provide no breakdown – unless more detailed information is available – of the turnover of the components of each asset (or liability) item related to the operating cycle. For example, receivables might include receivables from private sector customers, international customers and government agencies. These three categories can have very different collection periods (government agencies, for instance, are known to pay late).

You must ask yourself what degree of precision you want to achieve in your analysis of the company. If a general idea is enough, you might be satisfied with average ratios, as calculated above after verifying that:

- the business is not too seasonal;
- if it is seasonal, that the available data refer to the same point in time during the year. If this is your case, we advise you to express the ratios in terms of a percentage (receivables/sales), which does not imply a direct link with actual payment conditions.

If you need a more detailed analysis, you will have to look at the actual business volumes in the period just prior to the statement date. In this case, the daily sales figure will not be the annual sales divided by 365, but the last quarter's sales divided by 90, the last two months divided by 60, etc.

If you must perform an in-depth audit of outstandings in the balance sheet, averages are not enough. You must compare outstandings with the transactions that gave rise to them.

Section 11.3
READING BETWEEN THE LINES OF WORKING CAPITAL

Evaluating working capital is an important part of an analyst's job in continental Europe, because intercompany financing plays a prominent role in the economy. In Anglo-Saxon countries, this analysis is less important because working capital is much lower, either because it is usual practice to offer a discount for prompt payments (USA) or because companies have been used, for decades, to paying promptly.

1/ GROWTH OF THE COMPANY

In principle, the ratio of working capital to annual sales should remain stable.

If the permanent requirement equals 25% of annual sales and sales grow from €100m to €140m, the working capital requirement should grow by €10m (€40m × 25%).

Growth in business volume causes an increase in working capital. This increase appears, either implicitly or explicitly, in the cash flow statement.

Growth in the company's business tends to increase the amount of working capital. This increase represents an additional need that a business plan must take into account.

We might be tempted to think that working capital does not grow as fast as sales because certain items, such as minimum inventory levels, are not necessarily proportional to the level of business volume. Experience shows, however, that growth very often causes a sharp, sometimes poorly controlled, increase in working capital at least proportional to the growth in the company's sales volume.

In fact, a growing company is often confronted with **working capital that grows faster than sales**, for various reasons:

- management sometimes neglects to manage working capital rigorously, concentrating instead on strategy and on increasing sales;
- management often tends to integrate vertically, both upstream and downstream. Consequently, structural changes to working capital are introduced as it starts growing much more rapidly than sales, as we will explain later on.

When a company is growing, the increase in working capital constitutes a real use of funds, just as surely as capital expenditures do. For this reason, increases in working capital must be analysed and projected with equal care.

Efficient companies are characterised by controlled growth in working capital. Indeed, successful expansion often depends on the following two conditions:

- ensuring that the growth in working capital tracks the growth in sales rather than zooming ahead of it;
- creating a corporate culture that strives to contain working capital. If working capital grows unchecked, sooner or later it will lead to serious financial difficulties and compromise the company's independence.

Today, companies faced with slower growth in business manage working capital strictly through just-in-time inventory management, greater use of outsourcing, etc.

Note that **in inflationary periods, working capital increases** even if the quantities the company produces do not. This increase is primarily due to the rise in prices which, at constant payment terms, increases production costs and receivables.

The foregoing analysis sheds light on two models of growth. A company can:

- grow without changing its production cycle and its relative working capital;
- grow on the basis of:

  ○ a simple growth in volume sold;
  ○ a change in its manufacturing processes related, for example, to diversification into new products;
  ○ a change in the composition of the customer base, leading to a change in overall payment terms granted to customers. For example, if a growing part of sales is realised with international companies, receivables will take longer to collect.

In the first case, growth in sales will lead to proportional growth in working capital.

For example, imagine the company's sales rise from €100m to €140m and working capital is 72 days of sales. In absolute terms, working capital rises from €20m to €28m, or by 40%, the same as the percentage rise in sales. The company will have to finance an increase in working capital of €8m as a result of increasing its sales by €40m.

In the second case, this will depend on the production cycle of the new products.

In the third case, growth in sales can lead to a more-than-proportional increase in permanent working capital.

Using the figures from the same example, we suppose receivables used to represent 62 days of sales on average. Now suppose the 40% increase in sales results primarily from an increase in exports, to customers who are granted more generous payment terms. Receivables rise by 18 days to 80 days of sales on average. Because sales have increased, permanent working capital rises to 90 days (72+18) of sales, or 140 × 90/365 = €35m, representing an increase of 75% from its initial volume of €20m.

Consequently, the company will have to finance an additional working capital of €15m and will be confronted with a much bigger financing problem than the company in the first example.

2/ RECESSION

By analysing the working capital of a company facing a sudden drop in its sales, we can see that it reacts in stages.

Initially, the company does not adjust its production levels. Instead it tries other ways to shore up sales. The recession also leads to difficulty in controlling accounts receivable, because customers start having financial difficulties and stretch out their payments over time. The company's cash situation deteriorates, and it has trouble honouring its commercial obligations, so it secures more favourable payment terms from its suppliers. At the end of this first phase, working capital – the balance between the various items affected by divergent forces – stabilises at a higher level. This situation was experienced in particular by car manufacturers in late 2008.

In the second phase, the company begins to adopt measures to adjust its operating cycle to its new level of sales. It cuts back on production, trims raw material inventories and ratchets customer payment terms down to normal levels. By limiting purchases, accounts payable also decline. These measures, salutary in the short term, have the paradoxical effect of inflating working capital because certain items remain stubbornly high while accounts payable decline.

As a result, the company produces (and sells) below capacity, causing unit costs to rise and the bottom line to deteriorate.

Finally, in the third phase, the company returns to a sound footing:

* sales surpass production;
* the cap on purchases has stabilised raw material inventories. When purchases return to their normal level, the company again benefits from a "normal" level of supplier credit.

Against this background, working capital stabilises at a low level that is once again proportional to sales, but only after a crisis that might last as long as a year.

It is important to recognise that any contraction strategy, regardless of the method chosen, requires a certain period of psychological adjustment. Management must be convinced that the company is moving from a period of expansion to a period of recession. This psychological change may take several weeks, but once it is accomplished, the company can:

- decrease purchases;
- adjust production to actual sales;
- reduce supplier credit which the company had tried to maximise. Of course, this slows down reduction in working capital.

We have seldom seen a company take less than nine months to significantly reduce its working capital and improve the bottom line (unless it liquidates inventories at fire-sale prices).

During a recession, working capital has a paradoxical tendency to grow; then, despite restructuring measures, it still doesn't budge. It is only towards the end of the recession that working capital subsides and the company gains breathing space.

3/ COMPANY STRATEGY AND ITS IMPACT ON WORKING CAPITAL

Companies that expand vertically by acquiring suppliers or distributors lengthen their production cycle. In so doing, they increase their value added. But this very process also increases their working capital because the increased value added is incorporated in the various line items that make up working capital, notably receivables and finished goods inventories. Conversely, accounts payable reflect purchases made further upstream and therefore contain less value added. So they become proportionately lower.

4/ NEGATIVE WORKING CAPITAL

The operating cycles of companies with negative working capital are such that, thanks to a favourable timing mismatch, they collect funds prior to disbursing some payments. There are two basic scenarios:

- supplier credit is much greater than inventory turnover, while at the same time customers pay quickly, in some cases in cash;
- customers pay in advance. This is the case for companies that work on military contracts, collective catering companies, companies that sell subscriptions, etc. Nevertheless, these companies are sometimes required to lock up their excess cash for as long as the customer has not yet "consumed" the corresponding service. In this case, negative working capital offers a way of earning significant investment income rather than presenting a source of funding that can be freely used by the firm to finance its operations.

The companies in the examples below receive the proceeds of their sales before paying for all of their production costs, in particular their suppliers of raw materials or merchandise intended for resale. They are few in number and are concentrated in the following sectors:

- retail (food but also, to a lesser extent, non-food);
- companies that receive advance payments on work-in-progress, such as aerospace and telecoms contractors working for governments, and some companies operating in the public works sector;
- collective catering companies;

- mail-order companies or online retailers where the customer pays upon ordering;
- certain newspaper and magazine publishers, ISP or pay-TV channels, since a large part of their sales volume derives from subscriptions;
- companies whose suppliers are in a position of such weakness – printers or hauliers that face stiff competition, for example – that they are forced to offer inordinately long payment terms to their customers.

A low or negative working capital is a boon to a company looking to expand without recourse to external capital. Efficient companies, in particular in mass-market retailing, all benefit from low or negative working capital. Put another way, certain companies are adept at using intercompany credit to their best advantage.

The presence of negative working capital can, however, lead to management errors. We once saw an industrial group that was loathe to sell a loss-making division because it had a negative working capital. Selling the division would have shored up the group's profitability but would also have created a serious cash management problem, because the negative working capital of the unprofitable division was financing the working capital of the profitable divisions. Short-sightedness blinded the company to everything but the cash management problem it would have had immediately after the disposal.

5/ WORKING CAPITAL AS AN EXPRESSION OF BALANCE OF POWER

Economists have tried to understand the theoretical justification for intercompany credit, as represented by working capital. To begin with, they have found that there are certain minimum technical turnaround times. For example, a customer must verify that the delivery corresponds to his order and that the invoice is correct. Some time is also necessary to actually effect the payment.

But this explains only a small portion of intercompany credit, which varies greatly from one country to another (see page 192).

Several factors can explain the disparity.

- Cultural differences: in Germanic countries, the law stipulates that the title does not pass to the buyer until the seller is paid. This makes generous payment terms much less attractive for the buyer, because as long as his supplier is not paid, he cannot process the raw material.
- Historical factors: in France, Italy and Spain, bank credit was restricted for a long time. Companies whose businesses were not subject to credit restrictions (building, exports, energy, etc.) used their bank borrowing capacity to support companies subject to the restrictions by granting them generous payment terms. Tweaking payment terms was also a way of circumventing price controls in the Mediterranean countries.
- Technical factors: in the USA, suppliers often offer two-part trade credit, where a substantial discount is offered for relatively early payment, such as a 2% discount for payment made within 10 days. Most buyers take this discount. This discount explains the low level of accounts payable in US groups' balance sheets. As a by-product, failure of a buyer to take this discount could serve as a very strong and early signal of financial distress.

There are numerous theories that provide explanations for the provision of trade credit by suppliers.

Mian and Smith suggested that credit provisions will be more likely in circumstances where there is easier resale of the product being sold, since this will allow the seller to seize and resell the product if the buyer defaults.

Cunat argued that the provision of trade credit ties customers to particular suppliers, thereby increasing the scope for punishment of nonpayment.

Trade credit can be a substitute to the classical financial system, particularly in some developing countries. This will allow some sectors to grow faster.

Some industries may require trade credit as a guarantee for product quality.[2] Certainly some products, for example high-tech or newly-developed products, need more quality assurance for their inputs than others, such as commodities.

2 As in Long et al., 1993.

Furthermore, Dietsch has shown that supplier credit acts as a financial shock absorber for companies in difficulty. For commercial reasons, suppliers feel compelled to support companies whose collateral or financial strength is insufficient (or has become insufficient) to borrow from banks. Suppliers know that they will not have complete control over payment terms. They have unwittingly become bankers and, like bankers, they attempt to limit payment terms on the basis of the back-up represented by the customer's assets and capital.

That said, it is unhealthy for companies to offer overly generous payment terms to their customers. By so doing, they run a credit risk. Even though the corporate credit manager function is more and more common, even in small companies, credit managers are not in the best position to appreciate and manage this risk. Moreover, intercompany credit is one of the causes of the domino effect in corporate bankruptcies.

In conclusion, we reiterate the fact that intercompany credit is one of the most visible manifestations of the balance of power between customers and suppliers. The size of intercompany credit serves as an indication of the strength of the company's strategic position *vis-à-vis* its customers and suppliers. How else can we explain why 50% of industrial groups in the Eurostoxx 50 (i.e. the largest listed European groups) enjoy negative working capital?

Section 11.4
ANALYSING CAPITAL EXPENDITURES

The following three questions should guide your analysis of the company's investments:

- What is the state of the company's plant and equipment?
- What is the company's capital expenditure policy?
- What are the cash flows generated by these investments?

1/ ANALYSING THE COMPANY'S CURRENT PRODUCTION CAPACITY

The current state of the company's fixed assets is measured by the ratio

$$\frac{\text{Net fixed assets}}{\text{Gross fixed assets}^3}.$$

3 Net fixed assets are gross fixed assets minus cumulative depreciation.

A very low ratio (less than 25%) indicates that the company's plant and equipment are probably worn out. In the near term, the company will be able to generate robust margins because depreciation charges will be minimal. But don't be fooled, this situation cannot last forever.

In all likelihood, the company will soon have trouble because its manufacturing costs will be higher than those of its competitors who have modernised their production facilities or innovated. Such a company will soon lose market share and its profitability will decline.

If the ratio is close to 100%, the company's fixed assets are recent, and it will probably be able to reduce its capital expenditure in the next few years.

2/ ANALYSING THE COMPANY'S INVESTMENT POLICY

Through the production process, fixed assets are used up. The annual depreciation charge is supposed to reflect this wearing out. By comparing capital expenditure with depreciation charges, you can determine whether the company is:

- expanding its industrial base by increasing production capacity. In this case, capital expenditure is higher than depreciation as the company invests more than simply to compensate for the annual wearing out of fixed assets;
- maintaining its industrial base, replacing production capacity as necessary. In this case, capital expenditure approximately equals depreciation as the company invests just to compensate for the annual wearing out of fixed assets;
- underinvesting or divesting (capital expenditure below depreciation). This situation can only be temporary or the company's future will be in danger, unless the objective is to liquidate the company.

Comparing capital expenditure with net fixed assets at the beginning of the period gives you an idea of the size of the investment programme with respect to the company's existing production facilities. A company that invests an amount equal to 50% of its existing net fixed assets is building new facilities worth half what it has at the beginning of the year. This strategy carries certain risks:

- risk that economic conditions will take a turn for the worse;
- risk that production costs will be difficult to control (productivity deteriorates);
- technology risks, etc.

3/ ANALYSING THE CASH FLOWS GENERATED BY INVESTMENTS

The theoretical relationship between capital expenditures on the one hand and the cash flow from operating activities on the other is not simple. New fixed assets are combined with those already on the balance sheet, and together they generate the cash flow of the period. Consequently, there is no direct link between operating cash flow and the capital expenditure of the period.

Comparing cash flow from operating activities with capital expenditure makes sense only in the context of overall profitability and the dynamic equilibrium between sources and uses of funds.

The only reason to invest in fixed assets is to generate profits, i.e. positive cash flows. Any other objective turns finance on its head. You must therefore be very careful when comparing the trends in capital expenditure, cash flow and cash flow from operating activities. This analysis can be done by examining the cash flow statement.

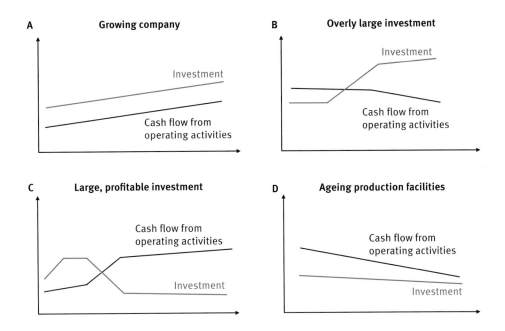

Any investment strategy must, sooner or later, result in an increase in cash flow from operating activities. If it doesn't, then the investments are not profitable enough. The company is heading for trouble or, more likely, is already in trouble.

Be on the lookout for companies that, for reasons of hubris, grossly overinvest, despite their cash flow from operating activities not growing at the same rate as their investments. Management has lost sight of the all-important criterion that is profitability.

All the above does not mean that capital expenditure should be financed by internal sources only. Our point is simply that a good investment policy grows cash flow at the same rate as capital expenditure. This leads to a virtuous circle of growth, a necessary condition for the company's financial equilibrium, as shown in graph A in the figure.

Graphs B, C and D illustrate other corporate situations. In D, investment is far below the company's cash flow from operations. You must compare investment with depreciation charges so as to answer the following questions:

- Is the company living off the assets it has already acquired (profit generated by existing fixed assets)?
- Is the company's production equipment ageing?
- Are the company's current capital expenditures appropriate, given the rate of technological innovation in the sector?

Naturally, the risk in this situation is that the company is "resting on its laurels", and that its technology is falling behind that of its competitors. This will eat into the company's profitability and, as a result, into its cash flow from operating activities at the very moment it will most need cash in order to make the investments necessary to close the gap *vis-à-vis* its rivals.

The most important piece of information to be gleaned from a cash flow statement is the relationship between capital expenditure and cash flow from operating activities and their respective growth rates.

Generally speaking, you must understand that there are certain logical inferences that can be made by looking at the company's investment policy. If its capital expenditure is very high, the company is embarking on a project to create significant new value rather than simply growing. Accordingly, future cash flow from operating activities will depend on the profitability of these new investments and is thus highly uncertain.

Lastly, ask yourself the following questions about the company's divestments. Do they represent recurrent transactions, such as the gradual replacement of a rental car company's fleet of vehicles, or are they one-off disposals? In the latter case, is the company's insufficient cash flow forcing the company to divest? Or is the company selling old, outdated assets in order to turn itself into a dynamic, strategically-rejuvenated company?

4 Financial statements for Indesit are shown on pages 54, 66 and 171.

Section 11.5
CASE STUDY: INDESIT[4]

1/ WORKING CAPITAL ANALYSIS

The average VAT rate of Indesit is not disclosed, and as it is difficult to estimate it since the group's activities span several continents, working capital ratios have been computed without taking VAT into account:

In days of net sales	2006	2007	2008	2009	2010
$\dfrac{\text{Operating working capital}}{\text{Net sales}} \times 365$	−3	−5	2	−20	−13
$\dfrac{\text{Inventories and work in progress}}{\text{Net sales}} \times 365$	40	35	43	39	41
$\dfrac{\text{Receivables}}{\text{Net sales}} \times 365$	64	55	53	55	63
$\dfrac{\text{Payables}}{\text{Net sales}} \times 365$	100	91	89	92	105

First of all, we should stress that, for such an industry, a working capital close to 0 is a very good achievement (−20 days for Electrolux, 87 for SEB). In particular, Indesit seems to have strong bargaining power *vis-à-vis* its suppliers.

Indesit had succeeded in reducing significantly its working capital in 2009 in order to generate cash. In 2010, the group could not reach the same achievement and the working capital was a bit less negative, despite a growth in sales. In particular, Indesit has to reduce pressure on its clients. The management of working capital within the group remains extremely sound, i.e. still largely negative.

2/ CAPITAL EXPENDITURE ANALYSIS

From a relatively high level (€186m) in 2005, Indesit's capital expenditures apparently decrease significantly, reaching net capital expenditure of €93m in 2007; appreciably below the depreciation level (€140m). The cycle reflects the high investments made in 2004 and 2005 to relocate part of the production to Poland and Russia. On average (€132m per year), the capital expenditure is close to the depreciation level so, over the long term, Indesit keeps a steady level of fixed assets although the volumes produced increase. This is a good performance which impacts favourably on its cash flows. But in 2009 and 2010, capex drops to €75m, i.e. close to half of the depreciation level. It is true that when demand drops sharply, one can do better than invest in production capacity, and reduce net debt for example! This situation is probably not sustainable over the long term and, if sales continue to grow, capex will have to pick up sooner or later, otherwise the equipment of the group will become outdated.

SUMMARY

The summary of this chapter can be downloaded from www.vernimmen.com.

A company's working capital is the balance of the accounts directly related to its operating cycle (essentially customer receivables, accounts payable and inventories). Calculated at the year-end closing date, it is not necessarily representative of the company's permanent requirement. Therefore, you must look at how it has evolved over time.

All of the components of working capital at a given point in time disappear shortly thereafter. Inventories are consumed, suppliers are paid, and receivables are collected. But even if these components are consumed, paid and collected, they are replaced by others. Working capital is therefore both liquid and permanent.

Working capital turnover ratios measure the average proportion of funds tied up in the operating cycle. The principal ratios are:

- days' sales outstanding: accounts receivable/sales (incl. VAT) × 365;

- days' payables outstanding: accounts payable/purchases (incl. VAT) × 365;

- days' inventory outstanding: inventories and work in progress/sales (excl. VAT) × 365;

- working capital turnover: working capital/sales (excl. VAT) × 365.

When a company grows, its working capital has a tendency to grow because inventories and accounts receivable (via payment terms) increase faster than sales. Paradoxically, working capital continues to grow during periods of recession because restrictive measures do not immediately deliver their desired effect. It is only at the end of the recession that working capital subsides and cash flow problems ease.

A low or negative working capital is a boon to a company looking to expand.

The level of working capital is an indication of the strength of the company's strategic position, because it reflects the balance of power between the company and its customers and suppliers.

We evaluate a company's investment policy by looking at the following three criteria:

- the extent to which production facilities are worn out, as measured by the net fixed assets/gross fixed assets ratio;

- the purpose of capital expenditure – build up fixed assets, maintain them or let them run down – is determined by whether capital expenditure is greater than, equal to or less than depreciation;

- analysis of the cash flow generated by investments. Any investment policy should, sooner or later, translate into increasing cash flows from operations. If not, the company will face financial difficulties.

QUESTIONS

1/ Can it be said that the working capital calculated on the balance sheet is representative of the company's permanent needs?

2/ If income is recorded on a company's books on the day it is received (and not on the invoice date) and costs on the date of payment, would this generate working capital? If so, how would this working capital differ from the working capital as calculated today?

3/ Is the permanent part of working capital liquid?

4/ Explain why, during a recession, working capital will decline at a slower pace than sales.

5/ How does working capital behave in an inflationary period?

6/ The financial director of a company makes the following comments: "The company performed remarkably well this year. You be the judge – our depreciation policy enabled us to generate 50% more EBITDA than last year. Our working capital has increased sharply, due to a more generous customer credit policy (three months instead of two) and to a significant increase in our inventories." What is your response? What advice would you give?

7/ The perfume division of Unilever has decided to launch a new perfume. During the first weeks following the launch, sales to retailers are high. Can the new perfume be considered a success?

8/ An aeronautics group has substantial inventories of unfinished goods. What consequences will this have? What measures would you suggest to improve this situation?

9/ Is calculating the ratio of non-operating working capital/sales a worthwhile exercise?

10/ Do you believe that Internet retail businesses carry high working capital?

11/ Do investments always take the form of capex?

12/ In what kind of sector is capex very low?

13/ In what sector is the largest investment in change in working capital?

More questions are waiting for you at www.vernimmen.com.

1/ The Belgian Van de Putte group has the following operating structure: sales = 100, raw materials used in the business = 30, direct production costs = 40, administrative costs = 20. Operating cycle: raw materials inventories = 15 days, length of production cycle = 1 month, inventories of finished products = 15 days. Payment terms: suppliers 2 months, customers 1 month, other costs paid in cash.

Assuming zero VAT, calculate working capital in days of sales. The production cycle lasts 1 month, which means that in-progress inventories represent 1 month of raw materials and 15 days of production costs.

2/ The operating details for Spalton plc are as follows:

○ permanent working capital equal to 25% of sales;
○ sales rise from 100 million in year 1 to 120 million in year 2;
○ EBITDA rises to 15% of sales in year 2.

Calculate operating cash flow (before financial expense and tax) in year 2.

3/ Calculation of working capital ratios.

Working capital for Moretti Spa over the last 5 years (at 31 December) was as follows:

(In €m)	2006	2007	2008	2009	2010
Inventories of finished goods	6.1	7.4	9.1	13	15.4
Trade and notes receivable	6.4	8.9	10.5	11.1	11.6
Trade and notes payable	2.1	3.5	3.5	3.8	3.4

The income statement includes the following data:

(In €m)	2006	2007	2008	2009	2010
Sales (excl. VAT)	32.8	44.7	49.4	48.9	50
Sales (incl. VAT)	38.9	52.6	58.1	57.4	57.2
Purchases (incl. VAT)	12.5	19.2	19.6	20.9	20.4

Calculate the different working capital ratios.

4/ Below are the operating terms and conditions of a trading company:

○ goods held for resale rotate four times a year;
○ cost of goods sold is equal to 60% of sales (excl. tax);
○ customers pay at 45 days from month-end;
○ suppliers are paid at 30 days;
○ salaries, which amount to 10% of pre-tax sales, are paid at the end of every month;
○ payroll taxes, which amount to 50% of salaries, are paid on the 15th of the following month;
○ operating charges other than purchases of goods for resale and staff costs are paid in cash;
○ VAT is payable at 19.6% on sales and purchases. VAT payable for month n equals the difference between VAT collected on sales in month n and VAT recoverable on sales in month n, and is paid at the latest on the 25th of the month (n + 1).

Using the above data, calculate the working capital of the company in days of sales (excl. VAT).

5/ Below are details of a distribution company's operating terms and conditions:

- days of goods held for resale: 24 days;
- supplier credit: 90 days;
- customer credit: 10 days;
- purchases: 75% of sales;
- no VAT.

Calculate normal working capital as a percentage of sales.

6/ Give your views of Air Liquide's investment policy since 1990, as represented in the following graph (data in €m):

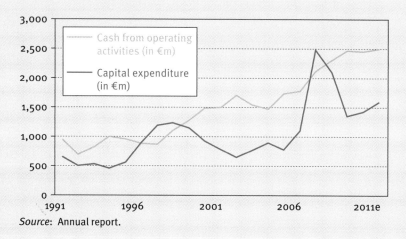

Source: Annual report.

Questions

1/ No, because of the seasonality of most business.
2/ Yes, it would, as working capital depends primarily on the time difference between payment to suppliers and payment from customers, which would not be substantially modified by a change in accounting rules; with an adjustment of working capital and shareholders' equity.
3/ Yes, because each item of working capital is sold, paid by the company or its suppliers.
4/ As a result of inertia.
5/ It tends to increase even if the number of products sold stays constant.
6/ Everything is mixed up. A depreciation charge does not affect EBITDA (as EBITDA is computed before depreciation charges). Working capital has increased considerably. Have a look at the change in net debt, which may be large and become a risk factor for the company. Change your CFO or offer him a Vernimmen!
7/ No, the retailers are getting in stock, but not necessarily selling any!
8/ Very high working capital. Downpayments by customers, prefinancing of series by state authorities, pass on to subcontractors, etc.
9/ Not really, given that non-operating working capital is such a catch-all category.
10/ No, as the client pays first and the product is delivered generally only a few weeks later.
11/ They can also take the form of operating losses.
12/ Sale of grey matter: advertising, consultancy, legal services.
13/ Cognac (7 years in barrels).

Exercises

A detailed Excel version of the solutions is available at www.vernimmen.com.

1/

Working capital component	% of sales	Time taken to shift goods or payment period	Value in days of sales
Raw materials	30%	15 days	4.5 days
+ Work in progress	30% × 30 days + 40% × 15 days		15 days
+ Inventories of finished products	90%	15 days	13.5 days
+ Trade receivables	100%	30 days	30 days
− Trade payables	30%	60 days	18 days
= Total			45 days

2/ *Operating cash flow (before taxes and financial expense) = EBITDA − Δ WC = 15% × 120 − 25% × (120−100) = €13m.*

3/

	2006	2007	2008	2009	2010
Working capital (WC)	10 400	12 800	16 100	20 300	23 600
WC in days of sales (excl. VAT)	116	105	119	152	172
Outstanding receivables in days of sales (incl. VAT)	60	62	66	71	74
Days of inventories	68	60	67	97	112
Days of payables in days of purchases (incl. tax)	61	67	65	66	61

The economy is in recession and the company has not yet adjusted production and is keeping sales up by offering customers better payment terms.

4/

Working capital component	% of sales	Time taken to shift goods or payment period	Value in days of sales
Inventories of goods for resale	60%	90 days	54 days
+ Trade receivables	119.60%	30/2 + 45 = 60 days	71.8 days
− Accounts payable	− 71.76%	30 days	21.5 days
− Personnel cost	10%	15 days	1.5 days
− Social security contribution payable	5%	30/2 + 15 = 30 days	1.5 days
− VAT payable	(19.6 − 19.6 × 60% = 7.84%)	30/2 + 25 = 40 days	3.1 days
= Total			98.1 days

5/

Working capital component	% of sales	Time taken to shift goods or payment period	Value in days of sales
Inventories of goods for resale	75%	24.3 days	18.2 days
+ Trade receivables	100%	10 days	10 days
− Accounts payable	75%	90 days	67.5 days
= Total			−39.2 days

6/ *Until 1995, Air Liquide reaps the benefits of capital expenditure prior to 1990 and generates cash flow which is stagnant but much higher than its capital expenditure. Between 1996 and 2000, seeking to achieve the growth it had previously recorded, Air Liquide lays out large amounts on capital expenditure, resulting in an increase in cash flow. After making these capital expenditures, Air Liquide can reduce the amount of its capital expenditure for a few years (1999–2003) and reap large amounts of cash from operating activities. When cash from operating activities starts to stagnate (2002–2004), Air Liquide increases again its capital expenditure with an exceptional amount in 2004 and cash flows pick up once more. In 2007, Air Liquide significantly invests again, while cash flows from operation increase significantly. In 2008–2009, Air Liquide is again in a position materially to reduce its capex.*

To get deeper into the analysis of working capital:

BIBLIOGRAPHY

B. Bardes, Délais de paiement et solde du crédit inter-entreprises de 1989 à 2002, *Bulletin de la Banque de France*, **132**, 69–82, December 2004.

B. Biais, Ch. Grolier, Trade credit and credit rationing, *The Review of Financial Studies*, **10**(4), 903–937, 1997.

V. Cunat, Inter-firm credit and industrial links, Mimeo, London School of Economics, 2000.

A.-F. Delaunay, M. Dietsch, Le crédit interentreprises joue un rôle d'amortisseur des tensions conjoncturelles, *Revue d'Economie Financière*, **54**, 121–136, October 1999.

M. Deloof, Does working capital management affect profitability of Belgian firms? *Journal of Business Finance & Accounting*, **30**(3–4), 573–585, April 2003.

KPMG, Etude comparée des dates de clôture en France et à l'international, 2010.

M. Long, I. Malitz, A. Ravid, Trade credit, quality guarantees, and product marketability, *Financial Management*, **22**(4), 117–127, Winter 1993.

C. Maxwell, L. Gitman, S. Smith, Working capital management and financial service consumption preferences of US and foreign firms: A comparison of 1979 & 1996 preferences, *Financial Management Association*, 46–52, Autumn–Winter 1998.

S. Mian, C. Smith, Accounts receivable management policy: Theory and evidence, *Journal of Finance*, **47**(1), 169–200, March 1992.

C. Ng, J. and R. Smith, Evidence on the determinants of credit terms used in interfirm trade, *Journal of Finance*, **54**(3), 1109–1129, June 1999.

H-H. Shin, L. Soenen, Efficiency of working capital management and corporate profitability, *Financial Management Association*, 37–45, Autumn–Winter 1998.

And on capex:

U.S. Census Bureau, Annual Capital Expenditures Survey, 2010.

M. Warusawitharana, Corporate asset purchases and sales: theory and evidence, *Journal of Financial Economics*, **87**(2), 471–497, 2008.

Chapter 12

FINANCING

Tell me how you're financed and I'll tell you who you are

When you evaluate how a company is financed, you must perform both dynamic and static analyses.

As we saw in the previous chapter, when it is founded, a company makes two types of investment. Firstly, it invests to acquire land, buildings, equipment, etc. Secondly, it makes operating investments, specifically startup costs and building up working capital.

To finance these investments, the company must raise either equity or debt financing. The investments, which initially generate negative cash flows, must generate positive cash flows over time. After subtracting returns to the providers of the company's financing (interest and dividends), as well as taxes, these cash flows must enable the company to repay its borrowings.

If the circle is a virtuous one, i.e. if the cash flows generated are enough to meet interest and dividend payments and repay debt, the company will gradually be able to grow and, as it repays its debt, it will be able to borrow more (the origin of the illusion that companies never repay their loans).

Conversely, the circle becomes a vicious one if the company's resources are constantly tied up in new investments or if cash flow from operating activities is chronically low. The company systematically needs to borrow to finance capital expenditure, and it may never be able to pay off its debt, not to mention pay dividends.

This is the dynamic approach.

- In parallel with the dynamic approach, you must look at the current state of the company's finances with two questions in mind:

    o Given the proportion of the company's assets financed by bank and other financial debt and the free cash flow generated by the company, can the company repay its debt?

    o Given the term structure of the company's debt, is the company running a high risk of illiquidity?

This is the static approach.

Section 12.1
A DYNAMIC ANALYSIS OF THE COMPANY'S FINANCING

To perform this analysis you will rely on the cash flow statement.

1/ THE FUNDAMENTAL CONCEPT OF CASH FLOW FROM OPERATING ACTIVITIES

The cash flow statement (see Chapter 5) is designed to separate operating activities from investing and financing activities. Accordingly, it shows cash flows from operating and investing activities and investments on the one hand and from financing activities on the other. This breakdown will be very useful to you when valuing the company and examining investment decisions.

The concept of cash flow from operating activities, as shown by the cash flow statement, is of the utmost importance. It depends on three fundamental parameters:

- the rate of growth in the company's business;
- the amount and nature of operating margins;
- the amount and nature of working capital.

An analysis of the cash flow statement is therefore the logical extension of the analysis of the company's margins and the changes in working capital.

Analysing the cash flow statement means analysing the profitability of the company from the point of view of its operating dynamics, rather than the value of its assets.

We once analysed a fast-growing company with high working capital. Its cash flow from operating activities was insufficient, but its inventories increased in value every year. We found that the company was turning a handsome net income, but its return on capital employed was poor, as most of its profit was made on capital gains on the value of its inventories. Because of this, the company was very vulnerable to any recession in its sector.

In this case, we analysed the cash flow statement and were able to show that the company's trade activity was not profitable and that the capital gains just barely covered its operating losses. It also became apparent that the company's growth process led to huge borrowings, making the company even more vulnerable in the event of a recession.

2/ FREE CASH FLOW AFTER INTEREST

Free cash flow after interest is equal to cash flows from operating activities minus cash flows from investments (capex net of disposal of fixed assets). It therefore includes the investment policy of the firm.

Free cash flow after interest measures, if negative, the financial resources that the company will have to find externally (from its shareholders or lenders) to meet the needs for cash generated by its operating and investment activities. If positive, the firm will be able to reduce its debt, to pay dividends without having to raise debt or even to accumulate cash for future needs. Free cash flow after interest will therefore set the tune for the financing policy.

3/ How is the company financed?

As an analyst, you must understand how the company finances its growth over the period in question. New equity capital? New debt? Reinvesting cash flow from operating activities? Asset disposals can contribute additional financial resources.

You should focus on three items for this analysis: equity capital issues, debt policy and dividend policy.

- Financing through new equity issuance: did the firm call for new equity from its shareholders during the period and, if yes, what was the use of it (to reduce debt, to finance a new capex programme)? You can also come across the opposite situation whereby the company buys back part of its shares; this is a way of returning cash to shareholders.[1] In this case, does the company want to alter its financial situation? Does it no longer have any investment opportunities?

- Financing through debt: analysing the net increase or decrease in the company's debt burden is a question of financial structure:
  - If the company is paying down debt, is it doing so in order to improve its financial structure? Has it run out of growth opportunities? Is it to pay back loans that were contracted when interest rates were high?
  - If the company is increasing its debt burden, is it taking advantage of unutilised debt capacity? Or is it financing a huge investment project or reducing its shareholders' equity and upsetting its financial equilibrium in the process?

- The dividend policy: as we will see in Chapter 38, the company's dividend policy is also an important aspect of its financial policy. It is a valuable piece of information when evaluating the company's strategy during periods of growth or recession:

  - Is the company's dividend policy consistent with its growth strategy?
  - Is the company's cash flow reinvestment policy in line with its capital expenditure programme?

You must compare the amount of dividends with the investments and cash flows from operating activities of the period. For a family-owned company, we would also advise increasing dividends by repayment of shareholders' loans, and any other unusual operating costs or payments that could be substitutes for dividend payments.

In conclusion, it is imperative that you analyse the cash flow statement to understand the dynamics of the company's cash flows.

In Section III of this book, we will examine the more complex reasoning processes that go into determining investment and financing strategies. For the moment, keep in mind that analysis of the financial statements alone can only result in elementary, common-sense rules.

As you will see later, we stand firmly **against** the following "principles":

- The amount of capital expenditure must be limited to the cash flow from operating activities. **No!** After reading Section III you will understand that the company should continue to invest in new projects until their marginal profitability is equal to the required rate of return. If it invests less, it is underinvesting; if it invests more, it is overinvesting, even if it has the cash to do so.

1 *See Chapter 38.*

- • The company can achieve equilibrium by having the "cash cow" divisions finance the "glamour"[2] divisions. **No!** With the development of financial markets, every division whose profitability is commensurate with its risk must be able to finance itself. A "cash cow" division should pay the cash flow it generates over to its providers of capital.

2 A glamour division is a fast-growing, high-margin division.

Studying the equilibrium between the company's various cash flows in order to set rules is tantamount to considering the company a world unto itself. This approach is diametrically opposed to financial theory. It goes without saying, however, that you must determine the investment cycle that the company's financing cycle can support. In particular, debt repayment ability remains paramount. We have already warned you about that in Chapter 2!

Section 12.2
A STATIC ANALYSIS OF THE COMPANY'S FINANCING

Focusing on a multi-year period, we have examined how the company's margins, working capital and capital expenditure programmes determine its various cash flows. We can now turn our attention to the company's absolute level of debt at a given point in time and to its capacity to meet its commitments while avoiding liquidity crises.

1/ CAN THE COMPANY REPAY ITS DEBTS?

The best way to answer this simple, fundamental question is to take the company's business plan and project future cash flow statements. These statements will show you whether the company generates enough cash flow from operating activities such that after financing its capital expenditure, it has enough left over to meet its debt repayment obligations without asking shareholders to reach into their pockets. If the company must indeed solicit additional equity capital, you must evaluate the market's appetite for such a capital increase. This will depend on who the current shareholders are. A company with a core shareholder will have an easier time than one whose shares are widely held, as this core shareholder, knowing the company well, may be in a position to underwrite the share issue. It will also depend on the value of equity capital (if it is near zero, maybe only a **vulture fund**[3] will be interested).

3 An investment fund that buys the debt of companies in difficulty or subscribes to equity issues with the aim of taking control of the company at a very low price.

Naturally, this assumes that you have access to the company's business plan, or that you can construct your own from scenarios of business growth, margins, changes in working capital and likely levels of capital expenditure. We will take a closer look at this approach in Chapter 32.

Analysts and lending banks have, in the meantime, adopted a "quick-and-dirty" way to appreciate the company's ability to repay its debt: the ratio of net debt to EBITDA. This is, in fact, the most often used financial covenant[4] in debt contracts! This highly empirical measure is nonetheless considered useful, because EBITDA is very close to cash flow from operating activities, give or take changes in working capital interests and income tax. A value of 3 is considered a critical level, below which the company should generally be able to meet its repayment obligations.

4 Clause in debt contracts restricting the freedom of the borrower till debt is above a certain level. For more on debt covenants, see Chapter 35.

If we were to oversimplify, we would say that a value of 3 signifies that the debt could be repaid in three years provided the company halted all capital expenditure and didn't pay corporate income tax during that period. Of course, no one would ask the company to pay off all its debt in the span of three years, but the idea is that it could if it had to.

Conversely, bank and other financial borrowings equal to more than 3 times EBITDA are considered a heavy debt load, and give rise to serious doubts about the company's ability to meet its repayment commitments as scheduled. As we will see in Chapter 45, LBOs can display this type of ratio. When the value of the ratio exceeds 5 or 6, the debt becomes "high-yield", the politically correct euphemism for "junk bonds".

Bankers are more willing to lend money to sectors with stable and highly predictable cash flows (food retail, utilities, real estate), even on the basis of a high net debt to EBITDA ratio, than to others where cash flows are more volatile (media, capital goods, electronics).

The following table shows trends in the net debt/EBITDA ratio posted by various different sectors in Europe between 1995–2012e.

NET DEBT/EBITDA RATIO FOR LEADING LISTED EUROPEAN COMPANIES

Sector	1995	2000	2005	2006	2007	2008	2009	2010	2011e	2012e
Aerospace & Defence	nm	1.2	0.7	0.4	0.3	0.4	0.3	0.1	0.1	nm
Automotive	0.2	0.4	nm	nm	nm	0.4	0.7	nm	nm	nm
Building Materials	1.4	2.3	2.2	2.0	2.2	2.8	2.9	2.6	2.1	1.6
Capital Goods	0.2	1.3	0.8	0.4	0.5	0.8	0.7	0.4	0.3	0.1
Consumer Goods	1.1	1.6	0.5	0.9	0.7	1.3	0.9	0.5	0.3	0.0
Food Retail	0.8	2.9	2.4	2.1	1.9	2.1	1.9	1.8	1.6	1.4
IT Services	1.8	nm	0.1	0.1	0.5	0.4	0.1	0.2	0.1	nm
Luxury Goods	0.8	2.4	1.3	0.8	0.9	1.0	0.7	0.4	0.4	0.1
Media	2.9	2.3	1.4	1.6	1.7	2.3	2.1	1.6	1.4	1.1
Mining	0.7	1.3	0.4	0.6	0.9	0.9	1.0	0.4	0.2	nm
Oil & Gas		0.6	0.3	0.4	0.4	0.4	0.9	0.8	0.5	0.5
Pharmaceuticals	0.2	nm	0.1	0.2	0.3	0.5	0.5	0.6	0.4	0.1
Steel		1.7	0.9	0.7	0.9	1.0	2.3	1.8	1.6	1.0
Telecom Operators	1.2	3.4	1.9	1.9	2.0	2.1	2.0	2.0	2.0	1.6
Utilities	3.3	2.2	1.9	1.8	2.3	2.7	2.9	2.8	2.8	2.7

Source: Exane BNP Paribas

Hotels/leisure and utilities are among the most highly leveraged sectors. One explanation is their capital intensity, which is strong. Another is the willingness of lenders to lend money to these sectors as they own real estate assets with a value independent of the business (a film theatre can be redeveloped into a commercial area) or with high long-term visibility on cash flows (concession contracts).

Similarly, analysts look at the interest coverage ratio, ICR (or debt service coverage or debt service ratio), i.e. the ratio of EBIT to net interest expense. A ratio of 3:1 is considered the critical level. Below this level, there are serious doubts as to the company's ability to meet its obligations as scheduled, as was the case for the transport sector post 9/11. Above it, the company's lenders can sleep more easily at night!

Rating agencies generally prefer to consider the ratio cash flow to net debt (they call our cash flow Funds From Operations or FFO). It is true that cash flow is closer than EBITDA to the actual capacity of the firm to repay its debt.

Until around 20 years ago, the company's ability to repay its loans was evaluated on the basis of its debt-to-equity ratio, or gearing, with a 1:1 ratio considered the critical point.

Certain companies can support bank and other financial debt in excess of shareholders' equity, specifically companies that generate high operating cash flow. EDF, the French electricity operator which generates robust cash flows from its nuclear plants, is an example. Conversely, other companies would be unable to support debt equivalent to more than 30% of their equity, because their margins are very thin. For example, the operating profit of Thomas Cook, the travel company, is, at best, only 2% of its sales revenue.

We advise against using the debt-to-equity ratio as a measure of the company's repayment capacity: shareholders' equity capital serves to repay loans only in the event of bankruptcy, not in the ordinary course of business.

2/ Is the company running a risk of illiquidity?

To understand the notion of liquidity, look at the company in the following manner: at a given point in time, the balance sheet shows the company's assets and commitments. This is what the company has done in the past. Without planning for liquidation, we nevertheless attempt to classify the assets and commitments based on how quickly they are transformed into cash. When will a particular commitment result in a cash disbursement? When will a particular asset translate into a cash receipt?

A company is illiquid when it can no longer meet its scheduled commitments.

To meet its commitments, either the company has assets it can monetise or it must contract new loans. Of course, new loans only postpone the day of reckoning until the new repayment date. By that time, the company will have to find new resources.

Illiquidity comes about when the maturity of the assets is greater than that of the liabilities. Suppose you took out a loan, to be repaid in six months, to buy a machine with a useful life of three years. The useful life of the machine is out of step with the scheduled repayment of the loan and the interest expenses on it. Consequently, there is a risk of illiquidity, particularly if there is no market to resell the machine at a decent price and if the activity is not profitable. Similarly, at the current asset level, if you borrow 3-month funds to finance inventories that turn over in more than three months, you are running the same risk.

The risk of illiquidity is the risk that assets will become liquid at a slower pace than the rate at which the liabilities will have to be paid, because the maturity of assets is longer. In a sense, liquidity measures the speed at which assets turn over compared with liabilities.

An illiquid company is not necessarily required to declare bankruptcy, but it must find new resources to bridge the gap. In so doing, it forfeits some of its independence, because it will be obliged to devote a portion of its new resources to past uses. In times of recession, it may have trouble doing so, and indeed be forced into bankruptcy.

Analysing liquidity means analysing the risk the company will have to "borrow from Peter to pay Paul". For each maturity, you must compare the company's cash needs with the resources it will have at its disposal.

We say that a balance sheet is liquid when, for each maturity, there are more assets being converted into cash (inventories sold, receivables paid, etc.) than there are liabilities coming due.

This graph shows, for each maturity, the cumulative amount of assets and liabilities coming due on or before that date.

LIQUIDITY

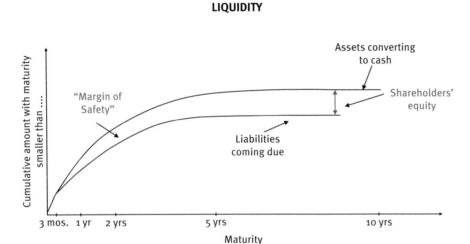

If, for a given maturity, cumulative assets are less than cumulative liabilities, the company will be unable to meet its obligations unless it finds a new source of funds. The company shown in this graph is not in this situation.

What we are measuring is the **company's maturity mismatch**, similar to that of a financial institution that borrows short-term funds to finance long-term assets.

(a) Liquidity ratios

To measure liquidity, then, we must compare the maturity of the company's assets to that of its liabilities. This rule gives rise to the following ratios, commonly used in loan covenants. They enable banks to monitor the risk of their borrowers.

- **Current ratio:**

$$\frac{Current\ assets\ (less\ than\ one\ year)}{Current\ liabilities\ (due\ in\ less\ than\ one\ year)}$$

This ratio measures whether the assets to be converted into cash in less than one year exceed the debts to be paid in less than one year.

- The **quick ratio** is another measure of the company's liquidity. It is the same as the current ratio, except that inventories are excluded from the calculation. Using the quick ratio is a way of recognising that a portion of inventories corresponds to the minimum the company requires for its ongoing activity. As such, they are tantamount to fixed assets. It also recognises that the company may not be able to liquidate the inventories it has on hand quickly enough in the event of an urgent cash need. Certain inventory items have value only to the extent they are used in the production process. The quick ratio (also called the acid test ratio) is calculated as follows:

$$\frac{Current\ assets\ (less\ than\ one\ year)\ excluding\ inventories}{Current\ liabilities\ (due\ in\ less\ than\ one\ year)}$$

A quick ratio below 1 means the company might have short-term liquidity problems as it owns less current assets than it owes to its short-term lenders. If the latter stop granting it payment facilities, it will need a cash injection from shareholders or long-term lenders or face bankruptcy.

- Finally, the **cash ratio** completes the set:

$$\frac{Cash\ and\ cash\ equivalents}{Current\ liabilities\ (due\ in\ less\ than\ one\ year)}$$

The cash ratio is generally very low. Its fluctuations often do not lend themselves to easy interpretation.

(b) More on the current ratio

Traditional financial analysis relies on the following rule:

A company must maintain a buffer between sources and uses of funds maturing in less than one year to cover risks inherent in its business (loss of inventory value, customers that fail to pay, decline in sales, business interruption costs that suddenly reduce shareholders' equity capital), because liabilities are not subject to such losses in value.

By maintaining a current ratio above one (more current assets than current liabilities), the company protects its creditors from uncertainties in the "gradual liquidation" of its current assets, namely in the sale of its inventories and the collection of its receivables. These uncertainties could otherwise prevent the company from honouring its obligations, such as paying its suppliers, servicing bank loans or paying taxes.

If we look at the long-term portion of the balance sheet, a current ratio above 1 means that sources of funds due in more than one year, deemed stable,[5] are greater than fixed assets, i.e. uses of funds "maturing" in more than one year. If the current ratio is below 1, then fixed assets are being financed partially by short-term borrowings or by a negative working capital. This situation can be dangerous. These sources of funds are liabilities that will very shortly become due, whereas fixed assets "liquidate" only gradually in the long term.

5 *Also called "permanent financing". This includes shareholders' equity, which is never due, and debts maturing after one year.*

The current ratio was the cornerstone of any financial analysis years ago. This was clearly excessive. The current ratio reflects the choice between short-term and long-term financing. In our view, this was a problem typical of the credit-based economy, as it existed in the 1970s in Continental Europe. Today, the choice is more between shareholders' equity capital and banking or financial debt, whatever its maturity. That said, **we still think it is unhealthy to finance a permanent working capital with very short-term resources. The company that does so will be defenceless in the event of a liquidity crisis, which could push it into bankruptcy.**

(c) Financing working capital

To the extent that working capital represents a permanent need, logic dictates that permanent financing should finance it. Since it remains constant for a constant business volume, we are even tempted to say that it should be financed by shareholders' equity. Indeed, companies with a high working capital are often largely funded by shareholders' equity. This is the case, for example, with big champagne companies, which often turn to the capital markets for equity funding.

Nevertheless, most companies would be in an unfavourable cash position if they had to finance their working capital strictly with long-term debt or shareholders' equity. Instead, they use the mechanism of revolving credits, which we will discuss in Chapter 22. For that matter, the fact that the components of working capital are self-renewing encourages companies to use revolving credit facilities in which customer receivables and inventories often collateralise the borrowings.

By their nature, revolving credit facilities are always in effect, and their risk is often tied directly to underlying transactions or collateralised by them (bill discounting, factoring, securitisation, etc.).

Full and permanent use of short-term revolving credit facilities can often be dangerous, because it:

- exhausts borrowing capacity;
- inflates interest expense unnecessarily;
- increases the volume of relatively inflexible commitments, which will restrict the company's ability to stabilise or restructure its activity.

Working capital is not only a question of financing. It can carry an operational risk as well. Financing through short-term borrowing solves the immediate cash management problem, but makes the company very vulnerable to any changes in its trade and financial environment. Such financing has provoked some spectacular bankruptcies or quasi bankruptcies (i.e. Vivendi Universal). Short-term borrowing does not exempt the company from strategic analysis of how its operating needs will change over time. This is a prerequisite to any financing strategy.

Companies that export a high proportion of their sales or that participate in construction and public works projects are risky inasmuch as they often have insufficient shareholders' equity compared with their total working capital. The difference is often financed by revolving credits, until one day, when the going gets rough . . .

In sum, you must pay attention to the true nature of working capital, and understand that a short-term loan that finances permanent working capital cannot be repaid by the operating cycle except by squeezing that cycle down or, in other words, by beginning to liquidate the company.

(d) Companies with negative working capital

Companies with a negative working capital raise a fundamental question for the financial analyst. Should they be allowed to reduce their shareholders' equity on the strength of their robust, positive cash position?

Can a company with a negative working capital maintain a financial structure with relatively little shareholders' equity? This would seem to be an anomaly in financial theory. On the practical level, we can make two observations.

Firstly, under normal operating conditions, the company's overall financing structure is more important and more telling than the absolute value of its negative working capital.

Let's look at companies A and B, whose balance sheets are as follows:

Company A			
Fixed assets	900	Shareholders' equity	800
Working capital	1000	Net debt	1100

Company B			
Fixed assets	125	Shareholders' equity	100
Cash & cash equiv.	105	Neg. working capital	130

Most of company A's assets, in particular its working capital, are financed by debt. As a result, the company is much more vulnerable than company B, where the working capital is well into negative territory and the fixed assets are mostly financed by shareholders' equity.

Secondly, a company with a negative working capital reacts much more quickly in times of crisis, such as recession. Inertia, which hinders positive working capital companies, is not as great.

Nevertheless, a negative working capital company runs two risks:

- The payment terms granted by its suppliers may suddenly change. This is a function of the balance of power between the company and its supplier, and unless there is an outside event, such as a change in the legislative environment, such risk is minimal. On the contrary, when a company with a negative working capital grows, its position *vis-à-vis* its suppliers tends to improve. Nevertheless, the tendency (including regulatory) to reduce payment periods has a mechanically negative impact on firms with negative working capital.
- A contraction in the company's business volume can put a serious dent in its financial structure.

Section 12.3
CASE STUDY: INDESIT[6]

6 *The financial statements for Indesit are on pages 54, 66 and 171.*

Cash flow from operating activity remained healthy in 2006–2007 (remaining over €200 million each year, even in 2005 when the activity slowed down slightly). Cash flows from operating activity were therefore sufficient to cover capital expenditure. In 2008, cash flows from operations (€50 million) no longer covered capital expenditure; this was due to the slowdown of operations and to the increasing working capital. The root-and-branch overhaul undertaken in 2009 brought cash flow from operations to a historic high (€333 million) whereas results were at a historic low. In 2010, the situation was back to normal and the cash flows from operations (even if lowered by a slight increase in working capital) covered capex (which remained low).

In 2006 and 2007, Indesit generated large enough free cash flows to distribute dividends and to reduce its net debt level significantly. In 2008, the debt level increased significantly but was then reduced in 2009 (€−257 million) thanks to cash flows from operations, limited capital expenditures and the cut in dividend payments. In 2010, the company reinitiated the payment of a modest dividend (three times lower than two years earlier); the group continued to reduce its debt burden.

The combination of a reduction in net debt and a slightly increasing EBITDA led to a sharp decrease in net debt level measured by the ratio net debt/EBITDA (from 2.0 in 2006 to 1.0 in 2010).

Analysing the balance sheet, the liquidity of the group in 2010 does not seem to be a problem, as short-term debt (€246 million) is in line with the available cash and cash equivalents (€240 million). In addition, digging a little further, we find that in 2010 the group has €425 million in undrawn committed credit lines. It should be noted, nevertheless, that most of this amount (€350 million) corresponds to a syndicated line with a term in 2011.

SUMMARY

The summary of this chapter can be downloaded from www.vernimmen.com.

Analysing how a company is financed can be performed either by looking at several fiscal years, or on the basis of the latest available balance sheet.

In the dynamic approach, your main analytical tool will be the cash flow statement. Cash flow from operating activities is the key metric.

Cash flow from operating activities depends on the growth rate of the business and on the size and nature of working capital. Cash flow from operating activities must cover capital expenditure, loan repayment and dividends. Otherwise, the company will have to borrow more to pay for its past use of funds.

The company uses shareholders' equity and bank or financial debts to finance its investments. These investments must gradually generate enough positive cash flow to repay debt and provide a return to shareholders.

In the static approach, analysis tries to answer the following two questions:

- Can the company repay its debts as scheduled? To answer this question, you must build projected cash flow statements, based on assumed rates of growth in sales, margins, working capital and capital expenditure. To perform a simplified analysis, you can calculate the net debt/EBITDA ratio. If the company is to have an acceptable capacity to meet its repayment commitments as scheduled, the ratio should not be in excess of 4. Similarly, the EBIT/debt service ratio should be at least equal to 3.

- Is the company running the risk of being illiquid? To answer this question, you must compare the dates at which the company's liabilities will come due and the dates at which its assets will be liquidated. Assets should mature before liabilities. If they do, the company will remain liquid.

QUESTIONS

1/ Why is it imperative to analyse the cash flow statement?

2/ Should capital expenditure levels depend on cash flow from operating activities?

3/ Your marketing manager suggests that you launch a marketing drive, giving some customers discounts and advantageous payment terms. State your views.

4/ Is financial expense included in cash flow from operating activities?

5/ On what conditions can a banker lend a company 7 times its EBITDA?

6/ Is a company with a current ratio below 1 illiquid?

7/ In your view, should short-term debt be separated out from medium- to long-term debt on the cash flow statement? Why?

8/ Short-term interest rates are currently very low and you are offered a 3-month loan. State your views.

9/ The debt-to-equity ratio of National Grid (which owns the high-voltage electricity transmission network in the UK and in New England) was around 2.4 in 2011. State your views.

More questions are waiting for you at www.vernimmen.com.

EXERCISES

1/ **Below are the key figures for the company Ivankovic over the last five years.**

	1	2	3	4	5
Fixed assets	100	110	120	130	140
Working capital	200	225	250	280	315
EBITDA	38	40	44	48	52
Depreciation and amortisation	10	10	11	12	13
Financial expense	14	15	17	19	22
Income tax expense	7	7.5	8	8	8.5
Dividends	5	5	5	6	6

Draw up the cash flow statement for years 2–5.
State your views.

2/ **Analyse and compare the summary cash flow statements of EDF Energies Nouvelles, Carrefour and Peugeot for 2008 and 2009.**

In € million	EDF Énergies Nouvelles		Carrefour		Peugeot	
Cash flow from operating activities	0	−43	4887	3740	62	3570
Capital expenditure	1007	1319	2596	2137	3243	2785[1]
Capital increase	540	0	0	0	0	0
Dividends paid	0	23	942	894	371	0
Decrease in net debt	−467	−1423	1349	192	−3552	913

1. Depreciation being equal to €3679 million.

3/ What is your view of Ringkvist AB?

Ringkvist AB	1	2	3
Cash flow from operating activities	400	700	1 600
Capital expenditure	1000	1300	1400
Asset disposals	0	0	0
Capital increase	300	300	0
Dividends paid	0	100	200
Decrease in net debt	−300	−400	0

4/ What is your view of Moser srl?

Moser srl	1	2	3
Cash flow from operating activities	400	300	−200
Capital expenditure	1000	1100	300
Asset disposals	0	0	300
Capital increase	300	0	600
Dividends	0	0	0
Decrease in net debt	−300	−800	400

5/ What is your view of the liquidity of this company?

7-year fixed assets	200	Shareholders' equity	100
3-year fixed assets	200	5-year debts	200
3-month inventories	300	1-year debts	300
2-month receivables	100	1-month debts	400
1-day liquidities	200		
Total	1000	Total	1000

Questions

1/ *In order to emphasise the dynamic of returns on investments.*
2/ *No, because financing can always be found for an investment that will bring returns, but sooner or later these returns must generate cash flows.*
3/ *This will have a double impact on cash flow from operating activities (drop in margins and increase in working capital).*
4/ *Yes, see Chapter 5.*
5/ *Only if he has excellent visibility on future EBITDA, high interest margin, in the context of a credit bubble and with a strict debt contract limiting the flexibility of the borrower.*
6/ *Potentially, as it has fewer current assets that will be transformed into cash within one year than liabilities maturing in less than one year.*
7/ *No, net decrease in debt provides more information (see Chapter 5).*
8/ *How would you pay off a loan in three months? You run the risk of not being able to raise new funds when your cheap loan matures.*
9/ *This level of debt can only be evaluated in relation to National Grid capacity to generate substantial cash flow. Most transmission companies generate high cash flows as capital expenditures have already been incurred.*

Exercises

A detailed Excel version of the solutions is available at www.vernimmen.com.

1/ *Cash flow statement*

	2	3	4	5
Cash flow	17.5	19	21	21.5
Change in working capital	25	25	30	35
Cash flow from operating activities	7.5	−6	−9	−13.5
Capital expenditures	20	21	22	23
Dividends paid	5	5	5	6
Decrease in net debt	−32.5	−32	−36	−42.5

The company Ivankovic is in a high-growth and high capital expenditure phase. Ivankovic is unable to control working capital, hence a large cash deficit. This deficit is covered by debt, leading to a sharp rise in financial expense. The financial situation of Ivankovic is worsening and, if there is a slump in the economy, Ivankovic might face bankruptcy.

2/ *EDF Energies Nouvelles is a young company. Its cash flow from operating activities is still negative and it needs to invest massively; given its high operating risk it decides to finance first with equity and then with debt.*
Carrefour is a mature company. Its cash flows from operating activities cover its capital expenditure and dividends; the group can even reduce its net debt.
In 2008, Peugeot faces a reduction in its cash flow from operating activities (due, in large part, to a sharp increase in working capital). Capital expenditures are therefore entirely financed with new debt. In 2009, the change in working capital reverses and the group can lower its debt level.

3/ *Ringkvist AB is in a virtuous circle of growth. The company is investing, the investments are generating in-flows, cash from operating activities thus increases every year, and the company does not need to borrow much. In period 3, Ringkvist AB generates enough cash through operating activities to finance its capital expenditures, pay dividends and stabilise its debt level.*

4/ *Moser srl is in a vicious circle. Cash flow from operating activities declines from year to year. Moser srl thus has to borrow heavily in year 2 to finance its capital expenditure. In year 3, the company experiences serious cash shortfalls, since cash generated by operating activities is negative. The company is forced to call on its shareholders to bail it out. It also launches a programme to refocus on its core business, which leads to asset disposals. Net capital expenditures are thus nil. Moser srl must reduce its debt.*

5/ *There is no guarantee of liquidity in one month (shortfall of 400 − 200 = 200), nor in one year (shortfall of 700 − 600 = 100), nor in five years (shortfall of 900 − 800 = 100). The company will have to restructure its debt quickly in order to postpone payment of instalments due.*

BIBLIOGRAPHY

H. Almeida, M. Campello, Financial Constraints, Asset Tangibility, and Corporate Investment, *Review of Financial Studies*, **20**(5), 1429–1460, September 2007.

R. Elsas, M. Flannery, J. Garfinkel, *Major Investments, Firm Financing Decisions, and Long Term Performance*, EFA 2004 Maastricht Meetings, Working Paper, May 2004.

A. Hackethal, R. Schmidt, *Financing Patterns: Measurement Concepts and Empirical Results*, University of Frankfurt – Department of Finance, Working Paper n125, 2004.

E. Morellec, Asset Liquidity, Capital Structure and Secured Debt, *Journal of Financial Economics*, **61**(2), 173–206, August 2001.

Chapter 13
RETURN ON CAPITAL EMPLOYED
AND RETURN ON EQUITY

The leverage effect is much ado about nothing

So far we have analysed:

- how a company can create wealth (margin analysis);
- what kind of investment is required to create wealth: capital expenditure and increase in working capital;
- how those investments are financed through debt or equity.

We now have everything we need to carry out an assessment of the company's efficiency, i.e. its profitability.

A company that delivers returns that are at least equal to those required by its shareholders and lenders will not experience financing problems in the long term, since it will be able to repay its debts and create value for its shareholders.

Hence the importance of this chapter, in which we attempt to measure the **book** profitability of companies.

Section 13.1
ANALYSIS OF CORPORATE PROFITABILITY

We can measure profitability only by studying returns in relation to the invested capital. If no capital is invested, there is no profitability to speak of.

Book profitability is the ratio of the wealth created (i.e. earnings) to the capital invested. **Profitability should not be confused with margins.** Margins represent the ratio of earnings to business volumes (i.e. sales or production), while profitability is the ratio of profits to the capital that had to be invested to generate the profits.

Above all, analysts should focus on the profitability of capital employed by studying the ratio of operating profit to capital employed, which is called return on capital employed (ROCE).

$$\text{Return on capital employed (ROCE)} = \frac{\text{Operating profit after tax}}{\text{Capital employed}}$$

Return on capital employed can also be considered as the **return on equity if net debt is zero**.

1 *Depending on whether capital expenditure during the period is regarded as having contributed to wealth creation or not.*

Much ink has been spilled over the issue of whether opening or closing capital employed[1] or an average of the two figures should be used. We will leave it up to readers to decide for themselves. That said, you should take care not to change the method you decide to use as you go along so that comparisons over longer periods are not skewed. The operating profit figure that should be used is the one we presented in Chapter 9, i.e. after employee profit-sharing, incentive payments and all the other revenues and charges that are assigned to the operating cycle.

Return on capital employed can be calculated by combining a margin and turnover rate as follows:

$$\frac{\text{Operating profit after tax}}{\text{Capital employed}} = \frac{\text{Operating profit after tax}}{\text{Sales}} \times \frac{\text{Sales}}{\text{Capital employed}}$$

The first ratio on the right-hand side – operating profit after tax/sales – corresponds to the operating margin generated by the company, while the second – sales/capital employed – reflects asset turnover or capital turn (the inverse of capital intensity), which indicates the amount of capital (capital employed) required to generate a given level of sales. Consequently, a "normal" return on capital employed may result from weak margins, but high asset turnover (and thus low capital intensity), e.g. in mass retailing. It may also stem from high margins, but low asset turnover (i.e. high capital intensity), e.g. whisky producers.

The following figure shows the ROCE and its components achieved by some leading groups during 2010:

ROCE AND ITS COMPONENTS

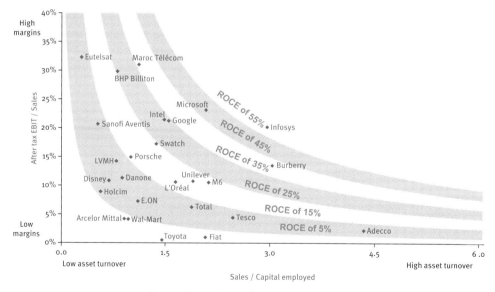

Source: Exane BNP Paribas, Annual reports

Adecco (temporary staffing) and Sanofi-Aventis (pharmacy) generate a similar return on capital employed, but their operating margins and asset turnover are entirely different. Sanofi-Aventis has a strong operating margin but a weak asset turnover (high level of accrued development costs) while Adecco has a smaller operating margin but a higher asset turnover (no inventories).

These figures are calculated after tax, which means that we calculate return on capital employed after tax at the normal rate and not by deducting the actual income tax as it takes into account the financial structure, the financial interest being deductible.

Analysts will have to decide for themselves whether, as we suggest here, they work on an after-tax basis. If so, they will have to calculate operating profit after theoretical tax (calculated based on the company's normalised tax rate), which is called NOPAT (net operating profit after tax).

Secondly, we can calculate the **return on equity (ROE)**, which is the ratio of net income to shareholders' equity.

$$\text{Return on equity} = \frac{\text{Net income}}{\text{Shareholders' equity}}$$

In practice, most financial analysts take goodwill impairment losses and non-recurring items out of net income before calculating return on equity.

Section 13.2

LEVERAGE EFFECT

1/ THE PRINCIPLE

The leverage effect explains a company's return on equity in terms of its return on capital employed and cost of debt.

In our approach, we considered the total amount of capital employed, including both equity and debt. This capital is invested in assets that form the company's capital employed and that are intended to generate earnings, as follows:

HOW THE WEALTH CREATED IS APPORTIONED

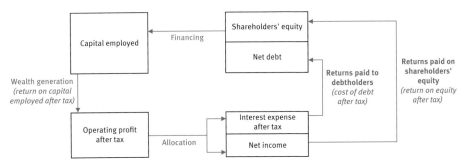

All the capital provided by lenders and shareholders is used to finance **all the uses of funds, i.e. the company's capital employed**. These uses of funds generate operating profit, which itself is apportioned between net financial expense (returns paid to debtholders) and net income attributable to shareholders.

If we compare a company's return on equity with its return on capital employed (after tax to remain consistent), we note that the difference is due only to its financial structure, apart from non-recurring items and items specific to consolidated accounts which we will deal with later on.

By definition, the leverage effect is the difference between return on equity and return on capital employed.

The leverage effect explains how it is possible for a company to deliver a return on equity exceeding the rate of return on all the capital invested in the business, i.e. its return on capital employed.

Readers should pause for a second to contemplate this corporate nirvana, which apparently consists in making more money than is actually generated by a company's industrial and commercial activities.

But before getting too carried away, readers should note that the leverage effect works both ways. Although it can lift a company's return on equity above return on capital employed, it can also depress it, turning the dream into a nightmare.

The leverage effect works as follows. When a company raises debt and invests the funds it has borrowed in its industrial and commercial activities, it generates operating profit that normally exceeds the interest expense due on its borrowings. If this is not the case, it is not worth investing, as we shall see at the beginning of Section II of this book. So, the company generates a surplus consisting of the difference between the return on capital employed and the cost of debt related to the borrowing. This surplus is attributable to shareholders and is added to shareholders' equity. The leverage effect of debt thus increases the return on equity. Hence its name.

Let's consider a company with capital employed of 100, generating a return of 10% after tax, which is financed entirely by equity. Its return on capital employed and return on equity both stand at 10%.

If the same company finances 30 of its capital employed with debt at an interest rate of 4% after tax and the remainder with equity, its return on equity is:

Operating profit after tax:	$10\% \times 100 = 10$
− Interest expense after tax:	$4\% \times 30 = 1.2$
= Net income after tax:	$= 8.8$

When divided by shareholders' equity of 70 (100 − 30), this yields a return on equity after tax of 12.6% (8.8/70), while the after-tax return on capital employed stands at 10%.

The borrowing of 30 that is invested in capital employed generates operating profit after tax of 3 which, after post-tax interest expense (1.2), is fully attributable for an amount of 1.8 to shareholders. This surplus amount (1.8) is added to operating profit generated by the equity-financed investments (70 × 10% = 7) to give net income of 7 + 1.8 = 8.8. The company's return on equity now stands at 8.8/70 = 12.6%.

The leverage effect of debt thus increases the company's return on equity by 2.6%, or the surplus generated (1.8) divided by shareholders' equity (1.8/70 = 2.6).

Debt can thus be used to boost a company's return on equity without any change in return on capital employed.

But readers will surely have noticed the prerequisite for the return on equity to increase when the company raises additional debt, i.e. **its ROCE must be higher than its cost of debt**. Otherwise, the company borrows at a higher rate than the returns it generates by investing the borrowed funds in its capital employed. This gives rise to a deficit, which reduces the rate of return generated by the company's equity. Its earnings decline, and the return on equity **dips below** its return on capital employed.

Let's go back to our company and assume that its return on capital employed falls to 3% after tax. In this scenario, its return on equity is as follows:

Operating profit after tax:	$100 \times 3\% = 3$
− Interest expense after tax:	$30 \times 4\% = 1.2$
= Net income after tax:	$= 1.8$

When divided by shareholders' equity of 70, this yields a return on equity after tax of 2.6% (1.8/70).

Once invested in tangible assets or working capital, the borrowing of 30 generates an operating profit after tax of 0.9 which, after deducting the 1.2 in interest charges, produces a deficit of 0.3 on the borrowed funds. This shortfall is thus deducted from net income, which will drop to $70 \times 3\% - 0.3 = 1.8$.

The original return on capital employed of 3% is thus reduced by 0.3/70 = 0.4% to give a return on equity of 2.6% after tax.

When the return on capital employed falls below the cost of debt, the leverage effect of debt shifts into reverse and reduces the return on equity, which in turn falls below return on capital employed.

2/ FORMULATING AN EQUATION

Before we go any further, we need to clarify the impact of tax on this line of reasoning.

Tax reduces earnings. All revenues give rise to taxation and all charges serve to reduce the tax bite (provided that the company is profitable). Consequently, each line of the income statement can thus be regarded as giving rise to either tax expense or a theoretical tax credit, with the actual tax charge payable being the net amount of the tax expense and credits. We can thus calculate an operating profit figure net of tax, by simply multiplying the operating profit before tax by a factor of (1 − rate of corporate income tax).

As a result, we can ensure the consistency of our calculations. Throughout this chapter, we have **worked on an after-tax basis** for all the key profit indicators, i.e. operating profit, net financial expense and net income (note that our reasoning would have been identical had we worked on a pre-tax basis).

Let's now formulate an equation encapsulating our conclusions. Net income is equal to the return on capital employed multiplied by shareholders' equity plus a surplus (or deficit) arising on net debt, which is equal to the net debt multiplied by the difference between the after-tax return on capital employed and the after-tax cost of debt.

Translating this formula into a profitability rather than an earnings-based equation, we come up with the following:

$$\text{Return on equity} = \frac{\text{Return on capital employed (after tax)}}{} + \left(\frac{\text{Return on capital employed (after tax)}}{} - \frac{\text{After tax cost of debt}}{}\right) \times \frac{\text{Net debt}}{\text{Shareholders' equity}}$$

or

$$\text{ROE} = \text{ROCE} + (\text{ROCE} - i) \times \frac{D}{E}$$

Readers should not let themselves get bogged down by this equation, which is based on an accounting tautology. The leverage effect is merely a straightforward factor that is used to account for return on equity, and nothing more.

The ratio of net debt to shareholders' equity is called financial leverage or gearing.

The leverage effect can thus be expressed as follows:

$$\frac{\text{Net debt}}{\text{Shareholders' equity}} \times \left(\text{Return on capital employed} - \text{After-tax cost of debt}\right)$$

Return on equity is thus equal to the return on capital employed plus the leverage effect.

Note that:

- the higher the company's return on capital employed relative to the cost of debt (e.g. if ROCE increases to 16% in our example, return on equity rises to 16% × 5.1% = 21.1%); or
- the higher the company's debt burden; the higher the leverage effect.

Naturally, the leverage effect goes into reverse once:

- return on capital employed falls below the cost of debt;
- the cost of debt is poorly forecast or suddenly soars because the company's debt carries a variable rate and interest rates are on the rise.

The leverage effect applies even when a company has negative net debt, i.e. when its short-term financial investments exceed the value of its debt. In such cases, return on equity equates to the average of return on equity and return on short-term investments weighted by shareholders' equity and short-term investments. The leverage effect can thus be calculated in exactly the same way, with i corresponding instead to the after-tax rate of return on short-term financial investments and showing a negative value because net debt is negative.

For instance, let's consider the case of Texas Instruments in 2010. Its shareholders' equity stood at $13.9bn and its net debt was a negative $7.1bn, while its short-term financial investments yielded 0.20% before tax. Its return on capital employed after applying an average tax rate of 31% stood at 47% based on its operating profit of \$4.6bn.[2] Return on equity thus stands at:

$$ROE = (4.6 + 0.2\% \times 7.1) \times (1-31\%)/13.9 = 47\% + (47\% - 0.2\%) \times -7.1/13.9 = 23\%$$

2 $4.6 \times (1-31\%)/$ $(13.9-7.1) = 47\%$

The reason for Texas Instruments' ROE being lower than its ROCE is clearly not that the group's cost of debt is higher than its return on capital employed! To put things simply, Texas Instruments is unable to secure returns on the financial markets for its surplus cash on a par with those generated by its manufacturing facilities. Consequently, it has to invest the funds at a rate below its return on capital employed, thus depressing its return on equity.

The following tables show trends in ROE and ROCE posted by various different sectors in Europe over the 1995–2012e period.

ROE FOR LISTED GROUPS (EUROPEAN GROUPS PER SECTOR)

Sector	1995	2000	2005	2006	2007	2008	2009	2010	2011e	2012e
Aerospace & Defence	9%	8%	13%	11%	13%	17%	13%	12%	13%	16%
Automotive	9%	8%	12%	12%	13%	10%	−5%	11%	13%	14%
Building Materials	12%	14%	14%	16%	17%	13%	6%	5%	7%	9%
Capital Goods	15%	22%	11%	13%	17%	17%	12%	15%	17%	17%
Consumer Goods	17%	21%	17%	17%	18%	16%	11%	14%	14%	15%
Food Retail	15%	16%	13%	13%	14%	14%	13%	14%	15%	15%
IT Services	4%	14%	12%	14%	13%	15%	11%	11%	12%	13%
Luxury Goods	12%	14%	15%	16%	17%	15%	12%	15%	14%	15%
Media	12%	5%	17%	18%	17%	16%	14%	15%	15%	16%
Mining	11%	16%	30%	33%	29%	27%	13%	23%	23%	20%
Oil & Gas		21%	25%	24%	21%	24%	12%	15%	16%	15%
Pharmaceuticals	19%	23%	21%	22%	22%	22%	26%	26%	25%	23%
Steel		9%	21%	21%	20%	18%	2%	7%	9%	11%
Telecom Operators	9%	3%	13%	14%	14%	15%	16%	15%	16%	16%
Utilities	9%	10%	15%	16%	14%	15%	13%	11%	10%	10%

Source: Exane BNP Paribas

ROCE FOR LISTED GROUPS (EUROPEAN GROUPS PER SECTOR)

Sector	1995	2000	2005	2006	2007	2008	2009	2010	2011e	2012e
Aerospace & Defence	5%	6%	10%	9%	12%	13%	9%	10%	11%	15%
Automotive	5%	5%	6%	7%	10%	6%	1%	11%	13%	15%
Building Materials	9%	8%	8%	9%	9%	8%	5%	5%	6%	7%
Capital Goods	10%	8%	11%	13%	15%	14%	11%	14%	15%	16%
Consumer Goods	13%	13%	15%	14%	13%	12%	10%	12%	13%	14%
Food Retail	12%	7%	8%	9%	10%	10%	10%	10%	11%	13%
IT Services	10%	12%	8%	8%	9%	11%	11%	11%	11%	13%
Luxury Goods	9%	9%	9%	11%	12%	11%	9%	13%	13%	14%
Media	7%	6%	12%	12%	13%	10%	10%	12%	12%	13%
Mining	8%	13%	22%	23%	19%	17%	10%	19%	22%	23%
Oil & Gas		14%	19%	17%	15%	18%	8%	8%	13%	12%
Pharmaceuticals	13%	16%	17%	17%	17%	18%	21%	21%	22%	22%
Steel		5%	13%	14%	13%	15%	1%	5%	6%	8%
Telecom Operators	8%	4%	9%	9%	9%	10%	10%	11%	11%	11%
Utilities	8%	5%	8%	9%	8%	8%	7%	6%	6%	6%

Source: Exane BNP Paribas

The reader may notice among other things the global improvement in ROCE since 2000 before it dropped again from 2008. Aerospace and defence and telecom operators have similar ROE at around 16% but very dissimilar ROCE (15% and 11% respectively). The explanation lies in the level of debt, which is generally high for telecoms operators as it is a capital-intensive sector and lower in the aerospace and defence industry, which exhibits poorer visibility.

3/ CALCULATING THE LEVERAGE EFFECT

(a) Presentation

To calculate the leverage effect and the return on equity, we recommend using the table shown below. The items needed for these calculations are listed below. We strongly recommend that readers should use the data shown in the tables on p. 235.
- On the income statement:
  - sales (S);
  - profit before tax and non-recurring items (PBT);
  - financial expense net of financial income (FE);
  - operating profit (EBIT).

- On the balance sheet:
  - fixed assets (FA);
  - working capital (WC) comprising both operating and non-operating working capital;
  - capital employed, i.e. the sum of the two previous lines, as well as the sum of the two following lines, since capital employed is financed by shareholders' equity and debt (CE);
  - shareholders' equity (E);
  - net debt encompassing all short-, medium- and long-term bank borrowings and debt less marketable securities, cash and equivalents (D).

Corporate income tax is abbreviated to T_c.

LEVERAGE EFFECT (e.g. Indesit)

Basic data	€m	2006	2007	2008	2009	2010
Sales (S)		3249	3438	3155	2613	2879
Profit before tax and non-recurring items (PBT)		132	166	95	67	150
+ Financial expense net of financial income (FE)		27	30	46	52	35
= Operating profit (EBIT)		158	197	141	119	184
Fixed assets (FA)		1254	1208	1080	1035	1046
+ Working capital (WC)		−28	−48	13	−160	−115
= CAPITAL EMPLOYED (CE)		1226	1160	1093	875	931
Shareholders' equity (E)		626	638	469	507	609
+ (restated) Net debt (D)		600	522	625	368	322
= CAPITAL INVESTED = CAPITAL EMPLOYED (CE)		1226	1160	1093	875	931
Corporate income tax (T_c)[1]		30%	30%	30%	50%	40%

(1) In practice, the analyst may prefer to use the actual rate based on the average taxation for the firm

Calculations

		2006	2007	2008	2009	2010
i	After tax cost of debt $= \dfrac{FE \times (1-T_c)}{D}$	3.1%	4.1%	5.1%	7.0%	6.4%
ROCE	Return on capital employed (after tax) $= \dfrac{EBIT \times (1-T_c) \text{ or NOPAT}}{CE}$	9.0%	11.9%	9.0%	6.8%	11.9%
ROCE − i	Return on capital employed (after tax) − after-tax cost of debt	5.9%	7.8%	3.9%	−0.2%	5.4%
D/E	Gearing	1.0	0.8	1.3	0.7	0.5
	Leverage effect $= (ROCE - i) \times \dfrac{D}{E}$	5.7%	6.4%	5.2%	−0.2%	2.9%
ROE	Return on equity $\text{ or } = \dfrac{PBT \times (1-T_c)}{E}$	14.7%	18.2%	14.2%	6.6%	14.8%

Results

		2006	2007	2008	2009	2010
	After tax operating margin (EBIT/S x (1−Tc))	3.4%	4.0%	3.1%	2.3%	3.8%
×	Capital employed turnover (S/CE)	2.6	3.0	2.9	3.0	3.1
=	**Return on capital employed (A)**	**9.0%**	**11.9%**	**9.0%**	**6.8%**	**11.9%**
	Return on capital employed − after-tax cost of debt (ROCE − *i*)	5.9%	7.8%	3.9%	−0.2%	5.4%
×	Gearing (*D/E*)	1.0	0.8	1.3	0.7	0.5
=	**Leverage effect (B)**	**5.7%**	**6.4%**	**5.2%**	**−0.2%**	**2.9%**
=	**Return On Equity (A + B)**	**14.7%**	**18.2%**	**14.2%**	**6.6%**	**14.8%**

(b) Practical problems

We recommend that readers use the balance sheets and income statements prepared during Chapters 4 and 9 as a starting point when filling in the previous table.

We cannot overemphasise the importance of the two following accounting equations:

Capital employed = shareholders' equity + net debt

Operating profit after tax = net income + net financial expense after tax.

Consequently, readers will arrive at the same return on equity figure whichever way they calculate it. It is worth remembering that using profit before tax and non-recurring items rather than net income eliminates the impact of non-recurring items.

Besides breaking down quasi-equity between debt and shareholders' equity, provisions between working capital and debt, etc., which we dealt with in Chapter 7, only two concrete problems arise when we calculate the leverage effect in consolidated financial statements: how to treat goodwill and associate companies.

The way goodwill is treated (see Chapter 6) has a significant impact on the results obtained. Setting off the entire amount of goodwill against shareholders' equity using the pooling of interests method causes a large chunk of capital employed and shareholders' equity to disappear from the balance sheet. As a result, the nominal returns on equity and on capital employed may look deceptively high when this type of merger accounting is used. Just because whole chunks of capital appear to have vanished into thin air from a balance sheet perspective does not mean that shareholders will give up their normal rate of return requirements on the capital that has done a perfectly legitimate disappearing act under certain accounting standards. The abolition of the pooling of interests method in IAS and US accounting standards is gradually eliminating this problem.

Likewise, goodwill amortisation when it is compulsory or impairment losses artificially reduce the capital that appears to be invested in the business. Consequently, we recommend that readers should, wherever possible, work with **gross** goodwill figures and add back to shareholders' equity the difference between gross and net goodwill to keep the balance sheet in equilibrium.[3] Likewise, we would advise working on the basis of operating profit and net profit before goodwill amortisation or impairment losses.

By doing so, readers will be able to conduct a rigorous assessment of a company's profitability. This area is explored further in Exercise 3 at the end of this chapter.

Consolidated accounts present another problem, which is how **income from associates[4] should be treated**. Should income from associates be considered as financial income or as a component of operating profit, bearing in mind that the latter approach implies adding an income after financial expense and tax to a operating profit (which is before tax)?

- The rationale for considering income from associates as financial income is that it equals the dividend that the group would receive if the associate company paid out 100% of its earnings. This first approach seems to fit a financial group that may sell one or other investment to reduce its debt.
- The rationale for considering income from associates as part of the operating profit is that income from associates derives from investments included in capital employed. This latter approach is geared more to an industrial group, for which such situations should be exceptional and temporary because the majority of industrial groups intend to control more than 50% of their subsidiaries.

That said, in a bid to improve the presentation of their accounts, certain groups park their least profitable assets and substantial debts in associate companies in which they own less than 40% and which are thus accounted for under the equity method. For instance, Coca-Cola boasted a headline return on capital employed of 14% in 2010. Note, however, that vital (bottling) assets worth $30bn are housed in less than 40%-owned associate companies, together with $11bn in bank and other borrowings. The return on capital employed generated by these assets stands at just 10% since internal transfer pricing[5] keeps most of the profits within the parent company. In such situations, where the letter of accounting standards is abided by but in our opinion not the

3 In the previous example involving Indesit, this adjustment was made as there was no goodwill written down.

4 For more on income from associates, see page 77, In the Indesit case study, the problem was disregarded as associates' book value is close to 0 with marginal contribution to results.

5 Price at which a product produced by one company is sold to another company belonging to the same group

spirit, analysts would be advised to examine the profitability of the parent and associate companies separately before forming an overall assessment. Adjusted for this accounting "trick", the group's return on capital employed comes to 11%, i.e. 3 points less than its face value.

Lastly, the tax rate may be affected by various deferred tax assets and liabilities arising from the restatement of individual financial statements for consolidation purposes. In practice, we recommend that readers choose an effective tax rate based on the company's average tax rate.

4/ COMPANIES WITH NEGATIVE CAPITAL EMPLOYED

Companies with negative capital employed usually have high negative working capital exceeding the size of their net fixed assets. This phenomenon is prevalent in certain specific sectors (contract catering, retailing, etc.) and this type of company typically posts a very high return on equity.

Of the two roles played by shareholders' equity, i.e. financing capital expenditure and acting as a guarantee for lenders, the former is not required by such companies. Only the latter role remains.

Consequently, return on capital employed needs to be calculated taking into account income from short-term financial investments (included in earnings) and the size of these investments (included in capital employed):

$$ROCE = \frac{(EBIT + Financial\ income) \times (1 - T_c)}{Capital\ employed + Short\text{-}term\ financial\ investments}$$

As a matter of fact, companies in this situation factor their financial income into the selling price of their products and services. Consequently, it would not make sense to calculate capital employed without taking short-term financial investments into account.

Section 13.3
USES AND LIMITATIONS OF THE LEVERAGE EFFECT

1/ LIMITATIONS OF BOOK PROFITABILITY INDICATORS

Book-based return on capital employed figures are naturally of great interest to financial analysts and managers alike. That said, they have much more limited appeal from a financial standpoint. The leverage effect equation always stands up to analysis, although sometimes some anomalous results are produced. For instance, the cost of debt calculated as the ratio of financial expense net of financial income to balance sheet debt may be plainly too high or too low. This simply means that the net debt shown on the balance sheet does not reflect average debt over the year, that the company is in reality much more (or less) indebted or that its debt is subject to seasonal fluctuations.

Attempts may be made to overcome this type of problem by using average or restated figures, particularly for fixed assets and shareholders' equity. But this approach is really feasible only for internal analysts with sufficient data at their disposal.

> It is thus important not to set too much store by implicit interest rates or the corresponding leverage effect when they are clearly anomalous.

For managers of a business or a profit centre, return on capital employed is one of the key performance and profitability indicators, particularly with the emergence of economic profit indicators, which compare the return on capital employed with the weighted average cost of capital (see Chapter 28).

From a financial standpoint, however, book-based returns on capital employed and returns on equity hold very limited appeal. Since book returns are prepared from the accounts, they do not reflect risks. As such, book returns should not be used in isolation as an objective for the company because this will prompt managers to take extremely unwise decisions.

As we have seen, it is easy to boost book returns on equity by gearing up the balance sheet and harnessing the leverage effect. The risk of the company is also increased without being reflected in the accounting-based formula.

> Return on capital employed and return on equity are accounting indicators used for historical analysis. In no circumstances whatsoever should they be used to project the future rates of return required by shareholders or all providers of funds.

If a company's book profitability is very high, shareholders require a lot less and will already have adjusted their valuation of shareholders' equity, whose market value is thus much higher than its book value. If a company's book profitability is very low, shareholders want much more and will already have marked down the market value of shareholders' equity to well below its book value.[6]

It is therefore essential to note that the book return on equity, return on capital employed and cost of debt do not reflect the rates of return required by shareholders, providers of funds or creditors respectively. These returns cannot be considered as financial performance indicators because they do not take into account the two key concepts of risk and valuation. Instead, they belong to the domains of financial analysis and control. We refer readers to Chapter 28 for a more detailed analysis.

Some analysts attempt to calculate return on capital employed by using the ratio of operating profit to market capitalisation plus the market value of debt. In our view, the theoretical basis for this type of approach is very shaky because an accounting profit indicator from the past is used in conjunction with an asset valuation based on expectations of future profits.

6 *For more on this point, see Chapter 27.*

2/ USES OF THE LEVERAGE EFFECT

The leverage effect sheds light on the origins of return on equity, i.e. whether it flows from operating performance (i.e. a good return on capital employed) or from a favourable financing structure harnessing the leverage effect. Our experience tells us that, **in the long term, only an increasing return on capital employed guarantees a steady rise in a company's return on equity.**

The main point of the leverage effect is to show how return on equity breaks down between the profitability of a company's industrial and commercial operations and its capital structure (i.e. the leverage effect).

Consider the profitability of the following groups:

RETURN ON EQUITY (%)

	2008	2009	2010	2011
Group A	15	16	18	20
Group B	15	15	15	15
Group C	40	40	40	40

RETURN ON CAPITAL EMPLOYED (AFTER TAX) (%)

	2008	2009	2010	2011
Group A	10	8	7	7
Group B	15	15	15	15
Group C	10	10	10	10

A superficial analysis may suggest that group C is a star performer owing to its stunningly high return on equity (40%), that group A is improving and that group B is rather disappointing by comparison.

But this analysis does not even scratch the surface of the reality! Group C generates its very high returns through the unbridled use of the leverage effect that weakens the whole company, while its return on capital employed is average. Group B has no debt and carries the least risk, while its return on capital employed is the highest. Group A's improvement is merely a mirage because it is attributable entirely to a stronger and stronger leverage effect while its return on capital employed is steadily declining, so group A is actually exposed to the greatest risks.

As we shall see in Section IV, the leverage effect is not very useful in finance because it does not create any value except in two very special cases:

- in times of rising inflation, real interest rates (i.e. after inflation) are negative, thereby eroding the wealth of a company's creditors who are repaid in a lender's depreciating currency to the great benefit of the shareholders;
- when companies have a very heavy debt burden (e.g. following an LBO, see Chapter 45), which obliges management to ensure that they perform well so that the cash flows generated are sufficient to cover the heavy debt servicing costs. In this type of situation, the leverage effect gives management a very strong incentive to do well, because the price of failure would be very high.

Section 13.4
CASE STUDY: INDESIT

Over the period, Indesit generates an ROE of 13%, which is decent even though one third of this rate is due to the leverage effect.

ROCE improves from 2005 to 2007. In 2008 and 2009 the performance is impacted by the downturn in the economy. ROCE falls to 6.6%, which is below the expectations of providers of funds but is not a surprise at this stage of the economic cycle. From 2010, ROCE is back to its 2006 high levels (11.9%).

SUMMARY

The summary of this chapter can be downloaded from www.vernimmen.com.

Return on capital employed (ROCE) is the book return generated by a company's operations. It is calculated as operating profit after normalised tax divided by capital employed or as the NOPAT margin (net operating profit after tax/sales) multiplied by asset turnover (sales/capital employed). Return on equity (ROE) is the ratio of net profit to shareholders' equity.

The leverage effect of debt is the difference between return on equity and return on capital employed. It derives from the difference between return on capital employed and the after-tax cost of debt and is influenced by the relative size of debt and equity on the balance sheet. From a mathematical standpoint, the leverage effect leads to the following accounting tautology:

$$ROE = ROCE + (ROCE - i) \times \frac{D}{E}$$

The leverage effect works both ways. Although it may boost return on equity to above the level of return on capital employed, it may also dilute it to a weaker level when the return on capital employed falls below the cost of debt.

Book return on capital employed, return on equity and cost of debt do not reflect the returns required by shareholders, providers of funds and creditors. These figures cannot be regarded as financial indicators because they do not take into account risk or valuation, two key parameters in finance. Instead, they reflect the historical book returns achieved and belong to the realms of financial analysis and control.

The leverage effect helps to identify the source of a good return on equity, which may come from either a healthy return on capital employed or merely from a company's capital structure, i.e. the leverage effect. This is its only real point.

In the long run, only a healthy return on capital employed will ensure a decent return on equity. As we shall see, the leverage effect does not create any value. Although it may boost return on equity, it leads to an increase in risk that is proportional to the additional profit.

QUESTIONS

1/ Why is capital employed equal to invested capital?

2/ What is the leverage effect?

3/ How is the leverage effect calculated?

4/ Why is the leverage effect equation an accounting tautology?

5/ According to the leverage effect equation, for the same after-tax ROCE of 10%, an increase in debt (costing 4% after tax) could improve the return on equity. State your views.

6/Why is goodwill a problem when calculating ROCE?

7/What is the basic purpose of the leverage effect?

8/Your financial director suggests that you increase debt to increase ROE. State your views.

9/What is the main problem with accounting profitability indicators such as ROE and ROCE?

10/Over a given period, interest rates are low, corporation tax rates are high and the economy is doing well. What consequences will this have on the financial structure of companies?

11/How would you view a sector with high margins and low capital intensity?

12/How would you view a sector with low margins and high capital intensity?

More questions are waiting for you at www.vernimmen.com.

EXERCISES

1/A businessman is hoping to get a 20% return on equity after tax. The business generates a 3% sales margin (after tax). Provide two possible combinations of financial structure, profitability and capital employed that could lead to the generation of a 20% return on equity (the cost of borrowing is 5% before tax, the tax rate is 40% and the company's capital employed is 1000).

2/Calculate the leverage effect for each year. What are your conclusions?

Millions of €	1	2	3	4	5
Shareholders' equity	100	115	320	300	240
Long- and medium-term debt	123	180	540	640	680
Financial expense before tax	11	18.5	29	63	83
Net income	14	16	(20)	(60)	(40)
Tax rate	35%	35%	35%	35%	35%

3/Calculate the ROCE and the ROE of L'Oréal and Carlsberg. You should include retirement benefits in the net debt and other long-term liabilities in working capital. There has been no amortisation or impairment of goodwill. The income tax rate is 32% for L'Oréal and 24% for Carlsberg.

2010	L'Oréal (in € bn)	Carlsberg (in DKR bn)
NET SALES	**19.5**	**60.1**
− Cost of sales	5.7	29.0
= GROSS MARGIN	13.8	31.1
− Selling and marketing costs	6.0	17.2
− General and administrative costs	4.0	4.0
− R&D costs	0.7	
± Other operating income and expense	−0.2	0.2
+ Income from associates	+ 0.3	0.1

= **RECURRING OPERATING PROFIT**	**3.2**	**10.2**
± Non-recurring items	0	−0.2
= **OPERATING PROFIT**	**3.2**	**10.0**
− Financial expense	0.0	3.2
+ Financial income	0.0	1.1
= PROFIT BEFORE TAX	3.2	7.8
− Income tax	0.9	1.9
− Minority interests	0.0	0.6
NET PROFIT ATTRIBUTABLE TO SHAREHOLDERS	**2.3**	**5.3**

	L'Oréal	Carlsberg
Goodwill	5.7	50.8
Other intangible fixed assets	2.2	37.0
Tangible fixed assets	2.7	32.4
Equity in associated companies	5.8	4.9
Other non-current assets	0.7	3.4
NON-CURRENT ASSETS (FIXED ASSETS)	**17.1**	**128.5**
Inventories	1.8	4.2
Trade receivables	2.7	5.7
Other operating receivables	0.9	2.9
Trade payables	3.2	9.4
Other operating payables	2.6	13.7
OPERATING WORKING CAPITAL (1)	−0.4	−10.3
NON-OPERATING WORKING CAPITAL (2)	0.0	0.0
WORKING CAPITAL (1+2)	**−0.4**	**−10.3**
SHAREHOLDERS' EQUITY GROUP SHARE	14.9	64.2
Minority interests in consolidated subsidiaries	0.0	5.4
SHAREHOLDERS' EQUITY	**14.9**	**69.6**
Retirement benefits	1.1	2.4
Deferred tax	0.5	9.9
Other long-term liabilities	0.2	2.4
LONG-TERM LIABILITIES (ex FIN. DEBT)	1.8	14.7
Medium- and long-term borrowings and liabilities	0.8	32.6
Bank overdrafts and short-term borrowings	0.8	4.0
Cash and equivalents	1.6	2.7
NET DEBT	**1.8**	**48.6**

4/Prove the leverage effect equation.

ANSWERS

Questions

1/ *Because accounts are balanced!*
2/ *The difference between return on equity and ROCE after tax.*
3/ *Leverage effect* $(ROCE - i) \times \frac{D}{E}$.
4/ *As it is based on total assets being exactly equal to total liabilities and equity.*
5/ *That is true but it also increases the risk to the shareholder.*

6/ Because if it had been impaired, reducing capital employed (see Chapter 6), it would have artificially increased book returns. Our advice is to look at the gross rather than the net figures (before impairment losses on this goodwill).

7/ It helps to identify the source of a good return on equity.

8/ Is ROCE higher than the cost of debt? What is the risk for shareholders?

9/ They do not factor in risk.

10/ An increase in the leverage effect. However, see Section III of this book.

11/ It's like Nirvana, high margins and low capex will generate high returns. New entrants will try to enter this sector and this will most likely reduce margins in the medium term.

12/ The sector needs to be restructured as it is not viable as such.

Exercises

A detailed Excel version of the solutions is available at www.vernimmen.com.

1/ Using the leverage effect equation the following can be determined:

	Solution 1	Solution 2
Capital employed	1000	1000
Net borrowings	750	0
Shareholders' equity	250	1000
Sales	1666.7	6666.7
Operating profit	120.8	333
Financial expense	37.5	0
Corporate income tax	33.3	133
Net income	50	200

2/

	1	2	3	4	5
ROCE after tax	9.5%	9.5%	0.7%	0.2%	3.0%
Leverage	1.23	1.57	1.69	2.13	2.83
Net cost of debt*	5.8%	6.7%	4.8%	9.7%	10.0%
Leverage effect	4.5%	4.4%	−6.9%	−20.2%	−19.7%
ROE	14%	13.9%	−6.2%	−20%	−16.7%

* Tax savings have only had a partial impact in the last three years.

When ROCE is above the after-tax cost of debt, debt boosts ROE. It depresses it when ROCE is lower than the after-tax cost of debt. This company is on the verge of bankruptcy.

3/ There is no one right answer. However, it is important to be consistent when calculating. Special attention should be paid:

When calculating ROCE:

○ Our advice is to take operating income before non-recurring items.

○ If capital employed includes long-term investments and investments in associates, operating income should be restated to include income on these assets. Here, operating profit includes income from associates, therefore to be consistent capital employed should include equity in associated companies. In any case, in our example, and given the small amounts, the difference between the ways of calculating would not be material.

○   *Whether to use recurring operating profit or total operating profit is another question. But if we use recurring operating profit, then the net result should also be restated for the calculation of ROE.*

○   *What tax rate to use? Marginal tax rate or actual tax rate? We tend to use actual tax rate, in particular for international groups which pay tax in different jurisdictions. But here again the key is to be consistent.*

When calculating ROE:

○   *ROE (group share) can be calculated by dividing net profits (group share) by shareholders' equity (group share). However, if the numerator includes minorities' shares, it will have to be divided by total shareholders' equity (including minority interests).*

	L'Oréal	Carlsberg
Capital employed	$17.1 - 5.8 - 0.4 - 0.2 = 10.7$	$128.5 - 4.9 - 2.4 = 99.6$
Operating income	3.2	10.0
Tax at 32% and 24% respectively	1.0	2.4
Return on capital employed after tax	20.3%	7.6%
Shareholders' equity, group share	14.9	64.2
Net earnings, group share	2.3	$5.3 + 0.2 = 5.5$
Return on equity, group share	15.4%	8.6%

Carlsberg has a modest ROCE (7.6% is probably close to cost of capital) and a stronger ROE (8.6%) because the company relies on debt (leverage of 0.7), taking advantage of a low after-tax cost of debt (4.8%).

L'Oréal has a ROCE of 20.3%. If its stake in Sanofi Aventis were considered as part of operating assets, the ROCE would be negatively impacted as this stake in Sanofi-Aventis (€5.8bn) generates only €0.3bn of income. As this stake is purely held for financial reasons, it should not be taken into account to compute ROCE. The leverage effect is negative given the negative debt level once the Sanofi stake is deducted from net debt.

4/ *Where:*

$$NI = \text{Net income}$$

$$EBIT = \text{Operating profit}$$

$$T_c = \text{Tax rate}$$

$$i = \text{After-tax cost of debt}$$

$$ROE = \frac{NI}{E} = \frac{EBIT \times (1 - T_c) - i \times D}{E} = \frac{EBIT \times (1 - T_c)}{E} - \frac{i \times D}{E}$$

$$= \frac{EBIT \times (1 - T_c) \times (E + D)}{E \times (E + D)} - \frac{i \times D}{E}$$

$$= \frac{EBIT \times (1 - T_c)}{E + D} + \frac{EBIT \times (1 - T_c)}{E + D} \times \frac{D}{E} - i \times \frac{D}{E}$$

whereas $ROCE = \dfrac{EBIT \times (1 - T_c)}{E + D}$ and so $ROE = ROCE + (ROCE - i) \times \dfrac{D}{E}$

BIBLIOGRAPHY

T. Andersson, C. Haslam, E. Lee, Financialized account: Restructuring and return on capital employed in the S&P 500, *Accounting Forum*, **30**, 21–41, June 2006.

G. Blazenko, Corporate Leverage and the Distribution of Equity Returns, *Journal of Business & Accounting*, **23**(8), 1097–1120, October 1996.

M. Campello, Z. Fluck, *Market Share, Financial Leverage and the Macroeconomy: Theory and Empirical Evidence*, University of Illinois, Working Paper, 3 February 2004.

A. Damodaran, *Return on Capital (ROC), Return on Invested Capital (ROIC) and Return on Equity (ROE): Measurement and Implications*, NYU working paper, 2008.

M. Dugan, D. Minyard, K. Shriver, A Re-examination of the Operating Leverage – Financial Leverage Tradeoff, *Quarterly Review of Economics & Finance*, **34**(3), 327–334, Fall 1994.

L. Lang, E. Ofek, R. Stulz, Leverage, Investment and Firm Growth, *Journal of Financial Economics*, **40**(1), 3–29, January 1996.

D. Nissim, S. Penman, Financial Statement Analysis of Leverage and how it Informs about Profitability and Price-to-book Ratios, *Review of Accounting Studies*, **8**(4), 531–560, 2003.

F. Reilly, The Impact of Inflation on ROE, Growth and Stock Prices, *Financial Services Review*, **6**(1), 1–17, 1997.

SECTION 1

Chapter 14
CONCLUSION OF FINANCIAL ANALYSIS

As one journey ends, another probably starts

By the time you complete a financial analysis, you must be able to answer the two following questions that served as the starting point for your investigations:

• Will the company be solvent? That is, will it be able to repay any loans it raised?
• Will it generate a higher rate of return than that required by those that have provided it with funds? That is, will it be able to create value?

Value creation and solvency are obviously not without links. A firm that creates value will most often be solvent and a company will most likely be insolvent because it has not succeeded in creating value.

Section 14.1
SOLVENCY

Here we return to the concept that we first introduced in Chapter 4.

A company is solvent when it is able to honour all its commitments by liquidating all of its assets, i.e. if it ceases its operations and puts all its assets up for sale.

Since, by definition, a company does not undertake to repay its shareholders, its equity represents a kind of life raft that will help keep it above water in the event of liquidation by absorbing any capital losses on assets and extraordinary losses.

Solvency thus depends on:

• the break-up value of a company's assets;
• the size of its debts.

Do assets have a value that is independent of a company's operations? The answer is probably "yes" for the showroom of a carmaker on 5th Avenue in New York and probably "no" as far as the tools and equipment at a heavy engineering plant are concerned.

Is there a secondary market for such assets? Here, the answer is affirmative for the fleet of cars owned by a car rental company, but probably negative for the technical installations of a foundry. To put things another way, will a company's assets fetch their book value or less? The second of these situations is the most common. It implies capital losses on top of liquidation costs (redundancy costs, etc.) that will eat into shareholders' equity and frequently push it into negative territory. In this case, lenders will be able to lay their hands on only a portion of what they are owed. As a result, they suffer a capital loss.

The solvency of a company thus depends on the level of shareholders' equity restated from a liquidation standpoint relative to the company's commitments and the nature of its business risks.

If a company posts a loss, its solvency deteriorates significantly owing to the resulting reduction in shareholders' equity and cumulative effects.

A loss-making company no longer benefits from the tax shield provided by debt.[1] As a result, it has to bear the full brunt of financial expense, which thus makes losses even deeper. Very frequently, companies raise additional debt to offset the decrease in their equity. Additional debt then increases financial expense and exacerbates losses, giving rise to the cumulative effects we referred to above.

If we measure solvency using the debt/equity ratio, we note that a company's solvency deteriorates very rapidly in the event of a crisis.

Let's consider a company with debt equal to its shareholders' equity. The market value of its debt and shareholders' equity is equal to their book value because its return on capital employed is the same as its cost of capital of 10%.

As a result of a crisis, the return on capital employed declines, leading to the following situation:

Year	0	1	2	3	4	5
Book value of capital employed	100	100	100	100	100	100
= Book value of equity	=50	=50	=47	=34	=25	=25
+ Net debt (costing 6%)	+50	+50	+53	+66	+75	+75
Return on capital employed	10%	0%	−10%	−5%	5%	10%
Operating profit after tax	10	0	−10	−5	5	10
− After-tax interest expense (tax rate of 35%)	−2	−3	−3	−4	−5	−5
= Net income	=8[2]	=−3	=−13	=−9	=0	=5
Market value of capital employed[3]	100	85	55	68	85	100
= Market value of equity	=50	=38	=15	=18	=25	=30
+ Market value of net debt	+50	+47	+40	+50	+60	+70

The company's evolution does not come as a surprise. The market value of capital employed falls by 45% at its lowest point because the previously normal return on capital employed turns negative. The market value of debt declines (from 100% to 75% of its nominal value) since the risk of non-repayment increases with the decline in return on capital employed and the growing size of its debt. Lastly, the market value of shareholders' equity collapses (by 70%).

Each year, the company has to increase its debt to cover the loss recorded in the previous year to keep its capital employed at the same level. From 1 at the start of our model, gearing soars to 3 by the end of year 5. In this scenario, its equity gets smaller and smaller, and its lenders will be very lucky to get their hands on the original amounts that they invested. This scenario shows how debt can spiral in the event of a crisis! Some

1 *We disregard the impact of carrybacks here, i.e. tax benefits which make it possible to reduce current tax liability against the losses of past periods.*

2 *In year 0, since the company is profitable, financial expense is only 2 given the income tax rate of 35% (rounded figures). In addition, to keep things simple, it is assumed that the entire amount of net income is paid out as a dividend.*

3 *Market value is observed rather than calculated.*

restructuring of equity and liabilities or, worse still, bankruptcy is bound to ensue with the additional losses caused by the disruption.

Had the same company been debt-free when the crisis began, its financial performance would have been entirely different, as shown by the following table:

Year	0	1	2	3	4	5
Book value of capital employed	100	100	100	100	100	100
= Book value of equity	=100	=100	=100	=90	=84	=84
+ Net debt	+0	+0	+0	+10	+16	+16
Return on capital employed	10%	0%	−10%	−5%	5%	10%
Operating profit after tax	10	0	−10	−5	5	10
− After tax interest expense (tax rate of 35%)	−0	−0	−0	−1	−1	−1
= Net income	=10[4]	=0	=+10	=−6	=4	=9
Market value of capital employed[5]	100	85	55	68	84	100
= Market value of equity	=100	=85	=55	=58	=68	=84
+ Market value of net debt	+0	+0	+0	+10	+16	+16

4 To keep things simple, it is assumed that the entire amount of net income is paid out as a dividend.

5 Market value is observed rather than calculated.

At the end of year 4, the company returns to profit and its shareholders' equity has been dented only moderately by the crisis.

Consequently, the first company, which is comparable to the second in all respects from an economic perspective, will not be able to secure financing and is thus probably doomed to failure as an independent economic entity.

For a long time, **net assets**, i.e. the difference between assets and total liabilities or assets net of debt, was the focal point for financial analysis. Net assets are thus an indicator that corresponds to shareholders' equity and are analysed in comparison to the company's total commitments.

Some financial analysts calculate net assets by subtracting goodwill (or even all intangible fixed assets), adding back unrealised capital gains (which may not be accounted for owing to the conservatism principle), with inventories possibly being valued at their replacement cost.

Broadly speaking, calculating net assets is an even trickier task with consolidated accounts owing to minority interests (which group assets do they own?) and goodwill (what assets does it relate to and what value, if any, does it have?). Consequently, we recommend that readers should work using the individual accounts of the various entities forming the group and then consolidate the net asset figures using the proportional method.

Section 14.2
VALUE CREATION

A company will be able to create value during a given period if the return on capital employed (after tax) that it generates exceeds the cost of the capital (i.e. equity and net debt) that it has raised to finance capital employed.

Readers will have to remain patient for a little while yet because we still have to explain how the rate of return required by shareholders and lenders can be measured. This subject is dealt with in Section III of this book. Chapter 27 covers the concept of value creation in greater depth, while Chapter 28 illustrates how it can be measured.

Section 14.3
FINANCIAL ANALYSIS WITHOUT THE RELEVANT ACCOUNTING DOCUMENTS

When a company's accounting documents are not available in due time (less than three months after year end), it is a sign that the business is in trouble. In many cases, the role of an analyst will then be to assess the scale of a company's losses to see whether it can be turned around or whether their size will doom it to failure.

In this case, the analysts will attempt to establish what proportion of the company's loans the lenders can hope to recover. We saw in Chapter 5 that cash flow statements establish a vital link between net income and the net decrease in debt.

It may perhaps surprise some readers to see that we have often used cash flow statements in reverse, i.e. to gauge the level of earnings by working back from the net decrease in debt.

It is essential to bear in mind the long period of time that may elapse before accounting information becomes available for companies in difficulty. In addition to the usual time lag, the information systems of struggling companies may be deficient and take even longer to produce accounting statements, which are obsolete by the time they are published because the company's difficulties have worsened in the meantime.

Consequently, the cash flow statement is a particularly useful tool for making rapid and timely assessments about the scale of a company's losses, which is the crux of the matter.

It is very easy to calculate the company's net debt. The components of working capital are easily determined (receivables and payables can be estimated from the balances of customer and supplier accounts, and inventories can be estimated based on a stock count). Capital expenditure, capital increases in cash and asset disposals can also be established very rapidly, even in a sub-par accounting system. We can thus prepare the cash flow statement in reverse to give an estimate of earnings.

A reverse cash flow statement can be used to provide a very rough estimate of a company's earnings, even before they have been reported.

In certain sectors,[6] cash is probably a better profitability indicator than earnings.

6 *Like construction, defence.*

When cash starts declining and the fall is not attributable to either heavy capital expenditure that is not financed by debt capital or a capital increase, to the repayment of borrowings, to an exceptional dividend distribution or to a change in the business environment, the company is operating at a loss, whether or not this is concealed by overstating inventories, reducing customer payment periods, etc.

If the decrease in cash cannot be accounted for by investing or financing activities, it can only come from deterioration in the company's profitability.

Section 14.4
Case study: Indesit

Is Indesit solvent at the close of 2010? Yes, as it has equity of €609m and intangible assets and goodwill of €332m. In addition, although the value of intangibles is always questionable, in the case of Indesit, the image of the group's brands leads us to think that there is clearly value in the intangibles.

Is Indesit creating value? Certainly with an after-tax return on capital employed of 11.9%, Indesit can, largely, provide investors with more than they require. Return on equity (14.8%) is also materially above the cost of equity (c. 10%).

This value creation is reflected in the market capitalisation (€782m) being significantly above the book value of equity.

SUMMARY

The summary of this chapter can be downloaded from www.vernimmen.com.

By the end of a financial analysis, readers must be able to answer the two following questions that served as the starting point for their investigations:

- Is the company solvent? Will it be able to repay all its creditors in full?

- Is the company creating any value for its shareholders?

A company is solvent when it is able to honour all its commitments by liquidating all of its assets, i.e. if it ceases its operations and puts all its assets up for sale. Net assets, i.e. the difference between assets and total liabilities, are the traditional measure of a company's solvency.

A company creates value if the return on capital employed (after tax) that it generates exceeds the cost of the capital (i.e. equity and net debt) that served to finance capital employed.

Lastly, we recommend that readers who need to carry out a rapid assessment of an ailing company where the accounts are not yet available build a cash flow statement in reverse. This reverse approach starts with reduction in net debt and works back towards net income, thus gauging the scale of losses that put the company's solvency and very survival in jeopardy.

QUESTIONS

1/ What risks do lenders run? How can lenders protect themselves against these risks?

2/ What is the ultimate guarantee that the lenders will be repaid?

3/ What is solvency?

4/ Is an insolvent company necessarily required to declare itself bankrupt?

5/ A company goes into debt with a one-day maturity in order to buy fixed-rate bonds. Is it running a liquidity risk? And a solvency risk? In what way does the risk manifest itself? What move in interest rates does this company expect?

6/ Is a company with negative net assets illiquid? Insolvent?

7/ It has been said that a solid financial structure is a guarantee of freedom and independence for a company. Is this true?

8/ Why is it difficult to determine the exact value of net assets in consolidated financial statements?

9/ Why is the concept of net book value useful?

10/ Do you assess solvency by analysing statutory or consolidated accounts?

11/ Do you assess liquidity by analysing statutory or consolidated accounts?

More questions are waiting for you at www.vernimmen.com.

EXERCISE

What is your view of the solvency of the following companies?

Groups	A	N	V
Intangibles	53	37 504	1679
Tangibles	2009	21 097	1739
Working capital	−306	7 945	−675
Shareholders' equity	381	54 916	1362
Net bank and other borrowings	1301	19 928	1625
Sales	4847	109 908	8664
EBITDA	−32	19 734	571
Operating profit	−310	15 676	−52

ANSWERS

Questions

1/ *The risk of default on payment. Request guarantees or ensure a high level of solvency.*
2/ *The value of shareholders' equity.*
3/ *The ability to repay its debts in full, even in the event of bankruptcy.*
4/ *Sooner or later it will probably have to do so.*
5/ *Yes; yes; inability to obtain further loans, capital losses; decline in interest rates.*
6/ *Possibly; yes.*
7/ *Yes, except when the share price is undervalued, in which case there is a risk of take-over (see Chapter 43).*
8/ *Because of minority interests.*
9/ *Because it shows the book value of all assets and liabilities.*
10/ *Analysing consolidated accounts as they will include all assets and debts of the group. Special attention should be given to heavily geared affiliates.*
11/ *Both in order to avoid the case of the parent company that bears a lot of debt with sub-sidiaries that do not have the capacity to pay sufficient dividends in the short term. In such cases, the parent company may have to sell some of its assets (on unfavourable terms).*

Exercise

A: *disastrous. EBITDA is negative. Given the operating loss equity will be lost in a few months. This company is on the verge of bankruptcy. This is Alitalia, the Italian airline, in 2007 just before its restructuring.*

N: *excellent situation. Financial leverage is low (1.0 x EBITDA). ROCE is good (13% after tax), the group is creating value. Even after deduction of all intangibles, equity remains positive. This is Nestlé in 2008 (it enjoys an AA rating, one of the best for a corporate).*

V: *weak situation. Equity seems very limited compared to intangibles. Debt level is high (2.8 x EBITDA) which becomes material. ROCE is negative, the group is destroying value. This is Valeo (an automotive supplier) in 2008.*

Section II
INVESTORS AND MARKETS

PART ONE
INVESTMENT DECISION RULES

Chapter 15
THE FINANCIAL MARKETS

Now let's step into the realm of finance

The introduction to this book discussed the role of financial securities in a market economy. This section will analyse the behaviour of the investor who buys those instruments that the financial manager is trying to sell. An investor is free to buy a security or not and, if he decides to buy it, he is then free to hold it or resell it in the secondary market.

The financial investor seeks two types of returns: the risk-free interest rate (which we call the time value of money) and a reward for risk-taking. This section looks at these two types of returns in detail but, first, here are some general observations about capital markets.

Section 15.1
THE RISE OF CAPITAL MARKETS

The primary role of a financial system is to bring together economic agents with surplus financial resources, such as households, and those with net financial needs, such as companies and governments. This relationship is illustrated below:

THE FINANCIAL SYSTEM

To use the terminology of John Gurley and Edward Shaw (1960), the parties can be brought together **directly** or **indirectly**.

In the first case, known as **direct finance**, the parties with excess financial resources directly finance those with financial needs. The financial system serves as a **broker**, matching the supply of funds with the corresponding demand. This is what happens when a small shareholder subscribes to a listed company's capital increase or when a bank places a corporate bond issue with individual investors.

In the second case, or **indirect finance**, financial intermediaries, such as banks, buy "securities" – i.e. loans – "issued" by companies. The banks in turn collect funds, in the form of demand or savings deposits, or issue their own securities that they place with

SECTION 2

investors. In this model, the financial system serves as a gatekeeper between suppliers and users of capital and performs the function of **intermediation**.

When you deposit money in a bank, the bank uses your money to make loans to companies. Similarly, when you buy bonds issued by a financial institution, you enable the institution to finance the needs of other industrial and commercial enterprises through loans. Lastly, when you buy an insurance policy, you and other investors pay premiums that the insurance company uses to invest in the bond market, the property market, etc.

This activity is called **intermediation**, and is very different from the role of a mere broker in the direct finance model.

With direct finance, the amounts that pass through the broker's hands do not appear on its balance sheet, because all the broker does is to put the investor and issuer in direct contact with each other. Only brokerage fees and commissions appear on a brokerage firm's profit and loss, or **income**, statement.

In intermediation, the situation is very different. The intermediary shows all resources on the liabilities side of its balance sheet, regardless of their nature: from deposits to bonds to shareholders' equity. Capital serves as the creditors' ultimate guarantee. On the assets side, the intermediary shows all uses of funds, regardless of their nature: loans, investments, etc. The intermediary earns a return on the funds it employs and pays interest on the resources. These cash flows appear in its income statement in the form of revenues and expenses. The difference, or spread, between the two constitutes the intermediary's earnings.

The intermediary's balance sheet and income statement thus function as holding tanks for both parties – those who have surplus capital and those who need it:

BANK BALANCE SHEET AND INCOME STATEMENT

Today's economy is experiencing **disintermediation**, characterised by the following phenomena:

- more companies are obtaining financing directly from capital markets; and
- more companies and individuals are investing directly in capital markets.

When capital markets (primary and secondary) are underdeveloped, an economy functions primarily on debt financing. Conversely, when capital markets are sufficiently well developed, companies are no longer restricted to debt, and they can then choose to increase their equity financing. Taking a page from John Hicks, it is possible to speak of **bank-based economies** and **market-based economies**.

In a **bank-based economy**, the capital market is underdeveloped and only a small portion of corporate financing needs are met through the issuance of securities. Therefore, bank financing predominates. Companies borrow heavily from banks, whose refinancing needs are mainly covered by the central bank.

The central bank tends to have a strong influence on the level of investment, and consequently on overall economic growth. In this scenario, interest rates represent the level desired by the government for reasons of economic policy, rather than an equilibrium point between supply and demand for loans.

A bank-based economy is viable only in an inflationary environment. When inflation is high, companies readily take on debt because they will repay their loans with devalued currency. In the meantime, after adjustments are made for inflation, companies pay real interest rates that are zero or negative. A company takes on considerable risk when it relies exclusively on debt, although inflation mitigates this risk. Inflation makes it possible to run this risk and, indeed, it encourages companies to take on more debt. The bank-based (or credit-based) economy and inflation are inextricably linked, but the system is flawed because the real return to investors is zero or negative. Their savings are insufficiently rewarded, particularly if they have invested in fixed-income vehicles.

The savings rate in a credit-based economy is usually low. The savings that do exist typically flow into tangible assets and real property (purchase of houses, land, etc.) that are reputed to offer protection against inflation. In this context, savings do not flow towards corporate needs. Lacking sufficient supply, the capital markets therefore remain embryonic. As a result, companies can finance their needs only by borrowing from banks, which in turn refinance themselves at the central bank. This process supports the inflation necessary to maintain a credit-based economy.

In such a context it would be unreasonable for a corporate not to take on some debt. It is, however, difficult to be wise when everybody else is behaving like a fool.

The lender's risk is that the corporate borrower will not generate enough cash flow to service the debt and repay the **principal**, or amount of the loan. Even if the borrower's financial condition is weak, the bank will not be required to book a provision against the loan so long as payments are made without incident.

In an economy with no secondary market, the investor's financial risk lies with the cash flows generated by his assets and their liquidity.

In a **market-based economy**, companies cover most of their financing needs by issuing financial securities (shares, bonds, commercial paper, etc.) directly to investors. A capital market economy is characterised by direct solicitation of investors' funds. Economic agents with surplus resources invest a large portion of their funds directly in the capital markets by buying companies' shares, bonds, commercial paper or other short-term negotiable debt. They do this either directly or through mutual funds. Intermediation gives way to the brokerage function, and the business model of financial institutions evolves towards the placement of companies' securities directly with investors.

In this economic model, bank loans are extended primarily to households in the form of consumer credit, mortgage loans, etc., as well as to small- and medium-sized enterprises that do not have access to the capital markets.

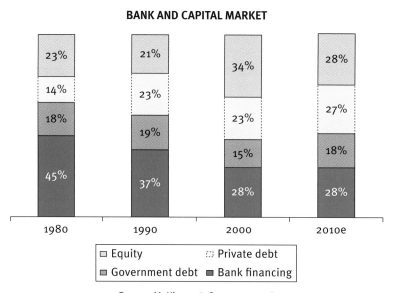

BANK AND CAPITAL MARKET

Source: McKinsey & Company 2008

The growing disintermediation has forced banks and other financial intermediaries to align their rates (which are the rates that they offer on deposits or charge on loans) with market rates. Slowly but surely, market forces tend to pervade all types of financial instruments.

For example, with the rise of the commercial paper market, banks regularly index short-term loans on money-market rates. Medium- and long-term lending have seen similar trends. Meanwhile, on the liabilities side, banks have seen some of their traditional, fixed-rate resources dry up. Consequently, the banks have had to step up their use of more expensive, market-rate sources of funds, such as certificates of deposit.[1]

Since the beginning of the 1980s, two trends have led to the rapid development of capital markets. First, real interest rates in the bond markets have turned positive. Second, budget deficits have been financed through the bond market, rather than through the money market.

In Chapter 1, the financial manager was described as a seller of financial securities. This is the result of European economies becoming capital market economies.

The risks encountered in a capital market economy are very different from those in a credit-based economy. These risks are tied to the **value of the security**, rather than to whether cash flows are received as planned. During a stock market crash, for example, a company's share price might sink even though its published earnings exceed projections.

The following graphs provide the best illustration of the rising importance of capital markets.

1 *Time deposits represented by a dematerialised negotiable debt security in the form of a bearer certificate.*

TOP 10 STOCK EXCHANGES BY NUMBER OF LISTED COMPANIES IN 2002 AND 2010

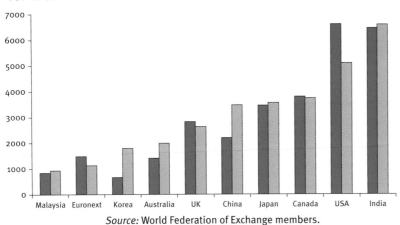

Source: World Federation of Exchange members.

... be it in terms of the number of listed companies ...

TOP 10 STOCK EXCHANGES BY MARKET CAPITALISATION IN 2002 AND 2010 (IN US$bn)

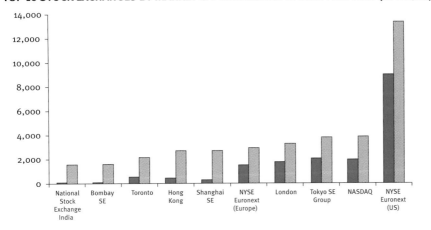

Source: World Federation of Exchanges members

transaction volumes are linked to the economic environment, even if the long-term trend shows a clear increase

VOLUME OF TRADES ON STOCK EXCHANGES (IN US$bn)

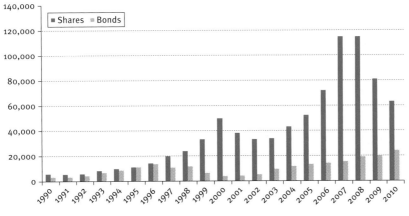

Source: World Federation of Exchange members.

... or market capitalisation

SECTION 2

Section 15.2
THE FUNCTIONS OF A FINANCIAL SYSTEM

The job of a financial system is to efficiently create financial liquidity for those investment projects that promise the highest profitability and that maximise collective utility.

However, unlike other types of markets, a financial system does more than just achieve equilibrium between supply and demand. A financial system allows investors to convert current revenues into future consumption. It also provides current resources for borrowers, at the cost of reduced future spending.

Robert Merton and Zvie Bodie have isolated **six essential functions** of a financial system:

1. means of payment;
2. financing;
3. saving and borrowing;
4. risk management;
5. information;
6. reducing or resolving conflict.

1. A financial system provides means of payment to facilitate transactions. Cheques, debit and credit cards, electronic transfers, etc. are all means of payment that individuals can use to facilitate the acquisition of goods and services. Imagine if everything could only be paid for with bills and coins!

2. A financial system provides a means of pooling funds for financing large, indivisible projects. A financial system is also a mechanism for subdividing the capital of a company so that investors can diversify their investments. If factory owners had to rely on just their own savings, they would very soon run out of investible funds. Indeed, without a financial system's support, Nestlé and British Telecom would not exist. The system enables the entrepreneur to gain access to the savings of millions of individuals, thereby diversifying and expanding his sources of financing. In return, the entrepreneur is expected to achieve a certain level of performance. Returning to our example of a factory, if you were to invest in your neighbour's steel plant, you might have trouble getting your money back if you should suddenly need it. A financial system enables investors to hold their assets in a much more liquid form: shares, bank accounts, etc.

3. A financial system distributes financial resources across time and space, as well as between different sectors of the economy. The financial system allows capital to be allocated in a myriad of ways. For example, young married couples can borrow to buy a house or people approaching retirement can save to offset future decreases in income. Even a developing nation can obtain resources to finance further development. And when an industrialised country generates more savings than it can absorb, it invests those surpluses through financial systems. In this way, "old economies" use their excess resources to finance "new economies".

4. A financial system provides tools for managing risk. It is particularly risky for an individual to invest all of his funds in a single company because, if the company goes bankrupt, he loses everything. By creating collective savings vehicles, such as mutual funds, brokers and other intermediaries enable individuals to reduce their risk by diversifying their exposure. Similarly, an insurance company pools the risk of millions of people and insures them against risks they would otherwise be unable to assume individually.

5. A financial system provides price information at very low cost. This facilitates decentralised decision-making. Asset prices and interest rates constitute information used by individuals in their decisions about how to consume, save or divide their funds among different assets. But research and analysis of the available information on the financial condition of the borrower is time-consuming, costly and typically beyond the scope of the layman. Yet when a financial institution does this work on behalf of thousands of investors, the cost is greatly reduced.

6. A financial system provides the means for reducing conflict between the parties to a contract. Contracting parties often have difficulty monitoring each other's behaviour. Sometimes conflicts arise because each party has different amounts of information and divergent contractual ties. For example, an investor gives money to a fund manager in the hope that he will manage the funds in the investor's best interests (and not his own!). If the fund manager does not uphold his end of the bargain, the market will lose confidence in him. Typically, the consequence of such behaviour is that he will be replaced by a more conscientious manager.

Section 15.3
THE RELATIONSHIP BETWEEN BANKS AND COMPANIES

Not so long ago, banks could be classified as:

- **Commercial banks** that schematically collected funds from individuals and lent to corporates.
- **Investment banks** that provided advisory services (mergers and acquisitions, wealth management) and played the role of a broker (placement of shares, of bonds) but without "using their balance sheet".

In the last fifteen years, large financial conglomerates have emerged both in the USA and Europe. This resulted from mega mergers between commercial banks and investment banks: BNP/Paribas, Citicorp/Travelers Group, Chase Manhattan/JP Morgan and, more recently, Merrill Lynch/Bank of America.

This trend, eased by changes in regulation (in particular in the US with the reform of the Glass–Steagall Act in 1999), shows a willingness of large banking groups to adopt the business model of a universal bank (also called "one-stop shopping") in a context of increasing internationalisation and complexity. This is particularly true for certain business lines like corporate finance or fund management, in which size constitutes a real competitive advantage.

Large banking groups now generally include the following business lines:

- **Retail banking**: for individuals and small and medium-sized corporates. Retail banks serve as intermediaries between those who have surplus funds and those who require financing. The banks collect resources from the former and lend capital to the latter. They have millions of clients and therefore adopt an industrial organisation. The larger the bank's portfolio, the lower the risk – thanks once again to the law of large numbers. After all, not everyone is likely to go bankrupt at the same time (even though mimetic behaviour and harsh competition may have led banks to forget about the fundamentals of risk analysis in 2006–2007).

Retail banking is an extremely competitive activity. After taking into account the cost of risk, profit margins are very thin. Bank loans are somewhat standard products, so it is relatively easy for customers to play one bank off against another to obtain more favourable terms.

Retail banks have developed ancillary services to add value to the products that they offer to their corporate customers. Accordingly, they offer a variety of means of payment to help companies move funds efficiently from one place to another. They also help clients to manage their cash flows (see Chapter 47) or their short-term investments.

A retail banking division also generally includes some specific financial services for individuals (consumer credit, etc.) or for corporates (factoring, leasing, etc.) as such services are used mostly by small- and medium-sized firms.

- **Corporate and investment banking (CIB)**: provides large corporates with sophisticated services. Such banks have, at most, a few thousand clients and offer primarily the following services:

   ○ **Access to equity markets (Equity Capital Market, ECM)**: investment banks help companies prepare and carry out initial public offerings on the stock market. Later on, investment banks can continue to help these companies by raising additional funds through capital increases. They also advise companies on the issuance of instruments that may one day become shares of stock, such as warrants and convertible bonds (see Chapter 25).
   ○ **Access to bond markets (Debt Capital Market, DCM)**: similarly, investment banks help large and medium-sized companies raise funds directly from investors through the issuance of bonds. The techniques of placing securities, and in particular the role of the investment bank in this type of transaction, will be discussed in Chapter 26. The investment bank's **trading room** is where its role as "matchmaker" between the investor and the issuer takes on its full meaning.
   ○ **Merger and acquisition (M&A) advisory services**: these investment banking services are not directly linked to corporate financing or the capital markets, although a public issue of bonds or shares often accompanies an acquisition.
   ○ **Bank financing**: syndicated loans, bilateral lines, structured financing; we will study these in Chapter 26.
   ○ **Access to foreign exchange, interest rate and commodities markets**: for the hedging of risk. The bank also uses these desks for speculating for its own account.

- **Asset management banking**: has its own clients – institutional investors and high net worth individuals – but also serves some of the retail banking clients through mutual funds. The asset management arm may sometimes use some of the products tailored by the investment banking division (hedging, order execution).

Besides these global banking groups operating across all banking activities, some players have focused on certain targeted services like mergers and acquisitions and asset management (Lazard, Rothschild) or specific geographical areas (Mediobanca).

The 2007–2010 crisis demonstrated the central role played by banks in the economy. They are suppliers of liquidity; they are also an indicator of investor risk aversion. The basic duty of a bank is to assess risk and repackage it while eliminating the diversifiable risk. Whatever their business model, the worst-managed players have been hit: Northern Rock, Fortis, Wachovia for retail banks; Bear Stearns, Lehman Brothers for investment banks; Citi for universal banks. There does not seem to be a better business model – some players are just better managed than others.

Section 15.4
THEORETICAL FRAMEWORK: EFFICIENT MARKETS

An efficient market is one in which the prices of financial securities at any time *rapidly* reflect *all available relevant* information. The terms "perfect market" or "market in equilibrium" are synonymous with "efficient market".

In an efficient market, prices instantly reflect the consequences of past events and all expectations about future events. As all known factors are already integrated into current prices, it is therefore impossible to predict future variations in the price of a financial instrument. Only new information will change the value of the security. Future information is, by definition, unpredictable, so changes in the price of a security are random. This is the origin of the **random walk** character of returns in the securities markets.

Competition between financial investors is so fierce that prices adjust to new information almost instantaneously. At every moment, a financial instrument trades at a price determined by its return and its risk.

Eugene Fama (1970) has developed the following three tests to determine whether a market is efficient.

1/ ABILITY TO PREDICT PRICES

In a **weak-form** efficient market, it is impossible to predict future returns. Existing prices already reflect all the information that can be gleaned from studying **past prices** and **trading volumes**, interest rates and returns. This is what is meant by the "weak form" of efficiency.

Extra returns can be obtained only if investors have future or privileged information. According to the weak-form of efficiency, the price of an asset is the sum of three components:

1. the last available price (P_{-1});
2. the expected return from the security (see Chapter 19); and
3. a random component due to new information that might be learned during the period in question. This component of random error is independent from past events and unpredictable in the future.

$$P_0 = P_{-1} + \text{Expected return} + \text{Random error}$$

When prices follow this model, they follow a random walk.
The efficient market hypothesis says that technical analysis has no practical value nor do martingales (martingales in the ordinary not mathematical sense).

For example, the notion that "if a stock rises three consecutive times, buy it; if it declines two consecutive times, sell it" is irrelevant. Similarly, the efficient market hypothesis says that models relating future returns to interest rates, dividend yields, the spread between short- and long-term interest rates or other parameters are equally worthless.

2/ THE MARKET RESPONSE TO SPECIFIC EVENTS

A **semi-strong** efficient market reflects all publicly available information, as found in annual reports, newspaper and magazine articles, prospectuses, announcements of new contracts, of a merger, of an increase in the dividend, etc.

Semi-strong efficiency is superior to weak-form efficiency because it requires that current prices include historical information (as assumed by the weak-form efficiency) *and* publicly available information. The latter, for example, is available in:

- financial statements;
- research on the company performed by external financial analysts; and
- company announcements.

This hypothesis can be empirically tested by studying the reaction of market prices to company events (**event studies**). In fact, the price of a stock reacts immediately to any announcement of relevant new information regarding a company. In an efficient market, no impact should be observable prior to the announcement, nor during the days following the announcement. In other words, prices should adjust rapidly only at the time any new information is announced.

On March 14, 2011 before market opening, Berkshire Hathaway, the investment vehicle of Warren Buffett, announced it would launch an agreed takeover bid on Lubrizol, a speciality chemical company. Lubrizol's share price immediately reached the offer price of $135 with a very high level of shares exchanged.

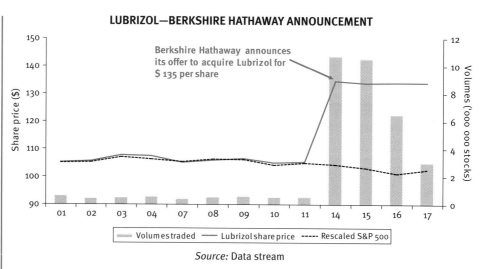

LUBRIZOL—BERKSHIRE HATHAWAY ANNOUNCEMENT

Berkshire Hathaway announces its offer to acquire Lubrizol for $135 per share

Volumes traded — Lubrizol share price ----- Rescaled S&P 500

Source: Data stream

In order to prevent investors with prior access to information from using it to their advantage (and therefore to the detriment of other investors), most stock market regulators suspend trading prior to a mid-session announcement of information that is highly likely to have a significant impact on the share price. Trading resumes a few hours later or the following day, so as to ensure that all interested parties receive the information. Then, when trading resumes, no investor has been short-changed.

3/ THE IMPACT OF INSIDER INFORMATION ON THE MARKET

In a **strongly** efficient financial market, investors with privileged or insider information or with a monopoly on certain information are unable to influence securities prices. This is the "strong form" of efficiency.

This holds true only when financial market regulators have the power to prohibit and punish the use of insider information.

In theory, professional investment managers have expert knowledge that is supposed to enable them to post better performances than the market average. However, without using any inside information, the efficient market hypothesis says that market experts have no edge over the layman. In fact, in an efficient market, the experts' performance is slightly below the market average, in a proportion directly related to the management fees they charge!

Actual markets approach the theory of an efficient market when:

- participants have low-cost access to all information;
- transaction costs are low;
- the market is liquid; and
- investors are rational.

Take the example of a stock whose price is expected to rise 10% tomorrow. In an efficient market, its price will rise today to a level consistent with the expected gain. "Tomorrow's" price will be discounted to today. Today's price becomes an estimate of the value of tomorrow's price.

In general, if we try to explain why financial markets have different degrees of efficiency, we could say that:

- **The lower transaction costs are, the more efficient a market is.** An efficient market must quickly allow equilibrium between supply and demand to be established. Transaction costs are a key factor in enabling supply and demand for securities and capital to adjust.

  Brokerage fees have an impact on how quickly a market reaches equilibrium. In an efficient market, transactions have no costs associated with them, neither underwriting costs (when securities are issued) nor trading costs (when securities are bought and sold).

  When other transaction-related factors are introduced, such as the time required for approving and publishing information, they can slow down the achievement of market equilibrium.

- **The more liquid a market is, the more efficient it is.** The more frequently a security is traded, the more quickly new information can be integrated into the share price. Conversely, illiquid securities are relatively slow in reflecting available information. Investors cannot benefit from the delays in information assimilation because the trading and transaction volumes are low.

  In general, it can be said that the less liquid a financial asset is, the higher the investor's required return is. Lower trading volume leads to greater uncertainty about the market price.

  Research into the significance of this phenomenon has demonstrated that there is a statistical relationship between liquidity and the required rate of return. This indicates the existence of a risk premium that varies inversely with the liquidity of the security. The premium is tantamount to a reward for putting up with illiquidity, i.e. when the market is not functioning efficiently. We will measure the size of this premium in Chapter 19.

- **The more rational investors are, the more efficient a market is.** Individuals are said to be rational when their actions are consistent with the information they receive. When good and unexpected news is announced, rational investors must buy a stock – not sell it. And for any given level of risk, rational investors must also try to maximise their potential gain.

Section 15.5
ANOTHER THEORETICAL FRAMEWORK UNDER CONSTRUCTION:
BEHAVIOURAL FINANCE

Since the end of the 1960s, a large number of research papers have focused on testing the efficiency of markets. It is probably the most tested assumption of finance! A number of "anomalies" that go against the efficiency of markets have been highlighted:

- **Excess volatility.** In 1985, De Bondt and Thaler published an article presenting robust evidence that investors **overreact** to news. Today, few would disagree that financial asset prices tend to be highly volatile. Shiller (2000) went a step further and claimed that financial markets are irrationally volatile.
- **Dual listing and closed-end funds.** Dual listings are shares of twin companies listed on two different markets. Their stream of dividends is, by definition, identical but we can observe that their price can differ over a long period of time. Similarly the price of a closed-end fund (made up of shares of listed companies) can differ from the sum of the value of its components. Conglomerate discount (see Chapter 40) cannot explain the magnitude of the discount for certain funds and certainly not the premium for some others. It is interesting to see that these discounts can prevail over a long period of time, therefore making any arbitrage (although easy to conceptualise) hard to put in place.
- **Dimension of companies.** There is some evidence that the compound annual return on the smallest companies is higher than on the biggest companies. Although the risk of these small stocks is also higher, it is not high enough to justify the extra return of these smaller capitalisation stocks. The reason for this excessive return is difficult to explain. Some researchers suggest that the superior historical return is compensation for the higher transaction costs of dealing with these securities.
- **Value vs. growth companies.** Stocks with low price-to-book and low price-to-earnings ratios are often called value stocks, whereas those with high values in these two ratios are called growth stocks. Value stocks are in the oil, motor, finance and utilities sectors and growth stocks are in the high-tech, telecommunications and information technology sectors. There is some evidence that historical returns on value stocks have exceeded those of growth stocks. A possible explanation for this anomaly is behavioural: investors can get overexcited about the growth prospects of firms with rapidly increasing earnings and, irrationally, pay high prices for them.
- **Calendar anomalies**. Recent research has revealed that there are predictable periods during the year when some stocks tend to outperform. Maybe the most frequently

observed anomaly is the outperformance of small stocks with respect to large stocks in one specific month of the year: January. As Shiller (2000) explains, the January effect is the most important reason that small stocks have obtained greater total returns than large stocks over the last 70 years. Similar to the January effect, and just as inexplicable, stocks tend to do much better (a) in the first few days of a month, and (b) on Fridays rather than on Mondays (the so-called weekend effect). Calendar anomalies are even more puzzling because they imply that the stock market is partially predictable and therefore possible to beat.

There seem to be some grounds to think that the efficient market theory is not valid. Nevertheless, Eugene Fama, one of the founders of this theory, defends it strongly. He calls into question the methodologies used to find anomalies (in particular for the over-reaction of markets).

Behavioural finance rejects the founding assumption of market efficiency: what if investors were not rational? It tries to build on other fields of social science to derive new conclusions. For example, economists will work with neuroscientists to understand individual economic choices. Finance researchers will be helped by psychologists to understand the actual behaviour of investors when they make an investment choice. This allows us to suppose that decisions are influenced by circumstances and the environment.

One of the first tests for understanding people's reasoning to make a choice is based on lotteries (gains with certain probabilities). The following attitudes can be observed:

- Gains and losses are not treated equally by investors: they will take risks when the probability of losing is high (they prefer a 50% chance of losing 100 to losing 50 for sure) whereas they will prefer a small gain if the probability is high (getting 50 for sure rather than a 50% chance of 100).
- If the difference (delta) in probability is narrow, the investor will choose the lottery with the highest return possible, but if the delta in probability is high, the investor will think in terms of weighted average return. This may generate some paradoxes: preferring BNP Paribas to UBS, UBS to Mediobanca but Mediobanca to BNP Paribas! This could drive an asset manager mad!

The lack of rationality of some investors would not be a problem if arbitrage made it possible to correct anomalies and if efficiency could be brought back rapidly. Unfortunately, anomalies can be observed over the long term.

The theory of mimicry is an illustration of behavioural finance. The economist André Orléan has distinguished three types of mimicry:

- *Normative mimicry* – which could also be called "conformism". Its impact on finance is limited and is beyond the scope of this text.
- *Informational mimicry* – which consists of imitating others because they supposedly know more. It constitutes a rational response to a problem of dissemination of information, provided the proportion of imitators in the group is not too high. Otherwise, even if it is not in line with objective economic data, imitation reinforces the most popular choice, which can then interfere with efficient dissemination of information.
- *Self-mimicry* – which attempts to predict the behaviour of the majority in order to imitate it. The "right" decision then depends on the collective behaviour of all other market participants and can become a self-fulfilling prophecy, i.e. an equilibrium that exists because everyone thinks it will exist. This behaviour departs from traditional economic analysis, which holds that financial value results from real economic value.

Mimicry can explain speculative bubbles.

Mimetic phenomena can be accentuated by **program trading**, which involves the computer programs used by some traders that rely on pre-programmed buy or sell decisions.

It is easy to criticise but harder to conclude. If some want to destroy efficient market theory (which implies no more CAPM or method to value financial products, etc.) they will have to propose a viable alternative. As of today, the models proposed by "behaviouralists" cannot be used (especially in corporate finance), they merely model the behaviour of investors towards investment decisions and products.

We can anticipate that in the future, the theoretical framework of finance will mix the rigorous approach of neoclassical theories (including the efficient market theory) with the more realistic understanding of the decision process of investors that behavioural finance will provide.

Section 15.6
Investors' behaviour

At any given point in time, each investor is either:

1. a hedger;
2. a speculator; or
3. an arbitrageur.

1/ Hedging

When an investor attempts to protect himself from risks he does not wish to assume he is said to be *hedging*. The term "to hedge" describes a general concept that underlies certain investment decisions, for example, the decision to match a long-term investment with long-term financing, to finance a risky industrial investment with equity rather than debt, etc.

This is simple, natural and healthy behaviour for non-financial managers. Hedging protects a manufacturing company's margin, i.e. the difference between revenue and expenses, from uncertainties in areas relating to technical expertise, human resources, sales and marketing, etc. Hedging allows the economic value of a project or line of business to be managed independently of fluctuations in the capital markets.

Accordingly, a European company that exports products to the United States may sell dollars forward against euros, guaranteeing itself a fixed exchange rate for its future dollar-denominated revenues. The company is then said to have hedged its exposure to fluctuations in currency exchange rates.

Similarly, a medium-term lender that refinances itself with resources of the same maturity has also hedged its interest-rate and liquidity exposure.

Companies can also structure their operations in such a way that they are automatically hedged without recourse to the financial markets. A French company that both produces and sells in the United States will not be exposed to exchange rate risk on all of its US revenues but only on the residual flows not covered by dollar-denominated costs. This is the only portion it will have to hedge.

Keep in mind, however, that hedging techniques are not always so simple, even if they are designed to produce the same end result.

An investor hedges when he does not wish to assume a calculated risk.

2/ SPECULATION

In contrast to hedging, which eliminates risk by transferring it to a party willing to assume it, speculation is the assumption of risk. A speculator takes a position when he makes a bet on the future value of an asset. If he thinks its price will rise, he buys it. If it rises, he wins the bet; if not, he loses. If he is to receive dollars in a month's time, he may take no action now because he thinks the dollar will rise in value between now and then. If he has long-term investments to make, he may finance them with short-term funds because he thinks that interest rates will decline in the meantime and he will be able to refinance at lower cost later. This behaviour is diametrically opposed to that of the hedger.

- Traders are professional speculators. They spend their time buying currencies, bonds, shares or options that they think will appreciate in value and they sell them when they think they are about to decline. Not surprisingly their motto is *"Buy low, sell high, play golf!"*
- **But the investor is also a speculator most of the time.** When an investor predicts cash flows, he is speculating about the future. This is a very important point, and you must be careful not to interpret "speculation" negatively. Every investor speculates when he invests, but his speculation is not necessarily reckless. It is founded on a conviction, a set of skills and an analysis of the risks involved. The only difference is that some investors speculate more heavily than others by assuming more risk.

People often criticise the financial markets for allowing speculation. Yet speculators play a fundamental role in the market, an economically healthy role, by assuming the risks that other participants do not want to accept. In this way, speculators minimise the risk borne by others.

Accordingly, a European manufacturing company with outstanding dollar-denominated debt that wants to protect itself against exchange rate risk (i.e. a rise in the value of the dollar vs. the euro) can transfer this risk by buying dollars forward from a speculator willing to take that risk. By buying dollars forward today, the company knows the exact dollar/euro exchange rate at which it will repay its loan. It has thus eliminated its exchange rate risk. Conversely, the speculator runs the risk of a fluctuation in the value of the dollar between the time he sells the dollars forward to the company and the time he delivers them, i.e. when the company's loan comes due.

Likewise, if a market's long-term financing needs are not satisfied, but there is a surplus of short-term savings, sooner or later a speculator will (fortunately) come along and assume the risk of borrowing short term in order to lend long term. In so doing, the speculator assumes intermediation risk.

Speculative bubbles are isolated events that should not put into question the utility and normal operation of the financial markets.

What, then, do people mean by a "speculative market"? A speculative market is a market in which all the participants are speculators. Market forces, divorced from economic reality, become self-sustaining because everyone is under the influence of the same phenomenon. Once a sufficient number of speculators think that a stock will rise, their purchases alone are enough to make the stock price rise. Their example prompts other speculators to follow suit, the price rises further, and so on. But at the first hint of a downward revision in expectations, the mechanism goes into reverse and the share price falls dramatically. When this happens, many speculators will try to liquidate positions in order to pay off loans contracted to buy shares in the first place, thereby further accentuating the downfall.

3/ ARBITRAGE

In contrast to the speculator, the arbitrageur is not in the business of assuming risk. Instead, he tries to earn a profit by exploiting tiny discrepancies which may appear on different markets that are not in equilibrium.

An arbitrageur will notice that Solvay shares are trading slightly lower in London than in Brussels. He will buy Solvay shares in London and sell them simultaneously (or nearly so) at a higher price in Brussels. By buying in London, the arbitrageur bids the price up in London; by selling them in Brussels, he drives the price down there. He or other arbitrageurs then repeat the process until the prices in the two markets are perfectly in line, or in equilibrium.

With no overall outlay of funds or assumption of risk, arbitrage consists of combining several transactions that ultimately yield a profit.

In principle, the arbitrageur assumes no risk, even though each separate transaction involves a certain degree of risk. In practice, arbitrageurs often take on a certain amount of risk as their behaviour is on the frontier between speculation and arbitrage. For arbitrage to be successful, the underlying securities must be liquid enough for the transactions to be executed simultaneously.

Arbitrage is of paramount importance in a market. By **destroying opportunities as it uncovers them**, arbitrage participates in the development of new markets by creating liquidity. It also eliminates the temporary imperfections that can appear from time to time. As soon as disequilibrium appears, arbitrageurs buy and sell assets and increase market liquidity. It is through their very actions that the disequilibrium is reduced to zero. Once equilibrium is reached, arbitrageurs stop trading and wait for the next opportunity.

Thanks to arbitrage, all prices for a given asset are equal at a given point in time. Arbitrage ensures fluidity between markets and contributes to their liquidity. It is the basic behaviour that guarantees market efficiency.

Throughout this book, you will see that financial miracles are impossible because arbitrage levels the playing field between assets exhibiting the same level of risk.

You should also be aware that the three types of behaviour described here do not correspond to three mutually exclusive categories of investors. A market participant who is primarily a speculator might carry out arbitrage activities or partially hedge his position. A hedger might decide to hedge only part of his position and speculate on the remaining portion, etc.

Moreover, these three types of behaviour exist simultaneously in every market. A market cannot function only with hedgers, because there will be no one to assume the risks they don't want to take. As we saw above, a market composed wholly of speculators is not viable either. Finally, a market consisting only of arbitrageurs would be even more difficult to imagine.

A market is fluid, liquid and displays the "right prices" when its participants include hedgers, speculators and arbitrageurs.

SUMMARY

SECTION 2

The summary of this chapter can be downloaded from www.vernimmen.com.

The job of a financial system is to bring together those economic agents with surplus funds and those with funding needs:

- either through the indirect finance model, wherein banks and other financial institutions perform the function of intermediation; or

- through the direct finance model, wherein the role of financial institutions is limited to that of a broker.

But a financial system also provides a variety of payment means, and it facilitates transactions because:

- the funds of many investors are pooled to finance large projects; and

- the equity capital of companies is subdivided into small units, enabling investors to diversify their portfolios.

A financial system also distributes financial resources across time and space, and between different sectors. It provides tools for managing risk, disseminates information at low cost, facilitates decentralised decision-making, and offers mechanisms for reducing conflict between the parties to a contract.

Financial markets are becoming more important every day, a phenomenon that goes hand-in-hand with their globalisation. The modern economy is no longer a credit-based economy, where bank loans are the predominant form of finance. Today it is rather a capital market economy, wherein companies solicit funding directly from investors via the issuance of shares and bonds.

Alongside their traditional lending function, banks have adapted to the new system by developing advisory services to facilitate corporate access to the financial markets, be they equity markets or bond markets.

Conceptually, markets are efficient when security prices always reflect all relevant available information. It has been demonstrated that the more liquid a market is, the more readily available information is, the lower transaction costs are and the more individuals act rationally, the more efficient the market is. The last of these factors probably constitutes the biggest hindrance to market efficiency because human beings cannot be reduced to a series of equations. Irrational human behaviour gives rise to mimicry and other anomalies, leading to speculative excesses that specialists in behavioural finance are still trying to comprehend and explain.

A financial market brings together three types of players:

- hedgers, who refuse to assume risk and instead wish to protect themselves from it;

- speculators, who assume varying degrees of risk; and

- arbitrageurs, who exploit market disequilibria and, in so doing, eliminate these discrepancies and therefore ensure market liquidity and efficiency.

The existence of these three types of players is necessary in a market to ensure that the corporates will be in a position to find financing and hedging products that they need at normal prices.

QUESTIONS

1/ Jérôme Kerviel was trying to use the discrepancy between the value of funds and their underlying components in duplicating the funds. This led to a €4.9 bn loss. Was this speculation, hedging or arbitrage?

2/ What is the economic function of speculation?

3/ Can you explain why a narrow-minded financial manager and a narrow-minded businessman will be unable to understand each other?

4/ How can the ordinary saver reduce the risk she faces?

5/ What conditions are necessary for arbitrage to work?

6/ What is the economic function of arbitrage?

7/ Can a market in which speculators are the only traders last indefinitely?

8/ Would you be speculating if you bought so-called risk-free government bonds? What type of risk is not present in "risk-free" bonds?

9/ Is it true that investors who bought Spanish real estate investment trusts at the peak of the bubble will not have lost anything as long as they hold onto their shares? State your views.

10/ What is a speculative market?

11/ What sort of regulatory mechanisms are in place to prevent speculative bubbles on:

- derivatives markets;
- secondary markets for debt securities;
- equity markets?

12/ Throughout the world, financial intermediaries can be split into two groups:

- brokers: they connect buyers with sellers. Trades can only be completed if the brokers find a buyer for each seller, and vice versa. Brokers work on commission.

○   market makers: when securities are sold to an investor, market makers buy them at a given price and try simultaneously or subsequently to sell them at a higher price. Their earnings are thus the difference between the sell price and the buy price.

In your view, is the price difference earned by market makers logically equal to, higher than or lower than the commissions earned by brokers?

13/ Yes or no?

	Yes	No
Provided that investors' demands are met, companies have access to unlimited funds		
The announcement of anticipated losses has an impact on the share price		
Manipulating accounting indicators has no impact on value		

14/ Which of the following statements in your view describe the inefficiency of a market? Which test demonstrates this?

(a) Tax-free US municipal bonds with a lower rate of return for the investor than government bonds which are taxed.

(b) Managers make higher than average profits by buying and selling shares in the company they work for.

(c) There is some correlation between the market rate of return during a given quarter and a company's expected change in profits the following quarter.

(d) Market watchers have observed that shares that have shot up in the recent past will go up again in the future.

(e) The market value of a company will tend to go up before the announcement of a takeover bid.

(f) Earnings on shares in a company whose profits have recently risen sharply will be high in the coming months.

(g) On average, earnings on shares that carry a risk are higher than earnings on shares that are relatively risk free.

15/ What is the purpose of behavioural finance?

16/ If financial markets are only occasionally efficient, is this of greater concern to small or large companies? Why?

More questions are waiting for you at www.vernimmen.com.

Questions

ANSWERS

1/ *In theory, as far as his superiors were concerned, he was executing arbitrage transactions. In reality, he was speculating without his superiors being aware of his actions.*

2/ *To take risks which intermediaries do not wish to take.*

3/ *The financial manager diversifies his risk. The businessman often cannot afford to do so.*

4/ *She can diversify her portfolio by buying shares in mutual funds or unit trusts.*

5/ *Trading costs must be low, all players must have access to all markets and there must be freedom of investment.*

6/ *To ensure market equilibrium and liquidity.*

7/ *No, because it is removed from economic reality.*

8/ *Yes, on changes in interest rates. The risk of the issuer going bankrupt.*

9/ *No, because assets have a market value at any point in time.*

10/ *A market controlled solely by speculators (it is removed from economic reality).*

11/ *Delivery of the underlying security on maturity, which forces equality of the trade price and the price of the underlying security. Repayment, which means that on maturity, the value of the debt security will be equal to the repayment amount. Economic value of the company.*

12/ *Higher, because the risk is higher.*

13/ *Yes, in theory, as investors are keen to invest in companies able to satisfy their requests for return. No, since it has been anticipated, the share had plenty of time to adjust itself before the official confirmation of the loss. Yes, as accounting window dressing does not, per se, affect cash flows which are the foundations of value.*

14/ *b, c, d, e, f: Inefficiency.*

15/ *It factors in the non-rational side of investors' behaviour.*

16/ *Small companies, since the limited number of investors interested in their shares means that their liquidity is low and that their share prices could shift away from a stable value for long periods.*

BIBLIOGRAPHY

For more on the macro-economic topics covered in this chapter:

J. Gurley, E. Shaw, *Money in a Theory of Finance*, The Brookings Institution, 1960.

J.R. Hicks, *Value and Capital*, 2nd edn, Oxford University Press, 1975.

McKinsey, *Global capital markets: Entering a new era*, McKinsey Global Institute, September 2009.

McKinsey, *Debt and deleveraging: The global credit bubble and its economic consequences*, McKinsey Global Institute, January 2010.

R.C. Merton, Z. Bodie *et al., The Global Financial System: A Functional Perspective*, Harvard Business School Press, Boston, 1995.

N. Naik, The many roles of financial markets, in G. Bickerstaffe (ed.), *Mastering Finance*, FT/ Pitman Publishing, London, 1998.

R. Rajan, L. Zingales, *Banks and markets: the changing character of European finance*, Working Paper, International Monetary Fund (IMF) and University of Chicago, 2008.

G. Soros, *The new paradigm for financial markets: the credit crisis of 2008 and what it means*, Public Affairs, 2008.

R. Stulz, The limits of financial globalization, *Journal of Finance*, **60**(4), 1529–1638, August 2005.

www.world-exchanges.org Website of International Federation of Stock Exchanges. Free download of monthly, quarterly and annual statistics regarding stock markets.

For more about efficient markets :

U. Bhattacharya, H. Daouk, The world price of insider trading, *Journal of Finance*, **57**(1), 75–108, February 2002.

C. Botosan, Evidence that greater disclosure lowers the cost of equity capital, *Journal of Applied Corporate Finance*, **12**(4), 60–69, Winter 2000.

E. Dimson, M. Mussavian, A brief history of market efficiency, *European Financial Management*, **4**(1), 91–103, March 1998.

E. Dimson, M. Mussavian, *Foundations of Finance*, Darmouth Publishing Company, 2000.

E. Fama, Efficient capital markets: A review of theory and empirical work, *Journal of Finance*, **25**(2), 383–417, May 1970.

E. Fama, Efficient capital markets II, *Journal of Finance*, **46**(5), 1575–1617, December 1991.

E. Fama, Market efficiency, long-term returns and behavioral finance, *Journal of Financial Economics*, **49**(3), 283–306, September 1998.

J. Fuller, M. Jensen, Just say no to Wall Street: Putting a stop to the earnings game, *Journal of Applied Corporate Finance*, **14**(4), 27–40, Winter 2002.

B. Malkiel, *A Random Walk Down Wall Street*, 10th edn, W.W. Norton & Company, New York, 2011.

M. Rubinstein, Rational markets: yes or no? The affirmative case, *Financial Analysts Journal*, **57**(3), 15–29, May–June 2001.

About empirical evidence and anomalies of efficient financial markets:

R. Banz, The relationship between return and market value of common stock, *Journal of Financial Economics*, **9**(1), 3–18, March 1981.

J. Fox, *The Myth of the Rational Market*, Harper Business, 2009.

M. Gibbons, H. Patrick, Day of the week effects and asset returns, *Journal of Business*, **54**(4), 579–596, October 1981.

D. Keim, Size-related anomalies and stock return seasonality: Further empirical evidence, *Journal of Financial Economics*, **12**(1), 13–32, June 1983.

T. Loughran, J. Ritter, The new issue puzzle, *Journal of Finance*, **50**(1), 23–51, March 1995.

T. Loughran, Book-to-market across firm size, exchange, and seasonality: Is there an effect? *Journal of Financial and Quantitative Analysis*, **32**(3), 249–268, September 1997.

R. Raghuram, *Has Financial Development Made the World Riskier?* NHBER Working Paper, 2005.

J. Ritter, The long-run performance of IPOs, *Journal of Finance*, **46**(1), 3–27, March 1991.

For those wanting to know more about behavioural finance:

M. Baker, R. Ruback, J. Wurgler, Behavioral corporate finance: A survey, in *Handbook of Corporate Finance, Empirical Corporate Finance*, E. Eckbo (Ed.), Elsevier/North Holland, 2007.

A. Barnea, H. Cronqvist, S. Siegel, Nature or nurture: What determines investor behaviour?, *Journal of Financial Economics*, **98**(3), 583–604, December 2010.

W. DeBondt, R. Thaler, Does the stock market overreact? *Journal of Finance*, **40**(3), 793–805, July 1985.

R. Fairchild, Behavioural corporate finance: existing research and future directions, *International Journal of Behavioral Accounting and Finance*, **1**(4), 277–293, April 2010.

J. Graham, C. Harvey, M. Puri, *Managerial attitudes and corporate actions*, Duke University working paper, 2009.

L. Pastor, R. Stambaugh, Mutual fund performance and seemingly unrelated assets, *Journal of Financial Economics*, **63**(3), 315–349, March 2002.

H. Shefrin, *Beyond Greed and Fear: Understanding Behavioral Finance and the Psychology of Investing*, Harvard Business School Press, 2000.

H. Shefrin, Behavioralizing finance, *Foundations and Trends in Finance*, **4**(1-2), 1–184, 2009.

R. Shiller, A. Banerjee, A simple model of herd behavior, *Quarterly Journal of Economics*, **107**(3), 797–817, August 1992.

R. Shiller, Conversation, information and herd behavior, *American Economic Review*, **85**(2), 181–185, May 1995.

R. Shiller, *Irrational Exuberance*, Princeton University Press, 2000.

V. Singal, *Beyond the Random Walk : A Guide to Stock Market Anomalies and Low Risk Investing*, Oxford University Press, 2006.

L. Von Mises, *Human Action*, Liberty Fund, Indianapolis, 2007.

SECTION 2

Chapter 16
THE TIME VALUE OF MONEY AND
NET PRESENT VALUE

A bird in the hand is worth two in the bush

For economic progress to be possible, there must be a universally applicable time value of money, even in a risk-free environment. This fundamental concept gives rise to the techniques of capitalisation, discounting and net present value, described below.

These are more than just tools, but actual reflexes that must be studied and acquired.

Section 16.1
CAPITALISATION

Consider an example of a businessman who invests €100 000 in his business at the end of 2002 and then sells it 10 years later for €1 800 000. In the meantime, he receives no income from his business, nor does he invest any additional funds into it. Here is a simple problem: given an initial outlay of €100 000 that becomes €1 800 000 in 10 years, and without any outside funds being invested in the business, what is the return on the businessman's investment?

His profit after 10 years was €1 700 000 (€1 800 000 – €100 000) on an initial outlay of €100 000. Hence, his return was (1 700 000/100 000) or 1700% over a period of 10 years.

Is this a good result or not?

Actually, the return is not quite as impressive as it first looks. To find the annual return, our first thought might be to divide the total return (1700%) by number of years (10) and say that the average return is 170% per year.

While this may look like a reasonable approach, it is in fact far from accurate. The value 170% has nothing to do with an annual return, which compares the funds invested and the funds recovered after 1 year. In the case above, there is no income for 10 years. Usually, calculating interest assumes a flow of revenue each year, which can then be reinvested, and which in turn begins producing additional interest.

To calculate returns over a period greater than one year, we cannot simply compare the end return to the initial outlay and divide by the number of years. This is incorrect reasoning.

There is only one sensible way to calculate the return on the above investment. First, it is necessary to seek the rate of return on a hypothetical investment that would generate income at the end of each year. After 10 years, the rate of return on the initial investment will have to have transformed €100 000 into €1 800 000. Further, the income generated must not be paid out, but rather it has to be reinvested (in which case the income is said to be **capitalised**).

Capitalising income means foregoing receipt of it. It then becomes capital and itself begins to produce interest during the following periods.

Therefore, we are now trying to calculate the annual return on an investment that grows from €100 000 into €1 800 000 after 10 years, with all annual income to be reinvested each year.

An initial attempt to solve this problem can be made using a rate of return equal to 10%. If, at the end of 2002, €100 000 is invested at that rate, it will produce 10% × €100 000, or €10 000 in interest in 2003.

This €10 000 will then be added to the initial capital outlay and begin, in turn, to produce interest. (Hence the term "to capitalise," which means to add to capital.) The capital thus becomes €110 000 and produces 10% × €110 000 in interest in 2004, i.e. €10 000 on the initial outlay plus €1000 on the interest from 2000 (10% × €10 000). As the interest is reinvested, the capital becomes €110 000 + €11 000, or €121 000, which will produce €12 100 in interest in 2005, and so on.

If we keep doing this until 2012, we obtain a final sum of €259 374, as shown in the table.

Year	Capital at the beginning of the period (€) (1)	Income (€) (2) = 10% × (1)	Capital at the end of the period (€) = (1) + (2)
2003	100 000	10 000	110 000
2004	110 000	11 000	121 000
2005	121 000	12 100	133 100
2006	133 100	13 310	146 410
2007	146 410	14 641	161 051
2008	161 051	16 105	177 156
2009	177 156	17 716	194 872
2010	194 872	19 487	214 359
2011	214 359	21 436	235 795
2012	235 795	23 579	259 374

Each year, interest is capitalised and itself produces interest. This is called **compound interest**. This is easy to express in a formula:

$$V_{2003} = V_{2002} + 10\% \times V_{2002} = V_{2002} \times (1 + 10\%)$$

Which can be generalised into the following:

$$V_n = V_{n-1} \times (1 + r)$$

where V is a sum and r the rate of return.

Hence, $V_{2003} = V_{2002} \times (1 + 10\%)$, but the same principle can also yield:

$$V_{2004} = V_{2003} \times (1 + 10\%)$$
$$V_{2005} = V_{2004} \times (1 + 10\%)$$
$$V_{2006} = V_{2005} \times (1 + 10\%)$$

All these equations can be consolidated into the following:

$$V_{2012} = V_{2002} \times (1 + 10\%)^{10}$$

Or, more generally:

Capitalisation formula

$$V_n = V_0 \times (1 + r)^n$$

---

where V_0 is the initial value of the investment, r is the rate of return and n is the duration of the investment in years.

This is a simple equation that gets us from the initial capital to the terminal capital. Terminal capital is a function of the rate, r, and the duration, n.

Now it is possible to determine the annual return. In the example, the annual rate of return is not 170%, but 33.5%[1] (which is not bad, all the same!). Therefore, *33.5%* is the rate on an investment that transforms €100 000 into €1 800 000 in 10 years, with annual income assumed to be reinvested every year at the same rate.

To calculate the return on an investment that does not distribute income, it is possible to reason by analogy. This is done using an investment that, over the same duration, transforms the same initial capital into the same terminal capital and produces annual income reinvested at the same rate of return. At 33.5%, annual income of €33 500 for 10 years (plus the initial investment of €100 000 paid back after the 10th year) is exactly the same as not receiving any income for 10 years and then receiving €1 800 000 in the 10th year.

[1] $33.5\% = \left(\dfrac{1,800,000}{100,000}\right)^{\frac{1}{10}} - 1$

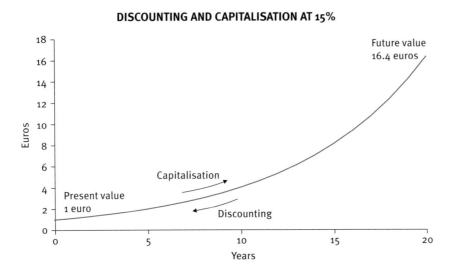

When no income is paid out, the terminal value rises considerably, quadrupling, for example, over 10 years at 15%, but rising 16.4-fold over 20 years at the same rate, as illustrated in this graph.

SECTION 2

Over a long period of time, the impact of a change in the capitalisation rate on the terminal value looks as follows:

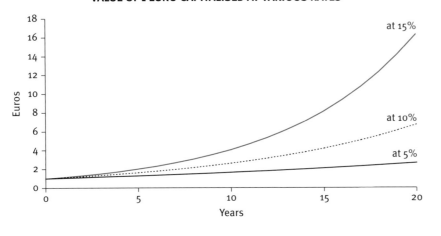

After 20 years, a sum capitalised at 15% is six times higher than a sum capitalised at one-third the rate (i.e. 5%).

This increase in terminal value is especially important in equity valuations. The example we gave earlier of the businessman selling his company after 10 years is typical. The lower the income he has received on his investment, the more he would expect to receive when selling it. Only a high valuation would give him a return that makes economic sense.

The lack of intermediate income must be offset by a high terminal valuation. The same line of reasoning applies to an industrial investment that does not produce any income during the first few years. The longer it takes it to produce its first income, the greater that income must be in order to produce a satisfactory return.

Tripling one's capital in 16 years, doubling it in 10 years or simply asking for a 7.177% annual return all amount to the same thing, since the rate of return is the same.

No distinction has been made in this chapter between income, reimbursement and actual cash flow. Regardless of whether income is paid out or reinvested, it has been shown that the slightest change in the timing of income modifies the rate of return.

To simplify, consider an investment of 100, which must be paid off at the end of year 1, with an interest accrued of 10. Suppose, however, that the borrower is negligent and the lender absent-minded, and the borrower repays the principal and the interest one year later than he should. The return on a well-managed investment that is equivalent to the so-called 10% on our absent-minded investor's loan can be expressed as:

$$V = V_0 \times (1+r)^2$$
$$\text{or} \quad 110 = 100 \times (1+r)^2$$
$$\text{hence} \quad r = 4.88\%$$

This return is less than half of the initially expected return!

It is not accounting and legal appearances that matter, but rather actual cash flows.

Any precise financial calculation must account for cash flow exactly at the moment when it is received and not just when it is due.

Section 16.2

DISCOUNTING

1/ WHAT DOES IT MEAN TO DISCOUNT A SUM?

To discount means to calculate the present value of a future cash flow.

Discounting into today's euros helps us compare a sum that will not be produced until later. Technically speaking, what is discounting?

To discount is to "depreciate" the future. It is to be more rigorous with future cash flows than present cash flows, because future cash flows cannot be spent or invested immediately. First, take tomorrow's cash flow and then apply to it a multiplier coefficient below 1, which is called a discounting factor. The discounting factor is used to express a future value as a present value, thus reflecting the depreciation brought on by time.

Consider an offer whereby someone will give you €1000 in 5 years. As you will not receive this sum for another 5 years, you can apply a discounting factor to it, for example, 0.6. The present, or today's, value of this future sum is then 600. Having discounted the future value to a present value, we can then compare it to other values. For example, it is preferable to receive 650 today rather than 1000 in 5 years, as the present value of 1000 5 years out is 600, and that is below 650.

Discounting makes it possible to compare sums received or paid out at different dates.

Discounting is based on the time value of money. After all, "time is money". Any sum received later is worth less than the same sum received today.

Remember that investors discount because **they demand a certain rate of return**. If a security pays you 110 in one year and you wish to see a return of 10% on your investment, the most you would pay today for the security (i.e. its present value) is 100. At this price (100) and for the amount you know you will receive in 1 year (110), you will get a return of 10% on your investment of 100. However, if a return of 11% is required on the investment, then the price you are willing to pay changes. In this case, you would be willing to pay no more than 99.1 for the security because the gain would have been 10.9 (or 11% of 99.1), which will still give you a final payment of 110.

Discounting is calculated with the required return of the investor. If the investment does not meet or exceed the investor's expectations, he will forego it and seek a better opportunity elsewhere.

Discounting converts a future value into a present value. This is the opposite result of capitalisation.

Discounting converts future values into present values, while capitalisation converts present values into future ones. Hence, to return to the example above, €1 800 000 in 10 years discounted at 33.5% is today worth €100 000. €100 000 today will be worth €1 800 000 when capitalised at 33.5%. over 10 years.

DISCOUNTING AND CAPITALISATION

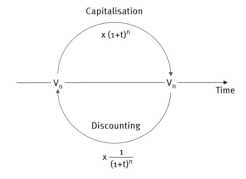

Discounting and capitalisation are thus two ways of expressing the same phenomenon: the time value of money.

2/ DISCOUNTING AND CAPITALISATION FACTORS

To discount a sum, the same mathematical formulas are used as those for capitalising a sum. Discounting calculates the sum in the opposite direction to capitalising.

To get from €100 000 today to €1 800 000 in 10 years, we multiply 100 000 by $(1 + 0.335)^{10}$, or 18. The number 18 is the **capitalisation factor**.

To get from €1 800 000 in 10 years to its present value today, we would have to multiply €1 800 000 by $(1/+0.335)^{10}$, or 0.056. 0.056 is the **discounting factor**, which is the inverse of the coefficient of capitalisation. The present value of €1 800 000 in 10 years at a 33.5% rate is €100 000.

More generally:

Discounting formula

$$V_0 = \frac{V_n}{(1+r)^n}$$

Which is the exact opposite of the capitalisation formula.

$1/(1+r)^n$ is the **discounting factor**, which depreciates V_n and converts it into a present value V_0. It remains below 1 as discounting rates are always positive.

Section 16.3
PRESENT VALUE AND NET PRESENT VALUE OF A FINANCIAL SECURITY

In the introductory chapter of this book, it was explained that a financial security is no more than a stream of future cash flows, to which we can then apply the notion of discounting. So, without being aware of it, you already knew how to calculate the value of a security!

1/ FROM THE PRESENT VALUE OF A SECURITY . . .

The present value (*PV*) of a security is the sum of its discounted cash flows; i.e.:

$$PV = \sum_{n=1}^{N} \frac{F_n}{(1+r)^n}$$

where F_n are the cash flows generated by the security, r is the applied discounting rate and n is the number of years for which the security is discounted.

All securities also have a **market value**, particularly on the secondary market. Market value is the price at which a security can be bought or sold.

Net present value (NPV) is the difference between present value and market value (V_0):

$$NPV = \sum_{n=1}^{N} \frac{F_n}{(1+r)^n} - V_0$$

If the net present value of a security is greater than its market value, then it will be worth more in the future than the market has presently valued it. Therefore you will probably want to invest in it, i.e. to invest in the upside potential of its value.

If, however, the security's present value is below its market value, you should sell it at once, for **its market value is sure to diminish**.

2/ . . . TO ITS FAIR VALUE

If an imbalance occurs between a security's market value and its present value, efficient markets will seek to re-establish balance and reduce net present value to zero. Investors acting on efficient markets seek out investments offering positive net present value, in order to realise that value. When they do so, they push net present value towards zero, ultimately arriving at the fair value of the security.

In efficient, fairly valued markets, net present values are zero, i.e. market value is equal to present value.

3/ APPLYING THE CONCEPT OF NET PRESENT VALUE TO OTHER INVESTMENTS

Up to this point, the discussion has been limited to financial securities. However, the concepts of present value and net present value can easily be applied to any investment, such as the construction of a new factory, the launch of a new product, the takeover of a competing company or any other asset that will generate positive and/or negative cash flows.

The concept of net present value can be interpreted in three different ways:

1. **the value created by an investment** – for example, if the investment requires an outlay of €100 and the present value of its future cash flow is €110, then the investor has become €10 wealthier;
2. **the maximum additional amount that the investor is willing to pay to make the investment** – if the investor pays up to €10 more, he/she has not necessarily made a bad deal, as he/she is paying up to €110 for an asset that is worth €110;
3. **the difference between the present value of the investment (€110) and its market value (€100).**

Section 16.4
THE NPV DECISION RULE

Calculating the NPV of a project is conceptually easy. There are basically two steps to be followed:

1. Write down the net cash flows that the investment will generate over its life.
2. Discount these cash flows at an interest rate that reflects the degree of risk inherent in the project.

The resulting sum of discounted cash flows equals the project's net present value. The **NPV decision rule** says to invest in projects when the present value is positive (greater than zero):

$$NPV > 0 \quad \text{invest}$$
$$NPV < 0 \quad \text{do not invest}$$

The NPV rule implies that firms should invest when the present value of future cash inflows exceeds the initial cost of the project. Why does the NPV rule lead to good investment decisions? The firm's primary goal is to maximise shareholder wealth. The discount rate r represents the highest rate of return (opportunity cost) that investors could obtain in the marketplace in an investment with equal risk. When the NPV of cash flow equals zero, the rate of return provided by the investment is exactly equal to investors' required return.

Section 16.5
WHAT DOES NET PRESENT VALUE DEPEND ON?

While net present value is obviously based on the amount and timing of cash flows, it is worth examining how it varies with the discounting rate.

The higher the discounting rate, the more future cash flow is depreciated and, therefore, the lower is the present value. **Net present value declines in inverse proportion to the discounting rate**, thus reflecting investor demand for a greater return (i.e. greater value attributed to time).

Take the following example of an asset (e.g. a financial security or a capital investment) with a market value of 2 and with cash flows as follows:

Year	1	2	3	4	5
Cash flow	0.8	0.8	0.8	0.8	0.8

A 20% discounting rate would produce the following discounting factors:

Year	1	2	3	4	5
Discounting factor	0.833	0.694	0.579	0.482	0.402
Present value of cash flow	0.67	0.56	0.46	0.39	0.32

As a result, the present value of this investment is about 2.4. As its market value is 2, its net present value is approximately 0.4.

If the discounting rate changes, the following values are obtained:

Discounting rate	0%	10%	20%	25%	30%	35%
Present value of the investment	4	3.03	2.39	2.15	1.95	1.78
Market value	2	2	2	2	2	2
Net present value	2	1.03	0.39	0.15	−0.05	−0.22

Which would then look like this graphically

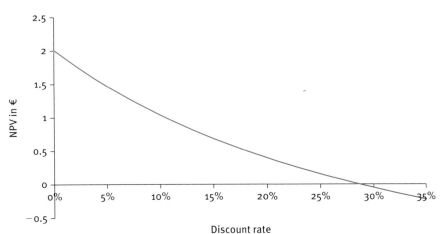

NET PRESENT VALUE AND THE DISCOUNT RATE

The higher the discounting rate (i.e. the higher the return demanded), the lower the net present value.

SECTION 2

The present value and net present value of an asset vary in inverse proportion to the discounting rate.

Section 16.6

SOME EXAMPLES OF SIMPLIFICATION OF PRESENT VALUE CALCULATIONS

For those occasions when you are without your favourite spreadsheet program, you may find the following formulas handy in calculating present value.

1/ THE VALUE OF AN ANNUITY F OVER N YEARS, BEGINNING IN YEAR 1

$$PV = \frac{F}{(1+r)} + \frac{F}{(1+r)^2} + \ldots + \frac{F}{(1+r)^N}$$

or:

$$PV = F \times \left[\frac{1}{(1+r)} + \frac{1}{(1+r)^2} + \ldots + \frac{1}{(1+r)^n} \right]$$

For the two formulas above, the sum of the geometric series can be expressed more simply as:

$$PV = \frac{F}{r} \times \left[1 - \frac{1}{(1+r)^{nv}} \right]$$

So, if $F = 0.8$, $r = 20\%$ and $n = 5$, then the present value is indeed 2.4.

Further $\dfrac{1}{r}\times\left[1-\dfrac{1}{(1+r)^{n}}\right]$ is equal to the sum of the first n discounting factors.

2/ THE VALUE OF A PERPETUITY

A **perpetuity** is a constant stream of cash flows without end. By adding this feature to the previous case, the formula then looks like this:

$$PV = \frac{F}{(1+r)} + \frac{F}{(1+r)^{2}} + \ldots + \frac{F}{(1+r)^{n}} + \ldots + \ldots$$

As n approaches infinity, this can be shortened to the following:

$$PV = \frac{F}{r}$$

The present value of a €100 perpetuity discounted back at 10% per year is thus:

$$PV = 100/0.10 = €1000$$

A €100 perpetuity discounted at 10% is worth €1000 in today's euros. If the investor demands a 20% return, the same perpetuity is worth €500.

3/ THE VALUE OF AN ANNUITY THAT GROWS AT RATE g FOR n YEARS

In this case, the F_{0} cash flow rises annually by g for n years.
Thus:

$$PV = \frac{F_{0}\times(1+g)}{(1+r)} + \ldots + \left[\frac{F_{0}\times(1+g)^{n}}{(1+r)^{n}}\right]$$

or:

$$PV = \frac{F_{0}\times(1+g)}{(r-g)} \times \left[1 - \frac{(1+g)^{n}}{(1+r)^{n}}\right]$$

Note: the first cash flow actually paid out is $F_{0}\times(1+g)$

Thus, a security that has just paid out 0.8, and with this 0.8 growing by 10% each year for the four following years has – at a discounting rate of 20% – a present value of:

$$PV = (0.8\times(1+10\%)/(20\%-10\%))\times(1-(1.10/1.20)^{4}) = 2.59$$

4/ THE VALUE OF A PERPETUITY THAT GROWS AT RATE g (GROWING PERPETUITY)

As n approaches infinity, the previous formula can be expressed as follows:

$$PV = \frac{F_0 \times (1+g)}{r-g} = \frac{F_1}{r-g}$$

As long as $r > g$.

The present value is thus equal to the next year's cash flow divided by the difference between the discounting rate and the annual growth rate.

For example, a security with an annual return of 0.8, growing by 10% annually to infinity has, at a rate of 20%, a $PV = 0.8/(0.2 - 0.1) = 8.0$.

SUMMARY

The summary of this chapter can be downloaded from www.vernimmen.com.

Capitalisation involves foregoing immediate spending of a given sum of money. By using the interest rate at which the money will be invested, the future amounts can be calculated. Thus, the future value of a sum of money can be determined by way of capitalisation.

Discounting involves calculating today's value of a future cash flow, what is known as the *present value*, on the basis of rates of return required by investors. By calculating the present value of a future sum, discounting can be used for comparing future cash flows that will not be received on the same date.

Discounting and capitalisation are two ways of expressing the same phenomenon: the time value of money.

Capitalisation is based on compound interest. $V_n = V_0 \times (1 + r)^n$

where V_0 is the initial value of the investment, r is the rate of return, n is the duration of the investment in years, $(1+r)^n$ is the capitalisation factor and V_n is the terminal value.

Discounting is the inverse of capitalisation. It is important to note that any precise financial calculation must account for cash flows at the moment when they are received or paid, and not when they are due.

Net present value (NPV) is the difference between present value and the value at which the security or share can be bought. Net present value measures the creation or destruction of value that could result from the purchase of a security or making an investment. When markets are in equilibrium, net present values are usually nil.

Changes in present value and net present value move in the opposite direction from changes in discount rates. The higher the discount rate, the lower the present value and net present value, and vice versa.

In many cases, calculating present value and net present value can be made a lot simpler through *ad hoc* formulas.

QUESTIONS

1/ Why should we discount?

2/ What is the discount factor equal to?

3/ On what should you base a choice between two equal discounted values?

4/ What is the simple link between the discount factor and the capitalisation factor?

5/ Why are capitalisation factors always greater than 1?

6/ Why are discount factors always less than 1?

7/ Should you discount even if there is no inflation and no risk? Why?

8/ Why does the graph on capitalisation show curves and not lines?

9/ Belgacom pays out big dividends. Should its share price rise faster or slower than the share price of Google which doesn't pay out any dividends? Why? Would it be better to have Belgacom stock options or Google stock options? Why?

10/ What is net present value equal to?

11/ The higher the rates of return, the larger present values will be. True or false?

12/ What mechanism pushes market value towards present value?

13/ Can net present value be negative? What does this mean?

14/ What does the discount rate correspond to in formulas for calculating present value and net present value?

15/ Are initial flows on an investment more often positive or negative? What about for final cash flows?

16/ A market is in equilibrium when present values are nil and net present values are positive. True or false?

17/ For the investment in Section 16.2, what is the maximum discount rate above which it would not be worthwhile for the investor?

18/ Can the growth rate to infinity of a cash flow be higher than the discount rate? Why?

19/ Could an investment made at a negative net present value result in the creation of value?

20/ Would you be more likely to find investments with positive net present value on financial markets or on industrial markets? Why?

21/ Which of the formulas in Section 16.6 is more appropriate for valuing a rented building, the Belgacom share price, a bond?

More questions are waiting for you at www.vernimmen.com.

1/ What is the present value of €100 received in 3 years at 5%, 10% and 20%?

2/ What is the present value at 10% of €100 received in 3 years, 5 years and 10 years? What are the discount factors?

3/ How much would €1000 be worth in 5 years, invested at 5%, 10% and 20%? Why is the sum invested at 20% not double that invested at 10%?

4/ How much would €1000 be worth in 5 years, 10 years and 20 years if invested at 8%? Why is the sum invested for 20 years not double that invested for 10 years?

5/ You are keen to obtain a helicopter pilot's licence. A club offers you lessons over two years, with a choice between the following payment terms:

- ○ you can either pay the full fees (€10 000) immediately with a 5% discount; or
- ○ you can make two equal annual payments, the first one due immediately.

At what interest rate would these two options work out at the same cost?

6/ What is the present value at 8% of €100 to be received in 3 years, 5 months and 17 days?

7/ How much would you have to invest today to have 100 in 8 years if the interest rate was 5%? What is the capitalisation factor?

8/ At 7%, would you rather have €100 today or €131.1 in 4 years' time? Why?

9/ Show that in order to double your money in one year, the interest rate would have to be around 75%/year.

10/ Show that in order to treble your money in N years, the interest rate would have to be around 125%/N.

11/ You are only prepared to forgo immediate spending if you get a 9% return on your investment. What would be the top price you would be prepared to pay for a security today that would pay you 121 in 2 years? If other investors were asking for 8%, what would happen?

12/ If instead of throwing his 30 pieces of silver away in 33 AD, Judas had invested them at 3% per annum, how much would his descendants get in 2010? Explain your views.

13/ You have the choice between buying a Francis Bacon painting for €100 000 which will be worth €125 000 in 4 years, and investing in government bonds at 6%. What would your choice be? Why?

14/ Given the level of risk, you require an 18% return on shares in Amazon.com. No dividends will be paid out for 5 years. What is the lowest price you could sell them at in 4 years' time, if you bought them for $14 a share today?

15/ Assume that a share in Zaleski has a market value of 897, with the following cash flow schedule:

Year	1	2	3	4	5
Cash flow	300	300	300	300	300

Calculate the NPV of the share at 5%, 10%, 20% and 25%. Plot your answers on a graph.

16/ What is the present value at 10% of a perpetual income of 100? And a perpetual income of 100 rising by 3% every year from the following year?

17/ What is the present value at 10% of €100 paid annually for 3 years? Same question for a perpetual income.

18/ An investment promises four annual payments of €52 over the next four years. You require an 8% return. How much would you be prepared to pay for this asset? The share is currently trading at €165. Would you be prepared to buy or to sell? Why? If you buy at that price, how much will you have gained? Will the rate of return on your investment be greater or less than 8%? Why? If you buy at €172, what will your return on this investment be? Why?

19/ Show that at 8% there is little difference between the value of a perpetual income and that of a security that offers a constant annual income equal to that of the perpetual income for only 40 years. Show that this will be even more correct if the rate of return is 15%.

20/ You have the opportunity to buy the right to park in a given parking place for 75 years, at a price of €300 000. You could also rent a parking place for €2000 a year, revised upwards by 2% every year. If the opportunity cost is 5%, which would you choose?

21/ You are the proud owner of the TV screening rights for the film *Singing in the Rain*. You sell the rights to screen the film on TV once every 2 years for €0.8m. What is the value of your asset? The film has just been screened. You make the assumption that screenings will be possible for 30 years or in perpetuity. The discount rate is 6%.

22/ You have found your dream house and you have the choice between renting it with a lease in perpetuity for €12 000 or buying it. At what purchase price would you be better off renting, if the loan you needed to buy the house costs you 7%, and the rent increases by 3% per year?

23/ Your current after-tax annual income is €50 000, which should increase by 4% per year until you retire. You believe that if you interrupt your professional career for 2 years to do an MBA, you could earn €65 000 after tax per year, with an annual increase of 5% until you retire. What is your present value if you retire in 40 years' time, and the discount rate is 4%? If the total cost of the MBA is €50 000 payable immediately, what is the net present value of this investment? Is it worth doing an MBA?

24/ Chile proposes a concession contract for the construction and operation of a motorway whereby the net present value at a rate of 10% is secured for the investor. The maturity of the concession depends on the time the investor takes to make up its NPV. Assume that the initial investment is 500 (year 0) and cash flows are 53 per year. What will the duration of the concession be? If cash flows drop to 51 per year, by how many years will the concession be extended?

Questions

1/ *So as to be able to compare a future value and a present value of a future inflow.*
2/ $1/(1 + t)^n$.
3/ *If the present values are equal, it makes no difference.*
4/ *One is the reverse of the other.*
5/ *Because interest rates are positive.*
6/ *Because interest rates are positive.*
7/ *Yes, because discounting is used to factor in an interest rate which remunerates the foregoing of immediate spending. Discounting is thus unrelated to inflation or risk.*
8/ *Because of capitalisation, which every year adds interest earned over the past year to the principal, and interest is earned on this interest in the future. This is called compound interest.*
9/ *The Google share price will have to rise more than that of Belgacom in order to make up for the lack of dividends. As stock options are options to buy shares at a fixed exercise price, their value will increase if the share price rises. So it would be better to have Google's stock options.*
10/ *To the difference between the present value and the market value of an asset.*
11/ *False, the opposite is true as the future is more depreciated.*
12/ *Arbitrage.*
13/ *Yes. The asset has been overvalued.*
14/ *To the required return on this asset.*
15/ *Negative, as we first invest to get positive cash flows in the future; positive.*
16/ *False, the opposite is true. NPV = 0 and PV > 0.*
17/ *Around 28%.*
18/ *No, because growth is not a process that can continue endlessly!*
19/ *No, unless you've made an error in your calculations of the cash flows or underestimated them.*
20/ *In industrial markets because arbitrage operations take longer to execute than in financial markets (building a factory takes longer than buying a share) and, therefore, disequilibrium is more frequent.*
21/ *The perpetuity for the rented building, the growing perpetuity for Belgacom, the value of an annuity for N years for the coupons of the bond.*

Exercises

A detailed Excel version of the solutions is available at www.vernimmen.com.

1/ $100/1.05^3 = €86.4$; $100/1.1^3 = €75.1$; $100/1.2^3 = €57.9$.
2/ *€75.1; €62.1; €38.6; 0.751; 0.621; 0.386.*
3/ *€1276, €1611, €2488. Because the principal (€1000) remains the same and interest more than doubles as a result of the process of compound interest.*
4/ *€1469, €2159 and €4661. Because the principal (€1000) remains the same and interest more than doubles as a result of the process of compound interest.*
5/ *11.1% per year.*
6/ *€76.6 as 3 years, 5 months and 17 days equals 3.463 years and $100/1.08^{3.463} = 76.6$.*
7/ *€67.7; €1.48.*
8/ *It makes absolutely no difference, because €100 capitalised at 7% a year would be worth €131.1 in 4 years.*
9/ *This is a good estimate. Over 5 years, a sum doubles at 14.87%, and 75%/5 = 15%.*
10/ *This is a good estimate. Over 5 years, a sum trebles at 24.57%, and 125%/5 = 25%.*
11/ *At 101.8 other investors are prepared to pay 103.7 and you cannot buy this security.*
12/ 7.18×10^{26} *pieces of silver (718 million billion billion pieces of silver!). Although mathematically possible, Judas's descendants would be unlikely to get anything at all, given the wars, revolutions, periods of inflation, state bankruptcies, etc. that have occurred since 33 AD!*

13/ €100 000 at 6% will be worth €126 248 in four years, which is more than €125 000, but if you're an art lover, it might be worth foregoing €1248 for the pleasure of admiring a Francis Bacon in the comfort of your own home for four years. There's more to life than money!

14/ $14 \times 1.18^4 = €27$.

15/ 402; 240; 109; 0; −90.

16/ 1000; 1429.

17/ €248.7; €1000.

18/ €172. Buy, because its present value is higher than its market value. €7. Greater than 8%, because at 8% it is worth €172, so if I buy at €165, I'll earn more. 8%.

19/ With income of 100, you get: 1250 and 1192, a difference of 5%. At 15%: 666.7 and 664.2, a difference of 0.4%. Barring other factors, income over a period exceeding 40 years no longer has a significant impact on present value.

20/ €2000 over 75 years growing at 2% would be worth €59 086, so it would be better to buy.

21/ €5.34m, €6.47m.

22/ €300 000.

23/ €1 923 077, €662 470, yes.

24/ 30 years, 11 years (41 years).

BIBLIOGRAPHY

The pioneering works on the net present value rule are:

I. Fisher, *The Theory of Interest*, Augustus M. Kelley Publishers, 1965. Reprinted from the 1930 edition.

J. Hirshleifer, On the theory of optimal investment decision, *Journal of Political Economy*, **66**(4), 329–352, August 1958.

F. Lutz, V. Lutz, *The Theory of the Investment of the Firm*, Princeton University Press, 1951.

J. Tobin, Liquidity preference as behaviour towards risk, *Review of Economic Studies*, **25**(1), 65–86, February 1958.

There are a number of financial calculation workbooks available which will help you get to grips with discounting calculations.

You could also consult:

E. Fama, M. Miller, *The Theory of Finance*, Holt, Rinehart and Winston, 1972.

SECTION 2

Chapter 17
THE INTERNAL RATE OF RETURN

A whimsical "nugget"

If net present value (NPV) is inversely proportional to the discounting rate, then there must exist a discounting rate that makes NPV equal to zero.

The discounting rate that makes net present value equal to zero is called the "internal rate of return (IRR)" or "yield to maturity".

To apply this concept to capital expenditure, simply replace "yield to maturity" by "IRR", as the two terms mean the same thing. It is just that one is applied to financial securities (yield to maturity) and the other to capital expenditure (IRR).

Section 17.1
HOW IS INTERNAL RATE OF RETURN DETERMINED?

To calculate IRR, make r the unknown and simply use the NPV formula again. The rate r is determined as follows:

$$NPV = 0, \text{or} \sum_{n=1}^{N} \frac{F_n}{(1+r)^n} = V_0$$

To use the same example from the previous chapter:

$$\frac{0.8}{(1+r)} + \frac{0.8}{(1+r)^2} + \ldots + \frac{0.8}{(1+r)^5} = 2$$

In other words, an investment's internal rate of return is the rate at which its market value is equal to the present value of the investment's future cash flows.

It is possible to use trial-and-error to determine IRR. This will result in an interest rate that gives a negative net present value and another that gives a positive net present value. These negative and positive values constitute a range of values which can be narrowed until the yield to maturity is found; in this case it is about 28.6%.

Obviously, this type of calculation is time consuming. It is much easier to just use a calculator or spreadsheet program with a function to determine the yield to maturity.

Section 17.2
INTERNAL RATE OF RETURN AS AN INVESTMENT CRITERION

The internal rate of return is frequently used in financial markets because it immediately tells the investor the return to be expected for a given level of risk. The investor can then compare this expected return to his required return rate, thereby simplifying the investment decision.

The decision-making rule is very simple: if an investment's internal rate of return is higher than the investor's required return, he will make the investment or buy the security. Otherwise, he will abandon the investment or sell the security.

In our example, since the internal rate of return (28.6%) is higher than the return demanded by the investor (20%), he should make the investment. If the market value of the same investment were 3 (and not 2), the internal rate of return would be 10.4%, and he should not invest.

An investment is worth making when its internal rate of return is equal to or greater than the investor's required return. An investment is not worth making when its internal rate of return is below the investor's required return.

Hence, at fair value, the internal rate of return is identical to the market return. In other words, net present value is nil.

Section 17.3
THE LIMITS OF THE INTERNAL RATE OF RETURN

With this new investment decision-making criterion, it is now necessary to consider how IRR can be used *vis-à-vis* net present value. It is also important to investigate whether or not these two criteria could somehow produce contradictory conclusions.

If it is a simple matter of whether or not to buy into a given investment, or whether or not to invest in a project, the two criteria produce exactly the same result, as shown in the example.

If the cash flow schedule is the same, then calculating the NPV by choosing the discounting rate and calculating the internal rate of return (and comparing it with the discounting rate) are two sides of the same mathematical coin.

1/ THE REINVESTMENT RATE AND THE MODIFIED IRR (MIRR)

Consider two investments A and B, with the following cash flows:

Year	1	2	3	4	5	6	7
Investment A	6	0.5					
Investment B	2	3	0	0	2.1	0	5.1

At a 5% discount rate, the present value of investment A is 6.17 and that of investment B 9.90. If investment A's market value is 5, its net present value is 1.17. If investment B's market value is 7.5, its net present value is 2.40.

Now calculate the IRR. It is 27.8% for investment *A* and 12.7% for investment *B*. Or, to sum up:

	NPV at 5%	IRR%
Investment *A*	1.17	27.8
Investment *B*	2.40	12.7

Investment *A* delivers a rate of return that is much higher than the required return (27.8% vs. 5%) during a short period of time. Investment *B*'s rate of return is much lower (12.7% vs. 27.8%), but is still higher than the 5% required return demanded and is delivered over a far longer period (seven years vs. two). Our NPV and internal rate of return models are telling us two different things. So should we buy investment *A* or investment *B*?

At first glance, investment *B* would appear to be the more attractive of the two. Its NPV is higher and it creates the most value: 2.40 vs. 1.17.

However, some might say that investment *A* is more attractive, as cash flows are received earlier than with investment *B* and therefore can be reinvested sooner in high-return projects. While that is theoretically possible, it is the strong (and optimistic) form of the theory because competition among investors and the mechanisms of arbitrage tend to move net present values towards zero. Net present values moving towards zero means that exceptional rates of return converge toward the required rate of return, thereby eliminating the possibility of long-lasting high-return projects.

Given the convergence of the exceptional rates toward required rates of return, it is more reasonable to suppose that cash flows from investment *A* will be reinvested at the required rate of return of 5%. The exceptional rate of 27.8% is unlikely to be recurrent. And this is exactly what happens if we adopt the NPV decision rule. The NPV in fact assumes that the reinvestment of interim cash flows is made at the required rate of return (k):

$$\left[\sum_{n=1}^{N} F_n \times \left(1+k\right)^{N-n}\right] \times \left(1+k\right)^{-N} - F_0 = \sum_{n=1}^{N} \frac{F_n}{\left(1+k\right)^n} - F_0$$

If we apply the same equation to the IRR, we observe that the reinvestment rate is simply the IRR again. However, in equilibrium, it is unreasonable to think that the company can continue to invest at the same rate of the (sometimes) exceptional IRR of a specific project. Instead it is much more reasonable to assume that, at best, the company can invest at the required rate of return.

However, a solution to the reinvestment rate problem of IRR is the **Modified IRR (MIRR)**.

MIRR is the rate of return that yields an NPV of zero when the initial outlay is compared with the terminal value of the project's net cash flows reinvested at the required rate of return.

Determining the MIRR requires two stages:

1. Calculate forward until the end of the project to determine the terminal value of the project by compounding all intermediate cash flows at the required rate of return.
2. Find the internal rate of return that equates the terminal value with the initial outlay.

So, by capitalising cash flow from investments A and B at the required rate of return (5%) up to period 7, we obtain from investment A in period 7: $6 \times 1.005^6 + 0.5 \times 1.05^5$, or 8.68. From investment B we obtain $2 \times 1.05^6 + 3 \times 1.05^5 + 2.1 \times 1.05^2 + 5.1$, or 13.9. The internal rate of return is 8.20% for investment A and 9.24% for investment B.

We have thus reconciled the NPV and internal rate of return models.

Some might say that it is not consistent to expect investment A to create more value than investment B, as only 5 has been invested in A vs. 7.5 for B. Even if we could buy an additional "half-share" of A, in order to equalise the purchase price, the NPV of our new investment in A would only be $1.17 \times 1.5 = 1.76$, which would still be less than investment B's NPV of 2.40. For the reasons discussed above, we are unlikely to find another investment with a return identical to that of investment A.

Instead, we should assume that the 2.5 in additional investment would produce the required rate of return (5%) for seven years. In this case, NPV would remain, by definition, at 1.17, whereas the internal rate of return of this investment would fall to 11%. NPV and the internal rate of return would once again lead us to conclude that investment B is the more attractive investment.

2/ MULTIPLE OR NO IRR

Consider the following investment:

Year	0	1	2
Cash flow	−1	7.2	−7.2

There are two annual rates of return! Which one should we choose? At 10%, the NPV of this investment is −0.40. So it is not worth realising, even though its internal rate of return is higher than the required rate of return.

The project has two IRRs, and we do not know which is the right one. There is no good reason to use one over the other. Investments with "unconventional" cash flow sequences are rare, but they can happen. Consider a firm that is cutting timber in a forest. The timber is cut, sold and the firm gets an immediate profit. But, when harvesting is complete, the firm may be forced to replant the forest at considerable expense.

Another example may be a strip-mining project, which normally requires a final investment to reclaim the land and satisfy the requirements of environmental legislation.

Consider now the following investment:

Year	0	1	2
Cash flow	3.2	−7.1	4.0

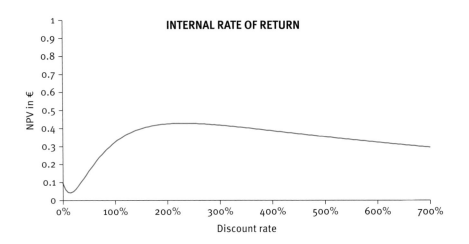

There is no internal rate of return that makes NPV zero! At 10%, the NPV of this investment is 0.05 and it is worth buying.

A project like this has no IRR. Thus, we have no benchmark for deciding if it is a good investment or not. Although the NPV remains positive for all the discount rates, it remains only *slightly* positive and the company may decide not to do it.

3/ INVESTING OR FINANCING?

Consider two projects with the following flows:

Project	F_0	F_1	IRR	NPV (15%)
A	−100	120	20%	€4.35
B	100	−120	20%	−€4.35

The flows are exactly the same but with opposite signs. The IRR of the two projects is the same (20%) but the NPV is positive for project A and negative for project B (both with a discount rate of 15%). According to the IRR rule, projects A and B have the same value; however, the NPV says that project A is preferable to project B.

Although an investment project with the cash flows of *B* may seem quite unusual, there are some situations where it is possible. For example, consider a business school conducting seminars and courses whereby the participants pay in advance. Large expenses (travelling expenses of external teachers, materials and salaries of teachers, etc.) are incurred at the seminar date or later on: thus cash inflows precede cash outflows.

Consider our trial-and-error method to calculate the IRR of project *B*:

F_0	F_1	k	NPV
100	−120	15%	−€4.35
100	−120	20%	€0.00
100	−120	30%	€7.69

The reader will surely have noticed that the net present value of project *B* is *negative* when the discount rate is below 20%. Conversely, the NPV is positive when the discount rate is above 20%.

The decision rule for this kind of project is exactly the opposite to the "traditional" IRR rule. In fact, you should **accept the project when the IRR is less than the discount rate and reject the project when the IRR is greater than the discount rate.**

Why has the rule ended up being inverted like this? The reason is clearly shown in the graph of the NPV profile of project *B*. The curve is upward sloping (similar to a loan), implying that NPV is *positively related* to the discount rate.

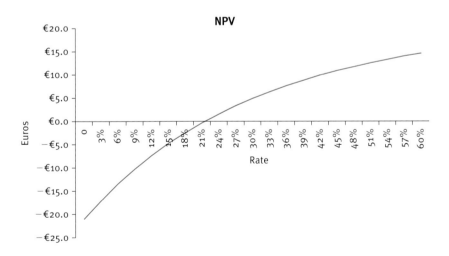

Intuitively, the "inverted IRR" rule makes sense. If the firm wants to obtain €100 immediately, it can either invest in project B or *borrow €100* from a bank, which will have to be repaid in the following period with an interest rate of 20%. Thus, the project is actually a substitute for borrowing.

4/ CHANGING DISCOUNT RATES

It is common to discount cash flows at a constant rate throughout a project's life. However, this may not be appropriate under certain circumstances. In fact, the required rate of return is a function of interest rates and of the uncertainty of cash flows, both of which can change substantially over time.

The necessity of using different discount rates can be overcome easily with the NPV criteria, whereby different discount rates can be set for each period. Conversely, the IRR method can only be compared with a single rate of return and cannot cope with changing discount rates.

5/ PROBLEMS SPECIFIC TO MUTUALLY EXCLUSIVE PROJECTS

Further problems may arise when a choice must be made among several investments (or securities), as is often the case in reality. Investments have different cash flow timetables that are all equally attractive. In this case, the investment decision is not about whether to invest or not, but rather it is about *which* investment to make. This situation refers to **mutually exclusive investments**. This occurs when there are two projects, A and B, and you can choose to accept A, accept B or reject both projects, *but it is impossible to accept both of them simultaneously.*

Why would a company decide to abandon one or more viable projects? Typically, the dilemma arises from **capital rationing** (the rationing can be imposed by market conditions or a management choice imposed on each division).

Mutually exclusive projects may give rise to two problems: the "scale problem" and the "timing problem", both of which will be examined next.

To understand the **scale problem**, consider two projects of different dimensions, one of which can be defined as a small-scale project, and the other as a large-scale project:

Project	F_0	F_1	IRR	NPV (10%)
Small-scale	−10	15	50%	€3.64
Large-scale	−100	120	20%	€9.09

The point of this example is that when considering two mutually exclusive investments, the financial manager typically concludes that the one offering the highest IRR is necessarily the one that should be chosen. If, in this case, we had to choose only one project, and we ranked them based on their IRRs, we would choose to invest in the small-scale project. However, the large-scale project generates a much higher NPV; this project thus creates more wealth for shareholders. The NPV tells us to undertake the large-scale project.

Why is there this conflict? The large-scale project is 10 times bigger than the small-scale project. Even though the latter provides a higher rate of return, the opportunity of making a much larger investment seems more attractive for shareholders.

For managers who prefer to use the IRR method, there is a solution to the scale problem. The approach is to calculate the IRR for an imaginary project with cash flows equal to the difference in cash flows between the large-scale and small-scale investments. This difference is defined as the *incremental project*.

The financial manager can use the incremental project's cash flows to determine the **incremental IRR**, i.e. the incremental return from choosing the large project instead of the small project:

	F_0	F_1	Incremental IRR	NPV (10%)
Incremental (large- to small-scale)	−90	105	17%	€5.45

If, as in this example, the incremental project's IRR is higher than the required rate of return, then the large-scale investment is better. If the inverse is true, then we should accept the small-scale project.

The logic of this approach works because both projects exceed the required rate of return. Therefore, this method is like equating the bigger-scale project to the sum of the small-scale project and the incremental project. Then it is possible to examine the incremental project's cash IRR, and if it also exceeds the required rate of return, we can accept the bigger project. If not, then we should opt for the small-scale project.

Why is this? If we accept the large-scale investment we are, in fact, making two investments, not just one. We are accepting one project with cash flows identical to those of the small-scale project and another with cash flows equal to those of the incremental project. Since both projects (small-scale and incremental) exceed the required rate of return, we may conclude that we are happy to undertake the incremental project *and* the small-scale project. The only way to do both is to accept the large-scale project.

The same decision obtained by comparing the incremental IRR with the required rate of return could also be obtained by:

- simply comparing the NPV of the two projects. The large-scale project has a higher NPV and is the preferred project according to the NPV rule; and
- estimating the incremental NPV. If it is positive, then the large-scale project is preferable. Vice versa, the smaller project is more attractive if the incremental NPV is negative.

In order to understand the **timing problem**, consider two projects with the same initial amount (ergo, no problem of scale). Project A is a marketing campaign that could push the sales of existing products. The cash inflows are immediate but disappear progressively. This can be defined as the "short-sighted" project. Project B is a new product development with big positive cash inflows expected at the end of the development process. This will be defined as the "far-sighted" project:

	0	1	2	3	IRR
Project A (Marketing campaign)	−10 000	8000	3000	1000	14%
Project B (New product development)	−10 000	0	2000	11 500	11%

According to the IRR method, project *A* is more attractive because it has a higher IRR (14% vs. 11%). The NPV profile of the two alternatives is:

THE NPV PROFILE

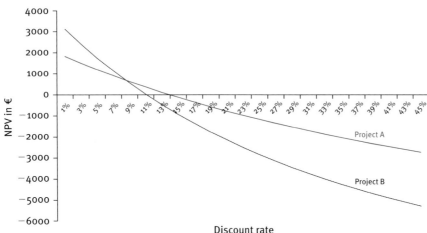

In the graph above, it can be seen that the NPV of project *B* is higher if the discount rate is low, say below 8%. When the discount rate is low, *B* has the higher NPV; when the discount rate is high, *A* has the higher NPV. If the discount rate is above 8% then the NPV of project *A* exceeds that of project *B*. The NPV of project *B* declines more rapidly than the NPV of project *A*. This occurs because the cash flows of *B* occur later.

In order to determine which project is more attractive, a comparison should be made between the NPVs of the two projects. The decision will then be a function of the discount rate.[1]

A naïve reliance on the IRR method can lead to decisions that favour investments with short-term payoffs. Perhaps this is one of the reasons behind the frequent criticism regarding managers of public corporations and their supposed "short-termism".

1 Alternatively, we could subtract the cash flows of A from the cash flows of B, and then calculate the incremental IRR: if the discount rate is lower than the incremental IRR we should accept project B.

Section 17.4
SOME MORE FINANCIAL MATHEMATICS:
INTEREST RATE AND YIELD TO MATURITY

1/ NOMINAL RATE OF RETURN AND YIELD TO MATURITY

Having considered the yield to maturity, it is now important to examine interest rates; for example, on a loan that you wish to take out. Where does the interest rate fit in this discussion?

Consider someone who wants to lend you €1000 today at 10% for five years. 10% means 10 per cent **per year** and constitutes the **nominal rate of return** of your loan. This rate will be the basis for calculating interest, proportional to the time elapsed and the amount borrowed. Assume that you will pay interest annually.

The first problem is how and when will you pay off the loan?

Repayment terms constitute the method of amortisation of the loan. Take the following example:

(a) Bullet repayment

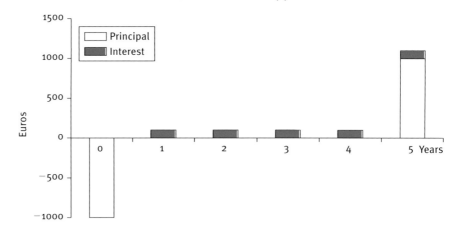

The entire loan is paid back at maturity.

The cash flow table would look like this:

Period	Principal still due	Interest	Amortisation of principal	Annuity
1	1000	100	0	100
2	1000	100	0	100
3	1000	100	0	100
4	1000	100	0	100
5	1000	100	1000	1100

Total debt service is the annual sum of interest and principal to be paid back. This is also called debt servicing at each due date.

(b) Constant amortisation

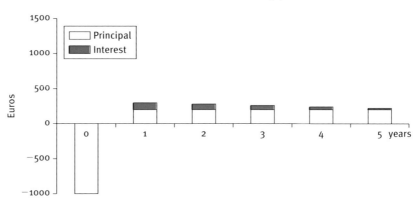

Each year, the borrower pays off a constant proportion of the principal, corresponding to $1/n$, where n is the initial maturity of the loan.

The cash flow table would look like this:

Period	Principal still due	Interest	Amortisation of principal	Annuity
1	1000	100	200	300
2	800	80	200	280
3	600	60	200	260
4	400	40	200	240
5	200	20	200	220

(c) Equal instalments

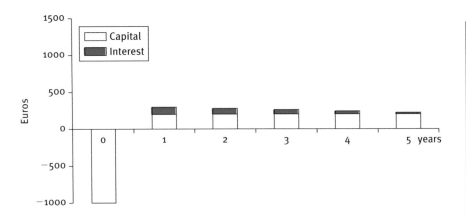

EQUAL INSTALMENTS (C)

The borrower may wish to pay off his loan by constant annuities, i.e. allocate a constant sum to interest and amortisation payments.

In the above cases, the borrower paid off either a constant sum in interest or a declining sum in interest. The principal was paid off in equal instalments.

Based on the discounting method described previously, consider a constant annuity A, such that the sum of the five discounted annuities is equal to the present value of the principal, or €1000:

$$1000 = \frac{A}{1.10} + \frac{A}{(1.10)^2} + \ldots + \frac{A}{(1.10)^5}$$

This means that **the NPV of the 10% loan is nil; in other words, the 10% nominal rate of interest is also the internal rate of return of the loan.**

Using the formula from Chapter 16, the previous formula can be expressed as follows:

$$1000 = \frac{A}{0.10} \times \left(1 - \frac{1}{(1.10)^5}\right)$$

$A = €263.80$. Hence, the following repayment schedule:

Period	Principal still due	Interest	Amortisation of principal	Annuity
1	1000	100	163.80	263.80
2	836.20	83.62	180.18	263.80
3	656.02	65.60	198.20	263.80
4	457.82	45.78	218.02	263.80
5	239.80	23.98	239.80	263.80

In this case, the interest for each period is indeed equivalent to 10% of the remaining principal (i.e. the nominal rate of return) and the loan is fully paid off in the fifth year. Internal rate of return and nominal rate of interest are identical, as calculation is on an annual basis and the repayment of principal coincides with the payment of interest.

Regardless of which side of the loan you are on, both work the same way. We start with invested (or borrowed) capital, which produces income (or incurs interest costs) at the end of each period. Eventually, the loan is then either paid back (leading to a decline in future revenues or in interest to be paid) or held on to, thus producing a constant flow of income (or a constant cost of interest).

(d) Interest and principal both paid when the loan matures

In this case, the borrower pays nothing until the loan matures.

The sum that the borrower will have to pay at maturity is none other than the future value of the sum borrowed, capitalised at the interest rate of the loan.

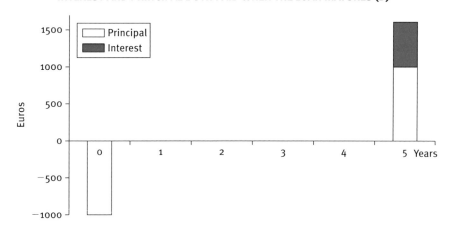

INTEREST AND PRINCIPAL BOTH PAID WHEN THE LOAN MATURES (D)

$$V = 1000 \times (1 + 10\%)^5 \text{ or } V = 1610.5$$

This is how the repayment schedule would look:

Period	Principal and interest still due	Amortisation of principal	Interest payments	Annuity
1	1100	0	0	0
2	1210	0	0	0
3	1331	0	0	0
4	1464.1	0	0	0
5	1610.51	1000	610.51	1610.51

This is a zero-coupon loan.

2/ EFFECTIVE ANNUAL RATE, NOMINAL RATES AND PROPORTIONAL RATES

This section will demonstrate that discounting has a much wider scope than might have appeared to be the case in the simple financial mathematics presented previously.

(a) The concept of effective annual rate

What happens when interest is paid not once but several times per year?

Suppose that somebody lends you money at 10% but says (somewhere in the fine print at the bottom of the page) that interest will have to be paid on a half-yearly basis. For example, suppose you borrowed €100 on 1 January and then had to pay €5 in interest on 1 July and €5 on 1 January of the following year, as well as the €100 in principal at the same date.

This is not the same as borrowing €100 and repaying €110 one year later. The nominal amount of interest may be the same (5+ 5 = 10), but the repayment schedule is not. In the first case, you will have to pay €5 on 1 July (just before leaving on summer holidays), which you could have kept until the following 1 January if using the second case. In the first case you pay €5, instead of investing it for six months as you could have done in the second.

As a result, the loan in the first case costs more than a loan at 10% with interest due annually. Its effective rate is not 10%, since interest is not being paid on the benchmark annual terms.

To avoid comparing apples and oranges, a financial officer must take into account the effective date of disbursement. We know that one euro today is not the same as one euro tomorrow. Obviously, the financial officer wants to postpone expenditure and accelerate receipts, thereby having the money work for him. So, naturally the repayment schedule matters when calculating the rate.

Which is the best approach to take? If the interest rate is 10%, with interest payable every six months, then the interest rate is 5% **for six months**. We then have to calculate **an effective annual rate** (and not for six months), which is our point of reference and our constant concern.

In our example, the lender receives €5 on 1 July which, compounded over six months, becomes 5 + (10% × 5) / 2 = €5.25 on the following 1 January, the date on which he receives the second €5 interest payment. So over one year, he will have received €10.25 in interest on a €100 investment.

Therefore, the effective annual rate is 10.25%. This is the real cost of the loan, since the return for the lender is equal to the cost for the borrower.

SECTION 2

If the nominal rate (r_a) is to be paid n times per year, then the effective annual rate (t) is obtained by compounding this nominal rate n times:

$$(1 + t) = (1 + r_a/n)^n$$

Formula for converting nominal rate into effective annual rate.

where n is the number of interest payments in the year and r_a/n the proportional rate during one period, or $t = (1 + r_a / n)^n - 1$.

In our example:

$$t = (1 + 10\% / 2)^2 - 1 = 10.25\%.$$

The effective interest rate is thus 10.25%, while the nominal rate is 10%.

It should be common sense that an investment at 10% paying interest every six months produces a higher return at year end than an investment paying interest annually. In the first case, interest is compounded after six months and thus produces interest on interest for the next six months. Obviously a loan on which interest is due every six months will cost more than one on which interest is charged annually.

It is essential to first calculate the effective annual rate before comparing investments (or loans) with different cash flow streams. The effective annual rate measures returns on the common basis of a year, thus making meaningful comparisons possible. This is not possible with nominal rates.

The table below gives the returns produced by an investment (a loan) at 10% with varying instalment frequencies:

Interest compounding period	Initial sum	Sum after one year	Effective annual rate (%)
Annual	100	110.000	10.000
Half-year	100	110.250	10.250
Quarterly	100	110.381	10.381
Monthly	100	110.471	10.471
Bimonthly	100	110.494	10.494
Weekly	100	110.506	10.506
Daily	100	110.516	10.516
Continuous[2]	100	110.517	10.517

2 The formula for continuously compounded interest is: $t = e^k - 1$. where e stands for 2.71828 and k is an interest rate, 10% in our example.

The effective annual rate can be calculated on any time scale. For example, a financial officer might wish to use continuous rates. This might mean, for example, a 10% rate producing €100, paid out evenly throughout the year on principal of €1000. The financial officer will use the annual equivalent rate as his reference rate for this investment

(b) The concept of proportional rate

In our example of a loan at 10%, we would say that the 5% rate over six months is **proportional** to the 10% rate over one year. More generally, two rates are proportional if they are in the same proportion to each other as the periods to which they apply.

10% per year is proportional to 5% per half-year or 2.5% per quarter, but 5% half-yearly is not equivalent to 10% annually. **Effective annual rate and proportional rates are therefore two completely different concepts that should not be confused.**

Proportional rates are of interest only when calculating the interest actually paid. In no way can they be evaluated with other proportional rates, as they are not comparable.

Proportional rates serve only to simplify calculations, but they hide the true cost of a loan. Only the effective annual rate (10.25%/year) gives the true cost, unlike the proportional rate (10%/year).

When the time span between two interest payment dates is less than one year, the proportional rate is lower than the effective annual rate (10% is less than 10.25%).

To avoid error, use the effective annual rate.

As we will see, the bond markets can be misleading since they reason in terms of nominal rate of return: paper is sold above or below par value, the number of days used in calculating interest can vary, there could be original issue discounts, and so on. And, most importantly, on the secondary market, a bond's present value depends on fluctuations in market interest rates.

In the rest of this book, unless otherwise specified, an interest rate or rate of return is assumed to be an effective annual rate.

SUMMARY

The summary of this chapter can be downloaded from www.vernimmen.com.

In this chapter we learned about the theoretical foundations of interest rates, which force financial managers to discount cash flows; i.e. to depreciate the flows in order to factor in the passage of time.

This led us to a definition of present value, the basic tool for valuing a financial investment, which must be compared to its market value. The difference between present value and the market value of an investment is net present value.

In a market in equilibrium, the net present value of a financial investment is nil because it is equal to its present value.

As the value of an investment and the discount rate are fundamentally linked, we also looked at the concept of yield to maturity (which cancels out NPV). Making an investment is only worth it when the yield to maturity is equal to or greater than the investor's required return. At fair value, internal rate of return is identical to the required return rate. In other words, net present value is nil.

The internal rate of return should be handled with care, as it is based on the implicit assumption that cash flows will be reinvested at the same rate. It should only be relied on for an investment decision concerning a single asset and not for choosing from among several assets, whether they are financial (e.g. an investment) or industrial (e.g. a mine, a machine, etc.). NPV should be used for such decisions.

Finally, some financial mathematics helped us look at the link between the nominal interest rate and the yield to maturity of an operation. The nominal (annual) rate of a loan is the rate used to calculate interest in proportion to the period of the loan and the capital borrowed. However, one must use the yield to maturity, which may differ from the apparent nominal rate, when interest is not paid on an annual basis.

QUESTIONS

1/ Why can't the internal rate of return be used for choosing between two investments?

2/ Does the interest rate depend on the terms of repayment of a loan or an investment?

3/ Does the interest rate depend on when cash flows occur?

4/ What are proportional rates?

5/ What is the internal rate of return?

6/ What are proportional rates used for? And the internal rate of return?

7/ On the same loan, is the total amount of interest payable more if the loan is repaid in fixed annual instalments, by constant amortisation or on maturity?

8/ If you believe that interest rates are going to rise, would you be better off choosing loans that are repayable on maturity or in fixed annual instalments?

9/ If the purchase price of an investment is positive and all subsequent cash flows are positive, show how there can only be a single yield to maturity.

10/ Is it better to make a small percentage on a very large amount or a large percentage on a small amount? Does this bring to mind one of the rules explained in this chapter?

11/ A very high yield to maturity over a very short period is preferable to a yield to maturity that is 2% higher than the required rate of return over 10 years. True or false?

More questions are waiting for you at www.vernimmen.com.

EXERCISES

1/ What interest rate on an investment would turn 120 into 172.8 over two years? What is the yield to maturity? What is the proportional rate over three months?

2/ What is the terminal value on an initial investment of 100 if the investor is seeking a 14% yield to maturity after 7 years?

3/ For how many years will 100 have to be invested to get 174.9 and a yield to maturity of 15%?

4/ You invest €1000 today at 6% with interest paid on a half-yearly basis for 4 years. What is the yield to maturity of this investment? How much will you have at the end of the 4-year period?

5/ Investment A can be bought for 4 and will earn 1 per year over 6 years. What is the yield to maturity? Investment B costs 6 and earns 2 over 2 years, then 1.5 over 3 years.

What is the yield to maturity? Which investment would you rather have? Why? Do you need to know what the minimum required rate of return is in order to make a decision?

6/ A company treasurer invests 100 for 18 months. The first bank he approaches offers to reinvest the funds at 0.8% per quarter, and the second bank at 1.6% per half-year. Without actually doing the calculation, show how the first bank's offer would be the best option. What are the two yields to maturity?

7/ A company treasurer invests €10 000 000 on the money market for 24 days. He gets back €10 019 745. What is the rate of return over 24 days? What is the yield to maturity?

8/ Draw up a repayment schedule for a loan of 100, with a yield to maturity of 7% over 4 years, showing repayment in fixed annual instalments and constant amortisation.

9/ Draw up a repayment schedule for a loan of 400, with a yield to maturity of 6.5% over 7 years with repayment deferred for 2 years, showing repayment in fixed annual instalments and constant amortisation.

10/ A bond issued at 98% of the nominal value is repaid at maturity at 108% after 10 years. Annual interest paid to subscribers is 7% of the nominal value. What is the yield to maturity of this bond? And what if it had been issued at 101%? So what is the rule?

11/ What is the discounted cost for the issuer of the bond described in question 10 if we factor in a 0.35% placement commission, an annual management fee of 2.5% of the coupon, a closing fee of 0.6% of the amount paid and an issue price of 98%?

12/ You sell your flat, valued at €300 000 for a down payment of €100 000 and 20 monthly payments of €11 000. What is the monthly interest rate for this transaction? What is the yield to maturity?

13/ Calculate the yield to maturity of the following investment, which can be purchased today for 1000:

Year	1	2	3	4	5
Cash flow	232	2088	232	−232	−927

Questions

1/ *Because it does not measure the value created.*
2/ *No, as it is applied at any moment to the remaining capital due.*
3/ *Yes, if cash flows are postponed in time, interest rate decreases.*
4/ *Rates that have a proportional relationship with the periods to which they relate.*
5/ *Rates that apply to different periods, but which transform the same sum in an identical manner over the same period.*
6/ *For calculating the interest that is paid out/earned. For calculating the yield to maturity.*
7/ *On maturity, because the principal is lent in full over the whole period.*
8/ *On maturity, so that you can take advantage for as long as possible of a low interest rate on the maximum amount of principal outstanding.*
9/ *At a discount rate equal to the yield to maturity, the present value of future cash flows is equal to the purchase price of the investment. If the discount rate increases, present value will drop and will never again be equal to the market price of the investment. If the discount rate decreases, present value will rise and will never again be equal to the market price of the investment. Accordingly, there is only a single yield to maturity.*
10/ *A small percentage on a very large amount. NPV is preferable to yield to maturity.*
11/ *False, because an investment with an acceptable yield to maturity over a long period creates more value than an investment with a very high yield to maturity but which is of little significance given the short period of the investment.*

Exercises

A detailed Excel version of the solutions is available at www.vernimmen.com.

1/ *44% over 2 years. 20%. 5% over 3 months.*

2/ *250.*

3/ *4 years.*

4/ *6.09%, €1266.7*

5/ *13%, 13.8%, a choice between these two securities cannot be based on yield to maturity. Only NPV can be relied on. Yes, you have to know what the required rate of return is.*

6/ *As the rates are proportional (0.8% over 3 months and 1.6% over 6 months), the first offer is better, since interest is capitalised after 3 months and not 6. 3.24% and 3.23%*

7/ *0.1975% over 24 days, 3.05%.*

8/ *Fixed annual instalments of 29.52, constant amortisation of 25/year and interest of 7, 5.25, 3.5 and 1.75.*

9/ *Fixed annual instalments of 109.2, constant amortisation of 90.74/year and interest of 29.5, 23.6, 17.7, 11.8 and 5.9.*

10/ *7.85% (don't forget interest for year 10), 7.42%, value and rates vary in opposite directions.*

11/ *8.12%.*

12/ *0.925%, 11.7%.*

13/ *There are 2: −15.1% and 48.3%*

BIBLIOGRAPHY

If you wish to learn more about internal rate of return and financial mathematics, you can consult:

Harvard Business School, *Net Present Value and Internal Rate of Return: Accounting for Time*, Harvard Business School Press, 2009.

E. Pilotte, Evaluating mutually exclusive projects of unequal lives and differing risks, *Financial Practice and Education*, **10**(2), 101–105, Fall/Winter 2000.

On capital rationing:

T. Mukherjee, H. Kent Baker, R. D'Mello, Capital rationing decisions of 'Fortune 500' firms – Part II, *Financial Practice and Education*, **10**(2), 69–77, Fall/Winter 2000.

H.M. Weingartner, Capital rationing: *n* authors in search of a plot, *Journal of Finance*, **32**(5), 1403–1432, December 1977.

Part Two
The risk of securities and the
required rate of return

After having covered the basics of finance (discounting, capitalisation, value and interest rates), it is time to delve deeper into another fundamental concept: risk. Risk is the uncertainty over future asset values and future returns. For better or for worse, without risk, finance would be quite boring!

Risk means uncertainty today over the cash flows and value of an asset tomorrow. Of course, it is possible to review all the factors that could have a negative or positive impact on an asset, quantify each one and measure the total impact on the asset's value. In reality, it is infinitely more practical to boil all the risks down to a single figure.

Chapter 18
RISK AND RETURN

The spice of finance

Investors who buy financial securities face risks because they do not know with certainty the future selling price of their securities, nor the cash flows they will receive in the meantime. This chapter will try to understand and measure this risk, and also examine its repercussions.

Section 18.1
SOURCES OF RISK

There are various risks involved in financial securities, including:

- **Industrial, commercial and labour risks, etc.**

  There are so many types of risk in this category that we cannot list them all here. They include: lack of competitiveness, emergence of new competitors, technological breakthroughs, an inadequate sales network, strikes and so on. These risks tend to lower cash flow expectations and thus have an immediate impact on the value of the stock.

- **Liquidity risk**

  This is the risk of not being able to sell a security at its fair value, as a result either of a liquidity discount or the complete absence of a market or buyers.

- **Solvency risk**

  This is the risk that a creditor will lose his entire investment if a debtor cannot repay him in full, even if the debtor's assets are liquidated. Traders call this **counterparty risk**.

- **Currency risk**

  Fluctuations in exchange rates can lead to a loss of value of assets denominated in foreign currencies. Similarly, higher exchange rates can increase the value of debt denominated in foreign currencies when translated into the company's reporting currency base.

- **Interest rate risk**

  The holder of financial securities is exposed to the risk of interest rate fluctuations. Even if the issuer fulfils his commitments entirely, there is still the risk of a capital loss or, at the very least, an opportunity loss.

- **Political risk**

    This includes risks created by a particular political situation or decisions by political authorities, such as nationalisation without sufficient compensation, revolution, exclusion from certain markets, discriminatory tax policies, inability to repatriate capital, etc.

- **Regulatory risk**

    A change in the law or in regulations can directly affect the return expected in a particular sector. Pharmaceuticals, banks and insurance companies, among others, tend to be on the front lines here.

- **Inflation risk**

    This is the risk that the investor will recover his investment with a depreciated currency, i.e. that he will receive a return below the inflation rate. A flagrant historical example is the hyperinflation in Germany in the 1920s.

- **The risk of a fraud**

    This is the risk that some parties to an investment will lie or cheat, i.e. by exploiting asymmetries of information in order to gain unfair advantage over other investors. The most common example is insider trading.

- **Natural disaster risks**

    These include storms, earthquakes, volcanic eruptions, cyclones, tidal waves, etc. which destroy assets.

- **Economic risk**

    This type of risk is characterised by bull or bear markets, anticipation of an acceleration or a slowdown in business activity or changes in labour productivity.

The list is nearly endless; however, at this point it is important to highlight two points:

- most financial analysis mentioned and developed in this book tends to generalise the concept of risk rather than analysing it in depth. So, given the extent to which markets are efficient and evaluate risk correctly, it is not necessary to redo what others have already done; and
- risk is always present. The so-called risk-free rate, to be discussed later, is simply a manner of speaking. **Risk is always present, and to say that risk can be eliminated is either to be excessively confident or be unable to think about the future – both very serious faults for an investor.**

Obviously, any serious investment study should begin with a precise analysis of the risks involved.

The knowledge gleaned from analysts with extensive experience in the business, mixed with common sense, allow us to classify risks into two categories:

- economic risks (political, natural, inflation, swindle and other risks), which threaten cash flows from investments and which come from the "real economy"; and
- financial risks (liquidity, currency, interest rate and other risks), which do not directly affect cash flow, but nonetheless do come into the financial sphere. These risks are due to external financial events, and not to the nature of the issuer.

Section 18.2
RISK AND FLUCTUATION IN THE VALUE OF A SECURITY

All of the aforementioned risks can penalise the financial performances of companies and their future cash flows. Obviously, if a risk materialises that seriously hurts company cash flows, investors will seek to sell their securities. Consequently the value of the security falls.

Moreover, if a company is exposed to significant risk, some investors will be reluctant to buy its securities. Even before risk materialises, investors' perceptions that a company's future cash flows are uncertain or volatile will serve to reduce the value of its securities.

Most modern finance is based on the premise that investors seek to reduce the uncertainty of their future cash flows. By its very nature, risk increases the uncertainty of an asset's future cash flow, and it therefore follows that such uncertainty will be priced into the market value of a security.

Investors consider risk only to the extent that it affects the value of the security. Risks can affect value by changing anticipations of cash flows or the rate at which these cash flows are discounted.

To begin with, it is important to realise that in corporate finance no fundamental distinction is made between the risk of asset revaluation and the risk of asset devaluation. That is to say, whether investors expect the value of an asset to rise or decrease is immaterial. It is the fact that risk exists in the first place that is of significance and affects how investors behave.

All risks, regardless of their nature, lead to fluctuations in the value of a financial security.

Consider, for example, a security with the following cash flows expected for years 1 to 4:

Year	1	2	3	4
Cash flow (in €)	100	120	150	190

Imagine the value of this security is estimated to be €2000 in 5 years. Assuming a 9% discounting rate, its value today would be:

$$\frac{100}{1.09} + \frac{120}{1.09^2} + \frac{150}{1.09^3} + \frac{190}{1.09^4} + \frac{2000}{1.09^5} = €1743$$

If a sudden sharp rise in interest rates raises the discounting rate to 13%, the value of the security becomes:

$$\frac{100}{1.13} + \frac{120}{1.13^2} + \frac{150}{1.13^3} + \frac{190}{1.13^4} + \frac{2000}{1.13^5} = €1488$$

The security's value has fallen by 15%. However, if the company comes out with a new product that raises projected cash flow by 20%, with no further change in the discounting rate, the security's value then becomes:

$$\frac{100 \times 1.20}{1.13} + \frac{120 \times 1.20}{1.13^2} + \frac{150 \times 1.20}{1.13^3} + \frac{190 \times 1.20}{1.13^4} + \frac{2000 \times 1.20}{1.13^5} = €1786$$

SECTION 2

The security's value increases for reasons specific to the company, not because of a rise of interest rates in the market.

Now, suppose that there is an improvement in the overall economic outlook that lowers the discounting rate to 10%. If there is no change in expected cash flows, the stock's value would be:

$$\frac{120}{1.10} + \frac{144}{1.10^2} + \frac{180}{1.10^3} + \frac{228}{1.10^4} + \frac{2400}{1.10^5} = €2009$$

Again, there has been no change in the stock's intrinsic characteristics and yet its value has risen by 12%.

If there is stiff price competition, then previous cash flow projections will have to be adjusted downward by 10%. If all cash flows fall by the same percentage and the discounting rate remains constant, the value of the company becomes:

$$2009 \times (1-10\%) = €1808$$

Once again, the security's value increases for reasons specific to the company, not because of a rise in the market.

In the previous example, a European investor would have lost 10% of his investment (from €2009 to €1808). If, in the interim, the euro had risen from $1.30 to $1.55, a US investor would have gained 7% (from $2612 to $2802).

A closer analysis shows that some securities are more volatile than others, i.e. their price fluctuates more widely. We say that these stocks are "riskier". **The riskier a stock is, the more volatile its price, and vice versa.** Conversely, the less risky a security is, the less volatile its price, and vice versa.

In a market economy, a security's risk is measured in terms of the volatility of its price (or of its rate of return). The greater the volatility, the greater the risk, and vice versa.

Volatility can be measured mathematically by **variance** and **standard deviation**.

RETURNS OF SOME FINANCIAL ASSETS SINCE 2000

Price trends of some financial assets since 1996 showing very different levels of volatility!

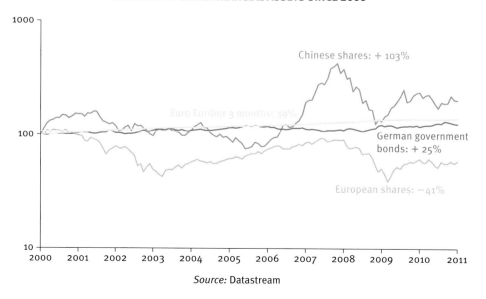

Source: Datastream

Typically, it is safe to assume that risk dissipates over the long term. The erratic fluctuations in the short term give way to the clear outperformance of equities over bonds, and bonds over money-market investments. The chart below tends to back up this point of view. It presents data on the **path of wealth** (POW) for the three asset classes. The POW measures the growth of 1€ invested in any given asset, assuming that all proceeds are reinvested in the same asset.

NOMINAL RETURNS IN UK SINCE 1900

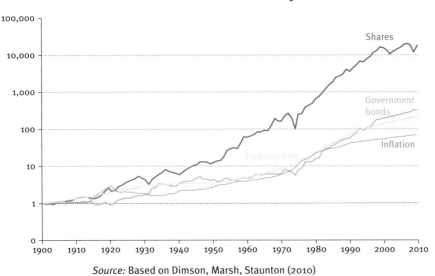

Source: Based on Dimson, Marsh, Staunton (2010)

Since 1900, UK stocks have grown by a factor of 286.9, hence an average annual return of 5.3% vs. 1.3% for bonds, 1.0% for money-market funds adjusted for inflation.

SECTION 2

As is easily seen from the chart, risk does dissipate, but only over the long term. In other words, an investor must be able to invest his funds and then do without them during this long-term timeframe. It sometimes requires strong nerves not to give in to the temptation to sell when prices collapse, as happened with stock markets in 1929, 1974, September 2001 and October–November 2008.

Since 1900, UK stocks have delivered an average annual return after inflation of 5.3%. Yet, during 38 of those years the returns were negative, in particular in 1974, when investors lost 57% on a representative portfolio of UK stocks.

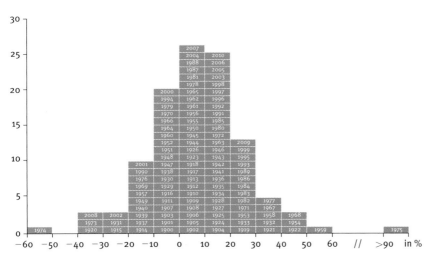

Source: Based on Dimson, Marsh and Staunton (2011)

If you are statistically inclined, you will recognise the "Gaussian" or "normal" distribution in this chart, showing the random walk of share prices underlying the theory of efficient markets. Nevertheless, extreme variations are more frequent than in a normal distribution law which questions the relevancy of this theory.

And in worst case scenarios, it must not be overlooked that some financial markets vanished entirely, including the Russian equity market after the First World War and 1917 revolution, the German bond market with the hyperinflation of 1921–23, and the Japanese and German equity markets in 1945. Over the stretch of one century, these may be exceptional events, but they have enormous repercussions when they do occur.

The degree of risk depends on the investment timeframe and tends to diminish over the long term. Yet rarely do investors have the means and stamina to think only of the long term and ignore short- to medium-term needs. Investors are only human, and there is definitely risk in the short and medium terms!

Section 18.3
Tools for measuring return and risk

1/ Expected return

To begin, it must be realised that a security's rate of return and the value of a financial security are actually two sides of the same coin. The rate of return will be considered first.

The holding-period return is calculated from the sum total of cash flows for a given investment, i.e. income, in the form of interest or dividends earned on the funds invested and the resulting capital gain or loss when the security is sold.

If just one period is examined, the return on a financial security can be expressed as follows:

$$F_1 / V_0 + (V_1 - V_0) / V_0 = \text{Income} + \text{Capital gain or loss}$$

Here F_1 is the income received by the investor during the period, V_0 is the value of the security at the beginning of the period and V_1 is the value of the security at the end of the period.

In an uncertain world, investors cannot calculate their returns in advance, as the value of the security is unknown at the end of the period. In some cases, the same is true for the income to be received during the period.

Therefore, investors use the concept of **expected return**, which is the average of possible returns weighted by their likelihood of occurring. Familiarity with the science of statistics should aid in understanding the notion of expected outcome.

Given security A with 12 chances out of 100 of showing a return of -22%, 74 chances out of 100 of showing a return of 6% and 14 chances out of 100 of showing a return of 16%, its expected return would then be:

$$-22\% \times \frac{12}{100} + 6\% \times \frac{74}{100} + 16\% \times \frac{14}{100}, \text{ or about } 4\%$$

More generally, expected return or expected outcome is equal to:

Expected return formula $E(r) = \sum_{t=1}^{n} r_t \times p_t = \bar{r}$

where r_t is a possible return and p_t the probability of it occurring.

2/ Variance, a risk-analysis tool

Intuitively, the greater the risk on an investment, the wider the variations in its return, and the more uncertain that return is. While the holder of a government bond is sure to receive his coupons (unless the government goes bankrupt!), this is far from true for the shareholder of an offshore oil drilling company. He could lose everything, show a decent return or hit the jackpot.

Therefore, the risk carried by a security can be looked at in terms of the dispersion of its possible returns around an average return. Consequently, risk can be measured mathematically by the variance of its return, i.e. by the sum of the squares of the deviation of each return from expected outcome, weighted by the likelihood of each of the possible returns occurring, or:

Risk formula $V(r) = \sum_{t=1}^{n} p_t \times (r_t - \bar{r})^2$

Standard deviation in returns is the most often used measure to evaluate the risk of an investment. Standard deviation is expressed as the square root of the variance:

$$\sigma(r) = \sqrt{V(r)}$$

The variance of investment A above is therefore:

$$\frac{12}{100} \times (-22\% - 4\%)^2 + \frac{74}{100} \times (6\% - 4\%)^2 + \frac{14}{100} \times (16\% - 4\%)^2$$

where $V(r) = 1\%$, which corresponds to a standard deviation of 10%.

In sum, to formalise the concepts of risk and return:

- expected outcome $E(r)$, is a measure of expected return; and
- standard deviation $\sigma(r)$ measures the average dispersion of returns around expected outcome, in other words, risk.

SECTION 2

Section 18.4
MARKET AND SPECIFIC RISK

Fluctuations in the value of a security can be due to:

* fluctuations in the entire market. The market could rise as a whole after an unexpected cut in interest rates, stronger than expected economic growth figures, etc. All stocks will then rise, although some will move more than others (see the figure below). The same thing can occur when the entire market moves downward; or
* factors specific to the company that do not affect the market as a whole, such as a major order, the bankruptcy of a competitor, a new regulation affecting the company's products, etc.

These two sources of fluctuation produce two types of risk: market risk and specific risk.

* **Market, systematic or undiversifiable risk** is due to trends in the entire economy, tax policy, interest rates, inflation, etc., and affects all securities. Remember, this is **the risk of the security correlated to market risk**. To varying degrees, market risk affects all securities. For example, if a nation switches to a 35-hour working week with no cut in wages, all companies will be affected. However, in such a case, it stands to reason that textile makers will be affected more than cement companies.
* **Specific, intrinsic or idiosyncratic risk** is independent of market-wide phenomena and is due to factors affecting just the one company, such as mismanagement, a factory fire, an invention that renders a company's main product line obsolete, etc. (In the next chapter, it will be shown how this risk can be eliminated by diversification.)

Market volatility can be economic or financial in origin, but it can also result from anticipation of flows (dividends, capital gains, etc.) or a variation in the cost of equity. For example, an overheating of the economy could raise the cost of equity (i.e. after an increase in the central bank rate) and reduce anticipated cash flows due to weaker demand. Together, these two factors could exert a double downward pressure on financial securities.

WHAT DIVERSIFICATION DOES

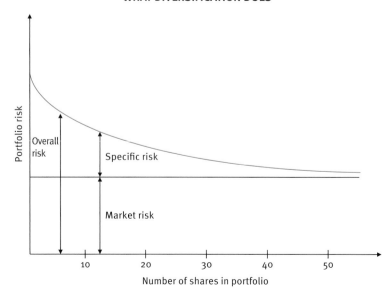

It is now possible to partition risk typologies according to their nature. There are some risks that only impact a small number of companies, e.g. project risk, competitive risk and industry risk. The latter refers to the impact that industrial policy can have on the performance of a specific industry.

Conversely, there are other risks that impact a much larger number of companies, e.g. interest rate risk, inflation risk and external shock risks. By their nature, these types of risk influence almost all companies in a country. Consider interest rate risk. It is reasonable to assume that an increase in interest rates will diminish the investments in fixed assets of *all* companies, because it affects different sectors and companies with varying levels of intensity.

Finally, there are some risks that lie between the two extremes. Their impact differs substantially among industries. A good example is currency risk, which is important for companies which have a significant proportion of their sales in foreign currencies.

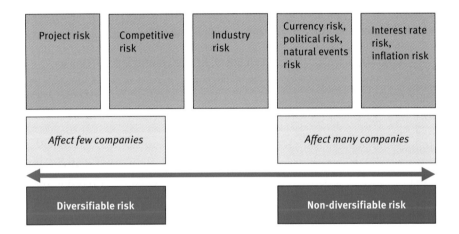

When an investor wants to know the contribution of risk to the portfolio rather than the total risk of an asset, what is the appropriate risk measure he should use? The standard deviation of a single asset is not the correct measure, because standard deviation measures the risk in isolation without considering the correlation with other assets. A better measure would be the **covariance** between the returns of the assets included in the portfolio.

Section 18.5
THE BETA COEFFICIENT

1/ THE BETA AS A MEASURE OF THE MARKET RISK OF A SINGLE SECURITY

Since market risk and specific risk are independent, they can be measured independently and we can apply Pythagoras's theorem (in more mathematical terms, the two risk vectors are orthogonal) to the overall risk of a single security:

$$(\text{Overall risk})^2 = (\text{Market risk})^2 + (\text{Specific risk})^2 \qquad (18.1)$$

The systematic risk presented by a financial security is frequently expressed in terms of its sensitivity to market fluctuations. This is done via a linear regression between periodic market returns (r_{M_t}) and the periodic returns of each security J: (r_{J_t}). This yields the regression line expressed in the following equation:

$$r_{J_t} = \alpha_J + \beta_J \times r_{M_t} + \varepsilon_{J_t}$$

β_J is a parameter specific to each investment J and it expresses the relationship between fluctuations in the value of J and the market. It is thus a coefficient of volatility or of sensitivity. We call it the **beta** or the **beta coefficient.**

A security's total risk is reflected in the standard deviation of its return, $\sigma(r_J)$.

A security's **market risk** is therefore equal to $\beta_J \times \sigma(r_M)$, where $\sigma(r_M)$ is the standard deviation of the market return. Therefore it is also proportional to the beta, i.e. the security's market-linked volatility. The higher the beta, the greater the market risk borne by the security. If $\beta > 1$, the security magnifies market fluctuations. Conversely, securities whose beta is below 1 are less affected by market fluctuations.

COMPARED EVOLUTION OF ERICSSON, HEINEKEN AND EUROSTOXX 50

The chart shows that the β of Ericsson is higher than that of Heineken.

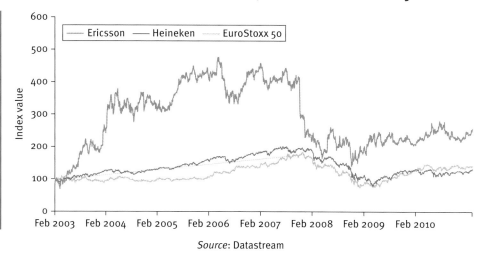

Source: Datastream

The **specific risk** of security J is equal to the standard deviation of the different residuals ε_{J_t} of the regression line, expressed as $\sigma(\varepsilon_J)$, i.e. the variations in the stock that are not tied to market variations.

In summary, proposition (1) can be expressed mathematically as follows:

$$\sigma^2(r_J) = \beta_J^2 \times \sigma^2(r_M) + \sigma^2(\varepsilon_J)$$

2/ Calculating beta

β measures a security's sensitivity to market risk. For security J, it is mathematically obtained by performing a regression analysis of security returns vs. market returns.

Hence:

$$\beta_J = \frac{\text{Cov}(r_J, r_M)}{V(r_M)}$$

Here $\text{Cov}(r_J, r_M)$ is the covariance of the return of security J with that of the market, and $V(r_M)$ is the variance of the market return. This can be represented as:

$$\beta_J = \frac{\sum_{i=1}^{n}\sum_{k=1}^{n} p_{i,k} \times (r_{J_i} - \overline{r_J}) \times (r_{M_k} - \overline{r_M})}{\sum_{i=1}^{n} p_i \times (r_{M_i} - \overline{r_M})^2}$$

More intuitively, β corresponds to the slope of the regression of the security's return vs. that of the market. The line we obtain is defined as the **characteristic line** of a security. As an example, we have calculated the β for Ericsson. It is 1.36, thus confirming the conclusion that might be drawn from a glance at the previous chart.

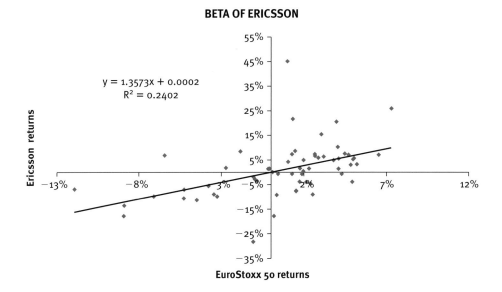

BETA OF ERICSSON

$y = 1.3573x + 0.0002$
$R^2 = 0.2402$

Ericsson returns

EuroStoxx 50 returns

The interpretation of beta from the figure is readily apparent. The graph tells us that Ericsson's returns are magnified 1.36 times over those of the market. When the market does well,

Ericsson is expected to do even better. When the market does poorly, Ericsson is expected to do even worse. As Ericsson's β is over 1, it is more volatile than the market and thus riskier.

RETURNS OF STOCKS – MARKET RETURNS

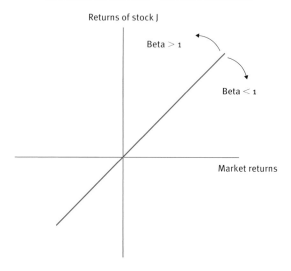

Now consider an investor who is debating whether or not to add Ericsson to his portfolio. Given that Ericsson has a magnification effect of 1.36, his reasoning will be affected by the fact that this stock will increase the risk of the portfolio.

3/ PARAMETERS BEHIND BETA

By definition, the market β is equal to 1. β of fixed-income securities ranges from about 0 to 0.5. The β of equities is usually higher than 0.5, and normally between 0.5 and 1.5. Very few companies have negative β and a β greater than 2 is quite exceptional.

To illustrate, the table below presents betas, as of 2011, of the members of the Dow Jones Industrial Average index:

BETA OF THE COMPONENTS OF THE DOW JONES INDEX

GROUP	BETA	GROUP	BETA	GROUP	BETA
WAL MART STORES	0.5	MERCK & CO.	0.8	INTEL	1.2
MCDONALDS	0.5	TRAVELERS COS.	0.9	CISCO SYSTEMS	1.2
PROCTER & GAMBLE	0.5	MICROSOFT	0.9	JP MORGAN CHASE & CO.	1.4
KRAFT FOODS	0.6	CHEVRON	0.9	BOEING	1.4
EXXON MOBIL	0.6	PFIZER	1.0	AMERICAN EXPRESS	1.6
COCA COLA	0.6	HEWLETT-PACKARD	1.0	E I DU PONT DE NEMOURS	1.7
JOHNSON & JOHNSON	0.7	3M	1.0	CATERPILLAR	1.9
INTERNATIONAL BUS.MCHS.	0.7	HOME DEPOT	1.1	GENERAL ELECTRIC	2.0
VERIZON COMMUNICATIONS	0.8	WALT DISNEY	1.2	ALCOA	2.2
AT&T	0.8	UNITED TECHNOLOGIES	1.2	BANK OF AMERICA	2.7

Source: Datastream

For a given security, the following parameters explain the value of beta:

(a) Sensitivity of the stock's sector to the state of the economy

The greater the effect of the state of the economy on a business sector, the higher is its β – temporary work is one such highly exposed sector. Another example is auto-makers, which tend to have a β close to 1. There is an old saying in North America, "As General Motors goes, so goes the economy". This serves to highlight how GM's financial health is to some extent a reflection of the health of the entire economy. Thus, beta analysis can show how GM will be directly affected by macroeconomic shifts in the economy.

(b) Cost structure

The greater the proportion of fixed costs to total costs, the higher the breakeven point, and the more volatile the cash flows. Companies that have a high ratio of fixed costs (such as cement makers) have a high β, while those with a low ratio of fixed costs (like mass-market service retailers) have a low β.

(c) Financial structure

The greater a company's debt, the greater its financing costs. Financing costs are fixed costs which increase a company's breakeven point and, hence, its earnings volatility. The heavier a company's debt or the more heavily leveraged the company is, the higher is the β of its shares.

(d) Visibility on company performance

The quality of management and the clarity and quantity of information the market has about a company will all have a direct influence on its beta. All other factors being equal, if a company gives out little or low quality information, the β of its stock will be higher as the market will factor the lack of visibility into the share price.

(e) Earnings growth

The higher the forecast rate of earnings growth, the higher the β. Most of a company's value in cash flows is far down the road and thus highly sensitive to any change in assumptions.

Section 18.6
PORTFOLIO RISK

1/ THE FORMULA APPROACH

Consider the following two stocks, Heineken and Ericsson, which have the following characteristics:

	Heineken %	Ericsson %
Expected return: $E(r)$	6	13
Risk: $\sigma(r)$	10	17

As is clear from this table, Ericsson offers a higher expected return while presenting a greater risk than Heineken. Inversely, Heineken offers a lower expected return but also presents less risk.

These two investments are not directly comparable. Investing in Ericsson means accepting more risk in exchange for a higher return, whereas investing in Heineken means playing it safe.

Therefore, there is no clear-cut basis by which to choose between Ericsson and Heineken. However, the problem can be looked at in another way: **would buying a combination of Ericsson and Heineken shares be preferable to buying just one or the other?**

It is likely that the investor will seek to diversify and create a **portfolio** made up of Ericsson shares (in a proportion of X_E) and Heineken shares (in a proportion of X_H). This way, he will expect a return equal to the weighted average return of each of these two stocks, or:

$$E(r_{E,H}) = X_E \times E(r_E) + X_H \times E(r_H)$$

where $X_E + X_H = 1$.

Depending on the proportion of Ericsson shares in the portfolio (X_E), the portfolio would look like this:

X_E (%)	0	25	33.3	50	66.7	75	100
$E(r_{E,H})$ (%)	6	7.8	8.3	9.5	10.7	11.3	13

The portfolio's variance is determined as follows:

$$\sigma^2(r_{E,H}) = X_E^2 \times \sigma^2(r_E) + X_H^2 \times \sigma^2(r_H) + 2X_E \times X_H \times \mathrm{cov}(r_E, r_H)$$

$\mathrm{Cov}(r_E, r_H)$ is the covariance. It measures the degree to which Ericsson and Heineken fluctuate together. It is equal to:

$$\mathrm{Cov}(r_E, r_H) = E\left[\left(r_E - E\left(r_E\right)\right) \times \left(r_H - E\left(r_H\right)\right)\right]$$

$$= \sum_{i=1}^{n}\sum_{j=1}^{m} p_{i,j} \times \left(r_E - \overline{r_E}\right) \times \left(r_H - \overline{r_H}\right)$$

$$= \rho_{E,H} \times \sigma\left(r_E\right) \times \sigma\left(r_H\right)$$

$p_{i,j}$ is the probability of joint occurrence and $\rho_{E,H}$ is the correlation coefficient of returns offered by Ericsson and Heineken. The correlation coefficient is a number between -1 (returns 100% inversely proportional to each other) and 1 (returns 100% proportional to each other). Correlation coefficients are usually positive, as most stocks rise together in a bullish market and fall together in a bearish market.

By plugging the variables back into our variance equation above, we obtain:

$$\sigma^2(r_{E,H}) = X_E^2 \times \sigma^2(r_E) + X_H^2 \times \sigma^2(r_H) + 2X_E \times X_H \times \rho_{E,H} \times \sigma(r_E) \times \sigma(r_H)$$

Given that:

$$-1 \le \rho_{E,H} \le 1$$

it is therefore possible to say:

$$\sigma^2(r_{E,H}) \le X_E^2 \times \sigma^2(r_E) + X_H^2 \times \sigma^2(r_H) + 2X_E \times X_H \times \sigma(r_E) \times \sigma(r_H)$$

or:

$$\sigma^2(r_{E,H}) \le \left(X_E \times \sigma(r_E) + X_H \times \sigma(r_H) \right)^2$$

As the above calculations show, the overall risk of a portfolio consisting of Ericsson and Heineken shares is less than the weighted average of the risks of the two stocks.

Assuming that $\rho_{E,H}$ is equal to 0.5 (from the figures in the above example), we obtain the following:

X (%)	0	25	33.3	50	66.7	75	100
$\sigma(r_{E,H})$ (%)	10.0	10.3	10.7	11.8	13.3	14.2	17.0

Hence, a portfolio consisting of 50% Ericsson and 50% Heineken has a standard deviation of 11.8% or less than the average of Ericsson and Heineken, which is (50% × 17%) + (50% × 10%) = 13.5%.

On a chart, it looks like this:

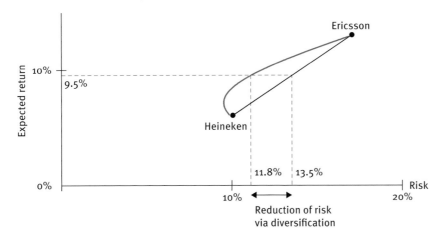

REDUCTION OF RISK VIA DIVERSIFICATION

Although fluctuations in Ericsson and Heineken stocks are positively correlated with each other, having both together in a portfolio creates a less risky profile than investing in them individually.

Only a correlation coefficient of 1 creates a portfolio risk that is equal to the average of its component risks.

CORRELATION BETWEEN DIFFERENT MARKETS

	France	Germany	Italy	Brazil	India	China	UK	USA
France	1.00	0.79	0.98	−0.13	0.05	0.37	0.92	0.95
Germany	0.79	1.00	0.69	0.43	0.57	0.69	0.90	0.91
Italy	0.98	0.69	1.00	−0.28	−0.10	0.27	0.85	0.90
Brazil	−0.13	0.43	−0.28	1.00	0.91	0.56	0.19	0.12
India	0.05	0.57	−0.10	0.91	1.00	0.61	0.36	0.28
China	0.37	0.69	0.27	0.56	0.61	1.00	0.41	0.46
UK	0.92	0.90	0.85	0.19	0.36	0.41	1.00	0.97
USA	0.95	0.91	0.90	0.12	0.28	0.46	0.97	1.00

Source: Datastream

There is a low correlation between technology sectors such as IT and more mature industries.

Globalisation has increased correlation among Western markets (period: 2006–2010). Emerging markets still bring diversification and are more correlated among themselves than with developed countries.

However, sector diversification is still highly efficient thanks to the low correlation coefficients among different industries:

CORRELATION BETWEEN DIFFERENT SECTORS

Sector	Bank	Car	Pharmacy	Oil & Gas	Construction	Web	Utilities	Food retailer	Tourism	Steel	Defence
Bank	1.00	0.91	0.91	0.74	0.83	0.60	0.72	0.39	0.89	0.57	0.76
Car	0.91	1.00	0.88	0.82	0.91	0.74	0.83	0.65	0.94	0.74	0.81
Pharmacy	0.91	0.88	1.00	0.70	0.80	0.73	0.72	0.58	0.91	0.63	0.72
Oil & Gas	0.74	0.82	0.70	1.00	0.93	0.69	0.92	0.63	0.80	0.90	0.92
Construction	0.83	0.91	0.80	0.93	1.00	0.72	0.96	0.71	0.91	0.88	0.93
Web	0.60	0.74	0.73	0.69	0.72	1.00	0.63	0.79	0.76	0.77	0.58
Utilities	0.72	0.83	0.72	0.92	0.96	0.63	1.00	0.72	0.85	0.89	0.95
Food retailer	0.39	0.65	0.58	0.63	0.71	0.79	0.72	1.00	0.70	0.85	0.60
Tourism	0.89	0.94	0.91	0.80	0.91	0.76	0.85	0.70	1.00	0.78	0.83
Steel	0.57	0.74	0.63	0.90	0.88	0.77	0.89	0.85	0.78	1.00	0.86
Defence	0.76	0.81	0.72	0.92	0.93	0.58	0.95	0.60	0.83	0.86	1.00

Source: Datastream

Diversification can:

* reduce risk for a given level of return; and/or
* improve return for a given level of risk.

2/ THE MATRIX APPROACH

It is possible to use matrices that contain all the elements of the variance of a portfolio in order to visually assess the elements of variance. The previous example yields the following table:

	E	H
E	$X_E^2 \times \sigma_E^2$	$X_E \times X_H \times \sigma_{H,E}$
H	$X_E \times X_H \times \sigma_{H,E}$	$X_H^2 \times \sigma_H^2$

The variance of a two-asset portfolio is the sum of the four elements contained in the matrix. Since the order in which we sum the assets is irrelevant, we may simply double the cell that contains the covariance, because they are exactly the same.

The matrix approach is a useful tool when the investor manages a portfolio of many assets. Consider the following example, with N assets that result in the following matrix:

Assets	A	B	C	...	N
A	$X_A^2 \times \sigma_A^2$	$X_A \times X_B \times \sigma_{A,B}$	$X_A \times X_C \times \sigma_{A,C}$	...	$X_A \times X_N \times \sigma_{A,N}$
B	$X_B \times X_A \times \sigma_{B,A}$	$X_B^2 \times \sigma_B^2$	$X_B \times X_C \times \sigma_{B,C}$	...	$X_B \times X_N \times \sigma_{B,N}$
C	$X_C \times X_A \times \sigma_{C,A}$	$X_C \times X_B \times \sigma_{C,B}$	$X_C^2 \times \sigma_C^2$	...	$X_C \times X_N \times \sigma_{C,N}$
...	...	...	...	...	...
N	$X_N \times X_A \times \sigma_{N,A}$	$X_N \times X_B \times \sigma_{N,B}$	$X_N \times X_C \times \sigma_{N,C}$	...	$X_N^2 \times \sigma_N^2$

Following the diagonal cells from the top left to the bottom right, it should be noted that the number of terms in the diagonal is always identical to the number of assets included in the portfolio. Consequently, the "group" of variances that can have an impact on the risk of the portfolio equals the number of assets included in the portfolio. The number of covariances is much more numerous, and it rapidly increases as we add assets to the portfolio.

What exactly does this result mean?

As with a portfolio of two assets, the variance of a portfolio of N assets is the sum of all the cells of the matrix. Thus, the variance of the portfolio is mostly influenced by covariances because their number exceeds that of variances.

Suppose that there is an equal weight for each asset included in the portfolio, i.e. each asset has a weight of 1/N. Then there will be N elements on the diagonal of variances and $N(N-1)$ – or $N^2 - N$ – terms in the other cells. The portfolio variance will then be given by:

$$\sigma_P^2 = N \times \left(\frac{1}{N}\right)^2 \overline{\text{var}} + \left(N^2 - N\right) \times \left(\frac{1}{N}\right)^2 \overline{\text{cov}}$$

SECTION 2

where $\overline{\text{var}}$ and $\overline{\text{cov}}$ indicate the average variance and covariance, respectively. It can then be simplified to:

$$\sigma_P^2 = \left(\frac{1}{N}\right)\overline{\text{var}} + \left(\frac{N^2 - N}{N}\right)\overline{\text{cov}}$$

$$\sigma_P^2 = \left(\frac{1}{N}\right)\overline{\text{var}} + \left(1 - \frac{1}{N}\right)\overline{\text{cov}}$$

This equation highlights the importance of the matrix approach because, if we increase the number of assets included in the portfolio, the variance of the portfolio converges towards the average covariance of the assets.

Ideally, if the covariance were zero, we could eliminate all risk from our portfolio. Unfortunately, financial assets tend to move together, thus the average covariance is positive.

Yet it is now possible to understand the real meaning of what was previously defined as "market risk". This is the risk measured by the covariance, and it represents the portion of risk that cannot be eliminated even after having taken advantage of diversification.

Section 18.7
CHOOSING AMONG SEVERAL RISKY ASSETS
AND THE EFFICIENT FRONTIER

This section will address the following questions: why is it correct to say that the beta of an asset should be measured in relation to the market portfolio? Above all, what is the market portfolio?

To begin, it is useful to study the impact of the correlation coefficient on diversification. Again, the same two securities will be analysed: Ericsson (E) and Heineken (H). By varying $\rho_{E,H}$, between -1 and $+1$, we obtain:

Proportion of E shares in portfolio (X_E) (%)		0	25	33.3	50	66.7	75	100
Return on the portfolio: $E(r_{E,H})$ (%)		6.0	7.8	8.3	9.5	10.7	11.3	13.0
Portfolio risk $\sigma(r_{E,H})$ (%)	$\rho_E,H = -1$	10.0	3.3	1.0	3.5	8.0	10.3	17.0
	$\rho_E,H = -0.5$	10.0	6.5	6.2	7.4	10.1	11.7	17.0
	$\rho_E,H = 0$	10.0	8.6	8.7	9.9	11.8	13.0	17.0
	$\rho_E,H = 0.3$	10.0	9.7	10.0	11.1	12.7	13.7	17.0
	$\rho_E,H = 0.5$	10.0	10.3	10.7	11.8	13.3	14.2	17.0
	$\rho_E,H = 1$	10.0	11.8	12.3	13.5	14.7	15.3	17.0

Note the following caveats:

- If Ericsson and Heineken were perfectly correlated (i.e. the correlation coefficient was 1), diversification would have no effect. All possible portfolios would lie on a line linking the risk/return point of Ericsson with that of Heineken. Risk would increase in direct proportion to Ericsson's stock added.

- If the two stocks were perfectly inversely correlated (correlation coefficient -1), diversification would be total. However, there is little chance of this occurring, as both companies are exposed to the same economic conditions.
- Generally speaking, Ericsson and Heineken are positively, but imperfectly, correlated and diversification is based on the desired amount of risk.

With a fixed correlation coefficient of 0.3, there are portfolios that offer different returns at the same level of risk. Thus, a portfolio consisting of two-thirds Heineken and one-third Ericsson shows the same risk (10%) as a portfolio consisting of just Heineken, but returns 8.3% vs. only 6% for Heineken.

There is no reason for an investor to choose a given combination if another offers a better (efficient) return at the same level of risk.

Efficient portfolios (such as a combination of Ericsson and Heineken shares) offer investors the best risk–return ratio (i.e. minimal risk for a given return).

IMPACT OF THE CORRELATION COEFFICIENT ON RISK AND RETURN

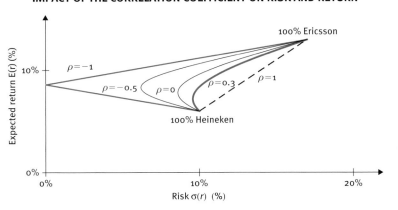

As long as the correlation coefficient is below 1, diversification will be efficient.

For any portfolio that does not lie on the **efficient frontier**, another can be found that, given the level of risk, offers a greater return or that, at the same return, entails less risk.

EFFICIENT FRONTIER

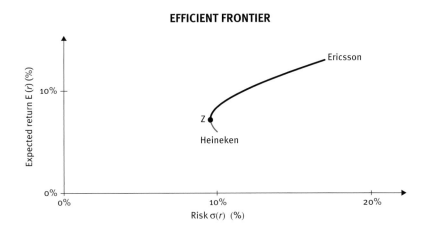

Efficient portfolios fall between Z and Ericsson. The portion of the curve between Z and Heineken is called the efficient frontier.

SECTION 2

All subjective elements aside, it is impossible to choose between portfolios that have different levels of risk. There is no universally optimum portfolio and therefore it is up to the investor to decide, based upon his appetite for risk. However, given the same level of risk, some portfolios are better than others. These are the efficient portfolios.

With a larger number of stocks, i.e. more than just two, the investor can improve his efficient frontier, as shown in the chart below.

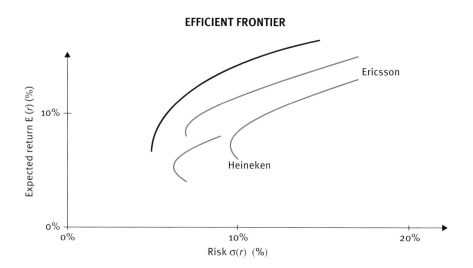

EFFICIENT FRONTIER

Section 18.8
CHOOSING BETWEEN SEVERAL RISKY ASSETS AND A RISK-FREE ASSET: THE CAPITAL MARKET LINE

1/ RISK-FREE ASSETS

By definition, **risk-free assets are those whose returns**, the risk-free rate (r_F), **are certain**. This is the case with a government bond, assuming of course that the government does not go bankrupt. The standard deviation of its return is thus zero.

If a portfolio has a risk-free asset F in proportion $(1 - X_H)$ and the portfolio consists exclusively of Heineken shares, then the portfolio's expected return $E(r_{H,F})$ will be equal to:

$$E(r_{H,F}) = (1 - X_H) \times r_F + X_H \times E(r_H) = r_F + (E(r_H) - r_F) \times X_H \qquad (18.2)$$

The portfolio's expected return is equal to the return of the risk-free asset, plus a risk premium, multiplied by the proportion of Heineken shares in the portfolio. The risk premium is the difference between the expected return on Heineken and the return on the risk-free asset.

How much risk does the portfolio carry? Its risk will simply be the risk of the Heineken stock, commensurate with its proportion in the portfolio, expressed as follows:

$$\sigma(r_{H,F}) = X_H \times \sigma(r_H) \qquad (18.3)$$

If the investor wants to increase his expected return, he will increase X_H. He could even borrow money at the risk-free rate and use the funds to buy Heineken stock, but the risk carried by his portfolio would rise commensurately.

By combining Equations (18.2) and (18.3), we can eliminate X_F, thus deriving the following equation:

$$E(r_{H,F}) = r_F + \frac{\sigma(r_{H,F})}{\sigma(r)} \times [E(r_H) - r_F]$$

This portfolio's expected return is equal to the risk-free rate, plus the difference between the expected return on Heineken and the risk-free rate. This difference is then weighted by the ratio of the portfolio's standard deviation to Heineken's standard deviation.

Continuing with the Heineken example, and assuming that r_F is 3%, with 50% of the portfolio consisting of a risk-free asset, the following is obtained:

$$E(r_{H,F}) = 3\% + (6\% - 3\%) \times 0.5 = 4.5\%$$
$$\sigma(r_{H,F}) = 0.50 \times 10\% = 5\%$$

Hence:

$$E(r_{H,F}) = 3\% + (5\% / 10\%) \times (6\% - 3\%) = 4.5\%$$

For a portfolio that includes a risk-free asset, there is a linear relationship between expected return and risk. To lower a portfolio's risk, simply liquidate some of the portfolio's stock and put the proceeds into a risk-free asset. To increase risk, it is only necessary to borrow at the risk-free rate and invest in a stock with risk.

2/ RISK-FREE ASSETS AND THE EFFICIENT FRONTIER

The risk–return profile can be chosen by combining risk-free assets and a stock portfolio (the alpha portfolio on the chart below). This new portfolio will be on a line that connects the risk-free rate to the efficient portfolio that has been chosen. In the chart below, the portfolio located on the efficient frontier, M, maximises utility. The line joining the risk-free rate to portfolio M is tangential to the efficient frontier.

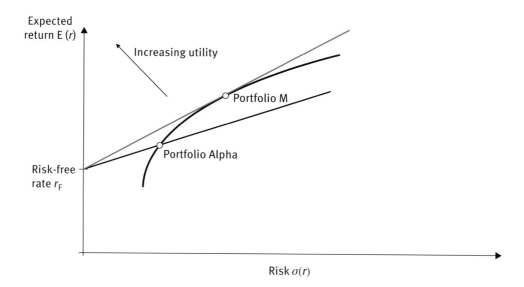

Investors' taste for risk can vary, yet the above graph demonstrates that the shrewd investor should be invested in portfolio M. It is then a matter of adjusting the risk exposure by adding or subtracting risk-free assets.

If all investors acquire the same portfolio, this portfolio must contain all existing shares. To understand why, suppose that stock i was not in portfolio M. In that case, nobody would want to buy it, since all investors hold portfolio M. Consequently, there would be no market for it and it would cease to exist.

The "market portfolio" includes all stocks at their market value. The market portfolio is thus weighted proportionally to the market capitalisation of a particular market.

The weighting of stock i in a market portfolio will necessarily be the value of the single security divided by the sum of all the assets. As we are assuming fair value, this will be the fair value of i.

3/ CAPITAL MARKET LINE

The expected return of a portfolio consisting of the market portfolio and the risk-free asset can be expressed by the following equation:

$$E(r_\mathrm{P}) = r_\mathrm{F} + \frac{\sigma_\mathrm{P}}{\sigma_\mathrm{M}} \times \left[E(r_\mathrm{M}) - r_\mathrm{F} \right]$$

where $E(r_\mathrm{P})$ is the portfolio's expected return; r_F, the risk-free rate; $E(r_\mathrm{M})$, the return on the market portfolio; σ_P, the portfolio's risk; and σ_M, the risk of the market portfolio.

This is the equation of the **capital market line**, which is graphically tangential to the efficient frontier containing the portfolio M. The reason is that if there was a more efficient combination of risk-free and risky assets, the weighting of the risky assets would depart from that of the market portfolio, and supply and demand for these stocks would seek a new equilibrium.

The most efficient portfolios in terms of return and risk will always be on the capital market line. The tangent point at M constitutes the optimal combination for *all* investors. If we introduce the assumption that all investors have **homogeneous expectations**, i.e. that they have the same opinions on expected returns and risk of financial assets, then the efficient frontier of risky assets will be the same for all of them. The capital market line is the same for all investors and thus each of them would hold a combination of the portfolio M and the risk-free asset.

With the assumption of homogeneous expectations, it is reasonable to say that the portfolio M includes all the assets weighted for their market capitalisation. This is defined as the **market portfolio**.[1] The market portfolio is the portfolio that all investors hold a fraction of, proportional to the market's capitalisation.

1 In practice, investors use wide-capitalisation market indexes as a proxy for the market portfolio.

The *capital market line* links the market portfolio M to the risk-free asset. For a given level of risk, no portfolio is better than those located on this line.

These portfolios consist of two types of investments:

- an investment in the risk-free rate and in the market portfolio, between $\sigma = 0$ and $\sigma = \sigma_M$; and
- an investment in the market portfolio financed partly by debt at the risk-free rate, beyond σ_M.

A rational investor will not take a position on individual stocks in the hope of obtaining a big return, but rather on the market as a whole. He will then choose his risk level by adjusting his debt level or by investing in risk-free assets. This is the **separation theorem**. According to this theorem the financial decision of an investor requires "two steps":

1. First, collect data and information on financial assets, estimate the expected risk and return for each of them, simulate sets of combinations of assets, build the efficient frontier of risky assets, link the risk-free asset with the efficient frontier, delineate the market portfolio (M).
2. Then choose how to allocate wealth between M and the risk-free assets. This decision is a function of personal preferences and attitude toward risk.

With this understanding of what a market portfolio is, it is now possible to answer the initial question of Section 18.7: why can we say that the beta of an asset should be measured in relation to the market portfolio? The answer is because all investors have a certain fraction of their wealth invested in the market portfolio. The additional risk of a new title should be computed measuring the covariance of that asset with the market portfolio.

Only portfolios located on a line passing through M and on a tangent to the efficient frontier are optimal. The others, such as portfolio Z, are suboptimal.

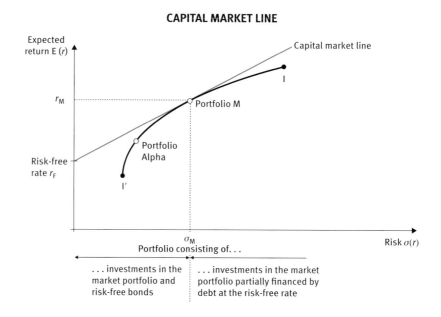

CAPITAL MARKET LINE

Section 18.9
HOW PORTFOLIO MANAGEMENT WORKS

The financial theory described so far seems to give a clear suggestion: invest only in highly diversified mutual funds and in government bonds.

The asset management industry is one of the most important industries in the modern economy, it manages €17 360 billion worldwide (one-third of this amount being invested in stock markets). Managers are employees of banks, insurance companies or independent.

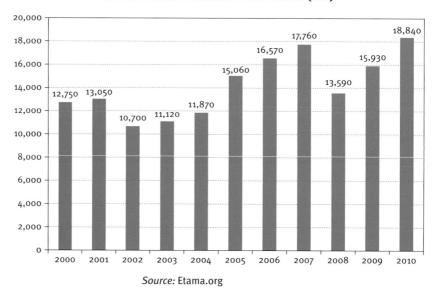

WORLDWIDE INVESTMENT FUND ASSETS (€bn)

Source: Etama.org

However, as our reader knows, not all investors subscribe to this theory. Some take other approaches, described below. Sometimes, investors combine different approaches.

The strategy that is closest to financial theory is index tracking. It consists in trying to follow the performance of a market index. Index tracking is an ideal tool for the investor who believes strongly in market efficiency. The development of this strategy has run in parallel to the diffusion of the portfolio theory. Hence, index tracking funds were created some 35 years ago with merely $6 million invested; they now account for $7000 billion under management. Index trackers can be listed on a market and are then called Exchange Traded Funds, or ETFs. Most stock markets now have a specific market segment for the listing of trackers. Over 2700 trackers are listed for a total amount of over $1600 billion.

In terms of portfolio management we shall consider the difference between a **top-down** and a **bottom-up** approach. In a top-down approach, investors focus on the asset class (shares, bonds, money-market funds) and the international markets in which they wish to invest (i.e. the individual securities chosen are of little importance). In a bottom-up approach (commonly known as stock-picking), investors choose stocks on the basis of their specific characteristics, not the sector in which they belong. The goal of the bottom-up approach is to find that rare pearl.

There are two types of stock-pickers:

- Investors who focus on fundamental analysis and seek to determine the intrinsic value of a stock. They believe that, sooner or later, market value will approach intrinsic value. These investors believe that all other price changes are temporary phenomena. Intrinsic value is what financial analysts seek to measure. A fundamental investor seeks to invest over the medium or long term and, like Warren Buffet, who is the most famous of them all, wait patiently for the market value to converge towards the intrinsic value, i.e. for the market to agree with them.
- Investors who focus on technical analysis, the so-called chartists, who do not seek to determine the value of a stock. Instead, these investors conduct detailed studies of trends in a stock's market value and transaction volumes in the hope of spotting short-term trends. Chartists prefer to analyse how the market perceives intrinsic value rather than looking at the stock's actual intrinsic value.

Chartists believe the market is predictable in the very short term, and this is often the attitude of traders and banks who take positions for very short periods, from a few hours to a few days.

Technical analysis is not based directly on any theory. It is based more on psychology than mathematics. Chartists believe that while investors are not perfectly rational, they at least are fixed in their way of reasoning, with predictable reactions to certain situations. Chartists look for these patterns of behaviour in price trends.

One method consists in calculating a moving average of prices over a certain number of days (generally 20). Chartists look for a price to break through its moving average, either upward or downward.

Another method is based on comparing a stock's prices with its highs and lows over a given period. This is used in identifying support and resistance levels:

- a support is a level that the price has very little chance of falling below; and
- a resistance is a level that the price has very little chance of rising above.

The fundamental investor believes that markets are predictable in the medium or long term, but certainly not in the short term. Chartists believe they are predictable in the short term, but not in the medium or long term. Believers in efficient markets espouse the notion that markets are never predictable.

2 Stocks that exhibit low price-to-book and low price-to-earnings ratios are value stocks, whereas those with high P/E and price-to-book ratios are called growth stocks.

Some fundamental investors seek out **growth stocks** (companies in sectors offering sustainable growth),[2] while others seek out **value stocks** (companies in more mature sectors that provide long-term performance). At the end of the spectrum, investors choose **income stocks** whose prices are relatively stable and provide the bulk of their returns from dividends. Asset managers have developed several types of funds targeted specifically at these types of investors: growth funds, value funds and mixed funds. These last, mixed funds, are actually a combination of the first two.

Another type of fund management has arisen recently, so-called **alternative management**, which is based on market declines, volatility, liquidity, time value and abnormal valuations, rather than on rising prices. An example of alternative management is the **hedge fund**, which is a speculative fund seeking high returns and relying heavily on derivatives, and options in particular. Hedge funds use leverage and commit capital in excess of their equity. Hedge funds offer additional diversification to "conventional" portfolios, as their results are in theory not linked to the performances of equity and bond markets. Short-seller funds, for example, bet that a stock will fall by borrowing shares at interest and selling them, then buying them back after their price falls and returning them to the borrower.

Institutional investors are taking a growing interest in hedge funds. As of end 2010, hedge funds had about $1700bn under management.

In recent years, hedge funds' risk-adjusted performance has been above that of traditional management. From 1990 to 2001, the average performance of a basket of hedge funds was 11.6%, vs. 7.9% for a basket of shares and 7.0% for bonds. It is important to note, however, that this greater return is in compensation for these funds' greater risk exposure.

Hedge funds may present some restrictions on investing (size, duration, etc.). Funds of funds allow a larger number of investors to invest in hedge funds. The fund of funds picks up the best hedge fund managers and packages their products to be offered to a wide number of investors.

Last but not least, private equity funds seek even higher returns (and thus encounter greater risks!) through leveraged buyout operations; our reader will learn more about this particular type of transaction in Chapter 45.

SUMMARY

The summary of this chapter can be downloaded from www.vernimmen.com.

There are various risks involved in financial securities. There are economic risks (political, inflation, etc.) which threaten cash flows from financial securities and which come from the "real economy", and there are financial risks (liquidity, currency, interest rate and other risks) which do not directly affect cash flow and come under the financial sphere.

All risks, regardless of their nature, lead to fluctuations in the value of a financial security.

In a market economy, a security's risk is measured in terms of the volatility of its price (or of its rate of return). The greater the volatility, the greater the risk, and vice versa.

We can break down the total risk of a financial security into the market-related risk (market or systematic risk) and a specific risk that is independent of the market (intrinsic or diversifiable risk). These two risks are totally independent.

The market risk of a security is dependent on its β coefficient, which measures the correlation between the return on the security and the market return. Mathematically, this is the regression line of the security's return vs. that of the market.

The β coefficient depends on:

- the sensitivity of the company's business sector;

- the economic situation;

- the company's operating cost structure (the higher the fixed costs, the higher the β),

- the financial structure (the greater the group's debts, the higher the β);

- the quality and quantity of information provided to the market (the greater visibility there is over future results, the lower the β); and

- earnings growth rates (the higher the growth rate, the higher the β).

Although the return on a portfolio of shares is equal to the average return on the shares within the portfolio, the risk of a portfolio is lower than the average risk of the shares making up that portfolio. This happens because returns on shares do not all vary to exactly the same degree, since correlation coefficients are rarely equal to 1.

As a result, some portfolios will deliver better returns than others. Those portfolios that are located on the portion of the curve known as the efficient frontier will deliver better returns than those portfolios which are not. However, given portfolios located on the efficient frontier curve, it is impossible to choose an optimal portfolio objectively from among them. The choice then becomes an individual one, and every investor chooses the portfolio according to his personal appetite for (or aversion to) risk.

By including risk-free assets, i.e. assets on which the return is guaranteed such as government bonds, it is possible to obtain portfolios that are even more efficient.

The inclusion of a risk-free asset in a portfolio leads to the creation of a new efficient frontier which is the line linking the risk-free asset to the market portfolio in the risk/returns space. This new line is called the capital market line. Investors are well advised to own shares in this market portfolio and to choose the level of risk that suits them by investing in risk-free assets or by going into debt. On this line, no portfolio could perform better, i.e. no portfolio could offer a better return for a given level of risk, or a lower risk for a given return.

Portfolio theory is generally applied in varying degrees, as demonstrated by the existence of investment strategies that favour certain securities rather than market portfolios.

QUESTIONS

1/ How is risk measured in a market economy?

2/ What does the β coefficient measure?

3/ In the graph on page 318, which is the most volatile asset? What motivates investors to enter this market?

4/ The β coefficient measures the specific risk of a security. True or false?

5/ Is the Heineken share more or less risky than the whole of the market? Why?

6/ Upon what is the β coefficient dependent?

7/ Why are market risk and specific risk totally independent?

8/ Will an increase in a company's debt reduce or increase the volatility of its share price?

9/ As a result of a change in the nature of its business, there is a relative rise in the proportion of fixed costs in a group's total costs. Will this affect the risk attached to its share price? If so, how?

10/ Explain why it is unhealthy for a company to invest its cash in shares.

11/ Is the β of a diversified conglomerate close to 1? Why?

12/ Internet companies have low fixed costs and low debt levels, yet their β coefficients are high. Why?

13/ Is the β coefficient of a group necessarily stable over time? Why?

14/ You buy a lottery ticket for €100 on which you could win €1 000 000, with a probability rate of 0.008%. Is this a risky investment? Could it be even riskier? How could you reduce the risk? Would this be a good investment?

15/ Why is standard deviation preferable to variance?

16/ What law of statistics explains that in the long term, risk disappears? State your views.

17/ You receive €100 000 which you decide to save for your old age. You are now 20. What sort of investment should you go for? Perform the same analysis as if it happened when you are 55 and 80.

18/ Do shares in Internet companies carry a greater or smaller risk than shares in large retail groups? Why?

19/ There are some sceptics who claim that financial analysis serves no purpose. Why? State your views.

20/ Why are negative β coefficients unusual?

21/ What can you say about a share for which the standard deviation of the return is high, and the β is low?

22/ Must the values of financial assets fluctuate in opposite directions in order to reduce risk? Why?

23/ What other concept does the capital market line bring to mind?

24/ Why does the market portfolio include all risky assets?

25/ Security A carries little risk and security B has great risk. Which would you choose if you wanted to take the least risk possible?

26/ The correlation coefficient between French equities and European equities developed as follows:

Years	1970–1979	1980–1989	1990–1999	2000–2009
Coefficient	0.43	0.42	0.73	0.996

Are you surprised by the table above? Does it prove that there is nothing to gain by geographic diversification? Does it reduce the importance of geographic diversification?

27/ Use the table on page 330 to determine which industrial sector makes the greatest contribution to reducing the risk of a portfolio.

28/ What is the only asset that can be used to precisely measure the levels of risk of a portfolio?

29/ What conditions are necessary for a risk-free asset to be free of risk? Provide an example. Is it really risk-free?

30/ Show that the market portfolio must be on the capital market line and on the portion of the curve called the efficient frontier (see Section 18.7).

31/ Why does this chapter provide an explanation of the development of mutual funds?

32/ Can the risk of a portfolio be greater than the individual risk of each of the securities it contains? Under what circumstances?

33/ Under what circumstances can the risk of a portfolio be less than the individual risk of each of the securities it contains?

34/ The greater the number of shares in a portfolio, the less the marginal contribution to diversification of an additional security will be. True or false?

35/ Will very wide diversification eliminate specific risk? And market risk?

More questions are waiting for you at www.vernimmen.com.

EXERCISES

1/ Calculate the return on the ENI share and on the Italian index over 13 months until 1 July 2008. To help you, you have a record of the share price and of the general index. What is the total risk of the ENI share? What is the β coefficient of ENI? What portion of the total risk of the ENI share is explained by market risk?

Period	Jan 10	Feb 10	Mar 10	Apr 10	May 10	Jun 10	Jul 10	Aug 10	Sep 10	Oct 10	Nov 10	Dec 10	Jan 11
ENI	16.93	16.57	17.37	16.86	15.2	15.19	15.69	15.67	15.83	16.19	15.50	16.34	17.30
Italian index	21896	21068	22847	21562	19544	19311	21021	19734	20505	21450	19105	20173	22050

2/ A portfolio gives a 10% return with a standard deviation of 18%. You would like the standard deviation to drop to 14%. What should you do? What should you do if you want the standard deviation to rise to 23%.

3/ Calculate the risk and returns of portfolio Z in Section 18.2. What is the proportion of Heineken shares and Ericsson shares in this portfolio?

4/ A portfolio gives a 10% return for a standard deviation of 18%. The shares in companies C and D have the following returns and standard deviations:

	C	D
Expected return (%)	10	20
Standard deviation (%)	15	30

The correlation between the return on these two shares is 25%.

(a) Calculate the expected return and the standard deviation for each of the following portfolios:

$$\alpha:100\%\,C; \quad \beta:75\%\,C + 25\%\,D; \quad \delta:50\%\,C + 50\%\,D; \quad \delta:25\%\,C + 75\%\,D;$$
$$\varepsilon:100\%\,D$$

(b) Plot your results on a graph. What are your conclusions?

ANSWERS

Questions

1/ *The volatility of the value of the asset is measured by the standard deviation of its rate of return.*

2/ *The correlation between the return on the security and the market return, the market risk of the security, the line of the regression of the security's return vs. that of the market.*

3/ *The Chinese shares carry the most risk, but they will also bring the highest returns.*

4/ *False, it measures the market risk of a security.*

5/ *It is difficult to give a very accurate answer, without knowing what the share's specific risk is.*

6/ *On the company's operating cost structure, its financial structure, its information policy and the growth rate of its earnings.*

7/ *One has an impact on all securities, the other on a given security.*

8/ *Yes, it will increase volatility due to the leverage effect, see Chapter 13.*

9/ *Yes, it will increase volatility due to the effect of the breakeven point, see Chapter 10.*

10/ *Because cash, by definition, should be available at all times, and share prices are very volatile.*

11/ *Usually yes, because conglomerates are highly diversified and are a bit like "mini markets" in their own right.*

12/ *Because of the very poor visibility we currently have over what is going to happen to Internet stocks.*

13/ *No, as the group's business and financial structure can change over the course of time, which will have a knock-on effect on the β.*

14/ Yes, very risky, because you have a 99.992% chance of losing your €100. Yes it could, if you used debt to finance the €100. If you bought all of the lottery tickets you would be sure of winning the €1 000 000, but that would cost you €100/ 0.008% = €1 250 000, which wouldn't be a very good investment.

15/ Because it's around 1, like returns, unlike variance which is around 2.

16/ The law of large numbers. The risk is never completely eliminated.

17/ Equities, bonds, money-market investments.

18/ A greater risk as the outlook is very uncertain, whereas the visibility over the earnings of large retail groups is very good.

19/ Financial analysis contributes very little, as it must be acted upon immediately and the results seen in the share price – financial analysis kills financial analysis. Financial analysis is necessary for market equilibrium (rationality).

20/ Because if they weren't, when markets went up, the price of most securities making up these markets would fall, which would be absurd.

21/ That it carries a specific risk which is very high.

22/ Of course not. The correlation must just not be equal to 1.

23/ The leverage effect.

24/ By definition.

25/ A combination of A and B, and not only security A, so that $\rho \pm 1$.

26/ No, because it reflects advances in European integration and globalisation, which both increase the synchronisation of economies. No, as long as correlation coefficients remain lower than 1, although they are now very close. Yes.

27/ The food retailer because correlation coefficients with the other sectors are lower.

28/ A risk-free asset.

29/ There must be no doubts about the solvency of the issuer, no risk vis-à-vis the rate at which the coupons can be reinvested, and protection against inflation. A zero-coupon government bond indexed to inflation. No, because there will always be a risk that the price will fluctuate before maturity.

30/ By construction, on the capital market line because this line is constructed from two points – itself and the risk-free asset. It is on the efficient frontier in Section 18.7 because, given its high level of diversity, risk is reduced to a minimum.

31/ Because a mutual fund is a reduced model of the market portfolio, which would be difficult to compile at an individual level.

32/ Yes, it is financed by debt.

33/ If it includes a large percentage of risk-free assets.

34/ True, because the portfolio is already very diversified.

35/ Yes, by definition. No, this would be impossible.

Exercises

A detailed Excel version of the solutions is available at www.vernimmen.com.

1/ Returns on the ENI share: $17.30/16.93 - 1 = 2.2\%$

Returns on the Italian index: $22\ 050/21\ 896 = 0.7\%$

$$\text{ENI risk } \sigma = 4.59\%$$

Index risk σ 7.35%; $\beta = 0.56$; 89.6% = (0.56 × 7.35%)/4.59%.

2/ Add more risk-free assets until they account for 4/18 of the portfolio. Use debt to finance an increase in the size of this portfolio by 5/18.

3/ *83% of Heineken shares and 17% of Ericsson shares. E(r) = 7.19% and σ = 9.57%.*

4/

	Expected return (%)	Standard deviation (%)
α	10.00	15.00
β	12.50	15.00
σ	15.00	18.37
δ	17.50	23.72
ε	20.00	30.00

BIBLIOGRAPHY

To learn more about the history of risk analysis:

P. Bernstein, *Against the Gods: The Remarkable Story of Risk,* John Wiley & Sons, Inc., 1998.

E. Dimson, P. Marsh, M. Staunton, *The Triumph of the Optimist. 101 Years of Global Investment Returns*, Princeton University Press, 2002.

E. Dimson, P. Marsh, M. Staunton, *Credit Suisse Global Investment Returns Yearbook 2010*, Credit Suisse, 2010.

M. Kritzman, What practitioners need to know . . . about time diversification, *Financial Analysts Journal*, **50**(1), 14–18, January–February 1994.

To learn more about the theoretical analysis of risk:

N. Barberis, Investing for the long run when returns are predictable, *Journal of Finance*, **55**(1), 225–264, February 2000.

E. Fama, M. Miller, *Theory of Finance*, Holt, Rinehart & Winston, 1971.

D. Hirshleifer, Investor psychology and asset pricing, *Journal of Finance*, **56**(4), 1533–1597, August 2001.

For more about asset management and investment strategies:

A. Damodaran, *Style Investing*, John Wiley & Sons, Inc., 2003.

B. Malkiel, A. Saha, Hedge funds: Risk and return, *Financial Analysts Journal*, **61**(6), 80–88, November–December 2005.

R. Wilson, *The Hedge Funds Handbook*, John Wiley & Sons, Inc., 2010.

www.hedgeindex.com

www.hedgeworld.com

Chapter 19
THE REQUIRED RATE OF RETURN

A ship in a harbour is safe but that is not what ships are built for

The previous chapter described the important concepts of risk, return and market portfolio. It also highlighted the notion of risk premium (i.e. the difference between the risk-free rate and the return on the market portfolio); this chapter continues to explore the risk premium in greater depth.

By seeking systematically to estimate the risk premium, i.e. in a fairly valued market, the question arises: what risk premium must be added to the risk-free rate to determine the required rate of return?

Investors must look at the big picture, first by investing in the market portfolio, then by borrowing or by investing in risk-free instruments commensurate with the level of risk they wish to assume. This approach allows them to assess an investment by merely determining the additional return and risk it adds to the market portfolio.

Investment risk is often broken down into its component parts, not necessarily in economic and financial terms, but rather into the volatility of the security itself and the volatility of the market as a whole.

We want to know how to get from r (the discounting rate used in calculating company value) to k (the return required by investors on a specific security).

Remember that this approach applies only if the investor owns a perfectly diversified portfolio. Here is why: the greater the risk assumed by the financial investor, the higher his required rate of return. However, if he makes just one investment and that turns out to be a failure, his required rate of return will matter little, as he will have lost everything.

With this in mind, it is easier to understand that risk premium is relevant only if the financial investor manages not just a single investment, but a diversified portfolio of investments. In this case, the failure of one investment should be offset by the return achieved by other investments, which should thereby produce a suitable return for the portfolio as a whole.

The concept of risk premium only makes sense when risk is spread over many investments.

Look at it this way:

- What is a bank if not a portfolio of loans and financial resources?

- What is a financial group if not a portfolio of industrial investments?

- What is a mutual fund if not a portfolio of securities?
- What is an insurance company if not a portfolio of statistical risks?

"Portfolio" and "diversification" are fundamental concepts in finance.

This is the main difference between an industrial investment and a financial investment.

An entrepreneur who sets up his own company does not act like a financial investor, as he owns just one investment. As his assets are not diversified, it is a matter of "life or death" for the firm that the investment succeeds. The law of averages in risk diversification does not apply to him.[1]

The financial investor, on the other hand, needs portfolio management tools to estimate the risk–return on each of his investments. Portfolio theory is not the main objective here, but it is useful to introduce some basic notions with which financial managers must be familiar.

1 *However, the very fact that he does not diversify his portfolio means that he must achieve strong performances in managing the company, as he has everything to lose. So he's likely to take steps to reduce risk.*

2 *See also Appendix 19.A for a formal derivation of the CAPM.*

SECTION 2

Section 19.1
RETURN REQUIRED BY INVESTORS: THE CAPM[2]

The CAPM (Capital Asset Pricing Model) was developed in the late 1950s and 1960s. Based on the work of Harry Markowitz, William Sharpe, John Lintner and Jack Treynor, it is now universally applied.

The CAPM is based on the assumption that investors act rationally and have at their disposal all relevant information on financial securities (see "efficient markets" in Chapter 15). Like the investor in Chapter 18, they seek to maximise their return, at a given level of risk.

From portfolio selection, we know that the investor:

1. Considers the efficient portfolios; that is, the portfolios that offer the highest return for a given level of risk (measured by the standard deviation).
2. Introduces the risk-free asset. The tangent point between the risk-free asset and the efficient frontier is the portfolio with the highest ratio of risk premium to standard deviation.
3. Holds the same portfolio as everybody else as long as there are **homogeneous expectations** among investors. This portfolio is the **market portfolio**.

From the analysis of risk of individual securities, it has been shown that:

1. The contribution of a stock to a portfolio depends on the stock's sensitivity to the returns of the portfolio.
2. The sensitivity to the returns of the market portfolio is known as beta (β).

The CAPM says that if all investors hold the market portfolio, the risk premium they will demand is proportional to market beta.

The expected return of an asset will then be a linear function of beta:

$$\text{Expected return on a financial asset} = \text{Risk-free rate} + \beta \times \left(\text{Expected return of market portfolio} - \text{Risk-free rate} \right)$$

Remember that in order to minimise total risk, investors seek to reduce that component which can be reduced, i.e. the specific risk. They do so by diversifying their portfolios.

As a result, when stocks are fairly valued, investors will receive a return only on the portion of risk that they cannot eliminate – the market risk, or the non-diversifiable risk. Indeed, in a market in which arbitrage is theoretically possible, they will not be amply remunerated for a risk that they could otherwise eliminate themselves by simply diversifying their portfolios.

Portfolio theory's essential contribution is to show that an investor's required rate of return is not linked to total risk, but solely to market risk. Conversely, in a fairly valued market, intrinsic, or diversifiable, risk is not remunerated.

This means that the required rate of return (k) is equal to the risk-free rate r_F,[3] plus the risk premium for the non-diversifiable risk, i.e. the market risk.

This can be expressed as follows:

> Required rate of return = risk-free rate + β × market risk premium, or:
>
> $$k = r_F + \beta \times (k_M - r_F)$$

Where k_M is the required rate of return for the market and β the sensitivity coefficient described previously.

Note that the coefficient β measures the non-diversifiable risk of an asset and not its total risk. So it is possible to have a stock that is, on the whole, highly risky but with a low β if it is only loosely correlated with the market.

The difference between the return expected on the market as a whole and the risk-free rate is called the **equity risk premium**. This averages 3–5% in developed economies, but is higher in emerging markets.

3 *For the risk-free rate, k_F is equal to r_F. The required rate of return is equal to the return that is actually received, as the asset has no risk.*

SECTION 2

1/ THE EXPECTED RISK PREMIUM OVER TIME

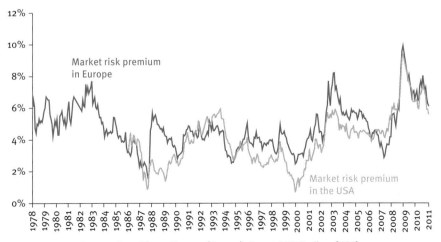

MARKET RISK PREMIUM IN EUROPE AND IN THE USA

Source: Associés en Finance (Europe), Exane BNP Paribas (USA).

Over the very long term (110 years!), the historical risk premium is as follows:

Belgium	2.6%	Spain	2.4%
France	3.3%	Switzerland	2.1%
Germany	5.4%	USA	4.2%
Italy	3.8%	UK	3.9%
Japan	5.1%	Europe	3.9%
South Africa	5.4%	World	3.7%

Source: Crédit Suisse Global Investment Returns Yearbook 2010.

Estimates of the equity market risk premium, i.e. the difference between the market return and the risk-free interest rate, are currently arrived at using two possible approaches:

- Either on the basis of forecast data (future free cash flows) and the current share price. In this case, we refer to the **expected or forward risk premium**, because it is based on investors' current expectations, both anticipated and not anticipated. The expected risk premium is not directly observable. However, it can be calculated by estimating the future cash flows of all the companies, and then finding the discount rate that equates those cash flows with current share prices from which we deduct the risk-free interest rate.
- Or on the basis of historical data relating to rates of returns received by investors over very long periods. In efficient markets, historical rates of return should be equal to future rates of return. In this case we refer to the **historical risk premium**, based on the very pleasing principle that, over the very long term, we end up getting what we ask for. The historical risk premium is equal to the annual performance of equity markets (including dividends) minus the risk-free rate.

To determine the risk premium for each stock, simply multiply the market risk premium by the stock's beta coefficient.

Hence, if the risk-free rate is 3.15% and the expected risk premium is 6.25%, a shareholder in the German airline Lufthansa will expect a return of $3.15\% + 1.31 \times 6.25\% = 11.34\%$, if Lufthansa's β is 1.31, while a shareholder in the British retail chain Tesco will expect: $3.15\% + 0.83 \times 6.25\% = 8.34\%$, as Tesco's β is 0.83.

A final remark. In the CAPM, the equilibrium risk premium is equal to the variance of the market portfolio times a weighted average of the degree of risk aversion of the holders of wealth (A):

$$E(r_{\mathrm{M}}) - r_{\mathrm{F}} = A \times \sigma_{\mathrm{M}}^2$$

A should be considered an index of the degree of risk aversion prevailing in the economy.

From a conceptual point of view, only the expected risk premium is acceptable for calculating a discount rate.

The price of an asset today can only correspond to expected discounted cash flows that it should generate given the rate of return required by the investor today. So, if the \$/€ exchange rate is currently 1.33, it is at this price that it is possible to buy or sell the dollar – not at 1.20, even though this is the average exchange rate over the previous years. The historical premium has, de facto, three drawbacks:

1. Given the volatility of annual returns recorded (annual returns of $= 20\%$ or $- 20\%$ are not rare), calculations have to be based on data over a very long period in order to reduce the standard deviation of observations and to arrive at a relevant average. Even over 75 years, the theoretical standard deviation of observations following a normal rule is 2.5%, which means that a premium of 5%, for example, has as much chance of being 2.5% as 5% or 7.5%. So UBS estimates that the risk premium for the USA calculated by Ibbotson since 1926, often cited and used (7.1% on arithmetical average and 5.2% on geometric average as of 2007), would change by one point if it were calculated from 1925 or 1927.

2. When markets are rising, the historic rate of return achieved increases; thus the risk premium – calculated as an average including recent years in which performances were good – rises while, because the market is performing so well, rates of return required by shareholders may be falling. Similarly, when markets are falling (2000–2003, 2007–2008), rates of return achieved are negative and bring down the historic average which takes them into account. At the same time, investors required returns rise.

3. Calculations of historical returns ignore the case of firms that went bankrupt over the period studied as this method only looks at the performance of share prices of firms still in existence today. However, the basis of a rate of return is the remuneration of the risk that a firm that goes bankrupt could generate only at a given moment. So it's hardly surprising that, using this method, we arrive at a higher risk premium (around 7%) than with the prospective method (just under 4% currently), as it ignores the case of investments with a -100% return (bankruptcy). It's a bit like including in a survey only those who have passed all of their A-levels to measure the average level of education of all 18-year-olds.

From a practical point of view, we believe that those using the historical approach to the risk premium, often driven by the fact that the current risk premium tends to be too volatile, forget that the risk-free interest rate can be even more volatile. Accordingly, proponents of the historical approach could, on the basis of the same argument of volatility, be justified in calculating the average risk-free interest rate over a long period. They don't do so because they probably realise the absurdity of the result based on a parameter, the risk-free interest rate, that is readily available in daily newspapers. In addition, it is inconsistent to calculate the risk premium using a given risk-free interest rate and in the formula of the CAPM, replacing r_F with a different figure from that used to calculate the risk premium (because most of the time we don't know what risk-free interest rate was used to calculate the risk premium). Finally, those with many years' experience in calculating expected risk premiums know that when interest rates rise, the risk premium tends to fall. Finally, the required rate of return doesn't rise as high as the performance of the risk-free interest rate might lead one to assume, as the risk premium absorbs part of the rate hike (and vice versa in the event of a fall in interest rates). All things considered, the rate of return required by the shareholder, calculated using expected risk premia, is less volatile than the rate of return calculated using a constant risk premium.

As there are several available sources for the expected risk premium over the very short term (a few days to a few weeks), averages of these various sources can be calculated over a period of a few (for example, three) months. Beware of the risk that the use of averages calculated over long periods could be disconnected from the market.

Section 19.2
PROPERTIES OF THE CAPM

1/ THE SECURITY MARKET LINE

4 *It differs from the capital market line, which has the total risk σ of the security on the x-axis, not the β coefficient.*

The French research house Associés en Finance publishes the securities market line[4] for the entire euro zone. It is calculated on the basis of the **expected return** on the *y*-axis and the **beta coefficient of each stock** on the *x*-axis.

Chapter 32 examines how the value of a stock can be expressed in terms of the flow of future dividends that it is expected to pay. These dividends are discounted at the rate required by the shareholder. The expected return is thus calculated by equating the current price of the stock to the discounted sum of dividends paid out by the company to infinity.

The securities market line is quite instructive. It helps determine the required rate of return on a security on the basis of the only risk that is remunerated, i.e. the market risk.

SECURITY MARKET LINE

Example from early 2011.

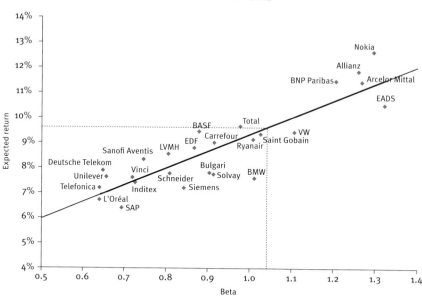

Source: Associés en Finance, 2011.

Shifts in the securities market line itself characterise the nature of changes in the markets and make it easier to understand them:

- a parallel shift, with no variation in slope (i.e. risk premium) reflects a change in the market brought on by a change in interest rates. For example, a cut in interest rates normally leads to a downward shift and thus a general appreciation of all stocks;

- a non-parallel shift (or pivoting) reflects a change in the risk premium and thus in the remuneration of risk. In this case, the riskiest stocks will move the most, whereas the least risky stocks may not be significantly affected.

In addition, the position of points *vis-à-vis* the market line serves as a decision-making tool. The above chart tells us that Deutsche Telekom offers too high an expected return for its risk. Investors will realise this and buy it, thus raising its price and lowering expected return. A stock that is "above" the securities market line is thus undervalued, while a stock that is "below" the securities market line (like EADS, the producer of Airbus) is overvalued.

But do not rush to place an order. Since this chart was printed, prices have had plenty of time to adjust.

2/ LINEARITY

An important property of the CAPM is that the measure of risk for individual assets is proportional to the weight of each security when the assets are combined into a portfolio.

Thus, for example, if an investor buys $a\%$ of asset X that has a systematic risk of β_X and places $1 - X$ of the total wealth in asset Y with a systematic risk of β_Y, then the beta of the portfolio would simply be the weighted average of the betas of single securities.

This property is extremely useful if we want to compute the beta of a diversified company. We could, in fact, consider the beta of single operating businesses and then weight each of them according to their relative market capitalisation (alternatively, we could use sales or other dimensions).

Section 19.3
THE LIMITS OF THE CAPM

The CAPM assumes that markets are efficient and it is without a doubt the most widely used model in modern finance. But financial analysts are always quick to criticise and thus this section appeases the critics by summarising how the CAPM presents some problems in practice.

1/ THE LIMITS OF DIVERSIFICATION

The CAPM is a development of portfolio theory and is based on the assumption that diversification helps to reduce risk (to the non-diversifiable risk). A study by Campbell *et al.* (2001) shows that diversification is increasingly complex and that, whereas in the 1970s a portfolio of 20 stocks reduced risk significantly, today at least 50 are required to achieve the same result.

This is due, among other things, to the greater volatility of individual stocks, although markets as a whole are no more volatile. Other reasons for this phenomenon are the arrival on the market of riskier companies, such as biotechnology, Internet and younger companies, and the dwindling prominence of conglomerates which, by nature, provided some diversification in and of themselves.

Meanwhile, the correlation between market return and return on individual stocks is falling. This may undermine the relevancy of the CAPM. Statistically, beta is becoming less and less relevant.

2/ DIFFICULTIES IN PRACTICAL APPLICATION OF THE CAPM

The first difficulty one encounters when using the CAPM is determining the risk-free rate which, all things considered, is just a theoretical concept.

The term "risk-free" means no risk of default and no coupon reinvestment risk. Zero-coupon government bonds come the closest to meeting this definition. However:

1. While governments' power to mint currency means that their risk of default is low, they still have some risk (the Argentine default in 2002 is one illustration).
2. In order to have zero reinvestment risk on the coupon, the reference period must be known.

In the case of an asset paying a return only once in five years, it may be easy to use the zero coupon rate produced by the yield curve as a risk-free rate (see Chapter 20). However, the single-period CAPM is often used to value assets whose cash flows are spread out over time. So, theoretically, we would have to use a different discounting rate for each of the periods. Each of these rates would have to be calculated with a different risk-free rate, thus complicating the use of the CAPM. In practice, this is done only to value bonds (see Chapter 21). For other assets, the risk-free rate at best reflects no more than the asset's duration.

Some apply the CAPM using short-term interest rates (the equity market premium is then obviously adjusted). This enables us to get rid of the problem of residual risk in government bonds but does not correspond to the actual average maturity of the future cash flows.

Richard Roll has pointed out that determining a market portfolio is not as easy as one would like to think. In theory, the market portfolio is not made up solely of stocks nor even just financial assets, but of all the assets that can be acquired. It is therefore impossible, in practice, to come up with a true market portfolio, especially when looking at it from an international point of view.

However, this is not an insurmountable obstacle. Indeed, in a portfolio already containing a large number of assets, the marginal contribution to return of a new asset is low. Portfolio diversification makes return and risk approach a limit – the return offered by a theoretically ideal market portfolio. So the market portfolio can be approximated with a portfolio containing "only" a large number of assets. Unfortunately, recent studies have shown that more and more assets must be included in a portfolio for it to be considered highly diversified.

However, we would still have to determine the return expected from the market portfolio. As the CAPM is used for making forecasts, it can also be used to calculate the return expected from a security based upon the return expected from the market portfolio, as well as the security's anticipated risk (its β). However, "anticipated" data cannot be observed directly in the market, and so forecasts must be made on the basis of historical data and macroeconomic data. For some countries, such as emerging nations, this is not easy!

3/ THE FORECAST β

The main criticism of beta is its instability over time. It boils down a large amount of information into a single figure, and this strength becomes its weakness.

The CAPM is used to make forecasts. It can be used to calculate expected return on the basis of anticipated risk. Therefore, it would be better to use a forecast β rather than an historical value, especially when the coefficient is not stable over time.

For this reason, calculations must often be adjusted to reflect the regularity of earnings and dividends, and visibility on the sector. Blume (1975) has sought to demonstrate a convergence of β towards 1 over the long term and has thus suggested the following adjustment to the standard equity β:

$$\beta_{Adjusted} = \beta_{Historic} \times \frac{2}{3} + \beta_{Market} \times \frac{1}{3}$$

Knowing that β_{Market} is 1, the value of β we get with the Blume adjustment is always closer to 1 than the historic β. This seems counter-intuitive to us as some sectors will always have a beta greater than 1. In addition, the recent crisis has demonstrated that, in difficult times, the gap between high β and low β increases.

4/ THE THEORETICAL LIMITS OF CAPM AND MARKETS AT FAIR VALUE

The CAPM assumes markets are fairly valued. But markets are not necessarily always at fair value. The fact that technical analysis has become so prominent on trading floors shows that market operators themselves have doubts about market efficiency (see Chapter 18).

Moreover, the theory of efficient markets in general, and the CAPM in particular, is based on the premise that market operators have rational expectations. To be applicable, the model must be accepted by everyone as being universally correct. The development of parallel theories shows that this is not necessarily the case.

The bias mentioned above has led the CAPM to be considered just one theoretical explanation for the functioning of the financial markets. Other theories and methods have been developed, but they have not (yet?) achieved the attractiveness of the CAPM, due to the simplicity of its concepts. We should not lose hope, as a study by Ferguson and Shockley (2003) posits that all weaknesses of the CAPM could be attributable to a mis-estimation of the market portfolio and that they would disappear if not only stocks but also bonds (and other investment opportunities) were included, as the theory suggests.

Section 19.4
MULTIFACTOR MODELS

1/ THE ARBITRAGE PRICING THEORY (APT)

In some ways, the APT (Arbitrage Pricing Theory) model is an extended version of the CAPM. The CAPM assumes that the return on a security is a function of its market risk and therefore depends on a single factor: market prices. The APT model, as proposed by Stephen Ross, assumes that the risk premium is a function of several variables, not just one, i.e. macroeconomic variables $(V_1, V_2, \ldots, V_n)$, as well as company "noise".

SECTION 2

So, for security J:

$$r_J = a + b_1 \times r_{V1} + b_2 \times r_{V2} + \ldots + b_n \times r_{Vn} + \text{Company-specific variable}$$

The model does not stipulate which V factors are to be used. Ross's original article uses the following factors, which are based on quantitative analyses:

- unanticipated variations in inflation;
- unanticipated variations in manufacturing output;
- unanticipated variations in the risk premium;
- changes in the yield curve.

The risk premium is then the sum of the risk premiums on each of the variables:

$$r_J - r_F = b_1 \times (r_{V1} - r_F) + b_2 \times (r_{V2} - r_F) + \ldots + b_n \times (r_{Vn} - r_F)$$

To use this model, we must first identify the relevant variables of a single security, the corresponding risk premiums, and then measure the security's sensitivity to these variables. For example, a chemical or paper company is more sensitive to overall economic growth than a maker of video games or a water distributor.

If all the b coefficients are zero, the risk premium is nil and the security's return is the risk-free rate.

In building a portfolio, an investor can adjust the various b values to obtain the desired level of risk. The most frequently used values are the difference between long-term and short-term government bond yields, changes in short-term interest rates, changes in effective exchange rates, changes in economic growth rates and unanticipated changes in inflation.

Comparing the APT model to the market portfolio, we can see that APT has replaced the notion (hard to measure in practice) of return expected by the market with a series of variables which, unfortunately, must still be determined. This is why APT is a portfolio management tool and not a tool for valuing stocks.

2/ THE FAMA–FRENCH MODEL

There are offshoots from the APT that have sought to explain historical returns by company-specific factors rather than the general macroeconomic factors in the APT. For example, Eugene Fama and Kenneth French (1995) have isolated three factors: market return (as in the CAPM), price/book value (see Chapter 32), and the gap in returns between large caps and small caps (which lends credence to the notion of a liquidity effect).

Other factors can be added to this list, including P/E, market capitalisation, yield and even past performance (which is a direct contradiction of efficient market theory). However, these are based on purely empirical approaches, not theoretical ones. While they criticise the CAPM, they offer no better alternative model.

3/ LIQUIDITY PREMIUM, SIZE PREMIUM AND INVESTOR PROTECTION

Among factors used in determining risk, the criteria by which liquidity can be measured (size, free float, transaction volumes, bid–ask spread) are often statistically significant. In other words, the required return on a security often appears to be a function of liquidity.

In order to avoid confusion, it is preferable to separate the liquidity premium due to free float, transaction volumes and bid–ask spread from the so-called "size premium". The size premium is the additional remuneration due to the higher risk and, therefore, the higher cost of capital, associated with the idea of the smaller size of the company and of the trading volume.

A number of studies have argued that the expected return and the cost of capital are inversely related to liquidity as represented by free float, transaction volume and bid–ask spread. If this is the case, an interesting consequence is that it is much easier to increase the liquidity of the firm's stock, while it can be quite difficult to lower the risk of a firm. Thus, it might be easier for a firm to lower its cost of capital through liquidity enhancement than through changing its risk profile.

What can corporations do in order to increase the liquidity of stocks? Mendelson and Amihud (2000) suggest two possible strategies:

1. They could try to bring in more uninformed investors. Stock splits may be useful in this regard.
2. They could disclose more information.

Ibbotson Associates has broken down the NYSE stock returns into deciles by size, as measured by the aggregate market value of the common equity. The results show that the excess returns over the basic general equity risk premium increase with decreasing size, as shown in the table below.

Decile	Beta	Size premium (beta adjusted) (%)	Biggest company by market value ($m)
Mid-cap, 3rd–5th dec.	1.13	1.34	6794
Low-cap, 6th–8th dec.	1.24	2.12	1776
Micro-cap, 9th–10th dec.	1.38	4.65	477

Source: Morningstar–SBBI, Valuation Edition 2011 Yearbook

If we expand the CAPM to also reflect the size effect, we can expand the cost of equity capital formula to add this factor:

$$k = r_F + \beta \times (k_M - r_F) + \text{Size premium}$$

Hamon and Jacquillat (1999) have demonstrated the existence of a liquidity premium in Europe, which is nil for large caps and significant for small caps. The liquidity premium should be added to the return derived from the CAPM to arrive at the total return expected by the shareholder. Hamon and Jacquillat use the term "market plane" (instead of securities market line). Under their model, expected return on a security is a linear equation with two parameters: the market premium and the liquidity premium. What is λ? Let us report the definition from the original article:

$$k = r_F + \beta \times (k_M - r_F) + \lambda \times \text{Liquidity premium}$$

In early 2011, Associés en Finance estimated the market plane parameters for euro-zone stocks at:

$$k = 3.15\% + \beta \times 6.25\% + \lambda \times 1.16\%$$

The liquidity premium, which is expected in addition to the required rate of return, finds its opposite number in the notion of "liquidity discount".

LIQUIDITY PREMIUM IN EUROPE

The liquidity premium was found in a study on the returns of several hundred European stocks.

Source: Associés en Finance.

There is also some evidence that the cost of equity goes up where insider-trading laws are not enforced and legal protection of minorities is flawed. The legal system governing investors and markets in a given country *can influence systematic risk* because it determines the level of protection given to minority shareholders and other financial claimants.

La Porta *et al.* (1998) report that companies in common law countries have higher valuations than companies in civil law countries. The median of medians of Tobin's Q is 1.23 for common law and 1.10 for civil law countries.

These results are consistent with the prediction that better shareholder protection is associated with higher corporate valuation. At the same time, the growth rate in sales is also higher for common law countries, suggesting that companies in those countries may be able to access better investment opportunities.

SUMMARY

The summary of this chapter can be downloaded from www.vernimmen.com.

This chapter has shown how to work out the cost of equity, i.e. the rate of return required on equity capital. The investor's required rate of return is not linked to total risk, but solely to market risk. Conversely, in a market in equilibrium, intrinsic – or diversifiable – risk is not remunerated.

The CAPM (Capital Asset Pricing Model) is used to determine the rate of return required by an investor.

Risk-free rate $= \beta \times$ market risk premium, or:

$$k = r_F + \beta \times (k_M - r_F).$$

Although the CAPM is used universally, it does have drawbacks that are either practical (for reliable determination of beta coefficients) or fundamental in nature (since it supposes that markets are in equilibrium). This criticism has led to the development of new models, such as the Arbitrage Pricing Theory (APT), and has highlighted the importance of the liquidity premium for groups with small free floats. Like the CAPM, the APT assumes that the required rate of return no longer depends on a single market rate; however, it considers a number of other variables too, such as the difference between government bonds and Treasury bills, unanticipated changes in the growth rate of the economy or the rate of inflation, etc.

SECTION 2

QUESTIONS

1/ Explain in a few lines why diversifiable risk cannot be remunerated on markets in equilibrium.

2/ Given that diversifiable risk is not remunerated, would it be worthwhile to diversify an investment?

3/ What is the rate of return required by the shareholder equal to?

4/ What is the drawback of the β coefficient?

5/ A shareholder requires a rate of return that is twice as high on a share with a β coefficient that is twice as high as that of another share. True or false?

6/ What does a low-risk premium indicate?

7/ On the graph on page 352, does the Bulgari share seem under- or overvalued to you? What about the Inditex (Zara) share?

8/ What is the strong point of the APT compared with the CAPM? And the weak point?

9/ Will liquidity premiums tend to rise or fall during a crash? Why?

10/ What does a reduced liquidity premium indicate?

11/The standard deviation of the earnings on State Bank of India shares is 40%, while for Siemens it is only 28%. However, State Bank of India has a β of 1.13 and Siemens of 1.7. Explain how this is possible.

12/Explain why an investor would be prepared to require a return lower than the risk-free rate for a share with a negative β.

13/How do you explain the fact that rates of return required by investors may be identical for two groups of totally different activities (oil and IT services, for example) as long as they have the same β?

14/An experiment was recently carried out where a child, an astrologer and a financial analyst were each given €10 000 to invest for eight years. Who do you think achieved the best results?

15/Mid-2010 we could see that large food processing groups (Danone, Kraft, Nestlé, Unilever) were valued at 17.1 times their expected results. For smaller groups in the same sector (LDC, Bonduelle, Bongrain) the ratio was only 12.5. State your views.

More questions are waiting for you at www.vernimmen.com.

EXERCISES

1/What rate of return should be required on the Bharti Airtel share, which has a β of 0.7, if the Rio Tinto share, which has a β of 1.1, returns 10% and is correctly valued, and the rate of a risk-free asset is 5%?

2/Are the following shares undervalued, correctly valued or overvalued? The rate for a risk-free asset is 5.5% and the market risk premium is 4%.

Share	Imperial Tobacco	Walmart	Volkswagen	ING	UBS
β	0.34	0.77	0.93	1.47	2.1
Rate of return	9%	8.2%	8%	10%	18%

3/You think that the Lapparent.com share will be worth €40 in one year. What price would you be prepared to pay today if the no-risk cash rate is 5%, the market rate of return is 9% and the β is 2.7?

4/Your portfolio has a β of 1.2, the no-risk cash rate is 5.6% and the risk premium is 3%. In this chapter you learned about the APT and were told that the two V factors are growth of GDP and unanticipated inflation. The equation for the model is: $r_j = 5.6\% + b_{j_1} \times 2\% + b_{j_2} 3\ 5\%$. Suppose that the sensitivity of your portfolio to GDP growth is 20.4, what is your portfolio's sensitivity to unanticipated inflation? You believe that a recession is looming and you wish to eliminate your portfolio's sensitivity to GDP growth but you still want to get the returns you expected. What happens to your portfolio's sensitivity to unanticipated inflation?

Questions

1/ Because if it were remunerated, this would be an "unwarranted" gain.

2/ Yes, in order to eliminate it, given that it is not remunerated.

3/ Risk-free rate + market risk premium.

4/ Its instability.

5/ No, because this would be forgetting the constant (the no-risk cash rate) in the equation for the required rate of return.

6/ That the market may be about to take a steep dive because risk is not being adequately rewarded.

7/ Overvalued, because the required rate of return, given the risk, is too low. It will thus rise, causing the share price to fall. Inditex is on the "securities market line" and is therefore correctly valued.

8/ Analysis of the market return in different components. The degree of precision required, because risk premiums by factor and the associated betas are difficult to estimate.

9/ To rise, because investors will only wish to invest in very liquid shares that they can sell immediately.

10/ A good thing for small companies, generally growing rapidly, which are in fashion at the time.

11/ The standard deviation is explained both by the market risk and the specific risk of the share, while the β only reflects the market risk of the share. State Bank of India thus has a very high specific risk.

12/ These types of shares are very rare and very valuable, because they go up when the market falls! Their marginal contribution to the reduction of a portfolio's risk is thus strong.

13/ Because what is important in the CAPM is not the specific risk but the market risk of each security.

14/ The child. If markets are really efficient, the answer is completely random.

15/ It is due to the liquidity premium as the required rate of return will be higher on smaller companies and their multiple of future earnings will be lower.

Exercises

A detailed Excel version of the solutions is available at www.vernimmen.com.

1/ Risk premium: $(10\% - 5\%)/1.1 = 4.54\%$. $k = 5\% + 0.7 \times 4.54\% = 8.2\%$.

2/ Undervalued: Imperial Tobacco, UBS. Correctly valued: Walmart. Overvalued: Volkswagen, ING.

3/ €40/ $(5\% + 2.7 \times (9\% - 5\%) + 1) = €34.54$.

4/ $r = 5.6\% + 1.2 \times 3\% = 9.2\% \cdot (9.2\% - 5.6\% + 2\% \times 0.4)/5\% = 0.88$
$(9.2\% - 5.6\%)/5\% = 0.72$.

BIBLIOGRAPHY

To read articles by the economists who developed the CAPM:

J. Lintner, The valuation of risk assets and the selection of risky investments in stock portfolios and capital budgets, *Review of Economics and Statistics*, **47**(1), 13–37, February 1965.

H. Markowitz, Portfolio selection, *Journal of Finance*, **7**(1), 77–91, March 1952.

W. Sharpe, Capital asset prices: A theory of market equilibrium under conditions of risk, *Journal of Finance*, **19**(3), 425–442, September 1964.

For an overview of the CAPM:

E. Fama, M. Miller, *The Theory of Finance*, Holt, Rinehart Winston, 1972.
A. Perold, The capital asset pricing model, *Journal of Economic Perspectives*, **18**(3), 3–24, Summer 2004.

For criticism on the limitations of the CAPM:

M. Blume, Betas and their regression tendencies, *Journal of Finance*, **30**(3), 785–795, June 1975.
J. Campbell, M. Lettau, B. Malkiel, Y. Xu, Have individual stocks become more volatile? An empirical exploration of idiosyncratic risk, *Journal of Finance*, **56**(1), 1–43, February 2001.
E. Fama, K. French, Size and book-to-market factors in earnings and returns, *Journal of Finance*, **50**(1), 131–155, March 1995.
N. Groenewold, P. Fraser, Forecasting beta: How does the "five-year rule of thumb" do?, *Journal of Business & Accounting*, **27**(7&8), 953–982, September/October 2000.
H. Markowitz, Market efficiency: A theoretical distinction and so what? *Financial Analysts Journal*, **61**(5), 17–30, September–October 2005.
R. Roll, A critique of the asset pricing theory's tests. Part I: On past and potential testability of the theory, *Journal of Financial Economics*, **4**(2), 129–179, March 1997.

For a rehabilitation of the CAPM:

M. Ferguson, R. Shockley, Equilibrium "anomalies", *Journal of Finance*, **58**(6), 2549–2580, December 2003.

For a historical approach to CAPM theory:

J. Burton, Revisiting the Capital Asset Pricing Model, *Dow Jones Asset Manager*, 20–28, May–June 1998.

For an overview of the APT:

M. Brennan, T. Chordia, A. Subrahmanyam, Alternative factor specifications, security characteristics, and the cross section of expected stock returns, *Journal of Financial Economics*, **49**(3), 345–373, September 1998.
E. Fama, K. French, The cross section of expected stock returns, *Journal of Finance*, **47**(2), 427–465, June 1992.
R. Petkova, Do the Fama–French factors proxy for innovations in predictive variables? *Journal of Finance*, **61**(2), 581–612, April 2006.
R. Roll, S. Ross, An empirical investigation of the Arbitrage Pricing Theory, *Journal of Finance*, **35**(5), 1073–1103, December 1980.
R. Roll, S. Ross, The Arbitrage Pricing Theory approach to strategic portfolio planning, *Financial Analysts Journal*, **40**(3), 14–26, May–June 1984.
S. Ross, The arbitrage theory of capital asset pricing, *Journal of Economic Theory*, **13**(3), 341–360, December 1976.
http://mba.tuck.dartmouth.edu/pages/faculty/ken.french/data_library.html is the website where it is possible to download the parameters of the Fama–French model.

On the liquidity premium:

E. Dimson, B. Hanke, The expected illiquidity premium: Evidence from equity index-linked bonds, *Review of Finance*, **8**(1), 19–47, January 2004.
J. Hamon, B. Jacquillat, Is there value-added information in liquidity and risk premiums? *European Financial Management*, **5**(3), 369–393, 1999.

J. Idier, C. Jardet, G. Le Fol, How liquid are markets: an application to stock markets, *Bankers, Markets and Investors*, **103**, 50–58, November–December 2009.

H. Mendelson, Y. Amihud, Asset pricing and the bid–ask spread, *Journal of Financial Economics*, **17**(2), 223–249, December 1986.

H. Mendelson, Y. Amihud, The liquidity route to a lower cost of capital, *Journal of Applied Corporate Finance*, **12**(4), 8–25, Winter 2000.

For a comprehensive review of risk premia:

W. Goetzmann, R. Ibbotson, *The Equity Risk Premium: Essays and Explorations*, Oxford University Press, 2006.

R. Mehra, *Handbook of the Equity Risk Premium*, Elsevier Sciences, 2007.

J. Siegel, *Stock for the Long Run*, 4th edn, McGraw Hill, 2007.

On risk premia:

R. Arnott, P. Bernstein, What risk premium is "normal"? *Financial Analysts Journal*, **58**(2), 64–85, March/April 2002.

S. Brown, W. Goetzmann, S. Ross, Survivorship bias, *Journal of Finance*, **50**(3), 853–873, July 1995.

J. Claus, J. Thomas, Equity premia as low as three percent? Evidence from analysts' earnings forecasts for domestic and international stock markets, *Journal of Finance*, **56**(5), 1629–1666, October 2001.

A. Damodoran, Estimating risk free rate, *www.damodaran.com*.

A. Damodoran, Estimating risk premiums, *www.damodaran.com*.

E. Dimson, P. Marsh, M. Staunton, *The Triumph of the Optimists. 101 Years of Investment Returns*, Princeton University Press, 2002.

F. Fama, K. French, The equity premium, *Journal of Finance*, **57**(2), 637–659, April 2002.

P. Fernandez, *The equity premium in 150 textbooks*, working paper IESE Business School, September 2009.

P. Fernandez, J. Del Campo, *Market risk premium used in 2010 by Professors: a survey with 1,500 answers*, working paper IESE Business School, May 2010.

W. Goetzmann, P. Jorion, Global Stock Markets in the Twentieth Century, *Journal of Finance*, **54**(3), 953–980, June 1999.

R. Ibbotson, P. Chen, Long-run stock returns: Participating in the real economy, *Financial Analysts Journal*, **59**(1), 88–98, January–February 2003.

M. Kritzman, *Puzzles of Finance. Six Practical Problems and their Remarkable Solutions*, John Wiley & Sons, Inc., 2002.

R. La Porta, F. Lopez de Silanes, A. Shleifer, R. Vishny, Law and Finance, *Journal of Political Economy*, **106**(6), 1113–1155, December 1998.

R. Mehra, The equity premium: Why is it a puzzle? *Financial Analysts Journal*, **59**(1), 54–69, January/February 2003.

For alternative techniques – DDM and P/E model:

T. Benninga, *Financial Modeling*, The MIT Press, 2008.

T. Copeland, T. Koller, J. Murrin, *Valuation*, John Wiley & Sons, Inc., 2000.

On chaos theory:

E. Peters, *Chaos and Order in Capital Markets*, 2nd edn, John Wiley & Sons, Inc., 1996.

SECTION 2

APPENDIX 19A: A FORMAL DERIVATION OF THE CAPM

The figure below shows the expected return and standard deviation of the market portfolio, M, the risk-free asset, r_F, and a generic risky asset I. The line connecting the risk-free asset and the market portfolio is the *capital market line*.

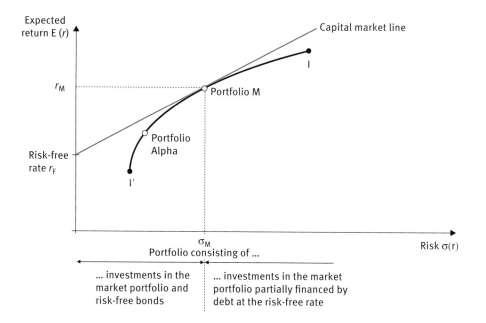

We know that when markets are in equilibrium, the prices of all financial assets must adjust until there is no excess demand. Prices, in other words, must be fixed at a level where the supply of assets equals their demand. Therefore, the market portfolio for market in equilibrium includes all marketable assets held in proportion to their value weights.

The proportion of a single asset in the market portfolio is given by:

$$w_i = \frac{\text{Market value of a single asset}}{\text{Market value of all assets}}$$

Thus, a generic portfolio (P) consisting of $a\%$ invested in the single (risky) asset I and $(1 - a\%)$ in the market portfolio will have the following mean and standard deviation:

$$E(r_P) = aE(r_i) + (1-a)E(r_M)$$

$$\sigma(r_P) = \left[a^2\, \sigma_i^2 + (1-a)^2\, \sigma_M^2 + 2a(1-a)\, \sigma_{iM} \right]^{1/2}$$

A crucial point is that the market portfolio already contains asset I held according to its market value weight because the market portfolio includes all assets held according to their market value weights.

The change in the mean and standard deviation with respect to the % of the portfolio, a, invested in asset I is determined as follows:

$$\frac{\partial E(r_P)}{\partial a} = E(r_i) - E(r_M)$$

$$\frac{\partial \sigma(r_P)}{\partial a} = \frac{1}{2}\left[a^2 \sigma_i^2 + (1-a)^2 \sigma_M^2 + 2a(1-a)\sigma_{iM}\right]^{-1/2}$$

$$\times \left[2a\sigma_i^2 - 2\sigma_M^2 + 2a\sigma_M^2 + 2\sigma_{iM} - 4a\sigma_{iM}\right]$$

Sharpe and Treynor's insight is that the $a\%$ is the excess demand for an individual risky asset. And we know that in equilibrium the excess demand for any asset must be zero. Therefore, if we evaluate the two equations above where excess demand equals zero, *we can determine the equilibrium price at point M (i.e. the only point where there is no excess demand)*. We obtain:

$$\left.\frac{\partial E(r_P)}{\partial a}\right|_{a=0} = E(r_i) - E(r_M)$$

$$\left.\frac{\partial \sigma(r_P)}{\partial a}\right|_{a=0} = \frac{1}{2}\left(\sigma_M^2\right)^{-1/2}\left(-2\sigma_M^2 + 2\sigma_{iM}\right) = \frac{\sigma_{iM} - \sigma_M^2}{\sigma_M}$$

The slope of the risk–return trade-off evaluated at M is:

$$\left.\frac{\partial E(r_P)/\partial a}{\partial \sigma(r_P)/\partial a}\right|_{a=0} = \frac{E(r_i) - E(r_M)}{(\sigma_{iM} - \sigma_M^2)/\sigma_M}$$

The final step is to recognise that the slope of the opportunity set IMI′ must also be equal to the slope of the capital market line r_FM. Since the slope of the capital market line is:

$$\frac{E(r_M) - r_F}{\sigma_M}$$

If we equate the slope of the risk–return tradeoff evaluated at M with the slope of the capital market line, we obtain:

$$\frac{E(r_M) - r_F}{\sigma_M} = \frac{E(r_i) - E(r_M)}{(\sigma_{iM} - \sigma_M^2)/\sigma_M}$$

Finally, we appropriately rearrange the equation by solving for $E(r_i)$:

$$E(r_i) = r_F + \left[E(r_M) - r_F\right]\frac{\sigma_{iM}}{\sigma_M^2}$$

This is the final equation of the **Capital Asset Pricing Model**: it states that the required rate of return on *any* asset is equal to the risk-free rate of return plus a risk premium. The latter is the *price* of the risk $[E(r_M) - r_F]$ multiplied by the quantity of risk (σ_{iM}/σ_M^2).

When shown graphically, this equation is also called the **security market line**.

Chapter 20

THE TERM STRUCTURE OF INTEREST RATES

Here comes a curveball

Conventional financial theory, portfolio theory and the CAPM, which were presented in Chapter 19, are concerned with the notion of interest rates and reducing it to the level of a factor that is exogenous to their models, namely the risk-free rate. But the risk-free rate is by no means a given variable, and there is no financial instrument in existence which allows investors to completely escape risk.

Moreover, because it is a single-period model, the CAPM draws no distinction between short-term and long-term interest rates. As has been discussed, a money-market fund does not offer the same annual rate of return as a 10-year bond. An entire body of financial research is devoted to understanding movements in interest rates and, in particular, how different maturities are linked. This is the study of how the yield curve is formed.

Section 20.1

FIXED-INCOME SECURITIES AND RISK

Investing in debt securities is not risk free, although it is much less risky than options or even stocks. There are at least four risks involved in debt securities:

- inflation risk;
- the risk of a change in interest rates if the security's maturity is different from the investment horizon;
- liquidity risk; and
- counterparty (or default) risk.

Counterparty risk is ignored in yield curves, because generally they are based on government debt, and therefore the risk is considered to be negligible (although recent economic events have shown that only a few countries really face no risk of bankruptcy). Liquidity risk is often neglected in analysing bonds with sufficient trading volumes. The two other risks play a more important part in interest rate structure.

1/ FIXED-INCOME INSTRUMENTS AND INFLATION

When an investor buys an Italian government zero-coupon bond and keeps it until maturity, he has sure and advance knowledge of the sum he will receive when the bond is redeemed (assuming that the state does not go bankrupt). However, he is not certain of that sum's future purchasing power.

Let us take the example of a zero-coupon bond redeemable for €1000 in January 2032. If you have paid €377 for this bond in January 2012, your return will be 5% per year if you keep the bond until maturity. In 2012, the market was pricing in long-term inflation at about 2.5%. This means that the price of an asset worth €1 in 2012 (subway ticket for example) should be worth €1.64 in 2032.[1] So you invested €377 today in your zero-coupon bond believing that you will be able to buy 610 subway tickets (1000/1.64) in 2032.

Unfortunately, if between 2012 and 2032 inflation is not 2.5% per year, but 4% per year, you will be able to buy just 456 tickets,[2] not 610. By investing in a long-term bond, you have frozen your nominal interest rate (5%), but not the interest rate after inflation that you will ultimately receive. This rate is called the real interest rate.

The relationship between nominal interest rates and real interest rates can be expressed as follows:

$$\text{Real interest rate} = \frac{1 + \text{Nominal interest rate}}{1 + \text{Inflation rate}} - 1$$

If inflation is not too high, the equation can be simplified as follows:

$$\text{Real interest rate} = \text{Nominal interest rate} - \text{Inflation rate}$$

2/ FIXED-INCOME SECURITIES AND THE TIMEFRAME FOR INVESTMENT

An investor who does not want to get trapped by an unexpected upturn in inflation can invest his €377 for one year, and then repeat the transaction every year. He will thus be sure that the rate at which he invests will reflect anticipation of inflation. Hence, if the one-year nominal rate is 4% (composed of a real rate of 2% and inflation of 2%) and if inflation rises to 2.5%, short-term rates will probably move to 4.5%. Repeated investment in short-term, fixed-income securities limits the risk of an unexpected upturn in inflation. Hence, our investor, with his €377 invested at 4% and with inflation of 2%, can buy 558 subway tickets in 20 years. This is true even if inflation rises to 2.5%, as the short-term rate would then be 4.5%, with the real long-term unchanged at 2%.

However, this strategy exposes the investor to trends in real short-term interest rates. It is possible that, with constant 1% inflation, real interest rates will move to 1%. The investor's nominal rate would then be 2% and in 20 years, even without any change in inflation, he would only be able to buy 459 subway tickets and not the 558 he was expecting.

1 $1.64 = 1 \times (1 + 2.5\%)^{20}$

2 $456 = 1000/ (1 + 4\%)^{20}$

SECTION 2

Investors also choose their investment timeframe on the basis of liquidity preferences. Repeated short-term investments secure a certain measure of liquidity in exchange for uncertainty about the ultimate rate of return. To secure a guaranteed return, an investor in long-term bonds must keep his bonds until maturity.

3/ Choosing risk

Thus, it can be seen that investors must choose their type of risk. They can elect to have the maturity of their investment coincide with their investment timeframe, and thus expose themselves to inflation risk (but not interest rate risk), or they can choose a short-term timeframe and renew their investment on a regular basis, and thus expose themselves to interest rates (but not inflation).

Depending upon the timeframe chosen, an investor will not consider short-term and long-term rates in the same way:

* The long-term investor is willing to receive a lower yield to maturity than a short-term investor who will have to renew constantly, considering that "normally" long-term rates are below short-term rates.
* The short-term investor, on the other hand, will consider it "normal" that short-term rates should be below long-term rates.

Only a bond with a redemption value and interest rate indexed to inflation can protect against unexpected changes in inflation and ensure fixed annual rate, as long as the issuer does not go bankrupt and the bond's maturity is the same as the investment timeframe.

Section 20.2
THE DIFFERENT INTEREST RATE CURVES

1/ How a bond breaks down

Consider a bond issued by India Motors on 24 February 2011 paying 4.25% annual interest on a €50 000 face value, i.e. €2125, and a 7-year maturity.

3 That is, the bond has only one final stream with both capital and capitalised interest.

Like any financial security, the India Motors bond is a cash flow timetable. But in another light, it can also be thought of as a **portfolio of zero-coupon bonds**.[3] This "portfolio" is based on a zero-coupon bond that matures 24 February 2012 with a redemption value of €2125, a zero-coupon bond that matures 24 February 2013 with a redemption value of €2125, and so on, concluding with a zero-coupon bond that matures 24 February 2018 with a redemption value of €52 125.

Each of these zero-coupon bonds can be valued individually. The sum of the values is equal to the value of the India Motors bond (otherwise arbitrage traders would quickly re-establish the equilibrium). The present value of our India Motors bond can thus be calculated as follows:

$$PV = \sum_{t=1}^{7} \frac{F_t}{(1+r_t)^t}$$

where F_t is the cash flows of year i (€2125 for the first 6 years and €52 125 for the 7th year) and r_t is the market rate for zero-coupon bonds with a maturity of N years. The single rates of interest on zero-coupon bonds are named **spot rates**. The series of spot rates, r_1, r_2 etc., is *one* way of expressing the **term structure** of interest rates.

Rather than discounting each of the payments at a different rate of interest, it could be possible to find a single rate of discount that would produce the same result. This rate is defined as **yield to maturity**, and it is in fact exactly the same as the internal rate of return but masquerading under another name!

2/ Curve of zero-coupon rates and swap curve

By charting the interest rate for the same categories of risk at all maturities, the investor obtains the yield curve that reflects the anticipation of all financial market operators.

However, if bond market data were used to calculate yields to maturity, then the coupons would introduce a bias. The yield curve shows the interest rate on instruments with different maturities and different coupons. Using a zero-coupon curve allows one to track overall changes in yields to maturity, while offering the advantage of describing more precisely the changes caused by market anticipation.

Zero-coupon bonds for each maturity have recently developed very quickly, although they are rarely listed and, when they are, they are too illiquid for their yield to maturity to be significant. So a zero-coupon yield curve is only based on listed and liquid bonds (such as government bonds). One method is commonly obtained with the **bootstrapping model**, which first studies bonds maturing in 1 year. Their yield to maturity is necessarily a zero-coupon yield (as there is only one cash flow, one year out). Then, by observing the price of a 2-year bond, we can figure the yield to maturity of a 2-year zero-coupon bond. The entire curve is obtained by repeating the calculation for each maturity.[4]

With the development of inflation-indexed government bonds, it should soon be possible to estimate the real yield curve on zero-coupon bonds. Inflation-indexed bonds are a financial innovation that disassociates two risks that had been intertwined: the coupon reinvestment risk and the inflation risk.

Interest rate swaps[5] allow banks to trade fixed-rate-based interest streams for variable-rate ones among themselves or with clients. This development has led to a much larger market than the one for government bonds, as many governments are seeking to reduce their debt. More and more often, yield curves are calculated on the basis of interest rate swaps, and these are becoming the benchmark.

3/ The various yield curves

The concept of premium helps explain why the interest rate of any financial asset is generally proportional to its maturity.

4 *That is, the bond has only one final stream with both capital and capitalised interest.*

5 *See Chapter 49.*

Hence, the so-called yield curve should have a configuration like those on the chart for March 2011.

SECTION 2

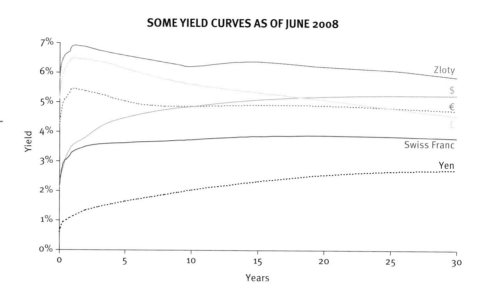

SOME YIELD CURVES AS OF JUNE 2008

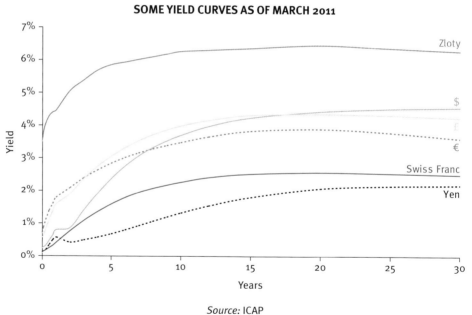

SOME YIELD CURVES AS OF MARCH 2011

Source: ICAP

Generally speaking, the yield curve reflects the market's anticipation regarding:

- long-term inflation;
- the central bank's monetary policy; and
- the country's issuing debt management policy.

Hence, during a period of economic recovery, the yield curve tends to be "normal" (i.e. long yields are higher than short yields). The steepness of the slope depends on:

- how strong an expected recovery is;
- what expectations the market has about the risk of inflation; and

- the extent to which the market expects a rapid tightening in central banks' intervention rates (to calm inflationary risks).

The curve's upward slope in 2011 is due to the extremely low levels reached by short-term rates, following central banks interventions to avoid a major economic downturn and to support the economy.

In contrast, when a recession follows a period of growth, the yield curve tends to reverse itself (with long-term rates falling below short-term rates). The steepness of the negative slope depends on:

- how strong expectations of recovery are;
- how credible the central bank's policy is (i.e. how firm the central banks are in fighting inflation); and
- the extent to which inflationary trends appear to be diminishing (despite the recession, if inflationary trends are very strong then long-term rates will tend to remain stable, and the curve could actually be flat for some time).

This is what could be observed in early 2008 when, due to the lack of liquidity, short-term euro and British pound interest rates were above long-term interest rates.

Lastly, when rates are low, the curve cannot remain flat for any length of time because investors will buy fixed-rate bonds. As long as investors expect that their capital gain, which is tied to falling long-term rates, is more than the cost of short-term financing, then they will continue to purchase the fixed-rate bonds. However, when long-term rates seem to have reached a lower limit, these expectations will disappear because investors will demand a differential between long-term and short-term rates' yield on their investment. This results in:

- either a rebound in long-term rates; or
- stable long-term rates if short-term rates fall because of central bank policies; and
- a steepening in the curve, the degree of which will depend on the currency.

We saw such a movement back to the upward slope at the end of 2008 for the Swiss franc.

Section 20.3
RELATIONSHIP BETWEEN INTEREST RATES AND MATURITIES

1/ RELATION BETWEEN INTEREST RATES AND MATURITIES

By no means are short-term and long-term rates completely disconnected. In fact, there is a fundamental and direct link between them.

About 20 years ago, this relationship was less apparent and common consensus favoured the **theory of segmentation**, which said that supply and demand balanced out across markets, with no connection among them, e.g. the long-term bond market and the short-term bond market.

As seen above, this theory is generally no longer valid, even though each investor will tend to focus on his own timeframe. It is worthwhile reviewing the basic mechanisms. For example, an investor who wishes to invest on a 2-year time basis has two options:

- he invests for two years at today's fixed rate, which is the interest rate for any two-year investment; or
- he invests the funds for one year, is paid the one-year interest rate at the end of the year, and then repeats the operation.

In a **risk-free environment**, these two investments would produce the same return, as the investor would already know the return that he would be offered on the market in one year for a one-year bond. As he also knows the current one-year rate, he can determine the return on a two-year zero-coupon bond.

$$(1 + {_0r_2})^2 = (1 + {_0r_1}) \times (1 + {_1r_1})$$

where ${_0r_2}$ is the current two-year rate, ${_1r_1}$ the one-year rate in one year and ${_0r_1}$ the current one-year rate.

The formula can be generalised for all one-year rates:

$$(1 + {_0r_N})^N = \prod_{t=0}^{N-1}(1 + {_ir_1})$$

The long-term rate (N years) in a risk-free environment is thus the geometric average of n one-year interest rates.

2/ TAKING LIQUIDITY INTO CONSIDERATION

The first theories to highlight the existence of a premium to reflect the relative lack of liquidity of long-term investments were the market **preferred habitat theory** and the **liquidity preference theory**.

In the mid-1960s, Modigliani and Sutch advanced the theory of preferred habitat, which says that investors prefer certain investment timeframes. Companies that wish to issue securities whose timeframe is considered undesirable will thus have to pay a premium to attract investors.

The theory of liquidity preference is based on the same assumption, but goes further in assuming that the preferred habitat of all investors is the short term. Investors preferring liquidity will require a liquidity premium if they are to invest for the long term.

Hence, long-term rates will be the geometric average of anticipation of short-term rates increased by a liquidity premium normally increasing with maturity.

Even if investors anticipate fixed short-term rates, the yield curve will slope upward due to the liquidity premia.

Section 20.4
A FLASHBACK

After having studied the yield curve, it is easier to understand that the discounting of all the cash flows from a fixed-income security at a single rate, regardless of the period when they are paid, is an oversimplification, although this is the method that will be used throughout this text for stocks and capital expenditure. It would be wrong to use it for fixed-income securities.

In order to be more rigorous, it is necessary to discount each flow with the interest rate of the yield curve corresponding to its maturity: the one-year rate for next year's income stream, the three-year rate for flows paid in three years, etc. Ultimately, yield to maturity is similar to an average of these different rates.

SUMMARY

The summary of this chapter can be downloaded from www.vernimmen.com.

The most prevalent risks associated with an investment in a debt security include the risk of default, the coupon reinvestment risk and the risk of inflation. Relying on financial analysis, the risk of default can be isolated and analysed separately. However, the other two risks lie at opposite ends of the risk scale. Investors factor them into the risk equation through a liquidity premium, which depends on the maturity of the debt security.

Rates of return on bonds with different maturity dates can be plotted on a graph known as the yield curve. In order to avoid distortions linked to coupon rates of bonds, it is better to analyse zero-coupon curves that can be reconstituted on the basis of the yield curve.

The shape of the yield curve depends on changes in expectations about short-term rates and the liquidity premium that investors will require for making a long-term investment. In a risk-free environment, the long-term rate at *n* years is a geometric average of short-term rates anticipated for future periods. Generally, there is a positive link between the interest rate of a financial asset and its duration, which is where the rising yield curves come from. However, the yield curve can also slope the other way, especially during a recession.

Different mathematical models are now seeking to model and anticipate the shape of yield curves and how they will change on the basis of simple parameters.

QUESTIONS

1/ What is the difference between the zero-coupon curve and the yield curve?

2/ Why is a yield curve showing higher long-term interest rates than short-term rates (rising curve) called a normal curve?

3/ What risk are we talking about when we say that government bonds are risk-free?

4/ What is the "reinvestment risk"?

5/ On a market where no zero-coupon bond is traded can you determine the interest rate at two years if you know the interest rate at one year? And then the rate for a three-year maturity?

6/ And if you do not know the interest rate at one year?

More questions are waiting for you at www.vernimmen.com.

SECTION 2

EXERCISE

You observe the following prices for different bonds (note that the coupons on all of them have just been paid and their face value is 100).

Bond	Maturity (years)	Annual coupon (%)	Price
1	1	7	99
2	2	9	99
3	3	8	95
4	4	7	89
5	5	10	97

(a) Calculate the return on each of these bonds.

(b) Reconstruct the zero-coupon curve at 5 years.

ANSWERS

Questions

1/ *The yield curve is drawn directly, taking into account the maturity but without adjusting the coupon of each bond. The zero-coupon curve is recalculated and can be used directly for valuing a security.*

2/ *The preference for liquidity means that in normal circumstances (i.e. when anticipated changes in the inflation rate do not interfere), long-term rates are higher than short-term rates.*

3/ *There is no economic risk of the issuer going bankrupt.*

4/ *The risk of reinvesting coupons and changes in the rate of inflation (risk of losing purchasing power).*

5/ *Knowing the interest rate at one year and the price of a bond with a two-year maturity, you can draw an equation with only the two-year interest rate unknown. Once you know the rate at two years, you can use a bond with a three-year maturity and the same methodology to derive the three-year interest rate.*

6/ *You will need to use the price of two different bonds with the same two-year maturity and have two equations with two unknown elements: the one-year and two-year interest rates.*

Exercise

A detailed Excel version of the solutions is available at www.vernimmen.com.

(a) 8.08%; 9.57%; 10.01%; 10.51%; 10.81%.

(b) 8.08%; 9.64%; 10.09%; 10.62%; 11.01%.

D. Backus, S. Foresi, C. Telmer, Discrete-time models of bond pricing, *National Bureau of Economic Research*, September 1998.

M. Brennan, E. Schwartz, Bond pricing and market efficiency, *Financial Analysts Journal*, **38**(5), 49–56, September/October 1982.

M. Choudhry, *Analysing and Interpreting the Yield Curve*, John Wiley & Sons, Inc., 2004.

P. Collin-Dufresne, B. Solnik, On the term structure of default premia in the swap and LIBOR markets, *The Journal of Finance*, **56**(3), 1095–1115, June 2001.

G. Costantinides, A theory of the nominal term structure of interest rates, *Review of Financial Studies*, **5**(4), 531–552, Winter 1992.

J. Cox, J. Ingersoll, S. Ross, A reexamination of traditional hypotheses about the term structure of interest rates, *Journal of Finance*, **36**(4), 769–799, September 1981.

E. Fama, The information in the term structure, *Journal of Financial Economics*, **4**(13), 509–528, December 1984.

E. Fama, The behaviour of interest rates, *Review of Financial Studies*, **19**(2), 359–379, Summer 2006.

D. Heath, R. Jarrow, A. Morton, Bond pricing and the term structure of interest rates, *Econometrica*, **60**(2), 225–262, March 1992.

J. Hicks, *Value and Capital*, 2nd edn, Oxford University Press, 1946.

T. Ho, S. Lee, Term structure movements and pricing interest rate contingent claims, *Journal of Finance*, **41**(5), 1011–1029, December 1986.

F. Lutz, The structure of interest rates, *Quarterly Journal of Economics*, **55**(1), 36–63, November 1940.

D. Meiselman, *The Term Structure of Interest Rates*, Prentice Hall, 1962.

F. Modigliani, R. Sutch, Innovations in interest rate policy, *American Economic Review*, **56**, 178–197, May 1966.

S. Nawalkha, G. Soto, *Term Structure Estimation*, working paper, 2009.

SECTION 2

PART THREE
FINANCIAL SECURITIES

In Chapter 1 we wrote that a financial manager helps secure a company's financing needs by selling securities to his investor clients. In the following chapters, you will learn more about such securities – debt, equity, options and hybrid – as well as how they are valued and sold to investors.

Chapter 21
BONDS

Or "rendering what is fixed, volatile, and what is volatile, fixed"

A debt security is a financial instrument representing the borrower's obligation to the lender from whom he has received funds. This obligation provides for a schedule of cash flows defining the terms of repayment of the funds and the lender's remuneration in the interval. The remuneration may be fixed during the life of the debt or floating if it is linked to a benchmark or index.

The reader should recognise the basic differences between debt (Chapters 21 and 22) and equity (Chapter 23).

- Debt:

  ○ has a remuneration which is independent of the company's results and is contractually set in advance. Except in some extreme cases (a missed payment or bankruptcy), the lender will receive the interest due to him regardless of whether the company's results are excellent, average or poor;

  ○ always has a repayment date, however far off, that is also set contractually. For the moment, we will set aside the rare case of perpetual debt;

  ○ is paid off ahead of equity when the company is liquidated and its assets sold off. The proceeds will first be used to pay off creditors, and only when they have been fully repaid will any surplus be paid to shareholders.

- Equity:

  ○ has a remuneration which depends on company earnings. If those earnings are bad, there is no dividend or capital gain;

  ○ carries no guarantee of repayment at any date, however far into the future. The only "way out" for an equity investor is to sell to another equity investor, who thus takes over ownership;

  ○ is remunerated last, in the event of bankruptcy, only after the creditors have been paid off. As you know, in most cases, the liquidation of assets is not enough to fully pay off creditors. Shareholders then have no recourse, as the company is no longer solvent and equity is negative!

In other words, shareholders are fully exposed to company risk, as creditors have the first claim on revenue streams generated by operating assets (free cash flow) and only once they have been paid what is owed to them will the rest be paid to shareholders.

In light of the above, it is natural that shareholders alone should have voting rights and thus the right to appoint management. They have a very direct interest in the operating assets being managed as efficiently as possible, i.e. in having cash flow as high as possible, so that there is something left over after the creditors have been paid off (interest and principal).

Voting rights are not a fourth difference between debt and equity. Rather, they are the logical continuation of the three differences listed above. **Shareholders come after creditors in their claim on cash flow and are thus exposed to company risk. They therefore have voting rights.**

1 *i.e the value of capital employed in the firm, for more details see Chapter 32.*

Hence, the higher the enterprise value,[1] the higher the equity value. As debt is not exposed to company risk (except in the event of bankruptcy), its value will be much less sensitive to variations in enterprise value.

Most debt securities started out as regular loans or credits, but evolved into **bonds** with the development of financial markets and **disintermediation** in the 1960s.

Unlike conventional bank loans, debt securities can be traded on secondary markets (stock exchanges, money markets, mortgage markets and interbank markets). Debt securities are bonds, commercial paper, Treasury bills and notes, certificates of deposit and mortgage-backed bonds or mortgage bonds. Furthermore, the current trend is to securitise loans to make them negotiable.

Disintermediation was not the only factor fuelling the growth of bond markets. The increasing difficulty of obtaining bank loans was another, as banks realised that the interest margin on such loans did not offer sufficient return on equity. This pushed companies to turn to bond markets to raise the funds banks had become reluctant to advance.

Companies accounted for 5% of euro-denominated outstanding in 2011.

SPLIT OF BONDS IN EUROS

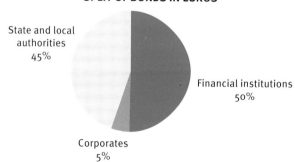

State and local authorities 45%

Financial institutions 50%

Corporates 5%

Source: European Union

2 *The graph includes only markets with the highest market value. Luxembourg is the main listing market for European bonds.*

Lastly, investors have welcomed the emergence of corporate bonds offering higher yields than government bonds. Of course, these higher returns come at the cost of higher risks.

The following graph illustrates the market value of bonds listed at the end of 2010.[2]

MARKET VALUE OF BONDS OUTSTANDING (€ bn)

Source: World Federation of Exchanges, SIFM, NYSE Euronext Paris

Many of the explanations and examples offered in this chapter deal with bonds, but they can easily be applied to all kinds of debt instruments. We shall take the example of the India Motors February 2011 bond issue with the following features.

INDIA MOTORS – 4.25% FEBRUARY 2011–FEBRUARY 2018 BOND ISSUE

Amount:	€300 000 000
Denomination:	€50 000
Issue price:	99.532% or €49 766 per bond, payable in one instalment on the settlement date.
Date of issue:	24 February 2011.
Settlement date:	24 February 2011.
Maturity:	7 years.
Annual coupon:	4.25%, i.e. €2125 per bond payable in one instalment on 24 February of each year, with the first payment on 24 February 2012.
Yield to maturity for the subscriber:	4.33% on the settlement date.
Average life:	7 years.
Normal redemption date:	The bonds will be redeemed in full on 24 February 2018 at par value.
Guarantee:	No guarantee.
Further issues (fungibility):	The issuer may, without prior permission from the bondholders, create and issue new bonds with the same features as the present bonds with the exception of the issue price and the first coupon payment date. The present bonds could thus be exchanged for the new bonds.
Rating:	BBB (Standard & Poor's) for this issue
Listing:	Luxembourg.

Section 21.1
BASIC CONCEPTS

1/ THE PRINCIPAL

(a) Nominal or face value

Loans that can be publicly traded are divided into a certain number of units giving the same rights for the same fraction of the debt. This is the nominal, face or par value, which, for bonds, is generally €1000 but is €50 000 in the India Motors case.

The nominal value is used to calculate the interest payments. In the simplest cases, it equals the amount of money the issuer received for each bond and that the issuer will repay upon redemption.

(b) Issue price

The issue price is the price at which the bonds are issued; that is, the price investors pay for each bond. *The India Motors bond was issued on 24 February 2011 at a price of €49 766, i.e. 99.532% of its face value.*

Depending on the characteristics of the issue, the issue price may be higher than the face value (issued at a premium), lower than the face value (issued at a discount) or equal to the face value (at par).

(c) Redemption

When a loan is amortised, it is said to be redeemed. In Chapter 17 we looked at the various ways a loan can be repaid:

- redemption at maturity, or on a bullet repayment basis. *This is the case of the India Motors issue*;
- redemption in equal slices (or series), or constant amortisation;
- redemption in fixed instalments.

Other methods exist, such as determining which bonds are redeemed by lottery . . . there is no end to financial creativity!

A **deferred redemption period** is a grace period, generally at the beginning of the bond's life, during which the issuer does not have to repay the principal.

The terms of the issue may also include provisions for **early redemption** (call options) or retraction (put options). A call option gives the issuer the right to buy back all or part of the issue prior to the maturity date, while a put option allows the bondholder to demand early repayment.

No such options are included in the India Motors issue.

A **redemption premium or discount** arises where the redemption value is higher or lower than the nominal value.

(d) Maturity of the bond

The life of a bond extends from its issue date to its final redemption date. Where the bond is redeemed in several instalments, the **average maturity** of the bond corresponds to the average of each of the repayment periods.

$$Average\ maturity = Average\ life = \frac{\sum_{t-1}^{N} t \times \text{Number of bonds redeemed during year } t}{\text{Total number of bonds to be redeemed}}$$

where t is the variable for the year and N the total number of periods.

The India Motors bonds have a maturity of 7 years.

(e) Guarantees

Repayment of the principal (and interest) on a bond borrowing can be guaranteed by the issuer, the parent company and less often for corporates by collateral (i.e. mortgages), pledges or warranties. Bonds are rarely secured, while commercial paper and certificates of deposit can, in theory, be secured but in fact never are.

The bonds issued by India Motors are not guaranteed.

2/ Income

(a) Issue date

The issue date is the date on which interest begins to accrue. It may or may not coincide with the **settlement date**, when investors actually pay for the bonds purchased.

Interest on the India Motors bond begins to accrue on the settlement date.

(b) Interest rate

The coupon or nominal rate is used to calculate the interest (or coupon in the case of a bond) payable to the lenders. Interest is calculated by multiplying the nominal rate by the nominal or par value of the bond.

On the India Motors issue, the coupon rate is 4.25% and the coupon payment €2125.

In addition to coupon payments, investors may also gain an additional remuneration if the issue price is lower than the par value. *On the India Motors issue, investors paid €49 766 for each bond, whereas interest was based on a par value of €50 000 and the bond will be redeemed at €50 000. In this case, the bond sold at a discount.*

(c) Periodicity of coupon payments

Coupon payments can be made every year, half-year, quarter, month or even more frequently. On certain borrowings, the interval is even longer, since the total compounded interest earned is paid only upon redemption. Such bonds are called **zero-coupon bonds**.

In some cases, the interest is **prepaid**; that is, the company pays the interest at the beginning of the period to which it relates. In general, however, the **accrued** interest is paid at the end of the period to which it relates.

The India Motors issue pays accrued interest on an annual basis.

The actual return on an investment (or the cost of a loan for the borrower) depends on a number of factors: the difference between the settlement date and the issue date, the issue premium/discount, the redemption premium/discount, the deferred redemption period and the coupon payment interval. As a result, the nominal rate is not very meaningful.

We have seen that the **yield to maturity** (see Chapter 17) cancels out the bond's present net value; that is, the difference between the issue price and the present value of future flows on the bond. **Note that for bonds, the yield to maturity (y) and the internal rate of return are identical.** This yield is calculated on the settlement date when investors pay for their bonds, and is always indicated in the prospectus for bond issues. The yield to maturity takes into account any timing differences between the right to receive income and the actual cash payment.

In the case of the India Motors bond issue:

$$99.532\,\% - \left(\sum_{i=1}^{7} \frac{4.25\,\%}{(1+y)^i} + \frac{100\,\%}{(1+y)^7} \right) = 0 \quad \text{i.e. } y = 4.33\%$$

The yield to maturity, before taxation and intermediaries' fees, represents:

- **for investors**, the rate of return they would receive by holding the bonds until maturity, assuming that the interest payments are reinvested at the same yield to maturity, which is a very strong assumption;
- **for the issuer**, the pre-tax actuarial cost of the loan.

From the point of view of the investor, the bond schedule must take into account intermediation costs and the tax status of the income earned. For the issuer, the gross cost to maturity is higher because of the commissions paid to intermediaries. This increases the actuarial cost of the borrowing. In addition, the issuer pays the intermediaries (**paying agents**) in charge of paying the interest and reimbursing the principal. Lastly, the issuer can deduct the coupon payments from its corporate income tax, thus reducing the actual cost of the loan.

The yield to maturity on a security is the *ex ante* **promised rate** at a moment in time. The lender will obtain this rate if he keeps the security until the maturity *and the lender doesn't default*. Thus, the promised rate is not necessarily the rate *actually* realised if the bond is held to maturity. The **realised rate** is the rate of discount that equates all payments actually received by investors, including the final principal payment, with the market price of the security at the time it was purchased. The difference between the two rates is known as the **loss rate** attributable to default. If default probability is a positive number, the **expected yield** on a security will be less than that promised.

1/ Spreads

The spread is the difference between the rate of return on a bond and that on a benchmark used by the market. In the euro area, the benchmark can be:

- a short-term rate, the 3- or 6-month Euribor, for floating rate debt;
- the Interest Rate Swap (IRS) rate or government bond yields for long-term debt.

The India Motors bond was issued with a spread of 135 basis points (1.35%) to mid swap rate, meaning that India Motors had to pay 1.35% more than banks per year to raise funds.

The spread is a key parameter for valuing bonds, particularly at the time of issue. It depends on the perceived credit quality of the issuer and the maturity of the issue, which are reflected in the credit rating and the guarantes given. Spreads are, of course, a relative concept, depending on the bonds being compared. The stronger the creditworthiness of the issuer and the market's appetite for risk, the lower the margin will be.[3]

3 *An interesting study on yield spreads in major financial areas is periodically published by the International Monetary Fund and can be freely obtained at www.imf.org.*

Spreads tend to widen markedly during a crisis (like in 2008-2010), both in absolute terms and relative to each other.

SECTION 2

SPREADS IN EUROPE

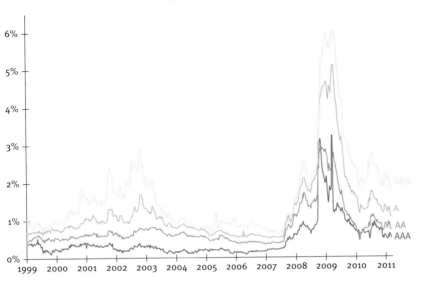

Source: Datastream

SPREADS IN THE USA

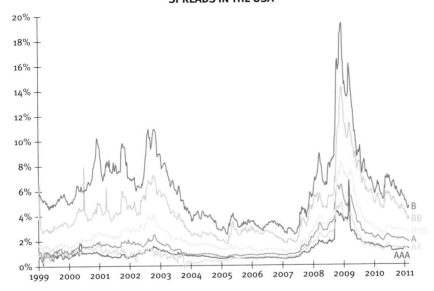

Source: Datastream

Spreads are so important that they have become the key criteria for both issuers and investors when they want to issue, sell or buy bonds.

2/ THE SECONDARY MARKET

Once the subscription period is over, the price at which the bonds were sold (their issue price) becomes a thing of the past. The value of the instrument begins to fluctuate on the secondary market. Consequently, the yield to maturity published in the prospectus applies only at the time of issue; after that, it fluctuates in step with the value of the bond.

Theoretically, changes in the bond's yield to maturity on the secondary market do not directly concern the borrower, since the cost of the debt was fixed when it was contracted.

For the borrower, the yield on the secondary market is merely an **opportunity cost**; that is, the **cost of refunding** for issuing new bonds. It represents the "real" cost of debt, but is not shown in the company accounts where the debt is recorded at its historical cost, regardless of any fluctuations in its value on the secondary market.

3/ LISTING TECHNIQUES

The price of bonds listed on stock markets is expressed as a percentage of the nominal value. In fact, they are treated as though the nominal value of each bond were €100. Thus, a bond with a nominal value of €50 000 will not be listed at €49 500 but at 99% (49 500/50 000 × 100). Similarly, a bond with a nominal value of €10 000 will be listed at 99%, rather than €9900.

This makes it easier to compare bond prices.

For the comparison to be relevant, the prices must not include the fraction of annual interest already accrued. Otherwise, the price of a bond with a 15% coupon would be 115 just before its coupon payment date and 100 just after. This is why bonds are quoted **net of accrued interest**. Bond tables thus show both the price expressed as a percentage of the nominal value and the fraction of accrued interest, which is also given as a percentage of the nominal value.

The table below indicates that on April 2011, the India Motors bond traded at 100.7% with an accrued interest of 0.42%. This means that at that date the bond cost €50 600, i.e.: €50 000 × (100.7% + 0.42%).

Price	Bond ticker	Gross YTM	Maturity	Maturity date	Modified duration	Duration	Accrued interest	Next coupon payment
100.7%	IN0010859686	4.13 %	6.90 years	24/02/18	5.86	6.10	0.42%	24/02/12

Certain debt securities, mainly fixed-rate Treasury notes with annual interest payments, are quoted at their yield to maturity. The two listing methods are rigorously equivalent and only require a simple calculation to switch from one to the other.

By now, you have probably realised that the price of a bond does not reflect its actual cost. A bond trading at 105% may be more or less expensive than a bond trading at 96%. **The yield to maturity is the most important criterion, allowing investors to evaluate various investment opportunities according to the degree of risk they are willing**

to accept and the length of their investment. However, it merely offers a temporary estimate of the **promised** return; this may be different from the **expected** return which incorporates the probability of default of the bond.

4/ FURTHER ISSUES AND ASSIMILATION

Having made one bond issue, the same company can later issue other bonds with the same features (time to maturity, coupon rate, coupon payment schedule, redemption price and guarantees, etc.) so that they are interchangeable. This enables the various issues to be grouped as one, for a larger total amount. This offers two advantages:

*   administrative expenses are reduced, since there is just one issue;
*   more importantly, the bonds are more liquid and therefore more easily traded on the secondary market. Their price is accordingly lower, as investors are willing to accept slightly lower interest rates on securities that are more liquid.

Bonds assimilated are issued with the same features as the bonds with which they are interchangeable. The only difference is in the issue price,[4] which is shaped by market conditions that are very likely to have changed since the original issue.

The India Motors bond provides for further (future fungible) issues.

Section 21.3
FLOATING-RATE BONDS

4 *In some cases, the first coupon payment is different while the issue price is identical: the bonds only become fungible after the first coupon payment.*

So far we have looked only at fixed-income debt securities. The cash flow schedule for these securities is laid down clearly when they are issued, whereas the securities that we will be describing in this section give rise to cash flows that are not totally fixed from the very outset, but follow preset rules.

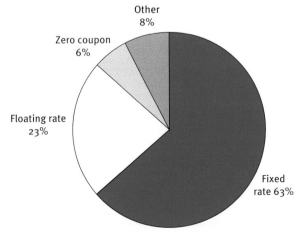

SPLIT OF BOND ISSUES IN 2010

Other 8%

Zero coupon 6%

Floating rate 23%

Fixed rate 63%

Source: European Commission-2011

SECTION 2

1/ THE MECHANICS OF THE COUPON

The coupon of a floating-rate bond is not fixed, but is indexed to an observable market rate, generally a short-term rate, such as a 6-month Euribor. In other words, the coupon rate is periodically reset based on some reference rate plus a spread. When each coupon is presented for payment, its value is calculated as a function of the market rate, based on the formula:

$$\text{Coupon}_t = (\text{Market rate}_t + \text{Spread}) \times \text{Par value}$$

This cancels out the interest rate risk since the issuer of the security is certain of paying interest at exactly the market rate at all times. Likewise, the investor is assured at all times of receiving a return in line with the market rate. Consequently, there is no reason for the price of a variable-rate bond to move very far from its par value unless the issuer's solvency becomes a concern.

Let's take the simple example of a fixed-rate bond indexed to the one-year rate that pays interest annually. On the day following payment of the coupon and in the year prior to its maturity date, the price of the bond can be calculated as follows (as a percentage of par value):

$$V = \frac{100 + r_1 \times 100}{1 + r_1} = 100$$

where r_1 is the one-year rate.

Here the price of the bond is 100% since the discount rate is the same as the rate used to calculate the coupon. Likewise, we could demonstrate that the price of the bond is 100% on each coupon payment date. The price of the bond will fluctuate in the same way as a short-term instrument in between coupon payment dates.

If the reference rate covers a period which is not the same as the interval between two coupon payments, the situation becomes slightly more complex. That said, since there is rarely a big difference between short-term rates, the price of the bond will clearly not fluctuate much over time.

The main factor that can push the price of a variable-rate bond well below its par value is a deterioration in the solvency of the issuer.

Consequently, floating-rate bonds are not highly volatile securities, even though their value is not always exactly 100%.

Three final points about the mechanics of the coupon of floating-rate securities:

- There is a distinction between a floating-rate security and what is sometimes referred to as a **variable-rate (or adjustable-rate) security** and the *frequency* at which the coupon rate is reset and the *reference rate*. A floating-rate security resets more than once a year, and the reference rate is a short-term rate. In contrast, a variable-rate security does not reset more than once a year, and the reference rate is a long-term interest rate.
- There are some issues whose coupon rate moves in the *opposite direction* of the interest-rate change. They are called **inverse floaters**.
- There are some securities whose coupon rate is equal to the reference rate as long as the reference rate is within a contractually specified range. If, at the reset rate, the reference rate is outside this range, the coupon rate is zero for that single period. These securities are called **range notes**.

2/ THE SPREAD

Like those issuing fixed-rate securities, companies issuing floating-rate securities need to pay investors a return that covers the counterparty (credit) risk. Consequently, a fixed margin **(spread)** is added to the variable percentage when the coupon is calculated. For instance, a company may issue a bond at 3-month Euribor + 0.45% (or 45 basis points). The size of this margin basically depends on the company's financial creditworthiness.

The spread is set once and for all when the bond is issued, but of course the company's risk profile may vary over time. This factor, which does not depend on interest rate trends, slightly increases the volatility of variable-debt securities.

The issue of credit risk is the same for a fixed-rate security as for a variable-income security.

3/ INDEX-LINKED SECURITIES

Floating rates, as described in the first paragraph of this section, are indexed to a market interest rate. Broadly speaking, however, a bond's coupons may be indexed to any index or price provided that it is clearly defined from a contractual standpoint. Such securities are known as **index-linked securities**.

For instance, most European countries have issued bonds indexed to inflation. The coupon paid each year, as well as the redemption price, is reset to take into account the rise in the price index since the bond was launched. As a result, the investor benefits from complete protection against inflation. With the advent of the euro, for example, the UK government issued a bond indexed to the rate of inflation in the United Kingdom. Likewise, Mexican companies have brought to market bonds linked to oil prices, while other companies have issued bonds indexed to their own share price.

To value this type of security, projections need to be made about the future value of the underlying index, which is never an easy task.

The following table shows the main reference rates in Europe.

REFERENCE RATES IN EUROPE

Reference rate	Definition	As at June 2011
EONIA (Euro Overnight Index Average)	European money-market rate. This is an average rate weighted by overnight transactions reported by a representative sample of European banks. Computed by the European Central Bank and published by Reuters.	1.075%
EURIBOR (European Interbank Offered Rate)	European money-market rate corresponding to the arithmetic mean of offered rates on the European banking market for a given maturity (between 1 week and 12 months). Sponsored by the European Banking Federation and published by Reuters, it is based on daily quotes provided by 64 European banks.	1.43% (3 months)
LIBOR (London Interbank Offered Rate)	Money-market rate observed in London corresponding to the arithmetic mean of offered rates on the London banking market for a given maturity (between 1 and 12 months) and given currency (euro, sterling, dollar, etc.).	1.381% (euro 3 months)
Interest Rate Swap (IRS)	The Interest Rate Swap (IRS) rate indicates the fixed interest rate that will equate the present value of the fixed-rate payments with the present value of the floating-rate payments in an interest-rate swap contract. The convention in the market is for the swap market makers to set the floating leg – normally at Euribor – and then quote the fixed rate that is payable for that maturity.	

A medium-term note (MTN) is essentially a plain vanilla[5] debt security (generally) with a fixed coupon and maturity date. MTNs are generally *non-callable, unsecured, senior debt securities* with *investment-grade* ratings. Notes can be issued either as bearer[6] or registered securities.[7]

There are two important differences between MTNs and corporate bonds:

- the distribution process (see Chapter 26): MTNs are normally sold *on a best-efforts basis* by financial intermediaries. Therefore the borrowing company is not guaranteed to place all its paper;[8]
- MTNs are usually sold in relatively small amounts on a *continuous basis*. This is a unique characteristic of MTNs: they are offered to investors continually over a period of time as part of an *MTN programme*.

Companies with MTN programmes have great flexibility in the types of securities they may issue. This flexibility concerns the coupon (fixed vs. floating), the embedded options and the maturities.

Despite their denomination, MTNs are not necessarily medium term. The single bonds issued in a programme can, in fact, range in maturity from 9 months to 30 years or more.

The total amount of debt issued in an MTN programme generally ranges from €100 million to €1 billion. The single issue size can be rather small and some issues have been for as little as €5 million!

1/ REASONS FOR ISSUING MTNs

An MTN programme is a series of issues over time, matching the issuer's funding requirements, and therefore should be preferred over a "traditional" bond by companies that do not need all the funding at once, nor for the full duration of the programme.

However, corporate bonds continue to be preferred when:

- funds are required immediately;
- issuers expect interest rates to rise in the near future and want to lock in a fixed rate for all the funding required;
- issuers want to minimise the cost of the issue. The all-in cost of a straight bond issue is generally lower than the all-in cost of an MTN programme. This reflects the economies of scale that may be achieved when issuing big amounts at once, as well as the greater secondary market liquidity of larger-sized issues. The liquidity premium associated with large volume issues is not known with certainty, but is estimated at around 5 to 10 basis points (Kitter, 1999).

Three major advantages can be reached through MTN programmes:

1. A high financial flexibility. This is often the most important reason behind the corporate treasury's decision to use this funding instrument, notwithstanding

the interest cost advantage of straight bonds. The major flexibility is with regards to the term to maturity of the issues. It is not rare to see issues with unconventional maturities, like 15 months, 4.5 years and so on. This makes MTNs the preferred instrument when the primary need of the issuer is to **match exactly the duration of assets with the duration of liabilities**.

2. A fast issue process of single issues, often less than a day.
3. Avoiding publicity, since often the distribution method is private placement. This characteristic is particularly relevant in times of turbulent markets, high volatility and financial distress of the company.

9 *Rule 415 (March 1982) permits delayed or continuous issuance of so-called shelf-registered corporate securities. Issuers register securities that may be sold for two years after the effective date of the registration without the requirement of another regist-ration statement each time new offerings are made. Thus shelf registration enables issuers to take advantage of brief periods of low interest rates by selling previously regis-tered securities at a moment's notice.*

COMPARATIVE CHARACTERISTICS OF BOND ISSUES IN THE INTERNATIONAL BOND MARKET

	Domestic markets	US market (Yankee bonds)	Eurobond market
Regulatory bodies	Official agency approval	SEC	Minimum regulatory control
Disclosure requirements	Variable	More detailed: • High initial and ongoing expense • Onerous to non-US firms	Determined by market prices
Issuing costs	Variable up to 4%	0.75% – 1.00%	0.2 – 0.5%
Rating requirements	Usually not	Yes	No, but commonly done
Exchange listing	Listing is usual	Listing is usual	Listing is usual
Queuing	Queuing is common	Queuing is not common	No formal process
Currency of denomination restrictions	Part of queuing (many countries have in the past or now restrict use of currency)	US does not restrict the use of US$	No restrictions
Speed of issuance	Variable	Relatively slow until Rule 415 *shelf registration*[9]	Usually fast (bought deal leads to fast issuance)

COMPARATIVE CHARACTERISTICS OF BOND ISSUES IN THE INTERNATIONAL BOND MARKET (cont.)

	Pros	Cons	Pros	Cons	Pros	Cons
Issuer incentives	+ Local visibility, diversification of funding sources	− Market may be small, queuing may prevail	+ Large market, great depth	− Disclosure is costly to foreigners, speed	+ Lower annual interest expenses, speed of placement	− Cannot sell issue in US until seasoned
Lender incentives	+ Diversified currency portfolio	− Reporting to tax authorities, withholding tax may apply	+ Great depth and liquidity, appeal of standardised information	− Reporting to tax authorities	+ Diversified currency portfolio, bearer bonds, no withholding tax	− Less liquidity and information disclosures

Section 21.5
THE VOLATILITY OF DEBT SECURITIES

The holder of a debt security may have regarded himself as protected having chosen this type of security, but he actually faces three types of risk:

- **interest rate risk** and **coupon reinvestment risk**, which affect almost solely fixed-rate securities;
- **credit risk**, which affects fixed-rate and variable-rate securities alike. We will consider this at greater length in the following section.

1/ CHANGES IN THE PRICE OF A FIXED-RATE BOND CAUSED BY INTEREST-RATE FLUCTUATIONS

(a) Definition

What would happen if, at the end of the subscription period for the India Motors 4.25% bond, the market interest rate rose to 5.25% (scenario 1) or fell to 3.25% (scenario 2)? In the first scenario, the bondholder would obviously attempt to sell the India Motors bond to buy securities yielding 5.25%. The price of the bond would fall such that the bond offered its buyer a yield to maturity of 5.25%. Conversely, if the market rate fell to 3.25%, holders of the India Motors bond would hold onto their bonds. Other investors would attempt to buy them, and the price of the bond would rise to a level at which the bond offered its buyer a yield to maturity of 3.25%.

An upward (or downward) change in interest rates therefore leads to a fall (or rise) in the present value of a fixed-rate bond, irrespective of the issuer's financial condition.

The value of a fixed-rate debt instrument is not fixed. It varies inversely with market rates: if interest rates rise, its value declines; if interest rates fall, its value appreciates.

As we have seen, if the yield on our India Motors bond rises to 4.33%, its price will move to 99.532.

But if its yield to maturity rises to 4.83% (a 0.5 point increase), its price will change to:

$$V = \sum_{i=1}^{7} \frac{4.25\,\%}{(1+4.83\,\%)^i} + \frac{100\,\%}{(1+4.83\%)^7} = 96.62\,\%, \text{ i.e. a decrease of } 2.93\%$$

This shows that holders of bonds face a risk to their capital, and this risk is by no means merely theoretical given the fluctuations in interest rates over the medium term:

LONG TERM AND SHORT TERM INTEREST RATES IN THE UK

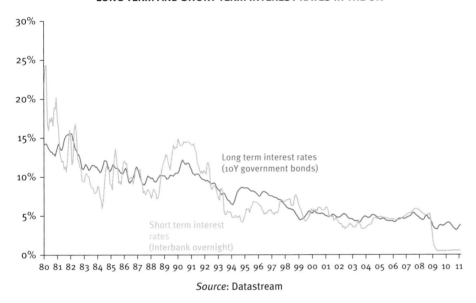

Source: Datastream

(b) Measures: modified duration and convexity

The modified duration of a bond measures the percentage change in its price for a given change in interest rates. The price of a bond with a modified duration of 4 will increase by 4% when interest rates fall from 7% to 6%, while the price of another bond with a modified duration of 3 will increase by just 3%.

From a mathematical standpoint, modified duration can be defined as the absolute value of the first derivative of a bond's price with respect to interest rates, divided by the price:

$$\text{Modified duration} = \frac{1}{V} \times \sum_{t=1}^{N} \frac{t \times F_t}{(1+r)^{t+1}}$$

where r is the market rate and F_t the cash flows generated by the bond.

Turning back to the example of the India Motors bond at its issuance date, we arrive at a modified duration of 5.94.

Modified duration is therefore a way of calculating the percentage change in the price of a bond for a given change in interest rates. It simply involves multiplying the change in interest rates by the bond's modified duration. A rise in interest rates from 4.33% to 4.83% therefore leads to a price decrease of 0.5% × 5.94 = 2.97%, i.e. from 99.532% to 99.532 × (1 − 2.97%) = 96.58%.

We note a discrepancy of 0.04% with the price calculated previously (96.62%). Modified duration is valid solely at the point where it is calculated (i.e. 4.33% here). The further we move away from this point, the more skewed it becomes. For instance, at a yield of 4.83% it is 5.73 rather than 5.94. This will skew calculation of the new price of the bond, but the distortion will be small if the fluctuation in interest rates is also limited in size. From a geometrical standpoint, the modified duration is the first derivative of price with respect to interest rates and it reflects the slope of the tangent to the price/yield curve. Since this forms part of a hyperbolic curve, the slope of the tangent is not constant and moves in line with interest rates.

(c) Parameters influencing modified duration

Let's consider the following three bonds:

Bond	A	B	C
Coupon	5%	5%	0%
Price	100	100	100
Yield to maturity	5%	5%	5%
Redemption price	100	100	432.2
Residual life	5 years	15 years	30 years

How much are these bonds worth in the event of interest rate fluctuations?

Market interest rates (%)	A	B	C
1	119.4	155.5	320.7
5	100	100	100
10	81.0	62.0	24.8
15	66.5	41.5	6.5

Note that **the longer the maturity of a bond, the greater its sensitivity to a change in interest rates**.

Modified duration is primarily a function of the maturity date. **The closer a bond gets to its maturity date, the closer its price moves towards its redemption value and the more its sensitivity to interest rates decreases.** Conversely, the longer it is until the bond matures, the greater its sensitivity to interest rate fluctuations.

Modified duration also depends on two other parameters, which are nonetheless of secondary importance to the time to maturity factor:

- **the bond's coupon rate**: the lower the coupon rate, the higher its modified duration;
- **market rates**: the lower the level of market rates, the higher a bond's modified duration.

Modified duration represents an investment tool used systematically by fixed-income portfolio managers. If they anticipate a decline in interest rates, they opt for bonds with a higher modified duration, i.e. a longer time to maturity and a very low coupon rate, or even zero-coupon bonds, to maximise their capital gains.

Conversely, if portfolio managers expect a rise in interest rates, they focus on bonds with a low modified duration (i.e. due to mature shortly and carrying a high coupon) in order to minimise their capital losses.

Convexity is the second derivative of price with respect to interest rates. **It measures the relative change in a bond's modified duration for a small fluctuation in interest rates.** Convexity expresses the speed of appreciation or the sluggishness of depreciation in the price of the bond if interest rates decline or rise.

2/ COUPON REINVESTMENT RISK

As we have seen, the holder of a bond does not know at what rate its coupons will be reinvested throughout the bond's lifetime. Only zero-coupon bonds afford protection against this risk, simply because they do not carry any coupons!

First of all, note that this risk factor is the mirror image of the previous one. If interest rates rise, the investor suffers a capital loss, but is able to reinvest coupon payments at a higher rate than the initial yield to maturity. Conversely, a fall in interest rates leads to a loss on the reinvestment of coupons and to a capital gain.

Intuitively, it seems clear that for any fixed-income debt portfolio or security, there is a period over which:

- the loss on the reinvestment of coupons will be offset by the capital gain on the sale of the bond if interest rates decline;
- the gain on the reinvestment of coupons will be offset by the capital loss on the sale of the bond if interest rates rise.

All in all, once this period ends, the overall value of the portfolio (i.e. bonds plus reinvested coupons) is the same, and the investors will have achieved a return on investment identical to the yield to maturity indicated when the bond was issued.

In such circumstances, the portfolio is said to be **immunised**, i.e. it is protected against the risk of fluctuations in interest rates (capital risk and coupon reinvestment risk).

This time period is known as the **duration** of a bond. It may be calculated at any time, either at issue or throughout the whole life of the bond.

For instance, an investor who wants to be assured of achieving a certain return on investment over a period of three years will choose a portfolio of debt securities with a duration of three years.

Note that the duration of a zero-coupon bond is equal to its remaining life.

In mathematical terms, duration is calculated as follows:

$$\text{Duration} = \frac{\displaystyle\sum_{t=1}^{N} \frac{t \times F_t}{(1+r)^t}}{\displaystyle\sum_{t=1}^{N} \frac{F_t}{(1+r)^t}}$$

Duration can be regarded as being akin to the discounted average life of all the cash flows of a bond (i.e. interest and capital). The numerator comprises the discounted cash flows weighted by the number of years to maturity, while the denominator reflects the present value of the debt.

The India Motors bond has a duration of 6.2 years at issue.

We can see that $5.94 \times (1 + 4.33\%) = 6.2$ *years.*

Turning our attention back to modified duration, we can say that it is explained by the duration of a bond, which brings together in a single concept the various determinants of modified duration, i.e. time to maturity, coupon rate and market rates.

Note, however, that duration is **barely used in practice** owing to the constant fluctuations in market rates and the constant shifts in investors' investment horizons.

Section 21.6
DEFAULT RISK AND THE ROLE OF RATING

1/ RATING AND DEFAULT RISK

Default risk can be measured on the basis of a traditional financial analysis of the borrower's situation or by using credit scoring, as we saw in Chapter 8. Specialised agencies, which analyse the risk of default, issue ratings which reflect the quality of the borrower's signature. There are three agencies that dominate the market – Standard & Poor's (*www.standardandpoors.com*), Moody's (*www.moodys.com*) and Fitch (*www.fitch.com*).

A number of scholars have investigated the main determinants of rating opinions. For corporate debt, higher ratings are generally associated with:

1. lower debt ratios;
2. higher ROCE;
3. lower variation in earnings;
4. larger companies;
5. higher interest coverage ratios;
6. lack of subordination.[10]

Although rating services have existed in the USA since the beginning of the 20th century, they are a more recent development in Europe (1980s and 1990s).

Rating agencies provide ratings for companies, banks, sovereign states and municipalities. They can decide to rate a specific issue or to give an absolute rating for the issuer (rating given to first-ranking debt). Rating agencies also distinguish between short- and long-term prospects.

Some examples of long-term debt ratings:

10 *Overall, these studies were able to explain from 60% to 90% of the ratings assigned by the rating agencies.*

Moody's	Standard & Poor's and Fitch	Definition	Examples (mid 2011)
Aaa	AAA	Best quality, lowest risk	Germany, USA, Rabobank, France
Aa	AA	High quality. Very strong ability to meet payment obligations	Total, Nestlé, city of Lyon, BNP Paribas, GE Capital, Belgium
A	A	Upper-medium grade obligations. Issuer has strong capacity to meet its obligations	Morgan Stanley, BASF, Botswana, Poland, Barclays
Baa	BBB	Medium grade. Issuer has satisfactory capacity to meet its obligations	Vivendi, Xstrata, Daimler, Eutelsat
Ba	BB	Speculative. Uncertainty of issuer's capacity to meet its obligations	Tata Motors, Piaggio, Pernod Ricard, Attijariwafa Bank
B	B	Issuer has poor capacity to meet its obligations	Cambodia, Ukraine, Toys 'R' Us, US Airways, Alcatel Lucent
Caa	CCC	Poor standing. Danger with respect to payment of interest and return of principal	Technicolor, Greece
Ca	CC	Highly speculative. Often in default	
C	C	Close to insolvency	
	D or SD	Insolvent!	Lehman Brothers, Metrogas

SECTION 2

Short-term debts:

Moody's	Standard & Poor's and Fitch	Definition	Examples (June 2011)
Prime 1	A-1	Superior ability to meet obligations	Air Liquide, AXA, France
Prime 2	A-2	Strong ability to repay obligations	Telefonica, Thales
Prime 3	A-3	Acceptable ability to repay obligations	PPR, Morocco
Not Prime	B	Speculative	Peugeot, Attijariwafa Bank, Lafarge
	C	Vulnerable	
	D	Insolvent	Lehman Brothers

Short-term rating is not independent from long-term rating, as seen in the diagram below: Rating services also add an **outlook** to the rating they give – stable, positive or negative – which indicates the likely trend of the rating over the two to three years ahead.

Short- and medium-term ratings may be modified by a + or – or a numerical modifier, which indicates the position of the company within its generic rating category.

CORRELATION BETWEEN RATING

Long term rating / Short term rating

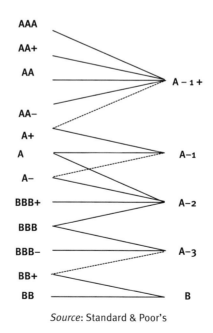

Source: Standard & Poor's

The **watchlist** alerts investors that an event such as an acquisition, disposal, merger, once it has been weighed into the analysis, is likely to lead to a change in the rating. A company on the watchlist is likely to be upgraded when the expected outcome is positive, downgraded when the expected outcome is negative and, when the agency is unable to determine the outcome, it indicates an unknown change.

Ratings between AAA and BBB are referred to as **Investment Grade**, and those between BB and D as **Speculative Grade** (or *Non Investment Grade*). The distinction between these two types of risk is important to investors, especially institutional investors, who often are not permitted to buy the risky speculative grade bonds!

The reader should avoid considering speculative grade bonds as a synonym for "junk bonds". The term "junk" originated in the mid-1970s to describe those corporate securities that lost their investment grade status due to a fundamental deterioration in the quality of their operating and financial performance (so called "fallen angels").

Since the late 1970s, this market began to include more newly issued or original issues that represented a source of capital for emerging or continuing growth companies, and those other companies which previously relied on private placements.

In Europe, rating agencies generally rate companies at their request, which enables them to access privileged information (medium-term plans, contacts with management). Rating agencies very rarely rate companies without management cooperation. When they do, the accuracy of the rating depends on the quality of the information about the company

CUMULATIVE AVERAGE DEFAULT RATE

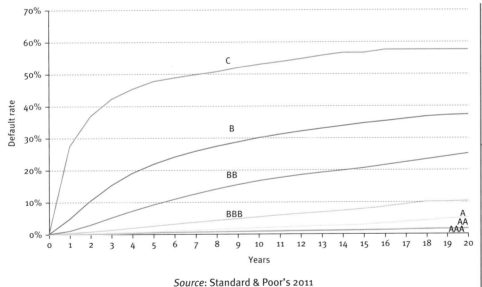

From the sample of international issuers rated by Standard & Poor's over 15 years, 0.8% of issuers rated AAA failed to pay an instalment on a loan, while 38% of issuers rated B defaulted.

Source: Standard & Poor's 2011

available on the market. If the company does not require a public rating immediately, it may ask to keep it **confidential**, and it is then referred to as a *shadow rating*.

Because the rating agencies work independently, they sometimes attach different ratings to a bond issue; this phenomenon is known as a **split rating**. The yield on a split-rated bond tends to be an average of yields for the higher and lower rating categories.

With the disappearance of exchange fluctuation exposure in Europe thanks to the introduction of the euro, investors no longer shy away from bonds issued in other eurozone countries, making it easier for them to diversify their portfolios. However, given that they

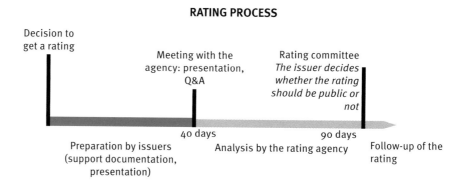

RATING PROCESS

are relatively less well-informed about the financial situation of these new investment targets, investors now rely on rating agencies much more than they did before the advent of the euro.

Moreover, the current opening up of the bond market to new issuers that are smaller and more of an unknown quantity, has led to an increase in this trend. This has long been established practice in the USA, where the range of issuers' ratings looms large.

The rating given to a company has a direct impact on the cost of the debt it has to pay.

A final comment. Academic research demonstrates that bond ratings can be predicted with a high degree of accuracy with publicly available data, leading some to question what value the agencies add beyond certification. However, it is true that bond yields are more and more associated with ratings than publicly available data alone, implying that the agencies seem to provide additional information, perhaps as a result of their contacts with management.

2/ EXPLAINING THE SPREAD ON CORPORATE BONDS

Is the relation between rating and corporate spread so strongly influenced by the default probability signalled by the class of rating of companies? The evidence is not so unanimous. An article by Elton *et al.* (2001) has explored the relative importance of the following factors in explaining corporate spreads in the USA:

1. expected default loss, because investors require a higher promised payment to compensate for the expected loss from defaults;
2. tax premium, because interest payments on corporate bonds are taxed in the USA at the state level whereas interest payments on government bonds are not;
3. risk premium, because a portion of the risk on corporate bonds is systematic rather than diversifiable.

These factors seem almost entirely to explain the spreads and expected default accounts for a surprisingly small fraction of the premium of corporate rates. A substantial portion

SECTION 2

of the spread is closely related to state taxes and – above all – to risk premiums for common stock.

Why should a systematic risk exist also for bonds? There are basically two reasons, as the authors point out:

- If expected default loss were to move with equity prices – while stock prices rise, default risk goes down and vice versa – it would introduce a systematic factor. However, the relationship between the economic cycle and yield spread is not always the same, depending on the sector to which the issuer belongs. Athanassakos and Carayannopoulos (2001) have demonstrated that while in the industrial and transportation sectors bond premia are generally higher during recessionary periods, the opposite is true for utilities. This may be the result of investors decreasing their demand for bonds in highly cyclical industries, while at the same time increasing the demand for instruments less affected by general economic conditions such as bonds issued by utilities.
- The compensation for risk required in capital markets changes over time. If changes in the required compensation for risk affect both corporate bonds and equities, then this would introduce a systematic factor.

SUMMARY

The summary of this chapter can be downloaded from www.vernimmen.com.

A debt security is a financial instrument representing the borrower's obligation to the lender from whom he has received funds. This obligation provides for a schedule of financial flows defining the terms of repayment of the funds and the lender's remuneration in the interval.

The price of a bond does not reflect its actual cost. The yield to maturity (which cancels out the bond's NPV – that is the difference between the issue price and the present value of future flows) is the only criterion allowing investors to evaluate the various investment opportunities, (according to risk and length of investment). On the secondary market, the yield to maturity is merely an opportunity cost for the issuer, i.e. the cost of refunding today.

The basic parameters for bonds are as follows:

- Nominal or face value.

- Issue price, with a possible premium on the nominal value.

- Redemption: redemption at maturity (known as a bullet repayment), constant amortisation or fixed instalments. The terms of the issue may also include provisions for early redemption (call options) or retraction (put options).

- Average life of bond: where the bond is redeemed in several instalments, the average life of the bond corresponds to the average of each of the repayment periods.

- Nominal rate: also known as the coupon rate and used to calculate interest payable.

- Issue/redemption premium/discount: the difference between the issue premium/ discount and the nominal value and the difference between the redemption premium/discount and the nominal value.

- Periodic coupon payments: frequency at which coupon payments are made. We talk of zero-coupon bonds when total compounded interest earned is paid only upon redemption.

The diversity of these parameters explains why the yield to maturity may differ from the coupon rate.

Floating-rate debt securities are exposed to the risk of interest rate fluctuations: the value of a fixed rate debt security increases when interest rates fall, and vice versa. This fluctuation is measured by:

- the modified duration, which measures the percentage change in the price of a bond for a small change in interest rates. Modified duration is a function of the maturity date, the nominal rate and the market rate;

- convexity, the second derivative of price with respect to interest rates, which expresses the speed of appreciation or the sluggishness of depreciation in the price of the bond if interest rates decline or rise;

- coupon reinvestment risk. There is a time period over which the portfolio is said to be immunised, i.e. it is protected against the risk of fluctuations in interest rates (capital risk and coupon reinvestment risk). This period is known as the duration of the bond, and is equal to the ratio of the discounted cash flows weighted by the number of years to maturity and the present value of the debt.

Fixed-rate securities have a coupon that is not fixed but indexed to an observable market rate (with a fixed margin that is added to the variable rate when the coupon is calculated). Variable-rate bonds are not very volatile securities, even though their value is not always exactly 100% of the nominal.

All debt securities are exposed to default risk which is assessed by rating agencies on the basis of ratings (AAA, AA, A, BBB, etc.) which depend on the volatility of the economic assets and the financial structure of the issuer. The result is a *spread* which is the difference between the bond's yield to maturity and that of a no-risk loan over an identical period. Obviously, the better the perceived solvency of the issuer, the lower the spread.

QUESTIONS

1/ What is face value? What is it used for?

2/ What is the difference between the average life and the duration of a bond? For what type of bond are the two equal?

3/ What is the yield to maturity of a bond? How is it computed?

4/ Is a bond more volatile on the day of issue or on the day of redemption?

5/ Is the value of a floating-rate bond always equal to 100%? Why?

6/ You are an investor anticipating a decrease in interest rates. Classify, by decreasing order of preference, these bonds:

(a) floating-rate bond to be redeemed (bullet) in 10 years;
(b) floating-rate bond to be redeemed (bullet) in 7 years;
(c) perpetuity with fixed rate

(d)   fixed-rate bond to be redeemed (bullet) in 5 years;

(e)   floating-rate bond with constant instalments with 5-year maturity;

(f)   floating-rate bond with constant amortisation with 5-year maturity.

7/ Why was the yield to maturity of India Motors's bond higher than the nominal rate at issue?

8/ True or false:

(a)   if interest rates increase, the price of fixed-rate bonds will fall;

(b)   if the nominal rate is higher than the yield to maturity, the bond will trade at less than 100% of face value;

(c)   a bond with a high coupon will be worth more than a bond with a low coupon;

(d)   the higher the duration, the higher the value of a bond.

9/ Does the investor's required rate of return for a bond increase with

(a)   inflation;

(b)   the proportion of debt in the financial structure of the corporate;

(c)   the maturity;

(d)   government bond rates;

(e)   the risk of the assets.

10/ The spread between a corporate bond yield to maturity and the Government bond rate to maturity corresponds to an option. What are its features?

11/ True or false:

(a)   the higher the duration, the lower the modified duration;

(b)   the longer the maturity, the higher the modified duration;

(c)   the higher the coupon, the higher the duration.

12/ In what situation can a floating-rate bond trade at much less than 100%?

More questions are waiting for you at www.vernimmen.com.

EXERCISES

1/ Butchery Withoutbones issued the following bond:

Amount: €125m

Issue price: 99.731%

Date of issue: 20 February 2010

Settlement date: 20 February 2010

Maturity: 7 years

Annual coupon: 5.5%, i.e. in one instalment on 20 February of each year, with the first payment on 20 February 2011.

Normal redemption date: The bonds will be redeemed in full on 20 February 2017 at par value.

(a)   Calculate the yield to maturity of the bond on issue, its modified duration and its duration.

(b)   On 21 February 2011, the yield to maturity on bonds comparable to the Butchery Withoutbones bond is 5%. Calculate the value, the modified duration and the duration on this date of the Butchery Withoutbones bond. What are your comments compared to previous results.

2/ In August 2010, Mineral Waters from Syldavia launched a two-tranche bond of the same size:

	Tranche A	Tranche B
Redemption	at maturity in 10 years	at maturity in 10 years
Interest rate	8% + 1.5 × (ABY − 8.3%)	8% − 1.5 × (ABY − 8.3%)
Interest rate floor/ceiling	0% − 16%	0% − 16%

ABY = average bond yield on Syldavian market

On the launch date of the bond, the ABY was 8.3%.

(a)   Analyse the behaviour of these two bonds for different ABYs.
(b)   If you thought that interest rates were going to rise, which tranche would you choose?
(c)   Did Mineral Waters from Syldavia borrow at a fixed or variable rate? What were they expecting interest rates to do?
(d)   What advantages did this bond have for Mineral Waters from Syldavia?

3/ On 21 February 2010, you see the following figures in Les échos de Moulinsart for Belgian Government zero-coupon bonds (which only pay a single coupon with the principal on maturity of a total amount of 100):

Maturity	Price
20 February 2011	96.25
20 February 2012	91.92
20 February 2013	87.38
20 February 2014	82.90
20 February 2015	78.35
20 February 2016	74.20
20 February 2017	70.13

(a)   Calculate the yield to maturity for each zero-coupon bond.
(b)   You estimate that the Butchery Withoutbones risk requires a spread of 58 basis points (0.58%) compared with government bonds. Calculate the value of the Butchery Withoutbones bond from Exercise 1.

Questions

1/ *It is the nominal value, it is used to compute the coupon and the amount that will be repaid.*
2/ *Duration is kind of a discounted average life (including coupons). Zero coupon?*
3/ *The rate that will make the net present value of future cash flows (coupons, repayment) equal to the present price of the bond.*
4/ *On the day of issue. On the day of redemption it will invariably be worth its redemption price.*
5/ *No, between two instalments it will trade as a short-term fixed-rate bond.*
6/ *(c), (d), (e), (f), (a) and (b) being equal.*
7/ *As the issue price is below the face value.*
8/ *True (a); False (b), (c), (d).*
9/ *True (a), (b), (c) (generally), (d), (e).*
10/ *It is the value of a put allowing the shareholders to sell the assets of the firm to the lenders if at maturity, the value of assets is below the redemption price of the debts.*
11/ *True (b); False (a), (c), (d).*
12/ *If the solvency of the issuer has deteriorated.*

Exercises

A detailed Excel version of the solutions is available at www.vernimmen.com.

1/ (a) *Yield to maturity = 5.547%; modified duration: 5.68; duration: 6.0 years.*
   (b) *The modified duration and the duration are reduced since the life of the bond is shorter, even though the market rate has dropped, which shows that the life factor impacts more on modified duration than the market rate factor. Value = 102.6, modified duration = 5.3, duration = 5.28 years.*

2/ (a) *The tranche A bond prices rise when the interest rate rises. The opposite happens for tranche B.*
   (b) *Tranche A.*
   (c) *A fixed rate of 8%, rising.*
   (d) *To be able to issue at a lower rate than the market rate (8% vs. 8.3%).*

3/ (a) *3.90%; 4.30%; 4.60%; 4.80%; 5%; 5.10%; 5.20%.*
   (b) *V = 98.79.*

BIBLIOGRAPHY

G. Athanassakos, P. Carayannopoulos, An empirical analysis of the relationship of bond yield spreads and macro-economic factors, *Applied Financial Economics*, **11**(2), 197–207, April 2001.

G. Bierwag, I. Fooladi, Duration analysis: An historical perspective, *Journal of Applied Finance*, **16**(2), 144–160, February 2006.

L. Chen, D. Lesmond, J. Wei, Corporate yield spreads and bond liquidity, *Journal of Finance*, **62**(1), 119–149, February 2007.

M. Choudry, *The Bond and Money Markets. Strategy, Trading and Analysis*, Butterworth-Heinemann, 2003.

A. Claes, M.J. De Ceuster, R. Polfliet, Anatomy of the Eurobond market: 1980–2000, *European Financial Management*, **8**(3), 373–386, 2002.

O. de la Grandville, *Bond Pricing and Portfolio Analysis: Protecting Investors in the Long Run*, The MIT Press, 2003.

A. Diaz, E. Navarro, Yield spread and term to maturity: Default vs. liquidity, *European Financial Management*, **8**(4), 449–478, December 2002.

E. Elton., M. Gruber, D. Agrawal, C. Mann, Explaining the rate spread on corporate bonds, *Journal of Finance*, **56**(1), 247–278, February 2001.

F. Fabozzi, *The Handbook of European Fixed Income Securities*, 8th edn, McGraw-Hill, 2007.

J. Finnerty, D. Emery, *Debt Management. A Practitioner's Guide*, Oxford University Press, 2001.

J. Hand, R. Holthausen, R.W. Leftwich, The effect of bond rating agency announcements on bond and stock prices, *Journal of Finance*, **47**(2), 733–752, June 1992.

G. Kitter, *Investment Mathematics for Finance and Treasury Professionals: A Practical Approach*, John Wiley & Sons, Inc., 1999.

B. Kopprasch, Duration: A practitioner's view, *Journal of Applied Finance*, **16**(2), 138–149, February 2006.

H. Langohr, P. Langohr, *The Rating Agencies and Their Credit Ratings: What They Are, How They Work, and Why They are Relevant*, John Wiley & Sons, Ltd, 2009.

F. Longstaff, S. Mithal, E. Neis, Corporate yield spreads: Default risk or liquidity? New evidence from the credit default swap market, *Journal of Finance*, **60**(5), 2213–2247, October 2005.

P. Veronesi, *Fixed Income Securities: Valuation, Risk, and Risk Management*, John Wiley & Sons, Inc., 2010.

And also

www.fitchratings.com.
www.moodys.com.
www.standardandpoors.com.

Chapter 22
OTHER DEBT PRODUCTS

What a choice!

In the previous chapter, we first presented the bond as a debt product and we illustrated the key features of a debt product through this simple security. The reader will now discover that there are actually a very large number of products that follow the same logic as that of a bond: remuneration independent from the financial performance of the firm and commitment to reimburse.

Before plunging headfirst into a discussion of existing products, we shall examine their general features and the investment selection criteria applied by corporate treasurers. We shall see further on that financing can be far more than just a financial resource and that it can raise quite complex issues. This is especially true with structured financing, which has shaken the foundations of capital structure policies. We will end the chapter with a roundup of investment products.

Section 22.1
SHORT-TERM MARKETABLE DEBT SECURITIES

The term bond (see previous chapter) is used to refer to marketable securities with maturity of over one year but firms can also issue shorter-term instruments.

Commercial paper refers to negotiable debt securities issued on the money market by companies for periods ranging from 1 day to 1 year. In practice, the average maturity of commercial paper is very short, between 1 and 3 months. Issuers can also launch variable-rate commercial paper linked with a variable-rate/fixed-rate swap (see Chapter 49) or paper denominated in US dollars with a euro swap, allowing them to separate the company's financing from interest or exchange-rate risk management.

Commercial paper enables companies to borrow directly from investors or other companies without going through the banking system at rates very close to those of the money market.

Obtaining at least a short-term credit rating for a commercial paper issue is optional but implicitly recommended, since companies are required to indicate whether they have called on a specialised rating agency and, if so, must disclose the rating given. Moreover, any issuer can ask a bank for a commitment to provide financing should the market situation make it impossible to renew the note. These backup lines came into their own at the end of 2008 when the commercial paper market virtually closed for several weeks following the bankruptcy of Lehman Brothers. Companies have to have such lines if they want their commercial paper issues to get an investment grade rating. Certain credit rating agencies, for example, will only keep their short-term rating of outstanding commercial paper at A1+ if 70% of the paper is covered by a backup line.

Two markets are active on the European level:

- The ECP (European Commercial Paper) market is based in London and is not regulated.
- The French TCN (*Titres de Créances Négociables*) on which French but also other European corporates issue. This market is regulated and under the supervision of French market authorities, and offers better secured and more flexible transactions (spot and overnight delivery).

Short-Term European Paper (STEP) is a label adopted in 2006 that has homogenised the documentation for the issue of short-term paper.

In addition to lower issue costs, commercial paper gives the company some autonomy *vis-à-vis* its bankers. It is very flexible in terms of maturity and rates, but less so in terms of issue amounts.

Lastly, regardless of their country of origin, companies can issue American commercial paper. Such issues are governed by Regulation 144A defining the terms and conditions of securities issues by foreign companies in the US (see Chapter 26).

Section 22.2
BANK DEBT PRODUCTS

Banks have developed a number of credit products that, contrary to market financing, are tailored to meet the specific needs of their clients.

1/ TYPES OF BUSINESS LOANS

Business loans (i.e. loans not linked to a specific asset) have two key characteristics: they are based on interest rates and take into account the overall risk to the company.

They are business loans because they are not granted for a specific purpose (investments, trade payables, inventories, etc.). There is no connection between the funds advanced and the company's disbursements. They can even be used to finance an investment already made.

This translates into two possible approaches:

- The company calculates how much it needs and negotiates with its bank to obtain the corresponding credit, for example a credit line, even if no investment is explicitly planned during the period.
- The bank determines the overall amount of financing required by the company based on investment volumes and changes in investment as well as working capital requirements and grants an overall loan to cover these requirements.

For companies, these loans are often a backup mechanism to meet any kind of cash payment.

Business loans are based on interest rates – in other words, cost, and the cheapest usually wins. They rarely come with ancillary services such as debt recovery, and are determined according to the maturity schedule and margin on the market rate.

These loans take into account **corporate risk**. The bank lending the funds agrees to take on the company's overall risk as reflected in its financial health. A profitable company will always obtain financing as long as it adopts a sufficiently prudent capital structure. In fact, the financial loan is guaranteed by the corporate manager's explicit compliance with a certain number of criteria, such as ratios, etc.

Financial loans are a type of credit that, in theory, is repaid by the cash flow generated by the company.

The credit line will either be negotiated with a single bank, in which case the term **bilateral loan** is used, or with a number of banks (usually for larger amounts) and the firm will then put in place a **club deal** or a **syndicated loan**.

Overdrafts on current accounts are the corporate treasurer's means of adjusting to temporary cash shortages but, given their high interest charges, they should not be used too frequently or for too long. Small enterprises can only obtain overdrafts against collateral, making the overdraft more of a secured loan.

Commercial loans are short-term loans that are easy to set up and therefore very popular.

The bank provides the funds for the period specified by the two parties. The interest rate is the bank's refinancing rate plus a margin negotiated between the two parties. It generally ranges from 0.10% to 1.50% per year depending on the borrower's creditworthiness since there are no other guarantees.

Commercial loans can be made in foreign currencies either because the company needs foreign currencies or because the lending rates are more attractive.

Alternatively, the firm can put in place a **revolving credit facility** (RCF) which is a confirmed short-term or mid-term credit line. When the line is put in place, the firm will not have debt on its balance sheet, but it will have the capacity to draw on the credit line when it needs it. On the undrawn amount, the corporate will only pay an engagement fee (between 0.1% and 1% of the amount depending on the credit quality of the firm and the maturity of the line).

If the firm has to finance a specific investment, it will put in place a **term loan** that will be less flexible than the RCF. Usually the borrower has the capacity to reimburse by anticipation but will not be allowed to re-borrow any of the repaid amounts.

A **bridge loan** is put in place to finance an investment quickly. A bridge loan can be reimbursed in the short term after a long-term financing has been put in place (long-term loan, equity issue, disposal of a subsidiary, etc.). This type of loan is costly as it presents a significant risk for the lender. Its development is highly dependent on the activity on the mergers and acquisitions market.

Syndicated loans are typically set up for facilities exceeding €50 million which a single bank does not want to take on alone. The lead bank (or banks depending on the amounts involved), known as the mandated lead arranger, will arrange the line and commit to undertake the full amount of the credit. It will then syndicate part of the loan to some 5 to 20 banks which will each lend part of the amount. The mandated lead arranger will receive an underwriting fee and the other banks a lower participation fee.

When the loan is put in place with the house banks of the firm with no further syndication of the loan, we use the term **club deal**.

What is the borrower's rationale for using this instrument?

- The potential to raise larger amounts than from a single bank.
- The possibility of making few visits to the market. This in turn determines lower fixed costs and scale economies.
- Enhanced visibility among a larger group of lenders.
- The tradability of syndicated loans. Their high liquidity determines lower rates.

The lender's rationale is driven by the following factors:

- Diversification of bank loan portfolios.
- Reduced risk of default against syndicate vs. a single bank.
- Access to deals/credits not otherwise available to some banks.
- Up-front fee income (to managers) + loan trading and derivative sales potential.

SYNDICATED LOANS (US$bn)

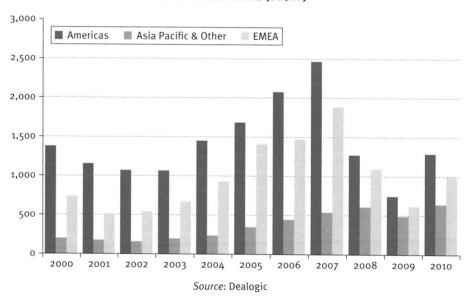

Source: Dealogic

Extending this concept leads us to the **master credit agreement**, which is a confirmed credit line between several banks offering a group (and by extension its subsidiaries) a raft of credit facilities ranging from overdrafts, commercial credit lines, backup lines, foreign currency advances or guarantees for commercial paper issues (see above). These master agreements take the form of a contract and give rise to an engagement commission on all credits authorised, in addition to the contractual remuneration of each line drawn down. Large groups use such master agreements as multi-currency and multi-company backup lines and umbrella lines, and secure financing from their usual banks according to market conditions. Smaller companies sometimes obtain similar financing from their banks. Engagement commissions are usually paid on these credit lines.

Master agreements take into account the borrower's organisation chart by organising and regulating its subsidiaries' access to the credit lines. At the local level, the business relationship between the company's representatives and the bank's branches may be based on the credit conditions set up at group level. Subsidiaries in other countries can draw on the same lines at the same conditions. Centralising credit facilities in this manner offers a number of advantages by:

- pooling cash between subsidiaries in different countries to minimise cash balance differentials;
- harmonising the financing costs of subsidiaries or divisions;
- centralising administrative and negotiating costs to achieve real economies of structure.

Master agreements are based on a network of underlying guarantees between the subsidiaries party to the agreement and the parent company. In particular, the parent company must provide a letter of credit for each subsidiary.

2/ FEATURES OF THE LOAN DOCUMENTATION

The loan documentation sets out:

- the amount, maturity and purpose of the loan (i.e. the use of funds);
- the way the amount will be cashed in by the firm (one single payment, upon request by the firm, etc.);
- the interest rate, fixed or floating, periodicity of interest payments, rules for the computation of interest, fees to be paid;
- the reimbursement or amortisation features;
- the potential early repayment options;
- the potential guarantees, pledges;
- the covenants.

Banks include a certain number of covenants in the loan agreements, chiefly regarding accounting ratios, financial decisions and share ownership. These covenants fall into four main categories:

- **Positive or affirmative covenants** are agreements to comply with certain capital structure or earnings ratios, to adopt a given legal structure or even to restructure.
- **Negative covenants** can limit the dividend payout, prevent the company from pledging certain assets to third parties (negative pledges) or from taking out new loans or engaging in certain equity transactions, such as share buy-backs.
- **Pari passu** clauses are covenants whereby the borrower agrees that the lender will benefit from any additional guarantees it may give on future credits.
- **Cross default** clauses specify that if the company defaults on another loan, the loan which has a cross default clause will become payable even if there is no breach of covenant or default of payment on this loan.

Section 22.3
FINANCING LINKED TO AN ASSET OF THE FIRM

1/ DISCOUNTING

There are several short-term financing techniques that bridge the cash flow gap between invoicing and collection and are backed by the corresponding trade receivable. They are the counterpart to trade credit (inter-company credit), which is widely used in some countries (continental Europe).

Discounting is a financing transaction whereby a company remits an unexpired commercial bill of exchange to the bank in return for an advance of the amount of the bill, less interest and fees.

The discounting bank becomes the owner of the bill and, ordinarily, is repaid when it presents the bill to its customer's customer for payment. If, at maturity, the bill remains unpaid, the bank turns to the company, which assumes the bankruptcy risk of its customer (such discounting is called discounting with recourse).

In principle, a company uses discounting to obtain financing based on the credit it extends to its own customers, which may be better known to the banking system than the company is. In this way, the company may be able to obtain better financing rates.

In discounting, the bank does not finance the company itself, but only certain receivables in its portfolio, i.e. the bills of exchange. For the bank, the risk is bound by a double guarantee: the credit quality of its customer backed by that of the issuer of the bill of exchange.

Under most accounting principles (including IFRS and US GAAP), discounted bills are reintegrated into accounts receivable and the bank advances are reported as debt.

For this reason, banks now also offer non-recourse discounting, which is a straight sale of customer receivables, under which the bank has no recourse to its customer if the bill remains unpaid at maturity. This technique allows the company to remove the receivables from its balance sheet and from its off-balance-sheet commitments and contingencies.

2/ FACTORING

Factoring is a credit transaction whereby a company holding an outstanding trade bill transfers it to its bank or a specialised financial institution in exchange for the payment of the bill, less interest and commissions. **Factoring companies or factors** specialise in buying a given portion of a company's trade receivables at a discount to the face value. The factoring company then collects the invoice payment directly from the debtors.

Factoring actually may include one or several of the following services to the firm:

- a financing with an attractive interest rate;
- the externalisation of receivables recovery;
- an insurance against unpaid bills;
- an off-balance-sheet financing.

Factoring is like discounting with additional services!

Banks increasingly offer non-recourse discounting services, which consist of an outright purchase of the trade receivables without recourse in the event of default. This technique removes contingent liabilities from the bank's on- and off-balance-sheet accounts.

3/ SECURITISATION

Securitisation was initially used by credit institutions looking to refinance part of their assets; in other words, to convert customer loans into negotiable securities.

Securitisation works as follows: a bank first selects mortgages or consumer loans, or unsecured loans such as credit card receivables, based on the quality of the collateral they offer or their level of risk. To reduce risk, the loans are then grouped into an SPV*so as to pool risks and take advantage of the law of large numbers. The SPV buys the loans and finances itself by issuing securities to outside investors: equity, mezzanine debt, subordinated debt, senior debt, commercial paper, etc., so as to offer different risk–return profiles to investors. Usually the vehicle is kept alive and "refilled" progressively by banks with new loans when old loans mature. The new entity, such as a debt securitisation fund receives the flow of interest and principal payments emanating from the loans it bought from the banks (or non-bank companies). The fund uses the proceeds to cover its obligations on the securities it has issued.

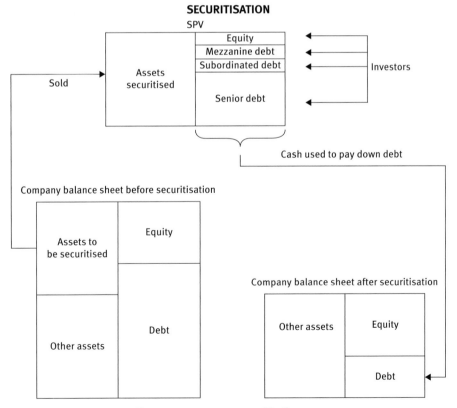

SECURITISATION

Source: www.europeansecuritisation.com

*Special Purpose Vehicle

To boost the rating of the securities, the SPV buys more loans than the volume of securities to be issued, the excess serving as enhancement. Alternatively, the SPV can take out an insurance policy with an insurance company. The SPV might also obtain a short-term line of credit to ensure the payment of interest in the event of a temporary interruption in the flow of interest and principal payments.

Most of the time, the securitisation vehicle subcontracts administration of the fund and recovery to one service provider and cash management to another. More complicated structures, often based on swaps (see Chapter 49), can also be used when the SPV does not need to reproduce the exact cash flows of the original loans. Instead, cash flows can be reorganised to satisfy the requirements of the various investors involved: no income stream, steady income stream, increasing income stream, etc.

With the help of securitisation specialists, some industrial companies regularly securitise accounts receivable, inventories, buildings or other assets. In short, the whole balance sheet can be made liquid. Once isolated, certain assets are of higher quality than the balance sheet as a whole, thus allowing the company to finance them at preferential rates. That said, the cost of these arrangements is higher than that of straight debt, especially for a high-quality borrower with an attractive cost of debt.

For example, Arcelor Mittal securitises its account receivables and Avis its rental fleet, while Glencore does the same thing with its lead, nickel, zinc, copper and aluminium inventories.

The subprime crisis has badly hurt securitisation of banks' assets due to a fear of finding subprime loans or debts of highly leveraged LBOs among the securitised assets. For industrial groups, the securitisation market is still open provided the SPV structure is crystal clear and its assets of undisputed quality.

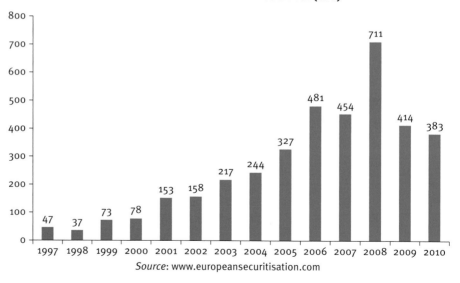

EUROPEAN SECURITISATION ISSUANCE (€bn)

Source: www.europeansecuritisation.com

4/ LEASES

In a lease contract the firm (lessee) commits itself to making fixed payments (usually monthly or semiannually) to the owner of the asset (lessor) for the right to use the asset.

These payments are either fully or partially tax-deductible, depending on how the lease is categorised for accounting purposes. The lessor is either the asset's manufacturer or an independent leasing company.

If the firm fails to make fixed payments it normally results in the loss of the asset and even bankruptcy, although the claim of the lessor is normally subordinated to other lenders.

The lease contract may take a number of different forms, but normally is categorised as either an operating or a financial lease.

For **operating leases**, the term of the lease contract is *shorter* than the economic life of the asset. Consequently, the present value of lease payments is normally lower than the market value of the asset. At the end of the contract the asset reverts back to the lessor, who can either offer to sell it to the lessee or lease it again to somebody else. In an operating lease, the lessee generally has the right to cancel the lease and return the asset to the lessor. Thus, the lessee bears little or no risk if the asset becomes obsolete.

A **financial (or capital) lease** normally lasts for the entire economic life of the asset. The present value of fixed payments tends to cover the market value of the asset. At the end of the contract, the lease can be renewed at a reduced rate or the lessee can buy the asset at a favourable price. This contract cannot be cancelled by the lessee.

From an accounting point of view, leasing an asset rather than buying it substitutes lease payments as a tax deduction for the payments that the firm would have claimed if it had owned the asset – depreciation and interest expenses on debt.

According to IFRS principles:

- Finance leases are those that transfer substantially all risks and rewards to the lessee.
- Lessees should capitalise a finance lease at the lower of the fair value and the present value of the minimum lease payments.
- Rental payments should be split into (i) a reduction of liability, and (ii) a finance charge designed to reduce in line with the liability.
- Lessees should calculate depreciation on leased assets using useful life, unless there is no reasonable certainty of eventual ownership. In the latter case, the shorter of useful life and lease term should be used.
- Lessees should expense operating lease payments.

There are different reasons a firm can prefer leasing.

1. The firm may not have the borrowing capacity to purchase an asset.
2. Operating leases provide a source of off-balance-sheet financing for heavily leveraged firms. However, this opportunity does not reduce the firm's financial risk. Lenders are, in fact, careful in considering the cash flow effects of lease payments.
3. The firm may want to avoid bond covenants.

5/ EXPORT CREDIT

Buyer's credit or **export credit** is used to finance export contracts of goods and/or services between an exporter and the buyer importing the goods/services. The banks granting the buyer's credit undertake to provide the borrower with the funds needed to pay the supplier directly according to the terms specified by the contract.

The borrower, in turn, gives the bank an irrevocable mandate to pay the funds only to the supplier. The agreement stipulates the interest rates, duration and repayment conditions of the loan, and any bank fees or penalties that may arise if the borrower fails to meet its obligations.

The credit agreement also specifies that the transaction is purely financial, since the borrower must repay the funds notwithstanding any disputes that may arise in the course of its business with the exporter. The advantages to the supplier are:

- insurance against payment default;
- the cost of the credit is not deducted from the contract while the risk level remains acceptable to the bank;
- the portion of the contract that must be paid upon maturity is not on the balance sheet.

Moreover, in most cases the first payments can be made before completion of the contract. There is thus less need to resort to cash or pre-financing loans. And lastly, if the sale is denominated in a foreign currency there is no need to worry about hedging the foreign exchange risk while the borrower makes his repayments.

Certain types of buyer's credit can also be used to finance major projects and thus resemble project financing, which we will discuss in Chapter 49.

SUMMARY

The summary of this chapter can be downloaded from www.vernimmen.com.

The main debt products are

- bonds (long-term market products);

- commercial paper (short-term market products);

- short-, medium- or long-term borrowings including RCF and term loans.

There are also other methods of financing based on assets of the firm:

- discounting and factoring;

- securitisation;

- leasing.

Export credit is not per se a debt product as it will not generate a cash-in for the firm but is a way of securing commercial relationships.

QUESTIONS

1/ What are the main features of a loan?

2/ Do banks take a risk when a firm issues commercial paper?

3/ What other financial product can export credit be associated with?

4/ What is the risk linked to discounting?

5/ Why are small companies restricted in the choice of a debt product?

6/ How do banks finance the loans they grant to corporates?

7/ What is the interest of an RCF for a firm?

8/ How can banks propose cheaper credit than bonds to corporates?

9/ What is the difference between discounting and factoring?

More questions are waiting for you at www.vernimmen.com.

ANSWERS

1/ *See chapter.*
2/ *Yes, as they grant backup lines.*
3/ *An insurance contract.*
4/ *Default of the client to pay.*
5/ *Limited amounts do not allow the issue of market products (as they would be too illiquid).*
6/ *Deposits, interbank market, bonds, equity.*
7/ *Secure access to funds.*
8/ *Better guarantees through covenants, additional expected services sold.*
9/ *Factoring is discounting with additional services.*

BIBLIOGRAPHY

J. Carter, R. Watson, *Asset Securitisation and Synthetic Structures: Innovations in the European Credit Markets*, Euromoney, 2006.
R. Contino, *The Complete Equipment-Leasing Handbook*, Amacom, 2006.
J. Finnerty, D. Emery, *Debt Management. A Practitioner's Guide*, Oxford University Press, 2001.
T. Lea, W. Trollope, *A Guide to Factoring and Invoice Discounting: The New Bankers*, Chapman & Hall, 2006.
I. Santos, Is the secondary loan market valuable for borrowers? *The Quarterly Review of Economics and Finance*, **49**(4), 1410–1428, November 2009.
A. Taylor, A. Sansone, *The Handbook of Loan Syndications and Trading*, McGraw-Hill, 2006.
www.afme.eu, European securitisation site.
www.loanradar.co.uk, site on syndicated loans in Europe.

Chapter 23
SHARES

One of a kind, or one of many?

A share or a stock is a security that is not redeemed – the investment can only be realised through a disposal – and whose revenue flows are uncertain. It is in compensation for these two disadvantages that shareholders have a say in managing the company via the voting rights attached to their shares.

The purpose of this chapter is to present the key parameters used in analysing stocks and show how the stock market operates. For a discussion of stock as a claim option on operating assets, refer to Chapter 35, and to find out more about stock as a claim on assets and commitments, see Chapter 32 on company valuation.

Section 23.1
BASIC CONCEPTS

This section presents the basic concepts for analysing the value of stocks, whether or not they are listed. Remember that past or future financial transactions could artificially skew the market value of a stock with no change in total equity value. When this happens, technical adjustments are necessary, as explained in Section 5 of this chapter. We will then assume that they have been done.

To familiarise ourselves with basic stock information, let's use the example of Indesit. Looking at the Yahoo! Page on Indesit on 27 May 2011, you would find more or less the following:

Last price	€7.51	52wk range	€7.5 – 10.0
Trade time	5:30 pm	Volume	489 875
Change	↑ 0.015 (+0.2%)	Average volume (3 m)	419 397
Previous close	€7.48501	Market capitalisation	€774m
Open	€7.58	P/E (11)	8.2
Bid	€7.45	EPS (11)	€0.92
Ask	€7.56	Dividend (paid in 10)	€0.27
Day's range	€7.45 – €7.58		

1/ VOTING RIGHTS

Shares are normally issued with one voting right each. For our purposes, this is more of a compensation for the risk assumed by the shareholder than a basic characteristic of stock.

A company can issue shares with limited or without voting rights. These are known under different names, such as preference shares, savings shares or simply non-voting shares.

At the other extreme, companies in some countries, such as the Netherlands and Sweden, issue several types of shares ("A" shares, "B" shares, etc.) having different numbers of voting rights. Some shareholders use this to strengthen their hold on a company, as we will see in Chapter 40.

2/ EARNINGS PER SHARE (EPS)

EPS is equal to net attributable profit divided by the total number of shares issued. EPS reflects the theoretical value creation during a given year, as net profit belongs to shareholders.

There is no absolute rule for presenting EPS. However, financial analysts generally base it on restated earnings, as shown below:

Net attributable profit:
− Exceptional (after-tax) profit
− Other non-recurring items not included in exceptional profit
+ Goodwill amortisation or impairment

Indesit's 2011 EPS was estimated mid-2011 to be €0.92 (it was €0.87 in 2010).

Some companies have outstanding equity-linked securities, such as convertible bonds, warrants and stock options. In this case, in addition to standard EPS, analysts calculate **fully diluted EPS**. We will show how they do this in Section 23.4.

3/ DIVIDEND PER SHARE (DPS)

Dividends are generally paid out from the net earnings for a given year but can be paid out of earnings that have been retained from previous years. Companies sometimes pay out a quarterly or half-year dividend.

In 2011 Indesit paid a €0.27 dividend per share on 2010 earnings (€0.14 was paid in 2010 on 2009 earnings).

Some shares – like preference shares – pay out higher dividends than other shares or have priority in dividend payments over those other shares. They are generally non-voting shares.

SECTION 2

4/ DIVIDEND YIELD

Dividend yield per share is the ratio of the last dividend paid out to the current share price:

$$\text{Dividend yield} = \frac{\text{Dividend per share}}{\text{Share price}} = \frac{DPS_0}{P_0}$$

The dividend yield on Indesit is 3.6%.

Yield is based on market value and never on book value.

The average yield on stocks listed on Western stock markets is currently about 3%.

DIVIDEND YIELD

	France	Germany	India	Italy	Japan	Netherlands	Spain	Switzerland	UK	USA
1990	2.8	1.8	1.0	2.5	0.4	3.7	3.5	1.7	4.3	3.3
1995	3.1	1.9	0.9	1.8	0.7	3.3	4.1	1.7	4.0	2.8
2000	1.8	1.3	1.1	1.6	0.6	1.7	1.7	1.2	2.4	1.1
2001	2.1	1.5	1.4	2.1	0.7	2.0	2.1	1.4	2.4	1.1
2002	2.6	2.0	2.0	2.8	0.9	3.0	1.8	1.9	3.0	1.3
2003	3.5	2.9	2.3	3.8	1.1	3.7	2.5	1.6	4.0	1.8
2004	3.3	2.0	1.4	3.4	0.9	3.3	2.3	1.5	3.4	1.5
2005	2.7	1.9	1.6	3.4	1.0	3.3	2.5	1.6	3.0	1.7
2006	2.6	2.0	1.6	3.0	0.9	2.8	2.3	1.5	3.0	1.7
2007	2.6	2.1	1.2	3.2	1.1	2.6	2.5	1.5	2.9	1.7
2008	3.0	2.1	0.8	3.7	1.5	3.3	2.7	2.0	3.2	1.8
2009	5.4	4.5	1.7	8.0	2.7	7.9	5.7	3.1	4.8	2.9
2010	3.7	3.1	1.0	5.0	1.8	3.4	4.4	2.2	3.3	1.9
2011	3.3	2.5	0.9	3.9	1.9	2.5	5.4	2.7	2.8	1.8

Source: Datastream

5/ PAYOUT RATIO

The payout ratio is the percentage of earnings from a given year that is distributed to shareholders in the form of dividends. It is calculated by dividing dividend by earnings for the given year:

$$\text{Payout ratio} = d = \frac{\text{Cash dividend}}{\text{Net income}}$$

When the payout ratio is above 100%, a company is distributing more than its earnings; it is tapping its reserves. Conversely, a payout close to 0% indicates that the company is reinvesting almost all its earnings into the business.

In 2011, European companies paid out an average of about 43% of their earnings.

It will be clear that the higher the payout ratio, the weaker future earnings growth will be. The reason for this is that the company will then have less funds to invest. As a result, fast-growing companies such as Solarworld and Google pay out little or none of their earnings, while a mature company will pay out a higher percentage of its earnings. Mature companies are said to have moved from the status of a **growth stock** to that of an **income stock (also called a yield stock), i.e. a company that pays out in dividends a large part of its net income, such as a utility**.

The dividend is legally drawn on parent company profits. However, it should be assessed on the basis of consolidated net attributable profit – the only meaningful figure, as in most cases the parent company is merely a holding company.

Indesit's payout ratio is 31% (it was 44% for financial year 2009).

6/ Cash flow per share

Cash flow per share has no theoretical basis, in that it does not constitute true creation of value.

Cash flow per share is nonetheless used for two reasons:

- when EPS is very low, it can be used for comparisons where EPS cannot;
- one of its components, depreciation, in some cases has little connection to real wear and tear and instead results from a tax strategy. Consolidated accounts fortunately offset this drawback.

Such calculations assume that cash flow provides a better picture of real earnings than reported earnings. However, cash flow is not equal to real earnings, only proportional to them.

When the expression price to cash flow is mentioned, it is best to check what exactly is included in the vague term "cash flow".

7/ Equity value (book value or net asset value) per share

Equity value (book value or net asset value) per share is the accounting estimate of the value of a share. While book value may appear to be directly comparable to equity value, it is determined on an entirely different basis – it is the result of strategies undertaken up to the date of the analysis and corresponds to the amount invested by the shareholders in the company (i.e. new shares issued and retained earnings).

Book value may or may not be restated. This is generally done only for financial institutions and holding companies.

8/ Cost of equity (expected rate of return)

According to the CAPM (see Chapter 19), the cost of equity is equal to the risk-free rate plus a risk premium that reflects the stock's market (or systematic) risk.

$$k_E = r_f + \beta \times (r_M - r_f)$$

9/ SHAREHOLDER RETURN (HISTORICAL RATE OF RETURN)

In a given year, shareholders receive a return in the form of dividends (dividend yield) and the increase in price or market value (capital gain):

$$\frac{P_1 - P_0}{P_0} + \frac{\text{Div}_1}{P_0}$$

Total shareholder return (TSR) is calculated in the same way, but over a longer period. It reflects the IRR of the investment in the stock.

10/ LIQUIDITY

A security is said to be liquid when it is possible to buy or sell a large number of shares on the market without it having too great an influence on the price. Liquidity is a typical measure of the relevance of a share price. It would not make much sense to analyse the price of a stock that is traded only once a week, for example.

A share price is relevant only if the stock is sufficiently liquid.

A share's liquidity is measured mainly in terms of free float, trade volumes and analyst coverage (number of analysts following the stock, quality and frequency of brokers' notes).

(a) Free float

The free float is the proportion of shares available to purely financial investors, to buy when the price looks low and sell when it looks high. Free float does not include shares that are kept for other reasons, i.e. control, sentimental attachment or "buy and hold" strategies. A skyrocketing share price could make sellers out of loyal shareholders, thus widening the free float.

Free float can be measured either in millions of euros or in percentage of total shares. It is becoming more common to use free-float-based indices, i.e. indices composed of the relative free float value of each company. The free float factor is normally given by the percentage of shares remaining after the block ownership and restricted shares adjustments are applied to the total number of shares:

Free float factor (%)
  = 100% − [Larger of block ownership and restricted shares adjustments (%)]

The free float market capitalisation is the portion of a stock's total market capitalisation that is available for trading:

Free float market capitalisation = Capitalisation free float factor × Total market

Thus it may happen that a company with a high total market value has a lower percentage in the free float index because the percentage of shares "free to float" is low. At the same time, mid-caps could increase their relevance in the indices if core shareholders hold a low portion of the entire equity.

(b) Volumes

Liquidity is also measured in terms of volumes traded daily. Here again, absolute value is the measure of liquidity, as a major institutional investor will first try to determine how long it will take to buy (or sell) the amount it has targeted. But volumes must also be expressed in terms of percentage of the total number of shares and even as a percentage of free float.

11/ MARKET CAPITALISATION

Market capitalisation is the market value of company equity. It is obtained by multiplying the total number of shares outstanding by the share price. However, rarely can the majority of the shares be bought at this price at the same time, for example, in an attempt to take control and appoint new management. Most often, a premium must be paid (see Chapters 32 and 43).

All too often, only the shares in free float are counted in determining market capitalisation. All shares must be included, as market cap is the market value of company equity and not of the free float.

On 27 May 2011, Indesit had a market cap of €774m.

12/ PRICE TO BOOK RATIO (PBR)

The PBR **(price to book ratio) measures the ratio between market value and book value:**

$$\text{PBR} = \frac{\text{Price per share}}{\text{Book value per share}} = \frac{\text{Market capitalisation}}{\text{Book value of equity (Net worth)}}$$

The PBR can be calculated either on a per share basis or for an entire company. Either way, the result is the same.

It may seem surprising to compare book value to market value which, as we have seen, results from a company's future cash flow. Even in the event of liquidation, equity value can be below book value (due, for example, to restructuring costs, accounting issues, etc.).

There is no direct link between book value and market value.

However, there is an economic link between book value and market value, as long as book value correctly reflects the market value of assets and liabilities.

It is not hard to show that a stock's PBR will be above 1 if its market value is above book value, when return on equity (ROE) is above the required rate of return (k_E). The reason for this is that if a company consistently achieves 15% ROE, and the share-holders require only 10%, a book value of 100 would mean an equity value of 150, and the shareholders will have achieved their required rate of return:

$$\frac{15\% \times 100}{150} = 10\%, \quad \text{and} \quad PBR = 1.5$$

However, the PBR will be below 1 if ROE is below the required rate of return (k_E).

A sector cannot show equity value below book value for long as sector consolidation will soon intervene and re-establish balance, assuming that markets are efficient. Nor can a sector have equity value higher than book value for long as new entrants will be attracted to the sector and bring down the abnormally high returns. Market equilibrium will thus have been re-established.

As an illustration, here are the PBRs seen on the main world markets since 1990.

	France	Germany	India	Italy	Japan	Netherlands	Spain	Switzerland	UK	USA
1990	1.9	2.3	2.7	1.8	4.0	1.7	0.9	1.4	1.5	2.0
1995	1.4	2.7	3.5	1.4	2.1	1.6	0.6	1.6	1.9	2.2
2000	2.9	2.8	3.0	2.3	2.7	3.1	2.7	2.9	2.8	4.3
2001	3.0	2.3	2.1	2.6	1.8	3.3	2.5	3.1	2.5	4.0
2002	2.6	2.1	1.5	2.0	1.7	3.2	2.6	3.0	2.4	3.5
2003	1.7	1.2	1.6	1.7	1.4	2.0	1.8	2.0	1.8	2.4
2004	1.9	1.6	2.7	1.8	1.5	1.9	2.0	2.2	2.1	2.8
2005	1.7	1.4	2.8	1.7	1.5	1.7	2.2	2.0	2.1	2.7
2006	1.9	1.7	2.8	1.9	1.8	1.9	2.3	2.3	2.3	2.6
2007	2.0	1.9	3.4	2.0	1.8	1.9	2.6	2.6	2.3	2.7
2008	2.1	2.4	4.7	1.8	1.6	1.7	2.7	2.9	2.1	3.1
2009	1.2	1.3	1.9	0.9	1.1	0.9	1.4	1.9	1.4	1.8
2010	1.4	1.5	3.1	1.1	1.1	1.2	1.7	2.1	1.6	2.0
2011	1.4	1.7	3.5	1.0	1.1	1.3	1.4	2.1	1.8	2.3

Source: Datastream

Section 23.2
Multiples

In order to understand the level of stock prices, investors must make some comparisons with comparable investments (similar stocks). By doing so, they can arbitrage between stocks taking into account their belief about the companies' qualities and the level of their prices. To achieve this objective, investors normally relate the stock price to a financial item.

There are two basic categories of multiples:

- those which allow a direct estimate of the market capitalisation. In this section, we will refer specifically to the price to earnings ratio (P/E);
- those which don't consider the capital structure of the company. These multiples allow the estimate of the value of the entire firm (firm or enterprise value) or, which

is the same, the market value of the capital employed. The EBIT multiple will be presented in this section. Since capital employed is financed by equity and net debt, the enterprise value must then be allocated between creditors (first) and shareholders. The following formula shows how to derive the value of equity from the enterprise value:

$$\text{Enterprise value} = \text{Value of net debt} + \text{Value of equity}$$

and

$$\text{Value of equity} = \text{Enterprise value} - \text{Value of net debt}$$

1/ EBIT MULTIPLE

(a) The principle

Investors interested in estimating the market value of a company's capital employed frequently find that the stock market believes that a fair value for similar companies could be, for example, 8 times their EBIT (or operating profit). With a pinch of salt, the investor can then decide to apply the same multiple to the EBIT of the company she is considering.

Investors name this ratio the **EBIT multiple**:

$$\text{EBIT multiple} = \frac{\text{Enterprise value}}{\text{Operating profit}}$$

Enterprise value is normally estimated by summing the market value of equity and the book value of net debt, assuming that the difference between the book value of debt and the corresponding market value is rarely enormous.

Where the comparison is made using companies with different fiscal positions (because they belong to different countries, for example), it is more appropriate to consider an operating profit net of taxes (net operating profit after tax or NOPAT). This result can be easily obtained by multiplying the operating profit by (1 – the corporate tax rate of the specific country).

A company whose value is 100 while the operating profit is 12.5 will be traded for 8× its operating profit. If the operating profit remains unchanged, and disregarding the terminal value, these figures imply that investors must wait 8 years before they can recover their investment. Conversely, if the operating profit increases, they will not have to wait so long. The following interpretation is consequently allowed: the EBIT multiple corresponds to the purchase price of €1 of the operating profit.

The reader might be interested in knowing why the EBIT multiple is so popular in practice and is preferred to multiples based on similar aggregates. The reason is very simple: the operating profit is the result generated by the capital employed. Net of taxes, the operating profit is the result generated by the company ready for distribution between financial creditors and shareholders.

In practice, when applying the multiple, financial analysts prefer using the operating profit of the current period or of the next period.

SECTION 2

(b) The multiple drivers

Although the EBIT multiple is a ratio that summarises a lot of information, its value is basically determined by three factors: the growth rate of the operating profit, the risk of the company and the level of interest rates.

1. **The growth rate of the operating profit**. There is a certain degree of correlation between the multiple and the expected growth of the operating profit. This is no surprise. Investors will be more willing to pay a higher price if the operating profit is expected to grow at a high rate. However, the reader should not forget that behind the growth of the operating profit are the growth of both revenues and operating margins.

    The following graph shows the relation between the medium-term growth rate of the operating profit of some European companies and their multiples.

EBIT MULTIPLE VS. GROWTH

2. **The risk of the capital employed**. The link between growth rate and multiples is not always verified in the market. Sometimes some companies show a low multiple and a high growth rate, and vice versa. This apparent anomaly can often be explained by considering the risk profile of the company. Analysts and investors in fact do not take the expected growth rate for granted. Thus, they tend to counterweight the effects of the growth rate with the robustness of these estimates.

All other things held equal, the higher the risk of the company, the lower the operating profit multiple; the lower the risk, the higher the multiple.

3. **The level of interest rates**. There is a strong inverse correlation between the level of interest rates and the EBIT multiple. This link is rather intuitive: our reader is, in fact, perfectly aware that high interest rates increase the returns expected by investors (think, for example, about the CAPM equation!), thus reducing the value of any asset.

All other things held equal, the higher the level of interest rates, the lower the operating profit multiple; the lower the interest rates, the higher the multiple.

Generally speaking, we can say that the level of the multiple can be frequently explained – at *a specific moment* – by the current level of interest rates in the economy.

2/ PRICE TO EARNINGS (P/E)

(a) The principle

Many market operators now value shares based on earnings per share (EPS) multiplied by the price to earnings (P/E) ratio.
P/E is equal to:

$$P/E = \frac{\text{Price per share}}{\text{EPS}}$$

Another way to put this is to consider the aggregate values:

$$P/E = \frac{\text{Market capitalisation}}{\text{Net income}}$$

EPS reflects theoretical value creation over a period of one year. Unlike a dividend, EPS is not a revenue stream.
As an illustration, here are the P/E ratios of the main markets since 1990.

	France	Germany	India	Italy	Japan	Netherlands	Spain	Switzerland	UK	USA
1990	11.5	14.9	21.1	16.0	60.6	11.5	11.4	12.6	12.4	14.3
1995	13.1	17.6	26.1	19.0	67.0	14.5	13.4	16.4	15.1	16.2
2000	24.5	25.6	21.1	28.0	83.1	31.9	24.0	21.0	26.7	30.6
2001	19.3	21.1	14.3	22.4	49.7	22.1	19.1	19.9	21.0	25.3
2002	18.0	18.2	10.2	16.7	40.8	16.1	15.2	20.7	19.9	27.8
2003	11.8	10.3	10.7	16.8	34.3	13.2	13.0	17.4	14.9	21.4
2004	16.0	12.2	15.8	15.7	38.5	15.5	16.0	21.4	16.5	23.1
2005	13.2	13.3	15.3	16.7	27.5	12.0	18.4	16.1	15.1	20.3
2006	15.2	14.4	17.2	19.4	34.9	13.5	19.3	18.5	14.5	18.5
2007	15.4	14.2	20.2	17.1	26.1	12.2	21.2	18.3	14.0	17.9
2008	14.0	13.6	27.7	12.9	25.2	11.1	12.7	13.9	13.2	18.0
2009	8.0	11.2	13.2	6.4	16.0	5.4	7.8	12.8	7.1	11.7
2010	21.0	26.8	22.8	18.9	34.2	23.4	12.2	17.7	12.4	21.8
2011	15.8	15.3	24.0	13.0	15.6	15.0	9.4	12.9	15.4	17.4

Source: Datastream

While there is no obligation to do so, P/E is based on estimated earnings for the current year. However, forward earnings are also considered; for example, $N + 1$ expresses the current market value of the stock vs. estimated earnings for the following year. For fast-growing companies or companies that are currently losing money, P/E_{N+1} or P/E_{N+2} are sometimes used, either to give a more representative figure (and thus avoid scaring the investor!) or because, in the case of loss-making companies, it is impossible to calculate P/E for year N.

The widespread use of P/E (which is implicitly assumed to be constant over time) to determine equity value has given rise to the myth of EPS as a financial criterion to assess a company's financial strategy. Such a decision might or might not be taken on the basis of its positive or negative impact on EPS. This is why P/E is so important, but it also has its limits, as we will demonstrate in Chapters 27, 28 and in Section IV.

P/E is conceptually similar to the EBIT multiple (or even more to the NOPAT multiple). The latter is a division of enterprise value by after-tax operating profit, while P/E is a division of market value by net profit.

Hence, many of the things we have said about the EBIT multiple also apply to P/E:

- Another way of understanding P/E is to note that it expresses market value on the basis of the number of years of earnings that are being bought. Thus, an equity value of 100, with earnings of 12.5 is valued at 8 times these earnings and the P/E is therefore 8. This means that if EPS remains constant, the investor will have to wait 8 years to recover his investment, while ignoring the residual value of the investment after 8 years, omitting the discount and assuming that he receives all of the EPS. If the EPS rises (falls), the investor will have to wait less (more) than 8 years.
- In an efficient market, the greater EPS growth, the higher the P/E, and vice versa.
- P/E is inversely proportional to interest rates: all other factors being equal, the higher the interest rates, the lower the P/Es and vice versa, again assuming efficient markets.
- The greater the perceived risk, the lower the P/E, and vice versa.

P/E is used in the same way as the EBIT multiple. To value a company, it is useful to set it alongside other companies that are as comparable as possible in terms of activity, growth prospects and risk, and then apply their P/E to it.

P/E reflects a risk that the EBIT multiple does not – financial structure – which comes on top of the risk presented by the operating assets.

P/E can only be used for valuation purposes if the comparable companies have the same EPS growth and the same risks on both the operating and financial levels.

(b) P/E and investors' required rate of return

Inverse P/E, also called earnings yield, is often mistakenly used in approximating investors' required rate of return. This should only be done in those very rare cases where earnings growth is nil and the company pays out 100% of its earnings. Here is our reasoning:

$$P = \frac{DPS}{k_E} = \frac{EPS}{k_E}$$

Then:

$$\frac{P}{E} = \frac{P}{EPS} = \frac{1}{k_E}$$

and, thus,

$$\frac{1}{\dfrac{P}{E}} = k_E$$

In most cases, companies are growing and the inverse P/E is below the required rate of return. Using the inverse P/E to approximate required rate of return would seriously underestimate the latter – a big mistake.

The P/E of a company with EPS of 12 that's trading at 240 would then be:

$$\frac{240}{12} = 20$$

The inverse P/E is just 5%, whereas the required return nowadays is probably about 10%.

For a mature company, the inverse P/E is above the shareholders' required rate of return. Using the inverse P/E to approximate required rate of return would overestimate the rate of return – another big mistake.

All in all, the inverse P/E reflects only an immediate accounting return for a new shareholder who has bought the share for V and who has a claim on EPS:

$$\text{Accounting rate of return} = \frac{EPS}{V} = \frac{1}{P/E}$$

- A very low return means that shareholders expect EPS growth to be strong enough to ultimately obtain a return commensurate with their required rate of return.
- A very high rate means that immediate return is uncertain and shareholders expect negative EPS growth to ultimately bring accounting return closer to their required rate of return.
- A normal rate, i.e. in line with the required rate of return, means that EPS growth is expected to be nil, and the investment is considered a perpetual annuity.

3/ OTHER MULTIPLES

Apart from the EBIT multiple and the P/E, investors and analysts sometimes use the following multiples.

(a) Sales multiple

Sometimes, the value of the firm is assessed in proportion to its sales, the ratio enterprise value/sales is then computed. This ratio is often used to derive the value of shops or very small companies.

SECTION 2

Using such multiples implies that the compared firms have the same type of profitability. It implies somehow a normative return over sales for firms in a certain sector.

We believe that sales multiples should not be used for mid-size or large companies as they completely disregard profitability. They have often been used in the past, in times of bull markets, to value Internet or biotech companies, for example, as such companies did not show a positive EBIT!

The same type of criticism can be levelled against multiples of numbers of subscribers, numbers of clicks . . . or other multiples of volume of activity. These multiples not only assume a comparable return over sales but also the same revenue per unit.

(b) EBITDA multiple

In some sectors such as the telecoms sector, depreciation can be a very high proportion of costs (15% of France Telecom's costs) as depreciation periods and methods can be largely subjective (even for companies applying the same accounting principles), the profile of EBIT can be impacted and may not be comparable from one company to another. In addition, accounting principles can set different rules for depreciation and amortisation. In such cases, analysts and investors tend to compute EBITDA multiples instead of EBIT multiples.

Although we understand the logic of it, we do not recommend generalising this approach to all sectors. As we will show with the following example, the use of the EBITDA multiple will lead to overvaluing low-margin companies and undervaluing high-margin companies.

	Group A	Group B
Sales	100	100
EBITDA	20	10
Depreciation	10	10
EBIT	10	0
Enterprise value	60	?

Group A is valued at 3 times its EBITDA. If we use this same multiple to value Group B, we derive an enterprise value for Group B of 30 (10×3). But if the cost structure of Group B remains the same in the future, its EBIT will never be positive; if that is the case, why should an investor pay a single cent for such a company? The value of such a firm should be nil. This is the result we find if we prefer the EBIT multiple to the EBITDA multiple.

(c) Free cash flow multiple

The free cash flow multiple is computed as: enterprise value/free cash flow to the firm (i.e. EBITDA – theoretical tax on EBIT – change in working capital – capex). Free cash flow is, in fact, the sum that can be redistributed to the providers of the firm's funds, therefore theoretically this multiple is highly relevant. It nevertheless suffers from its high volatility, in particular because the capex policy of the firm may show some huge differences from one year to another.

This ratio is therefore relevant mainly for mature sectors where capex is mainly maintenance capex.

Section 23.3
KEY MARKET DATA

We are now able to fill in the blanks of the chart below, but it will only make sense if you have first assessed the company's strategy and finances.

We have filled in the data for Indesit, whose ROE (14.7%) surpasses the rate of return required by its shareholders (about 10.4% mid-2011). Hence, equity value (€782 m) is greater than book value (€636m), and PBR is greater than one.

Moderate earnings growth explains why Indesit's P/E is low. At 30%, its payout is lower than average, but as is often the case with family-owned firms their dividend distribution policy is quite conservative.

Although Indesit's free-float is low (20%), the market for the stock is liquid (0.5% of total equity exchanged every day on average, good coverage by analysts) so the above comments apply here.[1]

1 *See Section 23.4.*

KEY MARKET DATA ON INDESIT

In Euros	Past		Current	Future
	2009	**2010**	**2011**	**2012**
Adjusted share price				
High	8.70	10.4	8.98	
Low	1.62	7.9	7.5	
Average or last	7.80	8.56	7.59	
Absolute data				
Number of fully diluted shares (m)	103	103	103	
Market capitalisation (bn)	803	882	782	
Equity, group share (bn)	506	609	636	705
Value of net debt (bn)	368	322	406	336
Enterprise value (bn)	1171	1204	1188	
Multiples				
Fully diluted EPS	0.32	0.87	0.92	0.97
EPS growth	−41%	+172%	+6%	+5%
P/E	24.4	9.8	8.3	
After-tax operating profit (m)	169	228	184	192
EBIT multiple	6.9	5.3	6.5	
Price/book ratio (PBV)	1.6	1.4	1.2	
Dividend				
Dividend per share (DPS)	0.14	0.27	0.27	0.27
DPS growth	nm	+93%	+0%	+0%
Net yield	1.8%	3.2%	3.6%	
Payout	44%	31%	29%	28%
Return				
Beta (β)	1.10	0.99	1.13	
Risk premium: $r_M - r_F$	6.8%	6.5%	6%	

In Euros	Past 2009	2010	Current 2011	Future 2012
Risk-free rate: r_F	4.0%	4.0%	3.2%	
Required rate of return: k_E	11.5%	10.4%	10.0%	
Return on equity: r_E	6.5%	14.7%	14.9%	
Actual return (capital gains and dividends)	82.0%	14%		
Free float	30%	30%	30%	

HOW TO CARRY OUT A STOCK MARKET ANALYSIS

A SHARE PRICE THAT IS CONSISTENT WITH FAIR VALUATION ...

- *Shareholding base / Free float*
- *Liquidity / Volumes*
- *Change in capital (shares issued / outstanding)*

... SHOULD MAKE IT POSSIBLE TO TRACE A STOCK MARKET HISTORY ...

Share price performance or change in market capitalisation:

- *Over a relevant period*
- *In absolute terms (volatility; possible cycles)*
- *In relative terms (compared with indices, and / or comparable stocks)*

... THAT IS IN LINE WITH THE FINANCIAL PERFORMANCE OF THE FIRM ...

- *Change in EPS and other relevant aggregates (EBITDA, EBIT, ...)*
- *Change in corresponding "multiples":*
  - *P/E ratio*
  - *EV / EBITDA, EV / EBIT, PBR*
- *Consistency between market evolution / market "multiples" and financial analysis (profitability / capital structure)*

... AND ITS DIVIDEND POLICY ...

Change in:

- *DPS*
- *Payout ratio*
- *Yield*

... MAKING IT POSSIBLE TO "QUALIFY" THE SHARE PROFILE ...

- *Volatility (Beta); correlation to indices*
- *Possible profile of the share:*
  - *Growth stock?*
  - *High yield / defensive stock?*
  - *Cyclical stock?*

> ...AND TO WORK OUT ITS CURRENT VALUE ON THE BASIS OF THE FIRM'S
> FUTURE PROSPECTS
>
> - *Forecasts for EPS, EBITDA, EBIT... (for example based on analysts' consensus)*
> - *Positioning / signification of current "multiples" compared with these forecasts*
> - *Relationship between return expected by the market (k_{CP}) and return on equity (ROE); impact on current PBR*
> - *Possibly, more comprehensive valuation (DCF, comparables, ...)*

Section 23.4
HOW TO PERFORM A STOCK MARKET ANALYSIS

In order to perform a stock market analysis, we advise our reader to follow the above battle plan tailored by Marc Vermeulen.

Section 23.5
ADJUSTING PER SHARE DATA FOR TECHNICAL FACTORS

1/ REWRITE HISTORY, IF NECESSARY

"Let's not mix apples with oranges." This old saying applies to the adjustment of per-share data after the detachment of rights and for free share awards and rights issues which, **from a technical point of view**, can modify the value of a stock.

Studying past share prices only makes sense if they are comparable; that is, if they have been adjusted for variations that are due solely to technical factors. Prices prior to the detachment of a right are adjusted by multiplying them by what is called the "adjustment coefficient".

(a) Free share awards

Suppose a company decides to double its equity by incorporating its reserves, and issues one new share for each existing share. Each shareholder is then the owner of twice as many shares without having paid in additional funds and with no change to the company's financial structure. The unit value of the shares has simply been divided into two.

Naturally, the company's equity value will not change, as two shares will be equal to one previously existing share. However, the share price before and after the operation will have to be adjusted to obtain a comparable series.

In this case, simply divide the shares existing after the free share award by two. The adjustment coefficient is 1/2.

More generally, if N' new shares are issued for N already existing shares, the adjustment coefficient is as follows:

$$\frac{N}{N+N'}$$

(b) A rights issue with an exercise price below the current share price

This is the second reason we might have to adjust past per-share data. We will go further into detail in Chapter 26, which deals with share offerings.

To subscribe to the new shares, investors must first buy one or more rights detached from previously existing shares, whose price is theoretically such that it doesn't matter whether they buy previous existing shares or use the rights to buy new ones. The detachment of the right from the existing shares makes an adjustment necessary.

For a rights issue, the adjustment coefficient is:

$$\frac{\text{Share price after detachment}}{\text{Share price before detachment}} = \frac{\text{Share price after detachment} - \text{Rights}}{\text{Share price before detachment}}$$

If P is the price of the already existing share, E the issue price of the new shares, N' the number of new shares and N the number of already existing shares, the adjustment coefficient will be equal to:

$$\frac{N \times P + N' \times E}{(N' + N) \times P}$$

More generally, the adjustment coefficient is equal to the price after detachment of the right (either the right to receive a free share or the right to buy a new one) divided by the price before detachment of the right. Henceforth, we will assume all prices to have been adjusted.

To make the adjustment, simply multiply all the share data (e.g. price, EPS, DPS, BV/S) before the detachment by this coefficient.

As you have seen, the adjustment consists in rewriting past stock performance to make it comparable to today and tomorrow, and not the reverse.

2/ THE IMPACT OF FUTURE TRANSACTIONS

When equity-linked securities (convertible bonds, mandatory convertibles, bonds with warrants attached, stock options, etc.) have been issued, financial managers must factor these potential new shares into their per-share data. Here again, we must adjust in order to obtain an average number of outstanding shares.

As there is at least potential dilution, we have to assume full conversion in calculating the per-share data (EPS, BV/S, etc.) on a fully diluted basis. This is easy to do for convertible bonds (CBs). Simply assume that the CBs have been converted. This increases the number of shares but lowers financing costs, as interest is no longer paid on the CBs.

For warrants (or stock options), two methods can be used. The **first method**, called the **treasury method**, is commonly used: it assumes investors will exercise their warrants in-the-money and the company will buy back its own shares with the proceeds. The company thus offsets some of the dilution caused by the exercise of the warrants. This is the method recommended by the IASB.

The following example will illustrate the method: on 1 September 2011, Loch Lomond Corporation decided to issue 100 000 equity warrants exercisable from 1 January 2012 to 1 January 2016 at one share at €240 per warrant.

In 2012, EPS is €10m (net income 2012) divided by 1 000 000 (number of shares), i.e. €10.

As of 31 December 2012, Loch Lomond's share price is €300, all the warrants are in the money and thus are assumed exercised: 100 000 new shares are issued. The exercise of the warrants raises the following sum for the company: 100 000 × €240 = €24 000 000.

The company could use this money to buy back 80 000 of its own shares trading at €300. Fully diluted EPS can be computed as follows:

$$2012 \text{ EPS} = 10\,000\,000/(1\,000\,000 + 100\,000 - 80\,000) = €9.80$$

Note that only in-the-money diluting securities are restated; out-the-money securities are not taken into account.

The **second method**, called the "**investment of funds method**", assumes that all investors will exercise their warrants and that the company will place the proceeds in a financial investment. Let's go back to that last example and use this method.

In this method, we assume all warrants are exercised by investors and the proceeds are invested at 3% after taxes[2] pending use in the company's industrial projects. Fully diluted EPS would be as follows:

$$\text{EPS} = \frac{100\,000 \times 240 \times 3\% + 10\,000\,000}{1\,000\,000 + 100\,000} = €9.75$$

As can be seen, the two methods produce different results as a direct consequence of the different uses of the cash proceeding from the exercise of warrants.

The treasury method can be considered to be the closest to the financial markets, as the main figure it uses is the company's share price. However, the treasury method assumes that the best investment for a company is to buy back its own shares.

2 *Depending on the case, we can assume either the company's average rate on short-term investment or the weighted average cost of capital.*

SECTION 2

SUMMARY

The summary of this chapter can be downloaded from www.vernimmen.com.

A stock market analysis of a firm should be performed after having checked the liquidity of the stock and understood the shareholder base. It is centred on stock market performance which should be compared to the financial performance of the firm, multiples (especially P/E), dividends and returns, compared with required returns.

Dividends are analysed by looking at returns (dividend on the share price) and the payout ratio (dividend on net profit).

The P/E (price to earnings ratio) is the ratio of the value of the share to EPS (earnings per share). Changes in P/E follow future EPS growth and move in the opposite direction from interest rates and risk (financial and operational).

It is only when the company pays out all of its profits and when financial and industrial markets are in equilibrium that inverse P/E (also called earnings yield) is equal to shareholders' required rate of return. Generally, the inverse P/E criterion results in an underestimation of shareholders' required rate of return.

The EBIT multiple is another valuation multiple which is computed as enterprise value (i.e. value of debt and equity) divided by EBIT.

It should be noted that a stock market analysis should be performed only after the market price has been adjusted for some past transaction, (stock split, rights issue); certain future events (conversion of convertible bonds, exercise of warrants or stock options) can also be taken into account.

QUESTIONS

1/Why is adjustment necessary?

2/Define growth stock and income stock.

3/What are the growth prospects for a company that pays out all of its profits?

4/Does a "high" P/E necessarily mean that the company is experiencing high growth?

5/What assumptions must be made for inverse P/E to provide an approximate estimate of required rate of return?

6/Will a change in required rate of return have a greater impact on a company that pays out 75% of its profits than a company that has a payout ratio of 5%, but which should increase to 75% in 25 years?

7/Will a share with a higher than average required rate of return for the same risk be undervalued or overvalued?

8/If dividend growth is higher per share than for the total amount of dividends paid out, what is this a sign of? If dividend growth is higher for the total amount of dividends paid out than the payout per share, what is this a sign of? What are your conclusions?

9/Is a company's earnings growth the most important criterion defining a growth stock?

10/What does a PBR that is much higher than 1 mean?

11/What are the three drivers of the level of EBIT multiple?

12/The higher the interest rates, the higher the EBIT multiple. True or False?

More questions are waiting for you at www.vernimmen.com.

EXERCISES

1/You buy a stock which has the following features:

- price: €500
- EPS: €33.3
- payout ratio: 25%
- projected EPS growth 15%

What will EPS have to be equal to in year 3 for you to get a 12% return on your investment? What will the share be worth then?

2/What is your view of the following companies?

Company	Share price	EPS (€)			EPS CAGR (2008 * 2010)	Beta	Payout	Yield	BV/S	P/E 2008
		2008	2009	2010						
Arcelor Mittal	23.5	11.20	1.1	3.2	−71.5%	1.32	88%	0.8%	38.2	2.1
M6	13.9	1.10	1.0	1.0	−11.2%	0.90	84%	6.1%	6.2	13.0
Iliad	77.1	2.4	3.6	5.1	111.6%	0.99	14%	0.4%	11.1	32.0

The risk-free rate is 3.7%. The market premium is 8.5%.

3/ For each of the following shares, provide an approximation of the missing figure (?) and then give your view of each share.

	Share A	Share B	Share C	Share D
P/E	10	25	7	50
Payout ratio d	95%	20%	20%	?
Annual EPS growth after 5 years: g	?	30%	5%	30%
Long-term debt/Shareholders' equity	0.15	0.20	0.25	8
ROE	10%	30%	?	90%
PBR	1	?	0.4	45

ANSWERS

Questions

1/ Because a share is no longer the same after a right has been detached.
2/ Growth stock: a stock which does not pay out much but is likely to in the future (high expectations of capital gains). Yield stock: stock that pays out a high dividend given the lack of investment opportunities (low expectations of capital gains).
3/ Zero, unless there is an improvement in productivity or an upturn in the economy.
4/ Generally yes, but not if the company is experiencing problems (drop in profits, antici-pated restructuring).
5/ That the company will pay out all of its profits in dividends, that profits will be constant and that the markets will be in equilibrium.
6/ No, on the contrary, the latter will be more sensitive as a result of the long period that will elapse before any inflows are received.
7/ Undervalued.
8/ Capital reductions. Capital increases.
9/ Yes, along with the rate of return on shareholders' equity.
10/ That the rate of return on shareholders' equity is much higher than that required by shareholders.
11/ EBIT growth rate, risk, interest rates.
12/ False, it is the other way round.

Exercises

A detailed Excel version of the solutions is available at www.vernimmen.com.

1/ P/E = 13.1 V = €665.

2/ Arcelor Mittal is a cyclical group, the earnings of which strongly decreased in 2009 but were anticipated to increase again in 2010. The group destroys value (PBR below 1), and its risk level is high (beta of 1.3). This risk combined with the drop in earnings explains the very low P/E (2.1). Arcelor Mittal paid a low dividend but, as earnings were also very low, the payout ratio appears to be high (88%).

M6 is a mature company with fairly stable results. Its risk is marginally below the mar-ket average (beta of 0.9). Its P/E reflects a low growth compensated by a low risk; it *is therefore close to the market average. M6 paid a high dividend as it does not need funds to invest for growth.*

Iliad is a fast-growing company, this is reflected in its high P/E and its low dividend policy. It is not a high-risk company and therefore, thanks to its high growth, P/E is high.

3/ *The g of A is very low at around 0%. PBR of B = P/E × ROE = 7.5. ROE of C=PBR/P/E=5.7%. The d of D: probably very low, given the amount of debt and the very high growth rate. A is very close to returning a profit, without growing. B is growing briskly with excellent returns. The returns achieved by C will not meet the requirements of its shareholders and it will have to pay out much more. D's returns on shareholders' equity are exceptional, which is explained by a very high leverage effect.*

For institutional aspects regarding stock markets, see *www.world-exchanges.org*, where the reader can find links to the 52 regulated stock exchanges belonging to the World Federation of Stock Exchanges.

BIBLIOGRAPHY

For institutional aspects regarding stock markets, see *www.world-exchanges.org*, where the reader can find links to the 52 regulated stock exchanges belonging to the World Federation of Stock Exchanges.

Chapter 24
OPTIONS

The haunted house or how to pay for being frightened!

In the previous chapters, we saw that when calculating net present value, the required rate of return includes a risk premium that is added to the time value of money. The study of options is useful from a purely financial point of view, as it highlights the notion of remuneration of risk.

True, options are more complex than shares or bonds. Moreover, in their daily use they have more to do with financial management than finance. However, we will see that many financial assets (contingency value rights, warrants and stock options) can be analysed as options or as the combination of an option and a less risky asset.[1]

Why do we place a chapter on options here, right in the middle of the financial securities a company can use to raise financing?

Some securities are *de facto* financial options. For example, we will show that a warrant can be compared to a call option.

Some securities have embedded options, i.e. options *incorporated* into the main contract. As we will see in the next chapter, a convertible bond can be seen as a combination of a conventional bond and an option.

Some securities can be usefully interpreted with the options framework. For example, equity capital can be conceptually analysed as a call option on the value of the firm, while a long-term loan is the sum of several short-term debts and an option on future trends in the yield curve.

We will also examine how options theory can be applied to major financial strategy decisions within a company.

Options are an effective tool of analysis whose applications are limited only by financial managers' imaginations.

This is why we have included them in our discussion of the basic concepts of finance.

The purpose of this chapter is not to make you a wizard in manipulating options or to teach you the techniques of speculation or hedging on options, but merely to show you how they work in practice.

1 *Have some fun by discovering the options hidden in any financial product!*

Section 24.1
DEFINITION AND THEORETICAL FOUNDATION OF OPTIONS

An option gives you the right to buy or sell an asset at a predetermined price during a predetermined period.

1/ SOME BASIC DEFINITIONS

There are **call** (buy) **options** and **put** (sell) **options**. The asset that can thereby be bought or sold is called the **underlying asset**. This can be either a financial asset (stock, bond, Treasury bond, forward contract, currency, stock index, etc.) or a physical one (a raw material or mining asset, for example).

The price at which the underlying asset can be bought or sold is called the **strike price**. The holder of an option may exercise it (i.e. buy the underlying asset if he holds a call option or sell it if he holds a put option) either at a given date (**exercise date**) or at any time during a period called the **exercise period,** depending on the type of option held (see below).

A distinction is made between "**US-style options**" (the holder can exercise his right at any moment during the exercise period) and "**European-style options**" (the holder can only exercise his right on the exercise date). Most listed options are "US-style" options, and they are found on both sides of the Atlantic, whereas most over-the-counter (OTC) options are "European-style".

Legally speaking, call options are a promise to sell made by the seller of the call option to the buyer of the call option.

Here are two examples:

Let's say Peter sells Helmut a call option on the insurance company Allianz having an €85 strike price and maturing in 9 months. For 9 months (US-style option) or after 9 months (European-style option), Helmut will have the right to buy one Allianz share at a price of €85, regardless of Allianz's share price at that moment. Helmut is not required to buy a share of Allianz from Peter, but if Helmut wants to, Peter must sell him one for €85.

Obviously, Helmut will exercise his option only if Allianz's share price is above €85. Otherwise, if he wants to buy an Allianz share, he will simply buy it on the market for less than €85.

Now let's say that Paul buys from Clara put options on $1 million in currency at an exchange rate of €1.1/$, exercisable 6 months from now. Paul may, in 6 months' time (if it's a European-style option) sell $1 million to Clara at €1.1/$, regardless of the dollar's exchange rate at that moment. Paul is not required to sell dollars to Clara but, if he wants to, Clara must buy them from him at the agreed price.

Obviously, Paul will only exercise his option if the dollar is trading below €1.1.

Legally speaking, put options are a promise to buy made by the seller of the put option to the buyer of the put option.

The above examples highlight the fundamentally asymmetric character of an option. An option contract does not grant the same rights or obligations to each side. **The buyer of any option has the right but not the obligation, whereas the seller of any option is obliged to follow through if the buyer requests.**

The value at which an option is bought or sold is sometimes called the **premium**. It is obviously paid by the buyer to the seller, who thereby obtains some financial compensation for a situation in which he has all the obligations and no rights.

Hence, a more precise definition of an option would be:

An option is a contract between two sides, under which one side gives the other side the right (but not the obligation) to buy from him (a call option) or to sell to him (a put option) an asset, in exchange for the payment of a premium.

This asset will be bought (or sold) at a predetermined price called the strike price, during a period of time (the exercise period for US-style options), or at a precise date (the exercise date for European-style options).

When the option matures, we can show the payouts for the buyer and the seller of the call option in the following way:

CALL OPTION

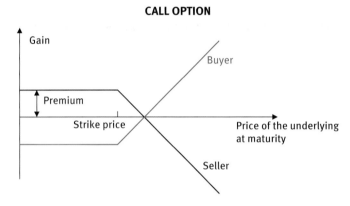

At maturity, if Allianz is trading at €90, Helmut will exercise his option and buy his Allianz share at €85. He can then sell it again if he wishes, and make €5 in profit (minus the premium he paid for the option).
    Similarly, for the put option:

PUT OPTION

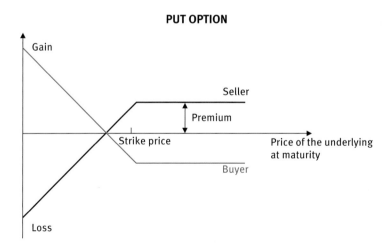

This diagram highlights the **asymmetry of risk** involved: the buyer of the option risks only the premium, while his profit is almost unlimited, while the seller's gain is limited, but his loss is potentially unlimited.

2/ The theoretical basis of options

In a risk-free environment, where we knew today with certainty what would happen tomorrow, options would not exist as they would be completely unnecessary.

If the future were known with certainty there would be no risk and all financial assets would bring in the same return, i.e. the risk-free rate. What purpose would an option have, i.e. the right to buy or sell, if we already knew what the price would be at maturity? What purpose would a call option on Siemens serve, at a strike price of €170, if we already knew that Siemens' share price would be below €160 at maturity and that the option would therefore not be exercised? And if we knew that, at maturity, Siemens' share price would be €250, the price of the option would be such that it would offer the risk-free rate, just like Siemens' shares, since the future would be known with certainty.

Options would not exist if the future were known with certainty.

In a risky environment, options remunerate the risk of an uncertain future. The basis of an option is therefore the remuneration of risk.

Options might therefore be called pure financial products, as they are merely remuneration of risk. There is no other basis to the value of an option.

More generally, all risk premiums are a sort of option.

Section 24.2
Mechanisms used in pricing options

Let's suppose that Felipe buys a call option on Solvay at a €50 strike price, maturing in 9 months, and simultaneously sells a put option on the same stock at a €50 strike maturing in 9 months. Assuming the funds paid for the call option are largely offset by the funds received for the sale of the put option, what will happen at maturity?

If Solvay is trading at above €50, Felipe will exercise his call option and pay €50. The put option will not be exercised, as his counterparty will prefer to sell Solvay at the market price.

If Solvay is trading below €50, Felipe will not exercise his call option, but the put option that he sold will be exercised and Felipe will have to buy Solvay at €50.

Hence, regardless of the price of the underlying asset, buying a call option and selling a put option on the same underlying asset, at the same maturity and at the same strike price is the same thing as a forward purchase of the underlying asset at maturity at the strike price.

In other words:

Buying a call option and selling a put option is a forward purchase of the underlying asset; we say there is put–call parity.

Assuming fairly valued markets, we can thus deduce that at the maturity of the exercise period:

Value at maturity of a call option – Value at maturity of a put option = Value at maturity of the underlying asset – strike price

It looks like this on a chart:

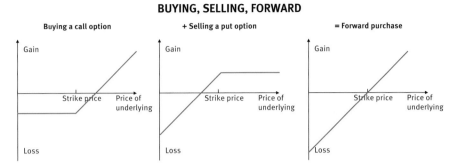

BUYING, SELLING, FORWARD

We can see that the profit (or loss) of this combination is indeed equal to the difference between the price of the underlying asset at maturity and the strike price.

Let's now consider the following transaction: Eugueni wants to buy Solvay stock, but does not have the funds necessary at his immediate disposal. However, he will be receiving €50 in 9 months, enough to make the purchase. He can thus borrow the present value of €50, 9 months out, and buy Solvay.

At maturity, the profit (or loss) on this transaction will thus be equal to the difference between the value of the Solvay shares and the repayment of the €50 loan.

So we are back to the previous case and can thus affirm that in value terms:

Buying a call option and selling a put option on the same underlying asset, at the same strike price, and at the same maturity, is like buying the underlying asset by borrowing the present value of the strike price, as long as the two options are European-style options and as long as there is no dividend payout in the interim.

We have used a stock for the underlying asset, but the above statement applies to any underlying asset (currencies, bonds, raw materials, etc.).

This can be expressed in eight different ways, which are all equivalent:

1. Buying a call option and selling a put option is like buying the underlying asset and borrowing at the risk-free rate.
2. Buying a call option and selling the underlying asset is like buying a put option and borrowing at the risk-free rate.
3. Buying a call option and investing in a risk-free asset is like buying the underlying asset and buying the put option.
4. Buying a put option and selling a call option is like investing in a risk-free asset and selling the underlying asset.
5. Buying a put option and buying the underlying asset is like buying a call option and investing in a risk-free asset, and we are back to point 3 above.
6. Buying a put option and borrowing at the risk-free rate is like buying a call option and selling the underlying asset, and we are back to point 2 above.

Also:

7. Buying a put option is like buying a call option and selling the underlying asset and investing in a risk-free asset.
8. Buying a call option is like buying a put option and buying the underlying asset and borrowing at the risk-free rate.

Points 7 and 8 show that we can "manufacture" a synthetic call option based on a put option and vice versa.

When we have three investment opportunities on an underlying asset, we can always recreate the fourth, as long as we can borrow and invest in the risk-free asset!

Section 24.3
ANALYSING OPTIONS

1/ INTRINSIC VALUE

Intrinsic value is the difference (if it is positive) between the price of the underlying asset and the option's strike price. For a put option, it's the opposite. In the rest of this chapter, unless otherwise mentioned, we will use call options as examples.

By definition, intrinsic value is never negative.

Let's take a call option on sterling, with a strike price of €1.5/£ and maturing at end-December. Let's say that it is now June and that the pound is trading at €1.6.

What is the option's value? The holder of the option may buy a pound for €1.5, while the pound is currently at €1.6.

This immediate possible gain is none other than the option's intrinsic value, which will be billed by the seller of the option to the buyer. The option will be worth at least €0.1.

Technically, a call option is said to be:

- **out of the money** when the price of the underlying asset is below the strike price (zero intrinsic value);
- **at the money** when the price of the underlying asset is equal to the strike price (zero intrinsic value);
- **in the money** when the price of the underlying asset is above the strike price (positive intrinsic value).

2/ TIME VALUE

Now let's imagine that sterling is trading at €1.4 in October. The option would be out of the money (€1.4 is less than the €1.5 strike price) and the holder would not exercise it. Does this mean that the option is worthless? No, because there is still a chance, however slight, that sterling will move over €1.5 by the end of December. This would make the option worth exercising. So the option has some value, even though it is not worth exercising right now. This is called **time value**.

For an in-the-money option, i.e. whose strike price (€1.5) is below the value of the underlying asset (let's now assume that £1 = €1.7), intrinsic value is €0.2. But this intrinsic value is not all of the option's value. Indeed, we have to add time value, which ultimately is just the anticipation that intrinsic value will be higher than it is currently. For there is always a probability that the price of the underlying asset will rise, thus making it more worthwhile to wait to exercise the option.

The anticipation of an even greater intrinsic value is called the time value of an option.

In more concrete terms, time value represents "everything that could happen" from now until the option matures.

Hence:

An option's value = intrinsic value + time value.[2]

VALUE OF A CALL OPTION

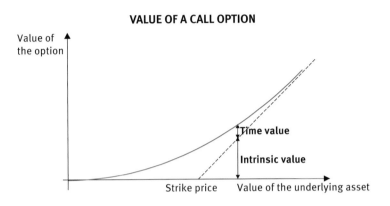

VALUE OF A PUT OPTION

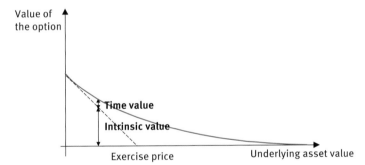

2 *The reader might remark that there is always a probability that the price of the underlying asset may decrease and that the time value could be negative as well. This cannot happen, for it would imply that the option price may be lower than its intrinsic price, which, as we have seen above, is impossible.*

Time value diminishes with the passage of time, as the closer we get to the maturity date, the less likely it is that the price of the underlying asset will exceed the strike price by that date. Time value vanishes on the date the option expires.

This means that an option is worth at least its intrinsic value, but is there an upper limit on the option's value?

In our example, the value **at maturity** of the call option on sterling is as follows:

*   If sterling is trading above €1.5, the option is worth the current price of sterling less €1.5, i.e. its intrinsic value, which is below the value of the underlying asset.
*   If sterling is below or equal to €1.5, the option will be worthless (i.e. no intrinsic value) and therefore even further below the price of the underlying asset.

This means that if the option's value is equal to the price of the underlying asset, all operators will sell the option to buy the underlying asset, as their gain will be greater in any case.

The value of a call option is always above its intrinsic value, as it possesses time value, but it is always below the value of the underlying asset.

SECTION 2

There are six criteria in determining the value of an option. We have already discussed one of them, the price of the underlying asset. The other five are:

- the strike price;
- the volatility of the underlying asset;
- the option's maturity;
- the risk-free rate;
- the dividend or coupon, if the underlying asset pays one out.

1/ STRIKE PRICE

Assuming the same value of the underlying asset, the higher the strike price, the lower the value of a call option.

Hence, and again assuming the same value for the underlying asset, the higher the strike price, the greater the value of a put option.

This is just common sense: the higher a call option's strike price, the less chance the price of the underlying asset will exceed it. It is thus normal that the value of this call option is lower. However, the price of the put option will rise as the underlying asset can be sold at a higher price.

The value of a call option (*call*) is inversely proportional to the strike price.

VALUE OF THE UNDERLYING ASSET

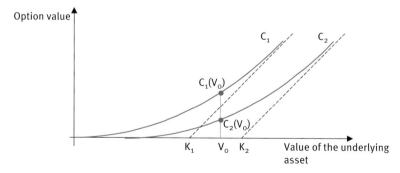

2/ VOLATILITY IN THE VALUE OF THE UNDERLYING ASSET

The value of both a call and a put option rises with the volatility in the value of the underlying asset.

Here again, this is easy to understand: the more volatile the underlying asset, the more likely it is to rise and fall sharply. In the first case, the return will be greater for the holder of a call option; in the second, it will be greater for the holder of a put option. As an option is nothing more than pure remuneration of risk, the greater that risk is, the greater the remuneration must be, and thus the option's value.

TIME VALUE RISES WITH THE VOLATILITY

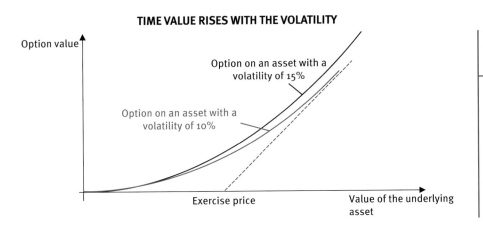

3/ THE TIME TO MATURITY

The further away maturity is, the greater the value of both a call and a put option.

You can easily see that the further away maturity is, the greater the likelihood of fluctuations in the price of the underlying asset. This raises the option's value.

THE FURTHER AWAY MATURITY

4/ THE RISK-FREE RATE

We have seen that the passage of time has a cost: the risk-free rate. The further away the maturity date on an option, the further away the payment of that cost. The holder of a call (put) option will thus have a cash advantage (disadvantage) that depends on the level of the risk-free rate.

The value of a call option increases with the risk-free rate, while the value of a put option is an inverse function of the risk-free rate.

The buyer of the call option pays the premium, but pays the strike price only when exercising the option. Everything happens as if he was buying on credit until "delivery". The amount borrowed is, in fact, the present value of the strike price discounted at the risk-free rate, as we have seen previously.

Interest rates have much less influence on the value of an option than the other five factors.

5/ Dividends or coupons

When the underlying asset is a stock or bond, the payment of a dividend or coupon lowers the value of the underlying asset. It thus lowers the value of a call option and raises the value of a put option. This is why some investors prefer to exercise their calls (on US-style options) before the payment of the dividend or coupon.

Section 24.5
Methods for pricing options

1/ Reasoning in terms of arbitrage (binomial method)

To model the value of an option, we cannot use traditional discounting of future cash flow at the required rate of return as we have for other financial securities, because of the risk involved. Cash flow depends on whether or not the option will be exercised and the risk varies constantly. Hence, the further the option is into the money, the higher its intrinsic value and the less risky it is.

Cox *et al.* (1979) thus had the idea of using arbitrage logic in comparing the profit generated with options, with a direct position on the underlying asset.

Let's take the example of a call option with a €105 strike price on a given stock (currently trading at €100) and for a given maturity.

Let's also assume that there are only two possibilities at the end of this period: either the stock is at €90 or it is at €110. At maturity, our option will be worth its intrinsic value, i.e. either €0 or €5, or €0 or €20 for four options.

We can try to obtain the same result (€0 or €20) in the same conditions using another combination of securities (a so-called **replicating portfolio**). If we achieve this result, the four call options and this other combination of securities should have the same value. If we can determine the value of this other combination of securities, we will have succeeded in valuing the call option.

To do so, let's say you borrow (at 5%, for example) a sum whose value (principal and interest) will be €90 at the end of the period concerned, and then buy a share for €100 today.

At the end of the period:

- either the share is worth €110, in which case the combination of buying the share and borrowing money is worth €110 – €90 = €20; or
- the share is worth €90, in which case the replicating portfolio is worth 90 – 90 = 0.

Since the two combinations – the purchase of four call options on the one hand, and borrowing funds and buying the share directly – produce the same cash flows, regardless of what happens to the share price, their values are identical. Otherwise, arbitrage traders would quickly intervene to re-establish the balance. So what is the original value of this combination? Let's look at it this way: €14.3 corresponds also to the value of the four call options. We thus deduce that the call option at a €105 strike is worth €3.58. We have valued the option using arbitrage theory.

Purchase of a share: €100
- borrowing of a sum that at maturity would be worth €90, hence, at 5%, 90/1.05
= €85.7
= Value: €14.3

"Delta" is the number of shares that must be bought to duplicate an option. In our example, four calls produce a profit equivalent to the purchase of one share. The option's delta is therefore 1/4, or 0.25.

More generally, delta is defined as the ratio between the variation in the option's value, and the variation in the price of the underlying asset.

Hence:

$$\delta = \frac{5-0}{110-90} = 0.25$$

We can therefore conclude that:

Value of a call option $= \delta \times$ (Price of the underlying asset – PV of capital borrowed)

Our example above obviously oversimplifies in assuming that the underlying asset can only have two values at the end of the period. However, now that we have understood the mechanism, we can go ahead and reproduce the model in backing up two periods (and not just one) before the option matures. This is called the binomial method, because there are two possible states at each step. By multiplying the number of periods or subdividing each period into subperiods, we can obtain a very large number of very small subperiods until we have a very large number of values for the stock at the option's maturity date, which is more realistic than the simplified schema that we developed above.

Here is what it looks like graphically:

VALUE OF UNDERLYING ASSET

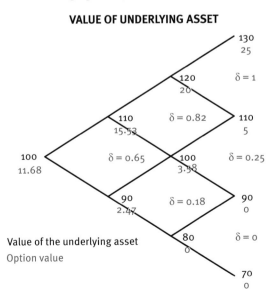

Value of the underlying asset
Option value

2/ The black–scholes model

In a now famous article, Fisher Black and Myron Scholes (1972) presented a model for pricing European-style options that is now used very widely. It is based on the construction of a portfolio composed of the underlying asset and a certain number of options such that the portfolio is insensitive to fluctuations in the price of the underlying asset. It can therefore return only the risk-free rate.

The Black–Scholes model is the continuous-time (the period approaches 0) version of the discrete-time binomial model. The model calculates the possible prices for the underlying asset at maturity, as well as their respective probabilities of occurrence, based on the fundamental assumption that this is a random variable with a log-normal distribution.

For a call option, the Black–Scholes formula is as follows:

$$\text{Value of the call option} = N(d_1) \times V - N(d_2) \times K \times e^{-T \times r_F}$$

with

$$d_1 = \frac{\ln\left(\dfrac{V}{K}\right) + \left(r_F + \dfrac{\sigma^2}{2}\right) \times T}{\sigma \times \sqrt{T}} \quad \text{and} \quad d_2 = d_1 - \sigma \times \sqrt{T}$$

where V is the current price of the underlying asset, $N(d)$ is a cumulative standard normal distribution (average = 0, standard deviation = 1), K is the option's strike price, e = exponential function, r_F is the continual annual risk-free rate, σ the instantaneous standard deviation of the return on the underlying asset, T the time remaining until maturity (in years), and ln the Naperian logarithm.

In practice, the instantaneous return is equal to the difference between the logarithm of the share price today and yesterday's share price.

$$r = \ln V_1 - \ln V_0$$

To cite an example: the value of a European-style 9-month call, with a strike price of €100, share price today of €90, a 3.2% risk-free rate and a 20% standard deviation of instantaneous return, is €3.3.

Comparing the model equation formula from page 449, you will see that $N(d_1)$ is the option's delta, while $Ke^{-T \times r_F}$ represents the present value of the strike price.

Hence:

$$\text{Call option's value} = V \times \delta - N(d_2) \times \text{Present value of the strike price.}$$

The model confirms that the value of a call option:

- rises with the current price of the underlying asset (V);
- falls with the strike price's net present value, which depends on the risk-free rate (r_F) and the time remaining till maturity $\sqrt{T}$;
- rises with the volatility σ, multiplied by the amount of time remaining till maturity.

The Black–Scholes model was initially designed for European-style stock options. The developers of the model used the following assumptions:

- no dividend payout throughout the option's life;
- constant volatility in the underlying asset over the life of the option, as well as the interest rate;
- liquidity of the underlying asset so that it can be bought and sold continuously, with no intermediation costs;
- that market participants behave rationally!

More complex models have been derived from Black and Scholes to surmount these practical constraints. The main ones are those of Garman and Kohlhagen (1983) for currency options and Merton (1976), which reflects the impact of the payment of a coupon during the life of a European-style option.

US-style options are more difficult to analyse and depend on whether or not the underlying share pays out a dividend:

- If the share pays no dividend, the holder of the option has no reason to exercise it before it matures. He will sell his option rather than exercise it, as exercising it will make it lose its time value. In this case, the value of the US-style call option is thus identical to the value of a European-style call option.
- If the share does pay a dividend, the holder of the call may find it worthwhile to exercise his option the day before the dividend is paid. To determine the precise value of such an option, we have to use an iterative method requiring some calculations developed by Roll (1977). However, we can simplify for a European-style call option on an underlying share that pays a dividend: the Black–Scholes model is applied to the share price minus the discounted dividend.

The formula for valuing the put option is as follows:

$$\text{Value of the put option} = N(-d_2) \times K \times e^{-T \times r_F} - N(d_1) \times V$$

Of the six criteria of an option's value, five are "given" (price of the underlying asset, strike price, maturity date, risk-free rate and, where applicable, the dividend); only one is unknown: volatility.

From a theoretical point of view, volatility would have to be constant for the Black–Scholes model to be applied with no risk of error, i.e. historical volatility (which is observed) and anticipated volatility would have to be equal. In practice, this is rarely the case: market operators adjust upward and downward the historical volatility that they calculated (over 20 days, one month, six months, etc.) to reflect their anticipation of the future stability or instability of the underlying asset. However, several classes of options (same underlying, but different maturity or strike price) can be listed for the same underlying asset. This allows us to observe the implied volatility of their quoted prices and thus value the options of another class.

This is how anticipated volatility is obtained and is used to value options. This practice is so entrenched that options market traders trade anticipation of volatility directly.

Anticipated volatility is then applied to models to calculate the value of the premium.

The Black–Scholes model can thus be used "backwards", i.e. by taking the option's market price as a given and calculating implied volatility. The operator can then price options by tweaking the price on the basis of his own anticipation. He buys options whose volatility looks too low and sells those whose implied volatility looks too high.

It is interesting to note that, despite these simplifying assumptions, the Black–Scholes model has been *de facto* adopted by market operators, each of them adapting it to the underlying asset concerned.

Section 24.6
TOOLS FOR MANAGING AN OPTIONS POSITION

Managing a portfolio of options (which can also be composed of underlying assets or the risk-free asset) requires some knowledge of four parameters of sensitivity that help us measure precisely the risks assumed and develop speculative, hedging and arbitrage strategies.

1/ THE IMPACT OF FLUCTUATIONS IN THE UNDERLYING ASSET: DELTA AND GAMMA

We have already discussed the delta, which measures the sensitivity of an option's value to fluctuations in the value of the underlying asset. For calls and puts that are significantly out of the money, the value of the option may not change much when the underlying asset moves up or down. As the price of the underlying asset moves to a level substantially above the strike for calls or below the strike for puts, the option becomes more valuable and more sensitive to changes in the underlying asset.

Mathematically, the delta is derived from the option's theoretical value *vis-à-vis* the price of the underlying asset and is thus always between 0 and 1, either positive or negative. Whether it is positive or negative depends on the type of option.

The delta of a call option is positive, since an increase in the price of the underlying asset increases the option's value.

The delta of a put option is negative, since a decrease in the price of the underlying asset lowers the option's value.

We have seen that, when using the Black–Scholes formula, the delta of a call option is equal to $N(d_1)$. The delta of a put option is equal to $N(d_1) - 1$. This index is prized by managers of options portfolios, as it links the option's value and the value of the underlying asset directly. Indeed, we have seen that the delta is, above all, an underlying equivalent: a delta of 0.25 tells us that a share is equivalent to 4 options. But above all, managers use the delta as an indicator of sensitivity: how much does the option's value vary in euros when the underlying asset varies by one euro?

The delta can also express probability of expiration in-the-money: a delta of 0.80 means that there is an 80% probability that the option will expire in-the-money.

Unfortunately, the delta itself varies with fluctuations in the underlying asset and with the passing of time.

The delta of a call option far in-the-money is very close to 1, as any variation in the underlying asset will show up directly in the option's value, which is essentially made up of intrinsic value.

Similarly, a call option that is far out-of-the-money is composed solely of its time value and a variation in the underlying asset has little influence on its value. Its delta is thus close to 0.

The delta of an at-the-money call option is close to 0.5, indicating that the option has as much chance as not of being exercised.

This is expressed in the following table:

	Out-of-the-money	At-the-money	In-the-money
Call option	$0 <$ delta < 0.5	delta $= 0.5$	$0.5 <$ delta < 1
Put option	$-0.5 <$ delta < 0	delta $= -0.5$	$-1 <$ delta < -0.5

Changes in the delta of an option create either a risk or an opportunity for investors and traders. Hence, the idea of measuring the sensitivity of delta to variations in the value of the underlying asset: **this is what gamma does**. Mathematically, it is none other than a derivative of the delta *vis-à-vis* the underlying asset, and is often called the delta of the delta!

The gamma of an option is largest near the strike price. A zero-gamma options position is completely immune against fluctuations in the value of the underlying asset.

2/ THE IMPACT OF TIME: THETA

Options are like people: they run down with time. Even if there is no change in the underlying asset price, the passage of time alone shows up in gains or losses for the option's holder.

Mathematically speaking, the theta is equal to the opposite of the derivative of the theoretical value of the option with respect to time. Theta measures how much an option loses in value if no other factors change.

3/ THE IMPACT OF VOLATILITY: VEGA

The vega can be defined as the rate of change in derivative of the theoretical value of the option *vis-à-vis* implied volatility. Vega is always positive for a call option, as for a put option, as we have seen that the time value of an option is an increasing function of volatility.

All other factors being equal, the closer an option is to being in the money (with maximum time value), the greater the impact of an increase in volatility.

While each of the tools presented here is highly useful in and of itself, combining them tells us even more. In practice, it is impossible to create a position that is neutral on all criteria at once. No return is possible when taking no risk. No pain, no gain! Hence, a delta-neutral position and a gamma-negative position must necessarily have a positive theta in order to be profitable.

4/ IMPLICIT VOLATILITY

From 1990, the CBOE (Chicago Board Options Exchange) has calculated the VIX, an index of the implicit volatility of the Standard & Poor's 100, using at-the-money options with a maturity shorter than 1 month. The options on the S&P 100 are sufficiently liquid to consider this index representative of the implicit volatility on the market.

SECTION 2

The following graph shows the evolution of VIX from its initial launch.

VOLATILITY OF US STOCKS (VIX ON S&P500)

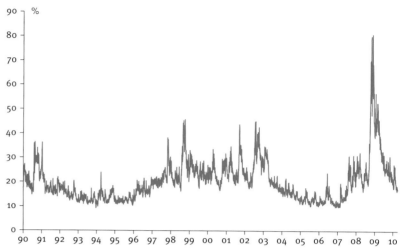

Source: Datastream (CBOE volatility Index on S&P100 until 31/2/2006 on S&P500 since)

5/ MODEL RISK

Options markets, whether organised (listed) or not (over the counter), have developed considerably since the mid-1970s, as a result of the need for hedging (of currency risks, interest rates, share prices, etc.), an appetite for speculation (an option allows its holder to take a position without having to advance big sums), and the increase in arbitrage trading.

In these conditions, a new type of approach to risk has developed on trading floors: model risk. The notion of model risk arose when some researchers noticed that the Black–Scholes model was biased, since (like many other models) it models share prices on the basis of a log-normal distribution. We have seen empirically that this type of distribution significantly minimises the impact of extreme price swings.

If returns actually followed a Gaussian distribution, the Dow Jones would change daily by more than 7% only once in 300 000 years. In the 20th century, there were 48 such changes, and there have been two since 2000. Recent studies have shown that the distribution of return has a configuration something like this.

REAL DISTRIBUTION VERSUS GAUSSIAN

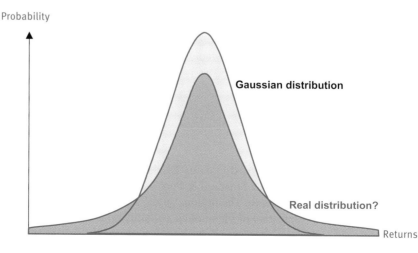

To simplify, we can say that the Black–Scholes model does not reflect the risk of a market crash.

This has given rise to the notion of model risk, as almost all banks use the Black–Scholes model (or a model derived from it). Financial research has uncovered risks that had hitherto been ignored.

An anomaly in the options market highlights the problems of the Black–Scholes model. When we determine the implied volatility of an underlying asset (the only factor not likely to be observed directly) based on the price of various options having the same underlying asset, we can see that we do not find a single figure. Hence, the implied volatility on options far out-of-the-money or far in-the-money is higher than the implied volatility recalculated on the basis of at-the-money options. This phenomenon is called the volatility smile (because when we draw volatility on a chart as a function of strike price, it looks like a smile).

We will see in the following chapters the many applications of options in corporate finance:

- to raise financing (see Chapter 25);
- to resolve conflicts between management and ownership or between ownership and lenders (see Chapter 35);
- to hedge risks and invest (see Chapter 49);
- to choose investments (see Chapter 31);
- to value assets (see Chapter 31);
- to value the equity of a company (see Chapter 35);
- to take over a company (see Chapter 43).

This gives you an idea of the importance of options.

SUMMARY

The summary of this chapter can be downloaded from www.vernimmen.com.

Options are very useful financial products to analyse complex corporate finance problems. You will soon see that the number of ways in which they can be used continues to grow! This is why this chapter is so important.

An option is a contract between two sides, under which one side gives the other the right (but not the obligation) to buy from him (a call option) or sell to him (a put option) an asset, in exchange for the payment of a premium. This asset will be bought (or sold) at a predetermined price called the strike price, during a period of time (the exercise period for US-style options), or at a precise date (the exercise date for European-style options). The basis of an option is the remuneration of risk. The option cannot exist in a risk-free environment and it thrives on risk.

The value of an option (call or put) can be broken down into an intrinsic value and a time value. The intrinsic value is the difference between the price of the underlying asset and the option's strike price. It can only be zero or positive. The time value is the premium on the intrinsic value, which remunerates passing time.

There are six criteria for determining the value of an option:

- the price of the underlying asset;
- the strike price;

- the volatility of the underlying asset;

- the option's maturity;

- the risk-free rate; and, if applicable,

- the dividend or the coupon if the underlying asset is a share or a bond that pays one or the other during the life of the option.

Models have been developed for valuing options, the main ones being the Black–Scholes and binomial models. They have been adapted over time to make them less restrictive and capable of factoring in specific features.

Lastly we looked at tools for managing an options position.

QUESTIONS

1/ Define a call or put option.

2/ What are the six criteria for determining the value of an option?

3/ What does the delta of an option indicate?

4/ What impact will a rise in volatility have on the value of a call option? And a drop in interest rates? And payment of a dividend? And the extension of the maturity of an option? And an upward revision of the strike price? And on the value of a call option?

5/ Can you set the sale of a call option off against the purchase of a put option on the same underlying asset at the same maturity?

6/ How would this investor find counterparties?

7/ Show how, in the end, the investor always pays too much for the option. Why is this statement absurd?

8/ Of the following four transactions, which carries the most risk?

   ○ purchase of a call option;
   ○ sale of a call option;
   ○ purchase of a put option;
   ○ sale of a put option.

   Why?

9/ Time value is the anticipation of intrinsic value being stronger than it is now. However, intrinsic value can drop. Why, then, can time value not be negative?

10/ In concrete terms, what does the difficulty in valuing an option boil down to?

11/ Why are options particularly well suited to arbitrage strategies? And speculation?

12/ Show how the purchase of an option and the sale of another option can protect you against the risk of a drop in the value of the underlying share, without costing you anything if you give up the profit on a possible rise in the value of the underlying asset over a given threshold.

13/If you hold stock options on the shares in your company, would you be pleased to see the company paying out large dividends? Why?

14/In your view, what is the main contribution of the Black–Scholes model?

More questions are waiting for you at www.vernimmen.com.

1/The Schauspielhaus in Berlin sells tickets thirty minutes before the start of every concert that has been sold out, known as *Nacheinlasskarten*.

Holders of these tickets are entitled to occupy any free seat in the concert hall thirty seconds before the concert starts. Buyers of these tickets wait at the doors giving access to the various categories of seats in the concert hall. Thirty seconds before the concert starts, they are allowed in and can occupy any free seat. If there are no free seats they have to leave the hall and are not allowed to try again for a different category of seat (in any event, the conductor has already raised his baton). If the legitimate ticket holder for the seat arrives before the concert starts, the holder of the *Nacheinlasskart* must give up his/her seat and leave the hall.

What is your view of this type of ticket? Be as specific as possible. Careful! This is a lot more complicated than you probably think it is.

2/You wish to value a call option on Google shares (which do not pay dividends) with a strike price of $600 and a 6-month duration. You do not know what volatility to factor in. Fortunately, 4-month options are listed at $30 for a strike price of $630. What is the implicit volatility of these options? The interest rate is 3% and Google shares are trading at $600. What is the value of this first option?

3/Redo the exercise above, assuming in the first case that Google shares rise to $700 or fall to $450. What is the impact on the value of the option? What basic feature of the option have you highlighted?

Questions

1/*An option is a promise to buy for a call and to sell for a put.*
2/*The strike price, the value of the underlying share, volatility, the interest rate, the maturity of the option and any dividend or coupon.*
3/*The hedge ratio and the probability that the option will expire in the money.*
4/*Rise, fall, fall, rise, fall. Rise, rise, rise, rise, rise.*
5/*No. The position obtained in this way would correspond to the sale, on maturity of the option, of the underlying asset.*
6/*By going onto the futures market.*
7/*See Section 24.1.*
8/*Sale of a call option (unlimited losses as the value of the asset is unlimited). The purchase of a put option is also very risky (but the loss is limited to the value of the underlying share minus the strike price).*

9/ *Because, in this case, the value of the option would be lower than the intrinsic value, resulting automatically in arbitrage (purchase of the option, exercise of the option, sale of the underlying share obtained).*

10/ *Determining the volatility to be used.*

11/ *Because, by combining them, you can reconstitute an underlying asset, as a result of their strong leverage effect.*

12/ *Sale of a call option with a strike price of 120, and using the price obtained on this option to purchase a put option at, say, 100. You will then be protected against a drop below 100, but will not benefit from a rise above 120.*

13/ *No, not at all, as this would reduce the value of the stock options.*

14/ *The method for calculating conditional assets, which enabled the "industrialisation" of options.*

Exercises

A detailed Excel version of the solutions is available at www.vernimmen.com.

1/ *This is a call option at a zero strike price combined with a put option at a zero strike price, the value of which depends on how many people arrive in time for the concert.*

2/ *29%, $53.2.*

3/ *$124.0, $4.5, the risk! Because a 17% rise in the value of Google's share will lead to a 133% rise in the value of the option, and a 25% drop in the value of the share will lead to a 92% fall in the value of the option.*

BIBLIOGRAPHY

Read the articles written by the founders of option valuation:

F. Black, M. Scholes, The valuation of option contracts and a test of market efficiency, *Journal of Finance*, **27**, 399–417, May 1972.

F. Black, M. Scholes, The pricing of options and corporate liabilities, *Journal of Political Economy*, **18**, 637–654, May–June 1973.

J. Cox, S. Ross, M. Rubinstein, Option pricing: A simplified approach, *Journal of Financial Economics*, **7**, 229–263, September 1979.

M. Garman, S. Kohlhagen, Foreign currency option values, *Journal of International Money and Finance*, December 1983.

R. Merton, Options pricing when underlying stock returns are discontinuous, *Journal of Financial Economics*, **3**, 125–144, January–March 1973.

R. Merton, Theory of rational option pricing, *Bell Journal of Economics and Management Services*, **4**, 637–654, Summer 1976.

R. Roll, An analytic valuation formula for unprotected American call options on stocks with known dividends, *Journal of Financial Economics*, 251–258, November 1977.

To find out more about options:

J. Cox, M. Rubinstein, *Options Markets*, Prentice Hall, 1985.

S. Figlewski, W. Silber, M. Subrahmanyam, *Financial Options. From Theory to Practice*, Irwin, 1990.

J. Hull, *Options, Futures and Other Derivatives*, 7th edn, Prentice Hall, 2009.

J. Hull, *Fundamentals of Futures and Options Markets*, 7th edn, Prentice Hall, 2010.

To learn more about the mechanics of option trading:

L. McMillan, *Options as a Strategic Investment*, 4th edn, New York Institute of Finance, 2002.
L. McMillan, *McMillan on Options*, 2nd edn, John Wiley & Sons, Inc., 2004.

To learn more about volatility:

L. Calvet, A. Fisher, *Multifractal Volatility, Theory, Forecasting, and Pricing*, Academic Press, 2008.
S. Gerlach, S. Ramaswamy, M. Scatigna, 150 years of financial markets volatility, *BIS Quarterly Review*, 77–91, September 2006.
J. Gatheral, *The Volatility Surface*, John Wiley & Sons, Inc., 2006.

For valuing stock options:

J. Hull, A. White, How to value employee stock options? *Financial Analysts Journal*, 1(60), 114–119, January–February 2004.

Chapter 25
HYBRID SECURITIES

It's a kind of magic

Before we begin the study of these different products, we caution the reader to bear in mind the following points.

- Some types of securities offer a lower interest rate in exchange for other advantages to the holder, and therefore give the impression of lowering the cost of financing to the company. It is an error to think this way. **In markets in equilibrium, all sources of financing have the same cost if one adjusts for the risk borne by the investor.**

- To know whether a source of financing is cheap or dear, one must look past the apparent cost to the overall valuation of the financing. **Only if securities have been issued at prices higher than market value can one say that the cost of financing is indeed lower.**

- With the exception of products that exactly match a particular market demand, these sophisticated hybrid securities are costly to issue and sell. As such, they are a signal to investors that the company, or its majority shareholder, is having trouble attracting investors, perhaps because it is experiencing other difficulties.

- By emphasising the fundamental asymmetry of information between issuer and investor, agency theory and signalling theory are both very useful for explaining the appeal of products of this kind.

- Lastly, it must not be forgotten that corporate finance is not immune to fashion. Investors have a great appetite for novelty, especially if it gives them the feeling of doing high finance!

Hybrid instruments – *essentially bonds with an equity component or "non-ordinary" shares* – are found in a multitude of guises. This generic heading encompasses a seemingly endless array of financial instruments, including convertible bonds, mandatory convertibles, reverse convertibles, preferred shares and LYONs.[1] Within each one of these instruments is found a wide range of variations and features. These include reset, negative pledge, screw and forced conversion clauses, as well as step-up coupons, call schedules, call options with soft and hard protection, etc.

The range of possibilities can seem bewildering, but it is this very flexibility that proves a huge attraction for investors, issuers and financial institutions. On the sell side, companies issue these securities and corporate service departments advise on the type of options to include in them. On the buy side, investment managers seek to build portfolios

1 *Liquid yield option notes.*

with limited risk exposure using these securities and hedge funds to use arbitrage opportunities between the convertible bond and the common share. Sometimes (more often than we might think), investors simply hedge part of the features of these products and turn them back to bonds or shares.

We will look first at products with embedded options (warrants, convertible bonds, mandatory convertibles), then at products that offer a preferential return (preference shares, bonds redeemable in shares, investment certificates), and lastly at exchangeable bonds.

Section 25.1
WARRANTS

1/ DEFINITION

A **warrant** is a security that allows the holder to subscribe to another newly issued security (share, bond, or even another warrant) during a given period, in a proportion and at a price fixed in advance.

Subscription warrants may be attached to an issue of shares or bonds, in which case the issue is said to be one of "shares cum warrants" or "bonds cum warrants". Attached warrants to buy shares may be called an "equity sweetener" or "equity kicker". Warrants can also be issued and distributed to existing shareholders at no charge. Once securities with attached warrants have been issued, the whole is split into its two component parts: the shares or bonds become traditional securities, and the warrants take on a life of their own. **The warrants are traded separately after issue.**

As an illustration, the advertising group Publicis issued equity subscription warrants in September 2002. One warrant in that issue allowed the holder to subscribe to one Publicis share at €30.5 from 24 September 2013 until 24 September 2022. In June 2011 the Publicis warrants were trading at €10.65, whereas Publicis shares were trading at €38.3.

As liquidity in the stock and bond markets has increased, financial institutions have taken the opportunity to issue warrants on existing securities independently of the company that issued the underlying shares. These securities are also called **covered warrants** because the issuing institution covers itself by buying the underlying securities on the market.

Warrants ordinarily involve a transaction between one investor and another and therefore play no direct role in financing a business. There being no limits to the imagination, some players have not hesitated in creating warrants on baskets of existing securities (such as indices). Thus, a warrant on a basket of different shares gives one the right to acquire during a given period of time a lot consisting of those shares, in proportions and at an overall price fixed in advance.

2/ VALUE

Conceptually, a warrant is similar to a call option sold by a company on shares in issue or to be issued. The exercise price of this option is the price at which the holder of the

2 *But perpetual warrants are not unknown.*

3 *Warrants and convertible bonds also affect accounting numbers because of the increase in the number of shares. This causes the firm's net income to be spread over a larger number of shares, thereby decreasing earnings per share. For this reason, firms capitalised with these instruments must report earnings on both a primary and a fully diluted basis. See Chapter 23.*

4 *How do we obtain the dilution factor? If the warrants are exercised, equity value will increase by the amount of the exercise money to $E + N_2K$. So the share price after the warrants exercise will be: Share price after exercise*

$$= \frac{E + N_2K}{N_1 + N_2}$$

At maturity, the value of the warrants will either be the share price minus the exercise price or zero, whichever is higher. Thus, analytically Warrant value at maturity

$$= \max\left(\frac{E + N_2K}{N_1 + N_2} - K, 0\right)$$

Warrant value at maturity

$$= \max\left(\frac{E + N_2K}{N_1 + N_2} - \frac{(N_1 + N_2)K}{N_1 + N_2}, 0\right)$$

Warrant value at maturity

$$= \max\left(\frac{E + N_2K - N_1X - N_2K}{N_1 + N_2}, 0\right)$$

Warrant value at maturity

$$= \frac{N_1}{N_1 + N_2}\max\left(\frac{E}{N_1} - K, 0\right)$$

warrant can acquire the underlying security; the expiry date of the option is the same as the expiry date of the warrant.

A warrant, however, has a few particular characteristics that must be taken into account in its valuation:

- It normally has a long life (typically 2–3 years),[2] which increases its time value and makes it more difficult to accept the assumption of constancy in interest rates and volatility used in the Black–Scholes model.
- The underlying asset is more likely to pay a periodic return during the time the warrant is held:

  ○ For an equity warrant, the payment of dividends on the underlying share lowers the value of that share and thereby reduces the value of the warrant. More generally, any transaction that changes the value of the share affects the value of the warrant.

  ○ For a debt warrant, the price of the underlying bond varies over time and, as we saw in Chapter 21, the closer a bond comes to maturity, the more its market price tends towards its redemption price. Its volatility gradually declines, making the Black–Scholes model, which assumes constant volatility, inapplicable as stated.

- Lastly, in the case of subscription warrants, the dilution associated with exercise of the warrants entails a gradual change in the value of the underlying security. When investors exercise warrants, the number of outstanding shares increases, and the issuing firm receives the strike price as a cash inflow. When investors exercise call options, no change in outstanding shares occurs as call options are options on shares that already exist and not on new shares to be issued; hence, the firm receives no cash.[3]

To get round these difficulties, traders use models derived from the binomial and Black–Scholes models, taking into account the fact that the exercise of warrants can create more shares and thus affect the stock price. This is the case with warrants, management options and convertible bonds. As a general rule, using an unadjusted option-pricing model to value these options will overstate their value.

Fortunately, there is a simple and reasonable solution if we want to continue to use the Black–Scholes formula. We must:

1. value a call option with characteristics similar to those of a warrant;
2. then multiply the call value by an adjustment factor for dilution.

If N_1 represents the number of "old shares" outstanding and N_2 represents the number of new shares issued as a result of the warrant being exercised, then the price of the warrant equals the price of an identical call option, C, multiplied by the following dilution factor $(N_1/N_1 + N_2)$:[4]

$$\text{Value of a warrant} = C \times \frac{N_1}{N_1 + N_2}$$

Agency theory offers an almost "psychological" approach to these hybrid securities. They are seen as a preferred means of resolving conflicts between shareholders, creditors and managers.

Take a bond with attached equity warrant as an example. A hybrid security of this kind may seem unnatural since it combines a low-risk asset (bond) with a high-risk asset (share).

However, there is something in it for each of the parties.

The company's **managers** benefit from the flexibility that warrants provide, since the company can set bounds on the date of the capital increase (by setting the subscription period of the warrant) and the amount of funds that will be raised (by setting the exercise price and the number of warrants per bond at appropriate levels). The amount of funds raised in the form of bonds can be completely different from the amount potentially raised later in the form of shares. Furthermore, the company may be able to use the funds from both sources for several years since the warrants may be exercised before the bonds are paid off.

A company that wants to accomplish the capital increase part of the issue quickly will set an exercise price barely above, or even below, the current value of the share. If it chooses, it can also move up the beginning of the subscription period. If it prefers to bring in a greater amount of funds, it will increase the number of warrants per bond (which must then have a lower yield to maturity if equilibrium is to be maintained) and/or raise the exercise price of the warrants.

Because it entails selling an option, though, the opportunity cost of a warrant can be substantial. Take the case of a company that has sold for €10 the right to buy one share at €100. Suppose that at the time this warrant becomes exercisable, the shares are trading at €210. A straight capital increase without a rights issue at a very slight discount to the share price would bring in, say, €205 per share, whereas exercise of the warrants will bring in €110 per share all told. The opportunity cost is €95 per share.

Lastly, stock market history has shown that exercise of warrants can never be taken for granted. In the euphoria of the speculative bubble, many Internet companies issued warrants with high exercise prices that were never exercised.

The holders of bonds with attached equity warrants, if they keep both securities, are both creditors and potential shareholders. As creditors, they benefit from a small but relatively certain yield; as potential shareholders, they have hope of realising a capital gain.

In a context of rising interest rates and falling share prices, however, holders of bonds cum warrants suffer the downside risks of both debt and equity securities instead of combining their advantages.

On the other hand, the holders of the bonds may be different from the holders of the warrants. The bonds may end up with investors preferring a fixed-rate security, while the warrants go to investors seeking a more volatile security.

In appearance only, **existing shareholders** retain their proportionate equity stake in the company. The warrant mechanism makes for gradual dilution over time. An issue of bonds with equity warrants allows existing shareholders to maintain their control over the company with a smaller outlay of funds, since they can buy the warrants and resell the bonds. If they do this, the securities they will end up holding will be much riskier overall because the bonds will no longer be there to cushion fluctuations in the value of the warrants.

The dilution problem is postponed, but when the warrants are exercised, they may have risen in value to such an extent that existing shareholders can pay for virtually all of their proportionate share of the capital increase by selling their warrants.

3/ PRACTICAL USES

Warrants are increasingly widely used in corporate finance. They are frequently issued in connection with equity issues. They may be distributed free of charge in a number of different situations.

- **A company in difficulty that wants to raise fresh capital.** Before going ahead with a capital increase, the company decides to make a bonus distribution of warrants to existing shareholders. In practice, the shareholders are giving themselves these warrants. They can then speculate more readily on the company's turnaround.
- **When creditors are cancelling debts due to them**, shareholders may give them equity warrants in return. The value of these warrants is virtually nil at the start, but if the company regains its footing, the warrants will rise in value and make up for some or all of the loss on the cancelled debts. A deal of this kind is the way to reconcile the normally divergent interests of creditors and shareholders. In modern finance, this technique replaces the "return to better fortune" clause in loan agreements.
- **In a tender offer** for shares of company A in exchange for shares of company B, shareholders of A may be offered not only shares of B but also warrants for shares of B.
- **In a leveraged buyout** (LBO, see Chapter 45), warrants may be used to offer an additional reward to holders of mezzanine debt or even to management (another instance of an "equity kicker").

The reader must nevertheless be wary of throwing in "free" equity warrants as a miracle remedy to ensure the success of a deal. It must not be forgotten that warrants entail potential dilution – and that in finance nothing is ever free!

Section 25.2
CONVERTIBLE BONDS

1/ DEFINITION

5 A convertible preferred stock can be converted into common stocks. The only difference with a convertible bond is that normally it has an infinite maturity.

A **convertible bond** is like a traditional bond except that it also gives the holder the right to exchange it for one or more shares of the issuing company during a conversion period set in advance. A convertible bond is similar to a bond cum warrant. The most important difference is that warrants can be separated into distinct securities and a convertible cannot[5] (directly, that is, but investors can hedge part of the product so in practice the two products are very similar).

This is a financial product of considerable flexibility. The interest rate can be fixed, variable, indexed, floating, adjustable or determined in some other way (also under the form of a zero coupon), and any amortisation schedule can be specified for return of principal.

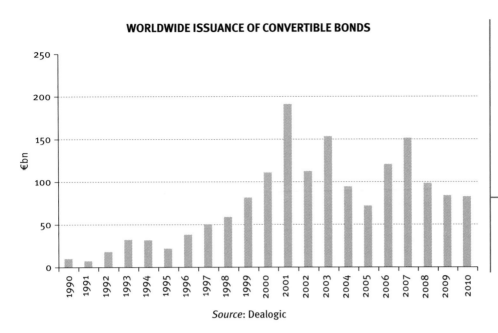

WORLDWIDE ISSUANCE OF CONVERTIBLE BONDS

Source: Dealogic

The flexibility of convertible bonds explains their great success in Europe, particularly when financial markets are depressed such as in 2001–2003; it seemed to grow again in 2007–2009.

As an example, in April 2010 Gecina (a French real estate company) issued a convertible bond with the following characteristics:

GECINA APRIL 2010 CONVERTIBLE BOND ISSUE (€320M)	
Issue price:	€111.05
Face value:	€111.05
Issue date:	9 April 2010
Maturity:	1 January 2016
Interest rate:	2.125% (€2.35 coupon)
Redemption price:	€111.05
Conversion ratio:	1 share for 1 bond
Conversion period:	From 1 January 2014 to 8th working day prior to the redemption date
Gecina share price at the time of issue:	€82.26

The **conversion period** is specified in the bond indenture or issue contract. It may begin on the issue date or later. It may run to the maturity date, or a decision may be forced if the company calls the bonds before maturity, in which case investors must choose between converting or redeeming them.

The bond may be convertible into one or more shares (1 share for each bond in our example). This ratio, called the **conversion ratio**,[6] is set at the time of issue. The

6 *Bond traders also speak of the conversion price of a convertible bond, which is calculated as the ratio of the face value of the bond to the conversion ratio.*

conversion ratio is adjusted for any equity issues or buy-backs, mergers, asset distributions or distributions of bonus shares in order to preserve the rights of holders of the convertibles as if they were shareholders at the time of issue.

The **conversion premium** is the amount by which the conversion price exceeds the current market price of the share. A conversion premium is typical. In our Gecina example, the conversion premium is 35%.[7] Since Gecina offered no redemption premium, its shares must rise 35% by the maturity date of the bonds for investors to be willing to convert their bonds into shares rather than redeem them for cash. The calculation is slightly different when a redemption premium is involved.

7 *111.05/82.26 − 1 = 35%.*

Some convertible bonds are issued with a **call provision** that allows the issuer to buy them back at a predetermined price. Holders must then choose between redeeming for cash or converting into shares. The indenture may provide for a minimum period of time during which the call provision may not be exercised ("hard non-call" period, usually at least one year) and/or set a condition for exercising the call provision, such as that the share price exceeds the conversion price by more than 25 or 30% ("soft call" provision).

In some cases, the issuer may, at conversion, provide either newly issued shares or existing shares held in portfolio – for example, following a share buy-back.

Convertible bonds must not be confused with the similar-sounding **exchangeable bonds**, which are pure debt securities from the point of view of investors. We are going to study them in Section 25.4.

2/ VALUE

8 *One complication in determining the value of a convertible bond is the call feature, typical of nearly all convertibles.*

The value of a convertible bond during its life is the sum of three components:[8]

1. the value of the straight bond alone is called the **investment value** (or just the **bond value**) of the convertible bond. It is calculated by discounting the future cash flows on the bond at the market interest rate, assuming no conversion;
2. the **conversion value**, which is what the bonds would be worth if they were immediately converted into the stock at current market price;
3. the **option value**. The value of a convertible generally exceeds both the straight bond and the conversion value because holders of convertibles have the option to wait and convert later on (time value of the option). The option to take advantage of whichever is greater in the future – the straight bond value or the conversion value – raises the value of the convertible over both the straight bond and the conversion value.

> Value of a convertible bond
>   = The greater of (Straight bond or Conversion value) + Option value

When the value of the firm is low, the value of the convertible tends to be mostly influenced by the value of the straight debt. The opposite happens when the value of the firm is very high: the value is mostly influenced by the conversion value. Graphically, we have:

VALUE OF A CONVERTIBLE BOND

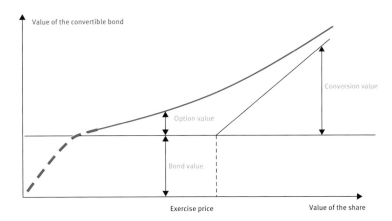

EXAMPLE OF A CONVERTIBLE BOND ISSUED BY AIR FRANCE KLM

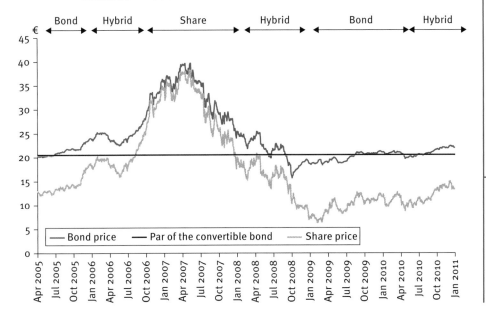

The convertible issued by Air France KLM in April 2005 behaved like a bond when first issued, but from October 2006 until October 2007 it had become virtually indistinguishable from the share. It now behaves like a "risky bond".

The attractiveness of convertible bonds to some investors is given by their "defensive" quality, since the bond value provides a *floor* to the price of the security while giving the opportunity for price appreciation if the underlying stock rises. The bond value thus represents a minimum value: the convertible will never be worth less than this floor value, even if the share price falls significantly. It also cushions the impact of a falling share price on the price of the convertible. Bear in mind, though, that investment value is not a fixed number but one that varies as a function of changes in interest rates.

Whenever the share price is well above the redemption value of the convertible, as in the "share" zone of the chart above, the convertible behaves more and more like the share because the probability that it will be converted into shares is very high.

In the "bond" zone, the convertible behaves essentially like a bond because, given the level and trend of the share price, the probability of conversion is low. The price of the convertible is close to its investment value.

In the "hybrid" zone, the value of the convertible reflects the simultaneous influence of both the level of interest rates and the price of the underlying security.

There can also be a high-risk zone for the convertible if the share price has fallen sharply. Heavy doubts appear as to the company's ability to repay its debts. The price of the convertible adjusts downward accordingly, until it offers a yield to maturity consistent with the risk of default by the issuer.

3/ THEORETICAL ANALYSIS

Unlike a bond with attached equity warrants, a convertible bond is an indivisible product. The straight bond cannot be sold separately from the call option.

For the investor, the convertible bond is often presented as a miracle product, with downside protection by virtue of its debt component and upside potential by virtue of its equity component.

In much the same fashion, the convertible bond is pitched to issuers as the panacea of corporate finance. Initially, it enables the company to issue debt at an interest rate lower than the normal market rate; at a later point, it may enable the company to issue fresh equity at a price higher than the current share price.

No, there are no miracles in finance. At best, one can find mirages, and this is one. If the company is able to issue bonds at an interest rate below its normal cost of debt, it is because it has agreed to issue shares in the future at a price (€111.05 in our Gecina example) *below* the share value at that time – necessarily below, or conversion would not take place. *Current shareholders will therefore be diluted on poor terms for them.* In addition, the argument of a lower rate is no longer 100% true for companies publishing accounts in IFRS, as under IFRS, the current interest rate at which they could issue an ordinary bond must be applied when recording associated interest expenses in the P&L, even if they actually pay a lower interest rate on their convertible bonds.

Similarly, if the investor is getting a call option on the share, it is because in return he accepts a lower rate of return on the bond than the issuer-specific risk would justify.

The apparent cost of the convertible bond is low only because its true cost is partly hidden. The company is selling investors call options, which they pay for by accepting a lower interest rate on the bonds than the company could normally obtain given its risk.

The cost of a convertible bond may be calculated in intuitive fashion as a weighted average of the cost of equity and the cost of debt. The weighting corresponds to the probability that the convertible will actually be converted. This probability is not hard to estimate if one assumes that returns on the share are normally distributed (then the expected yearly increase in share price is equal to the cost of equity less the dividend yield).

Equilibrium market theory is not of much help in explaining why convertible bonds, which are no more than a combination of two existing products, should themselves exist. Unsurprisingly, agency theory and signalling theory – together with the "matching hypothesis" – are far more useful in understanding the usefulness of convertibles.

- According to **agency theory**, a convertible bond is a mode of **resolving conflicts between shareholders and creditors**. The temptation of managers of leveraged companies is to undertake risky investments that increase shareholder wealth at the creditors' expense. With this fear in mind, creditors refuse to finance the company except via convertible bonds. Creditors will then have some protection, since the convertible gives them the option of becoming shareholders if there are transfers of value working against them as creditors. A heavily indebted company may have to pass up highly profitable investment projects if it cannot obtain bank financing that would not put too great a strain on its cash flow at the start. With its low apparent interest cost, the convertible bond is an attractive alternative. A convertible bond also helps in **resolving conflicts between shareholder-managers and outside shareholders**. A shareholder-manager of a company with convertible bonds outstanding will hesitate to divert company resources to private use at the expense of other shareholders, since he knows that would increase the probability of having to redeem the convertibles in cash. If the company is already carrying a sufficiently high debt load, redemption could put it in difficulty and threaten the manager's position, so he is deterred from taking such action.

- **The "matching" hypothesis** provides another contribution to the explanation of why convertible bonds exist. A young, fast-growing company or one with limited financial resources will avoid taking on too much debt, as its cash flow is likely to be highly variable and its cost of debt, given its short history, likewise high. In these cases, it makes sense to issue securities whose cash flows **match** those of the firm.

- A fast-growing company will have little inclination to issue more shares, either because it believes its shares are undervalued or because it **fears sending out a negative signal** (see Chapter 39). That leaves only convertible bonds. Investors, relieved that the signal associated with a capital increase has not been sent, will welcome an issue of convertibles. This is what the **signalling theory** assumes.

Taken together, these three explanations provide good reasons for issues of convertible bonds by smaller companies that are growing rapidly, are already heavily indebted or have assets that are quite risky. We could also add another explanation, which is commonly known as the **"backdoor equity" hypothesis.** Young, growing firms cannot usually issue debt because of the high financial distress costs. At the same time, they may be unwilling to issue equity if current stock prices are too low. Thus, convertible bonds could offer a good compromise solution. Convertible bonds cause expensive dilution, but it occurs when the firm can afford it![9]

The market for convertibles is also supplied by large groups (e.g. Air France KLM, Arcelor Mittal), which use it to raise funds from specialised investors that invest only in convertible bonds. For these large groups, convertibles offer **a way of diversifying the investor base** and raising money in large quantities more easily. Lastly, groups in financial difficulty will resort to issuing convertibles when the equity market is closed to them, as was the case for Gecina.

4/ CYCLICALITY OF THE CONVERTIBLE MARKET

From 2004 to 2008 only a few convertible issues were marketed, but in the early 2000s the convertible market was hot. It is, therefore, an interesting exercise to try to understand the market drivers in order to be able to read the market trends.

9 A similar rationale is offered by Mayers (1998). If a company has many real options it needs the capital in two stages: the first stage is used to prove that the real investment options may be worth pursuing; the second, to exploit the option effectively. Corporations may prefer to use convertible debt because it can be designed in such a way that investors can allow the firm to exercise (in providing equity) the real options only if they turn out to be valuable, or abandon the conversion option if the real option disappears (thus avoiding the overinvestment problem of companies with high liquidity and no good investment opportunities).

SECTION 2

Three types of drivers can explain hot convertible markets:

- The product in itself is easy to sell, it does not involve management (no roadshows or one-on-ones) and does not require the company to be rated. An issue can thus be made very rapidly, which is a clear plus in volatile markets. The reason for this is the reduced problems of information asymmetry between management and investors as investors are protected by the bond component.
- The equity market can sometimes be virtually closed and, in such periods, firms will try to issue products with equity content as convertible bonds. In addition, for a firm, selling a convertible means selling volatility (and therefore deriving a high price for the option part of the product), and accordingly, issuing convertibles will be attractive for the firm when markets are volatile (which is usually when the equity issues market is insufficiently open).
- When markets are bearish, the call component of old convertible issues tends to disappear, so investors will have appetite for new issues to renew their "real" convertible portfolios.
- Convertible bonds are bought almost equally by classical or specialised bond funds on one side and on the other side by hedge funds that buy the convertible and sell the underlying share (which they have usually borrowed). Hedge funds do not take a position on the changes in stock price but on the potential increase in stock volatility.

The price of the stock tends, therefore, to drop (by 2 to 4%) when a convertible issue is announced. The Gecina share price dropped by 2.6% on announcement of the issue. Who said that convertibles carried a low cost?

Section 25.3
PREFERENCE SHARES

The securities called **preference shares** (a definition prevailing in the United Kingdom) or **preferred shares** (a definition prevailing in the United States) enjoy economic advantages over ordinary shares, typically in return for a total or partial absence of voting rights.

1/ DEFINITION

Preference shares are created on the occasion of a capital increase by the decision of the shareholders at an (extraordinary where applicable) general meeting.

The advantages conferred on preference shares may include:

- a claim to a higher proportion of earnings than is paid out on other shares;
- priority in dividend distributions, meaning the dividend on preference shares must be paid before any ordinary dividend is paid on other shares;
- a cumulative dividend, so that if earnings are insufficient to pay the preference dividend in full, the amount not distributed becomes payable from future earnings;
- a firm cannot go into default if it misses paying some dividends;
- rating agencies and financial analysts consider preference shares a part of equity (thus improving the rating of the company).

At the same time, there are two important disadvantages in issuing preference shares.

- for the issuer – because the dividends may not be tax deductible;[10]
- for the investors – because they may have limited voting rights.

We should note here that the term "preferred securities" (often shortened to just "pre-ferreds"), is much broader in scope and may encompass convertible bonds and subordinated debt securities as well as preference shares without voting rights. The reader is advised to look closely at the detailed characteristics of any security called a "preferred" and not to assume that it is necessarily a preference share.

Special features can be added to preference shares to make them more attractive to investors or less risky to issuers:

- **adjustable rate preference share**: the dividend rate is pegged to an index rate, such as a Treasury bill or Treasury bond;
- **participating preference share**: the dividend is divided into a fixed and a variable component. The latter is generally set as a function of earnings;
- **trust preference share**: the dividend on these stocks is tax deductible like interest expenses. Firms issuing this security get the tax shield of debt and keep leverage low (because preference shares are treated like equity by analysts and rating agencies).

10 *This is not always true. In the United States, for example, companies do not have to pay taxes on 70% of the preferred dividends they receive on preference shares investments they have made in other firms. This tax saving might then be shared with the issuing company, enabling the company to bring the preferred dividend rate down.*

SECTION 2

2/ VALUE

It is complex to generalise the valuation formula of preference shares as the term covers products that can have very different features.

Preference shares will normally be valued just like ordinary shares (taking into account the potential higher dividend stream). The value of the preference share will be equal to the value of the ordinary share to which you need to:

- add the value of the advantages granted;
- deduct a liquidity discount (as the preference share will generally have low liquidity). This discount is almost always observed in trading prices;
- potentially deduct the value of the voting right.

As each of these elements is difficult to assess, the value of the preference share will be quite uncertain.

3/ THEORETICAL ANALYSIS

(a) For the company

Preference shares can enable a company which is in difficulty but has a good chance of recovering to attract investors by granting them special advantages.

Banks are often issuers of preference shares because these securities are classified by central banks as part of the bank's own funds for the purpose of determining its net capital. This is so even though the preference share pays a constant annual dividend expressed as a percentage of par value, which gives it a strong resemblance to a debt security. Analysts are not fooled; for their purpose, preference shares are reclassified as debt.

Against these advantages, preference shares also present several drawbacks:

1. They cost more than a traditional capital increase: the preference dividend is higher than the ordinary dividend, whereas the preference share itself is usually worth less than the ordinary share because of its lesser liquidity.
2. Their issuance entails complications that are avoided with an ordinary capital increase, such as calling a special shareholders' meeting.
3. Furthermore, understanding such issues can be quite difficult. Preference shares frequently trade at a steep discount to theoretical value because holders demand a big premium over market value before they will sell or exchange them.

(b) For current shareholders

For current shareholders, issuing preference shares makes sense only if those shares have no voting rights. When this is true, a capital increase can be accomplished without diluting their control of the company. A company with family shareholders may issue preference shares in order to attract outside financial investors without putting the family's power over the company in jeopardy.

But this advantage brings with it an additional cost for current shareholders and so appears to us quite illusory over the long term. It is just as if the company's cost of equity had been raised.

Today this product has virtually disappeared from stock markets, which prefer to see a single quoted share class for each company traded in substantial volume. These securities cease to exist either when the issuing company is taken over by another or when it offers to exchange the priority dividend shares for ordinary shares.

On the other hand, preference shares remain useful as a vehicle for financial investments in unlisted companies (particularly in LBOs) or in cross-border business combinations, as a means of equalising dividend flows between different shareholders in dual listed companies, as in the case of BHP Billiton, for example.

4/ BETWEEN PREFERENCE SHARES AND CONVERTIBLE DEBT: CONVERTIBLE PREFERRED STOCKS

Recent financial innovation has introduced a new distinct class of securities – convertible preferred securities – which are designed to provide issuers with the dual benefits of maintaining the dilution-limiting benefits of convertible debt while providing significant rating agency, balance sheet and, (in limited cases) regulatory equity content. In addition, all classes of convertible securities can be structured such that issuer interest payments are tax deductible.

11 Given these features, the after-tax cost of these securities tends to be higher than normal convertible debt.

Their main characteristics are: (1) deep subordination; (2) long-dated maturity; (3) multiyear dividend/interest deferral; (4) various common stock conversion features.[11]

Within the convertible preferred stock category, there are two primary security types:

- **Conventional convertible preferred**. Typically structured as either perpetual or 30-year preferred stock.
- **Mandatory convertible preferred stock**. Short-maturity preferred securities that automatically convert into common stock at maturity.

An important attribute of these securities is the amount of "equity" that rating agencies assign to the product. S&P tends to view this equity in percentage terms while Moody's assigns content in distinct groupings. The factors that influence the "amount" of equity are the following:

- the type of equity-linked product being used;
- the amount of other hybrid equity products on the issuer's balance sheet;
- the industry or sector of the issuer;
- management credibility.

Here is a spectrum of convertible alternatives:

CONVERTIBLE PREFERRED AND DEBT

Products	Common stock	CONVERTIBLE PREFERRED			CONVERTIBLE DEBT			Straight debt
		Mandatory convertible	Convertible preferred	Hybrid preferred securities	Convertible debt	Moderate high premium convertible debt	Zero coupon convertible debt	
Certainty of conversion	Certain	Certain/High		High		Medium	Very Low	None
Rating agency equity treatment	100%	Partial equity treatment			0%			

The reader may wonder why subordinated securities have been more successful than preference shares which have fairly similar features. We believe that there are two main reasons:

- The first is the fact that interest on subordinated debt is tax deductible, unlike dividends on preference shares.
- The second is the fact that the investors likely to be interested in these products do not have the same investor profile as those keen on preference shares. Subordinated securities are mainly placed with long-term investors (insurance companies, private banking clients) who are seeking attractive returns over the long term. Such investors are relatively indifferent to the low liquidity of the security (a feature subordinated securities and preference shares have in common).

On the other hand, recent history has shown that preference shares are difficult to value, difficult to get rid of if necessary and often heavily discounted because of their reduced liquidity compared with ordinary shares. Increasing the different types of bonds results in a better breakdown of demand from bond investors, which means they can be issued in better conditions. Increasing the different types of shares has the opposite effect, by reducing the liquidity of each line, when liquidity is the watchword of many investors in equity and not the chief concern of investors in bonds.

Subordinated securities seem to have found their place on the market. They are issued by companies seeking to strengthen their financial solidity without diluting their shareholdings and they come with a tax break. They are bought by long-term investors who are seeking comfortable returns but are prepared to take a certain amount of risk and to sacrifice the liquidity of their investment.

Section 25.4
OTHER HYBRID SECURITIES

Financial innovation has reduced the difference between the investment characteristics of debt and equity. Firms are able to issue securities that function very much like equity but which are frequently treated as debt for tax purposes. Much of this innovation represents "equity in drag" (Bulow *et al.*, 1990). Innovation has, in fact, eroded each of the traditional tests used for distinguishing debt and equity.

1/ MANDATORY CONVERTIBLES

Unlike convertible bonds, for which there is always some risk of non-conversion, **mandatory convertibles** are **necessarily** transformed into equity capital (unless the issuing company goes bankrupt in the meantime) since the issuer redeems them by delivering shares; no cash changes hands at redemption.

Mandatory convertibles are hybrid securities, which automatically convert into a predetermined number of shares dependent on the stock price at the time of conversion. They are closer to equity than debt because they redeem in shares instead of cash, and provide little downside protection (just the coupon payments). In addition, mandatory convertibles are often treated as equity on the balance sheet and regarded as equity by the rating agencies.

Mandatory convertibles are more established in the US than in Europe. They have emerged primarily as an opportunistic response to uninviting market conditions for direct equity issuance and have helped companies deleverage their balance sheets.

Mandatory convertibles appeal to investors looking for high yield and capital appreciation, although they have less downside protection than standard convertible bonds. As a result, we see interest from equity funds and outright investors but the main investors are hedge funds because they are able to significantly offset stock exposure.

In view of the ongoing pressure on corporates' balance sheets and the need to refinance upcoming redemptions, it is reasonable to expect further interest in mandatory convertible securities.

The value of a bond redeemable in shares is the present value of the interest payments on it plus the present value of the shares received upon redemption. In pure theory, this is equal to the value of the share increased by the present value of the interest and decreased by the present value of the dividends that will be paid before redemption. The discount rate for the interest is the required rate of return on a risky debt security, while the discount rate for the dividends is the company's cost of equity.

For tax purposes, bonds redeemable in shares are treated as bonds until they are redeemed, and subsequently as shares.

In recent years there has been a revival for mandatory convertibles and new features have been added to make this product more attractive for investors.

Mandatory convertibles are equity-linked hybrid securities such as PERCS (Preferred Equity Redemption Cumulative Stock) or DECS (Debt Exchangeable for Common Stock, or Dividend Enhanced Convertible Securities), which automatically convert to common stock on a prespecified date.

Mandatory convertibles have been designed with a variety of payoff structures, and carry different names depending on their payoff structure and the investment bank underwriting their issue: examples are Morgan Stanley's PERCS and PEPS, Merrill Lynch's PRIDES, Salomon Brothers' DECS and Goldman Sachs' ACES (for an explanation of these abbreviations, see Chemmanur *et al.*, 2004).

They have been issued by a number of companies, large and small, to raise capital: these include Texas Instruments, General Motors, Citicorp and Sears. In Europe, Lafarge used a similar product, a bond redeemable either in shares or in cash, when it acquired Blue Circle. This issue was, in reality, a capital increase conditional on the success of its bid for the target company. Legally, capital increases can never be conditional. This is also the structure used by AXA in 2003.

2/ Deeply subordinated debt

These financial instruments present the four following features, which are also presented by ordinary share capital and provide the undertaking with financial flexibility.

1. **Permanency**: the instrument must be perpetual, and early redemption features must be under the sole control of the issuer.
2. **Ranking**: in case of liquidation, the securities must rank senior only to share capital.
3. **Conditional payment of interest**: under certain conditions, such as non-payment of dividends to shareholders, payment of the coupon/dividend to investors must be left at the issuer's entire discretion. Such non-payment must not be considered as a default event, but as a cancellation of the remuneration, with no deferred remuneration (non-cumulative coupon). Moreover, should the payment endanger the solvency soundness of the undertaking, the non-payment must be compulsory. Step-up remuneration clauses, allowing an increase in the interest rate to be paid if the financial situation of the issuer deteriorates, are forbidden.
4. **Loss absorption mechanism**: the securities must give the issuer the ability, in addition to the non-payment of interest, to absorb potential losses by a reduction of the nominal value of the securities, in order to pursue its activity.

3/ Tracking stocks

A **tracking stock** is an issue of shares for which performance is indexed to the earnings of a subsidiary or division. Tracking stock is technically a class of the parent company's shares. It confers no right to vote on the decisions of the subsidiary that it supposedly represents. If the business is sold, however, the holder of tracking stock shares has the right to receive a portion of the capital gain.

There are three main reasons for issuing tracking stocks:

1. they allow investors to buy only those portions of the firm that they feel have the greatest potential or value;
2. they provide more transparency to investors on how well the firm is doing in different businesses;

3.   they enable a company to retain full control of a subsidiary while allowing the market to establish a value for it, thereby providing a ready currency for acquisitions.

This type of security is relatively well developed in the United States but extremely rare in Europe.

The value of a share of tracking stock is theoretically equal to what a share of the subsidiary would be worth if it were publicly traded. However, in the absence of effective control over the subsidiary, the legal complexity and the often low liquidity generally result in a sharp discount to the theoretical value.

4/ EXCHANGEABLE BONDS

An **exchangeable bond** is a bond issued by one company that is redeemable in the shares of a second company in which the first company holds an equity interest. Thus, while a convertible bond can be exchanged for specified amounts of common stock in the issuing firm, an exchangeable bond is an issue that can be exchanged for the common stock of a company other than the issuer of the bond.

At maturity, two cases are possible. If the price of the underlying shares has risen sufficiently, holders will exchange their bonds for the shares; the liability associated with the bonds will disappear from the first company's balance sheet, as will the asset associated with the shares. If the price has not risen enough, holders will redeem their bonds for cash, and the first company will still have the underlying shares. In neither case will there be any contribution of equity capital. An exchangeable bond is therefore like a collateralised loan with a call option for the holder on securities held in the company's portfolio.

For the investor, a bond issued by company X that is exchangeable for shares of company Y is very close to a convertible bond issued by Y. The only thing separating these two financial instruments is the default risk of X versus that of Y.

By way of example, in May 2009 Eurazeo (a French listed investment fund) issued a bond exchangeable for shares in Danone (for a total of 2% of Danone) in which Eurazeo held a stake of about 5%. Bonds are exchangeable with shares with a premium of 25% for 5 years. This issue raised €700 million for the group at an apparent interest rate of just 6.24%, so 6.5% less than the actual cost of debt for Eurazeo at that time. The *quid pro quo* is obviously twofold: for one thing, Eurazeo cannot be sure of having unloaded a part of its holding in Danone; for another, if it does succeed in disposing of that stake, it will have let it go at a price below its market value.

SUMMARY

The summary of this chapter can be downloaded from www.vernimmen.com.

Hybrid securities often seem to be equity, but that is not always the case. A convertible bond that is not converted remains a debt; a bond with attached warrants is, likewise, still a debt.

Many of these hybrids give the impression of lowering the company's cost of financing. Do not believe it! In markets in equilibrium, all sources of financing have the same cost when adjusted for the risk taken by the investor. It is not enough to look only at the apparent cost; the full cost of any source of financing must be understood and taken into account. Similarly, these securities give the impression of belonging to the world of high finance. More often than not, though, their use is a sign that the issuer is in trouble or is having difficulty placing ordinary equity or debt securities with investors.

Agency theory explains the existence of these products by showing their usefulness in resolving potential conflicts between shareholders and creditors or between shareholder-managers and outside shareholders. Signalling theory sees in them the mark of an undervalued, heavily indebted company that is unwilling to finance itself through a traditional capital increase.

A convertible bond is like a traditional bond, generally one bearing a fixed rate, except that it also gives the holder the right to exchange it for one or more shares (depending on the conversion ratio) of the issuing company during a conversion period set in advance. Its value is analysed as the sum of the value of the traditional bond and the value of a call option on the shares with an exercise price equal to the conversion price.

Convertible bonds are issued at lower coupon rates than traditional bonds. This is not an advantage for the issuing company but merely the compensation for the call option it has granted the investor "at no charge".

A subscription warrant is a security that allows the holder to subscribe during a given period, in a proportion and at a price fixed in advance, to another security. A subscription warrant may be attached to an issue of shares or bonds or distributed by itself "at no charge". Conceptually, a warrant is a form of call option sold by the company on shares to be issued. Issuing warrants enables a company to accomplish a capital increase by a process of gradual dilution.

Preference shares, mandatory convertibles, super-subordinated bonds and exchangeable bonds are other categories of hybrid securities.

SECTION 2

QUESTIONS

1/ Can any financial product normally make it possible to obtain resources at below market cost?

2/ Define: convertible bond, bond with equity warrants, preference share, investment certificate and bond redeemable in shares.

3/ The bond market yield is 7%. A company issues a bond with equity warrants at a gross yield to maturity of 3% assuming the warrants are not exercised. What is the cost of this product? What is the breakdown of that cost?

4/ Is a convertible bond more costly to the issuing company than a bond with equity warrants?

5/ Which is (are) the most appropriate financial product(s) for the following companies:

- a company that wants to raise fresh equity capital immediately but does not want to risk losing control;
- a company that wants to raise fresh equity capital immediately in which the state is the majority shareholder;
- a company with a very volatile share price that wants to gradually broaden its shareholder base;
- a company emerging from a period of difficulties whose future is still perceived by investors to be risky.

6/Rank convertible bonds, investment certificates, bonds with equity warrants, preference shares and new ordinary shares in terms of:

- actual or potential dilution;
- achieved rate of return;
- potential capital gain;
- cost to the issuing company.

7/Which product would *appear* to be a case of "tails I win, heads you lose"?

8/Show that if managers think their company's shares are undervalued, there is a better product to issue than a convertible bond.

9/Show that if managers think their company's shares are overvalued, there is a better product to issue than a convertible bond.

10/Given your answers to Questions 8 and 9, how do you explain the existence of convertible bonds?

11/True or false:

(a)   The higher the conversion premium, the higher the yield on a convertible bond.
(b)   The higher the volatility of the underlying share, the higher the conversion premium.
(c)   A rise in the payout ratio on the underlying share increases the probability of conversion before a convertible bond matures.
(d)   A convertible bond does not offer the same percentage of upside participation in the share price as the share itself, but in return it offers downside protection.

12/Why isn't a bond redeemable in shares attractive to financial investors?

13/Why is there a good chance that preference shares will be worth less than the same issuer's ordinary shares, despite the preferences accorded to them?

More questions are waiting for you at www.vernimmen.com.

EXERCISES

1/Company X has capital of 2 million shares that are currently trading at €2000 per share. On its balance sheet it has a liability for an issue of convertible bonds with the following characteristics:

- nominal value: €500m (500 000 convertible bonds of face value €1000 each);
- interest rate: 5%;
- conversion ratio: 1 for 1;

Company X expects to have a net profit of €300m next year.

(a) Calculate X's *fully diluted* earnings per share. The corporate income tax rate is 36.7%.

(b) Redo the same exercise, replacing the convertible bond with a bond with attached warrants to subscribe to one share of X at €2100. Assume the pre-tax rate of return on short-term investments is 8%. Use two different methods to make your calculations.

(c) What would be the result of the calculation in (b) above if X issued the bond with warrants to pay off another borrowing at a pre-tax interest rate of 8%? Assume that the expected net profit is after interest expense on the previous borrowing.

Questions

1/ *Normally no.*

2/ *See definitions in this chapter.*

3/ *One cannot say what the cost of this product is; the most one can say is that the cost consists of a minimum rate plus an option.*

4/ *There is no basis for affirming that either one is more costly than the other.*

5/ *Preference shares (but no one is fooled); investment certificates; convertible bonds; convertible bonds.*

6/ *In descending order of dilution: preference shares, investment certificates, ordinary shares, convertible bonds, bonds with equity warrants. In descending order of return: convertible bonds, bonds with equity warrants, preference shares, investment certificates, ordinary shares. In descending order of potential capital gain: ordinary shares, preference shares, investment certificates, bonds with equity warrants, convertible bonds. The cost to the company depends on the pricing!*

7/ *Convertible bond.*

8/ *Traditional bond that will be paid off by a capital increase once the share price has risen.*

9/ *Ordinary shares that will never have to be redeemed.*

10/ *By agency theory and signalling theory.*

11/ *True: (b) and (d); false: (a) and (c).*

12/ *Because it is simply a forward purchase of shares, payable immediately.*

13/ *Because of their lower liquidity; there are many fewer of them than there are of the ordinary shares.*

Exercise

A detailed Excel version of the solutions is available at www.vernimmen.com.

(a) *Saving on interest costs (after tax at 36.7%): €15.83m. Fully diluted EPS = €126.3.*

(b) *Invest proceeds in short term: fully diluted EPS = €141.3. Use proceeds to buy back shares: fully diluted EPS = €151.9.*

(c) *Gain on interest expense: (8% − 5%) × 0.6333 × 500 = €9.50 m; by the short-term investment method: fully diluted EPS = €145.1; by the share buy-back method: fully diluted EPS = €156.7.*

SECTION 2

BIBLIOGRAPHY

On convertible bonds:

M. Ammann, A. Kind, C. Wilde, Are convertible bonds underpriced? An analysis of the French market, *Journal of Banking & Finance*, **27**(4), 635–653, April 2003.

E. Arzac, PERCS, DECS and other mandatory convertibles, in D. Chew (Ed.), *The New Corporate Finance. Where Theory Meets Practice*, 3rd edn, McGraw Hill, 2000.

F. Bancel, U. Mittoo, Why do European firms issue convertible debt? *European Financial Management Journal*, **10**(2), 339–374, June 2004.

T. Chemmanur, D. Nandy, A. Yan, *Why issue mandatory convertibles? Theory and empirical evidence.* Downloadable from www.ssrn.com, 2004.

T. Chemmanur, What drives the issuance of puttable convertibles: risk-shifting, asymmetric information, or taxes? Financial Management, **39**(3), 1027–1067, Autumn 2010.

T. Ganshaw, D. Dillon, Convertible securities: A toolbox of flexible financial instruments for corporate issuers, *Journal of Applied Corporate Finance*, **13**(1), 22–30, Spring 2000.

C. Lewis, R. Rogalski, J. Seward, Understanding the design of convertible debt, *Journal of Applied Corporate Finance*, **11**(1), 45–53, Summer 1998.

D. Mayers, Why firms issue convertible bonds: The matching of financial and real investment options, *Journal of Financial Economics*, **47**(1), 83–102, January 1998.

A. Rai, Changes in risk characteristics of firms issuing hybrid securities: case of convertible bonds, *Accounting and Finance*, **45**(4), 635–651, December 2005.

W. Schoutens, J. de Spiegeleer, *The Handbook of Convertible Bonds*, John Wiley & Sons, Ltd, 2011.

J. Stein, Convertible bonds as backdoor equity financing, *Journal of Financial Economics*, **32**(1), 3–21, August 1992.

On tracking stocks:

M. Clayton, Y. Qian, Wealth Gains from Tracking Stocks: Long-run Performance and Ex-date Returns, *Financial Management*, **33**(3), 83–106, Autumn 2003.

D. Tompkins, Are tracking stocks on track? *Business Horizons*, 73–78, November–December 2000.

On exchangeable bonds:

F. Fabozzi, *The Handbook of Fixed Income Securities*, 8th edn, McGraw-Hill, 2008.

J.D. Finnerty, D.R. Emery, *Debt Management. A Practitioner's Guide*, Harvard Business School Press, 2001.

On hybrid securities and equity "in drag":

F. Black, M. Scholes, The pricing of options and corporate liabilities, *Journal of Political Economy*, **81**(3), 637–654, May–June 1973.

J. Bulow, L.H. Summers, V.P. Summers, Distinguishing debt from equity in the junk bond era, in J. Shoven, J. Waldfogel (eds) *Taxes and Corporate Restructurings*, Brooking Institution, 1990.

M. Fridson, Do high-yield bonds have an equity component? *Financial Management*, 82–84, Summer 1994.

M. Jensen, W. Meckling, The theory of the firm: Managerial behavior, agency costs, and capital structure, *Journal of Financial Economics*, **3**(4), 305–360, October 1976.

S. Myers, N. Majluf, Corporate financing and investment decisions when firms have information that investors do not have, *Journal of Financial Economics*, **13**(2), 187–221, June 1984.

I. Nelken, *Handbook of Hybrid Instruments: Convertible Bonds, Preferred Shares, Lyons, ELKS, DECS and other Mandatory Convertible Notes*, John Wiley & Sons, Inc., 2000.

SECTION 2

Chapter 26
SELECTING SECURITIES

Get 'em while they're hot!

Now that we have studied the properties of the various financial securities, let's see how companies sell them to investors. Bank finance was beautiful in its simplicity – whenever a company needed funds, it turned to its bank. Now that direct financing has become more common, companies can raise funds from a great many investors whom it does not necessarily know. That means they have to market their financing!

Section 26.1
GENERAL PRINCIPLES IN THE SALE OF SECURITIES

1/ THE PURPOSE OF OFFERINGS

The company's main goal in selling its securities to investors is to obtain the highest possible price.

For the sale to be successful, the company must offer investors a return or a potential capital gain. Otherwise, it will be harder to gain access to the market in the future.

The offering must be in line with this objective. The price of a security is equal to its present value, as long as all publicly available information has been priced in. This is the very basis of market efficiency. Conversely, asymmetric information is the main factor that can keep a company from selling an asset at its fair value.

Investors must therefore be given the information they need to make an investment decision. The company issuing securities and the bank(s) handling the offerings must provide investors with information. Depending on the type of offering, this can be in the form of:

- a mandatory legal written document called a prospectus;
- presentations by management via meetings/conference calls with investors or electronic road shows;
- valuations and comments by financial professionals on the deal and the issuer via notes by financial analysts and presentations to the bank's sales teams, for example.

A firm underwriting commitment by the bank(s) handling the transaction can provide additional reassurance to investors, because if the bank is willing to arrange and underwrite the offering, it must believe that the offering will succeed and that the price is "fair". After all, investors are also clients to whom the bank regularly offers shares.

In any offering the bank's exact positioning is always ambiguous. In theory it is mandated by the company that is issuing the securities and must therefore defend that company's interests to the fullest. But to do so, it must persuade the investors, who are its regular customers, to subscribe. It cannot afford to lead its clients astray. Ultimately, it defends the interests of both sides, not to mention its own!

Investor information needs and the complexity of the deal depend on the following:

- **The amount of information that is already available on the issuing company itself.** Clearly, an initial public offering of shares in a company unknown to the market will require a big effort to educate investors on the company's strategy, business, financial profile and perhaps even the sector in which it operates. This information is already contained in the share price of a publicly traded company, as that price reflects investor anticipation. This is why it is generally easier to offer shares in a company that is already listed.
- **Investor risk.** Investors need more information for shares than for bonds, which are less risky.
- **The type and number of investors targeted.** In addition to regulatory restrictions, it is generally more difficult for a European company to sell its securities in the US than in Europe, especially if the company and its industry are not known outside its home country (sometimes the opposite can occur, as in the oil services sector, for example). Meanwhile, a private placement with a few investors is simpler than a public offering.

COMPLEXITY OF THE DEAL

The type of offering will depend on the complexity and risk involved.

Complexity of the deal

Initial public offering

Secondary share offerings

Convertible bond issues

Bond issues

Block trades

2/ THE ROLE OF BANKS

The bank(s) in charge of an offering have four roles, the complexity of which depends on the type of offering:

1. **Arranging the deal**, i.e. choosing the type of offering on the basis of the goal sought: volume of securities to offer and in what form and timetable, choosing the market for the offering, contacts with market authorities, preparation of legal documents in liaison with specialised attorneys.

2. **Circulation of information**: an offering is often an opportunity for an issuer to report on its recent activity, prospects and strategy. The consistency of this information is checked by the bank and the lawyers in charge of the deal during a phase called "due diligence", which consists of interviews with the company's management. Information

is also gathered by the brokerage arm of the bank and then put out in research notes written by the bank's financial analysts. The bank also organises meetings between the issuer and investors in one or more markets (road shows or one-to-one meetings).

3. **Distribution of the paper**: the bank's sales teams approach their regular clients, the investors, to market the securities and take orders. The issue price is then set by the bank in liaison with the issuer or seller, and the securities are allocated to investors. An equilibrium price is established in the "after-market" phase. In the days after that, the bank may intervene in the market in order to facilitate exchanges of blocks among investors.

4. **Underwriting**: in some cases the bank provides the issuer (or seller) with a guarantee that the securities will find buyers at the agreed price. The bank thus assumes a certain market risk. The magnitude of this risk will depend on the type of guarantee and on the timing of the commitment.

Most offerings, especially public offerings,[1] require a **syndicate** made up of several banks. Depending on how involved it is in the deal, and in particular the degree of guarantee, any one bank may play the role of:

- **global coordinator**, who coordinates all aspects of an offering; global coordinators are also lead manager and usually serve as lead and book-runner as well. For fixed-income issues, the global coordinator is called the **arranger**;
- the **lead manager** is responsible for preparing and executing the deal. The lead helps choose the syndicate. One (or more) leads also serve as book-runners. The lead also takes part in allocating the securities to investors;
- **joint-leads** play an important role, but do not usually serve as book-runners;
- **co-leads** underwrite a significant portion of the securities but have no role in structuring the deal;
- **co-managers** play a more limited role in the transaction, normally just underwriting a small portion of securities.

For some transactions (a block trade of already existing shares or a bond issue), the banks may buy the securities from the seller (or issuer) and then sell them to investors. This is called a **bought deal**. Unsold securities go onto the bank's balance sheet.

A **firm underwriting** agreement carries less of a commitment than a bought deal. A firm underwriting is a commitment by the bank to buy the securities only if the offering fails to attract sufficient investor interest. In some cases, the bank may be released from its commitment in the event of *force majeure*.

Before agreeing to underwrite more complex deals, banks may wish to have some idea of investors' intentions. They do so via a process called **book-building**, which occurs at the same time that information is sent out and the securities are marketed. Volumes and prices from potential investors are listed in the book. This helps determine if the transaction is feasible and, if so, at what price. Only after the book-building process do banks choose whether or not to underwrite the deal. Book-building allows the banks running the transaction to limit their risk, by assuring them that investors are willing to buy the securities.

Book-building helps to determine, at a given moment, the best price for the seller and/or company and to allocate the securities on a more or less discretionary basis.

In simpler transactions such as the placement of blocks or the issue of convertible bonds, the bank will almost always get feedback from a limited number of investors on their interest in the transaction and on the pricing.

1 *That is, for a flotation on a regulated market or a public retail offer.*

SECTION 2

In some cases, the bank does not pledge that the transaction will go through successfully, only that it will make its best efforts to ensure that this happens. This is rare in a formal documented offer, as investor confidence could be sapped if there is no formal pledge that the deal will go through. As a result, best efforts is the rule only in offerings by smaller companies or in very special cases (companies in financial distress, for example).

In some transactions, the bank's commitment is half-way between an initial bought deal and a post-book-building bought deal. When a block of existing shares is being sold, a bank may make a "back-stop" or floor underwriting commitment, i.e. go through the book-building process but guarantee the seller a minimum price.

There are three techniques for adjusting the offering to anticipation of investor behaviour, as well as to their actual behaviour: **extension option**, **greenshoe** and **clawback**.

The extension option allows shareholders wanting to sell shares or the company issuing new shares to sell more shares than initially planned if demand turns out to be strong. The option is disclosed in the prospectus and can be exercised at the time of the allocation. The size of the transaction can be increased by 15% in the case of a share issue and 25% in the case of a secondary placement.

To stabilise the price after the transaction, the issuer or seller may give the bank the option of buying a number of shares over and above the shares offered to investors (as many as 15% more in a capital increase and 25% for block trades of existing shares). This is called a greenshoe (named after the first company to use it). The bank allocates all the securities to investors, including the greenshoe shares, i.e. more than the official offering. These additional shares are borrowed by the bank:

- If the price falls after the offering, the bank buys shares on the market up to the limit of the greenshoe. This supports the price. It then has 30 days to resell these shares if the price moves back up. If the price doesn't rise, the bank repays the loan using the shares it bought to support the price. In this case the greenshoe is not exercised.
- If the price moves up, the bank can resell the shares or, if the price rises immediately after the transaction, the bank no longer has the shares so it will pay back the loan by exercising the greenshoe. The company will thus have sold more shares than originally planned.

Greenshoes are used for secondary offerings (i.e. sale of existing shares), new share issues (the lead bank receives, free of charge, warrants that it may or may not exercise) or convertible bond issues (when it takes the form of a simple extension of the issue, decided two or three days after its launch).

An offering targeted at several categories of investors (institutional, retail, employees, etc.) will be split into several tranches reserved for each of them. The **clawback** clause gives the company some flexibility in the size of each tranche. Hence, if institutional demand is very heavy and retail demand very light, the clawback allows the shares initially allocated to retail investors to be reallocated to institutional investors.

If a large shareholder sells part of his shares through the transaction, the placement will be eased if this shareholder commits not to sell additional shares over a certain period of time (unless the bank coordinating the transaction gives the green light). This is called a **lock up** and lasts between a few months and a year.

To simplify the transaction, the bank may advise the company to target a limited number of investors, thus avoiding the rules governing a public offering, including supervision by market authorities, obligation to present information, etc. This is called a **private placement** and is possible on all types of products. Private placements are often used in offerings to US investors (generally under rule 144A), as the offering would otherwise be subject to extremely strict restrictions.

3/ ISSUE DISCOUNTS

Studies show that when a company is floated, its stock normally rises by an average of about 10–15% over its issue price, depending on the country, the timing and how the rise is calculated! Meanwhile, shares in a company that is already listed are usually offered at a discount ranging from 2–5% although the range varies profoundly according to different countries.

Country	Period	Sample size	Mean underpricing (%)
Australia	1976–1994	328	+15.2
Austria	1984–1996	67	+6.5
Belgium	1984–1990	28	+10.1
Brazil	1979–1992	66	+74.1
Canada	1971–1992	258	+5.4
Chile	1982–1997	55	+8.8
China	1990–1996	226 (A-shares)	+388.0
	1987–1995	57 (B-shares)	+37.1
Denmark	1989–1997	29	+8.0
	1984–1992	76	+3.9
Finland	1984–1997	102	+9.9
France	1984–1995	228 (Second Marché)	+20.9
	1992–1998	264	+13.2
Germany	1970–1993	180	+9.2
Greece	1987–1994	129	+51.7
Hong Kong	1980–1996	334	+15.9
India	1992–1994	386	+72.3
Indonesia	1989–1994	106	+15.1
Israel	1993–1994	28	+4.5
Italy	1985–1998	135	+20.3
Japan	1970–1996	975	+24.0
	1989–1995	456 (OTC market)	+15.7
Korea	1980–1990	347	+78.1
Malaysia	1990–1994	220	+72.6
Mexico	1987–1990	37	+33.0
Netherlands	1982–1991	72	+7.2
	1984–1994	64	+4.0
New Zealand	1979–1991	149	+28.8
Nigeria	1989–1993	63	+19.1
Norway	1984–1996	68	+12.5
Philippines	1987–1997	104	+22.7
Poland	1991–1998	149	+35.6
Portugal	1992–1998	21	+10.5
Singapore	1973–1992	128	+31.4
Spain	1985–1990	71	+10.8
Sweden	1979–1997	233	+29.3
Switzerland	1985–1994	55	+34.6
Taiwan	1971–1990	168	+45.0
Thailand	1988–1989	32	+56.73
Turkey	1990–1995	138	+13.6
UK	1959–1990	2133	+12.0
	1989–1996	385	+10.1
USA	1960–1997	13 910	+13.7

Source: Paleari (2000).

This discount is theoretically due to the asymmetry of information between the seller and the investors or intermediaries. One side knows more about the company's prospects, while the other side knows more about market demand. The transaction is therefore possible. It's all a matter of price! Selling securities generally sends out a negative signal, so the seller has to price his securities slightly below their true value to ensure the deal goes through and that investors are satisfied.

Some authors suggest that the discount is due to the "**winner's curse**" that pursues the winner of an auction. The winner, in fact, shouldn't be (economically) pleased about the win because it is clear that everybody else apparently thought the object's value was less than the price paid by the winner!

IPOs, after all, are similar to auctions. The IPO discount could then be due to the fact that there are both informed and uninformed investors. Uninformed investors cannot distinguish which issues are really attractive and thus are exposed to the winner's curse. This is why an average discount is offered, to guarantee an appropriate return for uninformed investors who will be receiving many shares of a "bad deal" and few shares of a "good deal".

Others suggest that the discount is a way of remunerating the banks underwriting the deal. The discount makes the issue easier to market, reduces their risk and allows them to meet institutional client demand.

The issue discount is another way to persuade investors to invest in a transaction that appears to carry some risk.

> The greater the asymmetry in information between an issuer and investors, and the lower the liquidity of the security, the greater is the issue discount. The issue discount will thus be high for an initial public offering, less for the sale of shares in an already listed company, low or non-existent for convertible bonds and totally absent for bonds.

So much for the major principles. Let's look now at how the main types of securities are offered. As you will see, the methods converge towards two main techniques: bought deals and book-building.

Section 26.2
INITIAL PUBLIC OFFERINGS

1/ HOW AN IPO WORKS

The purpose of this section is not to analyse the motivations, strategic or otherwise, of an initial public offering (IPO) but simply to describe how it works.

> IPOs are surely the most complex of transactions. They involve selling securities, about which prior information is extremely limited, to a large number of investors, including institutional and retail investors and employees.

An IPO can include a primary tranche (i.e. shares newly issued by the company) and/or a secondary tranche (i.e. existing shares). The techniques are the same for both tranches and, in fact, existing shares and new shares are bundled up in the same lot of shares to be offered.

However, the techniques vary depending on whether the shares are being offered to institutional investors, retail investors or employees.

2/ How IPOs are made

A number of techniques exist for floating a company. However, in the past few years, IPOs on regulated markets have almost all been in the same form: that of an **underwritten deal** with institutional investors and a **retail public offering** with retail investors.

(a) Underwriting

Offerings of securities to institutional investors are often underwritten. This is the main tranche in almost all IPOs. Under this system, one or more banks organise the marketing and sale of securities to investors via a phase of book-building. The price set after book-building will serve as a basis for setting the price of the retail public offering. Other techniques are used for the other tranches (employees and retail investors, in particular).

IPOs that make use of book-building take place in several phases.

The initial **review phase** is handled by the banks. This consists in assessing and preparing the legal and regulatory framework of the deal (choice of market for listing, whether to offer shares in the US, etc.); structuring the deal; supervising documentation (due diligence, prospectus), as well as underwriting and execution agreements; preparing financial analysis reports; designing a marketing campaign (i.e. the type and content of management presentations, programme of meetings between management and investors).

Then comes the **execution phase**, with the publishing of financial analysis notes by syndicate banks. This is a pre-marketing period lasting one to two weeks prior to the effective launch of the operation. The notes are presented to investors during "warm-up" meetings, which help test investor sentiment. Analysts' research notes cannot be published during the black-out period that precedes the launch. The terms of the transaction, particularly the price range, are set on the basis of conclusions from this pre-marketing exercise.

The marketing campaign itself then begins, and the offering is under way. During this period, full information is distributed via draft prospectuses (certified by market authorities), which may be national or international in scope. The prospectus includes all information on the company and the transaction. The offering is marketed within a price range of about 15%. Company managers are mobilised during this period for numerous meetings with investors (road shows) or for one-on-one meetings. The information given to investors is mainly on company results, markets and strategy.

In the meantime, investor intentions to subscribe in terms of volumes and prices are recorded in an order book, on the basis of the preliminary price range.

After this period, which can last 5–15 days, the sale price of the existing shares and/or newly issued shares is set. The price reflects market conditions, overall demand as reflected in the order book and the price sensitivity that investors may have expressed.

Not until after this phase might banks enter into a firm underwriting agreement. The shares are then immediately allocated, thus limiting the bank's risk. After allocation, investors are theoretically committed. However, up to the actual settlement and delivery of the shares (three days after the transaction), banks still face counterparty risk. There is also business risk in the form of an institutional investor who decides he does not wish to take delivery of the shares after all. In sum, the only risks the syndicate takes is that of a market crash between the moment the price is set and the moment when the shares are allocated, and that of stabilising the price for around a month after the transaction by buying shares on the market.

The guarantee given by the bank to the company is also implicitly a guarantee for the market. The bank determines a value after review of internal information. This partly resolves the problem of asymmetry of information. The signal is no longer negative, because a bank with access to internal information is taking the risk of buying the shares at a set price if the market does not.

The final prospectus (with the issue price) is sent out after the price is set and the subscription period is closed. The lead bank knows the quantity and quality of demand. The book-runner allocates the new shares to investors in concert with the issuer and/or seller, who can thus "choose" his shareholders to a certain extent.

The shares are allocated on the basis of certain criteria determined in advance. Allocation is discretionary but not arbitrary. The goal may be to favour US, European or local investors. Generally, the main goal in allocation is to have a balance between investors with different investment timing in order to ensure a stable aftermarket. The banks may steer the issuer to what it believes are quality investors, thus limiting excessive **flowback**, i.e. the massive sale of securities immediately after the offering.

In academic research, discretionary allocation and pricing have been interpreted in the following ways:

- Benveniste and Spindt claim that the most knowledgeable investors reveal the information they have (through their order in the order book) in exchange for a good allocation and a good pricing (IPO discount).
- In a second interpretation, the bank tries to favour long-term investors in order not to drive down the share price in the short term. In addition, the IPOed firm may wish to create a long-term shareholder base.
- In a third interpretation, the bank will use its power in the transaction to maximise its profits (which is sometimes against the interest of the firm being IPOed). The bank derives high profits from its large institutional clients (in particular thanks to trading revenues). They will, therefore, favour them in the primary transactions in granting large allocations and driving the pricing down. Such behaviour has sometimes been sanctioned by law.

Book-building offers several advantages, including greater flexibility. For one thing, the price can be adjusted as necessary during the marketing phase, which can sometimes last several weeks. Moreover, shareholders can still be chosen via discretionary allocation of shares.

BOOK BUILDING

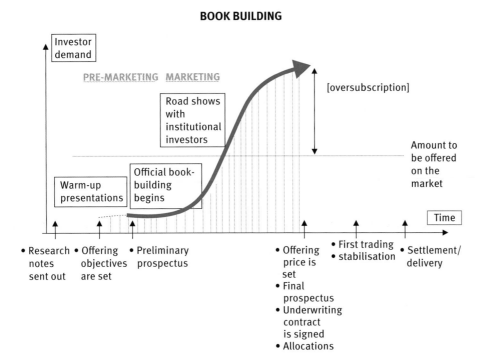

(b) How shares are offered to retail investors

In an underwritten deal, shares are allocated at the discretion of the lead, based on the order book, as well as on criteria announced in advance. However, when shares are being sold to retail investors, the issue is centralised by the market itself.

- **The retail public offering**

    In a retail public offering, a price range is set before the offering, but the exact price is set after the offering. The final price reflects market demand. French market authorities, for example, require a marketing period lasting at least three days, after which a draft prospectus is issued with the characteristics of the deal. Based on a price range, financial intermediaries collect orders from investors. The issue price is set jointly by the issuer and the syndicate lead and is generally equal to the underwriting price.[2] The final prospectus is then approved by the market authorities.

    With the agreement of the market authorities, the banks can adjust the price if they have previously reserved the right to do so but, in general, they must begin the process anew if the new price is outside of the initial range. Shares are allocated on the basis of orders if supply is equivalent to demand and can be reduced on the basis of predetermined criteria. Allocation of shares to the various categories of buyers is done on the same basis as the fixed price offer.

    Orders are filled on the basis of a percentage resulting from the comparison of supply and demand. Normally, at least 1% of the order is filled, but there may be provision

2 *Retail investors are generally offered a discount or are exempt from certain fees.*

for a minimum number of shares per order, so that broker fees do not end up swallowing any potential gain. Similarly, there are sometimes several categories of orders with different allocation priorities.

- **Fixed price offering**

  Under a fixed price offering, a certain number of shares are offered to the public at a preset price, which is generally identical to the price offered to institutional investors. The price is set after the book-building phase and is independent of market conditions. It is applied regardless of the number of shares requested. If it is far below what the market is willing to pay, the price will rise sharply in the days after the IPO and primary market buyers will have a capital gain to show for their initiative.

  The only difference between a fixed price offering and a retail public offering is how the price is set.

- **Minimum price offering**

  Under this technique, a number of shares are offered to the public at a certain price, under which they will not be sold. The local stock exchange centralises orders, in which buyers must specify a floor price, and tries to find a sufficiently wide price range at which orders can be allocated in a certain proportion (about 6%) if there is sufficient demand.

  In a minimum price offering, some orders may be shut out entirely, and orders at very high prices are paradoxically eliminated. This explains why the first quoted price is above the pre-set minimum price. If demand is too strong to quote the shares, trading is declared "limit up" and resumes at a higher price or another technique is used for the initial quotation.

- **An ordinary full listing**

  The principle of an ordinary full listing is simple: the shares are offered on the basis of the market's normal trading and quoting conditions. A minimum sale price is set, but buy orders are not centralised by the local stock exchange. Quotation is possible at a price normally no higher than 110% of the minimum price; at least 6% of the buy orders are filled (4% in exceptional cases). As in a minimum price offering, trading may be suspended "limit up" and resumed at a higher price. In addition, orders may have to be covered by sufficient funds (the goal being to discourage speculation).

3/ US LISTINGS FOR NON-US COMPANIES

Companies normally list their shares on their domestic stock market, where they are better known. However, they may wish to tap foreign investors to widen their shareholder base and could thus seek a foreign listing.

As can be seen from the chart below, this decision is not so unusual!

Since the American markets (NYSE and NASDAQ) are traditionally the preferred alternative for companies wanting to list, we focus our attention on US listing.

A company can list its shares on the US market via (1) a private placement, (2) American Depositary Receipts or (3) full listing.

NUMBER OF FOREIGN COMPANIES

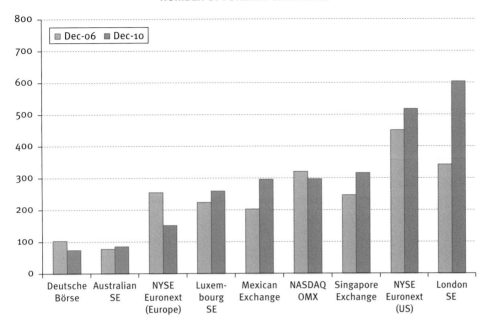

Source: World Federation of Exchanges

3 *American Depositary Receipts may be also called – generically – Depositary Receipts (DRs), or Rule 144A Depositary Receipts or Global Depositary Receipts (GDRs), which are the "private placement" discussed in the text. However, different names typically identify the market in which the Depositary Receipts are available:* **ADRs** *are publicly available to US investors on a national stock exchange or in the over-the-counter market;* **Rule 144A ADRs** *are privately placed and resold only to Qualified Institutional Buyers (QIBs) in the US QIB POR-TAL market; and* **GDRs** *are generally available in one or more markets outside the foreign company's home country, although these may also be known as ADRs.*

(a) Private placements

Under rule 144A, companies may opt for private placement of their shares, but they may only do so with US **Qualified Institutional Buyers** (QIBs). QIBs are then prohibited from selling their shares on the open market for two years, but can trade with other QIBs via the PORTAL system. Private placements are simply a means of gaining access to US investors, but do not allow a company to register its shares with the Securities Exchange Commission (SEC) or to quote them in the US.

This is the least restrictive way to raise capital on US markets, as private placements are not registered with the SEC and come under the 12g3-2(b) waiver. All the issuing company has to do is translate the information that it has provided to its domestic market.

(b) Indirect listing via American Depositary Receipt (ADR)

ADRs, also known as DRs or GDRs,[3] are negotiable instruments issued by a US bank and representing the shares that it has acquired in a foreign company listed on a non-US market – something like tracking stocks, except they are not issued by the company itself. ADRs are traded on a regulated market or an over-the-counter (OTC) market.

The ADR shares can be established either for existing shares already trading in the secondary market of the home country, or as part of a global offering of new shares.

There are several types of ADR:

- Level 1 ADRs are not traded on an organised market but only over the counter. They do not allow companies to raise funds on the US market, but nor do they require any particular information to be put out.
- Level 2 ADRs are listed on an organised market. This attracts some US pension funds, but requires the companies to publish a 20-F report every year. The 20-F is a more extensive document than a typical European annual report (it includes, for example, a table for converting from the company's accounting principles to US GAAP[4]). Companies are not allowed to raise funds with Level 2 ADRs.
- Level 3 ADRs provide the company with a listing (via its ADR) on an organised market, and also allow it to raise funds via a public offering. Level 3 accordingly requires full registration with the SEC (F-1). Moreover, the company is subject to strict obligations on information (based on the 20-F and 6-K). Among other things, the published documents must list plans for acquisitions or reorganisation, as well as a partial reconciliation of company accounts to US GAAP. Companies usually go this route when they have significant commercial interests in North America.

4 Companies following the IFRS norms will no longer be obliged to abide by this rule after 2009.

More than 3000 ADRs are listed from 50 different countries, including Axa, Alcatel-Lucent, Telefónica, Korea Electric Power, Nokia, BP and many others.

(c) Full listing

Companies can also list their ordinary shares in both their home countries and directly in the US. This gives them access to institutional investors whose by-laws do not allow them to buy shares outside the US.

The main difference between ordinary registered shares and ADRs is that ordinary registered shares carry lower transaction costs as there is no depositary. They are also more liquid and are less subject to arbitrage trading between domestic shares and ADRs.

Full listing is a relatively long and complex process suitable only for very large companies (UBS, Deutsche Telekom, Repsol YPF, etc.). Information to be disclosed includes full financial statements in US GAAP.

Section 26.3
Capital increases

A financial approach to capital increases is developed in Chapter 39.

1/ The different methods

The method chosen for a capital increase depends:

1. on whether or not the company is listed;
2. on how eager current shareholders are to subscribe.

(a) Listed companies

When the large majority of current shareholders are expected to subscribe to the capital increase and it is not necessary or desirable to bring in new shareholders, the transaction comes with pre-emptive subscription rights (the transaction is then called a rights issue). The issue price of the new shares is set and announced in advance and the offering then unfolds over several days. The price is set at a significant discount to the market price, so that the transaction will go through even if the share price drops in the run up to the listing of new shares. To avoid penalising existing shareholders, the issue comes with pre-emptive subscription rights, which are negotiable throughout the transaction period.

However, when current shareholders are not expected to subscribe or when the company wants to widen its shareholder base, no pre-emptive subscription rights are issued. The issue price is then not set until a marketing and pre-placement period has been completed, with a very slight discount to the share price at the end of this period. There are no pre-emptive subscription rights, but there may be a period during which current shareholders are given priority in subscribing.

(b) Unlisted companies

In this case, the issue price's discount will not be dictated by the fear that the share price will fluctuate during the operation (as the company is not listed), but rather by the wish of current shareholders to raise cash by selling the subscription rights they may have received.

If current shareholders do not wish to raise cash, the company will issue pre-emptive subscription rights at a price about equal to the share price, or may issue shares to identified investors that have been found via a private placement.[5]

WHICH METHOD SHOULD BE USED FOR CAPITAL INCREASE?

Rights issue subscribed mainly by:	Listed company	Unlisted company
Current shareholders	Pre-emptive subscription rights Steep discount to the market price	Pre-emptive subscription rights with a steep discount if current shareholders wish to raise cash Pre-emptive subscription rights with no discount or no pre-emptive rights if current shareholders do not want to raise cash
New shareholders	Offer without pre-emptive subscription rights (at a slight discount to the current share price) In some cases, a reserve rights issue	Pre-emptive subscription rights with a steep discount if shareholders want to raise cash Reserved rights issue if shareholders do not want cash

5 *In the rare case of a capital increase with no subscription rights and not reserved for identified investors, the price is based on an expert appraisal or is set at book value.*

Shares cannot be issued below par value (this is also the case for listed companies). Book value or an expert appraisal constitutes a floor value.

2/ RIGHTS ISSUE

A fixed-price rights issue with pre-emptive subscription rights (also called *privileged subscription* or *rights issues*) is the traditional issue preferred by small investors (or their representatives). Such issues acknowledge their loyalty or, conversely, allow them to raise a little cash by selling their subscription rights.

In some countries, such as the United States and Japan, rights issues are quite rare, while in Continental Europe they generally have to be sold by rights.

Such issues remain open for at least 10 trading days. Banks underwrite them at a price well below the current share price, generally at a discount of 15–30%. No bank will guarantee a price near the current market price because, the longer the subscription period, the greater the risk of a drop in price. It is at this price that the banks will buy up any shares that have not found takers.

A steep discount would be a considerable injustice to existing shareholders, as the new shareholders could buy shares at 20% below the current market price. Rights issues resolve this problem by allowing existing shareholders to buy a number of shares proportional to the number they already have. If existing shareholders use all their pre-emptive rights, i.e. buy the same proportion of new shares as they possess of existing shares, they should not care what price the new shares are offered at.

The price of the new shares plus the value of the pre-emptive subscription rights is equivalent to the stock's current market value (i.e. its share price if it is listed), even if the price of the new shares is below the current share price.

Even when existing shareholders do not wish to subscribe, the pre-emptive subscription rights keep them from being penalised, as they can sell the right on the first day it is detached.

(a) Definition

The subscription right is a right attached to each existing share allowing its holder to subscribe to the new share issue.

The subscription right offers the existing shareholder:

- the certainty of being able to take part in the capital increase in proportion with his current stake;
- the option of selling the right (which is listed separately for listed companies) throughout the operation. This negotiable right adjusts the issue price to the current share price.

The subscription right is similar to a call option whose underlying is the share, whose strike price is the issue price of the new shares and whose exercise period is that of the capital increase. Hence, its theoretical value is similar to that of a call option whose time value is very low, given its short maturity.

If the issue price and the current share price are the same, the subscription right's market value will be zero and its only value will be the priority it grants.

If the share price falls below the issue price, the rights issue will fail, as nobody will buy a share at more than its market price. The right then loses all value. Fortunately, the reverse occurs more frequently.

(b) Calculating the theoretical value of the subscription right

Let's take a company that has 1 000 000 shares outstanding, trading at €50 each. The company issues 100 000 new shares at €40 each, or one new share for each 10 existing ones. Each existing share will have one subscription right, and to buy a new share for €40, 10 subscription rights and €40 will be required.

After the new shares have been issued, an existing shareholder who holds one share and has sold his pre-emptive subscription rights must be in the same situation as an investor who has bought 10 pre-emptive subscription rights and one new share. So the share price after the deal should be equal to:

$$\text{Pre-deal price} - 1 \text{ pre-emptive right}$$

but also

$$\text{Issue price} + 10 \text{ pre-emptive subscription rights}$$

In our example:

$$\text{€50} - 1 \text{ pre-emptive right} = \text{€40} + 10 \text{ pre-emptive rights}$$

Hence

$$\text{The value of the right} = \text{€0.91}$$

The post-deal share price should be equal to:

$$\text{€50} - \text{€0.91} = \text{€40} + 10 \times \text{€0.91} = \text{€49.09}$$

It is easy to calculate the theoretical value of the subscription right:

$$\text{Subscription right} = \frac{\text{Value of the existing share} - \text{Issue price}}{1 + \text{Subscription parity}}$$

as it should make no difference to an investor whether he buys an existing share minus the right or the necessary number of rights plus one new share.

Mathematically, the value of the subscription right looks like this:

$$(V - E) \times \frac{N'}{N + N'}$$

where V is the pre-issue share price, E the issue price of the new shares, N' the number of new shares issued and N the number of existing shares.

We can see that this formula can be used to find the previous result.

The detachment of subscription rights is conceptually similar to a bonus share award. Hence, the existing shareholder may, if he wishes, sell some pre-emptive rights and use the cash and remaining rights to subscribe to new shares, without laying out new cash (see the exercise at the end of this chapter).

The theoretical value of the share, once the rights have been distributed, is equal to the price pre transaction less the value of the right. It is called the **theoretical ex-right price** or **TERP**.

(c) Advantages and drawbacks of pre-emptive rights

The subscription right is valid for at least 10 days – a relatively lengthy amount of time. The issue price therefore has to be well below the share price, so that if the share price does fall during the period, the deal can still go through. The value of the right (i.e. the difference between the share price and the issue price) will fall but will remain positive, as long as the share price, ex-rights, is above the issue price.

This is a double-edged sword as, once the deal is launched and the rights issued, nothing can delay the capital increase, even if the share price drops significantly during the deal. This is why the initial discount is so significant.

Complicating the transaction further is the fact that shareholders who do not possess a number of shares divisible by the subscription parity must sell or buy rights on the market so that they do. This can be difficult to do on international markets.

The fixed-price offer with subscription rights is poorly suited to the current strong market volatility. That's why it is meant mainly for existing shareholders and is not feasible in transactions equal to a large portion of market cap, because the new shares must be marketed aggressively to new shareholders.

Another potential complication is the large proportion of US investors among current shareholders who are sometimes unable to exercise their pre-emptive subscription rights.

3/ CAPITAL INCREASES WITHOUT PRE-EMPTIVE SUBSCRIPTION RIGHTS

In rights issues without pre-emptive subscription rights, the company also turns to a bank or a banking syndicate for the issue. But their role is more important in this case, as they must market the new shares to new investors. They generally underwrite the issue, as described above for IPOs. A retail public offering can be undertaken simultaneously. Alternatively, the bank can simply launch the transaction and centralise the orders without having gone through a book-building phase. The company may issue 10–15% more shares than expected, via a *greenshoe*, under which warrants are issued to the banks (see above).

Local regulations tend to limit the flexibility to issue shares without subscription rights so that the shareholder will not be diluted at an absurd price. Therefore, in most countries regulation fixes a maximum discount to the last price or a minimum issue price as a reference to a price average.

When new shares are issued with no pre-set price, current shareholders can be given first priority without necessarily receiving pre-emptive rights. Indeed, such a priority period is the rule when pre-emptive rights are not issued. However, unlike pre-emptive rights, the priority period cannot be bought or sold. However, priority periods have the disadvantage of lengthening the total transaction period, as they generally last a few trading days (this is the minimum amount of time to allow individual shareholders the time to subscribe).

Legally speaking, a public issue of new shares, with or without pre-emptive rights, is considered to have been completed when the banks have signed a contract on a firm underwriting of the transaction, regardless of whether or not the shares end up being fully subscribed.

4/ EQUITY LINES

The way an equity line works is that a company issues warrants to a bank which exercises them at the request of the company when it needs to raise equity. Equity lines smooth the impact of a capital increase over time. The shares issued when the warrants are exercised are immediately resold by the bank.

The strike price is the average price over a short period (5 days in recent operations) less a discount of about 10%. The number of warrants that can be issued at any one time depends on the stock's liquidity (equivalent to a fraction of the number of shares traded over the previous days), thus partly preventing the problem of overhang (i.e. the fear that the arrival of a large number of shares on the market will depress the share price).

Equity lines are suitable for young businesses where the stock performance history does not allow conventional rights issues. However, it opens the way to many uncertainties, particularly on the terms imposed on the banks in exercising warrants and reselling the shares.

Equity lines may be less convenient for low-liquidity shares and low market capitalisation because there could be strong pressure to reduce the price of the shares. This phenomenon has been defined as a "death spiral" in the US because it has determined the end of various new-economy companies.

5/ THE NEW EQUITY (OR ISSUES) PUZZLE

A study by Ritter and Loughran (1995) has compared how an investor would have fared buying stock in a company that made a seasoned equity offering vs. buying stock in similarly capitalised non-issuing firms ("**Seasoned Equity Offerings**", or SEOs, simply refers to a sale of additional stock by a company whose shares are already publicly traded.)

The authors studied 2680 companies that sold additional shares from 1970 to 1990. Each company that issued shares was compared to a company of equal market capitalisation that did not. As a result, two portfolios were created, each with the same number of companies and a similar market capitalisation. The only difference was that one portfolio was made up of stock-issuing companies, while the other – the reference portfolio – consisted only of non-issuing companies.

The average annual return of the issuing companies was a measly 7% a year. The non-issuing companies averaged a return of 15.3% annually. In each case, the timeframe studied was the 5 years following the date of the seasoned offering.

Other researchers have shown that many IPOs and SEOs start out well. Their stock price rises, but then over the following period (3–5 years) they perform far worse than the average stock. In fact, they underperform the rest of the market by around 30%. In academic circles this phenomenon is known as the "new equity puzzle".

Playing devil's advocate with their own study, Ritter and Loughran wondered if the poor performance of the issuing companies could have been due to something other than the fact that they had issued more stock. After all, the stock issuers' share prices had run up about 72%, on average, in the year preceding the second stock offering. Perhaps the subsequent slump merely evened out their returns.

Section 26.4
BLOCK TRADES OF SHARES

A block is a large number of shares that a shareholder wishes to sell on the market. Normally, only a small fraction of a company's shares are traded during the course of a normal day. Hence, a shareholder who wants to sell, for example 5% of a company's shares, cannot do so directly on the market. If he did, he could only do so over a long period and with the risk of driving down the share price. Blocks are sold via book-building and/or bought deals, which were described above.

1/ BOOK-BUILDING AND ACCELERATED BOOK-BUILDING

Like a rights issue, a block trade is done via book-building. However, while rights issues allow companies to raise significant funds for investment, a block trade does not raise any new capital or have any direct impact on the company's business.

Moreover, fewer shares are usually involved in a block trade than in a capital increase. Block trades are thus "simpler" deals than capital increases and require less marketing. Book-building is faster, top management is less involved or not involved at all, and the deal can sometimes be done within a few hours.

Bigger transactions involving a strategic shift (exit by a controlling shareholder, etc.) may require an intense marketing campaign, and the deal will be managed as if it were a rights issue.

Book-building can come with a public offer of sale when the company wants to allow retail investors to acquire shares, but only for the larger issues. Barring a waiver from Euronext, a retail offering is possible only if it involves at least 10% of the total outstanding shares or at least 20 times the average daily volumes during the previous 6 months.

Block trades use methods similar to those of IPOs, particularly in price setting. For example, prices can be set in advance or on the basis of terms set when the offering begins. However, in the latter case, no price range is required (but the price-setting mechanism and the maximum price must be spelled out). In the requisite filings with Euronext, the initiator can reserve the right to withdraw the offer if take-up is insufficient or increase the number of shares on offer by as much as 25% if demand is greater than expected.

2/ BOUGHT DEALS AND BACK-STOPS

When the seller initiates book-building or accelerated book-building, he has no guarantee that the transaction will go through. Nor does he know at what price the deal will be done. To solve this problem, he can ask the bank to buy the shares itself. The bank will then sell them to investors. This is called a "bought deal".

The bank is then taking a significant risk and will only buy the shares at a discount to the market price. In recent bought deals involving liquid stocks, this discount has ranged from 2% to 5%.

The way it works is this: the seller contacts a few banks one evening after the markets close. He may have mentioned to some banks a few days or weeks beforehand that he might be selling shares, thus ensuring better quality replies. The seller asks each bank the price it is willing to offer for the shares. Bids must be submitted within a few hours. The seller chooses the bank solely on the basis of price, and the shares are sold that very night. The bank must then organise its sales teams to resell the shares during the night in North America or Asia, taking advantage of the time difference, and then the following morning in Europe.

For the seller, bought deals offer the advantage of being certain that the deal will go through and at the price stated at the moment when it decides whether to sell. There are some disadvantages, however:

- the deal will generally be at a greater discount than in accelerated book-building;
- share performance can suffer, as the bank that has acquired the shares will want to sell them as quickly as possible, even if that means making the price fall;

In a very hot market, the seller may have the best of both worlds in transactions with a back-stop.

- The bank sets up an order book so that the firm can benefit from an increase in share price.
- The bank guarantees a minimum price. If all or part of the placement cannot be made at that price, the bank will buy the shares at the back-stop price.

Section 26.5
BONDS

As the bond market develops and becomes more international, investors need benchmarks to measure the risk of default by issuers they do not always know very well. Ratings have thus become crucial in bond offerings. Companies that do not have a rating from at least one agency are finding it increasingly difficult to issue bonds.

As we mentioned in Chapter 21, the corporate bond market can be separated between companies having a rating of at least BBB (investment grade) and companies rated BB or lower (below investment grade). When they want to issue bonds, the latter must offer higher interest rates. Such bonds are called "high-yield". The investment grade and high yield markets are separate, not just for the issuers, but also for investors and for the investment banks handling the offering.

1/ INVESTMENT GRADE BONDS

The euro switchover has naturally given rise to a pan-European bond market, and has allowed much larger issues than were previously possible on national markets. €1bn issues are no longer rare, and only issues of €10bn or more are exceptional.

Bond-offering techniques have thus evolved towards those used for shares, and market regulations have followed suit. For example, **competitive bidding** has gradually given way to book-building. Competitive bidding consists in a tender from banks. The issuer chooses the establishment that will head up the offering on the basis of the terms offered (mainly price). It thus takes the risk of giving the lead mandate to a bank that is overly aggressive on price. The reason this is risky is that prices of bonds on the secondary market may fall after the operation begins as the bonds were issued at too high a price (hence at an excessively low rate). Buyers will not like this and will demand a higher interest rate the next time the issuer comes to the primary market. Competitive bidding is similar to a bought deal and is often used by state-owned companies, as well as companies that have already tapped the bond markets.

Corporate bonds are generally placed via book-building.

Book-building helps avoid price weakness after launch, as the issue price (or spread) is not pre-set. The lead bank suggests a price range and sounds out investors to see what price they are willing to pay. Presentations to investors, one-on-one meetings and electronic road shows over the Internet or Bloomberg allow management to present its strategy.

The lead then builds a book of volumes and prices (either rate or spread) offered by each investor interested in the issue. There is little risk of miscalculation, as the issue price is set by the market. The period between when the price is set and the effective delivery of the shares is called the **grey market** (this is also the case for IPOs and rights issues). Shares are traded on the grey market without, technically, even existing. Transactions on the grey market are unwound after settlement and delivery and the first official quotations. The lead intervenes on the grey market to maintain the spread at which the issue has been priced. This is especially useful when an issue requires, or would benefit from, intense marketing. Companies wishing to market investors aggressively (notably to return to the market when they wish), will use book-building.

So there are some similarities between share and bond offerings. *However, the process is much shorter for bonds and can be extremely short, especially if a company is a frequent issuer, and if the issue is on its local market.* The process is longer for a first issue or if the company is targeting a large proportion of international investors.

A sample timetable for an issuer who has issued bonds in the past is shown in the diagram below:

TIMETABLE FOR A BOND ISSUES

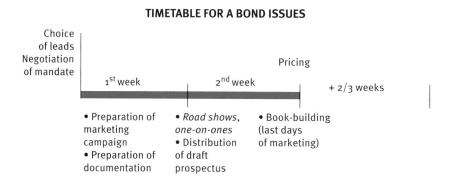

The role of the lead is not just to market the paper, but to advise the client, where applicable, in the obtaining of a rating. It determines the spread possible through comparisons with issuers having a similar profile and chooses the members of the syndicate to help sell the bonds to the largest number possible of investors.

When the company plans several issues in the medium term, it can put out an umbrella prospectus to cover all of them, under an issue of **EMTNs (euro medium-term notes)**. This allows the company to tap the markets very rapidly when it needs to or when the market is attractive.

Underwriting syndicates routinely stabilise the secondary market price for poorly received initial public offerings. Few debt IPOs suffer sharp price declines during the first few days of trading, in part because the syndicate imposes so-called "penalty bids" whose common aim is to discourage investors from immediately reselling their shares.

A number of studies have examined the determinants of the at-issue yield spread, which is an increasing function of the issue costs (the at-issue yield is measured by equating the net proceeds, after deducting the issue costs, with the present value of the coupon and principal payments). Datta *et al.* (1999), as well as other studies, documented that the at-issue yield spread is *negatively* related to credit rating and *positively* related to bond maturity. As issue costs are an important determinant of the at-issue yield spread, these findings imply similar relations for the issue costs.

Several studies have investigated the determinants of direct issue costs, which consist primarily of underwriter fees (e.g. Lee *et al.*, 1996; Altinkilic and Hansen, 2000). These studies generally find that the direct issue costs are positively related to bond maturity and are negatively related to issue size and credit quality.

2/ HIGH-YIELD BONDS

The high-yield bond market has developed in Europe only since the late 1990s. Until then, the financing needs of risky companies were covered exclusively by equity or bank loans.

By definition, high-yield, or non-investment grade, bonds are risky products.

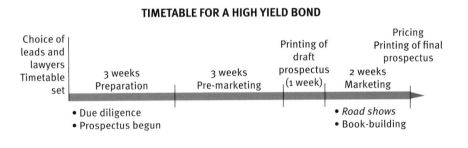

TIMETABLE FOR A HIGH YIELD BOND

High-yield issues take longer and require more aggressive marketing than a standard issue as there are fewer potential buyers.

3/ RULE 144A

As already explained, the US SEC approved Rule 144A in April 1990, an initiative that allowed for the immediate resale of private placements *among* **Qualified Institutional Buyers** (QIBs).[6] Rule 144A facilitates the resale of privately placed debt and equity securities and thus increases secondary trading among institutional investors.

Under this ruling, it is possible to resell privately placed bond securities to QIBs. Thus, large financial institutions can sell previously acquired private placements without having to register the securities or hold the securities for two years. The SEC rule has modified the two-year holding period requirement on privately placed securities by permitting QIBs to trade these positions among themselves.

6 A QIB, broadly defined, is a financial institution that owns and manages $100 million ($10 million in the case of a registered broker-dealer) or more in qualifying securities. For a banking institution to qualify as a QIB, a $25 million minimum net worth test must also be satisfied.

Thus, Rule 144A issues do not require SEC registration. By lifting the registration requirements for purchasers of 144A issues, the SEC sought to reduce regulatory costs and create a more liquid market for these restricted securities.

Rule 144A imposes less stringent disclosure and reporting requirements than a registered issue entails, so issuers can complete the offering fairly quickly. On the other hand, Rule 144A bonds have limited liquidity because only qualified institutional investors can buy and sell them. Despite this drawback, more companies have warmed up to Rule 144A.

Rule 144A is particularly important for foreign issuers. Under this rule, in fact, these firms have gained access to institutional investors without having to meet the strict disclosure standards required of US public companies. The Rule 144A market has evolved rapidly and now closely resembles the SEC-registered market in terms of underwriting practices, marketing, disclosure and credit rating requirements.

	Rule 144A offering	Public offering
Size	$250m–$1bn	$250m–$1bn
Rating	Two ratings are required	Two ratings are required
Spread	Credit spread usually slightly higher than public	Lowest credit spread
Syndicate composition	Usually 3 or more underwriters, depending on deal	Usually 3 or more underwriters, depending on deal
Covenants	Covenants similar to those required for a public issue	Loosest covenant structure
	Long preparation time needed before accessing the market	Long preparation time needed before accessing the market

Source: Adapted from Johnson (2000), p. 91

Given the growing convergence between the two forms, why should a company choose one form or the other? Basically there are two reasons:

1. the different average sizes; and
2. the desire not to report to the SEC on an ongoing basis.

While Rule 144A permits issuers to raise debt and equity capital, the total amount of capital raised via debt is nearly eight times the amount raised via equity.

Debt issuers pay a price – in the form of higher yields – for the convenience associated with Rule 144A offerings (Livingston and Zhou, 2002). Rule 144A issues, particularly those of private companies that do not file financial statements with the SEC, have substantially higher yields than their SEC-registered counterparts. Overall, they yield 19 basis points more than public bonds and 54 basis points more than private debt offerings. Investors apparently regard the lack of information about the issue as a risk factor and demand higher yields in return for the added uncertainty, which more dramatically affects private companies without SEC-mandated transparency.

Section 26.6
CONVERTIBLE AND EXCHANGEABLE BONDS

Convertible and exchangeable bonds are issued via accelerated book-building or bought deals.

Convertible bonds (CBs) (examined in Chapter 25) are a very specific product. They are first of all bonds paying interest and redeemed in cash at maturity. They are called convertibles, as the investor has the right to ask that the bond be redeemed not in cash but in shares, based on a parity set at issue, if the share price has risen enough by then. Holders of convertible bonds are entitled to all information put out by the issuer to its shareholders, while the share price tells them precisely how much the CB's option component is worth.

There is little problem of asymmetry of information between the investor and issuer in the case of a convertible bond, as the convertible's bond component protects the investor.

The only factor that could make an investor hesitate to invest in a convertible bond is the product's complexity. However, CBs are now well known to professional investors, and are sold mainly to specialised investors or *hedge funds*.

Section 26.7
SYNDICATED LOANS

Syndicated loans are not securities in their own right, but merely loans made to companies by several banks. A syndicated loan offering is nonetheless similar to a bond issue. The company first chooses the bank that will arrange the deal. This bank may do a bought deal of the entire loan and then syndicate it afterwards. The arranger is paid specifically for its advisory and placement role.

The main terms are negotiated between the arranger and the company and are put into a **term sheet**. Meanwhile, the bank and company choose a syndication strategy, as well as the banks (or financial institutions) that will be members of the syndicate.

After meetings with the company and a memorandum of information, the banks contacted will decide whether or not to take part in the syndicated loan. Once the syndicate is formed, the legal documentation is finalised. The entire process can take 2 months, between the choice of arranger and the delivery of funds.

Syndicated loans are closely dependent on the quality of the company's relationship with its banks. Syndicated loans do not often make much money for the banks when they are not the arranger, and they take part only as they wish to develop or maintain good relations with a client, to whom they can later market more lucrative transactions. Membership of a syndicate sometimes even comes with the stipulation that it will be remunerated through an implicit or explicit pledge from the company to choose the bank as the lead on its next market transaction or as advisory for its next M&A deal.

Syndication forms of a loan can be of three types:

1. **Underwritten deal**, whose major characteristics are:

    (a)   the lead manager(s) guarantee that funds will be provided;

(b)   the commitment of lenders can be of two types: *full commitment*, or committed for the entire amount; *partial commitment*, in which some commitment is contingent on market interest. Full commitment is an important competitive tool for lenders and it usually requires higher fees from the borrower.

2.   **Best-efforts deal.** The commitment is only of the lead manager(s). The remainder of funds is contingent on sufficient market interest. However, best efforts deals are quite rare because the commitment of lenders is a major value of the syndicated loan.

3.   **Club deal.** This is typical of smaller deals (< \$250m). They are pre-marketed within a group of relationship banks.

The members of a syndicate can have the following titles:

- **Lead manager/Arranger/Book-runner.** This is the bank that handles the loan design and the structuring of the syndicate. Thus, it: maintains the contact with the borrower; structures the credit terms so they meet the borrower's requirements; assists in preparing an information memorandum; provides counsel in preparing the credit agreement and related documents; arranges the bank syndicate.

- **Agent bank.** Often this is the lead bank or a co-lead manager bank which maintains a fiduciary relationship with the lending participants and coordinates two functions:

  ○   administrative functions – loan service payments;
  ○   coordination functions – when changes in terms are requested or when trouble looms.

- **Manager and co-managers.** The managing banks are appointed by the lead bank to help identify and organise a wider contingent of participating banks (*participants*) as the final bank lenders. Some of the lending banks participating with major amounts are referred to as *co*-managers; however, none of the responsibilities of the arranging and managing banks fall on them.

- **Participants (or selling group).** *Other* lenders who supply funds for pieces of the loan. In order to avoid confusion, it is useful to specify that all intermediaries that make up the syndicate participate in the funding, but they must also accomplish other tasks, while the selling group is engaged exclusively in the selling activity.

7 In the simplest transactions, called "club loans", there are only two layers of intermediaries: the lead-managing and the participating banks.

Although the final structure of the bank syndicate can vary substantially – depending on the type of finance it tries to accommodate – a typical bank syndicate could be structured as follows:[7]

STRUCTURE OF A BANK SYNDICATE

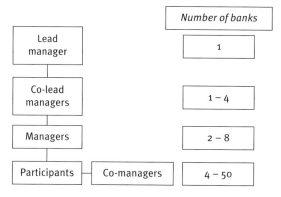

The syndication process normally develops in three steps:

1. **Preliminary contacts**: the borrower contacts the lender and gets the syndication mandate (sets pricing, terms, fees of loan, etc.).
2. **General syndication**: the lead manager canvasses the market for commitments and closes the phase once all funds are committed.
3. **Secondary syndication**: the lead manager prepares an information memorandum and a term sheet for the loan. Managers above the "hold target" sell off excess loan commitment to the "participants".

SUMMARY

The summary of this chapter can be downloaded from www.vernimmen.com.

The aim of all types of equity offerings is to sell the shares to investors at the highest price at any given time.

To achieve this, the large gap in the quantity and quality of information available to the issuer compared with that available to the investor must be reduced. One of the roles of banks in equity offerings is to inform investors by passing on information obtained from the issuer. The bank has three other roles: it must structure the deal, distribute the securities and generally provide the issuer with a guarantee at a given level.

There are two main types of equity placements:

* book-building;

* bought deals.

Book-building means that the bank or the banking syndicate will only commit itself to the deal if it knows that there is investor appetite for the shares. Following a phase of dissemination of information to investors, investor intentions to subscribe are recorded in an order book. It is only at this stage that the banks will sign a firm underwriting agreement, thus limiting the risk taken. For a bought deal, the banks will buy the securities from the issuer, and it is up to the banks to place the securities with investors as quickly as possible in order to limit the risk.

Initial public offerings are very complex transactions and involve the dissemination of appropriate information to a variety of investors. Two types of offering exist side by side. There is the underwritten deal, when the banking syndicate places the securities with institutional investors on the basis of the orders recorded in the order book. Generally, a retail public offering is made to retail investors at the same time: in a retail public offering, a price range is set before the offering, but the exact price is set after the offering. The final price reflects market demand. When the offer to retail investors is a fixed price offer, the issue price is pre-set. Generally identical to the price offered to institutional investors, it is totally independent of the market. Minimum price offerings and full listings using standard market procedures are rarely used these days.

There are two techniques for carrying out equity issues of companies that are already listed, depending on how eager existing shareholders are to subscribe to new shares. There is the fixed-price capital increase with pre-emptive subscription rights, or a capital increase without pre-emptive subscription rights but possibly with a period during which existing shareholders are given priority to subscribe.

For the former, the issue price is set at a significant discount to the market price. In addition, in order to avoid penalising existing shareholders, the issue comes with pre-emptive subscription rights, which are negotiable. Accordingly, the price of the new

SECTION 2

shares is equivalent to the stock's current market value even if the price of the new shares is below the current share price. A pre-emptive subscription right is akin to a call option.

A capital increase without a pre-emptive subscription right, for which shareholder approval is required, is an underwritten deal. The issue price is close to the market price. For unlisted companies, capital increases are carried out with or without pre-emptive subscription rights, with defined investors who have been identified following a private placement.

Block trades and issues of convertible bonds are carried out via book-building (or accelerated book-building which takes only a few hours) or via a bought deal.

The procedure a company uses to issue bonds depends first and foremost on the company's rating (whether the stock is investment grade – i.e. rated BBB or higher – or non-investment grade – i.e. lower than BBB). A company whose stock is rated as investment grade can invite banks to bid for the opportunity to carry out a bought deal, or opt for book-building. Whatever procedure is chosen, the deal is completed within a shortened time frame.

For non-investment grade companies, the placement procedure is closer to the capital increase procedure via book-building.

Convertible bonds, despite their apparent complexity, are products that are relatively easy to place as they offer substantial guarantees. They can be sold to investors within a relatively short period.

The procedure for placing a syndicated loan is similar to that for placing a bond issue with a limited number of investors. The banks involved are generally keen to develop a business relationship with the borrower.

QUESTIONS

1/ What is a prospectus used for?

2/ Why does it take longer to set up a share issue than a bond issue?

3/ What financial product can a greenshoe be compared to?

4/ Why is the timetable for a first issue for a company issuing a high-yield bond much longer than for the issue of a standard bond?

5/ Which placement procedure carries the most risk for a bank? Why?

6/ Describe two different methods used for calculating the value of a subscription right.

7/ Will a shareholder who subscribes a capital increase with a pre-emptive subscription right become poorer if the share price drops after the operation? Why?

8/ Which party is the bank that places the shares working for – the issuer or the investor subscribing to the shares?

9/ Which is more costly for an issuer – an underwritten deal or a bought deal? Why?

10/ Why can convertible bonds be placed so quickly?

11/ Immediately after bonds are placed on the market, the price rises. What is the good news for the issuer? And the bad news? Which is the most important?

More questions are waiting for you at www.vernimmen.com.

EXERCISE

In May 2010, Prudential had scheduled an issue of shares with subscription rights. 13 964 557 750 new shares were to be issued at a price of £1.04. Before the capital increase, the company's share capital was made up of 2 539 010 500 shares, which meant that eleven new shares were being issued for two existing shares. Before the capital increase, the share was trading at £5.42.

(a) Calculate the theoretical value of the pre-emptive subscription right.
(b) Calculate the theoretical ex-right price.
(c) If you own 1647 Prudential shares, what should you do before and after the capital increase so that your portfolio remains more or less as it is?

ANSWERS

Questions

1/ *For providing investors with a description of the company and the deal which will assist them in making a decision as to whether to invest or not.*
2/ *Because investors are taking a greater risk by investing in shares than in bonds. Further and better information is needed because of this risk.*
3/ *A call option held by the banks and sold by the company.*
4/ *Because a bond issued by a below investment grade company carries much more risk than a standard bond. The investor thus needs a lot more information on which to base an investment decision.*
5/ *A bought deal, as a risk is taken that the market will change before the shares can be sold.*
6/ *Equation described in the chapter and application of the Black–Scholes equation, which we study in Chapter 24.*
7/ *No, because the shareholder was able to acquire shares at a discount to the share price.*
8/ *For the issuer, but the bank must also ensure that investors are satisfied with the deal or it may lose its clients!*
9/ *Usually a bought deal, because it transfers the risk of the deal failing to the bank, and this has a cost.*
10/ *Because a convertible bond provides the same guarantees as a bond along with the possibility of making the same gains as a share. Investors buying them are thus taking a limited risk.*
11/ *Investors will be happy. A lower interest rate could have been paid. If the rise remains reasonable, the former, because it will be possible to retain an open financial market.*

Exercise

A detailed Excel version of the solutions is available at www.vernimmen.com.

(a) *£3.71.*
(b) *£1.71.*
(c) *Sell 1000 rights for £3710, buy 3558 shares with the 647 remaining rights plus £3700. You would then own 1647 + 3558 = 5205 shares worth £1.71 each (or £8921), compared with £8927 for 1647 shares before the capital increase. The difference of £6 being due to calculation roundings.*

BIBLIOGRAPHY

On book-building and IPOs:

L. Benveniste, W. Busaba, Bookbuilding versus fixed price: An analysis of competing strategies for marketing IPOs, *Journal of Financial and Quantitative Analysis*, **32**, 383–403, December 1997.

F. Cornelli, D. Goldreich, Bookbuilding and strategic allocation, *Journal of Finance*, **56**(6), 2337–2370, December 2001.

F. Cornelli, D. Goldreich, Bookbuilding: How informative is the order book? *Journal of Finance*, **58**(4), 1415–1443, August 2003.

F. Degeorges, F. Derrien, K. Womack, Auctioned IPOs: The US evidence, *Journal of Financial Economics*, **98**(2), 177–194, November 2010.

F. Derrien, K. Womack, Auction vs. book-building and the control of underpricing in hot IPO markets, *Review of Financial Studies*, **16**(1), 31–61, Spring 2003.

On IPO underpricing:

P. Dechow, A. Hutton, R. Sloan, Solving the new equity puzzle, in G. Bickerstaffe (Ed.), *Mastering Finance*, FT/Pitman Publishing, 175–183, 1998.

T. Loughran, J. Ritter, Why don't issuers get upset about leaving money on the table in IPOs? *Review of Financial Studies*, **15**(2), 413–444, July 2002.

M. Lowry, M. Officer, G. William Schwert, The variability of IPO initial returns, *Journal of Finance*, **65**(2), 425–465, April 2000.

J. Ritter, I. Welch, A review of IPO activity, pricing, and allocations, *Journal of Finance*, **57**(4), 1795–1828, August 2002.

K. Rock, Why new issues are underpriced, *Journal of Financial Economics*, **15**(1-2), 187–212, January–February 1986.

On share issues and IPOs:

R. Aggarwal, Stabilization activities by underwriters after initial public offerings, *Journal of Finance*, **55**(3), 1075–1103, June 2000.

L. Benveniste, P. Spindt, How investment bankers determine the offer price and allocation of new issues, *Journal of Financial Economics*, **24**(2), 343–361, October 1989.

J. Brau, S. Fawcett, Initial Public Offerings: An analysis of theory and practice, *Journal of Finance*, **1**(6), 399–436, February 2006.

P. Chollet, E. Ginglinger, The pricing of French unit seasoned equity offerings, *European Financial Management*, **7**(1), 23–38, March 2001.

F. Degeorge, F. Derrien, K. Womack, *Quid pro quo in IPOs: Why book-building is dominating auctions*, working paper, May 2004.

B. Eckbo, R. Masulis, O. Norli, Seasoned public offerings: Resolution of the new issues puzzle, *Journal of Financial Economics*, **56**(2), 251–291, May 2000.

C. Gondat-Larralde, K. James, IPO Pricing and share allocation: The importance of being ignorant, *Journal of Finance*, **63**(1), 449–478, January 2008.

T. Jenkinson, H. Jones, Bids and allocations in European IPO bookbuilding, *Journal of Finance*, **59**(5), 2309–2338, October 2004.

T. Jenkinson, H. Jones, IPO pricing and allocation: A survey of the view of constitutional Investors, *Review of Financial Studies*, **22**(4), 1477–1504, April 2009.

T. Jenkinson, H. Jones, Competitive IPOs, *European Financial Management*, **15**(4), 733–756, September 2009.

D. Kim, D. Palia, A. Saunders, Are initial returns and underwriting spreads in equity issues complements or substitutes? *Financial Management*, **39**(4), 1403–1423, Winter 2010.

M. Lowry, W. Schwert, IPO market cycles: Bubbles or sequential learning? *Journal of Finance*, **67**(3), 1171–1198, June 2002.

M. Lowry, W. Schwert, Is the IPO pricing process efficient? *Journal of Financial Economics*, **71**(1), 3–26, January 2004.

J. Ritter, T. Loughran, The new issues puzzle, *Journal of Finance*, **50**(1), 23–51, March 1995.
www.hoovers.com/global/ipoc/index.xhtml, for information on IPOs

On ADR:

A. Karolyi, Sourcing equity internationally with Depositary Receipt Offerings: Two exceptions that prove the rule, *Journal of Applied Corporate Finance*, **10**(4), 90–101, Winter 1998.

A. Karolyi, DaimlerChrysler AG, the truly global share, *Journal of Corporate Finance*, **9**(4), 409–430, September 2003.

D. Miller, The market reaction to international cross-listings: Evidence from Depositary Receipts, *Journal of Financial Economics*, **51**(1), 103–123, January 1999.

www.adrbnymellon.com, for information on ADRs.

On bonds:

O. Altinkilic, R.S. Hansen, Are there economies of scale in underwriting fees? Evidence of rising external financing costs, *Review of Financial Studies*, **13**, 191–218, 2000.

I. Lee, S. Lochhead, J. Ritter, Q. Zhao, The cost of raising capital, *Journal of Financial Research*, **19**, 59–74, 1996.

On Rule 144A:

G. Johnson, Yankee bonds and cross–border private placements: An update, *Journal of Applied Corporate Finance*, **13**(3), 80–91, Fall 2000.

M. Livingston, L. Zhou, The impact of Rule 144A debt offerings upon bond yields and underwriter fees, *Financial Management*, **31**(4), 5–27, Winter 2002.

On debt issues:

S. Datta, M. Datta, A. Patel, The market pricing of debt IPOs, *Journal of Applied Corporate Finance*, **12**(1), Spring 1999.

B. Emerick, W. White, The case for private placements: How sophisticated investors add value to corporate debt issuers, in D. Chew (Ed.), *The New Corporate Finance: Where Theory Meets Practice*, 2nd edn, McGraw Hill, 1999.

C. Godlewski, How to get a syndicated loan fast. The role of syndicate composition and organization, *Revue de l'association française de finance*, **31**(2), 51–92, Décembre 2010.

J. Helwege, P. Kleiman, The pricing of high-yield debt IPOs, *Journal of Fixed Income*, **8**(2), 61–68, September 1998.

R. Taggart, The growing role of junk bonds in corporate finance, in D. Chew (Ed.), *The New Corporate Finance: Where Theory Meets Practice*, 3rd edn, McGraw Hill, 2000.

SECTION 2

SECTION III
VALUE

This section presents the concepts and theories that underpin all important financial decisions. In particular, we will examine their impact on value, keeping in mind that basically to maximise a value, we must minimise a cost. The chapters in this section will introduce you to the investment decision processes within a firm and their impact on the overall value of the company.

Chapter 27

VALUE AND CORPORATE FINANCE

No, Sire, it's a revolution!

Section 27.1
THE PURPOSE OF FINANCE IS TO CREATE VALUE

1/ INVESTMENT AND VALUE

The accounting rules we looked at in Chapter 4 showed us that an investment is a use of funds, but not a reduction in the value of assets. We will now go one step further and adopt the viewpoint of the financial manager for whom a profitable investment is one that increases the value of capital employed.

We shall see that a key element in the theory of markets in equilibrium is the market value of capital employed. This theory underscores the direct link between the return on a company's investments and that required by investors buying the financial securities issued by the company.

The true measure of an investment policy is the effect it has on the value of capital employed. This concept is sometimes called "enterprise value", a term our reader should not confuse with the value of equity (capital employed less net debt). The two are far from the same!

Hence the importance of every investment decision, as it can lead to three different outcomes:

- Where the expected return on an investment is higher than that required by investors, the value of capital employed rises instantly. An investment of 100 that always yields 15% in a market requiring a 10% return is worth 150 (100 × 15%/10%). The value of capital employed thus immediately rises by 50.
- Where the expected return on the investment is equal to that required by investors, there is neither gain nor loss. The investors put in 100, the investment is worth 100 and no value has been created.
- Where the expected return on an investment is lower than that required by investors, they have incurred a loss. If, for example, they invested 100 in a project yielding 6%, the value of the project is only 60 (100 × 6%/10%), giving an immediate loss in value of 40.

- Value remains constant if the expected rate of return is equal to that required by the market.
- An immediate loss in value results if the return on the investment is lower than that required by the market.
- Value is effectively created if the expected rate of return is higher than that required by the market.

The resulting gain or loss is simply the positive or negative net present value that must be calculated when valuing any investment. All this means, in fact, is that if the investment was fairly priced, nothing changes for the investor. If it was "too expensive", investors take a loss, but if it was a good deal, they earn a profit.

The graph below shows that value is created (the value of capital employed exceeds its book value) when the economic return exceeds the weighted average cost of capital, i.e. the rate of return required by all suppliers of funds to the company.

VALUE CREATION FOR MAIN EUROPEAN TELECOM COMPANIES

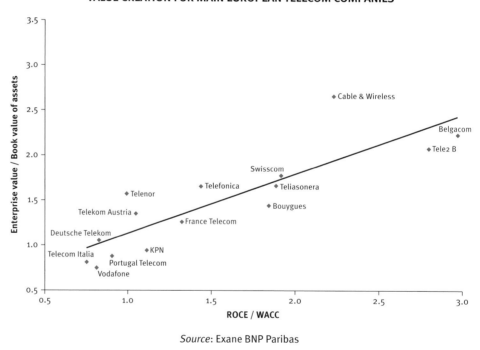

Source: Exane BNP Paribas

2/ THE RELATIONSHIP BETWEEN COMPANIES AND THE FINANCIAL WORLD

In the preceding chapters we examined the various financial securities that make up the debt issued by a company from the point of view of the investor. We shall now cross over to the other side to look at them from the issuing company's point of view.

- Each amount contributed by investors represents a **resource** for the company.
- The financial securities held by investors as assets are recorded as liabilities in the company's balance sheet.
- And, most importantly, the **rate of return** required by investors represents a financial cost to the company.

At the financial level, a company is a portfolio of assets financed by the securities issued on financial markets. Its liabilities, i.e. the securities issued and placed with investors, are merely a financial representation of the industrial or operating assets. The financial manager's job is to ensure that this representation is as transparent as possible.

What is the role of the investor?

Investors play an active role when securities are issued, because they can simply refuse to finance the company by not buying the securities. In other words, if the financial manager cannot come up with a product offering a risk/reward trade-off acceptable to the financial market, the lack of funding will eventually push the company into bankruptcy.

We shall see that when this happens, it is often too late. However, the financial system can impose a sanction that is far more immediate and effective: the valuation of the securities issued by the company.

The investor has the power not just to provide funds, but also to value the company's capital employed through the securities already in issue.

Financial markets continuously value the securities in issue. In the case of debt instruments, rating agencies assign a credit rating to the company, thus determining the value of its existing debt and the terms of future loans. Similarly, by valuing the shares issued the market is, in fact, valuing the company's equity.

So how does this mechanism work?

If a company cannot satisfy investors' risk/reward requirements, it is penalised by a lower valuation of its capital employed and, accordingly, its equity. Suppose a company offers the market an investment of 100 that is expected to yield 10 every year over a period long enough to be considered to perpetuity.[1] However, the actual yield is only 5. The disappointed investors who were expecting a 10% return will try to get rid of their investment. The equilibrium price will be 50, because at this price investors receive a return of 10% (5/50) and it is no longer in their interests to sell. But by now it is too late . . .

Investors who are unhappy with the offered risk/reward trade-off sell their securities, thus depressing the value of the securities issued and of capital employed, since the company's investments are not profitable enough with regard to their risk. True, the investor takes a hit, but it is sometimes wiser to cut one's losses . . .

In doing so, he is merely giving tit for tat: an unhappy investor will sell off his securities, thus lowering prices. Ultimately, this can lead to financing difficulties for the company.

The "financial sanction" affects first and foremost the valuation of the company via the valuation of its shares and debt securities.

As long as the company is operating normally, its various creditors are fairly well protected.[2] Most of the fluctuation in the value of its debt stems from changes in interest rates, so changes in the value of capital employed derive mainly from changes in the value of equity. We see why the valuation of equity is so important for any normally-developing company. This does not apply just to listed companies: unlisted companies are also affected whenever they envisage divestments, alliances, transfers or capital increases.

1 This strong assumption simplifies the calculation but it does not modify the reasoning.

2 Since there is always a risk, their required rate of return comprises a risk premium.

SECTION 3

The role of creditors looms large only when the company is in difficulty. The company then "belongs" to the creditors, and changes in the value of capital employed derive from changes in the value of the debt, by then generally lower than its nominal value. This is where the creditors come into play.

The valuation of capital employed, and therefore the valuation of equity, are the key variables of any financial policy, regardless of whether or not the company is listed.

3/ IMPLICATIONS

Since we consider that creating value is the overriding financial objective of a company, it follows that:

- A financial decision harms the company if it reduces the value of capital employed.
- A decision is beneficial to the company if it increases the value of capital employed.

A word of caution, however! Contrary to appearances, this does not mean that every good financial decision increases earnings or reduces costs.

Financial shortsightedness consists in failing to distinguish between cost and reduction in value, or between income and increase in value.

Remember, we are not in the realm of accounting, but in that of finance – in other words, value. An investment financed by cash from operations may increase earnings, but could still be insufficient with regard to the return expected by the investor who, as a result, has lost value.

Certain legal decisions, such as restricting a shareholder's voting rights, have no immediate impact on the company's cash, yet may reduce the value of the corresponding financial security and thus prove costly to the holder of the security.

We cannot emphasise this aspect enough and insist that you adopt this approach before immersing yourselves further in the raptures of financial theory.

Section 27.2
VALUE CREATION AND MARKETS IN EQUILIBRIUM

Corporate financial policy consists first and foremost of a set of principles necessary for taking decisions designed to maximise value for the providers of funds, in particular shareholders.

1/ A CLEAR THEORETICAL FOUNDATION

We have just said that a company is a portfolio of assets and liabilities, and that the concepts of cost and revenue should be seen within the overall framework of value. Financial management consists of assessing the value created for the company's fund providers.

Can the overall value of the company be determined by an optimal choice of assets and liabilities? If so, how can you be sure of making the right decisions to create value?

You may already have raised the following questions:

- Can the choice of financing alone increase the value of the firm, particularly when certain investors, such as banks, have allowed the company to incur more debt than would have been wise?
- Is capital employed financed half by debt and half by equity worth more than if it were financed wholly through equity?
- More generally, can the entrepreneur increase the value of capital employed – that is, influence the market's valuation of it – by either combining independent industrial and commercial investments or implementing a shrewd financing policy?

If your answer to all these questions is yes, you attribute considerable powers to financial managers. You consider them capable of creating value independently of their industrial and commercial assets.

And yet, the equilibrium theory of markets is very clear:

When looking at valuations, financial investors are not interested in the underlying financial engineering, because they could duplicate such operations themselves. This is called the **value additivity rule**.

We now provide a more formal explanation of the above rule, which is based on arbitrage. To this end, let us simplify things by imagining that there are just two options for the future: either the company does well or it does not. We shall assign an equal probability to each of these outcomes. We shall see how the free cash flow of three companies varies in our two states of the world:

FREE CASH FLOW

	State of the world: bad	State of the world: good
A	200	1000
B	400	500
G	600	1500

Note that the sum of the free cash flows of companies A and B is equal to that of company G. We shall demonstrate that the share price of company G is equal to the sum of the prices of shares B and A.[3] To do so, let us assume that this is not the case, and that $V_A + V_B > V_G$ (where V_A, V_B and V_G are the respective share prices of A, B and G).

You will see that no speculation is necessary here to earn money. Taking no risk, you sell short one share of A and one share of B and buy one share of G. You immediately receive $V_A + V_B - V_G > 0$; yet, regardless of the company's fortunes, the future negative flows of shares A and B (sold) and positive flows of share G (bought) will cancel each other out. You have realised a gain through arbitrage.

The same method can be used to demonstrate that $V_A + V_B < V_G$ is not possible in a market that is in equilibrium. We therefore deduce that $V_A + V_B = V_G$. It is thus clear that a diversified company, in our case G, is not worth more than the sum of its two divisions A and B.

3 We are assuming that companies A, B and G have the same number of shares.

Let us now look at the following three securities:

	FREE CASH FLOW	
Company	State of the world: bad	State of the world: good
C	100	1000
D	500	500
E	600	1500

According to the rule demonstrated above, $V_C + V_D = V_E$. Note that security D could be a debt security and C share capital. E would then be the capital employed. The value of capital employed of an indebted company $(V_{(C+D)})$ can be neither higher nor lower than that of the same company if it had no debt (V_E).

The additivity rule is borne out in terms of risk: if the company takes on debt, financial investors can stabilise their portfolios by adding less risky securities. Conversely, they can go into debt themselves in order to buy less risky securities. So why should they pay for an operation they can carry out themselves at no cost?

This reasoning applies to diversification as well. If its only goal is to create financial value without generating industrial and commercial synergies, there is no reason why investors should entrust the company with the diversification of their portfolio.

2/ ILLUSTRATION

Are some asset combinations worth more than the value of their individual components, regardless of any industrial synergies arising when some operations are common to several investment projects? In other words, is the whole worth more than the sum of its parts?

Or again, is the required rate of return lower simply because two investments are made at the same time? Company managers are fuzzy on this issue. They generally answer in the negative, although their actual investment decisions tend to imply the opposite. Take Alcan (a leading aluminium group), for example, which was bought by Rio Tinto in 2007. If financial synergies exist, one would have to conclude that the required rate of return in the economic press segment differs depending on whether the company is independent or part of a group. Alcan would therefore appear to be worth more as part of the Rio Tinto group than on a standalone basis.

The question is not as specious at it seems. In fact, it raises a fundamental issue. If the required return on Alcan has fallen since it became part of Rio Tinto, its financing costs will have declined as well, giving it a substantial, permanent and possibly decisive advantage over its competitors.

Diversifying corporate activities reduces risk, but does it also reduce the rate of return required by investors?

Suppose the required rate of return on a company producing a single product is 10%. The company decides to diversify by acquiring a company of the same size on which the required rate of return is 8%. Will the required rate of return on the new group be lower than $(10\% + 8\%) / 2 = 9\%$ because it carries less risk than the initial single-product company?

We must not be misled into believing that a lower degree of risk must be always matched by a lower required rate of return. On the contrary: **markets only remunerate systematic or market risks, i.e. those that cannot be eliminated by diversification**. We have seen that unsystematic or specific risks, which investors can eliminate by diversifying their portfolios, are not remunerated. Only non-diversifiable risks related to market fluctuations are remunerated. This point was discussed in Chapter 18.

Since diversifiable risks are not remunerated, **a company's value remains the same whether it is independent or part of a group**. Alcan is not worth more now that it has become a division of Rio Tinto. All else being equal, the required rate of return in the aluminium sector is the same whether the company is independent or belongs to a group.

On the other hand, Alcan's value will increase if, and only if, Rio Tinto's management allows it to improve its return on capital employed.

Purely financial diversification creates no value.

Value is created only when the sum of cash flows from the two investments is higher because they are both managed by the same group. This is the result of **industrial synergies** $(2 + 2 = 5)$, **and not financial synergies**, which do not exist.

The large groups that indulged in a spate of financial diversifications in the 1960s have since realised that these operations were unproductive and frequently loss-making. Diversification is a delicate art that can only succeed if the diversifying company already has expertise in the new business. Combining investments *per se* does not maximise value, unless industrial synergies exist. Otherwise, an investment is either "good" or "bad" depending on how it stacks up against the required rate of return.

In other words, managers must act on cash flows; **they cannot influence the discount rate applied to them** unless they reduce their risk exposure.

There is no connection between the required return on any investment and the portfolio in which the investment is held.

Unless it can draw on industrial synergies, the value of a company remains the same whether it is independent or part of a large group. The financial investor does not want to pay a premium in the form of lower returns for something he can do himself at no cost by diversifying his portfolio.

3/ A FIRST CONCLUSION

The value of the securities issued by a company is not connected to the underlying financial engineering. Instead, it simply reflects the market's reaction to the perceived profitability and risk of the industrial and commercial operations.

The equilibrium theory of markets leads us to a very simple and obvious rule, that of the additivity of value, which in practice is frequently neglected. Regardless of developments in financial criteria, in particular earnings per share, value cannot be created simply by adding (diversifying) or reducing value that is already in equilibrium.

SECTION 3

To ensure a flow of financing, financial managers have to transform their industrial and commercial assets into financial assets. This means that they have to sell the very substance of the company (future risk and returns) in a financial form.

Financial investors evaluate the securities offered or already issued according to their required rate of return. By valuing the company's share, they are, in fact, directly valuing the company's operating assets.

The valuation of the different securities has nothing to do with financial engineering; it is based on a valuation of the company's industrial and commercial assets.

We emphasise that this rule applies to listed and unlisted companies alike, a fact that the latter are forced to face at some point. Capital employed always has an equilibrium value, and the entrepreneur must ultimately recognise it.

This approach should be incorporated into the methodology of financial decision-making. Some strategies are based on maximising other types of value, for example nuisance value. They are particularly risky and are outside the conceptual framework of corporate finance. The first reflex when faced with any kind of financial decision is to analyse whether it will create or destroy value. If values are in equilibrium, financial decisions will be immaterial.

Does this mean that, ultimately, financing or diversification policies have no impact on value?

On the contrary, the equilibrium theory of markets represents a kind of ideal that is very useful for the financial professional but, like all ideals, tends to remain out of reach. In a way, it is the paradise that all financial managers strive for, while secretly hoping never to reach such a perfect state of boredom . . .

Our aim is not to encourage nihilism, merely a degree of humility.

Section 27.3
VALUE AND ORGANISATION THEORIES

1/ LIMITS OF THE EQUILIBRIUM THEORY OF MARKETS

The equilibrium theory of markets offers an overall framework, but it completely disregards the immediate interests of the various parties involved, even if their interests tend to converge in the medium term.

Paradoxically, the neoclassical theory emphasises the general interest while completely overlooking that of the individual parties.

We cannot rely on the equilibrium theory alone to explain corporate finance.

Since the equilibrium theory demonstrates that finance cannot change the size of the capital employed, but only how it is divided up, it follows that many financial problems stem from the struggle between the various players in the financial realm.

First and foremost we have the various parties providing funding to the company. To simplify matters, they can be divided into two categories: shareholders and creditors.

But we shall soon see that, in fact, each type of security issued gives rise to its own interest group: shareholders, preferred creditors, ordinary creditors, investors in hybrid products, etc. Further on in this chapter, we shall see that interests may even diverge within the same funding category.

One example should suffice. According to the equilibrium theory of markets, investing at the required rate of return does not change the value of capital employed. But if the investment is very risky and, therefore, potentially very profitable, creditors, who earn a fixed rate, will only see the increased risk without a corresponding increase in their return. The value of their claims thus decreases to the benefit of shareholders whose shares increase by the same amount, the value of capital employed remaining the same. And yet, this investment was made at its equilibrium price.

This is where the financial manager comes into play! His role is to distribute value between the various parties involved. **In fact, the financial manager must be a negotiator at heart**.

But let's not forget that the managers of the company are stakeholders as well. Since portfolio theory presupposes good diversification, there is a distinction between investors and managers, who have divergent interests with different levels of information (internal and external). This last point calls into question one of the basic tenets of the equilibrium theory, which is that all parties have access to the same information (see Chapter 15).

2/ SIGNALLING THEORY AND ASYMMETRIC INFORMATION

Signalling theory is based on two basic ideas:

- the same information is not available to all parties: the managers of a company may have more information than investors;
- even if the same information were available to all, it would not be perceived in the same way, a fact frequently observed in everyday life.

Thus, it is unrealistic to assume that information is fairly distributed to all parties at all times, i.e. that it is symmetrical as in the case of efficient markets. On the contrary, **asymmetric information** is the rule.

In short, perfect and equally-shared information is at best an objective, and most often an illusion.

This can clearly raise problems. Asymmetric information may lead investors to undervalue a company. As a result, its managers might hesitate to increase its capital because they consider the share price to be too low. This may mean that profitable investment opportunities are lost for lack of financing, or that the existing shareholders find their stake adversely diluted because the company has launched a capital increase anyway.

This is where the **communication policy** comes into its own. Basing financial decisions on financial criteria alone is not enough: managers also have to convince the markets that these decisions are wise.

As a result, pure financial expertise does not suffice if it is not matched by an ability to communicate and to shape market sentiment.

The cornerstone of the financial communications policy is the **signal** the managers of a company send to investors. Contrary to what many financial managers and CEOs believe, the signal is neither an official statement nor a confidential tip. **It is a real financial decision, taken freely and which may have negative financial consequences for the decision-maker if it turns out to be wrong.**

After all, investors are far from naive and they take each signal with the requisite pinch of salt. Three points merit attention:

- **Investors' first reaction is to ask themselves why the signal is being sent, since nothing comes for free in the financial world.** The signal will be perceived negatively if the issuer's interests are contrary to those of investors. For example, the sale of a company by its majority shareholder would, in theory, be a negative signal for the company's growth prospects. Managers must therefore persuade the buyer of the contrary or provide a convincing explanation for the disposal.

  Similarly, owner-managers cannot fool investors by praising the merits of a capital increase without subscribing to it!

  However, the market will consider the signal to be credible if it deems that it is in the issuer's interest that the signal be correct. This would be the case, for example, if the managers reinvest their own assets in the company . . .

- **The reputation of management and its communications policy** certainly play a role, but we must not overestimate their importance or lasting impact.
- **The market supervisory authorities stand ready to impose penalties** on the dissemination of misleading information or insider trading. If investors, particularly international investors, believe that supervision is effective, they will factor this into their decisions. That said, some managers may be tempted to send incorrect signals in order to obtain unwarranted advantages. For example, they could give overly optimistic guidance on their company's prospects in order to push up share prices. However, markets catch on to such misrepresentations quickly and react to incorrect signals by piling out of the stock.

In such a context, the "watchdog" role played by the market authorities is crucial and the recent past has shown that the authorities intend to assume it in full. Such rigour is essential if we are to have the best possible financial markets and the lowest possible financing costs.

Financial managers must therefore always consider how investors will react to their financial decisions. They cannot content themselves with wishful thinking, but must make a rational and detailed analysis of the situation to ensure that their communication is convincing.

Signalling theory says that corporate financial decisions (e.g. financing, dividend payout) are signals sent by the company's managers to investors. It examines the incentives that encourage good managers to issue the right signals and discourage managers of ailing companies from using these same signals to give a misleading picture of their company's financial health.

In sum, information asymmetry may lead to a share being priced at less than its objective value, with two consequences:

- investments are not maximised because the cost of financing is too high;
- the choice of financing is skewed in favour of sources (such as debt) where there is less information asymmetry.

Stephen Ross initiated the main studies in this field in 1977.

3/ AGENCY THEORY

Agency theory says that a company is not a single, unified entity. It considers a company to be a legal arrangement that is the culmination of a complex process in which the conflicting objectives of individuals, some of whom may represent other organisations, are resolved by means of a set of contractual relationships.

On this basis, a company's behaviour can be compared to that of a market, insofar as it is the result of a complex balancing process. Taken individually, the various stakeholders in the company have their own objectives and interests that may not necessarily be spontaneously reconcilable. As a result, conflicts may arise between them, especially since our modern corporate system requires that the suppliers of funds entrust the managers with the actual administration of the company.

Agency theory analyses the consequences of certain financial decisions in terms of risk, profitability and, more generally, the interests of the various parties. It shows that some decisions may go against the simple criteria of maximising the wealth of all parties to the benefit of just one of the suppliers of funds.

To simplify, we consider that an agency relationship exists between two parties when one of them, the agent, carries out an activity on behalf of the other, the principal. The agent has been given a mandate to act or take decisions on behalf of the principal. This is the essence of the agency relationship.

This very broad definition allows us to include a variety of domains, such as the resolution of conflicts between:

- executive shareholders/non-executive shareholders;
- non-shareholder executives/shareholders;
- creditors/shareholders.

Thus, shareholders give the company executives a mandate to manage to the best of their ability the funds that have been entrusted to them. However, their concern is that the executives could pursue objectives other than maximising the value of the equity, such as increasing the company's size at the cost of profitability, minimising the risk to capital employed by rejecting certain investments that would create value but could put the company in difficulty if they fail, etc.

One way of resolving such conflicts of interest is to use stock options, thus linking management compensation to share performance (see Chapter 42). This gives managers a financial incentive that coincides with that of their principal, the shareholders. Since stock options give the holders the right to buy or subscribe to shares at a fixed price, the managers have a financial incentive to see the price of their company's shares rise so that they receive significant capital gains. It is then in their interests to make the financial decisions that create the most value.

Debt plays a role as well since it has a constraining effect on managers and encourages them to maximise cash flows so that the company can meet its interest and principal payments. Failing this, the company risks bankruptcy and the managers lose their jobs. Maximising cash flows is in the interests of shareholders as well, since it raises the value of shareholders' equity. Thus, the interests of management and shareholders converge. Maybe debt is the modern whip! This is sometimes referred to as "the discipline of debt".

The diverging interests of the various parties generate a number of costs called "agency costs". These comprise:

- the cost of monitoring managers' efforts (control procedures, audit systems, performance-based compensation) to ensure that they correspond to the principal's objectives. Stock options represent an agency cost since they are exercised at less than the going market price for the stock;
- the costs incurred by the agents to vindicate themselves and reassure the principals that their management is effective, such as the publication of annual reports;
- residual costs.

Ang *et al.* (2000) have shown that the margins and asset turnover rates of small- and medium-sized American firms tend to be lower in companies managed by non-shareholding CEOs, and in which managers have little stake in the capital and many non-executive shareholders.

The main references in this field are Jensen and Meckling (1976), Grossman and Hart (1980) and Fama (1980). Their research aims to provide a scientific explanation of the relationship between managers and shareholders and its impact on corporate value.

Their main contribution is to try and compare financial theory and organisational theory.

This research forms the intellectual foundation on which the concept of **corporate governance** was built (see Chapter 42).

4/ FREE RIDERS

We saw above that the interests of the different types of providers of funds may diverge, but so may those of members of the same category.

The term "free rider" is used to describe the behaviour of an investor who benefits from transactions carried out by other investors in the same category without participating in these transactions himself.

This means, first, that there must be several – usually a large number – of investors in the same type of security and, second, that a specific operation is undertaken implying some sort of sacrifice, at least in terms of opportunity cost, on the part of the investors in these securities.

As a result, when considering a financial decision, one must examine whether free riders exist and what their interests might be.

Below are two examples:

- Responding to a takeover bid: if the offer is motivated by synergies between the bidding company and its target, the business combination will create value. This means that it is in the general interest of all parties for the bid to succeed and for the shareholders to tender their shares. However, it would be in the individual interest of these same shareholders to hold on to their shares in order to benefit fully from the future synergies.

- Bank A holds a small claim on a cash-strapped company that owes money to many other banks. It would be in the interests of the banks as a whole to grant additional loans to tide the company over until it can pay them back, but the interest of our individual bank would be to let the other banks, which have much larger exposure, advance the funds themselves. Bank A would thus hold a better-valued existing claim without incurring a discount on the new credits granted.

Section 27.4
HOW CAN WE CREATE VALUE?

Before we begin simulating different rates of return, we would like to emphasise once again that a project, investment or company can only realise extraordinary returns if it enjoys a strategic advantage. The equilibrium theory of markets tells us that under perfect competition, the net present value of a project should be nil. If a financial manager wants to advise on investment choices, he will no doubt have to make a number of calculations to estimate the future return of the investment. But he will also have to look at it from a strategic point of view, incorporating the various economic theories he has learnt.

A project's real profitability can only be explained in terms of economic rent – that is, a position in which the return obtained on investments is higher than the required rate of return given the degree of risk. The essence of all corporate strategies is to obtain economic rents – that is, to generate imperfections in the product market and/or in factors of production, thus creating barriers to entry that the corporate managers strive to exploit and defend.

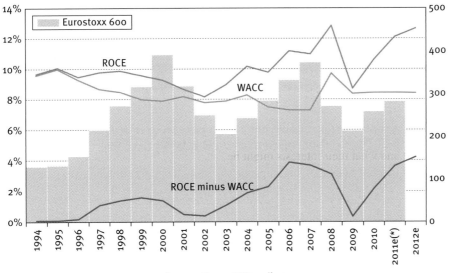

ROCE, WACC AND VALUE CREATION FOR THE MAIN EUROPEAN LISTED GROUPS

Source: Exane BNP paribas

The correlation is striking between the economic rent measured by the difference between ROCE and WACC on one hand, and stock market prices on the other hand.

The purpose of a financial strategy is to try to "skew" market mechanisms in order to secure an economic rent.

But don't fool yourself, economic rents do not last forever. Returns that are higher than the required rate, taking into account the risk exposure, inevitably attract the attention of competitors or of the anti-trust authorities, as in the case of Google. Sooner or later, deregulation and technological advances put an end to them. There are no impregnable fortresses, only those for which the right angle of attack has not yet been found.

A strategic analysis of the company is thus essential to put the figures in their economic and industrial context, as we explained in Chapter 8.

We insist on the consequences of a good strategy. When based on accurate forecasts, it immediately boosts the value of capital employed and, accordingly, the share price. This explains the difference between the book value of capital employed and its market value, which may vary by a factor of 1–10, and sometimes even more.

Rather than rising gradually as the returns on the investment accrue, the share price adjusts immediately so that the investor receives the exact required return, no more, no less. And if everything proceeds smoothly thereafter, the investment will generate the required return until expectations prove too optimistic or too pessimistic.

Section 27.5
VALUE AND TAXATION

Depending on the company's situation, certain types of securities may carry tax benefits. You are certainly aware that tax planning can generate savings, thereby creating value or at least preventing the loss of value. Reducing taxes is a form of value creation for investors and shareholders. All else being equal, an asset with tax-free flows is worth more than the same asset subject to taxation.

Better to have a liability with cash outflows that can be deducted from taxes than the same liability with outflows that are not deductible.

This goes without saying, and any CFO worthy of his title will do his best to reduce tax payments.

However, tax optimisation should not merely endeavour to reduce costs if this leads to higher risks. Financial managers must think in terms of value.

They must carefully examine the impact each financial decision will have on taxes. The main issues we shall be addressing in the subsequent chapters are:

- taxation of debt vs. equity;
- taxation of accelerated depreciation and one-off write-downs;
- taxation of capital gains vs. ordinary income (dividends or coupons);
- taxation of financial income and expenses;
- tax groups;
- usable or unusable tax-loss carryforwards.

SUMMARY

The summary of this chapter can be downloaded from www.vernimmen.com.

From a financial point of view, a company's aim is to create value, i.e. it should be able to make investments on which the rate of return is higher than the required rate of return, given the risk involved. If this condition is met, the share price or the value of the share will rise. If not, it will fall. The theory of markets in equilibrium teaches us that it is very difficult to create lasting value. Rates of return actually achieved tend, over the medium term, to meet required rates of return, given technological progress and deregulation, which reduce entry barriers and economic rents that all managers must strive to create and defend, even if sooner or later they will be eliminated. Similarly, diversification or debt cannot create value for the investor who can, at no cost on an individual level, diversify his portfolio or go into debt. Finally, **there is no connection between the required return on any investment and the portfolio in which the investment is held** – value can only be created by industrial synergies. **Financial synergies do not exist.**

It is important to understand that the creation of value is not just the outcome of a calculation of returns. It has an economic basis which is a sort of economic rent that comes out of a strategy, the purpose of which is to "skew" market mechanisms. Accordingly, the conceptual framework of the theory of markets in equilibrium alone fails to explain corporate finance.

Signal and agency theory were developed to make up for the shortcomings of the theory of markets in equilibrium.

Signal theory is based on the assumption that information is not equally available to all parties at the same time, and that information asymmetry is the rule. This can have disastrous consequences and result in very low valuations or a suboptimum investment policy. Accordingly, certain financial decisions, known as signals, are taken to shake up this information asymmetry. These signals can, however, have a negative financial impact on the party who initiates them if they turn out to be unfounded.

Agency theory calls into question the claim that all of the stakeholders in the company (shareholders, managers, creditors) have a single goal – to create value. Agency theory shows how, on the contrary, their interests may differ and some decisions (related to borrowing, for example) or products (stock options) come out of attempts at achieving convergence between the interests of managers and shareholders or at protecting creditors. Agency theory forms the intellectual basis of corporate governance.

SECTION 3

QUESTIONS

Questions

1/ Take the example on p. 517 and give a probability of 50% to the two states of the world. Calculate the value of *A*, *B* and *G*. Calculate the value of *C*, *D* and *E*. What are your conclusions?

2/ You offer investors the opportunity to invest 100, financed solely with equity. Assuming that no taxes are payable, projected constant annual profits to perpetuity are 25 (we assume that necessary capital expenditure is equal to depreciation, that change in working capital is nil and that all profits are paid out).

   (a) What is the rate of return required by the market on this investment?
   (b) The return on this investment only comes to 10 per year. If the required rate of return is not modified, what will the value of this share be on the secondary market?

(c) Same question if the return on the investment is 50 per year? And if profits are nil?
(d) What impact will all of the above scenarios have on the company?
(e) Is it possible to define a simple rule on the creation and destruction of value?

3/ What does it mean when a source of financing is cheap?

4/ When is value created?

- in the choice of investment;
- in the choice of financing?

5/ You are required to analyse a number of decisions and establish whether or not they will create value. You then have to decide whether value was, in fact, created or transferred on a general level, and, if so, who were the winners and who were the losers?

	Creation of value	Transfer of value
Set up an oligopoly		
Innovate		
Secure loans at a lower rate than the market rate		
Improve productivity		
Reduce income tax		

6/ Analyse the following financial decisions. Do they send out positive, negative or neutral signals?

Signal	+	−	=
Sale of company by managing shareholder			
Sale of company by non-managing shareholder			
Failure of a managing shareholder who has invested most of his wealth in the company to subscribe to an equity issue			
Failure of a capital investor to subscribe to an equity issue			
Increase in the dividend per share (DPS)			
A family-run company running up excessive debts			
Giving out free shares in order to maintain the dividend per share			
Giving subscription rights to all shareholders at a strike price that is twice the price at which the share is currently trading			

7/ What is synergy?

8/ Can we talk about financial synergy?

9/ What is a conglomerate discount? How can it be avoided?

10/ Show how the share price of a very profitable company which invests at a rate of return that is higher than the required rate of return can still drop.

11/ Reread Chapter 23 with your new insight into investment policy, especially the link between P/E and PBR, and the rate of return on the investment.

12/Should an investment have a higher expected rate of return than required rate of return? Generally will value always be created?

13/Show how the conglomerate discount leads to an increase in the cost of equity.

14/Can a signal be sent if there is no cash flow?

15/What is an economic rent? What is it based on?

16/A company that is close to insolvency carries out a capital increase. Is this a signal? Why? What criteria can you identify as being necessary for a decision to be described as a signal?

17/An increasing number of large groups now ask their top managers to invest a large amount of their personal wealth (often more than 40%) in company shares. What is the theory behind this type of behaviour? Why?

18/Can you explain why the behaviour described in Question 17 could have the secondary effect of encouraging managers to diversify their groups' activities?

More questions are waiting for you at www.vernimmen.com.

EXERCISE

Rawhajpoutalah Intl., an Indian tobacco company, has two divisions, A and B, for which the figures are as follows:

	Division A	Division B
Capital employed	1000	1000
Expected return	15%	15%
Net operating income	50	300

(a) What are the values for divisions A and B if you assume, for calculation purposes, that operating income is constant to perpetuity?

(b) The company pays out 50 and so finances its investments for 300. The company invests everything in division B at the same return on capital employed (30%). How much value is created?

(c) Same question if the 300 is invested in division A at the average rate of return of A (5%).

(d) Same question if the 300 is divided equally between A and B.

(e) What are your conclusions?

SECTION 3

ANSWERS

Questions

1/ 1/ V_A = 600, V_B = 450, V_G = 1050; V_C = 550, V_D = 500, V_E = 1050; $V_A + V_B = V_G$, $V_E − V_D = V_C$

2/ (a) 25%.

(b) 40.

(c) 200; 0.

(d) None.

(e) Value is created when the return is higher than the required rate of return; and vice versa.

3/ That the risk is underestimated by providers of funds.

4/ In the choice of investment: when an investment is made with a return that is higher than the required rate of return. In the choice of financing: when a company can finance its operations at a lower rate of return than usually required by the market for the same risk.

5/ Transfer of client value to shareholders. Creation of value. Transfer of creditors' value to shareholders. Creation of value. Creation of value.

6/ Signal: Negative. Neutral. Neutral. Negative. Positive. Positive. Positive. Neutral.

7/ Synergy results from a reduction in charges or an improvement in products that leads to the value of the whole being greater than the sum of the values of the parts.

8/ No.

9/ The fact that a conglomerate is worth more than the parts of which it is made up. By dismantling conglomerates.

10/ This is possible because of an error in anticipation (which was too high at the outset).

12/ This is the strength of a good corporate strategy, but obviously, if industrial markets are efficient, it is impossible. Macro-economically, this could be a simple transfer of value between the customers and the shareholders.

13/ If a conglomerate raises funds of 100 to invest in various assets, and if a discount of 25% is applicable, the 100 will only be worth 75 and it is at this price that new shares will be issued and not 100. This is where the higher cost of equity comes from.

14/ No, because a decision based on financial policy is only a signal if it has negative financial consequences for the management which took the decision if the signal turns out to be wrong.

15/ An economic rent is a situation in which it is possible to obtain a higher return on capital employed than the required rate of return given the risk, on the basis of a special strategic advantage. It is based on a (temporary) lack of equilibrium in the market.

16/ This cannot be interpreted as a signal because the company has no other choice than to carry out a capital increase if it wishes to avoid bankruptcy. A decision can only be qualified as a signal if it is taken freely and if there is a viable alternative.

17/ Agency theory, in order to reconcile management's financial criteria with those of the shareholders who have appointed them as managers.

18/ Because this severely limits the diversification of the personal portfolios of managers, who may wish to make up for this by diversifying the activities in which their groups are involved.

Exercise

A detailed Excel version of the solutions is available at www.vernimmen.com.

(a) V_A = 50/0.15 = 333.3; V_B = 300/0.15 = 2000.

(b) V_A unchanged; V_B = 390/0.15 = 2600; for 300 reinvested, creation of value = 300.

(c) V_B unchanged; V_A = 65/0.15 = 433.33; for 300 reinvested, destruction of value = 200.

(d) V_A = 57.5/0.15 = 383.33; V_B = 345/0.15 = 2300; for 300 reinvested, creation of value = 50.

(e) Tendency within conglomerates to spread the investment budget. This does not make for optimal returns.

For more on signal and agency theories:

A. Alchian, H. Demsetz, Production, information costs and economic organization, *American Economic Review*, **62**(5), 777–795, December 1972.

J. Ang, R. Cole, J. Wuhkin, Agency costs and ownership structure, *Journal of Finance*, **55**(1), 81–106, February 2000.

J. Coles, N. Daniel, L. Naveen, Managerial incentives and risk-taking, *Journal of Financial Economics*, **79**(2), 431–468, 2006.

E. Fama, Agency problems and the theory of the firm, *Journal of Political Economy*, **88**(2), 288–307, April 1980.

S. Grossman, O. Hart, Takeover bids, the free-rider problem and the theory of the corporation, *Bell Journal of Economics*, **11**(1), 42–64, Spring 1980.

M. Jensen, W. Meckling, Theory of the firm: Managerial behavior, agency costs and ownership structure, *Journal of Financial Economics*, **3**(4), 305–360, October 1976.

M. Jensen, Value maximization, stakeholder theory, and the corporate objective function, *Journal of Applied Corporate Finance*, **14**(3), 8–21, Autumn 2001.

S. Ross, The determination of capital structure: Incentive signalling approach, *The Bell Journal of Economics*, **8**(1), 23–40, Summer 1977.

S. Ross, Some notes on financial incentive signalling models, activity choice and risk preferences, *Journal of Finance*, **33**(3), 777–792, June 1978.

For more on corporate governance:

Chapter 42 of the Vernimmen!

www.ecgn.org, the website of European Corporate Governance, an institution which monitors the corporate governance practices around the world.

Stock options and more generally, other forms of variable compensation:

L. Bebchuk, J. Fried, *Paying for long term performance*, Harvard Law and Economics discussion paper No 658.

A. Morgan, A. Poulser, Linking pay to performance-compensation proposal in the S&P 500, *Journal of Financial Economics*, **62**(3), 489–523, December 2001.

BIBLIOGRAPHY

SECTION 3

Separating the wheat from the chaff

Creating value has become such an important issue in finance that a host of indicators have been developed to measure it. They come under a confusing array of acronyms – TSR, MVA, EVA, CFROI, ROCE-WACC – but most of these will probably be winnowed out in the years to come. Ultimately, they should be reduced to those few that best mirror and address the recent developments in cash flow statements.

The current profusion of indicators has its advantages, as normally we expect only the most reliable to survive. However, in practice some companies use the lack of clear guidelines and standards to choose indicators that best serve their interests at a given time, even if this involves the laborious task of changing indicators on a routine basis.

The chart below should help you find your way through the maze of indicators. It plots the chronological appearance of value measures according to three criteria: ease of manipulation, sensitivity to financial markets and category (accounting, economic or stock market indicators).

EVOLUTION OF FINANCIAL INDICATORS

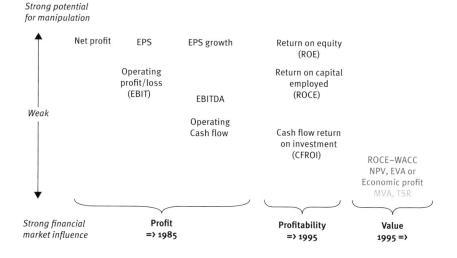

Section 28.1
OVERVIEW OF THE DIFFERENT CRITERIA

Predictably, the indicators cluster around a diagonal running from the upper left-hand corner down to the lower-right hand: this reflects companies' diminished ability to manipulate the indicators over time. Gradually, investors become more experienced and financial markets become more influential, and therefore are less prone to misinterpreting company data.

Value creation indicators fall into three categories:

- **Accounting indicators.** Until the mid-1980s, companies mainly communicated their **net profit/loss** or **earnings per share (EPS)**. Regrettably, this is a key accounting parameter that is also very easy to manipulate. This practice of massaging EPS is called "window dressing", or improving the presentation of the accounts by adjusting exceptional items, provisions, etc. The growing emphasis on operating profit or EBITDA represents an improvement because it considerably reduces the impact of exceptional items and non-cash expenses.

  The second-generation accounting indicators appeared as investors began to reason in terms of **profitability**, i.e. **efficiency**, by comparing return with the equity used. This ratio is called *return on equity*, or **ROE**. However, it is possible to leverage this value as well, since a company can boost its ROE by skilfully raising its debt level. Even though ROE might look more attractive, no "real" value has been created since the increased profitability is cancelled out by higher risk not reflected in accounting data.

  Since the return on capital employed (**ROCE**) indicator avoids this bias, it has tended to become the main measure of economic performance. Only in a few sectors of activity is it meaningless to use ROCE (such as in banking or insurance, where fixed assets and working capital are only a fraction of the assets). In those industries, return on equity (ROE) is widely used.

  While NPV and other economic indicators represent valuable tools for strategic analysis and a good basis for estimating the market value of companies, they are based on projections that are frequently difficult to assess. Unfortunately the cash flow for one single year is easy to manipulate and meaningless. Indeed, it is not intuitively interpretable. At the same time, we know that the major drivers of cash flows are the *growth of earnings and revenues* of the company and ROCE. By focusing attention on ROCE, there is a better intuitive grasp of how the company is performing. It is then easier to assess the firm's growth both over time and relative to its industry.

- **Accounting/financial indicators** emerged with the realisation that profitability *per se* cannot fully measure value because it does not factor in risks. To measure value, returns must also be compared with the cost of capital employed. Using the cost of financing a company, called the weighted average cost of capital, or WACC,[1] it is possible to assess whether value has been created (i.e. when return on capital employed is higher than the cost of capital employed) or destroyed (i.e. when return on capital employed is lower than the cost of capital employed).

  But companies can also go one step further by applying the calculation to capital employed at the beginning of the year in order to measure the value created

1 *See Chapter 30.*

over the period. The difference can then be expressed in currency units rather than as a percentage. This popular measure of value creation has been most notably developed in the **EVA**, or *economic value added*, model. It is also known as **economic profit**.

- **Financial indicators.** Yet the best of all indicators is undoubtedly *Net Present Value* (see **NPV**, Chapter 16), which provides the exact measure of value created. It has been repeatedly demonstrated that intrinsic value creation is the principal driver of *companies' market value*. But NPV has one drawback because it must be computed over several periods. For the external analyst who does not have access to all the necessary information, the NPV criterion becomes difficult to handle. The quick and easy solution is to use the above-mentioned ratios. It is important to remember that while the other ratios are simpler to use, they are also less precise and may prove misleading when not used with care.

- **Market indicators**: *Market Value Added* (**MVA**) and *Total Shareholder Return* (**TSR**) are highly sensitive to the stock market. MVA represents the difference between the value of equity and net debt and the book value of capital employed. It is expressed in currency units. TSR is expressed as a percentage and corresponds to the addition of the return on the share (dividends/value of the share) and the capital gains rate (capital gains during the period divided by the initial share value). It is the return earned by a shareholder who bought the share at the beginning of a period, earned dividends and then sold the share at the end of the period.

  A major weakness with these two measures is that they may show destruction in value because of declining investor expectations about future profits, even though the company's return on capital employed is higher than its cost of capital. This happened to L'Oréal, which saw its share price remain flat from 2000 to 2010. However, during this time, its ROCE was between 12 and 19% per year whereas its cost of capital was only about 8%. Conversely, in a bull market, a company with mediocre economic performances may have flattering TSR and MVA. In the long term, these highs and lows are smoothed out and TSR and MVA eventually reflect the company's modest performances. Yet in the meantime, there may be some major divergences between these indicators and company performance.

  These considerations prompted some stock exchange authorities to recommend making a clear distinction between economic indicators and measures of stock market value creation (TSR and MVA). The former measure the past year's performance, while the latter tend to reflect anticipation of future value creation. The measures of stock market value creation take into account the share price, which reflects this anticipation. Yet the different measures of economic performance and stock market value are complementary, rather than contradictory.

- Aside from accounting, economic and market indicators, companies frequently adopt a fourth category of performance variables known as **value drivers**. These are measured with a class of associated metrics called **key performance indicators (KPIs)**.

  Value drivers are at the root of business performance because they are frequently **leading indicators** of performance, while financial results (such as ROCE, for example) are lagging indicators. Management has a strong need to understand where the company is going in the future. KPIs can be either *operating* or *strategic* measures, for example in:

○ pharmaceutical companies ⇒ value driver: R&D pipeline;
○ packaged food division ⇒ market share; and
○ retailers ⇒ number of stores opened in a given year or number of new product categories introduced.

While it is worthwhile to mention value drivers at this juncture, the rest of this chapter will continue to focus on accounting, economic and market criteria. The reasons for leaving behind the discussion of value drivers are:

○ value drivers are highly company and industry specific. They are also innumerable. It would be highly impractical to try and dedicate appropriate attention to all of them here; and
○ value drivers are normally identified and adopted on a business unit by business unit basis. The scope of this text is more concerned with detailed examinations of corporate and company-wide measures at a higher level.

Section 28.2
NPV, THE ONLY RELIABLE CRITERION

It should now be clear that the concept of value corresponds perfectly to the measure of **net present value**. Financial management consists of constantly measuring the net present value of an investment, project, company or source of financing. Obviously, one should only allocate resources if the net present value is positive; in other words, if the market value is lower than the present value. **Net present value reflects how allocation of the company's resources has led to the creation or destruction of value.** On the one hand, there is a constant search for anticipated financial flows – while keeping in mind the uncertainty of these forecasts. On the other hand, it is necessary to consider the rate of return (k) required by the investors and shareholders providing the funds.

The value created is thus equal to the difference between the capital employed and its book value. Book value is the amount of funds invested in the company's operations.

Creation of value = enterprise value − book value of capital employed.

The creation of value reflects investors' expectations. Typically, this means that, over a certain period, the company will enjoy a rent with a present value allowing its capital employed to be worth more than its book value!

The same principle applies to choosing a source of financing for allocating resources. To do so, one must disregard the book value and determine instead the value of the financial security issued and deduct the required rate of return. This approach represents a shift from the explicit or accounting cost to the **financial cost, which is the return required on this category of security**. By minimising the cost of a source of financing, one is actually minimising the overall financial cost.

On its own, the concept of cost may be insufficient when analysing certain very complex products. In such cases, one must resort to the concept of present value. This is particularly true of hybrid securities.

A source of financing is considered cheap **only** if its net present value is negative.

Once again, the only reliable financial criterion is net present value.

SECTION 3

1/ ECONOMIC PROFIT OR ECONOMIC VALUE ADDED (EVA)

Economic profit is less ambitious than net present value. It only seeks to measure the wealth created by the company in each financial year. EVA factors in not just the cost of debt, such as in calculating net profit, but it also accounts for the cost of equity.

The innovative aspect of EVA is that it identifies the income level at which value is created. This is because EVA is calculated after deducting the capital charge, i.e. the remuneration of the funds contributed by creditors and shareholders.

Economic profit or EVA first measures the excess of ROCE over the weighted average cost of capital. Then, to determine the value created during the period, the ratio is multiplied by the book value of the **capital employed at the start of the reporting period**. Thus, a company that had an opening book value of capital employed of 100 and an after-tax return on capital employed of 12% with a WACC of only 10% will have earned 2% more than the required rate. It will have created a value of 2 on funds of 100 during the period.

$$EVA = \text{Capital employed} \times (ROCE - WACC)$$
$$EVA = NOPAT - WACC \times \text{Capital employed}$$

Economic profit is related to net present value, because NPV is the sum of the economic profits discounted at the weighted average cost of capital.

$$NPV = \sum_{i=0}^{\infty} \frac{\text{Economic profit}_i}{\left(1 + \text{weighted average cost of capital}\right)^i} = \sum_{i=0}^{\infty} \frac{EVA_i}{\left(1 + WACC\right)^i}$$

The table shows EVA for some European firms.

Company	EVA in 2010 (€m)	Company	EVA in 2010 (€m)
Nestlé	6 221	BIC	137
Roche	6 166	Michelin	67
AstraZeneca	5 977	NRJ	(8)
Telefonica	2 363	Bonduelle	(42)
ENI	2 280	Carlsberg	(218)
BASF	2 017	Carrefour	(240)
Shell	1 558	Peugeot	(325)
L'Oréal	1 014	Lafarge	(590)
Belgacom	644	Italcementi	(678)
E.ON	172	Heidelberg Cement	(766)
Heineken	162	Deutsche Telekom	(1 224)
Adidas	160	ArcelorMittal	(4 675)

Source : Exane BNP Paribas, Datastream

To calculate EVA, it is necessary to switch from an accounting to an economic reading of the company. This is done by restating certain items of capital employed as follows:

- The research and development costs expended by the company during the past five to ten years must be capitalised and added to fixed assets if they contributed to the development of the business for more than one year.
- The exceptional losses of previous years must be restated and added to capital employed insofar as they artificially reduce the company's capital.
- The goodwill recorded in the balance sheet must be taken as gross, i.e. corrected for cumulative amortisation or impairment, the badwill must be deducted from assets.

Of course, the profit and loss account (operating profit/loss and taxes) must be restated to ensure consistency with the capital employed calculated previously.

The firms that develop economic profit tools for companies generally have a long list of accounting adjustments that attest to their expertise. Such accounting expertise typically represents a barrier to entry for others seeking to perform the same analyses.

EVA's novelty also lies in its scope of application, since it enables a company to measure performance at all levels by applying an individual required rate of return to various units. It is a decentralised financial management tool.

Keep in mind these words of warning about EVA:

- If managers are judged based on EVA they will have a strong incentive to reduce invested capital. However, it can happen that the reduction in the invested capital is purely cosmetic.
- If managers are judged according to the current year's EVA, they will have a bias towards assets-in-place. As a result, they may be induced to abandon high-growth investments. Such behaviour in turn reduces the long-term economic value added that such investments may have otherwise added to the value of the company. A company can be tempted to maximise its EVA for a single year, at the cost of future EVA, by underinvesting or artificially reducing its working capital. In general, it is very difficult to find an annual measure of performance that truly reflects the creation of value. The only real measure of a company's ability to create value in the long term is the net present value of all future flows.
- If management's compensation is based on short-term EVA, managers may sacrifice future growth for current EVA.
- EVA will be overestimated for companies' divisions that are under-allocated capital, and underestimated for those divisions or business units that are over-allocated capital.
- Companies that undertake value-adding projects may end up with a lower value if the new projects increase the operating and financial risk and thus the cost of capital.
- Above all, EVA is an example of successful marketing and communication. Its promoters have taken a financial concept that has been around for a long time and reformulated it in easy-to-understand terms that can be explained at all organisational levels.

In short, we think there are good reasons for agreeing with Damodaran's opinion on EVA: ". . . economic value added is an approach skewed toward assets-in-place and away from future growth" (Damodaran, 2001, p. 821).

SECTION 3

2/ Net present value and EVA: A comparison

Economic value added is a throwback to the net present value rule. In fact, it can be demonstrated that the present value of the economic value added by a project over its life is the net present value of the project. In order to achieve this result, the project must have a salvage value of zero, and the present value of depreciation must be equal to the present value of initial investment, discounted back over the project's life. In other words, we must assume that the cash flow from depreciation is really the capital being returned to the firm.

3/ Cash flow return on investment (CFROI)

The original version of cash flow return on investment (CFROI) corresponds to the average of the internal rates of return on the company's existing investments. It measures the IRR earned by a firm's existing projects.

CFROI is the internal rate of return and it is equal to:

1. the company's *gross* capital employed (GCE), i.e. before depreciation and adjusted for inflation. GCE is computed by adding depreciation back to the book value of the assets to arrive at an estimate of the original investment in the assets. The gross investment must then be converted into current value by reflecting the inflation incurred since the asset was purchased; *and*
2. the *current* **year EBIT** $\times$ **(1 − Tax rate)** + **Depreciation and amortisation**. We define this measure as gross cash flow (GCF). GCF is then considered an annuity with the same length as the expected life of the assets (N); *and*
3. the expected value of the assets at the end of their life, in current values. This is defined as the **SV** (salvage value).

CASH FLOW RETURN ON INVESTMENT

Analytically, CFROI is the result of:

$$\text{GCF}(\text{PV of an annuity}, N \text{ years}, \text{CFROI}) + \text{SV}/(1 + \text{CFROI}) - \text{GCE} = 0$$

CFROI is then compared with the weighted average cost of capital. If CFROI is higher than WACC, the company is creating value; if it is lower, then the firm is destroying value.

There are two major differences between the CFROI and the "traditional" IRR:

1. The internal rate of return is based on incremental *future* cash flows. Conversely, the CFROI reconstructs an asset using both cash flows that have already occurred and cash flows that are yet to occur.
2. CFROI holds gross cash flows constant over a project's life and considers them an annuity with a length of N years and a rate equal to CFROI. IRR does not assume that after-tax cash flows are constant over time.

The CFROI is complex to calculate, and even more difficult to explain than ROCE to non-financial managers. As with EVA, the series of accounting adjustments required to calculate CFROI seem designed to convince users to call on the services of its creators, in this case Holt Value Associates, to implement the system. As a result, a simplified version of CFROI is frequently used, one which is more of an accounting measure than a financial one.

In general, there can be relevant differences between ROCE and CFROI when companies have:

- very long-lived fixed assets;
- a high incidence of fixed assets vs. working capital;
- very old or very new fixed assets; and/or
- irregular capital expenditure patterns.

However, it is possible to demonstrate that an increase in CFROI does not necessarily indicate a higher value of the firm because such a result may have come at the expense of lower growth and higher risk.

Section 28.4
MARKET CRITERIA

1/ CREATING STOCK MARKET VALUE (MARKET VALUE ADDED)

For listed companies, *market value added (MVA)* is equal to:

MVA = market capitalisation + net debt − book value of capital employed

In most cases, if no other information is available, we assume that net debt corresponds to its book value. Thus, the equation becomes simpler:

Value created = Market capitalisation + Book value of net debt

− (Book value of equity + Book value of debt)

= Market capitalisation − Book value of equity

2 *The market-to-capital ratio is a variation of MVA expressed as a ratio rather than a unit amount, because it is obtained by dividing the market capitalisation of debt and equity by the amount of capital invested.*

So, market value added is frequently considered to be the difference between market capitalisation and the book value of equity. This is the equivalent of the price-to-book ratio (PBR) discussed in Chapter 23.[2]

The table shows MVA for some large listed Indian companies as of May 2011.

Company	MVA 2010 (€m)	Company	MVA 2010 (€m)
Tata Consultancy	32 154	Wipro	14 118
Coal India	31 968	Bharat Heavy Electrical	11 627
Reliance Industries	20 990	ICICI Bank	10 364
Infosys	20 762	State Bank of India	10 222
Bharti Airtel	15 888	India Oil	4 000

Source: Datastream

SECTION 3

MVA, and particularly any change in MVA, constitutes a more relevant measure of value than just developments in share price. MVA assesses the increase in value with regard to the capital invested.

Inversely, MVA can raise measurement problems due to the use of accounting data.

It is easy to demonstrate the relationship between market value added and intrinsic value creation in equilibrium markets, since:

$$\text{Market value added} = \sum_{t=0}^{\infty} \frac{\text{Economic profit}_t}{\left(1 + \text{WACC}\right)^t}$$

Economic profit being equal to capital employed $\times$ (ROCE $-$ WACC). This is also equivalent to:

$$\text{Enterprise value} = \text{Book value of assets} + \sum_{t=0}^{\infty} \frac{\text{Economic profit}_t}{\left(1 + \text{WACC}\right)^t}$$

However, those who do not believe in market efficiency contend that MVA is flawed because it is based on market values that are often volatile and out of the management's control. Yet this volatility is an inescapable fact for all, as that is how the markets function.

2/ TOTAL SHAREHOLDER RETURN (TSR)

TSR is the return received by the shareholder who bought the share at the beginning of a period, earned dividends (which are generally assumed to have been reinvested in new shares) and values his portfolio with the last share price at the end of the period. In other words, TSR equals (share appreciation + dividends)/price at the beginning of the period.

In order for it to be meaningful, the TSR ratio is calculated on a yearly basis over a fairly long period of, say, 5–10 years. This smoothes out the impact of erratic market movements, e.g. the tech, media and telecom stock bubble of 2000 or the 2007–2010 crisis.

Below is a table of the total shareholder returns of several large European groups over the 1991–2010 period:

Company	TSR (1991 - 2010)	Company	TSR (1991 – 2010)
Nokia	41%	Nestlé	14%
Telefonica	21%	ING	12%
Ericsson	18%	Royal Dutch Shell	12%
HSBC	18%	E.ON	11%
Vodafone	18%	BP	11%
ENI	16%	GlaxoSmithKline	11%
Roche	15%	Crédit Suisse	11%
Siemens	14%	Deutsche Telekom	9%
Total	14%	Novartis	9%
BNP Paribas	14%	Royal Bank of Scotland	9%

Source : Exane BNP Paribas, Datastream

Since markets are not always in equilibrium, there may be times when the creation of both intrinsic value and market value are not automatically correlated. This is particularly true during bust (or boom) periods, when a company may earn more than the cost of its capital and yet still see the market value of its capital employed collapse.

Section 28.5
ACCOUNTING CRITERIA

Certain accounting indicators, like net profit, shareholders' equity and cash flow from operations, are more representative of a firm's financial strength. However, they are flawed and not appropriate for the purposes of financial analysis, mainly because:

* accounting items can be manipulated;
* they may not consider the time value of money and the opportunity cost of capital.

The same could be said of the criteria presented next in this section – earnings per share (**EPS**), the accounting rate of return and equity per share. However, they are systematically used as analytical criteria for all financial decisions, even at the board level.

Even so, are they really of any practical use?

Although EPS, the accounting rate of return and equity per share are primarily of an accounting nature and generally tend to ignore risks, they do have some merit and can impart useful information.

However it is inappropriate to believe that by artificially boosting them you have created value. Nor is it correct to assume that there is a constant and automatic link between improving these criteria and creating value. In order to maximise value, it is simply not enough to maximise these ratios, even if they are linked by a coefficient to value or the required rate of return.

1/ EARNINGS PER SHARE

Notwithstanding the comments just made about earnings per share (EPS), many financial managers continue to favour using it. Despite its limitations, it is still the most widespread multiple because it is directly connected to the share price via the price–earnings ratio. EPS's popularity is rooted in three misconceptions:

* the belief that earnings per share factors in the cost of equity and, therefore, the cost of risk;
* the belief that accounting data influence the value of the company. Changing accounting methods (for inventories, depreciation, goodwill, etc.) will not modify the company's value, even if it does change earnings per share; and
* the belief that any financial decision that lifts EPS will change value as well. This would imply that the P/E ratio[3] remains the same before and after the financial decision, which is frequently not the case. Thus, value is not a direct multiple of earnings per share, because the decision may affect investors' assessment of the company's risks and growth potential.

3 *The P/E ratio is equal to price/earnings per share. It measures the relative expense of a share.*

Consider Company A which, based upon its risks and growth and profitability prospects, has a P/E ratio of 20. Its net profit is 50. Company B has equity of 450 with net profit of 30, giving it a P/E of 15. Company A decides to acquire a controlling interest in Company B, paying a premium of 33% on B's value, i.e. a total of 600. Company A finances the acquisition entirely by taking on debt at an after-tax cost of 3%. Both Companies A and B are fairly valued with regards to their risk exposure. There are no industrial or commercial synergies that could increase the new group's earnings, and no goodwill.

Company A's net profit is thus:

Former net profit of A:	50
+ net profit of B:	30
− cost of financing:	18 = 600 × 3%
= New net profit of A:	62, or + 24%

Since A financed its acquisition of B entirely through debt, it still has the same number of shares. The increase in earnings per share is therefore equal to that in net profit; that is, 24%. This certainly seems like an extraordinary result! But has A really created value by buying B? The answer is no, since there are no synergies to speak of between A and B. Keep in mind that A paid 33% more than B's equilibrium price. In fact, Company A has destroyed value in proportion to this premium, i.e. 150, because it cannot be offset by synergies.

In fact, the explanation for the – apparent – paradox of a 24% rise in earnings per share matched by a destruction of value is that **the buyer's EPS has increased, because the P/E of the company bought by means of debt is higher than the after-tax cost of the debt**. Here, B has a P/E of 20 given the 33% premium paid by A on the acquisition. The inverse of 20 (5%) is much higher than the 3% after-tax cost of the debt for A.

At present low interest rates (4% net of taxes), an acquisition paid in cash must be based on a P/E ratio of more than 25 to have a negative impact on the EPS[4] of the buyer. Such a situation leaves plenty of margin to manoeuvre.

4 *Before amortisation of goodwill.*

Consider now Company C, which has equity of 1400 with net profit of 140, i.e. a P/E of 10. It merges with Company D, which has the same risk exposure, equity of 990 and a P/E of 18 (net profit of 55), with no control premium. Thanks to very strong industrial synergies, C is able to boost D's net profit by 50%. Without doubt, value has been created. And yet, it is not difficult to prove (see Exercise 1) that C's EPS dropped 7% after the merger. This is a mechanical effect due simply to the fact that D's P/E of 18 is higher than C's P/E of 10, because D has better earnings prospects than C.

At the risk of being repetitive, a word of warning about the widespread fallacy that EPS growth equals value creation. This has led to the misconception that, accordingly, EPS dilution means that value has been destroyed. This is a myth. EPS is an accounting metric, not a measure of value.

So, what was the net result of Company C's acquisition of Company D? **The question is not whether Company C's EPS has been enhanced or diluted, but whether it paid**

too much for D. In fact, it did not, since there was no control premium paid and industrial synergies were created. After the operation, C's share will trade at a higher P/E, as it should enjoy greater earnings growth thanks to the contribution from D's higher-growth businesses. In the end, the higher P/E ratio should more than compensate for the diluted EPS, lifting the share price. This is only logical considering that the industrial synergies created value.

In fact, EPS can be a reliable indicator of value creation under three conditions only:

- the risk on capital employed remains the same from one period to the next, or before and after operations such as mergers, capital increases or share buy backs, investments, etc.;
- earnings growth remains the same before and after any given operation; and
- the company's financial structure remains the same from one period to the next, or before and after a given operation.

If these three conditions are met, we can assume that EPS growth reflects the creation of value, and EPS dilution the destruction of value.

If just one of these conditions is lacking, there is no way to effectively evaluate EPS. It is not possible to infer that any increase in EPS reflects the creation of value, nor that a decrease is a destruction of value. In our example of a combination between A and B financed by debt, although A's EPS rose 24%, its risk increased sharply. Its position is no longer directly comparable with that before the acquisition of B.

Similarly, C's post-merger EPS cannot be compared with its EPS prior to the merger. While the merger did not change its financial structure, C's growth rate after the merger with D is different from what it was beforehand.

2/ ACCOUNTING RATES OF RETURN

Accounting rates of return comprise:

- return on equity (**ROE**);
- return on capital employed (**ROCE**), which was described in Chapter 13; and
- cash flow return on investment (**CFROI**), the simplified version of which compares EBITDA with gross capital employed, i.e. before amortisation and depreciation of fixed assets.

$$CFROI = \frac{EBITDA}{Capital\ employed}$$

This ratio is used particularly in business sectors wherein charges to depreciation do not necessarily reflect the normal deterioration of fixed assets, e.g. in the hotel business.

The main drawback of accounting rates of return on equity or capital employed is precisely that they are accounting measures. As shall be demonstrated below, these have their dangers.

Consider[5] Company X, which produces a single product and generates a return of 20% on capital employed amounting to 100. X operates in a highly profitable sector and is considering diversifying. Should it expect the present 20% rate of return to be generated on other possible projects? If it does, X will never diversify because it is unlikely that any other investments will meet these criteria.

5 *To simplify the discount calculation, we assume that the planned investments will generate a return to infinity.*

How can this problem be rationally approached? The company generates an accounting return of 20%. Suppose its shareholders and investors require a 10% return. Its market value is thus 20/10%, or 200.

The proposed investment amounts to 100 and generates a return of 15% on identical risks. The required rate of return is constant at 10%. We see that:

	Present operating profit	20% × 100 = 20
+	Operating profit on new investment	15% × 100 = 15
=	Total	35

This yields an enterprise value of 35/10% = 350 (+150), with a return on capital employed of 35/200 = 17.5%.

The value of the capital employed has increased by more than the amount invested (150 versus 100) because the profitability of Company X's investment is higher than the rate required by its shareholders and investors. Value has been created, and X was right to invest. And yet the return on capital employed fell by 20% to 17.5%, demonstrating that this criterion is not relevant.

In general, if the investment yields more than the required rate of return, the increase in the value of the company will exceed that of the sums invested.

The inverse example is Company Y, which has a return of 5% on capital employed of 100. Assuming the shareholders and investors require a 10% return as well, the value of Y's capital employed is 5/10% = 50.

The proposed investment amounts to 25 and yields a return of 8%. Since we have the same 10% required return, we get:

	Present operating profit	5% × 100 = 5
+	Operating profit on new investment	8% × 25 = 2
=	Total	7

This results in capital employed being valued at 7/10% = 70(+20), with a return of 7/125 = 5.6%

The value of Y's capital employed has indeed increased by 20, but this is still less than the increase of 25 in capital invested. Value has been destroyed. The return on the investment is just 8%, whereas the required rate is 10%. The company has lost money and should not have made the investment. And yet the return on capital employed rose from 5% to 5.6%.

Similarly, one could demonstrate that ROE increases after an acquisition funded by a share issue, when the target company's reverse 1/(P/E) is higher than the buyer's current ROE.

Financial managers should approach book rates of return with caution. These ratios are accounting measures, but not external measures. They assume that the company is operating in a closed system! The minimum criterion should be the return required by the financial system.

Setting aside all these accounting concepts, what are the implications for the financial concepts (k)?

Unfortunately, investors and corporate managers continue to view decision-making in terms of the impact on accounting measures, even though it has just been demonstrated that these criteria have little to say about the creation of value. True, accounting systems are a company's main source of information. However, financial managers need to focus first and foremost on how financial decisions affect value.

Section 28.6
PUTTING THINGS INTO PERSPECTIVE

1/ STRENGTHS AND WEAKNESSES OF FINANCIAL INDICATORS

As long as performance measures and their implementation remain so diversified, it is vital to have a good understanding of their respective flaws. By choosing one or another measure, companies can present their results in a more or less flattering light. Financial managers typically choose those measures that will demonstrate the creation, rather than the destruction, of value.

2/ CREATING VALUE OR VALUES?

Over the past 15 years, the concept of value creation has spread rapidly, to the point where no corporate communication can afford to disregard it. Increasingly, value is assessed not just as it pertains to shareholders, but to all the stakeholders in the company: shareholders, employees and clients alike.

Managers now talk of stakeholder value, customer capital and human capital just as they do of financial capital.

While these concepts are certainly very appealing, we believe they are rooted in two misconceptions:

1. The creation of value is sometimes rather hastily accused of leading to layoffs, plant closures, drastic cost reductions or disregard for environmental protection, labour law and human dignity. In fact, the opposite is true! A look at groups that have created sustainable value for their shareholders, frequently over long periods, shows that these same companies are at the forefront of innovation, constantly creating new markets, meeting new needs, hiring and training employees and inspiring loyalty and strong customer relationships. Just a few examples are L'Oréal, Johnson and Johnson, Singapore Airlines, Apple and BMW. Cost-cutting strategies can only be temporary and they cannot durably create shareholder value. Cost-cutting only works in the short term and only if it gives rise to a strategy of profitable growth.
2. Shareholders entrust their money to managers whose task is to multiply it. Financial directors must operate within the framework of a given corporate mission and with the shareholders' best interests in mind. When managers pursue other objectives, they betray the basic tenet upon which this pact is founded. More importantly, they are sure to fall short of all their objectives.

Ratio	Financial criteria	Financial/accounting criteria		Accounting criteria		Market criteria	
	Net present value	Economic profit	Cash flow return on investment	Earnings per share	Accounting rates of return	Market value added	Total shareholder return
Acronym	NPV	EVA	CFROI	EPS	ROE, ROCE	MVA	TSR
Strengths	The best criterion	Simple indicator leading to the concept of weighted average cost of capital	Not restricted to just one year.	Historical data. Simple.	Simple concepts.	Astoundingly simple. Reflects the total rather than annual value created.	Represents shareholder return in the medium to long term.
Weaknesses	Difficult to calculate for an external analyst	Restricted to one year. Difficult to evaluate changes over a period of time.	Complex calculations.	Does not factor in risks. Easily manipulated. Does not factor in the cost of equity.	Accounting measures, thus do not factor in risks. Restricted to one year. To be significant, must be compared with the required rate of return.	Subject to market volatility. Difficult to apply to unlisted companies.	Calculated over too short a period. Subject to market volatility.

We believe the words of **Milton Friedman** (1970) are still valid: "In a free-enterprise, private-property system, a corporate executive is an employee of the owners of the business. He has direct responsibility to his employers. That responsibility is to conduct the business in accordance with their desires, which generally will be to make as much money as possible while conforming to the basic rules of the society, both those embodied in law and those embodied in ethical custom. Of course, in some cases his employers may have a different objective. A group of persons might establish a corporation for an eleemosynary purpose – for example, a hospital or a school. The manager of such a corporation will not have money profit as his objective but the rendering of certain services. In either case, the key point is that, in his capacity as a corporate executive, the manager is the agent of the individuals who own the corporation or establish the eleemosynary institution, and his primary responsibility is to them."

Only by creating sustainable value can a company ensure that it has the means to finance growth, train and pay its employees properly, produce quality goods or services and respect the environment.

Fortunately, there is more to life than finance. Yet in finance, there is just one overriding objective – creating value – and only by meeting this objective can one achieve all the others.

SUMMARY

The summary of this chapter can be downloaded from www.vernimmen.com.

The tools used for measuring creation of value can be classified under four headings:

- Net present value is the only true **financial tool** for measuring value creation.

- **Financial/accounting tools**, which factor in returns required by investors (the weighted average cost of capital) and do not depend directly on the sometimes erratic price movements of markets. EVA, the popular term for economic profit, measures how much the shareholder has increased his wealth over and above standard remuneration. However, EVA has the drawback of being restricted to the financial period in question; EVA can thus be manipulated to yield maximum results in one period at the expense of subsequent periods.

- **Market tools**, which measure MVA (market value added), or the difference between the company's enterprise value and its book value, and TSR (total shareholder returns). TSR is the rate of shareholder returns given the increase in the value of the share and the dividends paid out. These market tools are only useful over the medium term, because to be meaningful they should avoid the market fluctuations that can distort economic reality.

- **Accounting indicators,** which have the main drawback of being designed for accounting purposes, i.e. they do not factor in risk or return on equity. They include earnings per share (EPS) linked to the value of the share by the price–earnings ratio (P/E), shareholders' equity linked to the value of the share by the price–book ratio (PBR), accounting profitability indicators (shareholders' equity, return on equity (ROE), return on capital employed (ROCE)) to be compared with the cost of equity (or the weighted average cost of capital, WACC).

A thorough understanding of the weaknesses of all of these tools is vital. Given the lack of a generally accepted standard measure for value creation, companies quite naturally rely on those criteria that show them off in the best light.

QUESTIONS

1/ What is the main drawback of accounting profitability indicators?

2/ Why do EVA adversaries describe it as a great marketing stunt?

3/ What is a TSR calculated over one year?

4/ Will a company that is making losses record positive economic profits or EVA?

5/ Can a company with a positive net profit show a negative economic profit?

6/ What is the sum of future EVA discounted to the cost of capital equal to?

7/ Subject to what conditions is it possible to compare EPS before and after a deal?

8/ What is your view of this quotation: "A series of positive EVA can only be a sign of two things: either of a monopoly that is more or less temporary (for example a high tech development) or a poor estimation of the cost of capital"?

9/ Is a drop in return on equity synonymous with value destruction? Why?

10/ Is a drop in return on capital employed (ROCE) synonymous with value destruction? Why?

11/ Can a company create value and have a negative TSR over one year? And over 10 years?

12/ What does TSR correspond to in terms of investment choice?

13/ If you were stranded on a desert island with only one criterion for measuring value creation, which would you want to use? Why?

14/ If EPS drops after a deal, does this necessarily imply value destruction?

15/ If EPS rises after a deal, does this necessarily imply value creation?

16/ Why does an accurate calculation of EVA or profitability mean that the balance sheet will have to be restated?

17/ What is the drawback of company rankings based on EVA?

18/ Do layoffs systematically lead to value creation?

19/ Can value be created by developing new products and new markets or by reducing costs?

20/ The hotel chain CIGA provides information to the market on value creation, measured by a ROCE calculated as the ratio between EBITDA and the historic value (i.e. gross before depreciation and amortisation) of capital employed. State your views.

More questions are waiting for you at www.vernimmen.com.

1/ Show that in the example on p. 542, C's EPS drops by 7% after the company merges with D.

2/ Use the figures provided in Section 1 (Chapters 4 and 9) and calculate the EVA and the MVA of Indesit in 2010. The weighted average cost of capital of Indesit is 9.2% and it has a market capitalisation of €782m. Suppose the tax rate is 40%. Why then, as the EVA and MVA of Indesit are positive, is its market value of equity down in 2010?

Questions

1/ *The very fact that they are accounting indicators and not part of the realm of value, since they do not factor in risk or the cost of equity.*

2/ *Take a concept that has existed for years, give it a new trendy name and the full media treatment and you've got EVA.*

3/ *Intellectual trickery! TSR only means something if it is calculated over at least five years in order to eliminate extreme market movements.*

4/ *No, because since it is making losses, it does not cover the cost of equity.*

5/ *Yes, if net profits do not cover the cost of equity.*

6/ *To NPV.*

7/ *Subject to the risk of capital employed, the capital structure and the growth rate remaining the same before and after the operation.*

8/ *It is quite true given the pressure from the competition.*

9/ *Not necessarily if there is a simultaneous drop in risk (capital employed, capital structure) and an improvement in growth prospects. If not, then yes.*

10/ *Same answer as for question 9 above.*

11/ *Over one year, yes. Much less likely over 10 years, since sudden fluctuations in prices that are not linked to the company's economic performance are set off against each other.*

12/ *The internal rate of return (IRR).*

13/ *Net present value, which is the best criterion.*

14/ *Not necessarily, if the growth rate after the deal is higher than before or if the risk related to capital structure and capital employed is reduced. If not, then yes.*

15/ *Not necessarily, if the growth rate after the deal is lower than before or if the risk related to capital structure and capital employed is increased. If not, then yes.*

16/ *In order to get away from the formal constraints of accounting which are heavily influenced by the principle of conservatism and to think more in terms of economic value.*

17/ *It focuses on an annual indicator and does not factor in an investment policy which could take over a year to yield results.*

18/ *No, on the contrary, the creation of value is built on the development of new products and new markets, which leads to an increase in headcount.*

19/ *In theory, by creating new products and markets, because the sky is the limit! Reducing costs is less effective as all possible cost-cutting options are soon exhausted.*

20/ *ROCE is usually calculated on the basis of operating profit/capital employed (in net book value, i.e. after depreciation and amortisation). CIGA calculates the numerator and the denominator after depreciation and amortisation, which is explained by the highly asset-based nature of its activity – a hotel is not written down economically even if it has been fully amortised.*

Exercises

A detailed Excel version of the solutions is available at www.vernimmen.com.

1/ *Profits rise from 140 to 140 + 55 + 27.5 = 222.5, or a multiplication by 222.5/140 = 1.59. The number of C's shares increases by 990/1400 = 70.7%, since D is paid in C's shares, or a multiplication by 1.707. EPS is multiplied by 1.59/1.707 = 93%, or a drop of 7%.*

$2/EVA\ 2010 = 2010\ operating\ profit \times (1 - tax\ rate) - capital\ employed \times 9.2\% = 184 \times (1 - 40\%) - 931 \times 9.2\% = €25m.\ MVA\ 2009 = 782 - 609 = €173m$

A positive MVA and EVA mean that investors believe that Indesit has created and will be able to create value in the future but this does not prevent them from reducing their estimates for future results and hence a lower stock price.

BIBLIOGRAPHY

For a general overview of value creation indicators:

Boston Consulting Group, *Shareholder Value Metrics, Shareholder Value Management*, Boston Consulting Group, 1996.

T. Copeland, What do practitioners want? *Journal of Applied Finance*, **12**(1), 5–11, Spring/Summer 2002.

T. Copeland, T. Koller, J. Murrin, *Valuation,* 3rd edn, John Wiley & Sons, Inc., 2000.

A. Damodaran, Value creation and enhancement: Back to the future, *Contemporary Finance Digest*, **2**, 5–51, Winter 1998.

A. Damodaran, *Corporate Finance: Theory and Practice*, 2nd edn, John Wiley & Sons, Inc., 2001.

R. Dobbs, T. Koller, Measuring long-term performance, *The McKinsey Quarterly*, special edition *Value and performance*, 17–27, 2005.

M. Friedman, The social responsibility of business is to increase its profits, *New York Times Magazine*, September 13, 1970.

B. Madden, *CFROI: A Total System Approach to Valuing a Firm*, Butterworth-Heinemann, 1998.

For more on EVA and economic profit:

R. Bernstein, An empirical analysis of EVA as a proxy for market value added, *Financial Practice and Education*, **7**, 41–49, 1997.

G. Stewart, *The Quest for Value*, Harper Business, 1991.

The reader can also consult an interesting monographic issue on "EVA and incentive compensation" in the *Journal of Applied Corporate Finance*, **12**(2), Summer 1999.

On TSR:

B. Deelder, M. Goedhart, A. Agrawal, A better way to understand TSR, *The McKinsey Quarterly*, **28**, 26–30, Summer 2008.

A history of return on investment and the cost of capital in the USA:

E. Fama, K. French, The corporate cost of capital and the return on corporate investment, *Journal of Finance*, **54**, 1939–1967, December 1999.

The impact of EPS accretion and dilution on stock prices:

G. Andrade, *Do Appearances Matter? The Impact of EPS Accretion and Dilution on Stock Prices.* Harvard Business School Working Paper 00–07.

SECTION 3

Chapter 29
INVESTMENT CRITERIA

Back to flows and financial analysis

SECTION 3

The "mathematics" we studied in Chapters 16 and 17, dealing with present value and internal rate of return, can also be applied to investment decisions and financial securities. These theories will not be covered again in detail, since the only real novelty is of a semantic nature. In the sections on financial securities, we calculated the yield to maturity. The same approach holds for analysing industrial investments, whereby we calculate a rate that takes the present value to zero. This is called the internal rate of return (IRR). **Internal rate of return and yield to maturity are thus the same.**

Net present value (NPV) measures the value created by the investment and is the best criterion for selecting or rejecting an investment, whether it is industrial or financial. When it is simply a matter of deciding whether or not to make an investment, NPV and IRR produce the same outcome. However, if the choice is between two mutually exclusive investments, net present value is more reliable than the internal rate of return.

This chapter will discuss:

- the cash flows to be factored into investment decisions, which are called **incremental cash flows**; and
- **other investment criteria** which are less relevant than NPV and IRR and have proven disappointing in the past. As future financial managers, you should nevertheless be aware of them, even if they are more pertinent to accounting work than financial management.

Section 29.1
THE PREDOMINANCE OF NPV AND THE IMPORTANCE OF IRR

Each investment has a **net present value (NPV), which is equal to the amount of value created**. Remember that the net present value of an investment is the value of the positive and negative cash flows arising from an investment, discounted at the rate of return required by the market. The rate of return is based upon the investment's risk.

From a financial standpoint, and if forecasts are correct, an investment with positive NPV is worth making since it will create value. Conversely, an investment with negative NPV should be avoided as it is expected to destroy value. Sometimes investments with negative NPV are made for strategic reasons, such as to protect a position in the industry sector or to open up new markets with strong, yet hard to quantify, growth potential. It must be kept in mind that if the NPV is really negative, it will certainly lead to the destruction of value. Sooner or later, projects with negative NPV have to be offset by other investments with positive NPV that create value. Without doing so, the company will be headed for ruin.

An investment with an NPV of zero will not create value, but it will not destroy value either. All other things being equal, decisions about projects with an NPV of zero are akin to tossing a coin in order to decide whether or not to go ahead.

The internal rate of return (IRR) is simply the rate of return on an investment. Given an investment's degree of risk, it is financially worthwhile if the IRR is higher than the required return. However, if the IRR is lower than the risk-based required rate of return, the investment will serve no financial purpose.

J. Graham and C. Harvey (2001) conducted a broad survey of corporate and financial managers to determine which tools and criteria they use when making financial decisions. They asked them to indicate how frequently they used several capital budgeting methods by ranking them on a scale ranging from 0 (never) to 4 (always). The findings showed that net present value and internal rate of return carry the greatest weight, and justifiably so. Some 75% of financial managers systematically value investments according to these two criteria.

Interestingly, large firms apply these criteria more often than small- and medium-sized companies, and MBA graduates use them systematically while older managers tend to rely on the payback ratio.

A much older study by Gitman and Forrester (1977) found that only 9.8% of large firms used NPV as their primary capital budgeting tool. By comparing those results with the more up-to-date work of Graham and Harvey, it is apparent that the popularity of the NPV method has grown significantly over time.

The third most frequently used decision criterion is the payback method, which is particularly popular among small firms. This and other criteria will be discussed later on in this chapter.

Bruner *et al.* (1998) surveyed 27 significant corporations and 10 financial advisers. Of these, 89% of corporations and 100% of advisers confirmed that they always use NPV as a primary tool in evaluating investment opportunities.

Dallocchio and Salvi (2000) conducted a survey of 56 CFOs and treasurers of multinational companies. When asked about the criteria they chose for valuing the M&A transactions of their company, 75% of respondents ranked NPV and IRR as the most popular approaches. These were followed by the payback method (20%) and economic value added (5%).

The strong popularity of NPV is widespread globally, as shown by other studies. Hall (2000) and Lumby (1991) have illustrated the diffusion of the NPV technique in South Africa and the United Kingdom, respectively.

Section 29.2
THE MAIN LINES OF REASONING

Any well-advised investment decision must respect the following six principles:

1. consider cash flows rather than accounting data;
2. reason in terms of incremental cash flows, considering only those associated with the project;

3.   reason in terms of opportunity;
4.   disregard the type of financing;
5.   consider taxation; and
6.   above all, be **consistent**.

1/ REASON IN TERMS OF CASH FLOWS

We have already seen that the return on an investment is assessed in terms of the resulting cash flows. One must therefore analyse the negative and positive cash flows, and not the accounting income and expenses. These accounting measures are irrelevant because they do not take into account working capital generated by the investment and include depreciation which is a non-cash item.

As a result, only cash flows are relevant in the financial analysis of investments.

2/ REASON IN TERMS OF INCREMENTAL FLOWS

When considering an investment, one must take into account all the flows it generates, and nothing else but these flows. It is crucial to assess all the consequences of an investment upon a company's cash position. Some of these are self-evident and easy to measure, and others are less so.

A movie theatre group plans to launch a new complex and substantial costs have already been incurred in its design. Should these be included in the investment programme's cash flows? The answer is no, since the costs have already been incurred regardless of whether or not the complex is actually built. These are **sunk costs**. Therefore, they should not be considered part of the investment expenditure.

It would be absurd to carry out an investment simply because the preparations were costly and one hopes to recoup funds that, in any case, have already been spent. The only valid reason for pursuing an investment is that it is likely to create value.

Now, if the personnel department has to administer an additional 20 employees hired for the new complex (e.g. 5% of its total workforce), should 5% of the department's costs be allocated to the new project? Again, the answer is no. With or without the new complex, the personnel department is part of overhead costs. Its operating expenses would only be affected if the planned investment generates additional costs – for example, recruitment expenses.

However, design and overheads will be priced into the ticket charged for entry to the new complex.

A perfume company is about to launch a new product line that may cut sales of its older perfumes by half. Should this decline be factored into the calculation of the investment's return? Yes, because the new product line will prompt a shift in consumer behaviour: the decline in cash flow from the older perfume stems directly from the introduction of this new product.

When estimating cash flows on an incremental basis, one only considers the future cash flows arising from the investment. Our objective is to calculate the investment's marginal contribution to the company's profitability.

SECTION 3

Nevertheless, we can mention that in certain very specific sectors with very low marginal costs, this reasoning may lead to overinvestment creating over capacity and therefore price wars.

3/ REASON IN TERMS OF OPPORTUNITY

For financial managers, an asset's value is its market value, which is the price at which it can be bought (investment decision) or sold (divestment decision). From this standpoint, its book or historic value is of no interest whatsoever, except for tax purposes (taxes payable on book capital gains, tax credit on capital losses, etc.).

The opportunity principle boils down to some very simple rules:

- if a company decides to hold on to a business, this implies that it should be prepared to buy that business (if it did not already own it) in identical operating circumstances; and
- if a company decides to hold on to a financial security that is trading at a given price, this security is identical to one that it should be prepared to buy (if it did not already own it) at the same price.

Financial managers are, in effect, "asset dealers". They must introduce this approach within their company, even if it means standing up to other managers who view their respective business operations as essential and viable. Only by systematically confronting these two viewpoints can a company balance its decision-making and management processes.

For example, if a project is carried out on company land that was previously unused, the land's after-tax resale value must be considered when valuing the investment. After all, in principle, the company can choose between selling the land and booking the after-tax sales price, or using the land for the new project. Note that the book value of the land does not enter into this line of reasoning.

Theoretically, a financial manager does not view any activity as essential, regardless of whether it is one of the company's core businesses or a potential new venture. The CFO must constantly be prepared to question each activity and reason in terms of:

- buying and selling assets; and
- entering or withdrawing from an economic sector of activity.

If we push our reasoning to the extreme, we could say that for financial managers an investment is never a necessity, but simply a "good or bad" opportunity.

4/ DISREGARD THE TYPE OF FINANCING

When comparing an investment's return with its cost of financing (what we will call weighted average cost of capital in Chapter 30), the two items must be considered separately.

In practice, since the discount rate is the cost of financing the investment (weighted average cost of capital), interest expense, repayments or dividends should not be included in the flows. **Only operating and investment flows are taken into account, but never financing flows. This is the same distinction that was made in Chapter 2.** Failure to do so would skew the project's net present value. This would also overstate its IRR, since the impact of financing would be included twice:

- first within the weighted average cost of capital for this investment which is its cost of financing; and
- second at the cash flow level.

Consider, for example, an investment with the following flows:

Year	0	1	2	3
Investment flows	− 100	15	15	115

The NPV of this investment is 7.2 (if cash flows are discounted at 12%) and its IRR is 15%. Now, assume that 20% of the investment was financed by debt at an annual after-tax cost of 6%. Then it is possible to deduct the debt flows from the investment flows and calculate its NPV and IRR:

Year	0	1	2	3
Investment flows	−100	15.0	15.0	115.0
Debt financing flows	20	−1.2	−1.2	−21.2
Net flows to equity	−80	13.8	13.8	93.8

With a rate of 12%, the NPV is 10.1 and the IRR is 17.2%. Now, if 50% of the investment were financed by debt, the NPV would rise to 14.4 and the IRR to 24%. At 80% debt-financing, NPV works out to 18.7 and the IRR to 51%.

This demonstrates that by taking on various degrees of debt, it is possible to manipulate the NPV and IRR. This is the same as using the financial leverage that was discussed in Chapter 12. However, this is a slippery slope. It can lead unwary companies to invest in projects whose low industrial profitability is offset by high debt, which in fact increases the risk considerably.

All that matters is the investment's return *per se*.

When debt increases, so does the required return on equity as the risk increases for shareholders, as we have seen in Chapter 12. It is not correct to continue valuing NPV at a constant discount rate of 12%. The discount rate has to be raised in conjunction with the level of debt. This corrects our reasoning and NPV remains constant. The IRR is now higher, but the minimum required return has risen as well to reflect the greater degree of risk of an investment financed by borrowings.

It would be absurd to believe that one can undertake an investment because it generates an IRR of 10% whereas the corresponding debt can be financed at a rate of 7%. In fact, the debt is only available because the company has equity that acts as collateral for creditors. Equity has to be remunerated, and this is not reflected in the 7% interest on the

SECTION 3

debt. No company can be fully financed by debt, and it is therefore impossible to establish a direct comparison between the cost of debt and the project's return.

5/ CONSIDER TAXATION

Clearly taxation is an issue because corporate executives endeavour to maximise their **after-tax** flows. Consider that:

- additional depreciation generates tax savings that must be factored into the equation;
- the cash flows generated by the investment give rise to taxes, which must be included as well; and
- certain tax shields offer tax credits, rebates, subsidies, allowances and other advantages for carrying out investment projects.

In practice, it is better to value a project using after-tax cash flows and an after-tax discount rate in order to factor in the various tax benefits from an investment. Therefore, the return required by investors and creditors is calculated after tax.

In cases where cash flows are discounted before tax, it is important to ascertain that all flows and components of weighted average cost of capital are considered before taxes as well.

When considering an investment, it is also necessary to look at the tax implications.

6/ BE CONSISTENT!

Finally, the best advice is to always be consistent. If the base of valuation is on constant euro values – that is, excluding inflation – be sure that the discount rate excludes inflation as well. We recommend using current euro values, because the discount rate already includes the market's inflation expectations.

If it is a pre-tax valuation, make sure the discount rate reflects the pre-tax required rate of return. We recommend using after-tax valuations because a world without taxes only exists in textbooks!

And if flows are denominated in a given currency, the discount rate must correspond to the interest rate in that currency as well.

Section 29.3
WHICH CASH FLOWS ARE IMPORTANT?

In practice, three types of cash flow must be considered when assessing an investment: **operating flows, investment flows and extraordinary flows**. Financial managers try to plan both the amount of a cash flow and its timing. In other words, they draw up projections of the cash flows on the investment.

Where the investment has a limited life, it is possible to anticipate its cash flows over the entire period. But, in general, the duration of an investment is not predetermined, and one assumes that at some point in the future it will be either wound up or sold. This means that the financial manager has to forecast all cash flows over a given period with an explicit forecast period, and reason in terms of *residual (or salvage) value* beyond that horizon. Although the discounted residual value is frequently very low since it is very far off in time, it should not be neglected. Its book value is generally zero, but its economic value may be quite significant since accounting depreciation may differ from economic depreciation. The residual value reflects the flows extending beyond the explicit investment horizon, and on into infinity. If some of the assets may be sold off, one must also factor in any taxes on capital gains.

1/ OPERATING FLOWS

The investment's contribution to total earnings before interest, taxes, depreciation and amortisation (EBITDA) must be calculated. It represents the difference between the additional income and expenses arising from the investment, excluding depreciation and amortisation.

Then from EBITDA, the **theoretical** tax on the additional operating profit must be deducted. The actual tax is then calculated by multiplying the effective tax rate with the differential on the operating profit, taking into account any tax loss carryforwards.

In other words:[1]

$$\text{Operating flows} = \text{EBITDA} - \text{EBIT} \times T_C$$

where T_c is the corporate tax rate.

2/ INVESTMENT FLOWS

The definition of investment is quite inclusive, ranging from investments in working capital to investments in fixed assets.

It is essential to deduct changes in working capital from EBITDA. Unfortunately, many people tend to forget this. In most cases, working capital is just a matter of a time lag. It builds up gradually, grows with the company and is retrieved when the business is discontinued. A euro capitalised today in working capital can be retrieved in ten years' time, but it will not be worth the same. Money invested in working capital is not lost. It is simply capitalised until the investment is discontinued. However, this capitalisation carries a cost, which is reflected in the discounted amount.

Investment in fixed assets comprises investment in production capacity and growth, whether in the form of tangible assets (machinery, land, buildings, etc.) or intangible assets (research and development, patents and licences, etc.) or financial assets (shares in subsidiaries) for external growth.

The calculation must be made for each period, as the investment is not necessarily restricted to just 1 year, nor spread evenly over the period. Once again, remember that our approach is based on cash and not accounting data. The investment flows must be recognised when they are paid, not when the decisions to make them were incurred. And finally, do not forget to reason in terms of net investment; that is, after any disposals, investment subsidies and other tax credits.

1 *The same result can be obtained with the following formula:*

Operating flows = EBIT $\times (1 + T_C)$ + Depreciation and Amortisation

SECTION 3

3/ Extraordinary flows

It may seem surprising to mention extraordinary items when projecting estimated cash flows. However, financial managers frequently know in advance that certain expenses that have not been booked under EBITDA (litigation, tax audits, etc.) will be disbursed in the near future. These expenses must all be included on an after-tax basis in the calculation of estimated free cash flow.

Extraordinary flows can usually be anticipated at the beginning of the period since they reflect known items. Beyond a two-year horizon, it is generally assumed that they will be zero.

This gives us the following cash flow table:

Periods	0	1	. . .	n
Incremental EBITDA	+	+	+	
− Incremental tax on operating profit		−	−	−
− Change in incremental working capital R		− −	−	+ +
− Investments	− − −	−	−	
+ Divestments after tax	+	+	+	+ +
− Extraordinary expenses		−		
= Cash flow to be discounted	− −	+	+	+ +

Section 29.4
Other investment criteria

1/ The payback period

The payback period is the time necessary to recover the initial outlay on an investment. Where annual cash flows are identical, the payback period is equal to:

$$\frac{\text{Investment}}{\text{Annual cash flow}}$$

For the following investment:

Period	0	1	2	3	4	5
Cash flows	−2.1	0.8	0.8	0.8	0.8	0.8

the payback period is $2.1/0.8 = 2.6$ years.

Where the annual flows are not identical, the cumulative cash flows are compared with the amount invested, as below:

Period	0	1	2	3	4	5
Cash flows	−1	0.3	0.4	0.4	0.5	0.2
Cumulative cash flows		0.3	0.7	1.1	1.6	1.8

The cumulative flow is 0.7 for period 2 and 1.1 for period 3. The payback period is thus 2–3 years. A linear interpolation gives us a payback period of 2.75 years.

Once the payback period has been calculated, it is compared with an arbitrary cut-off date determined by the financial manager. If the payback period is longer than the cut-off period, the investment should be rejected. Clearly, when the perceived risk on the investment is high, the company will look for a very short payback period in order to get its money back before it is too late!

The payback ratio is used as an indicator of an investment's risk and profitability. However, it can lead to the wrong decision, as shown in the example below of investments A and B.

	Flows in period 0	Flows in period 1	Flows in period 2	Flows in period 3	Recovery within	20% NPV
Investment A	−1000	500	400	600	2 years and 2 months	42
Investment B	−1000	500	500	100	2 years	−178

The payback rule would prompt us to choose investment B, even though investment A has positive NPV, but B does not. The payback rule can be misleading because it does not take all flows into account. It emphasises the liquidity of an investment rather than its value.

Moreover, because it considers that a euro today is worth the same as a euro tomorrow, the payback rule does not factor in the time value of money. To remedy this, one sometimes calculates a discounted payback period representing the time needed for the project to have positive NPV. Returning to the example, it then becomes:

Year	0	1	2	3	4	5
Cumulative present values	−2.1	−1.43	−0.88	−0.41	−0.03	0.29

The discounted payback period is now 4 years compared with 2.6 years before discounting. Discounted or not, the payback period is a risk indicator, since the shorter it is, the lower the risk of the investment. **That said, it ignores the most fundamental aspect of risk: the uncertainty of estimating liquidity flows.** Therefore, it is just an approximate indicator since it only measures liquidity.

However, the payback ratio is fully suited to productive investments that affect neither the company's level of activity nor its strategy. Its very simplicity encourages employees to suggest productivity improvements that can be seen to be profitable without having to perform lengthy calculations. It only requires common sense. However, calculating flows in innovative sectors can be something of a shot in the dark. Also, the payback rule tends to favour investments with a high turnover rate. As a result, it has come under quite a bit of criticism because it can only compare investments that are similar.

2/ RETURN ON CAPITAL EMPLOYED

The return on capital employed (ROCE) represents wealth created over the year divided by capital employed. Wealth created is equal to after-tax operating profit, while the capital employed is the sum of fixed assets and the working capital generated by the investment.

$$ROCE = \frac{\text{Operating income after tax}}{\text{Net average fixed assets} + \text{Net average working capital}}$$

This ratio has a strong accounting bias, and is frequently just a comparison between the project's operating profit and the average book value of fixed assets and working capital. The average accounting return can then be calculated, which is the annual ROCE over the life of the investment. The computation of ROCE takes into account the after-tax operating profit and capital employed (working capital plus the residual investment after depreciation).

Depreciation plays a detrimental role, as shown in the example below of an initial investment of 500 generating annual EBITDA of 433 for 5 years. With stable working capital of 500 and a 40% tax rate, the free cash flow projection is as follows:

	31/12/y	y + 1	y + 2	y + 3	y + 4	y + 5
EBITDA		433	433	433	433	433
Tax		−133	−133	−133	−133	−133
Changes in working capital	−500	0	0	0	0	+500
Investment	−500					
Free cash flow	−1000	+300	+300	+300	+300	+800

The investment's IRR works out at 23.75%. What is its return on capital employed?

Assuming the asset is depreciated on a straight-line basis over five years, it then gives:

	$y+1$	$y+2$	$y+3$	$y+4$	$y+5$
After-tax operating profit	200	200	200	200	200
Average net asset value (NAV) of investment	450	350	250	150	50
Average working capital	500	500	500	500	500
ROCE	21 %	24 %	27 %	31 %	36 %

If the declining balance method of depreciation is used (40%, 30%, 20%, 5% and 5%), this yields:

	$y+1$	$y+2$	$y+3$	$y+4$	$y+5$
After-tax operating profit	140	170	200	245	245
Average NAV of investment	400	225	100	37.5	12.5
Average working capital	500	500	500	500	500
ROCE	16%	23%	33%	46%	48%

So, what is the return on capital employed? In the first case, it averages 29.8% and in the second case it is 35%. Do you really believe that just changing an accounting method can influence the intrinsic profitability of a project? Of course not, and this example clearly illustrates the flaw inherent in the criteria.

Although the highest returns are usually obtained on projects with the longest durations, accounting rates of return do not take into account the dates of the flows. Hence, they generally tend to overstate returns. Another drawback with accounting rates of return is that they maximise rates without considering the corresponding risk.

On the surface, it may seem that there is no connection between return on capital employed and the internal rate of return. The first discounts flows while the second calculates book wealth. And yet, taken over a year, their outcomes are identical. An amount of 100 that increases to 110 a year later has an IRR of $100 = 110/(1+r)$, so $r = 10\%$ and an ROCE of 10/100, or 10%.

ROCE and IRR are equal over a given period of time. ROCE is therefore calculated by period, while IRR and NPV are computed for the entire life of the investment.

Although accounting rates of return should not be used as investment or financing criteria, they can be useful financial control tools.

Sooner or later, a discounted return has to be translated into an accounting rate of return. If not, the investment has not generated the anticipated ex-post return and has not achieved its purpose. We strongly advise you to question any differences between IRR and ROCE, i.e. are income flows distributed or retained, do profits arise unevenly over the period (starting out slowly or not at all and then gathering momentum), what is the terminal value, etc.?

3/ CAPITAL RATIONING AND THE PRESENT VALUE INDEX

Sometimes there is a strict capital constraint imposed on the firm, and it is faced with more NPV positive projects than it can afford. In order to determine which project to pursue, the best formula to use is the **present value index (PVI)**. This is the present value of cash inflows divided by the present value of cash outflow:

$$PVI = \frac{\text{Present value of inflows}}{\text{Present value of outflows}}$$

By using the PVI, financial managers can rank the different projects and then select the investment with the highest PVI – that is, the project with the highest NPV relative to the present value of outflows. After making this selection, if the total amount of capital available has not been fully exhausted, the managers should then invest in the project with the second-highest PVI, and so on until no more capital remains to invest.

More generally, the objective is to compare all combinations of x projects that meet the budget and find the one that maximises the *weighted average PVI:*

$$PVI = \frac{\text{PV outflows Project } A}{\text{Total funds available}} \times \left(PVI_A\right) + \ldots + \frac{\text{PV outflows Project } X}{\text{Total funds available}} \times \left(PVI_X\right)$$

SUMMARY

The summary of this chapter can be downloaded from www.vernimmen.com.

The criteria on which investment decisions are based include:

- first and foremost, net present value (NPV), which is the best criterion because it measures the value creation of the investment;

- the internal rate of return (IRR), which measures the yield to maturity of the investment; and

- if necessary and to simplify calculations, the payback ratio, which measures the amount of time needed to pay back the investment, and the return on capital employed (operating profit after tax for the period divided by capital employed for the period), which is more of a financial control tool.

The flows that are used for calculating NPV and IRR are free cash flows:

- EBITDA on the investment;

- corporate income tax calculated on the operating income of the investment;

- change in working capital created by the investment;

- capital expenditure (including any divestments).

    To avoid making errors, it is necessary to:

- reason only in terms of cash flow, not charges and revenues;

- reason in terms of incremental flows – i.e. consider the cash flows arising on the investment, all the cash flows arising on the investment and only the cash flows arising on the investment. This involves calculating the investment's marginal contribution to the company's cash flows;

- reason in terms of opportunity – i.e. in financial values and not in book values;

- disregard the way in which the investment was financed – flows used in the calculations never include financial income and expenditure, new loans and repayment of loans, capital increases and capital reductions or dividends;

- consider ordinary taxation (on operating profits) or exceptional taxes (on capital gains, subsidies, etc.); and

- finally, the best advice is to **be consistent!**

In the business world, the differences between practice and theory in investment decisions are diminishing. Financial managers now look increasingly at NPV and IRR when making investment decisions.

QUESTIONS

SECTION 3

1/When making an investment decision, should you reason:

- ○ in terms of cash flow?
- ○ marginally?
- ○ without regard to the type of financing?
- ○ with consideration for taxation?

2/Define the payback ratio.

3/What are the drawbacks of the payback ratio?

4/Define return on capital employed.

5/Can an investment decision be based on return on capital employed?

6/What purpose does the return on capital employed serve?

7/What roles do depreciation and amortisation play in the calculation of cash flows to be discounted?

8/What is the optimal depreciation method for a company that is not taxed? What about for a company that pays tax at the standard rate?

9/A company is planning to build a new plant to replace an older one that is to be demolished. What are the most important flows to consider?

(a) market value of the land and the older plant;
(b) demolition costs;
(c) costs of building an access road the previous year;
(d) production losses while an old plant is demolished and a new one is being built;
(e) depreciation of the plant;
(f) tax credits on the investment;
(g) part of the salary of the managing director;
(h) constitution of working capital?

10/When can investment in working capital be neglected?

11/Provide examples of investments where residual value must under no circumstances be neglected.

12/In an inflationary environment, how should you reason in evaluating an investment?

13/When operating cash flow is negative, should IRR and NPV be calculated including the interest expense on loans used to finance it?

14/Should an investment subsidy be included in investment flows or by reducing the discount rate?

More questions are waiting for you at www.vernimmen.com.

EXERCISES

1/ The following investment project is submitted to you:

- Project: extension of an industrial plant;
- purchase of equipment €20m;
- set-up costs €1.5m;
- useful life 8 years;
- residual value 0;
- increase in working capital €2.5m.

The project will result in an increase in EBITDA of €3m per year, over the 8 years during which the new asset is used. The equipment is depreciated over 5 years. The corporate income tax rate is 40%.

(a) Draw up the cash flow schedule for the project, on the basis of straight-line depreciation.
(b) Calculate each of the two cases:
  - net present value at 10%;
  - the internal rate of return of the project.

2/ A company is planning to replace a machine with a new, better-performing one. The figures for the investment are as follows:

- Purchase of new machine:
  - cost €2m;
  - useful life 5 years, residual value nil;
  - linear depreciation over 5 years;
  - savings on charges €0.8m per year.
- Sale of second-hand machine:
  - purchase cost €1.5m (machine bought the previous year);
  - linear depreciation over 5 years (residual value is nil);
  - net book value today €1.2m;
  - potential sale price €1.0m.

If the tax rate on profits and capital gains/losses is 40%, what is the "value" for the company of the new machine the company is planning to buy (this company's required rate of return is 12%)?

Calculate the net present value and the internal rate of return of the planned investment.

3/ Take the following project:

Period	0	1	2	3	4	5
Cash flow	−100	110	−30	25	50	100

What problem do you come up against when calculating the payback ratio? What is the NPV of this project at 10%? What is the internal rate of return?

4/ The Catalunia region is prepared to pay €2m to a private company to run a bus service three times a day between Lerida and Tarragona, for a period of 10 years. The initial outlay for the project is estimated at €0.8m, but annual operating losses (excluding depreciation) will amount to €0.2m. What is the NPV for this investment? If the private company's required rate of return is 10%, will it take up the contract? And if it is 15%?

5/ Industrial Electric plc estimates its needs for a component used in its products at 7000 units per year for the next 10 years. A subcontractor offers to supply the parts at €5 per unit.

Industrial Electric can make the part in its own workshops for €3 per unit, if it buys a new machine. A new machine would cost €78 000, have a useful life of 10 years and a residual value of nil. The company generally gets a 10% return (after tax) on its capital expenditure. It depreciates machinery on a straight-line basis and tax is levied at a rate of 35%.

Should the company accept the subcontractor's offer?

6/ A large oil company has been invited to get involved in a project to build a parking facility in the centre of Frankfurt. The project includes a 450-car public parking lot, a 200-car garage and a petrol station covering 1000 sq.m. It will take one year to build and a 30-year concession to run the facility will be granted by the municipality (after construction has been completed). Total capital expenditure will be €8 400 000 and working capital will be nil. The annual income statement for the project after the construction looks like this:

Costs		Revenues	
Operating costs	670 000	Parking places	1 680 000
Depreciation and amortisation	280 000	Garage	770 000
Income tax expense	1 000 000	Petrol station	800 000
Net profits	1 300 000		
	3 250 000		3 250 000

Calculate the average of the accounting returns on the project, the discounted payback ratio, the net present value at 10% and the internal rate of return. Why is the IRR not equal to the average of the annual returns on the project?

7/ A year ago, Robin plc invested in a machine to improve the manufacturing of one of its products. It has just discovered that a new machine has come onto the market which would improve performance more than the one it bought. The first machine cost €8000 a year ago, and is depreciated on a straight-line basis over 8 years (the same period as its useful life, after which it will be scrapped). If it were sold now, the company would get around €5000 (tax credit on the capital loss would be 40%).

The new machine costs €11 000 and would be depreciated for €10 500 on a straight-line basis over its useful life, estimated at 7 years. It could be sold at the end of its useful life for €500, which is what its book value would be.

The company is hoping to produce 100 000 units of its product annually for the next 7 years. With the equipment currently in use, the company's per unit cost price breaks down as follows: €0.14 per unit in direct labour costs, €0.10 for raw materials and €0.14 in general costs. The new machine will enable the company to cut direct labour costs to €0.12 per unit produced. The cost of raw materials will drop to €0.09 per unit thanks to a reduction in waste. General costs will remain at €0.14 per unit. All other factors will remain unchanged, in particular supplies, energy consumed and maintenance costs. Profits are taxed at 40%.

(a)   Draw up the cash flow schedule for the contemplated investment.
(b)   Calculate the discounted payback ratio on this investment.

8/Pincer plc is hoping to increase sales by granting its customers longer payment periods. Its annual sales currently stand at €1m and it gives its customers an average of 30 days to pay.

The company made the following assumptions when defining its customer credit policy.

Extension of payment period	Increase in sales
15 days	€40 000
30 days	€60 000
45 days	€70 000
60 days	€75 000

The sales price of a manufactured unit is €4 and the cost price is €3.2, including €1 in fixed costs. What policy should the company introduce if it requires a 20% return (before tax) on its capital invested (its inventories are financed through supplier credit)?

Pincer has also made the following forecasts for bad debts:

Extension of payment period	Bad debts (Sales)
15 days	2%
30 days	2.5%
45 days	3%
60 days	4%

Bad debts currently only account for 1.2% of debts. Which policy should the company introduce?

Questions

1/; 2/; 3/; 4/; 5/ and 6/ *see chapter.*
7/ *In calculating tax.*
8/ *It makes no difference. Depreciation is quicker.*
9/ *(a) yes; (b) yes; (c) no; (d) yes; (e) tax point of view; (f) yes; (g) no; (h) yes.*
10/ *When it is negligible!*
11/ *Investment in real estate.*
12/ *In current euro values.*
13/ *No, never, negative flows are part of capital expenditure in finance just as the purchase of a fixed asset is.*
14/ *In investment flows, because it is deducted from the flows to be invested and not from the risk, which remains the same.*

Exercises

A detailed Excel version of the solutions is available at www.vernimmen.com.

1/

Year	0	1	2	3	4	5	6	7	8
− investment flows	−21.5								
+ Δ EBITDA		3	3	3	3	3	3	3	3
− Δ working capital		2.5							−2.5
− Δ taxes		−0.4	−0.4	−0.4	−0.4	−0.4	1.2	1.2	1.2
= cash flows	−21.5	0.9	3.4	3.4	3.4	3.4	1.8	1.8	4.3

NPV = −6.9. IRR = 0.9%

2/

Year	0	1	2	3	4	5
− purchase of new machine	−2					
+ sale of old machine	1					
+ tax credit on capital loss	−0.2 × 40%					
+ cost savings after tax		0.8−60%	0.48	0.48	0.48	0.48
+ tax savings on incremental depreciation and amortisation		0.1−40%	0.04	0.04	0.04	0.04
= cash flows to be discounted	−0.92	0.52	0.52	0.52	0.52	0.64

NPV = 1. IRR = 50%

3/ *Difficult to calculate payback period as investment is made in two phases. NPV = 90.23. IRR = 42.64%*

4/ *At 10% no, at 15% yes.*

5/ *Yes, because the NPV on the investment is −€5310.*

6/ *1.58/(8.4 − 0)/2 = 60%, 7 years and 9 months. NPV at 10% = €6.5m. IRR = 18.7%. As the average accounting return is heavily influenced by the rate of the last year which is very high (464%) because the asset is practically fully depreciated.*

7/ *Figures for year 0: 5000 (sale of old machine) −11 000 (purchase of new machine) +800 (tax credit at 40% of capital loss on sale of old machine) = 5200. Years 1 to 7: (100 000 × 0.03 − (8000/8 − 10 500/7)) × 60% + (8000/8 − 10 500/7) = 2000. Year: 500. Payback ratio: around 3 years.*

8/ *(a) Extend the period to 30 because NPV would then be the highest at €9300 for one year.*
   (b) The 60-day period extension is the only one for which NPV is negative.

BIBLIOGRAPHY

For more on techniques used for making investment decisions:

H. Bierman, S. Smidt, *The Capital Budgeting Decision*, Macmillan Company, 1992.
T. Copeland, T. Koller, J. Murrin, *Valuation. Measuring and Managing the Value of Companies*, 3rd edn, John Wiley & Sons, Inc., 2000.
A. Damodaran, *Corporate Finance. Theory and Practice,* 2nd edn, John Wiley & Sons, Inc., 2002.

Surveys regarding the popularity of capital budgeting techniques:

R. Bruner, K. Eades, R. Harris, R. Higgins, Best practice in estimating the cost of capital: Survey and synthesis, *Financial Practice and Education*, 13–28, Spring/Summer 1998.
M. Dallocchio, A. Salvi, *Capital structure and dividend policies of European firms. A research survey*, SDA Bocconi working paper collection, 2000.
L. Gitman, J.R. Forrester, A survey of capital budgeting techniques used by major US firms, *Financial Management*, **6**, 66–71, 1977.
J. Graham, C. Harvey, The theory and practice of corporate finance: Evidence from the field, *Journal of Financial Economics*, **60**, 187–243, May 2001.
J.H. Hall, *An empirical investigation of the capital budgeting process*, working paper, University of Pretoria, 2000.
L. Lumby, *Investment Appraisal and Investment Decision*, 4th edn, Chapman & Hall, 1991.
E. Trahan, L. Gitman, Bridging the theory–practice gap in corporate finance: a survey of chief financial officers, *Quarterly Review of Economics and Finance*, **1**, 73–87, Spring 1995.

SECTION 3

Chapter 30
THE COST OF CAPITAL

Mirror, mirror on the wall . . .

Determining the cost of capital, or the weighted average cost of capital, is not a simple task, but it is one of the fundamentals of finance. The cost of capital has to be factored into investment decisions because it is the rate that is used for discounting cash flows for NPV or comparing with the IRR. Cost of capital is also used to determine enterprise value (see Chapter 32). Truly, its importance can hardly be understated.

But before reading on, it is imperative to understand the distinction between cost of capital, which is the weighted average cost of the capital contributed to the firm, and the cost of equity, which is just one component of the weighted average of the cost of capital.

Section 30.1
THE COST OF CAPITAL AND THE RISK OF ASSETS

The cost of capital is the minimum rate of return on the company's investments that can satisfy both shareholders (the cost of equity) and debtholders (the cost of debt). The cost of capital is thus the company's total cost of financing.

When markets are in equilibrium, any investor with a perfectly diversified portfolio holds a fraction of both the company's equity and its debt. This is known as the CAPM, as was discussed in Chapter 19. In other words, each investor holds a share of the company's operating assets, since this is equal to the sum of equity and net debt. Accordingly, each investor has some exposure to the risk arising from the company.

The rate of return required by investors thus depends on just one factor: **the risk arising from the assets-in-place**. This means that the cost of the company's financial resources – its cost of capital – is none other than the rate of return required by investors, which is a function of the risk on capital employed.

The cost of capital depends solely on the risk of the assets-in-place, specifically its systematic risk, since unsystematic or specific risks are not remunerated.

The cost of capital is thus shaped by the economic characteristics of each sector of activity. It rises when fixed costs are high or the business is cyclical, and falls when the business operates more on variable costs or is easily predictable.

Modigliani and Miller (1958) and Miller (1977)[1] were the first to state that the company's cost of capital is not a function of its capital structure (see Chapter 33). If the risk

1 *See Chapters 33 and 34.*

on capital employed is such that it requires a 12% rate of return, and if it is fully equity-financed, shareholders will expect a minimum 12% return. On the other hand, if it is fully debt-financed, creditors will again require a 12% rate of return since they incur the same risk with the operating assets as the shareholders in the previous example. Lastly, suppose financing is *equally* divided between debt and equity. If the cost of debt is 10%, then shareholders will require a 14% return on equity to achieve a weighted average of 12%, i.e. the remuneration justified by the 12% risk for capital employed or the cost of capital.

Assume that, in a perfect market, the company changes its capital structure – for example, by buying back some of its equity via the issue of new debt. In this case, an investor with a perfectly diversified portfolio who holds 1% of the company's equity and 1% of its debt and thus 1% of its capital employed will continue to hold 1% of capital employed, though now with a lower amount of equity because of the share buy-back and a higher percentage of net debt. The transaction is thus totally neutral for the investor. It will not affect the cost of capital, even if it is now divided between the cost of debt and the cost of equity, because the risk on capital employed remains unchanged.

As we have already discussed, the cost of capital is equal to the weighted average costs of net debt and of net equity. This will be examined in greater detail in the next section.

The cost of capital is not the weighted average of two separate costs. The overall riskiness of the company is represented by the cost of capital, whose two key components are debt and equity. The costs of equity and debt are a function of the risk of the assets, the cost of overall capital, and the respective weighting of each.

For purely practical reasons, however, the cost of capital is calculated by taking the costs of debt and equity together.

Section 30.2
ALTERNATIVE METHODS FOR ESTIMATING THE COST OF CAPITAL

The cost of capital can be calculated in three ways: directly, indirectly or via enterprise value.

1/ DIRECT CALCULATION VIA THE β OF ASSETS

Since a company's liabilities merely provide a "screen" between the asset side of the company and the financial market, the rate of return required to satisfy investors is equal to the risk-free rate plus a risk premium related to the company's activity.

Applying the CAPM gives us:

$$k = r_{\text{F}} + \beta_{\text{A}} \times \left(r_{\text{M}} - r_{\text{F}} \right)$$

where k is the weighted average cost of capital, r_{F} the risk-free rate, r_{M} the market rate of return and β_{A} the **beta of assets** or **unlevered beta;** that is, the β of a debt-free company.

Just as the beta of a security measures the deviation between its returns and those of the market, so too does the beta of an asset measure the deviation between its future cash flows and those of the market. Yet these two betas are not independent. A firm that invests in projects with a high β_A – in other words, projects that are risky – will have a high β_E on its shares because its profitability will fluctuate widely.

	Asset beta		Asset beta
Hotels	0.40	Advertising	0.68
Highways	0.40	IT (services)	0.69
Telecom operators	0.41	Internet	0.72
Consumer goods	0.51	Car parts	0.99
Beer	0.51	Retail – jewellery	1.08
Tobacco	0.51	Temporary recruitment	1.22
Food retail	0.56	Oil services	1.38
Food	0.59	Mining	1.39
IT (software)	0.65	Life insurance	1.44
All sectors[2]	**0.68**	IT (hardware)	1.70

Source: BNP Paribas Corporate Finance, Business Valuation Team, May 2011

2 *This figure is lower than 1 since it is not the β of all shares on the market that average 1 but the β excluding the impact of net debt.*

The β_A can be easily computed knowing that it is equal to the weighted average of the β of equity and the β of debt:

$$\beta_{Asset} = \beta_{Equity} \times \frac{V_E}{V_E + V_D} + \beta_{Debt} \times \frac{V_D}{V_E + V_D}$$

β_A can also be expressed as follows:

$$\beta_{Asset} = \frac{\beta_{Equity} + \beta_{Debt} \times \dfrac{V_D}{V_E}}{1 + \dfrac{V_D}{V_E}}$$

β_{Debt} corresponds to the beta of the net debt and it should be computed exactly the same way as the beta of equity, which is by regressing the returns on listed debt against market returns of the debt of the same credit quality. However, it is reasonable to assume that β_{Debt} is equal to zero for weakly-leveraged companies. Thus, the previous equation can be simplified as follows:

$$\beta_{Asset} = \frac{\beta_{Equity}}{1 + \dfrac{V_D}{V_E}}$$

We believe that it is not reasonable to simplify the analysis by assuming that $\beta_{Debt} = 0$ if the leverage of a company is not negligible. In fact, the higher the leverage the less the

SECTION 3

financial debt depends on the level of interest rates and the more will be linked to the specific characteristics of the company (fixed costs/variable costs) and its industry (cyclicality). In these cases, debt then begins to behave more like equity in terms of beta characteristics.

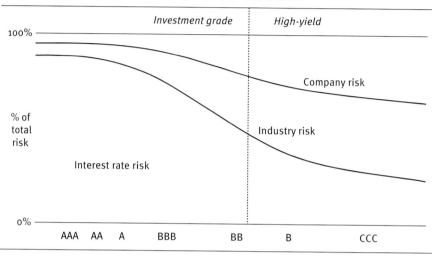

INVESTMENT GRADE – HIGH YIELD

Often, our readers will read that financial analysts prefer using the following formula:

$$\beta_A = \frac{\beta_{Equity}}{\left[1 + (1 - T_C) \times \dfrac{V_D}{V_E}\right]}$$

This way of computing β_A assumes two strong assumptions, following Modigliani and Miller's (1963) propositions:

1. the company can borrow at the risk-free rate, whatever its capital structure is;
2. the value of the firm is equal to the unlevered value plus the value of the tax shield of debt, computed as the product of the net debt multiplied by the corporate tax rate.

Although these two assumptions are useful for simplifying the analysis, they are frequently unrealistic. The first, because even the borrowing rate of companies with AAA rating includes a credit spread (0.3% for Microsoft, for example). The second, because the financial distress costs are not considered in the analysis, even if their magnitude is close to the value of the tax shield for highly levered companies.

2/ INDIRECT CALCULATION

In practice, to determine the rate of return required by all of the company's providers of funds, it is necessary to **calculate the cost of capital by valuing the various securities issued by the company**.

THE WEIGHTED AVERAGE COST OF CAPITAL

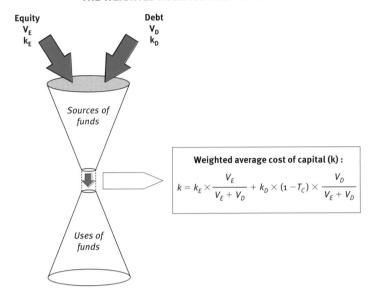

Thus, a company with equity financing of 100 at a rate of 10%, and debt financing of 50 at a pre-tax cost of 5%, has a cost of capital of 7.75% (with a 35% tax rate, T_c).

This is the most frequently used method to calculate the cost of capital. Nevertheless, beware of relying too much on spreadsheets to calculate the cost of capital, instead of getting your hands dirty by working on some examples yourself.

When performing simulations, it is all too tempting to change the company's capital structure while forgetting that the cost of equity and the cost of debt are not constant: they are a function of the company's structure. It is all too easy to reduce the cost of capital on paper by increasing the relative share of net debt, because debt is always cheaper than equity!

In the preceding example, if the share of debt is increased to 80% without changing either the cost of debt or equity, then the cost of capital works out to be 4.6%. **While the arithmetic may be correct, this is totally wrong financially.**

Do not forget that higher debt translates into a higher cost of both equity and net debt, as shown in the graph for food companies.

The cost of capital is related to the value of the securities and represents the amount the company would have to pay to refund all its liabilities, regardless of the cost of its current resources. As such, it symbolises the application of financial market logic to the corporation.

To calculate a company's cost of capital, we determine the rate of return required of each type of security and weight each rate according to its relative share in financing. This is none other than the WACC formula:

$$k = k_{\mathrm{E}} \times \frac{V_{\mathrm{E}}}{V_{\mathrm{E}} + V_{\mathrm{D}}} + k_{\mathrm{D}} \times \left(1 - T_{\mathrm{C}}\right) \times \frac{V_{\mathrm{D}}}{V_{\mathrm{E}} + V_{\mathrm{D}}}$$

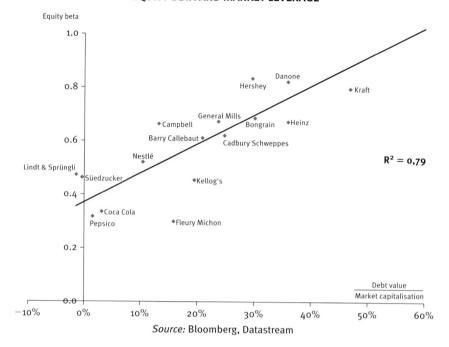

EQUITY BETA AND MARKET LEVERAGE

Source: Bloomberg, Datastream

3/ THE IMPLICIT CALCULATION BASED ON ENTERPRISE VALUE

The cost of capital can be estimated based on enterprise value and a projection of antici-pated future free cash flows, since:

$$V = V_E + V_D = \sum_{t=0}^{\infty} \frac{FCF_t}{(1+k)^t}$$

It is then necessary to solve the equation with k as the unknown factor. However, this calculation is rarely used because it is difficult to determine the market consensus for free cash flows.

4/ THE PITFALLS OF THE INDIRECT COST-OF-CAPITAL CALCULATION

(a) Expected rate of return or effective rate of return?

The cost of capital is a financial concept reflecting the *expected* rate of return **required or expected** by investors at a given point in time. It is not an accounting concept and should not be confused with the *ex post* return on capital employed, which is the **effective** rate of return.

Since it is not an accounting concept, the calculation of the cost of capital should be based on market rather than accounting data.

The cost of capital is neither an inverted P/E, nor the return on equity (ROE) nor the rate of return. Instead, it is the rate of return currently required by shareholders as measured by the CAPM:

$$k_E = r_F + b_E \times (r_M - r_F)$$

The cost of debt is not the cost of debt contracted 10 years, 1 year or 3 months ago. Nor is it the company's average cost of debt or the ratio of financial expenses to average debt for the year, as studied in Chapter 12, which covered the nominal cost of debt.

The cost of net debt is the rate at which the company could refinance its existing debt given its present economic position. It cannot be lower than the risk-free rate.

The tax savings generated by debt are represented by the factor $(1 - T_c)$ as applied to the cost of debt. Remember that cash flow was originally calculated at a marginal tax rate based on operating profit.

It is possible to estimate the rate at which the company can refinance its existing debt using four alternatives:

- use the interest rate paid by the company on a very recent bond issue or syndicated loan; or
- use the yield to maturity of traded debt of the company if any; or
- use the official rating of the company. If the company has a rating given by one of the recognised rating agencies (Standard & Poor's, Moody's, etc.), the analyst should simply use the yield to maturity (YTM) required by financial markets at the time of the valuation for similar securities belonging to that class of rating; or
- create an implicit or synthetic rating. In the case where the company has not got an official rating, then the analyst proceeds by giving the company an **implicit** (or **synthetic**) **rating**. The idea is very simple (albeit difficult when applied!): the analyst tries to replicate the style of analysis performed by rating agencies in order to arrive at a reasonable approximation of the rating that the company could have received from such an agency. Once we have the implicit rating, the analyst uses the yield to maturity required on financial markets for the obtained class of rating. The reader should refer to our website for an exhaustive description of the process of implicit ratings.

(b) Accounting or market values of equity and debt?

Shareholders base their required rate of return on the market value of equity; that is, the amount at which equity can be bought or sold, rather than using book values. The same reasoning applies to debtholders.

The choice of weighting is based on market values rather than book values.

This is consistent with the idea of selecting the required rate of return rather than the book rate of return. Using the book value of liabilities can be very misleading because it may significantly differ from the market value of equity and debt.

The yield to maturity shown in bond quotations in the financial press is based on the closing market price of a bond, not on its face value. Similarly, the implied cost of equity for a company's cost should be based on the market price per share at which it trades.

3 *Book return on 2010 equity.*
4 *Discounted rate of return on a borrowing listed at 131%.*
5 *This approach is inadequate if debt has options features like caps, floors, call provisions, convertibility options, and so on. In these cases we should use the option framework in order to value these derivatives (see Garbade, 2002).*

For example, the Nestlé shareholder does not require a 14%[3] return on book equity of CHF 62 billion, but a 6.9% return on market capitalisation of CHF 172 billion! Similarly, an investor buying Deutsche Telekom bonds with a nominal yield of 9.25% at a price of 131% of the nominal amount does not require a 9.25% return. Instead, he is looking for 6.6%.[4]

The market value of debt can be estimated without too much difficulty. The process is as follows:[5]

Step 1 Identify the annual contract payments.

Step 2 Determine the credit quality of debt. Credit ratings may be estimated from bond rating models that mimic the behaviour of rating agencies (i.e. an implicit rating).

Step 3 Estimate the yield to maturity for which debt would trade, by reference to current market yields with similar *ratings, maturity and coupons.*

Step 4 Calculate the present value of financing payments, discounting each annual promised payment with the estimated yield to maturity: The result should approximate the market value of debt.

Two comments:

1. This process can be readily applied to just single debt instruments and not only to the entire amount of debt.

2. Step 4 calculations can be simplified if contract payments are constant over time, in which case we can use the following formula:

Estimatedmarket value of debt

$$= \text{Annual interest expenses} \times \frac{(1 - 1/(1 + \text{current YTM})^{\text{maturity of debt}})}{\text{current YTM}}$$

Section 30.3
SOME PRACTICAL APPLICATIONS

1/ FOR THE INVESTMENT DECISION

When making an investment decision, and even if using the indirect method, it is not particularly difficult to calculate the cost of capital. If the company is publicly listed, the calculation is based on readily available market data. Average prices are often used to smooth out any erratic market swings. If the company is not listed, the calculation is based on the cost of capital of companies of comparable size and risk operating in the same sector of activity. If the peer sample has been well chosen, the resulting cost of capital will be the same as that of the unlisted company.

The trick is elsewhere; one should not mix up the cost of capital of the firm and the cost of capital of the project. The two are the same only if the risk level of the project is the same as that of the firm.

If the company is engaging in a greenfield project (e.g. a new oil field for an oil company), it should add to its cost of capital a premium of c. 2%.

If the company invests in a new sector or a new geography, it will not be able to use the cost of capital of the firm to assess the project. The risk of the project will have to be taken into account to determine the cost of capital to be used. The cost of capital will therefore reflect the industry and geographic risk of the project.

The cost of the funds that will be used to finance the project should never be treated as the cost of capital. If the project is financed by debt, the cost of capital to be used will be higher, as the cost of debt takes into account that the firm has equity to secure the repayment of the debt. Alternatively, if the project is financed by new equity, the cost of capital to be used is likely to be lower, as the higher overall equity will make it possible to reduce the risk borne by debt (and equity) holders.

One should not mix up the cost of financing of a project with its cost of capital. The cost of financing will most likely depend on the overall financial health of the firm whereas the cost of capital will only depend on the risk of the project.

2/ FOR VALUATION

The indirect method is less adapted to valuations, because to determine the value of equity one needs the cost of capital (see Chapter 32), and to calculate the cost of capital one needs the cost of equity! However, there are three ways to solve this dilemma:

* **use the parameters associated with a target capital structure**, while being careful to use the costs of equity and net debt that correspond to the target capital structure, and not the present costs;
* **state the equation of the value of equity** (knowing that you need the value of equity to derive the discount rate) and find, by successive approximation, the discount rate that fits. Excel does iterative calculations that will solve this issue. Some other practitioners first use a very rough estimate of the value of equity (derived by the comparables method, for example) and then refine their calculation depending on the results.
* **use the direct method.** The advantage of this alternative is that one avoids the frequent mistake of using costs of equity and debt that do not correspond to the capital structure in question.

3/ DIVERSIFIED COMPANIES

The overall cost of capital of a diversified company can be calculated similarly to a company with a single business. Conversely, the analyst should be cautious if the divisions do not show the same risk profile. In these cases, each division should be analysed separately according to its cost of capital; the weighted average costs of capital of different divisions would then represent the overall cost of capital for the company. As shown in Chapter 32, diversification does not reduce the cost of capital because it only considers systematic risk. As unsystematic risk can be eliminated by diversification; it does not affect the required rate of return.

SECTION 3

4/ MULTINATIONAL COMPANIES

A similar logic applies to companies operating in different countries. A British company investing in Russia, for example, should not use a discount rate based on British data just because its suppliers of funds are British. After all, the project's flows are affected by the Russian systematic risks (inflation, taxation, exchange rates, etc.), rather than the British systematic risk. Therefore, the company should correctly apply a beta reflecting the project's sensitivity to Russian systematic risk.

After the West-based company has invested in Russia, its cost of capital will probably be higher. The difference would be made up of two costs, a lower one for western Europe and a higher one for Russia, reflecting the different levels of systemic risk (political and macroeconomic) in the two regions.

This approach avoids the frequent error of discounting flows denominated in one currency using discount rates denominated in another currency.

5/ EMERGING MARKETS

In developing countries, calculating the cost of capital of an investment raises some practical problems. The risk-free rate of local government bonds is often just wishful thinking, since these countries have little solvency. The local risk-free rate and betas of local peer groups are rarely measured, let alone significant, given the limited size of financial markets in these countries.

We suggest Bancel and Perrotin's (1999) system for calculating the cost of capital in such cases:

	Government bond rate of the euro zone
+	Sovereign spread
+	$\beta_{Equity} \times$ European risk premium
=	Cost of capital in an emerging market

The sovereign *spread* represents the difference between bond yields issued on international markets (in euros or dollars) by the country in question vs. those offered by euro- or dollar-zone bonds. This yield represents the political risk in the emerging country. When the developing nation has not made any international issues, it is possible to use a bond issue by another state with the same credit rating as a benchmark.

When the sovereign spread reflects the fact that the state cannot be considered a risk-free borrower (like Ukraine in mid-2009), we advise using the spread of the best-rated borrower.

β_E is the beta coefficient of the sector of activity calculated in developed financial markets. This parameter measures the sensitivity of an industry's flows to the overall economic environment. It is shaped by the sector of activity, not the country.

Obviously, this rate must be applied to flows that have been converted from their local currencies into euros. If the flows are denominated in dollars, then remember to apply a USD rather than a euro benchmark.

For example, it is possible to calculate the cost of capital of a Chilean investment project based on the following assumptions: $\beta_E = 0.82$, r_F in the US = 5%, a Chilean government bond rate of 7.5%, a US risk premium of = 4%:

$$
\begin{aligned}
& \quad 5\% \\
+ & \quad 7.5\% - 5\% \\
+ & \quad 0.82 \times 4\% \\
= & \quad 10.78\% \text{ on flows denominated in dollars}
\end{aligned}
$$

If the project's flows are denominated in Chilean pesos, the cost of capital is converted from dollars into pesos as follows:

$$
\text{Cost of capital in pesos} = \frac{1 + \text{Cost of capital in US\$}}{\dfrac{1 + \text{Inflation rate in US}}{1 + \text{Inflation rate in Chile}}} - 1
$$

6/ COMPANIES WITH NEGATIVE NET FINANCIAL DEBT

For the purposes of this discussion, disregard negative net debt situations that occur when a company has sold a major asset in order to use the proceeds for another investment – such as the buy-back of shares, etc. – since such a situation is temporary.

Consider a group that, for structural reasons, has net cash of 2 with no banking or financial debt, and equity of 9.

Assume that the shareholders buying these shares understand that they are buying both operating assets with a given risk level and have a cash situation with virtually no risk. In other words, the risk on the share is lower than the risk on the company given the structurally positive net cash balance.

The cost of capital of this company can be estimated using the indirect method applying a **negative value** for V_D. So, in this example, if the cost of equity is 7% and net cash generates 2% after taxes:

$$
k = 7\% \times \frac{9}{9-2} + 2\% \times \frac{-2}{9-2} = 8.4\%
$$

To offer the 7% return required by shareholders, the company would have to invest in projects yielding at least 8.4%. The 7% cost of equity is the weighted average of the required 8.4% return on capital employed and the 2% on net cash.

The company's cost of capital is thus 8.4%.

The cost of capital for a company with a structurally positive cash balance does not differ from that of a company with the same capital employed but no cash. The cost of equity changes, but the cost of capital remains the same.

SECTION 3

Practitioners often use a cost of capital equal to the cost of equity when the firm holds net cash. This is a mistake unless you consider that shareholders do not take into account the security brought by the net cash.

Section 30.4
CAN CORPORATE MANAGERS INFLUENCE THE COST OF CAPITAL?

Chapters 33 and 34 demonstrate why there is little point in using debt and its tax advantages to lower the cost of capital. While net debt costs less than equity, it tends to increase the risk to shareholders, who retaliate by raising the required rate of return and consequently the cost of equity. Debt works to the advantage of the company, because the interest on the net debt can be deducted from its tax base (which it cannot do for dividends). The opposite tends to apply to investors.

In short, in a perfect world in which investors had diversified portfolios, one man's gain would be another man's loss.

Moreover, if debt really did reduce the cost of capital, one would have to wonder why highly efficient companies, such as Rolls Royce, Swatch Group, Toyota, Google and SAP are not levered, given that they have no reason to fear bankruptcy.

Since the cost of capital depends on the risk to the company, the only way it can be lowered is through risk-reducing measures, such as:

- Lowering the breakeven point by shifting from fixed to variable costs, i.e. subcontracting, outsourcing, etc. Unfortunately, the margins will probably decline accordingly.
- Improving the business's visibility and smoothing its cyclical nature, i.e. winning medium-term supply contracts with important clients. Here too, however, margins may be affected since, in exchange, the clients will demand price concessions.
- Diversifying the business does not help as it does not reduce market risk, but rather specific risk, which is the only one to be remunerated.
- Shifting from a risky activity (e.g. a biotech startup) in a high-risk country like Pakistan to a safer business in a more stable country (cheese production in Switzerland), will no doubt cut the cost of capital, but it will also lower profitability. In addition, it would have no impact on value, since it is simply a lateral move in the market.

In conclusion, managers have virtually no means of lowering the cost of capital while simultaneously creating value. Their only viable strategy is to improve the return on capital employed by increasing flows and reducing the amount of capital employed.

Similarly, increasing the risk for capital employed increases the cost of capital, but value will not be destroyed if profitability improves at the same time.

BOUYGUES–IMPACT OF BUSINESS

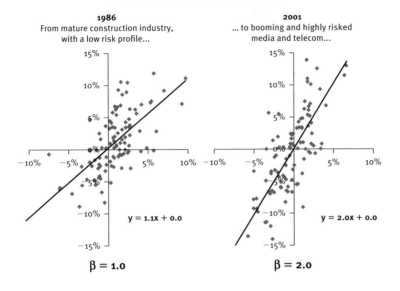

1986
From mature construction industry,
with a low risk profile...

y = 1.1x + 0.0

β = 1.0

2001
... to booming and highly risked
media and telecom...

y = 2.0x + 0.0

β = 2.0

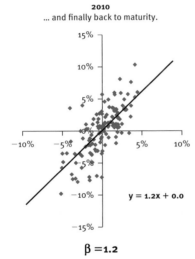

2010
... and finally back to maturity.

y = 1.2x + 0.0

β =1.2

Source: Datastream

The cost of capital of Bouygues increased as it launched media and telecom activities (riskier than its traditional construction operations) and then decreased as these operations matured.

Section 30.5
COST OF CAPITAL: A LOOK AT THE EVIDENCE

A study by Gitman and Vandenberg (2000) compares the cost of capital methodologies of major US corporations in 1997 and 1980. The results show that practitioners have substantially changed their practices for computing the cost of capital.

There is robust evidence that the gap between theory and practice is rapidly narrowing. Firms that use the required return from investors as the primary procedure for the cost of equity capital have increased from 35.6% to 70.3%. Conversely, the use of the historical dividend yields has a lower relevance. It is also important to note that 93% of firms estimating required shareholder return (64.9% out of 70.3%) use CAPM as the preferred cost of equity capital technique.

These results are consistent with those obtained by Graham and Harvey (2001). Their survey provides further evidence of the increasing popularity of the CAPM to calculate the cost of capital.

The most frequent response in 1997 was between 9 and 11% (for 44% of the firms), well below the corresponding response in 1980 (15–17%). The difference between the two values results mainly from the decline in interest rates in the United States. It may also be attributable to a reduction in average risk faced by responding firms.

A final study by Bruner *et al.* (1998) yielded results that are also consistent with previous ones. Here are the main results of their findings:

1. There are different alternatives in the risk-free rate choice. An almost equal percentage of analysts use 10- and 30-year Treasuries, while a lower percentage uses 3-month T-bills.
2. The majority of corporations use published sources for the beta estimation, while around 30% of respondents estimate it themselves.
3. Around 40% of firms use a fixed rate of 5–6% for the market risk premium, while a lower percentage (around 10%) uses a value between 4–4.5%. Around 50% of financial advisers who were interviewed claim to use a much higher rate of between 7–7.5%.

SUMMARY

The summary of this chapter can be downloaded from www.vernimmen.com.

The cost of capital or the weighted average cost of capital (WACC) is a fundamental concept in corporate finance. It is relied on for making investment decisions and for the valuation of businesses.

The cost of capital is not just the risk of capital employed. It exists before the capital structure is even fully assembled or finalised. In fact, creditors and shareholders will determine the rate of return they require on debt and equity on the basis of the capital structure and of the risk of capital employed.

Only for calculation purposes is the cost of capital often calculated as the weighted average cost of equity and debt.

The cost of capital can be calculated by:

*   using a direct method on the basis of the β of the capital employed; or

*   using an indirect method where it is equal to the weighted average of the values of the cost of equity and the cost of net debt; or

*   observing the value of capital employed, when this figure is available.

For a diversified company, there are as many costs of capital as there are sectors in which it operates. Similarly, every country or economic area has its own specific cost of capital, which is dependent upon the political landscape and macroeconomic risks.

For emerging countries, the methodology must be adapted to factor in both the lack of certain data (risk-free interest rate) and international parameters (the industry's β).

A company's negative net debt structure brings down the cost of its equity, but has no impact on the cost of capital which is the same as if the company had no cash.

Managers have very little margin for manoeuvre to create value in reducing their cost of capital, as if they lower the cost of capital they will most likely also lower their returns. The only hope that they have is of providing better information to the market.

SECTION 3

QUESTIONS

1/ When is the cost of capital equal to the cost of equity? Can the cost of capital be equal to the cost of debt?

2/ Why does the cost of capital constitute a direct link between return on capital expenditure and the returns required by capital investors?

3/ Why is the cost of capital not an accounting concept?

4/ What is the cost of capital equal to?

5/ Is the cost of equity equal to the dividend yield?

6/ How many costs of capital are there in a company that has diversified into different (business) sectors but not geographic areas? What about if it has done so within each of the company's divisions?

7/ Can a company that invests in projects on which the returns are lower than its cost of capital continue to obtain resources through cash flow? Through debt? Through capital increases?

8/ A listed company launches a takeover bid on another company at a price that is far too high. According to the cost of capital theory, what should the sanction be?

9/ Can diversification reduce the cost of capital?

10/ Does a firm have a low cost of capital because it is leveraged or did it become leveraged because it has a low cost of capital?

More questions are waiting for you at www.vernimmen.com.

EXERCISES

1/ What is the cost of equity of a company whose shares are trading at 30.2 and which pays a dividend of 5 over 5 years and 6 after 5 years?

2/ What is the cost of debt for a company whose debt at 11% has a nominal value of 1000, is trading at 1037.9 and has a life of 5 years (redemption at maturity)?

3/ Use the answers to questions 1 and 2 and calculate the cost of capital of this company. The company has issued 1000 shares, the corporate tax rate is 34%.

4/Calculate the cost of capital of a company for which the key figures are as follows:

	Equity	Debt
Book value	10 000	1000
Value	12 000	1000
Perpetual remuneration	1800	100

5/What is the net present value of the following perpetual investment before and after tax?

Cost: 100
Cash flow before tax: 26
Tax rate: 50%

Capital structure:

	Percentage (%)	Cost before tax (%)	Cost after tax (%)
Equity	60	24	24
Debt	40	16	8

Cyclone case study

The Cyclone group operates in three sectors: the sale of commercial shipping equipment, shipping of goods by sea between mainland India and Sri Lanka (the group owns two container ships), and a small shipyard which oversees the careenage of most of the boats in Sri Lanka.

The three divisions are listed on the Mumbai Stock Exchange.

	Equipment sales division	Maritime shipping division	Shipyard
Market capitalisation	2160	18 520	632
Shareholders' equity	1580	10 512	824
Net debt (estimated value)	812	−12	−1356
Sales	22 210	23 724	701
EBIT	405	1625	82
Net income	226	1057	−24
β_E observed	0.8	0.5	1.2
β_D estimated	0.1	0	0.3
Tax rate	35%	35%	35%

(a) What is your view of the financial health of this group (very simple financial analysis)?

(b) The required return for a risk-free investment is around 6.5% (before tax) and the average required return for the market portfolio is 11% (before tax). Calculate the overall cost of capital for this group.

1/ When debt is zero. Yes, but only if the company is carrying very heavy debts.

2/ By definition.

3/ Because it is the cost at which the company could reconstitute its liabilities today.

4/ To the required return on the capital employed.

5/ No, it is generally much higher.

6/ As many as there are divisions. Only one.

7/ Yes, unfortunately using cash flow. Yes, using debt if its debts are still low. With difficulty through a capital increase.

8/ Its value drops.

9/ No, as only the market risk is remunerated.

10/ It has a low cost of equity because its assets are not risky, it can therefore be financed largely by debt.

Exercises

A detailed Excel version of the solutions is available at www.vernimmen.com.

1/ 18.00%.

2/ 10.00%.

3/ 17.62%.

4/ 14.62%.

5/ Before tax: k = 20.8%; NPV = 25 After tax: k = 17.6%; NPV = −26.

Cyclone case study

(a) The group is economically cohesive (it is not a conglomerate). The shipping and equipment sales divisions are profitable, although the shipyard is not; however, it is a small division compared with the others. Overall, the group is profitable and carries very little debt. There is the possibility that the current capital allocation may not be optimal, given the co-existence of profitable divisions and a non-profitable division.

(b)

	Equipment sales division (%)	Maritime shipping division (%)	Shipyard (%)	Group (%)
k_E	10.10	8.75	11.90	8.98
k_D after tax	4.52	4.23	5.10	4.89
K	8.57	8.75	7.26	8.60

BIBLIOGRAPHY

Y. Amihud, H. Mendelson, The liquidity route to a lower cost of capital, *Journal of Applied Corporate Finance*, **12**(4), 8–25, Winter 2000.

M. Atias, F. Bancel, The cost of capital of greenfield projects, *The Vernimmen.com Newsletter*, **43**, 1–2, September 2009.

F. Bancel, Th. Perrotin, Le coût du capital dans les pays émergents, *Analyse Financière*, **119**, 76–88, June 1999.

SECTION 3

S. Benninga, *Corporate Valuation. A Valuation Approach,* McGraw Hill, 1997.

A. Bernardo, B. Chowdhry, A. Goyal, Growth options, betas and the cost of capital, *Financial Management,* **36**(2), 5–17, Summer 2007.

C. Botosan, Evidence that greater disclosure lowers the cost of equity capital, *Journal of Applied Corporate Finance,* **12**(4), 60–69, Winter 2000.

C. Botosan, Disclosure and the cost of capital: What do we know? *Accounting and Business Research, International Accounting Policy Forum,* 31–40, 2006.

D. Brounen, A. de Jong, K. Koedijk, Corporate finance in Europe: Confronting theory with practice, *Financial Management,* **33**, 71–101, Winter 2004.

D. Easley, M. O'Hara, Information and the cost of capital, *Journal of Finance,* **59**(4), 1553–1583, August 2004.

E. Fama, K. French, The corporate cost of capital and the return on corporate investment, *Journal of Finance,* **54**(6), 1939–1967, December 1999.

P. Fernandez, Levered and unlevered beta, *Journal of Applied Finance,* 2005.

K. Garbade, *Fixed Income Analytics,* MIT Press, 2002.

L. Jui, R. Merton, Z. Bodie, Does a firm's equity returns reflect the risk of its pension plan? *Journal of Financial Economics,* **81**(1), 1–16, July 2006.

Y. Le Fur, P. Quiry, The equity risk premium, *The Vernimmen.com Newsletter,* **26**, 1–4, July 2007.

E. de Mézerac, *Cost of Capital in Investment Decisions. From Theory to Practice,* VDM Verlag, 2009.

M. Miller, Debt and taxes, *Journal of Finance,* **32**(2), 261–276, May 1977.

F. Modigliani, M. Miller, The cost of capital, corporation finance and the theory of investment, *American Economic Review,* **53**, 261–297, June 1958.

F. Modigliani, M. Miller, Corporate income taxes and the cost of capital: A correction, *American Economic Review,* **53**(3), 433–443, June 1963.

S. Myers, Interactions of corporate financing and investment decisions – implication for capital budgeting, *Journal of Finance,* **29**(1), 1–25, March 1974.

S. Pratt, R. Grabowski, *Cost of Capital. Applications and examples,* 4th edn, John Wiley & Sons, Inc., 2010.

R. Schramm, H. Wang, Measuring the cost of capital in an international CAPM framework, *Journal of Applied Corporate Finance,* **12**(3), 63–72, Autumn 1999.

R. Stulz, Globalisation, corporate finance and the cost of capital, *Journal of Applied Corporate Finance,* **12**(3), 8–25, Autumn 1999.

For more on the evidence coming from the practice:

R. Bruner, K. Eades, R. Harris, R. Higgins, Best practices in estimating the cost of capital: Survey and synthesis, *Financial Practice and Education,* 13–29, Spring/Summer 1998.

L. Gitman, P. Vandenberg, Cost of capital techniques used by major US firms: 1997 vs. 1980, *Financial Practice and Education,* 54–68, Fall/Winter 2000.

J. Graham, C. Harvey, The theory and practice of corporate finance: Evidence from the field, *Journal of Financial Economics,* **60**, 187–243, May 2001.

The following websites provide information on the cost of capital:

Europe: *www.associes-finance.fr*
USA: *www.ibbotson.com, www.damodaran.com*

Chapter 31
RISK AND INVESTMENT ANALYSIS

When uncertainty creates value . . .

Valuing an investment by discounting future free cash flows at the weighted average cost of capital can provide some useful parameters for making investment decisions, but it does not adequately reflect the investors' exposure to risk. On its own, this technique does not take into account the many factors of uncertainty arising from industrial investments. Attempting to predict the future is too complicated (if not impossible!) to be done using mathematical criteria alone.

Accordingly, investors have developed a number of risk analysis techniques whose common objective is to *know more about a project* than just the information provided by the NPV. In fact, these techniques allow the investor to:

1. *know* the most important *sources of uncertainty* of a project and the quantitative impact of each of them. With this information, a manager can decide if it is necessary to conduct additional analysis, such as market research, product testing, logistics alternatives, and so on; and
2. *identify* a project's *key value drivers* so that the manager can accurately monitor these factors before, during and after an investment is made.

Nonetheless, these traditional approaches to risk analysis suffer from an important shortcoming: they don't consider *the value of flexibility*. Recently, options theory of investment decisions has begun to allow investors to assess some new concepts that are crucial to investment analysis.

Section 31.1
ASSESSING RISK THROUGH THE BUSINESS PLAN

The reader must realise that the business plan is the first stage in assessing the risks related to an investment. The purpose of the business plan is to model the firm's most probable future and it helps to identify the parameters that could significantly impact on a project's value. For example, in certain industries where sales prices are not very important, the model will be based on gross margins, which are more stable than turnover.

Establishing a business plan helps to determine the project's dependence upon factors over which investors have some influence, such as costs and/or sales price. It also outlines those factors that are beyond investors' control, such as raw material prices, exchange rates, etc. Obviously, the more the business plan depends upon exogenous factors, the riskier it becomes.

1/ SENSITIVITY ANALYSIS

One important risk analysis consists in determining how sensitive the investment is to different economic assumptions. This is done by *holding all other assumptions fixed* and then applying the present value to each different economic assumption. It is a technique that highlights the consequences of changes in *prices*, *volumes*, *rising costs* or *additional investments* on the value of projects.

To perform a sensitivity analysis, the investor:

1. fixes a base-case set of assumptions and calculates the NPV; and
2. allows one variable to change while holding the others constant, and recalculates the NPV based on these assumptions. Usually analysts develop both pessimistic and optimistic forecasts for each assumption, and then analysts move to a more complete range of possible values of the key drivers.

The sensitivity analysis requires a good understanding of the sector of activity and its specific constraints. The industrial analysis must be rounded off with a more financial analysis of the investment's sensitivity to the model's technical parameters, such as the discount rate or terminal value (growth rate to infinity, see Chapter 32).

Practitioners usually build a sensitivity matrix, which offers an overview of the sensitivity of the investment's NPV to the various assumptions.

2/ SCENARIO ANALYSIS AND MONTE CARLO SIMULATION

With a **scenario analysis**, the analyst calculates the project NPV assuming simultaneously a whole set of new assumptions, rather than adjusting one assumption at a time. For example, the analyst may foresee that if production volume falls short of expectations, operating costs per unit may also be higher than anticipated. In this case, two variables change at the same time. But as the reader can easily understand, in reality the situation may be much more complex.

Although scenario analysis is appealing, it can be very difficult to understand how different variables are related to each other. The problem is two-sided:

- What are the assumptions that move together? and
- What is the strength of their relationships?

As with sensitivity analysis, companies often build a base-case (or consensus) scenario and then move to optimistic and pessimistic scenarios.

An even more elaborate variation of scenario analysis is the **Monte Carlo simulation**, which is based on more sophisticated mathematical tools and software. It consists of isolating a number of the project's key variables or value drivers, such as turnover or margins, and allocating a probability distribution to each. The analyst enters all the assumptions about distributions of possible outcomes into a spreadsheet. The model then randomly samples from a table of predetermined probability distributions in order to identify the probability of each result.

Assigning probabilities to the investment's key variables is done in two stages:

1. First, influential factors are identified for each key variable. For example, with turnover, the analyst would also want to evaluate sales prices, market size, market share, etc.
2. It is then important to look at available information (long-run trends, statistical analysis, etc.) to determine the uncertainty profile of each key variable using the values given by the influential factors.

Generally, there are several types of key variables, such as simple variables (e.g. fixed costs), compound variables (e.g. turnover = market $\times$ market share) or variables resulting from more complex, econometric relationships.

The investment's net present value is shown as an uncertainty profile resulting from the probability distribution of the key variables, the random sampling of groups of variables, and the calculation of net present value in this scenario.

Repeating the process many times gives us a clear representation of the NPV risk profile.

Once the uncertainty profile has been created, the question is whether to accept or reject the project. The results of the Monte Carlo method are not as clear cut as present value, and a lot depends upon the risk/reward tradeoff that the investor is willing to accept. One important limitation of the method is the analysis of interdependence of the key variables; for example, how developments in costs are related to those in turnover, etc.

Section 31.2
THE CONTRIBUTION OF REAL OPTIONS

1/ THE LIMITS OF CONVENTIONAL ANALYSIS

Do not be confused by the variety of risk analysis techniques presented in the preceding section. In fact, all of these different techniques are based on the same principle. In the final analysis, simulations, the Monte Carlo or the certainty equivalent methods are just complex variations on the NPV criteria presented in Chapter 16.

Like NPV, conventional investment risk analyses are based on two fundamental assumptions:

*   the choice of the anticipated future flow scenario; and
*   the irreversible nature of the investment decision.

The second assumption brings up the limits of this type of analysis. Assuming that an investment is irreversible disregards the fact that corporate managers, once they get new information, generally have a number of options. They can abandon the investment halfway through if the project does not work out, they can postpone part of it or extend it if it has good development prospects, or use new technologies. The teams managing or implementing the projects constantly receive new information and can adapt to changing circumstances. In other words, **the conventional approach to investment decisions ignores a key feature of many investment projects, namely flexibility**.

It might be argued that the uncertainty of future flows has already been factored in via the mathematical hope criterion[1] and the discount rate, and therefore this should be enough to assess any opportunities to transform a project. However, it can be demonstrated that this is not necessarily so.

> The discount rate and concept of mathematical hope quantify the direct consequences of random events. However, they do not take into account the manager's ability to change strategies in response to these events.

2/ Real options

Industrial managers are not just passively exposed to risks. *In many cases, they are able to react to ongoing events*. They can increase, reduce or postpone their investment, and they exercise this right according to ongoing developments in prospective returns.

In fact, the industrial manager is in the same situation as the financial manager who can increase or decrease his position in a security given predetermined conditions.

Industrial managers who have some leeway in managing an investment project are in the same position as financial managers holding an option.[2]

The flexibility of an investment thus has a value that is not reflected in conventional analysis. **This value is simply that of the attached option.** Obviously, this option does not take the form of the financial security with which you have already become familiar. It has no legal existence. Instead, it relates to industrial assets and is called a **real option**.

> Real options relate to industrial investments. They represent the right, but not the obligation, to *change* an investment project, particularly when new information on its prospective returns becomes available.

The potential flexibility of an investment, and therefore of the attached real options, is not always easy to identify. Industrial investors frequently do not realise or do not want to admit (especially when using a traditional investment criterion) that they do have some margin for manoeuvre. This is why it is often called a **hidden option**.

3/ Real options categories

> The theory of real options is complex but, like any conceptual universe, it helps us to discuss and analyse problems.

1 *The mathematical hope is the expected value, i.e. the sum of the product of the probability of each event multiplied by the value of each event.*

2 *If you are not familiar with options, we advise you to read Chapter 24 before reading the rest of this chapter.*

Given the potential value of hidden options, it is tempting to consider all investment uncertainties as a potential source of value. But the specific features of option contracts must not be overlooked. The following three factors are necessary to ensure that an investment project actually offers real options:

- The project must have a degree of **uncertainty**. The higher the underlying volatility, the greater the value of an option. If the standard deviation of the flows on a project is low, the value of the options will be negligible.
- Investors must be able to get **more information** during the course of the project, and this information must be sufficiently precise to be useful.
- Once the new information has been obtained, it must be possible to change the project **significantly and irrevocably**. If the industrial manager cannot use the additional information to modify the project, he does not really have an option but is simply taking a chance. In addition, the initial investment decision must also have a certain degree of irreversibility. If it can be changed at no cost, then the option has no value. And lastly, since the value of a real option stems from the investor's ability to take action, any increase in **investment flexibility generates value**, since it can give rise to new options or increase the value of existing options.

Real options apply primarily to decisions to invest or divest, but they can appear at any stage of a company's development. As a result, the review in this text of options theory is a broad outline, and the list of the various categories of real options is far from exhaustive.

The option to launch a new project corresponds to a call option on a new business. Its strike price is the startup investment, a component that is very important in the valuation for many companies. In these cases, they are not valued on their own merits, but according to their ability to generate new investment opportunities, even though the nature and returns are still uncertain.

A good example of this principle is publishers who own digital rights. Since the business model of ebooks is still uncertain and the corresponding development costs are high, the value of a publisher is partly based on anticipated changes in the market in which the publisher operates. But the value also includes an option to develop in the new digital market, which still remains to be defined.

Similarly, R&D departments can be considered to be generators of real options embedded within the company. Any innovation represents the option to launch a new project or product. This is particularly true in the pharmaceutical industry. If the project is not profitable, this does not mean that the discovery has no value. It simply means that the discovery is out of the money. Yet this situation could change with further developments.

The option to develop or extend the business is comparable to the launch of a new project. However, during the initial investment phase decisions have to be made, such as whether to build a large factory to meet potentially strong demand or just a small plant to first test the waters.

A real options solution would be to build a small factory with an option to extend it if necessary. Flexibility is just as important in current operations as when deciding on the overall strategy of a project. Investments should be judged by their ability to offer recurring options throughout their lifecycle. Certain power stations, for example, can easily be adapted to run on coal or oil. This flexibility enhances their value, because they can be easily switched to a cheaper source of energy if prices fluctuate. Similarly, some auto plants need only a few adjustments in order to start producing different models.

The option to reduce or contract business is the opposite of the previous example. If the market proves smaller than expected, the investor can decide to cut back on production, thus reducing the corresponding variable costs. Indeed, he can also decide not to carry out part of the initial project, such as building a second plant. The implied sales price of the unrealised portion of the project consists of the savings on additional investments. This option can be described as a put option on a fraction of the project, even if the investment never actually materialises.

The option to postpone a project. The initial investment in the rights of an oil field is minimal in comparison with prospecting and extraction costs. It can thus be quite useful to defer the start of the project, for example until the business environment becomes more propitious (oil prices, operating costs, etc.). To a certain extent, this is similar to holding a well-known but not fully exploited brand.

> There is a certain time value in delaying the realisation of a project, since in the meantime better information about the project's income and expenses may become available. This enables a better assessment of the potential for value creation.

Nonetheless, the option to defer the project's start is valid only if the investor is able to secure ownership of the project from the outset. If not, his competitors may take on the project. In other words, the advantage of deferring the investment could be cancelled out by the risk of new market entrants.

Looking beyond the investment decision itself, **option models can be used to determine the optimal date for starting up a project**. In this case, the waiting period is similar to holding an American option on the project. The option's value corresponds to the price of ensuring future ownership of the project (land, patents, licence, etc.).

The option to defer progress on the project is a continuation of the previous example. Some projects consist of a series of investments rather than just one initial investment. Should investors receive information casting doubt on a project that has already been launched, they may decide to put subsequent investments on hold, thus effectively halting further development. In fact, investors hold an option on the project's further development at every call for more financing.

The option to abandon means that the industrial manager can decide to abandon the project at any time. Thus, hanging on to it today means keeping open the option to abandon at a later date. However, the reverse is not possible. This asymmetry is reflected in options theory, which assumes that a manager can sell his project at any time (but might not be able to buy it back once it is sold).

Such situations are analogous to the options theory of equity valuations that we will examine in Chapter 35. If the project is set up as a levered company, the option to abandon corresponds to shareholders' right to default. The value of this option is equal to that of equity, and it is exercised when the amount of outstanding debt is greater than the value of the project.

In the example below, the project includes an option to defer its launch (wait and see), an option to expand if it proves successful and an option to abandon it completely.

OPTION TO DEFER—OPTION TO EXPAND—OPTION TO ABANDON

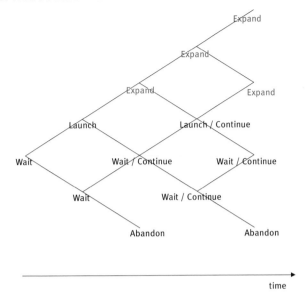

4/ THE EXPANDED NET PRESENT VALUE

Since options allow us to analyse the various risks and opportunities arising from an investment, the project can be assessed as a whole. This is done by taking into account its two components – anticipated flows and real options. Some authors call this the **expanded net present value (ENPV)**, which is the opposite of the "passive" NPV of a project with no options. Based on the preceding sections, this gives:

$$ENPV = NPV + Real\ option\ value$$

When a project is very complex with several real options, the various options cannot be valued separately since they are often conditional and interdependent. If the option to abandon the project is exercised, the option to reduce business obviously no longer exists and its value is nil. *As a result, there is no additional value on options that are interdependent.*

THE EXPANDED NET PRESENT VALUE

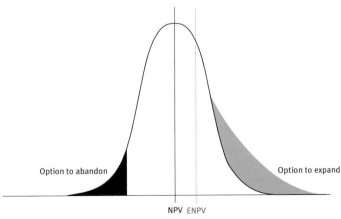

5/ EVALUATING REAL OPTIONS

Option theory sheds light on the valuation of real options by stating that uncertainty combined with flexibility adds value to an industrial project. How appealing! It tells us that the higher the underlying volatility, and thus the risk, the greater the value of an option. This appears counterintuitive compared with the net present value approach, but remember that this value is very unstable. The time value of an option decreases as it reaches its exercise date, since the uncertainty declines with the accumulation of information on the environment.

The uncertainty inherent in the flexibility of an industrial project creates value, because the unknown represents risk that has a time value. As time passes, this uncertainty declines as the discounted cash flows are adjusted with new information. The uncertainty is replaced with an intrinsic value that progressively incorporates the ever-changing expectations.

Consider the case of a software publisher who is offered the opportunity to buy a licence to market cell phone software for £5 million. If the publisher does not accept the deal right away, the licence will be offered to a rival. The software can be produced on the spot at a cost of £50 million.

If the software is produced immediately, the company should be able to generate £2 million in cash flows over the next year. The situation the following year, however, is far more uncertain, since one of the main telephone carriers is due to choose a new technological standard. If the standard chosen corresponds to that of the licence offered to our company, it can hope to generate a cash flow of £9 million per year. If another standard is chosen, the cash flows will plunge to £1 million per year. The management of our company estimates there is a 50% chance that the "right" standard will be chosen. As of the second year, the flows are expected to be constant to infinity.

The present value of the immediate launch of the product can easily be estimated with a discount rate of 10%. The anticipated flows are $0.5 \times 9 + 0.5 \times 1 = £5$ million from the second year on to infinity. Assuming that the first year's flows are disbursed (or received) immediately, the present value is $5/0.1 + 2 = £52$ million for a total cost of $50 + 5 = £55$ million. According to the NPV criteria, the project destroys £3 million in value and the company should reject the licensing offer. This would be a serious mistake!

If it buys the licence, the company can decide to produce the software whenever it wants to and can easily wait a year before investing in production. While this means giving up revenues of £2 million in the first year, the company will have the advantage of knowing which standard the telephone operator will have chosen. It can thus decide to produce only if the standard is suited to its product. If it is not, the company abandons the project and saves on development costs. The licence offered to the company thus includes a real option: the company is entitled to earn the flows on the project in exchange for investing in production.

The NPV approach assumes that the project will be launched immediately. That corresponds to the immediate exercise of the call option on the underlying instrument. This exercise destroys the time value. To assess the real value of the licence, we have to work out the value of the corresponding real option, i.e. the option of postponing development of the software.

When a company has a real option, using NPV or any other traditional investment criteria implies that it will exercise its option immediately. It is important to keep in mind that this is not necessarily the best solution or the only reality that the company/investor faces.

The value of an option can be determined by the binomial method, which we described in greater detail in Chapter 24.

Imagine that the company has bought the licence and put off producing the software for a year. It now knows what standard the carrier has chosen. If the standard suits its purposes, it can immediately start up production at an NPV of $9 \times (1 + 1/0.1) - 50 = £49$ million at that date. If the wrong standard is chosen, the NPV of developing the software falls to $1 \times (1 + 1 + 1/0.1) - 50 = -£39$ million, and the company drops the project (this investment is irreversible and has no hidden options). The value of the real option attached to the licence is thus £49 million for a favourable outcome and 0 for an unfavourable outcome. Using a risk-free discount rate of 5%, the calculation for the initial value of the option is £20.7 million, since:

CALCULATION FOR THE INITIAL VALUE OF THE OPTION

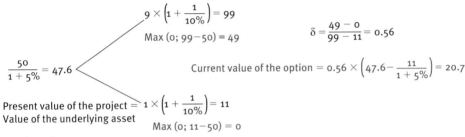

$$9 \times \left(1 + \frac{1}{10\%}\right) = 99$$

Max (0; 99−50) = 49

$$\delta = \frac{49 - 0}{99 - 11} = 0.56$$

$$\frac{50}{1 + 5\%} = 47.6$$

Current value of the option $= 0.56 \times \left(47.6 - \frac{11}{1 + 5\%}\right) = 20.7$

Present value of the project $= 1 \times \left(1 + \frac{1}{10\%}\right) = 11$
Value of the underlying asset

Max (0; 11−50) = 0

Option value

Here is another look at the licensing offer. The licence costs £5 million and the value of the real option is £20.7 million assuming development is postponed for one year. With this proviso, the company has been offered the equivalent of an immediate gain of $20.7 - 5 = £15.7$ million.

In this example, the difference between the two approaches is considerable. Legend has it that when an oil concession was once being auctioned off, one of the bidding companies offered a price that was less than a tenth that of its competitor, quite simply because he had "forgotten" to factor in the real options!

This example assumed just one binomial alternative but, when attempting to quantify the value of real options in an investment, one is faced by a myriad of alternatives. More generally, the binomial model uses the **replicating portfolio approach**: Suppose that we know the value of the option at the end of the period, both in the up- and in the down-state. We could simply obtain the value by discounting the expected value of the two returns at an appropriate discount rate. Although correct, this approach suffers two limitations:

- we do not know the probability of the up and down scenario. This problem can be overcome; and
- the discount rate is not the cost of capital we use in estimating the NPV of the project without flexibility. A real option has different payouts and different risks than the underlying project. Thus the cost of capital inappropriately reflects the riskiness of the cash flows of the project with flexibility.

It is sometimes possible to choose δ shares of a "traded" or twin (of the project with flexibility!) security (an asset named S, which is perfectly correlated with the option) and B euros of risk-free debt. Suppose that if the price goes up, the twin security price will be S_U (supposedly known), while if it goes down, it will be S_D (also known). In the up-state, the project with flexibility will return P_U (a figure that we are able to estimate as we will see later on) while in the down-state it will return P_D (also estimable). The result is two equations and two unknowns (B and δ):

$$\delta \times S_U + B \times (1 + r_F) = P_U$$

$$\delta \times S_D + B \times (1 + r_F) = P_D$$

The solution of this simple system is:

$$\delta = (P_U - P_D) / (S_U - S_D)$$

$$B = (P_U - \delta \times S_U) / (1 + r_F)$$

In each node, the present value of the project with flexibility is:

$$\delta \times PV \text{ of the project at the node} + B / (1 + r_F)$$

We then work backwards, node by node and in a similar way, to arrive at the present value of the project with real options, i.e. the expanded net present value.

The reader should be aware that the expanded net present value cannot be lower than the "passive" NPV.

But what is this security that is perfectly correlated (the twin!) with a project with real options? The trick is to use the project itself, taking the present value without flexibility, as the twin security. In other words, we use the present value of the passive project as an estimate of the price it would have if it were traded on the market. This solution is extremely reasonable and useful because, after all, the project with flexibility has the highest asset correlation with the no-flexibility project.

It is now possible to take all of these tools and create some order out of this line of reasoning. The approach for option valuation is a five-step process. Discussion of the process provides an opportunity to analyse a few other important concepts.

Step 1 Calculate the "passive" present value of the project, using the traditional discounted cash flow methods.

Step 2 Build a so-called event tree, i.e. the lattice that models the values of the "passive" investment. This tree does not contain decision nodes and simply models the evolution of the present value of the project.

The up and down movements can be determined by the following formulae:[3]

$$\text{Up movement} = U = e^{\sigma \sqrt{T}}$$

$$\text{Down movement} = D = e^{-\sigma \sqrt{T}}$$

3 *If we build the event tree with these up and down movements, we are building a geometric tree. The main characteristic is that it has multiplicative up and down movements that model a log-normal distribution of outcomes – whose returns can go to infinity on the up side and to zero on the down side.*

The corresponding probabilities of up and down movements are:

$$\text{Probability up} = (1 + r_F - D)/(U - D)$$

$$\text{Probability down} = 1 - \text{Probability up}$$

Step 3 Turn the event tree into a decision tree, by identifying the managerial flexibility and building it into the *appropriate* nodes of the tree, i.e. when the flexibility is effectively possible. For example, suppose that it is possible to expand the project and its payouts by 15% by spending an additional €10 at any time. Wherever the exercise of this option is possible in the event tree, multiply by 15%, and reduce by €10 the corresponding node on the original tree. For each node, then choose the maximum value between the original event tree and the tree with the incorporated flexibility.

Step 4 Use the replication portfolio approach to value the present value of the project with flexibility. Then the entire decision tree can be solved by working from the final branches backwards through time.

$$d \times \text{PV of the no-flexibility project at the node} + B/(1 + r_F)$$

Step 5 Calculate the expanded net present value by subtracting the initial investment from the present value of the project with flexibility.

Real options are calculated using quite sophisticated mathematical tools, which iterate the option's flows by a portfolio of financial assets, i.e. the foundation of the binomial method. Estimating volatility is always the most problematic issue regarding the concrete application of this methodology.

In practice, the information derived from the quantification of real options is frequently not very significant when compared with a highly positive NPV in the initial scenario. However, when NPV is negative at the outset, one always has to consider the flexibility of the project by resorting to real options.

In general, Copeland *et al.* sum up the practice quite succinctly: "For practitioners to use the option pricing approach, it must be relatively transparent and easy to understand" (Copeland *et al.*, 2010 p. 411). Likewise, the reader should avoid using extremely complicated valuation tools if they hamper an appropriate understanding of the value added by real options.

6/ CONCLUSION

The predominant appeal of real options theory is its factoring of the value of flexibility that the traditional approaches ignore. The traditional net present value approach assumes that there is only one possible outcome. It does not take into account possible adaptive actions that could be taken by corporate managers. Real options fill this gap.

But do not get carried away; applying this method can be quite difficult because:

- not everyone knows how to use the mathematical models. This can create problems in communicating findings; and
- estimating some of the required parameters, such as volatility, opportunity costs, etc. can be complicated.

If not properly applied, real options can give very high values. In turn, these can be used to justify the unjustifiable, e.g. stock prices during the Internet bubble in 2000 or 3G licences in 2001.

Their main advantage is that they force users to reason "outside of the box" and come up with new ideas.

We trust that the reader will not mind being told that the use of these tools by practitioners is inversely correlated to the place devoted to them in this chapter: virtually systematic for scenarios, less often for the Monte Carlo method and very rarely for real options.

SUMMARY

The summary of this chapter can be downloaded from www.vernimmen.com.

Traditional risk analysis methods are all based on the principle of net present value. They are applicable when all investment decisions are irreversible and projects have no flexibility.

With breakeven analysis, the manager or the analyst tries to understand the level of output and revenues that must be reached in order to break even. It is an important tool for a manager because it can set very clear targets. It is convenient to use this method by considering all fixed costs, including financial expenses.

Sensitivity analysis allows the manager to understand how sensitive the NPV is to changes in assumptions on key value drivers, while holding everything else constant.

Scenario analysis changes multiple assumptions simultaneously. In this manner, the analyst must make some effort in estimating which variables move together as well as the intensity of their relationship. Using the Monte Carlo method, a better idea of the prospects of flows can be obtained by allocating a probability distribution to each of them. Although powerful, the method is not so easy to interpret and can be misused.

The limitations of all these methods become evident when project managers are able to use new information to modify a project that is already underway, i.e. when there is a certain amount of flexibility. In such cases, the industrial manager is in the same situation as the financial manager who can increase or decrease his position in a security given predetermined conditions. An industrial manager can also be compared to a financial manager who holds an option. Flexibility of an investment has a value – the value of the option attached to it. This concrete property of a flexible investment is a real option.

Three factors are necessary to ensure that an investment project actually offers real options:

- there is some uncertainty surrounding the project;

- there is additional information arriving over the course of time; and

- it must be possible to make significant changes to the project on the basis of this information.

A number of different types of real options can be present in investment projects:

- the option to launch a new project;

- the option to expand, reduce or abandon the project; or

- the possibility to defer the project or delay the progress of work.

The study of investments on the basis of their net present value can be expanded, thanks to the concept of the real option. The result we obtain by including real options in the analysis is known as expanded net present value. This is the sum of the net present value of the project and the real options attached to the project. The uncertainty inherent in the flexibility of an industrial project creates value, but this uncertainty declines as time goes by. The uncertainty is replaced by the intrinsic value arising from the discounted flows adjusted for the new information.

QUESTIONS

1/ How does using different scenarios differ from simple cash flow discounting?

2/ In a simplified form, can the Monte Carlo method be implemented without a computer?

3/ What does the theory of options contribute to the valuing of an investment?

4/ Is the theory of options opposed to the theory of efficient markets?

5/ Can a project that contains significant real options be valued properly by the NPV criterion? By the construction of scenarios? By the Monte Carlo method? By the certainty equivalent method?

6/ Provide an example of a project where there is an option to abandon.

7/ Provide an example of a project where there is an option to expand.

8/ In practice, what is the most serious problem raised by real options?

9/ What makes the contribution of real options attractive for operations managers?

10/ How do you interpret the acquisition by EDF of plots of land adjacent to British Energy nuclear plants a few months before the UK privatised this company (knowing that this land was necessary for the modernisation of the plants)?

More questions are waiting for you at www.vernimmen.com.

EXERCISE

An Internet portal aimed at pet owners has just developed a nuclear sewing machine and offers you the opportunity to invest in the industrialisation of this product. The project will last 5 years, and for 4 years, you will not be paid a dividend. But if the company is floated on the stock exchange after 5 years (which is the plan) you will get €5m. The founders of the portal estimate that your initial investment will be about €2.5m.

What return will this project bring you?

SECTION 3

Given the project's risk, you decide that you require a return of more than 20%. What investment do you offer?

The founders, keen to obtain the €2.5m in question and believing firmly in the success of their project, offer you the following arrangement: you give them €2.5m and, if all goes well, you'll get €5m after 5 years. If the project fails, then they'll give you €1m after 5 years out of the €2.5m you invested. They believe that this reduces your risk considerably. How would you go about tackling this problem (without doing any calculations)?

ANSWERS

Questions

1/ *The assumptions are obvious.*
2/ *No.*
3/ *The valuation of management's margin for manoeuvre.*
4/ *No.*
5/ *No, no, no, no.*
6/ *Definitive closure of a mine.*
7/ *Buy a plot of land that is too big for the plant to be constructed, in order to be able to cater for a growing market.*
8/ *Valuing the alternatives.*
9/ *They highlight flexibility and the ability to adapt to a new environment.*
10/ *It's a real option that provides a certain gain: even though EDF did not win the auction, it would have been able to favourably negotiate the disposal of the land to the new owner of British Energy. It therefore increased the cost of British Energy for other bidders in the auction.*

Exercise

A detailed Excel version of this solution is available at www.vernimmen.com.

IRR = 14.87%. Around €2m. The founders' offer could be compared to a put option on the project with a strike price of €1m. The whole problem lies in the valuation of this option (the volatility of the value of the project must be evaluated). The founders value it at €0.5m. The option that they're "offering" you does, in fact, reduce your risk, since your loss is now limited to €1.5m compared with €2.5m previously.

BIBLIOGRAPHY

For more about sensitivity and simulations:

S. Benninga, *Financial Modelling*, 3rd edn, MIT Press, 2008.
J. Tjia, *Building financial models*, 2nd edn, McGraw-Hill, 2009.

For more about real options:

M. Amra, N. Kulatilaka, *Real Options*, Harvard Business School Press, 1998.
T. Copeland, T. Koller, D. Wessels, *Valuation*, 5th edn, John Wiley & Sons, Inc., 2010.
J. Cox, M. Rubinstein, S. Ross, Option pricing: A simplified approach, *Journal of Financial Economics*, 7(3), 229–263, September 1979.
A. Dixit, R. Pindyck, *Investment Under Uncertainty*, University Press, 1994.
A. Dixit, R. Pindyck, The option approach to capital investment, *Harvard Business Review*, May–June 1995.

M. Franc, G. Paepegaey, Factoring risk into the capital expenditure decision-making process, *The Vernimmen.com Newsletter*, **47**, 1–5, January 2010.

G. Guthrie, *Real Options in Theory and Practice,* Oxford University Press, 2009.

S. Myers, S. Turnbull, Capital budgeting and the capital asset pricing model: Good news and bad news, *Journal of Finance*, **32**(2), 321–333, May 1997.

L. Trigeorgis, A conceptual options framework for capital budgeting, *Advances in Futures and Options Research*, **3**, 145–167, 1998.

L. Trigeorgis, E. Schwartz, *Real Options and Investment under Uncertainty: Classical Readings and Recent Contributions*, MIT Press, September 2004.

www.puc-rio.br/marco.ind, real options in the oil & gas sector.

Chapter 32
VALUATION TECHNIQUES

Just how rosy is the future?

Perhaps without knowing it, you already have the knowledge of all the tools that you will need to value a company. You discovered what discounting was about in Chapter 16 and learnt all about the right discount rate to use in Chapters 19 and 30. Finally, the comparable method was explained in Chapter 23.

This chapter contains an in-depth look at the different valuation techniques and presents the problems (and solutions!) you will probably encounter when using them.

Nevertheless, we want to stress that valuation is not a simple use of mathematical formulae, it requires the valuator to have good accounting and tax skills. You will also need to fully understand the business model of the firm to be valued in order to assess the reliability of the business plan supporting the valuation. Reading this chapter will only be a first step towards becoming a good valuator and, in addition, a great deal of practice and application will be needed.

Section 32.1
OVERVIEW OF THE DIFFERENT METHODS

Generally, we want to value a company in order to determine the value of its shares or of its equity capital.

Broadly speaking, there are two methods used to value equity: the direct method and the indirect method. In the direct method, obviously, we value equity directly. In the indirect method, we first value the firm as a whole (what we call "enterprise" or "firm" value), then subtract the value of net debt to get the equity value.

INDIRECT AND DIRECT METHODS

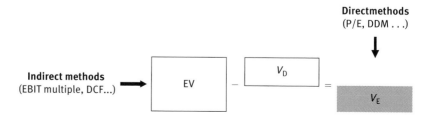

In addition, there are two approaches used in both the direct and indirect methods:

- The fundamental approach based on valuing either:
  - ○ a stream of dividends, which is the **Dividend Discount Model (DDM)**; or
  - ○ a stream of free cash flows, which is the **Discounted Cash Flow (DCF) method**.

  This approach attempts to determine the company's intrinsic value, in accordance with financial theory, by discounting cash flows to their present value using the required rate of return.

- The pragmatic approach of valuing the company by analogy with other assets or companies of the same type for which a value reference is available. This is the **peer comparison** method (often called the comparables method). Assuming markets are efficient, we should be able to infer the value of a company from the value of others.

	Indirect approach	**Direct approach**
Intrinsic value method (discounted present value of financial flows)	Present value of free cash flows discounted at the weighted average cost of capital (k) – value of net debt	Present value of dividends at the cost of equity: k_E
Peer comparison method (multiples of comparable companies)	EBIT multiple $\times$ EBIT – value of net debt	P/E $\times$ net income

The **sum-of-the-parts method** consists of valuing the company as the sum of its assets less its net debt. However, this is more a combination of the techniques used in the direct and indirect methods rather than a method in its own right.

Lastly, we mention options theory, whose applications we will see in Chapter 35. In practice, nearly no one values equity capital by analogy to a call option on the assets of the company. The concept of real options, however, had its practical heyday in 1999 and 2000 to explain the market values of "new economy" stocks. Needless to say, this method has since fallen out of favour.

If you remember the efficient market hypothesis, you are probably asking yourself why market value and discounted present value would ever differ. In this chapter we will take a look at the origin of the difference, and try to understand the reason for it and how long we think it will last. Ultimately, market values and discounted present values should converge.

Section 32.2
VALUATION BY DISCOUNTED CASH FLOW

The Discounted Cash Flow (DCF) method consists of applying the investment decision techniques (see Chapter 16) to the firm value calculation. We will focus on the **present value** of the cash flows from the investment. This is the **fundamental valuation method**. Its aim is to value the company as a whole (i.e. to determine the value of the capital employed, what we call enterprise value). After deducting the value of net debt, the remainder is the value of the company's shareholders' equity.

SECTION 3

As we have seen, the cash flows to be valued are the after-tax amounts produced by the firm. They should be discounted out to perpetuity at the company's weighted average cost of capital (see Chapter 30).

$$EV = \sum_{t=0}^{\infty} \frac{FCFF_t}{(1+k)^t}$$

In practice, we project specific cash flows over a certain number of years. This period is called the **explicit forecast period**. The length of this period varies depending on the sector. It can be as short as 2–3 years for a high-tech company, 5–7 years for a consumer goods company and as long as 20–30 years for a utility. For the years beyond the explicit forecast period, we establish a **terminal value**.

The value of the firm is the sum of the present value of after-tax cash flows over the explicit forecast period and the terminal value at the end of the explicit forecast period.

1/ SCHEDULE OF CASH FLOWS OVER THE EXPLICIT FORECAST PERIOD

As we saw in Chapter 29, free cash flows measure the cash-producing capacity of the company. Free cash flows are estimated as follows:

	Operating income (EBIT)
−	Normalised tax on operating income
+	Depreciation and amortisation
−	Capital expenditure
−	Change in working capital
=	Free cash flow to firm

You buy a company for its future, not its past, no matter how successful it has been. Consequently, future cash flows are based on projections. As they will vary depending on growth assumptions, the most cautious approach is to set up several scenarios. But for starters, are you the buyer or the seller? The answer will influence your valuation. The objective of negotiation is to reconcile the buyer's and seller's points of view. We have found in our experience that discounted cash flow analysis is a very useful discussion tool: the seller gets accustomed to the idea of selling his/her company and the buyer gets a better understanding of the company for sale.

It is all right for a business plan to be optimistic – our bet is that you have never seen a pessimistic one – the important thing is how it stands up to scrutiny. It should be assumed that competition will ultimately eat into margins, that increases in profitability will not be sustained indefinitely without additional investment or additional hiring, etc. Quantifying these crucial future developments means entering the inner sanctum of the company's strategy.

The length of the explicit forecast period will depend on the company's "visibility" – i.e. the period of time over which is it reasonable to establish projections. This period is necessarily limited. In 10 years' time, for example, probably only a small portion of the company's profits will be derived from the production facilities it currently owns or from its current product portfolio. The company will have become a heterogeneous mix of the assets it has today and those it will have acquired over the next 10 years.

The forecast period should therefore correspond to the time during which the company will live off its current configuration. If it is too short, the terminal value will be too large and the valuation problem will only be shifted in time. Unfortunately, this happens all too often. If it is too long (more than 10 years), the explicit forecast is reduced to an uninteresting theoretical extrapolation.

Let's look at Indesit's financial projections produced by the broker Exane BNP Paribas:[1]

in € m	2010	2011e	2012e	2013e	2014e	2015e
Profit and loss statement						
Turnover	2879	3064	3209	3314	3424	3492
EBITDA[2]	310	309	330	340	364	361
– Depreciation and amortisation	126	123	123	124	124	124
= EBIT	184	186	207	216	240	237
Balance sheet						
Fixed assets	1046	1063	1070	1076	1082	1088
+ Working capital	−115	−79	−71	−63	−58	−57
= Capital employed	931	984	999	1013	1024	1031
Operating margin after 40% tax	3.8%	3.6%	3.9%	3.9%	4.2%	4.1%
ROCE[3] after 40% tax	11.9%	11.3%	12.4%	12.8%	14.1%	13.8%

These projections are quite reasonable with operating margin expected to be lower by 1 to 2 points compared to its pre-crisis level. Over the period, the ROCE is projected to rise to 13.8% and on to a peak of 19.2% in 2015 which may seem quite aggressive given past performance.

Projected after-tax free cash flows are as follows:

in € m	2010	2011e	2012e	2013e	2014e	2015e
EBIT	184	186	207	216	240	237
– Corporate income tax at 40%	−74	−74	−83	−86	−96	−95
+ Depreciation and amortisation	126	123	123	124	124	124
– Capital expenditure	−75	−140	−130	−130	−130	−130
– Change in working capital	−44	−36	−8	−8	−5	−1
= Free cash flow	117	59	109	116	133	135

1 *It is not the business plan for the company but only projections made by a third party in early 2011. The financial analysis of the company was done in the first section of this book.*

2 *Earnings before interest, taxes, depreciation and amortisation.*

3 *Return on capital employed.*

SECTION 3

Using a weighted average cost of capital of 9.2%, the end-2010 present value of the free cash flows generated during the explicit forecast period is €415m.

2/ TERMINAL VALUE

It is very difficult to estimate a terminal value, because it represents the value at the date when existing business development projections will no longer have any meaning. Often analysts assume that the company enters a phase of maturity after the end of the explicit forecast period. **In this case, the terminal value can be based either on the capital employed or on the free cash flow in the last year of the explicit forecast period.**

The most commonly used terminal value formula is the Gordon–Shapiro formula. It consists of a normalised cash flow, or annuity, that grows at a rate (g) out to perpetuity:

$$\text{Value of the company at the end of the explicit forecast period} = \frac{\text{Normalised free cash flow}}{k - g}$$

However, the key challenge is in choosing the normalised free cash flow value and the perpetual growth rate. **The normalised free cash flow** must be consistent with the assumptions of the business plan. It depends on long-term growth, the company's investment strategy and the growth in the company's working capital. Lastly, normalised free cash flows may be different from the free cash flow in the last year of the explicit forecast period, because normalised cash flow is what the company will generate after the end of the explicit forecast period and will continue to generate to perpetuity.

Concerning the growth rate to perpetuity, do not get carried away:

- Apart from the normalised cash flow's growth rate to perpetuity, you must take a cold, hard look at your projected long-term growth in return on capital employed. How long can the economic profit it represents be sustained? How long will market growth last?
- Most importantly, the company's rate of growth to perpetuity cannot be significantly greater than the long-term growth rate of the economy as a whole. For example, if the anticipated long-term inflation rate is 2% and real GDP growth is expected to be 2%, then if you choose a growth rate g that is greater than 4%, you are implying that the company will not only outperform all of its rivals but also will eventually take control of the economy of the entire country or indeed of the entire world (trees do not grow to the sky)![4]

4 All the more so as in mature sectors, inflation is lower than in the economy in general.

In the case of Indesit, the normalised cash flow must be calculated for the year 2016, because we are looking for the present value at the end of 2015 of the cash flows expected in 2016 and every subsequent year to perpetuity. Given the necessity to invest if growth

SECTION 3

is to be maintained, you could use the following assumptions to determine the normalised cash flow:

Normalised cash flow

    Normalised 2016 EBIT
−   Corporate income tax at 40%
+   Depreciation and amortisation
−   Capital expenditure
−   Change in working capital
=   Normalised 2016 free cash flow

Using a rate of growth to perpetuity of 1.5%, we calculate a terminal value of €1779m. Discounted over 5 years, this gives us €1146m at the end of 2010. The enterprise value of Indesit is therefore €1146m + €415m or €1561m. Note that the terminal value of €1779m at end-2015 corresponds to a multiple of 7.5 times 2015 EBIT. This means that choosing a multiple of 7.4 is theoretically equivalent to applying a growth rate to perpetuity of 1.5% to the normalised cash flow and discounting it at the required rate of return of 9.2%.

Given a net debt of €322m, the equity value of Indesit works out, with this method, at €1239m.

Sometimes the terminal value is estimated based on a multiple of a measure of operating performance. This measure can be, among other things, turnover, EBITDA or EBIT. Generally, this "horizon multiple" is lower than an equivalent, currently observable, multiple. This is because it assumes that, all other things being equal, prospects for growth decrease with time, commanding a lower multiple. Nevertheless, since using this method to assess the terminal value implies mixing intrinsic values with comparative values, we strongly advise against it.

Computing the terminal value with a multiple prevents you from pondering over the level of ROCE that the company can maintain in the future.

Remember that if you compute a terminal value greater than book value, you are implying that the company will be able to maintain forever a return on capital employed in excess of its weighted average cost of capital. If you choose a lower value, you are implying that the company will enter a phase of decline after the explicit forecast period and that you think it will not be able to earn its cost of capital in the future. Lastly, if you assume that terminal value is equal to book value, you are implying that the company's economic profit[5] falls immediately to zero. This is the method of choice in the mining industry, for example, where we estimate a liquidation value by summing the scrap value of the various assets – land, buildings, equipment – less the costs of restoring the site.

Our experience tells us that no economic profit can be sustained forever. The company's expected return on capital employed must gradually converge towards its cost of capital. This is the case with Coca-Cola, Michelin or British Airways. Regardless of the calculation method, the terminal value must reflect this. To model this phenomenon, we recommend using a "cash flow fade" methodology. In this approach, you define a time period during which the company's return on capital employed diminishes, either because its margins shrink or because asset turnover declines. Ultimately, the ROCE falls down to

5 *NOPAT (EBIT after tax) – WACC × Capital employed.*

the weighted average cost of capital. At the end of this time period, the enterprise value is equal to the book value of capital employed.

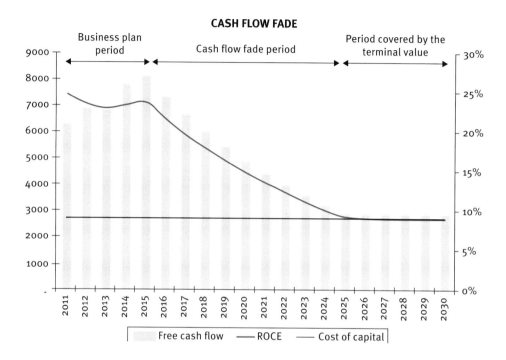

Readers will have to make choices: length of the cash flow fade period, speed of the convergence towards the cost of capital (form of the ROCE curve: convex, concave or a straight line as in our graph). They might also think that the company will be in a position to earn 1% or 2% more than its cost of capital due to the strength of its strategic position in its markets. Economic theory would not approve that!

This model can also be used for value-destroying companies. Sooner or later, there will be restructurings and bankruptcies triggering improvements in ROCE, but before applying the cash flow fade method the other way around, our readers would be well advised to ask themselves whether or not their company will be among the survivors!

3/ CHOOSING A DISCOUNT RATE

As we value cash flow to the firm, the discount rate is the **weighted average cost of capital (WACC)** or simply, the cost of capital. Calculating an accurate cost of capital is one of the key drivers of any valuation exercise, based on the discounted cash flow approach.

Certain industrial companies use normative discount rates, for example we have come across some groups for which all investments had to have a 15% return (no matter what the characteristics of the target were). Beware of such rates that do not yield market values. These rates could either result in the destruction of value by paying too much, or to opportunities being lost because the discount rate is too high compared to market practice.

The weighted average cost of capital is the minimum rate of return required by the company's fund providers, i.e. shareholders and lenders.

It is the overall cost of financing a company's activities that must be estimated.

The difficulty is in estimating the weighted average cost of capital in real-world conditions. You may want to turn back to Chapter 30 for a more detailed look at this topic.

4/ THE VALUE OF NET DEBT

Once you obtain the enterprise value using the above methodology, you must remove the value of net debt to derive equity value. Net debt is composed of financial debt net of cash, i.e. of all bank borrowings, bonds, debentures and other financial instruments[6] (short-, medium- or long-term), net of cash, cash equivalents and marketable securities.

6 *Including the value of hedging instruments, if any.*

Theoretically, the value of net debt is equal to the value of the future cash outflows (interest and principal payments) it represents, discounted at the market cost of similar borrowings. When all or part of the debt is listed or traded over the counter (listed bonds, syndicated loans), you can use the market value of the debt. You then subtract the market value of cash, cash equivalents and marketable securities. To illustrate this point, remember that, prior to its restructuring, Technicolor's debt was worth €1.8bn compared to a face value of €2.8bn. The difference of €1bn was equal to 5 times Technicolor's market cap.

The book value of net debt is often used as a first approximation of its present value. This approach makes sense especially when the debt was not contracted very long ago, or when it carries a variable rate and the company's risk profile has not fundamentally changed. If the interest rate or the risk of the company has changed significantly from when the debt was issued, then the market value of net debt is different from its book value. When the company's business is seasonal, year-end working capital may not reflect average requirements, and debt on the balance sheet at the end of the year may not represent real funding needs over the course of the year (see Chapter 11). Some companies also perform year-end "window-dressing" in order to show a very low level of net debt. In these cases, if you notice that interest expense does not correspond to debt balances,[7] you should restate the amount of debt by using a monthly average of outstanding net debt, for example.

7 *The interest rate calculated as interest in the income statement/net debt in the closing balance sheet does not reflect the actual interest rates paid on the ongoing debt during the year.*

5/ OTHER VALUATION ELEMENTS

(a) Provisions

Provisions must only be included if cash flows exclude them. If the business plan's EBIT does not reflect future charges for which provisions have been set aside – such as for restructuring, site closures, etc. – then the present value of the corresponding provisions on the balance sheet must be deducted from the value of the company.

Pension liabilities are a sticky problem (this is further developed in Chapter 7). How to handle them depends on how they were booked and, potentially, on the age pyramid of the company's workforce. You will have to examine the business plan to see whether it takes future pension payments into account and whether or not a large group of employees is to retire just after the end of the explicit forecast period.

Normally, pension liabilities should be treated as debt. Present value of future outflows for pension, net of pension assets, should be subtracted from the enterprise value.

With rare exceptions, deferred tax liabilities generally remain relatively stable. In practice, they are rarely paid out. Consequently, they are usually not considered debt equivalents.

(b) Unconsolidated or equity-accounted investments

If unconsolidated or equity-accounted financial investments are not reflected in the projected cash flows (via dividends received), you should add their value to the value of discounted cash flows. In this case, use the market value of these assets including, if relevant, tax on capital gains and losses.

For listed securities, use listed market value. Conversely, for minor, unlisted holdings, the book value is often used as a shortcut. However, if the company holds a significant stake in the associated company – this is sometimes the case for holdings booked using the equity method – you will have to value the affiliate separately. This may be a simple exercise, applying, for example, a sector-average P/E to the company's pro rata share of the net income of the affiliate. It can also be more detailed, by valuing the affiliate with a multi-criteria approach if the information is available.

(c) Tax-loss carryforwards

8 *Through a temporary lower corporate income tax.*

If tax loss carryforwards are not yet included in the business plan,[8] you will have to value any tax-loss carryforward separately, discounting tax savings until deficits are exhausted. We advise discounting savings at the cost of equity capital as they are directly linked to the earnings of the company and are as volatile (if not more so).

(d) Minority interests

Future free cash flows calculated on the basis of consolidated financial information will belong partly to the shareholders of the parent company and partly to minority shareholders in subsidiary companies, if any.

If minority interests are significant, you will have to take them into account by either:

- performing a separate DCF valuation of the subsidiaries in which some minority shareholders hold a stake and subtract from the enterprise value the minority share of the subsidiary;
- including only the group share in consolidated cash flows (which requires detailed information about the group subsidiaries).

Naturally, this assumes you have access to detailed information about the subsidiaries.

You can also use a multiple approach. Simplifying to the extreme, you could apply the group's implied P/E multiple to the minority shareholders' portion of net profit to get a first-blush estimate of the value of minority interests. Alternatively, you could apply the group's price-to-book ratio to the minority interests appearing on the balance sheet. In either case, we would not recommend using book value to value minority interests unless amounts are low.

(e) Dilution

You might be wondering what to do with instruments that give future access to company equity, such as convertible bonds, warrants and stock options. If these instruments have a market value, your best bet will be to subtract that value from the enterprise value of the company to derive the value of equity capital, just as you would for net debt. The number of shares to use in determining the value per share will then be the number of shares currently in circulation.

Alternatively, you could adjust the number of shares used to calculate value per share. This is the treasury stock method (see p. 434). Its drawback lies in ignoring the value of out-of-the money dilutive instruments.

6/ PROS AND CONS OF THE CASH FLOW APPROACH

The advantage of the discounted cash flow approach is that it quantifies the often implicit assumptions and projections of buyers and sellers. It also makes it easier to keep your feet closer to the ground during periods of market euphoria, excessively high valuations and astronomical multiples. It forces the valuation to be based on the company's real economic performance.

You might be tempted to think this method works only to estimate the value of the majority shareholder's stake and not for estimating the discounted value of a flow of dividends. You might even be tempted to go a step further and apply a **minority discount** to the present value of future cash flows for valuing a minority holding.

This is wrong. Applying a **minority discount** to the discounted cash flow method implies that you think **the majority shareholder is not managing the company fairly**. A discount is justified only if there are "losses in transmission" between free cash flow and dividends. This can be the case if the company's strategy regarding dividends, borrowing and new investment is unsatisfactory or oriented towards increasing the value of some other assets owned by the majority shareholder.

Minority discounts are inconsistent with the discounted cash flow method. Similarly, increasing the cash-flow based value can be justified only if the investor believes he can unlock synergies that will increase free cash flows.

Nevertheless, as satisfying as this method is in theory, it presents three major drawbacks:

1. It is very sensitive to assumptions and, consequently, the results it generates are very volatile. It is a rational method, but the difficulty in predicting the future brings significant uncertainty.
2. It sometimes depends too much on the terminal value, in which case the problem is only shifted to a later period. Often the terminal value accounts for more than 50% of the value of the company, compromising the method's validity. However, it is sometimes the only applicable method, such as in the case of a loss-making company for which multiples are inapplicable;
3. Lastly, it is not always easy to produce a business plan over a sufficiently long period of time. External analysts often find they lack critical information.

SECTION 3

7/ DISCOUNTING CASH FLOW AND DISCOUNTING DIVIDENDS

9 *That is, before 1995 in Europe and the USA.*

Before people grew accustomed to using the discounted free cash flow to firm method,[9] the dividend discounted model (DDM) was very popular: the value of a share is equal to the present value of all the cash flows that its owner is entitled to receive, namely the dividends, discounted at the cost of equity (k_E).

This method is rarely used today, because it is extremely complicated. The critical variable is the rate of growth in dividends. It is quite an arbitrary figure as, in the computation, this rate is not a function of any of the factors that give rise to it: marginal rate of return, payout ratio, gearing, etc.

This method is still used in very specific cases – for example, for companies in mature sectors with very good visibility and high payout ratios, such as utilities, concessions and real estate companies.

Using the same logic, one can compute the value of equity by discounting free cash flow to equity (and no longer to firm) at the cost of equity. Free cash flow to equity is money available for shareholders, i.e. free cash flow to the firm minus after-tax interest payments and plus change in net debt.

This method is not an easy one to carry out if there is regular change in the financial structure which prompts regular change in the cost of equity. But it is widely used to value banks, whose financial structures do not change much over time due to regulatory constraints.[10]

10 *Basel II, McDonough ratio.*

Section 32.3
MULTIPLE APPROACH OR PEER-GROUP COMPARISONS

1/ PRESENTATION

The peer comparison or multiples approach (or comparables, "comps" method) is based on three fundamental principles:

- the company is to be valued in its entirety;
- the company is valued at a multiple of its profit-generating capacity. The most commonly used are the P/E ratio, EBITDA and EBIT multiples;
- markets are efficient and comparisons are therefore justified.

The approach is global, because it is based not on the value of operating assets and liabilities *per se*, but on the overall returns they are expected to generate. The value of the company is derived by applying a certain multiplier to the company's profitability parameters. As we saw in Chapter 23, multiples depend on expected growth, risk and interest rates.

High expected growth, low risk in the company's sector and low interest rates will all push multiples higher.

The approach is comparative. At a given point in time and in a given country, companies are bought and sold at a specific price level, represented, for example, by an EBIT multiple. These prices are based on internal parameters and by the overall stock market context. Prices paid for companies acquired in Europe in 2010, for example, when EBIT multiples were relatively low (7/8 times on average) were not the same as for those acquired in 1980 when multiples hovered around four times EBIT, nor for those bought in 2000, when multiples were very high (c. 12 to 15 times).

Multiples can derive from a sample of comparable, listed companies or a sample of companies that have recently been sold. The latter sample has the virtue of representing actual transaction prices for the equity value of a company. These multiples are respectively called **market multiples or trading multiples** and **transaction multiples**, and we will look at them in turn. As these multiples result from comparing a market value with accounting figures, keep in mind that the two must be consistent. The enterprise value must be compared with operating data, such as turnover, EBITDA or EBIT. The value of equity capital must be compared with a figure after interest expense, such as net profit or cash flow.

2/ BUILDING A SAMPLE OF COMPARABLE COMPANIES

For market multiples, a peer group comparison consists of setting up a sample of comparable listed companies that have not only similar sector characteristics, but also similar operating characteristics, such as ROCE and expected growth rates. Given that the multiple is usually calculated on short-term projections, you should choose companies whose shares are liquid and are covered by a sufficient number of financial analysts.

3/ THE MENU OF MULTIPLES

There are two major groups of multiples: those based on the enterprise value (i.e. the value of capital employed) and those based on the value of equity.

Multiples based on the value of capital employed are multiples of operating balances before subtracting interest expense. We believe NOPAT is the best denominator, i.e. EBIT less corporate income taxes on EBIT. But many practitioners use EBIT, which is not a major problem provided corporate income tax rates are roughly the same for all the companies in the sample. The EBITDA multiple is also widely used.

Multiples based on the value of equity are multiples of operating balances after interest expense, principally net income (P/E multiple), as well as multiples of cash flow and multiples of underlying income – i.e. before non-recurring items.

4/ MULTIPLES BASED ON ENTERPRISE VALUE

Whatever multiple you choose, you will have to value the capital employed for each listed company in the sample. This value is the sum of the company's market capitalisation (or transaction value of equity for transaction multiples) and the value of its net debt at the valuation date and other adjustments presented.

In any case you need to be clear:

- the value of a minority stake will be added to the enterprise value if no dividend has been included in the company parameter (EBIT or EBITDA, which is normally the case), but not if it is included (net income);

11 *Which could
be the case under
IFRS.*

- the part of pension cost corresponding to the interest cost is not to be included in the EBIT or EBITDA[11] if pension assets minus pension liabilities have been added to enterprise value;
- etc.

You will then calculate the multiple for the comparable companies over three fiscal years: the current year, last year and next year. Note that we use the same value of capital employed in all three cases, as current market values should reflect anticipated changes in future operating results.[12]

12 *For more
on this, see the
Vernimmen.com
Newsletter no 24,
May 2007.*

(a) EBIT multiple

The EBIT multiple is the ratio of the value of capital employed to EBIT (operating income). It enables us to compare the genuine profit-generating capacity of the sample companies.

A company's genuine profit-generating capacity is the normalised operating profitability it can generate year after year, excluding exceptional gains and losses and other non-recurring items.

You may have to perform a series of restatements in order to derive this operating income (see Chapter 3 for a more detailed discussion).

Consider the following sample of listed companies comparable to Indesit, the characteristics of which in 2011 were as follows:

€m	Electrolux	Whirlpool	SEB	De Longhi
Market capitalisation (value of equity)	45 900	6800	3625	1308
+ Value of debt	709	3747	847	114
= Value of capital employed (A)	46 609	10 547	4472	1422
2011e Operating income (EBIT) (B)	7201	1393	459	208
2011e EBIT multiple (A/B)	6.5	7.6	9.7	6.8

The 2012 average pre-tax operating income (EBIT) multiple is 7.6 times. Applied to Indesit's 2012e operating income of €207m, comparable multiples would value Indesit's enterprise value at €1573m and equity at €1251m, taking into account €322m of debts.

(b) EBITDA multiple

The EBITDA multiple follows the same logic as the EBIT multiple. It has the merit of eliminating the sometimes significant differences in depreciation methods and periods. It is very frequently used by stock market analysts for companies in capital-intensive industries.

Be careful when using the EBITDA multiple, however, especially when the sample and the company to be valued have widely disparate levels of margins. In these cases, the EBITDA multiple tends to overvalue companies with low margins and undervalue companies with high margins, independently of depreciation policy. EBITDA does not capture certain (other) elements of profitability. Applying the sample's multiple therefore introduces a distortion.

(c) Other multiples

Operating multiples can also be calculated on the basis of other measures, such as turnover. Some industries have even more specific multiples, such as multiples of the number of subscribers, number of visitors or page views for Internet companies, tonnes of cement produced, etc. These multiples are particularly interesting when the return on capital employed of the companies in the sample is standard. Otherwise, results will be too widely dispersed. They are only meaningful for small businesses such as shops where there are a lot of transactions and where, in many countries, turnover gives a better view of the profitability than the official profit figure.

These multiples are generally used to value companies that are not yet profitable: they were widely used during the Internet bubble, for instance. They tend to ascribe far too much value to the company to be valued and we recommend that you avoid them.

5/ MULTIPLES BASED ON EQUITY VALUE

You may also decide to choose multiples based on operating balances after interest expense. These multiples include the P/E ratio, the cash flow multiple and the price-to-book ratio. All these multiples use market capitalisation at the valuation date (or price paid for the equity for transaction multiples) as their numerator. The denominators are net profit, cash flow and book equity, respectively. The net profit used by analysts is the company's bottom line, i.e. the net profit attributable to the group (after deduction of minority interests) restated to exclude non-recurring items and the depreciation of goodwill, so as to put the emphasis on recurrent profit-generating capacity.

Using the same sample of comparable comparisons for Indesit presented before, we notice that, in mid-2011, their average 2012e P/E ratio is 9.9:

Local currency	Electrolux	Whirlpool	SEB	De Longhi
Market capitalisation (A)	45 900	6800	3625	1308
2008 Net income (B)	5310	806	300	124
P/E ratio (A) / (B)	8.6	8.4	12.1	10.5

Applied to Indesit's 2012e net income of €119m, comparable multiples would value Indesit's equity at €1178m.

These multiples indirectly value the company's financial structure, thus creating distortions depending on whether or not the companies in the sample are indebted.

Consider the following two similarly-sized companies, Ann and Valeria, operating in the same sector and enjoying the same outlook for the future, with the following characteristics:

Company	Ann	Valeria
Operating income	150	177
− Interest expense	30	120
− Corporate income tax (40%)	48	23
= Net profit	72	34
Market capitalisation	1800	?
Value of debt (at 10% p.a.)	300	1200

Ann's P/E ratio is 25 (1800/72). As the two companies are comparable, we might be tempted to apply Ann's P/E ratio to Valeria's bottom line to obtain Valeria's market capitalisation – i.e. the market value of its shares, or $25 \times 34 = 850$.

Although it looks logical, this reasoning is flawed. Applying a P/E ratio of 25 to Valeria's net income is tantamount to applying a P/E of 25 to Valeria's NOPAT ($177 \times (1 - 40\%) = 106$) less a P/E of 25 applied to its after-tax interest expense ($120 \times (1 - 40\%) = 72$). After all, net income is equal to net operating profit after tax less interest expense after tax.

The first term ($25 \times$ NOPAT) should represent the enterprise value of Valeria, i.e. $25 \times 106 = 2650$.

The second term ($25 \times$ after-tax interest expense) should represent the value of debt to be subtracted from enterprise value to give the value of equity capital that we are seeking. However, $25 \times$ interest expense after tax is 1800, whereas the value of the debt is only 1200.

In this case, this type of reasoning would result in overstating the value of the debt (at 1800 instead of 1200) and then understating the value of the company's equity.

The proper reasoning is as follows: we first use the multiple of Ann's NOPAT to get Valeria's enterprise value. If Ann's market capitalisation is 1800 and its debt is worth 300, then its enterprise value is $1800 + 300$, or 2100. As Ann's NOPAT is $150 \times (1 - 40\%) = 90$, the multiple of Ann's NOPAT is $2100/90 = 23.3$. Valeria's enterprise value is therefore equal to 23.3 times its NOPAT, or $23.3 \times 106 = 2470$. We now subtract the value of the debt (1200) to obtain the value of equity capital, or 1270. This is not the same as 850!

These distortions are the reason why financial analysts use multiples of operating income (EBIT) or of operating income before depreciation and amortisation (EBITDA). This approach removes the bias introduced by different financial structures.

6/ TRANSACTION MULTIPLES

The approach is slightly different, but the method of calculation is the same. The sample is composed of information available on recent transactions in the same sector, such as the sale of a controlling block of shares, a merger, etc.

If we use the price paid by the acquirer, our multiple will contain the **control premium** the acquirer paid to obtain control of the target company. As such, the price includes the value of anticipated synergies. Using the listed share prices leads to a so-called minority value, which we now know is nothing other than the standalone value. In contrast, transaction multiples reflect majority value – i.e. the value including any control premium for synergies. For listed companies it has been empirically observed that control premiums are around 25% of pre-bid market prices (i.e. prices prior to the announcement of the tender offer).

You will find that it is often difficult to apply this method, because good information on truly comparable transactions is often lacking or incomplete (price paid not made public, unknown aggregates when the company is private, etc.).

7/ MEDIANS, MEANS AND REGRESSIONS

People often ask if they should value a company by multiplying its profit-generating capacity by the mean or the median of the multiples of the sample of comparable companies.

Our advice is to be wary of both means and medians, as they can mask wide disparities within the sample, and sometimes may contain extreme situations that should be excluded altogether. Try to understand why the differences exist in the first place rather than to bury them in a mean or median value that has little real significance. For example, look at the multiples of the companies in the sample as a function of their expected growth. Sometimes this can be a very useful tool in positioning the company to be valued in the context of the sample.

Some analysts perform linear regressions to find a relationship between, for example: the EBIT multiple and expected growth in EBIT; the multiple of turnover and the operating margin; the price-to-book ratio and the return on equity.[13]

13 *In particular when valuing a bank.*

This method allows us to position the company to be valued within the sample. The issue still pending is to find the most relevant criterion. R^2 indicates the significance of the regression line, and will be our guide in determining which criteria are the most relevant in the industry in question. Sometimes it allows you to choose a multiple outside the range of comparables' multiples simply because the company you are valuing has higher or lower expected growth than others you are comparing it with.

Section 32.4
THE SUM-OF-THE-PARTS METHOD (SOTP) OR NET ASSET VALUE (NAV)

The sum-of-the-parts method consists in valuing and summing up the company's different assets, divisions or subsidiaries and deducting liabilities. It is a method well suited for diversified groups or conglomerates for which consolidated accounts projections give too global a view.

The sum-of-the-parts method is simple. It consists in systematically studying the value of each asset and each liability on the company's balance sheet. For a variety of reasons – accounting, tax, historical – book values are often far from reality. They must therefore be restated and revalued before they can be assumed to reflect a true net asset value. The sum-of-the-parts method is an **additive method**. Revalued assets are summed, and the total of revalued liabilities is subtracted.

SECTION 3

14 *Not that of subsidiaries, as it has already been taken into account when valuing the subsidiaries.*

For diversified groups, the SOTP or NAV method implies valuing subsidiaries or activities pro rata the ownership level using either the DCF or the multiples of comparable companies method. Then, debt of the mother company[14] is deducted as well as the present value of central costs.

To apply this method properly, therefore, we must value each asset and each liability. Estimates must be consistent, even though the methods applied might be different.

1/ Type of approach

(a) General philosophy

Several basic types of value are used in the sum-of-the-parts method:

- **market value:** this is the value we could obtain by selling the asset. This value might seem indisputable from a theoretical point of view, but it virtually assumes that the buyer's goal is liquidation. This is rarely the case. Acquisitions are usually motivated by the promise of industrial or commercial synergies;
- **value in use:** this is the value of an asset that is used in the company's operations. It is a kind of market value at replacement cost;
- **liquidation value:** this is the value of an asset during a fire sale to get cash as soon as possible to avoid bankruptcy. It is market value minus a discount.

The sum-of-the-parts method is the easiest to use and the values it generates are the least questionable when the assets have a value on a market that is **independent of the company's operations**, such as the property market, the market for aeroplanes, etc. It is hard to put a figure on a new factory in a new industrial estate. The value of the inventories and vineyards of a wine company is easy to determine and relatively undisputed.

A wide variety of values is available when we apply the sum-of-the-parts method. Possible approaches are numerous. We can assume discontinuation of the business – either sudden or gradual – or that it will continue as a going concern, for example. The important thing is to be consistent, sticking to the same approach throughout the valuation process.

For example, this is how the broker Deutsche Bank valued the Daimler group in early 2011:

€ m	Valuation	Valuation method
Mercedes cars (100%)	22 000	EBITDA multiple
Mercedes trucks (100%)	21 000	EBITDA multiple
Van Bus (100%)	7000	EBITDA multiple
Financial services	5000	sustainable ROE/COE × Equity
Intercompany eliminations	−1000	
Other businesses	2183	
EADS (17.3%)	2526	Share of market cap
Tognum (25%)	573	Share of market cap
Renault (3.1%)	367	Share of market cap
Nissan (3.1%)	888	Share of market cap
Total assets	60 537	

€ m	Valuation	Valuation method
Pension underfunding	−5000	
Healthcare + other provisions	−2600	
Adjusted net cash	13 224	
Minorities	−1566	
Equity value	**64 595**	

(b) Tax implications

The acquirer's objectives will influence the way taxes are included (or not) in the sum-of-the-parts approach.

- If the objective is to liquidate or break up the target company into component parts, the acquirer will buy the assets directly, giving rise to capital gains or losses. The taxes (or tax credits) theoretically generated will then decrease (increase) the ultimate value of the asset.
- If the objective is to acquire some assets (and liabilities), and to run them as a going concern, then the assets will be revalued through the transaction. Increased depreciation will then lower income tax compared to liquidation or the breakup case above.[15]
- If the objective is to acquire a company and maintain it as a going concern (i.e. not discontinue its activities) and as a separate entity, the acquiring company buys the shares of the target company rather than the underlying assets. It cannot revalue the assets on its books and will depreciate them from a lower base than if it had acquired the assets directly. As a result, depreciation expense will be lower and taxes higher.

The theoretical tax impact of a capital gain or loss must be taken into account if the objective is to break up the company.

15 *Acquisition of assets will most often generate deductible depreciation whereas acquisition of shares of a company will generate goodwill, which in most European countries does not give rise to tax-deductible amortisation.*

SECTION 3

2/ TANGIBLE ASSETS

Production assets can be evaluated on the basis of replacement value, liquidation value, going-concern value or yet other values.

We do not intend to go into great detail here. Our main point is that in the sum-of-the-parts method it is important to determine an overall value for productive and commercial assets. Rather than trying to decompose assets into small units, you should reason on a general basis and consider sufficiently large groups of assets that have a standalone value (i.e. for which a market exists or that can operate on a standalone basis).

For example, it makes no sense to value the land on which a warehouse has been built. It makes more sense to value the combination of the land and the buildings on it. An appraiser will value the combination based on its potential productive capacity, not on the basis of its individual components. Of course, this is not the case if the objective is to reuse the land for something else, in which case you will want to deduct the cost of knocking down the warehouse.

3/ INVENTORIES

For industrial companies, valuing inventories usually does not pose a major problem, unless they contain products that are obsolete or in poor condition. In this case, we have to apply a discount to their book value, based on a routine inventory of the products.

In some situations, you will have to revalue the inventories of companies with long production cycles; the revaluation can lead to gains on inventories. This is often the case with champagne, cognac, whisky and spirits in general. Here again, revaluation will have an impact on income taxes. Remember that when you revalue inventories, you are **decreasing future profits**.

4/ INTANGIBLE ASSETS

It might seem paradoxical to value intangible assets, since their liquidation value has, for a long time, been considered to be low. It is now widely acknowledged, however, that the value of a company is partly determined by the real value of its intangible assets, be they brand names, a geographical location or other advantages.

The sum-of-the-parts approach makes no sense unless it takes into account the company's intangible assets.

Some noteworthy examples:

- **lease rights:** the present value of the difference between market rental rates and the rent paid by the company;
- **brands:** particularly hard to value but the importance of brands in valuation is growing.

In general, there are three methods for valuing brands:

Method 1   The first method asks how much would have to be spent in advertising expense, after tax, to rebuild the brand. This method leads to undervaluation of new and successful brands and overvaluation of older and failing brands.

Method 2   The second method calculates the present value of all royalty payments that will or could be received from the use of the brand by a third party. It is very sensitive to the chosen royalty rate.

Method 3   The third method consists in analysing the brand's fundamental utility. After all, the brand's *raison d'être* is to enable the company to sell more and at higher prices than would otherwise be possible without the brand name. Discounting this "excess profit" over a certain period of time should, after subtracting the related higher costs, yield an estimate of the value of the brand. Users of this method discount the incremental future operating income expected from the use of the brand and subtract the additional operating expense, working capital and investments, thereby isolating the value of the brand. We will not hide the fact that this approach, while intellectually appealing, is very difficult to apply in practice, because often there is no generic "control" product to use as a benchmark.

- **patents and technical know-how:** they are valued as brands but with the same difficulties.

5/ USEFULNESS OF SUM-OF-THE-PARTS VALUES

Sum-of-the-parts values can be deceptive as many people think they imply safe or reliable values. In fact, when we say that a company has a high net asset value, it means that from a free cash flow point of view, the company's terminal value is high compared with the value of intermediate cash flows. Consequently, the more "net asset value" a company has and the fewer cash flows it has, the more speculative and volatile its value is. Granted, its industrial risk may be lower, but most of the value derives from speculation about resale prices.

For this reason, the sum-of-the-parts method is useful for valuing small companies with no particular strategic value, or companies whose assets can be sold readily on a secondary market (aeroplanes, cinemas, etc . . .).

Section 32.5
COMPARISON OF VALUATION METHODS

1/ RECONCILING THE DIFFERENT METHODS OF VALUATION

If markets are efficient, all of the valuation methods discussed so far should lead to the same valuation. In reality, however, there are often differences among the sum-of-the-parts value, the DCF-based value and the peer-comparison value. You must analyse the source of these differences and **resist the temptation to average them**!

(a) Analysing the difference between sum-of-the-parts value and discounted cash flow value

If the sum-of-the-parts value is higher than the DCF value or the value derived from a comparison of multiples, then the company is being valued more for its past, its revalued equity capital, than for its outlook for future profitability. In this case, the company should not invest but divest, liquidating its assets to boost profitability and improve the allocation of its resources.

This strategy had its heyday in the 1980s and is back in fashion.[16] Companies were bought up on the open market, and then sold off piecemeal. The buyer realised a gain because the parts were worth more than the company as a whole. Far from a return to unbridled, 19th-century capitalism, these purely financial transactions represented a better allocation of resources as well as punishment for bad management.

If the sum-of-the-parts value is lower than the DCF value or the value derived from multiples, which is the usual case in an economy where companies have a lot of intangibles, then the company is very profitable and invests in projects with expected profitability greater than their cost of capital. The company has real expertise, a strong strategic positioning and enjoys high barriers to entry. But the chances are that it will not escape competitive pressure forever.

16 *Breakup of ABN Amro, Scottish & Newcastle, Hagemayer.*

(b) Comparison values versus DCF values

If the value obtained via peer comparison is greater than the DCF-based value (and if all the calculations are correct!), then the company's managers should be thinking about floating the company on the stock exchange, because financial investors have a more positive view of the company's risk profile and profitability outlook than its management or current shareholders. Conversely, if the value obtained by comparison is lower than the DCF value and if the business plan is reliable, it would be wiser to wait until more of the long-term growth potential in the company's business plan feeds through to its financial statements before launching an IPO; and perhaps do a Public to Private[17] if the company is already listed.

17 See p. 866.

If transaction multiples generate a significantly higher value than market multiples or the DCF model, then it would be better to organise a trade sale by soliciting bids from several industry participants. In short, look before you leap!

(c) Is there one valuation method for selling a company and another for buying it?

There is no technical reason why a seller should not use one valuation method and the buyer another:

*   A seller usually favours the DCF method as it is based upon a business plan which is rarely built on pessimistic assumptions! Most business plans are fathered by the management under instruction from selling shareholders. But in the back of his mind, a seller will not forget results obtained with a peer-comparison method as he will be very reluctant to sell at a lower multiple than the one obtained by a competitor a few months ago or the one he could get through an IPO.
*   A buyer will use the peer-comparison method to justify a lower price than that resulting from the DCF. He will claim that other buyers have paid 100 and there is no reason why he should pay 120 or 130. Nevertheless at the back of his mind, the buyer is thinking about his own business plan including synergies and new developments. He will soon be able to compute his own DCF to check whether the price he will pay is expected to create value for his own shareholders.

2/ THE LIFECYCLE THEORY OF COMPANY VALUE

Companies that have achieved a certain level of success will see their sum-of-the-parts and cash flow values differ throughout their lifecycle. Lifecycle is an important factor in determining the value of companies, as it was in determining the optimal capital structure and financing policies.

When the company is founded, its net asset value and cash flow value are identical; the company has not yet made any investments. After the first year or two of operations, net asset value may dip because of startup losses. Meanwhile, cash flow value is greater because it anticipates hopefully positive future profitability.

During the growth phase, net asset value will rise as all or part of the company's profits are reinvested and the company builds a customer base (the value of which does not appear in the accounts, however). Cash flow value also continues to rise and remains above the net asset value. The company's expertise has not yet become a tangible asset. It is still associated with the people who developed it.

At maturity, cash flow value will start growing more slowly or stop growing altogether, reflecting a normal profit trend. Nonetheless, the net asset value continues to grow, but more slowly because the company increases its payout ratio. Broadly speaking, net asset value and cash flow value are very close.

If the company then enters a phase of decline, its profits decline and the cash flow value slips below net asset value. The latter continues to grow but only very slowly, until the company starts posting losses. The net asset value falls. As for cash flow value, it is already very low. **The net asset value then becomes particularly speculative**.

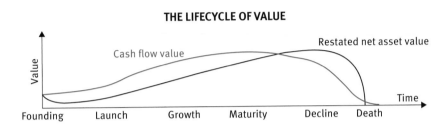

Net asset value and cash flow value evolve differently throughout the life of the company.

At any given point in time, it is very important to understand the reasons for the difference between the net asset value and the cash flow value, because this understanding gives important clues as to the situation and future prospects of the company.

You might now be thinking that our kaleidoscope of methods leads to as many **values** as there are images of the company:

- sum-of-the-parts, or net asset value;
- peer-comparison value;
- intrinsic value (i.e. DCF), etc.

We advise against calculating a wide variety of valuations, unless it is to show that you can prove anything when it comes to valuation. But you must not throw up your hands in despair either. Instead, try to understand each type of value, which corporate circumstances it applies to and what its implicit assumptions are. It is more important to determine ranges than to come up with precise values. Precision is the domain of negotiation, the goal of which is to arrive at an agreed **price**.

Lastly, remember that valuing a company means:

- taking a speculative stance not only on the future of the company, but also on its market conditions. The cash flow and comparison methods demonstrate this;
- implicitly extrapolating past results or expected near-term results far into the future, opening the door to exaggeration;
- sometimes forgetting that net asset value is not a good reference if the profitability of the company differs significantly from its investors' required return.

Shareholders' decisions to sell all or part of a company are based on the price they believe they can obtain compared to their set of calculated valuations.

SECTION 3

A newcomer to finance might think that the market for the purchase and sale of companies is a separate market with its own rules, its own equilibria, its own valuation methods and its own participants.

This is absolutely wrong. Indeed the market for corporate control is simply a segment of the financial market. The valuation methods used in this segment are based on the same principles as those used to measure the value of a financial instrument. Experience has proven that the higher the stock market, the higher the price of unlisted companies.

Participants in the market for corporate control think the same way as investors in the financial market. Of course, the smaller the company is, the more tenuous is the link. The value of a butcher's shop or a bakery is largely intangible and hard to measure, and thus has little in common with financial market values. But in reality, only appearances make the market for corporate control seem fundamentally different.

1/ STRATEGIC VALUE AND CONTROL PREMIUM

There is no real control value other than strategic value. We will develop this concept later. For a long time, the **control premium** was a widely-accepted notion that was virtually a pardon for dispossessing minority shareholders. When a company was valued at 100 and another company was willing to pay a premium of 20 to the controlling shareholder (holding 50.01% for example), minority shareholders were excluded from this advantageous offer.

The development of financial markets and financial market regulations has changed this: equality among shareholders is a sacrosanct principle in most countries. Shareholder agreements are a common method for expressing this principle in unlisted companies.

When control of a listed company changes hands, minority shareholders receive the same premium as that paid to the majority shareholder.

Nevertheless, entrepreneurs often have a diametrically opposed view. For them, minority shareholders are passive beneficiaries of the fruits of all the personal energy the managers/majority shareholders have invested in the company. It is difficult to convince entrepreneurs that the roles of management and shareholders can be separated and that they must be compensated differently – and especially that risk assumed by all types of shareholders must be rewarded.

What then is the basis for this premium which, in the case of listed companies, can often lift a purchase price to 20% or 30% more than current market price? The premium is still called a "control premium" even though it is now paid to minority shareholders as well as to the majority shareholder.

If we assume that markets are efficient, the existence of such a premium can be justified only if the new owners of the company obtain more value from it than did its previous owners. A control premium derives from the **industrial, commercial, administrative or tax synergies** the new majority shareholders hope to unlock. They hope to improve the acquired company's results by managing it better, pooling resources, combining businesses or taking advantage of economies of scale. These value-creating actions are reflected in the buyer's valuation. The trade buyer (i.e. an acquirer which already has industrial operations) wants to acquire the company so as to change the way it is run and, in doing so, create value.

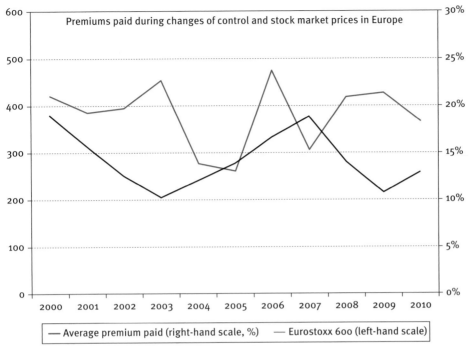

M&A ACTIVITY CONTROL PREMIUM

Premiums paid during changes of control and stock market prices in Europe

— Average premium paid (right-hand scale, %)   — Eurostoxx 600 (left-hand scale)

Source: Exane BNP Paribas, Datastream

The company is therefore worth more to a trade buyer than it is to a financial buyer (i.e. usually a venture capitalist fund which has no operations in the industry), who values the company on a **standalone** basis, as one investment opportunity among others, **independently of these synergies**.

The peculiarity of the market for corporate control arises from the existence of synergies that give rise to strategic value.

In this light, we now understand that the trade buyer's expectations are not the same as those of the financial investor. This difference can lead to a different valuation of the company. We call this **strategic value**.

Strategic value is the maximum value a trade buyer is prepared to pay for a company. It includes the value of projected free cash flows of the target on a standalone basis, plus the value of synergies from combining the company's businesses with those of the trade buyer. It also includes the value of expected improvement in the company's profitability compared to the business plan provided, if any.

We previously demonstrated that the value of a financial security is independent of the portfolio to which it belongs, but now we are confronted with an exception. Depending on whether a company belongs to one group of companies or another, it does not have the same value. Make sure you understand why this is the case. The difference in value derives from different cash flow projections, not from a difference in the discount rate applied to them, which is a characteristic of the company and identical for all investors. **The principles of value are the same for everyone, but strategic value is different for each trade buyer, because each of them places a different value on the synergies it believes it can unlock and on its ability to manage the business better than current management.**

SECTION 3

For this reason, a company's strategic value is often higher than its standalone value.

As the seller will also hope to benefit from the synergies, negotiation will focus on how the additional profitability the synergies are expected to generate will be shared between the buyer and the seller.

But some industrial groups go overboard, buying companies at twice their standalone value on the pretext that their strategic value is high or that establishing a presence in such-and-such geographic location is crucial. They are in for a rude awakening. Sometimes the market has already put a high price tag on the target company. Specifically, when the market anticipates merger synergies, speculation can drive the share price far above the company's strategic value, even if all synergies are realised. In other cases, a well-managed company may benefit little or even be hurt by teaming up with another company in the same industry, meaning either that there are no synergies to begin with or, worse, that they are negative.

2/ MINORITY DISCOUNTS AND PREMIUMS

We have often seen minority holdings valued with a discount, and you will quickly understand why we believe this is unjustified. A "minority discount" would imply that minority shareholders have proportionally less of a claim on the cash flows generated by the company than the majority shareholder. This is not true.

Whereas a control premium can (and must) be justified by subsequent synergies, there is no basis for a minority discount.

In fact, a shareholder who already has the majority of a company's shares may be forced to pay a premium to buy the shares held by minority shareholders. On average in Europe, the premium paid to buy out minorities is in the region of 20%, only marginally less than that paid to obtain control. Indeed, majority shareholders may be willing to pay such a premium if they need full control over the acquired company to implement certain synergies.

Having said that, the lack of liquidity associated with certain minority holdings, either because the company is not listed or because trading volumes are low compared with the size of the minority stake, can justify a discount. In this case, the discount does not really derive from the minority stake *per se*, but from its lack of liquidity.

Lack of liquidity may increase volatility of the share price. Therefore investors will discount an illiquid investment at a higher rate than a liquid one. The difference in values results in a liquidity discount.

SUMMARY

The summary of this chapter can be downloaded from www.vernimmen.com.

Discounted cash flow, or DCF, is based on the notion that the value of the company is equal to the amount of free cash flows expected to be generated by the company in the future and discounted at a rate commensurate with its risk profile. The discount rate applied is the weighted average cost of capital (WACC). DCF calculation is performed as follows:

- future free cash flows are discounted over the explicit forecast period, i.e. the period over which there is visibility on the company's operations;

- a discounted terminal value is calculated on the basis of an estimated growth rate carried to perpetuity;

- the value of equity is the difference between the enterprise value obtained above and the value of the company's net debt.

The peer group or multiples method is a comparative approach that sets off the company to be valued against other companies in the same sector. In this approach, the enterprise value of the company is estimated via a multiple of its profit-generating capacity before interest expense. EBIT and EBITDA multiples are among those commonly used. The multiple used in the comparison can be either a market multiple or a transaction multiple. The value of net debt is deducted from this enterprise value to get the value of equity. Equity can also be directly valued through a multiple of net income, cash flow or book equity.

The sum-of-the-parts method of valuation consists in valuing and summing up each of the company's assets, subsidiaries or divisions and subtracting liabilities. There are several types of net asset value, from liquidation value to going-concern value, and there are important tax considerations. Either capital gains or losses will be subject to tax or depreciable assets will be undervalued and yearly taxes higher. Calculating net asset value makes sense only if it includes the company's intangible assets, which can be particularly difficult to value.

No company valuation is complete without an analysis of the reasons for the differences in the results obtained by the various valuation methods. These differences give rise to decisions of financial engineering and evolve throughout the life of the company. To the financial manager, the market for corporate control is nothing but a segment of the broader capital market. From this principle it follows that there is no such thing as control value other than the strategic value deriving from synergies.

Industrial synergies generally make a company's strategic value higher than its financial or standalone value. The essence of negotiation lies in determining how the strategic value pie will be divided between the buyer and the seller, with both parties trying, unsurprisingly, to obtain the largest possible share.

QUESTIONS

1/ What is the most relevant cash flow when valuing a company using the discounted cash flow method?

2/ What sort of a discount can a minority shareholder get compared with a financial value? Show how the situation differs between a listed company and an unlisted company.

3/ What is a synergy?

4/ Logically, should a foreign investor with little knowledge of the country pay more or less for a company? Explain why foreign investors often offer the highest price. What is the role of the investment bank?

5/ Can you multiply a P/E ratio by the EBIT to get the equity value?

6/ Describe the type of company that has a financial value higher than its strategic value.

7/ Which method in your view would be best suited for valuing: a property management company; a holding company; mutual fund; a company in the aeronautics sector; a bicycle factory; a portfolio of movies?

SECTION 3

8/Can an asset have several values? Why?

9/Is a valuation of a cinema theatre or a chemist shop in terms of a number of weeks' sales a result of the sum-of-the-parts or the cash flow method?

10/What are the two determining factors when valuing a wine estate?

11/Which method should be used for estimating the value of a company in decline?

12/When a company is bought, is there a control premium?

13/Name the types of companies for which cash flow value is much higher than net asset value.

14/Can the purchase of a company by venture capitalists create value? And by trade buyers?

15/Has a reduction in working capital of 1% the same impact on a DCF as a 1% improvement in the EBIT margin?

16/Why can we say that the mean or the median figure is the choice of an indecisive person?

17/What is the popular saying on which the cash flow fade method is founded?

18/Should the buyer's costs be separated from the target company's costs in the cost savings that come out of a merger of two companies?

More questions are waiting for you at www.vernimmen.com.

EXERCISES

1/Megabyte plc is a high-tech company experiencing transitional problems. To get through this difficult period, management has decided on a €120m recapitalisation. In 5 years' time, the company should make net profits of €21m, and be valued at 30 times its profits. Assume that the discount rate is 25% and that there will be no cash flows generated for 5 years.

- What is the present value of shareholders' equity?
- What is the present value of shareholders' equity if profits of only €14m are expected in 5 years?
- What do you conclude from the above?

2/The table below shows the forecasts for Management plc (in millions of €):

Year	1	2	3	4	5
Sales	3960	4080	4200	4326	4458
Cost of goods sold	1782	1794	1806	1860	1917
Marketing costs	870	897	924	996	1026
Administrative costs	396	408	420	432	447
Depreciation and amortisation	330	315	300	300	300
EBIT (Operating income)	582	666	750	738	768

The company is expecting annual capital expenditure of €300m per year over the next 5 years; working capital will increase by €50m in years 1 and 2, and stabilise thereafter. The following information is also available:

- the company has net debts today of €2250m;
- the company's cost of equity is estimated at 10%, and the cost of debt at 6% (before tax);
- financing is split 2/3 equity and 1/3 debt;
- the tax rate is 37%;
- an increase in inflows of 2% to perpetuity can be expected from year 6.

Work out the value of Management plc using the DCF method.

3/ The mean multiple for the 2011 operating profits of comparable peers is 10, and the mean 2011 P/E is 15. Calculate the equity value of Pixi Spa. Key figures for the company are set out below.

	Millions of €
Net debt at 31 December 2010	100
2011e operating profits	60
2011e net profits	32

4/ You have to value Nestlé, the Swiss food group, using a peer-comparable method. In 2010, Nestlé earned an operating income of CHF 16.2bn and had, as of 31/12/2010, a net financial debt of CHF 1.3bn. Nestlé owned 30.5% of L'Oréal, consolidated using the equity method and whose market cap as of 31/12/10 was CHF 67bn. If the 2010 EBIT multiple of food groups was 14, what is your estimation of the equity value of Nestlé?

ANSWERS

Questions

1/ *Free cash flows.*
2/ *A liquidity discount only. For a private company, the liquidity issue for a minority share-holder will be much more important as probably no one will want to buy this minority stake (apart maybe from the majority shareholder!). Stock market for a minority share-holder provides some (if not perfect) liquidity.*
3/ *See p. 624.*
4/ *He/she should pay less because information asymmetry works against him/her. There is a price to be paid for strategic reasons (e.g. to enter a market). This is where the advisory banks come in – their role is to reduce information asymmetry.*
5/ *No, as the P/E ratio can only be used with net income.*
6/ *A company with a large market share, that is very well run and in a high-growth non-strategic market segment.*
7/ *DCF value, sum-of-the parts value, sum-of-the parts value, sum-of-the parts value, DCF value, DCF value.*
8/ *Yes, because an asset can have a value for an investor or a trade buyer that differs from its value within the company of which it is currently part.*
9/ *It looks like the sum-of-the-parts method but it is actually the normalised cash flow method.*
10/ *Inventories, quality of the estate's land.*

SECTION 3

11/ *Sum-of-the-parts value.*

12/ *Yes, due to expected synergy gains.*

13/ *Advertising and Internet companies, Louis Vuitton and Gucci.*

14/ *Yes, for an LBO. Yes. Improved management, more efficient allocation of resources and better sharing of information.*

15/ *Yes, if the improvement in margin is a one-off event that will last for only one year, as the reduction in working capital generates a change in cash flow for only one year. And no if the increase in margin is here to stay resulting in a permanent improvement in cash flows.*

16/ *Because you have to choose where to position the company to be valued among its peers and mean or median is the answer for those who do not know how to make a choice.*

17/ *Trees do not grow until they reach the sky – ROCE cannot be higher than WACC forever.*

18/ *No. At the end of the day it will be value creative for the new group. Who gets it (the acquirer or the target's shareholders) is a question of negotiation between them.*

Exercises

A detailed Excel version of the solutions is available at www.vernimmen.com.

1/ *Present value with profits of 21: €86.4m. Present value with profits of 14: €17.6m. A one-third drop in profits reduces the value by more than 80% – very high volatility of value.*

2/ *Cost of capital 7.9%. Enterprise value = €7387m. Equity value €5137m.*

Years	1	2	3	4	5	Terminal value
EBITDA	912	981	1050	1038	1068	
– Corporate income tax	216	246	279	273	285	
– Change in working capital	50	50	0	0	0	
– Capital expenditure	300	300	300	300	300	
= Free cash flows	346	385	471	465	483	8307

3/ *Equity value = €480m = 15 × €32m or 10 × €60m – €100m = €500m.*

4/ *Nestlé value of equity = 14 × 16.2 × 30.5% × 67 – 1.3 × CHF 245.9bn.*

BIBLIOGRAPHY

A. Cheng, R. McNamara, The valuation accuracy of the price-earnings and price-book benchmark valuation methods, *Review of Quantitative Finance and Accounting*, **15**(4), 349–370, December 2000.

T. Copeland, T. Koller, J. Murrin, *Valuation: Measuring and Managing the Value of Companies*, 5th edn, John Wiley & Sons, Inc., 2010.

A. Damodaran, *Damodaran on Valuation: Security Analysis for Investment and Corporate Finance*, 2nd edn, John Wiley & Sons, Inc., 2006.

A. Damodaran, *The Dark Side of Valuation*, 2nd edn, Financial Times/Prentice Hall, 2009.

A. Damodaran, *Volatility rules: Valuing emerging market companies*, Working paper, Stern School of Business, September 2009.

P. Fernandez, Company valuation methods. The most common errors in valuation, *Investment Management and Financial Innovations Journal*, **2**(2), 128–141, July 2005.

L. Kruschwitz, A. Löffler, *Discounted Cash Flow: A Theory of the Valuation of Firms*, John Wiley & Sons, Ltd., 2005.

Y. Le Fur, P. Quiry, What are EV/FCF multiples? *The Vernimmen.com Newsletter*, **6**, 6 May 2005.

Y. Le Fur, P. Quiry, When valuing shareholders' equity, should debt be taken at fair value? *The Vernimmen.com Newsletter*, **7**, 1–3, June 2005.

E. Lie, H. Lie, Multiples used to estimate corporate value, *Financial Analysts Journal*, **58**(2), 44–54, March 2002.

B.J. Madden, *CFROI Valuation*, Butterworth-Heinemann Finance, 1999.

E. Ofek, M. Richardson, Dotcom mania: The rise and fall of internet stock prices, *Journal of Finance*, **58**(3), 1113–1137, June 2003.

G.B. Stewart, J. Stern, *The Quest for Value*, Harpers, 1991.

R. Thomas, B. Gup, *The Valuation Handbook: Valuation Techniques from Today's Top Practitioners*, John Wiley & Sons, Inc., 2009.

SECTION 3

Section IV
Corporate financial policies

PART ONE
CAPITAL STRUCTURE POLICIES

Chapter 33

CAPITAL STRUCTURE AND THE THEORY
OF PERFECT CAPITAL MARKETS

Does paradise exist in the world of finance?

The central question of this chapter (and of the following one) is: is there an optimal capital structure? That is to say, is there a "right" combination of equity and debt that allows us to reduce the weighted average cost of capital and therefore to maximise the value of capital employed (enterprise value)?

Section 33.1
THE VALUE OF CAPITAL EMPLOYED

While accounting looks at a company by examining its past and focusing on its costs, finance is mainly a projection of the company into the future. Finance reflects not only risk but also – and above all – the value that results from the perception of risk and future returns.

In finance, everything is about the future – return, risk and value.

From now on, we will speak constantly of **value**. As we saw previously, by value we mean **the present value of future cash flows discounted at the rate of return required by investors**:

- equity (E) will be replaced by the **value of equity** (V_E);
- net debt (D) will be replaced by the value of net debt (V_D);
- capital employed (CE) will be replaced by enterprise value (EV), or firm value.

We will speak in terms of a financial assessment of the company (rather than the accounting assessment provided by the balance sheet). Our financial assessment will include only the market values of assets and liabilities:

ENTERPRISE VALUE or FIRM VALUE (EV)	VALUE OF NET DEBT (V_D)
	EQUITY VALUE (V_E)

As operating assets are financed by equity and net debt (which are accounting concepts), logically, a company's enterprise value will consist of the market value of net debt and the market value of equity (which are financial concepts). This chapter therefore reasons in terms of:

Enterprise value = Value of net debt + Equity value

Important: Enterprise value is sometimes confused with equity value. Equity value is the enterprise value remaining for shareholders after creditors have been paid. To avoid confusion, remember that **enterprise value is the sum of equity value and net debt value.**

In this book we refer to the market value of operating assets (industrial and commercial) as "enterprise value", which is the sum of the market value of equity (i.e. the company's market capitalisation if it is publicly traded) and the market value of net debt. Enterprise value and firm value are synonymous.

Similarly, we will reason not in terms of return on equity, but rather required rate of return, which was discussed in depth in Chapter 19. In other words, the accounting notions of **ROCE (return on capital employed), ROE (return on equity) and i (cost of debt)**, which are based on past observations, will give way to **WACC or k (required rate of return on capital employed), k_E (required rate of return on equity) and k_D (required rate of return of net debt)**, which are the returns required by those investors who are financing the company.

Note that we consider the weighted average cost of capital (or cost of capital), denoted k, to be the rate of return required by all the company's investors either to buy or to hold its securities. **It is the company's cost of financing and the minimum return its investments must generate in the medium term. If not, the company is heading for ruin.**

k_D is the rate of return required by lenders of a given company, k_E is the cost of equity required by the company's shareholders, and k is the weighted average rate of the two types of financing, equity and net debt (from now on referred to simply as debt). The weighting reflects the breakdown of equity and debt in enterprise value.

With V_D, the market value of net debt, and V_E the market value of equity, we get:

$$k = k_D \left(\frac{V_D}{V_D + V_E} \right) + k_E \times \left(\frac{V_E}{V_D + V_E} \right)$$

or, since the enterprise value is equal to that of net debt plus equity ($EV = V = V_E + V_D$):

$$k = k_D \times \left(\frac{V_D}{V} \right) + k_E \times \left(\frac{V_E}{V} \right)$$

If, for example, the rate of return required by the company's creditors is 5% and that required by shareholders 10% and the value of debt is equal to that of equity, the return required by all of the company's sources of funding will be 7.5%. Its weighted average cost of capital is thus 7.5%.

To simplify our calculations and demonstrations in this chapter, we shall assume infinite durations for all debt and investments. This enables us to apply perpetual bond analytics and, more importantly, to assume that the company's capital structure remains unchanged during the life of the project; income being distributed in full.

The assumption of an infinite horizon is just a convention designed to simplify our calculations and demonstrations, but they remain accurate within a limited time horizon (say, for simplicity, 15–20 years).

We shall start by assuming a tax-free environment, both for the company and the investor, in which neither income nor capital gains are taxed. In other words, heaven! Concretely, the optimal capital structure is one that minimises k, i.e. that maximises the enterprise value (V). Remember that the enterprise value results from discounting free cash flow at rate k. However, free cash flow is not related to the type of financing. The demonstrations below endeavour to measure and explain changes in k according to the company's capital structure.

Section 33.2
WHAT OUR GRANDPARENTS THOUGHT

According to conventional wisdom, there is an optimal capital structure that maximises enterprise value by the judicious use of debt and the leverage it offers. This enables the company to minimise its weighted average cost of capital – that is, the cost of financing.

Why do we say that? Because there is enough evidence showing that the leverage of companies is not highly volatile. If the leverage doesn't change so often it means that companies are generally satisfied with the level of debt they have in their capital structure.

We know that *ex ante* debt is always cheaper than equity ($k_D < k_E$) because it is less risky. Consequently, a moderate increase in debt will help reduce k, since a more expensive resource – equity – is being replaced by a cheaper one – debt. This is the practical application of the preceding formula and the use of leverage.

However, any increase in debt also increases the risk for the shareholder. Markets then demand a higher k_E the more debt we add in the capital structure. The increase in the expected rate of return on equity cancels out part (or all, if the firm becomes highly leveraged!) of the decrease in cost arising on the recourse to debt. More specifically, the traditional theory claims that a certain level of debt gives rise to a very real risk of bankruptcy. Rather than remaining constant, shareholders' perception of risk evolves in stages.

The risk accruing to shareholders increases in step with that of debt, prompting the market to demand a higher return on equity. This process continues until it has cancelled out the positive impact of the debt financing.

At this level of financial leverage, the company has achieved the optimal capital structure ensuring the lowest weighted average cost of capital and thus the highest enterprise value. Should the company continue to take on debt, the resulting gains would no longer offset the higher return required by the market.

Moreover, the cost of debt increases after a certain level because it becomes more risky. At this point, not only has the company's cost of equity increased, but also of that of its debt.

In short, the evidence from the "real world" shows that an optimal capital structure can be achieved with some – but not too much – leverage.

According to the traditional approach, an optimal capital structure can be achieved where the weighted average cost of capital is minimal.

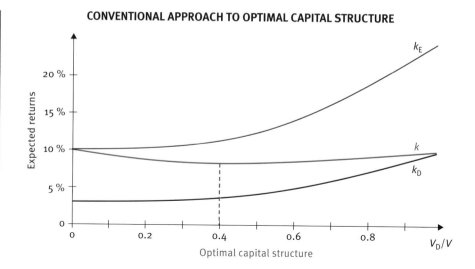

CONVENTIONAL APPROACH TO OPTIMAL CAPITAL STRUCTURE

In this example, the debt-to-equity ratio that minimises k is 0.4. The optimal capital structure is thus achieved with 40% debt financing and 60% equity financing.

The evidence from the capital structure can be explained with a theoretical model. This is a success. Why? Because if we have a model that explains the determinants of an optimal capital structure policy we can:

- *explain* **and interpret the behaviour of companies;**
- *predict* **where companies should position themselves and** *suggest* **these positions and an appropriate "convergence path".**

The common name of the model we are talking about is the (static) **"tradeoff model"**. It simply states that the optimal capital structure of a company is where benefits and costs of debt are best balanced.

This "thriller solution" – a startlingly simple conclusion – has been the result of a long evolution of financial theory, a story that started out with Franco Modigliani and Merton Miller in 1958 with a totally different result compared with the "real world" wisdom.

Section 33.3
THE CAPITAL STRUCTURE POLICY IN PERFECT FINANCIAL MARKETS

The perfect markets theory of capital structure contradicts the "real world" approach. It states that, barring any distortions, there is *no one* optimal capital structure.

We shall demonstrate this proposition by means of an example given by Franco Modigliani and Merton Miller (MM), who showed that, in a perfect market and without taxes, the traditional approach is incorrect. **If there is no optimal capital structure, the overall cost of equity (k or WACC) remains the same regardless of the firm's debt policy.**

SECTION 4

The main assumptions behind the theorem are:

1. companies can issue only two types of securities: risk-free debt and equity;
2. financial markets are frictionless;
3. there is no corporate and personal taxation;
4. there are no transaction costs;
5. firms cannot go bankrupt;
6. *insiders* and *outsiders* have the same set of information.

According to MM, investors can take on debt just like companies. So, in a perfect market, they have no reason to pay companies to do something they can handle themselves at no cost.

Imagine two companies that are completely identical except for their capital structure. The value of their respective debt and equity differs, but the sum of both, i.e. the enterprise value of each company, is the same. If the reverse were true, equilibrium would be restored by arbitrage.

We shall demonstrate this using the examples of companies X and Y, which are identical except that X is unlevered and Y carries debt of 80 000 at 5%. If the traditional approach were correct, Y's weighted average cost of capital would be lower than that of X and its enterprise value higher:

	Company X	Company Y
Operating profit: *EBIT*	20 000	20 000
Interest expense (at 5%): *IE*	0	4000
Net profit: *NP*	20 000	16 000
Dividend : $DIV = NP$[1]	20 000	16 000
Cost of equity: k_E	10%	12%
Equity: $V_E = DIV/k_E$[2]	200 000	133 333
Debt: $V_D = IE/k_D$[2]	0	80 000
Enterprise value: $V = V_E + V_D$	200 000	213 333
Weighted average cost of capital: $k = EBIT/V$[2]	10%	9.4%
Gearing : V_D/V_E	0%	60%

1 *To simplify calculations, the payout ratio is 100%.*

2 *To simplify calculations, we adopt an infinite horizon.*

Y's cost of equity is higher than that of X since Y's shareholders bear both the operating risk and that of the capital structure (debt), whereas X's shareholders incur only the same operating risk. As a matter of fact, the operating risk of X is the same as that of Y, as X and Y are identical but for their capital structures.

Modigliani and Miller demonstrated that Y's shareholders can achieve a higher return on their investment by buying shares of X, at no greater risk.

Thus, if a shareholder holding 1% of Y shares (equal to 1333) wants to obtain a better return on investment, he must:

- sell his Y shares . . .
- . . . **replicate** Y's debt/equity structure in proportion to his 1% stake; that is, borrow 1333 × 60% = 800 at 5%...
- . . . invest all this (800 + 1333 = 2133) in X shares.

SECTION 4

The shareholder's risk exposure is the same as before the operation: he is still exposed to operating risk, which is the same on X and Y, as well as to financial risk, since his exposure to Y's debt has been transferred to his personal borrowing. However, the personal wealth invested by our shareholder is still the same (1333).

Formerly, the investor received annual dividends of 160 from company Y (12% × 1333 or 1% of 16 000). Now, his net income on the same investment will be:

Dividends (company X)	2133 × 10% = 213
– Interest expense	800 × 5% = 40
= Net income	= 173

He is now earning 173 every year instead of the former 160, on the same personal amount invested and with the same level of risk.

Y's shareholders will thus sell their Y shares to invest in X shares, reducing the value of Y's equity and increasing that of X. This arbitrage will cease as soon as the enterprise values of the two companies come into line again.

Thus, barring any distortions, the enterprise value of a company must be independent of its financing policy.

Investing in a leveraged company is neither more expensive nor cheaper than in a company without debt; in other words, the investor should not pay twice, once when buying shares at enterprise value and again to reimburse the debt. The value of the debt is deducted from the price paid for the equity.

While obvious, this principle is frequently forgotten. And yet it should be easy to remember: the value of an asset, be it a factory, a painting, a subsidiary or a house, is the same regardless of whether it was financed by debt, equity or a combination of the two. As Merton Miller explained when receiving the Nobel Prize for Economics, "it is the size of the pizza that matters, not how many slices it is cut up into." Or, to restate this: the weighted average cost of capital does not depend on the sources of financing. True, it is the weighted average of the rates of return required by the various providers of funds, but this average is independent of its different components, which adjust to any changes in the financial structure.

Let's see a more practical implication. Take a company with an invested capital (working capital and fixed assets) of €500 000. The investments can generate a constant (and perpetual) operating income of €120 000. Suppose also that:

- the annual depreciation equals the new investments of each period;
- the annual variation of working capital is approximately zero;
- the payout ratio is 100%.

Let us limit the analysis to a range of leverage values between 0 and 25%. The cost of debt is 8%.

The following table shows the effects of debt on net income and on total cash flows (dividends + interest expenses), *when there is no taxation and no other distortions*:

$V_D/(V_D + V_E)$ market values	0%	5%	10%	15%	20%	25%
Operating income	120 000	120 000	120 000	120 000	120 000	120 000
Interest expenses	0	(4000)	(8000)	(12 000)	(16 000)	(20 000)
Operating income before taxes	**120 000**	**116 000**	**112 000**	**108 000**	**104 000**	**100 000**
Tax rate	0%					
Taxes	0	0	0	0	0	0
Net income	**120 000**	**116 000**	**112 000**	**108 000**	**104 000**	**100 000**
Dividends	120 000	116 000	112 000	108 000	104 000	100 000
Total cash flows	**120 000**	**120 000**	**120 000**	**120 000**	**120 000**	**120 000**

The total cash flows remain constant, regardless of the level of debt. In a *perfect* MM world, if we increase the proportion of debt in the capital structure, the only effect we obtain is a redistribution of the slices of the "pizza" from shareholders to creditors. The total value of the "pizza" doesn't change. That is:

$$V_L = V_U$$

This is the **first proposition** of the Modigliani Miller theorem in the absence of taxation. It simply states that, *in perfect financial markets*, the value of a levered company is exactly the same as an unlevered company.

The absence of any effect produced by changing leverage on total cash flows implies that the weighted average cost of capital (k) doesn't change, whatever the leverage.

In their article, Modigliani and Miller assumed that the cost of debt would remain constant as bankruptcy was not an option. In this context, how is it possible to obtain a constant k if k_D is constant too and thus if we increase the leverage we would expect a continuously decreasing k? The answer is simple: as leverage increases, risk for shareholders increases too and they require a higher cost of equity. The increased leverage is counterbalanced by the increase in cost of equity.

The following picture illustrates this circumstance. As can be seen, the cost of debt is represented by a horizontal line, since there are no financial distress costs. Since k is also uninfluenced by the degree of leverage, the cost of equity line must have the values shown in the picture so that k can remain unchanged.

When debt increases, so do both the risk to shareholders and the cost of equity. As a result, total shareholder wealth does not change.

SECTION 4

M&M VIEW ON CAPITAL STRUCTURE

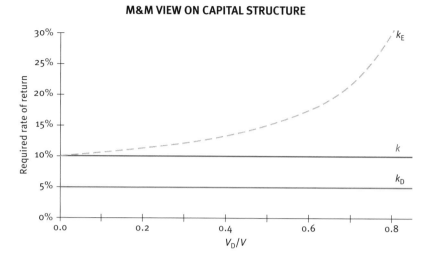

We can easily erase the assumption of no distress cost. In this case, Modigliani and Miller's proposition still stands: enterprise value does not depend on capital structure.

In this context, cost of debt (k^D) actually increases with leverage, as debtholders suffer an increasing risk of bankruptcy. Cost of equity obviously still increases with a higher level of debt but not as fast as in Modigliani and Miller's proposition, as shareholders are passing on part of the risk to debtholders.

MODERN THEORY OF CAPITAL STRUCTURE

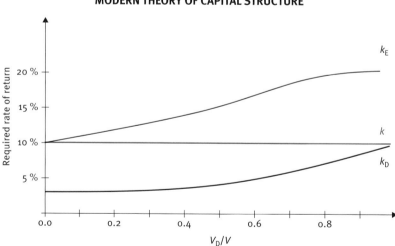

SUMMARY

The summary of this chapter can be downloaded from www.vernimmen.com.

Is there such a thing as an optimal capital structure, i.e. a way of splitting the financing of operating assets between debt and equity which would enhance the value of the operating assets and minimise the company's cost of capital? This is the central question that this chapter attempts to answer.

SECTION 4

The real world camp says yes, but without being able to prove it, or to set an ideal level of net debt and equity.

Modigliani and Miller said no in 1958, and showed how, if it were so, there would be arbitrages that re-established the balance.

For an investor with a perfectly diversified portfolio, and in a tax-free universe, there is no optimal capital structure. The following rules can be formed on the basis of the above:

- for any given investment policy and if no taxes are levied, value cannot be instantly created by the choice of a "good" capital structure;

- whether a given company is sold and the deal is paid in shares only, or whether the deal is paid in a whole range of different securities (shares, debt, hybrid shares), this will not change the value of its operating assets (excluding tax);

- in a world without taxes, the expected leverage effect is an illusion. The cost of capital (excluding tax) is linked to the company's assets and is independent from the method of financing.

But a world without taxes is a utopia, which is why the next chapter brings tax and other "distortions" into the equation.

QUESTIONS

1/ Why is the cost of equity for a company with no debt equal to the average weighted cost of capital?

2/ What is the cost of capital equal to?

3/ What are the two risks for a shareholder of an indebted company?

4/ Of the following decisions, which is the most important: An investment decision? A financing decision? Why?

5/ Explain what impact an increase in debt will have on the β of shares.

6/ What are Modigliani and Miller's theories based on?

7/ The fact that shareholders' expected returns rise with the level of debt does not run contrary to the approach taken by Modigliani and Miller. Why?

8/ Is the cost of capital an accounting or financial concept?

9/ Why can it be dangerous to use a spreadsheet to create simulations of the cost of capital?

10/ Can a company create value by going into debt?

11/ What is the cost of net debt of a company that has no more shareholders' equity equal to? And the cost of capital?

12/ What are we forgetting when we say that by increasing return on equity, the leverage effect of debt cannot increase value?

13/ True or false? "By reducing financial leverage, we reduce the cost of debt and the cost of equity and, accordingly, the weighted average cost of capital?" Why?

14/ True or false? "The more debt we incur, the higher the interest rate we are charged. Our shareholders also require a higher return. Additionally, if we want a low cost of capital, we have to have a low level of debt." Why?

More questions are waiting for you at www.vernimmen.com.

EXERCISES

1/ Sixty per cent of company *A*'s needs are equity-financed at a cost of 9%, and 40% are debt-financed at 5%. Excluding tax, what is the weighted average cost of capital of this company?

2/ In a tax-free world, companies *B* and *C* are similar in every respect, except their capital structures. *B* has no debts while *C* has debts of 24 000 at 5%. The companies have been valued as follows:

	Company B	Company C
Operating income	10 000	10 000
Financial expense	0	1200
Net income	10 000	8800
k_{SE}	8%	11%
V_{SE}	125 000	80 000
V_D	0	24 000
V	125 000	104 000
k	8%	9.62%
$V_D/(V_E + V_D)$	0%	23%
Payout	100%	100%

You own 1% of company B's shares. How much will you receive every year? Show how you can increase this amount without altering the amount of your investment or increasing the level of risk.

When will arbitrage cease? What will the P/E be for companies B and C?

3/ A company with no debts has a weighted average cost of capital of 8%.

(a) What is the cost of equity for this company?

(b) It decides to borrow 33.5% of the value of its operating assets at a rate of 5%, in order to finance a capital reduction of 33.5%. What is the cost of equity now?

(c) If the market risk premium is 4% and the β of the company's shares before it went into debt was 1.2, what is the new β of shares after the capital reduction?

(d) What is the β of the debt, if the β of the capital employed is equal to the average β of the capital employed and the debt weighted by the relative share of debt and equity in financing the capital employed.

$$\left(\beta = \beta_E \times \frac{V_E}{V_E + V_D} + \beta_D \frac{V_D}{V_D + V_E} \right)$$

4/ Deutsche Telekom and France Telecom have a similar economic risk. The beta of France Telecom shares is 1.4, and is 1.1 for Deutsche Telekom. If the no-risk cash rate is 3.5% and the risk premium is 6%, what are the shareholders' required returns? If the net debt/shareholders' equity ratio is 1.5 in value for France Telecom, what is it for Deutsche Telekom which has debts of 4% compared with 4.5% for France Telecom (imagine that this is a tax-free world)?

Questions

1/ Because shareholders' equity alone bears the risk of capital employed.
2/ To the average weighted by the values of the cost of equity and the cost of net debt.
3/ The risk of capital employed and the risk of capital structure.
4/ Investment, because it is easier to create value by making a good investment, and we learnt in this chapter that there is no such thing as good financing.
5/ Debt capital, increasing the risk of shares, increases the β.
6/ Arbitrage.
7/ Because the risk also increases.
8/ Financial, because only market values (rates and values) come into the calculation of the cost of capital.
9/ Because by modifying the relative weights of debt/shareholders' equity, we often forget that the cost of shareholders' equity and debt depends on this relative weight, and that they are not constant, no matter what the capital structure.
10/ No, this would be too good to be true and all companies would have huge debts.
11/ To the cost of shareholders' equity of a debt-free company in the same sector. Ditto.
12/ The risk of shareholders' equity increases and accordingly the returns required by shareholders increases at the same time.
13/ False, by reducing leverage, an "expensive" resource (shareholders' equity, the cost of which is reduced) replaces a "cheap" resource (debt, the cost of which is reduced). In sum, the weighted average cost of capital remains constant.
14/ False, the company is replacing an "expensive" resource (shareholders' equity) with a "cheap" resource (debt) even though the cost will rise. In sum, the weighted average cost of capital remains constant.

SECTION 4

Exercises

A detailed Excel version of the solutions is available at www.vernimmen.com.

1/ $k = 7.4\%$.

2/ *A shareholder of 1% of company B will receive the following sum every year: $1\% \times 125\ 000 \times 8\% = 100$. He sells his shares in company B and buys shares in company C. However, because the company is indebted, as a shareholder he carries a higher risk than before. If he wants to keep the same level of risk, he must put an equivalent amount into the debt underlying the shares he has bought in company C. Accordingly, if n is the percentage of 1250 paid for the shares in company C, $n \times 23.1\% = 1 - n$. The solution to this equation is $n = 1/(1 + 23.1\%) = 81\%$. Or, for assets totalling 1250: 19% is lent at 5% and 81% is invested in company C shares. Which is an income of $19\% \times 1250 \times 5\% + 81\% \times 1250 \times 11\% = 123$, more than the initial income of 100. Arbitrage will cease when the value of the capital employed of companies B and C is equal, for example 111 400, which gives an equity value for company C of $114\ 000 - 24\ 000 = 90\ 000$ and a P/E of 10.2 for company C and 11.4 for company B.*

3/ (a) $k_E = 8\%$. (b) $k_E = 9.5\%$. (c) $\beta = 1.57$. (d) $\beta_D = 0.45$.

4/ DT: $k_E = 10.1\%$; FT: $k_E = 11.9\%$; $V_D/V_E = 0.76$.

BIBLIOGRAPHY

A classic example of a conventional point of view:

B. Graham, L. Dodd, *Security Analysis*, 3th edn, McGraw Hill, 1951.

To read the seminal article by Modigliani and Miller:

F. Modigliani, M. Miller, The cost of capital, corporation finance and the theory of investment, *American Economic Review*, **47**, 261–297, June 1958.

For a general overview on capital structure that is still interesting to read:

J. Stiglitz, On the irrelevance of corporate financial policy, *American Economic Review*, **47**, 851–866, December 1974.

Chapter 34
CAPITAL STRUCTURE, TAXES AND
ORGANISATION THEORIES

There's no gain without pain

In the previous chapter we saw that the value of a firm is the same whether or not it has taken on debt. True, shareholders will pay less for the shares of a levered company, but they will have to pay back the debt (or buy it back, which amounts to the same thing) before obtaining access to the enterprise value. In the end, they will have paid, directly or indirectly, the same amount (value of equity plus repayment of net debt[1]); that is, the enterprise value.

1 *Again, we use net debt and debt synonymously.*

Now, what about the financial manager who must issue securities to finance the creation of enterprise value? It does not matter whether he issues only shares or a combination of bonds and shares, since again the proceeds will be the same – the enterprise value.

Enterprise value depends on future flows and how the related, non-diversifiable risks are perceived by the market.

But if that is the case, why diversify sources of financing? The preceding theory is certainly elegant, but it cannot fully explain how things actually work in real life.

In this chapter we look at **two basic explanations of real-life happenings**. First of all, within the same market logic, biases occur which may explain why companies borrow funds, and why they stop at a certain level. The fundamental factors from which these biases spring are *taxes and financial distress costs*. **Their joint analysis will give birth to the "tradeoff model".**

There are features of debt that can modify the optimal capital structure. Tradeoff models generally limit their attention to the pros and cons of tax shield and financial distress costs. We believe that the elements of the balance are more numerous than just these factors. Other factors may also be added:

- information asymmetries;
- disciplining role of debt;
- financial flexibility;
- agency costs;
- signalling aspects.

Maybe the main reasons for the interference between capital structure and investment are the divergent interests of the various financial partners regarding value creation and their differing levels of access to information. This lies at the core of the manager/shareholder relationship we shall examine in this chapter. A full chapter (Chapter 35) is devoted to an analysis of the capital structure resulting from a compromise between creditors and shareholders.

Rather than being simply a search for value, the choice of financing is far more an endeavour to reduce conflicts of interest between shareholders and managers or shareholders and lenders, as well as the information asymmetry between management and investors.

Section 34.1
The benefits of debt or the tradeoff model

1/ Corporate income taxes

Up to now, our reasoning was based on a tax-free world, which of course does not exist. The investor's net return can be 2–5 times (or more) lower than the pre-tax cash flows of an industrial investment.

It would therefore be foolhardy to ignore taxation, which forces financial managers to devote a considerable amount of their time to tax optimisation.

For financial managers, this chapter will cover familiar ground and our insistence on the importance of tax aspects in every financial decision will seem obvious.

But we ought not go to the other extreme and concentrate solely on tax variables. All too many decisions based entirely on tax considerations lead to ridiculous outcomes, such as insufficient earnings capacity. Tax deficits alone are no reason to buy a company!

In 1963, F. Modigliani and M. Miller (MM) pushed further their initial demonstration, but this time they factored in corporate income tax (*but no other taxes*) in an economy in which companies' financial expenses are tax deductible, but not dividends. This is pretty much the case in most countries.

The conclusion was unmistakable: once you factor in corporate income tax, there is more incentive to use debt rather than equity financing.

Interest expenses can be deducted from the company's tax base, so that creditors receive their coupon payments before they have been taxed. Dividends, on the other hand, are not deductible and are paid to shareholders after taxation.

Thus, a debt-free company with equity financing of 100 on which shareholders require a 10% return will have to generate profit of at least 15.4 in order to provide the required return of 10 after a 35% tax.

If, however, its financing is equally divided between debt at 5% interest and equity, a profit of 13.6 will be enough to satisfy shareholders despite the premium for the greater risk to shares created by the debt (i.e. 14.4%).

	Operating profit	13.6
–	Interest expense	2.5
=	Pre-tax profit	11.1
–	35% tax	3.9
=	Net profit	7.2 or 14.4% of 50

Allowing interest expenses to be deducted from companies' tax base is a kind of subsidy the state grants to companies with debt. **But to benefit from this tax shield, the company must generate a profit.**

A company that continually resorts to debt benefits from tax savings that must be factored into its enterprise value.

When corporate income taxes are levied, the enterprise value of the levered company is equal to that of an unlevered company plus the present value of the tax savings arising on the debt.

Take, for example, a company with an enterprise value of 100, of which 50 is financed by equity and 50 by perpetual debt at 5%. Interest expenses will be 2.5 each year. Assuming a 35% tax rate and an operating profit of more than 2.5 regardless of the year under review (an amount sufficient to benefit from the tax savings), the tax savings will be 35% × 2.5 or 0.88 for each year. The present value of this perpetual bond increases shareholders' wealth by 0.88/14.4% = 6.1 if 14.4% is the cost of equity. Taking the tax savings into account increases the value of equity by 12% to 56.1 (50 + 6.1).

TAX SAVINGS AS A PERCENTAGE OF EQUITY

V_D/V	k_E	Maturity of debt		
		5 years	10 years	Perpetuity
0%	10.0%[2]	0%	0%	0%
25%	11.5%	2%	3%	4%
33%	12.2%	3%	5%	5%
50%	14.4%	6%	9%	12%
66%	18.8%	10%	15%	18%

The longer the maturity of the debt and the larger the amount, the greater the present value of the tax savings.

2 *Based on a β of 1.1, a 4% risk premium and a risk-free rate of 5.6%. The other costs of equity are deducted from the formula on p. 570.*

The value of a levered company is equal to what it would be without the debt, plus the amount of savings generated by the tax shield.[3]

The question now is what discount rate should be applied to the tax savings generated by the deductibility of interest expense? Should we use the cost of debt, as Modigliani and Miller did in their article in 1963, the weighted average cost of capital or the cost of equity?

Using the cost of debt is justified if we are certain that the tax savings are permanent. In addition, this allows us to use a particularly simple formula:

3 *This is the basis of the APV method (adjusted present value).*

$$\text{Value of the tax savings} = \frac{T_C \times k_D \times V_D}{k_D} = T_C \times V_D$$

Nevertheless, there are good reasons to prefer to discount the savings at the cost of equity, since it would be difficult to assume that the company will continually carry the same debt, generate profits and be taxed at the same rate. Moreover, the tax savings accrue to

SECTION 4

the shareholders, so it should be reasonable to discount them at the rate of return required by those shareholders.

Bear in mind that these tax savings only apply if the company has sufficient earnings power and does not benefit from any other tax exemptions, such as tax loss carryforwards, etc.

2/ COSTS OF FINANCIAL DISTRESS

We have seen that the more debt a firm carries, the greater the risk that it will not be able to meet its commitments. If the worst comes to the worst, the company files for bankruptcy, which in the final analysis simply means that assets are reallocated to more profitable ventures.

In fact, the bankruptcy of an unprofitable company strengthens the sector and improves the profitability of the remaining firms and therefore their value. Bankruptcy is a useful mechanism which helps the market stay healthier by eliminating the least efficient companies.

The public authorities would do well to apply this reasoning. Better to let a troubled sector rid itself of its lame ducks than to keep them artificially afloat, which in turn creates difficulties for the healthy, efficient firms to the point where they, too, may become financially distressed.

For investors with a well-diversified portfolio, the cost of the bankruptcy will be nil, since when a company is discontinued, its assets (market share, customers, factories, etc.) are taken over by others who will manage them better. One man's loss is another man's gain! If the investor has a diversified portfolio, the capital losses will be offset by other capital gains.

In practice, however, markets are not perfect and we all know that even if bankruptcies are a means of reallocating resources, they carry a very real cost to those involved. These include:

- Direct costs:

    ○ redundancy payments;
    ○ legal fees;
    ○ administrative costs;
    ○ shareholders' efforts to receive a liquidation dividend.

- Indirect costs:

    ○ order cancellations (for fear they will not be honoured);
    ○ less trade credit (because it may not be repaid);
    ○ reduced productivity (strikes, underutilisation of production capacity);
    ○ no more access to financing (even for profitable projects); as well as
    ○ incalculable human costs.

One could say bankruptcy occurs when shareholders refuse to inject more funds once they have concluded that their initial investment is lost. In essence, they are handing the company over to its creditors, who then become the new shareholders. The creditors bear all the costs of the malfunctioning company, thus further reducing their chances of getting repaid.

Even without going to the extremes of bankruptcy, a highly levered company in financial distress faces certain costs that reduce its value. It may have to cut back on

R&D expenditure, maintenance, training or marketing expenses in order to meet its debt payments and will find it increasingly difficult to raise new funding, even for profitable investment projects.

After factoring all these costs into the equation, we can say that:

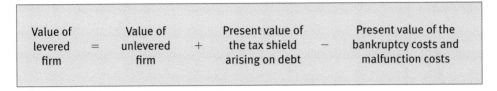

| Value of levered firm | = | Value of unlevered firm | + | Present value of the tax shield arising on debt | − | Present value of the bankruptcy costs and malfunction costs |

or, as illustrated by the following figure:

THE TRADE OFF MODEL

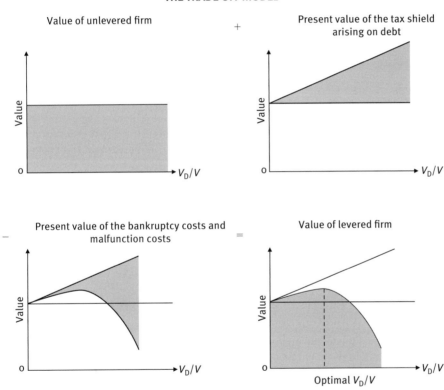

Because of the tax deduction, debt can, in fact, create value. A levered company may be worth more than if it had only equity financing. However, there are two good reasons why this advantage should not be overstated. Firstly, when a company with excessive debt is in financial distress, its tax advantage disappears, since it no longer generates sufficient profits. Secondly, the high debt level may lead to restructuring costs and lost investment opportunities if financing is no longer available. As a result, debt should not exceed a certain level.

The same reasoning applies to the weighted average cost of capital. When a company borrows funds, its cost of capital declines thanks to the tax savings on the interest payments, but if there is a risk of default, shareholders factor the bankruptcy costs into the cost of equity. This relationship can be observed by charting a given industry's cost of capital according to its credit rating.

WEIGHTED AVERAGE COST OF CAPITAL

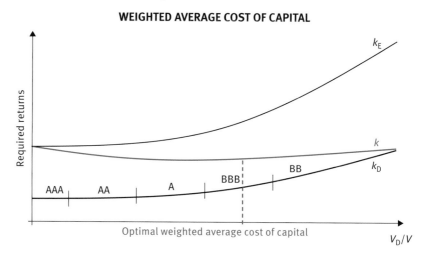

Paradoxically, this long detour brings us back to our starting point – the conventional approach which says "Some debt is fine, but not too much."[4]

4 *See Chapter 33.*

> The theoretical optimal debt ratio appears to be when the present value of the tax savings arising on additional borrowing is offset by the increase in the present value of financial distress and bankruptcy costs.

Section 34.2
A MORE GLOBAL AND RELEVANT APPROACH

1/ INTRODUCING PERSONAL TAXES, A MAJOR IMPROVEMENT
TO THE PREVIOUS REASONING

The personal taxes paid by investors can **reduce** and even **cancel out** the advantages of deducting interest payments on corporate debt.

Let us return to the example of the company at the beginning of the chapter. We shall assume that the dividends are not taxed at the personal investor's level but that – for the sake of simplicity – the interest income is taxed at 70% at the creditors' level.

If the company has no debt financing, it will still have to generate a pre-tax profit of at least 15.4 to satisfy shareholders' required rate of return. However, if its financing is 50 debt and 50 equity, the company will need to turn in a minimum profit before taxes and interest of 19.4. This will allow it to pay 8.3 of interest to its creditors, leaving them with a net revenue of 2.5 after the 70% tax, corresponding to their requested net return of 5% on 50. Corporate income tax will take out $35\% \times (19.4 - 8.3) = 3.9$, leaving $19.4 - 8.3 - 3.9 = 7.2$ for the shareholders who will get their requested 14.4% return after tax on 50. If, on the contrary, the company can only generate 15.4 instead of 19.4, there is a subtraction of value from shareholders to creditors (shareholders would get 4.6, equivalent to a 9.2% return).

Given the net expected return required by creditors – the introduction of the tax rate on interest income increases the total amount of money necessary to pay debt and subtracts resources to shareholders.

If the personal tax rate on interest income is cut to 30%, thus lower than the tax rate on corporate income, debt becomes cheaper, giving rise to (low) tax savings, although still less than Modigliani and Miller found in their 1963 article.

In 1977, Miller released a new study in which he revisited the observation made with Modigliani in 1958 that there is no one optimal capital structure. This time, however, he factored in both corporate **and personal taxes**.

Miller claimed that the taxes paid by investors can cancel out those paid by companies. This would mean that the value of the firm would remain the same regardless of the type of financing used. Again, there should be no optimal capital structure.

Miller based his argument on the assumption that equity income is not taxed, and that the tax rate on interest income is marginally equal to the corporate tax rate.

But these assumptions are shaky, since in reality investors are not all taxed at the same marginal rate and both equity returns and the capital gains on disposal of shares are taxed as well. In fact, Miller's objective was to demonstrate that real life is far more complicated than the simplified assumptions applied in the theories and models. The value of the tax shield is not so big as the 1963 article would have us believe. Suppose that, in addition to the corporate income tax (T_C) that there are also two other tax rates:

$$T_D = \text{personal tax rate on interest income;}$$
$$T_E = \text{personal tax rate on dividends.}$$

If we:

1. consider the cash flows net of all taxes that shareholders and creditors must pay to tax authorities;
2. sum them; and
3. rearrange terms,

the "complete" tax shield (G) is:

$$G = \left[1 - \frac{(1-T_C) \times (1-T_E)}{(1-T_D)} \right] \times V_D$$

The reader will immediately notice that if $T_E = T_D$ the tax shield turns back to the "original" $T_C - V_D$.

In our last example, if T_E is zero, $T_D = 30\%$ and $T_C = 35\%$, G is still positive but much lower because it equals only 0.0714 (or 7.14%).

If we include T_E in the analysis, two alternatives may be possible:

- if $T_E > T_D$ the tax shield is bigger than the basic case (i.e. the case with only corporate taxes);
- if $T_E < T_D$ the tax shield tends to be smaller than the basic case.

When personal taxes are introduced into the analysis, the firm's objective is no longer to minimise the corporate tax bill; the firm should minimise the present value of *all* taxes paid on corporate income (those paid by bondholders and shareholders).

SECTION 4

Once we factor in the tax credit granted before shareholders are taxed, the tax benefits on debt disappear although, since not all earnings are distributed, not all give rise to tax credits. Say a company has an enterprise value of 1000. Regardless of its type of financing, investors require a 6% return after corporate **and** personal income taxes. Bear in mind that this rate is not comparable with that determined by the CAPM ($r_F + \beta \times (r_M - r_F)$), which is calculated **before** personal taxation.

Let's take a country where (realistically) the main tax rates are:

- corporate tax: 34.43%;
- tax on dividends: 12%;
- capital gains tax: 12%;
- tax on interest income: 30%.

Now let us assume that the company has operating profit of 103. This corresponds to a cost of equity of 6% if it is entirely equity-financed.

Enterprise value	1000	1000	1000	1000
Equity	1000	750	500	250
Debt	0	250	500	750
Interest rate	–	4.5%	5.5%	8%
Operating profit	103	103	103	103
– Interest expense	0	11	28	60
= Pre-tax profit	103	92	75	43
– Corporate income tax at 34.4%	35	32	26	15
= Net profit	68	60	49	28
Personal income tax:				
On dividends/capital gains (12%)	8	7	6	3
On interest (30%)	0	3	8	18
Shareholders' net income	60	53	43	25
Shareholders' net return	6 %	7.1%	8.6%	10%
Creditors' net income	0	8	20	42
Creditors' net return	–	3.2%	4.0%	5.6%
Net income for investors	60	61	63	67
Total taxes	43	42	40	36

The net return of the investor, who is both shareholder and creditor of the firm, can be calculated depending on whether net debt represents 0%, 33.3%, 100% or 3 times the amount of equity.

The value created by debt must thus be measured in terms of the increase in net income for investors (shareholders and creditors). Our example shows that flows increase significantly only when the debt level is particularly high, well above the market average (around 33% of the enterprise value).

Miller's reasoning now becomes clearer. The table below shows that in certain countries, such as Morocco, the tax savings on corporate debt are more than offset by the personal taxes levied.

TAX RATES IN VARIOUS COUNTRIES (%)

Country	On dividends	On capital gains	On interest	On earnings
France	31.3%	31.3%	31.3%	34.4%
Germany	26.4%–28.0%	26.4%–28.0%	26.4%–28.0%	29.4%
India	0%	0% or 10%	0% to 30%	33.99%
Italy	12.5%	12.5%	12.5%–27.0%	31.4%
Morocco	10.0%	15.0%	20.0%	30.0%
Netherlands	30.0%	30.0%	30.0%	25.5%
Spain	21.0%	21.0%	21.0%	30.0%
Switzerland	22.0%–41.0%	0.0%	22.0–41.0%	12.5%–24.5%
Tunisia	0.0%	0.0%	0%–35.0%	30.0%
United Kingdom	42.5%	28.0%	50.0%	28.0%
United States	15.0%	15.0%	35.0%	39.5%

Bear in mind, too, that companies do not always use the tax advantages of debt since there are other options, such as accelerated depreciation, provisions, etc.

In 2000, Graham demonstrated that the value of the tax advantage of interest expenses is around 9.7%, and it goes down to 4.3% if personal taxation of investors is also considered. Almeida and Philippon (2007) have, on the other hand, estimated the bankruptcy costs; they believe the right percentage is around 4.5% – in brief, it seems that one effect "perfectly" compensates the other. In 2010, Van Binsbergen, Graham and Yang, and Korteweg found similar results.

What all this amounts to is that, while taxation is certainly a key parameter in absolute terms, it is unlikely to be the determinant of capital structure.

In fact, Modigliani and Miller's theory states the obvious: all economic players want to reduce their tax charge! A word of caution, however. Corporate managers who focus too narrowly on reducing tax charges may end up making the wrong decisions.

2/ INFORMATION ASYMMETRIES AND THE PECKING ORDER THEORY

The analysis of the impact of informational asymmetries on capital structure decisions requires the introduction of two new concepts: internal capital and external capital. **Internal capital** is represented by the cash flows generated internally or, more generically, by periodical income which is not distributed among shareholders; **external capital** is raised outside the firm, and can either be financial debt or equity from new shareholders.

The groups that operate within the company (directors, management, major shareholders, employees – in short, the "insiders") normally know more about the company than all other stakeholders ("outsiders"). These asymmetries tend to penalise the company when it needs to raise funds outside. External creditors receive a smaller set of information and do not believe that insiders find it convenient to share all the information they have. This, in turn, may have two forms:

1. a higher cost of capital;
2. a smaller amount of capital raised (capital rationing).

It is reasonable to assume that informational asymmetries are more relevant:

- for small companies;
- in startup phases;
- when the control of the company is in the hands of few shareholders.

Internal capital doesn't penalise the company either in terms of cost or in terms of quantity.

The major disadvantages of external capital are the additional cost of informational asymmetries and the dilution of control (for example, if shares are sold at a "bargain price" to new shareholders or if the debt contracts introduce covenants and guarantees).

The additional cost of informational asymmetries is higher if the new external capital is a share issue. All other things being equal, new debt thus has the comparative advantage of a lower cost and volume penalisation.

The evidence shows that the reaction of the market to the announcement of bond issues is:

- not necessarily negative;
- of limited amount;
- not always statistically significant, when the reaction is negative.

5 *See, for example, James and Smith (2003).*

The reaction of share prices may even be positive if the company announces the use of additional bank debt.[5] The reason may lie in the arm's length relationship that banks have with companies which should signal higher quality of information. The bank may know confidential information regarding its clients, control its liquidity or be part of their board of directors, all elements that justify a higher quality of companies that prefer to raise funds through the bank channel.

A totally different result is obtained when firms announce the issue of equity capital to new shareholders. These announcements are, in fact, generally viewed by the market as a bad signal and the evidence shows that the negative reaction tends to be statistically significant.

Having established that information asymmetry carries a cost, our next task is to determine what type of financing carries the lowest cost in this respect. The uncontested champion is, of course, internal financing, which requires no special procedures. Its advantage is simplicity.

Debt comes next, but only low-risk debt with plenty of guarantees (pledges) and covenants restricting the risk to creditors and thus making it more palatable to them. This is followed by riskier forms of debt and hybrid securities.

Capital increases come last, because they are automatically interpreted as a negative signal. To counter this, the information asymmetry must be reduced by means of road shows, one-to-one meetings, prospectuses and advertising campaigns. Investors have to be persuaded that the issue offers good value for money!

In an article published in 1984, Myers elaborates on a theory initially put forward by Donaldson in 1961, stating that, according to the **pecking order theory**, companies prioritise their sources of financing as follows:

- Internal financing heads their list of preferences. Companies adjust their dividend payout objectives to their investment opportunities.
- Since earnings and investment opportunities vary from year to year, companies may have to draw down their cash balances.
- If this is not enough and external financing becomes necessary, they issue risk-free debt. Credit lines are kept open to ensure that they can do so as needed.
- When a company cannot resort to traditional borrowings, it issues securities, starting with the least risky type and gradually moving up the scale.
- Lastly, when all else fails, the company issues equity.

As can be seen, although the corporate manager does not choose the type of financing arbitrarily, he does so without great enthusiasm, since they all carry the same cost relative to their risk.

The pecking order is determined by the law of least effort. Managers do not have to "raise" internal financing, and they will always endeavour to limit intermediation costs, which are the highest on share issues.

Let's take a look to see if companies really privilege internal capital. The following graph shows the evolution of the breakdown of financing of the top worldwide 1000 listed companies between 1993 and 2010.

The histograms represent the percentage of internal capital (cash flow) and external capital (new equity and the variation of the stock of debt) for the top 1200 groups representing 55% of the world equity market capitalisation:

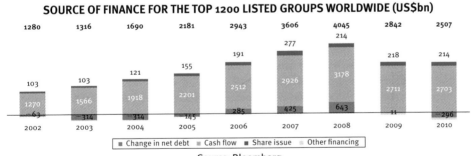

SOURCE OF FINANCE FOR THE TOP 1200 LISTED GROUPS WORLDWIDE (US$bn)

Source: Bloomberg

The picture suggests three major comments:

- Internal financing has always represented the major source of companies' financing. The average incidence (94%) of internal capital is consistent with the findings of Donaldson, who suggested that the behaviour of management is driven by two important factors:

  - Firms' survival. The need for preserving the life of the company induces the management to accumulate liquidity in excess and to keep the residual borrowing capacity unchanged.

○   Independence and self-sufficiency. The management prefers to be free to decide, regardless of external "influences", including capital markets. An appropriate reserve of liquidity could ease the achievement of this objective.

• Internal financing has not covered the entire amount of funds required by new investments. Each period thus shows a "financial gap" that needs to be filled with external capital.

• The financial gap has been mostly covered with debt and, if necessary, equity capital. However, the latter resource assumes a marginal role, consistent with the predictions of the pecking order model.

The evidence shown in the above graph seems to confirm the existence of a pecking order of financing choices.

A word of caution, however. The reader should never forget that internal capital has a cost like all other sources of financing, which can be estimated with the models presented in Chapters 19 and 30 where we discussed the cost of equity capital. So it is important to avoid considering internal capital as zero-cost or discretionary-cost capital. The cost of capital is always an *opportunity cost of capital*, and should be estimated by looking at the expected returns required (or obtained) by shareholders of similar (in terms of risk and duration) investments and companies.

3/ SIGNALLING AND DEBT POLICY

Signalling theory is based on the strong assumption that corporate managers are better informed about their companies than the suppliers of funding. This means that they are in a better position to foresee the company's future flows and know what state their company is in. Consequently, any signal they send indicating that flows will be better than expected or that risks will be lower may enable the investor to create value. Investors are therefore constantly on the watch for such signals. But for the signals to be credible there must be a penalty for the wrong signals in order to dissuade companies from deliberately misleading the market.

In the context of information asymmetry, markets would not understand why a corporate manager would borrow to undertake a very risky and unprofitable venture. After all, if the venture fails, he risks losing his job, or worse if the venture causes the company to fail. So debt is a strong signal for profitability, but even more for risk. It is unlikely that a CEO would resort to debt financing if he knew that in a worst-case scenario he would not be able to repay the debt.

Ross (1977) has demonstrated that any change in financing policy changes investors' perception of the company and is therefore a market signal.

It is thus obvious that an increase in debt increases the risk on equity. The managers of a company that has raised its gearing rate are, in effect, signalling to the markets that they are aware of the state of nature, that it is favourable and that they are confident that the company's performance will allow them to pay the additional financial expenses and pay back the new debt.

This signal carries its own penalty if it is wrong. If the signal is false, i.e. if the company's actual prospects are not good at all, the extra debt will create financial difficulties that will ultimately lead, in one form or another, to the dismissal of its executives.[6] In this scheme, managers have a strong incentive to send the correct signal by ensuring that the firm's debt corresponds to their understanding of its repayment capacity.

Ross has shown that, assuming managers have privileged information about their own company, they will send the correct signal on condition that the marginal gain derived from an incorrect signal is lower than the sanction suffered if the company is liquidated.

"They put their money where their mouths are." This explains why debt policies vary from one company to the other: they simply reflect the variable prospects of the individual companies.

6 *Note that a bad manager whose forecast of future flows was unintentionally wrong will be sanctioned just as much as one who deliberately sent the wrong signal.*

The actual capital structure of a firm is not necessarily a signal, but any change in it certainly is.

When a company announces a capital increase, research has shown that its share price generally drops by an average of 3%. The market reasons that corporate managers would not increase capital if, based on the inside information available to them, they thought it was undervalued, since this would dilute the existing shareholdings in unfavourable conditions. If there is no pressing reason for the capital increase, investors will infer that, based on their inside information, the managers consider the share price to be too high and that this is why the existing shareholders have accepted the capital increase. On the other hand, research has shown, too, that the announcement of a bond issue has no material impact on share prices.

It follows that the sale of a manager's stake in the company is a very negative signal. It reveals that he has internal information indicating that the value of future flows, taking risk into account, is lower than the proceeds he expects from the sale of his investment. Conversely, any increase in the stake, especially if financed by debt, constitutes a very positive signal for the market.

This explains why financial investors prefer to subscribe to capital increases rather than buy from existing shareholders. It is also the reason why every year in the US, the UK, France and many other countries, top managers and all directors must disclose the number of shares they hold or control in the companies they work for or of which they are board members.

4/ DEBT AS A MEANS OF CONTROLLING CORPORATE MANAGERS

Now let us examine the interests of non-shareholder executives. They may be tempted to shun debt in order to avoid the corresponding constraints, such as a higher breakeven threshold, interest payments and principal repayments. Corporate managers are highly risk averse and their natural inclination is to accumulate cash rather than resort to debt to finance investments. Debt financing avoids this trap, since the debt repayment prevents surplus cash from accumulating. Shareholders encourage debt as well because it stimulates performance. The more debt a company has, the higher its risk. In the event of financial difficulties, corporate executives may lose their jobs and the attendant compensation package and remuneration in kind. This threat is considered to be sufficiently dissuasive to encourage sound management, generating optimal liquidity to service the debt and engage in profitable investments.

The explicit cost of debt is a simple yet highly effective means of controlling a firm's management team. Large groups are well aware of the leverage this gives them and require the executives of their main subsidiaries to carry a level of "incentive debt" which is charged to the subsidiary.

Given that the parameters of debt are reflected in a company's cash situation while equity financing translates into capital gains or losses at shareholder level, management will be particularly intent on the success of its debt-financed investment projects. This is another, indirect, limitation of the perfect markets theory: **since the various forms of financing do not offer the same incentives to corporate executives, financing does indeed influence the choice of investment.**

This would indicate that a levered company is more flexible and responsive than an unlevered company. This hypothesis was tested and proven by Ofek, who shows that the more debt they carry, the faster listed US companies react to a crisis, by filing for bankruptcy, curtailing dividend payouts or reducing the payroll.

Debt is thus an internal means of controlling management preferred by shareholders. In Chapter 43 we shall see that another is the threat of a takeover bid.

However, the use of debt has its limits. When a group's corporate structure becomes totally unbalanced, debt no longer acts as an incentive for management. On the contrary, the corporate manager will be tempted to continue expanding via debt until his group has become too big to fail, like the Korean groups at the end of the 1990s. This risk is called "moral hazard".

With more empirical evidence, researchers have examined whether companies which have experienced a fast increase of leverage have become more efficient, as measured by profit margins and the return on invested capital.

This is the case with **leveraged buyouts, or LBOs**. An LBO is the acquisition, generally by management (MBO), of all a company's shares using borrowed funds. It becomes a **leveraged buildup** if it then uses debt to buy other companies in order to increase its standing in the sector. We look in more detail at LBOs in Chapter 45.

It is generally thought that the purpose of the funds devoted to LBOs is to use accounting leverage to obtain better returns. In fact, the success of LBOs cannot be attributed to accounting leverage, since we have already seen that this alone does not create value.

The real reason for the success of LBOs is that, when it has a stake in the company, management is far more committed to making the company a success. With management most often holding a share of the equity, resource allocation will be designed to benefit shareholders. Executives have a two-fold incentive: to enhance their existing or future (in the case of stock options) stake in the capital and to safeguard their jobs and reputation by ensuring that the company does not go broke. It thus becomes a classic case of the carrot and the stick!

The results reported by Palepu (1990) show an improvement – although quite limited – of the operating efficiency of companies subjected to leveraged buyouts. Similar results are discussed in Kaplan (1989) and Smith (1990).

Mature, highly profitable companies with few investments to make are the most likely candidates for an LBO. Jensen (1986) demonstrated that, in the absence of heavy debt, the executives of such companies will be strongly tempted to use the substantial free cash flow to grow to the detriment of profits by overinvesting or diversifying into other businesses, two strategies that destroy value.

The only value created by debt is the fact that it forces managers to improve enterprise value.

Some questions are still looking for an answer:

- Is the capital structure influenced by the lifecycle stage the company is going through?
- Is there a role for competitors in determining the capital structure of the firm?
- Why do managers sometimes prefer to use funding as a way to send signals to financial markets?
- What is the optimal maturity structure of debt? And the optimal percentage of floating debt? How much debt issued in different currencies should a company have?
- When a company wants to move towards its chosen debt/equity mix, should it reach that leverage rapidly or gradually?

In Chapter 36, we shall focus on these issues to illustrate how to reach an appropriate **design** of the capital structure of a company. After having explored the bulk of the theory, the time will come to examine details. But be patient, and take a look now at what options tell us before making wise capital structure choices.

SUMMARY

The summary of this chapter can be downloaded from www.vernimmen.com.

In this chapter we went beyond the simplified structure of perfect markets, and looked at a number of different factors (tax, bankruptcy costs, information asymmetry, conflicts of interest) which make analysis more complex, but also more relevant.

Modigliani and Miller demonstrated how, when corporate tax is included in the equation (financial expenses are tax deductible whereas dividends are not), debt financing becomes an attractive option. The optimal capital structure is thus one which includes a maximum amount of debt, and the value of a levered company is equal to what it would be without the debt, plus the amount of savings generated by the tax shield.

There are, however, two major drawbacks to this approach. Firstly, the higher a company's debts, the greater the probability of bankruptcy costs, whether direct or indirect (profitable investments that are not made). Secondly, if the personal tax situation of the investor is taken into account, this offsets the tax shield that debt enjoys at a corporate level. For individual taxpayers, the tax breaks on income on equity are better than they are for debt.

Problems stemming from information asymmetry between shareholders and investors have an obvious impact on the choice of capital structure. Managers believing that their companies are undervalued would prefer to increase debt levels rather than to issue new shares at a low price, and possibly carry out a capital increase once the share price has gone up. Similarly, a decision to use debt finance for a project is a sign of management's confidence in its ability to meet payments on the debt and an indirect sign that the project is likely to be profitable.

Pushing the information asymmetry problem to the limit brings us to the pecking order theory, which holds that managers choose sources of financing on the basis of the amount of intermediation costs and agency costs: cash flow, debt and only then a capital increase. Finally, according to agency theory, debt is analysed as an internal means of controlling management, which has to work hard to ensure that debt repayments are met. For a mature company making healthy profits but without major growth prospects,

SECTION 4

incurring large debts is a way of discouraging managers from spending cash on risky diversification projects or rash expansion projects, which both destroy value. The LBO, an innovation of the 1980s, is what has come out of this theory. LBOs create value, not on the basis of the accounting illusion of the leverage effect, but thanks to the high motivation of managers who are under pressure to repay debts, and who have a financial incentive to work harder as a result of the potentially very lucrative profit-sharing schemes that have been set up. This takes us a long way from the simplistic assumptions made in the first models designed by Modigliani and Miller!

QUESTIONS

1/ According to the approach by Modigliani and Miller (1963), how does the value of a levered company differ from the value of an unlevered company?

2/ What are the two drawbacks to Modigliani and Miller's 1963 theory?

3/ What is Modigliani and Miller's 1977 theory based on and what conclusions do they draw?

4/ Describe the tax breaks for debt financing and for equity financing.

5/ What are the latest tax trends with regard to sources of financing?

6/ What is the value of a levered company when there is a strong likelihood that it will file for bankruptcy?

7/ What is your view of the following statement: "X went bankrupt because its financial expenses amounted to 13% of its sales"?

8/ Why do managers tend to be wary of debt?

9/ Why is it a good thing for a highly profitable company that has reached maturity to carry a lot of debt?

10/ During the 1990s, interest rates in Europe were generally revised downwards. If Modigliani and Miller's 1963 theory was right, should debt levels of companies have increased or decreased? Debt levels actually fell. State your views.

11/ According to signal theory, should undervalued companies carry more or less debt than other companies? Why?

12/ If Modigliani and Miller's 1963 theory had been right, how much corporate income tax would the state have collected every year?

13/ In your view, after a failed takeover bid, will the debt-to-equity ratio of the target tend to rise or fall? Why?

14/ In your view, can the theories of capital structure described in this chapter be proven with as much certainty as, say, the put/call parity described in Chapter 24 that deals with options? Why?

15/ Is it better to calculate a leverage ratio on the basis of book values or market values of debt and equity to assess the level of risk taken by a company? Why?

16/Does the pecking order theory imply that the company has an optimal capital structure? What are the criteria for determining capital structure according to this approach?

17/If there was an optimal debt-to-equity ratio, should it be stable over time? Why?

18/An LBO fund is prepared to pay 3000 for operating assets if the financing is split equally between debt and equity, and 35 000 if the split is 75% debt and 25% equity. State your views.

More questions are waiting for you at www.vernimmen.com

EXERCISES

1/ 70% of company *A*'s needs are equity-financed at a cost of 10% and 30% debt-financed at 6%. What is the weighted average cost of capital of this company if the tax rate is 20%, 50% and 80%?

2/A company is totally financed by equity capital for a market value of 200m. The only tax it has to pay is corporate income tax at a rate of 40%. Calculate the value of this company if it borrows 50m at 6% to perpetuity, to be used to repay a part of shareholders' equity. Shareholders would then require an 11% return.

3/ Company *C* is financed by equity with a market value of 40 and by debt with a market value of 30. This debt is perpetual and its interest rate is 6%. The corporate income tax rate is 40%

(a) How much of C's enterprise value is due to debt? The shareholders' required rate of return is 11%.
(b) By how much will the enterprise value increase if the company borrows 5 on the same terms as previously (assume a required rate of return of 11% to simplify calculations)?
(c) By how much will the enterprise value fall if there is a change in the tax laws and in four years' time financial expenses will no longer be tax deductible?

4/ Redo the table on p.657 for Spain and Tunisia assuming two situations: no debt and 500 of debt at 7%. Assume the Tunisian tax rate on interest is 35%. State your views.

ANSWERS

SECTION 4

Questions

1/ *Difference: present value of tax saving due to the fact that financial expenses are tax deductible.*
2/ *The cost of bankruptcy and individual income tax.*
3/ *The individual tax payable by the investor cancels out the impact of the corporate tax payable. Conclusion: no optimal capital structure.*
4/ *Financial expenses are tax deductible. Tax credit.*
5/ *More favourable treatment for equity due to the drop in the corporate income tax rate, and heavier taxes on debt income for creditors.*
6/ *Value of unlevered company + present value of tax saving – present value of cost of filing for bankruptcy.*
7/ *This line of reasoning is false. A company goes bankrupt because its present and expected profits are inadequate compared with its risk, and not because it is carrying*

too much debt. If it is carrying too much debt, this is because its profits are too low, and not the other way round.

8/ Because by increasing the risk to which their companies are exposed, they increase their chances of losing their jobs.

9/ Because it can avoid using its free cash flows, it will not destroy value by diversifying or making unprofitable investments.

10/ Debt levels should have risen to set off the drop in interest rates so that tax-deductible financial expenses at least remained constant. Conclusion: either this theory does not stand up or there are other factors which explain the situation.

11/ More debt, because they are not keen to issue new equity while the value of their shareholders' equity is undervalued.

12/ Close to zero, since all companies would incur sufficient debts to reduce their tax bills to zero.

13/ Rise, as shareholders will increase pressure so that the company achieves better financial performance.

14/ No, because we are not dealing with mathematical certainties but with behaviour.

15/ Value, because if the company is very profitable, its equity capital will be worth much more than its book value. A more accurate assessment of the company's ability to meet its debt repayments will then be possible.

16/ No, because financial resources are used in a given order in line with requirements. The difference between operating inflows and investment outflows.

17/ No, because interest rates, tax rates, risk aversion, volatility of operating assets, the maturity of a sector, etc. change over time.

18/ A difference of this amount cannot simply be due to the tax break on debt. It is also difficult to believe that management would be more motivated by the higher level of debt (50/50 is already a high level). This can only be some sort of trap.

Exercises

1/ 8.44%; 7.9%; 7.36%.

2/ $200 + 50 \times 40\% \times 6\%/11\% = 210.9$.

3/ (a) $(30 \times 6\% \times 40\%)/11\% = 6.5$.

(b) The value increases by 1.1.

(c) Reduction of the value by 5.

4/

	Spain		Tunisia	
	D = 0	D = 500 at 7%	D = 0	D = 500 at 7%
Operating income	101.0	101.0	101.0	101.0
– Interest expense	0.0	35.0	0.0	35.0
= Pre-tax profit	101.0	66.0	101.0	66.0
– Income tax expense	30.3	19.8	30.3	19.8
= Net earnings	70.7	46.2	70.7	46.2
Income tax:				
on dividends/capital gains	12.7	8.3	0.0	0.0
on interest	0.0	6.3	0.0	12.3
Investors' net income	58.0	66.6	70.7	69.0
Total taxes	43.0	34.4	30.3	32.1

In Spain, debt receives more favourable tax treatment, while in Tunisia, equity enjoys better tax breaks.

Modigliani and Miller's main work on capital structure:

B. Grundy, Merton H. Miller, His contribution to financial economics, *Journal of Finance*, **56**(4), 1183–1206, August 2001.

M. Miller, Debt and taxes, *Journal of Finance*, **32**(2), 261–276, May 1977.

M. Miller, The M&M proposition 40 years later, *European Financial Management*, **4**(2), 113–120, July 1998.

F. Modigliani, M. Miller, Corporate income taxes and the cost of capital: A correction, *American Economic Review*, **53**(3), 433–443, June 1963.

Following on from the above work, on the problems of capital structure and taxes:

M. Arena, A. Roper, The effect of taxes on multinational debt location, *Journal of Corporate Finance*, **16**(5), 637–654, December 2010.

J. van Binsbergen, J. Graham, J. Yang, The cost of debt, *Journal of Finance*, **65**(6), 2089–2136, December 2010.

S. Byonn, How and when do firms adjust their capital structures toward targets?, *Journal of Finance*, **63**(6), 3069–3096, December 2008.

H. DeAngelo, R. Masulis, Optimal capital structure under corporate and personal taxation, *Journal of Financial Economics*, **8**(1), 3–29, March 1980.

E. Fama, K. French, Taxes, financing decisions and firm value, *Journal of Finance*, **53**(3), 819–843, June 1998.

D. Galai, Taxes, M&M propositions and government's implicit cost of capital in investment projects in the private sector, *European Financial Management*, **4**(2), 143–157, July 1998.

J. Graham, How big are the tax benefits of debt? *Journal of Finance*, **55**(5), 1901–1941, October 2000.

J. Graham, Taxes and corporate finance: A review, *Review of Financial Studies*, **16**(4), 1075–1129, Winter 2003.

R. Green, B. Hollifield, The personal tax advantages of equity, *Journal of Financial Economics*, **2**(67), 175–216, February 2003.

C. Hennessy, T. Whited, Debt dynamics, *Journal of Finance*, **3**(60), 1129–1165, June 2005.

H. Huizinga, L. Laeven, G. Nicodème, Capital structure and international debt shifting, *Journal of Financial Economics*, **88**(1), 80–108, April 2008.

A. Korteweg, The net benefits to leverage, *Journal of Finance*, **65**(6), 2137–2170, December 2010.

On the disciplining role of debt:

H. Almeida, Th. Philippon, The risk-adjusted cost of financial distress, *Journal of Finance*, **6**(62), 2557–2586, December 2007.

K.-H. Bae, J.-K Koo, J. Wang, Employee treatment and firm leverage: A test of the stakeholder theory of capital structure, *Journal of Financial Economics*, **100**(1), 130–153, April 2011.

J. Berk, R. Stanton, J. Zechner, Human capital, bankruptcy, and capital structure, *Journal of Finance*, **65**(3), 891–926, June 2010.

D. Denis, Leveraged recaps in the curbing of corporate overinvestment, *Journal of Applied Corporate Finance*, **6**(1), 60–71, Winter 1993.

E. Fama, What's different about bank loans? *Journal of Monetary Economics*, **15**(1), 29–39, January 1985.

M. Jensen, Agency costs of free cash flows, corporate finance and takeovers, *American Economic Review*, **76**(2), 323–329, May 1976.

S. Kaplan, The effects of management buy-outs on operating performance and value, *Journal of Financial Economics*, **24**(2), 217–254, October 1989.

C. Molina, Are firms underleveraged? An examination of the effect of leverage on default probabilities, *Journal of Finance*, **60**(3), 1427–1459, June 2005.

K. Palepu, Consequences of LBO, *Journal of Financial Economics*, **27**(1), 247–262, September 1990.

C. Smith, Corporate ownership structure and performance: The case of management buyouts, *Journal of Financial Economics*, **27**(1), 143–164, September 1990.

On financial asymmetries and pecking order theory:

D. Brounen, A. De Jong, K. Koedijk, Corporate finance in Europe: Confronting theory with practice, *Financial Management*, **33**(4), 71–101, Winter 2004.

G. Donaldson, *Corporate debt capacity: A study of corporate debt policy and the determination of corporate debt capacity*, Harvard University Division of Research, 1961.

C. James, D.C. Smith, Are banks still special? New evidence on their role in the corporate capital-raising process, in *The Revolution in Corporate Finance*, J. Stern and D. Chew (eds), Blackwell Publishing, 278–290, 2003.

S. Myers, Determinants of corporate borrowing, *Journal of Financial Economics*, **5**(2), 147–175, November 1977.

S. Myers, The capital structure puzzle, *Journal of Finance*, **39**(3), 575–592, July 1984.

S. Ross, The determination of financial structure: The incentive signaling approach, *Bell Journal of Economics*, **8**(1), 23–40, Summer 1977.

On the application of the theory of signals to capital structure:

H. Leland, Agency costs, risk management and capital structure, *Journal of Finance*, **53**(4), 1213–1243, August 1998.

S. Myers, The capital structure puzzle, *Journal of Finance*, **39**(3), 575–592, July 1984.

S. Myers, N. Majluf, Corporate financing and investment decisions when firms have information investors do not have, *Journal of Financial Economics*, **13**, 187–222, June 1984.

S. Ross, The determination of capital structure: The incentive signaling approach, *Bell Journal of Economics*, **8**(1), 23–40, Spring 1977.

To learn more about corporate debt policies:

D. Denis, V. Mihov, The choice among bank debt, non-bank private debt and public debt: Evidence from new corporate borrowings, *Journal of Financial Economics*, **70**(1), 3–28, January 2003.

M.-T. Marchisa, R. Mura, Financial flexibility, investment ability, and firm value: Evidence from firms with spare debt capacity, *Financial Management*, **39**(4), 1339–1365, Winter 2010.

S. Ravid, Debt maturity – a survey, *Financial Markets, Institutions & Instruments*, **5**(3), 1–69, March 1996.

On the costs of financial distress:

E. Altman, A further empirical investigation of the bankruptcy costs question, *Journal of Finance*, **39**(4), 589–609, September 1984.

E. Altman, *Default and Returns on High Yield Bonds through 1999 and Default Outlook for 2000–2002*, Working paper, New York University/Salomon Center 2000.

G. Andrade, S. Kaplan, How costly is financial (not economic) distress? Evidence from highly leveraged transactions that became distressed, *Journal of Finance*, **53**(5), 1443–1493, October 1998.

N. Baxter, Leverage, risk of ruin and the cost of capital, *Journal of Finance*, **22**(3), 395–403, September 1967.

J. Stiglitz, Some aspects of the pure theory of corporate finance: Bankruptcies and takeovers, *Bell Journal of Economics and Management Science*, **7**(1), 458–482, Autumn 1972.

S. Titman, The effect of capital structure on a firm's liquidation decision, *Journal of Financial Economics*, **13**(1), 137–151, March 1984.

On the application of agency theory to problems relating to capital structure:

M. Jensen, The agency costs of free cash flow, corporate finance, and takeovers, *American Economic Review*, **76**(2), 323–329, May 1986.

M. Jensen, W. Meckling, Theory of the firm: Managerial behavior agency costs and ownership structure, *Journal of Financial Economics*, **3**(4), 305–360, October 1976.

H. Leland, Agency costs, risk management and capital structure, *Journal of Finance*, **53**(4), 1213–1243, August 1998.

C. Mao, Interaction of debt agency problems and optimal capital structure: Theory and evidence, *Journal of Financial and Quantitative Analysis*, **2**(38), 399–423, June 2003.

E. Ofek, Capital structure and firm response to poor performance: an empirical investigation, *Journal of Financial Economics*, **34**(1), 3–30, August 1993.

And finally, some articles that summarise the topics covered in this chapter:

M. Barclay, C. Smith, The capital structure puzzle: Another look at the evidence, *Journal of Applied Corporate Finance*, **12**(1), 8–20, Spring 1999.

Z. Frank, V. Goyal, Capital structure decisions: which factors are reliably important?, *Financial Management*, **38**(1), 1–37, Spring 2009.

Chapter 35
DEBT, EQUITY AND OPTIONS THEORY

Light too bright to see by

The theories of corporate finance examined so far may have given the impression that the only difference between debt and equity is the required rate of return. However, **there is a big difference between the 10% return required by creditors and that required by shareholders**.

Shareholders simply hope to achieve this rate, which forms an average of rates that can be either positive or negative. The actual return can range from 0% to infinity, with the entire range of variations in between!

Creditors are assured of receiving the required rate, but never more. They can only hope to earn the 10% return but, with a few exceptions, this hope is almost always fulfilled. So here we have the first distinction between creditors and shareholders: the probability distribution of their remuneration is completely different.

That said, although the creditor's risk is very low, it is not nil. Capitalism is built on the concept of corporation, which legally **restricts shareholders' liability with respect to creditors**. When a company defaults, shareholders hold a "trump card" that allows them to hand the company, including its liabilities, over to the lenders.

The main financial innovation of the 19th century is the corporation.

In the rest of this chapter, *we will concentrate on the valuation of companies in which shareholders' responsibility is limited to the amount they have invested*. This applies to the vast majority of all companies in modern capitalism, be they corporations, limited liability companies or sole ownerships with limited liability.

This is the fundamental difference between shareholders and creditors: the former can lose their entire investment, but also hope for unlimited gains, while the latter will at best earn the flows programmed at the beginning of the contract.

Keep this in mind as we use options to analyse corporate structure and, more importantly, the relationship between shareholders and creditors.

Section 35.1
ANALYSING THE FIRM IN LIGHT OF OPTIONS THEORY

To keep our presentation simple, we shall take the example of a joint stock company in which enterprise value EV is divided between debt (V_D) and equity (V_E).

We shall also assume that the company has issued only one type of debt – zero-coupon bonds – redeemable upon maturity at full face value (principal and interest) for 100.

1/ EQUITY AND DEBT IN TERMS OF OPTIONS

Depending on the enterprise value when the debt matures, two outcomes are possible.

- The enterprise value is higher than the amount of debt to be redeemed (e.g. $EV = 120$). In this case, the shareholders let the company repay the lenders and take the residual value of 20.
- The enterprise value is lower than the amount of debt to be redeemed (e.g. $EV = 70$). The shareholders may then invoke their limited liability clause, forfeiting only their investment, and transfer the company to the lenders who will bear the difference between the enterprise value and their claim.

Now let us analyse this situation in terms of options. From an economic standpoint, shareholders have a call option (known as a European call if it can only be exercised at the end of its life) on the firm's assets. Its features are:

- **Underlying asset** = capital employed.
- **Exercise price** = amount of debt to be reimbursed (100).
- **Volatility** = volatility of the underlying assets, i.e. the capital employed.
- **Maturity** = expiration date.
- **Interest rate** = risk-free rate corresponding to the maturity of the option.

At the expiration date, shareholders exercise their call option and repay the lenders, or they abandon it. The value of the option is none other than the value of equity (V_E).

From the shareholder's point of view, when a company borrows funds, it is selling its "enterprise value" to its creditors, but with an option to buy it back (at the exercise price) when the debt matures. The shares of a levered company thus represent call options on the capital employed.

The lender, on the other hand, who has invested in the firm at no risk, *has sold the shareholders a put option on the capital employed*. We have just seen that in the event of default, the creditors may find themselves the unwilling owners of the company. Rather than recouping the amount they lent, they get only the value of the company back. In other words, they have "bought" the company in exchange for the outstanding amount of debt.

The features of the put option are:

- **Underlying asset** = capital employed.
- **Exercise price** = amount of debt redeemable upon maturity (100).
- **Volatility** = volatility of the underlying asset, i.e. the capital employed.
- **Maturity** = maturity of the debt.
- **Interest rate** = risk-free rate corresponding to the maturity of the option.

The sale of this (European-style) put option results in additional remuneration for the debtholder which, together with the risk-free rate, constitutes the total return. This is only fair, since the debtholder runs the risk that the shareholders will exercise their put option; in other words, that the company will not pay back the debt.

The value of this option is equal to the difference between the value of the loan computed by discounting its cash flows at the risk-free rate and its market value (discounted at a rate that takes into account the default risk, i.e. the cost of debt k_D). This is the risk premium that arises between any loan and its risk-free equivalent.

All this means is that the debtholder has lent the company 103 at an interest rate equal to the risk-free rate. The company should have received 103, but the value of the loan is only 100 after discounting the flows at the normal rate of return required in view of the company's risk, rather than the risk-free rate.

The company uses the balance of 3, which represents the price of the credit risk, to buy a put option on the capital employed. In short, the company receives 100 while the bank pays 100 for a risky claim since it has sold a put option for capital employed that the company, and therefore the shareholders, will exercise if its value is lower than that of the outstanding date at maturity. By exercising the option, the company, and thus its shareholders, discharges its debt by transferring ownership of the capital employed to the creditors.

Lending to a company is a means of investing in its assets at no risk. The lender sells the shareholders a put option at an exercise price that is equal to the debt to be repaid.

In conclusion, we see that, depending on the situation at the redemption date, one of the following two will apply:

- if $V_D < V$ the value of the call option is higher than 0, the value of the put option is zero and equity is positive,
- if $V_D > V$ the value of the call option is zero, the value of the put option is higher than 0 and the equity is worthless.

2/ AN OPTIONS APPROACH TO FINANCIAL SECURITIES

We have already seen that the additivity rule for equity and debt applies and that there is no connection between enterprise value and the type of financing:

$$\text{Enterprise value} = \text{equity} + \text{debt}$$

Based on the preceding developments, we deduce that:

> Value of equity = value of the call option on capital employed
> Value of debt = present value of debt at the risk-free rate
> — value of the put option
> Enterprise value = value of the call option
> + present value of debt at the risk-free rate
> — value of the put option

This brings us back to the fundamental equality between put and call options we examined in Chapter 24:

> Buying a call option + selling a put option
> = Buying the underlying asset + borrowing at the risk-free rate

This underscores the relationship between the value of a call on capital employed and the value of a put on the same capital employed:

> Value of equity = EV − present value of debt at the risk-free rate
> + value of the put on capital employed

Section 35.2
CONTRIBUTION OF OPTIONS THEORY TO THE VALUATION OF EQUITY

We have demonstrated that the value of a firm's equity is comparable to the value of a call option on its capital employed. The option's exercise price is the amount of debt to be repaid at maturity, the life of the option is that of the debt, and its underlying asset is the firm's capital employed.

This means that, at the valuation date, the value of equity is made up of an intrinsic value and a time value. The intrinsic value of the call option is the difference between the present value of capital employed and the debt to be repaid upon maturity. The time value corresponds to the difference between the total value of equity and the intrinsic value.

The main contribution of options theory to corporate finance is the concept of a time value for equity.

Take, for example, a company where the return on capital employed is lower than that required by investors in view of the related risk. The market value is thus lower than the book value.

If the debt were to mature today, the shareholders would exercise their put option since the capital employed is worth only 70 while the outstanding debt is 80. The company would have to file for bankruptcy. Fortunately, the debt is not redeemable today but only in, say, two years' time. By then, the enterprise value may have risen to over 80. In that case, equity will have an intrinsic value equal to the difference between the enterprise value at the redemption date and the amount to be redeemed (in our case, 80).

Today, however, the intrinsic value is zero and the present value of equity (8) can only be explained by the time value, which represents the hope that, when the debt matures two years hence, enterprise value will have risen enough to exceed the amount of debt to be repaid, giving the equity an intrinsic value.

As seen in the graphs below, a company's financial position can be considered from either the shareholders' or the creditors' standpoint.

By now you must be eager to apply your new-found knowledge of options to corporate finance!

(a) The time value of an option increases with the volatility of the underlying asset

The more economic or industrial risk on a company, the higher the volatility of its capital employed and the higher the time value of its equity. The options method is thus used to value large, risky projects financed by debt, such as the Channel tunnel, leisure parks, etc. or those with inherent volatility, such as biotech startups.

SECTION 4

(b) **The time value of an option depends on the position of the strike price relative to the market value of the underlying asset**

When the call option is out-of-the-money (enterprise value lower than outstanding debt), the company's equity has only time value. Shareholders hope for an improvement in the company, whose equity has no intrinsic value.

Decomposition of the value of the underlying asset.

DECOMPOSITION OF THE UNDERLYING ASSET VALUE

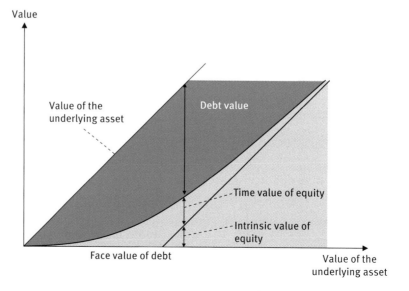

Intrinsic value of equity   Intrinsic value of equity

Equity value

Underlying asset value

Time value of equity

Value of put option on assets

Debt value discounted at risk free rate   Face value of debt

Debt value   Debt value

Shareholders' position.

SHAREHOLDERS' POSITION

Value

Value of the underlying asset

Debt value

Time value of equity

Intrinsic value of equity

Face value of debt

Value of the underlying asset

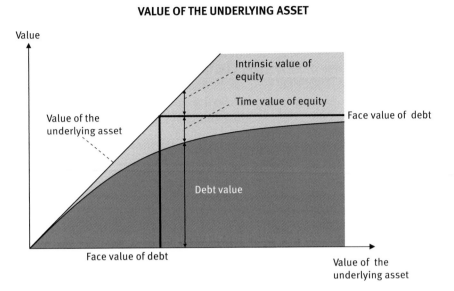

VALUE OF THE UNDERLYING ASSET

Debtholders' position

When the call option is at-the-money (enterprise value equal to debt at maturity), the time value of equity is at its highest and anything can happen. Using the options method to value equity is now particularly relevant, since it can quantify shareholders' anticipation.

When the call option is in-the-money (enterprise value higher than outstanding debt at maturity), the intrinsic value of equity quickly outweighs the time value. The risk on the debt held by the lenders decreases and becomes nearly non-existent when the enterprise value tends towards infinity. This brings us back to the traditional idea that the higher the enterprise value, the less risk creditors have of a default, and the more the cost of debt approaches the risk-free rate.

Using options theory to analyse liabilities is particularly helpful when a company is in financial distress.

The options method is therefore applied to companies that carry heavy debt or are very risky.

(c) The time value of an option increases with its maturity

This is why it is so important for companies in distress to reschedule debt payments, preferably at very long maturities.

The example below illustrates the use of options to value equity.

Take a company that has both debt and equity financing and let us assume its debt is 100, redeemable in one year. If, based on its degree of risk, the debt carries 6% interest, the amount to be repaid to creditors one year later is 106.

Traditional theory tells us that if the firm's value is 150 at the time of calculation, the value of equity – defined as the difference between enterprise value and the value of debt – will be $150 - 100 = 50$.

What happens if we apply options theory to this value?

We shall assume the risk-free rate is 5%. The discounted value of the debt + interest payment at the risk-free rate is 106/1.05, or 100.95.

The value of debt can be expressed as:

Value of debt = Value of debt at the risk-free rate – value of a put i.e. value of the put $= 100.95 - 100 = 0.95$.

We know that the value of equity breaks down into its intrinsic and time value:

	Value of equity	= 50
−	Intrinsic value = 150 − 106	= 44
=	Time value	= 6

You can see that, for this company with limited risk, the time value measuring the actual risk is far lower than the intrinsic value. Similarly, the value of the put, which acts as a risk premium, is very low as well.

Now, let's increase the risk to the capital employed and assume that the interest rate required by the creditors is 15% rather than 6%, corresponding to a 10% risk premium. The amount to be repaid in one year is thus 115.

The value of the debt discounted at the risk-free rate is 115/1.05, or 109.52. The value of the put is thus $109.52 - 100 = 9.52$.

Note that the risk premium for this company is much higher than in the preceding example, reflecting the increasing probability that the company will default on its debt.

The value of equity, which is still 50, breaks down into intrinsic value of 35 (150 − 115) and a time value of 15 (50 − 35). Since there is more risk than in our previous example, the time value accounts for a higher portion of the equity value.

Section 35.3
USING OPTIONS THEORY TO ANALYSE A COMPANY'S FINANCIAL DECISIONS

Options theory helps us understand how major corporate financial decisions (choice of capital structure, dividend payout, investment decisions, etc.) affect shareholders and creditors differently, and how they can result in a transfer of value between the two.

Example   Take the example of a holding company, Holding plc, which owns 100 ordinary shares of Daughter plc, listed at £2230. We shall assume that the liabilities of Holding plc comprise 100 shares and 300 bonds. Each of the latter is a zero-coupon bond with a redemption value of £1000 in 3 years' time. The creditors do not expect any coupon payments or changes in the capital structure before the debt redemption date.

The table below lists the closing prices for a call option on a Daughter plc share at various exercise prices:

Exercise price (£)	Value of a 3-year call option on Daughter plc (£)
2600	130
2800	80
3000	45
3200	31

The enterprise value of Holding plc is equal to the number of Daughter plc shares multiplied by their closing price, i.e. £223 000.

Consider each of the 100 shares booked under liabilities at Holding plc as being an option on its capital employed (the shares of Daughter plc), i.e. £223 000, with an exercise price that is equal to the amount of Holding plc debt outstanding, giving 300 bonds × £1000 = £300 000.

Each Holding plc share can thus be considered to be a call option with an exercise price of: £300 000/100 shares = £3000, and a maturity of 3 years.

According to the table above, Holding plc's equity value is thus £45 × 100 shares = £4500.

MARKET VALUE BALANCE SHEET OF HOLDING PLC

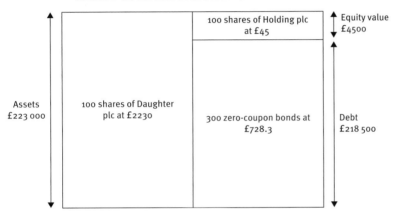

The value of debt is equal to the difference between the enterprise value (£223 000) and that of equity (£4500), i.e. £218 500.

One bond is therefore worth £728.3 (£218 500/300), corresponding to an implied yield of 11.1% (in fact: 728.3 = 1000/(1 + 0.111)³).

We will now discuss a few major financing or investment decisions in a context of **equilibrium** – that is, where the debt, shares and assets held are bought or sold at their fair value, **without the market having anticipated the decision**.

1/ INCREASING DEBT

Suppose the shareholders of Holding plc decide to issue 20 additional bonds and use the proceeds to reduce the company's equity by distributing an exceptional dividend. The overall exercise price corresponding to the redemption value of the debt at maturity is:

320 bonds × £1000 = £320 000 or £ 3200 per share

A look at the listed prices of the options shows us that at an exercise price of £3200, Holding plc's equity is valued as £31 ×100 shares = £3100, indicating that the value of its debt at the same date is: £219 900 (223 000 – 3100).

The new bondholders will thus pay £13 744 (20 bonds × £219 900/320 bonds), which will go to reduce the equity of Holding plc.

The shareholders consequently have £13 744 in cash and £3100 in shares, i.e. a total of £16 844 compared with the previous £4500. They have gained £12 344 to the detriment of the former creditors, who have seen the value of their claim fall from £218 500 to 300 bonds × £219 900/320 bonds, or £206 156.

Their loss (218 500 − 206 156 = £12 344) exactly mirrors the shareholders' gain. The implicit yield to maturity has risen to 13.3%, reflecting the fact that the borrowing has become riskier since it now finances a larger share of the same amount of capital employed.

Increasing the risk to creditors has enhanced the value of the shares, thereby reducing that of the bonds. The existing creditors have lost out because they were not able to anticipate the change in corporate structure and have been harmed by the dividend distribution.

Common (accounting) sense seems to indicate that distributing £13 744 in cash to shareholders should translate into an equivalent decrease in the value of their Holding plc shares. According to this reasoning, after the buy-back the Holding plc shares should have been revalued at −£9244 (£4500 − £13 744), but that cannot be!

Options theory solves this apparent paradox. It shows that when new debt is issued to reduce equity, the time value of the shares decreases less than the amount received by shareholders and remains positive. True, the likelihood that the value of Daughter plc shares will be higher than that of the redeemable debt upon maturity has lessened (since debt has increased), but it is still not nil, giving a time value that, while lower, is still positive.

Of course, this example is exaggerated. Such a decision would have catastrophic consequences for shareholders who would be taken to court by the creditors and lose all credibility in the eyes of the market. But it effectively illustrates the contribution of options theory to equity valuations.

Increasing debt increases the value of shareholders' investment to the detriment of the claims held by existing creditors. Thus, value is transferred from creditors to shareholders.

Conversely, when debt is reduced by a capital increase, the overall value of shares does not increase by the value of the shares issued. The old debt, which has become less risky, has, in fact, "confiscated" some of the value to the benefit of creditors and the detriment of shareholders.

2/ THE INVESTMENT DECISION

Now let us return to our initial scenario and assume that Holding plc manages to exchange the 100 shares of Daughter plc for 100 shares of a company with a higher risk profile called Risk plc, for £223 000 (100 × £2230).

Each share of Holding plc is equal to a call option on a Risk plc share with an exercise price of £3000 (300 × 1000/100).

Suppose the value of a call option on a Risk plc share is £140 with an exercise price of £3000 and an exercise date in 3 years' time.

The Holding plc shares are consequently worth £14 000.

Exchanging a low-risk asset (Daughter plc) for a highly volatile asset (Risk plc) has redistributed value to the benefit of shareholders, whose gain is £9500 (14 000 − 4500).

Their gain is offset by an equivalent loss to creditors, since the value of the debt has fallen from 218 500 to 223 000 − 14 000 = £209 000, i.e. a £9500 decline.

The higher risk led to an increase in the implicit yield to maturity of the bonds from 11.1% to 12.8%.

As in our previous examples, the transfer of value was only possible because creditors underestimated the power shareholders have over the company's investment decisions.

3/ Renegotiating the terms of debt

What if we now return to our initial situation and imagine that the company is able to reschedule its debt? This happens when creditors prefer to let a company in financial distress attempt a turnaround rather than precipitate its demise.

So let's assume the debt is due in 4, rather than the initial 3, years. A look at our options price list for Daughter plc shares with a 4-year maturity shows us that they carry a higher premium.

Exercise price (£)	Value of put on Daughter plc shares in 4 years (£)
2600	140 (versus 130)
2800	89 (versus 80)
3000	53 (versus 45)
3200	40 (versus 31)

This, of course, comes as no surprise to our attentive readers who remember learning in Chapter 24 that the value of an option increases with the length of its life.

The value of equity is thus £53 $\times$ 100 shares = £5300. A bond is therefore worth £725.7 (£217 700/300). Without having abandoned any flows, creditors' generosity will have cost them £800.

To sum up:

* Leveraging a company either to distribute dividends, reduce capital or to invest tends to increase the risk to creditors, transferring value from them to shareholders. The value of the shares diminishes less than the dividend payout and increases when the debt is used for investment purposes.
* Similarly, replacing non-risky with risky assets does not change enterprise value, but it does transfer value from creditors to shareholders.
* Lastly, rescheduling debt transfers value from creditors to shareholders, even if the interest rate remains the same.

This is called the expropriation effect, where some of the value of the claims is confiscated without any exchange of flows.

4/ Practical applications

As our readers may have understood, shareholders' equity is effectively only valued using the option models for distressed companies.

These theoretical developments have been the basis for the creation of models to assess the default risk of the firm. In particular, the consulting company KMV has developed well-known models from the work of Merton, Black and Scholes. Such models are used in particular by banks in the context of Basel II requirements.

Hedge funds have developed arbitrage strategies between debt and equity markets (capital structure arbitrage) based on this approach. These techniques use mainly credit default swaps (CDS).

Lastly, some borrowers hedge their credit risk by selling shares of the firm short. In doing so, they earn on one side what they may lose on the drop of value of their loan.

Section 35.4
ANALYSING THE FIRM'S LIQUIDITY

Until now, we have assumed that if, on maturity of its debt, the value of the firm's capital employed is higher than the debt, shareholders will subscribe a capital increase in order to enable it to pay off the debt.

In practice, more frequently, the company pays off part of its debt with its free cash flows and refinances the balance of its debt by taking out a new loan.

Most of the time, the sum of free cash flows is higher than the amount of debt to be repaid, but the flows generally are further off in time than the due date for the debt, and so are insufficient in the short term.

The duration (see page 396) of cash flows is generally longer than the duration of debt flows, which rarely exceed six to seven years.

The firm is then exposed to a double risk:

- the risk of the interest rate at which it is going, in the future, to refinance part of its current debt;
- a liquidity risk since, at the time when the firm is going to have to take out a new loan, market conditions may not allow it to if there is a major liquidity crisis underway (as was the case in late 2008/early 2009).

It is possible to hedge against these two risks, as we shall see in Chapter 49. Frequently however, the liquidity risk is unhedged, either because it is not always possible to hedge against it, or because the cost of hedging is seen as prohibitive, or possibly because situations of severe liquidity crises are so rare that it is not deemed necessary to hedge against this risk.

The difference between the duration of a firm's free cash flows and the duration of its debt (often a shorter period) constitutes an asset liability refinancing gap (ALRG).

Yann Aït-Mokhtar has shown that it is the same as a liability for a firm, as if it had put itself in the position of selling a borrower FRA (see page 931).

On maturity of its debt, the firm will only be able to make the repayment if it is able to find lenders that are prepared to lend to it, since its free cash flows will be insufficient to pay off the whole of the debt.

So what it has done is undertaken to take out future debt at an unknown interest rate in order to continue its activity. In normal times, this liability is worth a negligible amount as it is reasonable to expect that a healthy firm will have no problems in refinancing in the future. But in the event of a liquidity crisis and for firms with imminent debt repayment deadlines (a few months or quarters), this ALRG has a very high value.

It is equal to the existing uncertainty as to the possibility of the company being able to find the necessary financing.

So we can say:

$$\text{Value of capital employed}$$

$$- \text{ Value of net debt}$$

$$- \text{ Value of ALRG}$$

$$= \text{ Value of equity capital}$$

which corresponds to:

VALUE AND LIQUIDITY

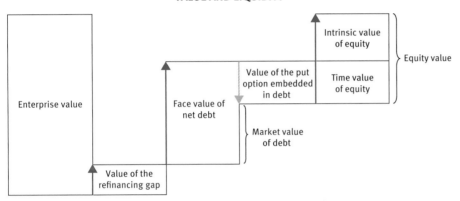

When investors start to worry about the ability of the company to refinance in the near future, the value of the ALRG increases, pushing down the value of equity. And the phenomenon can pick up speed if the current lenders try and hedge their risks by selling short the firm's shares, hoping to gain on this short-selling what they will lose as a result of the decline in the value of their debt.

When the firm is able to find refinancing for its debt, for example through a share issue, we see in some cases (Lafarge in 2009) an increase in the share price, which contradicts what we have seen up to now. On the one hand, the value of the share is negatively impacted by the transfer of value to the creditors, but on the other, it benefits fully from the disappearance of the ALRG. And if the latter were worth more than the discount on the debt, the net impact would be positive and the value of the share would rise.

Section 35.5
RESOLVING CONFLICTS BETWEEN SHAREHOLDERS AND CREDITORS

Creditors have a number of means at their disposal to protect themselves and overcome the asymmetry from which they suffer. They can be grouped under two main headings:

- hybrid financial securities;
- restrictive covenants.

1/ HYBRID FINANCIAL SECURITIES

Hybrid financial securities, combining features of both debt and equity – such as convertible bonds, bonds with equity warrants, participating loan stock, etc. – would not be necessary in a perfect market. By issuing such hybrid securities, shareholders are, in effect, giving creditors a call option on equity which neutralises the call option on equity creditors have granted shareholders.

In fact, should shareholders make investment or financing decisions that are detrimental to creditors, the latter can exercise their warrants or convert their bonds into shares, thus becoming shareholders themselves and, if all goes well, recouping in equity what they have lost in debt!

Jensen and Meckling (1976) have demonstrated that the issue of convertible bonds reduces the risk of the firm's assets being replaced by more risky assets that increase volatility and thus the value of the shares. The same reasoning is applied when "free" warrants are granted to creditors who agree to waive some of their claims during a corporate restructuring plan (see Chapter 25).

2/ RESTRICTIVE COVENANTS

We shall discuss the four main types of covenants, but our list is far from comprehensive. They can concern:

* corporate investment and production policies;
* dividend payments;
* net debt and subsequent debt issues;
* early redemption provisions.

(a) Corporate investment and production policies

The purpose of such covenants is chiefly to protect debtholders against the possibility that the firm will substitute more risky assets for the existing ones. Any investment in other companies, mergers, absorption or asset disposals are either restricted or subject to approval by the debtholders.

In some cases, the securities of certain subsidiaries or the equipment the issue served to finance are given as collateral (pledge). This restricts the possibility of asset substitution. Some covenants restrict the granting of certain assets as collateral for future debt (negative pledge).

The company may also be obliged to invest in certain projects, to continue holding certain assets, maintain its working capital or raise it above a certain threshold.

(b) Dividend payments

These covenants are designed to avoid the massive dividend distributions financed by increases in debt or asset disposals we discussed previously.

For example, they can link dividend distribution to a minimum level of equity during the life of the debt. Similarly, they frequently restrict or rule out the distribution of reserves or share buy-backs.

These clauses have the added advantage of imposing a minimum level of investment on shareholders in order to utilise the cash that cannot be distributed, thus reducing the risk of underinvestment.

(c) Net debt and subsequent debt issues

Any unforeseen, subsequent issue of equal or higher-ranking debt reduces value for existing debtholders. And yet it would not be in the interests of either the current bondholders or the shareholders to rule out any further debt issues. To protect themselves against a reduction in the value of their claims, debtholders can impose limits on the amount of net debt and the nature of the new debt issued based on certain ratios:

$$\frac{\text{Net finanical debt}}{\text{Equity}}, \quad \frac{\text{Operating income}}{\text{Interest expenses}},$$

$$\frac{\text{Net financial debt}}{\text{EBITDA}}, \quad \frac{\text{Receivables}}{\text{Payables}}, \text{ etc}\ldots$$

When these ratios exceed the predefined threshold, the debt immediately falls due.

It can also become payable when the ratios exceed these thresholds because of deteriorating corporate results rather than new borrowings.

In practice, these are chiefly *rendezvous* clauses that force the company to arrange a restructuring plan with its creditors to contain the risk to the latter, which increases with the financial distress of the company. In addition, waivers (i.e. the fact that banks may allow the borrower not to respect covenants) may be granted against a specific increase in rates or a waiver fee, thereby increasing the remuneration of the lender (as the borrower has become more risky).

(d) Early redemption clauses for all or part of the debt

In a context of information asymmetry, early redemption clauses are a means of dealing with the problem of overinvestment and asset substitution. Analysing equity as an option on the firm's value shows that paying a coupon or an annuity before the final repayment offers some protection to creditors and thus reduces share value.

In short, covenants are affirmative or negative pledges that entail the immediate repayment of the debt when not respected.

The main contribution of options theory to corporate finance is the concept of the time value of equity. The options approach is predicated on the physical separation of shareholders and debtholders, which has become standard practice.

You will have realised that this is very different from the simple accounting leverage effect that seemed to show that shareholders create wealth by investing at a higher rate than the cost of debt. The shareholder/debtholder relationship takes on an entirely different meaning where value is concerned. When risks change, the interests of the two parties may diverge radically without any exchange of flows between them or change in the overall value of the firm.

We hope to have impressed on you the importance of reasoning in terms of value and assessing all decisions not just on the basis of profits, but also risk. The use of options may now seem blindingly obvious to you, and we hope you always keep in mind the notion of risk transfers.

Please don't be discouraged by the difficulty of applying these formulas to real life. They are very efficient qualitative tools that will enable you to tackle the financial reengineering of a group with more imagination and creativity.

SUMMARY

The summary of this chapter can be downloaded from www.vernimmen.com.

It seems like stating the obvious when we say that the status of the creditor differs radically from that of the shareholder. The shareholder stands to gain a potentially unlimited amount and his risk is limited to his investment, while the creditor, who can also lose his investment, can only expect a fixed return.

This asymmetry brings options to mind. This chapter showed that there is more than one similarity.

The shareholders' equity of a levered company can be seen as a call option granted by creditors to shareholders on the company's operating assets. The strike price is the value of the debt and the maturity is the date on which the debt is payable. When the debt falls due, if the value of the operating assets is higher than the amount of the debt to be repaid, the shareholders exercise their call option on the operating assets, and pay the creditors the amount of the debt outstanding. If, however, the value of the operating assets is lower than the amount of the debt to be repaid, the shareholders decline to pay off the debt, and the creditors appropriate the operating assets.

Similarly, we can show that lending to a company is a means of investing in its assets at no risk. The lender sells the shareholders a put option at a strike price that is equal to the debt to be repaid.

Using this options-based approach we can break down the value of equity into intrinsic value and time value. Intrinsic value is the difference between the present value of capital employed and the debt to be repaid upon maturity. Time value is the hope that when the debt matures, enterprise value will have risen to exceed the amount of the debt to be repaid.

This leads to a better understanding of the impact of certain decisions on the financial situation of creditors and shareholders:

- a dividend payout financed by the sale of assets will increase creditors' risk, reduce the value of the debt owed to them, and at the same time increase the value of shareholders' equity;

- investing in high-risk projects (but for which the net value at the required rate of return is nil) does not result in an immediate change in enterprise value, but increases creditors' risk, reduces the value of debt and increases the value of shareholders' equity by the same amount;

- by financing its own investments (or carrying out a capital increase), the company increases enterprise value by this amount (if the return on the investment is equal to the required rate of return). Part of this additional value will go to the creditors, whose risk is reduced, to the detriment of shareholders, as the overall value of their shares will not rise by the amount of the funds invested or the capital increase.

All financial decisions must be examined from an overall point of view, but also in terms of the creation or destruction of value for the various stakeholders. A given financial decision could be neutral in terms of overall value, but could enhance the value of some financial securities at the expense of others.

1/When making a comparison with options, what does shareholders' equity correspond to?

2/When making a comparison with options, what does a credit risk correspond to?

3/For what type of company can we apply the options theory for the valuation of shareholders' equity?

4/According to this theory, can the value of a company's equity be nil?

5/Why is the application of this theory more efficient for companies in difficulty?

6/Is this view of the company opposed to the theory of markets in equilibrium?

7/Give an example of a decision where creditors are "expropriated" by shareholders, without the debt agreement being renegotiated. Explain.

8/Is the effect of expropriation a result of market inefficiency?

9/A company is in trouble as a result of low profits and excessive debts.

(a) Do you think that the creditors and the shareholders have the same concerns?

More specifically, in the event of the following:

- massive new investments carrying a very high risk but that will possibly lead to high returns which will enable the company to get back on its feet with a low level of profits;
- an increase in debt;
- an increase in shareholders' equity.

(b) Would your answer be different if the company were profitable and carrying very little debt?

(c) What financial product do these examples of creditor–shareholder relationships bring to mind?

10/What is a covenant? Provide a theoretical example of the usefulness of covenants.

11/Does a covenant represent a prevention against issuing new debt or does it ensure that shareholders/management will enter into discussions with creditors?

12/Can you give an example of a kind of company where shareholders' equity is made up of pure time value?

13/What is the role of debt in the management/shareholder relationship?

More questions are waiting for you at www.vernimmen.com.

EXERCISES

1/ The investment firm Verfinance owns 5000 shares in Uninet, a group involved in the maintenance products sector, worth 10 million. This asset is financed by a 5-year zero-coupon bond (issued today) whose redemption value is 6 million, and by equity for the balance.

The following table relating to the Uninet share appears in the financial press in the section on European call options:

Strike price	5-year option	7-year option
1200	1010	1085
1600	731	832
2000	510	627
2400	348	468

(a) Does the above table seem consistent to you?

(b) Can you value the shareholders' equity and the debt of Verfinance with the data you have?

(c) What could you do to increase the value of the company's shareholders' equity? Make several suggestions. Which would seem to be the most realistic to you? Why? Would you be creating value? Why? All in all, have you created value or transferred value?

2/ Companies A and B each have to pay 100 to their creditors in one year. The risk-free rate is 5% per year. Below are the key figures for companies A and B, before and after a capital increase of 50 that they are planning for the purpose of financing new investments:

	A		B	
	Before	After	Before	After
Enterprise value	100	150	100	150
Volatility of capital employed	10%	10%	40%	40%
Equity value	7	?	18	?
Value of debt	93	95.1	82	92.1
Implicit interest rate on debt	7.5%	5.2%	22%	8.6%

What is the equity value of A and B after the capital increase? Show that it is not in the interests of the shareholders of A or B to carry out a capital increase to finance investments. Does the capital increase create value? Show that, nevertheless, shareholders' wealth is increased. Do you think that the creditors would agree to finance new investments? Why? How do you explain this paradox?

3/ Take the figures for Holding plc (p. 676) and assume that the shareholders in the company decide to pay out a cash dividend of £13 380 totally financed by the sale of 63 shares in Daughter plc (£13 380/ £2230).

(a) What is the new value of Holding plc's equity, according to the options theory?

(b) What is the value of Holding plc's debt, according to the options theory? What is the yield to maturity?

(c) What is the result of the operation?

Questions

1/ To a call option on the operating assets, the strike price of which is the amount of debt to be repaid.

2/ To the risk-free assets minus a put option, the strike price of which is the amount of debt to be repaid.

3/ Companies in difficulty and high-risk companies.

4/ No, because there is always some hope, no matter how little, that the enterprise value will rise before the debt must be repaid, to above the amount to be repaid.

5/ Because the time value of their equity is higher.

6/ No, it is not incompatible.

7/ Investing at a fair price, but in a much more risky venture.

8/ No, only the lack of anticipation.

9/ (a) No, better for the shareholder, better for the shareholder, better for the shareholder.
(b) Fundamentally no, but the problem is considerably reduced.
(c) Options.

10/ A restriction that the creditors place on shareholders so that they cannot increase their risk.

11/ Covenants force management/shareholders to approach creditors to renegotiate loan agreements if they wish to exceed the limits set in these covenants.

12/ Companies in distressed situations close to bankruptcy.

13/ Control.

Exercises

A detailed Excel version of the solutions is available at www.vernimmen.com.

1/ (a) The table is consistent. The higher the strike, the lower the value of the option, the longer the maturity, the higher the price of the option.
(b) The shares can be compared to options on the assets (i.e. the Uninet shares). Strike price = 6m/5000 = 1200, maturity = same as debt = 5 years. Value of these options = 1010. Value of Verfinance's shareholders' equity = 1010 × 5000 = 5.05m. Value of debt = 4.95m.
(c) Capital reduction. "Exchange" Uninet shares for much more volatile shares. There would also be a transfer of value from creditors to shareholders, but no creation of net value.

2/ 54.9; 57.9. The capital increase of 50 will only increase the value of shareholders' equity by 47.9 for A and 39.9 for B. The capital increase creates value for the creditors (2.1 for A and 10.1 for B), but destroys the same amount of shareholder value. Accordingly, this is not a simple transfer of value. No, because unlike the capital increase, an increase in debt level will reduce the value of the debt.

3/ (a) Shareholders have a call option on 94 Daughter plc shares (100 − 6) with a strike price of 300 000 (300 bonds × 1000). This option is equal to 94% of an option of an asset made up of 100 Daughter plc shares (94/94%) and the strike price is equal to 319 149 (300 000/94%). The new value of shareholders' equity is thus: 94% × 31.6 × 100 shares = 2970. The value of the option − 31.6 − is calculated by linear interpolation on the basis of the table provided.
(b) The value of the debt will then be 94 × 2230 − 2970 = 206 650, a decrease of 11 850. The yield to maturity on the debt rises to 13.2%, which means an increase in the risk on Holding plc's debts.
(c) The shareholders will have 2970 worth of Holding plc shares and 13 380 in cash (dividends paid), a total of 16 350 compared with 4500 initially. Their gain of 11 850 (16 350 − 4500) is made at the expense of the creditors, who lose: 218 500 − 206 650 = 11 850.

BIBLIOGRAPHY

Black, Scholes and Merton were the first to analyse the value of shares and debts using options as a reference:

F. Black, M. Scholes, The pricing of options and corporate liabilities, *Journal of Political Economy*, **81**, 637–654, May/June 1973.

R. Merton, On the pricing of corporate debt: The risk structure of interest rates, *Journal of Finance*, **29**(2), 449–470, May 1974.

For an overall view of options theory applied to capital structure, see:

M. Chesney, R. Gibson-Asner, The investment policy and the pricing of equity in a levered firm: A re-examination of the contingent claims "valuation approach", *European Journal of Finance*, **5**, 95–107, June 1999.

D. Galai, R. Masulis, The option pricing model and the risk factor of stock, *Journal of Financial Economics*, **33**, 53–81, 1976.

K. Garbade, *Pricing Corporate Securities as Contingent Claims*, Stern School of Business, Unpublished manuscript, 1999.

R. Geske, H. Johnson, The valuation of corporate liabilities as compound options: A correction, *Journal of Financial and Quantitative Analysis*, **7**, 6–81, March 1979.

C. Hsia, Coherence of the modern theories of finance, *Financial Review*, Winter 1999.

J. Kalotay, Valuation of corporate securities: Applications of contingent claim analysis, in E. Altman and M. Subrahmanyam (eds), *Recent Advances in Corporate Finance*, Richard Irwin, 1985.

S. Mason, R. Merton, The role of contingent claims analysis in corporate finance, in E. Altman and M. Subrahmanyam (eds), *Recent Advances in Corporate Finance*, Richard Irwin, 1985.

J. Ogden, Determinants of the ratings and yields on corporate bonds: Tests of the contingent claim model, *Journal of Financial Research*, **10**, 329–340, 1986.

S.Y. Park, M. Subrahmanyam, Option features of corporate securities, in S. Figlewski, W. Silber, M. Subrahmanyam (eds), *Financial Options. From Theory to Practice*, Richard Irwin, 1990.

For a deeper insight:

Y. Aït Mokhtar, Cap Arb, Hidden value and investment opportunities, *Exane BNP Paribas Quantitative Research*, **63**, 1–4, March 2008.

K. Bhanot, A. Mello, Should corporate debt include a rating trigger? *Journal of Financial Economics*, **79**, 68–69, 2006.

J. Campbell, G. Taksler, Equity volatility and corporate bond yields, *Journal of Finance*, **6**(58), 2321–2349, December 2003.

M. Jensen, W. Meckling, The theory of the firm: Managerial behavior, agency costs and capital structure, *Journal of Financial Economics*, **3**(4), 305–360, October 1976.

H. Leland, Corporate debt value, bond covenants and optimal capital structure, *Journal of Finance*, **4**(49), 1213–1252, September 1994.

J. Turc, CDS vs. stock – the quest for the optimum hedge ratio, *Banques & Marchés*, **80**, 29–39, January–February 2006.

F. Yu, How profitable is capital structure arbitrage? *Financial Analysts Journal*, **5**(62), 47–62, September–October 2006.

SECTION 4

Chapter 36
WORKING OUT DETAILS: THE DESIGN
OF THE CAPITAL STRUCTURE

Steering a course between Scylla and Charybdis

By way of conclusion to the part on capital structure policy, we would like to reflect once again on the thread that runs throughout this set of chapters: the choice of a source of financing.

We begin by restating for the reader an obvious truth too often forgotten:

If the objective is value creation, the choice of investments is much more important than the choice of capital structure. Because financial markets are liquid, situations of disequilibrium on them do not last. Arbitrages inevitably occur to erase them. For this reason, it is very difficult to create value by issuing securities at a price higher than their value. In contrast, industrial markets are much more "viscous". Regulatory, technological and other barriers make arbitrages – building a new plant, launching a rival product, and so on – far slower and harder to implement than on a financial market, where all it takes is a telephone call or an online order.

An industrial business can therefore hope to find a strategy that secures it an economic rent – that is, a strategy that enables it to earn a return on investment higher than the required return adjusted for risk. If it can do so, it will create value. **But let it harbour no illusions as to permanence: sooner or later, that rent will erode and disappear.**

In other words, a company that has made investments at least as profitable as its providers of funds require will never have insurmountable financing problems. If need be, it can always restructure the liability side of its balance sheet and find new sources of funds. Inversely, a company whose assets are not sufficiently profitable will, sooner or later, have financing problems, even if it initially obtained financing on very favourable terms. How fast its financial position deteriorates will depend simply on the size of its debt.

Good financing can never make up for a bad investment.

Section 36.1
THE MAJOR CONCEPTS

1/ COST OF A SOURCE OF FINANCING

Several simple ideas can be stated in this context.

1. The cost of all sources of financing is given by the risk profile and the required return of the investment. Thus, a cement plant in Russia might require a 25% rate of return, and this will be the case whether it is financed by equity or debt and whether the investor is Russian, Swiss or Indonesian.

The required rate of return is basically independent of the method of financing and the nationality of the investor. It depends solely on the risk of the investment itself.

The following consequences ensue:

* It is generally not possible to link the financing to the investment.
* No "portfolio effect" can reduce this cost.
* Only the bearing of systematic risk will be rewarded.

It is therefore shortsighted to choose a source of financing based on what it appears to cost. To do so is to forget that all sources of financing will **cost the same, given the risk**.

2. For the purpose of managing the liability side of the company's balance sheet, it is a great mistake to take the apparent cost of a source of financing as its true cost.

We have too often heard it said that the cost of a capital increase was low, because the dividend yield on the shares was low, that internal financing costs nothing, that convertible bonds can lower a company's cost of financing, and so on. Statements of this kind confuse the accounting cost with the true financial cost.

A source of financing is a bargain only if, for whatever reason, it brings in more than its market value. A convertible bond can be a good deal for the issuer not because it carries a low coupon rate, but only if the option embedded in it can fetch more than its market value.

Let us dwell briefly on the error one commits by confusing apparent cost and true financial cost.

* The difference is minor for debt. It may arise from changes in market interest rates or, more rarely, from changes in default risk. In matters of financial organisation, debt has the merit that its accounting cost is close to its true cost; furthermore, that cost is visible on the books, since interest payments are an accounting expense.
* The error is greater for equity, inasmuch as the dividend yield on the share needs to be augmented for prospective growth.
* The error is extreme for internal financing, where, as we have seen, the apparent cost of reinvested cash flow is nil.
* The error is hard to evaluate for all forms of hybrid securities – and this is often the explanation for their success. But let the reader beware: the fact that such securities carry low yields does not mean their financial cost is low. As we have shown in the foregoing chapters, an analysis of the hybrid security using both present value and option valuation techniques is needed to identify the true cost of this financing source.

3. When it comes to a company's financing policy, the immediate direct consequences of its sources of financing cannot be neglected.

Debt, by virtue of the liability that it represents for timely payments of interest and principal, has a direct consequence on the company's cash flow. Debt can plunge the company into the ditch if its runs into difficulties; on the other hand, it can turn out to be a turbo-charger that enables the company to take off at high speed if it is successful.

Source	Instrument	Theoretical cost to be used in investment valuation	Cost according to financial theory	Apparent or explicit cost (accountability, cash flow)	Difference	Determinants of the difference
			(A)	(B)	(A) − (B)	
Debt			Market rate at which the company can refinance	Contractual rate	Small	Evolution of market interest rates; evolution of default risk
Equity	Share issue	The same for all products, it is a function of the systematic (non-diversifiable) risk of the investment	Expected return required by the market on shares with the same risk profile	Nil in income statement; apparent cost measured by the return	Significant	Expected dividend growth rate
	Self-financing			Nil in the income statement; no apparent cost	Very significant	Total absence of apparent cost
Hybrid products	Convertible bonds		Yield to maturity + value of the conversion option	Low yield to maturity (restated according to IFRS)	Medium	Value of conversion option
	Preference shares		Return should be slightly lower than the ordinary shares	Higher than ordinary shares and fixed throughout the life of the instrument	Small	They are shares for which a part of the value is guaranteed (present value of fixed dividends)
	Income bonds		Rate higher than the cost of debt	Mostly linked to the periodical income	Variable according to results	Variability of results

If a company is successful, the cost of a share issue will appear to be much higher, as shareholders will receive much higher dividends than they initially expected. They will notice, looking backwards, that the price of the share was cheap. On the contrary, if the firm is in financial distress, the cost of the share issue will be close to nil, as the company will not be able to pay the expected dividends. The same is rarely true for debt, as it only occurs if the financial distress of the firm leads debtholders to forgive part of their loans.

2/ IS THERE A "ONCE-AND-FOR-ALL" OPTIMAL CAPITAL STRUCTURE?

The answer is clear: no, the optimal capital structure is a firm-specific policy and changes across time.

At the same time, there are a few loose ideas on the subject that the reader will have absorbed. Otherwise, how could one explain why the notion of what constitutes a "good" or "balanced" capital structure should have "changed" so much, and so often, over the course of time?

- In the 1950s and 1960s, a good capital structure was one with little debt. Against a backdrop of economic stability, the accent was on securing the company's industrial and financial autonomy.
- In the 1970s, a good capital structure needed to show a "normal" level of debt – that is, not excessive relative to equity. In a context of strong economic growth and low or even negative real (inflation-adjusted) interest rates, the emphasis was on taking advantage of the financial leverage that debt provides.
- In the 1980s, a good capital structure needed to reflect a rebalancing of the structure of the business, characterised by gradual diminution of debt, improved profitability and heightened reliance on internal financing.
- In the early 1990s, in an environment of low investment and high real interest rates, there was no longer a choice: being in debt was not an option. A new "pecking order" (see Chapter 34) appeared. A company with cash but without opportunities to invest it at a high enough return would choose

  ○ first to pay down its debt;
  ○ then to buy back its shares;
  ○ lastly to raise its payout ratio. This move was last on the list because it mortgages the company's future: a rise in the dividend, unlike a share buy-back, implies a commitment of prospective earnings – the "ratchet" effect of the dividend.

- In the late 1990s, though, debt was back in favour if used either to finance acquisitions or to reduce equity. The reason: nominal interest rates at their lowest level in 30 years. But the euphoric climate of real growth and low inflation gave way, in the early 2000s, to economic crisis coupled with equity markets virtually closed to new issues, making it hard for companies that had just finished borrowing heavily to quickly rebalance their capital structures.
- The 2000s started with a financial crisis (burst of the Internet bubble) followed by an economic crisis that led to a closure of financial markets. This prevented firms from rebalancing their financial structure towards more equity. The lesson was learnt, as when the second economic crisis of the decade arrived in 2007–2008, corporates were lowly geared except for groups under LBO who suffered first. In all sectors, firms are trying to lower their debt level (low capex, reduction of working capital) as the timing of the upturn remains uncertain. Still, firms are seeking to secure undrawn, very attractive borrowing capacity in terms of interest rates and margins.

NET DEBT/BOOK EQUITY (MEDIAN RATIO)

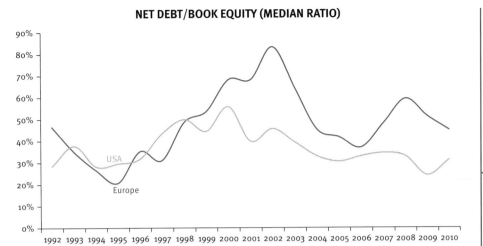

The great majority of companies had been paying down their debt for more than 10 years, thereby giving them considerable borrowing capacity they could use to get them through a difficult period.

NET DEBT/MARKET VALUE OF EQUITY (MEDIAN RATIO)

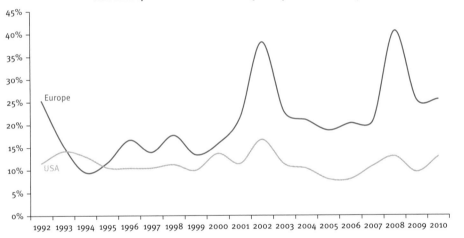

NET DEBT/EBITDA (MEDIAN RATIO)

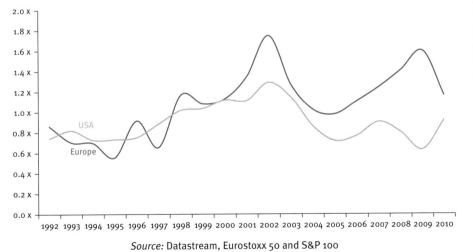

Source: Datastream, Eurostoxx 50 and S&P 100

SECTION 4

3/ CAPITAL STRUCTURE, INFLATION AND GROWTH

Because inflation is always a disequilibrium phenomenon, it is quite difficult to analyse from a financial standpoint. We can observe, however, that during a period of inflation and negative real interest rates, overinvestment and excessive borrowing lead to a general degradation of capital structures. Companies that invest reap the benefit of inflated profits: adjusted for inflation, the cost of financing is low. Shareholders can benefit from this phenomenon as well: a low rate of return on investment will be offset by the low cost of financing.

Companies' inclination to take on debt depends a great deal on the real interest rate and the real growth rate of the economy.

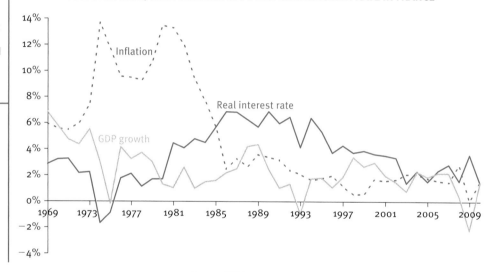

INFLATION RATE, REAL INTEREST RATE AND REAL GROWTH RATE IN FRANCE

Source: INSEE, Datastream

When inflation is accompanied by low real interest rates, companies are tempted to overinvest and pay for it by borrowing, thereby unbalancing their capital structure.

Disinflation leads to exactly the opposite behaviour: high real interest rates encourage companies to get rid of debt, all the more so given high rates are usually accompanied by anaemic economic activity and a business climate not conducive to borrowing.

4/ WHAT IS EQUITY FOR?

Let us begin by recalling the three fundamental differences between equity capital and debt capital.

*   There is no commitment to pay a periodic return on equity, whereas there is such a commitment on debt. The shareholder's reward depends solely on how well the business does, unlike the creditor's reward.

- There is no commitment to pay back the funds raised from shareholders, whereas there is such a commitment on funds borrowed from lenders.[1]

- If the company is liquidated, creditors will be paid in full before shareholders receive anything.

1 *Except for perpetual notes, which are extremely rare.*

Equity capital thus plays two roles. Its first function is of course to finance part of the investment in the business. The more important purpose, though, is to serve as a guarantee to the company's creditors that finance the other part of the investment. For this reason, the cost of equity includes a risk premium.

Whence the insurance aspect of equity capital (cf. discussion in Chapter 35 of equity as an option): like insurance, equity financing always costs too much until the accident crisis happens, in which case one is happy to have a lot of it. As we will see later, when a crisis does come, having considerable equity on the balance sheet gives a company time – time to survive and restructure when earnings are depressed, to introduce new products, to seize opportunities for external growth, and so on. By comparison, a company with considerable debt suffers greatly because it has fixed expenses (interest payments) and fixed maturities (principal repayment) that will drag it down further.

The amount of equity capital in a business is also an indicator of the level of risk shareholders are willing to run. In a crisis, the companies with the most leverage are the first to disappear.

Section 36.2
HOW TO CHOOSE A CAPITAL STRUCTURE

Graham and Harvey (2001) surveyed top executives and finance directors at 392 public groups to determine what criteria they use in taking a financing decision. According to their study – which will be further examined in Section 36.5 – the tax saving on debt was not an essential criterion in the choice of capital structure, nor was fear of substantial bankruptcy costs. Rather, concern about downgrading of the company's credit rating came top of the list. It is reassuring to see that the conclusions of the second Modigliani–Miller article (1963) are not prompting companies to focus on tax considerations in deciding whether or not to take on debt.

Even if companies say they have a fairly precise target for the level of their debt, more than half of all finance directors base their choice of financing on preserving **flexibility**.

Although some theoreticians and some finance professors emphasise the limitations of EPS dilution as a criterion – it is not automatically synonymous with destruction of value – among practitioners it remains the most important factor in deciding whether or not to undertake a capital increase. This criterion seems to us a bit outmoded, but we will address it nonetheless in a following section.

The reader will by now have grasped that capital structure is the result of complex compromises also determined by the:

- **need to keep flexibility;**
- **lifecycle of the company and the economic characteristics of the company's sector;**
- **risk aversion of shareholders and their wish not to be diluted;**
- **existence of opportunities or constraints on financial markets;**
- **need to preserve an adequate rating;**
- **the capital structure of competitors.**

1/ Financial flexibility

Having and retaining flexibility is of strong concern to finance directors. They know that choice of financing is a problem to be evaluated over time, not just at a given moment; a choice today can reduce the spectrum of possibilities for another choice to be made tomorrow.

Thus, taking on debt now will reduce borrowing capacity in the future, when a major investment – perhaps foreseeable, perhaps not – may be needed. If borrowing capacity is used up, the company will have no choice but to raise fresh equity. From time to time, though, the primary market in equities is closed because of depressed share prices (or can be opened at such high price conditions, as was the case at the end of 2008, that most issuers are discouraged from tapping this market). If this should be the case when the company needs funds, it may have to forgo the investment.

The equity capital market may not be open for new business during a crisis, when investors prefer to stick with safer debt securities. Debt markets are much less closed for business than is the equity capital market.

True, the markets for high-yield debt securities react as the equity markets do and may at times be closed to new issues. There are periods – such as the second half of 2001 and first half of 2002 or the last months of 2008 and the first months of 2009 – when the number of issues of shares and high-yield bonds has been extremely small.

Raising money today with a share issue, however, does not foreclose another capital increase at a later time. Moreover, an equity financing today will increase the borrowing capacity that can be mobilised tomorrow.

A sharp increase in debt reduces a company's financial flexibility, whereas a share issue increases its borrowing capacity.

The desire to retain flexibility prompts the company to carry less debt than the maximum level it deems bearable, so that it will at all times be in a position to take advantage of unexpected investment opportunities. Here again, we find the option concept applied to corporate finance.

In addition, the CFO will have taken pains to negotiate undrawn lines of credit with the company's bank; to have in hand all the shareholder authorisations needed to issue new debt or equity securities; and to have effective corporate communication on financial matters with rating agencies, financial analysts and investors.

Going beyond the debt–equity dichotomy, the quest for financial flexibility will require the CFO to open up different capital markets to the company. A company that has already issued securities on the bond market and keeps a dialogue going with bond investors can come back to this market very quickly if an investment opportunity appears.

The proliferation of financing sources – bilateral or syndicated bank loans, securitised receivables, bonds, convertibles, shares, and so on – allows the company to enhance its financial flexibility even further. But this strategy faces two limitations:

- issues on different markets have to be big enough to ensure sufficient liquidity for investors;
- multiple disparate sources of financing (possibly at different levels with a group structure) make the capital structure more complex and harder to manage (especially during liquidity crises).

Financial flexibility has a value, although it is difficult to estimate. We should bear in mind that the value of financial flexibility is reasonably linked to the number and the dimension of investment projects. If the company has a lot of investment opportunities and the average value of the investments is high, it should also have a high financial "reserve".

2/ LIFECYCLE OF THE COMPANY AND THE ECONOMIC CHARACTERISTICS OF THE COMPANY'S SECTOR

It is a mistake to think that the *tradeoff* model helps us to find an optimal leverage that doesn't change across time. The optimal capital structure is a concept that evolves from sector to sector – as discussed above – and from firm to firm.

Let's think about startup companies. They normally:

- have a high need of equity capital because of their:

    o lower tax shield capacity;
    o high financial distress costs (low tangible assets);
    o short history;

- need additional resources for new investments whose amount normally exceeds annual depreciation.

The necessity of funding with external resources is, in this case, quite high since internal sources (self-financing and liquidity) are insufficient to cover the amount of new investments in fixed assets and working capital.

At the same time, they must keep an adequate level of financial flexibility for facing the uncertain competitive dynamics of evolving sectors like, for example, advanced technologies. The capital structure of startup companies must then:

- try to match assets and liabilities;
- give the company a financial reserve for absorbing unfavourable reduction of cash flows;
- allow them to exploit real market opportunities.

Furthermore, it is reasonable to assume that the information asymmetries in the initial phases are high and that the use of external equity capital could dilute excessively the shares' value.

A startup will have a hard time getting any debt financing. It has no past and thus no credit history, and it probably has no tangible assets to pledge as security. The technological environment around it is probably quite unsettled, and its free cash flow is going to be negative for some time. For a lender, the level of specific risk is very high. The startup consequently has no choice but to seek equity financing.

At the other extreme, an established company in a market that has been around for years and is reaching maturity will have no difficulty attracting lenders. Its credit history is there, its assets are real and it is generating free cash flows (predictable with low forecast error) which are all the greater if the major investments have already been made. In short, it has everything a creditor craves. In contrast, an equity investor will find little to be enthusiastic about: not much growth, not much risk, thus not much profitability.

The evidence shows that bigger companies – living their maturity phase – tend to have higher leverage ratios, which confirms their high capacity for lowering the costs of debt thanks to their stability and higher fixed assets.

SECTION 4

Here we see the **lifecycle of financing sources.** An industrial venture is initially financed with equity. As the company becomes institutionalised and its risk diminishes, debt financing takes over, freeing up equity capital to be invested in emerging new sectors.

Similarly, in an industry with high fixed costs, a company will seek to finance itself mostly with equity, so as not to pile the fixed costs of debt (interest payments) on top of its fixed operating costs and to reduce its sensitivity to cyclical downswings. But sectors with high fixed costs – steel, cement, paper, energy, telecoms, etc. – are generally highly capital-intensive and thus require large investments, inevitably implying borrowing as well.

An industry such as retailing with high variable costs, on the other hand, can make the bet that debt entails, as the fixed costs of borrowing come on top of low fixed operating costs.

Lastly, the nature of the asset can influence the availability of financing to acquire it. A highly specific asset – that is, one with little value outside of a given production process – will be hard to finance with debt. Lenders will fear that if the company goes under, the asset's market value will not be sufficient to pay off their claims.

THE LIFECYCLE OF A COMPANY AND ITS CAPITAL STRUCTURE

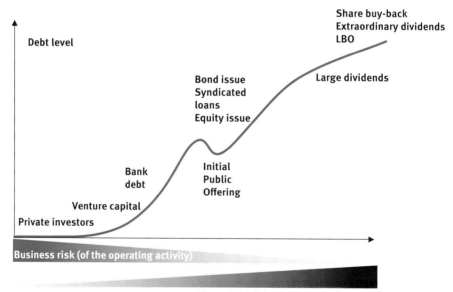

The major pros and cons of debt must be weighted by taking into account the different stage of companies:

	Startup	Growth	Maturity
Tax shield	Zero	Increases with earnings	High
Disciplining role of debt	Low, shareholders-managers	Increases, new external shareholders	Decreases, few new investments

	Startup	Growth	Maturity
Information asymmetries	High, business only an idea	Decreases, track record and credibility	Decreases, higher transparency
Financial distress costs	Very high	High	Declining
Agency costs	Very high	High	Declining
Need for financial flexibility	Very high	High	Low
Synthesis	**Costs of debt > benefits of debt**	**Relevant benefits from debt**	**Benefits of debt > Costs of debt**

3/ SHAREHOLDER PREFERENCES

If the company's shareholder base is made up of influential shareholders, majority or minority, their viewpoints will certainly have an impact on financing choices.

Some holders will block share issues that would dilute their stake because they are unable to take up their share of the rights. A company in this situation must then go deeply into debt. Others may have a marked aversion to debt because they have no desire to increase the level of risk they are bearing.

The choice of capital structure is also the choice of a level of risk that shareholders are willing to incur.

4/ OPPORTUNITIES AND CONSTRAINTS

Since markets are not systematically in equilibrium, opportunities can arise at a given moment. A steep runup in share prices will enable a company to undergo a capital increase on the cheap (sell shares at a very high price). The folly of a bank that says yes to every loan application and the sudden infatuation of investors for a particular kind of stock (Internet companies in early 2000) are other examples. Lastly, loopholes in tax regulations may create financing opportunities (think of subordinated perpetual notes in the 1980s), but unfortunately the tax administration never stays duped for long.

Let the reader not be intoxicated by opportunities. It is hard to base a financing policy on a succession of opportunities, which are, by definition, unpredictable. They can happen only on margin.

Furthermore, if the company at some point in time is enjoying exceptionally low-cost financing, investors, for their part, will have made a bad mistake. In their fury, they risk tarnishing the company's image, and it will be a long time before they can be counted on to put up new money. The startup that went public at the peak of the "new economy" boom on the stock market will surely have raised money at low cost, but how will it raise more capital a year later, after its share price has fallen by 70%?

On the contrary, the company may suffer **capital rationing** – that is, a situation in which capital markets cannot satisfy all the financing the companies ask. This may be due to credit restrictions that might occur in turbulent periods as a consequence of authorities' decisions or of banking systems' policies.

5/ THE RATING OF THE COMPANY

Ratings agencies have clearly gained in importance – especially in Europe – due mostly to the transition from an economy based mostly on banking intermediaries to one where the financial markets are becoming predominant.

Ratings are becoming one of the main concerns of CFOs. According to Kisgen (2007, p. 73): "many (if not most) companies devote considerable attention to credit ratings in designing their financial policy. A higher credit rating can translate into direct benefits for a company's shareholders, including an expansion of the pool of eligible investors, lower cost of debt capital, and more favorable terms from other corporate stakeholders reassured by the firm's implied staying power." Financial decisions are thus frequently taken based partly on their rating impact; or, more precisely, decisions having a negative rating impact will be adjusted accordingly. Some companies even set rating targets (Pepsi, Diageo and Vivendi, for example). This can seem paradoxical in two ways:

* although all financial communication is based on creating shareholder value, companies are much less likely to set share price targets than rating targets;
* in setting rating targets, companies have a new objective: that of preserving value for bondholders! This is praiseworthy and, in a financial market context, understandable, but has never been part of the bargain with bondholders.

We see several possible explanations for this paradox. First of all, a debt rating downgrade is clearly a major event for a group and goes well behind bondholder information. A downgrade is traumatic and messy and almost always leads to a fall in the share price. So, in seeking to preserve a financial rating, it is also shareholder value that management is protecting, at least in the short term.

A downgrade can also have an immediate cost if the company has issued a bond with a step-up in the coupon, i.e. a clause stating that the coupon will be increased in the event of a rating downgrade. Step-ups are meant to protect lenders against a downgrade and obviously make managers pay more attention to their debt rating.

A good debt rating guarantees a higher degree of financial flexibility. The higher the rating, the easier it is to tap the bond markets, as transactions are less dependent on market fluctuations. An investment grade company, for example, can almost always issue bonds, whereas market windows close regularly for companies that are below investment grade.

Some banks sell the concept of lower cost of capital (and, thus, enhanced value) as a function of rating – for example, obtaining the lowest possible cost of capital for a BBB rating. This is based on the tax savings brought about by financing costs but, beginning with a certain level of debt, the savings are cancelled out by the discounted value of the cost of bankruptcy. Our readers know that we are not great fans of this argument. It looks difficult to maintain that companies rated BBB can be valued significantly higher than others. The average company rating is closer to A, after all, and major groups such as Nestlé and AstraZeneca, which have stable cash flows, do not try to play leverage, preferring to hold onto their very strong rating. Similarly, setting out to obtain the best rating possible is getting things backwards. This minimises the cost of debt, but so what? If it also requires an exorbitant level of equity, the cost of capital has not necessarily been reduced.

There is a phenomenon that is even more perverse than setting a target rating: refusing to be rated or asking for a confidential "shadow rating". Being rated can be scary, and CFOs balance out the lack of flexibility created by the lack of rating (e.g. certain investors can no longer be tapped and the bond market is mostly closed off) with the potential lack of flexibility created by a poor rating.

In extreme cases, we have even seen companies that, in their initial rating process, tried to obtain the worst possible rating for their particular financial profile. They did this in order to gain some flexibility, i.e. some room for their situation to get marginally worse without undermining their rating. In this particular case, caution has a clear impact on value, as a lower rating means higher debt costs. But this is like an insurance premium that always looks too high until an accident strikes.

6/ Capital structure of competitors

- To have higher net debt than one's rivals is to bet heavily on the company's future profitability – that is, on the economy, the strategy, and so forth.
- To have higher net debt than one's rivals, other things being equal, is to be more vulnerable to a cyclical downturn, one that could lead to a shakeout in the sector and extinction of the weakest.

There is good evidence that the average capital structure of the sector is an important benchmark for the management when setting capital structure policies. Experience shows that business leaders are loath to imperil an industrial strategy by adopting a financing policy substantially different from their competitors'. If they have to take risks, they want them to be industrial or commercial risks, not financial risks. The rationale of this behaviour is clear: since all companies behave similarly, the average leverage indicates the sustainable level of financial risk belonging to the same sector!

Our opinion is that benchmarking on competitors is not contradictory with the precepts of the tradeoff model. Companies within the same sector – and in the same stage of the lifecycle – share the same basic economic and financial characteristics. Hence, financial policies shouldn't be so different.

Industries with high volatility of cash flows and low tangible assets are those where we expect leverage to be lower. On the contrary, in sectors where flows are stable and companies can provide high collateral, the use of debt should be higher.

The choice of capital structure is not absolute but *relative*: the real question is how to finance the business compared with the industry average – that is, compared with the company's competitors.

However, there are at least two situations where the simple replication of what competitors do could be erroneous:

- when the sector is made up of highly heterogeneous companies;
- when the sector is going through a restructuring phase.

With the analyses in hand, the person or body taking the financing decision will be able to do so with full knowledge of the facts. The investor will bear in mind that, statistically (and thus, for his diversified portfolio), his dream of multiplying his wealth through judicious use of debt will be the nightmare of the company in financial distress.

The financial success of a few tends to make one forget the failure of companies that did not survive because they were too much in debt.

Section 36.3
EFFECTS OF THE FINANCING CHOICE ON ACCOUNTING AND FINANCIAL CRITERIA

With this description of the key ideas in mind, the time has come for the reader to implement a choice of capital structure as part of a financing plan. To this end, we suggest that the following documents be at hand:

1. past financial statements: income statements, balance sheets, cash flow statements;
2. forecast financial statements and financing plan, constructed in the same form as past cash flow statements. These can be either mean forecasts or simulations based on several assumptions; the latter strikes us as the better solution. A simulation model will be very useful for establishing the probable future course of the company's capital structure, profitability, business conditions, and so on, given a set of assumptions. This kind of exercise is facilitated by using spreadsheet software and simulation assumptions that allow for a dynamic analysis;
3. to be fully prepared, the analyst will also want to have sector average ratios, which can be obtained from various industry studies.

An important task is then to study the consequences of a financing choice on pre-tax earnings. This traditional yardstick is not sufficient, though, if the financing plan calls for issuing new shares. When this is the case, the analyst will need to look at earnings per share and book value per share.

1/ IMPACT ON BREAKEVEN POINT

Other things equal, debt raises the company's breakeven point.

This is obvious inasmuch as interest payments constitute a *fixed cost* that cannot be reduced except by renegotiating the terms of the loan or filing for bankruptcy. Take, as an example, a company with fixed costs of 40 and variable costs of 0.5 per unit sold. If the selling price is 1, the breakeven point is 80 units. If the company finances an investment of 50 with debt at 6%, the breakeven point rises to 86 units because fixed costs have increased by 3 (interest expense on the borrowing). If the investment is financed with equity, the breakeven point stays at 80.

The problem is trickier when the interest rate is indexed to market rates but the interest payments are still a fixed cost in the sense of being independent of the level of activity.

Typically, interest rates rise when general economic activity is weakening. In such a case, it is important to test the sensitivity of the company's earnings to changes in interest rates. Take the previous example but suppose that the debt bears a floating rate. If the interest rate rises to 10%, the breakeven point goes to 90 units; if it rises to 15%, breakeven goes to 95.

In a period of difficult economic conditions and rising interest rates, the company's interest expense increases, raising its breakeven point and worsening its problems.

2/ IMPACT ON RETURN ON EQUITY

For a company with no debt, the return on equity is equal to the rate of return on capital employed. For a company with debt, one must add to the former a supplement (sometimes negative) for the effect of financial leverage (difference between ROCE and cost of debt, multiplied by the debt–equity ratio; see Chapter 13).

The analysis of the return on equity must therefore distinguish the part due to the economic return on capital employed from the part due to leverage. However, a static analysis is not sufficient. What is needed is to determine the sensitivity of return on equity to any change in financial leverage, cost of debt or return on capital employed.

3/ IMPACT ON EARNINGS PER SHARE

An investment financed by debt increases the company's net profit, and thus earnings per share, only if the after-tax return generated by its investments is greater than the after-tax cost of debt. If this is not the case, the company should not make the investments. If an investment is particularly sizeable and long-term, it may happen that its rate of return is less than the cost of debt for a period of time, but this must be a temporary situation.

To study these phenomena, companies are accustomed to analysing changes in earnings per share relative to operating profit (EBIT).

Example   Consider the example of a company which makes an investment of 200 in period 0 that will become fully operational in period 2. This investment is financed by a call to shareholders (case A) or by borrowing (case B). A simulation of the main parameters of profitability gives the results shown in the table below.

	Period 0	Period 1		Period 2	
		Case A	Case B	Case A (Equity)	Case B (Debt)
Operating profit (EBIT)	300	300	300	370	370
− Interest expense at 6%	0	0	12	0	12
= Pre-tax profit	300	300	288	370	358
− Income tax at 35%	105	105	101	130	125
= Net profit	195	195	187	242	233
Number of shares	100	120	100	120	100
Earnings per share	1.95	1.62	1.87	1.85	2.33

In period 2, earnings per share will be greater if the investment is financed by debt. In case B, the interest expense reduces EPS, but by less than the dilution due to the capital increase in case A.

This conclusion cannot be generalised, however. The chart below simulates various levels of EPS as a function of operating profit in period 2.

The reader will be able to verify that if operating profit is less than 340, the preceding assertion is reversed. However, a steep decline in earnings is required to produce this result.

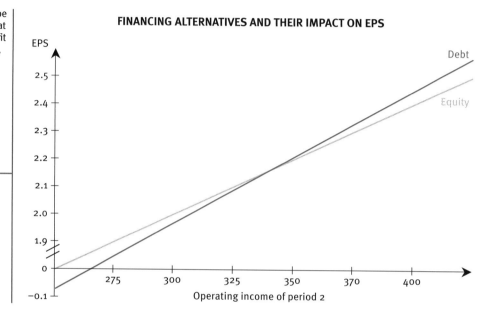

FINANCING ALTERNATIVES AND THEIR IMPACT ON EPS

Let's now discuss the limitation of the EPS analysis in more detail. We know that, as a first approximation, P/EPS can be considered a proxy of the reciprocal of the cost of equity. We also know that the price of a share is the result of earnings per share (measure of return) times the reciprocal of the cost of equity (measure of risk):

$$P = EPS \times \frac{P}{EPS}$$

Capital structure policies should then always be examined considering their impact on *price and value* rather than earnings per share. In a no-growth world, price is the result of earnings per share *and* perceived risk.

In short: beware! The faster growth of EPS with debt financing is a purely arithmetic result; it does not indicate greater value creation. It is due simply to the leverage effect, the counterpart of which is a higher level of risk to the shareholder.

An investment financed by debt increases EPS in year N if the company's marginal return on capital employed in year N is greater than the after-tax cost of debt.

An investment financed by equity in year N increases EPS in year $N + 1$ if the company's marginal return on capital employed in year $N + 1$ is greater than the reciprocal of P/E in year N.

4/ IMPACT ON SOLVENCY

Debt increases the company's risk of becoming insolvent. We refer the reader to the development of this topic in Chapter 14.

5/ IMPACT ON LIQUIDITY

The liquidity of the company is its ability to meet its financial obligations on time in the ordinary course of business, obtain new sources of financing and thereby ensure balance at all times between its income and expenditure.

In a truly serious financial crisis, companies can no longer obtain the financing they need, no matter how good they are. This is the case in a crash brought on by a panic. It is not possible to protect oneself against this risk, which fortunately is altogether exceptional. The more common liquidity risk occurs when a company is in trouble and can no longer issue securities that financial markets or banks will accept; investors have no confidence in the company at all, regardless of the merit of its investment projects.

Liquidity is therefore related to the term structure of financial resources. It is analysed both at the short-term level and at the level of repayment capacity for medium- and long-term debt. This leads to the use of traditional concepts and ratios that we have already seen: working capital, equity, debt, current assets/current liabilities, and so on.

For analysing the impact on liquidity, the simulation must bear on free cash flows. The analyst will need to simulate different levels of debt and repayment terms and test whether free cash flows are sufficient to pay off the borrowings without having to reschedule them.

Section 36.4
WORKING OUT THE DETAILS OF THE CAPITAL STRUCTURE

The capital structure policy is ideally a three-step process:

Step 1   The financial manager must decide the desired mix of debt and equity. This is the choice between the debt/equity mix.

Step 2   A firm that is not positioned at its optimal debt ratio should decide (if) and how to reach the optimal level.

Step 3   The financial manager is called to decide about the most appropriate financing vehicle for raising capital.

So far we have discussed thoroughly only the first step, which, however, is the most important because it underlies the financial equilibrium of the company. We shall now dedicate some attention to the other two steps.

1/ THE CONVERGENCE PATH

This second-step decision – the decision regarding if and how to get to the optimal level – involves the analysis of two joint aspects:

- The *speed* of convergence toward the optimal ratio. This decision is strictly firm-specific because different circumstances may influence it.
- The *alternative methods* that the company can use to achieve the desired result.

We shall now first discuss the reasons for which a company may decide *not to move* to the optimal debt ratio. Let's start our analysis with underlevered firms because this is the less problematic situation for a company (after all, it doesn't risk going bankrupt!). Companies may prefer to neglect the value maximising objective – which underlies the extended trade-off model and the optimal leverage – because the finance function may have different objectives. If the company prefers to increase income as much as possible or to maintain a high rating, the financial manager will try to keep the company underlevered.

Regarding the maximisation of net income, the rationale is quite clear: a company which carries low debt has a limited amount of interest expenses and thus a higher net income.

Less obvious is the emphasis that a company may put on maintaining a high rating, as explained, for example, by the treasurer of Pepsi who said:[2] "One of our financial aims at Pepsi is to minimise the amount of cash on our books. More precisely, our objective is to have zero excess cash on the books [. . .] *At the same time, we try to have the maximum amount of debt that we can while still maintaining our single-A credit rating.*"

Why? It is the treasurer yet again who provides us with an excellent rationale: "We want to be single-A because that gives us immediate access, under almost any conditions, to large amounts of cash at the best rates from all the commercial paper markets in the US, Europe and Japan." So, companies with a huge need for short-term debt and financial flexibility could decide to remain underlevered in order to keep their rating unchanged.

However, we think that maintaining a high grade rating doesn't necessarily conflict with the tradeoff objective. After all, it seems that these companies have a maximum leverage represented by the amount of debt they can raise without seeing their rating being lowered. Let's ask for some additional help from our treasurer: "We do have a capital structure or leverage target. And we arrive at that target by determining the largest leverage ratio consistent with our desired credit rating. Once we get to that leverage target, we try to stay there. How do we stay there? Mainly by using our excess cash to buy back stocks."[3]

A final reason that may be suggested to explain the underlevered choice is the desire of firms to avoid debt covenants that come with debt. Covenants tend to restrict the managerial flexibility and the degrees of freedom in exploiting the investment opportunities that may arise in the future.

More problematic is the opposite case regarding overlevered firms, because these firms face a high probability of default and bankruptcy. The "bankruptcy fear" may be overcome only if there is a counterbalancing force which may justify excessive debt ratios. This counterforce may be represented by governments and local authorities who may decide to shield firms from the costs associated with default or to back up loans made by banks to companies. In these cases, companies may decide voluntarily to remain overlevered.[4]

If the firm is aware that it is far from the optimal leverage and decides that it doesn't want to stay away from that point, the first important decision is the **speed of change**: gradual vs. immediate.

The most important advantage of moving rapidly toward the optimal point is that it is possible to benefit immediately from a lower cost of capital and a higher value. But the company must be sure of the calculation. In fact, the worst signal the management can send to the market is to discover that the optimal ratio was not exactly the one toward which the company has converged, but a different one. If the management is not confident about the optimal leverage of the firm, it would be better to move slowly and discover step-by-step the degree of precision of their calculations.

2 *Chew et al. (2003), p. 214.*

3 *Chew et al. (2003), p. 214.*

4 *This helps us to explain the undoubtedly excessive debt ratios of Korean firms during the 1990s and the reluctance of local companies to decrease leverage.*

SECTION 4

Underlevered firms (Palepu, 1986) may decide to change the capital structure rapidly if a takeover threat is high. In fact, many hostile acquisitions are financed with the unused debt capacity. Thus, firms with excess capacity tend to adapt to the optimal quickly in order to reduce the probability of takeover.

There are **five alternative methods** that can be used to change the debt–equity mix:

1. **Recapitalisation.** This is done by using new equity to retire debt (reduce leverage) or new debt to buy back equity (or pay a large dividend). This alternative is frequently a necessity for companies under takeover threat. Recapitalisations aimed at increasing the debt ratio in a fast and substantial way are called *leveraged recapitalisations*. On the contrary, *equity-for-debt swaps* are designed to reduce leverage with debt agreements by which lenders take an equity stake in the firm in exchange for a portion of debt in their possession.

2. **Divestitures.** The firm can change its debt ratio by selling part of the assets and using the proceeds of the sale to pay off debt or to reduce equity. Naturally, if the firm chooses this alternative it needs to select the assets to be divested with extreme care. On the one side, companies should, in principle, sell assets earning less than the cost of capital; on the other, the assets must also be attractive for potential buyers and the amount they are willing to pay for those assets. The move of Vivendi, while facing liquidity issues, to reduce debt through disposal, is a good example.

3. **Sale and leaseback.** This solution allows the company to sell assets to a leasing company, collect money, repay debt or equity while retaining possession of the assets by retaking them with a leasing from the leasing company. The company can thus reduce the capital employed and modify the debt/equity ratio with the proceeds of the sale. But it usually corresponds more to window-dressing than a real reduction of debt.

4. **Use of a different mix of financing for the new investments.** In this case, the company will change its leverage ratio *gradually*. The speed of change will be related to the amount of new investments, the incidence of their value on the existing investments and the difference between the debt ratio chosen for the new investment and the current debt ratio of the company.

5. **Changing the amount of cash returned to shareholders.** This means that a new dividend policy may alter the debt ratio of the company. If the firm uses earnings and cash flows to increase the dividend payout ratio or distributes extraordinary dividends, the debt ratio will go up because the company takes cash out of the firm and the firm becomes less valuable. This method normally implies a *gradual* change of the debt ratios.

The reader is surely aware that the five alternatives satisfy different needs. For the sake of simplicity, we can say that the first three methods are useful if there is an urgency for change because, for example, the company is under threat of a takeover or it is in serious financial distress.

If the company is neither under bankruptcy or takeover threat, alternatives 3 and 4 could be preferred because they leave the management the flexibility of deciding along the way if the optimal debt ratio is exactly what they calculated at the beginning of the change process.

SECTION 4

2/ THE MATURITY, BASIS AND THE CURRENCY STRUCTURE OF DEBT

Once the company has decided the amount of optimal debt, many other decisions are still to be taken. They basically concern the **design of debt**. Here we want to focus attention on three important aspects of the design:

1. **The maturity structure of debt** – that is, the amount of short- and long-term debt.
2. **The basis structure of debt** – i.e. the incidence of fixed- vs. floating-rate debt.
3. **The currency structure of debt** – that is, the amount of debt issued in foreign currencies. If the company has part of its revenues or cash flows in foreign currencies, it should decide if it wants to issue some debt in the same foreign currencies. By so doing, the company matches the inflows with the outflows and avoids currency risk.

Let's examine the basic coordinates of the problem. We know that the value of a firm is given by the present value of the cash flows generated by its assets and that this value changes cyclically over time. If we assume that the company is financed only with short-term debt which is not influenced by changes in macroeconomic variables, the situation would be the following:

FIRM VALUE OVER TIME WITH SHORT-TERM DEBT

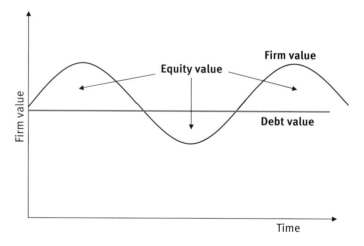

In some periods the company may suffer a serious bankruptcy problem, since the value of debt is higher than the value of the firm (and thus the equity value is negative). A company facing such a situation will surely try to borrow less and abandon the tax shields and the other advantages of debt.

If the firm can design financial debt so that the cash outflows of the service of debt match exactly the cash inflows, debt and equity value would follow a completely different dynamic:

FIRM VALUE OVER TIME WITH LONG-TERM DEBT

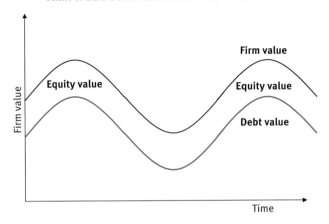

The debt value can be designed so that it moves according to the enterprise value. If the firm is successful in doing so, the equity value remains constantly positive. The bankruptcy probability is then reduced substantially and the company can have a higher debt capacity and a higher optimal debt ratio.

There is a simple (but strong!) principle that the financial manager can use if he wants to avoid additional risks: match as closely as possible cash outflows (due to the service of debt) with cash inflows. This principle can be termed the "matching principle" or the "hedging principle".

Perfect matching is, of course, not always achievable as desired, but the financial manager should do his best to inspire financial policies with this principle in mind if he wants to minimise the credit and financial risks.

We will now give the reader a basic "toolbox" to help him satisfy the "hedging principle".

(a) Debt maturity structure

The application of this principle to financing maturity choice requires matching the *duration of assets* with the *duration of liabilities*. This is the **cash-flow-matching approach**. While there are no particular difficulties in estimating the duration of debt, we could have problems in defining the duration of assets.

In this regard, the estimate of the duration of a project or assets can be done using the sequence of the expected operating cash flows (CF_t):

$$\text{Duration of assets} = \frac{dPV}{dr} = \frac{\left[\displaystyle\sum_{t=1}^{N} \frac{t \times CF_t}{(1+r)^t} + \frac{N \times TV}{(1+r)^N}\right]}{\left[\displaystyle\sum_{t=1}^{N} \frac{CF_t}{(1+r)^t} + \frac{TV}{(1+r)^N}\right]}$$

where r is the market (risk-free) interest rate, TV is the terminal value and N the horizon of analysis.

The duration of assets can be alternatively interpreted as:

1.   a measure of *when*, on average, the cash flows on the assets come due;
2.   a measure of *sensitivity* of asset value to a 1% change in interest rates.

An alternative – and conceptually better – measure of duration can be obtained by regressing the changes in asset value (for listed companies) or in the operating income (for listed, unlisted and short-lived companies) on interest rate changes:

$$\Delta \text{Asset value}_t = a + b \times \Delta \text{ Interest rate}_t$$

If we adopt this methodology, the coefficient b is a proxy for the duration of the assets (or of the operating income). "Regression methodology" is based on historical data and should always be used after controlling for the significance of the t-test of the coefficient b.

However, once the appropriate duration of the assets has been calculated, the company should try to have a maturity structure of its debt with a similar (*average*) duration.[5]

The most important consequence is that – no matter the direction of interest rate changes – the value of assets and liabilities will go up or down by the same amount. Equity value will then be unaffected by interest rates.

The strong interdependence between investments and liabilities has also been examined by the **agency costs** or **"incentive contracting" hypothesis** (Myers, 1977). According to this second approach, the optimal leverage of a company is a function of the growth opportunities that companies have in the different stages of their lifecycle. The agency cost hypothesis argues that shortening the effective maturity of debt can mitigate conflicts of interest. Using shorter-term debt forces managers to periodically generate information for investors to evaluate return and risk of major operating decisions. Investors will thus re-price the debt upon maturity based on new information. This approach mitigates asset substitution and underinvestment problems. Furthermore, short-term debt triggers effective monitoring by requiring periodic repayments of principal.

Companies with high growth opportunities should thus:

* use a higher amount of equity capital (to avoid the underinvestment problem);
* have a higher percentage of short-term debt, since the agency costs are higher for longer maturities. If the company wants to avoid the underinvestment problem, it could be more appropriate to raise debt which will mature before it exercises its growth option.

The empirical evidence on the incentive contracting hypothesis is not univocal. Barclay and Smith (1995, 1996) and Guedes and Opler (1996) have obtained results consistent with the hypothesis that companies with higher growth opportunities have a higher incidence of short-term debt. On the contrary, Stohs and Mauer (1996) and Scherr and Hulburt (2001) haven't found statistically robust evidence between the market-to-book ratio (a proxy of growth opportunities) and the debt maturity structure.

The third approach to the maturity choice is a **tax-based explanation** (Brick and Ravid, 1985). If the term structure of interest rates is not flat, then the long-term debt could be a better solution because coupons on long-term bonds are higher than coupons on short-term bonds and the tax benefit of debt is accelerated.

A recent article by Berger *et al.* (2005) examined the **role of credit risk and information asymmetries** in the debt maturity choice. This article is based on two

5 *The reader should also recall that duration is a linear operator, i.e. the average duration of two assets is simply a weighted average of the single duration.*

SECTION 4

theoretical models linking debt maturity to company ratings – the Flannery model and the Diamond model.

Flannery explained that debt maturity should be an upward-sloping function of the company's risk rating. It is better for a high-risk business to borrow over a period that is in line with its project (i.e. generally long term). In the case of short-term borrowing, the bank could make a quick assessment of the level of risk of a project, and require the corporate borrower to pay a very high interest rate to renew the loan (over and above the loan fees). Additionally, the company will not want to add to the financial risk involved in periodically renewing its loans to the risk of its project. By taking out a long-term loan, the company reveals the high-risk nature of its business, but avoids the costs of renewing the loan. A company involved in a low-risk business will, however, be prepared to bear these costs by taking out a short-term loan, which sends out a signal that it is a high quality enterprise.

According to Diamond, this relationship could not be valid for very high-risk businesses. Banks could refuse to grant them long-term loans but agree to short-term loans in order to obtain information on their projects. For both models, the relationship between risk and maturity is explained by information asymmetry.

The test carried out by the authors tends to confirm the Flannery model. When there is information asymmetry, corporate debt maturity increases with risk. The relationship will continue to slope upwards for very high-risk companies, contrary to predictions by Diamond. This happens when loans are for both small and large amounts. This study also shows that this relationship is indeed explained by information asymmetry. The impact of risk on maturity disappears when research is restricted to banks using techniques to reduce information asymmetry (especially small business credit scoring).

(b) Fixed vs. floating rate

The second important choice is whether the debt should be fixed or floating rate. This choice is more complex than one may initially think.

First of all, we note that the choice of interest rate is not directly linked with the choice of maturity of debt, as long-term debt can bear floating rates (this is generally the case for long-term bank loans) but also because, thanks to interest rate swaps, the firm can very easily change floating for fixed rates or the reverse.

To make this choice, the CFO will have to set some goals: minimise the cost of financing, minimise the risk, optimise the value, follow his anticipation . . .

Studies show that over a long period, firms that borrow short term (i.e. with floating rates) will bear a lower cost. Nevertheless, borrowing long term with fixed rates is perceived to be less risky, since, as the future interest expense is known in advance, there will be no nasty surprises in the P&L in the future. But one should keep in mind that when interest rates drop (generally in times of crisis), the value of fixed-rate debt will rise, therefore reducing the equity value. Even if, effectively, the P&L is not impacted.

Lastly, we should mention that the anticipation of CFOs of a future drop or increase in interest rates have, in practice, a heavy impact on their choice. Pretending to be good managers, they then speculate when they borrow at a fixed rate under the cover that they expect interest rates to increase.

(c) Currency structure

The hedging principle applies also to currency structure. The idea is that if companies have cash inflows from operating assets denominated in foreign currencies, the liabilities should be issued in the same proportion in the foreign currencies. Thus, a European company that expects 30% of its cash flows to be in US dollars should try to mitigate the currency risk by issuing 30% of debt in US dollars.

Section 36.5
CAPITAL STRUCTURE POLICIES: A LOOK AT THE EVIDENCE

It is now time to discover if the principles and the guidelines discussed in these chapters are consistent with the behaviour of financial management.

To this regard, we compare the Graham and Harvey survey (2001) with the survey of Bancel and Mittoo (2004). We have already mentioned the Graham and Harvey article. The Bancel and Mittoo study is basically a "replica" of Graham and Harvey applied to European companies. The authors surveyed managers in 16 European countries to examine the link between the theory and practice of capital structure across countries with different legal systems.

Generally speaking, it is surprising to discover that the two geographical areas are so alike.

In most of the cases, the answers given by the financial managers in the EU and USA tend to be the same.

This is, in fact, the case regarding the most important factors affecting the amount of debt: financial flexibility is the key issue in determining the capital structure choice in both areas. Similarly, the necessity of maintaining the credit rating unchanged is the second most important factor while the tax shield ranks third in Europe and fourth in the USA. There is little evidence about the influence of bankruptcy costs and industry norms of capital structure.

SECTION 4

(A) Capital structure choice is primarily driven by financial flexibility, credit rating and corporate tax shield

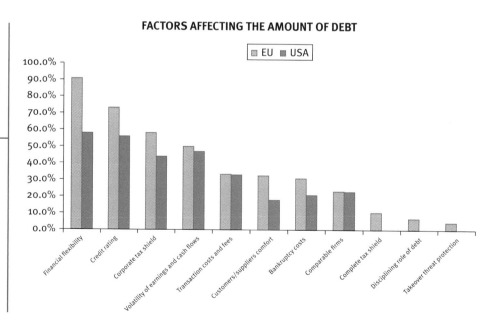

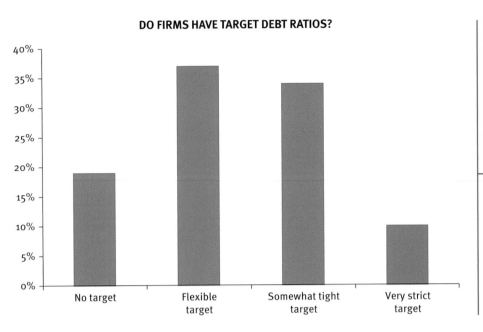

DO FIRMS HAVE TARGET DEBT RATIOS?

(B) The percentage of companies that do not have a target leverage are a minor fraction. It is, however, important to observe that the bulk of the answers regard a less flexible leverage target

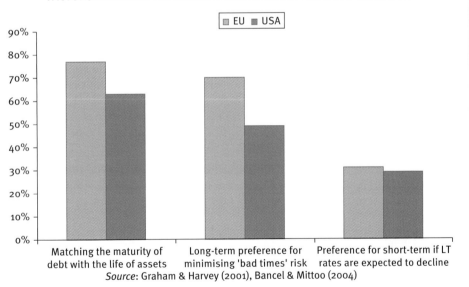

FACTORS AFFECTING THE CHOICE BETWEEN SHORT AND LONG-TERM DEBT

Source: Graham & Harvey (2001), Bancel & Mittoo (2004)

(C) The maturity structure decision is mainly driven by the matching principle and the will to avoid the refinancing risk that may occur if the company should raise debt in "bad times".

SECTION 4

The similarities between the capital structure determinants are consistent with the recent findings on capital structure of companies belonging to different countries and economic systems. Common wisdom has long held that, in relationship-based economies such as Germany, Italy and Japan, companies have higher leverage than companies in market-oriented economies, like the US and the UK. The higher leverage should, in turn, reduce the weighted average cost of capital and increase the competitiveness of companies.

The "folklore" of higher borrowing capacity comes from the strong relationship with banks. These institutions support companies when they are close to distress and exercise some control over investment policies to make sure they do not go awry. As a consequence, the costs of debt tend to disappear while the benefits remain. In short, companies in these countries tend to have a higher borrowing capacity.

This "folklore" has been questioned. According to Zingales and Rajan (1998), Japanese and German companies do not borrow more than US companies and, in fact, German as well as UK companies seem to borrow less than their international competitors.

SUMMARY

The summary of this chapter can be downloaded from www.vernimmen.com.

Whereas frequent disequilibria in industrial markets engender the hope of creating value through judicious investment, the same cannot be said of choosing a source of financing. Financial markets are typically close to equilibrium, and all sources of financing have the same cost to the company given their risk.

The cost of financing to buy an asset is equal to the rate of return required on that asset, regardless of whether the financing is debt or equity and regardless of the nationality of the investor.

It follows that the choice of source of financing is not made on the basis of its cost (since all sources have the same risk-adjusted cost!). Apparent cost must not be confused with financial cost (the true economic cost of a source of financing). The difference between apparent cost and financial cost is low for debt; it is attributable to the possibility of changes in the debt ratio and default risk. The difference is greater for equity owing to growth prospects; greater still for internal financing, where the explicit cost is nil; and difficult to evaluate for all hybrid securities. Lastly, a source of financing is cheap only if, for whatever reason, it has brought in more than its market value.

Because there is no optimal capital structure, the choice between debt and equity will depend on a number of considerations:

- Macroeconomic conditions. High real (inflation-adjusted) interest rates and low activity growth will prompt companies to deleverage. Inversely, rapid growth and/or low real interest rates will favour borrowing.

- The desire to retain a degree of financial flexibility so that any investment opportunities can be quickly seized. To this end, equity financing is preferred because it creates additional borrowing capacity and does not compromise future choices. Inversely, if current borrowing capacity is used up, the only source of financing left is equity; its availability depends on share prices holding up, which is never assured.

- The maturity of the industry and the capital structure of competitors. A startup will get no financing but equity because of its high specific risk, whereas an established company with sizeable free cash flows but little prospect of growth will be able to finance itself largely by borrowing. Companies in the same business sector often mimic each other (what matters is to be no more foolish than the next guy!).

- Shareholder preferences. Some will favour borrowing so as not to be diluted by a capital increase in which they cannot afford to participate. Others will favour equity so as not to increase their risk. It is all a question of risk aversion.

- Financing opportunities. These are, by definition, unpredictable, and it is hard to construct a rigorous financing policy around them. When they occur, they make it possible to raise funds at less than the normal cost – but at the expense of the investors who have deluded themselves.

The reader who performs simulations of the principal financial parameters, differentiating according to whether the company is using debt or equity financing, should be fully aware that such simulations mainly show the consequences of financial leverage:

- raising the breakeven point;

- accelerating EPS growth;

- increasing the rate of return on book equity;

- degrading solvency;

- affecting liquidity in a way that varies with the term of the debt.

Once the company has decided about the debt/equity mix, the financial manager should focus his attention on the other elements that define the "design" of the capital structure.

The most important factors determining the design of the capital structure are the maturity, basis and currency structure. The choices regarding these three aspects can be made following the same principle – the "matching" or "hedging" principle – according to which the optimal design of debt is the one that perfectly matches cash inflows and cash outflows.

QUESTIONS

1/ Can a good financing plan make up for a mediocre investment?

2/ What disorder afflicts the investor who mistakes the coupon rate on a convertible bond for its financial cost?

3/ A 17% rate of return is required on a certain asset. The acquisition of that asset is financed entirely by equity. What rate of return do shareholders require on it? If the asset were financed entirely by debt, what rate of return would lenders require on it?

4/ What is the source of financing for which the difference between financial cost and apparent cost is greatest?

5/ Would you advise a startup to seek debt financing? If yes, could it get it?

6/ Is there an optimal capital structure?

7/ Equity capital has two roles in a financing plan. What are they?

8/ Free subscription warrants are distributed to all the shareholders on a one-for-one basis. The value of each warrant is b. What is the value of the share after the warrant is detached, other things being equal?

9/ If a shareholder sells the warrant, what is he actually selling?

10/ In the final analysis, isn't the cheapest financial resource short-term borrowing?

11/ How do you reconcile these two statements:

- ○ "You can't make money without borrowing money."
- ○ "Borrowing can't create value."

12/ Will a company with ample growth opportunities tend to issue short-term, medium-term or long-term debt? Why?

13/ Give two examples of inflation profits. Under what conditions can they occur?

14/ If you believe a finance director's main concern is financial flexibility, would you expect a company ever to use up its borrowing capacity?

15/ Is a company destined always to be financed with equity capital?

16/ Why do startups go through several rounds of financing before they reach maturity? Couldn't they do it with a single big round?

17/ Can an entrepreneur with an industrial strategy be opportunistic in his financing choices over time?

18/ Why did European companies rid themselves of so much debt in 1980–1998? Why did they stop doing it in 1998–2002?

More questions are waiting for you at www.vernimmen.com.

EXERCISES

A company is considering the following investment:

Year	0	1	2	3	4	5
Cash flow	−100	−10	0	0	10	150

which can be financed with equity:

Year	0	1	2	3	4	5
Debt/Equity	30%	22%	22%	22%	22%	22%
EPS	10	8.25	9.1	10.3	11.8	13.6
EPS growth rate		−17.5%	+10%	+13%	+15%	+15%
Rate of return on equity	15%	11%	11%	11.4%	11.6%	12%

or with debt:

Year	0	1	2	3	4	5
Debt/Equity	30%	67%	67%	67%	67%	67%
EPS	10	9.3	10.4	12	14.1	16.5
EPS growth rate	−7%	+12%	+15%	+17%	+17%	+17%
Rate of return on equity	15%	14%	17%	18%	21%	22%

If the cost of capital is 10%, the shareholder-required rate of return is 12% and the cost of debt is 5%, do you think this investment should be financed with equity or with debt? Isn't there another question that should be asked first?

Questions

1/ No, because it is very difficult to create value at the level of the financing plan.
2/ Myopia, because he is not noticing that holders of convertible bonds expect the share price to rise so that they can convert them.
3/ 17%, 17%.
4/ Internal financing.
5/ No, because it would be far too risky for a startup, requiring certain outflows from uncertain inflows. Probably not.
6/ No!
7/ Providing part of the financing and providing security to lenders.
8/ Value of the share less b. The warrant is therefore not free.
9/ A share of the value above the exercise price and, of course, a time value as well.
10/ No, no and no!
11/ "You can't make money without borrowing money" applies to an investor with a poorly diversified portfolio; it's all or nothing if he goes into debt to leverage it. "Borrowing can't create value" applies to a perfectly diversified portfolio.
12/ Short-term, so as to be able to refinance on better terms as growth opportunities become profitable investments.
13/ Inventory profits and opportunity profits on investment realised sooner than expected. Provided the inflation rate is higher than the interest rate.
14/ No, because the finance director will always want to retain some room to manoeuvre, just in case.
15/ No, the less risky it becomes, the more readily it can be financed with debt.
16/ In order to profit from a valuation that rises between each round. No, because between each round, investors want to be sure that the business plan is panning out.
17/ No, because an industrial strategy can't wait for opportunities to arrive.
18/ High real interest rates and low investment. Because virtually all their debt had already been paid off, they could not go on deleveraging.

Exercise

A detailed Excel version of the solution is available at www.vernimmen.com.

The IRR on the investment is 8%, less than the cost of capital. The investment should not be made; the question of how to finance it is academic.

BIBLIOGRAPHY

M. Baker, J. Wurgler, Market timing and capital structure, *Journal of Finance*, **57**(1), 1–32, February 2002.

F. Bancel, U. Mittoo, The determinants of capital structure choice: A survey of European firms, *Financial Management*, **33**(4), 103–133, Winter 2004.

M. Barclay, C. Smith, The capital structure puzzle: Another look at the evidence, *Journal of Applied Corporate Finance*, **12**(1), 8–20, Summer 1999.

A. Berger *et al.*, *Loan sales and the cost of corporate borrowing*, IMF working paper, 05/201, 2005.

I. Brick, A. Ravid, On the relevance of debt maturity structure, *Journal of Finance*, **40**(5), December 1985.

D. Brounen, A. de Jong, K. Koedijk, Capital structure policies in Europe: Some evidence, *Journal of Banking and Finance*, **30**(5), 1409–1422, May 2006.

M. Campello, Capital structure and product market interactions: Evidence from business cycles, *Journal of Financial Economics*, **68**(3), 353–378, June 2003.

S. Chava, M. Roberts, How does financing impact investment? The role of debt covenants, *Journal of Finance*, **63**(5), 2085–2121, October 2008.

D. Chew *et al.*, Stern Stewart roundtable on capital structure and stock repurchase, in J. Stern and D. Chew (eds), *The Revolution in Corporate Finance*, 4th edn, Blackwell Publishing, 2003.

D. Diamond, Debt maturity structure and liquidity risk, *Quarterly Journal of Economics*, **106**(3), 709–737, August 1991.

European Central Bank, Corporate finance in the euro area, *Occasional Paper Series*, **63**, June 2007.

E. Fama, K. French, Financing decision: Who issues stock? *Journal of Financial Economics*, **76**(3), 549–582, June 2005.

M.J. Flannery, Debt maturity and the deadweight cost of leverage: Optimally financing banking firms, *American Economic Review*, **84**(1), 320–331, March 1994.

A. Gamba, A. Triantis, The value of financial flexibility, *Journal of Finance*, **63**(5), 2263–2296, October 2008.

J. Graham, C. Harvey, The theory and practice of corporate finance: Evidence from the field, *Journal of Financial Economics*, **63**(2–3), 187–243, May 2001.

B. Grundy, H. Merton Miller: His contribution to financial economics, *Journal of Finance*, **56**(4), 1183–1206, August 2001.

G. Hall, P. Hutchinson, N. Michaelas, Determinants of the capital structure of European SMEs, *Journal of Business Finance & Accounting*, **31**(5–6), 711–728, June 2004.

A. Hovakimian, T. Opler, S. Titman, The capital structure choice: New evidence from a dynamic trade-off model, *Journal of Applied Corporate Finance*, **15**(1), 24–30, Spring 2002.

A. Kayhan, S. Titman, Firms' histories and their capital structures, *Journal of Financial Economics*, **83**(1), 1–32, January 2007.

D. Kisgen, The influence of credit ratings on corporate capital structure decisions, *Journal of Applied Corporate Finance*, **19**(3), Summer 2007.

M. Leary, M. Roberts, Do firms rebalance their capital structures? *Journal of Finance*, **60**(6), 2575–2619, December 2005.

P. MacKay, G. Phillips, How does industry affect firm financial structure? *Review of Financial Studies*, **18**(4), 1433–1466, August 2005.

A. de Miguel, J. Pindado, Determinants of capital structure: New evidence from Spanish panel data, *Journal of Corporate Finance*, **7**(1), 77–99, 2001.

F. Modligliani, M. Miller, Corporate income taxes and the cost of capital: A correction, *American Economic Review*, **53**(3), 433–443, June 1963.

S. Myers, Determinants of Corporate Borrowing, *Journal of Financial Economics*, **5**(2), 147–175, November 1977.

S. Myers, Still searching for optimal capital structure, *Journal of Applied Corporate Finance*, **6**(1), 4–14, Spring 1993.

S. Myers, Financial architecture, *European Financial Magazine*, **5**(2), 133–141, July 1999.

S. Myers, Capital structure, *Journal of Economic Perspectives*, **15**(2), 81–102, Spring 2001.

K. Palepu, Predicting takeover targets: A methodological and empirical analysis, *Journal of Accounting and Economics*, **8**(1), 3–35, 1986.

J. Tierny, C. Smithson, Implementing economic capital in an industrial company: The case of Michelin, *Journal of Applied Corporate Finance*, **15**(4), 8–22, Summer 2003.

P. Vernimmen, Politique financière de l'entreprise, *Encyclopédie de Gestion*, Vol. 2, 2nd edn, 2325–2356, Economica, 1997.

L. Zingales, In search of new foundations, *Journal of Finance*, **55**(4), 1623–1653, August 2000.

L. Zingales, R. Rajan, Debt, folklore and cross-country differences in financial structure, *Journal of Applied Corporate Finance*, **10**(4), 102–107, Winter 1998.

On maturity, basis and currency structure:

M. Barclay, C. Smith, The maturity structure of corporate debt, *Journal of Finance*, **50**(2), 609–631, June 1995.

M. Barclay, C. Smith, On financial architecture: Leverage, maturity and priority, *Journal of Applied Corporate Finance*, **8**(4), 4–17, Winter 1996.

A. Damodaran, Financing innovations and capital structure choices, *Journal of Applied Corporate Finance*, **12**(1), 28–39, Spring 1999.

R. Greenwood, S. Hanson, J. Stein, A gap-filling theory of corporate debt maturity choice? *Journal of Finance*, **65**(3), 993–1028, June 2010.

J. Guedes, T. Opler, The determinants of the maturity of corporate debt issues, *Journal of Finance*, **51**(5), 1809–1833, December 1996.

G. Jun, F. Jen, Trade-off model of debt maturity structure, *Review of Quantitative Finance and Accounting*, **20**(1), 5–34, 2003.

J.R. Morris, On corporate debt maturity strategies, *Journal of Finance*, **31**(1), 29–37, March 1976.

M. Roberts, A. Sufi, Renegotiation of financial contracts: evidence from private credit agreements, *Journal of Financial Economics*, **93**(2), 159–184, August 2009.

F. Scherr, H. Hulburt, The debt maturity structure of small firms, *Financial Management*, **30**(1), 85–112, 2001.

C. Smithson, C. Smith, D. Wilford, *Managing Financial Risk*, Irwin, 1995.

M. Stohs, D. Mauer, Determinants of corporate debt maturity, *Journal of Business*, **69**(3), 279–312, July 1996.

SECTION 4

PART TWO
EQUITY CAPITAL

Equity capital policy is of such importance in corporate finance that it must be addressed in depth. The chapters in this part deal, in turn, with dividend policy, share buy-backs and share issues.

Chapter 37

RETURNING CASH TO SHAREHOLDERS

It's all grist to the mill

Net income has only two possible destinations: either it is reinvested in the business in the form of internal financing or it is redistributed to shareholders in dividends or share buy-backs.

In pure financial logic, all funds that cannot be reinvested yielding at least the appropriate cost of capital (i.e. the cost of capital that reflects the risk of the project) should be returned in one form or another, to shareholders.

In fact, when the capital structure of the firm already corresponds to the target fixed by shareholders and management, every cent left in the company in the form of cash will only yield the short-term interest rate, i.e. much less than the cost of equity. In this context, it is very likely that shareholders will value it at less than a cent given the low return provided. After all, shareholders do not need the firm to place cash at the bank. All in all, failure to comply with this rule will most likely lead to value destruction.

Additionally, the business risk should be financed through equity; otherwise, the firm is likely to face strong liquidity issues at the first downturn. Conversely, a company that has reached economic maturity with a strong strategic position may reduce its equity financing and select a higher gearing. The business cash flows have become sufficiently sound to support the cash requirements of debt.

Equity exists to support the business risk; therefore it is normal that once this risk is managed, debt takes over in the financing of the firm. The dividend policy is one of the main tools for achieving this objective but it can have other effects, as we will see.

Section 37.1
REINVESTED CASH FLOW AND THE VALUE OF EQUITY

1/ PRINCIPLES

An often-heard precept in finance says that a company ought to fund its development solely through internal financing – that is, by reinvesting its cash flow in the business.

This position seemingly corresponds to the interests of both its managers and its creditors, and indirectly to the interests of its shareholders:

- For shareholders, reinvesting cash flow in the business ought to translate into an increase in the value of their shares and thus into capital gains on those shares. In virtually all of the world's tax systems, capital gains are taxed less heavily than dividends. Other things being equal, shareholders will prefer to receive their returns in the form of capital gains. They will therefore look favourably on retention rather than distribution of periodic cash flows.
- By funding its development exclusively from internal sources, the company has no need to go to the capital markets – that is, to investors in shares or corporate bonds – or to banks. For this reason, its managers will have greater freedom of action. They, too, will look favourably on internal financing.
- Lastly, as we have seen, the company's creditors will prefer that it rely on internal financing because this will reduce the risk and increase the value of their claims on the company.

This precept is not wrong, but here we must emphasise the dangers of taking it to excess. A policy of *always* or *only* reinvesting internally generated cash flow postpones the financial reckoning that is indispensable to any policy. It is not good for a company to be cut off from the capital markets or for capital mobility to be artificially reduced, allowing investments to be made in unprofitable sectors. The company that follows such a policy in effect creates its own *internal capital market* independent of the outside financial markets. On that artificial market, rates of return may well be lower, and resources may accordingly be misallocated.

The sounder principle of finance is probably the one that calls for distributing all periodic earnings to shareholders and then going back to them to request funding for major projects. In the real world, however, this rule runs up against practical considerations – substantial tax and transaction costs and shareholder control issues – that make it difficult to apply.

In short, internal financing enjoys an extraordinarily positive image among those who own, manage or lend to the company. However, although internally generated cash flow belongs fundamentally to the shareholders, they have very little control over it. The result is that a policy of reinvesting cash flow can prove to be a time bomb for the company.

2/ INTERNAL FINANCING AND VALUE CREATION

We begin by revisiting a few truisms.

- The reader should fully appreciate that, given unchanged market conditions, the value of the company must increase by the amount of profit that it reinvests. This much occurs almost automatically, one might say. The performance of a strategy that seeks to create "shareholder value" is measured by the extent to which it **increases the value of shareholders' equity by more than the amount of reinvested earnings**.
- **The apparent cost of internal financing is nil.** This is certainly true in the short term, but what a trap it is in the long term to think this way! Does the reader know of

any good thing that is free, except for things available in unlimited quantity, which is clearly not the case with money? Reinvested cash flow indeed has a cost and, as we have learned from the theory of markets in equilibrium, that cost has a direct impact on the value of the company. It is an **opportunity cost**. Such a cost is, by nature, not directly observable – unlike the cost of debt, which is manifested in an immediate cash outflow. As we explained previously, retaining earnings rather than distributing them as dividends is financially equivalent to paying out all earnings and simultaneously raising new equity capital. **The cost of internal financing is therefore the same as the cost of a capital increase: to wit, the cost of equity.**

- Does this mean the company ought to require a rate of return equal to the cost of equity on the investments that it finances internally? No. As we saw in Chapter 30, it is a mistake to link the cost of any source of financing to the required rate of return on the investment that is being financed. Whatever the source or method of financing, the investment must earn at least the cost of capital.[1] By reinvesting earnings rather than borrowing, the company can reduce the proportion of debt in its capital structure and thereby lower its cost of debt. In equilibrium, this cost saving is added on top of the return yielded by the investment, to produce the return required by shareholders. Similarly, an investment financed by new debt needs to earn not the cost of debt, but the cost of capital, which is greater than the cost of debt. The excess goes to increase the return to the shareholders, who bear additional risk attributable to the new debt.

> 1 *At the same level of business risk as for the company's existing operating assets.*

- **Retained earnings add to the company's financial resources**, but they increase shareholder wealth only if the rate of return on new investments is greater than the weighted average cost of capital. If the rate of return is lower, each euro invested in the business will increase the value of the company by less than one euro, and shareholders will be worse off than if all the earnings had been distributed to them. This is the market's sanction for poor use of internal financing.

Consider the following company. The market value of its equity is 135, and its shareholders require a rate of return of 7.5%.

Year	Book value of equity	Net profit	Dividend (Div)	Market value of equity (V) P/E = 9	Gain in market value (ΔV)	Rate of return (ΔV + Div) /V
1	300.0	15.0	4.5	135.0		
2	310.5	15.6	4.7	140.4	5.4	7.2%
3	321.4	16.2	4.9	145.8	5.4	7.1%
4	332.7	16.8	6.7	151.2	5.4	8.0%

Annual returns on equity are close to 7.5%. Seemingly, shareholders are getting what they want. But are they?

To measure the harm done by ill-advised reinvestment of earnings, one need only compare the change in the book value of equity over 4 years (+32.7) with the change in market value (+16.2). For each €1 the shareholders reinvested in the company, they can hope to get back only €0.50. Of what they put in, fully half was lost – a steep cost in terms of forgone earnings.

SECTION 4

Think of reinvesting cash flow (internal financing) as a machine to transform energy (money) into work (value). When the return on reinvested cash flow is equal to the cost of capital, this machine has an energy yield of 1. Its energy yield falls below 1 whenever the return on incremental investment is below the required return. When that happens, there is a loss of energy; in other words, value is destroyed, not created.

Beware of "cathedrals built of steel and concrete" – companies that have reinvested to an extent not warranted by their profitability!

Reinvesting earnings automatically causes the book value of equity to grow. It does not cause symmetrical growth in the market value of the company unless the investments it finances are sufficiently profitable – that is, unless those investments earn more than the required rate of return given their risk. If they earn less, shareholders' equity will increase but shareholders' wealth will increase less than the amount of the reinvested funds. Shareholders would be better off if the funds that were reinvested had instead been distributed to them.

In our example, the market value of equity (151) is only about 45% of its book value (333). True, the rate of return on equity (5%) is, in this case, far below the cost of equity (7.5%).

More than a few unlisted mid-sized companies have engaged in excessive reinvestment of earnings in unprofitable endeavours, with no immediate visible consequence on the valuation of the business.

The owner-managers of such a company get a painful wake-up call when they find they can sell the business, which they may have spent their entire working lives building, only for less than the book value (restated or not) of the company's assets. The sanction imposed by the market is severe.

Only investment at least at the cost of capital can maintain the value of reinvested cash flow.

3/ INTERNAL FINANCING AND TAXATION

From a tax standpoint, reinvestment of earnings has long been considered a panacea for shareholders. It ought to translate into an increase in the value of their shares and thus into capital gains when they liquidate their holdings. Generally, capital gains are taxed less heavily than dividends.

Other things being equal, then, shareholders will prefer to receive their income in the form of capital gains and will favour reinvestment of earnings. Since the 1990s, however, as shareholders have become more of a force and taxes on dividends have been reduced in most European countries, this form of remuneration has become less attractive.

4/ INTERNAL FINANCING, SHAREHOLDERS AND LENDERS

We have seen (cf. the discussion of options theory in Chapter 35) that whenever a company becomes more risky, there is a transfer of value from creditors to shareholders.

Symmetrically, whenever a company pays down debt and moves into a lower risk class, shareholders lose and creditors gain.

Reinvestment of earnings can be thought of as a capital increase in which all shareholders are forced to participate.

This capital increase tends to diminish the risk borne by creditors and thus, in theory, makes them better off by increasing the value of their claims on the company.

The same reasoning applies in reverse to dividend distribution. The more a company pays out in dividends, the greater the transfer of value from creditors to shareholders. This is to be expected, since a high dividend policy is the inverse of a high earnings retention policy.

5/ INTERNAL FINANCING, SHAREHOLDERS AND MANAGERS

As we will see in Section 37.3 under the agency theory approach, internal financing represents a major issue in the relationship between shareholders and managers. Internal financing represents a blank cheque for managers without any control by shareholders. Internal financing is therefore one of the main sources of conflict between managers and shareholders.

Section 37.2
INTERNAL FINANCING AND RETURN CRITERIA

1/ INTERNAL FINANCING AND ORGANIC GROWTH

Growth of the equity of a firm that does not issue shares depends on its return on equity and its payout ratio.

Year	Book value of equity at beginning of year	Net profit (15% of equity)	Retained earnings	Book value of equity at end of year
1	100.0	15.0	10.0	110.0
2	110.0	16.5	11.0	121.0
3	121.0	18.2	12.1	133.1
4	133.1	20.0	13.3	146.4

A company with book value of equity of 100 and return on equity of 15% will make a profit of 15. If its payout ratio is 33.3%, it will retain two-thirds of its earnings – that is, 10. Book value of equity will increase from 100 to 110, an increase of 10%, in Year 1. If these rates are maintained, the results will be as shown in the table.

The book value of a company that raises no new money from its shareholders depends on its rate of return on equity and its dividend payout ratio.

The growth rate of book value is equal to the product of the rate of return on equity and the earnings retention ratio, which is the complement of the payout ratio.

We have:

$$g = \text{ROE} \times (1 - d)$$

2 *Note that in this section, since no new shares are issued, the growth rate of book value per share is always equal to the growth rate of book value.*

where g is the rate of growth of shareholders' equity,[2] ROE (return on equity) is the rate of return on the book value of equity and d is the dividend payout ratio.

This is merely to state the obvious, as the reader should be well aware.

In other words, given the company's rate of return on equity, its reinvestment policy determines the growth rate of the book value of its equity.

2/ Models of internal growth

If capital structure is held constant, growth in equity allows parallel growth in debt and thus in all long-term funds required for operations. We should make it clear that here we are talking about book values, not market values. In effect, the model assumes that there is a direct and systematic relation between the accounting value of shareholders' equity and the market value thereof; that is, the price-to-book ratio is constant.

At constant capital structure, growth in book equity determines growth in capital employed.

The preceding model can be generalised to companies with debt as well as equity capital. To do so, we need only recall that the rate of return on book value of equity is equal to the rate of return on capital employed adjusted for the positive or negative effect of financial leverage (gearing) due to the presence of debt.

$$ROE = ROCE + (ROCE - i) \times D / E$$

or:

$$g = \left[ROCE + \left(ROCE - i \right) \times \frac{D}{E} \right] \times \left(1 - d \right)$$

where g is the growth rate of the company's capital employed at constant capital structure and constant rate of return on capital employed (ROCE).

This is the **internal growth model**.

It is clear that the rates of growth of revenue, production, EBITDA and so on will be equal to the rate of growth of book equity if the following ratios stay constant:

$$\frac{Revenue}{Capital\ employed}, \frac{Production}{Capital\ employed}, \frac{EBITDA}{Capital\ employed}$$

Through the internal growth model, we establish a direct link between the rate of growth of the business and the rate of growth of capital employed.

To illustrate this important principle, we consider a company whose assets are financed 50% by equity and 50% by debt, the latter at an after-tax cost of 5%. Its after-tax return on capital employed is 15%, and 80% of earnings are reinvested. Accordingly, we have:

Period	Book equity at beginning of period	Net debt	Capital employed	Operating profit after tax	Interest expenses after tax	Net profit	Dividends	Retained earnings	Book equity at end of period
1	100	100	200	30	5	25	5	20	120
2	120	120	240	36	6	30	6	24	144
3	144	144	288	43.2	7.2	36	7.2	28.8	172.8

This gives us an average annual growth rate of book equity of:

$$g = \left[15\% + (15\% - 5\%) \times 1\right] \times 80\% = 20\%$$

The reader can verify that, if the company distributes half its earnings in dividends, the growth rate of the book value of equity falls to:

$$g = \left[15\% + (15\% - 5\%) \times 1\right] \times 50\% = 12.5\%$$

The growth rate of capital employed thus depends on the:

- rate of **return on capital employed**: the higher it is, the higher the growth rate of financial resources;
- **cost of debt**: the lower it is, the greater the leverage effect, and thus the higher the growth rate of capital employed;
- **capital structure**;
- **payout ratio.**

For the shareholder, the growth rate of capital employed by the company corresponds to the growth rate of book value per share, provided there are no capital increases. The same is true of the growth rate of earnings per share and dividend per share.

In a situation of equilibrium, then, shareholders' equity, debt, capital employed, net profit, book value per share, earnings per share and dividend per share all grow at the same pace, as illustrated in the example above. This equilibrium growth rate is commonly called the company's **growth potential.**

3/ ADDITIONAL ANALYSIS

The first of the models above – the internal growth model – assumes all the variables are growing at the same pace and also that returns on funds reinvested by organic growth are equal to returns on the initial assets. These are very strong assumptions.

A policy of reinvesting cash flow can be analysed only in terms of the *marginal* rate of return on reinvested earnings.

Suppose a company reinvests two-thirds of its earnings in projects that yield no return at all. We would observe the following situation:

Period	Book equity at beginning of period	Net profit	Return on equity	Dividends	Retained earnings	Book equity at end of period
1	100	15	15.0%	5	10	110 (+10.0%)
2	110	15 (+0%)	13.6%	5 (+0%)	10	120 (+9.1%)
3	120	15 (+0%)	12.5%	5 (+0%)	10	130 (+8.3%)

We see that if net profit and earnings per share do not increase, growth of shareholders' equity slows, and return on equity declines because the incremental return (on the reinvested funds) is zero.

If, on the other hand, the company reinvests two-thirds of its earnings in projects that yield 30%, or double the initial rate of return on equity, all the variables are now rising.

Period	Equity at beginning of period	Net profit	Rate of return on equity	Dividends	Retained earnings	Equity at end of period
1	100	15	15.0%	5	10	110 (+10.0%)
2	110	18 (+20%)	16.4%	6 (+20%)	12	122 (+10.9%)
3	122	21.6 (+20%)	17.7%	7.2 (+20%)	14.4	136.4 (+11.8%)

Although the rate of growth of book equity increases only slightly, the earnings growth rate immediately jumps to 20%. The rate of growth of net profit (and earnings per share) is linked to the *marginal* rate of return, not the *average*.

Here we see that there are multiplier effects on these parameters, as revealed by the following relation:

$$\frac{\text{Change in net profit}}{\text{Net profit}} = \frac{\text{Change in net profit}}{\text{Change in book equity}} \times \frac{\text{Change in book equity}}{\text{Net profit}}$$

This means that, barring a capital increase, the rate of growth of earnings (or earnings per share) is equal to the marginal rate of return on equity multiplied by the earnings retention ratio (1 – dividend payout ratio).

Similarly, it can be shown that the rate of growth of free cash flow can be deduced from the rate of growth of net profit:

$$\text{Change in net profit} = \text{Growth of free cash flows} \times \left(\frac{V_D}{V_E} \right)$$

This is another manifestation of the leverage effect.

Section 37.3
WHY RETURN CASH TO SHAREHOLDERS?

1/ DIVIDENDS AND EQUILIBRIUM MARKETS

In markets in equilibrium, payment of a dividend has no impact on the shareholder's wealth, and the shareholder is indifferent about receiving a dividend of one euro or a capital gain of one euro.

At equilibrium, by definition, the company is earning its cost of equity. Consider a company, Equilibrium plc, with share capital of €100 on which shareholders require a 10% return. Since we are in equilibrium, the company is making a net profit of €10. Either these earnings are paid out to shareholders in the form of dividends, or they are reinvested in the business at Equilibrium plc's 10% rate of return. Since that rate is exactly the rate that shareholders require, €10 of earnings reinvested will increase the value of Equilibrium plc by €10 – neither more nor less. Thus, either the shareholders collectively will have received €10 in cash, or the aggregate value of their shares will have increased by the same amount.

In markets in equilibrium, there are no good or bad dividend policies.

If the company pays out a high proportion of its earnings, its shares will be worth less but its shareholders will receive more cash. If it distributes less, its shares will be worth more (provided that it reinvests in projects that are sufficiently profitable) and its shareholders will receive less cash – but the shareholder, if he wishes, can make up the difference by selling some of his shares.

The chart below plots the share price of Unibail Rodamco, which on 7 October 2010 paid a special dividend of €20 in cash. The price of the shares adjusted immediately.

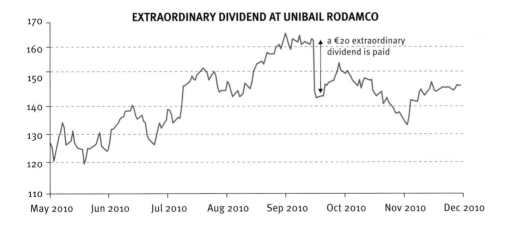

Source: Yahoo Finance

In a universe of markets in equilibrium, paying out more or less in dividends will have no effect on shareholder wealth.

Companies should thus not be concerned about dividend policy and should treat dividends as an adjustment to cash flow. This harks back to the Modigliani–Miller approach to financial policy: there is no way to create lasting value with merely a financing decision.

In any case, it's a fallacy to present the dividend distribution as a remuneration for shareholders, similar to the salary for the company's employees. The wealth of the employee increases with the salary. Conversely, the wealth of shareholders is not modified by the dividends they receive: while they are certainly happy about getting this periodical remuneration, on the other hand, they must consider that the value of their shares will fall by an equivalent amount.

Dividends do not enrich shareholders. They simply modify their wealth composition, like a transfer from the left to the right pocket.

What about firms that have never paid a dividend like UC Rusal (the Russian aluminium group) or Berkshire Hathaway (Warren Buffet's firm)? Have they never remunerated their shareholders? Of course they have and those firms have been very good investments for their shareholders. The return for shareholders comes from the increase in value of their portfolios (including dividends if any). The dividend is taken into account not because it represents a return for the shareholder but solely to compensate the drop in value of the share following the dividend payment.

2/ Dividends as signals

Equilibrium market theory has a hard time finding any good reason for dividends to be paid at all. Since they do exist in the real world, new explanations must be sought for the earnings distribution problem.

A justification for the existence of dividends is proposed by the theory of signalling, around which an entire literature has developed, mainly during the 1980s.

The dividend is a means of communication between the company and the market.

The financial information that investors get from companies may be biased by selective disclosure or even manipulative accounting. Managers are naturally inclined to present the company in the best possible light, even if the image they convey does not represent the exact truth. Companies that really are profitable will therefore seek to distinguish themselves from those that are not through policies that the latter cannot imitate because they lack the resources to do so. Paying dividends is one such policy because it requires the company to have cash. A company that is struggling is not able to imitate a company that is prospering.

For this reason, dividend policy is a means of signalling that cannot be faked, and managers use it to convince the market that the picture of the company they present is the true one.

Dividend policy is also a way for the company's managers to show the market that they have a plan for the future and are anticipating certain results. If a company maintains its dividend when its earnings have decreased, that signals to the market that the decline is only temporary and earnings growth will resume.

Dividends are paid a few months after the close of the year, therefore the level of the dividend depends on earnings during both the past and the current period. That level thus provides information – a signal – about expected earnings during the current period.

A dividend reduction, though, is not necessarily bad news for future earnings. It might also indicate that the company has a new opportunity and need to invest.

Thus, during the 1990s we saw a number of groups traditionally positioned in mature industries reorient themselves towards businesses with faster growth.

The strategic communication aspect of dividend policy is of crucial importance, especially when there is a change in policy. One trap to be avoided is having a dividend rise interpreted as signalling a scarcity of investment opportunities. A dividend cut can be justified to investors by a strategy of renewed growth.

3/ DIVIDENDS AND AGENCY THEORY

Creditors and managers are seen as having a common interest in favouring reinvestment of earnings. When profits are not distributed, "the money stays in the business", whereas shareholders "always want more".

If the manager directs free cash flow into unprofitable investments, his ego may be gratified by the size of the investment budget, or his position may become more secure if those investments carry low risk.

In addition, retained earnings are one source of financing about which not much dis closure is necessary. The cost of any informational asymmetry having to do with internal financing is therefore very low. It is not surprising that, as predicted by Jensen and observed in a study conducted by Harford (1999), companies that have cash available make less profitable investments than other companies. Money seems to burn a hole in managers' pockets.

There is a sanction, however, for taking reinvestment to excess: the takeover bid or *tender offer* in cash or shares.

If a management team performs poorly, the market's sanction will, sooner or later, take the form of a decline in the share price. If it lasts, the decline will expose the company to the risk of a takeover. Assuming the managers themselves do not hold enough of the company's shares to ensure that the tender offer succeeds or fails, a change of management may enable the company to get back on track, by once again making investments that earn more than the cost of capital, and thereby lead to a rise in the share price.

A formalisation of agency theory as applied to tender offers has been made by Michael Jensen (1986). The key to Jensen's approach is the notion of *free cash flow*.

Jensen defines the difference between the acquisition price and the new market value of the company as the value of the supervision provided by outside firms.

However, since Jensen's work was published, managers have been apparently much more careful when using their cash reserves. They now seem to be aware of the take-over threat which has stricken several ill-managed companies since 1980 (ITT, ABN Amro,. . .). Developing corporate governance principles[3] and share buy-back policies[4] are probably linked to this threat.

3 See Chapter 42.

4 See Chapter 38.

By requiring managers to pay out a fraction of the company's earnings to share-holders, dividend policy is a means of imposing "discipline" on those managers and forcing them to include in their reckoning the interest of the company's owners. A generous divi-dend policy will increase the company's dependence on either shareholders or lenders to finance the business.

In either case, those putting up the money have the power to say no. In the extreme, shareholders could demand that all earnings be paid out in dividends in order to reduce managers' latitude to act in ways that are not in the shareholders' interest. The company would then have to have regular rights issues, to which shareholders would decide whether to subscribe based on the profitability of the projects proposed to them by the managers. This is the virtuous cycle of finance.

Although attractive intellectually because it greatly reduces the problem of asymmetric information, this solution runs up against the high costs of carrying out a capital increase – not just the direct costs, but the cost in terms of management time as well.

Bear in mind also that creditors watch out for their interests and tend to oppose overly generous dividends that could increase their risk, as we saw in Chapter 35.

Even though the dividend is often quite small in relation to the value of equity capital (a few percent at most), it plays an important role. It is a signal from the company to the financial markets. It is an instrument for control of managers by the market, in that it deprives the company of some of the cash the managers would have been able to invest as they saw fit. If the managers still wish to invest that much cash, they will have to borrow; and because debt imposes a discipline of its own (repayment), this pushes them to be more efficient.

4/ BECAUSE SHAREHOLDERS WISH IT

Baker and Wurgler (2004) have demonstrated that in some periods shareholders demand dividends and are thus ready to pay higher prices for more generous shares. From 2002 we have been exactly in this situation. Whilst our readers know that dividends do not enrich shareholders (since the value of the shares falls correspondingly), shareholders may nonetheless be happy about receiving more dividends. A good example of this attitude was provided by John Rockefeller in the 1920s: "Do you know the only thing that I like? To cash in my dividends!"

Conversely, there are some periods when investors prefer companies that retain most of their earnings. In these cases, the stock market penalises generous shares, as happened in the second half of the 1990s: at the end of 1998, Telefonica announced the suppression of its dividend for financing its expansion in Latin America. At the announcement, the stock increased by 9%.

The reader may wonder why a series of opposite phases are often observed. We believe that there is no better answer than the existence of fads, even in finance. Waves of optimism lead to the reinvestment of earnings; conversely, pessimism pushes companies to distribute a higher portion of earnings.

5/ TO PROVIDE SHAREHOLDERS WITH CASH

This is particularly true for private companies, but can also apply to small listed companies with low liquidity on the market. Shareholders are human beings after all; they have needs and may need cash for day-to-day life.

Family-owned companies may need to pay a regular dividend to allow their shareholders to pay their annual taxes without having to sell part of their holding.

The summary of this chapter can be downloaded from www.vernimmen.com.

Internal financing by reinvestment of cash flow enjoys an excellent image: it reduces risk for the creditor and results in capital gains rather than more heavily taxed dividends for the shareholder. For managers, it is a resource they can mobilise without having to go to third parties; as such, it reduces the company's risk and increases the value of their stock options.

For the same reason, though, systematic reinvestment of cash flow can be dangerous. It is not appealing from a financial standpoint if it allows the company to finance investments that bring in less than the rate of return required given their risk. To do so is to destroy value. If the penalty for value destruction is delayed, as it often is because companies that reinvest excessively are cut off from the capital markets, the eventual sanction is all the harsher.

The trap for the unwitting is that internal financing has no explicit cost, whereas its true cost – which is an opportunity cost – is quite real.

Reinvesting cash flow makes possible organic growth at a rate equal to the rate of return on equity multiplied by the earnings retention ratio (1 minus the payout ratio). With constant financial leverage and a constant rate of return on capital employed, the organic growth rate is the same as the growth rate of book equity and capital employed. Lastly, the rate of growth of earnings per share is equal to the marginal rate of return on book equity multiplied by the earnings retention ratio.

Dividends as well as share buy-backs aim at giving back to shareholders funds that cannot be invested by the firm at the appropriate cost of capital. This then allows the firm to avoid value destruction. In macroeconomic terms, it makes it possible to reallocate funds from mature companies to startups and developing companies that require equity to finance their business risk.

Dividend payment can serve secondary goals:

- signalling that the firm has sufficient stable cash flow to support a high level of debt;

- reducing the flexibility of the management, who may otherwise invest in value-destroying projects;

- answering the wish of shareholders, who, depending on the environment, might be willing to pay more for high-payout firms or, on the contrary, low-dividend firms;

- granting shareholders cash, as they may need it.

SUMMARY

SECTION 4

QUESTIONS

1/ Why does internal financing enjoy such a positive image?

2/ Why is a policy of sticking strictly to internal financing unsound?

3/ What determines the rate of growth of capital employed?

4/ What should a company do if its rate of return on reinvested earnings is below the weighted average cost of capital?

5/ By what criterion should a policy of reinvesting cash flow be judged?

6/ In your opinion, which theory best explains the interest of internal financing from an overall standpoint?

7/ Show with an example why reinvestment of earnings by the company has no cost for a holder of call options on the company's shares.

8/ What is the market's sanction for over-reliance on internal financing?

9/ What kind of companies rely heavily on internal financing? What kind do not?

10/ Can internal financing lower the cost of capital?

11/ What are the advantages and drawbacks of 100% internal financing for family shareholders?

12/ Why is internal financing the financial resource with the lowest implementation cost?

13/ Under what condition is the dividend growth rate at least equal to the growth rate of free cash flow?

14/ On the day of the dividend payment, the value of the share drops by the amount of the dividend. Has the shareholder become poorer?

15/ Under what condition can you accept that a firm does not pay a dividend?

16/ A firm that used to pay no dividends announces its first dividend payment. How would you interpret this according to efficient market theory, signalling theory, agency theory?

17/ Do you think tobacco companies have high or low payout ratios? Why?

More questions are waiting for you at www.vernimmen.com.

SECTION 4

EXERCISES

1/ An entrepreneur is determined to retain control of his company and refuses to accept any outside investors. The company's return on capital employed is 10% after tax. He wishes to achieve growth of 25% a year. The cost of debt is 7% before tax, and the tax rate is 40%.

    (a) If he has no earnings distribution policy, what capital structure is he choosing implicitly?

    (b) If instead he has to pay out one-third of the company's earnings, what capital structure is he choosing?

    (c) If he chooses financial leverage (debt/equity) equal to 1, what is the implied normal growth rate of the company?

    (d) Which other parameters can he play with?

2/ Choose an example of "death spiral" deterioration of capital structure, with an initial positive leverage effect and then a negative leverage effect. Construct tables like those presented in this chapter.

Questions

1/ Because it reduces risk to creditors, results in capital gains rather than more heavily taxed dividends and increases the value of managers' stock options.

2/ It isolates the company from the capital markets.

3/ The rate of return on capital employed, the capital structure and the interest rate on debt.

4/ Pay out all its earnings.

5/ The marginal rate of return on investment.

6/ Agency theory.

7/ Holders of call options get no benefit from earnings paid out as dividends, but retained earnings increase the value of the shares and therefore the value of their options.

8/ A takeover bid.

9/ Growth companies with high rates of return. Mature companies that generate cash.

10/ No. Unless it changes the risk on capital employed, it has no impact on the cost of capital.

11/ Capital increases that could dilute the family's shareholding are avoided, but potential dividends are reduced.

12/ Because nobody else's agreement need be sought before going ahead with it.

13/ When the company has positive net debt.

14/ No, as the share price is lower but the shareholder has received in cash (the dividend) the same amount as compensation. Otherwise, there would be arbitrage.

15/ If its ROCE is above the cost of capital.

16/ No difference – reduction in agency costs as manager will have less flexibility – growth is slowing down.

17/ High, as growth opportunities are low (but also in order to drug shareholders like they drug their customers!).

Exercises

A detailed Excel version of the solutions is available at www.vernimmen.com.

1/ (a) $D/E = [(g/(1-d)) - r_{ce}]/(r_{ce} - i(1-40\%)) = 2.6$;

(b) $D/E = 4.7$;

(c) $g = 15.8\%$ if he pays no dividend, $g = 10.5\%$ if he pays out one-third of earnings;

(d) He can try to improve his rate of return on capital employed.

2/ Dubai is a good example of a death spiral with a high leverage effect. This Emirate financed fast growth mainly with debt. When the crisis arrived in 2008, its difficulties accelerated. It had to be saved from bankruptcy by Abu Dhabi.

Consider the following example of a company for which the leverage effect changes sign in year 4.

	Equity	Debt	Capital employed	Operating earnings after tax	Interest expenses after tax	Net profit	Dividends	Reinvested earnings	Equity at end of period
1	100	100	200	20	8	12	2	10	110
2	110	140	250	25	12	13	1	12	122
3	122	190	312	28	17	11	0	11	133
4	133	258	391	31	26	5	0	5	138
5	138	350	488	34	35	−1	0	−1	137
6	137	474	611	43	47	−4	0	−4	133

BIBLIOGRAPHY

Overview of the dividend policy problem:

K. Baker, *Dividends and Dividend Policy*, John Wiley & Sons, Inc., 2009.

F. Black, The dividend puzzle, *Journal of Portfolio Management*, **2**, 634–639, Summer 1976.

L. Brav, J. Graham, C. Harvey, R. Michaely, Payout policy in the 21st century, *Journal of Financial Economics*, **77**(3), 483–527, September 2005.

D. Denis, I. Osobov, Why do firms pay dividends? International evidence on the determinants of dividend policy, *Journal of Financial Economics*, **89**(1), 62–82, July 2008.

Equilibrium markets:

E. Fama, K. French, Testing trade-off and pecking order prediction about dividends and debt, *The Review of Financial Studies*, **15**(1), 1–33, Spring 2002.

M. Miller, F. Modigliani, Dividend policy, growth, and the valuation of shares, *Journal of Business*, **34**(4), 411–433, January 1961.

M. Miller, M. Scholes, Dividends and taxes, *Journal of Financial Economics*, **6**(4), 332–364, December 1978.

Empirical studies:

P. Asquith, D. Mullins, The impact of initiating dividend payments on shareholders' wealth, *Journal of Business*, **56**(1), 77–96, January 1983.

M. Baker, J. Wurgler, A catering theory of dividends, *Journal of Finance*, **59**(3), 1125–1165, June 2004.

M. Baker, J. Wurgler, Appearing and dividends: The link to catering incentives, *Journal of Financial Economics*, **73**(2), 271–288, August 2004.

F. Black, M. Scholes, The effect of dividend yield and dividend policy on common stock prices and returns, *Journal of Financial Economics*, **1**(1), 1–22, May 1974.

H. DeAngelo, L. DeAngelo, D. Skinner, Are dividends disappearing? Dividend concentration and the consolidation of earnings, *Journal of Financial Economics*, **72**(3), 425–456, December 2004.

H. DeAngelo, L. DeAngelo, The irrelevance of the MM dividend irrelevance theorem, *Journal of Financial Economics*, **79**(2), 293–315, 2006.

M. Desai, C. Fritz Foley, Dividend policy inside the multinational firms, *Financial Management*, **36**(1), 5–26, Spring 2007.

M. Desai, L. Jin, Institutional tax clienteles and payout policy, *Journal of Financial Economics*, forthcoming.

E. Fama, K. French, Disappearing dividends: Changing firm characteristics or lower propensity to pay? *Journal of Financial Economics*, **60**(1), 3–43, April 2001.

J. Graham, A. Kumar, Do dividend clientele exist? Evidence on dividend preferences of retail investors, *Journal of Financial Economics*, **61**(3), 1305–1336, June 2006.

Y. Grinstein, R. Michaeli, Institutional holdings and payout policy, *Journal of Finance*, **60**(3), 1389–1426, June 2005.

B. Julio, D. Ikenberry, Reappearing dividends, *Journal of Applied Corporate Finance*, **16**(4), 89–100, Fall 2004.

W. Li, E. Lie, Dividend changes and catering incentives, *Journal of Financial Economics*, **80**(2), 293–308, 2006.

J. Lintner, Distribution of incomes of corporations among dividends, retained earnings and taxes, *American Economic Review*, **46**(2), 97–116, May 1956.

Signalling theory:

J. Baskin, Dividend policy and the volatility of common stocks, *Journal of Portfolio Management*, **15**(3), 19–25, Summer 1989.

S. Benartzi, R. Michaely, R. Thaler, Do changes in dividends signal the future or the past? *Journal of Finance*, **52**(3), 1007–1034, July 1997.

A. Koch, A. Sun, Dividend changes and the persistence of part earnings changes, *Journal of Finance*, **49**(5), 2093–2118, October 2004.

M. Miller, The information content of dividends, in J. Bossons, R. Dornbush and S. Fisher (eds), *Macroeconomics: Essays in Honor of Franco Modigliani*, MIT Press, 1987.

A. Ofer, D. Siegel, Corporate financial policy, information and market expectations: An empirical investigation of dividends, *Journal of Finance*, **42**(4), 889–911, September 1987.

Agency theory:

S. Bhattacharya, Imperfect information, dividend policy and the bird in the hand fallacy, *Bell Journal of Economics*, **10**(1), 259–270, Summer 1979.

F. Easterbrook, Two agency-cost explanations of dividends, *American Economic Review*, **74**(4), 650–659, September 1984.

J. Harford, Corporate cash reserves and acquisitions, *Journal of Finance*, **54**(6), 1969–1997, December 1999.

P. Healy, K. Palepu, Earnings information conveyed by dividend initiations and omissions, *Journal of Financial Economics*, **21**(2), 149–176, September 1988.

M. Jensen, Agency costs of free cash flow, corporate finance and takeovers, *American Economic Review*, **76**(2), 323–329, May 1986.

M. Jensen, W. Meckling, A theory of the firm: Managerial behavior, agency cost and ownership structure, *Journal of Financial Economics*, **3**(4), 305–360, October 1976.

R. Lambert, W. Lanen, D. Larcker, Executive stock option plans and corporate dividend policy, *Journal of Financial and Quantitative Analysis*, **24**(4), 406–425, December 1989.

R. La Porta, F. Lopez-de-Silanes, A. Shleifer, Agency problems and dividend policies around the world, *Journal of Finance*, **55**(1), 1–33, February 2000.

S. Myers, Outside equity, *Journal of Finance*, **55**(3), 1005–1037, June 2000.

SECTION 4

Chapter 38

DISTRIBUTION IN PRACTICE:

DIVIDENDS AND SHARE BUY-BACKS

Now, give the money back

The topics addressed in this chapter are the logical complement of the preceding chapter. Distribution of cash can take the form of ordinary dividend payments, but also of exceptional dividends, share buy-backs or capital reductions.

Section 38.1
DIVIDENDS

1/ PAYOUT RATIO AND DIVIDEND GROWTH RATE

In practice, when dividends are paid, the two key criteria are:

* the rate of growth of dividends per share;
* the **payout ratio** (d), represented by

$$d = \frac{\text{Dividend}}{\text{Net profit}}$$

All other criteria are irrelevant, frequently inaccurate and possibly misleading. For example, it is absurd to take the ratio of the dividend to the par value of the share, since par value often has little to do with equity value.

Hence the difficulty for a company of meeting a dividend yield objective. It is the shareholder who, when evaluating the company, determines the desired yield, not the other way round.

In this regard, numerous tests have been performed to show that investors systematically re-evaluate a company when the amount of the dividend is made public.

In Europe, a payout ratio lower than 20% is considered to be a low dividend policy, whereas one greater than 60% is deemed high. The average in 2008 was about 40%.

PAYOUT RATIO FOR LARGE LISTED EUROPEAN COMPANIES IN 2010

0% < *d* < 20%		20% < *d* < 30%		30% < *d* < 40%		40% < *d* < 50%		50% < *d* < 100%	
Alcatel-Lucent	0%	Havas	21%	Publicis	31%	Carrefour	41%	Sodexo	51%
Ryanair	0%	Delhaize	22%	Heineken	31%	Metro	41%	Telecom Italia	52%
British Airways	0%	Italcementi	24%	Siemens	32%	Hermés	41%	Vivendi Universal	52%
Faurecia	0%	Arkema	24%	Philips	32%	Axa	42%	Casino	53%
BMW	0%	Eiffage	25%	Thales	34%	Repsol	43%	Veolia	55%
EADS	6%	Thyssenkrupp	25%	Essilor	34%	Dexia	44%	STMicroelectronics	56%
Heidelberg Cement	13%	Michelin	25%	Bayer	35%	JC Decaux	44%	Telefonica	57%
Air France – KLM	16%	Fiat	26%	Royal Dutch Shell	35%	Danone	45%	Société Générale	59%
Sacyr-Vallehermoso	17%	Continental	27%	Saint-Gobain	36%	Suez	45%	Belgacom	60%
Volkswagen	17%	Norbert Dentressangle	28%	Nokia	36%	BASF	46%	Energias de Portugal	63%
Ciments Français	18%	Beiersdorf	28%	LVMH	38%	PPR	48%	Bulgari	65%
Adidas	19%	Peugeot	28%	BNP Paribas	39%	Vinci	49%	Endesa	68%
Salzgiltsr	20%	Porsche	29%	Total	39%	Lagardére	49%	France Telecom	69%
Grupc Ferrcvial	20%	SAP	29%	Lafarge	40%	Air Liquide	50%	M6	80%
ArcelorMittal	20%	Allianz	30%	L'Oréal	40%	E.ON	50%	TF1	96%

Source: Exane BNP Paribas

SECTION 4

In 2010, only 62 out of the 600 largest listed companies in Europe had paid no dividend (twice as many as the previous year).

The payout ratio and the dividend growth rate (per share) are the only concrete parameters that are useful in analysing dividend policy.

As John Lintner (1956) has established, managers have a payout ratio target expressed in terms of future earnings, an absolute reference. For example, managers set an objective of distributing 45% of the company's earnings and try to keep fluctuations in the unit dividend as small as possible in the face of significant variations in earnings.

Lintner tested his model with actual corporate dividends and found a coefficient of determination (R^2) of 85%. In other words, 85% of the variation in dividend changes year to year was explained by this compact mathematical model. Importantly, the intercept term was significant and positive. This evidence indicated that managers consciously do avoid dividend cuts even when earnings decline, consistent with Lintner's impression from his interviews.

Lintner's results show us that managers do try to do what they normally describe verbally. They:

1. stabilise dividends with gradual, sustainable increases whenever possible;
2. establish an appropriate target payout ratio; and
3. avoid dividend cuts, if at all possible.

In 2010, payout ratios in Europe and the United States were quite high (over 50%), but the explanation has more to do with poor earnings than with any change in dividend policy. To avoid a cut in dividend per share, managers allowed the payout ratio to rise temporarily.

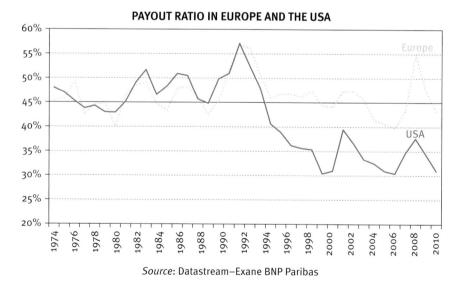

PAYOUT RATIO IN EUROPE AND THE USA

Source: Datastream–Exane BNP Paribas

Some degree of regularity is desirable, either in earnings growth or in dividends paid out, so the company must necessarily choose an objective for the profile of dividends over time. For this purpose, dividend profiles can be classified in the following three categories.

*   If earnings growth is regular, dividend policy is of lesser importance and the company can cut its payout ratio without risk.

- If earnings are cyclical owing to the nature of the business sector, it is important for the dividend to be kept steady. The company needs to retain enough room to manoeuvre to ensure that phases of steady dividends are followed by phases of rising dividends.
- Lastly, a dividend that varies frequently conveys no useful information to the investor and may even suggest that the company's management has no coherent strategy for doing business in its sector. A profile of this kind can hardly have any beneficial effect on the share price.

A dividend policy must be credible – that is, consistent with the earnings that the company achieves. In the long term, no dividend profile, regardless of how smooth it is, can have favourable effects unless it appears sustainable. In other words, it must not be inconsistent or incompatible with the earnings profile.

Compare, for example, the dividend and earnings profiles since 1980 of two industrial groups: Nestlé (a growth company) and Ford (a cyclical one):

NESTLE-EPS AND DPS IN CHF

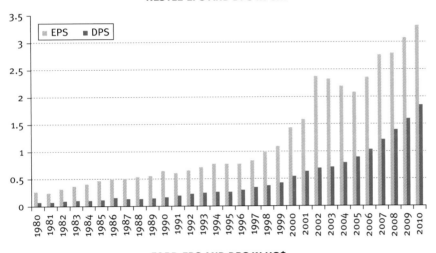

FORD-EPS AND DPS IN US$

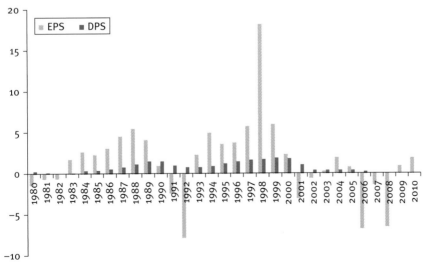

SECTION 4

On the stock market, a high payout ratio implies low price volatility, other things being equal. This is easily demonstrated with the dividend discount valuation model. The share price of a company that pays out all its earnings in dividends will behave much like the price of a bond.

> Here we re-encounter the concept of *duration*. The security with the highest duration will also have the highest volatility. A high payout ratio tends to reduce duration and thereby makes the share price less volatile.

Of course, the payout ratio is not the only determinant of a share's volatility.

For a company, paying out little or none of its earnings translates into growth in book value, an increase in market value and thus eventually into capital gains. To realise those gains, though, the shareholder has to sell. If selling the company's shares is a "crime" – and some managers come close to regarding it as one – then a low-dividend policy is an inducement to crime. A family-owned company that pays low dividends risks weakening its control.

A high-dividend policy, on the other hand, is certainly one way of retaining the loyalty of shareholders that have got used to the income and forget about the value. This tends to be particularly true of family shareholders without management roles in the company.

A financial holding company that wishes to pay dividends must either have received dividends itself from the companies in which it holds stakes or have realised potential capital gains by selling off some assets. One euro of dividends received goes directly onto the income statement and can therefore be redistributed. One euro of capital gain, in contrast, must be realised before it can go into earnings. There has to be a sale.

2/ HOW DIVIDENDS ARE PAID

(a) Advance dividend

This practice consists in paying a fraction of the forthcoming dividend in advance, hence the name. The decision is taken by the board of directors or the executive board and need not be approved by the AGM. An advance dividend offers a way of smoothing cash inflows to shareholders and cash outflows from the company. The advance is typically paid in December or January (midway between two annual dividend dates) and represents between a quarter and a half of the annual dividend.

In the United States, Canada and the United Kingdom, intra-annual dividends are common.

(b) Dividend paid in shares

1 *If its by-laws allow, a company may distribute shares that it holds in portfolio in place of a cash dividend. This is not the same as paying the dividend in its own shares.*

Companies may offer shareholders a choice of receiving dividends in cash or in shares of the company.[1] The decision is taken by shareholders at the ordinary general meeting at which the accounts of the year are approved. However, the company's by-laws must specifically allow such a choice.

Paying the dividend in shares allows the company to make a distribution of earnings while retaining the corresponding cash funds.

There is generally no tax advantage for shares issued in payment of dividends. The value of the shares received is taxed as if it were paid in cash. A shareholder who chooses to be paid in the form of shares must therefore pay tax on the dividend without having received any cash, which may present a problem.

Offering to pay dividends in shares may lead to some limited redistribution of ownership among the shareholders, since some will accept and others will decline.

A share dividend represents no special financial advantage for shareholders other than the ability to reinvest dividends at no charge and generally at a slight discount to the market price (at most 10%). Some investors have no compunctions about taking payment of their dividends in shares and immediately selling those shares in order to pocket the discount. Manipulation of this kind drives down the price. For this reason, the practice, although quite popular in the early 1990s, had practically disappeared.[2] It returned in 2008 with the economic crisis as firms tried to lower their cash out and strengthen their equity while avoiding cutting dividends.

(c) Preferential dividend

To reward loyal shareholders that have held their shares for over a certain period (e.g. more than two years), some companies (for example, Air Liquide) have instituted the practice of paying a preferential dividend. A preferential dividend can be established only by decision of an extraordinary general meeting.

Lastly, we should mention once again preference shares, which have a higher dividend than ordinary shares.

2 The practice made a comeback in 2008 as several banks wanted to preserve their cash reserves amid the subprime crisis and thereafter wanted to increase their solvency given new banking regulations (Basel III).

Section 38.2
Exceptional dividends, share buy-backs and capital reduction

A company may, in certain circumstances, buy back its own shares and either keep them on the balance sheet or cancel them, in which case there is said to be a **capital decrease** or **capital reduction**. Even when shares are repurchased but not cancelled, analysts will (in their own calculations) reduce the number of shares in circulation by the quantity of shares bought back.

Neglecting taxes, if one supposes that the company buys back shares from all shareholders in proportion to their holdings and then cancels those shares, the resulting share buy-back is strictly identical to the payment of a dividend. Cash is transferred from the company to the shareholders with no change in the structure of ownership.

As we shall see below, however, an actual capital reduction is most often not even for all shareholders. Furthermore, a share buy-back or capital reduction is likely to be a more exceptional event than payment of dividends, which is supposed to take place regularly every year.

1/ Exceptional dividend

The exceptional dividend is a dividend of an exceptionally high amount compared to the ordinary dividend. It is obviously not paid on a regular basis and usually corresponds to an exceptional event within the business life of the company (disposal of a large subsidiary,

SECTION 4

end of a lawsuit, etc.). The €20 dividend from Unibail Rodamco that we mentioned in the previous chapter was an exceptional dividend.

2/ SHARE BUY-BACKS

Only listed firms can buy their own shares back on the market. Depending on countries, the buy-backs have to be authorised by shareholders and can be limited in volume (for example, a maximum of 10% of the shares every year or 18 months) and in price (a maximum share buy-back price is set). Generally, the shares bought back will be cancelled but they can also be kept by the company (as treasury stocks) to be handed over in case of acquisition, for the exercise of stock options or for the conversion of convertible bonds.

Under US GAAP and IFRS, treasury stocks are deducted from the amount of shareholders' equity.

3/ CAPITAL REDUCTION

We will not be talking here of capital decreases that occur following an accounting determination that the book value of equity is insufficient. A capital reduction in this context may be required by law or undertaken voluntarily (to lower the par value of the share and make possible a new issue of shares as part of a recapitalisation). **Since capital decreases of this kind do not result in an outflow of cash, they are altogether different, a matter of law and accounting rather than finance.**

A capital reduction corresponding to a distribution of cash can be accomplished:

- By reducing the par value of all shares, thereby automatically reducing authorised capital.
- By **tender offer**. In practice the board of directors, using an authorisation that must have been granted to it at an extraordinary general meeting, makes an offer to all shareholders to buy all or part of their shares at a certain price during a certain period (usually about one month). If too many shares are tendered under the offer, the company scales back all the surrender requests in proportion. If too few are tendered, it cancels the shares that are tendered. If management decides on a tender offer, it has the option of considering the traditional fixed-price offering or the *Dutch auction method*. In Dutch auctions, the firm no longer offers to repurchase shares at a single price, but rather announces a *range* of prices. Each shareholder thus must specify an acceptable selling price within the prescribed range set by the company. If he chooses a high selling price, he will increase the proceeds provided the shares are accepted by the company, but he reduces the probability that shares will be accepted for repurchase. At the end of the offer period, the firm tabulates the received offers, and determines the lowest price that allows repurchasing the desired number of shares.
- In some countries, a share buy-back can be accomplished by issuing **put warrants** to each shareholder, each warrant giving the holder the right to sell one share to the company at a specified price. Such a warrant is a put option issued by the company.

A capital decrease changes the capital structure and thereby increases the risk borne by creditors. To protect the latter, law generally allows creditors to require additional guarantees or call their loans early, although they cannot block the operation outright.

4/ THE IMPACT ON THE COMPANY AND ITS RATIOS

Consider a company with book value of equity of €400m, one million shares outstanding and earnings of €20m. Suppose that it reduces its share capital by 20% by buying back its own shares at their market value, in one case at €200 per share and in another case at €800 per share. It pays for the buy-back by borrowing at 3% after tax (or by liquidating short-term investments earning 3%, which amounts to the same thing).

BEFORE						
Price per share	Book value of equity	Market value of equity	Earnings	Book value per share	EPS	P/E
€200	€400m	€200m	€20m	€400	€20	10
€800	€400m	€800m	€20m	€400	€20	40

AFTER						
Price per share	Book value of equity	Market value of equity	Earnings	Book value per share	EPS	P/E
€200	€360m	€160m	€18.8m	€450+12.5%	€23.5+17.5%	8.5
€800	€240m	€640m	€15.2m	€300−25%	€19−5%	42.1

After the transaction, the book value of equity has decreased by the amount of funds spent on the repurchase – €40 million in one case, €160 million in the other – and so has the market value. Going forward, earnings are reduced by the additional interest charges. The relevant analysis, however, is at the per-share level. The repurchase is made at the current share price (or at current value, if the company is not quoted), possibly increased by a premium of 5% or 10% to induce holders to tender their shares under the offer.

With repurchase at €200, earnings per share increase by 17.5%, whereas book value per share increases by 12.5%. With repurchase at €800, earnings per share decrease by 5% whereas book value per share decreases by 25%.

More generally, repurchase of shares by the company results in:

- an increase in earnings per share (accretion) whenever the reciprocal of P/E is greater than the after-tax rate of interest paid on incremental debt (or earned on short-term debt securities). If E/P is less than the rate of interest, there is a decrease in earnings per share (dilution).
- an increase in the book value of equity per share whenever book value per share before the purchase is greater than the purchase price per share.

The transaction is thus the inverse of a share issue, which should come as no surprise to the reader.

Bear in mind that, although the calculation of the change in earnings per share is of interest, it is not an indicator of value creation. The real issue is not whether a capital decrease will mechanically dilute earnings per share, but whether:

- the price at which the shares are repurchased is less than their estimated value;
- the increase in the debt burden will translate into better performance by management; and
- the marginal rate of return on the funds returned to shareholders by the buyback was less than the cost of capital.

These are the three sources of value creation in a capital decrease.

We frequently see it argued that a capital decrease, by replacing a more costly form of financing (equity) with a less costly one (debt), lowers the weighted average cost of capital. The reader who has absorbed the lessons of Modigliani and Miller and understands that cost of capital is independent from capital structure (remember "the size of a pizza is the same no matter how you slice it"?) may be indulgent. To err is human; only to persist in error is diabolical!

A capital decrease, by itself, does not reduce a company's cost of capital and thus cannot create value. At best, it can avoid value destruction by preventing the company from investing cash at less than the cost of equity.

Only if the company manages to buy back its shares at less than they are worth could it hope to create value. The theory of markets in equilibrium leaves little hope of being able to do this.

Share buy-backs are becoming a normal way of reallocating cash from mature businesses to newer sectors or faster-growing companies.

As an illustration, here are the top 20 share buy-backs in 2010 in Europe:

	Group	€m		Group	€m
1	Nestlé	8 585	11	KPN	1 000
2	Royal Bank of Scotland	3 564	12	Telefonica	883
3	Swedish Match	2 271	13	BAE Systems	613
4	AstraZeneca	1 962	14	Roche	560
5	Deutsche Bank	1 847	15	GDF Suez	491
6	Credit Suisse	1 518	16	Deutsche Telekom	400
7	TDC	1 209	17	BBVA	389
8	Novo Nordisk	1 184	18	Ahold	386
9	Barclays	1 152	19	Heineken	381
10	UBS	1 054	20	Essilor	349

Source: Datastream and company reports.

Section 38.3
THE CHOICE BETWEEN DIVIDENDS, SHARE
BUY-BACKS AND CAPITAL REDUCTION

Dividends, share buy-backs and capital reductions are all ways to return cash to share-holders, but as they have different impacts on a company's parameters one cannot be used instead of another. For instance, in Europe share buy-backs amounted to almost nothing in the mid-1990s, while they reached about €100bn in 2007 and then dropped sharply in 2008 and 2009:

DIVIDENDS AND SHARE BUY-BACKS OF THE 600 LARGEST LISTED EUROPEAN COMPANIES (€bn)

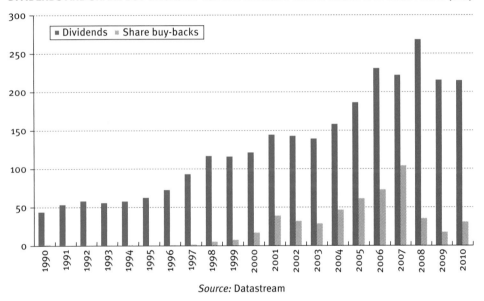

Source: Datastream

Five criteria can be used to understand the choice of the best technique for distributing the excess cash, given the desired objective.

1/ FLEXIBILITY

It is difficult to modify radically and rapidly the dividend level. Any change in the dividend policy raises concerns about the future evolution of the business model and creates expectations regarding the medium-term sustainability of the new level of dividends. This is the major reason for which changes in the dividend policy generally occur very slowly and produce effects on the capital structure only after some periods.

Conversely, the capital reduction and the extraordinary dividends are specific *una tantum* decisions, and investors do not expect any regularity regarding them. They can perfectly fit situations where the company wants to distribute the cash generated by an important asset or intends to modifiy the capital structure rapidly.

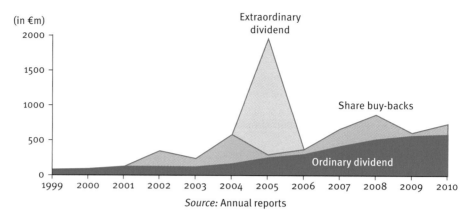

RETURNING CASH TO SHAREHOLDERS: THE EXAMPLE OF BOUYGUES

Source: Annual reports

Besides the regular annual ordinary dividend, Bouygues returns excess cash flows in the form of share buy-backs. In 2005 when it sold its water distribution arm, given the lack of material investment opportunity, Bouygues distributed an extraordinary dividend of €1.6bn.

2/ SIGNALLING

All financial decisions send signals to investors, and thus the company must ponder the expected perception investors may have following the adoption of a specific financial decision.

Applying this principle to dividends, we can reasonably say that the most neutral solution is represented by the extraordinay dividend: it is non-recurring and it does not imply any judgement on the value of the stock. Moreover, it benefits all investors.

Changes in ordinary dividends and capital reductions, however, are clearly perceived as signals sent to the market: in the former case, regarding the level of future earnings; in the latter case, regarding the stock price because a company would not buy a portion of its shares if the management believed that the shares were overvalued.

Jagannathan *et al.* have demonstrated that share buy-back gives little information about future results compared to dividends. While companies that increase dividends show an improvement of results, a similar conclusion cannot be reached with share buy-backs. The distribution of dividends contains a commitment from the management to maintaining the same level of dividend (or increasing them) for a certain number of periods; share buy-backs do not imply an analogous commitment. Thus, cyclical companies are more inclined to use share buy-backs than non-cyclical companies.

3/ IMPACT ON THE SHAREHOLDERS' STRUCTURE

Ordinary and extraordinary dividends do not affect the shareholding structure because they do not modify the number of outstanding shares. On the contrary, capital reduction and share buy-backs affect the shareholders' composition because some shareholders may simply decide not to participate in the capital reduction or to sell their shares in case of a share buy-back. Their percentage of control increases.

As an example, consider the case of Peugeot. Starting from 1999, the controlling family has regularly bought back shares of the company, for a total amount of €2884m, which has allowed them to increase their percentage to 30.3%, compared to the initial 22.7%.

4/ IMPACT ON STOCK OPTIONS

According to the current legislation of some countries, the capital reduction realised by buying back shares at a high price requires an adjustment of the exercise price of the stock options with a neutral effect on stock option holders.

However, some legal systems do not regulate similar adjustments in case of ordinary dividends and extraordinary dividends. Since the extraordinary dividend can strongly reduce the stock price, the absence of any adjustment of the exercise price of the stock options explains why this instrument is not favoured by the management.

The strong decrease in the number of companies distributing a dividend (66% in 1978 vs. 21% in 1999) in America in the last decade, can also be at least partially explained by the increasing popularity of share buy-backs, probably pushed up by the managers holding stock options.

In fact, the distribution of a dividend mechanically reduces the stock price, thus decreasing the probability of a high capital gain for stock option holders. The share buy-back does not generate this negative effect on the value of the stock options. It also leaves unsophisticated investors believing that the stock price will go up.

5/ TAX ISSUES

Tax is naturally an important element that requires close attention. For individual investors belonging to the top classes of personal income, generally speaking the lower taxation is on the capital gains rather than the ordinary dividends. This evidence pushes the shareholders to consider share repurchase more favourably.

In the United States, taxation on dividends for individual investors has been considerably sweetened since 2003, and now stands at 15%. This has restored the attractiveness of periodical dividends and penalised capital gains, which, in fact, are now the dominant way of distributing cash in the United States.

SECTION 4

SUMMARY

The summary of this chapter can be downloaded from www.vernimmen.com.

Within the framework of equilibrium market theory, dividend policy has little importance. The shareholder is indifferent about receiving a dividend and letting the company reinvest the cash in assets that will earn the rate of return he requires. His wealth is the same in either case.

Signalling theory interprets dividends as information communicated by managers to investors about future earnings. A rise in the dividend signals good news; a cut signals bad news.

Agency theory interprets dividends as a means of mitigating conflicts between owners and managers. Paying a dividend reduces the amount of cash that managers are able to invest without much control on the part of shareholders. On the other hand, paying a dividend aggravates conflicts between owners and lenders when the amount of that dividend is significant.

All things considered, dividend policy should be judged on the basis of the company's marginal rate of return on capital employed. If that rate is above the weighted average cost of capital, the dividend can be low or nil because the company is creating value when it reinvests its earnings. If the marginal rate of return is below the cost of capital, shareholders are better off if the company distributes all its earnings to them.

As long as the company has opportunities to invest at a satisfactory return, managers set a target dividend payout ratio that will be higher or lower depending on whether the company has reached maturity or is still growing. Fluctuations in net earnings can be smoothed over in the per-share dividend so that it does not move erratically and send the wrong signal to investors.

The reader should not forget that, to some extent, dividend policy determines the composition of the shareholder body: paying no dividends leads to low loyalty on the part of shareholders, who must regularly sell shares to meet their needs for cash.

A capital decrease can take the form of either a reduction in the par value of all shares via distribution to shareholders of the corresponding amount of cash, or a buy-back of shares in which shareholders are free to participate or not, as they see fit.

A capital decrease may be undertaken for several different purposes: to return funds to shareholders when managers are unable to find investment projects meeting the shareholders' return requirements; to signal an undervalued share price; as an indirect means of increasing the percentage of control held by shareholders that do not take part in the buy-back; or to distribute cash to shareholders at a lower tax cost than by paying a dividend.

The reduction in equity capital produces an increase in earnings per share if the reciprocal of the share's P/E ratio is higher than the after-tax interest rate paid on incremental debt (or forgone on short-term investments). But make no mistake, this has only a remote association with value creation.

Debt-financed capital decreases are economically sound when they allow equity capital to be reallocated away from companies that have reached maturity and achieved predictable cash flows, towards newer companies that are still growing. They are a means of preventing overinvestment and haphazard diversification. However, they lead to value creation only if one or more of the following hold: the added debt burden forces managers to achieve better performance; the shares are bought back at a price below their true value; or the funds returned to shareholders would have earned less than the cost of capital if kept in the company.

QUESTIONS

1/What are the two criteria by which a dividend policy should be judged?

2/Does an increase in the dividend result in an increase in the value of the share?

3/Given tax neutrality, would you prefer to receive dividends or realise capital gains?

4/According to signalling theory, what is indicated by maintaining the per-share dividend following a capital increase by incorporation of reserves?

5/ Is there a cost to the company of issuing bonus shares? Does such an issue change shareholder wealth? What purpose does it serve?

6/ Does a high dividend provide assurance of a stable share price? Why?

7/ Can a company have a target dividend yield for its shareholders? Why or why not?

8/ What is the natural temptation of a company that is required to pay out 100% of its earnings, in terms of how much earnings it records?

9/ Is a manager who holds stock options in favour of a high-dividend policy? Why or why not?

10/ What signal is sent by paying a dividend in shares?

11/ Explain why a sharp increase in dividend often results in a decrease in the value of the company's borrowings.

12/ What is the impact of a debt-heavy capital structure on the payout ratio?

13/ In what circumstances does a company have a good reason to undertake a capital decrease?

14/ Forgetting tax considerations, can a capital decrease enhance the value of the company's operating assets? The value of its shares?

15/ What difference do you see between payment of dividends and capital reduction?

16/ What is the necessary condition for a share buy-back to increase earnings per share? To increase the book value of equity capital per share?

17/ What does a share buy-back programme mean for the company's creditors?

18/ Under what conditions might a fast-growing company with opportunities to invest at a rate of return higher than its cost of capital have a capital decrease?

19/ Does a manager who holds stock options in the company prefer buy-backs or dividends? Why?

More questions are waiting for you at www.vernimmen.com.

SECTION 4

EXERCISES

1/ On 18 February 2011, you observe the following data on Yahoo! Finance:

- Vodafone share price: £180
- Net dividend per share: £8.89
- Earnings per share: £15.35

Calculate Vodafone's payout ratio and the gross yield and net yield on the company's shares. What do you think?

2/ What do you think of the dividend policies of the following companies?

		2006	2007	2008	2009	2010	2011	2012
A	EPS	100	115	131	150	160	165	167
	DPS	20	23	26	30	35	41	60
B	EPS	350	402	458	524	559	577	584
	DPS	70	80	92	105	112	115	117
C	EPS	100	50	0	−50	−50	0	50
	DPS	5	5	5	5	5	5	6
D	EPS	500	520	550	600	500	400	300
	DPS	100	80	70	100	120	150	200

3/ Gassoumi plc has the following characteristics:

- Net earnings: £100m
- Number of shares: 1 000 000
- Market price per share: £1000
- Book value of equity: £1200m
- EPS: £100
- Book value per share: £1200

The company decides to take advantage of a sudden stock market slump by buying back a quarter of its shares at a price of £500 per share. Its after-tax cost of debt is 5%.

Calculate EPS and book value per share. Same question if the buy-back price is £1500 per share. What do you conclude?

4/ Rowak plc is a Syldavian industrial company listed on the Klow stock exchange. The number of shares in issue has been constant over the period at one million. The corporate income tax rate is 33%.

(a) Calculate Rowak's after-tax ROCE and ROE in each year. What do you think?
(b) What do you think of the fact that Rowak has never paid a dividend?
(c) In early September 2009, the company's market capitalisation is 200 million, and its managers believe the shares are worth 150 each. Rowak's chairman proposes to the board of directors that 50 million be devoted to buying back (and cancelling) outstanding shares. The programme is to be financed by borrowing at 10% before tax. The board of directors refuses. Why, in your opinion?
(d) In December 2011, the company's market capitalisation has fallen to 90 million (still with the same number of shares in issue) and the estimated value of the share is 120. Rowak's chairman puts forward his proposal again. What do you think now?

(figures in millions)	Revenue	Net profit	Pre-tax interest expenses	Book value of equity	Net debt	Market capitalisation
2006	170	8	9	50	60	55
2007	130	10	10	60	70	90
2008	170	11	10	71	75	152
2009	220	13	9	84	76	195
2010	230	13	7	97	70	210
2011	240	13	6	110	65	200

Questions

1/ Dividend growth rate and payout ratio.

2/ Not according to equilibrium market theory, but it could be a positive signal.

3/ According to equilibrium market theory, you should not care; according to agency theory, you should prefer dividends.

4/ The company expects to maintain its profitability.

5/ The company does not gain or lose. An issue of bonus shares does not increase shareholder wealth. It can improve liquidity by increasing the number of shares in circulation. It can be a positive signal if the dividend per share is maintained.

6/ A high dividend helps to ensure stability of the share price but in no way guarantees it.

7/ No, because the shareholder determines what yield he chooses to receive.

8/ Conceal earnings to avoid having to pay them out in dividends and thereby maximise internal financing.

9/ No, because high dividends hold down the price of the shares on which the manager holds stock options.

10/ The company does not have the cash to pay a cash dividend!

11/ Because there is a transfer of value from creditors, whose claims on the company become riskier, to shareholders.

12/ Reduces the payout ratio because there are periodic interest and principal payments to be made.

13/ Whenever the marginal rate of return on its investments is less than the rate of return required by its shareholders.

14/ There will be a reduction in the informational asymmetry and a consequent increase in value.

15/ Fundamentally, the two are the same, but the dividend goes to all shareholders whereas the capital reduction may be reserved for only some of them. The tax treatment may also be different.

16/ EPS increases whenever the reciprocal of P/E is higher than the after-tax interest rate on debt (or short-term investments). Depends on the ratio of price to book value (PBR).

17/ An increase in risk borne by them.

18/ If its shares are particularly undervalued.

19/ He prefers buy-backs because paying a dividend reduces the value of the shares and therefore the value of his stock options.

Exercises

A detailed Excel version of the solutions is available at www.vernimmen.com.

1/ $d = 8.89/15.35 = 58\%$, dividend yield: $8.89/180 = 4.9\%$. Relatively high distribution policy of a group at maturity with some debt still to service.

2/ A fast growth has been slowing, payout ratio increasing. This is fairly logical.

B same growth pattern, but payout ratio is constant. This is surprising because the marginal rate of return has become very low (1.5% in 2012) and is surely below the cost of capital.

C cyclical company that keeps its dividend per share steady. Payout ratio is very low at the top of the cycle (5%) and very high at the bottom (<100%).

D No coherent dividend policy at all.

3/ At a cost of £500 per share – repurchase amount: £125m. Associated interest costs = £6.25m. EPS after the repurchase = £125. Book value per share = £1433. At a cost of £1500 per share: EPS = £108.3; book value per share = £1100.

4/ (a)

	2006	2007	2008	2009	2010	2011
ROE	12.7	12.8	12.1	11.9	10.6	9.7
ROCE	16	16.7	15.5	15.5	13.4	11.8

Returns on equity and capital employed have declined, reducing the leverage effect and the company's financial risk.

(b)

	2007	2008	2009	2010	2011
Δ Earnings/Δ Equity	20%	9.1%	15.4%	0	0

The dividend policy Rowak has been following (no dividend) was consistent with its situation until 2009 since it was getting adequate returns on reinvested earnings. This is no longer the case. Earnings are not growing, and shareholders are becoming relatively poorer.

(c) *Why would you want to pay 200 for shares that you believe are worth 150?*

(d) *The proposal makes sense now because a gross disequilibrium in the market means the shares can be bought back at a price below their estimated value.*

BIBLIOGRAPHY

Empirical studies:

P. Asquith, D. Mullins, The impact of initiating dividend payments on shareholders' wealth, *Journal of Business*, **56**, 77–96, January 1983.

M. Baker, J. Wurgler, A catering theory of dividends, *Journal of Finance*, **59**, 1125–1165, June 2004.

M. Baker, J. Wurgler, Appearing and dividends: The link to catering incentives, *Journal of Financial Economics*, **73**, 271–288, August 2004.

F. Black, M. Scholes, The effect of dividend yield and dividend policy on common stock prices and returns, *Journal of Financial Economics*, **1**(1), 1–22, May 1974.

J.B. Chay, J. Suh, Payout policy and cash flow uncertainty, *Journal of Financial Economics*, **93**(1), 88–107, July 2009.

H. DeAngelo, L. DeAngelo, D. Skinner, Are dividends disappearing? Dividend concentration and the consolidation of earnings, *Journal of Financial Economics*, **72**, 425–456, December 2004.

H. DeAngelo, L. DeAngelo, The irrelevance of the MM dividend irrelevance theorem, *Journal of Financial Economics*, **79**(2), 293–315, 2006.

M. Desai, C. Fritz Foley, Dividend policy inside the multinational firm, *Financial Management*, **36**(1), 5–26, Spring 2007.

Economist, The dividend puzzle, 9 January 2003.

E. Fama, K. French, Disappearing dividends: Changing firm characteristics or lower propensity to pay? *Journal of Financial Economics*, **60**, 3–43, April 2001.

J. Graham, A. Kumar, Do dividend clientele exist? Evidence on dividend preferences of retail investors, *Journal of Financial Economics*, **61**(3), 1305–1336, June 2006.

Y. Grinstein, R. Michaeli, Institutional holdings and payout policy, *Journal of Finance*, **60**(3), 1389–1426, June 2005.

SECTION 4

B. Julio, D. Ikenberry, Reappearing dividends, *Journal of Applied Corporate Finance*, **16**(4), 89–100, Fall 2004.

W. Li, E. Lie, Dividend changes and catering incentives, *Journal of Financial Economics*, **80**(2), 293–308, 2006.

J. Lintner, Distribution of incomes of corporations among dividends, retained earnings and taxes, *American Economic Review*, **46**(2), 97–116, May 1956.

D. Skinner, The evolving relation between earnings, dividends, and stock repurchases, *Journal of Financial Economics*, **87**(3), 582–609, March 2008.

H. Von Eije, W. Megginson, Dividends and share repurchases in the European Union, *Journal of Financial Economics*, **89**(2), 347–374, August 2008.

Share buybacks:

L. Dann, Common stock repurchases: An analysis of returns to bondholders and stockholders, *Journal of Financial Economics*, **9**, 113–138, June 1981.

A. Dittmar, Why do firms repurchase stocks? *Journal of Business*, **73**(3), 331–355, July 2000.

E. Ginglinger, J. Hamon, Actual share repurchase, timing and liquidity, *Journal of Banking and Finance*, **31**(3), 915–938, March 2007.

G. Grullon, D. Ikenberry, What do we know about stock repurchases? *Journal of Applied Corporate Finance*, **13**(1), 31–51, Spring 2000.

G. Grullon, R. Michaely, Dividends, share repurchases and the substitution hypothesis, *Journal of Finance*, **57**, 1649–1684, August 2002.

G. Grullon, R. Michaely, The information content of share repurchase programs, *Journal of Finance*, **59**(2), 651–680, April 2004.

B. Hausch, D. Logue, J. Seward, Dutch auction share repurchases: Theory and evidence, in D. Chew (Ed.), *The New Corporate Finance. Where Theory Meets Practice*, 2nd edn, McGraw Hill, 1999.

M. Jagannathan, C. Stephens, M. Weisbach, Financial flexibility and the choice between dividends and stock repurchases, *Journal of Financial Economics*, **57**, 355–384, September 2000.

R. Masulis, Stock repurchase by tender offer: An analysis of the cause of common stock price changes, *Journal of Finance*, **35**(2), 305–319, May 1980.

W. Maxwell, C. Stephens, The wealth effects of repurchases on bondholders, *Journal of Finance*, **58**, 895–919, April 2003.

W. McNally, Open market stock repurchase signaling, *Financial Management*, **28**(2), 55–67, Summer 1999.

B. Soter, E. Brigham, P. Evanson, The dividend cut "heard round the world": The case of FPL, in D. Chew (Ed.), *The New Corporate Finance. Where Theory Meets Practice*, 2nd edn, McGraw Hill, 1999.

T. Vermaelen, Repurchases tender offers, signaling and managerial incentives, *Journal of Financial and Quantitative Analysis*, **19**(2), 163–181, June 1984.

Other articles:

T. Koller, S. Foushee, Much ado about dividends, *McKinsey Quarterly*, **2**, 157–159, 2003.

SECTION 4

Chapter 39
SHARE ISSUES

There are no victories at bargain prices

The previous chapters have already begun our study of equity financing. This chapter analyses the consequences for the shareholder of a share issue (or capital increase). Capital increases resulting from mergers and acquisitions will be dealt with in Chapter 44.

Section 39.1
A DEFINITION OF A SHARE ISSUE

1/ A SHARE ISSUE IS A SALE OF SHARES . . .

A share issue is, first of all, a **sale of shares**. But who is the seller? The **current share-holder**. The paradox is that the seller receives no money. As we shall see in this chapter, **to avoid diluting his stake in the company at the time of a share issue, the shareholder must subscribe to the same proportion of the new issue that he holds of the pre-existing shares**. Only if he subscribes to more than that is he (from the standpoint of his own portfolio) buying additional control; if less, he is selling control.

Up to now, we have presented market value as a sanction on the company's management, an external judgement that the company can ignore so long as its shareholders are not selling out and it is not asking them to stump up more money. A share issue, which conceptually is a sale of shares at market value, has the effect of reintroducing this value-sanction via the company's treasury, i.e. its cash balance. **For the first time, market value, previously an external datum, interferes in the management of the company.**

2/ . . . THE PROCEEDS OF WHICH GO TO THE COMPANY, AND THUS INDIRECTLY TO ALL OF ITS INVESTORS, . . .

This may seem paradoxical, but it is not. The proceeds of the capital increase indeed go to the company. Shareholders will benefit to the extent that the additional funds enable the company to develop its business and thereby increase its earnings. Creditors will see their claims on the company made less risky and therefore more valuable.

3/ . . . WHICH IMPLIES SHARING BETWEEN OLD AND NEW SHAREHOLDERS

When a company issues bonds or takes out a loan from a bank, it is selling a "financial product". It is contracting to pay interest at a fixed or indexed rate and repay what it has borrowed on a specified schedule. As long as it meets its contractual obligations, the company does not lose its *autonomy*.

In contrast, when a company issues new shares, the old shareholders are agreeing to share their rights to the company's equity capital (which is increased by the proceeds of the issue), their rights to its future earnings and their control over the company itself with the new shareholders.

A capital increase is simply a sale of shares. It implies sharing the parameters of the company. The magnitude of this sharing depends on the market value of the equity capital, but it applies to a cake made larger by the proceeds of the capital increase.

To illustrate, consider company E with equity capital worth $1000m split between two shareholders, F (80%) and G (20%).

If G sells his entire shareholding ($200m) to H, neither the value nor the proportion of F's equity in the company is changed. If, on the other hand, H is a new shareholder brought in by means of an issue of new shares, he will have to put in $250m to obtain a 20% interest, rather than $200m as previously, since the value of equity after a capital increase of $250m is $1250m $(100 + 250)$. The new shareholder's interest is indeed 20% of the larger amount. **Percentage interests should always be reckoned on the value including the newly issued shares.**

After this share issue has been added to the $1000m base, the value of F's shareholding in the company is the same as it was ($800m) but his ownership percentage has decreased from 80% to 64% (800/1250), while G's has decreased from 20% to 16%.

We see that if a shareholder does not participate in a capital increase, his percentage interest declines. This effect is called **dilution**.

In contrast, if the share issue is reserved entirely for F, his percentage interest in the company rises from 80% to 84% (1050/1250), and the equity interest of all other shareholder(s) is necessarily diluted.

Lastly, if F and G each take part in the share issue in exact proportion to their current shareholding, **the market value of equity no longer matters** in this one particular case. Their ownership percentages remain the same, and each puts up the same amount of funds for new shares regardless of the market value. This is illustrated in the table below[1] for equity values of $500m, $1000m and $2000m. In effect, F and G are selling new shares to themselves.

1 *The figures in parentheses indicate cash flows: positive means an inflow; negative an outflow.*

SECTION 4

($ million)	Value of equity in E	Value of shares held by F	Value of shares held by G	Value of shares held by H
Before share issue	1000	800 or 80%	200 or 20%	
G sells 20% of the shares to H for 200	1000	800 or 80%	0 or 0% (+200)	200 or 20% (−200)
H subscribes to a cash share issue of 250	1250	800 or 64%	200 or 16%	250 or 20% (−250)

($ million)	Value of equity in E	Value of shares held by F	Value of shares held by G	Value of shares held by H
G sells 20% of the shares to F for 200	1000	1000 or 100% (−200)	0 or 0% (+200)	
F subscribes to a cash share issue of 250	1250	1050 or 84% (−250)	200 or 16%	
F and G subscribe to a share issue increase of 250 in proportion to their ownership percentage at different initial values of equity (1000, 2000 and 500, respectively)	1250	1000 or 80% (−200)	250 or 20% (−50)	
	2250	1800 or 80% (−200)	450 or 20% (−50)	
	750	600 or 80% (−200)	150 or 20% (−50)	

Section 39.2
SHARE ISSUES AND FINANCE THEORY

1/ SHARE ISSUES AND MARKETS IN EQUILIBRIUM

A share issue is analysed first and foremost as a sale of new shares at a certain price. If that price is equal to the true value of the share, there is no creation of value, nor is any current shareholder made worse off. This is an obvious point that is easily lost sight of in the analysis of financial criteria that we will get to later on.

If the new shares are sold at a high price (more than their value), the company will have benefited from a low-cost source of financing to the detriment of its most recent shareholders. The Internet companies that were able to raise money on very advantageous terms until early 2000 can be cited as an example.

Recall that the cost entailed by a share issue is neither the immediate return on the stock nor the accounting rate of return on equity. It is the rate of return required by shareholders given the market valuation of the stock (see Chapter 19 for the determination of cost of equity).

As we have seen, however, this cost is eminently variable. The sanction for not meeting it is that, other things being equal, the value of the share will decline. The company will be worth less, but in the short term there will be no impact on its treasury.

2/ TAXATION

A cash share issue generally results in immediate deleveraging, making the capital structure less advantageous from a tax standpoint. But the equity injection is usually part of a plan to achieve a new capital structure. For this reason, the tax factor is not a fundamental parameter of a share issue.

3/ SHAREHOLDERS AND CREDITORS

For a company in financial distress, a share issue results in a transfer of value from shareholders to creditors, since the new money put in by the former enhances the value of the claims held by the latter. According to the contingent claims model, the creditors of a "risky" business are able to appropriate most of the increase in the company's value due to an injection of additional funds by shareholders. The value of the put option sold by creditors to shareholders has a lower value. This is the reason why recovery plans for troubled companies always link any new equity financing to prior or concomitant concessions on the part of lenders.

Recapitalisation increases the intrinsic value of the equity and thereby reduces the riskiness of the company, thus increasing the value of its debt as well. Creditors run less risk by holding that debt. This effect is perceptible, though, only if the value of debt is close to the value of operating assets – that is, only if the debt is fairly high risk.

4/ SHAREHOLDERS AND MANAGERS

A capital increase is generally a highly salutary thing to do because it helps to reduce the asymmetry of information between shareholders and managers. A call on the market for fresh capital is accompanied by a series of disclosures on the financial health of the company and the profitability of the investments that will be financed by the issue of new shares. This practice effectively clears management of suspicion and reduces the agency costs of divergence between their interest and the interest of outside shareholders. A share issue thus encourages managers to manage in a way that maximises the shareholders' interest.

The reader will already have applied the line of reasoning above, so familiar has it become by now. What is new here is the conflict between old and new shareholders, under the cover of the oft-repeated hypocrisy that "we are all partners" in the same company.

5/ SHARE ISSUE AS A SIGNAL

If one assumes that managers look out for the interests of current shareholders, it is hard to see how they could propose an issue of new shares when the share price is undervalued.

If one believes in asymmetry of information, a share issue ought to be a signal that the share price is overvalued. A share issue may be a sign that managers believe the company's future cash flows will be less than what is reflected in the current share price. The management team takes advantage of the overvaluation by issuing new shares. The funds provided by this issue will then serve not to finance new investments but to make up for the cash shortfall due to lower-than-expected operating cash flows.

Furthermore, as we have already noted, a share issue implies a change in capital structure. Following the injection of new funds, financial leverage is appreciably decreased. The company's risk diminishes, and there is a transfer of value from shareholders to creditors; the value of the company's shares does not increase by the full value of the funds that are raised.

SECTION 4

In practice, the announcement of a capital increase produces a downward adjustment of 3–5% in the share price. Only the old shareholders suffer this diminution of value. Three major explanations have been proposed for this irregularity:

- Some claim that this effect is due to the negative consequences of the share issue on the company's accounting ratios (cf. Section 39.4). We do not think so.
- Others explain it by invoking a market mechanism: a product sells for a bit less when there is a larger quantity of it; "you catch more flies with honey than with vinegar".
- Lastly, still others explain it as being due to the negative signal that a share issue sends. The reader who wants to raise fresh capital for his company should take this effect into account and be able to respond in advance to the criticisms.

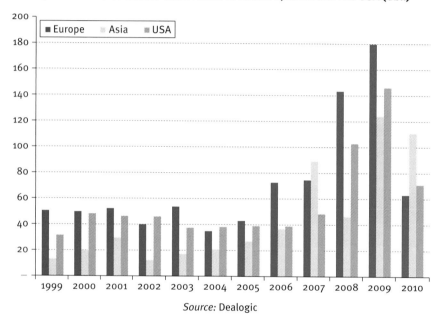

EQUITY ISSUES OF LISTED COMPANIES IN EUROPE, ASIA AND THE USA (€ bn)

Source: Dealogic

Section 39.3
OLD AND NEW SHAREHOLDERS

1/ DILUTION OF CONTROL

Returning to the examples given above, we see that there is dilution of control – that is, reduction in the percentage equity interest of certain shareholders, whenever those shareholders do not subscribe to an issue of new shares in proportion to their current shareholding.

The dilution is greatest for any shareholder who does not participate at all in the capital increase. It is nil for any shareholder who subscribes in proportion to his holding. By convention, we will say that:

Dilution of control is the reduction of rights in the company sustained by a shareholder for which the share issue entails neither an outflow nor an inflow of funds.

Recall that if new shares are issued at a price significantly below their value, current shareholders will usually have pre-emptive subscription rights that enable them to buy the new shares at that price. This right of first refusal is itself tradeable and can be acquired by investors who would like to become shareholders on the occasion of the capital increase.

In the absence of subscription rights, the calculation of dilution of control by a share issue is straightforward:

$$\frac{\text{Number of new shares}}{\text{Number of old shares} + \text{Number of new shares}}$$

When the issue of shares is made with an issue of pre-emptive subscription rights, this calculation no longer holds.

With a rights issue of this kind, we have to distinguish between three measures of dilution. *The most important of these is **real dilution**, which is equivalent to what we just now called dilution (with no modifier) in the absence of pre-emptive subscription rights.*

(a) Apparent dilution

Any capital increase with subscription rights gives rise to **apparent dilution** (sometimes called "overall dilution"), which is expressed by the ratio:

$$\frac{\text{Number of new shares}}{\text{Number of old shares} + \text{Number of new shares}} = \frac{N'}{N + N'}$$

In the case of a rights issue, this degree of dilution is only apparent because it is the result of two distinct transactions:

- a share issue in the strict sense; and
- a detachment of subscription rights, which is analysed as a distribution of bonus shares.

As we saw in Chapter 26, subscription rights enable current shareholders to participate partially in the capital increase with no outlay of funds. As a result, the dilution of their ownership is not as great as the apparent dilution would make it appear.

We therefore need to calculate only the dilution due solely to the capital increase, independently of the subscription rights mechanism. This degree of dilution is called **real dilution** and, in the analysis of the share issue, real dilution is what we are interested in knowing.

(b) Real dilution

Real dilution is the dilution of control that occurs when the share issue is cash-neutral for a shareholder who, on balance, neither pays nor receives any funds: the shareholder sells a portion of his subscription rights in order to buy new shares.

Method 1 The simplest way to calculate real dilution is to reckon on an aggregate basis rather than per share. Real dilution is then calculated as follows:

$$\text{Real dilution} = \frac{\text{Proceeds of capital increase}}{\text{Value of equity before capital increase} + \text{Proceeds of capital increase}}$$

Method 2 Regardless of the formal issue price, the existence of subscription rights ensures that the capital increase will always be subscribed at the company's market value. Every new shareholder will have to pay the issue price and the price of one or more rights in order to obtain one new share. Therefore, to calculate real dilution eliminating the bias due to subscription rights, one need only assume that the issue price is equal to the market value of the shares.

The theoretical number n' of shares that would have been issued under these conditions is:

$$n' = \frac{\text{Proceeds of the issue}}{\text{Market value of each share}}$$

Real dilution is then equal to $n'/(N + n')$ where n' is the number of shares that would have brought in the same funds if the issue price had been equal to the market value.

(c) Technical dilution

Technical dilution is apparent dilution less real dilution. It is due to the distribution of "free" bonus shares that automatically accompanies any capital increase via a rights issue.

Technical dilution represents the additional dilution attributable to the sale of sub-scription rights by shareholders who take the occasion of the capital increase to reduce their investment in the company.

As with any distribution of bonus shares, the various parameters of the company – earnings per share, dividend per share, value of the share – must be adjusted to correct for this technical aspect of the operation, which in no way changes the value of the company.

2/ ANTICIPATION MECHANISM

Take the example of a highly profitable company, entirely equity-financed, that now has investments of 100. With these investments, the company is on track to be worth 400 in 4 years, which corresponds to an annual rate of return on equity of 41.4%. Suppose that this company can invest an additional 100 at a rate of return similar to that on its current investments. To finance this additional capital requirement, it must sell new shares. Suppose also that the shareholder-required rate of return is 10%.

Before the company announces the share issue and before the market anticipates it, the value of its equity capital 4 years hence is going to be 400, which, discounted at 10%, is 273 today.

If, upon the announcement of the capital increase, management succeeds in convincing the market that the company will indeed be worth 800 in 4 years, which is 546 today, the value accruing to current shareholders is 546 – 100 = 446. There is thus instantaneous value creation of 173 (446 – 273) for the old shareholders.

The anticipation mechanism operates in such a way that new shareholders will not receive an excess rate of return. They will get only the return they require, which is 10%. If the intended use of funds is clearly indicated when the capital increase is announced, the share price *before* the capital increase will reflect the investment opportunities, and only the old shareholders will benefit from the value creation arising from them.

Some share prices that show very high P/E ratios are merely reflecting anticipation of exceptional investment opportunities. The 400 of added value in this example is already priced in. The reader will himself be able to observe companies whose share prices are at times so high that they cannot correspond to growth opportunities financed in the traditional way by operating cash flow and borrowing. The shareholders of these companies have placed a bet on the internal and external growth opportunities the company may be able to seize, as it may have done in the past, financed in part by issuing new shares.

Section 39.4
SHARE ISSUES AND FINANCIAL CRITERIA

In this section, we reckon only in terms of adjusted figures. The reader is referred to Chapter 23 for the calculation of the share price adjusted for a rights issue. The example we use is the capital increase by Carlsberg in June 2008.

CARLSBERG CAPITAL INCREASE

Pre-increase data	
Number of shares:	76.3m
Share price:	DKK674
Market capitalisation:	DKK51.4bn
Book value of equity:	DKK18.6bn
Earnings per share, 2007:	DKK25.3

Post-increase data	
Number of new shares issued:	76.3m
Issue price:	DKK400
Proceeds of the issue:	DKK30.5bn
Pre-emptive subscription right:	one for every old share held
Eligibility date of new shares:	1 January 2008
For information:	€1 = DKK7.5

Accountants and lawyers are accustomed to apportioning the proceeds of a capital increase between the increase in authorised capital (the number of new shares issued multiplied by the par value of the share; for Carlsberg, the par value is DKK20, and the increase in authorised capital is therefore DKK1.5bn) and the increase in the share premium account (the remainder). Since the reader knows how to distinguish between the DKK1.5bn and the DKK30.5bn, we are confident he will know how to distinguish between the two meanings of "capital increase".

1/ SHARE ISSUE AND EARNINGS PER SHARE

A capital increase will change earnings per share instantaneously. If EPS decreases, there is said to be **dilution** of earnings; if it increases, there is said to be **accretion** (or the operation is said to be "earnings-enhancing", which may sound better). This dilution has nothing in common with the dilution of Section 39.1 but the name and is calculated differently. The one has to do with a shareholder's percentage of ownership, the other with earnings per share.

Consider Carlsberg, the shares of which carry a midrange P/E (26.6) warranted by the company's moderate risk and reasonable growth prospects, and Company A, where very weak prospects of EPS growth justify a low P/E (10). For both companies, shareholders require an after-tax rate of return on equity of 9%, and we will assume that both Carlsberg and Company A invest the funds raised by a capital increase at 9%; there is neither creation nor destruction of value on this occasion. For both, the value of equity capital therefore increases by the amount of the capital increase.

Carlsberg and Company A each increase the number of shares by 100% and raise DKK30.5bn which, invested at 9%, will increase their net earnings by DKK2.75bn. The impact of the capital increase will be as shown in the table below.

(in DKK)	Before capital increase					After capital increase			
	Market value of equity	P/E	Earnings	Number of shares	EPS	Market value of equity	Earnings	Number of shares	EPS
Carlsberg	51.4bn	26.6	1.9bn	76.3m	25.3	81.9bn	4.65bn	152.6m	30.5 (+20%)
Company A	51.4bn	10	5.14bn	76.3m	67.4	81.9bn	7.89bn	152.6m	51.7 (−23%)

Carlsberg's EPS increases by 20% but the operation does not create value. Similarly, Company A's EPS decreases by 23% but the operation does not destroy value. This demonstrates once again that earnings per share are not a reliable indicator of value creation or destruction. These changes are merely mechanical and depend fundamentally on:

• the company's P/E ratio; and
• the rate of return on the investments made with the proceeds of the share issue.

More generally, the rule the reader will want to retain is that any capital increase will:

• **dilute** EPS whenever the reciprocal of P/E is greater than the rate of return on the investments financed by the share issue;
• **be neutral** whenever the reciprocal of P/E is equal to this incremental return; and
• increase or **"enhance"** EPS whenever the reciprocal of P/E is less than incremental return.

It can easily be demonstrated that the earnings dilution occasioned by a capital increase at the market price is equal to:

$$\text{Change in EPS} = P\,/\,E \times \frac{\text{Capital raised}}{\text{Market capitalisation after capital increase}}$$

$$\times \left(\text{After-tax rate of return} - \frac{E}{P} \right)$$

For Carlsberg, any investment that generates a return per year greater than 3.8% (the reciprocal of P/E of 26.6) will increase earnings per share, whereas for Company A the bar is set higher at 10% (reciprocal of 10). Hence the appeal of issuing new shares when P/Es are high, even though no value is created.

In the short term, it is rare for funds raised by a capital increase to earn the required rate of return immediately, either because they are sitting in the bank waiting for the investments to be made or because some period of time must elapse before the achieved rate of return reaches the required level. Consequently, it is not rare for EPS to decrease following a capital increase – but this does not necessarily mean that value is being destroyed.

Three measures of EPS dilution might be distinguished here:

1. Instantaneous dilution with no reinvestment of the funds raised. This is seldom calculated because it holds no interest.
2. Dilution assuming investment of the funds at the risk-free rate of interest. This is the measure that financial analysts generally calculate.
3. Dilution with reinvestment of the funds. This is obviously the measure of most interest, but it is difficult to get hold of because it requires forecasting the rate of return on future investments.

In the long term, EPS dilution should normally be offset by the earnings generated by the investment financed by the capital increase. It is therefore necessary to study the expected rate of return on that investment, for it will determine the future course of the company's value.

With the wisdom that derives from experience, and notwithstanding what any theory might indicate, we could almost say that whenever P/Es are high, it is a crime for a company not to issue new shares!

2/ SHARE ISSUE AND VALUE OF EQUITY CAPITAL

To say that the book value of a company's equity increases after a capital increase is to state the obvious, since the proceeds of the share issue are included in that book value.

It is of more interest to compare the percentage increase in book value with the ratio of the proceeds of the capital increase to the market value of equity and to calculate the growth in value per share.

Let us go back to the example of Carlsberg and make several different assumptions about market value (only the last of which is true). In all cases, we set the proceeds of the capital increase at the actual percentage level, which is 60% of the group's market capitalisation before the transaction.

(in DKKbn)	Case 1	Case 2	Case 3 (real)
Book value of equity	18.6	18.6	18.6
Market value of equity	30	40	51.4
Capital increase	18	24	30.5
Dilution	37%[2]	37%	37%
Increase in book value	+97%	+129%	+164%

2 $18/(18 + 30)$.

At constant capital structure, the increase in equity allows a parallel increase in debt and thus in the company's overall financial resources. This phenomenon is all the more important when the company is profitable and its market value is greater than its book value. Here we link up again to the PBR (price-to-book ratio) notion that we examined in Chapter 23.

A capital increase may increase a company's financial power considerably, with relatively little dilution of control.

- If market value of equity coincides with book value, the dilution of control will be accompanied by a similar increase in the company's overall financial resources.
- If market value is greater than book value, the dilution of control will be countered by a greater increase in financial resources.
- If market value is less than book value, the dilution of control will be accompanied by a lesser increase in financial resources.

3/ BOOK VALUE PER SHARE

Let us continue with the example of Carlsberg, this time changing the issue price of the new shares but keeping the size of the issue at 76.3m shares.

Issue price	100	244	400
Book value per share before share issue	243.8	243.8	243.8
Book value per share after share issue	171.9 (−30%)	243.9 (0%)	321.89 (+32%)

At the time of a share issue, book value per share increases if the share price is greater, and decreases if the share price is less, than book value before the capital increase. This is self-evident since in the one case the issue price is higher than book value per share and in the other it is lower.

This increase or decrease also applies to the rights of the old shareholders in respect of the book value of equity.

Consider a fast-growing company worth €40m with a book value of €1m. If it carries out a €40m capital increase that doubles its market value, the old shareholders' equity rights are multiplied by 20.5 (from €1m to €20.5m)! For them, the capital increase locks in what was previously just a potential. If the company were to be wound up right after the capital increase, the old shareholders would have a right to €20.5m when they had put in only €1m, whereas the new shareholders would have a right to €20.5m when they had put in €40m. In a way, this imbalance is the "price of admission" when investing in such a profitable company – but also one entailing high risk, as shown, for example, by the Internet companies.

Book value per share is diluted for old shareholders if the market value of the company's shares is less than the book value (PBR $<$ 1). It is increased if market value is greater than book value (PBR $>$ 1).

SUMMARY

The summary of this chapter can be downloaded from www.vernimmen.com.

A share issue is a sale of shares, the proceeds of which go to the company and thus indirectly to all shareholders who will therefore share future cash flows.

In the theory of markets in equilibrium, the cost of a capital increase is equal to the cost of equity given the valuation of the shares. This is neither the dividend yield nor, except very rarely, the earnings yield (reciprocal of P/E). It is a forward-looking cost and one to which there is no firm commitment on the company's part. (*Ex post*, it may be quite different: exorbitantly high or actually negative.) Value is created for old shareholders if the capital increase captures the value creation stemming from the new funds.

Other theoretical approaches provide a wealth of insights. A capital increase tends to benefit lenders to the detriment of shareholders insofar as the market re-rates the company's debt to reflect the reduced risk of its share issue. A capital increase tends to favour old shareholders over new, via a transfer of value, if the rate of return on new investments is correctly anticipated. The *a priori* negative signal that any capital increase sends – namely, that the shares are overvalued – has to be countered (signalling theory). A capital increase is a subject of acrimonious discussions between managers and shareholders. It entails a temporary reduction in informational asymmetry (agency theory).

The reduction in equity rights of a shareholder that neither puts in nor takes out funds on the occasion of a capital increase is called real dilution. In the case of a rights issue, real dilution is different from apparent or overall dilution.

This dilution of power and control is to be distinguished from the dilution (or its opposite) in the company's financial parameters in the short term. Any share issue increases EPS when the reciprocal of P/E is less than the after-tax rate of return on reinvested funds. Book value per share is diluted for old shareholders if the company's market capitalisation is less than its book value.

QUESTIONS

1/ What is important in a capital increase where each shareholder takes his proportionate share of the issue?

2/ What is dilution of control?

3/ When are there three different measures of dilution of control? What are they?

4/ What is the purpose of subscription rights? What is their theoretical value?

5/ At what price is a capital increase effected when made with an issue of subscription rights? When made without?

6/ How can a company be sold by means of a capital increase?

SECTION 4

7/What is the consequence of a capital increase on EPS in the short term? In the long term?

8/Should there be an issue of new shares whenever the share price is overvalued?

9/Why are the most profitable companies the ones that gain the most by issuing new shares?

10/When an investment bank underwrites an issue of new shares, it charges the issuing company a commission. How is this commission analysed using options theory?

11/Does a capital increase with pre-emptive subscription rights signal overvaluation of the shares more strongly than one without?

EXERCISES

1/(a) A company has a market value of €100m divided into 1 million shares. It proposes to raise funds equivalent to 25% of its value by issuing new shares at €75. Calculate the value of the subscription right, the apparent, technical and real dilutions, the adjustment coefficient and the subscription ratio.

(b) A shareholder holds 90 shares of the company above. Show the bonus share aspect inherent in a capital increase of this kind.

(c) If the shareholder does not subscribe to the new issue, what is his new ownership percentage? Calculate it in two different ways.

(d) Show that if all shareholders subscribe to the capital increase, the issue price does not matter.

(e) What is EPS after the capital increase if previously it was €10?

(f) If the book value of equity was €80m before the capital increase, what is the percentage increase in it? What is the book value per share before the operation? What is it after the operation?

(g) Answer questions (a) through (f) again assuming that, after a sharp run-up in share prices, the market value of the company has doubled. The amount of the capital increase is still €25m, but the issue price rises to €150. What conclusions do you draw?

2/Case study: Saint Gobain share issue in June 2009.

Issue of 109.3m new shares, or 2 new for every 7 old, with pre-emptive subscription rights

Number of shares before the capital increase:	382.6m
Issue price:	€14
Eligibility date of new shares:	1 January 2009
Latest price:	€27.75
Issue proceeds (gross):	€1.5bn.

(a) Compare consolidated shareholders' equity (€14.3bn) with the amount of the capital increase, the amount of the latter to market capitalisation before the operation. What do you conclude?

(b) Calculate the real dilution entailed by the capital increase.

(c) Calculate the share that new shareholders will hold in the capital and the shareholders' equity of Saint Gobain.

(d) What is your conclusion?

Questions

1/ *Not much.*

2/ *Reduction in the equity rights of shareholders that do not subscribe to the capital increase in proportion to their current shareholding.*

3/ *When there is a capital increase along with an issue of pre-emptive subscription rights. Apparent dilution (ignoring the value of the rights), real dilution (the one that matters) and technical dilution (solely attributable to the rights).*

4/ *Subscription rights ensure that the old shareholders can take part in the share issue if they wish.*

5/ *At market value. At the price guaranteed by the bank underwriting the share issue.*

6/ *By having a very large capital increase with a very small issue premium.*

7/ *Generally, dilution. It depends on the returns generated by the projects that are financed.*

8/ *In theory, yes. In practice, this is quite difficult to do.*

9/ *Because this is the virtuous circle of the share issue.*

10/ *The commission represents the price of the put option that the company buys from the bank. In effect, the company is buying the right to sell the newly issued shares to the bank at the guaranteed price.*

11/ *Yes, because the substantial discount provides a cushion against a sharp drop in the market price and because the banks were unwilling to get caught up in a process that would have led to them guaranteeing a price close to the market price.*

Exercises

A detailed Excel version of the solutions is available at www.vernimmen.com.

1/ (a) *Subscription right = 6.25, apparent dilution = 25, real dilution = 20, technical dilution = 5, adjustment coefficient = 0.9375, subscription ratio = 1 new for 3 old.*

(b) *The shareholder has 90 subscription rights. If he sells 72 of them and keeps 18, he will be able to buy 6 new shares without expending any cash. This is equivalent to receiving 6 bonus shares.*

(c) $(90 + 6)/(1\,000\,000 + 333\,333) = 0.0072 = (90/1\,000\,000) \times (1 - 20\%)$.

(d) *Since the control percentages are unchanged and the amount of the increase is fixed, the price has no effect.*

(e) *Before the funds raised are invested, EPS falls to 7.5.*

(f) *Book value of equity increases by 31.25%. Book value per share drops from €80 before to €78.75 after.*

(g) *Subscription right = 7.14, apparent dilution = 14.3, real dilution = 11.1, adjustment coefficient = 0.9643, subscription ratio = 1 new for 6 old. Book value per share after: €90.*

2/ *Saint-Gobain case study.*

(a) *The share issue increases the market cap by 14% and the book shareholders' equity by 10%.*

(b) *Apparent dilution is $109.3/(109.3 + 382.6) = 22\%$ but real dilution is $1.5/(1.5 + 10.6) = 12\%$.*

(c) $109.3/(109.3 + 382.6) = 22\%$ *of capital and* $1.5/(1.5 + 14.3) = 9\%$ *of equity.*

(d) *As Saint Gobain's prospects have been significantly hit by the crisis, the new shareholders enter the capital at a discount compared to book equity.*

BIBLIOGRAPHY

P. Asquith, D. Mullins, Equity issues and offering dilution, *Journal of Financial Economics*, **15**(1), 61–89, January–February 1986.

H. DeAngelo, L. DeAngelo, R. Stulz, Seasoned equity offerings, market timing and the corporate life-cycle? *Journal of Financial Economics*, **95**(3), 275–295, March–February 2010.

A. Dittmar, A. Thakor, Why do firms issue equity? *Journal of Finance*, **62**(1), 1–54, February 2007.

A. Kalay, A. Shimrat, Firm value and seasoned equity issues: Price pressure, wealth redistribution, or negative information, *Journal of Financial Economics*, **19**(1), 109–126, September 1987.

T. Loughran, J. Ritter, The new issues puzzle, *Journal of Finance*, **50**(1), 23–51, March 1995.

R. Masulis, A. Korwar, Seasoned equity offerings: An empirical investigation, *Journal of Financial Economics*, **15**(1), 91–118, January–February 1986.

S. Myers, N. Majluf, Corporate financing and investment decisions when firms have information that investors do not have, *Journal of Financial Economics*, **13**(2), 187–221, June 1984.

Section V
FINANCIAL MANAGEMENT

Part One
Corporate governance and financial engineering

In this part, we will examine the issues an investment banker deals with on a daily basis when assisting a company in its strategic decisions which include:

* organising a group;
* launching an IPO;[1]
* selling assets, a subsidiary or the company;
* merging or demerging;
* restructuring and more.

In short, the stuff that all-nighters are made of! As the reader will soon realise, financial engineering raises and solves many questions of corporate governance.

1 *Initial public offering.*

Chapter 40
CHOICE OF CORPORATE STRUCTURE

What a cast of characters!

Section 40.1
SHAREHOLDER STRUCTURE

Our objective in this section is to demonstrate the importance of a company's shareholder structure. While the study of finance generally includes a clear description of why it is important to value a company and its equity, analysis of who owns its shares and how shareholders are organised is often neglected. Yet in practice, this is where investment bankers often look first.

There are several reasons for looking closely at the shareholder base of a company. Firstly, the shareholders theoretically determine the company's strategy, but we must understand who really has power in the company, the shareholders or the managers. You will undoubtedly recognise the mark of "agency theory". This theory provides a theoretical explanation of shareholder–manager problems.

Secondly, we must know the objectives of the shareholders when they are also the managers. Wealth? Power? Fame? In some cases, the shareholder is also a customer or supplier of the company. In an agricultural cooperative, for example, the shareholders are upstream in the production process. The cooperative company becomes a tool serving the needs of the producers, rather than a profit centre in its own right. This is probably why many agricultural cooperatives are not very profitable.

Lastly, disagreement between shareholders can paralyse a company, particularly a family-owned company.

1/ DEFINITION OF SHAREHOLDER STRUCTURE

The shareholder structure (or shareholder base) is the percentage ownership and the percentage of voting rights held by different shareholders. When a company issues shares with multiple voting rights or non-voting preference shares or represents a cascade of holding companies, these two concepts are separate and distinct. A shareholder with 33% of the shares with double-voting rights will have more control over a company where the remaining shares are widely held than will a shareholder with 45% of the shares with single voting rights if two other shareholders hold 25% and 30%. A shareholder who holds 20% of a company's shares directly and 40% of the shares of a company that holds the other 80%, will have rights to 52% of the company's earnings but will be in the minority for decision-taking. In the case of companies that issue equity-linked instruments (convertible bonds, warrants, stock options) attention must be paid to the number of shares currently outstanding vs. the fully-diluted number of potential shares.

Shareholder structure is the study of how power is distributed among the different shareholders and potential shareholders.

Lastly, without placing much importance on them, we should mention **nominee** (warehousing) **agreements**. Under a nominee agreement, the "real" shareholders sell their shares to a "nominee" and make a commitment to repurchase them at a specific price, usually in an effort to remain anonymous. A shareholder may enter into a nominee agreement for one of several reasons: transaction confidentiality, group restructuring or deconsolidation, etc. Conceptually, the nominee extends credit to the shareholder and bears counterparty and market risk. If the issuer runs into trouble during the life of the nominee agreement, the original shareholder will be loath to buy back the shares at a price that no longer reflects reality. As a result, nominee agreements are difficult to enforce. Moreover, they can be invalidated if they create an inequality among shareholders. We do not recommend the use of nominee agreements.

2/ General framework

Theoretically, in all jurisdictions, the ultimate decision-making power lies with the shareholders of a company. They exercise it through the assembly of a shareholders Annual General Meeting (AGM). Nevertheless, the types of decisions can differ from one country to another. Generally, shareholders decide on:

- appointment of board members;
- appointment of auditors;
- approval of annual accounts;
- distribution of dividends;
- changes in articles of association (i.e. the constitution of a company);
- mergers;
- capital increases and share buy-backs;
- dissolution (i.e. the end of the company).

In most countries – depending on the type of decision – there are two types of shareholder vote: ordinary and extraordinary.

At an Ordinary General Meeting (OGM) of shareholders, shareholders vote on matters requiring a simple majority of voting shares. These include decisions regarding the ordinary course of the company's business such as approving the financial statements, payment of dividends and appointment and removal of members of the board of directors.

At an Extraordinary General Meeting (EGM) of shareholders, shareholders vote on matters that require a change in the company's operating and financial policies: changes in the articles of association, share issues, mergers, asset contributions, demergers, share buy-backs, etc. These decisions require a qualified majority. Depending on the country and on the legal form of the company this qualified majority is generally two-thirds or three-quarters of outstanding voting rights.

The main levels of control of a company in various countries are as follows:

	Supermajority	Type of decision
Brazil	1/2	Changes in the object of the company Merger, demerger Dissolution Changes in preferred share characteristics
China	2/3	Increase or reduction of the registered capital Merger, split-up Dissolution of the company Change of the company form
France	2/3	Changes in the articles of association Merger, demerger Capital increase and decrease Dissolution
Germany	3/4	Changes in the articles of association Reduction and increase of capital Major structural decisions Merger or transformation of the company
India	3/4	Merger
Italy	—	Defined in the articles of association
Netherlands	2/3	Restrictions in pre-emption rights Capital reduction
Russia	3/4	Changes in the articles of association Reorganisation of the company Liquidation Reduction and increase in capital Purchase of own shares Approval of a deal representing more than 50% of the company's assets
Spain	—	Defined in the articles of association
Switzerland	2/3	Changes in purpose Issue of shares with increased voting powers Limitations of pre-emption rights Change of location Dissolution
UK	3/4	Altering the articles of association Disapplying members' statutory pre-emption rights on issues of further shares for cash Capital decrease Approving the giving of financial assistance/purchase of own shares by a private company or, off market, by a public company Procuring the winding up of a company by the court Voluntarily winding up a company
USA	—	Defined on a state level and frequently in the articles of association

SECTION 5

Shareholders holding less than the blocking minority (if this concept exists in the country) of a company that has another large shareholder have a limited number of options open to them. They cannot change the company objectives or the way it is managed. At best, they can force compliance with disclosure rules, or call for an audit or an EGM.

Their power is most often limited to being that of a nay-sayer. In other words, a small shareholder can be a thorn in management's side, but no more. Nevertheless, the voice of the minority shareholder has become a lot louder and a number of them have formed associations to defend their interests. Shareholder activism has become a defence tool where the law had failed to provide one.

It should be noted that in some countries (Sweden, Norway, Portugal) minority shareholders can force the payment of a minimum dividend.

A shareholder who holds a blocking minority (one-quarter or third of the shares plus one share depending on the country and the legal form of the company) can veto any decision taken in an extraordinary shareholders meeting that would change the company's articles of association, company objects or called-up share capital.

A blocking minority is in a particularly strong position when the company is in trouble, because it is then that the need for operational and financial restructuring is the most pressing. The power of blocking minority shareholders can also be decisive in periods of rapid growth, when the company needs additional capital.

The notion of a blocking minority is closely linked to exerting control over changes in the company's articles of association. Consequently, the more specific and inflexible the articles of association are, the more power the holder of a blocking minority wields.

A blocking minority does not give its holder control over decisions taken at ordinary shareholders meetings (dividend payout, etc.). It gives veto power, not direct power.

3/ The different types of shareholders

(a) The family-owned company

By "family-owned" we mean that the shareholders have been made up of members of the same family for several generations and, often through a holding company, exert significant influence over management. This is still the dominant model in Europe. The following table shows the shareholder base of the 50 largest companies by market capitalisation in several countries (2010).

However, this type of shareholder structure is on the decline for several reasons:

Shareholding	Germany	Spain	USA	France	Italy	UK
Widely spread	36%	20%	90%	42%	18%	78%
Family (and non-listed)	18%	20%	8%	30%	38%	12%
State and local authorities	8%	2%	0%	16%	16%	2%
Other listed firm	16%	32%	2%	4%	14%	6%
Financial institution	16%	20%	0%	6%	10%	2%
Other	6%	6%	0%	2%	4%	0%

Source: Company data, Thomson One Banker

SECTION 5

- some new or capital-intensive industries, such as telecoms, media and energy/utilities, require so much capital that a family-owned structure is not viable. Indeed, family ownership is more suited to consumer goods, retailing, services, processing, etc.;
- financial markets have matured and financial savings are now properly rewarded, so that, with rare exceptions, diversification is a better investment strategy than concentration on a specific risk (see Section II of this book);
- increasingly, family-owned companies are being managed on the basis of financial criteria, prompting the family group either to exit the capital or to dilute the family's interests in a larger pool of investors that it no longer controls.

Lastly, there are generally no tax incentives for a company to remain family-owned. In fact, family members who are passive investors in the company may be penalised through inheritance taxes and wealth taxes.

(b) Business angels

Business angels are generally former executives or majority shareholders. They invest a few tens or hundreds of thousand of euros, bringing advice and their networks to help entrepreneurs to launch their companies. Some get lucky, like the business angels that financed Facebook when it was based in a Harvard University student's room. Their failure rate is very high as they invest at the most risky stage of a company's life.

(c) Private equity funds

Today, private equity funds, financed by insurance companies, pension funds or wealthy investors, play a major role. In most cases these funds specialise in a certain type of investment: venture capital, development capital and LBOs, which correspond to a company's different stages of maturity.

Venture capital funds focus on bringing seed capital, i.e. equity, to startups to finance their early developments, or to struggling companies, buying their debts to take them over and restructure them.

Development capital funds give an acquisitive company in a consolidating market the financial resources it needs to achieve its goals.

LBO funds invest in companies put up for sale by a group looking to refocus on its core business or by a family-held group faced with succession problems, or help a company whose shares are depressed (in the opinion of the management) to delist itself in a **public to private** (P-to-P) transaction. LBO funds are keen to get full control over a company in order to reap all of the rewards and also to make it possible to restructure the company as they think best, without having to worry about the interests of minority shareholders. Therefore, they usually prefer the target companies not to be listed (or to be delisted if the target was public) but the fund itself can be listed.

Managed by teams of investment professionals whose compensation is linked to performance, these funds have a limited life span (no more than 10 years). Before the fund is closed, the companies that the fund has acquired are resold, floated on the stock exchange or the fund's investments are taken over by another fund.

Some private equity funds take a minority stake in listed companies, a PIPE (private investment in public equity), helping the management to revitalise the company so as to make a capital gain. Thus, in 2006, Blackstone bought a 4.5% stake in Deutsche Telekom for $3.3bn.

Private equity funds are playing a growing role in the economy and are a real alternative to a listing on the stock exchange. They solve agency problems by putting in place strict reporting from the management which is incentivised through management packages and the pressure of debt[1] (LBO funds).

1 *See Chapter 45 devoted to LBOs.*

They also bring a cash culture to optimise working capital management and limit capital expenditure to reasonably value-creating investments. Private equity funds are ready to bring additional equity to finance acquisitions with an industrial logic. They also bring to management a capacity to listen, to advise and to exchange, which is far greater than that provided by most institutional investors. They are professional shareholders who have only one aim – to create value – and they do not hesitate to align the management of companies they invest in with that objective.

(d) Institutional investors

Institutional investors are banks, insurance companies, pension funds and unit trusts that manage money on behalf of private individuals.

Collectively they can be the longest-standing shareholder of many listed companies and play mainly a passive role. However, new regulations on corporate governance may push them to vote at annual general meetings to defeat some resolutions they do not like (share issue without pre-emption rights, voting limits, stock option plans that are too generous, etc.).

Some of them have started to play a far more active role and are called **activist funds**. They publicly put pressure on underperforming management teams, suggesting corrective measures to improve value creation. One of them, TCI, prompted the dismantling of ABN-Amro in 2007.

(e) Financial holding companies

Large European financial holding companies such as Deutsche Bank, Paribas, Mediobanca, Société Générale de Belgique, etc. played a major role in creating and financing large groups. In a sense, they played the role of (then-deficient) capital markets. Their gradual disappearance or mutation has led to the breakup of core shareholder groups and cross-shareholdings. Today, in emerging countries (Korea, India, Colombia), large industrial and financial conglomerates play their role (Samsung, Tata, Votorantim, etc.).

(f) Employee-shareholders

Many companies have invited their employees to become shareholders. In most of these cases, employees hold a small proportion of the shares, although the majority in a few cases. This shareholder group, loyal and non-volatile, lends a degree of stability to the capital and, in general, strengthens the position of the majority shareholder, if any, and of the management. The main schemes to incentivise employees are:

- **Direct ownership.** Employees and management can invest directly in the shares of the company. In LBOs, private equity sponsors bring the management into the shareholding structure to minimise agency costs.
- **Employee stock ownership programmes (ESOPs).** ESOPs consist in granting shares to employees as a form of compensation. Alternatively, the shares are acquired by shareholders but the firm will offer free shares so as to encourage employees to invest in the shares of the company. The shares will be held by a trust (or employee savings plan) for the employees. Such programmes can include lock-up clauses to maintain the incentive aspect and limit flow-back (see Chapter 26). In this way, the shares allocated to each employee will vest (i.e. become available) gradually over time.
- **Stock options.** Stock options are a right to subscribe to new shares or new shares held by the company as treasury stocks at a certain point in time.

For service companies and fast-growing companies, it is key to incentivise employees and management with shares or stock options, as the key assets of such companies are their people. For other companies, offering stock to employees can be part of a broader effort to improve employee relations (all types of companies) and promote the company's image internally. The success of such a policy largely depends on the overall corporate mood. In large companies, employees can hold up to 10% (Saint-Gobain 7.8%). Lehman, the US investment bank, was one of the listed companies with the largest employee shareholdings (c. 25%) when it went into meltdown in 2008.

Regardless of the type of company and its motivation for making employees shareholders, you should keep in mind that the special relationship between the company and the employee-shareholder cannot last forever. Prudent investment principles dictate that the employee should not invest too heavily in the shares of the company that pays their salaries, because in so doing they, in fact, compound the "everyday life" risks they are running.[2]

Basically, the company should be particularly fast-growing and safe before the employee agrees to a long-term participation in the fruits of its expansion. Most often, this condition is not met. Moreover, just because employees hold stock options does not mean they will be loyal or long-term shareholders. The LBO models we will study in Chapter 45 become dangerous when they make a majority of the employees shareholders. In a crisis, the employees may be keener to protect their jobs than to vote for a painful restructuring. When limited to a small number of employees, however, LBOs create a stable, internal group of shareholders.

2 *Enron's and Lehman's employees can confirm this!*

(g) Governments

In Europe and the USA, governments' role as the major shareholders of listed groups is fading, even if they are still majority shareholders of large industry players (Deutsche Bahn, EDF, SNCF) or playing a key role in some groups like Deutsche Telekom, EADS, ENI. State ownership had a period of revival thanks to the economic crisis, as some groups were taken over to avoid collapses (General Motors, RBS), or funds were injected through equity issues to reinforce financial institutions (Citi, ING, etc.).

At the same time, **sovereign wealth funds**, mostly created by emerging countries and financed thanks to reserves from staples, are gaining importance as long-term shareholders. They are normally very financially minded, but their opacity, their size (often above

SECTION 5

€50bn or €100bn) and their strong connections with mostly undemocratic states are worrying to some. As of December 2010, they had c. \$4200bn under management. The most well known include Abu Dhabi Investment Authority (ADIA, \$627bn), the Government Pension Fund of Norway (\$512bn), Saudi Arabian Monetary Agency (SAMA, \$439bn), Government of Singapore Investment Corporation (GIC) and Temasek in Singapore (\$380bn), China Investment Company (CIC, \$332bn), Kuwait Investment Authority (KIA, \$203bn), the Reserve Fund of Russia (\$142bn), etc. They are majority shareholders of a number of firms (Travelodge, Tussauds, Aston Martin, P&O, etc.) and minority shareholders in some listed firms such as the London Stock Exchange, KKR, Carlyle, Daimler, Lagardère, etc.

4/ Joint ventures

Most technological or industrial alliances take place through **joint ventures**, often held 50/50, or through joint partnerships that perform services at cost for the benefit of their shareholders.

These often-ephemeral companies can easily fall victim to boardroom paralysis. When business is booming, one or both of the partners may want to take it over entirely. Conversely, when the joint venture's fortunes are fading, both partners may be looking for the exit.

Preparing the potential future exit of one partner is key when creating a JV. Joint venture agreements often have **exit clauses** intended to resolve conflicts. Some examples are:

- a buy-sell provision, also called a **Dutch clause** or a **shotgun clause**. For example, shareholder A offers to sell his shares at a price X to shareholder B. Either B agrees to buy the shares at price X or, if he refuses, he must offer his stake to A at the same price X. Another form calls for a simple auction among shareholders;
- an appraisal clause, which states that the price of a transaction between shareholders shall be determined by independent appraisal.

In sum, the joint venture company – like any company – must have a coherent strategy and set of objectives. A 50/50 sharing arrangement injects numerous difficult-to-resolve problems into the management equation.

5/ Shareholders' agreement

Minority shareholders can protect their interests by concluding a shareholders' agreement with other shareholders.

A shareholders' agreement is a legal document signed by several shareholders to define their future relationships and complement the company's articles of association.

Most of the time, the shareholders' agreement is confidential except for listed companies in countries which require its publication in order for it to be valid.

They mainly contain two sets of clauses:

- clauses that organise corporate governance such as breakdown of directors' seats, nomination of the Chairman, of the CEO, of the auditors; how major decisions are taken, including capex; financing, dividend policy, acquisitions, share issues; how to vote during annual general meetings; what kind of information is disclosed to shareholders, etc;

- clauses that organise the sale or purchase of shares in the future: lock up, right of first refusal if one shareholder wants to exit, tag-along (to force the disposal of 100% of the capital if one of the majority shareholders wishes to exit) or drag-along (to allow minority shareholders to benefit from the same transaction conditions if the majority shareholder is selling), caps and floors, etc.

As we will see below, the stock exchange probably offers the minority shareholder the best protection.

Section 40.2
HOW TO STRENGTHEN CONTROL OVER A COMPANY

Defensive measures for maintaining control of a company always carry a cost. From a purely financial point of view, this is perfectly normal: there are no free lunches!

Measures to preserve control are not only costly to put in place but also effectively preclude the company from accessing certain financial instruments. These costs are borne by current shareholders and ultimately by the company itself in the form of a higher cost of capital.

With this in mind, let us now take a look at the various takeover defences. We will see that they vary greatly depending on the country, on the existence or absence of a regulatory framework and on the powers granted to companies and their executives. Certain countries, such as the UK and, to a lesser extent, France and Italy, regulate anti-takeover measures strictly, while others, such as Germany and the USA, allow companies much more leeway.

Broadly speaking, countries where financial markets play a significant role in evaluating management performance, because companies are more widely held, have more stringent regulations. This is the case in the UK and France.

Conversely, countries where capital is concentrated in relatively few hands have either more flexible regulation or no regulation at all. This goes hand-in-hand with the articles of association of the companies, which ensure existing management a high level of protection. In Germany, half of the seats on the board of directors are reserved for employees, and board members can be replaced only by a 75% majority vote.

Paradoxically, when the market's power to inflict punishment on companies is unchecked, companies and their executives may feel such insecurity that they agree to protect themselves via the articles of association. Sometimes this contractual protection is to the detriment of the company's welfare and of free market principles. This practice is common in the US.

The extremely long discussions over the European Directive on public offers (which was finally adopted in 2004) demonstrate precisely this difficulty: how to coax very different stock market regulations from one country to another toward a common standard. In the UK, the sanctity of the market is the rule, whereas Germany prizes its respect for employee rights. France stands somewhere between the two. The Directive attempts to generalise certain guiding principles. In particular, it states that management should have only limited ability to implement defensive measures without prior consultation with shareholders.

Defensive measures fall into four categories:

- Separate management control from financial control:

    - different classes of shares: shares with multiple voting rights and non-voting shares;
    - holding companies;
    - limited partnerships.

- Control shareholder changes:

    - right of approval;
    - pre-emption rights.

- Strengthen the position of loyal shareholders:

    - reserved capital increases;
    - share buy-backs and cancellations;
    - mergers and other tie-ups;
    - employee shareholdings;
    - warrants.

- Exploit legal and regulatory protection:

    - regulations;
    - voting caps;
    - strategic assets;
    - change of control provisions.

1/ SEPARATING MANAGEMENT CONTROL FROM FINANCIAL CONTROL

(a) Different classes of shares: shares with multiple voting rights and non-voting shares

As an exception to the general rule, under which the number of votes attributed to each share must be directly proportional to the percentage of the capital it represents (principle of one share, one vote), companies in some countries have the right to issue multiple-voting shares or non-voting shares.

In the Netherlands, the USA and the Scandinavian countries, dual classes of shares are not infrequent. The company issues two (or more) types of shares (generally named A shares and B shares) with the same financial rights but with different voting rights.

French corporate law provides for the possibility of double-voting shares but, contrary to dual-class shares, all shareholders can benefit from the double-voting rights if they hold the shares for a certain time.

Multiple-voting shares can be particularly powerful; for example the Ford family has 40% of voting rights while it holds only 4% of the shares. Google and Facebook have also put in place this type of capital structure. These dual-class shares can appear as unfair and contrary to the principle that the person who provides the capital gets the power in a company. Some countries (Italy, Spain, Belgium and Germany) have outlawed dual-class shares.

Issuing non-voting shares is similar to issuing dual-class shares because some of the shareholders will bring capital without getting voting power. Nevertheless, issuing non-voting shares is a more widely spread practice than issuing dual-class shares. Actually, in compensation for giving up their voting rights, holders of non-voting shares usually get preferential treatment regarding dividends (fixed dividend, increased dividend compared to ordinary shareholders, etc.). Accordingly, non-voting (preference) shares are not perceived as unfair but as a different arbitrage for the investor between return, risk and power in the company.

(b) Holding companies

Holding companies can be useful but their intensive use leads to complex, multi-tiered shareholding structures. As you might imagine, they present both advantages and disadvantages.

Suppose an investor holds 51% of a holding company, which in turn holds 51% of a second holding company, which in turn holds 51% of an industrial company. Although he holds only 13% of the capital of this industrial company, the investor uses a cascade of holding companies to maintain control of the industrial company.

A holding company allows a shareholder to maintain control over a company, because a structure with a holding disperses the minority shareholders. Even if the industrial company were floated on the stock exchange, the minority shareholders in the different holding companies would not be able to sell their stakes.

Maximum marginal personal income tax is generally higher than income taxes on dividends from a subsidiary. Therefore, a holding company structure allows the controlling shareholder to draw off dividends with a minimum tax bite and use them to buy more shares in the industrial company.

Technically, a holding company can "trap" minority shareholders; in practice, this situation often leads to an ongoing conflict between shareholders. For this reason, holding companies are usually based on a group of core shareholders intimately involved in the management of the company.

A two-tiered holding company structure often exists, where:

- a holding company controls the operating company;
- a top holding company holds the controlling holding company. The shareholders of the top holding company are the core group. This top holding company's main purpose is to buy back the shares of minority shareholders seeking to sell some of their shares.

Often, a holding company is formed to represent the family shareholders prior to an IPO. For example, Portman Baela SL is a holding company formed to hold the del Pino family's stakes in Ferrovial.

(c) Limited share partnerships (LSP)

A limited share partnership introduces a complete separation between management and financial ownership of the company.

A limited share partnership is a company where the share capital is divided into shares, but with two types of partners:

- several limited partners with the status of shareholders, whose liability is limited to the amount of their investment in the company. A limited share partnership is akin to a public limited company in this respect;

- one or more general partners, who are jointly liable, to an unlimited extent, for the debts of the company. Senior executives of the company are usually general partners, with limited partners being barred from the executive suite.

The company's articles of association determine how present and future executives are to be chosen. These top managers have the most extensive powers to act on behalf of the company in all circumstances. They can be fired only under the terms specified in the articles of association. In some countries, the general partners can limit their financial liability by setting up a (limited liability) family holding company. In addition, the LSP structure allows a change in management control of the operating company to take place within the holding company. For example, a father can hand over the reins to his son, while the holding company continues to perform its management functions.

Thus, theoretically, the chief executive of a limited share partnership can enjoy absolute and irrevocable power to manage the company without owning a single share. Management control does not derive from financial control as in a public limited company, but from the stipulations of the by-laws, in accordance with applicable law. Several large listed companies have adopted limited share partnership form, including Merck KGaA, Michelin and Hermès.

2/ CONTROLLING SHAREHOLDER CHANGES

(a) Right of approval

The right of approval, written into a company's articles of association, enables a company to avoid "undesirable" shareholders. This clause is frequently found in family-owned companies or in companies with a delicate balance between shareholders. The right of approval governs the relationship between partners or shareholders of the company; be careful not to confuse it with the type of approval required to purchase certain companies (see below).

Technically, the right of approval clause requires all partners to obtain the approval of the company prior to selling any of their shares. The company must render its decision within a specified time period. If no decision is rendered, the approval is deemed granted.

If it refuses, the company, its board of directors, executive committee, senior executives or a third party must buy back the shares within a specified period of time, or the shareholder can consummate the initially planned sale.

The purchase price is set by agreement between the parties, or in the event that no agreement is reached, by independent appraisal.

Right of approval clauses might not be applied when shares are sold between shareholders or between a shareholder, his spouse or his ascendants and descendants.

(b) Pre-emption rights

Equivalent to the right of approval, the pre-emption clause gives a category of shareholders or all shareholders a priority right to acquire any shares offered for sale. Companies whose existing shareholders want to increase their stake or control changes in the capital use this clause. The board of directors, the chief executive or any other authorised person can decide how shares are divided amongst the shareholders.

Technically, pre-emption rights procedures are similar to those governing the right of approval.

Most of the time, pre-emption rights do not apply in the case of inherited shares, liquidation of a married couple's community property, or if a shareholder sells shares to his spouse, ascendants or descendants.

Right of approval and pre-emption right clauses constitute a means of controlling changes in the shareholder structure of a company. If the clause is written into the articles of association and applies to all shareholders, it can prevent any undesirable third party from obtaining control of the company. These clauses cannot block a sale of shares indefinitely, however. The existing shareholders must always find a solution that allows a sale to take place if they do not wish to buy.

3/ STRENGTHENING THE POSITION OF LOYAL SHAREHOLDERS

(a) Reserved share issues

In some countries, a company can issue new shares on terms that are highly dilutive for the existing shareholders. For example, to fend off a challenge from ACS, the German construction group Hochtief, issued 9% of its share capital to the sovereign wealth fund Qatar Holding in December 2010.

The new shares can be purchased either for cash or for contributed assets. For example, a family holding company can contribute assets to the operating company to strengthen its control over this company.

(b) Mergers

Mergers are, first and foremost, a method for achieving strategic and industrial goals. As far as controlling the capital of a company is concerned, a merger can have the same effect as a reserved capital increase, by diluting the stake of a hostile shareholder or bringing in a new friendly shareholder. We will look at the technical aspects in Chapter 44.

The risk, of course, is that the new shareholders, initially brought in to support existing management, will gradually take over control of the company.

(c) Share buy-backs and cancellations

This technique, which we studied in Chapter 38 as a financial technique, can also be used to strengthen control over the capital of a company. The company offers to repurchase a portion of outstanding shares with the intention of cancelling them. As a result, the percentage ownership of the shareholders who do not subscribe to the repurchase offer increases. In fact, a company can regularly repurchase shares. For example, Peugeot regularly uses this method in order to strengthen the control of the family shareholders.

(d) Employee shareholdings

Employee-shareholders generally have a tendency to defend a company's independence when there is a threat of a change in control. A company that has taken advantage of the legislation favouring different employee share-ownership schemes can generally count on a few percentage points of support in its effort to maintain the existing equilibrium in its capital. In 2007, for example, the employee-shareholders of the construction group Eiffage rallied behind management in its effort to see off Sacyr's rampant bid.

SECTION 5

(e) Warrants

The company issues warrants to certain investors. If a change in control threatens the company, investors exercise their warrants and become shareholders. This issue of new shares will make a takeover more difficult, because the new shares dilute the ownership stake of all other shareholders. The strike price of the warrant is usually very attractive but the warrants can only be exercised if a takeover bid is launched on the company.

This type of provision is common in the Netherlands (ING or Philips), France (Pernod Ricard, GDF Suez) and in the US.

4/ LEGAL AND REGULATORY PROTECTION

(a) Regulations

Certain investments or takeovers require approval from a government agency or other body with vetoing power. In most countries, sectors where there are needs for specific approval are:

* media;
* financial institutions;
* activities related to defence (for national security reasons).

Golden shares are special shares that enable governments to prevent another shareholder from increasing its stake above a certain threshold, or the company from selling certain of its assets (Total, Telecom Italia, Eni and Cameroon Airlines are some examples).

(b) Voting caps

In principle, the very idea of limiting the right to vote that accompanies a share of stock contradicts the principle of "one share, one vote". Nevertheless, in most countries, companies can limit the vote of any shareholder to a specific percentage of the capital. In some cases, the limit falls away once the shareholder reaches a very large portion of the capital (e.g. 50% or 2/3).

For example, Danone's articles of association stipulate that no shareholder may cast more than 6% of all single voting rights and no more than 12% of all double-voting rights at a shareholders' meeting, unless she owns more than two-thirds of the shares. Voting caps are commonly used in Europe, specifically in Switzerland (12 firms out of the 50 largest use them), France, Belgium, the Netherlands and Spain. Nestlé, Total, Alcatel Lucent and Novartis all use voting caps.

This is a very effective defence. It prevents an outsider from taking control of a company with only 20% or 30% of the capital. If he truly wants to take control, he has to "ante up" and bid for all of the shares. We can see that this technique is particularly useful for companies of a certain size. It makes sense only for companies that do not have a strong core shareholder.

(c) Strategic assets (poison pills)

Strategic assets can be patents, brand names or subsidiaries comprising most of the business or generating most of the profits of a group. In some cases the company does not actually own the assets but simply uses them under licence. In other cases these assets are located in a subsidiary with a partner who automatically gains control should control of the parent company change hands. Often contested as misuse of corporate property, poison pill arrangements are very difficult to implement, and in practice are generally ineffective.

(d) Change of control provisions

Some contracts may include a clause whereby the contract becomes void if one of the control provisions over one of the principles of the contract changes. The existence of such clauses in vital contracts for the company (distribution contract, bank debt contract, commercial contract) will render its takeover much more complex.

Some "golden parachute" clauses in employment contracts allow some employees to leave the company with a significant amount of money in the event of a change of control.

Section 40.3
ORGANISING A DIVERSIFIED GROUP

Imagine you were suddenly at the helm of a diversified industrial group. What sort of organisation should you choose? Should you set up a separate company for each major business unit with a holding company overseeing them, or a single legal entity with several divisions?

1/ LISTING SUBSIDIARIES

Listing certain subsidiaries brings in minority shareholders and increases the capital available to the group while offering investors a slice of the assets that interest them the most. The same reasoning holds for bringing financial investors into the capital of the subsidiaries.

Opinions vary widely on this topic. The company gains access to equity financing without fundamentally changing the capital structure of the group. Carried too far, however, the parent company becomes a financial holding company with the problem of the holding company discount.

We note, however, that in certain sectors of the economy, legislation requires the presence of a financial partner or a public listing. In Luxembourg, for example, a shareholder may not hold more than 25% of the capital of a radio station; in France, no-one may own more than 49% of a free-to-air TV channel. Researchers have shown that the share price performance of the subsidiary improves when the parent company's stake falls below 50%! A company that creates a new subsidiary and sells a stake on the stock exchange is said to perform a **carve-out**.

Depending on market conditions, valuations and strategies, sometimes it will be advantageous to list subsidiaries and bring in minority shareholders and sometimes it will be better to do the opposite and delist a subsidiary. Many companies – EDF and Iberdrola, to name just two – listed their wind power or similar subsidiaries in 2007. This was to take advantage of the high multiples the market was ascribing to the sector in the hope of paying for future acquisitions with the shares of their newly-listed subsidiaries rather than with cash. This strategy works well when valuations are high because when acquisitions are paid in paper, the question of price becomes one of parity. At the same time, many more mature companies – Générali, Allianz and Lafarge stand out as examples – bought out minority shareholders in their listed subsidiaries. Moral: nothing is irreversible.

2/ CASCADE STRUCTURE

As a newly-minted CEO, you may be tempted to structure your group as a Russian Matryushka doll, like Groupe Arnault and LVMH or Olivetti and Telecom Italia, or like the current Albert Frère group:

At each level, it makes sense to create a new company only if it will house different businesses. The most profitable activities must be as close as possible to the controlling

SIMPLIFIED ORGANISATION CHART OF THE FRERE GROUP

Although the group controls 21% of Lafarge, the Frère family's financial interest in the cement group is only 1.5%.

Source: Annual reports

holding company. Otherwise, if it is the company at the bottom of the "cascade", cash flow will have trouble reaching the controlling holding company, and shareholders will have the impression their money is working for free!

What are the advantages and disadvantages of such a cascade structure?

The **multiplier effect** is maximised. With capital of 100, you can control a set of businesses with a capital of 2500! Even more leverage can be obtained if intermediate structures borrow, but we strongly recommend against this practice. As they do not hold the operating assets directly and depend solely on dividends for their livelihood, borrowing would make the intermediate structures even more fragile. Remember that a chain is only as strong as its weakest link.

These cascade companies generally trade at a deep discount (between 20% and 50%). If a parent company wants to participate in its subsidiary's capital increase in order to maintain control over it, it must, in turn, carry out a capital increase. But because of the holding company discount, the new shares of the holding company will be issued at a heavy discount, increasing its cost of capital. In effect, the cost of capital for a parent holding company which has stock that trades at a 50% discount is twice the cost of capital of the operating subsidiary.

These structures have fallen a bit out of fashion. Investors are afraid of being caught on the least liquid and most fragile part of the ladder and suffering an accumulation of discounts.

Section 40.4
FINANCIAL SECURITIES' DISCOUNTS

When a financial security trades at a discount – i.e. when the market value of the security is less than the value as we have defined it throughout this book – the market is inefficient. For example, if you cannot sell a bond for more than 80 when its discounted present value is 100.

Some of the features or structures that we have seen through this chapter can generate discounts.

1/ HOLDING COMPANY DISCOUNTS

A holding company owns minority or majority investments in listed or unlisted companies either for purely financial reasons or for the purpose of control.

A holding company trades at a discount when its market capitalisation is less than the sum of the investments it holds. This is usually the case. For example, the holding company holds assets worth 100, but the stock market values the holding company at only 80. Consequently, the investor who buys the holding company's stock will think he is buying something "at a discount", because he is paying 80 for something that is worth 100. The market value of the holding company will never reach 100 unless something happens to eliminate the discount, such as a merger between the holding company and its operating subsidiary.

The size of the discount varies with prevailing stock market conditions. In bull markets, holding company discounts tend to contract, while in bear markets they can widen to more than 30%.

Here are four reasons for this phenomenon:

- the portfolio of assets of the holding company is imposed on investors who cannot choose it;
- the free float of the holding company is usually smaller than that of the companies in which it is invested, making the holding's shares less liquid;
- tax inefficiencies. Capital gains on the shares held by the holding company may be taxed twice: first at the holding company level, then at the level of the shareholders. Moreover, it takes time for the flow of dividends to come from the operating company up to the ultimate holding company;
- administrative inefficiencies: the holding company has its own administrative costs which, discounted over a long period, constitute a liability to be subtracted from the value of the investments it holds. Imagine a holding company valued at €2bn with administrative costs of €10m p.a. If those costs are projected to infinity and discounted at 8% p.a., their present value is €125m before tax, or 6.25% of the value of the holding company.

These factors can generally explain a statistical discount up to the 15–25% range. Beyond that, the discount is probably more indicative of a power struggle between investors and holding companies. The former want to get rid of the latter and finance the operating assets directly. The disappearance of many listed holding companies over the last few years, such as Olivetti and IFI in Italy, Eurafrance in France, Cobepa and Electrabel in Belgium or Companie Financière Michelin in Switzerland, has demonstrated how effective investor pressure can be.

2/ CONGLOMERATE DISCOUNTS

A conglomerate is a group active in several, diverse businesses. Whether the group combines water and telephones or missiles and magazines, the market value of the conglomerate is usually less than the sum of the values of the assets the conglomerate holds. The difference, the **conglomerate discount**, generally reflects investors' fears that resources will be poorly allocated. In other words, the group might reduce emphasis on profitable investments in order to support ailing divisions in which the profitability is mediocre or below their cost of capital.

Moreover, investors now want "pure play" stocks and prefer to diversify their holdings themselves. In a conglomerate, investors cannot select the company's portfolio of assets; they are, in fact, stuck with the holding company's choice. As in the case of holding companies, head office costs absorb some of the value of the conglomerate. Finally, a company can suffer both a conglomerate and a holding company discount if some of the company's activities are lodged in a listed subsidiary.

3 *See Chapter 44.*
4 *See Chapter 43.*

A persistent conglomerate discount usually leads to a spin-off[3] or a hostile takeover bid.[4]

Some conglomerates are valued without a discount (General Electric, Bouygues) because investors are convinced that they are efficiently managed.

The summary of this chapter can be downloaded from www.vernimmen.com.

Shareholder structure explains how power is distributed among a company's different shareholders or groups of shareholders. Major shareholder categories are as follows:

- employee-shareholders. Normally these shareholders are loyal and non-volatile, lending a degree of stability to the capital;

- family shareholders. This model is in decline. New industries require too much capital for a family-owned structure to be viable. Funding requirements make capital markets become increasingly important;

- financial investors and investment funds, whose objectives vary: business angels, LBO funds, institutional investors, venture capitalists, etc;

- governments, the importance of which is rising due to sovereign wealth funds mainly originating from emerging markets.

Defensive measures for maintaining control of a company's capital carry a cost, because they prevent investors from taking advantage of the potential opportunities a takeover might.

These measures include:

- separating management control from financial control through double-voting shares, holding companies, limited share partnerships, investment certificates and non-voting shares;

- controlling shareholder changes through right of approval clauses or pre-emption rights;

- strengthening the position of loyal shareholders by carrying out reserved capital increases, buying back shares, merging, encouraging employees to become shareholders and issuing warrants;

- exploiting legal and regulatory opportunities: specific regulations, voting rights limitations and poison pills.

Tax considerations aside, whether a group is made up of subsidiaries or divisions depends on control and organisational factors. Listing certain subsidiaries gives the group access to additional equity capital without changing the shareholder structure of the group. But such carve-outs risk transforming the parent company into a financial holding company.

Lastly, remember that shares with low market liquidity, shares of a holding company or conglomerate or shares without voting rights often trade at discounted values. These discounts increase the cost of capital.

SUMMARY

QUESTIONS

1/What techniques can be used for choosing shareholders?

2/What sort of general meeting must be held to approve capital transactions?

3/What power does a shareholder with a blocking minority have?

4/What purpose does a "Dutch clause" serve?

5/Why can management compensation in the form of stock create value?

SECTION 5

6/ How would compensating employees in stock run contrary to financial theory?

7/ What advantages are there in buying 100% of the capital of a limited share partnership?

8/ Why do so many conglomerates continue to survive, despite the loss of value they generate? Can this situation last?

9/ What is the advantage of cascade structures for the majority shareholder? And for other shareholders?

10/ What is the difference between a holding company discount and a conglomerate discount?

11/ A company manager has a 55% stake in his unlisted company, in which a competitor also has a 32% stake. The former is keen to dilute the shareholding of the latter, without diluting his own stake at the same time. What should he do?

12/ Why is the shareholding of a family-run business unstable in the long term? What is the likely future of such a business? How can this process be slowed down?

13/ Two managers have a 25% and 75% stake respectively in a company. They are keen to bring in a capital investor with the minimum dilution to their shareholdings. How should they go about solving this problem?

More questions are waiting for you at www.vernimmen.com.

EXERCISE

Provide a description of the shareholdings and management in the following situations:

- ○ Company 1: capital split between investors each holding the blocking minority;
- ○ Company 2: large group holding absolute majority, rest widely held;
- ○ Company 3: no shareholder has more than 5% of shareholders' equity;
- ○ Company 4: trade buyer with blocking minority, capital investor with shareholding significant but below blocking minority, rest widely held;
- ○ Company 5: trade buyer just below simple majority, rest widely held.

ANSWERS

Questions

1/ *Approval, pre-emption, A and B shares, etc.*
2/ *Extraordinary General Meeting (where applicable).*
3/ *Blocking decisions at EGMs.*
4/ *Limiting strategic divergence among shareholders.*
5/ *Because it permits reduction of agency costs.*
6/ *Their risks are not diversified.*
7/ *None (see chapter).*
8/ *It is in the interest of management – power, prestige. No, because sooner or later there will be pressure from shareholders.*
9/ *Secure control with limited resources. None.*
10/ *See chapter.*

11/ *Reserved capital increase if some minority shareholders vote with him so as to get the EGM's approval, contribution of assets, etc.*

12/ *The principle of portfolio diversification renders the principle of a family shareholding structure unstable. It will be sold to pay taxes (wealth and inheritance taxes). Provide them with tax breaks.*

13/ *By creating a holding company or issuing convertible bonds.*

Exercise

Stable shareholding structure – Companies 2, 4 and 5.
Unstable shareholding structure – Companies 1 and 3.
Managers: 1 – highly controlled. 2 – stable. 3 – only risk is risk of a takeover bid. 4 – stable (but risk of takeover bid could exist, depending on relationship with capital investor. 5 – stable (risk of takeover bid not excluded).

BIBLIOGRAPHY

On group structure:

R. Aggarwal, A. Samwick, Why do managers diversify their firms? Agency reconsidered, *Journal of Finance*, **58**(1), 71–118, February 2003.

A. Boone, D. Haushalter, W. Mikkelson, An investigation of the gains from specialized equity claims, *Financial Management*, **32**(3), 67–83, Autumn 2003.

A. Boot, R. Gopalan, A. Thakor, The entrepreneur's choice between private and public ownership, *Journal of Finance*, **61**(2), 803–836, April 2006.

B. Cornell, Q. Liu, The parent company puzzle: When is the whole worth less than one of the parts? *Journal of Corporate Finance*, **7**(4), 341–366, December 2001.

H. Cronqvist, M. Nilsson, Agency costs of controlling minority shareholders, *Journal of Financial Quantitative Analysis*, **38**(4), 695–719, December 2003.

P. Dussauge, B. Garrette, *Cooperative Strategy, Competing Successfully through Strategic Alliances*, John Wiley & Sons, Inc., 1999.

J. Rauh, Own company stock in defined contribution pension plans. A takeover defense? *Journal of Financial Economics*, **81**(2), 379–410, August 2006.

Shearman & Sterling, ISS, ECGI, *Report on the Proportionality Principle in the European Union*, 2007.

On shareholding structure:

H. Almeida, D. Wolfenzon, A theory of pyramidal ownership and family business groups, *Journal of Finance*, **61**(6), 2637–2680, December 2006.

A. Brav, J. Wei, F. Partnoy, R. Thomas, Hedge fund activism, corporate governance and firm performance, *Journal of Finance*, **63**(4), 1729–1775, August 2008.

M. Faccio, L. Lang, The ultimate ownership – of western European corporations, *Journal of Financial Economics*, **65**(3), 365–395, September 2002.

J. Hellwege, Ch. Pirinski, R. Stulz, Why do firms become widely held? An analysis of the dynamics of corporate ownership, *Journal of Finance*, **62**(3), 995–1028, June 2007.

M. Jensen, Eclipse of the public corporation, *Harvard Business Review*, **67**, 61–74, September 1989.

B. Maury, Family ownership and firm performance: Empirical evidence from Western European corporations, *Journal of Corporate Finance*, **12**(12), 321–341, January 2006.

R. Morck *et al. History of Corporate Ownership: The Rise and Fall of a Great Business Family*, NBER, 2004.

S. Myers, Outside equity, *Journal of Finance*, **55**(3), 1005–1037, June 2000.

B. Villalonga, R. Amit, How do family ownership, control and management affect firm value? *Journal of Financial Economics*, **80**(2), 385–417, May 2006.

B. Villalonga, R. Amit, Family control of firms and industries, *Financial Management*, **39**(3), 863–904, Autumn 2010.

Chapter 41
INITIAL PUBLIC OFFERINGS (IPOs)

Welcome to the wonderful world of listed companies!

Theoretically, the principles of financial management that we have developed throughout this book find their full expression in the share price of the company. They apply to unlisted companies as well, but for a listed company, market approval or disapproval, expressed through the share price, is immediate. Today, a stock exchange listing offers distinct benefits for large groups: **it enables financial managers to access capital markets and have a direct understanding of the market value of their companies**.

When you see that several billion euros can change hands on financial markets in the course of a few hours (when the financial markets are not in crisis!), you understand that markets constitute a very efficient way of exchanging shares compared to the complex negotiations necessary to obtain private financing.

"Paper", i.e. financial securities, can be placed on financial markets so quickly because:

- financial analysts periodically publish studies reviewing company fundamentals, reinforcing the market's efficiency;
- listing on an organised market enables financial managers to "sell" the company in the form of securities that are bought and sold solely as a function of profitability and risk. Poor management is punished by poor share price performance or worse – from management's point of view – by a takeover offer;
- listed companies must publish up-to-date financial information and file an annual report (or equivalent) with the market authority.

IPOs WORLDWIDE (US$bn)

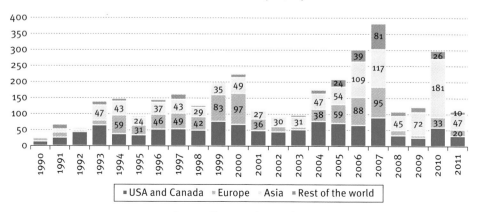

Source: Thomson One Banker

Section 41.1
TO BE OR NOT TO BE LISTED

Whether or not to float a company on the stock exchange is a question that concerns, first and foremost, **the shareholders** rather than the company. But technically, it is the company that requests a listing on the stock exchange.

An initial public offering (IPO) is always to the advantage of the minority shareholders.

When a company is listed, its shareholders' investments become more **liquid**, but the difference for shareholders between a listed company and a non-listed company is not always that significant. Companies listed on the market gain liquidity at the time of the listing, since a significant part of the equity is floated. But thereafter, for small or medium-sized companies, only a few shares are usually traded every day, unless the market "falls in love" with the company and a long-term relationship begins.

In addition to real or potential liquidity, a stock market listing gives the minority shareholder a level of protection that no shareholders' agreement can provide. The company must publish certain information; the market also expects a consistent dividend policy. If the majority shareholders sell their stake, the rights of minority shareholders are protected (see Chapter 43).

Conversely, a listing complicates life for the majority shareholder. It is true that liquidity gives him the opportunity to sell some of his shares in the market without losing control of the company. Listing can also allow the majority shareholder to get rid of a bothersome or restless minority shareholder by providing a forum for the minority shareholders to sell their shares in an orderly manner. But in return, a majority shareholder will no longer be able to ignore financial parameters such as P/E multiples, EPS, dividends per share, etc. (see Chapter 23) when determining strategy.

Once a majority shareholder has taken the company public, investors will judge the company on its ability to create value and communicate financial information properly. Delisting a company to take it private again is a long, drawn-out process. So, for management, being listed results in a lot more restrictions in terms of transparency and communication.

For the company, a stock market listing presents several advantages:

- the company becomes widely known to other stakeholders (customers, suppliers, etc.). If the company communicates well, the listing constitutes a superb form of "free" advertising, on an international scale;
- the company can tap the financial markets for additional funding and acquire other companies, using its shares as currency. This constitutes invaluable flexibility for the company;
- in a group, a parent company can obtain a market value for a subsidiary by listing it (we will then speak of a carve-out), in the hope that the value will be high enough to have a positive impact on the value of the parent company's shares;
- the company finds it easier to involve employees in the success of the company, incentivising them through stock options, stock-based bonuses, etc.

Now for the warning flags: a stock market listing does not guarantee happy shareholders. If only a small percentage of the shares are traded, or if total market capitalisation is low, i.e. less than €500m, large institutional investors will not be interested, especially if the company is not included in a benchmark index. Volatility on the shares will be relatively high because the presence of just a few buyers (or sellers) will easily drive up (down) the share price significantly. In countries like France and the United Kingdom, the authorities have created tax or regulatory incentives (for insurance companies) to encourage investment in such small- and mid-cap companies.

Section 41.2
PREPARATION OF AN IPO

It usually takes at least six months between the time the shareholders decide to list a company and the first trading in its shares.

This six-month period provides an opportunity for management to revisit some financial decisions made in the past that were appropriate for an unlisted, family-owned company or for a wholly-owned subsidiary of a group, but which would not be suitable for a listed company with minority shareholders, such as:

* prepare accounts in line with accounting standards required for listed companies which may be different from the ones used by private companies, and introduce reporting procedures that cover the whole of the entity to be listed;
* review the group's legal structure in order to ensure that vital assets (brands, patents, customer portfolios, etc.) are fully owned by the group and that the group's legal form and articles of association are compatible with listing (no simplified joint-stock companies and no pre-emptive rights or special agreements in the articles);
* review the group's operating structure ensuring that it is an independent group with its own means of functioning and that it does not retain the structure of a division of a group or a family-run business (terminate employment contracts with non-operational family members, take out necessary insurance policies, draw up management agreements, etc.);
* draw up a shareholders' agreement if there is no such existing agreement (see Chapter 40);
* introduce corporate governance appropriate for a listed company (independent directors, control procedures, board of director committees, etc. – see Chapter 42);
* review the company's financial structure in order to ensure that it is similar to that of other listed companies in the same sector. This applies particularly to companies under LBO which will have to partially deleverage, at the latest at the time of listing;
* adopt a well-thought-out dividends policy that is sustainable over the long term and that will not compromise the group's development (see Chapter 37);
* introduce a scheme for providing employees with access to the company's shares through the allocation of free shares and/or stock options, etc. (see Chapter 40);
* define the company strategy in a form that is simple and easy to communicate, which will become the equity story to be told to the market at the time of listing.

From the start of this phase, the company should seek the assistance of an investment bank, which will act as a link between the company and the market. The company will also have to retain the services of a law firm, an accounting firm and possibly a PR agency.

10 LARGEST IPOs WORLDWIDE IN 2010

Rank	Company	Exchange Nationality	Industry	Deal Value (in €m)
1	Agricultural Bank of China Ltd	Hong Kong; China	Finance	17,646
2	AIA Group Ltd	Hong Kong	Insurance	14,772
3	General Motors Co	United States; Canada	Auto/Truck	13,361
4	Dai-ichi Life Insurance Co Ltd	Japan	Insurance	8,234
5	Petronas Chemicals Group Bhd	Malaysia	Chemicals	3,475
6	Samsung Life Insurance Co Ltd	South Korea	Insurance	3,307
7	QR National Ltd	Australia	Transportation	2,924
8	Enel Green Power SpA	Spain; Italy	Utility & Energy	2,466
9	Coal India Ltd	India	Mining	2,464
10	China Everbright Bank Co Ltd	China	Finance	2,437

Source: Dealogic

Section 41.3
EXECUTION OF THE IPO

1/ CHOOSING A MARKET

With rare exception, the natural market for the listing is the company's home country. This is where the company is best known to local investors, who are the most likely to give it the highest value. There are obviously a few exceptions, such as L'Occitane, which elected for a Hong Kong listing (given that the company's activity is highly developed in Asia). But only a very small number of companies from major European countries are not listed in their home country.

The next question is whether there should be a second listing on a foreign market. Listing on a foreign market generally constitutes a constraint on a company, because it requires additional financial reporting. Accordingly, with a listing on a foreign market, come direct and indirect costs without any guarantee of greater liquidity or a higher valuation of the company.

Only groups from emerging countries, when their local market is underdeveloped (Russia, Latin America, etc.), have a clear advantage to get from a secondary listing in New York, London, Paris or Hong Kong. The Russian aluminium group, Rusal, is a good example, with its parallel listing in Paris and Hong Kong.

2/ SIZING THE IPO

Over and above the choice of a (or several) stock market(s) for listing, a certain number of parameters will have to be fixed, including the size of the IPO and the choice between a primary offer (share issue), a secondary offer (sale of shares by existing shareholders) or a mix of the two.

These decisions will be made based on the following:

- whether existing shareholders want to convert all or part of their stakes into cash;
- whether the company needs funds to finance its growth or to deleverage;

SECTION 5

- the need to put a sufficient number of shares on the market so that the share can offer a certain amount of liquidity;
- the need to limit the negative signal of the transaction.

These constraints can sometimes turn out to be contradictory. For example, the sale of all of the existing shares on the market by existing shareholders is rarely considered, as this would send a very negative signal to the market. So, when the IPO includes the sale by one or more major shareholders of some of their shares, they will generally be asked to undertake to hold onto the shares that have not been sold for a given period (6 to 12 months) so as to avoid any heavy impact on the market if they were to sell large volumes of shares immediately after the IPO. This undertaking, or lock-up clause, acts as a reassurance to the market and tempers the negative signal of the operation.

It may also be a good idea to combine the sale of shares by existing shareholders with a capital increase, even if the company has no immediate need of funds. The message sent by an IPO through a capital increase is, by definition, more positive. The newly-listed company will be able to speed up its development and to tap a new source of funding, which is why most IPOs are partly primary, whether to a larger or smaller degree.

3/ IPO TECHNIQUES

The different techniques for carrying out an IPO, whether aimed at institutional or retail investors, are discussed in Chapter 26.

Section 41.4
UNDERPRICING OF IPOs

If statistics are to be believed, the share price of a newly-floated company generally rises by around 9% (UK) and 15 to 16% (USA or France) on the IPO price in the days following flotation (see Chapter 26). It would also appear that this discount at which shares are sold or issued at the time of an IPO is volatile over time, compared with a balanced value – high in the 1960s, lower in the 1970s to 1980s, and then high again in the 2000s. Following research, many different explanations for this discount have been put forward. The main ones are:

- This underpricing is theoretically due to the asymmetry of information between the seller and the investors or intermediaries. The former has more information on the company's prospects while the latter have a good idea of market demand. A deal is therefore possible, but price is paramount.
- In this asymmetrical situation, signal theory says that the sale of shares by the shareholders is a negative signal, so the seller has to "leave some money on the table" in return for ensuring that the IPO goes off smoothly and to investors' satisfaction.
- Some explanations are more complex and are based on the degree of information that the various investors have on the true value of the company. Institutional investors will generally have better information and a more in-depth understanding of companies that are about to arrive on the market. Such "informed" investors will only be interested in good deals and will not be tempted by overvalued IPOs. Less well-informed

investors, who will thus be involved in all operations, will find that they are better served in unattractive operations. They will not be as present on more attractive deals. If the average IPO were not underpriced, less well-informed investors would be excluded and would end up abandoning the market. In seeking to retain these investors, who provide valuable and necessary liquidity to the market, IPOs are carried out at a discount.

- There are some who argue (not very convincingly) that underpricing can limit the risk of legal disputes with investors who would feel as if they had been swindled because they'd made a bad investment.

Section 41.5
PUBLIC TO PRIVATE

A company (or the shareholders) will first start considering a public to private move when the reasons why it decided to list its shares in the first place, for the most part, become irrelevant. It has to weigh the cost of listing – direct costs: stock exchange fees, publication of annual reports, meetings with analysts, employment of investor relations staff – and indirect costs: requirement to disclose more information to the public and to competitors, market influence on strategy, management's time spent talking to the market, etc. against the benefits of listing when deciding whether the company should remain listed or not. This is especially the case if:

- the company no longer needs large amounts of outside equity and shareholders themselves are able to meet any equity requirements it may have. The company no longer has any ambition to raise capital on the market or to pay for acquisitions in shares;
- the stock exchange no longer provides minority shareholders with sufficient liquidity (which is often rapidly the case for smaller companies which only really benefit from liquidity at the time of their IPO). Listing then becomes a theoretical issue and institutional investors lose interest in the share;
- the company no longer needs the stock exchange in order to increase awareness of its products or services.

The second type of reason why companies delist is financial. Large shareholders, whether majority shareholders or not, may consider that the share price does not reflect the intrinsic value of the company. Turning a problem into an opportunity, such shareholders could offer minority shareholders an exit, thus giving them a larger share of the creation of future value.

A public tender offer must be launched in order to delist a company. Delisting is possible if the majority shareholder exceeds a threshold, often 90% or 95%, as it is then obliged to acquire the rest of the shares. This is known as a squeeze-out. In practice, this amounts to forcing minority shareholders to sell any outstanding shares. Because this is a form of property expropriation, the price of the operation is analysed very closely by the market regulator. In most countries, a fairness opinion has to be drawn up by an independent, qualified financial expert.

But let's not delude ourselves – no matter how the company's share has performed, minority shareholders will insist that the price they're offered reflects the intrinsic value of their shares. If it doesn't, they won't tender their shares in the offer. Accordingly, it is not surprising to note that, even though there is no change in control, tender offers launched for the purpose of delisting a company are made at a premium that is equivalent to the premium paid for takeovers.

If investors are below the squeeze-out threshold, they first have to launch an offer on the company's shares, hoping to go above the squeeze-out threshold so as to be able to take the company private. This is a P-to-P, public-to-private, deal.

Being listed is never a dead-end, as a company can become private again and come back on to the stock exchange years later.

SUMMARY

The summary of this chapter can be downloaded from www.vernimmen.com.

A stock market listing provides shareholders with access to a certain liquidity for their investment in the company. However, this is only real for large corporates, or only at the time of the IPO for smaller companies. Listing enables the company to access new sources of funding, to raise its corporate profile and to incentivise managers and employees. Company strategy must, however, be linked to financial parameters.

An IPO is a complex process that generally takes around six months to complete. During the preparation phase, the whole of the company's legal, operational and financial structure has to be reviewed, its corporate governance needs to be adapted, financial statements may have to be drawn up in line with the relevant accounting principles and a strategy has to be defined in the form of an equity story for the market.

A company is generally listed in its country of origin. The choice of the market segment on which the company will be listed will be determined by the size of the company and by any constraints weighing on it.

The number of shares offered on the market will depend on the sizing of the IPO, which will also determine whether the shares will be shares sold by existing shareholders and/or new shares in the company's capital that are issued at the time. This will depend on the company's requirements, on what the shareholders want and on market constraints.

At the time of the IPO, shares are generally sold on the market at a discount of between 10 to 20% compared with the first listed price. Different theoretical explanations, based mainly on information asymmetry, have been put forward to explain this.

Delisting may be a good option when the company no longer requires funds or when liquidity has become too low. Delisting can also be a complex process and an independent expert has to be brought in to draw up a fairness opinion on the squeeze-out price.

QUESTIONS

1/ Give reasons why a company would want to list on the stock exchange.

2/ Why might shareholders prefer to sell their stakes in a company through an IPO rather than a straight sale to an investor?

3/ Why would a company with an 85% stake in a subsidiary launch a takeover bid for the remaining shares?

4/ Why do companies that list their shares on the stock market have, more often than not, to change their corporate governance?

SECTION 5

5/Why is it difficult for a sole shareholder to sell 100% of his shares when the company undertakes an IPO?

6/In response to a question about his expectations of Hermès's new financial strategy at the time of its IPO, Jean-Louis Dumas, Hermès's CEO, replied that he hoped that his grandchildren would be proud of him. Comment.

7/What are the risks run by a company that carries out an IPO just because IPOs are fashionable?

8/What are the risks of an IPO?

9/What will a company with a large number of shareholders and which does not want to get a listing on the stock exchange have to do sooner or later?

More questions are waiting for you at www.vernimmen.com.

EXERCISE

A subsidiary of PPR, CFAO is a leading specialised distributor of automobile and pharmaceutical products in Africa. CFAO operates in 34 countries, including 31 African countries, and has over 10 000 employees.

Description of the initial public offering of CFAO on Euronext Paris:

Price range: between €24.80 and €29.00 per share.

– Size of the offer: 35 650 000 existing shares (57.94% of share capital) sold by the PPR Group.

– Value of the offer between €768.8m and €899.0m on the basis of the price bracket.

– Greenshoe option on a maximum of 4 650 000 existing shares.

– Close of offering scheduled for December 1, 2009.

Income statement (millions of euros)	2006	2007	2008	2009(e)	2010(e)
Sales	2219	2535	2864	2571	2700
– Operating costs	(2016)	(2278)	(2557)	(2323)	(2414)
= EBITDA	204	257	307	248	286
– Depreciation	(27)	(31)	(37)	(40)	(42)
= Operating income	177	226	270	208	244
+ Financial income	(19)	(20)	(21)	(22)	(23)
+ Non-recurring items	10	9	9	(4)	0
= Pre-tax profit	168	215	257	182	221
– Income tax	(57)	(76)	(90)	(62)	(76)
Share of income from firms accounted for under the equity method	3	3	4	4	5
= Net profit	114	142	171	124	150
– Minority interests	(31)	(36)	(43)	(28)	(32)
= Net earnings, group share	83	106	129	96	118

Cash flow statement	2006	2007	2008
Cash flow from operating activities (1)	116	151	63
Cash flow from investing activities (2)	(58)	(66)	(71)
– Dividends	(93)	(71)	(209)
= Decrease (increase) in net debt	(36)	14	(217)

Balance sheet	2006	2007	2008
Fixed assets(1)	374	430	464
Working capital (2)	318	315	451
Capital employed = (1) + (2)	692	745	915
Shareholders' equity (3)	550	617	570
Net debt (4)	142	128	345
Invested capital = (3) + (4)	692	745	915

Dividend policy	2006	2007	2008	2009(e)	2010(e)
Net earnings, group share (€m)	83	106	129	96	118
Earnings per share (EPS in €)	1.4	1.7	2.1	1.6	1.9
Dividend per share (€)	0.8	2.9	1.3	0.8	1.0
Payout ratio	61%	170%	60%	50%	50%

What are your views on the company's dividend policy before and after the IPO?

What impact will the IPO have on CFAO's balance sheet and on its income statement?

What benefits could this transaction have for CFAO?

Why did PPR decide to IPO CFAO through the sale of a large portion of its shares?

ANSWERS

Questions

1/ *Gain access to new sources of funding. Increase its visibility* vis-à-vis *its customers, suppliers and employees. Make it easier to incentivise employees and management. Provide shareholders with liquidity (especially if there are minority shareholders).*

2/ *There might not be a buyer prepared to pay a control premium. This enables the shareholder to sell only a minority stake, thus holding on to majority control, while cashing in part of his shares.*

3/ *In order to get rid of minority shareholders and to implement group synergies.*

4/ *Because there are now outside shareholders and an obligation to follow the rules applied to listed companies.*

5/ *Because of the very negative signal that this would send out.*

6/ *This highlights the conflict between the very financial approach of minority shareholders and a wider approach of managing shareholders. The two are not irreconcilable, as Hermès shares have been an excellent investment since they were listed on the stock exchange.*

7/ *The risk of severe disappointment as there will be no advantage for the company compared with all of the restrictions involved in listing.*

8/ *In the short term, failure during the course of the process as stock markets fall and the possible price of the placement could seem very low to existing shareholders. Over the longer term, a change in the group's culture, and a change in control (takeover bid).*

9/ *Sooner or later, the company will have to be sold in order to provide shareholders with liquidity or an internal stock exchange will have to be organised among shareholders so that those wishing to sell their shares can do so without having to sell to third parties.*

Exercise

Before the IPO, the dividend policy was not very cohesive and depended largely on the needs of the single shareholder. After the IPO, it seems as though the company has sought to adopt a clearer and more easily readable policy, paying out 50% of its profits.

As the IPO was carried out solely through the sale of shares by PPR, it will have no impact on CFAO's balance sheet or income statement.

The benefits of listing for CFAO would be the enhancement of its visibility vis-à-vis its customers and access to new means of funding.

Perhaps PPR was unable to find a buyer for a majority stake in CFAO or perhaps it wanted to retain exposure to CFAO's value creation while at the same time cashing in part of its stake, either to pay off debt and/or to reinvest in its luxury division.

BIBLIOGRAPHY

For more about taking companies public:

F. Bancel, U. Mittoo, Why do European firms go public?, *European Financial Management*, **15**(4), 844–884, September 2009.

S. Benninga, M. Helmantel, O. Sarig, The timing of initial public offerings, *Journal of Financial Economics*, **75**(1), 115–132, January 2005.

A. Boot, R. Gopalan, A. Thakor, The entrepreneur's choice between private and public ownership, *Journal of Finance*, **61**(2), 803–836, April 2006.

J. Brau, S. Fawcett, Initial public offerings: An analysis of theory and practice, *Journal of Finance*, **61**(1), 399–436, February 2006.

J. Chod, E. Lyandres, Strategic IPOs and product market competition, *Journal of Financial Economics*, **100**(1), 45–67, April 2011.

A. Hovakimian, I. Hutton, Merger-motivated IPOs, *Financial Management*, **39**(4), 1547–1573, Winter 2010.

H. Hsu, A. Reed, J. Rocholl, The new game in town: competitive effects of IPOs, *Journal of Finance*, **65**(2), 495–528, April 2010.

M. Lowry, Why does IPO volume fluctuate so much? *Journal of Financial Economics*, **67**(1), 3–40, January 2003.

L. Pastor, P. Veronesi, Rational IPO waves, *Journal of Finance*, **60**(4), 1713–1757, August 2005.

A. Subrahmanyam, S. Titman, The going public decision and the development of financial markets, *Journal of Finance*, **54**(3), 1045–1082, June 1999.

On discounts on IPOs:

D. Chambers, E. Dimson, IPO underpricing over the very long run, *Journal of Finance*, **64**(3), 1407–1444, June 2009.

F. Derrien, IPO pricing in "hot" market conditions: who leave money on the table?, *Journal of Finance*, **60**(1), 487–521, February 2005.

SECTION 5

A. Ellul, M. Pagaro, IPO underpricing and after-market liquidity, *Review of Financial Studies*, **2**(19), 381–421, Summer 2006.

J. Ritter, I. Welch, A review of IPO activity, pricing, and allocations, *Journal of Finance*, **57**(4), 1795–1828, August 2002.

K. Rock, Why new issues are underpriced, *Journal of Financial Economics*, **15**(1–2), 187–212, January–February 1986.

Chapter 42
CORPORATE GOVERNANCE

Or on being politically correct

You may be surprised to find a chapter on corporate governance in a corporate finance textbook. Corporate governance is not, strictly speaking, a financial issue and is based on the legal considerations underlying the framework within which a company is run. However, as you may, by now, have come to expect, we approach the subject mainly from the angle of value. In other words, we attempt to find answers to the question "Will good corporate governance foster the creation of value and will poor corporate governance necessarily destroy value?"

The idea of corporate governance first arose in the 1990s and has been given a boost by the eruption of several major financial scandals in 2001–2003 (Enron, Worldcom, Parmalat). More fundamentally, corporate governance is a natural by-product of the changing economy. For example, a change in the shareholding structure of firms (with a shift away from family-owned firms to a more widely-held shareholding structure made up of institutional and retail investors) leaves management with greater freedom. The issue of shareholder control over management has thus become more pressing. Corporate governance was first introduced at listed companies in the UK and the USA (where firms are generally more widely held) before spreading to countries where the frequent cohabitation of family shareholders and minority shareholders also raises issues of corporate governance.

Section 42.1
WHAT DOES CORPORATE GOVERNANCE MEAN?

1/ DEFINITION

Broadly speaking, corporate governance is the organisation of the control over, and management of, a firm. It covers:

- the definition of the legal framework of the firm: specifically, the organisation, the functioning, the rights and responsibilities of shareholders' meetings and the corporate bodies responsible for oversight (board of directors or executive board and supervisory board);
- the rules for appointing managers and directors;
- management rules and any conflicts of interest;

- the organisation of control over the management and the running of the company: internal controls, regulatory controls, auditing;
- the rights and responsibilities of other stakeholders (lenders, customers, suppliers, employees);
- the disclosure of financial information on the firm and the role and responsibility of external analysts: financial analysts, rating agencies and legal and financial advisors.

In a more narrow definition, the term "corporate governance" is used to describe the link that exists between shareholders and management. From this point of view, developments in corporate governance mainly involve the role and functioning of boards of directors or supervisory boards.

1 Based on the OECD approach.

We would suggest[1] that corporate governance covers all of the mechanisms and procedures surrounding decisions relating to the creation and sharing of value. They concern four main areas: shareholders' rights, transparency of information, organs of management and control and the alignment of compensation.

At this stage, we'd like to emphasise that corporate governance is a system that necessarily differs from one firm to the next, depending on its shareholding structure and its nationality. Strictly speaking, it is a bit of a misnomer to refer to "good" or "bad" corporate governance. There is only corporate governance that in practice inspires investors' confidence (or not) on the way in which decisions are taken within the firm, based on whether the following five principles are respected: efficiency, responsibility, transparency, fairness and ethics.

2/ RECOMMENDATIONS AND GUIDELINES

It should always be remembered that the organisation of corporate governance is determined, first and foremost, by company law, which defines the field of possibilities. The legal framework is constantly being updated and refined in line with the evolution of corporate governance. For example, in the USA, the Sarbanes–Oxley Act has reinforced the responsibility of management and also led to a root-and-branch overhaul of how accountants are overseen.

Over the years, a number of recommendations and guidelines have been added to the purely regulatory and legislative framework, in the form of reports and best practice codes (commissioned and/or drafted by employer bodies, investor associations, governments and government agencies, stock exchanges, etc. in various countries). It is important to note that these codes remain recommendations and guidelines only[2] and are not legally binding laws or regulations.

2 In some countries, such as the UK and France, listed companies are required to disclose whether or not they implement codes of corporate governance, which is clearly a very strong incentive for them to do so!

The the main recommendations and guidelines in terms of corporate governance all focus on key issues: transparency in the way that the board and management operate, the role, composition and functioning of the board and the exercise of shareholder power at general meetings.

However, each country has its own very specific features when it comes to companies and their shareholders:

- employee rights in Germany (and also in Denmark, Austria and Sweden);
- the role of banks in Germany and Japan;

- cross-shareholdings in Italy;
- very widely-held shareholdings in the UK or USA;
- etc.

(a) Transparency

The first recommendation is for transparency in the way the company's management and supervisory bodies operate.

There has been a huge increase in transparency in the way the boards of listed groups operate over the last 15 years.

For example, this is the way transparency evolved in France.

TRANSPARENCY FOR THE TOP 40 LISTED GROUPS IN FRANCE

	1995	1999	2004	2010
Firms disclosing the number of board meetings per year	0	34	40	40
Average number of board meetings	3	5.6	7	8.8
Number of boards with internal regulations	0	15	40	40
Number of boards with a board of directors' charter	n/a	n/a	10	37
Number of boards that carry out assessments of their performance	0	0	21	40

Source: Korn/Ferry International and AMF.

Transparency surrounding the compensation of managers and directors is also recommended. For a long time, this was a taboo subject, and most listed companies have only recently started disclosing clear figures on the compensation paid to their managers and directors. As we saw in Chapter 27, the way in which firms compensate management plays a key role in reducing conflict between shareholders and managers.

With the granting of variable compensation or stock options, managers have a financial interest that coincides with that of shareholders, to whom they are accountable. Since stock options are options to buy or subscribe to shares at a fixed price, managers have a direct financial stake in the financial performance of the company, i.e. the higher the share price, the larger their capital gains will be. Accordingly, there is a major incentive to make decisions that will create value.[3]

Stock options are not, however, a cure-all, as the short-term vision they encourage may sometimes tempt management to conceal certain facts when disclosing financial information and, in extreme cases, they may even consider committing fraud. This has resulted in the development of alternative products, such as the granting of free shares, the payment of part of their compensation in shares, etc.

3 For an explanation of the accounting treatment of stock options, see Chapter 7.

Between 1/3 (in France) and 2/3 (in the USA) of management compensation of large firms is linked to economic performance and share price.

SECTION 5

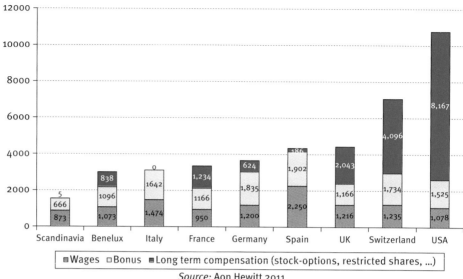

CEO COMPENSATION IN 2010 FOR COMPANIES WITH SALES OF AROUND €5bn (in €000)

■ Wages   □ Bonus   ■ Long term compensation (stock-options, restricted shares, …)

Source: Aon Hewitt 2011

The principle of transparency also applies to transactions carried out by management in the shares of the company. These have to be made public due to the signals that they may give out.

In certain countries (e.g. the US) there is pressure from the market for management compensation to be voted on at shareholders general meetings. This is referred to as the "Say on Pay"

(b) The role of an independent board

Corporate governance codes all recommend that a firm's corporate strategy be defined by a body (board of directors or supervisory board) which enjoys a certain degree of independence from management.

Independence is achieved by limiting the number of managers who sit on the board, and by setting a minimum number of independent directors.

For example, in the United Kingdom the latest recommendation is that at least half of the directors of listed companies should be independent. There are very few companies with no or hardly any independent directors on the board. One such example is Ubisoft, the video games company, with the founding family controlling 13% of the capital and occupying five out of six seats on the board.

The definition of the term "independent director" is the subject of much controversy. The Bouton report defines an independent director as follows: "Directors are independent when they have no link of any nature whatsoever with the company, the group or management, which could compromise them in the exercise of their free will." Even though this definition makes it clear that a member of management or a shareholder representative would not be considered independent, it allows for a great deal of leeway, which means that deciding whether or not a director is indeed independent is not as easy as it might appear.

The importance given to the need for independent directors on the board tends to overshadow the importance of other more vital matters, such as their competence, their availability and their courage when it comes to standing up to management. These qualities are indispensable throughout the financial year, whereas their independence only becomes an issue in situations of conflict of interest, which fortunately are the exception rather than the rule.

Lawyers will surely forgive us for pointing out that the development of corporate governance has brought an end to the idea of the board of directors as an entity invested with the widest of powers, authorised to act in all circumstances in the name of the company. This gives the impression that the board was responsible for running the company, which was quite simply never the case. This erroneous idea put management in a position where it was able to call all of the shots. These days, boards are designed to determine the direction the company will take and to oversee the implementation of corporate strategy. This is a much more modest mandate, but also a lot more realistic. The board is asked to come up with fewer but better goods.

(c) The functioning of the board and the creation of directors' committees

Corporate governance codes insist on the creation of special committees which are instructed by the board to draw up reports. These committees generally include:

- an audit committee (inspects the accounts, monitors the internal audit, selects the external auditors);
- a compensation committee (managers, sometimes directors);
- a selections or appointments committee (paves the way for the succession of the managing director and/or CEO, puts forward proposals for new directors);
- a strategic and/or financial committee (large capex plans, mergers and acquisitions, financing issues).

(d) The exercise of shareholder power during general meetings

It is clear that anything that stands in the way of the exercise of shareholder power will be an obstacle to good corporate governance. Such obstacles can come in various forms:

- the existence of shares with multiple voting rights that may enable minority shareholders with only a tiny stake in the capital to impose their views by wielding their extra voting rights. One such example occurred as recently as 2004, when the Wallenberg family and Industrivärden were able to control 66% of the voting rights in Ericsson, when they held only 7.3% of the share capital, thanks to the existence of *A* shares (with 1000 voting rights attached to each share) and *B* shares (with only one voting right attached);
- the existence of preferred shares with no voting rights attached.[4] The control held by the Pesenti family over Italcementi is facilitated by the existence of preferred shares with a priority dividend but no voting rights attached, accounting for 37% of the share capital;
- the restriction of voting rights in meetings by introducing caps on the number of votes cast during general meetings. For example, at Danone, a single investor cannot represent more than 6% or 12%[5] of the voting rights;[6]
- administrative or material restrictions on exercising voting rights by proxy or by postal vote.

4 *See Chapter 25.*

5 *Depending on whether the shares the investor holds carry double-voting rights or not.*

6 *This restriction will no longer apply if, following a takeover, a third party is in possession of more than 66.7% of the shares.*

SECTION 5

On the other side, making it compulsory for institutional shareholders to vote in general meetings of shareholders, or allowing shareholders to vote without having to freeze their shares a few weeks before the meeting, have clearly improved voting habits and enhanced shareholder democracy.

3/ A ONE-TIER OR A TWO-TIER BOARD: AN UNRESOLVED ISSUE

The way in which power within the board is organised is, in itself, a much debated topic. The need for a body that is independent from the management of the company remains an open question. We can observe three main types of organisation:

- board of directors with a chief executive officer acting also as chairman of the board. This means that a great deal of power is concentrated in the hands of one person who is head of the board and who also manages the company. This is known as a one-tier structure and is in place at groups such as Exxon Mobil, Roche and Telefónica;
- board of directors with an executive or a non-executive chairman and a separate chief executive officer. This sort of dual structure has been adopted by Infosys, Sony and Vodafone;
- supervisory board and executive board: this two-tier structure is in place at Peugeot and Philips.

7 *Other structures also possible but less common.*

8 *Compulsory if the listed company has more than 3% employee shareholding.*

9 *Board of auditors also necessary.*

Country	Main type of board	Separation of management and board	Employee representation on board
Belgium	One-tier[7]	Optional	No
France	One-tier[7]	Optional	Can be provided for in articles of association[8]
Germany	Two-tier	Yes	Yes
Italy	One-tier[9]	Optional	No
Japan	One-tier	Optional	No
Netherlands	Two-tier[7]	Yes	Consultative
Portugal	One-tier[7]	Optional	No
Spain	One-tier	Optional	No
Sweden	One-tier	Yes	Yes
Switzerland	One-tier	Optional	No
UK	One-tier	Optional	No
USA	One-tier[7]	Optional	No

Source: International comparison of selected corporate governance guidelines and codes of best practice, Weil, Gotshal **and** Manges, September 2007.

A board on which the control and management roles are exercised by two different people should, in theory, be more effective in controlling management on behalf of the shareholders. Is this always the case in practice? The answer is no, because it all depends on the quality and the probity of the men and women involved. Enron had a chairman and chief executive officer, and Google has a chief executive officer also acting as chairman of the board. The former went bankrupt in a very spectacular way as a result of fraud and the latter is seen as a model for creating value for its shareholders.

So it's much better to have an outstanding manager, and possibly even compromise a bit when it comes to corporate governance, by giving the manager the job of both running the company and chairing the board, rather than to have a poor manager. Even if extremely well controlled by the chairman of the board, a poor manager will remain a poor manager!

An additional question arises when it comes to the choice of the chairman of the board: can he be the former CEO? Certainly not in the UK, as if this were the case, the margin for manoeuvre of the new CEO would be restricted as the chairman will be tempted to keep some kind of management role. But in France or Germany, for example, this is often the case, on the basis of the fact that the new chairman's experience and knowledge of the company will be highly valuable. The split between the two functions often comes at the time of succession, so that the new CEO can prove his skills. Sooner or later, the two functions are generally brought back together.

IS THE CHAIRMAN OF THE BOARD OF DIRECTORS THE FORMER CEO IN EUROPE?

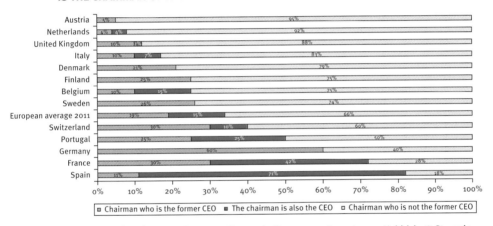

Source: Challeging Board Performance European Corporate Governance Report 2011, Heidricks & Struggle

> There is no straight answer to the question of whether it is best to combine the functions of management and control. Each case has to be assessed on its merits, taking into account the shareholder structure and the personality of the managers. Nothing is set in stone.

It cannot be denied that great strides forward have been taken in the area of corporate governance, even if there is still progress to be made in some emerging countries with less experience in dealing with listed companies and minority shareholders. Associations of minority shareholders, or minority shareholder defence firms, which also provide shareholders with advice on how to vote in general meetings, have often acted as a major stimulus in this regard.

The fact that, in developed countries, many groups have simplified their structures has made this a lot easier:

- these days, it is usually only the parent company that is listed, which eliminates the possibility of conflicts of interest between the parent company and minority shareholders of its subsidiaries.[10]

10 *Take the example of Allianz and Generali which have bought out the minority shareholders of most of their listed subsidiaries, making them wholly-owned subsidiaries.*

SECTION 5

- cross-holdings between groups which used to swap directors have been unwound;[11]
- assets used by the group but which belong to the founders have been contributed to the group;
- etc.

It's now up to researchers to determine whether this simplification was the cause or the consequence of the spread of corporate governance.

Section 42.2
CORPORATE GOVERNANCE AND FINANCIAL THEORIES

1/ THEORY OF MARKETS IN EQUILIBRIUM

The classic theory is of little or no help in understanding corporate governance. What it does is reduce the company to a black box, and draws no distinction between the interests of the different parties involved in the company.

2/ AGENCY THEORY

Agency theory is the main intellectual foundation of corporate governance. The need to set up a system of corporate governance arises from the relationship of agency that binds shareholders and managers. Corporate governance is the main means of controlling management available to shareholders. What corporate governance aims to do is to structure the decision-making powers of management so that individual managers are not able to allocate revenues to themselves at the expense of the company's shareholders, its creditors and employees and, more generally, society as a whole.

Given the information asymmetry that exists between management and shareholders, corporate governance also covers financial communication in the very broadest sense of the term, including information provided to shareholders, work done by auditors, etc.

A good system of corporate governance, i.e. a good set of rules, should make it possible to:

- limit existing or potential conflicts of interest between shareholders and management;
- limit information asymmetry by ensuring transparency of management with regard to shareholders.

12 *See Chapter 34.*

13 *See Chapter 43.*

Corporate governance can help to resolve potential conflicts between shareholders and management in the same way as stock options, restrictions arising from a large debt[12] or a hostile takeover bid[13] do. The difference is that corporate governance is a preventative measure.

Unsurprisingly, agency theory shows that in firms where there are few potential conflicts of interest between shareholders and management and where information asymmetry is low, i.e. in small and medium-sized companies where, more often than not, the manager and shareholder is one and the same person, corporate governance is not an issue.

3/ ENTRENCHMENT THEORY

Agency theory suggests mechanisms for controlling and increasing the efficiency of management. Entrenchment theory[14] is based on the premise, somewhat fallacious but sometimes very real, that mechanisms are not always enough to force management to run the company in line with the interests of shareholders. Some managers' decisions are influenced by their desire to hold onto their jobs and to eliminate any competition.[15] Their (main) aim is to make it very expensive for the company to replace them, which enables them to increase their powers and their discretionary authority. This is where the word "entrenchment" comes from. Managerial entrenchment and corporate governance do not make good bedfellows. But we live in a world that is less than perfect, and perhaps entrenchment is just a natural reaction on the part of management when corporate governance starts to play a major role in the firm.

Section 42.3
VALUE AND CORPORATE GOVERNANCE

An initial response to the question "Does good corporate governance lead to value creation?" is provided by a survey of institutional investors carried out by McKinsey.[16] The investors surveyed stated that they would be prepared to pay more for shares in a company with a good system of corporate governance in place. The premium investors are prepared to pay in countries where the legal environment already provides substantial investor protection is modest (12–14% in Europe and North America), but it is very high in emerging countries (30% in Eastern Europe and Africa).

The very large number of studies on the subject focus on the problem of coming up with a definition of good corporate governance. Existing studies merely rely on ratings provided by specialised agencies to back up their conclusions, which in our view provides no new insight into the subject.

Their results[17] show that good corporate governance does lead to the creation of shareholder value. Bauer, Guenster and Otten have shown that the shares of groups listed on the FTSE 300 that were given a good rating for their corporate governance (by the agency Deminor) performed significantly better than groups with "weak" corporate governance. These results tie in with results for US companies put forward by Gompers.

The results are all the more revealing when one considers that local law does not guarantee satisfactory corporate governance. For example, it would appear that a Russian group that adopts (and communicates) an efficient system of corporate governance will create value.[18]

More generally, Anderson and Reeb in the USA, and Harbula in France have shown that the financial performances of companies with one main shareholder (for example, a family) are better than average. But the best-performing companies are those with one major shareholder and also a fairly large free float. Ideally, the main shareholder should hold a stake of between 30 and 50% in the company's share capital. This may seem counter-intuitive in as far as family-owned companies are generally less transparent and comply less willingly with the rules of corporate governance.

On the other hand, majority or dominant shareholders are very motivated to ensure that their firms are successful, given that such firms often represent both the tools of their trade

14 *Initially developed by A. Shleifer and R. Vishny.*

15 *When Alcatel and Lucent merged, Serge Tchuruk and Patricia Russo, respectively chairman and CEO of Alcatel-Lucent, negotiated a clause in their contracts that excluded their dismissal by the board of directors unless it was approved by 10 out of 12 directors (themselves not included).*

16 *McKinsey Investor Opinion Survey, 2002.*

17 *See bibliography.*

18 *See the work done by Black (2001).*

SECTION 5

19 *Relevant documents should be submitted to the board in good time to enable them to study them, the members of the audit committee should have an understanding of finance and accounting, directors with a conflict of interest on a given issue should not be involved in decisions relating to this issue, etc.*

and their entire fortune! This is the reason why the only French company that declined to bid in the auction for UMTS licences at the height of the Internet boom was a family-owned company (Bouygues), reticence that clearly paid off as far as its minority shareholders were concerned. The minority shareholders of France Télécom (a state-controlled company at that time) and Vivendi Universal (a widely-held company) probably wish that their managers had been a little less gung ho!

We can thus see that there are limits to the systemisation of corporate governance, even though compliance with a certain number of basically simple, common sense rules[19] will help prevent disreputable behaviour on the part of managers and the inequitable treatment of minority shareholders.

Research has shown that the best guarantee for the creation of shareholder value is the strong motivation of the management team, rather than a perfect system of corporate governance. If a company manages to achieve both at the same time, so much the better, but let's get our priorities straight!

To conclude, we shouldn't lose sight of the fact that it is too soon yet to say whether the introduction of recent innovations in terms of corporate governance has really made a difference. Research focuses mostly on the correlation between good corporate governance and high valuations. Very few studies have been able to demonstrate any real correlation between corporate governance and the long-term financial performance of the company. But then nobody has shown that corporate governance has a negative impact on financial performance either!

SUMMARY

The summary of this chapter can be downloaded from www.vernimmen.com.

Broadly speaking, corporate governance is the organisation of the control over, and management of, a firm. A narrower definition of corporate governance covers the relationship between the firm's shareholders and management, mainly involving the functioning of the board of directors or the supervisory board.

Corporate governance is determined, first and foremost, by company law, but there are also a number of reports and best practice codes that complement the recommendations and guidelines contained in the strictly legal framework.

These recommendations and guidelines, most of which are contained in all of the reports, deal with subjects such as transparency in the functioning of the board of directors, the choice of directors, the role and independence of the board, and the setting up of specialised committees to help the board in its work.

Corporate governance is one of the main means of reducing agency costs arising out of the potentially damaging relationship between shareholders and management.

Studies on corporate governance and value tend to demonstrate that good corporate governance will create value. This is even more the case for large firms based in countries where the legal framework is very loose. For small firms, the cost of introducing a sophisticated system of corporate governance can be prohibitive. Generally, there is less need for such a system in smaller firms where the managers are often the main shareholders (which prevents conflicts of interest) and there are very rarely minority shareholders.

1/ Which financial theory best explains the development of corporate governance?

2/ Why has corporate governance mainly developed at listed companies?

3/ How do stock options help in aligning the interests of managers with those of shareholders? What are their limitations?

4/ Name a firm where practically all of the directors were independent, which did not prevent it from experiencing severe financial difficulties in 2002, the result of a lack of control over managers.

5/ What is the danger when a board has specialised committees?

6/ What should an overworked director who has only been able to attend every other board meeting do?

7/ What is the most important – an independent director, a hardworking director, a competent and courageous director? What is the ideal?

8/ In which countries is it more important for a firm to have a system of corporate governance in place?

9/ What is the link between corporate governance and the cost of capital?

10/ Does the regular rotation of a firm's statutory auditors improve corporate governance?

11/ Is corporate governance relevant at companies over which the state exercises full control?

12/ What are your views on a firm that replaces its one-tier board with a two-tier board and then, a few years later, reverts to a one-tier board, like Suez did, or which asks its chief executive officer to be chairman of the board as well before reverting to the previous system a few years later, like Nestlé did?

13/ Is it a good idea, with a view to providing directors with better information, for the auditor to be a director of the company as well?

14/ What are the pros and cons of separating the position of chairman of the board from that of CEO?

More questions are waiting for you at www.vernimmen.com.

1/ *Agency theory.*
2/ *Agency costs are lower at unlisted companies (less widely-held capital, shareholders closer to management). It could be too expensive for small firms to introduce sophisticated corporate governance systems.*
3/ *They provide an incentive to managers to create value for shareholders of which they will capture a part through their stock options. Drawbacks are focusing management's attention on the value of their stock options and not on the value of the share: no dividend, high risk taken, especially since they were given for free to managers and not acquired.*

4/ *Enron.*

5/ *The other directors may not always assume their full responsibility and the committee may turn into a decision-making body instead of a body that prepares all of the directors for making decisions.*

6/ *Resign. The position of director is not a just a fancy title, it's a job like any other.*

7/ *A competent and courageous director. If possible, all four!*

8/ *In countries where ownership rights are less secure, i.e. emerging countries.*

9/ *Good corporate governance should reduce the cost of capital, because it eliminates the risk of poor management and/or fraud, which would penalise minority shareholders.*

10/ *On paper, yes, because it means that a new set of eyes will be looking at recurrent problems. But this has not been borne out by academic research.*

11/ *Yes, there is no reason why not, since conflicts of interest can also exist between the state and the managers of state-run companies.*

12/ *It's an intelligent move, demonstrating the ability to adapt to change. Sometimes a change in structure is needed when there's a new manager at the head of a group.*

13/ *No, as a matter of fact, it's not allowed. Nobody can be a judge and a party to the project.*

14/ *Separating the role of control and management, of long-term decisions and day-to-day management doubles the number of corporate officers. Personal conflicts may arise which make it unmanageable.*

BIBLIOGRAPHY

On corporate governance:

R. Aggarwal, I. Erel, M. Ferreira, P. Matos, Does governance travel around the world? Evidence from institutional investors, *Journal of Financial Economics*, **100**(1), 154–181, April 2011

H. Baker, R. Anderson, *Corporate Governance: A Synthesis of Theory, Research, and Practice*, (Robert W. Kolb Series), John Wiley & Sons, Inc., 2010

R. Chara, *Boards that Deliver*, Jossey-Bass, 2005.

T. Clarke, *International Corporate Governance: A Comparative Approach*, 2nd edn, Routledge, 2011.

H. Demsetz, The structure of ownership and the theory of the firm, *The Journal of Law & Economics*, **26**(2), 375–390, June 1983.

S. Gillian, Recent developments in corporate governance: An overview, *Journal of Corporate Finance*, **12**(3), 381–402, June 2006.

M. Jensen, W. Meckling, Theory of the firm: Managerial behavior, agency costs and ownership structure, *Journal of Financial Economics*, **3**(4), 305–360, October 1976.

R. La Porta, F. Lopez de Silanes, A. Shleifer and R. Vishny, Law and finance, *Journal of Political Economy*, **106**(6), 1133–1155, December 1998.

Y. Le Fur, P. Quiry, New developments in corporate governance, *The vernimmen.com Newsletter*, **37**, 1–4, December 2008.

F. Lipman, L. Lipman, *Corporate Governance: Best Practices*, John Wiley & Sons, Inc., 2006.

R. Monks, N. Minow, *Corporate Governance*, 4th edn, John Wiley & Sons, Inc., 2008.

R. Mork, *A History of Corporate Governance around the World: Family Business Groups to Professional Managers*, University of Chicago Press, 2007.

Weil, Gotshal, Manges, *International comparisons of selected corporate governance guidelines and codes of best practice*, Powerpoint presentation, March 2007.

www.ecgi.org, the website of the European Corporate Governance Institute.

www.icgn.org, the website of the International Corporate Governance Network.

www.oecd.org, the website of the OECD which devotes a large section to corporate governance issues.

SECTION 5

On stock options and variable remuneration:

R. Fahlenbrach, A. Low, R. Stulz, Why do firms appoint CEOs as outside directors? *Journal of Financial Economics*, **97**(1), 12–32, July 2010.

A. Morgan, A. Poulser, Linking pay to performance-compensation proposal in the S&P 500, *Journal of Financial Economics*, **62**(3), 489–523, December 2001.

On directors and managers:

B.D. Nguyen, *Does the Rolodex Matter? Corporate Elite's Small World and the Effectiveness of Boards of Directors*, working paper, 2011.

B.D. Nguyen, K.M. Nielsen, The value of independent directors: evidence from sudden death, *Journal of Financial Economics*, **98**(3), 550–567, December 2010.

A. Shleifer, R.W. Vishny, Management entrenchment: The case of manager-specific investments, *Journal of Financial Economics*, **25**(1), 123–139, 1989.

www.boardmember.com, an information resource for senior officers and directors of publicly traded corporations

On value and corporate governance:

R. Albuquerue, N. Wang, Agency conflicts, reinvestments and asset pricing, *Journal of Finance*, **63**(1), 1–40, February 2008.

R.C. Anderson, D.M. Reeb, Founding-family ownership and firm performance: Evidence from the S&P 500, *The Journal of Finance*, **58**(3), 1301–1328, June 2003.

R. Bauer, N. Guenster, R. Otten, Empirical evidence on corporate governance in Europe. The effect on stock returns, firm value and performance, *Journal of Asset Management*, **5**(2), 91–104, August 2004.

L. Bebchuk, A. Cohen, A. Ferrell, What Matters in Corporate Governance, *Review of Financial Studies*, **22**(2), 783–827, February 2009.

S. Bhagat, B. Bolton, Corporate governance and firm performance, *Journal of Corporate Finance*, **14**(3), 257–273, June 2008.

B. Black, The corporate governance behavior and market value of Russian firms, *Emerging Markets Review*, **2**(2), 89–108, 2001.

V. Chhaochharia, Y. Grinstein, Corporate governance and firm value – The impact of the 2002 Governance Rules, *Journal of Finance*, **62**(4), 1789–1825, August 2007.

J. Core, W. Guay, T. Rusticus, Does weak corporate governance cause stock returns? An examination of firm operating performance and analysts' expectations, *Journal of Finance*, **61**(2), 655–687, April 2006.

C. Doidge, G. Karolyi, R. Stulz, Why do countries matter so much for corporate governance? *Journal of Financial Economics*, **86**(1), 1–39, October 2007.

A. Durnev, E. Han Kim, To steal or not to steal: Firm attributes, legal environment and valuation, *Journal of Finance*, **60**(3), 1461–1493, June 2005.

P. Gompers, J. Ishii, A. Metrick, Corporate governance and equity prices, *The Quarterly Journal of Economics*, **118**(1), 107–155, February 2003.

P. Harbula, The ownership structure, governance and performance of French companies, *Journal of Applied Corporate Finance*, **19**(1), 88–101, Winter 2007.

R. La Porta, F. Lopez de Silanes, A. Shleifer, R. Vishny, Investor protection and corporate valuation, *Journal of Finance*, **57**(3), 1147–1170, June 2002.

R. Stulz, R. Williamson, Culture, openness, and finance, *Journal of Financial Economics*, **70**(3), 313–349, December 2003.

SECTION 5

A peek behind the scenes of investment banking

At any given time, a company can have several valuations, depending on the point of view of the buyer and the seller and their expectations of future profits and synergies. This variety sets the stage for negotiation but, needless to say, a transaction will take place only if common ground can be found – i.e. if the seller's minimum price does not exceed the buyer's maximum price.

The art of negotiation consists of allocating the value of the anticipated synergies between the buyer and the seller, and in finding an equilibrium between their respective positions, so that both come away with a good deal. The seller receives more than the value for the company on a standalone basis because he pockets part of the value of the synergies the buyer hopes to unlock. Similarly, the buyer pays out part of the value of the synergies, but has still not paid more than the company is worth to him.

Transactions can also result from erroneous valuations. A seller might think his company has reached a peak, for example, and the buyer that it still has growth potential. But generally, out-and-out deception is rarer than you might think. It's usually only in hindsight that we say we made a killing and that the party on the other side of the transaction was totally wrong!

In this chapter we will focus on the acquisition of one company by another. We will not consider industrial alliances, i.e. commercial or technology agreements negotiated directly between two companies which do not involve a transaction of the equity of either of them. Before examining the various negotiation tactics and the purchase of a listed company, let us first take a look at the merger and acquisition phenomenon and the economic justification behind a merger.

Section 43.1
THE RISE OF MERGERS AND ACQUISITIONS

1/ MERGER AND ACQUISITION WAVES

Acquisitions can be paid for either in cash or in shares. Generally speaking, share transactions predominate when corporate valuations are high, as they were in 1999–2000, because absolute values do not have to be determined.

WORLDWIDE MERGER ACTIVITY (US$bn)

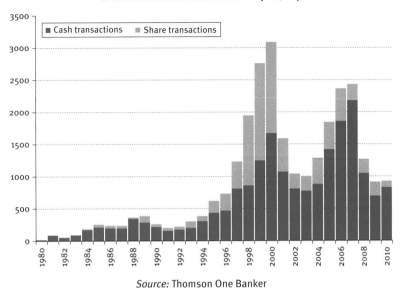

Source: Thomson One Banker

Conversely, when the market is bearish, cash payments are more attractive to both parties. The seller receives cold, hard cash which will not lose value as shares might, while the buyer is reluctant to issue new shares at prices he/she considers to be a discount to their intrinsic value.

As shown in the above graph, mergers and acquisitions tend to come in waves:

- In the 1960s conglomerates were all the rage. ITT, Gulf & Western, Fiat, Schneider and many others rose to prominence during this period. The parent company was supposedly able to manage the acquired subsidiaries better, plus meet their capital needs. Most transactions were paid for with shares.
- In the 1980s, most acquisitions were paid for in cash. Many of the big conglomerates formed in the 1960s were broken up. They had become less efficient, poorly managed and valued at less than the sum of the values of their subsidiaries.
- In the 1990s and 2000s, companies within the same sector joined forces, generally in share transactions: Procter & Gamble–Gillette, Pfizer–Wyeth, Arcelor–Mittal, Cadbury–Kraft, etc.

Shleifer and Vishny (2003) explain this phenomenon by saying that, in a given market at a given time, there are overvalued and undervalued companies. In this instance, the former bids to acquire the latter. The bid depresses the acquirer's valuation but also keeps this overvalued firm from falling too far or too fast when investors realise that the company is overvalued. AOL's acquisition of Time Warner was a case in point. The merger wave ends when there are no more undervalued firms left, because they have all been bought up (end of the 1980s) or because there are no more overvalued firms (2001, 2003).

Putting the purely financial elements aside, the determinants of mergers and acquisitions can be macroeconomic, microeconomic or human factors, as we will now see.

2/ Macroeconomic factors

Periods of innovation and technological change are often followed by merger waves. During the innovation period (computers in the 1970s, renewable energies today), many new companies are founded. Inevitably, however, the growth outlook for the growth and survival of these startups fades, leading to a period of consolidation (Microsoft trying to buy Yahoo!). Moreover, startups' heavy financing needs may prompt them to seek the support of a major group that, in turn, can take advantage of the growth in the startups' business (Google buys You Tube). Many companies are undergoing a change in market scope. Thirty years ago, their market was national; now they find they must operate in a regional (European) or more often worldwide context (Arcelor Mittal is an example). Adapting to this change requires massive investment in both physical and human capital, leading to much higher financing needs (pharmaceuticals). Lastly, as competition increases, companies that have not yet merged must grow rapidly in order to keep up with their now larger rivals. Critical mass becomes important (e.g. Tabacalera–Seita and then Altadis–Imperial Tobacco).

Legislative changes have fostered restructuring in many industries. A broad trend towards deregulation began in the 1980s in the US and the UK, profoundly changing many sectors of the economy, from air transport to financial services to telecommunications. In Europe, a single market is being implemented in conjunction with a policy of deregulation in banking, energy and telecommunications. European governments further scale back their presence in the economy by privatising many publicly-held companies. In many cases, these companies then became active participants in mergers and acquisitions (ENI, EDF, Deutsche Telekom, Tabacalera).

The increasing importance of financial markets has played a fundamental role in corporate restructuring. In the space of 30 years, European economies have evolved from primarily credit-based systems, where banks were the main suppliers of funds, to financial market systems, characterised by disintermediation (see Chapter 15). Not surprisingly, this change happened in conjunction with a shift in power from banks and other financial companies (Paribas, Mediobanca, Deutsche Bank, etc.) to investors. Accordingly, shareholders are exerting pressure on corporate managers to produce returns in line with their expectations:

- in the event of disappointing performance, shareholders can sell their shares and, in doing this, they depress the share price. Ultimately, this can lead to a restructuring (Daimler Chrysler) or a takeover (ABN Amro, Telecom Italia);
- conversely, companies must convince the market that their acquisitions (EDF/British Energy) are economically justified.

In conclusion, the financial and regulatory environment is a determining factor in economic consolidation. Industrial and technological changes naturally prompt companies to merge with each other. The decline in real growth in Europe has made it more difficult for firms to grow organically. In response, managers in search of new growth drivers try to combine with another company.

3/ MICROECONOMIC FACTORS

By increasing their size and production volumes, companies reduce their unit costs. Long ago, BCG found that when cumulative production volume for manufacturing companies doubles, the unit price declines by around 20%. On this basis, an acquisition constitutes a shortcut to economies of scale, in particular in R&D, administrative or distribution costs (Pernod Ricard/Allied Domecq). Moreover, higher volume puts a company in a better position to negotiate lower costs with its suppliers or higher prices with its customers (Vale/Inco).

Mergers can increase a company's market share and boost its revenues dramatically. To the extent the companies address complementary markets, merging will enable them to broaden their overall scope. Complementarity comes in two forms:

*   geographic (British Airways–Iberia). The two groups benefit from their respective presence in different regions;
*   product (Volvo–Zhejiang Geely). The group can offer a full palette of services to its customers.

Although riskier than organic growth, mergers and acquisitions allow a company to save valuable time. In growing sectors of the economy, speed – the first mover advantage – is often a critical success factor. Once the sector matures, it becomes more difficult and more expensive to chip away at competitors' market shares, so acquisitions become a matter of choice (Commerzbank–Dresdner Bank). When a company is expanding internationally or entering a new business, acquiring an existing company is a way to circumvent barriers to entry, both in terms of market recognition (L'Oréal–The Body Shop) and expertise (Google–Double-Click).

By gaining additional stature, a company can more easily take new risks in a worldwide environment. The transition from a domestic market focus to worldwide competition requires that companies invest much more. The financial and human risks become too great for a medium-sized company (oil and gas exploration, pharmaceutical research). An acquisition instantly boosts the company's financial resources and reduces risk, facilitating decisions about the company's future.

The need for cash, either because groups are in difficulties (Hertz sold by Ford) or because they regularly need to make capital gains (LBO funds) is another reason why M&A deals happen.

4/ HUMAN FACTORS

In addition to the economic criteria prompting companies to merge, there is also the human factor. Many companies founded between 1945 and 1970, which were often controlled by a single shareholder-manager, are now encountering, not surprisingly, problems of succession. In some cases, another family member takes over (Swatch, Fiat). In other cases, the company must be sold if it is to survive (Yves Saint-Laurent).

5/ THE LARGER CONTEXT

THE LIFECYCLE OF THE FIRM

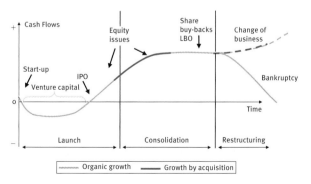

Mergers and acquisitions, although tricky to manage, are part of the lifecycle of a company and are a useful growth tool.

SECTION 5

Mergers are no panacea, however. Approximately one out of two fail because the promised synergies never materialise.

Synergies are often overestimated; their cost and time to implement underestimated. For example, making information systems compatible or restructuring staff can be notoriously difficult.

Numerous research works have measured the value created by an M&A deal and how this value is shared between shareholders of the buyer and of the target. They demonstrate that value is created for the target's shareholders because of the control premium paid. For the buyer's shareholders, the results are more mixed, even if they tend to show a recent improvement compared to the end of the 1990s where it was widely assumed that two-thirds of mergers were failing. Excluding some resounding failures (acquisition of Chrysler by Daimler[1] or the AOL–Time Warner merger) which heavily bias the results, M&A deals would appear value creative because of some largely successful deals such as Santander–Abbey National, Air France–KLM, NBC–Universal. Quality and speediness of the integration process are the key factors for successful M&A deals.

1 *The share price of Daimler was divided by 3 between the acquisition of Chrysler and its sale in 2007.*

Section 43.2
CHOOSING A NEGOTIATING STRATEGY

A negotiating strategy aims at achieving a price objective set in accordance with the financial value derived from our valuation work presented in Chapter 32. But price is not everything. The seller might also want to limit the guarantees he grants, retain managerial control, ensure that his employees' future is safe, etc.

Depending on the number of potential acquirers, the necessary degree of confidentiality, the timing and the seller's demands, there is a wide range of possible negotiating strategies. We present below the two extremes: private negotiation and auction. Academic researchers[2] have established that none of these strategies is better than another. Our personal experience tells us the same thing: the context dictates the choice of a strategy.

2 *See Boone and Mulherin (2007).*

1/ PRIVATE NEGOTIATION

The seller or his advisor contacts a small number of potential acquirers to gauge their interest. After signing a confidentiality agreement (or non-disclosure agreement, "NDA"), the potential acquirers might receive an information memorandum describing the company's industrial, financial and human resource elements. Discussions then begin. It is important that each potential acquirer believe he is not alone, even if in reality he is. In principle, this technique requires extreme confidentiality. Psychological rather than practical barriers to the transaction necessitate the high degree of confidentiality.

To preserve confidentiality, the seller often prefers to hire a specialist, most often an investment banker, to find potential acquirers and keep all discussions under wraps. Such specialists are usually paid a success fee that can be proportional to the size of the transaction. Strictly speaking, there are no typical negotiating procedures. Every transaction is different. The only absolute rule about negotiating strategies is that the negotiator must have a strategy.

The advantage of private negotiation is a high level of confidentiality. In many cases, there is no paper trail at all.

The discussion focuses on:

- how much control the seller will give up (and the status of any remaining minority shareholders);
- the price;
- the payment terms;
- any conditions precedent;
- representations and warranties; and
- any contractual relationship that might remain between the seller and the target company after the transaction.

As you might expect, price remains the essential question in the negotiating process. Everything that might have been said during the course of the negotiations falls away, leaving one all-important parameter: price. We now take a look at the various agreements and clauses that play a role in private negotiation.

(a) Memorandum of understanding (MOU) or letter of intent (LOI)

When a framework for the negotiations has been defined, a memorandum of understanding is often signed to open the way to a transaction. A memorandum of understanding is a moral, not a legal, commitment. Often, once the MOU is signed, the management of the acquiring company presents it to its board of directors to obtain permission to pursue the negotiations.

The memorandum of understanding is not useful when each party has made a firm commitment to negotiate. In this case, the negotiation of a memorandum of understanding slows down the process rather than accelerating it.

(b) Agreement in principle

The next step might be an agreement in principle, spelling out the terms and conditions of the sale. The commitments of each party are irrevocable, unless there are conditions precedent such as approval of the regulatory authorities. The agreement in principle can take many forms.

(c) Financial sweeteners

In many cases, specific financial arrangements are needed to get over psychological, tax, legal or financial barriers. These arrangements do not change the value of the company.

These arrangements cannot transform a bad transaction into a good one. They serve only to bring the parties to the transaction closer together.

Sometimes, for psychological reasons, the seller refuses to go below some purely symbolic value. If he draws a line in the sand at 200, for example, whereas the buyer does not want to pay more than 190, a schedule spreading out payments over time sometimes does the trick. The seller will receive 100 this year and 100 next year. This is 190.9 if discounted at 10%, but it is still 200 to his way of thinking. Recognise that we are out of the realm of finance here and into the confines of psychology, and that this arrangement fools only those who want to be fooled.

This type of financial arrangement is window-dressing to hide the real price. Often companies build elaborate structures in the early stages of negotiation, only to simplify them little by little as they get used to the idea of buying or selling the company. Far from being a magical solution, such sweeteners give each party time to gravitate towards the other. In these cases it is only a stage, albeit a necessary one.

The following techniques are part of the investment banker's stock in trade:

- set up a special-purpose holding company to buy the company, lever up the company with debt, then have the seller reinvest part of the funds in the hope of obtaining a second gain (this is an LBO[3] see Chapter 45);

- have the buyer pay for part of the purchase price in shares, which can then be sold in the market if the buyer's shares are listed;
- pay for part of the purchase price with IOUs;
- link part of the purchase price to the sale price of a non-strategic asset the buyer does not wish to keep;
- an earnout clause, which links part of the transaction price to the acquired company's future financial performance. The clause can take one of two forms:

  ○ either the buyer takes full control of the target company at a minimum price, which can only be revised upwards; or
  ○ he buys a portion of the company at a fixed price and the rest at a future date, with the price dependent on the company's future profits. The index can be a multiple of EBIT, EBITDA or pre-tax profit.

- Earnout provisions are very common in transactions involving service companies (advertising agencies, investment banks), where people are key assets. Deferral of part of the price will entice them to stay and facilitate the integration process.

2/ AUCTION

In an auction, the company is offered for sale under a predetermined schedule to several potential buyers who are competing with each other. The objective is to choose the one offering the highest price. An auction is often private, but it can also be announced in the press or by a court decision.

Private auctions are run by an investment bank in the following manner. Once the decision is taken to sell the company, the seller asks an audit firm to produce a Vendor Due Diligence (VDD, also called a Long Form Report), to provide a clear view of the weak points of the asset from legal, tax, accounting, regulatory, . . . points of view. The VDD will be communicated to buyers later on in the process. For the moment, a brief summary of the company is prepared (a "teaser"). It is sent, together with a non-disclosure agreement, to a large number of potentially-interested companies and financial investors.

In the next stage (often called "Phase I"), once the potential buyers sign the non-disclosure agreement,[4] they receive additional information, gathered in an information memorandum ("info memo"). Then they submit a non-binding offer indicating the price, its financing, any conditions precedent and eventually their intentions regarding the future strategy for the target company.

At that point of time ("Phase II") either:

- a "short list" of up to half a dozen candidates at most is drawn up. They receive still more information and possibly a schedule of visits to the company's industrial sites and meetings with management. Often a **data room** is set up,[5] where all economic, financial and legal information concerning the target company is available for perusal. Access to the data room is very restricted, for example no copies can be made. At the end of this stage, potential investors submit binding offers; or

- **exclusive negotiations** are opened for a few days. For a given period of time, the potential buyer is the only candidate. At the end of the exclusive period, the buyer must submit a binding offer (in excess of a certain figure) or withdraw from the negotiations.

Together with the binding offers, the seller will ask the bidder(s) to propose a markup (comments) to the disposal agreement (called the Share Purchase Agreement,[6] SPA) previously provided by the seller. The ultimate selection of the buyer depends, naturally, on the binding offer, but also on the buyer's comments on the share purchase.

An auction can lead to a high price because buyers are in competition with each other. In addition, it makes it easier for the seller's representatives to prove that they did everything in their power to obtain the highest possible price for the company, be it:

- the executive who wants to sell a subsidiary;
- a majority shareholder whose actions might be challenged by minority shareholders; or
- the investment banker in charge of the transaction.

Moreover, an auction is faster, because the seller, not the buyer, sets the pace. Competition sometimes generates a price that is well in excess of expectations.

However, the auction creates confidentiality problems. Many people have access to the basic data, and denying rumours of a transaction becomes difficult, so the process must move quickly. Also, as the technique is based on price only, it is exposed to some risks, such as several potential buyers teaming up with the intention of splitting the assets among them. Lastly, should the process fail, the company's credibility will suffer. The company must have an uncontested strategic value and a sound financial condition. The worst result is the one of an auction process which turns sour because financial results are not up to the estimations produced a few weeks before, leaving only one buyer who knows he is now the only buyer.

5 Nowadays mostly on the Internet: it is then an electronic data room.

6 Or Sell and Purchase Agreement.

STEPS OF AN M&A PROCESS

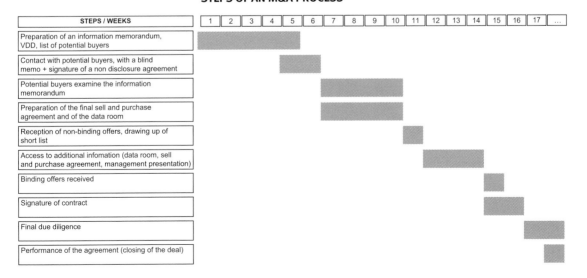

STEPS / WEEKS	1	2	3	4	5	6	7	8	9	10	11	12	13	14	15	16	17	...
Preparation of an information memorandum, VDD, list of potential buyers																		
Contact with potential buyers, with a blind memo + signature of a non disclosure agreement																		
Potential buyers examine the information memorandum																		
Preparation of the final sell and purchase agreement and of the data room																		
Reception of non-binding offers, drawing up of short list																		
Access to additional infomation (data room, sell and purchase agreement, management presentation)																		
Binding offers received																		
Signature of contract																		
Final due diligence																		
Performance of the agreement (closing of the deal)																		

SECTION 5

A well-processed auction can take 3–5 months between intention to sell and the closing. It is sometimes shorter when an investment fund sells on to another fund.

3/ THE OUTCOME OF NEGOTIATIONS

In the end, whatever negotiating method was used, the seller is left with a single potential buyer who can then impose certain conditions. Should the negotiations fall apart at this stage, it could spell trouble for the seller because he would have to go back to the other potential buyers, hat in hand. So the seller is in a position of weakness when it comes to finalising the negotiations. The principal remaining element is the representations and warranties provisions that are part of the share purchase agreement.

Representations and warranties ("reps & warranties") are particularly important because they give confidence to the buyer that the profitability of the company has not been misrepresented. It is a way of securing the value of assets and liabilities of the target company as the contract does not provide a detailed valuation.

Representations and warranties are not intended to protect the buyer against an overvaluation of the company. They are intended to certify that **all of the means of production are indeed under the company's control and that there are no hidden liabilities**.

Well-worded representations and warranties clauses should guarantee to the buyer:

- the substance of fixed assets (and not their value);
- the real nature and the value of inventories (assuming that the buyer and the seller have agreed on a valuation method);
- the real nature of other elements of working capital;
- the amount and nature of all of the company's other commitments, whether they are on the balance sheet (such as debts) or not.

The representations and warranties clause is generally divided into two parts.

In the first part (representations), the seller makes commitments related to the **substance** of the company that is to be sold.

The seller generally states that the target company and its subsidiaries are properly registered, that all the fixed assets on the balance sheet, including brands and patents, or used by the company in the ordinary course of business actually exist. As such, representations and warranties do not guarantee the book value of the fixed assets, but their existence.

7 Generally Accepted Accounting Principles.

The seller declares that inventories have been booked in accordance with industry standards and the demands of the tax authorities, that depreciation and provisions have been calculated according to GAAP.[7] The seller declares that the company is up to date in tax payments, salaries and other accruals and that there are no prejudicial contracts with suppliers, customers or employees. All elements already communicated to the buyer, in particular exceptional items such as special contracts, guarantees, etc., are annexed to the clause and excluded from it because the buyer is already aware of them.

Lastly, the seller guarantees that during the transitional period – i.e. between the last statement date and the sale date – the company was managed in a prudent manner. In particular, he certifies that no dividends were distributed or assets sold, except for those agreed with the buyer during the period, that no investments in excess of a certain amount were undertaken, nor contracts altered, etc.

In the second part of the clause (warranties), the seller guarantees the amount of the company's equity capital as of the most recent statement date (statements annexed to the agreement). The seller agrees to indemnify the buyer against any decrease caused by events that took place prior to the sale date. The guarantee remains in effect for a given period of time and is capped at a specified amount. This clause is often accompanied by a holdback (part of the purchase price is put in an escrow account[8]) or a bank guarantee.

The representations and warranties clauses are the main addition to the sale agreement but, depending on the agreement, there may be many other additions, so long as they are legally valid – i.e. not contrary to company law, tax law or stock market regulations requiring equal treatment of all shareholders. A non-exhaustive list would include:

- means of payment;
- status and future role of managers and executives;
- agreements with remaining shareholders;
- audit of the company's books. On this score, we recommend against realising an audit before the two parties have reached an agreement. An audit often detects problems in the company, poisoning the atmosphere, and can serve as a pretext to abandoning the transaction.

Of course, the parties to the contracts should also call upon legal experts to ensure that each clause is legally enforceable.

The final step is the actual consummation of the deal. It often takes place at a later date, because certain conditions must be met first: accounting, legal or tax audit, restructuring, approval of domestic or foreign competition commissioners, etc.

8 A special bank account for the deposit of funds, to which the beneficiary's access is a subject of the fulfilment of certain conditions.

4/ THE DUAL-TRACK PROCESS

In order to improve its negotiation position or because the likely outcome of the sale process is unclear, the seller may decide to pursue a dual-track process: it will launch a sale process and the preparation of an IPO in parallel. At the latest possible moment,[9] it will choose to sell to the one offering the best price, be it the stock market or a buyer.

9 Even the day before the IPO takes place, as Eurazéo did when it sold Fraikin to CVC.

Section 43.3
TAKING OVER A LISTED COMPANY

For a public company, the negotiation cannot take place between two parties in the same way as for a private company. The transaction has to take into account the treatment of minority shareholders.

Local regulations aim to protect minority shareholders in order to develop financial markets. The main target of these regulations is to guarantee a transparent and equal treatment for all shareholders.

In order to acquire a listed company, the buyer needs to secure shares from a large number of minority shareholders. It would be too difficult and time-consuming to acquire shares on the open market; therefore the buyer usually makes a public offer (takeover bid) to all shareholders to buy their shares.

Each country has regulations governing takeovers of companies listed on domestic stock exchanges. The degree of constraint varies from one country to another.

1/ Stake-building

To succeed in acquiring a listed company the first step can be to start building a block in the company. This can be done on the open market by buying shares.

In order to prevent the acquirer from taking control of a company in that way, most market regulations require investors in a listed company to publicly declare when they pass certain thresholds in the capital of a company. If the acquirer fails to declare these shares, voting rights are lost.

The first threshold is most often 5% (USA, France, Belgium, Poland, Netherlands . . .).

Regulatory disclosure requirements allow minority shareholders to monitor stake-building and prevent an acquirer from getting control of a company little by little. These requirements are also helpful for the management to monitor the shareholder structure of the company. By-laws can set additional thresholds to be declared (generally lower thresholds than required by law).

Regulatory threshold disclosure requirements are the following:

China	5% and multiples of 5% above
France	5%, 10%, 20%, 25%, 30%, 33.3%, 50%, 66.6%, 90% and 95%
Germany	3%, 5%, 10%, 15%, 20%, 25%, 30%, 50%, 75%
India	5%, 10%, 14%, 54%, 74%
Italy	2%, 5%, 10% and multiples of 5% above up to 50%, 66.6%, 75%, 90% and 95%
Netherlands	5%, 10%, 15%, 20%, 25%, 30%, 40%, 50%, 60%, 75% and 95%
Spain	3%, 5% and multiples of 5% thereafter
Switzerland	3%, 5%, 10%, 15%, 20%, 25%, 33.3%, 50%, 66.6%
UK	3% and multiples of 1% above
US	5% and multiples of 1% above

2/ Type of offer

It is very unusual for an acquirer to gain control of a public company without launching a public offer on the target. Such offers are made to all shareholders over a certain period of time (2–10 weeks depending on the country). Public offers can be split between:

- share offers or cash offers;
- voluntary or mandatory offers;
- hostile or recommended offers.

(a) Cash or share offers

The table below summarises the criteria relevant for assessing whether a bidder wants to propose shares or cash in a public offer:

	Payment in cash	**Payment in shares**	**Comments**
Signal from buyer's point of view	Positive: buyer's stock is undervalued. Debt financing: positive signal	Negative: buyer's stock is overvalued	
Signal from seller's point of view	None	Positive: the seller is taking some of the risk of the deal	
Allocation of synergies	Target company's shareholders benefit from synergies only via the premium they receive	Target company's shareholders participate fully in future synergies	In a friendly share exchange offer, the premium might be minimal if the expected synergies are high
Psychological effects	Cash lends credibility to the bid and increases its psychological value	Payment in shares has a "friendly" character	
Purchaser's financial structure	Increases gearing	Decreases gearing	The size of the deal sometimes requires payment in shares
Impact on purchaser's share price	After the impact of the announcement, no direct link between the purchaser's and target's share price	Immediate link between purchaser's and target's share price, maintained throughout the bid period	A share exchange offer gains credibility when the two companies' share prices align with the announced exchange ratio.
Shareholder structure	No impact unless the deal is later on refinanced through a share issue	Shareholders of the target become shareholders of the enlarged group	Sometimes, shareholders of the target get control of the new group in a share for share offer
Accounting effects	Increases EPS and its growth rate if the inverse of the target's P/E including any premium is greater than the after-tax cost of debt of the acquirer	Increases EPS if the purchaser's P/E is higher than the target's, premium included	EPS is not a real indicator of value creation, see Chapter 28
Purchaser's tax situation	Interest expense deductible	No impact, except capital gain if treasury shares are used	Taxation is not a determining factor
Seller's tax situation	Taxable gain	Gain on sale can be carried forward	
Index weighting	No change	Higher weighting in index (greater market capitalisation)	In the case of a share exchange, possible re-rating owing to size effect

In practice, the choice is not so black and white. The purchaser can offer a combination of cash and shares (mix offers), cash as an alternative to shares, or launch a "mix and match" offer, as we will see. The purchaser's investment banker plays a key role in helping to choose the type of bid, the premium offered, how the bid is communicated to investors, etc.

(b) Hostile or recommended offers

The success or failure of an offer can depend largely on the attitude of the target's management and the board of directors towards the offer.

To maximise the chances of success, the terms of an offer are generally negotiated with the management prior to the announcement, and then recommended by the board of the company. The offer is then qualified friendly or recommended.

In some cases, the management of the target is not aware of the launch of an offer; it is then called an unsolicited offer. Facing this sudden event the board has to convene and to decide whether the offer is acceptable or not. If the board rejects the offer, it becomes hostile. This does not mean that the offer will not succeed but just that the bidder will have to fight management and the current board of directors during the offer period to convince shareholders.

Most unsolicited offers end up as recommended offers, but only after the bidder has sweetened the offer in one way or another (generally by offering a higher price).

(c) Voluntary or mandatory offers

The concept of the mandatory offer does not exist in every country. Nevertheless, in most countries, when a buyer passes a certain threshold or acquires the control of the target, he is required by stock exchange regulation to offer to buy back all the shareholders' shares. It is one of the founding rules of stock exchange regulations. It should be noted that in the US, there is no mandatory offer and an acquirer can theoretically buy a majority of the capital of a listed company without having to launch an offer to the minority shareholders.

Generally, the constraints for a mandatory offer are tighter than for a voluntary offer. For example, in the UK the mandatory offer will be in cash, or at least a cash alternative will be provided. Obviously the conditions of the offer that the acquirer is allowed to set in a mandatory offer are limited because they are defined by the regulations.

3/ CERTAINTY OF THE OFFER

It would be very disruptive for the market if an acquirer were to launch an offer and withdraw it a few days later. All market regulations try to ensure that when a public offer is launched, shareholders are actually given the opportunity to tender their shares.

Therefore, market regulation requires that the offer is funded when it is launched. Full funding ensures that the market does not run the risk of a buyer falling short of financing when the offer is a success! This funding usually takes the form of a guarantee by a bank (generally the bank presenting the offer commits that if the acquirer does not have the funds the bank will pay for the shares).

Another principle is that offers should be unconditional. In particular, the bidder cannot set conditions to the execution of the offer that remains in his hands (as an example, an offer cannot be conditional upon board approval of the acquirer). Nevertheless, in most countries, the offer can be subject to a minimum acceptance (which generally cannot be too high) and regulatory approval (including anti-trust). In a few countries (the UK, the Netherlands, the US), the offer can be subject to a material adverse change (MAC) clause which can only be invoked in extreme cases.[10]

10 *In a UK takeover bid situation, 9/11 was not deemed to be such a case.*

4/ Documentation and market authority role

The main role of market authorities is to guarantee the equal treatment of all shareholders and the transparency of the process.

In that regard, market authorities will have a key role in public offers:

- They set (and often control) the standard content of the offer document. This document must contain all relevant information allowing the target's shareholders to take a proper decision.
- They supervise the process timetable.
- In most countries their green light is necessary for the launch of the offer (they therefore control the price offered).

5/ Defensive measures

In theory, a company whose shares are being secretly bought up on the stock market generally has a greater variety and number of defensive measures available to it than a company that is the target of a takeover bid. The reason behind this disparity is the secrecy surrounding shares bought up on the market compared with rules of equality and transparency applied to takeover bids.

If a company becomes aware that its shares are being bought up on the market, it is entitled to invoke all of the means of shareholder control described in Chapter 42. It can also get "friendly" investors to buy up its shares in order to increase the percentage of shares held by "friends" and push up its share price, thus making it more expensive for the hostile party to buy as many shares as it needs. Of course the company will also need to have the time required to carry out all of these transactions, which generally involve waiting periods.

In the case of a takeover bid, there are fewer defensive measures available and they also depend on regulations in force in each country. In some countries (the UK and the Netherlands), all defensive measures taken during a takeover period (excluding attempts to identify other bidders) must be ratified by an EGM held during the offer period. Proxies granted by the general meeting of shareholders to the board prior to the offer period may be suspended. In some countries, any decision taken by the corporate and management bodies before the offer period that has not been fully or partially implemented, which does not fall within the normal course of business and which is likely to cause the offer to fail, must be approved or confirmed by the general meeting of the target's shareholders.

Furthermore, in some countries, as soon as the takeover bid has been launched, the parties involved are required to ensure that the interests of the target's employees are taken into account, to ensure that all shareholders are treated equally and that no upheaval on the stock markets is caused, to act in good faith and to comply with all regulations governing takeover bids.

Generally, a company has limited means for defending itself against takeover bids.

The target company can either defend itself by embarking on an information campaign, explaining to shareholders and to the media how it will be able to create greater value in the future than the premium being offered by the predator, or it can use more active defensive measures, such as:

- finding a third party ready to launch a competing takeover bid;
- launching its own takeover bid on the hostile bidder;
- getting "friends" to buy up its shares;
- carrying out a capital increase or buying or selling businesses;
- warrants;
- legal action.

If the hostile bidder attempts to neutralise some of these defensive measures during the offer period, the company will have to hold an EGM to authorise them. This can be a difficult process. Some shareholders may have already sold their shares to hedge funds that are betting on the success of the takeover bid, and will thus vote against the defensive measures. Others may fear that the defensive measures will be too effective and will wipe out the takeover premium.

A competing takeover bid must be filed a few days before the close of the initial bid. The price offered should be at least a few percentage points higher than the initial bid. There's always the possibility that the initial bidder will make a higher bid, so there's no guarantee that the competing offer will succeed. Likewise, the "**white knight**" can sometimes turn grey or black when the rescue offer actually succeeds. We saw this when the German group E.On came to the "rescue" of Endesa which was "under attack" by the Spanish group Gas Natural[11] and when Alcan fell into the arms of Rio Tinto.

A share purchase or exchange offer by the target on the hostile bidder, known as a Pac-Man defence, is only possible if the hostile bidder itself is listed and if its shares are widely held. In such cases, industrial projects are not that different given that an offer by X on Y results in the same economic whole as an offer by Y on X. This marks the start of a communications war (advertisements, press releases, meetings with investors), with each camp explaining why it would be better placed to manage the new whole than the other.

The buying up of shares by "friends" is often highly regulated and generally has to be declared to the market authority which monitors any acting in concert or which may force the "friend" to file a counter offer!

A capital increase or the issue of marketable securities is often only possible if this has been authorised by the general meeting of shareholders prior to the takeover bid, because generally there won't be enough time to convene an EGM to fit in with the offer timetable. In any event, a reserved issue is often not allowed.

Warrants, described in Chapter 40, are a strong dissuasive element. The negative consequences of warrants being issued for the company launching a hostile takeover bid mean that it is generally prepared to negotiate with the target – neutralisation of the warrants in exchange for a higher offer price.

US experience has shown that "poison pill" warrants strengthen the negotiating position of the target's management, although they don't ensure its independence. If warrants are, in fact, issued, the matter of director responsibility will be raised, since the directors will effectively have caused shareholders to lose out on an opportunity to get a higher price for their shares.

Legal action could be taken to ensure that market regulations are complied with or on the basis of misleading information if the prospectus issued by the hostile bidder appears to criticise the target's management. There is also the possibility of reporting the

11 *Before it was pipped to the post by Enel and Acciona.*

SECTION 5

hostile bidder for abuse of a dominant position or insider trading if unusual trades are made before the offer is launched, for failing to comply with the principle of equality of shareholders or for failing to protect the interests of employees if the target has made risky acquisitions during the offer period. The real aim of any legal proceedings is to gain time for the target's management given that, in general, it takes a few months for the courts to issue rulings on the facts of a case.

6/ The larger context

The various anti-takeover measures generally force the bidder to sweeten his offer, but rarely to abandon it. What can happen is that an initially hostile bid can turn into a friendly merger (Imperial Tobacco–Altadis, RBS-Santander-Fortis–ABN Amro). Whether a hostile offer is successful or a white knight comes to the rescue, events invariably lead to the loss of the target company's independence.

Which, then, are the most effective defensive measures? In recent bids involving large companies, those that have taken the initiative far upstream have been at a clear advantage. A good defence involves ensuring that the company is always in a position to seize opportunities, to anticipate danger and to operate from a position of strength so as to be able to counterattack if need be.

In our view, loyal shareholders can be the best defence. What makes them loyal? Good financial performance, candid financial communication, a share price that reflects the company's value and skilled managers who respect the principles of shareholder value and corporate governance.

7/ Summary of some national regulations

The table below summarises the principal rules applicable to takeover bids in some countries:

Country	Regulator	Threshold for mandatory bid	Minimum percentage mandatory bid must encompass	Bid conditions allowed?	Bid validity after approval	Squeeze-out[12] possible?
China	China Securities Regulatory Commission *www.csrc.gov.cn*	30%	5%		30 days	No. Minority shareholders have the right to sell to the buyer after an offer giving him at least 75% of shares, at the offer price

[12] That is, possibility for the majority shareholder to force the buy-back of minority shareholders and delist the company if minority shareholders represent only a small part of the capital.

Country	Regulator	Threshold for mandatory bid	Minimum percentage mandatory bid must encompass	Bid conditions allowed?	Bid validity after approval	Squeeze-out[12] possible?
France	AMF, Autorité des Marchés Financiers www.amf-france.org	30% of shares or voting rights, 2% p.a. between 30% and 50% of shares or voting rights	100% of shares and equity-linked securities	Usual suspects[13]. None if bid mandatory	25–35 trading days	Yes if > 95% of voting rights and shares
Germany	BAFin, Budesanstalt für Finanzdien- stle- istungsauf- sicht www.bafin.de	30% of voting rights	100%	Usual supects[13] None if manda- tory bid	4–10 weeks	Yes, if > 95% of shares
India	Security and Exchange Board of India www.sebi.gov.in	15% of shares or voting rights	20% at least	Minimum accep- tance	20 days	No
Italy	CONSOB, Commissione Nazionale per le Società e la Borsa www .consob.it	30% of shares, 3% p.a. be- yond 30% up to 50%	100% of vot- ing shares	Usual suspects[13]	15–40 trading days	Yes, if > 95% of voting rights and shares
Netherlands	AFM, Actoriteit Financiele Markten www.afm.nl	30% of voting rights	100% of shares and equity-linked securities	Minimum accep- tance	> 23 trading days and > 30 if hostile	Yes if > 95%
Spain	CNMV, Comision Nacional de los Mercados de Valores www.cnmv.es	30% and 50% or less if right to nominate more than half of the directors or any increase of 5% between 30% and 50%	100%	Usual suspects[13]	4–11 weeks	Yes if > 90% of the voting rights
Switzerland	COPA, Commission des Offres Publiques d'Achat www. takeover.ch	33.3% of voting rights[14]	100% of shares	Usual suspects[13]	20–40 trading days	Yes, if > 98% of voting rights
UK	Takeover Panel www. thetake overpanel. org.uk	30% of voting rights and any increase between 30% and 50%	100% of shares and all instruments convertible or exchangeable into shares	Usual suspects[13] and MAC clause that must be approved by regulator	21–60 trading days	Yes, if > 90% of the shares
USA	SEC, Security Exchange Commission www.sec.gov	None	None	Usual suspects[13] and MAC clause	> 20 trading days	Yes with normal or super ma- jority

---

[13] Minimum acceptance, anti-trust authorisations, authorisation of shareholders to issue shares.

[14] No threshold (opt-out) or a threshold up to 49% if the by-laws of the target company permit.

8/ EUROPEAN DIRECTIVE ON PUBLIC OFFERS

The popularity of cross-border takeovers led the EU to issue a directive on public offers (on which it had been working for 15 years before it was finally voted on in 2004).

The text is rather general in nature and leaves considerable flexibility for translation into national legislation.

The directive first sets forth some basic principles:

*   Shareholders in the same category must be treated equally.
*   Shareholders must have enough time and information to decide whether the takeover bid is well founded.
*   Management of the target company must act in the interest of the company and allow shareholders the opportunity to make up their own minds on the takeover bid.
*   Manipulation of share prices is naturally banned.
*   A bid must have secured financing before being announced.
*   The bid must not keep the target company from operating properly.

In addition to basic principles, the directive sets precise rules in certain areas. Here are the main subjects:

*   the principle of a mandatory takeover bid;
*   anti-takeover defences;
*   the principle of mandatory buy-out and mandatory squeeze-out;
*   available information;
*   takeover law.

(a) Mandatory takeover bids

The directive lays down the principle that a shareholder who has assumed effective control over a company must bid for all equity-linked securities. It is up to individual countries to set a threshold of voting rights that constitutes effective control.

The directive states very specifically the floor price of a mandatory bid: the highest price paid by the new controlling shareholder in the 6–12 months prior to the bid (the exact period is set by national regulations).

A mandatory bid can be in either cash or shares (if the shares are listed and are liquid).

(b) Anti-takeover defences

The issue of limiting anti-takeover defences, poison pills and the like has been more controversial. Some countries feared that, by limiting anti-takeover defences, Europe would be at a disadvantage to the US, which does allow such practices. Consequently, the European directive left European states free to:

*   ban or not to ban the boards of target companies from taking anti-takeover defensive measures during the bid, such as poison pills, massive issuing of shares, etc., without approval from an extraordinary general meeting;
*   suspend or not to suspend during an offer, shareholders' agreements or articles of association limiting voting rights, transfers of shares, shares with multiple voting rights, rights of approval or of first refusal;

SECTION 5

15 *European law strictly limits national government leeway on golden shares. Golden shares are nonetheless still possible in some sectors and special cases, such as the defence industry.*

- authorise target to put in place anti-takeover measures without the approval of its shareholders if the buyer does not need a similar approval from its own shareholders to put in place similar measures at its own level.

Multiple voting rights and/or restrictions on voting rights disappear as of the first general shareholders' meeting after a bid that has given a bidder a qualified majority of the company. This does not apply to golden shares that have been deemed compatible with European law.[15]

(c) Squeeze-outs and mandatory buy-outs

The directive lays down the principle of the right to make a squeeze-out offer by shareholders (up to national legislation to decide):

- having obtained at least 90% of a company's shares (individual countries have the option of raising the threshold to 95%); or
- having obtained at least 90% of the shares in the course of a bid for all the shares.

The price of a squeeze-out can be the same as that of the mandatory bid or of a voluntary bid that has obtained more than 90% of the shares. In parallel, a minority of shareholders can ask for a buy-out (in the same cases that allow a squeeze-out).

SUMMARY

The summary of this chapter can be downloaded from www.vernimmen.com.

M&A deals tend to come in waves. Their determinants are macroeconomic (globalisation, deregulation, technological evolutions), microeconomic (search for size, for new markets, gains of time) or human (succession issues).

The art of negotiation consists of allocating the value of the synergies expected from a merger or acquisition between the buyer and the seller. There are two basic methods of conducting the negotiations:

- private negotiation, which preserves a high level of confidentiality, while excluding offers that might have been received had the process been wider;

- a private auction, which heightens the competition between buyers, but is more restrictive for the seller.

Regardless of the chosen procedure, certain elements are common to every deal:

- memorandums of understanding and agreements in principle serve to describe the general agreement found between the parties and are a milestone along the path to full commitment of the parties to the deal;

- representations and warranties guarantee to the buyer that all of the means of production belong to the company and that there are no hidden liabilities; the seller certifies substantive aspects of the company and the amount of equity capital;

- in some cases, earnout clauses link a portion of the purchase price to the company's future profits;

- the final outcome of negotiations is the signing of a share purchase agreement.

SECTION 5

Stake-building can be the first step to acquiring control over a listed company. But it can be slow and faces the requirement of declaring the crossing of thresholds.

A public offer is the usual way to acquire a listed company. It is based on two fundamental principles: transparency and equal treatment of shareholders. It can be in cash or in shares, hostile or friendly, voluntary or mandatory.

In each country, the acquisition of listed companies is conducted under the supervision of a stock market watchdog.

QUESTIONS

1/What are the advantages and drawbacks of private negotiation?

2/What are the advantages and drawbacks of a private sale by auction?

3/What is the advantage of a public purchase or share exchange offer for a minority shareholder?

4/What advantages does a public offer have for the acquirer over an acquisition on the market? What are the drawbacks?

5/Can a company launch an offer to buy another company that is for sale without having any real intention of closing the deal? Why? What protection is there for the seller?

6/What will be key to making an M&A deal a successful event in a company's history?

7/Why are earnout clauses so popular with companies in the service sector?

8/All things being equal, what is the downside of a deal being kept highly confidential?

9/When is it a good idea to go for a private auction?

10/How can a buyer be protected against any hidden liabilities and debts that the target may have?

11/What is the purpose of representations and warranties? What are the limits of such clauses?

12/What is the logical result of a successful hostile stake building on the market?

13/What concern of market authorities is addressed by a suspension of trading after notice of an offer has been filed?

14/Why are defence mechanisms against hostile takeover bids very strictly regulated?

15/On the basis of financial theory, how can the role of an investment bank in a deal be summarised?

More questions are waiting for you at www.vernimmen.com.

ANSWERS

1/ *Advantage: negotiations are kept confidential. Drawback: potential candidates may be left out.*

2/ *Advantage: organisation of a market. Drawback: lack of confidentiality.*

3/ *The minority shareholder is protected as he will be able to sell his shares at the same price as the majority shareholder.*

4/ *The acquirer does not cause the share price to rise. The drawback is that if a stock market battle unfolds, he will not be in such a good position.*

5/ *Yes. To obtain information. Memorandums of understanding and of agreement, confidentiality agreements.*

6/ *The integration process post acquisition.*

7/ *The deal itself can have an unpredictable impact on human resources – the company's main assets.*

8/ *The sale price might be lower.*

9/ *When the business for sale is very profitable, and attractive to both trade buyers and financial investors.*

10/ *General warranties.*

11/ *It provides a guarantee for the assets and liabilities of the company. Under no circumstances can such a clause guarantee the fairness of the price paid for the business.*

12/ *A takeover bid.*

13/ *The fair and equal dissemination of information.*

14/ *Anti-takeover measures can deprive shareholders of the capital gains that come out of the free process of auctions.*

15/ *Management of information asymmetry.*

BIBLIOGRAPHY

To know more about M&A deals:

A. Boone, J.H. Mulherin, How are firms sold? *Journal of Finance*, **62**(2), 847–875, April 2007.

M. Sirower, *The Synergy Trap*, Free Press, 1997.

J. Weston, M. Mitchell, H. Mulherin, *Takeovers, Restructuring and Corporate Governance*, 5th edn, Prentice Hall, 2010.

www.iclg.co.uk, main aspects of anti-trust and takeover rules for 50 countries.

For research works on M&A deals:

A. Agrawal, J. Jaffe, The post-merger performance puzzle, *Advances in Mergers and Acquisitions*, **1**, 7–41, 2000.

N. Aktas, E. de Bodt, R. Roll, Negotiations under threat of an auction, *Journal of Financial Economics*, **98**(2), 241–255, November 2010.

G. Andrade, M. Mitchell, E. Stafford, New evidence and perspectives on mergers, *Journal of Economic Perspectives*, **2**(15), 103–120, Spring 2001.

G. Andrade, E. Stafford, Investigating the economic role of mergers, *Journal of Corporate Finance*, **10**(1), 1–36, January 2004.

A. Chevalier, E. Redor, The determinants of payment method choice in cross-border acquisitions, *Bankers, Markets and Investors*, **106**, 4–14, May-June 2010.

M. Danielson, J. Karpoff, Do pills poison operating performance? *Journal of Corporate Finance*, **12**(3), 536–559, June 2006.

M. Dong, D. Hirshleifer, S. Richardson, S.H. Teoh, Does investors' misvaluation drive the takeover market? *Journal of Finance*, **61**(2), 725–762, April 2006.

G. Emery, J. Switzer, Expected market reaction and the choice of method of payment for acquisitions, *Financial Management*, **28**(4), 73–86, Winter 1999.

M. Faccio, R. Masulis, The choice of payment method in European mergers & acquisitions, *Journal of Finance*, **60**(3), 1345–1388, June 2005.

S. Grossman, O. Hart, Takeover bids, the free rider problem, and the theory of the corporation, *Bell Journal of Economics*, **11**(1), 42–64, Spring 1980.

G. Hubbard, P. Darius, A reexamination of the conglomerate merger wave in the 1960s, *Journal of Finance*, **54**(3), 1131–1152, June 1999.

M. Jensen, Agency costs of free cash flow, corporate finance, and takeovers, *American Economic Review*, **76**(2), 323–329, May 1986.

M. Jensen, R.S. Ruback, The market for corporate control: The scientific evidence, *Journal of Financial Economics*, **11**(1), 5–50, April 1983.

R. Rau, T. Vermaelen, Glamour, value and the post-acquisition performance of acquiring firms, *Journal of Financial Economics*, **49**(2), 223–254, August 1998.

M. Rhodes-Kropf, S. Viswanathan, Market valuation and merger waves, *Journal of Finance*, **59**(6), 2685–2718, December 2004.

R. Roll, The hubris hypothesis of corporate takeovers, *Journal of Business*, **59**(2), 197–216, April 1986.

S. Rossi, P. Volpin, Cross-country determinants of mergers and acquisitions, *Journal of Financial Economics*, **74**(2), 277–304, November 2004.

G. Schwert, Hostility in takeovers: In the eyes of the beholder? *Journal of Finance*, **55**(6), 2599–2640, December 2000.

A. Shleifer, R. Vishny, Stock market driven acquisition, *Journal of Financial Economics*, **70**(3), 295–311, December 2003.

M. Sirower, A. Rappaport, Stock or cash, *Harvard Business Review*, **77**, 147–158, November–December 1999.

M. Straska, G. Waller, Do antitakeover provisions harm shareholders? *Journal of Corporate Finance*, **16**(4), 487–497, September 2010.

To measure the relevancy of M&A deals:

G. Alexandridis, D. Petmezas, N.G. Travlos, Gains from mergers and acquisitions around the world: New evidence, *Financial Management,* **39**(4), 1671–1695, Winter 2010.

S. Bhagat, M. Dong, D. Hirshleifer, R. Noah, Do tender offers create value? New methods and evidence, *Journal of Financial Economics*, **76**(1), 3–60, April 2005.

T. Hoenh, European M&A: How do deals affect shareholder value? *PWC UK Economic Outlook*, 23–27, July 2006.

I. Loughran, A. Vijh, Do long-term shareholders benefit from corporate acquisitions? *Journal of Finance*, **52**(5), 1765–1790, December 1997.

M. Martynova, S. Oosting, L. Renneboog, The long-term operating performance of European mergers and acquisitions, in *International Mergers and Acquisitions Activity since 1990: Recent Research and Quantitative Analysis* , 79–116, Elsevier, 2007.

S. Moellers, F. Schlingemann, R. Stulz, Firm size and the gains from acquisitions, *Journal of Financial Economics*, **73**(2), 201–228, August 2004.

S. Moellers, F. Schlingemann, R. Stulz, Wealth destruction on a massive scale? A study of acquiring-firm returns in the recent merger wave, *Journal of Finance*, **60**(2), 757–782, April 2005.

P. Savor, Q. Lu, Do stock mergers create value for acquirers?, *Journal of Finance*, **64**(3), 1061–1098, June 2009.

To get information on M&A deals:

www.thomsonmergernews.com

Chapter 44
MERGERS AND DEMERGERS

When the financial manager celebrates a wedding (or a divorce!)

At first glance, this chapter might seem to repeat the previous ones in that selling a company almost always leads to linking it up with another. In everyday language we often talk of the merger of two companies, when in reality one company typically takes control of the other, using the methods described in Chapter 43. In fact, all that we have previously said about synergies and company valuations will be used in this chapter. **The only fundamental difference we introduce here is that 100% of the seller's consideration will be in shares of the acquiring company and not in cash.**

In addition, because markets nowadays prefer "pure-play" companies, demergers have come back into fashion. We will take a look at them in Section 44.3.

Section 44.1
ALL-SHARE DEALS

In this section, we will examine the general case of two separate companies that decide to pool their operations and redistribute roles. Before the business combination can be consummated, questions of valuation and power-sharing among the shareholders of the new entity must be resolved. Financially, the essential distinguishing feature among mergers and acquisitions is the nature of the consideration paid: 100% cash, a combination of cash and shares or 100% shares. Our discussion will focus on the last of these forms. Finally, we will not address the case of a company that merges with an already wholly-owned subsidiary, which raises only accounting, tax and legal issues and no financial issues.

1/ THE DIFFERENT TECHNIQUES

(a) Legal merger

A legal merger is a transaction by which two or more companies combine to form a single legal entity. In most cases, one company absorbs the other. The shareholders of the acquired company become shareholders of the acquiring company and the acquired company ceases to exist as a separate legal entity.

A legal merger is a combination of the assets and liabilities of two or more companies into a single legal entity.

From legal and tax points of view, this type of business combination is treated as a contribution of assets and liabilities, paid in new shares issued to the ex-shareholders of the acquired company. This type of transaction is often used in group restructuring, and it is rare to see two listed companies merge, as most of the time one launches an offer on the other. The opposite example is the merger between Procter & Gamble and Gillette in 2005 on the basis of 0.9774 Procter shares for every Gillette share.

(b) Contribution of shares

Consider the shareholders of companies A and B. Shareholders of company B, be they individuals or legal entities, can enter into a deal with company A wherein they **exchange their shares** of B for shares of A. In this case, companies A and B continue to exist, with B becoming a subsidiary of A and the shareholders of B becoming shareholders of A.

Financially and economically, the transaction is very close to the sale of all or part of company B funded by an equivalent issue of new company A shares, reserved for the shareholders of company B.

For listed companies, the most common approach for achieving this result is a share exchange offer, as described in Chapter 43.

(c) Asset contribution

In a **contribution** (or transfer) **of assets**, company B contributes a portion (or sometimes all) of its assets (and liabilities) to company A in return for shares issued by company A.

In a legal merger, the shareholders of company B receive shares of company A. In a transfer of assets, however, company B, not the shareholders thereof, receives the shares of company A. The position of company B shareholders is therefore radically different, depending on whether the transaction is a legal merger or a simple transfer of assets. In the transfer of assets, company B remains and becomes a shareholder of company A. Shareholders of B do not become direct shareholders of company A. In the legal merger, shareholders of B become direct shareholders of company A.

If company B contributes all of its assets to A, B becomes a holding company and, depending on the amount of the assets it has contributed, can take control of A. This procedure is often used in corporate restructurings to transfer certain activities to subsidiaries.

Economically, there is no difference between these transactions. The group created by bringing together A and B is economically identical regardless of how the business combination is effected.

As an example of asset contribution, you can have a look at the Vivendi Games–Activision transaction in 2008. Vivendi contributed its video games assets (mostly the online game *World of Warcraft*) to Activision in exchange for 54% of the new Activision.

STRUCTURES FOR BUSINESS COMBINATIONS

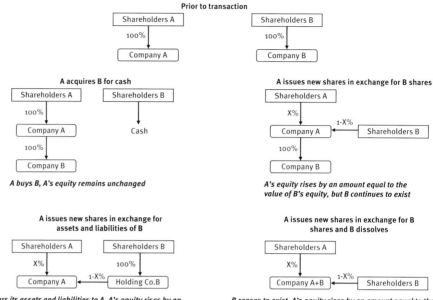

A buys B, A's equity remains unchanged

A's equity rises by an amount equal to the value of B's equity, but B continues to exist

B transfers its assets and liabilities to A. A's equity rises by an amount equal to the value of B's equity. The shareholders of B remain shareholders of B, which is now a holding company

B ceases to exist. A's equity rises by an amount equal to the value of B's equity

2/ ANALYSIS OF THE DIFFERENT TECHNIQUES

For simplicity's sake, we will assume that the shares of both companies are fairly priced and that the merger does not create any industrial or commercial synergies. Consequently, there is no value creation as a result of the merger.

(a) From the point of view of the company

Companies *A* and *B* have the following characteristics:

(in €m)	Enterprise value	Value of shareholders' equity agreed in the merger
Company *A*	900	450
Company *B*	1000	750

Depending on the method used, the post-transaction situation is as follows:

(in €m)	A acquires B shares for cash[1]	A issues new shares in exchange for B shares and dissolves B	A issues new shares in exchange for B shares and B becomes a 100% subsidiary of A	A issues new shares in exchange for assets and liabilities of B
Value of A's new capital employed (now A + B)	1900	1900	1900	1900
Value of A's shareholders' equity	450	1200	1200	1200
Percentage of A held by A shareholders	100%	37.5%	37.5%	37.5%
Percentage of A held by B shareholders	—	62.5%	62.5%	62.5%[2]

1 *The acquisition of* B *is financed by debt, not a capital increase.*

2 *In fact, company* B, *not its shareholders, holds 62.5% of* A.

Enterprise value and consolidated operating income are the same in each scenario. Economically, each transaction represents the same business combination of companies A and B.

Financially, however, the situation is very different, even putting aside accounting issues. If A pays for the acquisition in shares, the shareholders' equity of A is increased by the shareholders' equity of B. If A purchases B for cash, the value of A's shareholders' equity does not increase.

It can be noted that when the target is a listed company, a 100% successful share exchange offer is financially equivalent to a legal merger.

We reiterate that our reasoning here is strictly arithmetic and we are not taking into account any impact the transaction may have on the value of the two companies. If the two companies were already correctly priced before the transaction and there are no synergies their value will remain the same. If not, there will be a change in value. **The financial mechanics (sale, share exchange, etc.) have no impact on the economics of a business combination.**

That said, there is one important financial difference: an acquisition paid for in cash does not increase a group's financial clout (i.e. future investment capacity), but an all-share transaction creates a group with financial means which tend to be the sum of that of the two constituent companies.

From the point of view of the acquiring company, the only difference between a share exchange and a cash acquisition is in the financial clout of the new group.

In terms of value creation, our rules still hold, unless there are synergies or market inefficiencies.

(b) From the point of view of shareholders

A cash acquisition changes the portfolio of the acquired company's shareholders, because they now hold cash in place of the shares they previously held.

Conversely, it does not change the portfolio of the acquiring company's shareholders, nor their stake in the company.

An **all-share transaction** is symmetrical for the shareholders of A and B. No one receives any cash. When the dust settles, they all hold claims on a new company born out of the two previous companies. Note that their claims on the merged company would have been exactly the same if B had absorbed A. In fact, who absorbs whom is not so important; it is the percentage ownership the shareholders end up with that is important. Moreover, it is common for one company to take control of another by letting itself be "absorbed" by its "target".

Merger synergies are not shared in the same way. In a cash acquisition, selling shareholders pocket a portion of the value of synergies immediately (depending on the outcome of the negotiation). The selling shareholders do not bear any risk of implementation of the synergies. In an all-share transaction, however, the value creation (or destruction) of combining the two businesses will be shared according to the relative values negotiated by the two sets of shareholders.

In a cash acquisition, shareholders of the acquiring company alone assume the combination execution risks. In an all-share transaction, the risks are shared by the two groups of shareholders.

For the shareholders of company B, **a contribution of shares**, with B remaining a subsidiary of A, has the same effect as a legal merger of the two companies. An **asset contribution** of company B to company A is also very similar to a legal merger. The only difference is that, in an asset contribution, the claim of company B's ex-shareholders on company A is via company B, which becomes a holding company of company A.

3/ PROS AND CONS OF PAYING IN SHARES

In contrast to a cash acquisition, there is no cash outflow in an all-share deal, be it an exchange of shares, an asset contribution in return for shares or a demerger with a distribution of shares in a new company. The transaction does not generate any cash that can be used by shareholders of the acquired company to pay capital gains taxes. For this reason, it is important for these transactions to be treated as "tax free".

What is the advantage of paying in shares? The efficient markets hypothesis, which analyses a merger as an acquisition followed by a capital increase, does not provide a satisfactory answer. Sometimes company managers want to change the ownership structure of the company so as to dilute an unwelcome shareholder's stake, constitute a group of core shareholders or increase their power by increasing the company's size or prestige. More importantly, paying in shares enables the company to skirt the question of financing and merge even with very large companies. Some critics say that companies paying in shares are paying for their acquisitions with "funny money"; we think that depends on post-merger ownership structure and share liquidity. And, most importantly, it depends on the ability of the merged company to harness anticipated synergies and create value. In Chapter 43, we provide a table setting out the pros and cons of payment in shares vs. cash.

Section 44.2
THE MECHANICS OF ALL-SHARE TRANSACTIONS

1/ RELATIVE VALUE RATIO AND EXCHANGE RATIO

In practice, a non-cash merger requires first that the target company be valued. Then the acquiring company must be valued, since it must issue new shares to the target's shareholders. The ratio of shareholders' equity value of company A to shareholders' equity value of company B is called the **relative value**. To determine relative values, a full valuation of the two companies to be merged is generally performed according to the methods described in Chapter 32. Such a valuation is usually done on a standalone basis, with synergies valued separately.

Let us take another look at companies A and B, with the following key figures:

(in €m)	Value of shareholders' equity[3]	Value of shareholders' equity agreed in the merger
A (acquirer)	450	450
B (target)	680	750

3 *Market capitalisation if the companies are listed.*

The difference between the 750 agreed and the 680 is nothing but the result of a negotiation. B has succeeded in convincing A that either its market valuation underestimated its intrinsic value or that A's market cap was over optimistic. Remember that during the negotiation of the relative value ratio, the companies will usually gather much more information than what has been made public.

In our example, the relative value ratio is 1.67 (750/450). In other words, B is deemed to be worth 1.67 times A. The agreed relative value ratio gives the ex-shareholders of A $1/(1 + 1.67)$ or 37.5% of the shares of the new company and the ex-shareholders of B $1.67/(1 + 1.67)$ or 62.5%.

If the relative value ratio were 1.5 – i.e. close to the ratio of the market capitalisation of the two companies – the ownership structure of the two shareholder groups would be different (40%/60%).

The relative value agreed between the two companies determines who will own how much of the new company. As a result, this ratio will define the power each shareholder will wield after the transaction.

Once relative values have been determined, often after long, protracted negotiations, the **exchange ratio** is a direct result thereof. It is the ratio of the number of shares of company A to be tendered for each company B share received.

Once again, let's assume the following characteristics for companies A and B:

	Value of shareholders' equity agreed in merger (€)	Number of shares	Value per share
A (acquirer)	450m	4 500 000	100
B (acquiree)	750m	3 750 000	a

SECTION 5

In exchange for contribution of capital of 750m, A issues 7 500 000 (= 750m/100) new shares to the shareholders of B. Company B's 3 750 000 outstanding shares will be exchanged for the 7 500 000 newly-issued A shares. The exchange ratio is therefore 1 B share for 2 A shares (or 1 for 2).

Once relative values are determined, calculating the exchange ratio is a simple matter:

$$\text{Exchange ratio} = \text{Relative value ratio} \times \frac{\text{Pre-merger number of } A \text{ shares}}{\text{Pre-merger number of } B \text{ shares}}$$

(... A shares for one B share)		(B is worth ... times A)	
2	=	1.67	× 4 500 000/3 750 000

The difficulty is not so much in determining the per-share value of the acquired company as in establishing the **relationship that will serve as the basis for the exchange**. There is flexibility for the parties to set the value of shares as long as the exchange ratio is kept. We're not interested in calculating absolute shareholder equity values, but relative values. We often observe that the parties will both inflate values of their companies, but at the end of the negotiation all that matters is the relative value!

It is customary in the mergers and acquisitions business to examine the impact of the exchange ratio on the performance metrics generally monitored by the market. The most frequently-used measures are net income, cash flow, dividends, market capitalisation and sometimes book value[4] ...

2/ DILUTION OR ACCRETION CRITERIA

To help refine our analysis, let us suppose companies A and B have the following key financial elements:

(in €m)	Sales	Net income	Book equity	Value of shareholders' equity
A	1500	15	250	450
B	5000	35	450	680

Putting aside for one moment potential industrial and commercial synergies, the financial elements of the new company A + B resulting from the merger with B are as follows:

(in €m)	Sales	Net income	Book equity	Value of shareholders' equity
Group A + B	6500	50	700	1130

In theory, the value of the new entity's shareholders' equity should be the sum of the value of the shareholders' equity of A and B. In practice, it is higher or lower than this amount, depending on how advantageous investors believe the merger is.

Using the agreed relative value ratio of 1.67, our performance measures for the new group are as follows:

(in €m)	Group net income	Group book equity	Theoretical value of group shareholders' equity
The ex-shareholders of A have a claim on:	18.75	262.5	423.75
vs. before the transaction:	15	250	450
The ex-shareholders of B have a claim on:	31.25	437.5	706.25
vs. before the transaction:	35	450	680
TOTAL Before transaction	50	700	1130
After transaction	50	700	1130

As a result of the agreed relative value ratio, the ex-shareholders of B suffer a **dilution** (reduction) in book equity, as their portion declines from 450m to 437.5m, and in their share of the net income of the new entity. At the same time, they enjoy an **accretion** in their share of the new group's theoretical market capitalisation from 680m to 706.25m. Naturally, the situation is the opposite for the ex-shareholders of A.

When A absorbs B via a share exchange, if the relative value of (B/A) is less than the relative ratio calculated for a given reference metric (value of shareholders' equity, book value, net income, etc.), the ex-shareholders of A enjoy an accretion in value for that metric.

On the other hand, when the agreed relative value of (B/A) is higher than the reference metric, A's shareholders will suffer dilution for that metric.

Turning our attention now to the earnings per share of companies A and B, we observe the following:

	Value of shareholders' equity (€m)	Net income (in €m)	P/E[5]	Number of shares (million)	Earnings per share
Company A	450	15	30	4.5	3.33
Company B	680	35	19.4	3.75	9.33

5 *Price/earnings ratio.*

On the basis of the relative value ratio agreed in the merger (750/450), the earnings per share of the new group A now stand at $(15 + 45)/(4.5 + 7.5)$ or 4.17 per share. EPS has risen from 3.33 to 4.17, representing an increase of more than 25%. The reason is that the portion of earnings deriving from ex-company B is purchased with shares valued at A's P/E multiple of 30 (450/15), whereas B is valued at a P/E multiple of 21 (750/35). Company A has issued a number of shares that is relatively low compared with the additional net income that B has contributed to A's initial net income.

Earnings per share (before acquisition accounting) automatically increase when the P/E of the acquiring company is greater than the P/E of the acquired company (and vice versa).

The reasoning is similar for other performance metrics, such as cash flow per share.

3/ SYNERGIES

As an all-share merger consists conceptually of a purchase followed by a reserved capital increase, the sharing of synergies is a subject of negotiation just as it is in the case of a cash purchase.

In our example, let us suppose that synergies between A and B will increase the after-tax income of the merged group by €10m from the first year onwards.

The big unknown is the credit and the value investors will ascribe to these synergies:

* 300m – i.e. a valuation based on A's P/E multiple of 30;
* 194m – i.e. a valuation based on B's P/E multiple of 19.4;
* 226m – i.e. a valuation based on a P/E multiple of 22.6, the average of the P/Es of A and B;
* some other value.

Two factors lead us to believe that investors will attribute a value that is lower than these estimates:

* The amount of synergies announced at the time of the merger is only an estimate and the announcers have an interest in maximising it to induce shareholders to approve the transaction. In practice, making a merger or an acquisition work is a managerial challenge. You have to motivate employees who may previously have been competitors to work together, create a new corporate culture, avoid losing customers who want to maintain a wide variety of suppliers, etc. Experience has shown that

  ○ more than half of all mergers fail on this score;
  ○ actual synergies are slower in coming;
  ○ the amount of synergies is lower than originally announced.

* Sooner or later, the company will not be the only one in the industry to merge. Because mergers and acquisitions tend to come in waves, rival companies will be tempted to merge for the same reasons: to unlock synergies and remain competitive. As competition also consolidates, all market participants will be able to lower prices or refrain from raising them, to the joy of the consumer. As a result, the group that first benefited from merger synergies will be forced to give back some of its gains to its customers, employees and suppliers.

A study of the world's largest mergers and acquisitions shows that the P/E multiple at which the market values synergies when they are announced is well below that of both the acquiring company and the target.

Based on this information, let's assume that the investors in our example value the €10m p.a. in synergies at a P/E of 12, or €120m.

The value of shareholders' equity of the new group is therefore:

$$450 + 680 + 120 = 1250m$$

Value is created in the amount of $1250 - 1130 = 120m$. This is not financial value creation, but the result of the merger itself, which leads to cost savings or revenue enhancements. The €120m synergy pie will be shared between the shareholders of A and B.

At the extreme, the shareholders of A might value B at 800m. In other words, they might attribute the full present value of the synergies to the shareholders of B. The relative value ratio would then be at its maximum, 1.78.[6] Note that in setting the relative value ratio at 1.67, they had already offered the ex-shareholders of B 84%[7] of the value of the synergies!

The relative value ratios of 1.19[8] and 1.78 constitute the upper and lower boundaries of the negotiable range. If they agree on 1.19, the shareholders of A will have kept all of the value of the synergies for themselves. Conversely, at 1.78, all of the synergies accrue to the shareholders of B.

The relative value choice determines the relative ownership stake of the two groups of shareholders, A's and B's, in the post-merger group, which ranges from 45.6%/54.4% to 36%/64%. The difference is significant!

Determining the value of potential synergies is a crucial negotiating stage. It determines the maximum merger premium that company A will be willing to pay to the shareholders of B:

- large enough to encourage shareholders of B to approve the merger;
- small enough to still be value creating for A's shareholders.

4/ THE "BOOTSTRAP GAME"

Until now, we have assumed that the market capitalisation of the new group will remain equal to the sum of the two initial market capitalisations. In practice, a merger often causes an adjustment in the P/E, called a **rerating** (or a derating!). As a result, significant transfers of value occur to and between the groups of shareholders. These value transfers often offset a sacrifice with respect to the post-merger ownership stake or a post-merger performance metric.

If we assume that the new group A continues to enjoy a P/E ratio of 30 (ignoring synergies), as did the pre-merger company A, its market capitalisation will be 1500m. The ex-shareholders of A, who appeared to give up some relative value with regard to the post-merger market cap metric, see the value of their share of the new group rise to 562.5m,[9] whereas they previously owned 100% of a company that was worth only 450m. As for the ex-shareholders of B, they now hold 62.5% of the new group, a stake worth 937.5m, vs. 100% of a company previously valued at only 680m.

Whereas it seemed A's shareholders came out losing, in fact it's a win–win situation. The transaction is a money machine! The limits of this model are clear, however. A's pre-merger P/E of 30 was the P/E ratio of a growth company. Group A will maintain its level of growth after the merger only if it can light a fire under B and convince investors that the new group also merits a P/E ratio of 30.

This model works only if company A keeps growing through acquisition, "kissing" larger and larger "sleeping beauties" and bringing them back to life. If not, the P/E ratio of the new group will simply correspond to the weighted average of the P/E ratios of the merged companies.[10]

You have probably noticed by now that it is advantageous to have a high share price, and hence a high P/E ratio. They allow you to issue highly-valued paper to carry out acquisitions at relatively low cost, all the while posting automatic increases in earnings per share. You undoubtedly also know how to recognise an accelerating treadmill when you see one . . .

The higher a company's P/E ratio is, the more attractive it is for the company to make acquisitions.

6 $(680 + 120)/450$.

7 $(62.5\% \times 1250 - 680)/120$.

8 $680/(450 + 120)$.

9 $3.75\% \times 1500$.

10 *This is a variant of the tale Warren Buffett told Berkshire Hathaway shareholders in his February 1982 letter to shareholders.* http://www.berkshirehathaway.com/letters/1981.html

The potential immediate rerating after the merger does not guarantee creation of shareholder value. In the long run, only the new group's economic performance will enable it to maintain its high P/E multiple.

5/ Which way should the merger go?

Is *A* going to absorb *B* or the reverse? Several factors have to be taken into account.

Whether the company is listed or not is a factor, since in a merger between a listed and unlisted company, it is likely that the listed company will take over the unlisted one in order to simplify administrative procedures and to avoid an exchange of shares for the hundreds, thousands or even hundreds of thousands of shareholders of the listed company.

There are, of course, legal considerations when agreements signed by the acquired company contain a change of control clause, for example in the concessions sector or for loan agreements, with some loans falling due immediately.[11]

There are also psychological reasons why sometimes it makes more sense to continue trading under the name or structure of an entity which has been in existence for a very long time and which has great sentimental value for management and shareholders. In such cases, it is the oldest structure that becomes the acquiring company.

There are also some managers who believe that they will be in a better position within the new structure if their company is the acquiring rather than the acquired company. There are others who wish to make a symbolic statement about where the power lies.

Then there are those who are obsessed with EPS who are keen for the acquiring company to be the one with the highest P/E ratio, so the merger will be accretive in terms of EPS. Our readers know how cautious we are when it comes to EPS.[12]

In some countries, the tax issue is the main factor in deciding which way the merger should go. The acquired company loses all of its tax loss carryforwards, while the acquiring company is allowed to hold onto its own. Elsewhere, it is possible for the company resulting from the merger of two companies to hold onto the tax loss carryforwards of the company that is acquired, provided that the merger is not being carried out solely for tax reasons. This reduces the importance of the tax issue in deciding who should take over whom.

11 *This is how TF1 was able to take full control over Eurosport after its partner Canal was merged into Vivendi Universal.*

12 *See Chapter 28.*

Section 44.3
Demergers and split-offs

Demergers are not uncommon in countries where their tax treatment is not punitive.

1/ Principles

The principle of a demerger is simple. A group with several divisions, in most cases two, decides to separate them into distinct companies. The shares of the newly-created companies are distributed to the shareholders in exchange for shares of the parent group. The shareholders, who are the same as the shareholders of the original group, now own shares in two or more companies and can buy or sell them as they see fit.

There are two basic types of transactions, depending on whether, once approved, the transaction applies to all shareholders or gives shareholders the option of participating.

- A **demerger** is a separation of the activities of a group: the original shareholders become the shareholders of the separated companies. The transaction can be carried out by distributing the shares of a subsidiary in the form of a dividend (a spin-off), or by dissolving the parent company and distributing the shares of the ex-subsidiaries to the shareholders (a split-up). Immediately after the transaction, the shareholders of the demerged companies are the same, but ownership evolves very quickly thereafter.
- In a **split-off**, shareholders have the option to exchange their shares in the parent company for shares in a subsidiary. To avoid unnecessary holdings of treasury shares, the shares tendered are cancelled. A split-off is a share repurchase paid for with shares in a subsidiary rather than in cash. If all shareholders tender their shares, the split-off is identical to a demerger. If the offer is relatively unsuccessful, the parent company remains a shareholder of the subsidiary.

2/ WHY DEMERGE?

Broadly speaking, studies on demergers have shown that the shares of the separated companies outperform the market, both in the short and long term.

In the context of the efficient markets hypothesis and agency theory, demergers are an answer to conglomerate discounts (see Chapter 40). In this sense, a demerger creates value, because it solves the following problems:

- Allocation of capital within a conglomerate is suboptimal, benefiting divisions in difficulty and penalising healthy ones, making it harder for the latter to grow.
- The market values primary businesses correctly but undervalues secondary businesses.
- The market has trouble understanding conglomerates, a problem made worse by the fact that virtually all financial analysts are specialised by industry. With the number of listed companies constantly growing and investment possibilities therefore expanding, investors prefer simplicity. In addition, large conglomerates communicate less about smaller divisions, thus increasing the information asymmetry.
- Lack of motivation of managers of non-core divisions.
- Small base of investors interested by all the businesses of the group.
- The conglomerate has operating costs that add to the costs of the operating units without creating value.

Demergers expose the newly-created companies to potential takeovers. Prior to the demerger, the company might have been too big or too diverse. Potential acquirers might not have been interested in all of its businesses. And the process of acquiring the entire company and then selling off the unwanted businesses is cumbersome and risky. A demerger creates smaller, pure-play companies, which are more attractive in the takeover market. Empirically, it has been shown that demerged subsidiaries do not always outperform. This is the case when the parent company has completely divested its interest in the new company or has itself become subject to a takeover bid.

Lastly lenders are not great fans of demergers. By reducing the diversity of activities and consequently potentially increasing the volatility of cash flows, they increase the risk for lenders. At one extreme, the value of their debt decreases if the transaction is structured in such a way that one of the new companies carries all the debt, while the other is financed by equity capital only.

In practice, however, debtholders are rarely spoiled that way. Loan agreements and bond indentures generally stipulate that, in the event of a demerger, the loan or the bonds become immediately due and payable.

Consequently they are in a position to negotiate demerger terms that are not unfavourable to them. This explains why empirical studies have shown that, on average, demergers lead to no transfer of value from creditors to shareholders.

Because of their complexity and the detailed preparation they require, demergers are less frequent than mergers. Examples of demergers include Cadbury (confectionery) and Dr Pepper (drinks), Bayer (pharmaceuticals) and Lanxess (chemicals), Total (oil) and Arkema (chemicals), Electrolux (appliances) and Husqvarna (outdoor power products), Julius Baer (wealth management) and GAM Holding (asset management) and for split-offs, General Motors and Delphi, Procter & Gamble and Folger (coffee), Sequana (paper) and SGS (certification).

In a study published in 2004, Veld and Veld-Merkoulova show evidence based on a European sample of demergers that demergers do create value. As demonstrated in some US studies, the abnormal returns following the announcement of a demerger are on average around 2–4% (depending on the sample used).

Demerging is not a panacea. If one of the demerged businesses is too small, its shares will suffer a deep liquidity discount. And not all conglomerates are financial failures: General Electric and Bouygues are two prominent examples to the contrary.

If we wanted to be cynical, we might say that demergers represent the triumph of sloth (investors and analysts do not take time to understand complex groups) and selfishness (managers want to finance only the high-performance businesses).

But they are also the triumph of modern financial theory, which says that enterprises that bring together unrelated businesses without creating value will not stay as a group indefinitely.

SUMMARY

The summary of this chapter can be downloaded from www.vernimmen.com.

Business combinations, commonly referred to as mergers and acquisitions, can take many forms. The most important distinction among them is the method of payment: (i) cash or cash and shares or (ii) 100% in shares.

All-share deals can take several forms:

- **legal merger**: two or more companies are combined to form a single company. In general, one company is dissolved and absorbed into the other;

- **contribution of shares**: the shareholders of company *B* exchange their shares for shares of company *A*;

- **asset contribution**: company *B* transfers a portion of its assets to company *A* in exchange for shares issued by company *A*.

The economics of the business combination are independent of the financial arrangements. That said, in an all-share deal the resources of the two entities are added together, increasing the merged company's financial capacity, compared with what it would have been after the conclusion of a cash deal. Also, in an all-share deal, all the shareholders of the resulting group share the risks of the merger. When the deal is negotiated, the companies are valued and the **relative value ratio** and **exchange ratio** are set. The exchange ratio is the number of shares of the acquiring company that will be exchanged for the tendered shares of the acquired company. The relative value ratio determines the position of each group of shareholders in the newly-merged group.

The higher a company's P/E ratio is, the more tempted it will be to carry out acquisitions by issuing shares, because its earnings per share will automatically increase. But be careful! No value is automatically created. The increase in EPS is only a mathematical result deriving from the difference between the P/E ratios of the acquirer and the acquiree. At the same time, the P/E ratio of the new entity declines, because the market capitalisations of the new group should theoretically correspond to the sum of the market capitalisation of the two companies prior to the merger. Sometimes the new company's P/E ratio stays the same as the acquiring company's P/E ratio. We call this the "magic kiss" effect, because it implies that the company has only to "wake up" the "sleeping beauty" it has acquired. In each case, the value of the merger synergies is added to the value of the new company. How they are shared by the two groups of shareholders determines the premium the acquiring company will pay to the target's shareholders to persuade them to participate in the deal.

A demerger is a simple concept. A diversified group decides to separate several business divisions into distinct companies and to distribute the shares of the new companies to shareholders in return for shares of the parent group. It is often an answer to too low a valuation for a group with too far-flung activities.

The value created by a demerger can be analysed as follows:

- unlocking the value trapped in the conglomerate discount (efficient markets hypothesis);

- increasing the motivation of the managers of the newly independent company (agency theory).

A demerger results in companies being more exposed to takeover bids.

QUESTIONS

1/ What is the fundamental difference between a merger and a sale:

- for the shareholder of the acquired company?
- for the acquiring company?
- for the shareholder of the acquiring company?
- for the acquired company?

2/ Unlike what happens when a company is sold, when companies merge, their shareholders' equity is added together. Why?

3/ In your view, what are the possible reasons behind a merger? And a demerger?

4/ Ignoring tax issues, would a shareholder with a 51% controlling interest in a company be better off buying another company or merging with it?

5/ Is the dilution of EPS that follows all mergers generally greater or less than that which follows a standard share issue?

6/Why is the determination of the exchange ratio important?

7/What is the difference between the relative value ratio and the exchange ratio?

8/When negotiating, is agreement first reached on the relative value or on the calculation method?

9/Why do shareholders in an acquired company agree to the dilution of their shareholdings after completion of the merger?

10/Where does the creation of value lie in a merger?

11/Why are the legal procedures related to mergers so onerous?

12/In what circumstances can a demerger lead to creation of shareholder value? And value for creditors.

13/Can the success of a merger be judged by comparing the market performance of the new entity with that of the reference index?

14/Can the success of a merger be judged by looking at the change in share price of the companies when the merger is announced?

More questions are waiting for you at www.vernimmen.com.

EXERCISES

1/Alpha AG is wholly owned by Mr Alpha and Beta AG is wholly owned by Mr Beta. The key figures for the two companies are as follows:

	Net profit	Equity value	Book equity
Alpha	60	750	800
Beta	30	1500	400

Alpha acquires Beta. Calculate the shareholdings (as a percentage) of Mr Alpha and Mr Beta using net profits, equity value and book equity. What are your conclusions?

2/Below are the key figures for Gamma plc and Delta plc:

	Net profit	Book equity	P/E	Number of shares
Gamma	20	60	50	2000
Delta	40	300	8	1000

(a) Gamma acquires Delta. The criterion selected for calculation purposes is equity value. Calculate the old and new EPS, equity per share and the percentage of the shareholdings of the former shareholders of Gamma in the new entity.
(b) Redo the calculations with a P/E for Gamma of only 15, and then 6.
(c) What are the minimum and maximum relative values if the synergies that come out of the merger increase the profits of the new group by 10, and if the new group is valued on the basis of a P/E of 21? What would the ratios be then?
(d) What is the value of Epsilon, the new name for the merged Gamma and Delta (still with synergies of 10) if it is valued on the basis of a P/E of 50?
(e) What is the value created and what does it represent?

Questions

1/ *The shareholder of the acquired company receives shares instead of cash. The acquiring company issues shares instead of reducing cash (or incurring debt), its shareholding structure is modified. The shareholder of the acquiring company loses some control, but the risk is shared. The acquired company no longer exists as a separate legal entity.*

2/ *By definition, since assets and liabilities are pooled together.*

3/ *Synergies, defence against an unwelcome attack. Reduction of the conglomerate discount, focus on core business, defence against an unwelcome attack.*

4/ *Having the company buy the target, so as not to lose its controlling interest in it.*

5/ *This isn't where the problem lies. What's important is to know whether the merger will create value and not whether EPS will be diluted.*

6/ *Because it is the basis for sharing the creation of value and sharing power inside the new group.*

7/ *Relative value is the value of one of the companies compared with the other. Exchange ratio is the number of shares in the acquiring company that are exchanged for one share in the acquired company.*

8/ *On relative value and then on the calculation methods which would lead to the determination of the agreed relative value. On the surface, it looks like the opposite is true.*

9/ *Because they form part of a larger whole that is likely to generate synergies and because the merger could result in the P/E of the new entity being revalued.*

10/ *In the synergies created.*

11/ *In order to ensure the equal treatment of shareholders – the rights of all shareholders should be respected.*

12/ *When there is a conglomerate discount that will disappear. Rarely for creditors.*

13/ *Not in isolation. The initial business plans drawn up by companies should be taken into account.*

14/ *Yes, thanks to the efficiency of markets.*

Exercises

A detailed Excel version of the solutions is available at www.vernimmen.com.

1/

	Net profits	Value	Shareholders' equity
Mr Alpha's share	2/3	1/3	2/3
Mr Beta's share	1/3	2/3	1/3

The criteria selected are crucial.

2/ (a) and (b)

	Old (for Gamma)	New (P/E = 50)	New (P/E = 15)	New (P/E = 6)
EPS	0.01	0.0227	0.0145	0.0082
Equity per share	0.03	0.136	0.087	0.049
% of control held by Gamma shareholders	100% of Gamma	75.8%	48.4%	27.3%

The higher a company's P/E, the more it will get out of a merger.

(c) *If Gamma shareholders get all of the synergies: relative value of 3.59 and exchange ratio of 0.557 Gamma shares for 1 Delta share. If Gamma shareholders sell all of the synergies: relative value of 2.13 and exchange ratio of 0.940 Gamma shares for 1 Delta share.*

(d) *Value of the whole* $= 50 \times (40 + 20 + 10) = 3500$.

(e) *Wealth created* $= 2180$. *The wealth created is a result of synergies (500) and the revaluation of Delta (1680).*

BIBLIOGRAPHY

On value creation and mergers:

M. Bradley, A. Desai, E. Kim, Synergetic gains from corporate acquisitions and their division between the stockholders of target and acquiring firms, *Journal of Financial Economics*, **21**(1), 3–40, February 1988.

Z. Fluck, A. Lynch, Why do firms merge and then divest? A theory of financial synergy, *The Journal of Business*, **72**(3), 319–346, July 1999.

P. Healy, K. Palepu, R. Ruback, Does corporate performance improve after mergers?, *Journal of Financial Economics*, **31**(2), 135–175, April 1992.

U. Hege, S. Lovo, M. Slovin, Equity and cash in intercorporate asset sales: theory and evidence, *Review of Financial Studies*, **22**(2), 681–714, 2009.

U. Hege, E. Sushka, Equity or cash? The signal sent by the way you pay, *Harvard Business Review*, **87**(5), 22, May 2009.

W. Megginson, A. Morgan, L. Nail, The determinants of positive long-term performance in strategic mergers: Corporate focus and cash, *Journal of Banking and Finance*, **28**(3), 523–552, March 2004.

M. Rhodes-Kropf, S. Viswanathan, Market valuation and merger waves, *Journal of Finance*, **59**(6), 2685–2718, December 2004.

M. Sirower, *The Synergy Trap*, Free Press, 1997.

On demergers:

P. Anslinger, S. Klepper, S. Subramaniam, Breaking up is good to do, *McKinsey Quarterly*, **1**, 16–27, 1999.

T. Chemmanur, A. Yan, A Theory of Corporate Spin-offs, *Journal of Financial Economics*, **72**(2), 259–290, May 2004.

P. Cusatis, J. Miles, J. Woolridge, Restructuring through spin-offs, *Journal of Financial Economics*, **33**(3), 293–311, June 1993.

H. Desai, P. Jain, Firm performance and focus: Long-run stock market performance following spin-offs, *Journal of Financial Economics*, **54**(1), 75–101, October 1999.

S. Krishnaswami, V. Subramaniam, Information asymmetry, valuation, and the corporate spin-off decision, *Journal of Financial Economics*, **53**(1), 73–112, July 1999.

H. Leland, Financial synergies and the optimal scope of the firm: Implication for mergers spin-offs and structured finance, *Journal of Finance*, **62**(2), 765–807, April 2007.

W. Maxwell, R. Rao, Do spin-offs expropriate wealth from bondholders? *The Journal of Finance*, **58**(5), 2087–2108, October 2003.

V. Mehrotra, W. Mikkelson, M. Partch, The design of financial policies in corporate spin-offs, *The Review of Financial Studies*, **16**(4), 1359–1388, Winter 2003.

R. Parrino, Spin-offs and wealth transfers: The Marriott case, *Journal of Financial Economics*, **43**(2), 241–274, February 1997.

J.D. Rosenfeld, Additional evidence on the relation between divestiture announcements and shareholder wealth, *Journal of Finance*, **39**(5), 1437–1448, December 1984.

C. Veld, Y. Veld-Merkoulova, Do spin-offs create value? The European case, *Journal of Banking & Finance*, **28**(5), 1111–1135, May 2004.

Chapter 45
LEVERAGED BUYOUTS (LBOS)

Leverage on management!

A leveraged buyout (LBO) is the acquisition of a company by one or several private equity funds which finance their purchase mainly by debt. Most of the time, LBOs bring improvements in operating performance as the management is highly motivated (high potential for capital gains) and under pressure to rapidly pay down the debt incurred.

Why are financial investors willing to pay more for a company than a trade buyer investor? Are they miracle workers? Watch out for smoke and mirrors. Value is not always created where you think it will be. Agency theory will be very useful, as the main innovation of LBOs is a new corporate governance, which, in certain cases, is more efficient than that of listed or family companies.

In the course of this chapter we will use as an example the leveraged buyout of Spotless, a producer of specialty cleaning products, bought by Axa Private Equity.[1]

Section 45.1
LBO STRUCTURES

1/ PRINCIPLE

The basic principle is to create a holding company, the sole purpose of which is to hold financial securities. The holding company borrows money to buy another company, often called the "target". The holding company will pay interest on its debt and pay back the principal from the cash flows generated by the target. In LBO jargon, the holding company is often called *NewCo* or *HoldCo*.

Operating assets are the same after the transaction as they were before it. Only the financial structure of the group changes. Equity capital is sharply reduced and the previous shareholders sell part or all of their holding.

From a strictly accounting point of view, this setup makes it possible to benefit from the effect of financial gearing (see Chapter 13).

Now let us take a look at the example of Spotless, sold in early 2010 by the LBO fund BC Partners for an enterprise value of €623m. Spotless generated 2009 sales of €350m and an EBITDA of €65m. The acquiring holding company was set up with €374m of equity and €271m of debt.

1 *We have based this example on publicly available information, and for some of the figures have either simplified the reality or made some estimates. It should be considered as illustrative and does not reflect the reality or the exact state of the company.*

LBO STRUCTURE - SPOTLESS

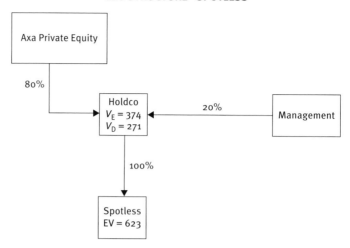

We assume that the pre-tax cost of debt is 6%. The balance sheets are as follows:

Revalued balance sheet		Holdco's unconsolidated balance sheet		Group's consolidated balance sheet	
Operating assets €623m	Shareholders' equity €623m	Share of Spotless €623m	Shareholders' equity €374m	Operating assets €623m	Shareholders' equity €352m
		Cash *€22m	Debt €271m		Debt €271m

* To pay transaction fees

Note that consolidated shareholders' equity, on a revalued basis, is now 43% lower than it was prior to the LBO.

An LBO leads to a massive destruction of equity.

The profit and loss statement, meanwhile, is as follows:

(in €m)	Spotless	Holdco	Consolidated
Earnings before interest and tax	60	39[2]	60
− Interest expense	0	16	16
− Income tax at 35%	21	0	−15[3]
= Net income	39	23	29

2 *Assuming 100% payout.*

3 *Assuming tax consolidation treatment.*

2/ TYPES OF LBO TRANSACTIONS

Leveraged buyout or *LBO* is the term for a variety of transactions in which an external financial investor uses leverage to purchase a company. Depending on how management is included in the takeover arrangements, LBOs fall into the following categories:

- a **(leveraged) management buyout** or **(L)MBO**, is a transaction undertaken by the existing management together with some or all of the company's employees;
- if a new management is put in place it will be called a **management buyin** or **MBI**;

- when outside managers are brought in to reinforce the existing management, the transaction is called a **BIMBO**, i.e. a combination of a *buyin* and a management *buyout*. This is the most common type of LBO in the UK;
- the term **leveraged build-up (LBU)** is used to describe an LBO in which the new group continues to acquire companies in its sector so as to create industrial synergies. These acquisitions are financed primarily with debt;
- an **owner buyout** (OBO) is a transaction undertaken by the largest shareholder to gain full control over the company.

3/ TAX ISSUES

Obtaining tax consolidation between the holding company and the target is one of the drivers of the overall structure, as it allows financial costs paid by the holding company to be offset against pre-tax profits of the target company, reducing the overall corporate income tax paid.

In some countries, it is possible to merge the holding company and the target company soon after the completion of the LBO. In other countries this is not the case, as the local tax administration argues it is contrary to the target's interest to bear such a debt load. Provided tax consolidation is possible between the target and Holdco, this has no material consequence. If tax consolidation is not possible because, for example, the Holdco stake in the target company has not reached the required minimum threshold, then a debt push down may be necessary.

In order to perform a debt push down, the target company pays an extraordinary dividend to Holdco or carries out a share buy-back financed by debt, allowing Holdco to transfer part of its debt to the target company where financial expenses can be offset against taxable profits. If the target company is still listed, an independent financial expert is likely to be asked to deliver a **solvency opinion** testifying that the target debt load does not prevent it from properly operating in the foreseeable future.

4/ EXIT STRATEGIES

The average LBO lifetime is short. Financial investors generally keep the investment for 2–5 years. There are several exit strategies:

- Sale to a trade buyer. Our general comment here is that in most cases financial investors bought the company because it had not attracted trade buyers at the right price. When the time has arrived for the exit of the financial buyer, either the market or the company will have had to have changed for a trade buyer to be interested. The private equity firm Astorg exited its investment in Geoservices in 2010 through a sale to trade buyer Schlumberger.
- Initial Public Offering. This strategy must be implemented in stages, and it does not allow the sellers to obtain a control premium; most of the time they suffer from an IPO discount. It is more attractive for senior management than a trade sale. At end-2006, Hertz was IPOed by Clayton Dubillier & Rice, and Carlyle; in 2010, Medica was listed in France.
- Sale to another financial investor, who, in turn, sets up another LBO. These "secondary" LBOs are becoming more and more common. Spotless is a fourth LBO.

- A leveraged recapitalisation. After a few years of debt reduction thanks to cash flow generation, the target takes on additional debt with the purpose of either paying a large dividend or repurchasing shares. The result is a far more financially leveraged company.

LBO EXITS IN THE UK

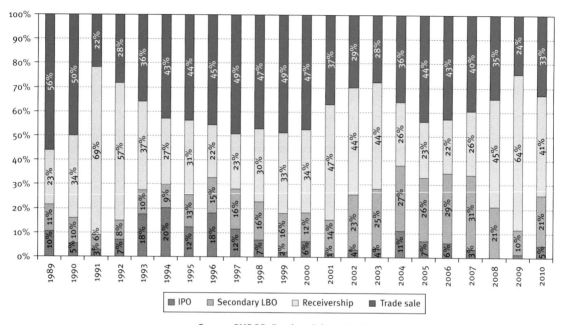

Source: CMBOR, Barclays Private Equity

If the company has grown or become more profitable on the financial investors' watch, it will be easier for them to exit. Improvement may take the form of a successful redundancy or cost-cutting plan or a series of bolt-on acquisitions in the sector. Size is important if flotation is the goal, because small companies are often undervalued on the stock market, if they manage to get listed at all.

The problem emerges when the target company's profits do not allow a large enough dividend payment to the parent company, which is then unable to pay its bank interest charges or repay its debt in a timely fashion. Apart from recapitalising the company, renegotiating with creditors is the traditional solution (interest rates, covenants, repayment schedule), but in some countries creditors cannot secure their loans with the assets of the subsidiary as long as the loans are extended to the holding company.

Section 45.2
THE PLAYERS

1/ POTENTIAL TARGETS

The transactions we have just examined are feasible only with certain types of target companies. Companies for which income streams are volatile by nature, such as trading companies, do not have access to LBO financing. The same is true for companies requiring heavy capital expenditure, such as certain high-tech companies.

The target company must generate profits and cash flows that are sufficiently large and stable over time to meet the holding company's interest and debt payments. The target must not have burdensome investment needs. Mature companies that are relatively shielded from variations in the business cycle make the best candidates: food, retail, water, building materials, real estate, cinema theatres and business listings providers are all prime candidates.

THE WORLD'S 10 LARGEST LBOs

Target	Date	Sector	Equity sponsor	Value ($bn)
TXU	February 2007	Energy	KKR/TPG	45
Equity Office	November 2006	Real Estate	Blackstone	36
HCA	July 2006	Health	Bain/KKR	33
RJR Nabisco	October 1988	Food	KKR	30
Kinder Morgan	August 2006	Energy	Carlyle	27
Harrah's Entertainment	December 2006	Casino	Apollo/TPG	27
First Data	September 2007	Technology	KKR	27
Clear Channel	November 2006	Media	Bain/Thomas Lee	27
Freescale	September 2006	Technology	TPG/Blackstone/Permira	17
Albertsons	January 2006	Retail	Cerberus	17

Source: Thomson Financial

The group's LBO financing already packs a hefty financial risk, so the industrial risks had better be limited. Targets are usually drawn from sectors with high barriers to entry and minimal substitution risk. Targets are often positioned on niche markets and control a significant portion of them, like Spotless.

Traditionally, LBO targets are "cash cows" but, more recently, there has been a movement towards companies exhibiting higher growth or operating in sectors with opportunities for consolidation.

As the risk aversion of investors decreases, some private equity funds have carried out LBOs in more difficult sectors or specialised in heavy turn-around situations (Chrysler). The mid-2007 crisis and the sudden disappearance of LBOs larger than €500m is likely to prompt a return to the basics: targets with high, stable and predictable cash flows able to pay down their debt with a reasonable degree of confidence.

2/ THE SELLERS

Around half of all LBOs are carried out on family-owned companies. An LBO solves the succession problem as the majority shareholders may be reluctant to sell to a competitor, may prefer to sell to their faithful and dedicated management team and/or as the stock exchange exit may be close at that time (Thomson Learning). In 20% of cases,[4] a large group wishing to refocus on a core business sells a subsidiary or a division via

4 *In number, but a larger percentage in amount.*

an LBO. Some sectors are so concentrated that only LBO funds can buy a target as the anti-trust authorities would never allow a competitor to buy it or would impose severe disposals making such an acquisition unpalatable to many trade buyers (Pro Sieben Sat 1, in German TV). The larger transactions fall into the latter category (Hertz sold by Ford).

But more and more frequently (30%), targets are companies already under an LBO, sold by one private equity investor to another one, for the second, third or more times, such as Spotless.

Finally, some listed companies that are undervalued (often because of liquidity issues or because of lack of attention from the investment community because of their size), sometimes opt for "**public-to-private**" (**P-to-P**) LBOs. In the process, the company is delisted from the stock exchange. Despite the fact that these transactions are complex to structure and generate high execution risk, they are becoming more and more common thanks to the drop in market values. The LBO on Boots Alliance was the largest worldwide P-to-P in 2007.

3/ LBO FUNDS ARE THE EQUITY INVESTORS

Setting up an LBO requires specific expertise, and certain investment funds specialise in them. These are called *private equity sponsors*, because they invest in the equity capital of unlisted companies.

LBOs are particularly risky because of their high gearing. Investors will therefore undoubtedly require high returns. Indeed, required returns are often in the region of 25% p.a. In addition, in order to eliminate diversifiable risk, these specialised investment funds often invest in several LBOs.

In Europe alone, there are over 100 LBO funds in operation. The US and UK LBO markets are more mature than those of Continental Europe. The Asian market is nascent. For this reason, Anglo-Saxon funds such as BC Partners, Blackstone, Candover, Carlyle, Cinven, CVC, Hicks Muse and KKR dominate the market, particularly when it comes to large transactions. In the meantime, the purely European funds, such as Eurazéo, Industrie Kapital and PAI are holding their own, generally specialising in certain sectors or geographic areas.

To reduce their risk, LBO funds also invest alongside another LBO fund (they form a consortium) or an industrial company (sometimes the seller) with a minority stake. In this case, the industrial company contributes its knowledge of the business and the LBO fund its expertise in financial engineering, the legal framework and taxation.

Most of the private equity sponsors contribute equity for between 40% and 50% of the total financing. Not so long ago, their contribution was between 30% and 40% and sometimes as low as 20%! Materially, LBO funds are organised in the form of a management company that is held by partners who manage funds raised from institutional investors[5] or high net worth individuals.

5 *Pension funds, insurance companies, banks, sovereign wealth funds.*

When a fund has invested nearly all of the equity it has raised, another fund is launched. Each fund is required to return to investors all of the proceeds of divestments as these are made, and the ultimate aim is for the fund to be liquidated after a given number of years.

The management company, in other words the partners of the LBO funds, is paid on the basis of a percentage of the funds invested (c. 2% of invested funds) and a percentage of the capital gains made (often close to 20% of the capital gain),[6] known as **carried interest**.

Some funds decide to list their shares on the stock market, like Blackstone did in June 2007,[7] while others such as Wendel and Eurazéo are listed for historical reasons.

6 *Sometimes above a minimum return rate.*

7 *Just before the LBO market ground to a sudden halt.*

4/ THE LENDERS

For smaller transactions (less than €10m), there is a single bank lender, often the target company's main bank.

For larger transactions, debt financing is more complex. The LBO fund negotiates the debt structure and conditions with a pool of bankers. Most of the time, bankers propose a financing to all candidates (even the one advising the seller). This is **staple financing**. The high degree of financial gearing requires not only traditional bank financing, but also subordinated lending and **mezzanine debt**, which lie between traditional financing and shareholders' equity. This results in a four-tier structure: traditional, secured loans called **senior debt**, to be repaid first, **subordinated** or **junior debt** to be repaid after the senior debt, mezzanine financing, the repayment of which is subordinated to the repayment of the junior and senior debt and, last in line, shareholders' equity. Sometimes, shareholders of the target grant a vendor loan to the LBO fund (part of the price of which payment is deferred) to help finance the transaction. Assets of the target can also be securitised[8] to raise more financing. Lastly in the halcyon days of LBOs (2005 till mid-2007) other products were created but they have since disappeared (equity bridge, interim facility agreement . . .).

8 *For more, see Chapter 22.*

(a) Senior debt

Senior debt generally totals 3–4 times the target's EBITDA.[9] It is composed of several tranches, from least to most risky:

9 *Earnings Before Interest, Taxes, Depreciation and Amortisation. For more, see Chapter 3.*

- tranche A is repaid in equal instalments over 6 to 7 years;
- tranches B and C are repaid over a longer period (7/8 years for the B tranche and 8/9 years for the C tranche) after the A tranche has been amortised.

Each tranche has a specific interest rate, depending on its characteristics (tranches B and C will be more expensive than tranche A because they are repaid after and are therefore more risky). Until mid-2007, the cost of senior LBO financing was 200 to 300 basis points[10] over government bond yields. Since then, and because of the subprime crisis, you have to add around 200 basis points to these figures.

10 *100 basis points = 1%.*

When the debt amount is high, the loan will be syndicated to several banks (see Chapter 26). Until mid-2007, collateralised debt obligation (CDO) funds were created, which subscribed or bought tranches of LBO debt whose shareholders were mainly insurance companies, hedge funds and pension funds. When the LBO market reached its climax mid-2007, 80% of the senior debt in the USA was subscribed by institutional investors directly or through CDO funds, and 55% in Europe. Since then, these figures have slumped.

(b) Junior or subordinated debt

High-yield bond issues are sometimes used to finance LBOs, but this technique is reserved for the largest transactions so as to ensure sufficient liquidity. In practice the lower limit is around €100m.

An advantage of this type of financing is that it carries a bullet repayment and a maturity of 8–10 years. In accordance with the principle of subordination, the bonds are repaid only after the senior debt is repaid.

Given the associated risk, high-yield LBO debt, as the name suggests, offers investors high interest rates. They were as much as 800 basis points over government bond yields until mid-2007. Since then they have disappeared.

(c) Mezzanine debt

Mezzanine debt also comes under the heading of (deeply) subordinated debt, but is unlisted and provided by specialised funds. Returns on mezzanine debt take three forms: a relatively low interest rate (5–6%) paid in cash; a deferred interest or payment in kind (PIK) for 5–8%; and a share in any capital gain when the LBO fund sells its stake.

As we saw in Chapter 25, certain instruments accommodate this financing need admirably. These "hybrid" securities include convertible bonds, mandatory convertibles, warrants, bonds with warrants attached, etc.

11 *See p. 382.*

Most of the time, mezzanine debt is made of bullet bonds[11] with warrants attached. Mezzanine financing is a true mixture of debt and shareholders' equity. Indeed mezzaniners demand returns more akin to the realm of equity investors, often approaching 15% p.a.

Given the associated risk, investors in mezzanine debt – "mezzaniners" – demand not only a high return, but also a say in management. Accordingly, they are sometimes represented on the board of directors.

LBO FINANCING

LBO financing spreads the risk of the project among several types of instruments, from the least risky (senior debt) to the most risky (common shares). The risk profile of each instrument corresponds to the preferences of a different type of investor.

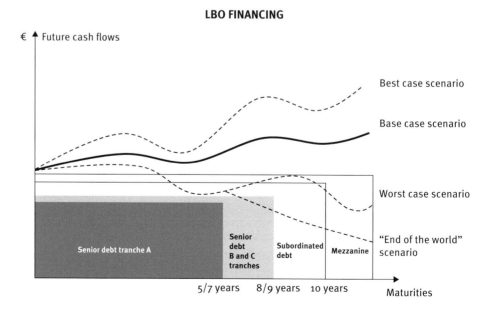

Subordinated and mezzanine debt offer the following advantages:

- they allow the company to lift gearing beyond the level acceptable for bank lending;
- they are longer term than traditional loans and a portion of the higher interest rate is paid through a potential dilution. The holders of mezzanine debt often benefit from call options or warrants on the shares of the holding company;
- they make upstreaming of cash flow from the target company to the holding company more flexible. Mezzanine debt has its own specific terms for repayment, and often for interest payments as well. Payments to holders of mezzanine debt are subordinated to the payments on senior and junior debt;
- they make possible a financing structure that would be impossible by using only equity capital and senior debt.

(d) Securitisation

Increasingly, LBOs are partly financed by securitisation (see Chapter 22). Securitised assets include receivables and/or inventories, when there is a secondary market for them.

A new technique, the securitisation buyout, has arisen in the UK. It is similar to standard securitisation of receivables, but aims to securitise the cash flows from the entire operating cycle.

(e) Other financing

Banks that finance LBOs are extremely inventive: the most complex structures can include, or did up to the summer of 2007, up to 10 different types of debt.

This has led to the development of a tranche of bank debt that falls in between senior debt and mezzanine debt – **second lien debt**, which is first ranking but long-term debt, and **interim facility agreements** which enable the LBO to go ahead even before the legal paperwork (often running to hundreds of pages) has been finalised and fully negotiated. Interim facility agreements are very short-term debts that are refinanced using LBO loans.

The pinnacle of inventiveness was reached with the **equity bridge**. Here, the lending banks behind the LBO guarantee a part of the equity used in structuring the buyout, pending a syndication of these shares with other LBO funds. One would be hard pressed to find a more efficient way of increasing the risk of lenders!

The financing of Holdco is generally topped up by financing at the level of the operating company:

- either through a **revolving credit facility** (RCF) which can help the company deal with any seasonal fluctuation in its working capital requirements; or
- an **acquisition facility**, which is a line of credit granted by the bank for small future acquisitions.

(f) The larger context

Up until the summer of 2007, investors' increasing appetite for risk meant that they were prepared not only to increase their investments in LBO funds, some of which had funds under management of over $15bn, but also to take out more and more LBO debt, which

12 *Debt securities issued by a special purpose vehicle which buys and holds bonds issued by corporations or banks (collateralised bond obligations) or bank loans (collateralised loan obligations). CDOs and CLOs provided liquidity for securities that weren't automatically liquid. It was used by banks to refinance themselves with investors wanting to take a risk on a debt portfolio.*

banks ceded back to them, either directly or indirectly, via CDOs or CLOs[12]. The role of LBO banks had more or less turned into a role of structuring and distributing funds. This is how a typical LBO structure changed:

Late 1990s		Early 2007		2011	
Equity:	35%	Equity:	20%	Equity:	40%−60%
Mezzanine debt:	10%	Pik or mezzanine debt:	5%	Mezzanine debt:	0−10%
		High-yield bond:	15%		
		Second lien:	5%		
Senior debt:	55%	Senior debt:	55%	Senior debt:	40%−50%
• Tranche A, 7 years amortisable		• Tranche A, 7 years amortisable			
• Tranche B, 8 years		• Tranche B, 8 years			
		• Tranche C, 9 years			
Revolving credit		Revolving credit or securitisation		Revolving credit	
		Capex line		Capex line	

Up until 2007, the prices of the target companies acquired under LBOs rose in comparison to their EBITDA:

As an example, Spotless was bought in early 2010 at 9.6 × its EBITDA of 2009 and the LBO was financed with debt of 42%, representing 4.2 times the EBITDA.

LBO FINANCING RATIOS TO EBITDA

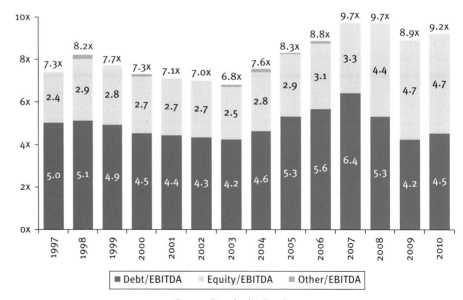

Source: Standard & Poor's

WEIGHTED AVERAGE SPREAD ON SENIOR LBO DEBT – TRANCHE B AND C IN EUROPE (basis points)

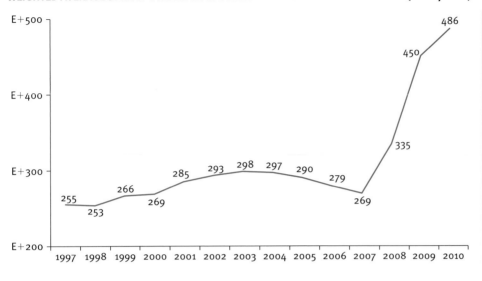

In a nutshell, the stage was set for a brutal crisis!

Source: Standard & Poor's

5/ THE MANAGERS OF A COMPANY UNDER AN LBO

The managers of a company under an LBO may be the historical managers of the company or new managers appointed by the LBO fund. Regardless of their background, they are responsible for implementing a clearly defined business plan that was drawn up with the LBO fund when it took over the target. The business plan makes provision for operational improvements, investment plans and/or disposals, with a focus on cash generation because, as the reader is no doubt aware, cash is what is needed for paying back debts!

LBO funds tend to ask managers to invest large amounts of their own cash in the company, and even to take out loans to be able to do so, in order to ensure that management's interests are closely aligned with those of the fund. Investments could be in the form of warrants, convertible bonds or shares, providing managers with a second leverage effect, which, if the business plan bears fruit, will result in a 5- to 10-fold or even greater increase in their investment. On the other hand, if the business plan fails, they will lose everything. So, only in the event of success will the management team get a partial share of the capital gains and a higher IRR on its investment than that of the LBO funds. This arrangement is known as the **management package**.

In some cases, following several successful LBOs, the management team can, as a result of this highly motivating remuneration scheme, take control of the company,[13] having seen its initial stake multiplied several times.

13 *Of small or medium size.*

Section 45.3
LBOs AND FINANCIAL THEORY

LBOs have gained considerable popularity since the mid-1980s, even though the market is cyclical and experienced a dry spell in the early 1990s and a big slump in 2007.

LBOs IN EUROPE SINCE 1982

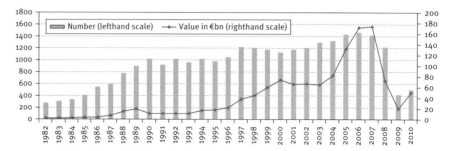

Source: CMBOR[14]/Barclays Private Equity/Deloitte & Touche

14 *Centre for Management Buy Out Research.*

Experience has shown that LBOs are often done at the same price or at an even higher price than what a trade buyer would be willing to pay. Yet the trade buyer, assuming he plans to unlock industrial and commercial synergies, should be able to pay more. How can we explain the widespread success of LBOs? Do they create value? How can we explain the difference between the pre-LBO value and the LBO purchase price?

At first, we might be tempted to think that there is value created because increased leverage reduces tax payments. But the efficient markets hypothesis casts serious doubts on this explanation, even though financial markets are not, in reality, always perfect. To begin with, the present value of the tax savings generated by the new debt service must be reduced by the present value of bankruptcy costs. Secondly, the arguments in Chapter 34 have led us to believe that the savings might not be so great after all. Hence, the attractions of leverage are not enough to explain the success of the LBO.

We might also think that a new, more dynamic management team will not hesitate to restructure the company to achieve productivity gains and that this would justify the premium. But this would not be consistent with the fact that the LBOs that keep the existing management team create as much value as the others.

Agency theory provides a relevant explanation. The high debt level prompts shareholders to keep a close eye on management. Shareholders will closely monitor operating performance and require monthly in-depth reporting. Management is put under pressure by the threat of bankruptcy if the company does not generate enough cash flow to rapidly pay down debt. At the same time, managers systematically become – either directly or potentially – shareholders themselves via their management package, so they have a strong incentive to manage the company to the best of their abilities.

Management, motivated by a potentially big payoff and put under pressure by a heavy debt burden, will manage the company in the most efficient manner possible, increasing cash flows and hence the value of the company. It's the carrot-and-stick approach!

15 *See interview with Philippe Santini (Managing a company under LBO), The Vernimmen.com Newsletter, June 2007.*

Kaplan has demonstrated through the study of many LBOs that their operating performance, compared with that of peer companies, is much better (cash flow generation, return on capital employed) and that they are able to outgrow the average company and create jobs.[15] This is one example where there is a clear interference of financial structure with operating performance.

LBO transactions greatly reduce agency problems and in so doing, create value. Their corporate governance policies are different from those of listed groups and family companies, and in many cases are more efficient.

LBOs give fluidity to markets, helping industrial groups to restructure their portfolio of assets. They play a bigger role than IPOs which are not always possible (equity markets are regularly shut down) or realistic (small and medium-sized companies in some countries are, in fact, practically banned from the stock exchange).

SUMMARY

The summary of this chapter can be downloaded from www.vernimmen.com.

A leveraged buyout is a transaction whereby the purchase of a company is financed primarily with borrowed funds. A holding company contracts the debt and purchases the target company. The company's cash flow is regularly funnelled upstream to the holding company via dividends to enable the latter to pay interest and reimburse the loans.

An LBO is often a solution in a family succession situation or when a large group wants to sell off a division. It can also be a way for a company to delist itself when it is undervalued in the market.

The target company in an LBO may keep the current management in place or hire a new management team. Equity capital is provided by specialised funds, the LBO funds. The structure depends on several layers of debt – senior, junior, mezzanine – with different repayment priorities. As priority declines, risk and expected returns increase.

Increased gearing and the deductibility of interest expense do not satisfactorily explain why value is created in an LBO. Instead, it appears that the heavier debt burden motivates management to do a better job managing the company, of which they are often destined to become shareholders themselves. This is agency theory in action. LBO funds bring different and, most of the time, more efficient corporate governance policies than those of family companies or listed groups: they focus management teams on cash flow generation and value creation. This is why a company can remain under LBO for years, with one LBO fund selling it to another.

QUESTIONS

1/ Explain why an LBO is a type of capital reduction.

2/ What risks are involved in an LBO?

3/ Can mezzanine financing in the context of an LBO be compared with equity or debt?

4/ In the context of an LBO, does the holder of senior debt take more or less risk than the holder of junior debt?

5/ Can an LBO be carried out on a startup company?

6/ In a secondary LBO, can an LBO fund accept that the management team does not reinvest part of the capital gains achieved on the first LBO in the new LBO? Why?

7/ What are the different possible exit routes after an LBO?

8/ How does corporate governance of an LBO differ from that of a listed company with no major shareholder?

9/ How does corporate governance of an LBO differ from that of most unlisted family companies?

SECTION 5

10/ What are the pros and cons of being a shareholder of a listed LBO fund compared to being a shareholder of a private one?

11/ What are the three types of risks that the shareholder of an LBO fund runs?

12/ Can an LBO work without debt?

13/ Can someone remain an LBO manager for more than 10 years?

More questions are waiting for you at www.vernimmen.com.

ANSWERS

1/ *Because shareholders' equity is mostly replaced by debt.*
2/ *The risk that debts will outweigh cash flows generated.*
3/ *With debt, because sooner or later it has to be repaid.*
4/ *Less risk because the holder of senior debt is repaid before the holder of junior debt.*
5/ *No, because a startup company's cash flows are much too volatile to allow it to carry debt.*
6/ *No, an LBO fund requires around 50% of the capital gains to be reinvested to keep management's motivation high.*
7/ *IPO, sale to a trade buyer, a secondary buyout, bankruptcy, a recapitalisation.*
8/ *Strong financial incentives for managers, constraint of the debt to be paid down, regular business discussions with shareholders (LBO fund representatives).*
9/ *Meritocracy is the rule of the game, not being a member of the founding family.*
10/ *The share of the LBO fund can be sold on the market; but it trades at a significant discount to the restated net asset value.*
11/ *Business risk, financial risk linked to the highly geared structure, risk linked to the lack of liquidity of the investment.*
12/ *No, as there is neither the pressure linked to the debt burden nor the hope for very high returns thanks to the leverage.*
13/ *No, as it would mean very high pressure for a very long time, and lack of motivation as he would have already become very rich.*

BIBLIOGRAPHY

To go into more detail:

B. Burrough, J. Helyar, *Barbarians at the Gate*, Harper Business Essentials, 2003.

R. Elitzur, P. Halpern, R. Kieschnick, W. Rotenberg, Management incentives and the structure of management buy-outs, *Journal of Economic Behaviour and Organization*, **35**(3), 347–367, August 1998.

EVCA, *Private Equity Fund Structures in Europe*, European Private Equity and Venture Capital Association, 2006.

M. Jensen, Eclipse of the public corporation, *Harvard Business Review*, **67**, 61–74, September 1989.

S. Kaplan, The staying power of leveraged buyouts, *Journal of Financial Economics*, **29**(2), 287–313, October 1991.

Y. Le Fur, P. Quiry, Challenge ahead for LBOs, *The Vernimmen.com Newsletter*, **13 and 14**, February and March 2006.

Y. Le Fur, P. Quiry, What is debt push down? *The Vernimmen.com Newsletter*, **29**, December 2007.

P. Povel, R. Singh, Stapled Finance, *Journal of Finance*, **65**(3), 927–953, June 2010.

P. Santini, Managing a company under LBO, *The Vernimmen.com Newsletter*, **25**, 1–4, June 2007.

www.evca.com, site of the European Private Equity and Venture Capital Association.

www.nottingham.ac.uk/business/cmbor, The Centre for Management Buy-out Research's website.

To study the value creation of LBOs:

V. Acharya, M. Hahn, C. Kehoe, *Corporate* Governance and Value Creation: Evidence from *Private Equity* (February 17, 2010). Working paper available at http://ssrn.com/abstract=1324016

A.K. Achleitner, Value creation in private equity, *Centre for Entrepreneurial and Financial Studies – Capital Dynamics*, 2009.

BCG-IESE, *The advantage of persistence: how the best private-equity firms "beat the fade"*, 2008.

S. Guo, E. Hotchkiss, W. Song, Do Buyouts (Still) Create Value, *Journal of Finance*, **66**(2), 479–517, April 2011.

S. Kaplan, The effects of management buy-outs on operating performance and value, *Journal of Financial Economics*, **24**(2), 217–254, October 1989.

Y. Le Fur, P. Quiry, Creating and sharing values in LBOs, *The Vernimmen.com Newsletter*, **51**, 1–4, June 2010.

D. Pindur, *Value Creation in Successful LBOs*, DUV, 2007.

Chapter 46
BANKRUPTCY AND RESTRUCTURING

Women and children first!

Every economic system needs mechanisms to ensure the optimal use of resources. Bankruptcy is the primary instrument for reallocating means of production from inefficient to efficient firms.

Theoretically, bankruptcy shakes out the bad apples from sectors in difficulty and allows profitable groups to prosper. Without efficient bankruptcy procedures, financial crises are longer and deeper.

A bankruptcy process can allow a company to reorganise, often requiring asset sales, a change in ownership and partial debt forgiveness on the part of creditors. In other cases, bankruptcy leads to liquidation – the death of the company.

Generally speaking, bankruptcy is triggered when a company can no longer meet its short-term commitments and thus faces a liquidity crisis. Nevertheless, the exact definition of the financial distress leading the company to file for bankruptcy may differ from one jurisdiction to another.

Bankruptcy is a critical juncture in the life of the firm. Not only does the bankruptcy require that each of the company's stakeholders make specific choices, but the very possibility of bankruptcy has an impact on the investment and financing strategies of healthy companies.

Section 46.1
CAUSES OF BANKRUPTCY

Companies do not encounter financial difficulties because they have too much debt, but because they are not profitable enough. A heavy debt burden does no more than accelerate financial difficulties.

The problems generally stem from an ill-conceived strategy, or because that strategy is not implemented properly for its sector (costs are too high, for example). As a result, profitability falls short of creditor expectations. If the company does not have a heavy debt burden, it can limp along for a certain period of time. Otherwise, financial difficulties rapidly start appearing.

Generally speaking, financial difficulties result either from a market problem, a cost problem or a combination of the two. The company may have been caught unawares by market changes and its products might not suit market demands (e.g. Smoby, a producer of wooden toys, Silicon Graphics). Alternatively, the market may be too small for the number of companies competing in it (e.g., online book sales, satellite TV platforms in various countries). Ballooning costs compared with those of rivals can also lead to bankruptcy. General Motors, for example, was uncompetitive against other carmakers. Eurotunnel, meanwhile, spent twice the budgeted amount on digging the tunnel between France and the UK.

Nevertheless, a profitable company can encounter financial difficulties, too. For example, if a company's debt is primarily short term, it may have trouble rolling it over if liquidity is lacking on the financial markets. In this case, the most rational solution is to restructure the company's debt.

One of the fundamental goals of financial analysis as it is practised in commercial banks, whose main business is making loans to companies, is to identify the companies most likely to go belly up in the near or medium term and not lend to them. Numerous standardised tools have been developed to help banks identify bankruptcy risks as early as possible. This is the goal of credit scoring, which we analysed in Chapter 8.

Rating agencies also estimate the probability that a company will go bankrupt in the short or long term (bankruptcies as a function of rating were presented in Chapter 21).

BANKRUPTCY RATE OF COMPANIES RATED BY MOODY'S

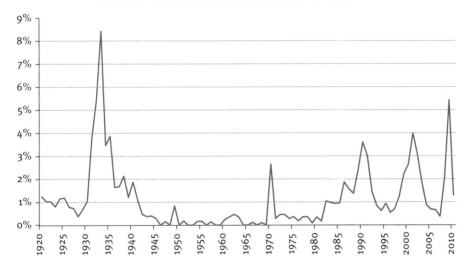

Source: Moody's 2011

1/ THE DIFFERENT BANKRUPTCY PROCEDURES

The bankruptcy process is one of the legal mechanisms that is the least standardised and homogenised around the world. Virtually all countries have different systems. In addition, legislation is generally recent and evolves rapidly.

Nevertheless, among the different procedures, some patterns can be found. In a nutshell, there are two different types of bankruptcy procedure. The process will be either "creditor (lender) friendly" or "debtor (company) friendly". But all processes have the same ultimate goals, although they may rank differently:

- paying-down the liabilities of the firm;
- minimising the disruptive impact on the industry;
- minimising the social impact.

A creditor-oriented process clearly sets the reimbursement of creditors as the main target of the bankruptcy process. In addition, the seniority of debt is of high importance and is therefore recognised in the procedure. In this type of procedure, creditors gain control, or at least retain substantial powers in the process. This type of process generally results in the liquidation of the firm. Bankruptcy procedure in the United Kingdom clearly falls into this category.

Such a regulation may seem unfair and too tough but it aims at preventing financial distress rather than solving it in the least disruptive way for the whole economy. In such countries, firms exercise a kind of self-discipline and tend to keep their level of debt reasonable in order to avoid financial distress. As a counterpart, creditors are more confident when granting loans, and money is more readily available to companies. For those supporting this type of process, the smaller number of bankruptcies in countries with stringent regulations (and an efficient judicial system) is evidence that this self-regulation works.

At the other end of the spectrum, some jurisdictions will give the maximum chance to the company to restructure. These procedures will generally allow management to stay in place and give sufficient time to come up with a restructuring plan. Countries with this approach include the USA (Chapter 11) and France.

To summarise, the following criteria help define a bankruptcy procedure:

- Does the procedure allow restructuring or does it systematically lead to liquidation (most jurisdictions design two distinct procedures)?
- Does management stay in place or not?
- Does the procedure include secured debts? In some countries, secured debts (i.e. debts that are guaranteed by specific assets) and related assets are excluded from the process and treated separately, allowing greater certainty in the repayment. In such countries, securing a debt by a pledge on an asset gives strong guarantees.
- Do creditors take the lead, or at least have a say in the outcome of the process? In most jurisdictions, creditors vote on the plan that is proposed to them as the outcome of the bankruptcy process. They sometimes have even greater power and are allowed to name a trustee who will liquidate the assets to pay down debt. But in some countries (e.g. France) they are generally not even consulted.

	France	Germany	India	Italy	UK	USA
Type	Debtor (borrower) friendly	Creditor (lender) friendly	Creditor (lender) friendly	Debtor (borrower) friendly	Creditor (lender) friendly	Debtor (borrower) friendly
Possible restructuring	Yes	Yes (rare)	Yes	Yes	Rare after opening of a proceeding	Yes
Management can stay in place	Yes*	Yes*	No	***	No	Yes
Lenders vote on restructuring/ liquidation plan	No	Yes	Yes	Yes**	Yes	Yes

	France	Germany	India	Italy	UK	USA
Priority rule	Salaries; tax, other social liabilities; part of secured debts; proceeding charges; other secured debts; other debts	Proceeding charges; secured debts; other debts	Secured debts and employees proceeding charges; tax and social liabilities; unsecured debts	Proceeding charges; preferential creditors (inc. tax and social) and secured creditors; unsecured creditors	Proceeding charges; secured debts on specific assets; tax and social security; other secured debts; other debts	Secured debts granted after filing; employee benefit and tax claims; unsecured debts

*Assisted by court-designated trustee.

**Yes in the case of restructuring (pre-emptive arrangement) but only consultative committee in case of liquidation.

***No in the case of liquidation.

2/ POTENTIAL INEFFICIENCIES IN THE BANKRUPTCY PROCEDURE

Depending on the severity of the bankruptcy process and in particular whether or not it allows and promotes restructurings, two opposite inefficiencies may arise. The process may:

- allow restructuring of an inefficient firm that destroys value. This could be an issue as such restructuring may destabilise the whole industry;
- lead to liquidation of efficient companies. A firm can be caught in a bankruptcy procedure because of a liquidity problem. In this case, liquidation could be value destroying.

3/ RESTRUCTURING PLANS

It is important to understand that not all financial difficulties lead to voluntary or court-mandated reorganisation or liquidation, which is often costly, lengthy and sometimes ineffective. The first step is usually private negotiation between the company (shareholders and/or managers) and its creditors. The more numerous the company's sources of funding – common shareholders, preferred shareholders, convertible bond holders, creditors, etc. – the more complex the negotiations.

Barring private negotiation, the potential conflicts between the various parties necessitate the intervention of a judge.

The business plan submitted by the company in financial distress is a key element in estimating its ability to generate the cash flows needed to pay off creditors.

A restructuring plan requires sacrifices from all of the company's stakeholders. It generally includes a recapitalisation, often funded primarily by the company's existing shareholders, and renegotiation of the company's debt. Creditors are often asked to give up some of their claims, accept a moratorium on interest payments and/or reschedule principal payments.

Creditors and shareholders are naturally at odds with each other in a restructuring. To bring them all on board, the renegotiated debt agreements sometimes include clawback provisions, whereby the principal initially foregone will be repaid if the company's future profits exceed a certain level. Alternatively, creditors might be granted share warrants. If the restructuring is successful, warrants enable the creditors to reap part of the benefits.

To succeed, financial restructuring must be accompanied by operational restructuring. As part of the effort to improve productivity, operational restructuring is very likely to involve head count reductions. Certain businesses might be sold or discontinued. Note that restructuring a company in difficulty can sometimes be a vicious circle. Faced with a liquidity crisis, the company must sell off its most profitable operations. But as it must do so quickly, it sells them for less than their fair value. The profitability of the remaining assets is therefore impaired, paving the way to new financial difficulties.

Section 46.2
BANKRUPTCY AND FINANCIAL THEORY

1/ THE EFFICIENT MARKETS HYPOTHESIS

In the efficient markets hypothesis, bankruptcy is nothing more than a reallocation of assets and liabilities to more efficient companies. It should not have an impact on investor wealth, because investors all hold perfectly diversified portfolios. Bankruptcy, therefore, is simply a reallocation of the portfolio.

The reality of bankruptcy is, however, much more complicated than a simple redistribution. Bankruptcy costs amount to a significant percentage of the total value of the company. By bankruptcy costs, we mean not only the direct costs, such as the cost of court proceedings, but also the indirect costs. These include loss of credibility *vis-à-vis* customers and suppliers, loss of certain business opportunities, etc. Economists have tried to measure these costs, but because of the complexity of the task, their results have been applicable only in isolated cases and are not statistically meaningful. According to these researchers (Stanley and Girth, 1971; Warner, 1977; Weiss, 1990; Andrade and Kaplan, 1998), bankruptcy costs range from 3% to 20% of the enterprise value of the company.

Bankruptcy costs have an impact on a company's choice of financial structure. A company that takes on a lot of debt increases its risk of going bankrupt, and investors will discount the value of its assets by the present value of the bankruptcy costs. Potential bankruptcy costs thus reduce the tax advantage of borrowing that stems from the deductibility of interest expense.

2/ SIGNAL THEORY AND AGENCY THEORY

The possibility of bankruptcy is a key element of signalling theory. An aggressive borrowing strategy sends a positive signal to the market, because company managers are showing their belief that future cash flows will be sufficient to meet the company's commitments. But this signal is credible only because there is also the threat of sanctions: if managers are wrong, the company goes bankrupt and incurs the related costs.

Moreover, conflicts between shareholders and creditors, as predicted by agency theory, appear only when the company is close to the financial precipice. When the company is in good health, creditors are indifferent to shareholder decisions. But any decision that makes bankruptcy more likely, even if this decision is highly likely to create value overall for the company, will be perceived negatively by the creditors.

Let's look at an example. Rainbow Ltd. manufactures umbrellas and is expected to generate just one cash flow. To avoid having to calculate present values, we assume the company will receive the cash flow tomorrow. Tomorrow's cash flow will be one of two values, depending on the weather. Rainbow has borrowings and will have to pay 50 to its creditors tomorrow (principal and interest).

Weather	Rain	Shine
Cash flow	100	50
Payment of principal and interest	–50	–50
Shareholders' portion of cash flow (equity)	50	0

Rainbow now has an investment opportunity requiring an outlay of 40 and returning cash flow of 100 in case of rainy weather and –10 in case of sunny weather. The investment project appears to have a positive net present value. Let's see what happens if the investment is financed with additional borrowings.

Weather	Rain	Shine
Cash flow	200	40
Payment of principal and interest	–90	–40 (whereas 90 was due)
Shareholders' portion of cash flow (equity)	110	0

Even though the investment project has a positive net present value, Rainbow's creditors will oppose the project because it endangers the repayment of part of their loans. Shareholders will, of course, try to undertake risky projects as it will more than double the value of the equity.

It can be demonstrated that when a company is close to bankruptcy, all financial decisions constitute a potential transfer of value between shareholders and creditors. Any decision that increases the company's overall risk profile (risky investment project, increase in debt coupled with a share buy-back) will transfer value from creditors to shareholders. Decisions that lower the risk of the company (e.g., capital increase) will transfer value from shareholders to creditors. As we showed in Chapter 35, these value transfers can be modelled using options theory.

Conflicts between shareholders and creditors and between senior and junior creditors also influence the decisions taken when the company is already in bankruptcy. On the one hand, creditors want to accelerate the procedure and liquidate assets quickly, because the value of assets rapidly decreases when the company is "in the tank". On the other hand, shareholders and managers want to avoid liquidation for as long as possible because it signifies the end of all hope of turning the company around, without any financial reward. For managers, it means they will lose their jobs and their reputations will suffer. At the same time, managers, shareholders and creditors would all like to avoid the inefficiencies linked with liquidation. This common objective can make their disparate interests converge.

The table below shows the average hope for repayment in the case of bankruptcy, depending on the ranking of the debt.

Whereas senior creditors get, on average, 60% of their money back, most junior creditors will receive less than 25% of their initial lending.

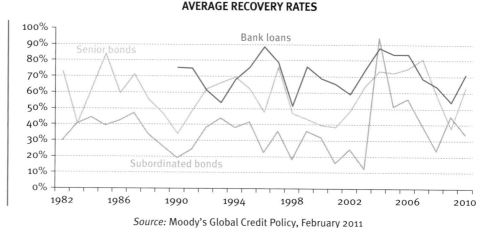

AVERAGE RECOVERY RATES

Source: Moody's Global Credit Policy, February 2011

3/ FREE RIDERS

Lastly, a company in financial difficulties gives rise to the free rider problem (see Chapter 27). For example, a small bank participating in a large syndicated loan may prefer to see the other banks renegotiate their loans, while keeping the terms of its loan unchanged.

Free rider problems will often arise when creditors are in different situations in terms of commitment or of ranking of their debt.

It has been observed that the number of bankruptcies is greater in countries with mature financial markets. The proposed explanation is that, in those countries, the companies are more likely to have public or syndicated debt and therefore a large number of creditors. In addition, with sophisticated markets, firms are more likely to have several types of debt: secured loans, senior debt, convertibles, subordinated, etc. In this context it may appear to be very difficult to restructure the firm privately (i.e. to find an agreement with a large number of parties with often conflicting interests such as hedge funds, vulture funds, trade suppliers, commercial banks, etc.), hence a bankruptcy process is the favoured route.

This is especially true when a lender has already hedged itself though a credit default swap[1] and will earn more from bankruptcy (recover 100% of its claims thanks to the CDS) than in a reorganisation (will get less than 100%).

In bank financing-based countries, firms have strong relationships with banks. In the case of financial distress, banks are likely to organise the restructuring privately. This is often the case in Germany or in France where bilateral relationships between banks and corporates are stronger than in the Anglo-Saxon world.

1 *For more, see Chapter 49.*

4/ THE LIMITS OF LIMITED LIABILITY

Modern economies are based largely on the concept of limited liability, under which a shareholder's commitment can never exceed the amount invested in the company. It is this rule that gives rise to the conflicts between creditors and shareholders and all other theoretical ramifications on this theme (agency theory).

In bankruptcy, managers can be required to cover liabilities in the event of gross negligence. In such cases, they can be forced to pay back creditors out of their own pockets, once the value of the company's assets is exhausted. So when majority shareholders are also the managers of the company, their responsibility is no longer limited to their investment. Such cases are outside the framework of the pure financial decision situations we have studied here.

Section 46.3
AN ILLUSTRATIVE EXAMPLE OF FINANCIAL RESTRUCTURING

We have chosen to illustrate the process of financial restructuring using, as an example, Eurotunnel, the company that owns and operates the Channel tunnel between France and the UK, and the financial distress it experienced in 2006 and 2007. The case and figures have been intentionally simplified and could therefore appear to have been altered.

Back in 1986, Eurotunnel decided to take on debt rather than equity: it raised 4.7 times more debt (€7.6bn) than equity (€1.6bn) to finance the construction of the tunnel. The construction cost 80% more than expected (€16.7bn) and opened 1 year behind schedule. As a consequence, even after several equity issues, Eurotunnel had to bear a monumental debt (around €10bn) resulting in an unbearable amount of interest, which always exceeded its free cash flows.

A new CEO, appointed in 2005, started to improve the operating structure, reducing the number of employees, optimising the tunnel's capacity and changing the marketing strategy. He then started negotiations with creditors knowing that Eurotunnel would be unable to meet its financial commitments by early 2007.

The CEO stated repeatedly that he would not hesitate to declare Eurotunnel bankrupt, highlighting the fact that creditors, generally the most junior, would lose their entire investment in the process. Very basically, creditors were either senior (€3.7bn of debt) or junior (€5.4bn, such as bondholders). The CEO first had to convince creditors that, given the cash flow projections, a reasonable amount of debt could not exceed €4bn. His next task was to persuade the creditors to share the effort that had to be made by playing one category off against the other, always bearing in mind that shareholders, whose approval was compulsory, could veto a deal that would be too harsh on them, pushing the company into liquidation. He was helped by French bankruptcy law which does not allow creditors to automatically seize assets in the event of bankruptcy. After having spent the whole of 2006 in negotiations, an agreement was reached and approved by shareholders and creditors alike. But to reach this deal, the CEO had to seek the protection of the Paris Court, allowing Eurotunnel to suspend the payment of debts during the negotiation phase, and a receiver was appointed to help him.

The restructuring involved:

- the issue of a long-term loan of €4.2bn, of which €3.7bn was used to reimburse the senior debt. This new loan was at a lower interest rate and over a longer period of time than the old senior debt and it was compatible with the cash flow projections of Eurotunnel. The first debt repayment was postponed from 2007 to 2013 with the main repayments between 2018 and 2043;
- the transformation of the junior debt in mandatory convertible bonds into Eurotunnel shares. In addition, junior debtholders received some cash (€0.4bn) and warrants to subscribe in the future to new Eurotunnel shares at a price of €0.01 per share;
- of the €4.2bn loan, €0.1bn was left as a financial reserve;

- the issue of free warrants to shareholders parallel to those distributed to junior debtholders (55% for the former and 45% for the latter).

Eurotunnel shareholders were to receive 28% of the equity of the restructured group after conversion of the mandatory convertible bonds into new shares and warrants exercise.

Basically, bondholders and other junior debtholders gave up all their claims to become owners of the group and received some cash. Prior to the plan, the debt (senior and junior) was trading at c. 44% of face value. The new loan is trading close to 100% of face value. Before restructuring, the market capitalisation of Eurotunnel was €0.7bn; after restructuring it increased by the exercise of warrants to c. €1.3bn.

For the shareholders and creditors the financial impact of the plan was as follows:

	Before restructuring (December 2005)	After restructuring (June 2007)
Senior creditors	Nominal value: €3.7bn Market value: below nominal	€3.7bn
Junior creditors	Nominal value: €5.4bn Market value: below 40% (i.e. €2.2bn)	€2.6bn, of which mandatory convertible bonds for €1.7bn, warrants for €0.5bn and cash for €0.4bn
Shareholders	€0.7bn	€1.3bn, of which value of the shares for €0.7bn + value of warrants: €0.6bn

The CEO should be complimented on the good job he did for his shareholders. Junior creditors were in a weak negotiating position, as, in the event of liquidation, senior creditors would be allocated most of the assets because the face value of their claims was close to the value of the assets. However, we should not forget that, before restructuring, Eurotunnel shares were trading at 97% below the IPO price!

SUMMARY

The summary of this chapter can be downloaded from www.vernimmen.com.

Bankruptcy is triggered when a company can no longer meet its short-term commitments and thus faces a liquidity crisis. This situation does not arise because the company has too much debt, but because it is not profitable enough. A heavy debt burden does no more than hasten the onset of financial difficulties.

The bankruptcy process is one of the legal mechanisms that is the least standardised and homogenised around the world. Virtually all countries have a different system. Depending on the country, the process will be either "creditor (lender) friendly" or "debtor (company) friendly". But all processes have the same goals, although they might rank differently:

- paying-down the liabilities of the firm;

- minimising the disruptive impact on the industry;

- minimising the social impact.

The bankruptcy process can generate two types of inefficiencies:

- allowing restructuring of an inefficient firm that destroys value;

- initiating the liquidation of efficient companies.

Prior to court proceedings, a company experiencing financial difficulties can try to implement a restructuring plan. The plan generally includes a recapitalisation and renegotiation of the company's debt.

Bankruptcy generates both direct (court proceedings, lawyers, fees, etc.) and indirect costs (loss of credibility *vis-à-vis* customers and suppliers, loss of certain business opportunities, etc.). These costs have an impact on a company's choice of financial structure.

Financial distress will generate conflict between shareholders and creditors (agency theory), and conflict among creditors (free rider issues).

QUESTIONS

1/ Why do companies go bankrupt?

2/ What risks do you take if you buy a subsidiary of a group that you know is in financial distress?

3/ Do the same types of conflict arise in the event of the bankruptcy of a partnership and that of a limited company? Why?

4/ How, in some countries, can bankruptcy play a role in the survival of the company?

5/ How do bankruptcy costs impact on the tax breaks available on debt?

6/ Why are companies that are emerging from bankruptcy proceedings often strong competitors?

7/ Why are companies in France that are emerging from bankruptcy proceedings rarely strong competitors?

8/ Can a company with no debts go bankrupt? Can it destroy value?

9/ Why is a company able to get back on its feet financially during the bankruptcy period?

10/ Why do creditors agree to grant loans to companies during the bankruptcy period?

11/ What are the pros of a creditor-friendly bankruptcy procedure for shareholders?

12/ Name countries which have debtor-friendly bankruptcy procedures.

More questions are waiting for you at www.vernimmen.com.

EXERCISE

1/ The Landmark car park will be shutting down tomorrow after having generated a final cash flow. It has debts of 500 used to finance its activities. Depending on whether the economic situation is good or bad (there is an equal probability of either), the flows are as follows:

Economic situation	–	+
Operating cash flow	500	1000
Payment of debt	−500	−500
Shareholders' portion of cash flow	0	500

SECTION 5

The company is offered an investment yielding 0 if things go badly (−) and 300 if things go well (+).

(a) What is the initial value of the debt? And of shareholders' equity?
(b) What is the objective value of the investment project? At what price would investors be prepared to invest? Does your answer depend on the way this investment is financed?
(c) What conditions would new creditors set for financing this new investment?
(d) Are conflicts that arise between shareholders and creditors a result of the way in which the company finances investments?

2/ Alok Malpani and Sons is a high-tech group in financial distress. Its key financials are as follows:

(in €m)	2008	2009	2010
Sales	8026	5208	3018
Operating income	130	(168)	(100)
Financial expense	(330)	(144)	(62)
Restructuring costs	(1020)	(314)	
Net income	(1220)	(626)	(162)
Fixed assets		122	72
Working capital		614	330
Shareholders' equity		(620)	(784)
Subordinated debt		616	616
Senior debt		740	570

The Alok Malpani and Sons shares are trading at €24. The company's share capital is divided into 8 910 000 shares. The value of the senior debt can be estimated at half of its face value and the value of the subordinated debt at 21% of its face value.

The following rescue plan has been submitted to all of the investors in the company:

○   Shareholder subscription to a capital increase of 15 500 000 new shares at a price of €20 per share, totalling €310m.
○   Partial repayment and conversion of the subordinated debt into capital: issue of 3 850 000 new shares and repayment of €36.96m.
○   Waiver of €160m of debts by senior creditors. In exchange, 1 250 000 warrants entitling holders to subscribe after 3 years to 1 share per warrant at a price of €25 per share. The value of these warrants is estimated at €4 per warrant. The proceeds of the capital increase that are left over after partial repayment of the subordinated debt will be used to repay the senior creditors.

(a) What is your view of the financial health of this company?
(b) Calculate the value of the different securities used to finance the capital employed.
(c) Calculate how much the various lenders will have before and after the rescue plan. Assume the negotiated amount of the face value of the senior debt will be 80% after the plan.
(d) Who are the key beneficiaries of this plan?

Questions

1/ *Because their return on capital employed is too low and they do not generate enough free cash flow.*

2/ *The risk that the sale may be declared invalid, as it took place during the period immediately preceding the bankruptcy.*

3/ *No, because in partnerships, partners' liability is not limited to their contributions.*

4/ *It puts the counter back to zero for all contracts.*

5/ *The present value of the cost of bankruptcy is deducted from the enterprise value. The more debts a company has, the higher the bankruptcy costs.*

6/ *Because a portion of their charges may have been renegotiated and revised downwards (rent, personnel expenses, miscellaneous charges).*

7/ *Because in France, public policy is weighted heavily in favour of job preservation, and the recovery plan that saves the largest number of jobs is likely to be the one selected by the bankruptcy courts, even if, in the long term, it leads to the demise of the company.*

8/ *No, since it doesn't owe anything (or practically nothing). Yes, if it invests at a rate of return below that required by shareholders.*

9/ *Because in most jurisdictions, repayments on old debts are frozen, and customers continue to pay their debts.*

10/ *Because their new debts will be paid off before the old debts if the company is liquidated.*

11/ *Managers will try to postpone bankruptcy for as long as possible.*

12/ *USA, France.*

Exercises

A detailed Excel version of the solutions is available at www.vernimmen.com.

1/ (a) $V_d = 500$, $V_e = 250$.

(b) *150; nearly 300 if it is debt financed; 150 if it is equity financed.*

(c) *They would want to be certain that they will be reimbursed first (i.e. their credit is ranked higher than that of existing creditors).*

(d) *Yes, but only because the company was close to bankruptcy at the outset.*

2/ (a) *The group is in very poor shape financially, and its returns are far too low. The disposal of the most attractive assets that became necessary to meet cash needs merely served to accelerate the group's plunge into bankruptcy. The business is shrinking away.*

(b) *Value of shareholders' equity = €213.84m.*
Value of subordinated debt = €129.36m.
Value of senior debt = €285m.
Value of capital employed = €628.2m.

(c) *Value of senior creditors' assets = $(310 - 36.94) + (570 - 160 - 310 + 36.94) \times 80\% + 1.25 \times 4 = €387.61m$.*
Value of shareholders' equity = $628.2 - (570 - 160 - 310 + 36.94) \times 80\% - 1.25 \times 4 = 513.65$.
Value of a share = $513.65/(8.91 + 15.5 + 3.85) = €18.2$
Shareholders' wealth without capital increase = €162.2m (compared with €213.83m before plan).
Subordinated creditors' assets = $36.94 + 3.85 \times 18.2 = €107m$ (compared with €129.36m before).
Wealth of shareholders who subscribed to the capital increase = $15.5 \times 18.2 = €282.1m$ (for €310m invested).

(d) *The creditors.*

BIBLIOGRAPHY

E. Altman, E. Hotchkiss, *Corporate Financial Distress and Bankruptcy: Predict and Avoid Bankruptcy, analyze and invest in distressed debt,* 3rd edn, John Wiley & Sons, Inc., 2005.

G. Andrade, S. Kaplan, How costly is financial (not economic) distress? Evidence from highly leveraged transactions that became distressed, *Journal of Finance*, **53**(5), 1443–1493, October 1998.

E. Berkovitch, R. Israel, Optimal bankruptcy laws across different economic systems, *Review of Financial Studies*, **12**(2), 347–377, Summer 1999.

A. Bris, I. Welch, N. Zhu, The costs of bankruptcy: Chapter 7 liquidation versus Chapter 11 reorganization, *Journal of Finance*, **61**(3), 1253–1306, June 2006.

J. Campbell, J. Hilscher, J. Szilagyi, In search of distress risk, *Journal of Finance*, **63**(6), 2899–2939, December 2008.

S. Claessens, L. Klapper, *Bankruptcy Around the World – Explanation of its Relative Use*, World Bank Development Research Group, July 2002.

S. Davydenko, J. Franks, Do bankruptcy codes matter? A study of defaults in France, Germany, and the UK, *Journal of Finance*, **63**(2), 565–608, April 2008.

S. Djankov, O. Hart, C. McLiesh, A. Shleifer, *Debt Enforcement Around the World*, *Journal of Political Economy*, **116**(6), 1105–1149, December 2008.

I. Hashi, The economics of bankruptcy, reorganization, and liquidation – Lessons for East European transition economies, *Russian and East European Finance and Trade*, **33**(4), 6–34, July/August 1999.

U. Hege, Workouts, court-supervised reorganization and the choice between private and public debt, *Journal of Corporate Finance*, **9**(2), 233–269, March 2003.

J. McConnell, D. Denis, *Corporate Restructuring*, Edward Elgar Publishing, 2005.

C. Molina, L. Preve, Trade receivables policy of distressed firms and its effect on the costs of financial distress, *Financial Management*, **38**(3), 663–686, Autumn 2009.

D.T. Stanley, M. Girth, *Bankruptcy: Problem, Process, Reform*, Brookings Institution, Washington, 1971.

J. Warner, Bankruptcy costs: Some evidence, *Journal of Finance*, **32**(2), 337–347, May 1977.

L. Weiss, Bankruptcy resolution, direct costs and violation of priority of claims, *Journal of Financial Economics*, **27**(2), 285–314, October 1990.

M. White, The corporate bankruptcy decision, *Journal of Economic Perspective*, **3**(2), 129–151, October 1989.

G. Zhang, Emerging from Chapter 11 bankruptcy: Is it good news or bad news for industry competitors? *Financial Management*, **39**(4), 1719–1742, Winter 2010.

PART TWO
MANAGING CASH FLOWS, WORKING CAPITAL AND FINANCIAL RISKS

In this part, we aim to analyse the day-to-day management of a company's financial resources in terms of three main components:

* management of cash flows and treasury, which we will examine in Chapter 47;
* management of working capital (Chapter 48); and
* management of financial risks, particularly interest rate, exchange rate, liquidity, credit risks and the risk of fluctuations in raw materials prices, which is described in Chapter 49.

These components were traditionally managed by distinct corporate functions, i.e. treasury and risk management. That said, they have now generally been pooled under the responsibility of the corporate treasurer, given the interlinkage between them. The treasurer's role is to oversee:

* a centralised treasury unit responsible for managing cash flows and monitoring working capital;
* a financing unit responsible for securing funds and negotiating borrowing terms with banks;
* a front-office unit handling market transactions as well as interest rate and exchange rate risks; and
* in large groups, a joint administrative unit ("back office") that processes transactions for all units.

Chapter 47
MANAGING CASH FLOWS

A balancing act . . .

Cash flow management is the traditional role of the treasury function. It handles cash inflows and outflows, as well as intra-group fund transfers. With the development of information systems, this function is usually automated. As a result, the treasurer merely designs or chooses a model, and then supervises the day-to-day operations. Nonetheless, we need to take a closer look at the basic mechanics of the treasury function to understand the relevance and the impact of the different options.

Sections 47.1 and 47.2 explain the basic concepts of cash flow management, as well as its main tools. These factors are common to both small companies and multinational groups. Conversely, the cash pooling units described in Section 47.3 remain the sole preserve of groups. In Section 47.4 we describe the products that the treasurer might use to invest the firm's residual cash in hand.

Section 47.1
THE BASICS

1/ VALUE DATING

From the treasurer's standpoint, the balance of cash flows is not the same as that recorded in the company's accounts or that shown on a bank statement. An example can illustrate these differences.

Example *A*, a company headquartered in Amsterdam, issues a cheque for €1000 on 15 April to its supplier *R* in Rotterdam. Three different people will record the same amount, but not necessarily on the same date:

- *A*'s accountant, for whom the issue of the cheque theoretically makes the sum of €1000 unavailable as soon as the cheque has been issued;
- *A*'s banker, who records the €1000 cheque when it is presented for payment by *R*'s bank. He then debits the amount from the company's account based on this date;
- *A*'s treasurer, for whom the €1000 remains available until the cheque has been debited from the relevant bank account. The date of debit depends on when the cheque is cashed in by the supplier and how long the payment process takes.

There may be a difference of several days between these three dates, which determines movements in the three separate balances.

1 *Note that the concept of value date is not universal.*

Cash management based on value dates[1] is built on an analysis from the treasurer's standpoint. The company is interested only in the periods during which funds are actually available. Positive balances can then be invested or used, while negative balances generate real interest expense.

The date from which a bank makes incoming funds available to its customers does not correspond exactly to the payment date. As a result, a **value date** can be defined as follows:

- **for an interest-bearing account**, it represents the date from which an amount credited to the account bears interest following a collection of funds; and the date from which an amount debited from the account stops bearing interest following a disbursement of funds;

2 *Also called transactional account, current account, checking account.*

- **for a demand deposit account**,[2] it represents the date from which an amount credited to the account may be withdrawn without the account holder having to pay overdraft interest charges (in the event that the withdrawal would make the account show a debit balance) following a collection; and the date from which an amount debited from the account becomes unavailable following a disbursement.

Under this system, it is therefore obvious that:

- a credit amount is given a value date after the credit date for accounting purposes;
- a debit amount is given a value date prior to the debit date for accounting purposes.

Let us consider, for example, the deposit of the €1000 cheque received by R when the sum is paid into an account. We will assume that the cash in process is assigned a value date 3 calendar days later and that on the day following the deposit R makes a withdrawal of €300 in cash, with a value date of 1 day.

VALUE DATES

Although the initial account balance is zero, R's account is in debit on a value date basis and in credit from an accounting standpoint.

	€1000 cheque paid in	€300 in cash withdrawn	Value date
	D	**D+1**	**D+3**
Account balance	1000	700	
Balance on a value date basis	−300		700

Although the account balance always remains in credit from an accounting standpoint, the balance from a value date standpoint shows a debit of €300 until D + 3. The company will therefore incur interest expense, even though its financial statements show a credit balance.

Consequently, a payment transaction generally leads to a debit for the company on a value date basis several days prior to the date of the transaction for accounting purposes. Value dates are thus a **way of charging for banking services** and covering the corresponding administrative costs. Nonetheless, value dates penalise large debits, the cost of which is no higher from an administrative standpoint than that of debit transactions for smaller amounts.

2/ ACCOUNT BALANCING

Company bank current accounts are intended simply to cover day-to-day cash management. They offer borrowing and investment conditions that are far from satisfactory:

- the cost of an overdraft is much higher than that of any other type of borrowing;
- the interest rate paid on credit balances is low or zero and is well below the level that can be obtained on the financial markets.

It is therefore easy to understand why it makes little sense for the company to run a permanent credit or debit balance on a bank account. **A company generally has several accounts with various different banks.** An international group may have several hundred accounts in numerous different currencies, although the current trend is towards a reduction in the number of accounts operated by businesses.

One of the treasurer's primary tasks is to avoid financial expense (or reduced financial income) deriving from the fact that some accounts are in credit while others show a debit balance. The practice of **account balancing** is based on the following two principles:

- avoiding the simultaneous existence of debit and credit balances by transferring funds from accounts in credit to those in debit;
- channelling cash outflows and cash inflows so as to arrive at a balanced overall cash position.

In the account balancing process, cash surpluses are pooled daily into a concentration account through interbank transfers and are used to finance accounts in debit.

Although the savings achieved in this way have been a decisive factor in the emergence of the treasury function over the past few decades, only small companies still have to face this type of problem. Banks offer account balancing services, whereby they automatically make the requisite transfers to optimise the balance of company accounts.

3/ BANK CHARGES

The return on equity[3] generated by a bank from a customer needs to be analysed by considering all the services, loans and other products the bank offers, including some:

- not charged for and thus representing unprofitable activities for the bank (e.g. cheques deposited by retail customers);
- charged for over and above their actual cost, notably using charging systems that do not reflect the nature of the transaction processed.

The banking industry is continuously reorganising its system of bank charges. The current trend is for it to cover its administrative processing costs by charging fees and to establish the cost of money (i.e. the cost of the capital lent to customers) by linking interest rates to the financial markets. Given the integration between banking activities (loans, payment services and investment products), banks generally apply **flat rate charges**.

3 *When a bank lends some money, it "uses part of the bank equity" because it has to constitute a minimum solvency ratio (equity/weighted assets).*

Section 47.2

CASH MANAGEMENT

1/ CASH BUDGETING

The cash budget shows not only the cash flows that have already taken place, but also all the receipts and disbursements that the company plans to make. These cash inflows and outflows may be related to the company's investment, operating or financing cycles.

The cash budget, showing the amount and duration of expected cash surpluses and deficits, serves two purposes:

- to ensure that the credit lines in place are sufficient to cover any funding requirements;
- to define the likely uses of loans by major categories (e.g. the need to discount based on the company's portfolio of trade bills and drafts).

Planning cash requirements and resources is a way of adapting borrowing and investment facilities to actual needs and, first and foremost, of managing a company's interest expense. It is easy to see that a better rate loan can be negotiated if the need is forecast several months in advance. Likewise, a treasury investment will be more profitable over a predetermined period, during which the company can commit not to use the funds.

The cash budget is a **forward-looking management chart showing supply and demand for liquidity within the company**. It allows the treasurer to manage interest expense as efficiently as possible by harnessing competition not only among different banks, but also with investors on the financial markets.

2/ FORECASTING HORIZONS

Different budgets cover different forecasting horizons for the company. Budgets can be used to distinguish between the degree of accuracy users are entitled to expect from the treasurer's projections.

Companies forecast cash flows by major categories over long-term periods and refine their projections as cash flows draw closer in time. Thanks to the various services offered by banks, budgets do not need to be 100% accurate, but can focus on achieving the relevant degree of precision for the period they cover.

An annual cash budget is generally drawn up at the start of the year based on the expected profit and loss account which has to be translated into cash flows. The top priority at this point is for cash flow figures to be consistent and material in relation to the company's business activities. At this stage, cash flows are classified by category rather than by type of payment.

These projections are then refined over periods ranging from 1 to 6 months to yield rolling cash budgets, usually for monthly periods. These documents are used to update the annual budgets based on the real level of cash inflows and outflows, rather than using expected profit and loss accounts.

Day-to-day forecasting represents the final stage in the process. This is the basic task of all treasurers and the basis on which their effectiveness is assessed. Because of the precision required, day-to-day forecasting gives rise to complex problems:

- it covers all the movements affecting the company's cash position;
- each bank account needs to be analysed;
- it is carried out on a value date basis;
- it exploits the differences between the payment methods used;
- as far as possible, it distinguishes between cash flows on a category-by-category basis.

The following table summarises these various aspects.

	BANK No. 1 Account value dates				
	Monday	Tuesday	Wednesday	Thursday	Friday
Bills presented for payment					
Cheques issued					
Transfers issued					
Standing orders paid					
Cash withdrawals					
Overdraft interest charges paid					
Sundry transactions					
(1) TOTAL DISBURSEMENTS					

	BANK No. 1 Account value dates				
	Monday	Tuesday	Wednesday	Thursday	Friday
Customer bills presented for collection					
Cheques paid in					
Standing orders received					
Transfers received					
Interest on treasury placements					
Sundry transactions					
(2) TOTAL RECEIPTS					
(2) − (1) = DAILY BALANCE ON A VALUE DATE BASIS					

Day-to-day forecasting has been made much easier by IT systems. Thanks to the ERP[4] and other IT systems used by most companies, the information received by the various parts of the business is processed directly and can be used to forecast future disbursements instantaneously. As a result, cash budgeting is linked to the availability of **information** and thus of the characteristics of the **payment methods** used.

4 *Enterprise Resources Planning*

3/ THE IMPACT OF PAYMENT METHODS

The various payment methods available raise complex problems and may give rise to uncertainties that are inherent in day-to-day cash forecasting. There are two main types of uncertainty:

SECTION 5

- **Is the forecast timing of receipts correct?** A cheque may have been collected by a sales agent without having immediately been paid into the relevant account. It may not be possible to forecast exactly when a client will pay down its debt by bank transfer.
- **When will expenditure give rise to actual cash disbursements?** It is impossible to say exactly when the creditor will collect the payment that has been handed over (e.g. cheque, bill of exchange or promissory note).

From a cash budgeting standpoint, payment methods are more attractive where one of the two participants in the transaction possesses the initiative both in terms of **setting up the payment** and **triggering the transfer of funds**. Where a company has this initiative, it has **much greater certainty** regarding the value dates for the transfer.

The following table shows an analysis of the various different payment methods used by companies from this standpoint. It does not take into account the risk of non-payment by a debtor (e.g. not enough funds in the account, insufficient account details, refusal to pay). This risk is self-evident and applies to all payment methods.

	Initiative for setting up transfer	Initiative for completing the fund transfer	Utility for cash budgeting
Cheque	Debtor	Creditor	None
Paper bill of exchange[5]	Creditor	Creditor	Helpful to both parties insofar as the deadlines are met by the creditors
Electronic bill of exchange[6]	Creditor	Creditor	
Paper promissory note[7]	Debtor	Creditor	
Electronic promissory note[8]	Debtor	Creditor	
Transfer[9]	Debtor	Debtor	Debtor
Debit[10]	Creditor	Creditor	Creditor

From this standpoint, establishing the actual date on which cheques will be paid represents the major problem facing treasurers. Postal delays and the time taken by the creditor to record the cheque in its accounts and to hand it over to its bank affect the debit date. Consequently, treasurers endeavour to:

- process cheques for small amounts globally, to arrive at a statistical rule for collection dates, if possible by periods (10th, 20th, end-of-month);
- monitor large cheques individually to get to know the collection habits of the main creditors – e.g. public authorities (social security, tax, customs, etc.), large suppliers and contractors.

Large companies negotiate with their banks so that they are debited with a value date of $D + 1$ for their cheques, where D is the day on which the cheques arrive at the clearing-house. As a result, they know in the morning which cheques will be debited with that day's value date.

Although their due date is generally known, domiciled bills[11] and notes can also cause problems. If the creditor is slow to collect the relevant amounts, the debtor, which sets aside sufficient funds in its account to cover payment on the relevant date, is obliged to freeze the funds in an account that does not pay any interest. Once again, it is in the

---

5 *Written document in which the supplier asks the customer to pay the amount due to its bank, a third party or him/herself, on the due date.*

6 *Electronic bill of exchange on a magnetic strip.*

7 *Written document, in which the customer acknowledges its debt and undertakes to pay the supplier on the due date.*

8 *Electronic promissory note on a magnetic strip.*

9 *Order given by the customer to its bank to debit a sum from its account and to credit another account.*

10 *Payment method, whereby a debtor asks its creditor to issue standing orders and its bank to pay the standing orders.*

11 *An invoice that must be paid at a particular place.*

interests of the debtor company to work out a statistical rule for the collection of domiciled bills and notes and to get to know the collection habits of its main suppliers.

The treasurer's experience is invaluable, especially when it comes to forecasting the behaviour of customers (payment dates) and of creditors (collection dates for the payment methods issued).

Aside from the problems caused by forecasting uncertainties, payment methods do not all have the same flexibility in terms of domiciliation – i.e. the choice of account to credit or debit. The customer cheques received by a company may be paid into an account chosen by the treasurer. The same does not apply to standing orders and transfers, where the account details must usually be agreed in advance and for a certain period of time. This lack of flexibility makes it harder to balance accounts. Lastly, the various payment methods have different value dates. The treasurer needs to take the different value dates into account very carefully in order to manage his or her account balances on a value date basis.

BREAKDOWN OF PAYMENT TOOLS IN 2009

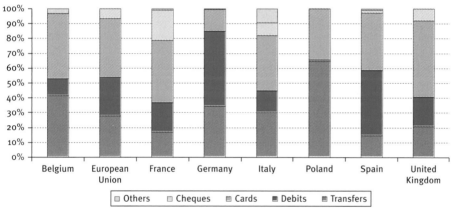

Each country has its own history and payment habits In Europe; these are far from being unified.

Source: European Central Bank

At the initiative of the European Union and of the European Central Bank, harmonisation of payment methods is under way in the euro zone (Single Euro Payment Area or SEPA), allowing companies or individuals to transfer money (from 2008) and debits (2010) as easily and as quickly and at the same cost as if the transfer were between two towns in the same country.

4/ OPTIMISING CASH MANAGEMENT

Our survey of account balancing naturally leads us to the concept of **zero cash**, the nirvana of corporate treasurers, which keeps interest expense down to a bare minimum.

Even so, this aim can never be completely achieved. A treasurer always has to deal with some unpredictable movements, be they disbursements or collections. The greater the number or volume of unpredictable movements, the more imprecise cash budgeting will be and the harder it is to optimise. That said, several techniques may be used to improve cash management significantly.

(a) Behavioural analysis

The same type of analysis as performed for payment methods can also yield direct benefits for cash management. The company establishes collection times based on the habits of its suppliers. A statistical average for collection times is then calculated. Any deviations from the normal pattern are usually offset where an account sees a large number of transactions. **This enables the company to manage the cash balance on each account to "cover" payments forecast with a certain delay** of up to 4 or 5 days **for value date purposes**.

Optimising forecasts using behavioural studies directly leads to the optimisation of cash flow management.

In any case, payments will always be covered by the overdraft facilities agreed with banks, the only risk for the company being that it will run an overdraft for some, limited, period and thus pay higher interest expense.

(b) Intercompany agreements

Since efficient treasury management can unlock tangible savings, it is normal for companies that have commercial relationships to get together to maximise these gains. Various types of contract have been developed to facilitate and increase the reliability of payments between companies. Some companies have attempted to demonstrate to their customers the mutual benefits of harmonisation of their cash management procedures and negotiated special agreements. In a bid to minimise interest expense attributable to the use of short-term borrowings, others offer discounts to their customers for swift payment. Nonetheless, this approach has drawbacks because, for obvious commercial reasons, it is hard to apply the stipulated penalties when contracts are not respected.

(c) Lockbox systems

Under the lockbox system, the creditor asks its debtors to send their payments directly to a PO box that is emptied regularly by its bank. The funds are immediately paid into the banking system, without first being processed by the creditor's accounting department.

When the creditor's and debtor's banks are located in the same place, cheques can easily be cleared on the spot. Such clearing represents another substantial time saving.

(d) Checking bank terms

The complexity of bank charges and the various different items on which they are based makes them hard to check. This task is thus an integral part of a treasurer's job.

Companies implement systematic procedures to verify all the aspects of bank charges. In particular, treasurers are keen to get their banks to ensure that all payments are credited or debited with a value date of $D + 1$, with any gains or losses being set off against the corresponding cash volumes on a monthly or quarterly basis. The conditions used to calculate interest payments and transaction charges may be verified by reconciling the documents issued by the bank (particularly interest-rate scales and overdraft interest charges) with internal cash monitoring systems. Flat-rate charges may be checked on a test basis. The most common bank errors occur when standard terms and conditions are applied rather than the specific terms negotiated. In addition, failure to meet the counter opening times (which determine the day on which a transaction is deemed to have been executed) and mistakes in credit and debit interest are also the source of potential bank errors.

Section 47.3
PLACEMENT OF CASH

Financial novices may wonder why debt-burdened companies do not use their cash to reduce debt. There are two good reasons for this:

*   Paying back debt in advance can be costly because of early repayment penalties, or unwise if the debt was contracted at a rate that is lower than rates prevailing today.
*   Keeping cash on hand enables the company to seize investment opportunities quickly and without constraints or to withstand changes in the economic environment. Some research papers[12] have demonstrated that companies with strong growth or volatile cash flows tend to have more free cash than average. Conversely, companies that have access to financial markets or excellent credit ratings have less cash than average.

12 *Opler et al. (1999).*

Obviously, all financing products used by companies have a mirror image as investment products, since the two operations are symmetrical. The corporate treasurer's role in investing the company's cash is nevertheless somewhat specific because the purpose of the company is not to make profits by engaging in risky financial investments. This is why specific products have been created to meet this criterion.

Remember that all investment policies are based on anticipated developments in the bank balances of each account managed by the company or, if it is a group, on consolidated, multicurrency forecasts. The treasurer cannot decide to make an investment without first estimating its amount and the duration. Any mistake, and the treasurer is forced to choose between two alternatives:

*   either having to resort to new loans to meet the financial shortage created if too much cash was invested, thus generating a loss (negative margin) on the difference between lending and borrowing rates (i.e. the interest rate spread); or
*   having to retrieve the amounts invested and incur the attendant penalties, lost interest or, in certain cases such as bond investments, risk of a capital loss.

Since corporate treasurers rarely know exactly how much cash they will have available for a given period, their main concern when choosing an investment is its liquidity – that is, how fast it can be converted back into cash. **For an investment to be cashed in immediately, it must have an active secondary market or a redemption clause that can be activated at any time.**

The corporate treasurer's first concern in investing cash is liquidity.

Of course, if an investment can be terminated at any time, its rate of return is uncertain since the exit price is uncertain. A 91-day Treasury bill at a nominal rate of 4% can be sold at will, but its actual rate of return will depend on whether the bill was sold for more or less than its nominal value. However, if the rate of return is set in advance, it is virtually impossible to exit the investment before its maturity since there is no secondary market or redemption clause, or if there is, only at a prohibitive cost.

The treasurer's second concern – security – is thus closely linked to the first. Security is measured in terms of the risk on the interest and principal.

When making this tradeoff between liquidity and security, the treasurer will, of course, try to obtain the **best return** taking into consideration **tax issues**, since various investment products may be subject to different tax regimes.

1/ INVESTMENT PRODUCTS WITH NO SECONDARY MARKET

Interest-bearing current accounts are the simplest way to earn interest on cash. Nevertheless, interest paid by banks on such accounts is usually significantly lower than what the money market offers.

Time deposits are fixed-term deposits on an interest-bearing bank account that are governed by a letter signed by the account holder. The interest on deposits with maturity of at least 1 month is negotiated between the bank and the client. It can be at a fixed rate or indexed to the money market. No interest is paid if the client withdraws the funds before the agreed maturity date.

Cash certificates are time deposits that take the physical form of a bearer or registered certificate.

Repos (repurchase agreements) are agreements whereby institutional investors or companies can exchange cash for securities for a fixed period of time (a securities for cash agreement is called a "reverse repo"). At the end of the contract, which can take various legal forms, the securities are returned to their original owner. All title and rights to the securities are transferred to the buyer of the securities for the duration of the contract.

The remuneration of the buyer of the securities can be determined at the outset according to how the contract will be unwound. The agreement can be adapted to various requirements. The only risk is that the borrower of the cash (the repo seller) will default.

Repo sellers hold equity or bond portfolios, while repo buyers are looking for cash revenues. From the buyer's point of view, a repo is basically an alternative solution when a time deposit is not feasible, for example for periods of less than 1 month. A repo allows the seller to obtain cash immediately by pledging securities with the assurance that it can buy them back.

Since the procedure is fairly unwieldy, it is only used for large amounts, well above €2m. This means that it competes with negotiable debt securities, such as commercial paper. However, the development of money market mutual funds investing in repos has lowered the €2m threshold and opened up the market to a larger number of companies.

The principle of **securities lending** is similar to that of repurchase agreements. It enables a company with a large cash surplus or listed investments to improve the yield on its financial instruments by entrusting them to institutional investors. These investors use them in the course of forward transactions while paying to the original owner (the company) the income arising on the securities and a borrowing fee. No cash changes hands in the course of the transaction. The incremental return thus stems from the remuneration of default risk on the part of the institutional investors borrowing the securities.

2/ INVESTMENT PRODUCTS WITH A SECONDARY MARKET

Treasury bills and notes are issued by governments at monthly or weekly auctions for periods ranging from 2 weeks to 5 years. They are the safest of all investments given the creditworthiness of the issuer (governments), but their other features make them less flexible and competitive. However, the substantial amount of outstanding negotiable Treasury bills and notes ensures sufficient liquidity, even for large volumes. These instruments can be a fairly good vehicle for short-term investments.

Certificates of deposit ("CDs") are quite simply time deposits represented by a dematerialised negotiable debt security in the form of a bearer certificate or order issued by an authorised financial institution. Certificates of deposit are issued in minimum amounts for periods ranging from 1 day to 1 year with fixed maturity dates. In fact, they are a form of short-term investment. CDs are issued by banks, for which they are a frequent means of refinancing, on a continuous basis depending on demand. Before the financial crisis of 2008, their yield was very close to that of the money market, and their main advantage is that they can be traded on the secondary market, thus avoiding the heavy penalties of cashing in time deposits before their maturity date. The flip side is that they carry an interest-rate risk.

We described the main characteristics of commercial paper and medium-term negotiable notes in Chapter 22.

Money-market or cash mutual funds are funds that issue or buy back their shares at the request of investors at prices that must be published daily. The return on a money-market capitalisation mutual fund arises on the daily appreciation in net asset value (NAV). This return is similar to that of the money market. Depending on the mutual fund's stated objective, the increase in net asset value is more or less steady. A very regular progression can only be obtained at the cost of profitability.

In order to meet its objectives, each cash mutual fund invests in a selection of Treasury bills, certificates of deposit, commercial paper, repos, variable- or fixed-rate bonds with a short residual maturity. Its investment policy is backed by quite sophisticated interest-rate risk management.

The subprime crisis has been a healthy (but costly!) reminder for some treasurers that an increase in return cannot be obtained without an increase in risk. Some money-market funds, nicknamed "turbo" or "dynamic", had invested part of their portfolio in subprime securities to boost their returns. During the summer of 2007 and thereafter, their performances suffered severely and most of them have lost most of their customers.

Securitisation vehicles are special-purpose vehicles created to take over the claims sold by a credit institution or company engaging in a securitisation transaction (see Chapter 22). In exchange, these vehicles issue units that the institution sells to investors.

In theory, **bond** investments should yield higher returns than money market or money-market indexed investments. However, interest-rate fluctuations generate capital risks on bond portfolios that must be hedged, unless the treasurer has opted for variable-rate bonds. Investing in bonds therefore calls for a certain degree of technical know-how and constant monitoring of the market. Only a limited number of treasurers have the resources to invest directly in bonds.

The high yields arising on investing surplus cash in the **equity** market over long periods become far more uncertain on shorter horizons, when the capital risk exposure is very high, well above that of a bond investment. Treasurers must keep a constant eye on the secondary market, and sharp market swings have rendered the few treasurers still investing in the equity market extremely cautious. However, treasurers may be charged with monitoring portfolios of equity interests.

Section 47.4
CASH MANAGEMENT WITHIN A GROUP

Managing the cash positions of the subsidiaries of a group is akin to managing the individual bank accounts held by each subsidiary. Prior to any balancing between subsidiaries at group level, each subsidiary balances its own accounts. Consequently, managing the cash position of a group adds an additional layer of data processing and decision-making based on principles that are exactly the same as those explained in Sections 47.1 and 47.2 for individual companies (i.e. group subsidiaries or SMEs[13]).

13 *Small and medium-sized enterprises.*

1/ CENTRALISED CASH MANAGEMENT

The methods explained in the previous sections show the scale of the task facing a treasury department. It therefore seems natural to centralise cash management on a group-wide basis, a technique known as cash pooling, since it allows a group to take responsibility for all the liquidity requirements of its subsidiaries.

The cash positions of the subsidiaries (lenders or borrowers) can thus be pooled in the same way as the various accounts of a single company, thereby creating a genuine internal money market. The group will thus save on all the additional costs deriving from the inefficiencies of the financial markets (bank charges, brokerage fees, differences between lending and borrowing rates, etc.). In particular, cash pooling enables a group to hold on to the borrowing/lending margin that banks are normally able to charge.

Cash pooling balances the accounts of a group's subsidiaries, thereby saving on the interest expense.

This is not the only benefit of pooling. It gives a relatively big group comprising a large number of small companies the option of tapping financial markets. Information-related costs and brokerage fees on an organised market may prevent a large number of subsidiaries from receiving the same financing or investment conditions as the group as a whole. With the introduction of cash pooling, the corporate treasurer satisfies in the markets the financing needs of the group. The treasurer then organises an internal refinancing of each subsidiary on the same financing terms that the group receives.

Cash pooling has numerous advantages. The manager's workload is not proportional to the number of transactions or the size of the funds under management. Consequently, there is no need to double the size of a department handling the cash needs of twice the number of companies. The skills of existing teams will nevertheless need to be enhanced. Likewise, investment in systems (hardware, software, communication systems, etc.) can be reduced when they are pooled within a single central department. Information gathering costs can yield the same type of saving. Consequently, cash pooling offers scope for genuine "industrial" economies of scale.

The compelling logic of having such a unit sometimes masks its *raison d'être* because, although the creation of a cash pooling unit may be justified for very good reasons, it may also lead to an unwise financial strategy and possibly even management errors. Notably, cash pooling will give rise to an internal debt market totally disconnected from the assets being financed. Certain corporate financiers may still be heard to claim that they have secured better financing or investment terms by leveraging the group's size or the size of the funds under management. But such claims do not stand up to analysis because the level of risk associated with investments alone determines their financing cost in a market economy. If the integration of a company within a larger group enables it to secure better financing terms, this improvement will be to the detriment of the overall entity's borrowing costs. We recommend that any readers still tempted to believe in financial economies of scale take another look at the analysis in Chapter 27.

In theory, once a company has achieved the critical mass needed to give it access to the financial markets, any economies of scale generated by cash pooling are "industrial" rather than financial.

That said, rating agencies estimate that diversification of activities is good for lenders. You might cry foul at seeing the remuneration of a diversifiable risk! That's the way it is. Cash pooling may create a mass effect, leading certain banks concerned solely with their market share to overlook the link between risk and profitability!

A prerequisite for cash pooling is the existence of an efficient system transmitting information between the parent company and its subsidiaries (or between the head office and decentralised units). The system requires the subsidiaries to send their forecasts to the head office in real time. The rapidity of fund movements – i.e. the unit's efficiency – depends on the quality of these forecasts, as well as on that of the corporate information system.

Lastly, a high degree of centralisation reduces the subsidiaries' ability to take initiatives. The limited responsibilities granted to local cash managers may encourage them not to optimise their own management, when it comes to either conducting behavioural analysis of payments or controlling internal parameters. Local borrowing opportunities at competitive rates may therefore go begging. To avoid demotivating the subsidiaries' treasurers, they may be given greater responsibility for local cash management.

2/ THE DIFFERENT TYPES AND DEGREES OF CENTRALISATION

Looking beyond its unifying nature in theory, there are many different ways of pooling a group's cash resources in practice, ranging from the outright elimination of the subsidiaries' cash management departments to highly decentralised management. There are two major types of organisation, which reflect two opposite approaches:

- Most common is the centralisation of balances and liquidity, which involves the group-wide pooling of cash from the subsidiaries' bank accounts. The group balances the accounts of its subsidiaries just as the subsidiaries balance their bank accounts. There are a number of different variations on this system.
- Significantly rarer is the centralisation of cash flows, under which the group's cash management department not only receives all incoming payments, but may also even

make all the disbursements. The department deals with issues such as due dates for customer payments and customer payment risks, reducing the role of any subsidiary to providing information and forecasting. This type of organisation may be described as hypercentralised.

The centralisation of cash balances can be dictated from above or carried out upon request of the subsidiary. In the latter case, each subsidiary decides to use the group's cash or external resources in line with the rates charged, thereby creating competition between the banks, the market and internal funds. This flexibility can help alleviate any demotivation caused by the centralisation of cash management.

In addition, coherent cash management requires the definition of uniform banking terms and conditions within a group. In particular, fund transfers between subsidiaries should not be subject to value dating.

Notional pooling provides a relatively flexible way of exploiting the benefits of cash pooling. With notional pooling, subsidiaries' account balances are never actually balanced, but the group's bank recalculates credit or debit interest based on the fictitious balance of the overall entity. This method yields exactly the same result as if the accounts had been perfectly balanced, **but the fund transfers are never carried out in practice**. As a result, this method leaves subsidiaries some room for manoeuvre and does not impact on their independence.

A high-risk subsidiary thus receives financing on exactly the same terms as the group as a whole, while the group can benefit from limited liability from a legal standpoint by declaring its subsidiary bankrupt. Notional pooling prevents a bank from adjusting its charges, thus introducing additional restrictions and setting reciprocal guarantees between each of the companies participating in the pooling arrangements. This network of contracts may prove to be extremely complex to manage.

NOTIONAL POOLING AND THE RISK OF BANKRUPTCY

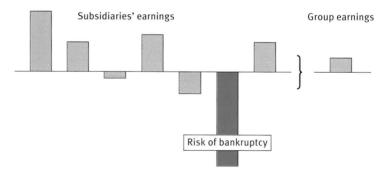

Consequently, cash balances are more commonly pooled by means of the daily balancing of the subsidiaries' positions. The **zero balance account (ZBA)** concept requires subsidiaries to balance their position (i.e. the balance of their bank accounts) each day by using the concentration accounts managed at group or subgroup level. The banks offer automated balancing systems and can perform all these tasks on behalf of companies. The use of ZBA requires a set of legal agreements between the parent company and each subsidiary (cash management agreements) which must be negotiated at arms' length so as not to raise any legal or tax issues.

To sum up, the degree of centralisation of cash management and the method used by a group do not depend on financial criteria only. The three key factors are as follows:

- the group's managerial culture – e.g. notional pooling is more suited to highly decentralised organisations than daily position balancing;
- regulations and tax systems in the relevant countries;
- the cost of banking services. While position balancing is carried out by the group, notional pooling is the task of the bank.

3/ INTERNATIONAL CASH MANAGEMENT

The problems arising with cash pooling are particularly acute in an international environment. That said, international cash management techniques are exactly the same as those used at national level – i.e. pooling on demand, notional pooling, account balancing.

Regulatory differences make the direct pooling of account balances of foreign subsidiaries a tricky task. Indeed, many groups find that they cannot do without the services of local banks, which are able to collect payments throughout a given zone. Consequently, multinational groups tend to apply a two-tier pooling system. A local concentration bank performs the initial pooling process within each country, and an international banking group, called an overlay bank, then handles the international pooling process.

INTERNATIONAL CASH POOLING

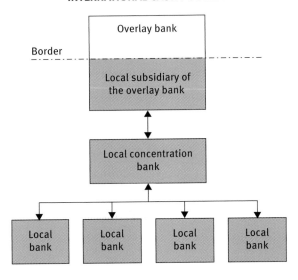

The international bank sends the funds across the border,[14] as shown in the chart above, which helps to dispense with a large number of regulatory problems.

At the local level, centralisation can be tailored to the specific regulatory requirements in each country, while at a higher level the international bank can carry out both notional pooling and daily account balancing. Lastly, it can manage the subsidiaries' interest and exchange rate risks (see Chapter 49) by offering exchange rate and interest

14 *For currencies that are freely convertible.*

rate guarantees. The structure set up can be used to manage all the group's financial issues rather than just the cash management aspects.

Within the Eurozone, the interconnection of payment systems under the aegis of the European Central Bank has made it possible to carry out fund transfers in real time, more cheaply and without having to face the issue of value dating. In the Eurozone, cash pooling may thus be carried out with the assistance of a single concentration bank in each country with cross-border transfers not presenting any problems.

Some groups have created a payment factory which pays off all the group's suppliers on behalf of all the subsidiaries, which reduces the number of transfers when subsidiaries have common suppliers.

4/ Cash management of a group experiencing financial difficulties

We ought to mention that all of the techniques and products discussed in this chapter work best for a group in good financial health and which accordingly has easy access to the debt market.

The treasurer of a group whose finances are stretched also has to manage its cash, with as much if not more care and attention, although the goals of such a treasurer will obviously be a lot different from those of the treasurer of a more financially sound group. Instead of seeking to optimise financial expenses, the treasurer will want to secure the group's financing.

Accordingly, he will maximise the amount of loans granted, even if this means taking out more short-term debt than is actually needed to meet short-term requirements.

When the going gets tough, the group will be able to draw on all of its credit lines as long as it is still meeting its financial covenants[15] and place the funds in short-term investments. So, if the situation gets worse, the group will not run the risk of having its credit lines cut off by the banks. The banks will be forced to work with the company in order to turn it around financially.

Looking after a company's cash turns out to be more of an operational monitoring job than an optimisation one. In fact, and paradoxically, the treasurer succeeds in managing the company's cash only thanks to its short-term investments.

This situation could raise the cost of debt for the company, but this additional cost is no more than a form of insurance against a liquidity risk!

15 See Chapter 22.

Section 47.5
The changing role of the treasurer

Technological developments have resulted in greater integration and automation in the management of a company's cash, and have also facilitated the centralisation of the process.

Large groups appear to be centralising cash management as much as they possibly can (which has no impact outside the group). However, this was just a start, and many groups have now also started centralising trade payables. In the near future, we could see the centralisation of both payables and receivables. This would be rather more difficult to set up as it requires the cooperation of customers who will have to send their payment, not to the company that has supplied it with the goods or services it has ordered, but to another company.

Some groups view cash management as a strategic function. Others see it as a complex administrative function that generates additional risks. Some large groups have, quite simply, outsourced the cash management function, either to banks or to consulting firms offering off-the-shelf solutions for outsourced cash management. However, since the early 2000s, there has also been an increase in the number of groups centralising their cash management.

With the development and greater security of the Internet, SMEs that do a lot of business on the international market have been able to set up efficient systems at a lower cost.

SUMMARY

The summary of this chapter can be downloaded from www.vernimmen.com.

A treasurer's job is to perform the following tasks:

- forecast trends in the credit and debit balances of the company's accounts;

- keep dormant funds to a minimum;

- invest excess cash as efficiently as possible;

- finance borrowing requirements as cheaply as possible.

Cash balances for treasury purposes are not the same as the balances shown in a company's accounts or the accounting balance of its assets held by the bank. In particular, treasurers must take account of value dating. The value date is the date from which a credited amount accrues interest when paid into an interest-bearing account or becomes available when paid into a demand account.

The aim of the cash budget is to determine the amount and duration of cash requirements and surpluses. The cash budget shows all the receipts and all the disbursements that the business expects to collect or make. Day-to-day forecasting, which takes into account value dating, requires paying considerable attention to the payment methods used. Forecasts are more reliable when the treasurer has the initiative both for setting up a payment and for carrying out the fund transfer.

Account balancing is the final stage in the liquidity management process. It eliminates the additional costs deriving from differences between borrowing and investment rates. Lastly, optimised cash management entails the acceleration of the collection process and the extension of suppliers' payment deadlines.

Cash pooling – the centralisation of subsidiaries' account balances within a group – is comparable to the process of balancing all of a subsidiary's accounts. Pooling is generally backed up by an integrated information system and a group-wide agreement concerning banking terms and conditions. At international level, regulatory difficulties concerning cross-border transfers prevent the direct balancing of subsidiaries' accounts. Instead, the initial pooling process is carried out by a local bank in each country, and then the resulting balances are pooled by an international banking group.

The corporate treasurer's first concern when investing cash is liquidity. The treasurer's second concern – security – is thus closely linked to the first. Security is measured in terms of the risk on the interest and principal. Products that can be used can be split between products with a secondary market (Treasury bills, money market funds, etc.) or without (time deposit, repos, etc.).

QUESTIONS

1/ What are the three key objectives of a corporate treasurer?

2/ What are the three cash positions for a company?

3/ What is a value date?

4/ What is a concentration account?

5/ What is the main difference between national group pooling and international group pooling?

6/ Does perfect daily balancing of accounts cost more or less than perfect notional pooling?

7/ Is the risk of bankruptcy of a subsidiary an obstacle to cash pooling for a group which balances its accounts daily?

8/ What is the main argument against full cash pooling for a group?

9/ What sort of cash organisation is generally in place for highly decentralised groups?

10/ What common practice is the principal of value dates based on?

11/ Is an investment that can be quickly sold on a vast market without risk?

12/ Can an investment yield more than a debt? What is then the consequence?

13/ Why do treasurers avoid investing their cash in shares?

14/ In 2006, ABN Amro created a new financial product, the Constant Proportion Debt Obligation, rated AAA by Standard & Poor's and yielding 1% to 2% more than a AAA-rated bond. What do you think?

More questions are waiting for you at www.vernimmen.com.

ANSWERS

1/ *To reduce dormant funds to a minimum, to optimise the cost of financing and investing, to optimise the cost of risk management.*
2/ *Value dating accounts, financial statements, company's bank accounts.*
3/ *The date from which a credit amount starts to bear interest and a debit amount ceases to bear interest.*
4/ *An account used for balancing cash positions.*
5/ *The level of pooling.*
6/ *In both cases: no financial expenses.*
7/ *No.*
8/ *Lower levels of accountability for subsidiaries.*
9/ *Cash pools that can be used upon request.*
10/ *Clearing cheques.*
11/ *No, as the liquidity risk does not erase all the other risks which may result in a change in value.*
12/ *Yes, but its risk is higher.*
13/ *High short- and medium-term risk.*
14/ *It was either a fabulous arbitrage opportunity or an investment with a higher risk than apparent. In early 2008, CPDOs were valued at 40–75% of face value. Their risk, counterparty of their return, had been severely underestimated.*

BIBLIOGRAPHY

T. Bates, K. Kahle, R. Stulz, Why do US firms hold so much more cash than they used to do?, *Journal of Finance*, **64**(5), 1985–2021, October 2009.

W. J. Baumol, The transactions demand for cash: An inventory theoretic approach, *Quarterly Journal of Economics*, **66**, 545–566, November 1952.

S. Bragg, *Treasury Management: The practitioner's guide*, John Wiley and Sons, Inc., 2010.

E. Detragiache, P. Garella, L. Guiso, Multiple versus single banking relationships: Theory and evidence, *Journal of Finance*, **55**(3), 1133–1161, June 2000.

European Central Bank, *Statistics on payments – Data for 2009*, 13 September 2010.

M. Faulkender, R. Wang, Corporate financial policy and the value of cash, *Journal of Finance*, **61**(4), 1957–1990, August 2006.

J. Graham, C. Harvey, The theory and practice of corporate finance: Evidence from the field, *Journal of Financial Economics*, **60**(2–3), 179–185, May–June 2001.

T. Opler, L. Pinkowitz, R. Stulz, R. Williamson, The determinants and implications of corporate cash holdings, *Journal of Financial Economics*, **52**(1), 3–46, April 1999.

L. Van den Wierlen, *International Cash Management*, 2nd edn, Riskmatrix, 2006.

www.treasurers.org: website of the Association of Corporate Treasurers

Chapter 48
MANAGING WORKING CAPITAL

Is it supply management or is it strategy? It's finance, General!

On aggregate in continental Europe, working capital represents large amounts (c. 15% on capital employed). Customer credits (and symmetrically, supplier credits), which are commercial loans between companies, amount to more than three times the amount of short-term loans granted to corporates.

The similarity between the amount of working capital and that of net debt is not completely coincidental, as often these two items behave in concert. An increase in working capital means an increase in net debt, as a large number of companies can testify following their experiences in late 2008. A drop in working capital often means a drop in net debt, as a large number of companies can testify following their experiences in 2009.

Having said that, working capital management does not involve reducing it at all costs in a simplistic fashion, as it also contributes to the overall equilibrium of the company. An often overlooked fact.

Finally, the problems and the amounts of working capital are not identical for all sectors. There is a world of difference between industry (management of work-in-progress, credit limits for major customers, etc.) and the services sector.

Section 48.1
A BIT OF COMMON SENSE

Working capital is an investment, like any other, even if on occasion there is less choice involved (for example, when a customer "forgets" to pay by the due date and turns the supplier into its unwilling banker). As an investment, it should be managed lucidly and properly. Reducing it in order to reduce the company's need for funds and to improve its earnings is a possibility, but it is not the only possibility.

From the company's point of view, what is working capital?

- first and foremost, it's part of commercial conquest. We all know that payment periods form part of the terms of a commercial contract. Try and set up a business in Greece, where contractual payment periods are 73 days with average periods often stretching to 107 days, by asking to be paid at 30 days like in Scandinavia! Similarly, keeping stock levels high reduces the risk of losing an order because supplies are not available. Consumers will remember the sense of annoyance and frustration felt in the spring of 2009 at the empty shelves of a number of retailers;[1]

- next, it's a source of financing when it reduces and a source of financing requirement when it increases. One might be tempted to assume that the stakes are not the same when the very short-term interest rates stand at 0.4% per year, as they did in the spring of 2010, or at 10% per year, as they did between 1990 and 1993.[2] This is a false assumption. The problem is not so much the cost of money, as to make money available by reducing working capital in order to invest, to repay debt or to constitute a war chest. The problem is also not having money when the company needs it. In other words, managing working capital is a timeless problem, even if some situations are better than others for highlighting the issue;

- finally, it is a source of risk. The risk that customers will pay late, will only pay partially or not at all because they have gone bankrupt, which could in turn create problems for the company and create a series of domino-like bankruptcies. It is to alleviate this risk that the European authorities have introduced statutory provisions to reduce payment periods to 45 days end of month or 60 days after the invoice is issued. There is also the risk of the loss of value for obsolescence of certain goods (news journals, cut flowers, yoghurts, etc.).

From a more economic point of view, working capital can be:

- a tool for helping customers or suppliers who are already experiencing problems as a result of a liquidity crisis. For example, in late 2008/early 2009, Peugeot and Renault, which had received cash support from the government, in turn helped their main subcontractors, which were experiencing a liquidity crisis, by reducing their payment periods. This wasn't a question of altruism, it was in Peugeot and Renault's best interests, in order to avoid the bankruptcy of their suppliers, which would have threatened the continuity of their supplies;

- a source of value creation in periods of negative interest rates, for sectors with high levels of inventories, through inflation gains.[3] In other words, good management of working capital in this case means not managing it!

- a source of speculation (and hence of risk) when the company overstocks raw materials, the price of which it is expecting will rise substantially over the coming months.

Working capital results from the company's strategy. For example, when a company decides to get involved upstream in order to secure its supplies (Arcelor Mittal owns iron ore mines that provide it with 45% of its consumption), or downstream in order to fill the gaps in a retail network that is patchy or not yet established (SEB runs over 1000 shops in 41 emerging countries such as China and Turkey), then working capital is necessarily increased. Similarly, when the company decides, like Indesit did, to outsource part of its production to Eastern Europe, South-East Asia or China, then margins rise (or don't fall), but working capital increases, since these subcontractors just don't have the financial structure necessary to grant Greek-style payment periods![4]

The level of working capital is also the result of a financial arbitrage between margins and costs. We know of a magazine group that pays cash for its paper supplies. It is able to purchase its paper at a knock-down price as it is in a very good position to negotiate discounts, at a higher rate than that at which it could invest its cash, from suppliers whose need for cash is constant given the extent of their investments. Our magazine publisher's working capital is mediocre (practically no supplier credit), but its margins are outstanding!

1 *And ours when we see that the Vernimmen is only available in 10 days on Amazon!*

2 *See page 393.*

3 *See page 694.*

4 *Without taking into account the fact that purchases are made by whole container or that more is bought in order to avoid stock outs (more than one month's delay).*

SECTION 5

Another example is the public works sector, which is structured around customer advances which more or less cover the cost of the works, and more for the best of them. Working capital is low, but then so are margins. You can't expect your customer to give you everything!

In other words, you can buy cash.

The company grants discounts so that customers will pay quickly, which means that working capital is good and that cash is quite plentiful but also that margins will decline. This is why in the USA, it is standard to offer customers the option of paying at 30 days or of paying at 10 days and getting a 2% discount. As the yield to maturity of this commercial offer is 44.6%, very few buyers are able to resist the temptation! (And those who do send out a signal of a pitiful financial situation which may alarm suppliers). Sales, when they are exceptional, are also a way of buying cash.

> The slide-rule will often depend on the situation. In periods of crisis, cash will be king and, accordingly, working capital will be managed very tightly. When times are good, the focus will be on growing sales and margins, at the expense of working capital.

There are four ways of approaching working capital management:

- tighten control over waste: stop the payments department from paying suppliers early, sell off stocks with low turnover rates and consider phasing out the production of such items. These measures are relatively easy to put in place and will not require a major overhaul of the company;
- take a close look at more structural elements that will require a change in behaviour or organisation. This could mean indexing the variable compensation of sales reps, not to orders taken but to actual payments or margins made, reorganising production chains in order to reduce buffer stocks, shifting from a mass procedure to a process procedure,[5] or introducing other structural changes. These changes are a lot more complex to put into place and will require the active cooperation of a number of departments, which more often than not will mean the involvement of general management;
- carry out an arbitrage between margins and working capital in order to buy or sell cash;
- create a false appearance, by reducing working capital on the balance sheet using factoring, securitisation, discounting, etc. But let's not fool ourselves – working capital has not really been reduced, it has only been partly financed, and this part disappears from view in the same way that poverty is invisible in Potemkin villages. These are financing techniques that are discussed in Chapter 22.

5 *Which often means rebalancing part of the company's stocks, like the carmakers did in the 1980s. See Chapter 8.*

Only the first two above ways of approaching working capital management will lead to the generation of cash without weighing heavily on the cost structure.

Working capital management is also a cultural issue. We saw in Chapter 11 that payment periods in Europe differ widely from one country to the next.

Some companies have a more developed cash culture than others, either because of the financial difficulties they have had to face in the past (carmakers in the 1980s), the influence of their shareholders (LBO funds make cash an essential lever of their culture[6]) or the approach of a manager (former financial director), which have made them sensitive to cash from a very early stage. Other firms have less of a cash culture because financial conditions make cash less of a pressing problem or because their culture is far removed

6 *See Chapter 45.*

from such pre-occupations (engineering firms, firms involved primarily in research and development, etc.).

In other words, if a cash culture is to take hold within a company, as an add-on to other cultures rather than a replacement, it will require a long learning period, patience, diplomacy, and above all, the support of general management, as it often leads to a root-and-branch overhaul of established practices with which staff are familiar and comfortable.

Finally, even though all employees can be expected to try to enhance their performance and improve their weak points, we can't help being a bit sceptical. Division managers are rarely superhuman. If we set division managers multiple targets of growing the market shares of their products, increasing margins, ensuring good relationships between labour and management and seeing to it that their divisions comply with corporate culture, and then we also ask them to innovate and to reduce their working capital over and above the obvious waste that needs to be avoided, then we are perhaps asking too much of them. These multiple objectives could hamper managers in the performance of their tasks with the risk that they are unable to perform properly and fail to achieve any of their goals.

We know of a multinational firm that has become a leader in its field as a result of innovation and highly effective marketing. Its margins are enviable and its after tax return on capital employed is just under 20%, yet its working capital can hardly be described as good. Is it possible to be good at everything all of the time?

This rather existential question has, unfortunately, to give way to the more mundane. The following sections look at the operational ways of reducing working capital. This may seem to be a bit dull, but it is the nuts and bolts of the field. Stay with us and be patient. There is more excitement and financial fireworks in store in the next and final chapter!

Section 48.2
MANAGING RECEIVABLES

Managing receivables involves:

- negotiating better payment terms (general terms and conditions);
- speeding up the payment of receivables while respecting contractual terms and conditions;
- securing the payment of receivables in order to avoid bad debts.

The last two points are intertwined as the risk of default increases in direct proportion to the length of the payment period. Payment periods for groups in eastern Europe are 50% longer than in Scandinavia, and the rate of default on payment is three times higher. Payment periods for Spanish and Greek groups are three times longer than in Scandinavia, and, here, the default rate is twice as high.

1/ SPEEDING UP THE PAYMENT OF TRADE RECEIVABLES

It is estimated that around 10% of invoices remain unpaid on their due date. What can be done to reduce this figure to 5% which is considered to be a healthy situation?

Payment periods are often described as the result of four factors:

PAYMENT PERIODS

The general terms and conditions of sale make provision for payment periods that are set by the company and are in line with it strategy, standard industry practice and local customs.

When sales reps offer exceptional terms and conditions of payment, this means that the financial manager has made sure that the customer is paying a higher price or purchasing a larger volume. If this is not the case, then sales reps will have to go back on their word, which is never easy with a customer who has been allowed to slide into bad habits! This is why it is best not to let sales reps make decisions on exceptional terms and conditions.

When customers fail to meet payment in full and on time, they are bending the rules and stretching the terms and conditions of sale which they signed up to. The EU Directive of June 2000 on the reduction of payment periods makes provisions for penalties for such infringements – late payment interest calculated at the Central European Bank rate + 10 points (11% in June 2010) and which cannot be less than three times the official interest rate (1.95%). In certain countries, the law also makes provision for civil and criminal penalties (fines). Even though suppliers are under an obligation to apply them, they may think twice before doing so, given the potential negative consequences of such action.

In order to avoid ending up in this situation, it is in the company's best interests to:

- contact customers 15 to 30 days before invoices are due in order to remind them that payment is due and to check that there are no problems with the invoice.

    If there are any problems, corrective measures should be taken immediately (for example, a new invoice with the correct invoice number should be issued). Such reminders should preferably be made by telephone if they are to be more effective. They must be adapted to the type of customer (large companies vs. small businesses) and should target the largest outstanding amounts. Payment reminders also provide an opportunity to check that all invoices sent to a particular client are up to date. It is estimated that c. 30% of groups with sales exceeding €300m do not carry out such reminders;

- identify customers that are systematically late payers or that regularly come up with stalling tactics in order to delay payment;

- identify customers who have long and complicated internal invoice payment approval systems, for example a customer with multiple delivery sites for payments that are centralised and paid by batch (invoices approved for payment received after the 20th of the month are paid on the 10th of the following month, etc.);

- set up a procedure for identifying swift and efficient dispute settlement. Customers that dispute invoices don't pay them. It is estimated that it takes, on average, 30 minutes to settle a dispute and that two-thirds of disputes are settled as soon as the first action is taken. Dispute settlement is all the more necessary since an unpaid invoice will often be an obstacle to new orders from the same customer, even if nothing is being done to understand and resolve the cause of the dispute. It is estimated that c. 35% of groups do not have a process for eradicating disputes;
- send out written reminders at the latest 15 days after the invoice is due, followed by a second reminder 15 days after that, and a final reminder 15 days after the second reminder, before taking legal action or handing over the debt to a debt collection agency.

Delays resulting from the internal malfunctioning of the company are, in theory, the easiest to remedy, even though this often involves overhauling the company's administrative processes, while always keeping in mind the play-off between costs and efficiency. It's also a good idea to look at the time it takes for invoices to be issued because the payment period starts as of the date of the invoice, even if the product or service has already been provided. Checks should be carried out to ensure that the invoice bears the correct address and that the quantity invoiced is identical to the quantity ordered.

2/ SECURING THE PAYMENT OF TRADE RECEIVABLES

As a defaulting customer can cause a company to go bankrupt, it is in the company's best interests to protect its receivables from any risk in this regard.

There are several simple measures that can be put in place:

- setting of a maximum credit limit for each major customer. In practice, two credit limits are often put in place, with the lower one triggering an alarm when it is breached, leading to an investigation into the customer's solvency. If the second credit limit is breached, then orders will no longer be taken from this customer, unless it agrees to pay on delivery or agrees to reservation of ownership clauses[7] for as long as it has not paid its commercial debt.

    It is estimated that 55% of groups with sales exceeding €300m have not set credit limits for each customer;
- spot checks on the solvency of customers because a customer that is solvent today may not be solvent tomorrow. Such checks can be carried out by analysing the customer's accounts and checking its rating with professionals involved in commercial information (Coface, Altares, Dun & Bradstreet, Credit Safe, etc.);
- preparation of sales reps' prospecting campaigns by carrying out advance checks on the solvency of targets. This is good practice in order to avoid payment problems in the short term, but also from a long-term point of view as the most solvent companies often turn out to be the best customers with the best payment practices;
- use of the most secure payment methods such as confirmed export letters of credit[8] or requirement of a downpayment on ordering.

This is the province of the **credit manager**, generally attached to the finance department, who is responsible for trade receivables, customer risks and collection and is also required to optimise performance, working alongside the sales departments.

7 *Enabling the company that has not yet been paid to automatically recover its asset if the customer goes bankrupt, without having to join the queue of creditors.*

8 *See Chapter 22.*

SECTION 5

At a later stage, the credit manager may have to make use of the services of collection firms (Intrum Justitia, Coface, Pouey, etc.) which handle the recovery of unpaid debts on behalf of companies, either amicably or through the courts.

In order to avoid such situations, the company can take out credit insurance. This is an insurance policy which guarantees the reimbursement of the unpaid debt by the credit insurer (Coface, Atradius, Euler Hermes, Zurich, Sace) in exchange for an insurance premium of between 0.10% and 2% of sales covered.[9] It is rare that full compensation is paid out as the company will still have to pay the insurance excess, which will be between 10 and 30% of the amount of the debt. The insurance payout is made either when the purchaser of the company's goods is declared insolvent or at the end of the lead time before payment. In order to avoid carrying only the risks that the company knows are bad risks (adverse selection), insurance companies often insist on covering the whole of the company's customer portfolio. Credit insurers provide three services:

9 Excluding very risky export regions and excluding very long periods for major export works.

- the prevention of receivables risk through solvency analyses and the provision of centralised commercial information which they update on an ongoing basis;
- recovery of unpaid invoices;
- compensation on guaranteed debts it has not been possible to recover.

Credit managers also have other tools at their disposal to protect the company against defaulting customers:

- **bank guarantees**: the banks of certain problem customers are sometimes prepared to provide a bank guarantee that they will meet their payments;
- techniques used in international trade such as the irrevocable and confirmed **documentary credit**[10] (very popular in high-risk countries);
- non-recourse factoring,[11] allowing a company to sell trade receivables.

10 See Chapter 22.

11 See Chapter 22.

Section 48.3
Managing trade payables

This item is often neglected as company buyers are often more keen to negotiate good prices than to negotiate advantageous payment periods.

All the more so since the development of credit insurance. If a company's supplier has taken out credit insurance to cover its receivables, and if the company pays after the contractual payment period and the supplier declares a default on payment to the insurance company, the company will be identified as a bad payer by the insurance company and this news will spread very quickly on the market.

Management of trade payables will mainly involve:

- a review of payment periods negotiated with each supplier. The company will often discover that it has a wide range of payment periods as a result of decentralisation. Even at companies where purchasing negotiations are centralised, payment periods are not dealt with as the focus is often only on prices fixed for the whole of the group. In such cases, the company should negotiate with its biggest suppliers and try to align all payment periods with the longest periods that are already in place. The company can try and force smaller suppliers to accept such longer payment periods;
- a comparison of theory (contractual payment periods) and practice (the actual period after which the company pays) will highlight situations in which the company pays

earlier than it should. Often, if lack of discipline and incompetence are eliminated as causes, the reason for this is that different dates appear in the terms of payment in the contract, on the order and even on the invoice. Sometimes companies pay on the 15th of the month, amounts that are due between the 15th and the 30th and on the 30th of the month, amounts that are due between the 1st and the 15th of the following month. There are other times when the supplier delivers the goods or service earlier than planned, and sends off the invoice immediately;

- a review of the procedure for validating the receipt of deliveries will help to prevent late validation of deliveries which, in the best of cases, generates delays in invoice accounting and hence payment delays, which could result in heavy penalties. In the worst of cases, new orders will be triggered as the stocks in the system could appear to be abnormally low!

- finally, disputes should be dealt with quickly as they will not result in any extension of the contractual payment period.

Section 48.4
INVENTORY MANAGEMENT

According to Walbert and Cabelli, the ability of a company to manage its inventories well is dependent on several parameters and on how well the company manages these:

- its ability to correctly forecast the level of activity in advance, which is highly dependent on the sector;
- its ability to carry out cross analyses between product families and customer families, in order to be able to work out suitable supplies and storage policies;
- its ability to reduce its supply periods;
- its ability to transform its stocks rapidly from raw materials into finished products, and then to sell them (called optimisation of the production process);
- its ability to monitor stock levels;
- its ability to obtain a service rate[12] high enough to avoid stockouts.

At any given moment, the company will have several types of inventories:

- safety stocks:

  o buffer stocks set up in order to mitigate the uncertainty linked to demand or to supply;
  o anticipation inventories set up in anticipation of future demand;

- structural stocks:

  o cyclical stocks linked to the size of manufacturing batches;
  o pending stocks, pending the next transformation operation;
  o in-process stocks, in the process of being transformed;
  o and stocks in transit between two entities.

Experience has shown that when a company takes a serious look at its inventory levels, it can achieve impressive results. In 2009, SEB reduced its inventories by 23%, cutting them from 70 to 54 days of sales. Carrefour has set itself the target of reducing inventories from 22 to 11 days! Progress in logistics and IT management have played a large role in

12 *Calculated as the number of error-free orders delivered on time/number of orders.*

these improvements. However, it would be fallacious to believe that it is always best to keep inventories low. Inventories remain an investment which results from a play-off of financial cost versus the flexibility gained.

As for the management of receivables, managing inventories involves action to combat waste and more structural action.

Action to combat waste includes:

- selling off dormant inventories for which orders have not been placed for more than a year;

13 *Which you can download from www.vernimmen. com.*

- systematically using the **Wilson formula** for determining the optimal quantity to order. The Wilson formula[13] consists in playing off the cost of placing the order (administrative cost, discount in line with size of order) against the cost of storage (financial cost of tying up capital, storage and risk);
- reducing uncertainty over supplies by analysing delivery periods and the reliability of the various suppliers or even setting up partnerships with some suppliers (as is the case in the automotive industry);
- integrating sales forecasts into the stock management tool;
- determining the inventories policy on the basis of service rates to be provided to customers.

Structural measures include:

14 *See Chapter 8.*

- shifting from a mass production mode to a process mode,[14] which is not without cost as the firm will lose flexibility and run the risk of breaks in production; or shifting from a workshop production mode to a mass production mode;
- including performance-based targets in the calculation of the variable remuneration of stock managers (only 20% of groups have such systems in place);
- optimising the location of stock and of picking processes at factories, in order to reduce in-transit inventory;
- working on sales forecasts so as to reduce buffer stocks and anticipation inventories, which may involve working more closely with the firm's main customers or working out precise statistics in order to be in a better position to determine the seasonality or the cyclical nature of sales;
- simplifying the range of products offered by reducing varieties which increase the number of unit stocks.

SUMMARY

The summary of this chapter can be downloaded from www.vernimmen.com.

Working capital is an investment, like any other, and accordingly, it has to be managed. Management of working capital does not necessarily mean reducing it at all costs. Working capital is the result of a play-off between liquidity and margins.

Over and above waste, which is relatively simple to eliminate but which requires determination and an ongoing effort, working capital can only be reduced at the expense of EBIT or at the cost of investing in modifying the firm's economic model.

In crisis periods, the firm will focus on reducing working capital in order to generate cash which is useful for paying down debt or self-financing projects. The impact on margins is less of an issue.

During economically good times, the firm will focus more on sales and margins than on working capital.

All of the techniques and tools for managing working capital were described in this chapter.

Financial managers will not be able to put in place measures for managing working capital without the close collaboration of operational managers responsible for purchasing, stocks, logistics, production, sales and human resources, over whom financial managers have no authority. Over and above the fight against waste, managing working capital often quickly leads to strategic decisions involving the firm's commercial, production and logistics policies.

Financial managers will, this time internally, have an opportunity to demonstrate their teaching skills and negotiating talents.

QUESTIONS

1/ For how long can factories be shut down while surplus stocks are absorbed?

2/ Why does managing working capital involve both supply management and strategy?

3/ Why do LBO funds set so much store by the management of working capital?

4/ In what conditions is excessive working capital not the sign of poor management?

5/ A customer suddenly increases his orders from you. What is your reaction?

6/ You are late in paying an invoice. You have not received a reminder. What do you conclude?

7/ What are the three documents that prove the existence of a debt and which are indispensable for sending out an effective reminder?

8/ Is the securitisation of trade receivables or inventories a way of managing working capital?

9/ What are the services provided by credit insurance?

10/ Why would a company, knowing that its suppliers had taken out credit insurance for part of the trade payables it owes, be well advised to pay by the due date?

11/ A client has the choice of paying at 10 days with a 2% discount or at 60 days, and it chooses the latter option. What does this signal?

12/ Why is there a correlation between payment period and rate of customer default?

13/ Is managing working capital only the business of the financial manager? Why?

14/ What could a group be tempted to do, if it fears that at the close of its financial year, it will be unable to meet its debt covenants, resulting in the restructuring or possibly even the calling in of this debt?

More questions are waiting for you at www.vernimmen.com.

SECTION 5

SECTION 5

Exercises

1/Provide a simple example to illustrate that upstream integration increases working capital.

2/Provide a simple example to illustrate that downstream integration increases working capital.

3/Show how the figure 44.6% (mentioned on page 912) is calculated.

4/A company makes annual sales of €10m (excl. VAT) and is subject to VAT at a rate of 19.6%. Its actual collection time is 75 days. What is the average outstanding amount receivable? The payment period has to be reduced to 60 days for legal reasons. How much extra cash will this mean for the company? What is the impact on the income statement if the company is currently borrowing at 6%?

5/A company posts monthly sales of €100 000 with a customer for which its gross margin is 25%. How long after the start of the relationship with this customer can the customer go bankrupt without the company making any net losses, given the gross margin made and the total loss of trade payables that remain unpaid? The payment period is 2 months.

Answers

Questions

1/*Some factories take a long time to shut down or start up again. It takes a lot longer to start up a blast furnace than it does to start up a sewing machine!*

2/*It involves strategy, because it depends on the commercial, production and financial strategy of the firm – arbitrage, margin and volume vs. cash. It involves supply management, as this is the continuation of small actions and decisions to be implemented.*

3/*Because by tightening up its working capital, the firm generates cash which will enable it to reimburse part of its debt and improve the IRR of the LBO fund.*

4/*If this situation is desired and the result of a conscious decision, and not something the company has to reluctantly bear. If, in exchange, the company receives more orders and records higher margins.*

5/*Has this customer failed to pay a competitor, which is now refusing to make more deliveries? This may be why the customer has increased orders from you.*

6/*Your supplier is badly organised and/or rich!*

7/*The order slip and the delivery slip signed by the customer, the invoice.*

8/*No, merely a way of financing working capital.*

9/*The analysis of the solvency of customers/prospects, the recovery of bad debts, compensation for receivables that are not recovered.*

10/*Because the market will find out very quickly if the firm is a bad payer via the credit insurer, which will pass on this information to its other clients.*

11/*Either that it has no cash or that its marginal cost of debt is higher than 15.9%, which is not a good sign of its future prospects!*

12/*Because a customer who pays late does not necessarily do so on purpose, but also does so because of liquidity problems, which indicates a high risk of bankruptcy.*

13/*No, because it also involves the commercial, marketing, production/logistics managers, and even the general manager, who have to make choices and decisions, playing various factors off against others.*

14/*It can buy cash by temporarily reducing its working capital in order to reduce its net debt.*

Exercises

A detailed Excel version of the solutions is available at www.vernimmen.com.

1/ *A factory pays all of its suppliers 900 on day 1, and receives 980 from its retailer customer on day 60. The retailer pays its supplier (the factory) 980 and 100 to other suppliers on day 60, and receives 1100 from its customers on day 90.*

For 60 days, the factory has a cash deficit of 900, which is its working capital, and makes a margin of 80. For 30 days, the retailer has a cash deficit of 1080, which is its working capital, and makes a margin of 1100 − 980 − 100 = 20.

If the factory buys the retailer, it carries working capital of 900 over 90 days and of 100 over 30 days, or an average of 933 over 90 days compared with 900 over 60 days.

Its working capital has thus increased.

2/ *Let's take the above example again. This time, let's say that the retailer buys the factory.*

It carries 1080 over 30 days.

Now it has to carry 900 over 90 days and 100 over 30 days, or an average of 933 over 90 days.

Its working capital has thus increased.

3/ $98 = 100/(1 + t)20/365$ *so* $t = 44.6\%$.

4/ $10 \times 1.196 \times 75/365 = €2.5m$.
Cash gain:
$10 \times 1.196 \times 60/365 − €2.5m = €0.49m$.
Savings in terms of financial expense:
$€0.49m \times 6\% = €29\,000$.

5/ *Monthly margin:*
$100\,000 \times 25\% = €25\,000$.
Company's financial risk:
$100\,000 \times (1 − 25\%) \times 3$ *months* $= €225\,000$.
$225/25 = 9$ *months of margins collected.*
Period of $9 + 3$ months of margins not collected $= 1$ year.

A 2-month payment period means 3 months of invoices, as customers generally go bankrupt just before a payment is due and not just after they have paid.

BIBLIOGRAPHY

Ernst & Young, *All tied up*, Working management report, 2009.

M. Hill, G. Kelly, M. Highfield, Net operating working capital behavior: A first look, *Financial Management*, **39**(2), 783–805, Summer 2010.

Intrum Justitia, *European payment index 2008*, May 2009.

C. Molina, L. Preve, Trade receivables policy of distressed firms and its effect on the costs of financial distress, *Financial Management*, **68**(3), 663–686, Autumn 2009.

R. Smid, Unlocking value from your sheet through working capital management, *Journal of Payment Strategy & Systems*, **2**(2), 127–137, January 2008.

J. Tennent, Working capital management, in *Guide to Financial Management*, Economist Intelligence Unit, 2008, Chapter 14.

SECTION 5

Chapter 49
MANAGING FINANCIAL RISKS

Forbidden, but useful, tools...

In recent years investors, regulators and management have increasingly focused their attention on risk management. We have thus seen:

- tighter regulatory frameworks (e.g. with the Sarbanes–Oxley Act in the US in 2002) that impose communication on risk identification and risk management;
- greater pressure from the market for increased transparency. In this context, the recommendation for good corporate governance suggests a reinforced role for directors, in particular through risk and audit committees;
- management awareness of risk management issues has led to the creation or the increased role of risk management departments (internal audit, risk managers, . . .).

A recent trend in risk management consisted in splitting up the risks and managing them with products that allow finer and more flexible hedging.

Section 49.1
INTRODUCTION TO RISK MANAGEMENT

1/ DEFINITION OF RISK

The key features of risk are:

- intensity of the possible loss on the amount of the exposure;
- frequency, which is the likelihood of this loss occurring (insurers talk about loss probability).

Risk can be classified into four major categories:

- Risk fundamentally linked to market changes (interest and exchange rates, raw material prices). The likelihood of occurrence of fundamental risk, i.e. the probability that the market will move against the interests of the company, is mechanically close to 50%. The intensity of the loss will depend on the volatility of the market in question.
- Loss probability refers to the likelihood of the loss occurring on a recurrent basis (such as losses on bad debts, the unknown losses suffered by mass market retailers on marked-down products, damage caused to vehicles by car rental companies, etc.).

This is more of a statistical cost than a risk. The real risk is the possibility that a probable loss will occur more suddenly than usual, hence its name.

• Volatility risk is a risk that materialises during an exceptional year (fire in a hypermarket). This sort of risk should always be covered.

• A disaster risk materialises once a century (for example, the explosion at the BP oil refinery in the Gulf of Mexico) but it can have a very high level of intensity. It is difficult to cover[1] and it is not unusual for the risk of a disaster occurring to be only partially covered, or not covered at all, given the fact that it is very unlikely to occur.

1 *Excluding market products such as cat bonds, where the coupon or redemption price is drastically cut in the event of an occurrence of a disaster suffered by the issuer.*

2/ RISK MANAGEMENT STEPS

The different steps involved in risk management are as follows:

Identification: the map-making work involved in risks. Once the intensity and probability of the risk has been identified and determined, it can be classified.

Determination of existing internal controls which will help to mitigate the risk. This step involves assessing and testing existing internal controls (adequacy and efficiency). Controls should, in fact, lead to the substantial reduction (and generally at a low cost) of most risks, acting as a sort of filter. So it would be counterproductive for a company to insure its losses on receivables if it hadn't put in place basic controls to ensure their recovery (monitoring of outstanding payables, sending out reminders, etc.).

Prevention is often the best form of internal control. There is the very telling example of the manager of a transport firm who sent all of his drivers off for driving lessons in order to reduce the firm's accident rate.

Determination of a residual risk and assessment: internal control generally manages and eliminates a large part of the risk that is easy to master. This leaves the company in a position where it can determine the residual risk. It then only has to assess the potential impact which will be a determining factor in the final phase.

Definition of a management strategy: this involves finding the answers to two key questions:

○ Am I in a position to manage this risk internally? If so, what is the cost?
○ Are there any tools that can be used to hedge against this risk? If so, what is the cost?

Managers will rely on an assessment of the relationship between the level of hedging and the cost of each strategy to help them come to a decision. However, the choice of whether to cover a risk or not is not a simple yes or no decision, as it may first appear. Often, the best solution turns out to be an intelligent combination of a number of options.

However, issues relating to corporate image and communication may interfere with this purely economic reasoning. For example, a company may have to opt for more expensive hedging if this ties in with its image as a good corporate citizen. There are also some financial directors who may question whether the company should take out insurance against certain risks that will need to be booked at fair value (as required under IAS 39) and which would be likely to introduce high levels of volatility onto the income statement!

Insuring against risks helps to limit the volatility of earnings and cash flows. Nevertheless, the reader, who will by now have developed the reasoning of a skilled theoretician, could quite rightly point out that, as the risks covered are by nature diversified

2 *See Chapter 18.*

risks, eliminating them through insurance is not remunerated by the investor in the form of a lower required rate of return.[2] In other words, the coverage does not create value. This is true from a purely logical point of view of efficient markets.

Looking at the issue in terms of agency theory, it is clear that managers should reduce the volatility of cash flows. Even if the coverage decision does not create value, a company that is less exposed to the ups and downs of the market is, from a manager's point of view, in a more comfortable position. Comprehensive insurance will enable management to implement a long-term strategy, by reducing the likelihood of bankruptcy and reducing the personal risk of managers.

3/ THE DIFFERENT TYPES OF RISK

Risks run by companies can be split into five categories:

- **Market risk** is exposure to unfavourable trends in product prices, interest rates, exchange rates, raw material prices or stock prices. Market risk occurs at various levels:

  - a position (a debt, for example, or an expected receipt of revenue in foreign currencies, etc.);
  - a business activity (purchases paid in a currency other than that in which the products are sold, etc.); or
  - a portfolio (short- and long-term financial holdings).

- **Counterparty or credit risk.** This is the risk of loss on an outstanding receivable or, more generally, on a debt that is not paid on time. It naturally depends on three parameters: the amount of the debt, the likelihood of default and the portion of the debt that will be collected in the event of a default.

- **Liquidity risk** is the impossibility at a given moment of meeting a debt payment, because:

  - the company no longer has assets that can rapidly be turned into cash;
  - a financial crisis (a market crash, for example) has made it very difficult to liquidate assets, except at a very great loss in value; or
  - it is impossible to find investors willing to offer new funding.

- **Operating risks:** these are risks of losses caused by errors on the part of employees, systems and processes, or by external events, they include:

  - risk of deterioration of industrial facilities (accident, fire, explosion, etc.) that may also cover the risk of a temporary halt in business;
  - technological risk: am I in a position to identify/anticipate the arrival of new technology which will make my own technology redundant?
  - climate risks that may be of vital importance in some sectors, such as agriculture (how can cereal growers protect their harvests from the vagaries of the weather?) or the leisure sector (what sort of insurance should producers of outdoor concerts take out?);
  - environmental risks: how can I ensure that I'm in a position to protect the environment from the potentially harmful impact of my activity? Am I in a position to certify that I comply with all environmental statutes and regulations in force?

- **Political, regulatory and legal risks:** these are risks that impact on the immediate environment of the company and that could substantially modify its competitive situation and even the business model itself.

Section 49.2
MEASURING FINANCIAL RISKS

Different financial risks are measured in very different ways. Measurement is:

- quite sophisticated for market risks, for example, with the notion of position and value at risk (VaR), and for liquidity risks;
- less sophisticated for counterparty risks;
- quite unsatisfactory for political risks.

Most risk measurement tools were initially developed by banks – whose activities make them highly exposed to financial risks – before being gradually adopted by other companies.

1/ POSITION AND MEASUREMENT OF MARKET RISKS

Market risk is exposure to fluctuations in value of an asset called the underlying asset. An operator's **position** is the residual market exposure on his balance sheet at any given moment.

When an operator has bought more in an underlying asset than he has sold, he is **long** (for interest or exchange rate a long position is when the underlying asset is worth more than the corresponding liability). It is possible, for example, to be long in euros, long in bonds or long 3 months out (i.e. having lent more than borrowed 3 months out). The market risk on a long position is the risk of a fall in market value of the underlying asset (or an increase in interest rates).

On the other hand, when an operator has sold more in the underlying asset than he has bought, he is said to be **short**. The market risk on a short position is the risk of an increase in market value of the underlying asset (or a fall in interest rates).

The notion of position is very important for banks operating on the fixed-income and currency markets. Generally speaking, traders are allowed to keep a given amount in an open position, depending on their anticipation. However, clients buy and sell products constantly, each time modifying traders' positions. At a given moment, a trader could even have a position that runs counter to his anticipation. Whenever this is the case, he can close out his position (by realising a transaction that cancels out his position) in the interbank market.

2/ COMPANIES' MARKET POSITIONS

Like banks, at any given moment an industrial company can have positions *vis-à-vis* the various categories of risk (the most common being currency and interest rate risk). Such positions do not generally arise from the company's choice or a purchase of derivatives, but are rather a natural consequence of its business activities, financing and the geographical location of its subsidiaries. A company's aggregate position results from the following three items:

- its commercial position;
- its financial position;
- its accounting position.

Let us first consider currency risk. Exposure to currency risk arises first of all from the purchases and sales of currencies that a company makes in the course of carrying out its business activities. Let us say, for example, that a Eurozone company is due to receive $10m in dollars in 6 months, and has no dollar payables at the same date. That company is said to be long in 6-month dollars. Depending on the company's business cycle, the actual timeframe can range from a few days to several years (if the order backlog is equivalent to several years of revenues). The company must therefore quantify its total currency risk exposure by setting receipts against expenditure, currency by currency, at the level of existing billings and forecast billings. By doing so, it obtains its **commercial currency position**.

However, the company's commercial exchange position goes well beyond the one-off transaction described above. Take, for example, a company such as Airbus, which gets its revenues in dollars but pays its costs in euros. Even if it hedges against foreign exchange losses on its orders, it will still be exposed over the long term to fluctuating exchange rates. The group cannot hedge against possible losses several years in advance on sales that it has not yet made!

Its commercial position is thus structural and it is obvious that this position is even more precarious when the company's competitors are not in the same position. Boeing, for example, earns its revenues and pays its costs in dollars.

There is also a risk in holding financial assets and liabilities denominated in foreign currencies. If our Eurozone company has raised funds in dollars, it is now short in dollars, as some of its liabilities are denominated in dollars with nothing to offset them on the asset side. The main sources of this risk are: (1) loans, borrowings and current accounts denominated in foreign currencies, with their related interest charges; and (2) investments in foreign currencies. Taken as a whole, these risks express companies' **financial currency position**.

The third component of currency risk is **accounting currency risk**, which arises from the consolidation of foreign subsidiaries. Equity denominated in foreign currencies, dividend flows, financial investments denominated in foreign currencies and currency translation difference[3] give rise to accounting currency risk. Note, however, that this is reflected in the currency translation differential in the consolidated accounts and therefore has no impact on net income.

The same thing can apply to the interest rate risk. The **commercial interest rate risk** depends on the level of inflation of the currencies in which the goods are bought and sold, while the **financial interest rate** is obviously tied directly to the terms a company has obtained for its borrowings and investments. Floating-rate borrowings, for example, expose companies to an increase in the benchmark rate, while fixed-rate borrowings expose them to opportunity cost if they cannot take advantage of a possible cut in rates.

In addition to currencies and interest rates, other market-related risks require companies to take positions. In many sectors, for example, raw material prices are a key factor. A company can have a strategically important position on oil, coffee, semiconductors or electricity markets, for example.

3 *That is, the use of an average exchange rate for the P&L and the closing rate for the balance sheet.*

3/ VALUE AT RISK (VaR) AND CORPORATE VALUE AT RISK

VaR (value at risk) is a finer measure of market risk. It represents an investor's maximum potential loss on the value of an asset or a portfolio of financial assets and liabilities, based on the investment timeframe and a confidence interval. This potential loss is calculated on the basis of historical data or deduced from normal statistical laws.

Hence, a portfolio worth €100m, with a VaR of €2.5m at 95% (calculated on a monthly basis) has just a 5% chance of shrinking more than €2.5m in one month.

VaR is often used by financial establishments as a tool in managing risk.

VaR is beginning to be used by major industrial groups. TeleDanmark, for example, includes it in its annual reports. However, VaR has two drawbacks:

- it assumes that the markets follow normal distribution laws, an assumption that underestimates the frequency of extreme values;
- it tells us absolutely nothing about the potential loss that could occur when stepping outside the confidence interval. Based on the above example, how much can be lost in those 5% of cases: €2.6m, €10m or €100m? VaR tells us nothing on this point, but stress scenarios can then be implemented.

In the same way, some firms compute earnings at risk, cash flows at risk and corporate value at risk to measure the impact of adverse effects on earnings, cash flows and value over a longer period than for banks: from several months up to a year.

4/ MEASURING OTHER FINANCIAL RISKS

Liquidity risk is measured by comparing contractual debt maturities with estimated future cash flow, via either a cash flow statement or curves such as those presented on p. 219. Contracts carrying clauses on the company's financial ratios or ratings must not be included under debt maturing in more than 1 year because a worsening in the company's ratios or a downgrade could trigger early repayment of outstanding loans.

In addition to conventional financial analysis techniques and credit scoring, credit and counterparty risk is measured mainly via tests that break down risks. Such tests include the proportion of the company's top 10 clients in total receivables, number of clients with credit lines above a certain level, etc.

The measure of political risk is still in its infancy.

Section 49.3
PRINCIPLES OF FINANCIAL RISK MANAGEMENT

Financial risk management comes in four forms:

- self-hedging, a seemingly passive stance that is taken only by a few, very large, companies and only on some of their risks;
- locking in prices or rates for a future transaction, which has the drawback of preventing the company from benefiting from a favourable shift in prices or rates;

- insurance, which consists in paying a premium in some form to a third party, which will then assume the risk, if it materialises; this approach allows the company to benefit from a favourable shift in prices or rates;
- immediate disposal of a risky asset or liability.

1/ Self-hedging

Self-hedging is only a strategy for hedging against risk when it is deliberately chosen by the company or when there is no other alternative (uninsurable risks). It can be structured to a greater or lesser extent. At one extreme, we get risk taking (no hedging after the risk has been analysed) and at the other, the setting up of a captive insurance scheme.

Self-hedging consists, in fact, in not hedging a risk. This is a reasonable strategy but only for very large groups. Such groups assume that the law of averages applies to them and that they are therefore certain to experience some negative events on a regular basis, such as devaluations, customer bankruptcy, etc. Risk thus becomes a certainty and, hence, a cost. Self-hedging is based on the principle that a company has no interest in passing on the risk (and the profit) to a third party. Rather than paying what amounts to an insurance premium, the company provisions a sum each year to meet claims that will inevitably occur, thus becoming its own insurer.

The risk can be diminished, but not eliminated, by natural hedges. A European company, for example, that sells in the US will also produce there, so that its costs can be in dollars rather than euros. It will take on debt in the US rather than in Europe, to set dollar-denominated liabilities against dollar-denominated assets.

> Self-hedging is a strategy adopted by either irresponsible companies or a limited number of very large companies who serve as their own insurance company!

One sophisticated procedure consists in setting up a **captive insurance company**, which will invest the premiums thus saved to build up reserves in order to meet future claims. In the meantime, some of the risk can be sold on the reinsurance market.[4]

4 *The reinsurance market allows insurers to transfer part of their risks to other insurance companies, called reinsurance companies, which act as insurers for insurers.*

Setting up a **captive insurance** scheme is a complex operation, which takes the company into the realms of insurance. A captive insurance company is an insurance or reinsurance company that belongs to an industrial or commercial company, whose core business is not insurance. The purpose of the company's existence is to insure the risks of the group to which it belongs. This sort of setup sometimes becomes necessary because of the shortcomings of traditional insurance:

- some groups may be tempted to reduce risk prevention measures when they know that the insurance company will pay out if anything goes wrong;
- coverage capacities are limited and some risks are no longer insurable, for example gradual pollution or asbestos-related damage;
- good risks end up making up for bad risks.

The scheme works as follows: the captive insurance company collects premiums from the industrial or commercial company and its subsidiaries, and covers their insurance losses.

Like all insurance companies, it reinsures part of its risks with international reinsurance companies. A captive insurance setup has the following advantages:

- much greater efficiency (involvement in its own loss profile, exclusion of credit risk, reduction of overinsurance, tailor-made policies);
- access to the reinsurance market;
- greater independence from insurance companies (having them compete against each other);
- reduction in vulnerability to cycles on the insurance market;
- possibility of tax optimisation;
- spreading the impact of losses over several financial years.

There is also the option of alternative risk financing. Well-known for their fertile imaginations, insurers have come up with products that make it possible to spread the impact of insurance losses on the income statement. The insured pays an annual premium and, if a loss occurs, the premium is adjusted, if necessary, to cover the cost of the loss. IFRS has killed off these products, which did not transfer risk but merely allowed the consequences of a loss to be spread over several financial years.

2/ LOCKING IN FUTURE PRICES OR RATES THROUGH FORWARD TRANSACTIONS

Forward transactions can fully eliminate risk by locking in now the price or rate at which a transaction will be made in the future. This costs the company nothing but does prevent it from benefiting from a favourable shift in price or rates.

Forward transactions sometimes defy conventional logic, as they allow one to "sell" what one does not yet possess or to "buy" a product before it is available. However, they are not abstractions divorced from economic reality. As we will show, forward transactions can be broken down into the simple, familiar operations of spot purchasing or selling, borrowing and lending.

(a) Forward currency transactions

Let us take the example of a US company that is to receive €100m in euros in 3 months. Let's say the euro is currently trading at $1.5198. Unless the company treasurer is speculating on a rise in the euro, he wants to lock in today the exchange rate at which he will be able to sell these euros. So he offers to sell euros now that he will not receive for another 3 months. This is the essence of the forward transaction. Although forward transactions are common practice, it is worth looking at how they are calculated.

The transaction is tantamount to borrowing today the present value in euros of the sum that will be received in 3 months, exchanging it at the current rate and investing the corresponding amount in dollars for the same maturity.

Assume A is the amount in euros received by the company; N, the number of days between today and the date of receipt; R, the euro borrowing rate; and $R_\$$, the dollar interest rate.

The amount borrowed today in euros is simply the value A, discounted at rate R_ϵ:

$$PV = A / (1 + (R_\epsilon \times N / 360))$$

This amount is then exchanged at the RS spot rate and invested in dollars at rate $R_\$$. Future value is thus expressed as:

$$FV = RS \times PV \times (1 + (R_\$ \times N / 360))$$

Thus:

$$FV = A \times RS \times \frac{1 + R_\$ \times \dfrac{N}{360}}{1 + R_\epsilon \times \dfrac{N}{360}}$$

The forward rate (F_R) is that which equalises the future value in euros and the amount A.

Thus:

$$F_R = RS \times \frac{1 + R_\$ \times \dfrac{N}{360}}{1 + R_\epsilon \times \dfrac{N}{360}}$$

If $RS = \$1.5198$, $N = 90$ days, $R_\$ = 3.03\%$ and $R_\epsilon = 4.38\%$, we obtain a forward selling price of \$1.5147.

A forward purchase of euros, in which the company treasurer pledges to buy euros in the future, is tantamount to the treasurer's buying the euros today while borrowing their corresponding value in dollars for the same period. The euros that have been bought are also invested during this time at the euro interest rate.

The forward exchange rate of a currency is based on the spot price and the interest rate differential between the foreign currency and the benchmark currency during the period covered by the transaction.

In our example, as interest rates are higher in euros than in dollars, the forward euro-into-dollar exchange rate is lower than the spot rate. The difference is called **swap points**. In our example, swap points come to 51.[5] Swap points can be seen as compensation demanded by the treasurer in the forward transaction for borrowing in a high-yielding currency (the euro in our example), and investing in a low-yielding currency (the dollar in our example) up to the moment when the transaction is unwound. More generally, if the benchmark currency offers a lower interest rate than the foreign currency, the forward rate will be below the spot rate. Currency A is said to be at discount *vis-à-vis* currency B if A offers higher interest rates than B during the period concerned.

Similarly, currency A is said to be at premium *vis-à-vis* currency B if interest rates on A are below interest rates on B during the period concerned.

As in any forward transaction, treasurers know at what price they will be able to buy or sell their currencies, but will be unable to take advantage of any later opportunities. For example, if a treasurer sold his €100m forward at \$1.5147, and the euro is trading at \$1.5500 dollars at maturity, he will have to keep his word (unless he wants to break the futures contract, in which case he will have to pay a penalty) and bear an opportunity cost equal to \$0.0353 per euro sold.

5 $51 = 5198 - 5147.$

(b) Forward-forward rate and FRAs

Let us say our company treasurer learns that his company plans to install a new IT system, which will require a considerable outlay in equipment and software in 3 months. His cash flow projections show that, in 3 months, he will have to borrow €20m for 6 months.

On the euro money market, spot interest rates are as follows:

3 months	21/4% – 25/16%
6 months	21/4% – 25/16%
9 months	25/16% – 23/8%

How can the treasurer hedge against a rise in short-term rates over the next 3 months? Armed with his knowledge of the yield curve, he can use the procedures discussed below to lock in the 6-month rate as it will be in 3 months.

He decides to borrow €20m today for 9 months and to reinvest it for the first 3 months. Assuming that he works directly at money market conditions, in 9 months he will have to pay back:

$$20 \times (1 + 23/8\% \times 9/12) = €20.35625m$$

But his 3-month investment turns €20m into:

$$20 \times (1 + 21/4\% \times 3/12) = €20.11250$$

The implied rate obtained is called the forward-forward rate and is expressed as follows:

$$T(3.6) = ((20.35625 - 20.11250)/20.11250) \times (12/6) = 2.424\%$$

Our treasurer was thus able to hedge his exchange rate risk but has borrowed €20m from his bank, €20m that he will not be using for 3 months. Hence, he must bear the corresponding intermediation costs. **His company's balance sheet and income statement will be affected by this transaction.**

Now let's imagine that the bank finds out about our treasurer's concerns and offers him the following product:

- in 3 months' time, if the 6-month (floating benchmark) rate is above 2.424% (the guaranteed rate), the bank pledges to pay him the difference between the market rate and 2.424% on a predetermined principal.
- in 3 months' time, if the 6-month (floating benchmark) rate is below 2.424% (the guaranteed rate), the company will have to pay the bank the difference between 2.424% and the market rate on the same predetermined principal.

This is called a **forward rate agreement**, or **FRA**. An FRA allows the treasurer to hedge against fluctuations in rates, without the amount of the transaction being actually borrowed or lent.

If, in 3 months' time, the 6-month rate is 2.5%, our treasurer will borrow €20m at this high rate but will receive, on the same amount, the pro-rated difference between 2.5% and 2.424%. The actual cost of the loan will therefore be 2.424%. Similarly, if the 6-month rate is 1.5%, the treasurer will have borrowed on favourable terms, but will have to pay the pro-rated difference between 2.424% and 1.5%.

The same reasoning applies if the treasurer wishes to invest any surplus funds. Such a transaction would involve an FRA lending, as opposed to the FRA borrowing described above.

Forward rate agreements are used to lock in an interest rate for a future transaction.

The **notional amount** is the theoretical amount to which the difference between the guaranteed rate and the floating rate is applied. The notional amount is never exchanged between the buyer and seller of an FRA. The interest rate differential is not paid at the maturity of the underlying loan but is discounted and paid at the maturity of the FRA.

An FRA is free of charge but, of course, the "purchase" of an FRA and the "sale" of an FRA are not made at the same interest rate. As in all financial products, a margin separates the rate charged on a 6-month loan in 3 months' time, and the rate at which that money can be invested over the same period of time.

Banks are key operators on the FRA market and offer companies the opportunity to buy or sell FRAs with maturities generally shorter than 1 year.

(c) Swaps

In its broadest sense, a swap is an exchange of financial assets or flows between two entities during a certain period of time. Both operators must, of course, believe the transaction to be to their advantage.

"Swap" in everyday parlance means an exchange of financial flows (calculated on the basis of a theoretical benchmark called a notional) between two entities during a given period of time. Such financial flows can be:

- currency swap without principal;
- interest rate swaps (IRS);
- currency swaps (with principal).

Unlike financial assets, financial flows are traded over the counter with no impact on the balance sheet, and allow the parties to modify the exchange or interest rate terms (or both simultaneously) on current or future assets or liabilities.

Interest rate swaps are a long-term portfolio of FRAs (from 1 to 15 years).

As with FRAs, the principle is to compare a floating rate and a guaranteed rate and to make up the difference without an exchange of principal. Interest rate swaps are especially suited for managing a company's long-term currency exposure.

For a company with long-term debt at 7% (at fixed rates) and wishing to benefit from the fall in interest rates that it expects, the simplest solution is to receive the fixed rate (7%) on a notional amount and to pay the floating rate on the same amount.

SECTION 5

INTEREST RATE SWAP

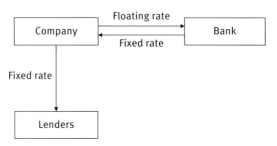

That is:

Fixed rate + Fixed rate – Floating rate = – Floating rate tantamount to our company's borrowing the notional at a floating rate for the duration of the swap without its lenders seeing any change in their debts. After the first year, if the variable benchmark rate (Libor,[6] Euribor,[7] etc.) is 6%, the company will have paid its creditors an interest rate of 7%, but will receive 1% of the swap's notional amount. Its effective rate will be 6%.

The transaction described is a swap of fixed for floating rates, and all sorts of combinations are possible:

- swapping a fixed rate for fixed rate (in the same currency);
- swapping floating rate 1 for floating rate 2 (called benchmark switching);
- swapping a fixed rate in currency 1 for a fixed rate in currency 2;
- swapping a fixed rate in currency 1 for a floating rate in currency 2;
- swapping a floating rate in currency 1 for a floating rate in currency 2.

These last three swaps come with an exchange of principal, as the two parties use different currencies. This exchange is generally done at the beginning and at the maturity of the swap at the same exchange rate. More sophisticated swaps make it possible to separate the benchmark rates from the currencies concerned.

The swaps market has experienced a considerable boom, and banks are key players. Company treasurers appreciate the flexibility of swaps, which allow them to choose the duration, the floating benchmark rate and the notional amount. Note, finally, that a swap between a bank and a company can be liquidated at any moment by calculating the present value of future cash flows at the market rate and comparing it to the initial notional amount. Swaps are also frequently used to manage interest rate risk on floating- or fixed-rate assets.

The difficulties that some emerging countries had in paying off their debt led to a boom in asset (and debt) swaps. They were meant to prevent too many risks from being heaped on the shoulders of a single debtor. The swaps work by allowing creditors to exchange one debt for another of the same type. Each country is rated in terms of percentage of the nominal of the debt. Ratings can range from almost 0 (default) to 100% for the safest borrowers.

The concept of the swap has been enlarged with **total return swaps**. Two players swap the revenues and change in value of two different assets they own during a certain period of time. One of the assets is generally a short-term loan, the other one can be a share price index, a block of shares, a portfolio of bonds, etc.

3/ INSURANCE

Insurance allows companies to pay a premium to a third party, which assumes the risk if that risk materialises. If it doesn't, companies can benefit from a favourable trend in the parameter hedged (exchange rate, interest rates, solvency of a debtor, etc.).

Conceptually, insurance is based on the technique of options; the insurance premium paid corresponds to the value of the option purchased.

As we saw in Chapter 24, an option gives its holder the right to buy or sell an underlying asset at a specified price on a specified date, or to forego this right if the market offers

6 *London inter bank offered rate.*

7 *European inter bank offered rate.*

better opportunities. See Chapter 24 for background, valuation and conditions in which options are used.

Options are an ideal management tool for company treasurers, as they help guarantee a price while still leaving some leeway. But, as our reader has learned, there are no miracles in finance and the **option premium is the price of this freedom**. Its cost can be prohibitive, particularly in the case of companies operating businesses with low sales margins.

Major international banks are market makers on all sorts of markets. Below we present the most commonly used options.

(a) Currency options

Currency options allow their holders to lock in an exchange rate in a particular currency, while retaining the choice of realising a transaction at the spot market rate if it is more favourable. Of course, the strike price has to be compared with the forward rate and not the spot rate. Banks can theoretically list all types of options, although European-style options are the main ones traded.

While standardised contracts are listed, treasurers generally prefer the over-the-counter variety, as they are more flexible for choosing an amount (which can correspond exactly to the amount of the flow for companies), dates and strike prices. Options can be used in many ways. Some companies buy only options that are far out of the money and thus carry low premiums; in doing do, they seek to hedge against extreme events such as devaluations. Other companies set the strike price in line with their commercial needs or perhaps their anticipation.

Given the often high cost of the premium, several imaginative (and risky) products have been developed, including lookback options, options on options and barrier options.

Average strike options[8] can be used to buy or sell currencies on the basis of the average exchange rate during the life of the option. The premium is thus lower, as less risk is taken by the seller and the buyer has a lower return potential.

Lookback options are options where the strike price is fixed at the lowest price reached by the underlying asset during the life of the call option, and at its highest price for a put option. This kind of option cancels all opportunity cost, consequently its premium is high.

Options on options are quite useful for companies bidding on a foreign project. The bid is made on the basis of a certain exchange rate, but let's say the rate has moved the wrong way by the time the company wins the contract. Options on options allow the company to hedge its currency exposure as soon as it submits its bid, by giving it the right to buy a currency option with a strike price close to the benchmark rate. If the company is not chosen for the bid, it simply gives up its option on option. As the value of an option is below the value of the underlying asset, the value of an option on an option will be low.

Barrier options are surely the most frequently traded exotic products on the market. A barrier is a limit price which, when exceeded, knocks in or knocks out the option (i.e. creates or cancels the option). This reduces the risk to the seller and thus the premium to the buyer. For example, if the euro is trading at $1.5, US company treasurers who know they will have to buy euros in the future can ensure that they'll get a certain exchange rate by buying a euro call at $1.46, for example; and then, to reduce the premium, placing the

8 *Also called Asian options.*

knock out barrier at $1.35. If the euro falls below $1.35 at any time during the life of the option, treasurers will find themselves without a hedge (but the market will have moved in their direction and at that moment the futures price will be far below the level at which they bought their options).

It's easy to imagine various combinations of barrier options (e.g. knock-out barrier above the current price or the knock-in barrier below; options at various strike prices: one activated at the level where the other is deactivated, etc.). When a bank offers a new currency product with a strange earnings profile (a staircase profile, for example), it is generally the combination of one (or several) barrier option(s) with other standard market products.

Barrier options are attractive but require careful management as treasurers must constantly keep up with exchange rates in order to maintain their hedging situation (and to rehedge, if the option is knocked out). Moreover, their own risk-management tools would not necessarily tell them the exact consequences of these products or their implied specifications.

(b) Interest rate options

The rules that apply to options in general obviously apply to interest rate options. For the financial market, the exact nature of the underlying asset is irrelevant to either the design or valuation of the option. As a result, many products are built around identical concepts and their degree of popularity is often a simple matter of fashion.

A **cap** allows borrowers to set a ceiling interest rate above which they no longer wish to borrow and they will receive the difference between the market rate and cap rate.

A **floor** allows lenders to set a minimum interest rate below which they do not wish to lend and they will receive the difference between the floor rate and the market rate.

A **collar or rate tunnel** involves both the purchase of a cap and the sale of a floor. This sets a zone of fluctuation in interest rates below which operators must pay the difference in rates between the market rate and the floor rate and above which the counterparty pays the differential. This combination reduces the cost of hedging, as the premium of the cap is paid partly or totally by the sale of the floor.

Do not be intimidated by these products, as the cap is none other than a call option on an FRA borrower. Similarly, the floor is just a call option on an FRA lender. In a sense, these products are long options on interest rates that give the implicit right to buy or sell bonds at a certain price. As we have seen, these products allow operators to set a borrowing or lending rate *vis-à-vis* the counterparty. These options are frequently used by operators to take positions on the long part of the yield curve.

Swaptions are options on swaps, and can be used to buy or sell the right to conclude a swap over a certain duration. The underlying swap is stated at the outset and is defined by its notional amount, maturity and the fixed and floating rate that are used as benchmarks.

Some banks have combined swaps with *swaptions* to produce what they call swaps that can be cancelled at no cost. Do not be too impressed by the lack of cost. This product is none other than a swap combined with an option to sell a swap. The premium of the option is not paid in cash but factored into the calculation of the swap rate.

Barrier interest rate options are similar to barrier currency options:

- either the option exists only if the benchmark rate reaches the barrier rate; or
- the option is knocked in only if the benchmark rate exceeds a set limit.

The presence of barriers reduces the option's premium. Company treasurers can combine these options with other products into a custom-made hedge. Like barrier currency options, barrier interest rate options often require careful management.

(c) Confirmed credit lines

In exchange for a commitment fee, a company can obtain short- and medium-term confirmed credit lines from banks, on which it can draw at any time for its cash needs. A confirmed credit line is like an option to take out a loan.

(d) Credit insurance

Insurance companies specialising in appraising default risk (Euler-Hermès, Atradius, Coface, etc.) guarantee companies payment of a debt in exchange for a premium equivalent to about 0.3% of the nominal.

(e) Credit derivatives

Credit derivatives, which emerged in 1995, are used to unlink the management of a credit risk on an asset or liability from the ownership of that asset or liability.

Developed and used first of all by financial institutions, credit derivatives are beginning to be used by major industrial and commercial groups. The purpose of these products is mainly to reduce the credit risk on some clients, which may account for an excessive portion of the credit portfolio. They can also be used to protect against a negative trend in margins on a future loan. Companies are marginal players on this market (less than 10% of volume, this share does not seem to be increasing).

Credit derivatives work very much like interest-rate or currency options. Only the nature of the risk covered is different – the risk of default or rating downgrade instead of interest rate or currency risk.

The most conventional form of credit derivative is the credit default swap (or CDS). In these agreements one side buys protection against the default of its counterparty by paying a third party regularly and receiving from it the predetermined amount in the event of default. The credit risk is thus transferred from the buyer of protection (a company, an investor, a bank) to a third party (an investor, an insurance company, …) in exchange for some compensation.

Credit derivatives are traded over the counter and play the same economic role as an insurance contract.

Meanwhile, a second category of derivatives has developed which is not an "insurance" type product but a "forward" type of product. Using these, companies can, from the start, set the spread of a bond to be issued in the future. The spread of an issue is thus bought and sold at a preset level. And, of course, wherever forward purchasing or selling exists, financial intermediaries will come up with the corresponding options. We thus end up with an insurance product called an option on future spreads!

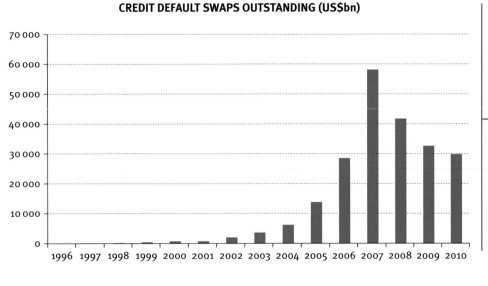

CREDIT DEFAULT SWAPS OUTSTANDING (US$bn)

Source: British Bankers' Association, International Swaps and Derivatives Association

Exponential development ... until collapse in 2008, credit derivatives cover an existing risk ... or can be used to speculate.

(f) Political risk insurance

Political risk insurance is offered by specialised companies, such as Unistrat-Coface, Hermès and Sace, which can cover 90–95% of the value of an investment for as long as 15 years in most parts of the world. Risks normally covered include expropriation, nationalisation, confiscation and changes in legislation covering foreign investments. Initially the domain of public or quasi-public organisations, political risk insurance is increasingly being offered by the private sector.

4/ OUTRIGHT DISPOSAL OF THE RISKY ASSET OR LIABILITY

Outright disposal is a last-gasp measure that obviously does not unlink the ownership of the asset (or liability) from the management of its risk. Measures include securitisation (see Chapter 22), defeasance[9] and non-recourse factoring (see Chapter 22).

Section 49.4
ORGANISED MARKETS – OTC MARKETS

9 In defeasance, the borrower simultaneously sells debt and a portfolio of assets to a special-purpose vehicle. The portfolio of assets is designed to meet interest payments and repay the principal of the debt.

1/ STANDARDISATION OF CONTRACTS

In the forward transactions we looked at in Section 49.3, two operators concluded a contract, each exposing himself to a counterparty risk if the other was in default at the delivery of the currency, for example, or before the maturity of the swap. Moreover, other operators were ignorant of the terms of these over-the-counter transactions, and

SECTION 5

the product's liquidity was unreliable. Liquidity is closely tied to the product's specificity, and usually dependent on the willingness of the counterparty to unwind the transaction.

It is because of these drawbacks that investors turn to standardised products that can be bought and sold on an organised market, such as a stock on the stock exchange. The futures and options markets have responded to this demand by offering:

- a fully liquid, listed product;
- with a clearing house; and
- specialised traders who act as intermediaries and ensure that the market functions properly.

Moreover, these markets offer the option of taking large positions with a small cash outlay, and on standardised maturities.

A future is a **firm** commitment to buy or sell an agreed upon quantity of an asset at an agreed upon price on an agreed upon date. All futures have the following specifications:

- the underlying asset is a benchmark for market operators: Euronext-Liffe, for example, offers:
  - ○ a notional contract on £100 000 in UK government bonds at 6% maturing in 10 years;
  - ○ a notional contract on €1 000 000 3-month Euribor;
  - ○ a contract on the MSCI Euro Index; or
  - ○ a contract on cocoa, robusta coffee or wheat.
- the amount of each contract is standardised;
- quotations are standardised;
- few maturities, generally at the end of March, June, September and December.

Let's take the example of a 3-month Euribor traded on Euronext-Liffe, which has a €1m notional value. The contract matures on the 20th day of March, June, September and December. It is listed in the form of 100 minus 3-month Euribor and can thus be compared immediately with bond prices. The initial deposit is €500 per contract and the minimum fluctuation is 0.001%.

The high degree of standardisation in futures ensures fungibility of contracts and market liquidity.

Liquidity is often greater on futures than on the underlying asset, as, unlike the underlying assets, futures volumes are not limited by the amount actually in issue.

The Eurex in Germany/Switzerland, the Euronext-Liffe (UK, France, Benelux and Portugal), the Chicago Board of Trade and Chicago Mercantile Exchange offer contracts for managing interest rates and commodity prices.

As listed contracts have become more liquid, standardised options have emerged on these contracts, which allow financial institutions and companies to take positions on the volatility of contract prices. Organised currency risk management markets are still in their infancy, as the dominance of banks in forward currency transactions constitutes an obstacle to the development of contracts of this type.

2/ Unwinding of contracts

In theory, when a contract matures, the buyer buys the agreed quantity of underlying asset and pays the agreed price. Meanwhile, the seller of the contract receives the agreed price and delivers the agreed quantity of underlying asset. This is the mechanism of delivery. For futures markets to be viable and to function properly, there must be at least the theoretical possibility of delivery. Possibility of physical delivery prevents the contract prices from being fully disconnected from price trends in the underlying asset. In other words, the value of the contract at maturity is equal to the value of the underlying asset at that time.

Let's take the example of an investor who, on 21 March, buys cocoa contracts maturing in July. Assume that the contract price is £2487 per tonne vs. a spot market price of £2500. Assume that, at the end of July, cocoa is quoted at £2600. By using futures contracts, our investor has bought the tonne of cocoa in July at £2487, whereas it is trading at £2600 on the market. Arbitrage trading makes the futures and spot prices converge at maturity. Let's assume that futures contracts were priced below the spot price. Investors would then snatch up these contracts at less than £2600 to instantly obtain (as the contract has now matured) cocoa that they can resell immediately for £2600. On the other hand, if the futures contracts were priced above £2600, no investor in his right mind would buy any (after all, who would buy cocoa for more than £2600 via futures contracts, when they can buy at £2600 on the spot market?).

The value of a future at maturity is equal to the value of the underlying asset. The theoretical possibility of delivery prevents the contract price from coming unlinked from the price of the underlying asset at maturity.

However, prior to maturity, the difference between the spot price and future price, called the "base", varies and is only rarely reduced to zero.

So much for the theory. In reality, in more than 95% of cases, no underlying asset is delivered, as this would be costly and administratively complicated. Let's look again at the example of the investor who bought contracts on cocoa at £2487 on 21 March and sells them at the end of July instead of taking delivery of the cocoa, since for him the result is the same. Indeed, what price would these futures be priced at except the cocoa spot price of £2600, which is also the futures price, since we are at maturity? Once the transaction is unwound, he will buy the cocoa on the spot market at £2600. This will cost him a total of £2487 (purchase of the contracts) − £2600 (reselling of the contracts) + £2600 (purchase of the cocoa), i.e. £2487 per tonne.

The mechanism of delivery exists only to allow arbitrage trading if, by chance, the price of contracts at maturity moves away from the price of the underlying asset. This is rather rare, as the markets regulate themselves. At maturity, buyers of contracts sell them to the sellers at a price that is equivalent to the price of the underlying asset at the time.

The purchase of a futures contract is normally unwound by selling it. The sale of a futures contract is normally unwound by buying it back.

3/ Eliminating counterparty risks

Derivatives markets offer considerable possibilities to investors, as long as everyone meets their commitments. The possibility of them not doing so is called counterparty risk.

And such a risk, while small, does exist. For example, a contract could be so unfavourable for an operator that he might decide not to deliver the securities or funds promised, preferring to expose himself to a long legal process rather than suffer immediate losses. And even when everyone is operating in good faith, could not the bankruptcy of one operator create a domino effect, jeopardising several other commitments and considerable sums?

Unless specific measures are in place, counterparty risk should certainly be considered the main market risk. But, in fact, markets are organised to address this concern.

Derivatives market authorities may, at any time, demand that all buyers and sellers prove they are financially able to assume the risks they have taken on (i.e. they can bear the losses already incurred and even those that are possible the next day). They do so through the mechanism of the **clearing, deposits** and **margin calls**. The clearing house is, in fact, the sole counterparty of all market operators.

The buyer is not buying from the seller, but from the clearing house. The seller is not selling to the buyer, but to the clearing house. All operators are dealing with an organisation whose financial weight, reputation and functioning rules guarantee that all contracts will be honoured.

Clearing authorities watch over positions and demand a deposit on the day that a contract is concluded. This deposit normally covers two days of maximum loss.

Daily price movements create potential losses and gains, relative to the transaction price. Each day, the clearing house credits or debits the account of each operator for this potential gain or loss. When it is a loss, the clearing house makes a **margin call** – i.e. it demands an additional payment from the operator. Hence, the operator's account is always in the black at least by the amount of the initial deposit. If the operator does not meet a margin call, the clearing house closes out his position and uses the deposit to cover the loss. For potential gains, the clearing house pays out a margin. When the contract has exceeded the clearing house's maximum regulatory amount, price quotation is stopped and the clearing house makes further margin calls before quotation resumes.

Margin calls are an integral component of derivatives markets. By limiting the amount of the initial deposit, margins provide considerable leverage to investors. Let's take the example of the cocoa contract above and try to work out the transaction's profitability. Our investor used futures contracts to buy July cocoa for £2487/tonne. At maturity it quotes at £2600 on the spot market, hence a £113 gain for a very limited outlay (just the deposit of £75). The return is considerable: 113/75 = 151%, whereas cocoa has gone up just (2600 – 2487)/2487 = 4.54%. **Here is an example of the steep leverage of futures, but leverage can also work in reverse.**

Such steep leverage explains why counterparty risk is never totally eliminated, despite precautions that are normally quite effective. Margin calls limit the extent of potential defaults to the losses that are incurred in one day, while the initial deposit is meant to cover unexpected events. However, the amounts at stake can, in a few hours, reach sums so high that all operators are shaken. Even if this happens only once in a while, no clearing house has ever gone bust, even in the 2008 financial crisis. On the contrary, new clearing houses are expected to be created for OTC-traded products, like credit derivative swaps, so as to avoid the trouble caused on markets by the collapses of Lehman and AIG.

Futures are a zero-sum game, as what one operator earns, another loses. The aggregate of market operators gets neither richer nor poorer (when excluding intermediation fees).

Let's take the above example of a tonne of cocoa quoted at £2600 at end-July. We saw that the investor who bought contracts on 21 March has earned £113 per tonne. On the other side, the operator who sold those contracts on 21 March must deliver cocoa at the end of July for £2487, even though it is priced at £2600. He will thus lose £113, the exact amount that his counterparty has earned.

A zero-sum game, not a senseless game.

This is not only a zero-sum game but also a worthwhile game. Derivatives markets are there not to create wealth, but to spread risk and to improve the liquidity of the financial markets. On the whole, there is no wealth creation.

GLOBAL MARKET FOR DERIVATIVES (ALL CONTRACT TYPES, US$tn)

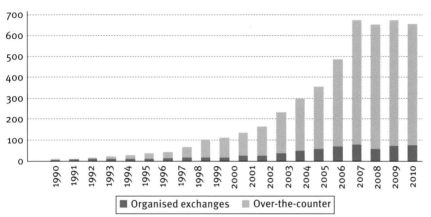

OTC markets are much larger than organised markets due to interest swaps but this may change as a consequence of the 2008 financial crisis.

Source: Bank for International Settlements (BIS)

Section 49.5
RISK MANAGEMENT: THE EXAMPLE OF PROJECT FINANCING

Bankers' imaginations know no bounds when creating specialised bank financing packages that combine funding with accounting, tax, legal or financial advantages. Sometimes the lenders are taking the global risk of the group in the form of subordinated debts (see Chapter 22). In other cases they may be only taking the risk of one project of the group which is most of the time isolated into a separate entity.

1/ PRINCIPLE AND TECHNIQUES

Project financing is used to raise funds for large-scale projects with costs running into the hundreds of millions of euros, such as oil extraction, mining, oil refineries, purchase of methane tankers, the construction of power plants or works of art.

Lenders base their decision to extend such financing on an assessment of the project itself rather than the borrower, and on the projected cash flows generated by the project that will repay the credit. They rely on the project's assets as collateral for the debt.

This type of financing was first used in the early 1930s by American banks to extend financing to oil prospectors who could not offer the guarantees required for standard loans. The banks drew up loan contracts in which a fraction of the oil still in the ground was given as collateral and part of the future sales were set aside to repay the loan.

With this financial innovation, bankers moved beyond their traditional sphere of financing to become more involved, albeit with a number of precautions, in the actual risk arising on the project.

But it is all too easy to become intoxicated by the sophistication and magnitude of such financial structures and their potential returns. Remember that the bank is taking on far more risk than with a conventional loan, and could well find itself at the head of a fleet of super oil tankers or the owner of an amusement park of uncertain market value. Lastly, the parent company cannot completely wash its hands of the financial risk inherent in the project, and banks will try to get the parent company's financial guarantee, just in case.

When considering project financing, it is essential to look closely at the professional expertise and reputation of the contractor. The project's returns, and thus its ability to repay the loan, often depend on the contractor's ability to control a frequently long and complex construction process in which cost overruns and missed deadlines are far from rare. Project financing is not just a matter of applying a standard technique. Each individual project must be analysed in detail to determine the optimal financing structure so that the project can be completed under the best possible financial conditions.

The financiers, the future manager of the project and the contractor(s) are grouped in a pool taking the form of a company set up specifically for the project. This company is the vehicle for the bank financing.

Clearly, project financing cannot be applied to new technologies which have uncertain operating cash flows, since the loan repayment depends on these cash flows. Similarly, the operator must have acknowledged expertise in operating the project, and the project's political environment must be stable to ensure that operations proceed smoothly. Only thus can investors and banks be assured that the loan will be repaid as planned.

In addition to investors and banks, two other players can take on an important role in project finance:

10 *European Bank for Reconstruction and Development*

- international financial organisations such as the World Bank and regional development banks like the EBRD,[10] especially if the project is located in a developing country. These institutions may lend funds directly or guarantee the loans extended by the other banks;
- export facilitating organisations like Coface in France or EBRD in the UK or Sace in Italy, which underwrite both the financial and the commercial risks arising on the project.

2/ RISKS AND HOW THEY ARE HEDGED

The risks on large projects arise during three quite distinct stages:

- when the project is being set up;
- during construction;
- during operations.

Contrary to appearances, risks arise as soon as the project is in the planning stage. Analysing a major project can take up to several years and requires considerable expertise and numerous technical and financial feasibility studies. All this can be quite costly. At this stage, no one is sure that the project will actually materialise. Moreover, when there is a call for tenders, the potential investors are not even sure that their bid will be retained.

But, of course, the greatest risk occurs during construction, since any loss can only be recouped once the facilities are up and running!

Some of the main risks incurred during the construction phase are:

- Cost overruns or delays. These are par for the course on large projects that are complex and lengthy. Such risks can be covered by specific insurance that can make up for the lack of income subject to the payment of additional premiums. Any claims benefits are paid directly to the lenders of the funds, or to both borrowers and lenders. Another method is for the contractor to undertake to cover all or part of any cost overruns and to pay an indemnity in the event of delayed delivery. In exchange, the contractor may be paid a premium for early completion.
- Non-completion of work, which is covered by performance bonds and contract guarantees, which unconditionally guarantee that the industrial unit will be built on schedule and with the required output capacity and production quality.
- "Economic upheavals" imposed by the government (e.g. car factories in Indonesia, dams in Nigeria, with initial strong support by local governments which was withdrawn later on because of cash shortages or a change of government) and arbitrary acts of government, such as changes in regulations.
- Natural catastrophes that are not normally covered by conventional insurance policies.

As a result, the financing is released according to expert assessments of the progress made on the project.

Risk exposure culminates between the end of construction and the start of operations. At this point, all funds have been released but the activity that will generate the flows to repay them has not yet begun and its future is still uncertain. Moreover, a new risk emerges when the installations are delivered to the client, since they must be shown to comply with the contract and the client's specifications. Because of the risk that the client may refuse to accept the installations, the contract usually provides for an independent arbitrator, generally a specialised international firm, to verify that the work delivered is in conformity with the contract.

Once the plant has come on stream, anticipated returns may be affected by:

- Operating risks *per se*: faulty design of the facilities, rising operating or procurement costs. When this occurs, the profit and loss account diverges from the business plan presented to creditors to convince them to extend financing. Lenders can hedge against this risk by requiring long-term sales contracts, such as:
  - take or pay: these contracts link the owner of the facilities (typically for the extraction and/or transformation of energy products) and the future users whose need for it is more or less urgent. The users agree to pay a certain amount that will cover both interest and principal payments, irrespective of whether the product is delivered and of any cases of *force majeure*;
  - take and pay: this clause is far less restrictive than take or pay, since clients simply agree to take delivery of the products or to use the installations if they have been delivered and are in perfect operating condition.
- Market risks. These risks may arise when the market proves smaller than expected, the product becomes obsolete or the conditions in which it is marketed change. They can be contained, although never completely eliminated, by careful study of the sales

contracts, in particular the revision and cancellation clauses which are the linchpin of project financing, as well as detailed market research.

- Foreign exchange risks are usually eliminated by denominating the loan in the same currency as the flows arising on the project or through swap contracts (see above).
- Abandonment risk arises when the interests of the industrial manager and the bankers diverge. For example, the former may want to bail out as soon as the return on capital employed appears insufficient, while the latter will only reach this conclusion when cash flow turns negative. Here again, the project financing contract must lay down clear rules on how decisions affecting the future of the project are to be taken.
- Political risks, for which no guarantees exist but which can be partly underwritten by state agencies.

SUMMARY

The summary of this chapter can be downloaded from www.vernimmen.com.

Managing risk inside a company has become a hot issue: regulations are much stricter, investors ask for more transparency and top management spends more time on it.

Risk management requires identification of risks, setting up controls, measuring the residual risk and lastly choosing a hedging strategy.

Risk is characterised by frequency and intensity.

We can identify five major risks:

- market risk – i.e. exposure of the company to unfavourable changes in interest and exchange rates or prices of raw materials or shares;

- counterparty risk – i.e. the loss of repayments of a debt in the event of default of the creditor;

- liquidity risk – i.e. the inability of a company to make its payments by their due date;

- operating risk – i.e. the losses caused by errors on the part of employees, systems and processes;

- political risk which impacts on importers, exporters and companies that invest abroad.

Market risks are accurately measured with the notion of position and value at risk (VaR). Liquidity is measured by comparing debt repayment and expected cash receipts. Techniques for measuring other risks are still in their infancy.

When confronted with risk, a company can:

- decide to do nothing and take its own hedging measures. This will only apply to small risks or some very large corporates;

- lock in prices or rates for a future transaction by means of forwardation;

- insure against the risk by paying a premium to a third party which will then assume the risk if it materialises. This is the same idea that underlies options;

- immediately dispose of the risky asset or liability (securitisation, defeasance, factoring, etc.).

The same types of product (forward buying, put options, swaps, etc.) have been developed to cover the four different risks and are traded either on the OTC markets or on stock exchanges. On the OTC market, the company can find products that are perfectly suited to its needs, but there is the counterparty risk of the third party that provides the hedging. This problem is eliminated on the futures and options markets, although the price paid is reduced flexibility in tailoring products to companies' needs.

QUESTIONS

1/ What are the five financial risks that companies are exposed to?

2/ Describe four ways for a company to deal with risk.

3/ Use arbitrage to calculate forward selling of yen against euros at 3 months. What information do you need to do the calculation?

4/ What is an FRA?

5/ A Portuguese company imports maize from Mexico, which it in turn exports to Canada. The company pays and is paid at 3 months (the maize is, in fact, shipped direct from Mexico to Canada). Should it buy or sell a peso call option or a put option against the Canadian dollar?

6/ What is a future?

7/ What are the differences between OTC forward transactions and futures?

8/ What role does a clearing house play?

9/ Can credit derivatives be based on options?

10/ Does a derivative product have to be sufficiently liquid to be attractive?

11/ Can you provide examples of hedging products used by individuals?

12/ What category of derivative products would personal injury insurance fit into?

13/ Should corporate treasurers take advantage of any arbitrages that they detect on the markets?

14/ Should traders take advantage of any arbitrages that they detect on the markets?

15/ Excluding any costs, can a company hedge against all of its risks, taking the risk of opportunity into account? And the trader?

16/ A company is hedging more than its actual position. In doing so what is it actually doing?

More questions are waiting for you at www.vernimmen.com.

Exercises

1/ Calculate the future buy and sell price, at 3 months (dollar against euro) using the following information:

- the 3-month euro rate is equal to 4 6/8 – 4 7/8%;
- the 3-month dollar rate is equal to 3 7/8 – 4%;
- the euro is currently trading at $1.0210/20.

2/ Calculate the 6-month interest rate of the dollar on the basis of the following information:

- the 6-month euro rate is equal to 4 4/8 – 4 5/8%;
- the euro is currently trading at $1.0210/20;
- the euro is trading at 6 months at $1.0150/60.

3/ A market trader is offering a $500m loan agreement in 3 months, for a period of 3 months on the following terms: 3 3/4% – 3 7/8%. Using the information provided in Questions 1 and 2, can you identify an arbitrage opportunity? What is the potential gain for the arbitrageur?

4/ Is an arbitrage of this sort really without risk?

5/ If a corporate treasurer finds himself in the situation described above, should he execute the arbitrage?

Answers

Questions

1/ *Market, liquidity, political, operational and counterparty risk.*
2/ *Self-hedging, locking in prices or interest rates now, taking out insurance, disposing of the risky asset or liability.*
3/ *See chapter. Three-month yen borrowing rate. Three-month euro investment rate. Yen/ euro spot price.*
4/ *See chapter.*
5/ *Purchase of a call option.*
6/ *A forward buy or sell contract.*
7/ *Futures market = organised market.*
8/ *Eliminating counterparty risk.*
9/ *Yes.*
10/ *No – it is an OTC product.*
11/ *All insurance policies.*
12/ *A floor.*
13/ *No, there is no such thing as a perfect arbitrage, and there is always an element of speculation. Accordingly, it does not fall within the remit of a corporate treasurer.*
14/ *Yes of course – that's what traders do.*
15/ *No, because it cannot wind up its business. Yes, because he can wind up his commitments.*
16/ *It is speculating.*

Exercises

A detailed Excel version of the solutions is available at www.vernimmen.com.

1/ *Three-month forward euro exchange rate: 1.0185 – $1.0201.*
2/ *Six-month dollar interest rate 3.099% – 3.623%.*

3/ *You should borrow $495.2m at 6 months at 3.623%, invest it at 3 7/8% in dollars for 3 months (you will have $500m in 3 months) and buy the traders' contract. The value of the arbitrage gain is $514 380 to be cashed in with no risk at maturity of the contract.*

4/ *No, there is always the counterparty risk of the trader offering the contract.*

5/ *No, because there is no way of measuring counterparty risk or any of the other market inefficiencies. For the corporate treasurer, this transaction would amount to financial speculation and, accordingly, would not form part of the ordinary course of the company's business.*

BIBLIOGRAPHY

On the theory behind the purpose and practice of hedging:

T. Adam, C. Fernando, Hedging, speculation and shareholder value, *Journal of Financial Economics*, **81**(2), 283–309, August 2006.

K. Ben Khediri, D. Folus, Hedging and financing decisions, *Bankers, Markets & Investors*, **98**, 28–38, January–February 2009.

G. Brown, Managing foreign exchange risk with derivatives, *Journal of Financial Economics*, **60**(2–3), 401–448, May 2001.

G. Brown, K. Bjerre Toft, How firms should hedge, *The Review of Financial Studies*, **15**(4), 1283–1324, Autumn 2002.

M. Faulkender, Hedging or market timing? Selecting the interest rate exposure of corporate debt, *Journal of Finance*, **60**(2), 187–243, May 2001.

G. Gay, C.-M. Lin, S. Smith, Corporate derivatives use and the cost of equity, *Journal of Banking and Finance*, forthcoming, 2011

J. Graham, C. Harvey, The theory and practice of corporate finance: Evidence from the field, *Journal of Financial Economics*, **60**(2–3), 187–243, May 2001.

P. Mackay, S. Moeller, The value of corporate risk management, *Journal of Finance*, **62**(3), 1379–1419, June 2007.

B. Rountree, J. Weston, G. Allayannis, Do investors value smooth performance?, *Journal of Financial Economics*, **90**(3), 237–251, December 2008.

J. Vickery, How and why do small firms manage interest rate risk? *Journal of Financial Economics*, **87**(2), 446–470, 2008.

And for more about credit derivatives:

G. Chacko, A. Sjöman, H. Motahashi, V. Dessain, *Credit Derivatives: A Primer on Credit Risk, Modelling and Instruments*, Wharton School Publishing, 2006.

R. Douglas, *Credit Derivatives Strategies: New Thinking on Managing Risk and Return*, Bloomberg Press, 2007.

A. Lipton, A. Rennie, *The Oxford Handbook of Credit Derivatives*, Oxford University Press, 2011.

http://www.credit-deriv.com

On the transfer of alternative risks:

K. Froot, The market for catastrophe risk: A clinical examination, *Journal of Financial Economics*, **60**(2–3), 529–571, May 2001.

On value at risk:

C. Alexander, *Value-at-Risk Models*, John Wiley & Sons, Ltd, 2009.

P. Jorion, *Value at Risk*, 3rd edn, McGraw Hill, 2006.

M. Leippold, Don't rely on VaR, *Euromoney*, 36–49, November 2004.

www.gloriamundi.org

SECTION 5

On political risk:

M. Bouchet, E. Clark, B. Groslambert, *Country Risk Assessment: A Guide to Global Investment Strategy*, John Wiley & Sons, Inc., 2003.

For a global view on risk:

www.riskcenter.com

Epilogue—Finance and Strategy

It's only au revoir!

We sincerely hope that after reading the 49 chapters of this book, you have not come away with the impression that finance is the most important function of the company!

Experience has shown that groups managed exclusively and excessively on the basis of finance cannot survive. For example, Havas, the leading European media group in the early 1990s (television, radio, advertising hoarding, publishing, professional press, etc.) disappeared in less than eight years, condemned to immobility by the dictatorship of EPS, by regular capital dilutions of subsidiaries aimed at generating exceptional profits that were supposedly recurrent, and by financial shareholders that were too preoccupied with neutralising each other to see that, in a changing world, Havas alone had remained static. Hanson in the UK and ITT in the USA experienced the same fate and for the same reasons.

On the other hand, an industrial strategy without healthy finances is also doomed to failure. This is what happened to RBS, after its acquisition of ABN Amro, mainly financed by debt. Pooling together two second-tier investment banks with some complementary strengths (LBO financing, emerging markets, etc.) to try to create a top tier one was not a bad idea in itself. But it was in the Autumn of 2007! The financing resulted in too low a solvency position for the combined group, which was only sustainable in a very good economic environment. This does not mean that a CFO should never become the CEO of a group. Many of the skills that CFOs have to display prepare them well for the position of CEO. However, it is important that former CFOs shed their old skins and adopt a new approach for this new position. The former CFO of Saatchi & Saatchi created WPP, becoming its CEO, and WPP went on to become the largest advertising group in the world within the space of 20 years.

So, we have a healthy situation when the company's financial policy plays second fiddle to its strategy. Strategy is, of course, guided by financial criteria (generate returns on investments higher than the cost of capital), but it remains of pre-eminent importance compared to financial policy.

As corporate strategy is determined by the company's shareholders, and as it depends, even though few will admit it, on the macro-economic context, financial policy is a function of corporate strategy, of shareholders and also of the macro-economic environment.

Section 1
CORPORATE STRATEGIES

Corporate strategy can take a number of different forms (diversification, refocusing on a business line, upstream or downstream integration, winning market share, internationalisation, etc.), and leverages internal or external growth. It is one of the visible sides of the invisible hand.

1/ A FINANCIAL READING OF STRATEGY

For a financial manager, these strategies, whatever they are, have a single goal – to enable the company to set itself apart on a competitive market in order to generate income, enabling it to generate higher earnings than its competitors, which in fact are no longer able to compete at the same level. Brands, patents, industrial barriers to entry (minimum size of factories, large advertising budgets, etc.) and legal barriers to entry (concessions, authorisations, etc.) are merely the instruments used to achieve this goal. For a financial manager, the most important role of an industrial manager is to analyse the economic, industrial, commercial, technological and competitive environment of the company, in order to develop a policy that will lead to higher earnings.

But, like Sisyphus, the entrepreneur must continually redo today what was done yesterday. High returns will always attract new players to the sector. These new entrants will seek to get around or demolish the barriers to entry that protect the high earnings. Sooner or later they'll succeed, which will lead to the reduction of margins following the resulting intensification of competition.

When risk is remunerated at too high a rate (for example, the luxury sector), new competitors will enter the sector, which will bring down earnings. When risk is remunerated at too low a rate, companies will abandon the sector, some firms will go bankrupt, the sector will consolidate or integrate (car parts makers, airline companies), which over time will reduce competition and increase earnings. We find here the same line of reasoning we saw for financial securities on which returns are too high or too low, given their risks.

On industrial markets, as on financial markets, a necessary relationship arises between risk and return. On financial markets, which, by definition, are a lot more liquid than industrial markets, the balance between risk and return is established a lot earlier than on industrial markets. Entering an industrial market involves a lot more than merely buying a share, as on financial markets, and exiting is a lot more complicated than selling a share.

Accordingly, there are some sectors where earnings generated may, over the long term, be higher than normal earnings, given the risk. However, let's not delude ourselves – even if adjustments often take a long time, sooner or later they take place, and abnormally high earnings will disappear, regardless of the strategy pursued by the company (see, for example, Coca-Cola[1]).

1 *See page 236.*

2/ STRATEGIES BASED ON INTERNAL GROWTH

The aim of an internal growth policy is to develop the activity and the profits of a company by leveraging its resources and capacities, without carrying out acquisitions of third companies. The company either plays the innovation card, in order to set itself apart from is competitors, or the cost-cutting card. These two strategies can be combined. Initially, a new market is created thanks to new products or new functionalities (for example, Apple with the IPod, IPad and IPhone), then the cost price is reduced (low-cost air travel, laptops).

Achieving the lowest possible cost prices enables the company to fight against the competition, even to eliminate it or to prevent it from entering its sector. Accordingly, the main aim of the industrial policy must be to minimise the cost price of stock keeping units of manufactured products.

In this context, corporate strategy consulting firms, and in particular BCG, demonstrated in the 1960s, on the basis of sector studies, that a statistical relationship exists between the accumulated volume of production and the unit cost. The greater the accumulated volume of production, the lower the unit cost will be.

The rather simplistic nature of the relationship has elicited some criticism. Nevertheless, in the majority of cases, all sectors can be "caricatured", at a given time, by an experience curve on which companies are found at a more or less low level. This type of relationship highlights the importance of the company's growth rate, compared to that of its competitors, and, more generally, compared to its sector. The more a company grows compared to its sector (i.e. the more it increases its market share), the lower its industrial costs will be, and the better it will be able to withstand competition, and thus to survive. What it does is set up a barrier to entry to new competitors in the form of low earnings prospects. New competitors are obliged to align their retail prices more or less with those of the company already on the market, while their cost prices will obviously be much higher. This results in low, or even negative, margins! Thanks to the size of its market share, the company succeeds in dissuading new competitors from entering the market (e.g. Internet access providers). This model holds especially true for sectors that are undergoing rapid development.

Over and above the experience curve, researchers have also observed that an innovation or a new strategic activity field will result in phased growth. The growth rate is initially low, then becomes very sharp before falling to a lower level again in the maturity phase, and becoming negative in the phase of decline. There are specific financial strategies that correspond to each phase of this lifecycle. For example, during the launch phase, the company will require a lot of financing and will have to make use of equity capital. On the other hand, during the maturity phase, the aim is to milk the rent, and debt is very useful at this stage.

The role of the financial manager here is to provide the company with the financial resources it needs for this internal growth policy. In order to implement this strategy, the company sets a target growth rate for the activity, which, to be achieved, requires spending on R&D (innovation), marketing (aggressive sales policy) and on tangible and operating elements (cost price), which is why financing is needed. These financing requirements can be partially, fully or excessively covered by resources that the company generates (its earnings). From a financial point of view, an internal growth strategy will necessarily involve an analysis of the relationship between the growth rate of the operations (measured by the change in sales) and the company's profitability, as we saw in Chapter 37.

We showed that the internal growth rate that the company can bear, without calling on its shareholders or modifying its financial structure, is equal to the return on equity (ROE) multiplied by (1 – payout ratio).

Accordingly, the role of financial policy is to:

- better manage the company's need for funds, by ensuring that their growth rate does not exceed that of the activity, through very tight inventory control, customer monitoring, best practice in the use of supplier credit and avoiding investments that are not directly productive;
- ensure that ROE is high, notwithstanding a possibly low ROCE (due to heavy investments), by using the leverage effect;
- reduce the cost of credit through rigorous debt management;
- possibly open up the capital (entry of new shareholders) on the basis of a high valuation.

Although, for the purposes of internal growth, industrial policy involves upstream spending in order to reduce production unit costs or bring out innovation after innovation, financial policy, on the other hand, requires rigour and continuity.

3/ STRATEGIES BASED ON EXTERNAL GROWTH

On the other hand, an external growth industrial policy is based mainly on opportunities that arise – the opportunity that a given company is for sale and can be bought, which will require the mobilisation of substantial financial resources within a short timeframe. In these cases, the aim of a financial policy behind an industrial strategy of external growth is to provide the company with access to large reserves of cash, either existing (share issues, bank loans, bonds, etc.) or potential (confirmed but undrawn credit lines, high share prices that will facilitate possible share issues or share exchanges if a merger takes place, etc.). There is the example of Nestlé in June 2011, which had around €13bn in cash, was able to sell its L'Oréal shares which brought in around €15bn and had been authorised by its shareholders to carry out capital increases up to a maximum amount of €4bn, without counting its undrawn credit lines for €7bn.

4/ THE IMPACT OF STRATEGY ON BREAKEVEN POINT

As we saw in Chapter 10, the notion of breakeven point is very important because it links profit sensitivity to a variation in activity. The closer a company gets to its breakeven point, the more sensitive it is to a drop in sales. On the other hand, the further off the company is from breakeven, the less sensitive it is to a change in its activity. It is thus more financially stable.

Accordingly, any strategy, whatever it may be, should be appreciated on the basis of its implications for the company's breakeven point.

If the strategy results in raising it faster than the level of activity increases, the company runs a heightened industrial risk. If, on the other hand, the strategy lowers the breakeven point, the company's industrial risk decreases, unless there is a more rapid fall off in activity.

This strategy cannot be considered independently from the sector in which the company operates. If the sector is cyclical, the company must minimise its fixed costs in order to remain as far from its breakeven point as possible, and to be able to withstand the unavoidable downturns in the cycle. In some sectors, upstream integration (control over suppliers) is a mistake, as it considerably raises the level of the company's breakeven point and, accordingly, of its industrial risk. On the other hand, in a growing sector, industrialisation is not a bad idea, as generally, the activity will grow faster than the increase in the level of breakeven. But care should be taken not to make mistakes when assessing the duration of the period of growth.

We are not certain that steelmakers that acquired iron ore and coal mines, such as Arcelor Mittal, made the best decision. They focused on controlling a portion of the raw materials they require in order to reduce their sensitivity to price when the economic situation is good, as if this would remain the case over the long term. In doing so, they were forgetting the key factor underlying the steel industry – its permanently cyclical nature, with its highs and its lows. During downturns, raw materials are abundant and cheap, although fixed costs still have to be met.

Section 2
SHAREHOLDERS

Legally, the shareholders are the owners of the company and take the decisions relating to strategy and financial policy. Accordingly, shareholders are another pillar of financial policy.

Theory has shown us (see Chapter 19) that, for a given level of risk, the maximum return is achieved when the investor is fully diversified and owns a fraction of each existing financial asset. In such circumstances, the shareholder will be indifferent to the company's strategy and financial policy.

Practice differs somewhat from theory, as investors are rarely fully diversified. In fact, diverse situations may arise.

We'll just mention three:

- there is a majority shareholder who is frequently the manager;
- there is a minority shareholder who is the manager;
- none of the minority shareholders can, or wish to, become the manager, so shareholders are forced to hand over the management of the company to an external manager.

1/ THE FAMILY-RUN COMPANY

Along with the confusion between the status of the manager and that of the main shareholder, there is also the overlap between the personal assets of the manager and the assets of the company, even though these can be legally separated through a limited liability company. In these circumstances, the company's financial policy is merely a tool for achieving the aims of the shareholder whose undiversified portfolio does nothing to put into practice the teachings of theory! Convinced that their activity is the best area for investment, such shareholders also do very little to diversify their family businesses (Gerdau, AB InBev, etc.).

On the other hand, why have groups such as LVMH, Reliance and Italmobiliare diversified? Unable to diversify their own assets, which has resulted in their selling control of the family business, the family shareholders have diversified their businesses and retained control over them.

For the family-run business, the dilemma is often between growth, control and risk. A company that wishes to grow but whose shareholders wish to avoid being diluted by capital increases to which they are unable to subscribe, is condemned to borrowing and will be fragile in times of crisis (Heidelberg Cement, Porsche, etc.). Alternatively, it will not grow, may be marginalised on its market and go bankrupt or be bought out.

Audacious, but wise, entrepreneurs will convince their families of the necessity of diluting control, in order to give the company the equity capital it needs to enable it to implement its strategy. And if the strategy is well managed, they will be able to retain control which no-one will dispute, notwithstanding their small (10 to 20%), but well-valued, stake. This is the wager won by the Pernod and Ricard families, which, in the space of 35 years, turned the French Pastis leader (with a stock market value of €280m and controlled by the Pernod and Ricard families) into the second largest spirits group in the world, with a stock market value of €18bn, and in which they now hold only14.3% of the shares.

There are, of course, companies with margins so high that they are able to finance their own growth without taking out too much debt or without issuing shares that will dilute the founding shareholders too much (Google, JCDecaux, etc.), but these are the exception rather than the rule.

The fifth section of this book may have convinced readers that the resources of financial engineering can always be used to put off the fatal moment by disconnecting the share capital from voting rights, by bringing minority shareholders into the subsidiaries or the controlling holding company. But let's not fool ourselves. Although these financial arrangements help to save time and to relaunch the development of a group, they always come at a cost, which takes the form of a discount on the share or, which amounts to the same thing, a higher cost of capital. They lead away from the basic principle of one share, one voting right. In the long run, they could end up blocking the way forward. Our experience has shown that in such cases they should be scrapped. Pernod Ricard no longer has treasury shares held by one of its controlled subsidiaries, L'Oréal no longer has shares without voting rights or with double-voting rights, Axa no longer has a controlling holding company that owns its brand.

2/ THE COMPANY WITH A MINORITY MANAGING SHAREHOLDER

Financial theory is no more applicable when the manager is a minority shareholder. The situation can be relatively complex. The aim of minority managers is to retain control over their companies and also to retain control over their status as managers. They often use financial policy in order to secure the loyalty of their shareholders, by paying out generous dividends, preferring debt to capital increases which would reduce their control over the company, as they generally do not have the financial resources to subscribe to them, etc.

3/ THE COMPANY WITHOUT A MANAGER SHAREHOLDER

The problem is quite different when the manager is not a shareholder or only holds a tiny stake in the capital. Such managers could pursue goals that are different from those of the shareholders who have given them a mandate to manage the company, involving power, material advantages, popularity in the media, etc. In some extreme cases, the goals of the manager could run contrary to those of the shareholders. In terms of financial policy, such managers could:

- be tempted to pay out high dividends in order to hypnotise shareholders and get them to forget the value of their shares (which will have little chance of increasing);
- be reticent to take out debt, knowing that debt will increase the risk of the company going bankrupt which will result in the loss of their jobs;
- be reluctant to carry out share issues that would bring in new shareholders who may challenge their mandates.

The Board of Directors, if it is doing its job properly, should prevent such practices, even if this means getting rid of the manager (Bank of America, SAP).

Section 3
THE MACROECONOMIC ENVIRONMENT

There are three parameters that have a fundamental influence on the company's strategy and on its financial policy:

- the growth rate in volume of the economy which serves as a backdrop against which the company performs its activity;
- the risk-free interest rate which is used as a basis for determining the cost of equity and the cost of debt;
- the rate of inflation which reduces the growth and interest rate for the firm, the real required rate for firms, which can pass inflation on to their customers.

The interaction of these three parameters is more important than their individual impact.

This means that we could have a context of high growth in volumes, rising inflation and negative interest rates, like in Europe during the 1960s or China in the middle of the 2000s. Companies would then be pushed towards borrowing, overproduction and overinvestment which results in inflation profits.[2]

2 *See page 694.*

Groups could be set up, which, on the basis of their size and their profts, appear to be powerful, but which, in reality, are fragile due to their financial structure, especially if they have become accustomed to the drug of inflation, which doesn't last. It disappeared suddenly in the late 1970s in Europe and the USA, when governments raised real interest rates to levels of above 5%, at the cost of a severe economic crisis.

Currently, weak (in the best of cases in developed countries!) economic growth, the fall in inflation and relatively high interest rates caused by risk premiums or spreads that are still high, make debt expensive (real interest rates above 4%) which is pushing companies to deleverage, even if this means selling assets that are more or less peripheral and putting strategy on hold until times improve!

The return of inflation in a few years is being predicted, the result of the massive amounts of cash that have recently been injected into the economy. Perhaps, but because the deleveraging is massive (banks, households, companies, hedge funds and now governments), nothing is certain.

We'll see in good time, and, as we said at the beginning of this epilogue, 'It's only au revoir!"

Top 20 Largest Listed Companies

Benelux (in €bn)   **First twenty by market capitalisation**

Group	Market Capitalisation	Beta	Price to book ratio (PBR) 2010	PER 2011	Revenues or net banking income 2010	Net income 2010	Headcount 2010
1 AB Inbev	64	0.73	2.7	15.4	24.8	3.5	114,313
2 Unilever	62	0.53	4.3	14.3	44.3	4.5	165,000
3 ArcelorMittal	35	1.58	0.8	11.5	53.4	2.6	273,811
4 ING Group	31	2.14	0.7	5.5	54.4	3.9	107,106
5 Heineken	23	0.48	2.3	14.1	16.1	1.4	65,730
6 Philips	18	1.13	1.1	11.4	25.4	1.6	119,001
7 KPN	15	0.35	4.5	8.1	13.4	1.8	30,599
8 Reed	14	0.54	4.8	11.2	7.1	1.2	31,000
9 Ahold	11	0.35	1.8	10.6	29.5	0.9	122,027
10 ASML	11	1.13	4.2	7.7	4.5	1.0	6,548
11 Akzo Nobel	11	0.92	1.2	12.2	14.6	0.8	55,590
12 RTL	11	0.90	2.1	13.7	5.6	0.6	9,788
13 GBL	10	0.91	0.7	14.1	0.7	0.6	34
14 Reinet Investments	10	0.53	1.0	n.s.	0.3	0.2	n.s.
15 KBC	10	2.40	0.8	5.1	8.4	1.7	52,110
16 Solvay	9	1.01	1.4	23.3	7.1	0.4	16,785
17 Aegon	9	1.87	0.3	7.4	31.6	1.6	27,474
18 DSM	8	0.94	1.4	11.7	9.1	0.5	21,911
19 Belgacom	8	0.45	2.6	10.3	6.6	0.8	16,308
20 Colruyt	7	0.19	4.9	17.3	6.8	0.3	21,149

Source: Datastream, Bloomberg, company data, Thomson Financial, in 2011.

Brazil (in €bn)   **First twenty by market capitalisation**

Group	Market Capitalisation	Beta	Price to book ratio (PBR) 2010	PER 2011	Revenues or net banking income 2010	Net income 2010	Headcount 2010
1 Petrobras	143	1.05	0.8	8.1	92.9	15.3	80,492
2 Vale	125	1.07	2.1	6.0	31.1	12.0	70,785
3 Itau Unibanco	66	1.03	2.7	10.6	19.7	5.7	108,000
4 Ambev	61	0.41	6.3	18.7	11.0	3.4	44,900
5 Banco Bradesco	48	0.94	2.4	10.5	15.6	4.3	95,248
6 Banco do Brasil	34	0.99	1.6	6.9	22.5	4.6	109,026
7 Itausa	23	1.03	1.8	9.0	2.3	1.9	125,000
8 OGX Petroleo	22	0.93	5.5	n.s.	n.s.	−0.1	213
9 Cia Siderurgica Nacional	14	1.30	4.1	8.8	6.3	1.1	19,000
10 Eletrobras	14	0.89	0.5	9.2	11.9	1.0	24,967
11 Souza Cruz	13	0.30	13.9	18.5	2.4	0.6	7,100
12 Vivo	12	0.58	2.8	12.3	7.9	0.8	13,419
13 Gerdau	12	1.36	1.3	11.1	13.7	0.9	40,000
14 Brazil Foods	11	0.65	1.6	17.9	9.9	0.4	113,000
15 BMF&Bovespa	10	1.24	1.1	16.1	0.8	0.7	1,559
16 Telesp	10	0.23	2.0	11.4	6.9	1.0	6,171
17 CPFL Energia	10	0.35	3.4	13.6	5.2	0.7	7,924
18 Cielo	10	0.61	18.5	12.6	1.9	1.0	1,089
19 Telemar NL	9	0.79	0.9	11.1	12.8	0.8	28,465
20 CCR	9	0.52	6.6	19.2	2.0	0.3	6,197

Source: Datastream, Bloomberg, company data, Thomson Financial, in 2011.

China (in €bn)

Group	Market Capitalisation	Beta	Price to book ratio (PBR) 2010	PER 2011	Revenues or net banking income 2010	Net income 2010	Headcount 2010
1 Petrochina	203	0.83	2.1	12.2	154.9	14.8	539,168
2 ICBC	170	0.69	1.9	7.6	40.2	17.5	389,827
3 China Construction Bank	154	0.74	1.8	7.6	34.4	14.3	301,537
4 Agricultural Bank of China	99	0.71	4.3	7.5	25.6	10.0	444,447
5 Bank of China	98	0.69	1.5	7.3	29.2	11.0	262,566
6 Sinopec	70	1.10	1.5	8.5	202.2	7.5	371,333
7 China Shenhua Energy	61	1.38	2.9	13.1	15.6	4.0	62,286
8 China Life Insurance	58	0.99	2.5	13.5	33.6	3.6	104,535
9 Ping An Insurance	44	1.05	3.3	16.1	14.9	1.8	128,808
10 Bank of Communications	36	1.03	1.4	6.6	10.5	4.1	79,122
11 China Merchants Bank	32	1.05	2.1	8.4	7.6	2.7	1,711
12 Kweichow Moutai	21	0.26	10.9	27.4	1.1	0.5	9,149
13 China Pacific Insurance	21	0.94	2.3	16.9	12.7	0.9	67,000
14 Shanghai Pudong	20	1.14	1.5	7.5	5.3	2.0	21,877
15 Citic Securities	20	1.07	1.6	7.9	6.0	2.3	24,180
16 SAIC Motor	17	0.97	2.4	9.5	32.3	1.5	4,373
17 China Minsheng Banking	16	0.97	1.5	7.0	5.8	1.9	26,039
18 Yanzhou Coal Mining	16	1.45	4.5	16.1	3.6	1.0	49,633
19 Industrial Bank	15	1.33	1.6	5.8	4.6	2.0	22,004
20 CEB Bank	15	1.62	1.7	8.8	3.2	1.4	19,217

Source: Datastream, Bloomberg, company data, Thomson Financial, in 2011.

Germany (in €bn)

Group	Market capitalisation	Beta	Price to book ratio (PBR) 2010	PER 2011	Revenues or net banking income 2010	Net income 2010	Headcount 2010
1 Siemens	85	1.12	2.9	11.5	76.0	5.1	405 000
2 BASF	59	1.25	2.8	10.3	63.9	5.3	102 956
3 Volkswagen	55	0.93	1.2	n.s.	126.9	6.8	368 500
4 SAP	53	0.73	5.2	16.2	12.5	2.7	47 584
5 Daimler	52	1.44	1.4	9.4	97.8	4.2	256 407
6 Bayer	47	0.94	2.5	12.2	35.1	3.5	108 400
7 Deutsche Telekom	45	0.51	1.0	13.9	62.4	3.4	259 920
8 Allianz	44	1.06	1.0	8.4	106.5	5.1	153 203
9 E.On	39	0.95	0.9	10.8	92.9	4.9	88 227
10 BMW	39	1.18	1.6	9.6	60.5	3.2	96 230
11 Deutsche Bank	38	1.21	0.8	7.0	28.6	2.3	77 053
12 Audi	26	0.36	2.3	11.6	35.4	2.6	55 608
13 RWE	23	0.79	1.6	8.2	53.3	3.8	70 726
14 Munich Re	20	0.73	0.9	18.4	45.5	2.4	47 249
15 Linde	20	0.75	1.8	15.8	12.9	1.2	47 731
16 Henkel	19	0.60	2.7	n.s.	15.1	1.1	49 262
17 Thyssen Krupp	17	1.31	1.8	15.3	42.6	0.7	187 495
18 Merck	17	0.39	1.6	10.1	9.3	1.5	33 062
19 Commerzbank	17	1.01	0.5	9.1	12.8	1.5	62 671
20 Deutsche Post	16	1.02	1.5	11.0	51.5	2.9	451 515

Source: Datastream, Bloomberg, Thomson Financial, company data, in 2011.

France (in €bn)   **First twenty by market capitalisation**

Group	Market Capitalisation	Beta	Price to book ratio (PBR) 2010	PER 2011	Revenues or net banking income 2010	Net income 2010	Headcount 2010
1 Total	94	0.92	1.5	7.2	159.3	10.3	96,387
2 Sanofi	72	0.72	1.4	8.2	30.4	9.2	104,867
3 BNP Paribas	65	1.47	0.9	7.4	43.9	7.8	205,300
4 LVMH	59	0.88	3.4	20.0	20.3	3.0	69,896
5 GDF Suez	58	0.98	0.9	12.4	84.5	3.9	242,714
6 L'Oréal	53	0.63	3.5	19.9	19.5	2.4	64,643
7 EDF	52	0.81	1.7	15.5	65.2	4.0	164,250
8 France Télécom	42	0.61	1.4	9.4	45.5	5.4	167,148
9 AXA	34	1.54	0.7	7.2	91.0	4.3	103,432
10 Danone	33	0.53	2.6	16.9	17.0	1.7	80,976
11 Schneider Electric	31	1.14	2.1	13.4	19.6	1.9	116,065
12 Société Générale	31	1.63	0.6	7.0	26.4	3.9	160,144
13 Air Liquide	27	0.91	3.1	17.5	13.5	1.4	43,000
14 Crédit Agricole	26	1.60	0.6	6.2	20.1	2.0	89,172
15 Vinci	25	1.16	2.5	12.9	33.4	1.8	161,746
16 Saint Gobain	24	1.45	1.4	13.2	40.1	1.3	189,876
17 Vivendi	24	0.98	1.0	8.1	28.9	2.7	48,284
18 Carrefour	21	0.57	2.2	12.8	90.1	1.4	475,976
19 Christian Dior	19	0.94	2.5	15.5	21.1	1.3	80,510
20 Hermès	19	0.60	8.7	38.0	2.4	0.4	8,057

Source: Datastream, Bloomberg, company data, Thomson Financial, in 2011.

India (in €bn)   **First twenty by market capitalisation**

Group	Market Capitalisation	Beta	Price to book ratio (PBR) 2010	PER 2011	Revenues or net banking income 2010	Net income 2010	Headcount 2010
1 Reliance Industries	47	1.05	1.8	12.8	40.7	3.1	24,679
2 Coal India	38	0.73	6.3	17.2	8.3	1.8	397,138
3 Oil & Natural Gas Corp.	37	0.74	2.4	9.2	18.0	3.4	33,035
4 Tata Consultancy	35	0.77	12.3	22.0	5.7	1.3	143,761
5 Infosys Technologies	25	0.74	5.9	19.9	4.2	1.0	104,850
6 ITC	23	0.38	10.2	25.1	3.4	0.8	23,473
7 State Bank of India	23	1.29	1.8	9.2	12.2	1.6	205,896
8 NTPC	22	0.73	2.3	15.0	8.8	1.4	24,713
9 Bharti Airtel	22	0.81	3.6	17.9	9.1	0.9	24,538
10 ICICI Bank	19	1.47	2.2	17.6	1.6	0.9	56,969
11 HDFC Bank	17	0.87	5.0	22.1	2.3	0.6	52,687
12 Wipro	17	0.78	5.9	18.4	4.8	0.8	97,810
13 Larsen & Toubro	16	1.14	4.9	20.1	7.9	0.7	37,357
14 NMDC	16	1.22	7.3	12.4	1.9	1.1	5,652
15 Housing Development Finance Corporation	15	1.06	5.2	23.2	0.9	0.7	1,490
16 Bharat Heavy Electricals	14	0.85	5.9	13.7	6.4	0.9	45,666
17 MMTC	14	1.08	58.2	n.s.	7.5	0.0	1,882
18 Indian Oil	12	0.35	1.5	8.8	43.7	1.2	33,998
19 Hindustan Unilever	11	0.37	26.0	28.1	3.0	0.3	15,000
20 Adani	10	1.07	5.1	17.4	4.0	0.4	505

Source: Datastream, Bloomberg, company data, Thomson Financial, in 2011.

Italy (in €bn) **First twenty by market capitalisation**

Group	Market Capitalisation	Beta	Price to book ratio (PBR) 2010	PER 2011	Revenues or net banking income 2010	Net income 2010	Headcount 2010
1 Eni	67	0.82	1.2	7.4	98.4	6.9	78,648
2 Enel	45	0.83	1.2	10.0	71.9	4.4	81,208
3 Unicredit	30	1.54	0.5	9.7	26.3	1.6	165,062
4 Intesa Sanpaolo	29	1.44	0.4	8.7	16.6	2.3	103,718
5 Generali	24	1.20	1.3	10.3	73.2	1.7	85,322
6 Tenaris	20	0.87	2.9	17.2	5.4	0.8	22,591
7 Telecom Italia	18	0.88	0.7	7.8	27.6	3.0	71,384
8 Saipem	16	1.07	4.0	17.7	11.2	0.8	36,224
9 Snam Rete Gas	15	0.36	2.3	13.3	3.5	1.1	6,187
10 Fiat Industrial	11	0.47	3.0	15.7	21.3	0.3	61,243
11 Luxottica	10	0.60	3.2	20.5	5.8	0.4	60,800
12 Atlantia	10	0.80	3.0	13.0	3.8	0.7	10,021
13 Enel Green Power	10	0.50	1.4	20.9	2.2	0.5	2,685
14 Fiat	9	1.31	0.8	22.4	35.9	0.3	190,014
15 Terna	7	0.38	2.5	15.7	1.6	0.5	3,447
16 Mediobanca	7	1.06	1.0	11.5	2.0	n.s.	3,244
17 Banca Monte Dei Paschi	6	1.08	0.3	10.6	5.6	0.6	32,475
18 Exor	5	1.14	0.9	18.5	59.0	0.2	16,950
19 Finmeccanica	5	0.81	0.7	7.6	18.7	0.7	73,056
20 Parmalat	4	0.42	1.3	23.2	4.3	0.3	13,788

Source: Datastream, Bloomberg, company data, Thomson Financial, in 2011.

Japan (in €bn) **First twenty by market capitalisation**

Group	Market Capitalisation	Beta	Price to book ratio (PBR) 2010	PER 2011	Revenues or net banking income 2010	Net income 2010	Headcount 2010
1 Toyota	95	1.21	1.0	24.0	161.9	3.5	320,808
2 NTT Docomo	55	0.41	1.3	11.9	36.0	4.2	21,831
3 NTT	47	0.50	0.6	9.2	87.9	4.3	196,296
4 Honda	47	1.17	1.2	14.1	76.2	4.6	181,876
5 Mitsubishi UFJ	45	1.29	0.6	8.3	38.6	5.0	84,780
6 Canon	44	1.12	1.8	20.0	31.6	2.1	168,879
7 Nissan	30	1.37	1.1	13.6	74.8	2.7	160,422
8 Softbank	28	1.04	5.3	13.2	25.6	1.6	21,048
9 Mitsubishi	28	1.28	1.0	6.4	164.0	4.0	60,095
10 Sumitomo Mitsui	28	1.36	0.7	7.9	32.8	4.1	48,079
11 Japan Tobacco	26	0.88	2.0	16.6	52.8	1.2	47,977
12 Takeda	26	0.50	1.4	11.8	12.1	2.1	19,362
13 Fanuc	25	1.08	2.7	17.0	3.8	1.0	4,914
14 Mizuho	23	1.44	0.7	6.9	23.2	3.5	50,191
15 Nintendo	22	0.80	1.8	21.9	8.7	0.7	4,130
16 KDDI	22	0.64	1.1	10.0	29.3	2.2	16,967
17 Denso	21	1.22	1.2	20.7	26.7	1.2	119,919
18 Mitsui	21	1.33	1.0	5.2	84.8	2.6	39,864
19 Komatsu	20	1.26	2.5	11.8	15.7	1.3	39,855
20 Panasonic	19	1.28	0.8	34.5	74.1	0.6	292,250

Source: Datastream, Bloomberg, company data, Thomson Financial, in 2011.

Morocco - Lebanon - Tunisia (in €bn) **First twenty by market capitalisation**

Group	Market Capitalisation	Beta	Price to book ratio (PBR) 2010	PER 2011	Revenues or net banking income 2010	Net income 2010	Headcount 2010
1 Maroc Telecom	11.4	0.64	6.8	13.8	2.8	0.8	13,942
2 Attijariwafa Bank	6.5	1.04	2.8	16.5	1.3	0.4	6,473
3 BMCE Bank	3.1	0.91	5.6	43.2	0.6	0.0	4,900
4 Lafarge Maroc	2.8	1.27	5.0	15.8	0.5	0.1	972
5 Groupe Addoha	2.5	1.44	3.4	22.8	0.7	0.2	500
6 Banque Centrale Populaire	2.4	0.91	2.5	16.3	0.9	0.2	10,076
7 CGI	2.4	2.49	6.1	43.9	0.2	0.0	n.s.
8 Solidere	2.0	1.70	1.7	n.s.	0.3	0.1	n.s.
9 Bank Audi	1.8	0.92	1.1	n.s.	0.5	0.2	4,668
10 Ciment du Maroc	1.4	1.59	3.1	14.2	0.3	0.1	1,080
11 Blom Bank	1.3	0.59	1.1	6.4	0.4	0.2	3,559
12 BMCI	1.2	1.45	1.8	16.6	0.2	0.1	400
13 Centrale Laitière	1.1	0.55	6.8	18.8	0.5	0.1	2,694
14 Byblos Bank	1.1	0.91	0.6	6.4	0.3	0.1	2,433
15 Wafa Assurances	0.9	1.10	3.6	22.4	0.4	0.0	427
16 Holcim Maroc	0.9	1.40	5.1	15.2	0.3	0.1	n.s.
17 Alliances	0.7	2.23	3.1	19.2	0.3	0.0	n.s.
18 Consumar	0.7	0.65	2.9	16.9	0.7	0.1	2,500
19 Poulina	0.7	0.94	3.1	n.s.	0.6	0.0	8,575
20 Managem	0.7	1.63	11.0	n.s.	0.3	0.0	2,390

Source: Datastream, Bloomberg, company data, Thomson Financial, in 2011.

Russia (in €bn) **First twenty by market capitalisation**

Group	Market Capitalisation	Beta	Price to book ratio (PBR) 2010	PER 2011	Revenues or net banking income 2010	Net income 2010	Headcount 2010
1 Gazprom	122	1.11	0.8	4.3	89.2	24.0	386,000
2 Rosneft	65	1.10	1.6	8.1	43.5	7.2	159,771
3 Sberbank	54	1.19	2.3	7.8	15.0	4.1	252,398
4 Lukoil	37	0.89	0.9	4.7	72.5	6.2	143,400
5 TNK-BP	34	0.35	2.2	7.3	31.0	4.9	n.s.
6 Norilsk Nickel	33	1.12	3.3	9.4	7.0	1.8	83,900
7 Novatek	27	0.82	8.1	NA	2.7	0.9	4,019
8 Surgutneftegas	27	0.87	0.8	8.9	13.6	2.9	n.s.
9 VTB Bank	23	1.10	1.7	8.8	5.3	1.4	40,447
10 Novolipetsk Steel	15	1.07	2.1	18.6	4.8	0.2	59,400
11 Gazprom Neft	15	0.79	1.1	4.8	22.6	2.2	64,895
12 UC Rusal	15	1.20	1.9	7.0	7.6	2.0	75,820
13 Uralkali	13	1.02	10.5	33.7	1.2	0.4	13,200
14 Severstal	13	1.22	2.7	8.2	9.4	0.9	26,568
15 Mobile Telesystems	12	0.62	4.5	n.s.	8.5	1.0	36,136
16 Federal Grid Company	12	1.06	0.6	14.0	1.9	1.0	11,933
17 Rushydro	10	0.75	0.8	9.2	10.4	0.9	5,426
18 Tatneft	9	1.02	1.2	6.5	10.6	1.1	71,000
19 Mechel	9	1.14	2.7	8.0	6.7	0.5	79,972
20 Polyus Gold	9	0.77	3.8	20.1	1.3	0.3	20,054

Source: Datastream, Bloomberg, company data, Thomson Financial, in 2011.

Spain (in €bn)   **First twenty by market capitalisation**

Group	Market Capitalisation	Beta	Price to book ratio (PBR) 2010	PER 2011	Revenues or net banking income 2010	Net income 2010	Headcount 2010
1 Telefonica	75	0.73	3.1	9.1	60.7	7.6	257,426
2 Banco Santander	67	1.40	0.9	7.6	42.0	8.2	169,460
3 Inditex	38	0.58	6.0	20.4	12.5	1.7	89,112
4 BBVA	36	1.50	1.0	7.4	20.9	4.6	103,721
5 Iberdrola	35	0.95	1.1	12.0	30.4	2.9	32,711
6 Repsol	27	0.88	1.1	10.7	60.4	2.4	41,014
7 Endesa	25	0.76	1.4	11.4	29.6	2.2	26,770
8 Caixa	17	0.74	1.3	11.0	6.4	1.4	1,818
9 Iberdrola Renovables	13	0.76	1.1	29.8	2.2	0.4	1,991
10 Gas Natural	12	0.85	1.1	10.4	19.6	1.5	18,314
11 Abertis	12	0.81	2.8	15.8	4.1	0.7	12,484
12 Grupo ACS	10	0.72	1.8	10.5	15.4	0.9	142,085
13 Mapfre	8	1.03	1.2	7.8	17.0	0.9	35,225
14 Cepsa	7	0.31	1.3	14.1	22.1	0.4	11,807
15 Amadeus	6	0.14	8.3	13.3	2.7	0.4	7,751
16 Ferrovial	6	1.08	1.2	43.0	12.2	−0.1	100,059
17 Red Electrica de Espana	6	0.73	3.5	12.5	1.4	0.4	1,679
18 Banco Popular	5	1.24	0.6	10.7	3.2	0.6	14,431
19 Acciona	5	1.00	0.8	25.0	6.3	0.2	33,112
20 Zardoya Otis	4	0.59	16.5	20.3	0.9	0.2	5,854

Source: Datastream, Bloomberg, company data, Thomson Financial, in 2011.

Switzerland (in €bn)   **First twenty by market capitalisation**

Group	Market Capitalisation	Beta	Price to book ratio (PBR) 2010	PER 2011	Revenues or net banking income 2010	Net income 2010	Headcount 2010
1 Nestlé	154	0.64	3.0	16.4	90.1	9.2	278,000
2 Novartis	120	0.78	2.1	11.2	34.8	8.1	99,834
3 Roche	106	0.82	13.2	11.1	39.0	9.0	81,507
4 UBS	50	1.72	1.3	8.6	26.3	5.9	65,233
5 ABB	42	1.47	4.1	17.2	21.7	2.0	116,000
6 Crédit Suisse	35	1.37	1.3	7.8	25.8	4.2	47,600
7 Zurich Financial Services	27	1.07	1.2	9.7	46.6	2.4	56,668
8 Richemont	23	1.44	3.6	18.3	6.9	1.1	19,571
9 Syngenta	22	0.99	4.2	17.2	8.0	1.1	26,688
10 Swatch	18	1.24	3.2	17.5	5.0	0.9	23,562
11 Holcim	18	1.38	1.2	16.3	17.8	1.0	81,498
12 Swisscom	17	0.40	3.2	10.4	9.8	1.5	19,479
13 Swiss Reinsurance	15	1.75	0.7	19.3	15.7	0.7	10,552
14 Synthes	14	0.77	3.1	20.1	2.5	0.6	10,705
15 Kuehne & Nagel	13	0.98	6.7	22.2	16.6	0.5	60,538
16 SGS Surveillance	11	0.62	5.9	20.3	3.9	0.5	58,818
17 Schindler	10	0.88	4.6	18.0	6.7	0.6	43,437
18 Adecco	9	1.52	2.3	15.5	18.7	0.5	28,508
19 Alpiq	7	0.41	1.1	14.9	11.6	0.5	10,795
20 Givaudan	7	0.66	2.5	15.8	3.5	0.4	8,501

Source: Datastream, Bloomberg, company data, Thomson Financial, in 2011.

United Kingdom (in €bn) First twenty by market capitalisation

Group	Market Capitalisation	Beta	Price to book ratio (PBR) 2010	PER 2011	Revenues or net banking income 2010	Net income 2010	Headcount 2010
1 BHP Billiton	164	1.64	4.6	9.6	36.7	8.7	40,990
2 Shell	157	1.00	1.5	8.5	256.0	13.0	101,000
3 HSBC	129	0.98	1.3	11.3	44.5	8.9	289,485
4 BP	101	1.15	1.5	6.4	206.7	14.3	80,300
5 Rio Tinto	99	1.89	1.8	7.3	39.4	9.7	74,262
6 Vodafone	99	0.63	1.1	10.5	52.5	10.0	79,097
7 Glaxosmithkline	78	0.45	8.4	11.5	32.5	7.7	99,913
8 Unilever	62	0.53	4.3	14.3	44.3	4.5	165,000
9 British American Tobacco	62	0.61	6.0	14.2	17.0	4.0	95,710
10 BG Group	55	1.02	2.8	17.0	12.7	3.0	6,191
11 RBS	53	1.89	0.3	14.6	36.5	1.5	184,500
12 AstraZeneca	50	0.37	3.2	7.4	23.1	6.7	62,700
13 Xstrata	48	2.16	1.7	8.2	21.2	3.6	37,845
14 Anglo American	46	1.61	2.0	7.9	19.4	3.5	107,000
15 Standard Chartered	44	1.23	1.7	13.2	11.2	2.9	77,326
16 Lloyds Banking	41	1.74	0.8	12.6	27.1	1.8	132,000
17 SABMiller	41	0.94	2.9	17.0	13.5	2.1	68,635
18 Barclays	39	1.58	0.7	9.0	36.0	3.4	144,200
19 Tesco	38	0.43	2.3	11.6	69.8	3.3	468,508
20 Diageo	37	0.58	8.0	16.3	11.2	2.1	24,270

Source: Datastream, Bloomberg, company data, Thomson Financial, in 2011.

United States (in €bn) First twenty by market capitalisation

Group	Market Capitalisation	Beta	Price to book ratio (PBR) 2010	PER 2011	Revenues or net banking income 2010	Net income 2010	Headcount 2010
1 Exxon Mobil	286	0.85	2.8	9.5	266.6	21.2	80,700
2 Apple	224	1.02	6.7	14.1	45.4	9.7	36,800
3 Microsoft	147	0.94	4.7	9.7	43.5	13.0	93,000
4 Chevron	147	1.10	2.0	8.1	137.9	13.1	64,000
5 General Electric	145	1.49	1.8	14.5	104.5	8.6	304,000
6 IBM	142	0.81	9.0	12.8	69.5	10.3	399,409
7 Berkshire Hathaway	136	0.56	1.2	18.9	94.7	7.7	222,000
8 Wal Mart Stores	134	0.46	2.8	12.4	293.4	10.4	2,100,000
9 Procter & Gamble	130	0.42	3.2	17.0	54.9	8.9	135,000
10 AT & T	130	0.60	1.7	13.4	86.4	9.5	282,720
11 Johnson & Johnson	128	0.52	3.3	13.6	42.8	9.2	115,500
12 Oracle	120	1.18	5.5	15.7	18.8	5.9	86,000
13 JP Morgan Chase	120	1.24	1.0	8.8	72.9	11.0	222,316
14 Google	119	1.17	3.7	15.6	15.3	6.7	19,835
15 Pfizer	118	0.85	2.0	9.6	47.2	12.5	116,500
16 Coca Cola	106	0.48	4.9	17.3	24.4	5.7	92,800
17 Wells Fargo & Co	104	1.38	1.3	10.3	59.3	8.1	267,300
18 Philip Morris	89	0.75	36.7	15.6	18.9	5.0	77,300
19 Bank of America	85	1.43	0.6	11.1	76.7	7.1	284,000
20 Citi Group	84	1.38	0.7	9.8	60.2	7.4	269,000

Source: Datastream, Bloomberg, company data, Thomson Financial, in 2011.

Contents

Part Two   Financial analysis and forecasting

Index